WEBSTER'S
NEW
THESAURUS

CONCISE EDITION

© Geddes & Grosset Ltd., New Lanark, Scotland 1990

Published by Russell, Geddes & Grosset, Windsor Court,
New York, N.Y., U.S.A.

Printed in U.S.A.

This book is not published by the original publishers of
WEBSTER'S THESAURUS or by their successors.

Contents

Preface

What is a thesaurus?

Clearly it is a kind of dictionary; but whereas an ordinary dictionary gives the meanings of a word, a thesaurus supplies alternatives for it. It is the essential companion for anyone who wants to create something satisfying out of words — a quick, convenient source of synonymous and related terms that will help the user to express himself in as precise, succinct, and yet varied a manner as possible.

It is 130 years since Peter Mark Roget published his *Thesaurus*. His purpose was to provide the reader not only with synonyms for a word, but, more generally, with a wide choice of expressions relevant to a particular concept. His method was to classify these within a framework of ideas on seventeenth-century philosophical and scientific principles. This meant that a very full alphabetical index was needed to open up the classified lists to the user. It was probably the complications of this system that ensured the continued popularity of the more 'user-friendly' type of word-finding book already in production in Roget's time — the simple alphabetical list of words, each followed by its own group of synonyms. More recently there has emerged the type of thesaurus that, while preserving the alphabetical arrangement, acknowledges the value of Roget's approach by supplying with each entry related vocabulary on a rather broader, more comprehensive basis than that of mere synonymity.

This thesaurus belongs to this last type — it contains 18,000 of the commonest, most synonym-rich words in the language, alphabetically listed, each with a plentiful supply of alternative and connected expressions; selected antonyms have also been added wherever appropriate. It has all the recognized usefulness of any thesaurus, and will be of inestimable value to all its users, particularly to dictionary connoisseurs and word-game enthusiasts, as a mine of useful, interesting and diverting items of vocabulary.

What are the advantages of a thesaurus?

To a regular thesaurus-user they become ever more apparent. A thesaurus jogs the memory — it offers help to the person struggling to encapsulate his meaning in a forgotten *mot juste* that might remain tantalizingly on the tip of his tongue. It is indispensable to the student, the journalist, writer and reporter; and to the businessman who wishes to express himself accurately, effectively and concisely. A thesaurus is fun to use, and with the fun comes the opportunity to enhance one's personal command of words and increase one's general knowledge; words that may not be well known to the reader will trigger off investigations in his dictionary and lead him to explore the remoter corners of the language. Finally, a thesaurus is a tool that the word-gamester — compiler, player or solver — cannot do without.

The thing one notices about a thesaurus is that it rarely yields completely interchangeable alternatives for a word — but this is one of its beauties. What it gives is a list of possibles that have more or less of a particular ingredient, are more or less formal, are more or less euphonious, that, in short, have more or less of the precise flavor sought by the user. English has its international origins largely to thank for its richness and subtle variety, and a thesaurus of English words, with their diversity of shape, size, sound and association, will surely yield that ideal, unmistakably usable expression to fit a particular context.

The bias towards abstract terms in the main text has been balanced by the addition of a section that is a virtual newcomer to this type of thesaurus: an appendix of concrete and technical terms, collected alphabetically into categories such as architecture, furniture, vehicles, garments, rhetorical terms, legal terms, anatomical terms. There are also useful lists of collective nouns, names for collectors and enthusiasts, ranks in the armed forces, and wine-bottle sizes. Such words do not fit readily into synonym lists but may be no less sought-after for that. A list of the categories included appears on the Contents page.

A second appendix contains words listed by suffix. The dictionary has been combed to produce exhaustive lists of -ologies, -ocracies, -ographies, -philias, -phobias, -manias, -therapies, -hoods, -doms and some seventy other such groups. This is another innovative and intriguing addition to the standard thesaurus. These two appendices will be invaluable extras not only for the crossword-solver, but for all types of thesaurus-user.

A

abandon *v.* abdicate, back-pedal, cede, chuck, desert, desist, discontinue, ditch, drop, evacuate, forgo, forsake, give up, jilt, leave, leave behind, leave in the lurch, quit, relinquish, renounce, repudiate, resign, scrap, sink, surrender, vacate, waive, withdraw from, yield.

antonyms continue, persist, support.

n. dash, recklessness, unrestraint, wantonness, wildness.

antonym restraint.

abandoned *adj.* cast aside, cast away, cast out, corrupt, debauched, depraved, derelict, deserted, desolate, discarded, dissipated, dissolute, dropped, forlorn, forsaken, jilted, left, neglected, outcast, profligate, rejected, relinquished, reprobate, scorned, sinful, unoccupied, vacant, wanton, wicked.

antonyms cherished, restrained.

abase *v.* belittle, cast down, debase, degrade, demean, discredit, disgrace, dishonor, downgrade, humble, humiliate, lower, malign, mortify, reduce, vitiate.

antonyms elevate, honor.

abashed *adj.* affronted, ashamed, astounded, bewildered, chagrined, confounded, confused, cowed, discomfited, discomposed, disconcerted, discountenanced, discouraged, dismayed, dum(b)founded, embarrassed, floored, humbled, humiliated, mortified, nonplused, perturbed, shamefaced, taken aback.

antonyms at ease, audacious, composed.

abate *v.* alleviate, appease, attenuate, bate, decline, decrease, deduct, diminish, discount, dull, dwindle, ease, ebb, fade, fall off, lessen, let up, mitigate, moderate, mollify, pacify, quell, rebate, reduce, relieve, remit, sink, slacken, slake, slow, subside, subtract, taper off, wane, weaken.

antonyms increase, strengthen.

abbreviate *v.* abridge, abstract, clip, compress, condense, contract, curtail, cut, digest, epitomize, lessen, précis, reduce, shorten, shrink, summarize, trim, truncate.

antonyms amplify, extend.

abbreviation *n.* abridgment, abstract, abstraction, clipping, compendium, compression, condensation, conspectus, contraction, curtailment, digest, epitome, précis, reduction, résumé, shortening, summarization, summary, summation, synopsis, trimming, truncation.

antonyms expansion, extension.

abdicate *v.* abandon, abjure, abnegate, cede, demit, forgo, give up, quit, relinquish, renounce, repudiate, resign, retire, surrender, vacate, yield.

abduct *v.* abduce, appropriate, carry off, kidnap, lay hold of, make off with, rape, run away with, run off with, seduce, seize, snatch, spirit away.

abduction *n.* appropriation, enlevement, kidnap, rape, seduction, seizure, theft.

aberrant *adj.* abnormal, anomalous, atypical, corrupt, corrupted, defective, degenerate, depraved, deviant, different, divergent, eccentric, egregious, erroneous, incongruous, irregular, odd, peculiar, perverse, perverted, queer, quirky, rambling, roving, straying, untypical, wandering, wrong.

antonyms normal, straight.

aberration *n.* aberrancy, abnormality, anomaly, defect,

delusion, deviation, divergence, eccentricity, freak, hallucination, illusion, irregularity, lapse, nonconformity, oddity, peculiarity, quirk, rambling, rogue, straying, vagary, wandering.

antonym conformity.

abet *v.* aid, assist, back, condone, connive, egg on, encourage, goad, help, incite, promote, prompt, sanction, second, spur, succor, support, sustain, uphold, urge.

antonym discourage.

abeyance *n.* adjournment, deferral, discontinuation, inactivity, intermission, lull, postponement, recess, remission, reservation, suspension, waiting.

antonyms activity, continuation.

abhor *v.* abominate, despise, detest, execrate, hate, loathe, recoil from, shrink from, shudder at, spurn.

antonyms adore, love.

abhorrent *adj.* abominable, absonant, despiteful, detestable, disgusting, distasteful, execrable, hated, hateful, heinous, horrible, horrid, loathsome, nauseating, obnoxious, odious, offensive, repellent, repugnant, repulsive, revolting.

antonym attractive.

abide *v.* accept, bear, brook, continue, endure, last, outlive, persist, put up with, remain, stand, stay, stomach, submit to, suffer, survive, tarry, tolerate.

antonyms dispute, quit.

ability *n.* adeptness, adroitness, aptitude, capability, capacity, competence, competency, deftness, dexterity, endowment, energy, expertise, expertness, facility, faculty, flair, forte, genius, gift, knack, know-how, long suit, nous, potentiality, power, proficiency, qualification, savoir-faire, savvy, skill, strength, talent, touch.

antonyms inability, incompetence.

abject *adj.* base, contemptible, cringing, debased, degenerate, degraded, deplorable, despicable, dishonorable, execrable, fawning, forlorn, groveling, hopeless, humiliating, ignoble, ignominious, low, mean, miserable, outcast, pathetic, pitiable, servile, slavish, sordid, submissive, vile, worthless, wretched.

antonym exalted.

able *adj.* accomplished, adept, adequate, adroit, capable, clever, competent, deft, dexterous, effective, efficient, experienced, expert, fit, fitted, gifted, ingenious, masterful, masterly, powerful, practiced, proficient, qualified, skilful, skilled, strong, talented.

antonyms incapable, incompetent.

able-bodied *adj.* firm, fit, hale, hardy, healthy, hearty, lusty, powerful, robust, sound, stalwart, staunch, stout, strapping, strong, sturdy, tough, vigorous.

antonyms delicate, infirm.

abnegation *n.* abandonment, abjuration, abstinence, acquiescence, continence, disallowance, eschewal, forbearance, giving up, refusal, rejection, relinquishment, renunciation, sacrifice, self-denial, submission, surrender, temperance.

antonyms acceptance, support.

abnormal *adj.* aberrant, anomalous, atypical, curious, deviant, different, divergent, eccentric, erratic, exceptional, extraordinary, irregular, monstrous, odd, paranormal, peculiar, queer, singular, strange, uncanny, uncommon, unexpected, unnatural, untypical, unusual, wayward, weird.

antonyms normal, straight.

abode *n.* domicile, dwelling, dwelling-place, habitat,

habitation, home, house, lodging, pad, place, quarters, residence.

abolish v. abrogate, annihilate, annul, blot out, cancel, destroy, do away with, eliminate, end, eradicate, expunge, exterminate, extinguish, extirpate, get rid of, invalidate, kibosh, nullify, obliterate, overthrow, overturn, put an end to, put the kibosh on, quash, repeal, repudiate, rescind, revoke, sink, stamp out, subvert, suppress, terminate, vitiate, void, wipe out.
antonyms continue, retain.

abolition n. abolishment, abrogation, annihilation, annulment, cancellation, destruction, dissolution, elimination, end, ending, eradication, expunction, extermination, extinction, extirpation, invalidation, nullification, obliteration, overthrow, overturning, quashing, repeal, repudiation, rescission, revocation, subversion, suppression, termination, vitiation, voiding, withdrawal.
antonyms continuance, retention.

abominable adj. abhorrent, accursed, appalling, atrocious, base, beastly, contemptible, despicable, detestable, disgusting, execrable, foul, hateful, heinous, hellish, horrible, horrid, loathsome, nauseating, nauseous, nefast, obnoxious, odious, repellent, reprehensible, repugnant, repulsive, revolting, terrible, vile, villainous, wretched.
antonyms delightful, desirable.

abomination n. abhorrence, anathema, animosity, animus, antipathy, aversion, bête noire, bugbear, curse, detestation, disgrace, disgust, distaste, evil, execration, hate, hatred, horror, hostility, loathing, odium, offence, plague, repugnance, revulsion, torment.
antonyms adoration, delight.

abort v. arrest, call off, check, end, fail, frustrate, halt, miscarry, nullify, stop, terminate, thwart.
antonym continue.

abortion n. aborticide, disappointment, failure, feticide, fiasco, freak, frustration, misadventure, misbirth, miscarriage, monster, monstrosity, termination, thwarting.
antonyms continuation, success.

abortive adj. barren, bootless, failed, failing, fruitless, futile, idle, ineffective, ineffectual, misborn, miscarried, sterile, unavailing, unproductive, unsuccessful, useless, vain.
antonym successful.

abound v. be plentiful, brim over, crowd, exuberate, flourish, increase, infest, luxuriate, overflow, proliferate, run riot, superabound, swarm, swell, teem, thrive.
antonym be in short supply.

about prep. adjacent to, all over, anent, around, as regards, beside, busy with, circa, close to, concerned with, concerning, connected with, encircling, encompassing, engaged on, in respect to, in the matter of, near, nearby, on, over, re, referring to, regarding, relating to, relative to, respecting, round, surrounding, through, throughout, touching, with reference to, with regard to, with respect to.
adv. active, almost, approaching, approximately, around, astir, close to, from place to place, here and there, hither and thither, in motion, in the region of, more or less, nearing, nearly, present, roughly, stirring, to and fro.

about-turn n. about-face, apostasy, backtrack, enantiod-romia, reversal, right-about (face), switch, turnabout, turn(a)round, U-turn, volte-face.

above prep. atop, before, beyond, exceeding, higher than, in excess of, on top of, over, prior to, superior to, surpassing, upon.
antonyms below, under.
adv. aloft, atop, earlier, heavenwards, in heaven, on high, overhead, supra.
antonym below.
adj. above-mentioned, above-stated, aforementioned, aforesaid, earlier, foregoing, preceding, previous, prior.

above-board adj. candid, fair, fair and square, forthright, frank, guileless, honest, honorable, legitimate, on the level, open, overt, reputable, square, straight, straightforward, true, trustworthy, truthful, upright, veracious.
antonyms shady, underhand.

abrasion n. abrading, chafe, chafing, erosion, friction, grating, graze, grinding, levigation, rubbing, scouring, scrape, scraping, scratch, scratching, scuff, scuffing, trituration, wearing away, wearing down.

abrasive adj. abradant, annoying, attritional, biting, caustic, chafing, erodent, erosive, frictional, galling, grating, hurtful, irritating, nasty, rough, scraping, scratching, scratchy, scuffing, sharp, unpleasant.
antonyms pleasant, smooth.

abreast adj. acquainted, au courant, au fait, conversant, familiar, in the picture, in touch, informed, knowledgeable, on the ball, up to date.
antonyms out of touch, unaware.

abridge v. abbreviate, abstract, circumscribe, clip, compress, concentrate, condense, contract, curtail, cut, cut down, decrease, digest, diminish, dock, epitomize, lessen, lop, précis, prune, reduce, shorten, summarize, synopsize, trim, truncate.
antonyms amplify, pad.

abridgment n. abbreviation, abrégé, abstract, compendium, compression, concentration, condensation, conspectus, contraction, curtailment, cutting, decrease, digest, diminishing, diminution, epitome, lessening, limitation, outline, précis, pruning, reduction, restriction, résumé, shortening, summary, synopsis, truncation.
antonyms expansion, padding.

abroad adv. about, at large, away, circulating, current, elsewhere, extensively, far, far and wide, forth, in circulation, in foreign parts, out, out of the country, out-of-doors, outside, overseas, publicly, widely.

abrupt adj. blunt, brief, brisk, broken, brusque, curt, direct, disconnected, discontinuous, discourteous, gruff, hasty, headlong, hurried, impolite, irregular, jerky, precipitate, precipitous, prerupt, quick, rapid, rough, rude, sharp, sheer, short, snappy, steep, sudden, surprising, swift, terse, unannounced, unceremonious, uncivil, uneven, unexpected, unforeseen, ungracious.
antonyms ceremonious, expansive, leisurely.

abscond v. absquatulate, beat it, bolt, clear out, decamp, disappear, do a bunk, escape, flee, flit, fly, hightail it, make off, quit, run off, scram, skedaddle, skip, take French leave, vamoose.

absence n. absenteeism, absent-mindedness, abstraction, dearth, default, defect, deficiency, distraction, inattention, lack, need, non-appearance, non-attendance, non-existence, omission, paucity, preoccupation, privation, reverie, scarcity, truancy, unavailability, vacancy, vacuity, want.

antonyms existence, presence.

absent *adj.* absent-minded, absorbed, abstracted, away, bemused, blank, day-dreaming, distracted, distrait(e), dreamy, elsewhere, empty, faraway, gone, heedless, inattentive, lacking, missing, musing, non-existent, not present, oblivious, out, preoccupied, truant, unavailable, unaware, unconscious, unheeding, unthinking, vacant, vague, wanting, withdrawn, wool-gathering.

antonyms aware, present.

absent-minded *adj.* absent, absorbed, abstracted, bemused, distracted, distrait(e), dreaming, dreamy, engrossed, faraway, forgetful, heedless, impractical, inattentive, musing, oblivious, otherwordly, pensive, preoccupied, scatterbrained, unaware, unconscious, unheeding, unthinking, withdrawn, wool-gathering.

antonyms matter-of-fact, attentive, practical.

absolute *adj.* absolutist, actual, almighty, arbitrary, autarchical, autocratic, autonomous, categorical, certain, complete, conclusive, consummate, decided, decisive, definite, definitive, despotic, dictatorial, downright, entire, exact, exhaustive, final, flawless, free, full, genuine, independent, indubitable, infallible, omnipotent, out-and-out, outright, peremptory, perfect, positive, precise, pure, sheer, sovereign, supreme, sure, terminative, thorough, total, totalitarian, tyrannical, unadulterated, unalloyed, unambiguous, unbounded, unconditional, uncontrolled, undivided, unequivocal, unlimited, unmitigated, unmixed, unqualified, unquestionable, unrestrained, unrestricted, utter.

antonyms conditional, partial.

absolutely *adv.* actually, arbitrarily, autocratically, autonomously, bang, categorically, certainly, completely, conclusively, consummately, dead, decidedly, decisively, definitely, despotically, diametrically, dictatorially, entirely, exactly, exhaustively, finally, fully, genuinely, indubitably, infallibly, peremptorily, perfectly, positively, precisely, purely, sovereignly, supremely, surely, thoroughly, totally, truly, tyrannically, unambiguously, unconditionally, unequivocally, unmitigatedly, unquestionably, unrestrainedly, utterly, wholly.

absolution *n.* acquittal, acquittance, amnesty, compurgation, deliverance, discharge, dispensation, emancipation, exculpation, exemption, exoneration, forgiveness, forgiving, freeing, indulgence, liberation, mercy, pardon, purgation, redemption, release, remission, shriving, vindication.

antonym condemnation.

absolve *v.* acquit, clear, deliver, discharge, emancipate, exculpate, excuse, exempt, exonerate, forgive, free, justify, let off, liberate, loose, pardon, ransom, redeem, release, remit, set free, shrive, vindicate.

antonym charge.

absorb *v.* apprehend, assimilate, captivate, consume, co-opt, devour, digest, drink in, engage, engross, engulf, enthral(l), enwrap, exhaust, fascinate, fill (up), fix, grip, hold, imbibe, immerse, incorporate, ingest, involve, monopolize, occupy, osmose, preoccupy, receive, retain, rivet, soak up, sorb, submerge, suck up, take in, understand, utilize.

antonyms dissipate, exude.

absorbing *adj.* amusing, arresting, captivating, compulsive, diverting, engrossing, entertaining, enthralling, fascinating, gripping, interesting, intriguing, preoccupying, riveting, spellbinding, unputdownable.

antonyms boring, off-putting.

abstain *v.* avoid, cease, decline, deny, desist, eschew, forbear, forgo, give up, keep from, refrain, refuse, reject, renounce, resist, shun, stop, swear off, withhold.

antonym indulge.

abstemious *adj.* abstinent, ascetic, austere, continent, disciplined, frugal, moderate, restrained, self-denying, self-disciplined, sober, sparing, temperate.

antonyms gluttonous, intemperate, luxurious.

abstinence *n.* abstemiousness, abstinency, asceticism, avoidance, continence, forbearance, frugality, moderation, nephalism, non-indulgence, refraining, self-denial, self-discipline, self-restraint, soberness, sobriety, teetotalism, temperance.

antonym self-indulgence.

abstract *adj.* abstruse, academic, arcane, complex, conceptual, deep, discrete, general, generalized, hypothetical, indefinite, intellectual, metaphysical, non-concrete, occult, philosophical, profound, recondite, separate, subtle, theoretic, theoretical, unpractical, unrealistic.

antonym concrete.

n. abbreviation, abridgment, abstractive, compendium, compression, condensation, conspectus, digest, epitome, essence, outline, précis, recapitulation, résumé, summary, synopsis.

v. abbreviate, abridge, compress, condense, detach, digest, dissociate, epitomize, extract, isolate, outline, précis, purloin, remove, separate, shorten, steal, summarize, withdraw.

antonyms expand, insert.

abstraction *n.* absence, absent-mindedness, absorption, bemusedness, concept, conception, dissociation, distraction, dream, dreaminess, formula, generalization, generality, hypothesis, idea, inattention, notion, pensiveness, preoccupation, remoteness, separation, theorem, theory, thought, withdrawal, wool-gathering.

abstruse *adj.* abstract, arcane, complex, cryptic, dark, deep, devious, difficult, enigmatic, esoteric, hermetic, hidden, incomprehensible, mysterious, mystical, obscure, occult, perplexing, profound, puzzling, recondite, subtle, tortuous, unfathomable, unobvious, vague.

antonyms concrete, obvious.

absurd *adj.* anomalous, comical, crazy, daft, derisory, fantastic, farcical, foolish, funny, humorous, idiotic, illogical, implausible, incongruous, irrational, laughable, ludicrous, meaningless, nonsensical, paradoxical, preposterous, ridiculous, risible, senseless, silly, stupid, unreasonable, untenable.

antonyms logical, rational, sensible.

absurdity *n.* comicality, craziness, daftness, farce, farcicality, farcicalness, fatuity, fatuousness, folly, foolery, foolishness, idiocy, illogicality, illogicalness, incongruity, irrationality, joke, ludicrousness, meaninglessness, nonsense, nonsensicality, preposterousness, ridiculousness, senselessness, silliness, stupidity, unreasonableness.

abundance *n.* affluence, ampleness, amplitude, bonanza, bounty, copiousness, exuberance, fortune, fullness, glut, heap, lavishness, luxuriance, luxuriancy, milk and

honey, munificence, oodles, opulence, plenitude, plenteousness, plenty, pleroma, plethora, prodigality, profusion, riches, richness, scads, uberty, wealth.
antonyms dearth, scarcity.

abundant *adj.* ample, bounteous, bountiful, copious, exuberant, filled, full, generous, in plenty, lavish, luxuriant, overflowing, plenteous, plentiful, prodigal, profuse, rank, rich, superabundant, teeming, uberous, unstinted, well-provided, well-supplied.
antonyms scarce, sparse.

abuse *v.* batter, calumniate, castigate, curse, damage, deceive, defame, denigrate, disparage, exploit, harm, hurt, ill-treat, impose on, injure, insult, inveigh against, libel, malign, maltreat, manhandle, mar, misapply, miscall, misemploy, misuse, molest, objurgate, oppress, oppugn, revile, scold, slander, slate, smear, spoil, swear at, take advantage of, traduce, upbraid, vilify, violate, vituperate, wrong.
antonyms cherish, compliment, praise.

n. affront, blame, calumniation, calumny, castigation, censure, contumely, curses, cursing, damage, defamation, denigration, derision, diatribe, disparagement, execration, exploitation, flyting, harm, hurt, ill-treatment, imposition, injury, insults, invective, libel, malediction, maltreatment, manhandling, misapplication, misconduct, misdeed, misuse, obloquy, offence, oppression, opprobrium, reproach, revilement, scolding, sin, slander, spoiling, swearing, tirade, traducement, upbraiding, vilification, violation, vitriol, vituperation, wrong, wrong-doing.
antonyms attention, care.

abusive *adj.* brutal, calumniating, calumnious, castigating, censorious, contumelious, cruel, defamatory, denigrating, derisive, derogatory, destructive, disparaging, harmful, hurtful, injurious, insulting, invective, libellous, maligning, objurgatory, offensive, opprobrious, pejorative, reproachful, reviling, rough, rude, scathing, scolding, slanderous, traducing, upbraiding, vilifying, vituperative.
antonym complimentary.

abysmal *adj.* abyssal, bottomless, boundless, complete, deep, endless, extreme, immeasurable, incalculable, infinite, profound, thorough, unending, unfathomable, vast, yawning.

academic *adj.* abstract, bookish, collegiate, conjectural, donnish, educational, erudite, highbrow, hypothetical, impractical, instructional, learned, lettered, literary, notional, pedagogical, scholarly, scholastic, speculative, studious, theoretical, well-read.

n. academe, academician, don, fellow, lecturer, man of letters, master, pedant, professor, pundit, savant, scholar, scholastic, schoolman, student, tutor.

accede *v.* accept, acquiesce, admit, agree, assent, assume, attain, capitulate, comply, concede, concur, consent, defer, endorse, grant, inherit, submit, succeed (to), yield.
antonyms demur, object.

accelerate *v.* advance, antedate, dispatch, expedite, facilitate, festinate, forward, further, hasten, hurry, pick up speed, precipitate, promote, quicken, speed, speed up, spur, step on the gas, step on the juice, step up, stimulate.
antonyms delay, slow down.

accent *n.* accentuation, arsis, articulation, beat, cadence, emphasis, enunciation, force, ictus, inflection, inten-

sity, intonation, modulation, pitch, pronunciation, pulsation, pulse, rhythm, stress, thesis, timbre, tonality, tone.

v. accentuate, emphasize, stress, underline, underscore.

accept *v.* abide by, accede, acknowledge, acquiesce, acquire, admit, adopt, affirm, agree to, approve, assume, avow, bear, believe, bow to, brook, concur with, consent to, co-operate with, defer to, gain, get, have, jump at, obtain, put up with, receive, recognize, secure, stand, stomach, submit to, suffer, swallow, take, take on, tolerate, undertake, wear, yield to.
antonyms demur, reject.

acceptable *adj.* adequate, admissible, agreeable, all right, conventional, correct, delightful, desirable, done, grateful, gratifying, moderate, passable, pleasant, pleasing, satisfactory, standard, suitable, tolerable, unexceptionable, unobjectionable, welcome.
antonyms unsatisfactory, unwelcome.

access *n.* adit, admission, admittance, approach, avenue, course, door, entering, entrance, entrée, entry, gateway, increase, ingress, key, onset, passage, passageway, path, road, upsurge, upsurgence.
antonyms egress, outlet.

accessible *adj.* achievable, affable, approachable, at hand, attainable, available, come-at-able, conversable, cordial, exposed, friendly, get-at-able, handy, informal, liable, near, nearby, obtainable, on hand, open, possible, procurable, reachable, ready, sociable, subject, susceptible, vulnerable, wide-open.
antonym inaccessible.

accessory *n.* abettor, accompaniment, accomplice, addition, adjunct, adjuvant, adornment, aid, appendage, assistant, associate, attachment, colleague, component, confederate, conniver, convenience, decoration, embellishment, extension, extra, frill, help, helper, particeps criminis, partner, supplement, trim, trimming.

adj. abetting, additional, adjuvant, adventitious, aiding, ancillary, assisting, auxiliary, contributory, extra, incidental, secondary, subordinate, subsidiary, supplemental, supplementary.

accident *n.* blow, calamity, casualty, chance, collision, contingency, contretemps, crash, disaster, fate, fluke, fortuity, fortune, happenstance, hazard, luck, misadventure, miscarriage, mischance, misfortune, mishap, pile-up, prang, serendipity, shunt.

accidental *adj.* adventitious, adventive, casual, chance, contingent, fluky, fortuitous, haphazard, inadvertent, incidental, random, serendipitous, unanticipated, uncalculated, uncertain, unexpected, unforeseen, unintended, unintentional, unlooked-for, unplanned, unpremeditated, unwitting.
antonyms intentional, premeditated.

acclaim *v.* announce, applaud, approve, celebrate, cheer, clap, commend, crown, declare, eulogize, exalt, extol, hail, honor, laud, praise, salute, welcome.
antonym demean.

n. acclamation, applause, approbation, approval, celebration, cheering, clapping, commendation, eulogizing, eulogy, exaltation, honor, laudation, ovation, plaudits, praise, welcome.
antonyms brickbats, criticism, vituperation.

accommodate *v.* acclimatize, accustom, adapt, adjust, afford, aid, assist, attune, billet, board, cater for, comply, compose, conform, domicile, entertain, fit, furnish, harbor, harmonize, help, house, lodge, modify, oblige, provide, put up, quarter, reconcile, serve, settle, shelter, supply.

accommodating *adj.* complaisant, considerate, co-operative, friendly, helpful, hospitable, indulgent, kind, obliging, polite, sympathetic, unselfish, willing.
antonym disobliging.

accommodation[1] *n.* adaptation, adjustment, assistance, compliance, composition, compromise, conformity, fitting, harmonization, harmony, help, modification, reconciliation, settlement.

accommodation[2] *n.* bed and breakfast, billet, board, digs, domicile, dwelling, harboring, house, housing, lodgings, quartering, quarters, residence, shelter, sheltering.

accompany *v.* attend, belong to, chaperon, co-exist, coincide, complement, conduct, consort, convoy, escort, follow, go with, occur with, squire, supplement, usher.

accomplice *n.* abettor, accessory, ally, assistant, associate, coadjutor, collaborator, colleague, confederate, conspirator, helper, helpmate, henchman, mate, particeps criminis, participator, partner, practisant.

accomplish *v.* achieve, attain, bring about, bring off, carry out, compass, complete, conclude, consummate, discharge, do, effect, effectuate, engineer, execute, finish, fulfil, manage, obtain, perform, produce, realize.

accomplished *adj.* adept, adroit, consummate, cultivated, expert, facile, gifted, masterly, polished, practiced, professional, proficient, skilful, skilled, talented.
antonym inexpert.

accomplishment *n.* ability, achievement, act, aptitude, art, attainment, capability, carrying out, completion, conclusion, consummation, coup, deed, discharge, doing, effecting, execution, exploit, faculty, feat, finishing, forte, fruition, fulfilment, futurition, gift, management, perfection, performance, production, proficiency, realization, skill, stroke, talent, triumph.

accord *v.* agree, allow, assent, bestow, concede, concur, confer, conform, correspond, endow, fit, give, grant, harmonize, jibe, match, present, render, suit, tally, tender, vouchsafe.
antonym disagree.

n. accordance, agreement, assent, concert, concurrence, conformity, congruence, congruity, consort, correspondence, harmony, rapport, symmetry, sympathy, unanimity, unity.
antonym discord.

accordingly *adv.* appropriately, as a result, as requested, consequently, correspondingly, ergo, fitly, hence, in accord with, in accordance, in consequence, properly, so, suitably, therefore, thus.

according to after, after the manner of, agreeably to, commensurate with, consistent with, in accordance with, in compliance with, in conformity with, in keeping with, in line with, in obedience to, in proportion, in relation, in the light of, in the manner of, obedient to.

account[1] *n.* advantage, basis, benefit, cause, chronicle, communiqué, concern, consequence, consideration, description, detail, distinction, esteem, estimation, explanation, ground, grounds, history, honor, import, importance, interest, memoir, merit, motive, narration, narrative, note, performance, portrayal, presentation, profit, rank, reason, recital, reckoning, record, regard,

relation, report, reputation, repute, sake, score, significance, sketch, standing, statement, story, tale, use, value, version, worth, write-up.

v. adjudge, appraise, assess, believe, consider, count, deem, esteem, estimate, explain, gauge, hold, judge, rate, reckon, regard, think, value, weigh.

account for answer for, clarify, clear up, destroy, elucidate, explain, illuminate, incapacitate, justify, kill, put paid to, rationalize, vindicate.

account[2] *n.* balance, bill, book, books, charge, check, computation, inventory, invoice, journal, ledger, reckoning, register, score, statement, tab, tally, tick.

accountable *adj.* amenable, answerable, blamable, bound, charged with, liable, obligated, obliged, responsible.

accredit *v.* appoint, approve, ascribe, assign, attribute, authorize, certificate, certify, commission, credit, depute, empower, enable, endorse, entrust, guarantee, license, okay, qualify, recognize, sanction, vouch for.

accrue *v.* accumulate, amass, arise, be added, build up, collect, emanate, enlarge, ensue, fall due, flow, follow, gather, grow, increase, issue, proceed, redound, result, spring up.

accumulate *v.* accrue, agglomerate, aggregate, amass, assemble, build up, collect, cumulate, gather, grow, hoard, increase, multiply, pile up, stash, stockpile, store.
antonyms diffuse, disseminate.

accumulation *n.* accretion, aggregation, assemblage, augmentation, backlog, build-up, collection, conglomeration, gathering, growth, heap, hoard, increase, mass, pile, reserve, stack, stock, stockpile, store.

accurate *adj.* authentic, careful, close, correct, exact, factual, faithful, faultless, just, letter-perfect, mathematical, meticulous, minute, nice, perfect, precise, proper, regular, right, rigorous, scrupulous, sound, spot-on, strict, true, truthful, unerring, veracious, veridical, well-aimed, well-directed, well-judged, word-perfect.
antonyms inaccurate, wrong.

accursed *adj.* abominable, anathematized, bedeviled, bewitched, blighted, condemned, cursed, damned, despicable, detestable, doomed, execrable, foredoomed, hateful, hellish, hopeless, horrible, ill-fated, ill-omened, jinxed, luckless, ruined, star-crossed, undone, unfortunate, unholy, unlucky, wretched.
antonym blessed.

accusation *n.* accusal, allegation, arraignment, attribution, charge, citation, complaint, crimination, delation, denunciation, gravamen, impeachment, imputation, incrimination, indictment, plaint, recrimination.

accuse *v.* allege, arraign, attaint, attribute, blame, censure, charge, cite, criminate, delate, denounce, impeach, impugn, impute, incriminate, indict, inform against, recriminate, tax.

accustom *v.* acclimatize, acculturate, acquaint, adapt, adjust, discipline, exercise, familiarize, habituate, harden, inure, season, train.

ache *v.* agonize, covet, crave, desire, grieve, hanker, hunger, hurt, itch, long, mourn, need, pain, pine, pound, rack, smart, sorrow, suffer, throb, twinge, yearn.

n. anguish, craving, desire, grief, hankering, hunger, hurt, itch, longing, misery, mourning, need, pain, pang, pining, pounding, smart, smarting, soreness, sorrow, suffering, throb, throbbing, yearning.

achieve *v.* accomplish, acquire, attain, bring about, carry out, compass, complete, consummate, do, earn, effect, effectuate, execute, finish, fulfil, gain, get, manage, obtain, perform, procure, produce, reach, realize, score, strike, succeed, win.

antonyms fail, miss.

achievement *n.* accomplishment, acquirement, act, attainment, completion, deed, effort, execution, exploit, feat, fruition, fulfilment, magnum opus, performance, production, qualification, realization, stroke, success.

acid *adj.* acerbic, acidulous, acrid, astringent, biting, bitter, caustic, corrosive, cutting, harsh, hurtful, ill-natured, incisive, mordant, morose, pungent, sharp, sour, stinging, tart, trenchant, vinegarish, vinegary, vitriolic.

acid test crucial test, touchstone, verification.

acknowledge *v.* accede, accept, acquiesce, address, admit, affirm, agree to, allow, answer, attest, avouch, concede, confess, confirm, declare, endorse, grant, greet, hail, notice, own, profess, react to, recognize, reply to, respond to, return, salute, vouch for, witness, yield.

acme *n.* apex, apogee, climax, crest, crown, culmination, height, high point, maximum, optimum, peak, pinnacle, sublimation, sublimity, summit, top, vertex, zenith.

antonym nadir.

acquaint *v.* accustom, advise, announce, apprize, brief, disclose, divulge, enlighten, familiarize, inform, notify, reveal, tell.

acquaintance *n.* associate, association, awareness, chum, cognizance, colleague, companionship, confrère, consociate, contact, conversance, conversancy, experience, familiarity, fellowship, intimacy, knowledge, relationship, understanding.

acquiesce *v.* accede, accept, agree, allow, approve, assent, comply, concur, conform, consent, defer, give in, submit, yield.

antonyms disagree, object.

acquire *v.* achieve, amass, appropriate, attain, buy, collect, cop, earn, gain, gather, get, net, obtain, pick up, procure, realize, receive, secure, win.

antonyms forfeit, forgo, relinquish.

acquirements *n.* accomplishments, achievements, acquisitions, attainments, attributes, culture, erudition, knowledge, learning, mastery, qualifications, skills.

acquisition *n.* accession, achievement, acquest, acquirement, appropriation, attainment, buy, gain, gaining, learning, obtainment, possession, prize, procurement, property, purchase, pursuit, securing, take-over.

acquisitive *adj.* avaricious, avid, covetous, grabbing, grasping, greedy, insatiable, mercenary, possessive, predatory, rapacious, voracious.

antonym generous.

acquit *v.* absolve, bear, behave, clear, comport, conduct, deliver, discharge, dismiss, exculpate, excuse, exonerate, free, fulfil, liberate, pay, pay off, perform, release, relieve, repay, reprieve, satisfy, settle, vindicate.

antonym convict.

acrid *adj.* acerbic, acid, acrimonious, astringent, biting, bitter, burning, caustic, cutting, harsh, incisive, irritating, malicious, mordant, nasty, pungent, sarcastic, sardonic, sharp, stinging, tart, trenchant, venomous, virulent, vitriolic.

acrimonious *adj.* abusive, acerbic, astringent, atrabilious, biting, bitter, caustic, censorious, churlish, crabbed, cutting, ill-tempered, irascible, mordant, peevish, petulant, pungent, rancorous, sarcastic, severe, sharp, spiteful, splenetic, tart, testy, trenchant, virulent, waspish.

antonyms irenic, kindly, peaceable.

acrobat *n.* aerialist, balancer, contortionist, equilibrist, funambulist, gymnast, somersaulter, stunt-girl, stuntman, tumbler, voltigeur.

act *n.* accomplishment, achievement, action, affectation, attitude, bill, blow, counterfeit, decree, deed, dissimulation, doing, edict, enactment, enterprise, execution, exertion, exploit, fake, feat, feigning, front, gest, gig, law, make-believe, maneuver, measure, move, operation, ordinance, performance, pose, posture, pretense, proceeding, resolution, routine, sham, show, sketch, spiel, stance, statute, step, stroke, transaction, turn, undertaking.

v. acquit, act out, affect, assume, bear, behave, carry, carry out, characterize, comport, conduct, counterfeit, dissimulate, do, enact, execute, exert, feign, function, go about, imitate, impersonate, make, mime, mimic, move, operate, perform, personate, personify, play, portray, pose, posture, pretend, put on, react, represent, seem, serve, sham, simulate, strike, take effect, undertake, work.

act up carry on, cause trouble, give bother, give trouble, horse around, make waves, malfunction, mess about, misbehave, muck about, play up, rock the boat.

act (up)on affect, alter, carry out, change, comply with, conform to, execute, follow, fulfil, heed, influence, modify, obey, sway, transform, yield to.

acting *adj.* interim, pro tem, provisional, reserve, standby, stop-gap, substitute, supply, surrogate, temporary. *n.* affectation, assuming, bluff, characterization, counterfeiting, dissimulation, dramatics, enacting, feigning, histrionicism, histrionics, histrionism, imitating, imitation, impersonation, imposture, melodrama, performance, performing, play-acting, playing, portrayal, portraying, posing, posturing, pretense, pretending, putting on, seeming, shamming, stagecraft, theatre, theatricals.

action *n.* accomplishment, achievement, act, activity, affray, agency, battle, case, cause, clash, combat, conflict, contest, deed, effect, effort, encounter, endeavor, energy, engagement, enterprise, exercise, exertion, exploit, feat, fight, fighting, force, fray, functioning, influence, lawsuit, litigation, liveliness, mechanism, motion, move, movement, operation, performance, power, proceeding, process, prosecution, skirmish, sortie, spirit, stop, stroke, suit, undertaking, vigor, vim, vitality, warfare, work, working, works.

actions *n.* address, air, bearing, behavior, comportment, conduct, demeanor, deportment, manners, mien, port, ways.

activate *v.* actuate, animate, arouse, bestir, energize, excite, fire, galvanize, impel, initiate, mobilize, motivate, move, prompt, propel, rouse, set in motion, set off, start, stimulate, stir, switch on, trigger.

antonyms arrest, deactivate, stop.

active *adj.* acting, activist, aggressive, agile, alert, ambitious, animated, assertive, assiduous, astir, bustling, busy, committed, deedy, devoted, diligent, doing, effectual, energetic, engaged, enterprising, enthusiastic, forceful, forward, full, functioning, hard-working, in force, in operation, industrious, involved, light-footed, live, lively, militant, moving, nimble, occupied, on the go, on the move, operate, quick, running, sedulous, spirited, sprightly, spry, stirabout, stirring, strenuous, through-going, vibrant, vigorous, vital, vivacious, working, zealous.

antonyms dormant, inactive, inert, passive.

activity *n.* act, action, activeness, animation, avocation, bustle, commotion, deed, endeavor, enterprise, exercise, exertion, hobby, hurly-burly, hustle, industry, interest, job, kerfuffle, labor, life, liveliness, motion, movement, occupation, pastime, project, pursuit, scheme, stir, task, undertaking, venture, work.

actor *n.* actress, agent, artist, comedian, doer, executor, factor, functionary, guiser, ham, hamfatter, histrio, histrion, impersonator, masquerader, mime, mummer, operative, operator, participant, participator, performer, perpetrator, personator, play-actor, player, practitioner, Roscius, Thespian, tragedian, trouper, worker.

actual *adj.* absolute, authentic, bona fide, categorical, certain, concrete, confirmed, corporeal, current, de facto, definite, existent, extant, factual, genuine, indisputable, indubitable, legitimate, live, living, material, physical, positive, present, present-day, prevailing, real, realistic, substantial, tangible, thingy, true, truthful, unquestionable, verified, veritable.

antonyms apparent, imaginary, theoretical.

actuality *n.* corporeality, fact, factuality, historicity, materiality, reality, realness, substance, substantiality, truth, verity.

acute[1] *adj.* astute, canny, clever, critical, crucial, cutting, dangerous, decisive, discerning, discriminating, distressing, essential, excruciating, exquisite, extreme, fierce, grave, important, incisive, ingenious, insightful, intense, intuitive, judicious, keen, lancinating, observant, overpowering, overwhelming, penetrating, perceptive, percipient, perspicacious, piercing, poignant, pointed, powerful, racking, sagacious, sapient, sensitive, serious, severe, sharp, shooting, shrewd, shrill, smart, stabbing, subtle, sudden, urgent, violent, vital.

antonyms chronic, mild, obtuse.

acute[2] *adj.* acicular, apiculate, cuspate, cuspidate, needle-shaped, peaked, pointed, sharp, sharpened.

antonym obtuse.

adamant *adj.* adamantine, determined, firm, fixed, flinty, hard, immovable, impenetrable, indestructible, inexorable, inflexible, infrangible, insistent, intransigent, obdurate, resolute, rigid, rock-like, rocky, set, steely, stiff, stony, stubborn, tough, unbending, unbreakable, uncompromising, unrelenting, unshakable, unyielding.

antonyms flexible, pliant, yielding.

adapt *v.* acclimatize, accommodate, adjust, alter, apply, attemper, change, comply, conform, contemper, convert, customize, familiarize, fashion, fit, habituate, harmonize, match, metamorphose, modify, prepare, proportion, qualify, refashion, remodel, shape, suit, tailor.

add *v.* adjoin, affix, amplify, annex, append, attach, augment, combine, compute, count, include, join, reckon, subjoin, sum up, superimpose, supplement, tack on, tot up, total.

antonym subtract.

add up add, amount, be consistent, be plausible, be reasonable, come to, compute, count, count up, hang together, hold water, imply, indicate, make sense, mean, reckon, reveal, ring true, signify, stand to reason, sum up, tally, tot up, total.

addict *n.* acid-head, adherent, buff, devotee, dope-fiend, enthusiast, fan, fiend, follower, freak, head, hop-head, junkie, mainliner, nut, pot-head, tripper, user.

address[1] *n.* abode, department, direction, domicile, dwelling, home, house, inscription, location, lodging, place, residence, situation, superscription, whereabouts.

address[2] *n.* adroitness, air, allocution, application, art, bearing, declamation, deftness, dexterity, discourse, discretion, dispatch, disquisition, dissertation, expedition, expertise, expertness, facility, harangue, ingenuity, lecture, manner, oration, sermon, skilfulness, skill, speech, tact, talk.

v. accost, address (oneself) to, apostrophize, apply (oneself) to, approach, attend to, bespeak, button-hole, concentrate on, devote (oneself) to, discourse, engage in, focus on, greet, hail, harangue, invoke, lecture, orate, salute, sermonize, speak, speak to, take care of, talk, talk to, turn to, undertake.

adept *adj.* able, accomplished, ace, adroit, deft, dexterous, experienced, expert, masterful, masterly, nimble, polished, practiced, proficient, skilful, skilled, versed.

antonyms bungling, incompetent, inept.

n. ace, dab hand, dabster, deacon, don, expert, genius, maestro, mahatma, master, old hand, pastmaster, wizard.

antonyms bungler, incompetent.

adequate *adj.* able, acceptable, capable, commensurate, competent, condign, efficacious, enough, fair, fit, passable, presentable, requisite, respectable, satisfactory, serviceable, sufficient, suitable, tolerable.

antonyms inadequate, insufficient.

adhere *v.* abide by, accrete, agree, attach, cement, cleave, cleave to, cling, coalesce, cohere, combine, comply with, fasten, fix, follow, fulfil, glue, heed, hold, hold fast, join, keep, link, maintain, mind, obey, observe, paste, respect, stand by, stick, stick fast, support, unite.

adherent *n.* admirer, advocate, aficionado, devotee, disciple, enthusiast, fan, follower, freak, hanger-on, henchman, nut, partisan, satellite, sectary, supporter, upholder, votary.

adhesive *adj.* adherent, adhering, attaching, clinging, cohesive, emplastic, gluey, glutinous, gummy, holding, mucilaginous, sticking, sticky, tacky, tenacious.

n. cement, glue, gum, mountant, mucilage, paste, tape.

adjacent *adj.* abutting, adjoining, alongside, beside, bordering, close, conterminant, conterminate, conterminous, contiguous, juxtaposed, near, neighboring, next, proximate, touching, vicinal.

adjoin *v.* abut, add, affix, annex, append, approximate, attach, border, combine, communicate with, connect, couple, impinge, interconnect, join, juxtapose, link, meet, neighbor, touch, unite, verge.

adjourn *v.* continue, defer, delay, discontinue, interrupt, postpone, prorogue, put off, recess, stay, suspend.

antonym convene.

adjust *v.* acclimatize, accommodate, accustom, adapt, alter, arrange, balance, change, coapt, compose, concert, conform, convert, dispose, fine-tune, fit, fix, har-

monize, jiggle, measure, modify, order, proportion, reconcile, rectify, redress, refashion, regulate, remodel, reshape, set, settle, shape, square, suit, temper, tune.
antonyms derange, disarrange, upset.

administer *v.* adhibit, apply, assign, conduct, contribute, control, direct, disburse, dispense, dispose, distribute, dole out, execute, give, govern, head, impose, lead, manage, measure out, mete out, officiate, organize, oversee, perform, preside over, provide, regulate, rule, run, superintend, supervise, supply.

administration *n.* adhibition, administering, application, conduct, control, direction, directorship, disbursement, dispensation, disposal, distribution, execution, executive, governing, governing body, government, leadership, management, ministry, organization, overseeing, performance, provision, regime, regulation, rule, ruling, running, settlement, superintendence, supervision, supply, term of office.

admirable *adj.* choice, commendable, creditable, deserving, estimable, excellent, exquisite, fine, laudable, meritorious, praiseworthy, rare, respected, superior, valuable, wonderful, worthy.
antonym despicable.

admiration *n.* adoration, affection, amazement, appreciation, approbation, approval, astonishment, awe, delight, esteem, fureur, idolism, pleasure, praise, regard, respect, reverence, surprise, veneration, wonder, wonderment, worship.
antonym contempt.

admire *v.* adore, applaud, appreciate, approve, esteem, iconize, idolize, laud, praise, prize, respect, revere, value, venerate, worship.
antonym despise.

admissible *adj.* acceptable, allowable, allowed, equitable, justifiable, lawful, legitimate, licit, passable, permissible, permitted, tolerable, tolerated.
antonyms illegitimate, inadmissible.

admission *n.* acceptance, access, acknowledgment, adhibition, admittance, admitting, affirmation, allowance, avowal, concession, confession, declaration, disclosure, divulgence, entrance, entrée, entry, exposé, granting, inclusion, ingress, initiation, introduction, owning, profession, revelation.
antonyms denial, exclusion.

admit *v.* accept, acknowledge, adhibit, affirm, agree, allow, allow to enter, avow, concede, confess, declare, disclose, divulge, give access, grant, initiate, introduce, intromit, let, let in, permit, profess, receive, recognize, reveal, take in.
antonyms exclude, gainsay.

admittance *n.* acceptance, access, admitting, allowing, entrance, entrée, entry, ingress, letting in, passage, reception.

admonish *v.* advise, berate, caution, censure, check, chide, counsel, enjoin, exhort, forewarn, rebuke, reprehend, reprimand, reproach, reprove, scold, upbraid, warn.

admonition *n.* advice, berating, caution, censure, counsel, pi-jaw, rebuke, reprehension, reprimand, reproach, reproof, scolding, warning.

ado *n.* agitation, bother, business, bustle, ceremony, commotion, confusion, delay, disturbance, excitement, ferment, flurry, fuss, hassle, hurly-burly, kerfuffle, labor, pother, stir, to-do, trouble, tumult, turmoil.
antonyms calm, tranquility.

adolescence *n.* boyhood, boyishness, childishness, development, girlhood, girlishness, immaturity, juvenescence, juvenility, minority, puberty, puerility, teens, transition, youth, youthfulness.
antonym senescence.

adopt *v.* accept, affect, appropriate, approve, assume, back, choose, embrace, endorse, espouse, follow, foster, maintain, ratify, sanction, select, support, take in, take on, take up.
antonyms disown, repudiate.

adoration *n.* admiration, esteem, estimation, exaltation, glorification, honor, idolatry, idolization, love, magnification, reverence, veneration, worship.
antonyms abhorrence, detestation.

adore *v.* admire, cherish, dote on, esteem, exalt, glorify, honor, idolatrize, idolize, love, magnify, revere, reverence, venerate, worship.
antonyms abhor, hate.

adorn *v.* adonize, apparel, array, beautify, bedeck, bedight, bedizen, begem, bejewel, bestick, crown, deck, decorate, dight, doll up, embellish, emblazon, enhance, enrich, furbish, garnish, gild, grace, impearl, miniate, ornament, tart up, trick out, trim.

adrift *adj.* aimless, amiss, anchorless, astray, at sea, directionless, goalless, insecure, off course, purposeless, rootless, rudderless, unsettled, wrong.
antonyms anchored, stable.

adroit *adj.* able, adept, apt, artful, clever, cunning, deft, dexterous, expert, habile, ingenious, masterful, neat, nimble, proficient, quick, resourceful, skilful, skilled, slick.
antonyms clumsy, inept, maladroit.

adult *adj.* developed, full-grown, fully grown, grown-up, mature, of age, ripe, ripened.
antonym immature.

advance *v.* accelerate, adduce, allege, ameliorate, assist, benefit, bring forward, cite, elevate, expedite, facilitate, foster, furnish, further, go ahead, go forward, grow, hasten, improve, increase, lend, move on, multiply, offer, pay beforehand, present, press on, proceed, proffer, profit, progress, promote, prosper, provide, raise, send forward, speed, submit, suggest, supply, thrive, upgrade.
antonyms impede, retard, retreat.

n. advancement, amelioration, betterment, breakthrough, credit, deposit, development, down payment, furtherance, gain, growth, headway, improvement, increase, loan, preferment, prepayment, profit, progress, promotion, retainer, rise, step.
antonym recession.

adj. beforehand, early, foremost, forward, in front, leading, preliminary, prior.

advantage *n.* account, aid, ascendancy, asset, assistances, avail, benefit, blessing, boon, boot, convenience, dominance, edge, expediency, fruit, gain, good, help, hold, interest, lead, leverage, precedence, pre-eminence, profit, purchase, service, start, superiority, sway, upper hand, use, usefulness, utility, welfare.
antonyms disadvantage, hindrance.

adventure *n.* chance, contingency, enterprise, experience, exploit, gest, hazard, incident, occurrence, risk, speculation, undertaking, venture.

adventurous *adj.* adventuresome, audacious, bold, dangerous, daredevil, daring, dauntless, doughty, enterprising, foolhardy, game, hazardous, headstrong, impetuous, intrepid, perilous, plucky, rash, reckless, risky, spunky, swashbuckling, temerarious, venturesome.

antonyms cautious, chary, prudent.

adversary *n.* antagonist, assailant, attacker, competitor, contestant, enemy, foe, foeman, opponent, opposer, rival.

antonyms ally, supporter.

adverse *adj.* antagonistic, conflicting, contrary, counter, counter-productive, detrimental, disadvantageous, hostile, hurtful, inauspicious, inexpedient, inimical, injurious, inopportune, negative, noxious, opposing, opposite, reluctant, repugnant, uncongenial, unfavorable, unfortunate, unfriendly, unlucky, unpropitious, untoward, unwilling.

antonyms advantageous, propitious.

adversity *n.* affliction, bad luck, blight, calamity, catastrophe, contretemps, disaster, distress, hard times, hardship, ill-fortune, ill-luck, mischance, misery, misfortune, mishap, reverse, sorrow, suffering, trial, tribulation, trouble, woe, wretchedness.

antonym prosperity.

advertise *v.* advise, announce, apprize, blazon, broadcast, bruit, declare, display, flaunt, herald, inform, make known, notify, plug, praise, proclaim, promote, promulgate, publicize, publish, puff, push, tout, trumpet.

advertisement *n.* ad, advert, announcement, bill, blurb, circular, commercial, display, handbill, handout, hype, leaflet, notice, placard, plug, poster, promotion, propaganda, propagation, publicity, puff, puffery.

advice *n.* admonition, caution, communication, conseil, counsel, direction, do's and don'ts, guidance, help, information, injunction, instruction, intelligence, memorandum, notice, notification, opinion, recommendation, rede, suggestion, view, warning, wisdom, word.

advisable *adj.* advantageous, appropriate, apt, beneficial, correct, desirable, expedient, fit, fitting, judicious, meet, politic, profitable, proper, prudent, recommended, seemly, sensible, sound, suggested, suitable, wise.

antonyms inadvisable, injudicious.

advise *v.* acquaint, apprize, bethink, caution, commend, counsel, enjoin, forewarn, guide, inform, instruct, make known, notify, recommend, report, suggest, teach, tell, tutor, urge, warn.

adviser *n.* admonitor, aide, authority, coach, confidant, consultant, counsel, counselor, éminence grise, guide, helper, instructor, lawyer, mentor, monitor, preceptor, righthand man, solicitor, teacher, therapist, tutor.

advocate *v.* adopt, advise, argue for, campaign for, champion, countenance, defend, encourage, endorse, espouse, favor, justify, patronize, plead for, press for, promote, propose, recommend, subscribe to, support, uphold, urge.

antonyms deprecate, disparage, impugn.

n. apologist, apostle, attorney, backer, barrister, campaigner, champion, counsel, counselor, defender, interceder, intercessor, lawyer, mediator, paraclete, patron, pleader, promoter, proponent, proposer, solicitor, speaker, spokesman, supporter, upholder, vindicator.

antonyms critic, opponent.

affable *adj.* agreeable, amiable, amicable, approachable, benevolent, benign, civil, congenial, cordial, courteous, expansive, free, friendly, genial, good-humored, good-natured, gracious, kindly, mild, obliging, open, pleasant, sociable, suave, urbane, warm.

antonyms cool, reserved, reticent, unfriendly.

affair *n.* activity, adventure, amour, amourette, business, circumstance, concern, connection, episode, event, happening, incident, interest, intrigue, liaison, matter, occurrence, operation, organization, party, proceeding, project, question, reception, relationship, responsibility, romance, subject, topic, transaction, undertaking.

affect[1] *v.* act on, agitate, alter, apply to, attack, bear upon, change, concern, disturb, grieve, grip, impinge upon, impress, influence, interest, involve, melt, modify, move, overcome, penetrate, pertain to, perturb, prevail over, regard, relate to, seize, soften, stir, strike, sway, touch, transform, trouble, upset.

affect[2] *v.* adopt, aspire to, assume, contrive, counterfeit, fake, feign, imitate, pretend, profess, put on, sham, simulate.

affected[1] *adj.* afflicted, agitated, altered, changed, concerned, damaged, distressed, gripped, hurt, impaired, impressed, influenced, injured, melted, moved, perturbed, smitten, stimulated, stirred, swayed, touched, troubled, upset.

affected[2] *adj.* alembicated, artificial, assumed, bogus, chichi, conceited, contrived, counterfeit, debby, euphuistic, fake, feigned, fussy, greenery-yallery, hyperaesthesic, hyperaesthetic, insincere, lah-di-dah, literose, mannered, mincing, minikin, namby-pamby, niminy-piminy, phoney, pompous, precious, pretended, pretentious, put-on, sham, simulated, spurious, stiff, studied, unnatural.

antonyms genuine, natural.

affection *n.* amity, attachment, care, desire, devotion, favor, feeling, fondness, friendliness, good will, inclination, kindness, liking, love, partiality, passion, penchant, predilection, predisposition, proclivity, propensity, regard, tenderness, warmth.

antonyms antipathy, dislike.

affectionate *adj.* amiable, amorous, attached, caring, cordial, devoted, doting, fond, friendly, kind, loving, passionate, responsive, solicitous, tender, warm, warmhearted.

antonyms cold, undemonstrative.

affirm *v.* assert, asseverate, attest, aver, avouch, avow, certify, confirm, corroborate, declare, depose, endorse, maintain, pronounce, ratify, state, swear, testify, witness.

afflict *v.* beset, burden, distress, grieve, harass, harm, harrow, hurt, oppress, pain, plague, rack, smite, strike, torment, torture, trouble, try, visit, wound, wring.

antonyms comfort, solace.

affliction *n.* adversity, calamity, cross, curse, depression, disaster, disease, distress, grief, hardship, illness, misery, misfortune, ordeal, pain, plague, scourge, sickness, sorrow, suffering, torment, trial, tribulation, trouble, visitation, woe, wretchedness.

antonyms comfort, consolation, solace.

affluent *adj.* comfortable, flourishing, flush, loaded, moneyed, opulent, pecunious, prosperous, rich, wealthy, well-heeled, well-off, well-to-do.

antonyms impecunious, impoverished, poor.

afford *v.* bear, bestow, cope with, engender, furnish,

generate, give, grant, impart, manage, offer, produce, provide, render, spare, stand, supply, sustain, yield.

affront v. abuse, anger, annoy, displease, gall, incense, insult, irritate, nettle, offend, outrage, pique, provoke, slight, snub, vex.

antonyms appease, compliment.

n. abuse, discourtesy, disrespect, facer, indignity, injury, insult, offense, outrage, provocation, rudeness, slap in the face, slight, slur, snub, vexation, wrong.

antonym compliment.

afraid adj. aghast, alarmed, anxious, apprehensive, cowardly, diffident, distrustful, faint-hearted, fearful, frightened, intimidated, nervous, regretful, reluctant, scared, sorry, suspicious, timid, timorous, tremulous, unhappy.

antonyms confident, unafraid.

after prep. afterwards, as a result of, behind, below, following, in consequence of, later, post, subsequent to, subsequently, succeeding, thereafter.

antonym before.

again adv. afresh, also, anew, another time, au contraire, besides, bis, conversely, da capo, de integro, de novo, ditto, encore, furthermore, in addition, moreover, on the contrary, on the other hand, once more.

against prep. abutting, across, adjacent to, athwart, close up to, confronting, contra, counter to, facing, fronting, hostile to, in contact with, in contrast to, in defiance of, in exchange for, in opposition to, in the face of, on, opposed to, opposing, opposite to, resisting, touching, versus.

antonyms for, pro.

age n. aeon, agedness, anility, caducity, date, day, days, decline, decrepitude, dotage, duration, elderliness, epoch, era, generation, lifetime, majority, maturity, old age, period, senescence, senility, seniority, span, the sere and yellow, time, years.

antonyms salad days, youth.

v. decline, degenerate, deteriorate, grow old, mature, mellow, obsolesce, ripen, season.

aged adj. advanced, age-old, ancient, antiquated, antique, decrepit, elderly, geriatric, gray, hoary, old, patriarchal, senescent, sere, superannuated, time-worn, venerable, worn-out.

antonyms young, youthful.

agency n. action, activity, bureau, business, department, effect, effectuation, efficiency, finger, force, handling, influence, instrumentality, intercession, intervention, means, mechanism, mediation, medium, office, offices, operation, organization, power, work, workings.

agent n. actor, agency, author, cause, channel, delegate, deputy, doer, emissary, envoy, executor, factor, force, functionary, go-between, instrument, intermediary, legate, means, middleman, mover, negotiator, operative, operator, organ, performer, power, practisant, rep, representative, substitute, surrogate, vehicle, vicar, worker.

aggravate v. annoy, exacerbate, exaggerate, exasperate, harass, hassle, heighten, incense, increase, inflame, intensify, irk, irritate, magnify, needle, nettle, peeve, pester, provoke, tease, vex, worsen.

antonyms alleviate, appease, mollify.

aggregate n. accumulation, agglomeration, aggregation, amount, assemblage, body, bulk, collection, combination, entirety, generality, heap, herd, lump, mass, mixture, pile, sum, throng, total, totality, whole.

adj. accumulated, added, assembled, collected, collective, combined, complete, composite, corporate, cumulative, mixed, total, united.

antonyms individual, particular.

v. accumulate, add up, agglomerate, amass, amount to, assemble, cluster, collect, combine, conglomerate, heap, mix, pile, total.

aggression n. aggressiveness, antagonism, assault, attack, bellicosity, belligerence, combativeness, destructiveness, encroachment, hostility, impingement, incursion, injury, intrusion, invasion, jingoism, militancy, offence, offensive, onslaught, provocation, pugnacity, raid.

aggressive adj. argumentative, assertive, bellicose, belligerent, bold, butch, combative, contentious, destructive, disputatious, dynamic, energetic, enterprising, forceful, go-ahead, hostile, intrusive, invasive, jingoistic, militant, offensive, provocative, pugnacious, pushful, pushing, pushy, quarrelsome, scrappy, vigorous, zealous.

antonyms peaceable, submissive.

aghast adj. afraid, amazed, appalled, astonished, astounded, awestruck, confounded, dismayed, frightened, horrified, horror-struck, shocked, startled, stunned, stupefied, terrified, thunder-struck.

agile adj. active, acute, adroit, alert, brisk, clever, fleet, flexible, limber, lissome, lithe, lively, mobile, nimble, prompt, quick, quick-witted, sharp, smart, sprightly, spry, supple, swift.

antonyms clumsy, stiff, torpid.

agility n. activity, acuteness, adroitness, alertness, briskness, cleverness, flexibility, lissomeness, litheness, liveliness, mobility, nimbleness, promptitude, promptness, quickness, quick-wittedness, sharpness, sprightliness, spryness, suppleness, swiftness.

antonyms sluggishness, stiffness, torpidity.

agitate v. alarm, arouse, beat, churn, confuse, convulse, discompose, disconcert, disquiet, distract, disturb, excite, ferment, flurry, fluster, incite, inflame, perturb, rattle, rock, rouse, ruffle, shake, stimulate, stir, toss, trouble, unnerve, unsettle, upset, work up, worry.

antonyms calm, tranquilize.

agitated adj. anxious, discomposed, distracted, feverish, flurried, flustered, in a lather, insecure, jumpy, nervous, perturbed, restive, restless, ruffled, tumultuous, twitchy, uneasy, unnerved, unsettled, upset, wrought-up.

antonyms calm, composed.

agony n. affliction, anguish, distress, misery, pain, pangs, paroxysm, spasm, suffering, throes, torment, torture, tribulation, woe, wretchedness.

agree v. accede, accord, acquiesce, admit, allow, answer, assent, chime, coincide, comply, concede, concord, concur, conform, consent, consort, contract, correspond, cotton, covenant, engage, fadge, fit, fix, get on, grant, harmonize, homologate, jibe, match, permit, promise, see eye to eye, settle, side with, square, suit, tally, yield.

antonyms conflict, disagree.

agreeable adj. acceptable, acquiescent, amenable, amicable, appropriate, approving, attractive, befitting, compatible, complying, concurring, conformable, congenial, consenting, consistent, d'accord, delectable, delightful, enjoyable, fitting, gemütlich, gratifying, in accord, likable, palatable, pleasant, pleasing, pleasurable, proper, responsive, satisfying, suitable, sympathetic, well-disposed, willing.

antonyms disagreeable, distasteful, incompatible, nasty.

agreement[1] *n.* acceptance, accord, accordance, adherence, affinity, analogy, closing, compact, compatibility, complaisance, compliance, concert, concord, concordat, concurrence, conformity, congruence, congruity, consentience, consistency, consonance, consort, convention, correspondence, harmony, modus vivendi, preconcert, resemblance, respondence, similarity, suitableness, sympathy, unanimity, union, unison.

antonym disagreement.

agreement[2] *n.* arrangement, bargain, compact, concordat, contract, covenant, deal, pact, settlement, treaty, understanding.

agriculture *n.* agribusiness, agronomics, agronomy, cultivation, culture, farming, geoponics, husbandry, tillage.

ahead *adj., adv.* advanced, along, at an advantage, at the head, before, earlier on, forwards, in advance, in front, in the forefront, in the lead, in the vanguard, leading, onwards, superior, to the fore, winning.

aid *v.* abet, accommodate, adminiculate, assist, befriend, boost, ease, encourage, expedite, facilitate, favor, help, oblige, promote, prop, rally round, relieve, second, serve, subsidize, succor, support, sustain.

antonyms impede, obstruct.

n. a leg up, adminicle, aidance, assistance, assistant, benefit, contribution, donation, encouragement, favor, help, helper, patronage, prop, relief, service, sponsorship, subsidy, subvention, succor, support, supporter.

antonyms impediment, obstruction.

ail *v.* afflict, annoy, be indisposed, bother, decline, distress, droop, fail, irritate, languish, pain, pine, sicken, trouble, upset, weaken, worry.

antonyms comfort, flourish.

ailing *adj.* debilitated, diseased, feeble, frail, ill, indisposed, infirm, invalid, languishing, off-color, out of sorts, peaky, poorly, sick, sickly, suffering, under the weather, unsound, unwell, weak, weakly.

antonyms flourishing, healthy.

ailment *n.* affliction, complaint, disability, disease, disorder, illness, indisposition, infection, infirmity, malady, sickness, weakness.

aim *v.* address, aspire, attempt, beam, design, direct, draw a bead, endeavor, essay, head for, intend, level, mean, plan, point, propose, purpose, resolve, seek, set one's sights on, sight, strive, take aim, target, train, try, want, wish, zero in on.

n. ambition, aspiration, course, desideratum, design, desire, direction, dream, end, goal, hope, intent, intention, mark, motive, object, objective, plan, purpose, scheme, target, telos, wish.

aimless *adj.* chance, desultory, directionless, erratic, feckless, frivolous, goalless, haphazard, irresolute, pointless, purposeless, rambling, random, stray, undirected, unguided, unmotivated, unpredictable, vagrant, wayward.

antonyms determined, positive, purposeful.

air *n.* ambience, ambient, appearance, aria, atmosphere, aura, bearing, blast, breath, breeze, character, demeanor, draught, effect, ether, feeling, flavor, heavens, impression, lay, look, manner, melody, mood, motif, oxygen, puff, quality, sky, song, strain, style, theme, tone, tune, waft, whiff, wind, zephyr.

v. aerate, broadcast, circulate, communicate, declare, disclose, display, disseminate, divulge, exhibit, expose, express, freshen, give vent to, make known, make public, parade, proclaim, publicize, publish, reveal, tell, utter, vaunt, ventilate, voice.

airy *adj.* aerial, blithe, blowy, bodiless, breezy, buoyant, cheerful, cheery, debonair, delicate, disembodied, drafty, ethereal, fanciful, flimsy, fresh, frolicsome, gay, graceful, gusty, happy, high-spirited, illusory, imaginary, immaterial, incorporeal, insouciant, insubstantial, jaunty, light, light-hearted, lively, lofty, merry, nimble, nonchalant, offhand, open, roomy, spacious, spectral, sportive, sprightly, trifling, uncluttered, unreal, unsubstantial, vaporous, visionary, weightless, well-ventilated, windy.

antonyms close, heavy, oppressive, stuffy.

aisle *n.* alleyway, ambulatory, corridor, deambulatory, division, gangway, lane, passage, passageway, path, walkway.

akin *adj.* affiliated, agnate, alike, allied, analogous, cognate, comparable, congenial, connected, consanguineous, consonant, corresponding, kin, kindred, like, parallel, related, similar.

antonym alien.

alarm *v.* affright, agitate, daunt, dismay, distress, frighten, give (someone) a turn, panic, put the wind up (someone), scare, startle, terrify, terrorize, unnerve.

antonyms calm, reassure, soothe.

n. alarm-bell, alert, anxiety, apprehension, bell, consternation, danger signal, dismay, distress, distress signal, fear, fright, horror, larum, larum-bell, nervousness, panic, scare, siren, terror, tocsin, trepidation, unease, uneasiness, warning.

antonym composure.

alarming *adj.* daunting, direful, dismaying, distressing, disturbing, dreadful, frightening, ominous, scaring, shocking, startling, terrifying, threatening, unnerving.

antonym reassuring.

alcoholic *adj.* ardent, brewed, distilled, fermented, hard, inebriant, inebriating, intoxicating, spirituous, strong, vinous.

n. bibber, boozer, dipso, dipsomaniac, drunk, drunkard, hard drinker, inebriate, lush, piss artist, soak, sot, sponge, tippler, toper, tosspot, wino.

alert *adj.* active, agile, attentive, brisk, careful, circumspect, heedful, lively, nimble, observant, on the ball, on the lookout, on the qui vive, perceptive, prepared, quick, ready, sharp-eyed, sharp-witted, spirited, sprightly, vigilant, wary, watchful, wide-awake.

antonyms listless, slow.

n. alarm, signal, siren, tocsin, warning.

v. alarm, forewarn, inform, notify, signal, tip off, warn.

alias *n.* allonym, anonym, assumed name, false name, nickname, nom de guerre, nom de plume, pen name, pseudonym, soubriquet, stage name.

adv. alias dictus, also, also called, also known as, formerly, otherwise, otherwise called.

alibi *n.* cover-up, defence, excuse, explanation, justification, plea, pretext, reason, story.

alien *adj.* adverse, antagonistic, conflicting, contrary, estranged, exotic, extraneous, foreign, inappropriate, incompatible, incongruous, inimical, opposed, outlandish, remote, repugnant, separated, strange, unfamiliar.

antonym akin.

n. emigrant, foreigner, immigrant, metic, newcomer, outlander, outsider, stranger.

antonym native.

alight[1] *v.* come down, come to rest, debark, descend, detrain, disembark, disentrain, dismount, get down, get off, land, light, perch, settle, touch down.

antonyms ascend, board, rise.

alight[2] *adj.* ablaze, afire, aflame, blazing, bright, brilliant, burning, fiery, flaming, flaring, ignited, illuminated, illumined, lighted, lit, lit up, on fire, radiant, shining.

antonym dark.

alive *adj.* active, alert, animate, animated, awake, breathing, brisk, cheerful, eager, energetic, existent, existing, extant, functioning, having life, in existence, in force, life-like, live, lively, living, operative, quick, real, spirited, sprightly, spry, subsisting, vibrant, vigorous, vital, vivacious, zestful.

antonyms dead, lifeless.

alive with abounding in, bristling with, bustling with, buzzing with, crawling with, crowded with, infested with, lousy with, overflowing with, overrun by, stiff with, swarming with, teeming with, thronged with.

allay *v.* allege, alleviate, appease, assuage, blunt, calm, check, compose, diminish, dull, ease, lessen, lull, mitigate, moderate, mollify, pacify, quell, quiet, reduce, relieve, slake, smooth, soften, soothe, subdue, tranquilize.

antonyms exacerbate, intensify.

allege *v.* adduce, advance, affirm, assert, asseverate, attest, aver, avow, charge, claim, contend, declare, depose, hold, insist, maintain, plead, profess, put forward, state.

allegiance *n.* adherence, constancy, devotion, duty, faithfulness, fealty, fidelity, friendship, homage, loyalty, obedience, obligation, support.

antonyms disloyalty, enmity.

allegory *n.* analogy, apologue, comparison, emblem, fable, metaphor, myth, parable, story, symbol, symbolism, tale.

alleviate *v.* abate, allay, assuage, blunt, check, cushion, deaden, diminish, dull, ease, lessen, lighten, mitigate, moderate, modify, mollify, palliate, quell, quench, quiet, reduce, relieve, slacken, slake, smooth, soften, soothe, subdue, temper.

antonym aggravate.

alley *n.* alleyway, back street, close, entry, gate, lane, mall, passage, passageway, pathway, walk.

alliance *n.* affiliation, affinity, agreement, association, bloc, bond, cartel, coalition, combination, compact, concordat, confederacy, confederation, conglomerate, connection, consociation, consortium, faction, federation, guild, league, marriage, pact, partnership, syndicate, treaty, union.

antonyms divorce, enmity, estrangement, hostility.

allot *v.* allocate, apportion, appropriate, assign, budget, designate, dispense, distribute, earmark, grant, mete, render, set aside, share out.

allow *v.* accord, acknowledge, acquiesce, admeasure, admit, allocate, allot, apportion, approve, assign, authorize, bear, brook, concede, confess, deduct, endure, give, give leave, grant, let, own, permit, provide, put up with, remit, sanction, spare, stand, suffer, tolerate.

antonyms deny, forbid.

allow for arrange for, bear in mind, consider, foresee,

include, keep in mind, keep in view, make allowances for, make concessions for, make provision for, plan for, provide for, take into account.

antonym discount.

allowance *n.* admission, allocation, allotment, amount, annuity, apportionment, concession, deduction, discount, emolument, grant, lot, measure, pension, portion, quota, ration, rebate, reduction, remittance, sanction, share, stint, stipend, subsidy, sufferance, tolerance, weighting, X-factor.

allude *v.* adumbrate, advert, cite, glance, hint, imply, infer, insinuate, intimate, mention, refer, remark, speak of, suggest, touch upon.

allure *v.* attract, beguile, cajole, captivate, charm, coax, decoy, disarm, enchant, enrapture, entice, entrance, fascinate, interest, inveigle, lead on, lure, persuade, seduce, tempt, win over.

antonym repel.

n. appeal, attraction, captivation, charm, enchantment, enticement, fascination, glamor, lure, magnetism, persuasion, seductiveness, temptation.

ally *n.* abettor, accessory, accomplice, associate, coadjutor, collaborator, colleague, confederate, confrere, consort, co-worker, friend, helper, helpmate, leaguer, partner, side-kick.

antonyms antagonist, enemy.

v. affiliate, amalgamate, associate, band together, collaborate, combine, confederate, conjoin, connect, fraternize, join, join forces, league, marry, team up, unify, unite.

antonym estrange.

almighty *adj.* absolute, all-powerful, awful, desperate, enormous, excessive, great, intense, invincible, loud, omnipotent, overpowering, overwhelming, plenipotent, severe, supreme, terrible, unlimited.

antonyms impotent, insignificant, weak.

almost *adv.* about, all but, approaching, approximately, as good as, close to, just about, nearing, nearly, not far from, not quite, practically, towards, virtually, well-nigh.

alms *n.* benefaction, beneficence, bounty, charity, donation, gift, largess(e), offerings, relief.

alone *adj., adv.* abandoned, apart, by itself, by oneself, deserted, desolate, detached, discrete, forlorn, forsaken, incomparable, isolated, just, lonely, lonesome, matchless, mere, nonpareil, on one's own, only, peerless, separate, simply, single, single-handed, singular, sole, solitary, unaccompanied, unaided, unassisted, unattended, uncombined, unconnected, unequaled, unescorted, unique, unparalleled, unsurpassed.

aloof *adj.* chilly, cold, cool, detached, distant, forbidding, formal, haughty, inaccessible, indifferent, offish, remote, reserved, reticent, stand-offish, supercilious, unapproachable, uncompanionable, unforthcoming, unfriendly, uninterested, unresponsive, unsociable, unsympathetic.

antonyms concerned, sociable.

also *adv.* additionally, along with, and, as well, as well as, besides, ditto, further, furthermore, in addition, including, moreover, plus, therewithal, to boot, too.

alter *v.* adapt, adjust, amend, bushel, castrate, change, convert, diversify, emend, metamorphose, modify, qualify, recast, reform, remodel, reshape, revise, shift, take liberties with, transform, transmute, transpose, turn, vary.

antonym fix.

alteration *n.* adaptation, adjustment, amendment, castration, change, conversion, difference, diversification, emendation, interchanging, metamorphosis, modification, reciprocation, reformation, remodeling, reshaping, revision, rotation, shift, transfiguration, transformation, transmutation, transposition, variance, variation, vicissitude.

antonym fixity.

altercation *n.* argument, bickering, clash, contention, controversy, debate, disagreement, discord, dispute, dissension, fracas, logomachy, quarrel, row, sparring, squabble, wrangle.

alternate *v.* alter, change, fluctuate, follow one another, interchange, intersperse, oscillate, reciprocate, rotate, substitute, take turns, transpose, vary.

adj. alternating, alternative, another, different, every other, every second, interchanging, reciprocal, reciprocating, reciprocative, rotating, second, substitute.

alternative *n.* back-up, choice, option, other, preference, recourse, selection, substitute.

adj. alternate, another, different, fall-back, fringe, other, second, substitute, unconventional, unorthodox.

although *conj.* admitting that, albeit, conceding that, even if, even supposing, even though, granted that, howbeit, notwithstanding, though, while.

altitude *n.* elevation, height, loftiness, stature, tallness.

antonym depth.

altogether *adv.* absolutely, all in all, all told, as a whole, collectively, completely, entirely, fully, generally, holus-bolus, in all, in general, in sum, in toto, on the whole, perfectly, quite, thoroughly, totally, utterly, wholesale, wholly.

altruism *n.* considerateness, disinterestedness, generosity, humanity, philanthropy, public spirit, self-abnegation, self-sacrifice, social conscience, unself, unselfishness.

antonym selfishness.

always *adv.* aye, consistently, constantly, continually, endlessly, eternally, ever, everlastingly, evermore, every time, forever, in perpetuum, invariably, perpetually, regularly, repeatedly, sempiternally, unceasingly, unfailingly, without exception.

antonym never.

amalgamate *v.* alloy, ally, blend, coalesce, coalize, combine, commingle, compound, fuse, homogenize, incorporate, integrate, intermix, merge, mingle, synthesize, unify, unite.

antonym separate.

amass *v.* accumulate, agglomerate, agglutinate, aggregate, assemble, collect, compile, foregather, garner, gather, heap up, hoard, pile up, rake up, scrape together.

amateur *n.* buff, dabbler, dilettante, do-it-yourselfer, fancier, ham, layman, non-professional.

antonym professional.

amaze *v.* alarm, astonish, astound, bewilder, confound, daze, disconcert, dismay, dumbfound, electrify, flabbergast, floor, shock, stagger, startle, stun, stupefy, surprise, wow.

ambiguous *adj.* ambivalent, amphibolic, amphibological, amphibolous, confused, confusing, cryptic, Delphic, double-barrelled, double-meaning, doubtful, dubious, enigmatic, enigmatical, equivocal, inconclusive, indefinite, indeterminate, louche, multivocal, obscure, oracular, puzzling, uncertain, unclear, vague, woolly.

antonyms clear.

ambition *n.* aim, aspiration, avidity, craving, design, desire, dream, drive, eagerness, end, enterprise, goal, hankering, hope, hunger, ideal, intent, longing, object, objective, purpose, push, striving, target, wish, yearning, zeal.

antonyms apathy, diffidence.

ambitious *adj.* arduous, aspiring, assertive, avid, bold, challenging, demanding, desirous, difficult, driving, eager, elaborate, energetic, enterprising, enthusiastic, exacting, fervid, formidable, go-ahead, grandiose, hard, hopeful, impressive, industrious, intent, keen, pretentious, purposeful, pushy, severe, strenuous, striving, zealous.

antonym unassuming.

amble *v.* dawdle, drift, meander, mosey, perambulate, promenade, ramble, saunter, stroll, toddle, walk, wander.

antonyms march, stride.

ambush *n.* ambuscade, concealment, cover, emboscata, hiding, hiding-place, retreat, shelter, snare, trap, waylaying.

v. ambuscade, bushwhack, ensnare, entrap, surprise, trap, waylay.

amend *v.* adjust, alter, ameliorate, better, change, correct, emend, emendate, enhance, fix, improve, mend, modify, qualify, rectify, redress, reform, remedy, repair, revise.

antonyms impair, worsen.

amends *n.* atonement, compensation, expiation, indemnification, indemnity, mitigation, quittance, recompense, redress, reparation, requital, restitution, restoration, satisfaction.

amiable *adj.* accessible, affable, agreeable, approachable, attractive, benign, biddable, charming, cheerful, companionable, complaisant, congenial, conversable, delightful, engaging, friendly, gemütlich, genial, good-humored, good-natured, good-tempered, kind, kindly, likable, lovable, obliging, pleasant, pleasing, sociable, sweet, winning, winsome.

antonyms hostile, unfriendly.

amid *conj.* amidst, among, amongst, in the middle of, in the midst of, in the thick of, surrounded by.

amiss *adj.* awry, defective, erroneous, fallacious, false, faulty, improper, inaccurate, inappropriate, incorrect, out of order, unsuitable, untoward, wonky, wrong.

adv. ill, imperfect, imprecise, out of kilter.

antonyms right, well.

among *prep.* amid, amidst, amongst, between, in the middle of, in the midst of, in the thick of, midst, mongst, surrounded by, together with, with.

amorous *adj.* affectionate, amatory, ardent, attached, doting, enamored, erotic, fond, impassioned, in love, lovesick, loving, lustful, passionate, randy, tender, uxorious.

antonyms cold, indifferent.

amount *n.* addition, aggregate, bulk, entirety, expanse, extent, lot, magnitude, mass, measure, number, quantity, quantum, quota, sum, sum total, supply, total, volume, whole.

amount to add up to, aggregate, approximate to, be equivalent to, be tantamount to, become, come to, equal, grow, mean, purport, run to, total.

ample *adj*. abundant, big, bountiful, broad, capacious, commodious, considerable, copious, expansive, extensive, full, generous, goodly, great, handsome, large, lavish, liberal, munificent, plenteous, plentiful, plenty, profuse, rich, roomy, spacious, substantial, sufficient, unrestricted, voluminous, wide.
antonyms insufficient, meager.

amplify *v*. add to, augment, boost, broaden, bulk out, deepen, develop, dilate, elaborate, enhance, enlarge, expand, expatiate, extend, fill out, heighten, increase, intensify, lengthen, magnify, raise, strengthen, supplement, widen.
antonym reduce.

amuse *v*. absorb, beguile, charm, cheer, cheer up, delight, disport, divert, engross, enliven, entertain, enthral, gladden, interest, occupy, please, popjoy, recreate, regale, relax, slay, tickle.
antonym bore.

amusement *n*. beguilement, delight, disportment, distraction, diversion, enjoyment, entertainment, fun, game, gladdening, hilarity, hobby, interest, joke, lark, laughter, merriment, mirth, pastime, pleasure, prank, recreation, regalement, sport.
antonyms bore, boredom.

amusing *adj*. amusive, charming, cheerful, cheering, comical, delightful, diverting, droll, enjoyable, entertaining, facetious, funny, gladdening, hilarious, humorous, interesting, jocular, jolly, killing, laughable, lively, ludicrous, merry, pleasant, pleasing, risible, sportive, witty.
antonym boring.

analogous *adj*. agreeing, akin, alike, comparable, correlative, corresponding, equivalent, homologous, like, matching, parallel, reciprocal, related, resembling, similar.
antonym disparate.

analysis *n*. anatomization, anatomy, assay, breakdown, dissection, dissolution, division, enquiry, estimation, evaluation, examination, exegesis, explanation, explication, exposition, interpretation, investigation, judgment, opinion, reasoning, reduction, resolution, review, scrutiny, separation, sifting, study, test.

analyze *v*. anatomize, assay, break down, consider, dissect, dissolve, divide, estimate, evaluate, examine, interpret, investigate, judge, reduce, resolve, review, scrutinize, separate, sift, study, test.

ancestral *adj*. atavistic, avital, familial, genealogical, genetic, hereditary, lineal, parental.

ancestry *n*. ancestors, antecedents, antecessors, blood, derivation, descent, extraction, family, forebears, forefathers, genealogy, heredity, heritage, house, line, lineage, origin, parentage, pedigree, progenitors, race, roots, stirps, stock.

anchor *n*. grapnel, kedge, killick, mainstay, mud-hook, pillar of strength, prop, security, staff, support.
v. affix, attach, fasten, fix, make fast, moor.

ancient *adj*. aged, age-old, antediluvian, antiquated, antique, archaic, bygone, démodé, early, fossilized, hoary, immemorial, obsolete, old, olden, old-fashioned, original, outmoded, out-of-date, preadamic, prehistoric, primeval, primordial, pristine, superannuated, time-worn, venerable, world-old.
antonym modern.

anecdote *n*. exemplum, fable, reminiscence, sketch, story, tale, yarn.

anemic *adj*. ashen, bloodless, chalky, characterless, colorless, dull, enervated, exsanguine, exsanguin(e)ous, feeble, frail, ineffectual, infirm, insipid, pale, pallid, pasty, sallow, sickly, spiritless, toneless, wan, weak, whey-faced.
antonyms full-blooded, ruddy, sanguine.

anesthetic *n*. analgesic, anodyne, narcotic, opiate, painkiller, palliative, sedative, soporific, stupefacient, stupefactive.

anesthetize *v*. benumb, deaden, desensitize, dope, dull, etherize, lull, mull, numb, stupefy.

angel *n*. archangel, backer, benefactor, cherub, darling, divine messenger, fairy godmother, guardian spirit, ideal, paragon, principality, saint, seraph, supporter, treasure.
antonyms devil, fiend.

angelic *adj*. adorable, beatific, beautiful, celestial, cherubic, divine, entrancing, ethereal, exemplary, heavenly, holy, innocent, lovely, pious, pure, saintly, seraphic, unworldly, virtuous.
antonyms devilish, fiendish.

anger *n*. annoyance, antagonism, bad blood, bile, bitterness, choler, dander, displeasure, dudgeon, exasperation, fury, gall, indignation, ire, irritability, irritation, monkey, outrage, passion, pique, rage, rancor, resentment, spleen, temper, vexation, wrath.
antonym forbearance.
v. affront, aggravate, annoy, antagonize, bother, bug, displease, enrage, exasperate, fret, frustrate, gall, incense, infuriate, irk, irritate, madden, miff, needle, nettle, offend, outrage, pique, provoke, rile, ruffle, vex.
antonyms appease, calm, please.

angry *adj*. aggravated, annoyed, antagonized, bitter, burned up, choked, choleric, chuffed, disgruntled, displeased, enraged, exasperated, furious, heated, hot, incensed, indignant, infuriated, irascible, irate, ireful, irked, irritable, irritated, mad, miffed, needled, nettled, outraged, passionate, piqued, provoked, raging, rancorous, ratty, red-headed, resentful, riled, shirty, splenetic, stomachful, tumultuous, uptight, waxy, wrathful, wroth.
antonyms calm, content.

anguish *n*. agony, angst, anxiety, desolation, distress, dole, dolor, grief, heartache, heartbreak, misery, pain, pang, rack, sorrow, suffering, torment, torture, tribulation, woe, wretchedness.
antonyms happiness, solace.

animal *n*. barbarian, beast, brute, creature, critter, cur, hound, mammal, monster, pig, savage, swine.
adj. bestial, bodily, brutish, carnal, faunal, feral, ferine, fleshly, gross, inhuman, instinctive, physical, piggish, savage, sensual, wild, zoic.

animate *v*. activate, arouse, embolden, encourage, energize, enliven, excite, fire, galvanize, goad, impel, incite, inspire, inspirit, instigate, invest, invigorate, irradiate, kindle, move, quicken, reactivate, revive, revivify, rouse, spark, spur, stimulate, stir, suffuse, urge, vitalize, vivify.
antonyms dull, inhibit.
adj. alive, breathing, conscious, live, living, sentient.
antonyms dull, spiritless.

animated *adj*. active, airy, alive, ardent, brisk, buoyant, eager, ebullient, energetic, enthusiastic, excited, fervent, gay, glowing, impassioned, lively, passionate,

quick, radiant, spirited, sprightly, vehement, vibrant, vigorous, vital, vivacious, vivid, zestful.
antonyms inert, sluggish.

animosity *n.* acrimony, animus, antagonism, antipathy, bad blood, bitterness, enmity, feud, feuding, hate, hatred, hostility, ill-will, loathing, malevolence, malice, malignity, odium, rancor, resentment, spite.
antonym goodwill.

annex *v.* acquire, add, adjoin, affix, append, appropriate, arrogate, attach, connect, conquer, expropriate, fasten, incorporate, join, occupy, purloin, seize, subjoin, tack, take over, unite, usurp.
n. addendum, additament, addition, adjunct, appendix, attachment, supplement.

annihilate *v.* abolish, assassinate, destroy, eliminate, eradicate, erase, exterminate, extinguish, extirpate, liquidate, murder, nullify, obliterate, raze, rub out, thrash, trounce, wipe out.

announce *v.* advertise, blazon, broadcast, declare, disclose, divulge, intimate, leak, make known, notify, preconize, proclaim, promulgate, propound, publicize, publish, report, reveal, state.
antonym suppress.

announcement *n.* advertisement, broadcast, bulletin, communiqué, declaration, disclosure, dispatch, divulgation, divulgence, intimation, notification, proclamation, promulgation, publication, report, revelation, statement.

annoy *v.* aggravate, anger, badger, bore, bother, bug, chagrin, contrary, displease, disturb, exasperate, fash, gall, get, give the pigs, harass, harm, harry, hip, hump, incommode, irk, irritate, madden, molest, needle, nettle, peeve, pester, pique, plague, provoke, rile, ruffle, tease, trouble, vex.
antonyms gratify, please.

annulment *n.* abolition, abrogation, cancellation, cassation, countermanding, disannulment, invalidation, negation, nullification, quashing, recall, repeal, rescindment, rescission, retraction, reversal, revocation, suspension, voiding.
antonyms enactment, restoration.

anoint *v.* anele, bless, consecrate, daub, dedicate, embrocate, grease, hallow, lard, lubricate, oil, rub, sanctify, smear.

answer *n.* acknowledgment, apology, comeback, counterbuff, countercharge, defence, explanation, outcome, plea, reaction, rebuttal, reciprocation, refutation, rejoinder, reply, report, resolution, response, retaliation, retort, return, riposte, solution, vindication.
v. acknowledge, agree, balance, conform, correlate, correspond, do, echo, explain, fill, fit, fulfil, match up to, meet, pass, qualify, react, reciprocate, refute, rejoin, reply, resolve, respond, retaliate, retort, return, satisfy, serve, solve, succeed, suffice, suit, work.

antagonism *n.* animosity, animus, antipathy, competition, conflict, contention, discord, dissension, friction, hostility, ill-feeling, ill-will, opposition, rivalry.
antonyms rapport, sympathy.

antagonist *n.* adversary, competitor, contender, contestant, disputant, enemy, foe, opponent, opposer, rival.
antonyms ally, supporter.

anthology *n.* analects, choice, collection, compendium, compilation, digest, divan, florilegium, garland, miscellany, selection, spicilegium, treasury.

anticipate *v.* antedate, apprehend, await, bank on, beat to it, count upon, earlierize, expect, forecast, foredate, foresee, forestall, foretaste, foretell, forethink, hope for, intercept, look for, look forward to, predict, pre-empt, prevent.

anticipation *n.* apprehension, awaiting, expectancy, expectation, foresight, foretaste, forethought, forewarning, hope, preconception, premonition, prescience, presentiment, prodrome, prolepsis.

antics *n.* buffoonery, capers, clownery, clowning, didoes, doings, escapades, foolery, foolishness, frolics, larks, mischief, monkey tricks, playfulness, pranks, silliness, skylarking, stunts, tomfoolery, tricks, zanyism.

antipathy *n.* abhorrence, allergy, animosity, animus, antagonism, aversion, bad blood, contrariety, disgust, dislike, distaste, enmity, hate, hatred, hostility, ill-will, incompatibility, loathing, odium, opposition, rancor, repugnance, repulsion, resentment.
antonyms rapport, sympathy.

antiquated *adj.* anachronistic, ancient, antediluvian, antique, archaic, dated, démodé, elderly, fogeyish, fossilized, obsolete, old, old hat, old-fashioned, old-fogeyish, outdated, outmoded, out-of-date, outworn, passé, quaint, superannuated, unfashionable.
antonyms forward-looking, modern.

antique *adj.* aged, ancient, antiquarian, archaic, elderly, obsolete, old, old-fashioned, outdated, quaint, superannuated, vintage.
n. antiquity, bibelot, bygone, curio, curiosity, heirloom, knick-knack, museum-piece, object of virtu, period piece, rarity, relic.

anxiety *n.* angst, anxiousness, apprehension, care, concern, craving, desire, disquiet, disquietude, distress, dread, dysthymia, eagerness, foreboding, fretfulness, impatience, keenness, misgiving, nervousness, presentiment, restlessness, solicitude, suspense, tension, torment, torture, unease, uneasiness, watchfulness, willingness, worriment, worry.
antonym composure.

anxious *adj.* afraid, angst-ridden, apprehensive, avid, careful, concerned, desirous, disquieted, distressed, disturbed, eager, expectant, fearful, fretful, impatient, in suspense, intent, itching, keen, nervous, on tenterhooks, overwrought, restless, solicitous, taut, tense, tormented, tortured, troubled, uneasy, unquiet, watchful, worried, yearning.
antonym composed.

apartment *n.* accommodation, chambers, compartment, condominium, flat, living quarters, lodgings, maisonette, pad, penthouse, quarters, room, rooms, suite, tenement.

apathy *n.* accidie, acedia, coldness, coolness, emotionlessness, impassibility, impassivity, incuriousness, indifference, inertia, insensibility, lethargy, listlessness, passiveness, passivity, phlegm, sluggishness, torpor, unconcern, unfeelingness, uninterestedness, unresponsiveness.
antonyms concern, warmth.

aperture *n.* breach, chink, cleft, crack, eye, eyelet, fissure, foramen, gap, hole, interstice, opening, orifice, passage, perforation, rent, rift, slit, slot, space, vent.

apex *n.* acme, apogee, climax, consummation, crest, crown, crowning point, culmination, fastigium, height, high point, peak, pinnacle, point, summit, tip, top, vertex, zenith.

antonym nadir.

apologetic *adj.* compunctious, conscience-stricken, contrite, excusatory, penitent, regretful, remorseful, repentant, rueful, sorry.
antonym defiant.

apology *n.* acknowledgment, apologia, confession, defence, excuse, explanation, extenuation, justification, palliation, plea, semblance, substitute, travesty, vindication.
antonym defiance.

apostate *n.* defector, deserter, heretic, recidivist, recreant, renegade, renegado, runagate, tergiversator, traitor, turncoat.
antonyms adherent, convert, loyalist.
adj. disloyal, faithless, false, heretical, perfidious, recreant, renegade, traitorous, treacherous, unfaithful, unorthodox, untrue.
antonym faithful.

apostle *n.* advocate, champion, crusader, evangelist, exponent, herald, messenger, missionary, pioneer, preacher, promoter, propagandist, propagator, proponent, proselytizer.

appal *v.* alarm, astound, daunt, disconcert, disgust, dishearten, dismay, frighten, harrow, horrify, intimidate, outrage, petrify, scare, shock, terrify, unnerve.
antonyms encourage, reassure.

appalling *adj.* alarming, astounding, awful, daunting, dire, disheartening, dismaying, dreadful, fearful, frightening, frightful, ghastly, grim, harrowing, hideous, horrible, horrid, horrific, horrifying, intimidating, loathsome, petrifying, scaring, shocking, startling, terrible, terrifying, unnerving, wretched.
antonym reassuring.

apparatus *n.* appliance, bureaucracy, contraption, device, equipment, framework, gadget, gear, gismo, hierarchy, implements, machine, machinery, materials, means, mechanism, network, organization, outfit, set-up, structure, system, tackle, tools, utensils.

apparel *n.* accouterments, array, attire, clothes, clothing, costume, dress, equipment, garb, garments, garniture, gear, guise, habiliments, habit, outfit, raiment, rig-out, robes, suit, trappings, vestiture, vestments, wardrobe, weeds.

apparent *adj.* clear, conspicuous, declared, discernible, distinct, evident, indubitable, manifest, marked, noticeable, obvious, on paper, open, ostensible, outward, overt, patent, perceptible, plain, seeming, specious, superficial, unmistakable, visible.
antonyms obscure, real.

apparition *n.* chimera, eidolon, ghost, manifestation, materialization, phantasm, phantom, presence, revenant, shade, specter, spirit, spook, umbra, vision, visitant, visitation, wraith.

appeal[1] *n.* adjuration, application, entreaty, imploration, invocation, orison, petition, plea, prayer, request, solicitation, suit, supplication.
v. address, adjure, apply, ask, beg, beseech, call, call upon, entreat, implore, invoke, petition, plead, pray, refer, request, resort to, solicit, sue, supplicate.

appeal[2] *n.* allure, attraction, attractiveness, beauty, charisma, charm, enchantment, fascination, interest, magnetism, winsomeness.
v. allure, attract, charm, draw, engage, entice, fascinate, interest, invite, lure, please, tempt.

appear *v.* act, arise, arrive, attend, be published, bob up,

come into sight, come into view, come out, come to light, crop up, develop, emerge, enter, issue, leak out, look, loom, materialize, occur, perform, play, rise, seem, show, show up, surface, take part, transpire, turn out, turn up.
antonym disappear.

appearance *n.* advent, air, appearing, arrival, aspect, bearing, brow, cast, character, coming, début, demeanor, emergence, expression, face, facies, favor, figure, form, front, guise, illusion, image, impression, introduction, look, looks, manner, mien, physiognomy, presence, pretense, seeming, semblance, show, the cut of one's jib.
antonyms disappearance, reality.

appease *v.* allay, assuage, blunt, calm, compose, conciliate, diminish, ease, give a sop to, humor, lessen, lull, mitigate, mollify, pacify, placate, propitiate, quell, quench, quiet, reconcile, satisfy, soften, soothe, subdue, tranquilize.
antonym aggravate.

append *v.* add, adjoin, affix, annex, attach, conjoin, fasten, join, subjoin, tack on.

appendage *n.* accessory, addendum, addition, adjunct, affix, ancillary, annexe, appendix, appurtenance, attachment, auxiliary, excrescence, extremity, limb, member, projection, prosthesis, protuberance, supplement, tab, tag.

appertaining *adj.* applicable, applying, belonging, characteristic, connected, germane, pertinent, related, relevant.

appetite *n.* appetence, appetency, craving, demand, desire, eagerness, hankering, hunger, inclination, keenness, liking, limosis, longing, orexis, passion, predilection, proclivity, propensity, relish, stomach, taste, willingness, yearning, zeal, zest.
antonym distaste.

appetizer *n.* antipasto, apéritif, bonne bouche, canapé, cocktail, foretaste, hors d'oeuvre, preview, sample, taste, taster, tidbit, whet.

applaud *v.* acclaim, approve, cheer, clap, commend, compliment, congratulate, encourage, eulogize, extol, laud, ovate, praise.
antonyms censure, disparage.

appliance *n.* apparatus, contraption, contrivance, device, gadget, gismo, implement, instrument, machine, mechanism, tool.

applicable *adj.* apposite, appropriate, apropos, apt, befitting, fit, fitting, germane, legitimate, pertinent, proper, related, relevant, suitable, suited, useful, valid.
antonym inapplicable.

apply[1] *v.* adhibit, administer, appose, assign, bring into play, bring to bear, direct, employ, engage, execute, exercise, implement, ply, practice, resort to, set, use, utilize, wield.

apply[2] *v.* appertain, be relevant, fit, have force, pertain, refer, relate, suit.

apply[3] *v.* anoint, cover with, lay on, paint, place, put on, rub, smear, spread on, use.

apply[4] *v.* appeal, ask for, claim, indent for, inquire, petition, put in, request, requisition, solicit, sue.

apply[5] *v.* address, bend, buckle down, commit, concentrate, dedicate, devote, direct, give, persevere, settle down, study, throw.

appoint *v.* allot, arrange, assign, charge, choose, command, commission, constitute, co-opt, decide, decree, delegate, designate, destine, detail, determine, devote, direct, elect, engage, enjoin, equip, establish, fit out, fix, furnish, install, name, nominate, ordain, outfit, plenish, provide, select, set, settle, supply.

antonyms dismiss, reject.

appointment *n.* allotment, arrangement, assignation, assignment, choice, choosing, commissioning, consultation, date, delegation, election, engagement, installation, interview, job, meeting, naming, nomination, office, place, position, post, rendezvous, selection, session, situation, station, tryst.

appraise *v.* assay, assess, estimate, evaluate, examine, gauge, inspect, judge, price, rate, review, size up, survey, valuate, value.

appreciate[1] *v.* acknowledge, admire, be sensible of, be sensitive to, cherish, comprehend, dig, do justice to, enjoy, esteem, estimate, know, like, perceive, prize, realize, recognize, regard, relish, respect, savor, sympathize with, take kindly to, treasure, understand, value.

antonyms despise, overlook.

appreciate[2] *v.* enhance, gain, grow, improve, increase, inflate, mount, rise, strengthen.

antonym depreciate.

apprehend[1] *v.* arrest, bust, capture, catch, collar, detain, get, grab, nab, nick, pinch, run in, seize, take.

apprehend[2] *v.* appreciate, believe, comprehend, conceive, consider, discern, grasp, imagine, know, perceive, realize, recognize, see, twig, understand.

apprehension[1] *n.* arrest, capture, catching, seizure, taking.

apprehension[2] *n.* alarm, anxiety, apprehensiveness, awareness, belief, comprehension, concept, conception, concern, conjecture, discernment, disquiet, doubt, dread, fear, foreboding, grasp, idea, impression, intellect, intellection, intelligence, ken, knowledge, misgiving, mistrust, nervousness, notion, opinion, perception, premonition, presentiment, qualm, sentiment, suspicion, thought, understanding, unease, uneasiness, uptake, view, worry.

apprehensive *adj.* afraid, alarmed, anxious, concerned, disquieted, distrustful, disturbed, doubtful, fearful, mistrustful, nervous, solicitous, suspicious, uneasy, worried.

antonym confident.

apprentice *n.* beginner, cub, learner, neophyte, newcomer, novice, probationer, pupil, recruit, starter, student, trainee, tyro.

antonym expert.

approach *v.* advance, anear, appeal to, apply to, approximate, be like, begin, broach, catch up, come close, come near to, commence, compare with, draw near, embark on, gain on, introduce, make advances, make overtures, meet, mention, near, reach, resemble, set about, sound out, undertake.

n. access, advance, advent, appeal, application, approximation, arrival, attitude, avenue, course, doorway, entrance, gesture, invitation, landfall, likeness, manner, means, method, mode, modus operandi, motion, nearing, offer, overture, passage, procedure, proposal, proposition, resemblance, road, semblance, style, system, technique, threshold, way.

appropriate *adj.* applicable, apposite, appurtenant, apropos, apt, becoming, befitting, belonging, condign, congruous, correct, felicitous, fit, fitting, germane, meet, merited, opportune, pertinent, proper, relevant,

right, seasonable, seemly, spot-on, suitable, timely, to the point, well-chosen, well-suited, well-timed.

antonym inappropriate.

v. allocate, allot, annex, apportion, arrogate, assign, assume, commandeer, confiscate, devote, earmark, embezzle, expropriate, filch, impound, impropriate, misappropriate, pilfer, pocket, possess oneself of, preempt, purloin, seize, set apart, steal, take, usurp.

approval *n.* acclaim, acclamation, acquiescence, admiration, adoption, agreement, applause, appreciation, approbation, approof, assent, authorization, blessing, certification, commendation, compliance, concurrence, confirmation, consent, countenance, endorsement, esteem, favor, go-ahead, good opinion, green light, honor, imprimatur, leave, licence, liking, mandate, OK, permission, plaudits, praise, ratification, recommendation, regard, respect, sanction, support, validation.

antonym disapproval.

approve *v.* accede to, accept, acclaim, admire, adopt, advocate, agree to, allow, applaud, appreciate, assent to, authorize, back, bless, commend, comply with, concur in, confirm, consent to, countenance, dig, endorse, esteem, favor, homologate, like, mandate, OK, pass, permit, praise, ratify, recommend, regard, respect, rubber-stamp, sanction, second, support, take kindly to, uphold, validate.

antonym disapproval.

approximate *adj.* close, comparable, conjectural, estimated, extrapolated, guessed, inexact, like, loose, near, relative, rough, similar, verging on.

antonym exact.

v. approach, be tantamount to, border on, resemble, verge on.

apt *adj.* accurate, adept, applicable, apposite, appropriate, apropos, astute, befitting, bright, clever, condign, correct, disposed, expert, fair, fit, fitting, germane, gifted, given, inclined, ingenious, intelligent, liable, likely, meet, pertinent, prompt, prone, proper, quick, ready, relevant, seasonable, seemly, sharp, skilful, smart, spot-on, suitable, talented, teachable, tending, timely.

antonym inapt.

aptitude *n.* ability, aptness, bent, capability, capacity, cleverness, disposition, facility, faculty, flair, gift, inclination, intelligence, knack, leaning, penchant, predilection, proclivity, proficiency, proneness, propensity, quickness, talent, tendency.

antonym inaptitude.

aptness *n.* ability, accuracy, applicability, appositeness, appropriateness, aptitude, becomingness, bent, capability, capacity, cleverness, condignness, congruousness, correctness, disposition, facility, faculty, felicitousness, felicity, fitness, fittingness, flair, germaneness, gift, inclination, intelligence, knack, leaning, liability, likelihood, likeliness, opportuneness, pertinence, predilection, proclivity, proficiency, proneness, propensity, properness, quickness, readiness, relevance, rightness, seemliness, suitability, talent, tendency, timeliness.

arbitrary *adj.* absolute, autocratic, capricious, chance, despotic, dictatorial, discretionary, dogmatic, domineering, erratic, fanciful, high-handed, imperious, inconsistent, instinctive, magisterial, optional, overbearing, peremptory, personal, random, subjective,

summary, tyrannical, tyrannous, unreasonable, unreasoned, unsupported, whimsical, wilful.
antonyms circumspect, rational, reasoned.

architecture *n.* architectonics, arrangement, building, composition, construction, design, framework, make-up, planning, structure, style.

ardent *adj.* amorous, avid, devoted, eager, enthusiastic, fervent, fervid, fierce, fiery, hot, hot-blooded, impassioned, intense, keen, lusty, passionate, perfervid, spirited, vehement, warm, zealous.
antonym dispassionate.

ardor *n.* animation, avidity, devotion, eagerness, earnestness, empressement, enthusiasm, feeling, fervor, fire, heat, intensity, keenness, lust, passion, spirit, vehemence, warmth, zeal, zest.
antonyms coolness, indifference.

arduous *adj.* backbreaking, burdensome, daunting, difficult, exhausting, fatiguing, formidable, grueling, hard, harsh, herculean, laborious, onerous, punishing, rigorous, severe, strenuous, taxing, tiring, toilsome, tough, troublesome, trying, uphill, wearisome.
antonym easy.

area *n.* arena, bailiwick, ball-park, breadth, canvas, compass, department, district, domain, environs, expanse, extent, field, locality, neighborhood, part, patch, portion, province, range, realm, region, scope, section, sector, size, sphere, stretch, terrain, territory, tract, width, zone.

argue *v.* altercate, argufy, assert, bicker, chop logic, claim, contend, convince, debate, demonstrate, denote, disagree, discuss, dispute, evidence, evince, exhibit, expostulate, fall out, fence, feud, fight, haggle, hold, imply, indicate, join issue, logicize, maintain, manifest, moot, persuade, plead, prevail upon, prove, quarrel, question, reason, remonstrate, show, squabble, suggest, talk into, wrangle.

argument *n.* abstract, altercation, argumentation, assertion, barney, beef, bickering, case, claim, clash, contention, controversy, debate, defence, demonstration, dialectic, difference, disagreement, discussion, dispute, exposition, expostulation, feud, fight, gist, ground, lemma, logic, logomachy, outline, plea, pleading, plot, polemic, quarrel, questioning, quodlibet, reason, reasoning, remonstrance, remonstration, row, set-to, shouting-match, squabble, story, story line, subject, summary, synopsis, theme, thesis, wrangle.

arid *adj.* baked, barren, boring, colorless, desert, desiccated, dreary, droughty, dry, dull, empty, flat, infertile, jejune, lifeless, moistureless, monotonous, parched, spiritless, sterile, tedious, torrid, torrefied, uninspired, uninteresting, unproductive, vapid, waste, waterless.
antonyms fertile, lively.

arise *v.* appear, ascend, begin, climb, come to light, commence, crop up, derive, emanate, emerge, ensue, flow, follow, get up, go up, grow, happen, issue, lift, mount, occur, originate, proceed, result, rise, set in, soar, spring, stand up, start, stem, tower, wake up.

aristocrat *n.* eupatrid, grand seigneur, grande dame, grandee, lady, lord, lordling, nob, noble, nobleman, noblewoman, optimate, patrician, peer, peeress, swell, toff.
antonym commoner.

arm¹ *n.* appendage, authority, bough, brachium, branch,

channel, department, detachment, division, estuary, extension, firth, inlet, limb, offshoot, projection, section, sector, sound, strait, sway, tributary, upper limb.

arm² *v.* accouter, ammunition, array, brace, empanoply, equip, forearm, fortify, furnish, gird, issue with, munition, outfit, prepare, prime, protect, provide, reinforce, rig, steel, strengthen, supply.

army *n.* armed force, array, arrière-ban, cohorts, gang, horde, host, land forces, legions, military, militia, mob, multitude, pack, soldiers, soldiery, swarm, the junior service, throng, troops.

aroma *n.* bouquet, fragrance, fumet(te), odor, perfume, redolence, savor, scent, smell.

arouse *v.* agitate, animate, awaken, bestir, call forth, disentrance, enliven, evoke, excite, foment, foster, galvanize, goad, incite, inflame, instigate, kindle, move, prompt, provoke, quicken, rouse, sharpen, spark, spur, startle, stimulate, stir up, summon up, wake up, waken, warm, whet, whip up.
antonyms calm, lull, quieten.

arraign *v.* accuse, attack, call to account, charge, denounce, impeach, impugn, incriminate, indict, prosecute.

arrange¹ *v.* adjust, align, array, categorize, class, classify, collocate, concert, construct, contrive, co-ordinate, design, determine, devise, dispose, distribute, fettle, file, fix, form, group, lay out, marshal, methodize, order, organise, plan, position, prepare, project, range, rank, regulate, schedule, set out, settle, sift, sort, sort out, stage-manage, style, swing, systematize, tidy, trim.

arrange² *v.* adapt, harmonize, instrument, orchestrate, score, set.

arrangement¹ *n.* adjustment, agreement, alignment, array, Ausgleich, battery, classification, compact, compromise, construction, deal, design, display, disposition, form, grouping, layout, line-up, marshaling, method, modus vivendi, order, ordering, organization, plan, planning, preconcert, preparation, provision, ranging, rank, schedule, scheme, settlement, set-up, spacing, structure, system, tabulation, taxis, terms.

arrangement² *n.* adaptation, harmonization, instrumentation, interpretation, orchestration, score, setting, version.

array *n.* apparel, arrangement, assemblage, attire, battery, clothes, collection, display, disposition, dress, equipage, exhibition, exposition, finery, formation, garb, garments, line-up, marshaling, muster, order, parade, raiment, regalia, robes, show, supply.

v. accouter, adorn, align, apparel, arrange, assemble, attire, bedeck, bedizen, caparison, clothe, deck, decorate, display, dispose, draw up, dress, equip, exhibit, form up, garb, group, habilitate, line up, marshal, muster, order, outfit, parade, range, rig out, robe, show, supply, trick out, wrap.

arrest *v.* absorb, apprehend, block, bust, capture, catch, check, collar, delay, detain, divert, end, engage, engross, fascinate, grip, halt, hinder, hold, impede, inhibit, interrupt, intrigue, lay, nab, nick, nip, obstruct, occupy, pinch, prevent, restrain, retard, run in, seize, slow, stall, stanch, stay, stem, stop, suppress.
n. apprehension, blockage, bust, caption, capture, cessation, check, cop, delay, detention, end, halt, hindrance, inhibition, interruption, obstruction, preven-

tion, restraint, seizure, stalling, stay, stoppage, suppression, suspension.

arrival *n.* accession, advent, appearance, approach, caller, comer, coming, débutant(e), entrance, entrant, happening, incomer, landfall, newcomer, occurrence, visitant, visitor.

antonym departure.

arrive *v.* alight, appear, attain, befall, come, enter, fetch, get to the top, happen, land, make it, materialize, occur, reach, show, show up, succeed, turn up.

antonyms depart.

arrogance *n.* airs, conceit, conceitedness, condescension, contempt, contemptuousness, contumely, disdain, disdainfulness, haughtiness, hauteur, high-handedness, hubris, imperiousness, insolence, loftiness, lordliness, morgue, presumption, presumptuousness, pretension, pretentiousness, pride, scorn, scornfulness, superciliousness, superiority, uppishness.

antonym humility.

arrogant *adj.* assuming, conceited, condescending, contemptuous, contumelious, disdainful, fastuous, haughty, high and mighty, high-handed, hubristic, imperious, insolent, lordly, on the high ropes, overbearing, overweening, presumptuous, proud, scornful, supercilious, superior, uppish.

antonym humble.

art *n.* address, adroitness, aptitude, artfulness, artifice, artistry, artwork, astuteness, contrivance, craft, craftiness, craftsmanship, cunning, deceit, dexterity, draughtsmanship, drawing, expertise, facility, finesse, guile, ingenuity, knack, knowledge, mastery, method, métier, painting, profession, sculpture, skill, slyness, subtlety, trade, trick, trickery, virtu, virtuosity, visuals, wiliness.

artful *adj.* adept, adroit, canny, clever, crafty, cunning, deceitful, designing, devious, dexterous, fly, foxy, ingenious, masterly, politic, resourceful, rusé, scheming, sharp, shrewd, skilful, sly, smart, subtle, tricksy, tricky, vulpine, wily.

antonyms artless, ingenuous, naïve.

article *n.* account, bit, clause, commodity, composition, constituent, count, detail, discourse, division, element, essay, feature, head, heading, item, matter, object, paper, paragraph, part, particular, piece, point, portion, report, review, section, story, thing, unit.

artifice *n.* adroitness, artfulness, chicanery, cleverness, contrivance, cozenage, craft, craftiness, cunning, deception, deftness, device, dodge, duplicity, expedient, facility, finesse, fraud, guile, hoax, invention, machination, maneuver, manipulation, ruse, scheme, shift, skill, slyness, stratagem, strategy, subterfuge, subtlety, tactic, trick, trickery, wile.

artificial *adj.* affected, assumed, bogus, contrived, counterfeit, ersatz, factitious, fake, false, feigned, forced, hyped up, imitation, insincere, made-up, manmade, mannered, manufactured, meretricious, mock, non-natural, phony, plastic, pretended, pseudo, sham, simulated, specious, spurious, stagey, synthetic, unnatural.

antonyms genuine, natural.

artisan *n.* artificer, craftsman, expert, handicraftsman, journeyman, mechanic, operative, technician, workman.

artist *n.* colorist, craftsman, draughtsman, expert, maestro, master, painter, portraitist, portrait-painter, sculptor, water-colorist.

artless *adj.* candid, childlike, direct, frank, genuine, guileless, honest, humble, ingenuous, innocent, naïf, naïve, naked, natural, open, plain, primitive, pure, simple, sincere, straightforward, true, trustful, trusting, unadorned, unaffected, uncontrived, undesigning, unpretentious, unsophisticated, unwary, unworldly.

antonym artful.

ascend *v.* climb, float up, fly up, go up, lift off, mount, move up, rise, scale, slope upwards, soar, take off, tower.

antonym descend.

ascertain *v.* confirm, detect, determine, discover, establish, find out, fix, identify, learn, locate, make certain, settle, verify.

ascribe *v.* accredit, arrogate, assign, attribute, chalk up to, charge, credit, impute, put down.

ashamed *adj.* abashed, apologetic, bashful, blushing, chagrined, confused, conscience-stricken, crestfallen, discomfited, discomposed, distressed, embarrassed, guilty, hesitant, humbled, humiliated, modest, mortified, prudish, red in the face, redfaced, reluctant, remorseful, self-conscious, shamefaced, sheepish, shy, sorry, unwilling, verecund.

antonyms defiant, shameless.

ask *v.* appeal, apply, beg, beseech, bid, catechize, claim, clamor, crave, demand, enquire, entreat, implore, importune, indent, interrogate, invite, order, petition, plead, pray, press, query, question, quiz, request, require, seek, solicit, sue, summon, supplicate.

askance *adv.* contemptuously, disapprovingly, disdainfully, distrustfully, doubtfully, dubiously, indirectly, mistrustfully, obliquely, sceptically, scornfully, sideways, suspiciously.

askew *adv., adj.* aglee, agley, aslant, asymmetric, awry, cock-eyed, crooked, crookedly, lopsided, oblique, off-center, out of line, skew, skew-whiff, squint.

asleep *adj.* benumbed, comatose, dead to the world, dormant, dormient, dozing, fast asleep, inactive, inert, napping, numb, reposing, sleeping, slumbering, snoozing, sound asleep, unconscious.

aspect *n.* air, angle, appearance, attitude, bearing, condition, countenance, demeanor, direction, elevation, exposure, expression, face, facet, feature, look, manner, mien, outlook, physiognomy, point of view, position, prospect, scene, side, situation, standpoint, view, visage.

aspersion *n.* abuse, animadversion, calumny, censure, criticism, defamation, denigration, derogation, detraction, disparagement, mud-slinging, obloquy, reproach, slander, slur, smear, traducement, vilification, vituperation.

antonyms commendation, compliment.

asphyxiate *v.* burke, choke, garrotte, smother, stifle, strangle, strangulate, suffocate, throttle.

aspirant *n.* applicant, aspirer, candidate, competitor, contestant, hopeful, postulant, seeker, striver, suitor.

aspire *v.* aim, crave, desire, dream, ettle, hanker, hope, intend, long, purpose, pursue, seek, wish, yearn.

aspiring *adj.* ambitious, aspirant, eager, endeavoring, enterprising, hopeful, keen, longing, optimistic, striving, wishful, would-be.

ass[1] *n.* blockhead, bonehead, cretin, dolt, dope, dunce, fool, half-wit, idiot, moron, nincompoop, ninny, nitwit, numskull, schmuck, simpleton, twerp, twit.

ass² n. burro, cardophagus, cuddy, donkey, hinny, jack-ass, jenny, Jerusalem pony, moke, mule.

assail v. abuse, assault, attack, belabor, berate, beset, bombard, charge, criticize, encounter, fall upon, impugn, invade, lay into, malign, maltreat, pelt, revile, set about, set upon, strike, vilify.

assassinate v. dispatch, eliminate, hit, kill, liquidate, murder, rub out, slay.

assault n. aggression, attack, blitz, charge, incursion, invasion, offensive, onset, onslaught, raid, storm, storming, strike.

v. assail, attack, beset, charge, fall on, hit, invade, lay violent hands on, set upon, storm, strike.

assemble v. accumulate, amass, build, collect, compose, congregate, construct, convene, convocate, convoke, erect, fabricate, flock, forgather, gather, group, join up, levy, make, manufacture, marshal, meet, mobilize, muster, muster (up), piece, rally, round up, set up, summon, together.

antonym disperse.

assembly n. agora, assemblage, ball, body, building, caucus, collection, company, conclave, concourse, conference, congregation, congress, consistory, construction, convention, convocation, council, crowd, diet, divan, ecclesia, erection, fabrication, fitting, flock, gathering, group, indaba, joining, levy, manufacture, mass, meeting, moot, multitude, panegyry, rally, reception, setting up, soirée, synod, throng.

assent v. accede, accept, acquiesce, agree, allow, approve, comply, concede, concur, consent, grant, permit, sanction, submit, subscribe, yield.

antonym disagree.

n. acceptance, accession, accord, acquiescence, agreement, approval, capitulation, compliance, concession, concurrence, consent, permission, sanction, submission.

assert v. advance, affirm, allege, asseverate, attest, aver, avouch, avow, claim, constate, contend, declare, defend, dogmatize, insist, lay down, maintain, predicate, press, profess, promote, pronounce, protest, state, stress, swear, testify to, thrust forward, uphold, vindicate.

antonym deny.

assertion n. affirmance, affirmation, allegation, asseveration, attestation, averment, avowal, claim, constatation, contention, declaration, dictum, gratis dictum, ipse dixit, predication, profession, pronouncement, statement, vindication, vouch, word.

antonym denial.

assess v. appraise, compute, consider, demand, determine, estimate, evaluate, fix, gauge, impose, investigate, judge, levy, rate, reckon, review, size up, tax, value, weigh.

asset n. advantage, aid, benefit, blessing, help, plus, resource, service, strength, virtue.

antonym liability.

assign v. accredit, adjudge, allocate, allot, apart, appoint, apportion, arrogate, ascribe, attribute, choose, consign, delegate, designate, determine, dispense, distribute, fix, give, grant, name, nominate, put down, select, set, specify, stipulate.

assignment n. allocation, allotment, appointment, apportionment, ascription, attribution, charge, com-

mission, consignment, delegation, designation, determination, dispensation, distribution, duty, errand, giving, grant, imposition, job, mission, nomination, position, post, responsibility, selection, specification, task.

assimilate v. absorb, accept, acclimatize, accommodate, acculturate, accustom, adapt, adjust, blend, conform, digest, fit, homogenize, imbibe, incorporate, ingest, intermix, learn, merge, mingle, take in, tolerate.

antonym reject.

assist v. abet, accommodate, aid, back, benefit, bestead, boost, collaborate, co-operate, enable, expedite, facilitate, further, help, rally round, reinforce, relieve, second, serve, succor, support, sustain.

antonym thwart.

assistance n. a leg up, abetment, accommodation, adjutancy, aid, backing, benefit, boost, collaboration, comfort, co-operation, furtherance, help, reinforcement, relief, succor, support, sustainment.

antonym hindrance.

assistant n. abettor, accessory, accomplice, adjutant, aide, ally, ancillary, associate, auxiliary, backer, coadjutor, collaborator, colleague, confederate, co-operator, Girl Friday, helper, helpmate, henchman, Man Friday, partner, Person Friday, right-hand man, second, subordinate, subsidiary, supporter.

associate v. accompany, affiliate, ally, amalgamate, combine, company, confederate, conjoin, connect, consort, correlate, couple, fraternize, hang around, hobnob, identify, join, league, link, mingle, mix, pair, relate, socialize, unite, yoke.

n. affiliate, ally, assistant, bedfellow, coadjutor, collaborator, colleague, companion, compeer, comrade, confederate, confrère, co-worker, fellow, follower, friend, leaguer, mate, partner, peer, side-kick.

association n. affiliation, alliance, analogy, band, blend, bloc, bond, cartel, clique, club, coalition, combination, combine, companionship, company, compound, comradeship, concomitance, confederacy, confederation, connection, consociation, consortium, conspiracy, co-operative, corporation, correlation, familiarity, federation, fellowship, fraternization, fraternity, friendship, Gesellschaft, group, intimacy, joining, juxtaposition, league, linkage, mixture, organization, pairing, partnership, relation, relations, relationship, resemblance, society, syndicate, syndication, tie, trust, union, Verein.

assortment n. arrangement, array, assemblage, categorization, choice, classification, collection, disposition, distribution, diversity, farrago, grading, grouping, hotchpotch, jumble, medley, mélange, miscellany, mishmash, mixture, olio, olla-podrida, pot-pourri, ranging, salad, salmagundi, selection, sift, sifting, sorting, variety.

assuage v. allay, alleviate, appease, calm, dull, ease, lessen, lighten, lower, lull, mitigate, moderate, mollify, pacify, palliate, quench, quieten, reduce, relieve, satisfy, slake, soften, soothe, still, temper, tranquilize.

antonym exacerbate.

assume v. accept, acquire, adopt, affect, appropriate, arrogate, believe, commandeer, counterfeit, deduce, don, embrace, expect, expropriate, fancy, feign, guess, imagine, infer, opine, postulate, pre-empt, premise, presume, presuppose, pretend to, put on, seize, sham, shoulder, simulate, strike, suppose, surmise, suspect, take, take for granted, take on, take over, take up, think, understand, undertake, usurp.

assumption *n.* acceptance, acquisition, adoption, appropriation, arrogance, arrogation, audacity, belief, bumptiousness, conceit, conjecture, expectation, expropriation, fancy, guess, guesswork, hypothesis, impudence, inference, postulate, postulation, pre-emption, premise, premiss, presumption, presumptuousness, presupposition, pride, seizure, self-importance, supposition, surmise, suspicion, theory, understanding, undertaking, usurpation.

assurance *n.* affirmation, aplomb, assertion, asseveration, assuredness, audacity, boldness, certainty, certitude, chutzpah, confidence, conviction, coolness, courage, declaration, firmness, gall, guarantee, nerve, oath, pledge, plerophory, poise, positiveness, profession, promise, protestation, security, self-confidence, self-reliance, sureness, vow, word.

antonym uncertainty.

assure *v.* affirm, attest, boost, certify, clinch, comfort, confirm, convince, embolden, encourage, ensure, guarantee, hearten, persuade, pledge, promise, reassure, seal, secure, soothe, strengthen, swear, tell, vow, warrant.

astonish *v.* amaze, astound, baffle, bewilder, confound, daze, dumbfound, electrify, flabbergast, floor, nonplus, shock, stagger, startle, stun, stupefy, surprise, wow.

astound *v.* abash, amaze, astonish, baffle, bewilder, confound, daze, dumbfound, electrify, flabbergast, overwhelm, shake, shock, stagger, stun, stupefy, surprise, wow.

astute *adj.* acute, adroit, artful, astucious, calculating, canny, clever, crafty, cunning, discerning, fly, foxy, intelligent, keen, knowing, penetrating, perceptive, percipient, perspicacious, politic, prudent, sagacious, sharp, shrewd, sly, subtle, wily, wise.

antonym stupid.

asunder *adv.* apart, in half, in pieces, in twain, in two, into pieces, to bits, to pieces.

asylum *n.* bedlam, bughouse, cover, funny farm, harbor, haven, hospital, institution, loony-bin, madhouse, mental hospital, nuthouse, preserve, refuge, reserve, retreat, safety, sanctuary, shelter.

athletic *adj.* active, brawny, energetic, fit, husky, muscular, powerful, robust, sinewy, strapping, strong, sturdy, thewy, vigorous, well-knit, well-proportioned, wiry.

antonym puny.

atone *v.* aby(e), compensate, expiate, make amends, make up for, offset, pay for, propitiate, recompense, reconcile, redeem, redress, remedy.

atrocious *adj.* abominable, barbaric, brutal, cruel, diabolical, execrable, fell, fiendish, flagitious, ghastly, grievous, heinous, hideous, horrible, horrifying, infamous, infernal, inhuman, monstrous, piacular, ruthless, savage, shocking, terrible, vicious, vile, villainous, wicked.

attach *v.* add, adhere, adhibit, affix, annex, append, articulate, ascribe, assign, associate, attract, attribute, belong, bind, captivate, combine, connect, couple, fasten, fix, impute, join, link, place, put, relate to, secure, stick, tie, unite, weld.

antonyms detach, unfasten.

attachment *n.* accessory, accouterment, adapter, addition, adhesion, adhibition, adjunct, affection,

affinity, appendage, appurtenance, attraction, bond, codicil, cohesion, confiscation, connection, connector, coupling, devotion, esteem, extension, extra, fastener, fastening, fidelity, fitting, fixture, fondness, friendship, joint, junction, liking, link, love, loyalty, partiality, predilection, regard, seizure, supplement, tenderness, tie.

attack *n.* abuse, access, aggression, assailment, assault, battery, blitz, bombardment, bout, broadside, censure, charge, convulsion, criticism, fit, foray, impugnment, incursion, inroad, invasion, invective, kamikaze, offensive, onset, onslaught, paroxysm, raid, rush, seizure, spasm, spell, strike, stroke.

v. abuse, assail, assault, belabor, berate, blame, censure, charge, chastise, criticize, denounce, do over, fake, fall on, flay, have one's knife in, impugn, invade, inveigh against, lash, lay into, light into, make at, malign, mob, put the boot in, raid, rate, revile, rush, set about, set on, snipe, storm, strafe, strike, vilify, visit, wade into.

attain *v.* accomplish, achieve, acquire, arrive at, bag, compass, complete, earn, effect, fulfil, gain, get, grasp, net, obtain, procure, reach, realize, reap, secure, touch, win.

attainment *n.* ability, accomplishment, achievement, acquirement, acquisition, aptitude, art, capability, competence, completion, consummation, facility, feat, fulfilment, gift, mastery, procurement, proficiency, reaching, realization, skill, success, talent.

attempt *n.* assault, assay, attack, bash, bid, coup d'essai, crack, effort, endeavor, essay, experiment, go, move, push, shot, shy, stab, struggle, trial, try, undertaking, venture.

v. aspire, endeavor, essay, experiment, have a bash, have a crack, have a go, have a shot, seek, strive, tackle, try, try one's hand at, try one's luck at, undertake, venture.

attend *v.* accompany, appear, arise from, assist, be all ears, be present, care for, chaperon, companion, convoy, escort, follow, frequent, give ear, guard, hear, hearken, heed, help, lend an ear, listen, look after, mark, mind, minister to, note, notice, nurse, observe, pay attention, pay heed, pin back one's ears, regard, result from, serve, squire, succor, take care of, tend, usher, visit, wait upon, watch.

attendant *n.* accompanier, acolyte, aide, assistant, auxiliary, batman, bed captain, chaperon, companion, custodian, equerry, escort, famulus, flunkey, follower, ghillie, guard, guide, helper, jäger, lackey, lady-help, lady-in-waiting, lady's-maid, livery-servant, marshal, menial, page, poursuivant, retainer, servant, steward, underling, usher, waiter.

adj. accessory, accompanying, associated, attached, concomitant, consequent, incidental, related, resultant, subsequent.

attention *n.* advertence, advertency, alertness, attentiveness, awareness, care, civility, concentration, concern, consciousness, consideration, contemplation, courtesy, deference, ear, gallantry, heed, heedfulness, intentness, mindfulness, ministration, notice, observation, politeness, recognition, regard, respect, service, thought, thoughtfulness, treatment, vigilance.

antonyms disregard, inattention.

attentive *adj.* accommodating, advertent, alert, awake, careful, civil, concentrating, conscientious, considerate, courteous, deferential, devoted, gallant, gracious, heedful, intent, kind, mindful, obliging, observant, polite, regardant, studious, thoughtful, vigilant, watchful.

antonyms heedless, inattentive, inconsiderate.

attest *v.* adjure, affirm, assert, authenticate, aver, certify, confirm, corroborate, declare, demonstrate, depose, display, endorse, evidence, evince, exhibit, manifest, prove, ratify, seal, show, substantiate, swear, testify, verify, vouch, warrant, witness.

attire *n.* accouterments, apparel, array, clothes, clothing, costume, dress, finery, garb, garments, gear, get-up, habiliments, habit, outfit, raiment, rig-out, robes, togs, uniform, vestment, wear, weeds.

v. accouter, adorn, apparel, array, caparison, clothe, costume, deck out, dress, equip, garb, habilitate, outfit, prepare, rig out, robe, turn out.

attitude *n.* affectation, air, Anschauung, approach, aspect, bearing, carriage, condition, demeanor, disposition, feeling, manner, mien, mood, opinion, outlook, perspective, point of view, pose, position, posture, stance, view, Weltanschauung.

attractive *adj.* agreeable, alluring, appealing, appetible, beautiful, beddable, captivating, catching, catchy, charming, comely, enchanting, engaging, enticing, epigamous, fair, fascinating, fetching, glamorous, good-looking, gorgeous, handsome, interesting, inviting, jolie laide, lovely, magnetic, nubile, personable, pleasant, pleasing, prepossessing, pretty, seductive, snazzy, stunning, taky, tempting, toothsome, voluptuous, winning, winsome.

antonyms repellent, unattractive.

attribute *v.* accredit, apply, arrogate, ascribe, assign, blame, charge, credit, impute, put down, refer.

n. affection, aspect, character, characteristic, facet, feature, idiosyncrasy, mark, note, peculiarity, point, property, quality, quirk, sign, symbol, trait, virtue.

auction *n.* cant, roup, sale, vendue.

audacious *adj.* adventurous, assuming, assured, bold, brave, brazen, cheeky, courageous, dare-devil, daring, dauntless, death-defying, der-doing, disrespectful, enterprising, fearless, forward, impertinent, impudent, insolent, intrepid, pert, plucky, presumptuous, rash, reckless, risky, rude, shameless, unabashed, valiant, venturesome.

antonyms cautious, reserved, timid.

audacity *n.* adventurousness, assurance, audaciousness, boldness, brass neck, bravery, brazenness, cheek, chutzpah, courage, daring, dauntlessness, defiance, derring-do, disrespectfulness, effrontery, enterprise, fearlessness, foolhardiness, forwardness, gall, guts, impertinence, impudence, insolence, intrepidity, nerve, pertness, presumption, rashness, recklessness, rudeness, shamelessness, valor, venturesomeness.

antonyms caution, reserve, timidity.

audible *adj.* appreciable, clear, detectable, discernible, distinct, hearable, perceptible, recognizable.

antonym inaudible.

augment *v.* add to, amplify, boost, dilate, eke out, enhance, enlarge, expand, extend, grow, heighten, increase, inflate, intensify, magnify, multiply, raise, reinforce, strengthen, supplement, swell.

antonym decrease.

auspicious *adj.* bright, cheerful, encouraging, favorable, felicitous, fortunate, happy, hopeful, lucky, opportune, optimistic, promising, propitious, prosperous, rosy, white.

antonyms inauspicious, ominous.

austere *adj.* abstemious, abstinent, ascetic, astringent, bitter, bleak, chaste, cold, conservative, continent, Dantean, Dantesque, economical, exacting, forbidding, formal, grave, grim, hard, harsh, plain, puritanical, restrained, rigid, rigorous, self-denying, self-disciplined, serious, severe, simple, sober, solemn, sour, spare, Spartan, stark, stern, strict, stringent, unadorned, unembellished, unornamented, unrelenting.

antonyms elaborate, extravagant, genial.

authentic *adj.* accurate, actual, authoritative, bona fide, certain, dependable, dinkum, factual, faithful, genuine, honest, kosher, legitimate, original, pure, real, reliable, simon-pure, true, true-to-life, trustworthy, valid, veracious, veritable.

antonyms counterfeit, inauthentic, spurious.

authenticate *v.* accredit, attest, authorize, avouch, certify, confirm, corroborate, endorse, guarantee, validate, verify, vouch for, warrant.

author *n.* architect, begetter, composer, creator, designer, fabricator, fashioner, father, forger, founder, framer, initiator, inventor, maker, mover, originator, paper-stainer, parent, pen, penman, penwoman, planner, prime mover, producer, volumist, writer.

authoritative *adj.* accepted, accurate, approved, assured, authentic, authorized, cathedratic, commanding, confident, convincing, decisive, definitive, dependable, factual, faithful, learned, legitimate, magisterial, magistrial, masterly, official, reliable, sanctioned, scholarly, sound, sovereign, true, trustworthy, truthful, valid, veritable.

antonym unreliable.

authority[1] *n.* administration, ascendancy, attestation, authorization, avowal, charge, command, control, declaration, domination, dominion, evidence, force, government, imperium, influence, jurisdiction, justification, licence, management, might, officialdom, permission, permit, power, prerogative, profession, right, rule, sanction, sovereignty, statement, strength, supremacy, sway, testimony, textbook, warrant, weight, word.

authority[2] *n.* arbiter, bible, connoisseur, expert, judge, master, professional, pundit, sage, scholar, specialist.

autocrat *n.* absolutist, authoritarian, Caesar, cham, despot, dictator, fascist, Hitler, panjandrum, totalitarian, tyrant.

automatic *adj.* automated, certain, habitual, inescapable, inevitable, instinctive, involuntary, mechanical, mechanized, natural, necessary, perfunctory, push-button, reflex, robot, robot-like, routine, self-acting, self-activating, self-moving, self-propelling, self-regulating, spontaneous, unavoidable, unbidden, unconscious, unthinking, unwilled, vegetative.

automobile *n.* armored car, convertible, coupe, fastback, gocart, hot rod, jeep, land-rover, limousine, racing car, roadster, sedan, sports car, station wagon.

auxiliary *adj.* accessory, adjuvant, adminicular, aiding, ancillary, assistant, assisting, back-up, emergency, helping, reserve, secondary, subsidiary, substitute, supplementary, supporting, supportive.

n. accessory, accomplice, adminicle, ally, ancillary,

assistant, associate, companion, confederate, foederatus, helper, partner, reserve, subordinate, supporter.

avail *v.* advance, advantage, aid, assist, benefit, boot, dow, exploit, help, make the most of, profit, serve, work.

n. advantage, aid, assistance, benefit, boot, good, help, profit, purpose, service, use, value.

available *adj.* accessible, at hand, attainable, convenient, disengaged, free, handy, obtainable, on hand, on tap, procurable, ready, to hand, vacant, within reach.

antonym unavailable.

avarice *n.* acquisitiveness, cheese-paring, covetousness, cupidity, greed, greediness, meanness, miserliness, niggardliness, parsimoniousness, parsimony, penny-pinching, penuriousness, predatoriness, rapacity, stinginess, tight-fistedness.

antonym generosity.

average *n.* mean, mediocrity, medium, midpoint, norm, par, rule, run, standard.

antonyms exception, extreme.

adj. common, commonplace, everyday, fair, general, indifferent, intermediate, mean, medial, median, mediocre, medium, middle, middling, moderate, normal, ordinary, passable, regular, run-of-the-mill, satisfactory, so-so, standard, tolerable, typical, undistinguished, unexceptional, unremarkable, usual.

antonyms exceptional, extreme.

averse *adj.* antagonistic, antipathetic, disapproving, disinclined, hostile, ill-disposed, inimical, loath, opposed, reluctant, unfavorable, unwilling.

antonyms sympathetic, willing.

aversion *n.* abhorrence, abomination, anathema, animosity, antagonism, antipathy, detestation, disapproval, disgust, disinclination, dislike, distaste, hate, hatred, horror, hostility, loathing, odium, opposition, phobia, phobism, reluctance, repugnance, repulsion, revulsion, unwillingness.

antonyms liking, sympathy.

avert *v.* avoid, deflect, evade, fend off, forestall, frustrate, obviate, parry, preclude, prevent, stave off, turn, turn aside, turn away, ward off.

avid *adj.* acquisitive, ardent, avaricious, covetous, dedicated, devoted, eager, earnest, enthusiastic, fanatical, fervent, grasping, greedy, hungry, insatiable, intense, keen, passionate, rapacious, ravenous, thirsty, voracious, zealous.

antonym indifferent.

avocation *n.* business, calling, distraction, diversion, employment, hobby, interest, job, occupation, pastime, profession, pursuit, recreation, relaxation, sideline, trade, vocation, work.

avoid *v.* abstain from, avert, balk, bypass, circumvent, dodge, duck, elude, escape, eschew, evade, evite, funk, get out of, obviate, prevent, refrain from, shirk, shun, side-step, steer clear of.

award *v.* accord, adjudge, allot, allow, apportion, assign, bestow, confer, determine, dispense, distribute, endow, gift, give, grant, present.

n. adjudication, allotment, allowance, bestowal, conferment, conferral, decision, decoration, dispensation, endowment, gift, grant, judgment, order, presentation, prize, trophy.

aware *adj.* acquainted, alive to, appreciative, apprized, attentive, au courant, cognizant, conscient, conscious, conversant, enlightened, familiar, heedful, hep, hip,

informed, knowing, knowledgeable, mindful, observant, on the ball, on the qui vive, sensible, sensitive, sentient, sharp, shrewd.

antonyms insensitive, unaware.

awe *n.* admiration, amazement, apprehension, astonishment, dread, fear, respect, reverence, terror, veneration, wonder, wonderment.

antonym contempt.

v. amaze, astonish, cow, daunt, frighten, horrify, impress, intimidate, overwhelm, stun, terrify.

awful *adj.* abysmal, alarming, amazing, atrocious, august, awe-inspiring, awesome, blood-curdling, dire, dread, dreadful, eldritch, fearful, fearsome, frightful, ghastly, gruesome, harrowing, hideous, horrendous, horrible, horrific, horrifying, majestic, nasty, portentous, shocking, solemn, spine-chilling, terrible, tremendous, ugly, unpleasant.

awkward *adj.* annoying, bloody-minded, blundering, bungling, chancy, clownish, clumsy, coarse, compromising, cubbish, cumbersome, delicate, difficult, disobliging, embarrassed, embarrassing, exasperating, farouche, fiddly, gauche, gawky, graceless, ham-fisted, ham-handed, hazardous, ill at ease, inconvenient, inelegant, inept, inexpedient, inexpert, inopportune, intractable, intransigent, irritable, left-handed, maladroit, obstinate, painful, perplexing, perverse, prickly, risky, rude, spastic, sticky, stubborn, thorny, ticklish, touchy, troublesome, trying, uncomfortable, unco-operative, unco-ordinated, uncouth, ungainly, ungraceful, unhandy, unhelpful, unmanageable, unpleasant, unrefined, unskilful, untimely, untoward, unwieldy, vexatious, vexing.

antonyms amenable, convenient, elegant, graceful, straightforward.

awry *adv.*, *adj.* aglee, amiss, askew, asymmetrical, cockeyed, crooked, misaligned, oblique, off-center, out of kilter, skew-whiff, twisted, uneven, unevenly, wonky, wrong.

antonyms straight, symmetrical.

axiom *n.* adage, aphorism, apophthegm, byword, dictum, fundamental, gnome, maxim, postulate, precept, principle, truism, truth.

B

babble *v.* blab, burble, cackle, chatter, gabble, gibber, gurgle, jabber, mumble, murmur, mutter, prate, prattle, purl, twattle.

n. burble, clamor, drivel, gabble, gibberish, lallation, lalling, murmur, purl, purling, twattle.

baby *n.* babe, bairn, child, infant, nursling, papoose, suckling, tiny, toddler, wean, weanling, youngling.

adj. diminutive, dwarf, Lilliputian, little, midget, mini, miniature, minute, pygmy, small, small-scale, tiny, toy, wee.

v. cocker, coddle, cosset, humor, indulge, mollycoddle, overindulge, pamper, pander to, pet, spoil, spoon-feed.

babyish *adj.* baby, childish, foolish, immature, infantile, jejune, juvenile, naïve, namby-pamby, puerile, silly, sissy, soft, spoilt.

antonyms mature, precocious.

back[1] *v.* advocate, assist, boost, buttress, champion, countenance, countersign, encourage, endorse, favor,

finance, sanction, second, side with, sponsor, subsidize, support, sustain, underwrite.
antonym discourage.

back up aid, assist, bolster, champion, confirm, corroborate, endorse, reinforce, second, substantiate, support.
antonym let down.

back² *n.* backside, end, hind part, hindquarters, posterior, rear, reverse, stern, tail, tail end, tergum, verso.
adj. end, hind, hindmost, posterior, rear, reverse, tail.

back³ *v.* backtrack, recede, recoil, regress, retire, retreat, reverse, withdraw.

back⁴ *adj.* delayed, earlier, elapsed, former, outdated, overdue, past, previous, prior, superseded.

backbiting *n.* abuse, aspersion, bitchiness, calumniation, calumny, cattiness, criticism, defamation, denigration, detraction, disparagement, gossip, malice, revilement, scandalmongering, slagging, slander, spite, spitefulness, vilification, vituperation.
antonym praise.

backbone *n.* basis, bottle, character, core, courage, determination, firmness, foundation, grit, hardihood, mainstay, mettle, nerve, pluck, power, resolution, resolve, spine, stamina, staunchness, steadfastness, strength, support, tenacity, toughness, vertebral column, will.
antonyms spinelessness, weakness.

backbreaking *adj.* arduous, crushing, exhausting, grueling, hard, heavy, killing, laborious, punishing, strenuous, tiring, toilsome, wearing, wearisome.
antonym easy.

backer *n.* advocate, benefactor, bottle-holder, champion, patron, promoter, second, seconder, sponsor, subscriber, supporter, underwriter, well-wisher.

backfire *v.* boomerang, come home to roost, fail, flop, miscarry, rebound, recoil, ricochet.

background *n.* breeding, circumstances, credentials, culture, dossier, education, environment, experience, fond, grounding, history, milieu, preparation, record, surroundings, tradition, upbringing.

backing *n.* accompaniment, advocacy, aid, assistance, championing, championship, encouragement, endorsement, favor, funds, grant, helpers, moral support, patronage, sanction, seconding, sponsorship, subsidy, support.

backlash *n.* backfire, boomerang, counterblast, kickback, reaction, recoil, repercussion, reprisal, resentment, response, retaliation.

backlog *n.* accumulation, excess, hoard, leeway, mountain, reserve, reserves, resources, stock, supply.

backslide *v.* apostatize, default, defect, fall from grace, lapse, regress, relapse, renegue, retrogress, revert, sin, slip, stray, weaken.
antonym persevere.

backward *adj.* bashful, behind, behindhand, diffident, dull, hesitant, hesitating, immature, late, reluctant, retarded, shy, slow, sluggish, stupid, subnormal, tardy, underdeveloped, unwilling, wavering.
antonyms forward, precocious.

bad *adj.* adverse, ailing, base, blameworthy, conscience-stricken, contrite, corrupt, criminal, damaging, dangerous, decayed, defective, deficient, deleterious, delinquent, despondent, detrimental, disastrous, discouraged, discouraging, diseased, disobedient, distressed, distressing, evil, fallacious, faulty, gloomy,

grave, grim, grotty, guilty, harmful, harsh, ill, illaudable, immoral, imperfect, inadequate, incorrect, inferior, injurious, mean, melancholy, mischievous, mouldy, naughty, noxious, off, offensive, onkus, painful, piacular, poor, putrid, rancid, regretful, remorseful, ropy, rotten, rueful, ruinous, sad, serious, severe, shoddy, sick, sinful, somber, sorry, sour, spoilt, stormy, substandard, terrible, troubled, unfortunate, unhealthy, unpleasant, unruly, unsatisfactory, unwell, upset, vile, wicked, wrong.

badger *v.* bait, bully, bullyrag, chivvy, goad, harass, harry, hassle, hound, importune, nag, pester, plague, torment.

baffle *v.* amaze, astound, balk, bamboozle, bemuse, bewilder, check, confound, confuse, daze, defeat, disconcert, dumbfound, flabbergast, floor, flummox, foil, frustrate, hinder, mystify, nonplus, perplex, puzzle, stump, stun, stymie, thwart, upset.
antonyms enlighten, help.

bag *v.* acquire, appropriate, capture, catch, commandeer, corner, gain, get, grab, kill, land, obtain, reserve, shoot, take, trap.
n. carrier, container, dorlach, Dorothy bag, dressing-case, Gladstone bag, grab-bag, grip, gripsack, handbag, haversack, hold-all, holder, pack, poke, reticule, rucksack, sack, satchel, satchet, scrip, shoulder-bag, tote-bag, valise.

bail *n.* bond, guarantee, guaranty, pledge, security, surety, warranty.

bait *n.* allurement, attraction, bribe, carrot, decoy, enticement, inducement, lure, temptation.
antonym disincentive.
v. annoy, gall, goad, harass, hound, irk, irritate, needle, persecute, provoke, tease, torment.

balance *v.* adjust, assess, calculate, compare, compute, consider, counteract, counterbalance, counterpoise, deliberate, equalize, equate, equilibrate, equipoise, equiponderate, estimate, evaluate, level, librate, match, neutralize, offset, parallel, poise, settle, square, stabilize, steady, tally, total, weigh.
antonyms overbalance, unbalance.
n. composure, correspondence, difference, equality, equanimity, equilibrium, equipoise, equity, equivalence, evenness, parity, poise, remainder, residue, rest, self-possession, stability, stasis, steadiness, surplus, symmetry.
antonyms imbalance, instability.

bald *adj.* bald-headed, baldpated, bare, barren, bleak, depilated, direct, downright, exposed, forthright, glabrate, glabrous, hairless, naked, outright, peeled, plain, severe, simple, stark, straight, straightforward, treeless, unadorned, uncompromising, uncovered, undisguised, unvarnished.
antonyms adorned, hirsute.

baleful *adj.* deadly, destructive, evil, fell, harmful, hurtful, injurious, malevolent, malignant, menacing, mournful, noxious, ominous, pernicious, ruinous, sad, sinister, venomous, woeful.
antonyms auspicious, favorable.

balk, baulk *v.* baffle, bar, boggle, check, counteract, defeat, demur, disconcert, dodge, evade, flinch, foil, forestall, frustrate, hesitate, hinder, jib, make difficulties, obstruct, prevent, recoil, refuse, resist, shirk, shrink, stall, thwart.

ball¹ *n.* bauble, bobble, bullet, clew, conglomeration, drop, globe, globule, orb, pellet, pill, shot, slug, sphere, spheroid.

ball² n. assembly, carnival, dance, dinner-dance, fandango, hop, masquerade, party, ridotto, rout, soirée.

ballad n. carol, composition, ditty, folk-song, lay, poem, pop-song, shanty, song.

ballet n. ballet-dancing, dancing, leg-business.

balloon v. bag, belly, billow, blow up, bulge, dilate, distend, enlarge, expand, inflate, puff out, swell.

ballot n. election, plebiscite, poll, polling, referendum, vote, voting.

balmy¹ adj. clement, gentle, mild, pleasant, soft, summery, temperate.
antonym inclement.

balmy² adj. barmy, crazy, daft, dippy, dotty, foolish, idiotic, insane, loony, mad, nuts, nutty, odd, round the bend, silly, stupid.
antonyms rational, sane, sensible.

ban v. anathematize, banish, bar, debar, disallow, exclude, forbid, interdict, ostracize, outlaw, prohibit, proscribe, restrict, suppress.
antonym permit.
n. anathematization, boycott, censorship, condemnation, curse, denunciation, embargo, interdiction, outlawry, prohibition, proscription, restriction, stoppage, suppression, taboo.
antonyms dispensation, permission.

banal adj. boring, clichéd, cliché-ridden, commonplace, corny, empty, everyday, hackneyed, humdrum, jejune, old hat, ordinary, pedestrian, platitudinous, stale, stereotyped, stock, threadbare, tired, trite, unimaginative, unoriginal, vapid.
antonym original.

band¹ n. bandage, bandeau, belt, binding, bond, chain, cincture, cord, fascia, fetter, fillet, ligature, manacle, ribbon, shackle, strap, strip, swath, tape, tie, vitta.

band² n. association, body, clique, club, combo, company, coterie, crew, ensemble, flock, gang, group, herd, horde, orchestra, party, range, society, troop, waits.
v. affiliate, ally, amalgamate, collaborate, consolidate, federate, gather, group, join, merge, unite.
antonyms disband, disperse.

bandit n. brigand, buccaneer, cowboy, dacoit, desperado, footpad, freebooter, gangster, gunman, highwayman, hijacker, marauder, outlaw, pirate, racketeer, robber, ruffian, thief.

bang n. blow, boom, box, bump, clang, clap, clash, collision, crash, cuff, detonation, explosion, hit, knock, noise, peal, pop, punch, report, shot, slam, smack, stroke, thud, thump, wallop, whack.
v. bash, boom, bump, burst, clang, clatter, crash, detonate, drum, echo, explode, hammer, knock, peal, pound, pummel, rap, resound, slam, stamp, strike, thump, thunder.
adv. directly, hard, headlong, noisily, plumb, precisely, right, slap, smack, straight, suddenly.

banish v. ban, bar, blacklist, debar, deport, discard, dislodge, dismiss, dispel, eject, eliminate, eradicate, evict, exclude, excommunicate, exile, expatriate, expel, get rid of, ostracize, oust, outlaw, remove, shut out, transport.
antonyms recall, welcome.

bank¹ n. accumulation, cache, depository, fund, hoard,

pool, repository, reserve, reservoir, savings, stock, stockpile, store, storehouse, treasury.
v. accumulate, deposit, keep, save, stockpile, store.
antonym spend.

bank² n. acclivity, banking, brink, bund, earthwork, edge, embankment, fail-dike, heap, margin, mass, mound, pile, rampart, ridge, rivage, shallow, shoal, shore, side, slope, tilt.
v. accumulate, aggrade, amass, camber, cant, drift, heap, incline, mass, mound, pile, pitch, slant, slope, stack, tilt, tip.

bank³ n. array, bench, echelon, file, group, line, rank, row, sequence, series, succession, tier, train.

banner n. banderol(e), bannerol, burgee, colors, ensign, fanion, flag, gonfalon, labarum, oriflamme, pennant, pennon, standard, streamer, vexillum.

banquet n. binge, dinner, feast, meal, repast, revel, treat, wayzgoose.

banter n. badinage, chaff, chaffing, cross-talk, derision, dicacity, jesting, joking, kidding, mockery, persiflage, pleasantry, quiz, raillery, repartee, ribbing, ridicule, word play.

bar¹ n. barricade, barrier, batten, check, cross-piece, deterrent, deterrment, hindrance, impediment, obstacle, obstruction, overslaugh, paling, pole, preventive, rail, railing, rod, shaft, stake, stanchion, stick, stop.
v. ban, barricade, blackball, bolt, debar, exclude, fasten, forbid, hinder, latch, lock, obstruct, preclude, prevent, prohibit, restrain, secure.

bar² n. bierkeller, boozer, canteen, counter, dive, doggery, dram-shop, estaminet, exchange, gin-palace, gin-shop, groggery, grogshop, honky-tonk, howff, inn, joint, lounge, nineteenth hole, pub, public house, saloon, tavern, vaults, watering-hole.

bar³ n. advocates, attorneys, barristers, bench, counsel, court, courtroom, dock, law court, tribunal.

bar⁴ n. block, chunk, ingot, lump, nugget, slab, wedge.

barbarian n. ape, boor, brute, clod, hooligan, hottentot, hun, ignoramus, illiterate, lout, lowbrow, oaf, philistine, ruffian, savage, tramontane, vandal, vulgarian, yahoo.
adj. boorish, brutish, coarse, crude, lowbrow, philistine, rough, tramontane, uncivilized, uncouth, uncultivated, uncultured, unsophisticated, vulgar.

barbarous adj. barbarian, barbaric, brutal, brutish, coarse, crude, cruel, ferocious, heartless, heathenish, ignorant, inhuman, monstrous, philistine, primitive, rough, rude, ruthless, savage, uncivilized, uncouth, uncultured, unlettered, unrefined, vicious, vulgar, wild.
antonyms civilized, cultured, educated.

bare adj. austere, bald, barren, basic, blank, defoliate, defoliated, denudated, denuded, disfurnished, empty, essential, explicit, exposed, hard, lacking, literal, mean, naked, napless, nude, open, peeled, plain, poor, scanty, scarce, severe, sheer, shorn, simple, spare, stark, stripped, unadorned, unarmed, unclad, unclothed, uncovered, undisguised, undressed, unembellished, unforested, unfurnished, unprovided, unsheathed, untimbered, unvarnished, unwooded, vacant, void, wanting, woodless.

barefaced adj. arrant, audacious, bald, blatant, bold, brash, brazen, flagrant, glaring, impudent, insolent, manifest, naked, obvious, open, palpable, patent, shameless, transparent, unabashed, unconcealed.

barely[1] *adv.* almost, hardly, just, scarcely, sparingly, sparsely.

barely[2] *adv.* explicitly, nakedly, openly, plainly.

bargain *n.* agreement, arrangement, compact, contract, discount, giveaway, negotiation, pact, pledge, promise, reduction, snip, steal, stipulation, transaction, treaty, understanding.

v. agree, barter, broke, buy, chaffer, contract, covenant, deal, dicker, haggle, higgle, negotiate, promise, sell, stipulate, trade, traffic, transact.

bargain for anticipate, consider, contemplate, expect, foresee, imagine, include, look for, plan for, reckon on.

baroque *adj.* bizarre, bold, convoluted, elaborate, extravagant, exuberant, fanciful, fantastic, flamboyant, florid, grotesque, ornate, overdecorated, overwrought, rococo, vigorous, whimsical.

antonym plain.

barren *adj.* arid, boring, childless, desert, desolate dry, dull, empty, flat, fruitless, infecund, infertile, jejune, lackluster, pointless, profitless, stale, sterile, unbearing, unfruitful, uninformative, uninspiring, uninstructive, uninteresting, unproductive, unprolific, unrewarding, useless, vapid, waste.

antonyms fertile, productive, useful.

barricade *n.* barrier, blockade, bulwark, fence, obstruction, palisade, protection, rampart, screen, stockade.

v. bar, block, blockade, defend, fortify, obstruct, palisade, protect, screen.

barrier *n.* bail, bar, barricade, blockade, boom, boundary, bulkhead, check, difficulty, ditch, drawback, fence, fortification, handicap, hindrance, hurdle, impediment, limitation, obstacle, obstruction, railing, rampart, restriction, stop, stumbling-block, transverse, wall.

barter *v.* bargain, chaffer, deal, dicker, exchange, haggle, higgle, negotiate, sell, swap, switch, trade, traffic, truck.

base[1] *n.* basis, bed, bottom, camp, center, core, essence, essential, foot, foundation, fundamental, groundwork, headquarters, heart, home, key, origin, pedestal, plinth, post, principal, rest, root, settlement, socle, source, stand, standard, starting-point, station, substrate, substructure, support, underpinning, understructure.

v. build, construct, depend, derive, establish, found, ground, hinge, locate, station.

base[2] *adj.* abject, contemptible, corrupt, counterfeit, depraved, disgraceful, disreputable, dog, evil, groveling, humble, ignoble, ignominious, immoral, infamous, low, lowly, low-minded, low-thoughted, mean, menial, miserable, paltry, pitiful, poor, scandalous, servile, shameful, slavish, sordid, sorry, valueless, vile, villainous, vulgar, wicked, worthless, wretched.

base[3] *adj.* adulterated, alloyed, artificial, bastard, counterfeit, debased, fake, forged, fraudulent, impure, inferior, pinchbeck, spurious.

bashful *adj.* abashed, backward, blushing, confused, coy, diffident, embarrassed, hesitant, inhibited, modest, nervous, reserved, reticent, retiring, self-conscious, self-effacing, shamefaced, sheepish, shrinking, shy, timid, timorous, unforthcoming, verecund.

antonym confident.

basic *adj.* central, elementary, essential, fundamental,

important, indispensable, inherent, intrinsic, key, necessary, primary, radical, root, underlying, vital.

antonyms inessential, peripheral.

basis *n.* approach, base, bottom, core, essential, fond, footing, foundation, fundamental, ground, groundwork, heart, keynote, pedestal, premise, principle, support, thrust.

bask *v.* apricate, delight in, enjoy, laze, lie, lounge, luxuriate, relax, relish, revel, savor, sunbathe, wallow.

bastion *n.* bulwark, citadel, defence, fastness, fortress, mainstay, pillar, prop, redoubt, rock, stronghold, support, tower of strength.

batch *n.* amount, assemblage, assortment, bunch, collection, consignment, contingent, group, lot, pack, parcel, quantity, set.

bath *n.* ablution, bathtub, cleansing, douche, douse, hamman, Jacuzzi®, scrubbing, shower, soak, tub, wash.

v. bathe, clean, douse, lave, shower, soak, tub, wash.

bathe *v.* cleanse, cover, dook, dunk, encompass, flood, immerse, moisten, rinse, soak, steep, stew, suffuse, swim, wash, wet.

n. dip, dook, rinse, soak, swim, wash.

bathos *n.* anticlimax, comedown, let-down.

battalion *n.* army, brigade, company, contingent, division, force, herd, horde, host, legion, mass, multitude, phalanx, platoon, regiment, squadron, throng.

batten *v.* barricade, board up, clamp down, fasten, fix, nail down, secure, tighten.

batter *v.* abuse, assault, bash, beat, belabor, bruise, buffet, crush, dash, deface, demolish, destroy, disfigure, distress, hurt, injure, lash, maltreat, mangle, manhandle, mar, maul, pelt, pound, pummel, ruin, shatter, smash, thrash, wallop.

battery *n.* artillery, assault, attack, barrage, beating, cannon, cannonry, emplacements, guns, mayhem, onslaught, progression, sequence, series, set, thrashing, violence.

battle *n.* action, affray, attack, campaign, clash, combat, conflict, contest, controversy, crusade, debate, disagreement, dispute, encounter, engagement, fight, fray, hostilities, row, skirmish, strife, struggle, war, warfare.

v. agitate, argue, campaign, clamor, combat, contend, contest, crusade, dispute, feud, fight, strive, struggle, war.

bauble *n.* bagatelle, flamfew, gewgaw, gimcrack, kickshaw, knick-knack, plaything, tinsel, toy, trifle, trinket.

bawd *n.* brothel-keeper, madam, panderess, pimp, procuress.

bawdy *adj.* blue, coarse, dirty, erotic, gross, improper, indecent, indecorous, indelicate, lascivious, lecherous, lewd, libidinous, licentious, lustful, obscene, pornographic, prurient, ribald, risqué, rude, salacious, smutty, suggestive, vulgar.

antonyms chaste, clean.

bawl *v.* bellow, blubber, call, caterwaul, clamor, cry, halloo, howl, roar, shout, sob, squall, vociferate, wail, waul, weep, yell.

bay[1] *n.* arm, bight, cove, embayment, fjord, gulf, inlet, reach.

bay[2] *n.* alcove, booth, carrel, compartment, cubicle, embrasure, niche, nook, opening, recess, stall.

bay[3] *v.* bark, bawl, bell, bellow, cry, holler, howl, roar.

bazaar *n.* agora, alcaicería, alcázar, bring-and-buy, exchange, fair, fête, market, market-place, mart, sale.

beach *n.* coast, foreshore, lido, littoral, margin, plage, riviera, sand, sands, seaboard, seashore, seaside, shingle, shore, strand, water's edge.

beachcomber *n.* Autolycus, forager, loafer, loiterer, scavenger, scrounger, wayfarer.

beacon *n.* beam, bonfire, fanal, flare, lighthouse, pharos, rocket, sign, signal, watch-fire.

bead *n.* blob, bubble, dot, drop, droplet, glob, globule, pearl, pellet, pill, spherule.

beak *n.* bill, bow, mandibles, neb, nib, nose, nozzle, proboscis, projection, prow, ram, rostrum, snout, stem.

beam *n.* arbor, bar, boom, girder, gleam, glimmer, glint, glow, joist, plank, radiation, rafter, ray, shaft, spar, stanchion, stream, support, timber.

v. broadcast, effulge, emit, fulgurate, glare, glimmer, glitter, glow, grin, laugh, radiate, shine, smile, transmit.

beaming *adj.* beautiful, bright, brilliant, cheerful, effulgent, flashing, gleaming, glistening, glittering, glowing, grinning, happy, joyful, lambent, radiant, refulgent, scintillating, shining, smiling, sparkling, sunny.

antonyms lowering, sullen.

bear¹ *v.* abide, admit, allow, beget, bring, brook, carry, cherish, convey, endure, entertain, exhibit, hack, harbor, have, hold, maintain, move, permit, possess, put up with, shoulder, stomach, suffer, support, sustain, take, tolerate, tote, transport, undergo, uphold, weather, weigh upon.

bear² *v.* breed, bring forth, develop, drop, engender, generate, give birth to, give up, produce, propagate, yield.

bearable *adj.* acceptable, endurable, livable(-with), manageable, sufferable, supportable, sustainable, tolerable.

bearing *n.* air, application, aspect, attitude, behavior, carriage, comportment, connection, course, demeanor, deportment, direction, import, manner, mien, pertinence, poise, posture, presence, reference, relation, relevance, significance.

bearings *n.* aim, course, direction, inclination, location, orientation, position, situation, tack, track, way, whereabouts.

beast *n.* animal, ape, barbarian, brute, creature, devil, fiend, monster, pig, sadist, savage, swine.

beastly *adj.* barbarous, bestial, brutal, brutish, coarse, cruel, depraved, disagreeable, foul, inhuman, mean, monstrous, nasty, repulsive, rotten, sadistic, savage, sensual, swinish, terrible, unpleasant, vile.

beat¹ *v.* bang, bash, baste, bastinade, bastinado, batter, belabor, belabour, bethwack, bless, bludgeon, bruise, buffet, cane, contuse, cudgel, curry, ding, drub, dunt, fashion, flog, forge, form, fustigate, hammer, hit, impinge, knobble, knock, knout, knubble, lam, lash, lay into, malleate, maul, mill, model, nubble, pelt, pound, punch, shape, slat, strap, strike, swipe, tan, thrash, thwack, trounce, vapulate, verberate, warm, welt, whale, wham, whip, work.

n. blow, hit, lash, punch, shake, slap, strike, swing, thump.

adj. exhausted, fatigued, jiggered, tired, wearied, worn out, zonked.

beat² *v.* best, conquer, defeat, excel, hammer, outdo,

outrun, outstrip, overcome, overwhelm, slaughter, subdue, surpass, trounce, vanquish.

beat³ *v.* flutter, palpitate, patter, pound, pulsate, pulse, quake, quiver, race, shake, throb, thump, tremble, vibrate.

n. accent, cadence, flutter, measure, meter, palpitation, pulsation, pulse, rhyme, rhythm, stress, throb, time.

beat⁴ *n.* circuit, course, journey, path, round, rounds, route, territory, way.

beaten¹ *adj.* baffled, cowed, defeated, disappointed, disheartened, frustrated, overcome, ruined, surpassed, thwarted, vanquished, worsted.

beaten² *adj.* fashioned, forged, formed, hammered, malleated, shaped, stamped, worked.

beaten³ *adj.* blended, foamy, frothy, mixed, pounded, stirred, tenderized, whipped, whisked.

beating *n.* belting, caning, chastisement, conquest, corporal punishment, defeat, downfall, dressing, drubbing, flogging, lamming, overthrow, rout, ruin, slapping, smacking, thrashing, vapulation, verberation, warming, whaling, whipping.

adj. pounding, pulsatile, pulsating, pulsative, pulsatory, pulsing, racing, throbbing, thumping.

beau *n.* admirer, Adonis, boyfriend, cavalier, coxcomb, dandy, escort, fancy man, fiancé, fop, gallant, Jack-a-dandy, ladies' man, lover, popinjay, suitor, swain, sweetheart, swell.

beautiful *adj.* alluring, appealing, attractive, beau, beauteous, belle, charming, comely, delightful, exquisite, fair, fine, good-looking, gorgeous, graceful, handsome, lovely, pleasing, pulchritudinous, radiant, ravishing, stunning.

antonyms plain, ugly.

beauty¹ *n.* allure, attractiveness, bloom, charm, comeliness, elegance, excellence, exquisitness, fairness, glamor, grace, handsomeness, loveliness, pleasure, pulchritude, seemliness, symmetry.

antonym ugliness.

beauty² *n.* belle, charmer, corker, cracker, femme fatale, goddess, good-looker, knockout, lovely, siren, stunner, Venus.

antonym frump.

becalmed *adj.* at a standstill, idle, motionless, still, stranded, stuck.

because *conj.* as, by reason of, for, forasmuch, forwhy, in that, inasmuch as, on account of, owing to, since, thanks to.

beckon *v.* allure, attract, bid, call, coax, decoy, draw, entice, gesticulate, gesture, invite, lure, motion, nod, pull, signal, summon, tempt, waft.

become *v.* befit, behove, embellish, enhance, fit, flatter, grace, harmonize, ornament, set off, suit.

becoming *adj.* appropriate, attractive, befitting, charming, comely, comme il faut, compatible, congruous, decent, decorous, enhancing, fit, fitting, flattering, graceful, maidenly, meet, neat, pretty, proper, seemly, suitable, tasteful, worthy.

antonym unbecoming.

bed¹ *n.* bedstead, berth, bunk, cot, couch, divan, kip, mattress, pallet, palliasse, sack, the downy.

bed² *n.* base, border, bottom, channel, foundation, garden, groundwork, layer, matrix, patch, plot, row, stratus, strip, substratum, wadi, watercourse.

v. base, embed, establish, fix, found, ground, implant, insert, plant, settle.

bedeck v. adorn, array, beautify, bedight, bedizen, decorate, embellish, festoon, garnish, ornament, trick out, trim.
antonym strip.

bedevil v. afflict, annoy, besiege, confound, distress, fret, frustrate, harass, irk, irritate, pester, plague, tease, torment, torture, trouble, vex, worry.

bedlam n. anarchy, babel, chaos, clamor, commotion, confusion, furore, hubbub, hullabaloo, madhouse, noise, pandemonium, tumult, turmoil, uproar.
antonym calm.

bedraggled adj. dirty, disheveled, disordered, messy, muddied, muddy, scruffy, slovenly, sodden, soiled, stained, sullied, unkempt, untidy.
antonym tidy.

beef[1] n. beefiness, brawn, bulk, flesh, fleshiness, heftiness, muscle, robustness, sinew, strength.

beef[2] n. complaint, criticism, dispute, dissatisfaction, grievance, gripe, grouse, grumble, objection, protest.
v. complain, criticize, gripe, grumble, moan, object.
antonym approve.

beefy adj. brawny, bulky, burly, corpulent, fat, fleshy, heavy, hefty, hulking, muscular, plump, podgy, pudgy, rotund, stalwart, stocky, strapping, sturdy.
antonym slight.

befall v. arrive, betide, chance, ensue, fall, follow, happen, materialize, occur, supervene, take place.

before adv. ahead, earlier, formerly, in advance, in front, previously, sooner.
antonyms after, later.
prep. ahead of, earlier than, in advance of, in anticipation of, in front of, in preparation for, previous to, prior to, sooner than.
conj. in case, rather than.

befriend v. aid, assist, back, benefit, comfort, encourage, favor, help, patronize, stand by, succor, support, sustain, take a liking to, take under one's wing, uphold, welcome.
antonym neglect.

befuddled adj. baffled, bewildered, confused, dazed, fuddled, groggy, hazy, inebriated, intoxicated, muddled, woozy.
antonym lucid.

beg v. beseech, cadge, crave, desire, entreat, fleech, implore, importune, petition, plead, pray, prog, request, require, schnorr, scrounge, shool, skelder, solicit, sponge on, supplicate, touch.

beget v. breed, bring, cause, create, effect, engender, father, gender, generate, get, give rise to, occasion, procreate, produce, propagate, result in, sire, spawn.

beggar[1] n. Abraham-man, bankrupt, beadsman, besognio, bluegown, cadger, canter, derelict, down-and-out, hobo, lazzarone, mendicant, pauper, schnorrer, scrounger, sponger, starveling, supplicant, toe-rag, toe-ragger, tramp, vagrant.

beggar[2] v. baffle, challenge, defy, exceed, surpass, transcend.

begin v. activate, actuate, appear, arise, commence, crop up, dawn, emerge, happen, inaugurate, initiate, instigate, institute, introduce, originate, prepare, set about, set in, spring, start.
antonyms end, finish.

beginner n. abecedarian, alphabetarian, amateur, apprentice, cheechako, cub, fledgling, freshman, greenhorn, initiate, Johnny-raw, learner, neophyte, novice,

recruit, rookie, rooky, starter, student, tenderfoot, tiro, trainee.
antonyms expert, old hand, veteran.

beginning n. birth, commencement, embryo, establishment, fons et origo, fountainhead, germ, inauguration, inception, inchoation, initiation, introduction, onset, opening, origin, outset, preface, prelude, prime, rise, root, rudiments, seed, source, start, starting point.
antonyms end, finish.
adj. early, elementary, inaugural, inauguratory, inceptive, inchoative, incipient, initial, introductory, nascent, primal, primary, primeval.

begrudge v. covet, envy, grudge, mind, resent, stint.
antonym allow.

beguiling adj. alluring, appealing, attractive, bewitching, captivating, charming, diverting, enchanting, entertaining, enticing, interesting, intriguing.
antonyms offensive, repulsive.

behalf n. account, advantage, authority, benefit, defense, good, interest, name, part, profit, sake, side, support.

behave v. acquit, act, bear, comport, conduct, demean, deport, function, operate, perform, react, respond, run, work.

behavior n. action, actions, bearing, carriage, comportment, conduct, dealings, demeanor, deportment, doings, functioning, habits, manner, manners, operation, performance, reaction, response, ways.

behead v. decapitate, decollate, execute, guillotine, unhead.

behest n. authority, bidding, charge, command, commandment, decree, dictate, direction, fiat, injunction, instruction, mandate, order, ordinance, precept, wish.

behind prep. after, backing, causing, following, for, initiating, instigating, later than, responsible for, supporting.
adv. after, afterwards, behindhand, en arrière, following, in arrears, in debt, in the wake of, next, overdue, subsequently.
n. ass, backside, bottom, butt, buttocks, derrière, fanny, posterior, prat, rear, rump, seat, sit-upon, tail, tush.

behold v. consider, contemplate, descry, discern, espy, eye, look at, note, observe, perceive, regard, scan, survey, view, watch, witness.
interj. ecce, lo, look, mark, observe, see, voici, voilà, watch.

being[1] n. actuality, animation, entity, essence, existence, haecceity, life, living, nature, quiddity, reality, soul, spirit, substance.

being[2] n. animal, beast, body, creature, human being, individual, mortal, sentient, thing.

belabor v. attack, bash, batter, beat, belt, berate, castigate, censure, chastise, criticize, flay, flog, lambast, lay into, thrash, whip.

belated adj. behind-hand, delayed, late, overdue, retarded, tardy, unpunctual.
antonyms punctual, timely.

belch v. burp, discharge, disgorge, emit, eruct, eructate, erupt, gush, hiccup, spew, vent.
n. burp, eructation, eruption, hiccup.

beleaguered adj. badgered, beset, besieged, bothered, harassed, hedged about, hedged in, persecuted, plagued, surrounded, vexed, worried.

belie v. conceal, confute, contradict, deceive, deny, disguise, disprove, falsify, gainsay, mislead, misrepresent, negate, refute, repudiate, run counter to, understate.

antonym attest.

belief *n.* assurance, confidence, conviction, credence, credit, credo, creed, doctrine, dogma, expectation, faith, feeling, ideology, impression, intuition, ism, judgment, notion, opinion, persuasion, presumption, principle, principles, reliance, sureness, surety, tenet, theory, trust, view.

antonym disbelief.

believe *v.* accept, assume, be under the impression, conjecture, consider, count on, credit, deem, depend on, gather, guess, hold, imagine, judge, maintain, postulate, presume, reckon, rely on, speculate, suppose, swallow, swear by, think, trust, wear.

antonym disbelieve.

believer *n.* adherent, catechumen, convert, devotee, disciple, follower, proselyte, supporter, upholder, votary, zealot.

antonyms apostate, sceptic, unbeliever.

belittle *v.* decry, deprecate, depreciate, deride, derogate, detract, diminish, dismiss, disparage, downgrade, lessen, minimize, ridicule, run down, scorn, underestimate, underrate, undervalue, vilipend.

antonym exaggerate.

belligerent *adj.* aggressive, antagonistic, argumentative, bellicose, bullying, combative, contentious, forceful, militant, pugnacious, quarrelsome, violent, warlike, warring.

antonym peaceable.

bellow *v.* bell, call, clamor, cry, howl, roar, scream, shout, shriek, troat, yell.

belly *n.* abdomen, bowels, bread-basket, corporation, gut, guts, insides, paunch, pot, sound-board, stomach, tummy, uterus, venter, vitals, womb.

v. bag, balloon, billow, blow up, bulge, dilate, distend, expand, fill out, inflate, swell.

antonyms deflate, shrink.

belonging *n.* acceptance, affinity, association, attachment, closeness, compatibility, fellow-feeling, fellowship, inclusion, kinship, link, linkage, loyalty, rapport, relationship.

antonym antipathy.

belongings *n.* accouterments, chattels, effects, gear, goods, impedimenta, paraphernalia, possessions, stuff, things, traps.

beloved *adj.* admired, adored, cherished, darling, dear, dearest, favorite, loved, pet, precious, prized, revered, sweet, treasured.

n. adored, darling, dear, dearest, favorite, inamorata, inamorato, lover, pet, precious, sweet, sweetheart.

below *adv.* beneath, down, infra, lower, lower down, under, underneath.

prep. inferior to, lesser than, 'neath, subject to, subordinate to, under, underneath, unworthy of.

belt[1] *n.* area, band, ceinture, cincture, cingulum, cummerbund, district, girdle, girth, layer, region, sash, strait, stretch, strip, swathe, tract, waistband, zone, zonule, zonulet.

v. circle, encircle, girdle, ring, surround.

belt[2] *v.* bolt, career, charge, dash, hurry, race, rush, speed.

bemoan *v.* bewail, deplore, grieve for, lament, mourn, regret, rue, sigh for, sorrow over, weep for.

antonym gloat.

bend *v.* aim, bow, brace, buckle, compel, constrain, contort, couch, crankle, crimp, crouch, curve, deflect, direct, dispose, diverge, embow, fasten, flex, incline, incurvate, incurve, influence, lean, mold, nerve, persuade, shape, stoop, string, subdue, submit, sway, swerve, turn, twist, veer, warp, yield.

n. angle, arc, bight, bought, bow, corner, crank, crook, curvature, curve, elbow, flexure, genu, hook, incurvation, incurvature, incurve, inflexure, loop, turn, twist, zigzag.

beneath *adv.* below, lower, lower down, under, underneath.

prep. below, inferior to, infra dig(nitatem), lower than, 'neath, subject to, subordinate to, unbefitting, under, underneath, unworthy of.

benediction *n.* beatitude, Benedictus, benison, blessing, consecration, favor, grace, invocation, orison, prayer, thanksgiving.

antonyms anathema, curse, execration.

beneficial *adj.* advantageous, benign, benignant, edifying, favorable, gainful, healthful, helpful, improving, nourishing, nutritious, profitable, restorative, rewarding, salubrious, salutary, serviceable, useful, valuable, wholesome.

antonym harmful.

benefit *n.* advantage, aid, asset, assistance, avail, betterment, blessing, boon, favor, gain, good, help, interest, profit, service, use, weal, welfare.

antonym harm.

v. advance, advantage, aid, ameliorate, amend, assist, avail, better, enhance, further, improve, profit, promote, serve.

antonyms harm, hinder, undermine.

benevolence *n.* altruism, benignity, bounty, charity, compassion, fellow-feeling, generosity, goodness, goodwill, humanity, kind-heartedness, kindliness, kindness, munificence, sympathy.

antonym meanness.

benevolent *adj.* altruistic, beneficent, benign, bounteous, bountiful, caring, charitable, compassionate, considerate, generous, good-will, humane, humanitarian, kind, kind-hearted, kindly, liberal, loving, philanthropic, solicitous, well-disposed.

antonym mean.

bent *adj.* angled, arched, bowed, coudé, criminal, crooked, curved, dishonest, doubled, falcate, folded, homosexual, hunched, inbent, inflexed, retorted, retroverted, stolen, stooped, twisted, untrustworthy.

antonym straight.

n. ability, aptitude, capacity, facility, faculty, flair, forte, gift, inclination, knack, leaning, penchant, preference, proclivity, propensity, talent, tendency.

berate *v.* castigate, censure, chastise, chide, criticize, flyte, jump down the throat of, rail at, rate, rebuke, reprimand, reproach, reprove, revile, scold, tell off, upbraid, vituperate.

antonym praise.

beseech *v.* adjure, ask, beg, call on, conjure, crave, desire, entreat, implore, importune, obsecrate, petition, plead, pray, solicit, sue, supplicate.

beset *v.* assail, attack, badger, bamboozle, bedevil, besiege, embarrass, encircle, enclose, encompass, entangle, environ, faze, harass, hassle, hem in, perplex, pester, plague, surround.

beside *prep.* abreast of, abutting on, adjacent, bordering on, close to, near, neighboring, next door to, next to, overlooking, upsides with.

besides *adv.* additionally, also, as well, extra, further, furthermore, in addition, into the bargain, moreover, otherwise, to boot, too, withal.

prep. apart from, in addition to, other than, over and above.

besiege *v.* assail, badger, belay, beleaguer, beset, blockade, bother, confine, dun, encircle, encompass, environ, harass, harry, hound, importune, nag, pester, plague, surround, trouble.

bespeak *v.* attest, betoken, demonstrate, denote, display, evidence, evince, exhibit, forebode, foretell, imply, indicate, predict, proclaim, reveal, show, signify, suggest, testify to.

best *adj.* advantageous, apt, correct, excellent, finest, first, first-class, first-rate, foremost, greatest, highest, incomparable, largest, leading, makeless, matchless, nonpareil, optimal, optimum, outstanding, perfect, pre-eminent, preferable, principal, right, superlative, supreme, transcendent, unequaled, unsurpassed.

antonym worst.

adv. excellently, exceptionally, extremely, greatly, superlatively, surpassingly.

antonym worst.

n. choice, cream, crème de la crème, élite, favorite, finest, first, flower, hardest, nonpareil, pick, prime, the tops, top, utmost.

antonym worst.

v. beat, conquer, defeat, get the better of, have the laugh of, lick, outclass, outdo, outwit, surpass, thrash, trounce, vanquish, worst.

bestial *adj.* animal, barbaric, barbarous, beastly, brutal, brutish, carnal, degraded, depraved, feral, gross, inhuman, savage, sensual, sordid, subhuman, swinish, vile.

antonyms civilized, humane.

bestow *v.* accord, allot, apportion, award, bequeath, commit, confer, donate, dower, endow, entrust, give, grant, impart, lavish, lend, present, transmit, wreak.

antonym deprive.

bet *n.* accumulator, ante, bid, flutter, gamble, hazard, pledge, risk, speculation, stake, venture, wager.

v. ante, bid, chance, gamble, hazard, lay, pledge, punt, risk, speculate, stake, venture, wager.

betray *v.* abandon, beguile, corrupt, deceive, delude, desert, disclose, discover, divulge, dob in, doublecross, dupe, ensnare, entrap, evince, expose, forsake, give away, grass, inform on, jilt, manifest, mislead, reveal, seduce, sell, sell down the river, sell out, shop, show, tell, testify against, turn state's evidence, undo.

antonyms defend, fulfil, protect.

betrothal *n.* engagement, espousal, fiançailles, handfast, plight, promise, troth, vow.

better *adj.* bigger, cured, finer, fitter, greater, healthier, improving, larger, longer, on the mend, preferable, progressing, recovered, recovering, restored, stronger, superior, surpassing, worthier.

antonym worse.

v. advance, ameliorate, amend, beat, cap, correct, enhance, exceed, excel, forward, further, go one further than, improve, improve on, increase, meliorate, mend, outdo, outstrip, overtake, overtop, promote, raise, rectify, redress, reform, strengthen, surpass, top, transcend.

antonyms deteriorate, worsen.

between *prep.* amidst, among, amongst, betwixt, inter-, mid.

beware *v.* avoid, give a wide berth to, guard against, heed, look out, mind, shun, steer clear of, take heed, watch out.

antonyms brave, dare.

bewilder *v.* baffle, bamboozle, befuddle, bemuse, buffalo, confound, confuse, daze, disconcert, disorient, fuddle, maze, muddle, mystify, perplex, puzzle, stupefy, tie in knots.

bewitch *v.* allure, attract, beguile, captivate, charm, elfshoot, enchant, enrapture, ensorcell, entrance, fascinate, forspeak, hex, hoodoo, hypnotize, jinx, obsess, possess, spellbind, voodoo, witch.

beyond *prep.* above, across, apart from, away from, before, further than, out of range, out of reach of, over, past, remote from, superior to, yonder.

bias *n.* angle, bent, bigotry, distortion, editorialization, favoritism, inclination, intolerance, leaning, one-sidedness, parti pris, partiality, penchant, predilection, predisposition, prejudice, proclivity, proneness, propensity, slant, tendency, tendentiousness, turn, unfairness, viewiness.

antonyms fairness, impartiality.

v. angle, distort, earwig, editorialize, influence, jaundice, load, load the dice, predispose, prejudice, slant, sway, twist, warp, weight.

bibulous *adj.* alcoholic, crapulous, dipsomaniac, drunken, inebriate, intemperate, sottish, thirsty, tipsy.

antonyms sober, temperate.

bicker *v.* altercate, argue, clash, disagree, dispute, feud, fight, quarrel, row, scrap, spar, squabble, wrangle.

antonym agree.

bid *v.* ask, call, charge, command, desire, direct, enjoin, greet, instruct, invite, offer, proclaim, propose, request, require, say, solicit, summon, tell, wish.

n. advance, amount, ante, attempt, crack, effort, endeavor, go, offer, price, proposal, proposition, submission, sum, tender, try, venture.

bidding *n.* behest, call, charge, command, demand, dictate, direction, injunction, instruction, invitation, order, request, requirement, summons.

big *adj.* adult, altruistic, beefy, benevolent, boastful, bombastic, bulky, burly, buxom, colossal, considerable, corpulent, elder, elephantine, eminent, enormous, extensive, gargantuan, generous, gigantic, gracious, great, grown, grown-up, heroic, huge, hulking, immense, important, influential, large, leading, lofty, magnanimous, main, mammoth, man-sized, massive, mature, mighty, momentous, noble, paramount, plonking, ponderous, powerful, prime, principal, prodigious, prominent, serious, significant, sizable, spacious, stout, substantial, titanic, tolerant, unselfish, valuable, vast, voluminous, weighty.

antonyms little, small.

bigot *n.* chauvinist, dogmatist, fanatic, racist, religionist, sectarian, sexist, verkrampte, zealot.

antonyms humanitarian, liberal.

bigoted *adj.* biased, blinkered, chauvinist, closed, dogmatic, illiberal, intolerant, narrow, narrow-minded, obstinate, opinionated, prejudiced, sectarian, twisted, verkrampte, warped.

antonyms broad-minded, enlightened, liberal.

bilious *adj.* choleric, crabby, cross, crotchety, grouchy, grumpy, irritable, liverish, nauseated, out of sorts, peevish, queasy, sick, sickly, testy.

bilk v. balk, bamboozle, cheat, con, cozen, deceive, defraud, do, do out of, fleece, foil, rook, sting, swindle, thwart, trick.

bill¹ n. account, advertisement, battels, broadsheet, broadside, bulletin, card, catalog, charges, check, chit, circular, greenback, handbill, hand-out, inventory, invoice, leaflet, legislation, list, listing, measure, note, notice, placard, playbill, poster, program, proposal, reckoning, roster, schedule, score, sheet, statement, syllabus, tab, tally.
v. advertise, announce, charge, debit, invoice, list, post, reckon, record.

bill² n. beak, mandible, neb, nib, rostrum.

billow v. balloon, belly, expand, fill out, heave, puff out, roll, seethe, spread, surge, swell, undulate.

bind v. astrict, astringe, attach, bandage, border, cinch, clamp, colligate, compel, complain, confine, constipate, constrain, cover, detain, dress, edge, encase, engage, fasten, finish, force, glue, hamper, harden, hinder, hitch, indenture, lash, necessitate, obligate, oblige, prescribe, require, restrain, restrict, rope, seal, secure, stick, strap, swathe, thirl, tie, trim, truss, wrap.
n. bore, difficulty, dilemma, embarrassment, hole, impasse, nuisance, predicament, quandary.

binding adj. compulsory, conclusive, imperative, indissoluble, irrevocable, mandatory, necessary, obligatory, permanent, requisite, strict, unalterable, unbreakable.
n. bandage, border, covering, deligation, edging, stricture, syndesis, tape, trimming, wrapping.

birth n. ancestry, background, beginning, birthright, blood, breeding, childbirth, delivery, derivation, descent, emergence, extraction, family, fell, genealogy, genesis, geniture, line, lineage, nativity, nobility, origin, parentage, parturition, pedigree, race, rise, source, stirps, stock, strain.

biscuit n. cake, cookie, cracker, hardtack, rusk, wafer.

bit n. atom, chip, crumb, fragment, grain, instant, iota, jiffy, jot, mammock, minute, mite, moment, morsel, part, period, piece, scrap, second, segment, sippet, slice, snippet, speck, spell, tick, time, tittle, while, whit.

bite v. burn, champ, chew, clamp, corrode, crunch, crush, cut, gnaw, knap, masticate, nibble, nip, pierce, pinch, rend, seize, smart, snap, sting, tear, tingle, wound.
n. edge, food, grip, kick, morsel, morsure, mouthful, nip, piece, pinch, piquancy, prick, punch, pungency, refreshment, smarting, snack, spice, sting, taste, wound.

biting adj. astringent, bitter, blighting, caustic, cold, cutting, cynical, freezing, harsh, hurtful, incisive, mordant, nipping, penetrating, piercing, raw, sarcastic, scathing, severe, sharp, stinging, tart, trenchant, withering.
antonyms bland, mild.

bitter adj. acerb, acerbic, acid, acrid, acrimonious, astringent, begrudging, biting, calamitous, crabbed, cruel, cynical, dire, distressing, embittered, fierce, freezing, galling, grievous, harsh, hateful, heartbreaking, hostile, intense, ironic, jaundiced, merciless, morose, odious, painful, poignant, rancorous, raw, resentful, ruthless, sarcastic, savage, severe, sharp,

sore, sour, stinging, sullen, tart, unsweetened, vexatious, vinegary, waspish.
antonyms contented, genial, sweet.

bizarre adj. abnormal, comical, curious, deviant, eccentric, extraordinary, extravagant, fantastic, freakish, grotesque, ludicrous, odd, off-beat, outlandish, outré, peculiar, quaint, queer, ridiculous, strange, unusual, way-out, weird.
antonym normal.

black adj. angry, atrocious, bad, begrimed, coal-black, coaly, dark, darksome, depressing, dingy, dirty, dismal, doleful, dusky, ebony, evil, filthy, funereal, furious, gloomy, grim, grimy, grubby, hopeless, horrible, hostile, inky, jet, jet-black, jetty, lugubrious, menacing, moonless, morel, mournful, murky, nefarious, ominous, overcast, pitchy, raven, resentful, sable, sad, sloe, soiled, somber, sooty, stained, starless, Stygian, sullen, swarthy, threatening, thunderous, villainous, wicked.
v. ban, bar, blacklist, boycott, taboo.

blackball v. ban, bar, blacklist, debar, exclude, expel, ostracize, oust, pip, reject, repudiate, snub, veto.

blacken v. befoul, begrime, besmirch, calumniate, cloud, darken, decry, defame, defile, denigrate, detract, dishonor, malign, revile, slander, smear, smirch, smudge, soil, stain, sully, taint, tarnish, traduce, vilify.
antonyms enhance, praise.

blackmail n. blood-sucking, chantage, exaction, extortion, hush money, intimidation, milking, pay-off, protection, ransom.
v. bleed, bribe, coerce, compel, demand, force, hold to ransom, lean on, milk, put the black on, squeeze, threaten.

blackout n. censorship, coma, concealment, cover-up, faint, oblivion, power cut, secrecy, suppression, swoon, syncope, unconsciousness.

bladder n. aveole, bag, bursa, cecum, capsule, cell, cyst, pocket, pouch, receptacle, sac, theca, utricle, vesica, vesicle, vesicula.

blade n. dagger, edge, knife, rapier, scalpel, sword, vane.

blame n. accountability, accusation, animadversion, castigation, censure, charge, complaint, condemnation, criticism, culpability, discommendation, fault, guilt, incrimination, liability, obloquy, onus, rap, recrimination, reprimand, reproach, reproof, responsibility, stick, stricture.
v. accuse, admonish, censure, charge, chide, condemn, criticize, disapprove, discommend, dispraise, find fault with, rebuke, reprehend, reprimand, reproach, reprove, tax, upbraid.
antonym exonerate.

blameless adj. above reproach, clean, clear, faultless, guiltless, immaculate, impeccable, inculpable, innocent, irreprehensible, irreproachable, irreprovable, perfect, sinless, stainless, unblamable, unblemished, unimpeachable, unspotted, unsullied, untarnished, upright, virtuous.
antonym guilty.

blanch v. bleach, blench, drain, etiolate, fade, pale, wan, whiten.
antonyms blush, color, redden.

bland adv. affable, amiable, balmy, boring, calm, characterless, congenial, courteous, demulcent, dull, fair-spoken, flat, friendly, gentle, gracious, humdrum, hypo-allergenic, impassive, inscrutable, insipid, mild, mollifying, monotonous, nondescript, non-irritant, smooth, soft, soothing, suave, tasteless, tedious, temperate, unexciting, uninspiring, uninteresting, urbane, vapid, weak.

antonyms piquant, sharp.

blandishments *n.* blarney, cajolery, coaxing, compliments, enticements, fawning, flattery, inducements, ingratiation, inveiglement, lip-salve, persuasiveness, soft soap, sweet talk, sycophancy, wheedling.

blank *adj.* apathetic, bare, bewildered, clean, clear, confounded, confused, deadpan, disconcerted, dull, dumbfounded, empty, expressionless, featureless, glazed, hollow, immobile, impassive, inane, inscrutable, lifeless, muddled, nonplused, plain, poker-faced, sheer, spotless, staring, uncomprehending, unfilled, unmarked, unrhymed, vacant, vacuous, vague, void, white.

n. break, emptiness, gap, nothingness, space, tabula rasa, vacancy, vacuity, vacuum, void.

blanket *n.* carpet, cloak, coat, coating, cover, covering, coverlet, envelope, film, housing, layer, mackinaw, manta, mantle, rug, sheet, wrapper, wrapping.

adj. across-the-board, all-embracing, all-inclusive, comprehensive, inclusive, overall, sweeping, wide-ranging.

v. cloak, cloud, coat, conceal, cover, deaden, eclipse, hide, mask, muffle, obscure, surround.

blare *v.* blast, boom, clamor, clang, honk, hoot, peal, resound, ring, roar, scream, shriek, toot, trumpet.

blasphemous *adj.* execrative, godless, hubristic, impious, imprecatory, irreligious, irreverent, profane, sacrilegious, ungodly.

blasphemy *n.* curse, cursing, defilement, desecration, execration, expletive, hubris, impiety, impiousness, imprecation, irreverence, outrage, profanation, profaneness, profanity, sacrilege, swearing, violation.

blast[1] *n.* blare, blow, boom, honk, hoot, peal, roar, scream, shriek, sound, wail.

blast[2] *n.* bang, bluster, burst, clap, crack, crash, detonation, discharge, draught, eruption, explosion, flatus, gale, gust, hail, outburst, salvo, squall, storm, tempest, volley.

v. assail, attack, blight, blow up, burst, castigate, demolish, destroy, explode, flay, kill, lash, ruin, shatter, shrivel, storm at, wither.

blasted *adj.* blighted, desolated, destroyed, devastated, ravaged, ruined, scorched, shattered, wasted, withered.

blatant *adj.* arrant, bald, barefaced, brazen, clamorous, conspicuous, egregious, flagrant, flaunting, glaring, harsh, loud, naked, noisy, obtrusive, obvious, ostentatious, outright, overt, prominent, pronounced, sheer, unmitigated.

blather *n.* blether, chatter, chatterbox, chatterer, chitchat, claptrap, drivel, gibberish, gibble-gabble, gobbledegook, jabbering, loquacity, moonshine, nonsense, prattle, prattler, twaddle.

v. blabber, chatter, gab, gabble, haver, jabber, prattle.

bleach *v.* blanch, decolorise, etiolate, fade, lighten, pale, peroxide, whiten.

bleak *adj.* bare, barren, blae, blasted, cheerless, chilly, cold, colorless, comfortless, delightless, depressing, desolate, discouraging, disheartening, dismal, dreary, empty, exposed, gaunt, gloomy, grim, hopeless, joyless, leaden, loveless, open, raw, somber, unsheltered, weather-beaten, windswept, windy.

antonyms cheerful, congenial.

bleary *adj.* blurred, blurry, cloudy, dim, fogged, foggy, fuzzy, hazy, indistinct, misty, muddy, murky, obscured, rheumy, watery.

bleed *v.* blackmail, deplete, drain, exhaust, exploit, extort, extract, extravasate, exude, fleece, flow, gush, hemorrhage, leech, milk, ooze, reduce, run, sap, seep, spurt, squeeze, suck dry, trickle, weep.

blemish *n.* birthmark, blot, blotch, blur, botch, defect, deformity, disfigurement, disgrace, dishonor, fault, flaw, imperfection, mackle, macula, maculation, mark, naevus, smudge, speck, spot, stain, taint.

v. besmirch, blot, blotch, blur, damage, deface, disfigure, flaw, impair, injure, maculate, mar, mark, smirch, smudge, spoil, spot, stain, sully, taint, tarnish.

blend *v.* amalgamate, coalesce, combine, complement, compound, contemper, fit, fuse, harmonize, intermix, meld, merge, mingle, mix, synthesize, unite.

antonym separate.

n. alloy, amalgam, amalgamation, combination, composite, compound, concoction, fusion, interunion, meld, mix, mixture, synthesis, union.

bless *v.* anoint, approve, bestow, consecrate, countenance, dedicate, endow, exalt, extol, favor, glorify, grace, hallow, magnify, ordain, praise, provide, sanctify, thank.

antonyms condemn, curse.

blessed *adj.* adored, beatified, blissful, contented, divine, endowed, favored, fortunate, glad, hallowed, happy, holy, joyful, joyous, lucky, prosperous, revered, sacred, sanctified.

antonym cursed.

blessing *n.* advantage, approbation, approval, authority, backing, benedicite, benediction, benefit, benison, boon, bounty, commendation, concurrence, consecration, consent, countenance, dedication, favor, fortune, gain, gift, godsend, grace, help, invocation, kindness, leave, permission, profit, sanction, service, support, thanksgiving, windfall.

antonyms blight, condemnation, curse.

blight *n.* affliction, bane, cancer, canker, check, contamination, corruption, curse, decay, depression, disease, evil, fungus, infestation, mildew, pest, pestilence, plague, pollution, rot, scourge, set-back, woe.

antonyms blessing, boon.

v. annihilate, blast, crush, dash, destroy, disappoint, frustrate, injure, mar, ruin, shatter, shrivel, spoil, undermine, wither, wreck.

antonym bless.

blind *adj.* amaurotic, beetle-eyed, blinkered, careless, closed, concealed, dark, dim, eyeless, hasty, heedless, hidden, ignorant, impetuous, inattentive, inconsiderate, indifferent, indiscriminate, injudicious, insensate, insensitive, irrational, mindless, neglectful, oblivious, obscured, obstructed, prejudiced, purblind, rash, reckless, sand-blind, senseless, sightless, stone-blind, thoughtless, unaware, uncontrollable, uncritical, undiscerning, unobservant, unobserving, unreasoning, unseeing, unsighted, unthinking, violent, visionless, wild.

antonyms aware, clear, sighted.

n. camouflage, cloak, cover, cover-up, distraction,

façade, feint, front, mask, masquerade, screen, smoke-screen.

blink v. bat, condone, connive at, disregard, flash, flicker, flutter, gleam, glimmer, glimpse, ignore, nictate, nictitate, overlook, peer, pink, scintillate, shine, sparkle, squint, twinkle, wink.

bliss n. beatitude, blessedness, blissfulness, ecstasy, euphoria, felicity, gladness, happiness, heaven, joy, nirvana, paradise, rapture.
antonyms damnation, misery.

blister n. abscess, bleb, boil, bubble, bulla, canker, carbuncle, cyst, furuncle, papilla, papula, papule, pimple, pompholyx, pustule, sore, swelling, ulcer, vesicle, vesicula, welt, wen.

blithe adj. animated, buoyant, carefree, careless, casual, cheerful, cheery, debonair, gay, gladsome, happy, heedless, jaunty, light-hearted, lightsome, lively, merry, mirthful, nonchalant, sprightly, sunny, thoughtless, unconcerned, untroubled, vivacious.
antonym morose.

bloated adj. blown up, bombastic, dilated, distended, dropsical, edematous, enlarged, expanded, inflated, sated, swollen, tumescent, tumid, turgid.
antonyms shriveled, shrunken, thin.

blob n. ball, bead, bobble, bubble, dab, dew-drop, drop, droplet, glob, globule, gob, lump, mass, pearl, pellet, pill, spot.

block n. bar, barrier, blockage, brick, cake, chunk, cube, delay, hang-up, hindrance, hunk, impediment, ingot, jam, let, lump, mass, obstacle, obstruction, piece, resistance, stoppage, tranche.
v. arrest, bar, check, choke, clog, close, dam up, deter, halt, hinder, impede, obstruct, obturate, oppilate, plug, scotch, stonewall, stop, stop up, thwart, trig.

blockade n. barricade, barrier, beleaguerment, closure, encirclement, obstruction, restriction, siege, stoppage.

blockhead n. bonehead, boodle, chump, dolt, dullard, dunce, fool, idiot, ignoramus, jobernowl, klutz, leather-head, loggerhead, log-head, noodle, numskull, pigsconce, pinhead, pot-head, thickhead, thick-skull.
antonyms brain, genius.

blood n. ancestry, anger, birth, bloodshed, consanguinity, descendants, descent, extraction, family, kindred, kinship, lineage, murder, relations, relationship, temper, temperament.

bloodcurdling adj. appalling, chilling, dreadful, eldritch, fearful, frightening, hair-raising, horrendous, horrible, horrid, horrifying, scaring, spine-chilling, terrifying, weird.

bloodshed n. bloodletting, butchery, carnage, gore, killing, massacre, murder, slaughter, slaying.

bloodthirsty adj. barbaric, barbarous, brutal, cruel, ferocious, inhuman, murderous, ruthless, sanguinary, savage, slaughterous, vicious, warlike.

bloody adj. bleeding, bloodstained, blooming, brutal, cruel, ferocious, fierce, gaping, murderous, raw, sanguinary, sanguine, sanguineous, sanguinolent, savage.

bloom n. beauty, blossom, blossoming, blow, blush, bud, efflorescence, florescence, flourishing, flower, flush, freshness, glaucescence, glow, health, heyday, luster, perfection, prime, radiance, rosiness, vigor.
v. blossom, blow, bud, burgeon, develop, flourish, grow, open, prosper, sprout, succeed, thrive, wax.
antonym wither.

blooming adj. blossoming, bonny, florescent, flowering, healthful, healthy, rosy, ruddy.
antonym ailing.

blossom n. bloom, bud, floret, flower, flowers.
v. bloom, blow, burgeon, develop, effloresce, flourish, flower, grow, mature, progress, prosper, thrive.
antonym wither.

blot n. blemish, blotch, defect, disgrace, fault, flaw, mackle, macula, mark, patch, smear, smudge, speck, splodge, spot, stain, taint.
v. bespatter, blur, disfigure, disgrace, maculate, mar, mark, smudge, spoil, spot, stain, sully, taint, tarnish.

blow[1] v. bear, blare, blast, breathe, buffet, drive, exhale, fan, fling, flow, flutter, mouth, pant, pipe, play, puff, rush, sound, stream, sweep, toot, trumpet, vibrate, waft, whirl, whisk, wind.
n. blast, draft, flurry, gale, gust, puff, squall, tempest, wind.

blow[2] n. affliction, bang, bash, bat, belt, biff, bombshell, bop, box, buff, buffet, calamity, catastrophe, clap, clip, clout, clump, comedown, concussion, counterbluff, crack, disappointment, disaster, douse, haymaker, hit, jab, jolt, knock, knuckle sandwich, misfortune, oner, poke, punch, rap, reverse, setback, shock, siserary, slap, slat, slosh, smack, sock, sockdologer, souse, stroke, swash, swat, swipe, thump, upset, wallop, wap, welt, whack, whang, winder.

blue[1] adj. aquamarine, azure, cerulean, cobalt, cyan, indigo, navy, sapphire, turquoise, ultramarine, watchet.

blue[2] adj. black, bleak, dejected, depressed, despondent, dismal, dispirited, doleful, down in the dumps, downcast, down-hearted, fed up, gloomy, glum, low, melancholy, miserable, morose, sad, unhappy.
antonym cheerful.

blue[3] adv. bawdy, coarse, dirty, improper, indecent, lewd, naughty, near the bone, near the knuckle, obscene, offensive, pornographic, risqué, smutty, vulgar.
antonym decent.

blueprint n. archetype, design, draft, guide, model, outline, pattern, pilot, plan, project, prototype, sketch.

blues n. blue devils, dejection, depression, despondency, doldrums, dumps, gloom, gloominess, glumness, melancholy, miseries, moodiness.
antonym euphoria.

bluff[1] n. bank, brow, cliff, crag, escarp, escarpment, foreland, headland, height, knoll, peak, precipice, promontory, ridge, scarp, slope.
adj. affable, blunt, candid, direct, downright, frank, genial, good-natured, hearty, open, outspoken, plainspoken, straightforward.
antonyms diplomatic, refined.

bluff[2] v. bamboozle, blind, deceive, defraud, delude, fake, feign, grift, hoodwink, humbug, lie, mislead, pretend, sham.
n. bluster, boast, braggadocio, bravado, deceit, deception, fake, fanfaronade, feint, fraud, grift, humbug, idle boast, lie, pretence, sham, show, subterfuge, trick.

blunder n. bêtise, bevue, bloomer, boner, boob, booboo, bungle, clanger, clinker, error, fault, faux pas, floater, fluff, gaffe, gaucherie, goof, howler, impropriety, inaccuracy, indiscretion, mistake, oversight, pratfall, slip, slip-up, solecism.
v. blow it, botch, bumble, bungle, err, flounder, flub,

fluff, fumble, goof, miscalculate, misjudge, mismanage, muff it, slip up, stumble.

blunt *adj.* abrupt, bluff, brusque, candid, curt, direct, discourteous, downright, dull, dulled, edgeless, explicit, forthright, frank, honest, impolite, insensitive, obtuse, outspoken, plain-spoken, pointless, retuse, rounded, rude, straightforward, stubbed, stumpy, tactless, thick, trenchant, unceremonious, uncivil, unpolished, unsharpened.

antonyms sharp, tactful.

v. abate, allay, alleviate, anesthetize, bate, dampen, deaden, disedge, dull, hebetate, numb, obtund, palliate, rebate, retund, soften, stupefy, unedge, weaken.

antonyms intensify, sharpen.

blur *v.* becloud, befog, blear, blemish, blot, blotch, cloud, darken, dim, fog, mask, obfuscate, obscure, scumble, smear, smutch, soften, spot, stain.

n. blear, blot, blotch, cloudiness, confusion, dimness, fog, fuzziness, haze, indistinctness, muddle, obscurity, smear, smudge, spot, stain.

blush *v.* color, crimson, flush, glow, mantle, redden.

antonym blanch.

n. color, erubescence, flush, glow, reddening, rosiness, ruddiness, suffusion.

board¹ *n.* beam, clapboard, deal, lath, panel, plank, sheet, slab, slat, timber, two-by-four.

board² commons, food, grub, meals, provisions, rations, repasts, table, victuals.

v. accommodate, bed, billet, feed, house, lodge, put up, quarter, room, table.

board³ *n.* advisers, chamber, commission, committee, conclave, council, directorate, directors, jury, panel, trustees.

board⁴ *v.* catch, embark, embus, emplane, enter, entrain, mount.

boast *v.* be all mouth, blazon, blow, bluster, bounce, brag, claim, crow, exaggerate, exhibit, gasconade, possess, puff, rodomontade, show off, strut, swagger, talk big, trumpet, vaunt.

antonym deprecate.

n. avowal, brag, claim, fanfaronade, gasconade, gem, joy, pride, rodomontade, swank, treasure, vaunt.

body¹ *n.* being, bod, build, bulk, cadaver, carcass, consistency, corpse, corpus, creature, density, essence, figure, firmness, form, frame, human, individual, mass, material, matter, mortal, opacity, person, physique, relics, remains, richness, shape, solidity, stiff, substance, substantiality, tabernacle, torso, trunk.

body² *n.* association, band, bevy, bloc, cartel, collection, company, confederation, congress, corporation, crowd, group, horde, majority, mass, mob, multitude, society, syndicate, throng.

bogus *adj.* artificial, counterfeit, dummy, ersatz, fake, false, forged, fraudulent, imitation, phony, pinchbeck, pseudo, sham, spoof, spurious, unauthentic.

antonym genuine.

boil¹ *v.* agitate, brew, bubble, churn, decoct, effervesce, erupt, explode, fizz, foam, froth, fulminate, fume, gurgle, mantle, parboil, rage, rave, seethe, simmer, sizzle, spume, steam, stew, storm, wallop.

boil down abridge, abstract, concentrate, condense, decrease, digest, distil, epitomize, reduce, summarize, synopsize.

boil² *n.* abscess, anthrax, bleb, blister, carbuncle,

furuncle, gathering, gumboil, inflammation, papule, parulis, pimple, pock, pustule, tumor, ulcer, whelk.

boisterous *adj.* blusterous, blustery, bouncy, clamorous, disorderly, exuberant, gusty, impetuous, loud, noisy, obstreperous, rackety, raging, rambunctious, riotous, roisting, rollicking, rough, rowdy, rumbustious, squally, tempestuous, termagant, tumultous, turbulent, unrestrained, unruly, uproarious, vociferous, wild.

antonyms calm, quiet, restrained.

bold *adj.* adventurous, audacious, brash, brave, brazen, bright, cheeky, colorful, confident, conspicuous, courageous, daring, dauntless, enterprising, extrovert, eye-catching, fearless, flamboyant, flashy, forceful, forward, fresh, gallant, heroic, impudent, insolent, intrepid, jazzy, lively, loud, malapert, outgoing, pert, plucky, prominent, pronounced, saucy, shameless, showy, spirited, striking, strong, unabashed, unashamed, unbashful, valiant, valorous, venturesome, vivid.

antonyms diffident, restrained.

bolt *n.* arrow, bar, bound, catch, dart, dash, elopement, escape, fastener, flight, flit, latch, lock, missile, peg, pin, projectile, rivet, rod, rush, shaft, sneck, sprint, thunderbolt.

v. abscond, bar, bound, cram, dart, dash, devour, discharge, elope, escape, expel, fasten, fetter, flee, fly, gobble, gorge, gulp, guzzle, hurtle, jump, latch, leap, lock, run, rush, secure, spring, sprint, stuff, wolf.

bomb *n.* A-bomb, bombshell, charge, egg, explosive, grenade, mine, missile, mortar-bomb, petrol bomb, projectile, rocket, shell, torpedo.

v. attack, blow up, bombard, collapse, come a cropper, come to grief, destroy, fail, flop, misfire, shell, strafe, torpedo.

bond *n.* affiliation, affinity, agreement, attachment, band, binding, chain, compact, connection, contract, copula, cord, covenant, fastening, fetter, ligament, ligature, link, manacle, obligation, pledge, promise, relation, shackle, tie, union, vinculum, word.

v. bind, connect, fasten, fuse, glue, gum, paste, seal, unite.

bondage *n.* captivity, confinement, durance, duress, enslavement, enthralment, imprisonment, incarceration, restraint, serfdom, servitude, slavery, subjection, subjugation, subservience, thraldom, vassalage, yoke.

antonyms freedom, independence.

book *n.* album booklet, codex, companion, diary, hornbook, incunable, incunabulum, jotter, lectionary, manual, manuscript, notebook, pad, paperback, publication, roll, scroll, textbook, tome, tract, volume, work.

v. arrange, arrest, bag, charter, engage, enter, insert, list, log, note, organize, post, procure, program, record, register, reserve, schedule.

antonym cancel.

boom¹ *v.* bang, blare, blast, crash, explode, resound, reverberate, roar, roll, rumble, sound, thunder.

n. bang, blast, burst, clang, clap, crash, explosion, reverberation, roar, rumble, thunder.

boom² *v.* develop, escalate, expand, explode, flourish, gain, go from strength to strength, grow, increase, intensify, prosper, spurt, strengthen, succeed, swell, thrive.

antonyms collapse, fail.

n. advance, boost, development, escalation, expansion,

explosion, gain, growth, improvement, increase, jump, spurt, upsurge, upturn.

antonyms collapse, failure.

boon *n.* advantage, benefaction, benefit, blessing, donation, favor, gift, godsend, grant, gratification, gratuity, kindness, petition, present, windfall.

antonyms blight, disadvantage.

boor *n.* barbarian, brute, bumpkin, churl, clodhopper, goop, Goth, hayseed, hedgehog, hick, hog, lout, oaf, peasant, philistine, rube, rustic, vulgarian, yokel.

antonyms aesthete, charmer.

boorish *adj.* awkward, barbaric, bearish, churlish, clodhopping, clownish, coarse, crude, gross, gruff, ill-bred, inconsiderate, loutish, lubberly, lumpen, oafish, rude, ruffianly, rustic, slobbish, uncivilized, uncouth, uneducated, unrefined, vulgar.

antonyms cultured, polite, refined.

boost *n.* addition, advancement, ego-trip, encouragement, enhancement, expansion, fillip, heave, help, hoist, hype, improvement, increase, increment, jump, lift, praise, promotion, push, rise, supplement, thrust.

antonyms blow, setback.

v. advance, advertise, aid, amplify, assist, augment, bolster, develop, elevate, encourage, enhance, enlarge, expand, foster, further, heave, heighten, hoist, improve, increase, inspire, jack up, lift, plug, praise, promote, push, raise, supplement, support, sustain, thrust.

antonyms hinder, undermine.

boot[1] *n.* bootee, galosh, gumshoe, jackboot, loafer, moccasin, mule, overshoe, platform, pump, riding-boot, rubber, sneaker, top-boot, wader, wellington.

v. bounce, dismiss, eject, expel, fire, give the bum's rush, give the heave, kick, kick out, knock, oust, punt, sack, shove.

boot[2] *v.* advantage, aid, avail, benefit, help, profit, serve.

bootless *adj.* barren, fruitless, futile, ineffective, on a hiding to nothing, pointless, profitless, sterile, unavailing, unproductive, unsuccessful, useless, vain, worthless.

antonyms profitable, useful.

bootlicking *n.* ass-licking, back-scratching, crawling, cringing, deference, faggery, fagging, fawning, flattery, groveling, heepishness, ingratiation, lackeying, obsequiousness, servility, sycophancy, toadying.

booty *n.* boodle, bunce, gains, haul, loot, pickings, pillage, plunder, spoil, spoils, swag, takings, winnings.

border *n.* borderline, bound, boundary, bounds, brim, brink, circumference, confine, confines, demarcation, edge, fringe, frontier, hem, limit, limits, lip, list, march, margin, perimeter, periphery, rand, rim, screed, selvage, skirt, surround, trimming, valance, verge.

adj. boundary, circumscriptive, dividing, frontier, limitary, limitrophe, marginal, perimeter, separating, side.

borderline *adj.* ambivalent, doubtful, iffy, indecisive, indefinite, indeterminate, marginal, problematic, uncertain.

antonyms certain, definite.

bore[1] *v.* burrow, countermine, drill, gouge, mine, penetrate, perforate, pierce, sap, sink, thrill, tunnel, undermine.

bore[2] *v.* annoy, bother, bug, fatigue, irk, irritate, jade, pester, tire, trouble, vex, weary, worry.

antonyms charm, interest.

n. annoyance, bind, bother, drag, dullard, headache, nuisance, pain, pain in the neck, pest, schmo, terebrant, trial, vexation, vieux jeu, yawn.

antonym pleasure.

boredom *n.* acedia, apathy, doldrums, dullness, ennui, flatness, irksomeness, listlessness, monotony, sameness, tediousness, tedium, vapors, weariness, wearisomeness, world-weariness.

antonym interest.

boring *adj.* commonplace, dead, dreary, dry, dull, ennuying, flat, ho-hum, humdrum, insipid, irksome, monotonous, repetitious, routine, stale, stupid, tedious, tiresome, tiring, trite, unamusing, undiverting, unedifying, uneventful, unexciting, unfunny, unimaginative, uninspired, uninteresting, unvaried, unwitty, vapid, wearisome.

antonyms interesting, original.

borrow *v.* adopt, ape, appropriate, cadge, copy, crib, derive, draw, echo, filch, imitate, list, mimic, obtain, pilfer, pirate, plagiarize, scrounge, sponge, steal, take, use, usurp.

bosom *n.* breast, bust, center, chest, circle, core, heart, midst, protection, sanctuary, shelter.

adj. boon, cherished, close, confidential, dear, favorite, inseparable, intimate.

boss[1] *n.* administrator, baron, captain, chief, director, employer, executive, foreman, gaffer, governor, head, leader, manager, master, overseer, owner, superintendent, supervisor, supremo.

v. administrate, command, control, direct, employ, manage, oversee, run, superintend, supervise.

boss[2] *n.* knob, knub, knubble, nub, nubble, omphalos, point, protuberance, stud, tip, umbo.

bossy *adj.* arrogant, authoritarian, autocratic, demanding, despotic, dictatorial, domineering, exacting, hectoring, high-handed, imperious, insistent, lordly, oppressive, overbearing, tyrannical.

antonym unassertive.

botch *v.* blunder, bungle, butcher, cobble, corpse, do carelessly, flub, fudge, fumble, goof, louse up, mar, mend, mess, mismanage, muff, patch, ruin, screw up, spoil.

antonyms accomplish, succeed.

n. balls-up, blunder, bungle, cock-up, failure, farce, hash, mess, miscarriage, muddle, shambles.

antonym success.

bother *v.* alarm, annoy, bore, chivvy, concern, dismay, distress, disturb, dog, harass, harry, hassle, inconvenience, irk, irritate, molest, nag, pester, plague, pother, pudder, trouble, upset, vex, worry.

n. aggravation, annoyance, bustle, consternation, difficulty, flurry, fuss, hassle, inconvenience, irritation, kerfuffle, molestation, nuisance, palaver, perplexity, pest, pother, problem, pudder, strain, trouble, vexation, worry.

bothersome *adj.* aggravating, annoying, boring, distressing, exasperating, inconvenient, infuriating, irksome, irritating, laborious, tedious, tiresome, troublesome, vexatious, vexing, wearisome.

bottom *n.* ass, backside, base, basis, behind, bum, butt, buttocks, core, depths, derrière, essence, floor, foot, foundation, fundament, fundus, ground, groundwork, heart, nadir, origin, pedestal, plinth, posterior, principle, rear, rear end, root, rump, seat, sit-upon, socle, sole, source, substance, substratum, substructure, support, tail, underneath, underside, understratum.

bounce *v.* bob, bound, bump, dap, dismiss, eject, expel, jounce, jump, kick out, leap, oust, rebound, recoil, resile, ricochet, spring, throw out.

n. animation, bound, dap, dynamism, ebullience, elasticity, energy, exuberance, give, go, life, liveliness, pep, rebound, recoil, resilience, spring, springiness, vigor, vitality, vivacity, zip.

bound[1] *adj.* bandaged, beholden, cased, certain, chained, committed, compelled, constrained, destined, doomed, duty-bound, fastened, fated, fixed, forced, held, liable, manacled, obligated, obliged, pinioned, pledged, required, restricted, secured, sure, tied, tied up.

bound[2] *v.* bob, bounce, caper, frisk, gallumph, gambol, hurdle, jump, leap, lope, loup, lunge, pounce, prance, skip, spring, vault.

n. bob, bounce, caper, dance, frisk, gambado, gambol, jump, leap, lope, loup, lunge, pounce, prance, scamper, skip, spring, vault.

boundary *n.* abuttal, barrier, border, borderline, bounds, bourne, brink, confines, demarcation, edge, extremity, fringe, frontier, junction, limes, limits, line, march, margin, mete, perimeter, termination, verge.

adj. border, demarcation, frontier, limitary, limitrophe, perimeter.

boundless *adj.* countless, endless, illimitable, immeasurable, immense, incalculable, indefatigable, inexhaustible, infinite, interminable, interminate, limitless, measureless, prodigious, unbounded, unconfined, unending, unflagging, unlimited, untold, vast.

antonym limited.

bounty *n.* allowance, almsgiving, annuity, assistance, beneficence, benevolence, bonus, charity, donation, generosity, gift, grace, grant, gratuity, kindness, largesse, liberality, philanthropy, premium, present, recompense, reward.

bourgeois *adj.* Biedermeier, circumscribed, commonplace, conformist, conservative, conventional, dull, hide-bound, humdrum, kitsch, materialistic, middleclass, pedestrian, tawdry, traditional, trite, trivial, unadventurous, unimaginative, uninspired, unoriginal, vulgar.

antonyms bohemian, original, unconventional.

n. conformist, petit bourgeois, philistine, plebeian, stick-in-the-mud.

antonyms bohemian, nonconformist.

bout *n.* battle, competition, contest, course, encounter, engagement, fight, fit, go, heat, match, period, round, run, session, set-to, spell, spree, stint, stretch, struggle, term, time, turn, venue.

bow[1] *v.* accept, acquiesce, bend, bob, capitulate, comply, concede, conquer, consent, crush, curtsey, defer, depress, droop, genuflect, give in, incline, kowtow, nod, overpower, stoop, subdue, subjugate, submit, surrender, vanquish, yield.

n. acknowledgment, bending, bob, curtsey, genuflexion, inclination, kowtow, nod, obeisance, salaam, salutation.

bow out abandon, back out, bunk off, chicken out, defect, desert, give up, opt out, pull out, quit, resign, retire, stand down, step down, withdraw.

bow[2] *n.* beak, head, prow, rostrum, stem.

bowels *n.* belly, center, core, depths, entrails, guts,

heart, hold, innards, inside, insides, interior, intestines, middle, viscera, vitals.

bowl[1] *n.* basin, container, cruse, dish, pan, porringer, receptacle, sink, tureen, vessel.

bowl[2] *n.* jack, wood.

v. fling, hurl, pitch, revolve, roll, rotate, spin, throw, trundle, whirl.

bowl over amaze, astonish, astound, dumbfound, fell, flabbergast, floor, stagger, startle, stun, surprise, topple, unbalance.

bowl[3] *n.* amphitheater, arena, auditorium, coliseum, field, ground, hall, hippodrome, stadium.

box[1] *n.* bijou, carton, case, casket, chest, coffer, coffin, coffret, consignment, container, coop, fund, pack, package, portmanteau, present, pyx, pyxis, receptacle, trunk.

v. case, embox, encase, pack, package, wrap.

box[2] *v.* buffet, butt, clout, cuff, fight, hit, punch, slap, sock, spar, strike, thwack, wallop, whack, wham, whang.

n. blow, buffet, clout, cuff, punch, slap, stroke, thump, wallop, wham, whang.

boy *n.* callant, cub, dandiprat, fellow, gamin, gossoon, halfling, imp, junior, kid, lad, loon, loonie, man-child, nipper, puppy, schoolboy, spalpeen, stripling, urchin, whippersnapper, youngster, youth.

boycott *v.* ban, bar, black, blackball, blacklist, cold-shoulder, disallow, embargo, exclude, ignore, ostracize, outlaw, prohibit, proscribe, refuse, reject, spurn.

antonyms encourage, support.

boyfriend *n.* admirer, beau, date, fancy man, fellow, inamorato, lover, man, steady, suitor, swain, sweetheart, young man.

brace[1] *n.* binder, bracer, bracket, buttress, cleat, corset, nogging, prop, reinforcement, shoring, stanchion, stay, strap, strut, support, truss.

v. bandage, bind, bolster, buttress, fasten, fortify, prop, reinforce, shore (up), steady, strap, strengthen, support, tie, tighten.

brace[2] *n.* couple, doubleton, duo, pair, twosome.

bracing *adj.* brisk, crisp, energetic, energizing, enlivening, exhilarating, fortifying, fresh, invigorating, refreshing, restorative, reviving, rousing, stimulating, strengthening, tonic, vigorous.

antonym debilitating.

brag *v.* bluster, boast, crow, fanfaronade, rodomontade, swagger, talk big, trumpet, vapor, vaunt.

antonym deprecate.

braid *v.* entwine, interlace, intertwine, interweave, lace, plait, ravel, twine, twist, weave, wind.

antonyms undo, untwist.

brain[1] *n.* boffin, egghead, expert, genius, highbrow, intellect, intellectual, mastermind, prodigy, pundit, sage, savant, scholar, wizard.

antonym simpleton.

brain[2] *n.* cerebrum, gray matter, intellect, mind, sensorium, sensory.

brake *n.* check, constraint, control, curb, drag, rein, restraint, restriction, retardment.

v. check, decelerate, drag, halt, moderate, pull up, retard, slacken, slow, stop.

antonym accelerate.

branch *n.* arm, bough, chapter, department, division, grain, limb, lodge, office, offshoot, part, prong, ramification, ramus, section, shoot, sprig, subdivision, subsection, whip, wing, witty.

branch out bifurcate, broaden out, develop, divaricate, diversify, enlarge, expand, extend, increase, move on, multiply, proliferate, ramify, vary.

brand *n*. brand-name, class, emblem, grade, hallmark, kind, label, line, logo, make, mark, marker, marque, quality, sign, sort, species, stamp, symbol, trademark, type, variety.

v. burn, censure, denounce, discredit, disgrace, label, mark, scar, stain, stamp, stigmatize, taint, type.

brave *adj*. audacious, bold, courageous, daring, dauntless, doughty, fearless, fine, gallant, game, glorious, hardy, heroic, indomitable, intrepid, plucky, resolute, resplendent, splendid, stalwart, stoic, stoical, stouthearted, unafraid, undaunted, unflinching, valiant, valorous.

antonyms cowardly, timid.

v. accost, bear, beard, challenge, confront, dare, defy, encounter, endure, face, face up to, stand up to, suffer, withstand.

antonyms capitulate, crumple.

brawl *n*. affray, altercation, argument, bagarre, battle, broil, bust-up, clash, disorder, dispute, dog-fight, Donnybrook, dust-up, fight, fracas, fray, free-for-all, mêlée, punch-up, quarrel, row, ruckus, rumpus, scrap, scuffle, squabble, tumult, uproar, wrangle.

v. altercate, argue, battle, come to blows, dispute, fight, flyte, quarrel, row, scrap, scuffle, squabble, tussle, wrangle, wrestle.

brawn *n*. beef, beefiness, brawniness, bulk, bulkiness, flesh, meat, might, muscle, muscles, muscularity, power, robustness, sinews, strength, thews.

brazen *adj*. assured, audacious, barefaced, blatant, bold, brash, brassy, defiant, flagrant, forward, immodest, impudent, insolent, malapert, pert, saucy, shameless, unabashed, unashamed.

antonym shamefaced.

breach *n*. alienation, aperture, break, break-up, chasm, cleft, contravention, crack, crevice, difference, disaffection, disagreement, discontinuity, disobedience, disruption, dissension, dissociation, division, estrangement, fissure, gap, hole, infraction, infringement, lapse, offence, opening, parting, quarrel, rent, rift, rupture, schism, scission, scissure, secession, separation, severance, split, transgression, trespass, variance, violation.

break *v*. abandon, absorb, announce, appear, bankrupt, batter, beat, better, breach, burst, bust, contravene, cow, crack, crash, cripple, cushion, cut, dash, defeat, degrade, demolish, demoralize, destroy, diminish, discharge, disclose, discontinue, disintegrate, disobey, dispirit, disregard, divide, divulge, emerge, enervate, enfeeble, erupt, escape, exceed, excel, explode, flee, flout, fly, fract, fracture, fragment, go phut, happen, humiliate, impair, impart, incapacitate, inform, infract, infringe, interrupt, jigger, knacker, knap, lessen, moderate, modify, occur, outdo, outstrip, part, pause, proclaim, reduce, rend, rest, retard, reveal, ruin, separate, sever, shatter, shiver, smash, snap, soften, splinter, split, stave, stop, subdue, surpass, suspend, tame, tear, tell, transgress, undermine, undo, violate, weaken, worst.

n. abruption, advantage, alienation, breach, breather, chance, cleft, crack, crevice, disaffection, discontinuity, dispute, disruption, divergence, division, estrangement, fissure, fortune, fracture, gap, gash, halt, hiatus, hole, interlude, intermission, interruption, interval, lapse, let-up, lull, opening, opportunity, pause, quarrel, recess, rent, respite, rest, rift, rupture, schism, separation, split, suspension, tear, time-out.

breed *v*. arouse, bear, beget, bring forth, bring up, cause, create, cultivate, develop, discipline, educate, engender, foster, generate, hatch, induce, instruct, make, multiply, nourish, nurture, occasion, originate, procreate, produce, propagate, raise, rear, reproduce, train.

n. family, ilk, kind, line, lineage, pedigree, progeny, race, sort, species, stamp, stock, strain, type, variety.

breeze *n*. air, breath, cat's-paw, draft, flurry, gale, gust, waft, whiff, wind, zephyr.

v. flit, glide, hurry, sail, sally, sweep, trip, wander.

breezy *adj*. airy, animated, blithe, blowing, blowy, blustery, bright, buoyant, carefree, careless, casual, cheerful, debonair, easy-going, exhilarating, fresh, gusty, informal, insouciant, jaunty, light, light-hearted, lively, nonchalant, sprightly, squally, sunny, untroubled, vivacious, windy.

antonyms calm, staid.

brevity *n*. abruptness, briefness, brusqueness, conciseness, concision, crispness, curtness, economy, ephemerality, evanescence, fugacity, impermanence, incisiveness, laconicism, laconism, pithiness, shortness, succinctness, summariness, terseness, transience, transitoriness.

antonyms longevity, permanence, verbosity.

brew *v*. boil, build up, concoct, contrive, cook, decoct, develop, devise, excite, ferment, foment, gather, hatch, infuse, mix, plan, plot, prepare, project, scheme, seethe, soak, steep, stew.

n. beverage, blend, bouillon, brewage, broth, concoction, distillation, drink, fermentation, gruel, infusion, liquor, mixture, potion, preparation, stew.

bribe *n*. allurement, back-hander, baksheesh, boodle, dash, enticement, graft, grease, hush money, incentive, inducement, kickback, pay-off, payola, protection money, refresher, slush fund, sweetener.

v. buy off, buy over, corrupt, reward, square, suborn.

bridle *v*. check, contain, control, curb, govern, master, moderate, rein in, repress, restrain, subdue.

brief *adj*. abrupt, aphoristic, blunt, brusque, capsular, compendious, compressed, concise, crisp, cursory, curt, ephemeral, fast, fleeting, fugacious, fugitive, hasty, laconic, limited, momentary, passing, pithy, quick, sharp, short, short-lived, succinct, surly, swift, temporary, terse, thumbnail, transient, transitory.

antonyms long, long-lived, verbose.

n. advice, argument, briefing, case, contention, data, defense, demonstration, directions, directive, dossier, instructions, mandate, orders, outline, précis, remit, summary.

v. advise, direct, explain, fill in, gen up, guide, inform, instruct, prepare, prime.

brigand *n*. bandit, cateran, dacoit, desperado, footpad, freebooter, gangster, haiduk, heister, highwayman, klepht, marauder, outlaw, plunderer, robber, ruffian.

bright *adj*. ablaze, acute, astute, auspicious, beaming, blazing, brainy, breezy, brilliant, burnished, cheerful, clear, clear-headed, clever, cloudless, dazzling, effulgent, encouraging, excellent, favorable, flashing, fulgent, gay, genial, glad, glaring, gleaming, glistening, glittering, glorious, glowing, golden, happy, hopeful, illuminated, illustrious, ingenious, intelligent, intense, inventive, jolly, joyful, joyous, keen, lambent, lamping, light-hearted, limpid, lively, lucent, lucid, luculent, luminous, lustrous, magnificent, merry, observant, optimistic, pellucid, perceptive, percipient, perspicacious, polished, prefulgent, promising, propitious, prosperous, quick, quick-witted, radiant, resplendent, rosy, scintillating, sharp, sheeny, shimmering, shining, smart, sparkling, splendid, sunny, translucent, transparent, twinkling, unclouded, undulled, untarnished, vivacious, vivid, wide-awake.

antonyms depressing, dull, stupid.

brilliant *adj.* ablaze, accomplished, adroit, animated, astute, blazing, brainy, bright, celebrated, clever, coruscating, dazzling, effulgent, eminent, exceptional, expert, famous, gemmy, gifted, glaring, glittering, glorious, glossy, illustrious, ingenious, intellectual, intelligent, intense, inventive, lambent, luminous, magnificent, masterly, outstanding, quick, refulgent, scintillating, shining, showy, skilful, sparkling, splendid, star, star-like, superb, talented, vivacious, vivid, witty.

antonyms dull, restrained, stupid, undistinguished.

brim *n.* border, brink, circumference, edge, lip, marge, margin, perimeter, periphery, rim, skirt, verge.

bring *v.* accompany, accustom, add, attract, bear, carry, cause, command, conduct, convey, convince, create, deliver, dispose, draw, earn, effect, engender, escort, fetch, force, gather, generate, get, gross, guide, induce, inflict, influence, introduce, lead, make, move, net, occasion, persuade, produce, prompt, return, sway, take, transfer, transport, usher, wreak, yield.

brink *n.* bank, border, boundary, brim, edge, extremity, fringe, limit, lip, marge, margin, point, rim, skirt, threshold, verge, waterside.

brisk *adj.* active, agile, alert, allegro, bracing, bright, brushy, bustling, busy, crank, crisp, effervescing, energetic, exhilarating, expeditious, fresh, galliard, invigorating, keen, lively, nimble, nippy, no-nonsense, prompt, quick, refreshing, sharp, snappy, speedy, spirited, sprightly, spry, stimulating, vigorous.

antonym sluggish.

briskly *adv.* abruptly, actively, allegro, brightly, decisively, efficiently, energetically, expeditiously, incisively, nimbly, promptly, quickly, rapidly, readily, smartly, vigorously.

antonym sluggishly.

bristle *n.* barb, hair, prickle, spine, stubble, thorn, vibrissa, whisker.

v. bridle, draw oneself up, horripilate, prickle, react, rise, seethe, spit.

brittle *adj.* anxious, breakable, crackly, crisp, crumbling, crumbly, curt, delicate, edgy, fragile, frail, frangible, friable, frush, irritable, nervous, nervy, shattery, shivery, short, tense.

antonyms durable, resilient, sturdy.

broach *v.* crack open, introduce, launch into, mention, pierce, propose, puncture, raise, start, suggest, tap, uncork, utter.

broad *adj.* all-embracing, ample, beamy, blue, capacious, catholic, coarse, comprehensive, eclectic, encyclopedic, enlightened, expansive, extensive, far-reaching, general, generous, gross, improper, inclus-

ive, indecent, indelicate, large, latitudinous, roomy, spacious, square, sweeping, tolerant, universal, unlimited, unrefined, vast, voluminous, vulgar, wide, wide-ranging, widespread.

antonym narrow.

broadcast *v.* advertise, air, announce, beam, cable, circulate, disseminate, proclaim, promulgate, publicize, publish, radio, relay, report, show, spread, televise, transmit.

n. program, relay, show, telecast, transmission.

broaden *v.* augment, branch out, develop, diversify, enlarge, enlighten, expand, extend, increase, open up, spread, stretch, supplement, swell, thicken, widen.

broad-minded *adj.* catholic, cosmopolitan, dispassionate, enlightened, flexible, free-thinking, indulgent, liberal, open-minded, permissive, receptive, tolerant, unbiased, unprejudiced, verligte.

brochure *n.* advertisement, booklet, broadsheet, broadside, circular, folder, handbill, hand-out, leaflet, pamphlet.

broil *n.* affray, altercation, argument, brawl, brouhaha, dispute, disturbance, fracas, fray, imbroglio, quarrel, scrimmage, scrum, stramash, strife, tumult, wrangle.

broken *adj.* bankrupt, beaten, betrayed, browbeaten, burst, crippled, crushed, defeated, defective, demolished, demoralized, destroyed, disconnected, discontinuous, dishonored, disjointed, dismantled, dispersed, disregarded, disturbed, down, dud, duff, erratic, exhausted, faulty, feeble, forgotten, fracted, fractured, fragmentary, fragmented, halting, hesitating, humbled, ignored, imperfect, incoherent, incomplete, infirm, infringed, intermittent, interrupted, isolated, jiggered, kaput, knackered, oppressed, out of order, overpowered, prerupt, rent, retracted, routed, ruined, run-down, ruptured, separated, severed, shattered, shivered, spasmodic, spent, stammering, subdued, tamed, traduced, transgressed, uncertain, vanquished, variegated, weak.

broken-hearted *adj.* crestfallen, dejected, desolate, despairing, despondent, devastated, disappointed, disconsolate, grief-stricken, hard-hit, heartbroken, heartsick, heartsore, inconsolable, miserable, mournful, prostrated, sorrowful, unhappy, wretched.

bromide *n.* anodyne, banality, cliché, commonplace, platitude, stereotype, truism.

brooch *n.* badge, breastpin, clasp, clip, pin, prop.

brood *v.* agonize, cover, dwell on, fret, go over, hatch, incubate, meditate, mope, mull over, muse, ponder, rehearse, repine, ruminate.

n. birth, chicks, children, clutch, family, hatch, issue, litter, nide, offspring, progeny, spawn, young.

brook[1] *n.* beck, burn, channel, freshet, gill, inlet, mill, rill, rivulet, runnel, stream, streamlet, watercourse.

brook[2] *v.* abide, accept, allow, bear, countenance, endure, permit, stand, stomach, submit to, suffer, support, swallow, thole, tolerate, withstand.

brother *n.* associate, blood-brother, brer, chum, colleague, companion, compeer, comrade, confrère, cousin, fellow, fellow-creature, friar, friend, kin, kinsman, mate, monk, pal, partner, relation, relative, religieux, religious, sibling.

brotherhood *n.* affiliation, alliance, association, clan, clique, community, confederacy, confederation, confraternity, confrèrie, coterie, fraternity, guild, league, society, union.

brotherly adj. affectionate, amicable, benevolent, caring, concerned, cordial, fraternal, friendly, kind, loving, neighborly, philanthropic, supervisory, sympathetic.
antonyms callous, unbrotherly.

brow n. appearance, aspect, bearing, brink, cliff, countenance, crown, edge, eyebrow, face, forehead, front, mien, peak, ridge, rim, summit, temples, tip, top, verge, visage.

browbeat v. awe, batter, bludgeon, bulldoze, bully, coerce, cow, domineer, dragoon, hector, hound, intimidate, oppress, overbear, threaten, tyrannize.
antonym coax.

brown adj. auburn, bay, brick, bronze, bronzed, browned, brunette, chestnut, chocolate, coffee, dark, donkey, dun, dusky, fuscous, ginger, hazel, mahogany, russet, rust, rusty, sunburnt, tan, tanned, tawny, titian, toasted, umber, vandyke brown.

brown study absence, absent-mindedness, absorption, abstraction, contemplation, meditation, musing, pensiveness, preoccupation, reflection, reverie, rumination.

browse v. crop, dip into, eat, feed, flick through, graze, leaf through, nibble, pasture, peruse, scan, skim, survey.

bruise v. blacken, blemish, contund, contuse, crush, discolor, grieve, hurt, injure, insult, mar, mark, offend, pound, pulverize, stain, wound.
n. blemish, contusion, discoloration, injury, mark, rainbow, shiner, swelling.

brunt n. burden, force, impact, impetus, pressure, shock, strain, stress, thrust, violence, weight.

brush¹ n. besom, broom, sweeper.
v. buff, burnish, caress, clean, contact, flick, glance, graze, kiss, paint, polish, rub, scrape, shine, stroke, sweep, touch, wash.

brush² n. brushwood, bushes, frith, ground cover, scrub, shrubs, thicket, undergrowth, underwood.

brush³ n. clash, conflict, confrontation, dust-up, encounter, fight, fracas, incident, run-in, scrap, set-to, skirmish, tussle.

brush-off n. cold shoulder, discouragement, dismissal, go-by, rebuff, refusal, rejection, repudiation, repulse, slight, snub.
antonym encouragement.

brusque adj. abrupt, blunt, curt, discourteous, gruff, hasty, impolite, sharp, short, surly, tactless, tart, terse, uncivil, undiplomatic.
antonyms courteous, tactful.

brutal adj. animal, barbarous, bearish, beastly, bestial, bloodthirsty, boarish, brute, brutish, callous, carnal, coarse, crude, cruel, doggish, ferocious, gruff, harsh, heartless, impolite, inhuman, inhumane, insensitive, merciless, pitiless, remorseless, rough, rude, ruthless, savage, sensual, severe, uncivil, uncivilized, unfeeling, unmannerly, unsympathetic, vicious.
antonyms humane, kindly.

brute n. animal, barbarian, beast, bête, boor, creature, devil, fiend, lout, monster, ogre, sadist, savage, swine.
antonym gentleman.
adj. bestial, bodily, carnal, coarse, depraved, fleshly, gross, instinctive, mindless, physical, senseless, sensual, unthinking.
antonym refined.

bubble¹ n. ball, bead, bladder, blister, blob, drop, droplet, globule, vesicle.

v. babble, boil, burble, effervesce, fizz, foam, froth, gurgle, murmur, percolate, purl, ripple, seethe, sparkle, trickle, trill, wallop.

bubble² n. bagatelle, delusion, fantasy, fraud, illusion, sting, toy, trifle, vanity.

buccaneer n. corsair, filibuster, freebooter, pirate, privateer, sea-robber, sea-rover, sea-wolf.

buck¹ n. beau, blade, blood, coxcomb, dandy, fop, gallant, playboy, popinjay, spark, swell.

buck² v. bound, cheer, dislodge, encourage, gladden, gratify, hearten, inspirit, jerk, jump, leap, please, prance, spring, start, throw, unseat, vault.

bucket n. bail, barrel, basin, can, cask, kibble, pail, pan, pitcher, vessel.

buckle n. bend, bulge, catch, clasp, clip, contortion, distortion, fastener, hasp, kink, twist, warp.
v. bend, bulge, catch, cave in, clasp, close, collapse, connect, contort, crumple, distort, fasten, fold, hitch, hook, secure, twist, warp, wrinkle.

bud n. embryo, germ, knosp, shoot, sprig, sprout.
v. burgeon, develop, grow, pullulate, shoot, sprout.
antonyms waste away, wither.

budge v. bend, change, convince, dislodge, give (way), inch, influence, move, persuade, propel, push, remove, roll, shift, slide, stir, sway, yield.

budget n. allocation, allotment, allowance, cost, estimate, finances, fonds, funds, means, resources.
v. allocate, apportion, cost, estimate, plan, ration.

buff¹ adj. fawn, fulvid, fulvous, khaki, sandy, straw, tan, yellowish, yellowish-brown.
v. brush, burnish, polish, polish up, rub, shine, smooth.

buff² n. addict, admirer, aficionado, bug, cognoscente, connoisseur, devotee, enthusiast, expert, fan, fiend, freak.

buffet¹ n. café, cafeteria, counter, snack-bar, snack-counter.

buffet² v. bang, batter, beat, box, bump, clobber, clout, cuff, flail, hit, jar, knock, pound, pummel, push, rap, shove, slap, strike, thump, wallop.
n. bang, blow, box, bump, clout, cuff, jar, jolt, knock, push, rap, shove, slap, smack, thump, wallop.

buffoon n. clown, comedian, comic, droll, fool, goliard, harlequin, jester, joker, merry-andrew, mountebank, scaramouch, schmuck, tomfool, vice, wag, zany.

bug n. addict, admirer, bacterium, blemish, buff, catch, craze, defect, disease, enthusiast, error, fad, failing, fan, fault, fiend, flaw, freak, germ, gremlin, imperfection, infection, mania, micro-organism, obsession, rage, snarl-up, virus.
v. annoy, badger, bother, disturb, get, harass, irk, irritate, needle, nettle, pester, plague, vex.

bugbear n. anathema, bane, bête noire, bloody-bones, bogey, bugaboo, devil, dread, fiend, horror, Mumbo-jumbo, nightmare, pet hate, poker, rawhead.

build v. assemble, augment, base, begin, big, constitute, construct, develop, edify, enlarge, erect, escalate, establish, extend, fabricate, form, formulate, found, improve, inaugurate, increase, initiate, institute, intensify, knock together, make, originate, raise, strengthen.
antonyms destroy, knock down, lessen, weaken.
n. body, figure, form, frame, physique, shape, size, structure.

building n. architecture, construction, domicile, dwelling, edifice, erection, fabric, fabrication, house, pile, structure.

antonym destruction.

build-up *n.* accretion, accumulation, ballyhoo, development, enlargement, escalation, expansion, gain, growth, heap, hype, increase, load, mass, plug, promotion, publicity, puff, stack, stockpile, store.

antonyms decrease, reduction.

bulge *n.* belly, boost, bump, distension, hump, increase, intensification, lump, projection, protrusion, protuberance, rise, surge, swelling, upsurge.

v. bag, belly, bulb, dilate, distend, enlarge, expand, hump, project, protrude, sag, strout, swell.

bulk *n.* amplitude, bigness, body, dimensions, extensity, extent, generality, immensity, largeness, magnitude, majority, mass, most, plurality, preponderance, size, substance, volume, weight.

bulky *adj.* big, colossal, cumbersome, enormous, heavy, hefty, huge, hulking, immense, large, lumping, mammoth, massive, massy, ponderous, substantial, unmanageable, unwieldy, volumed, voluminous, weighty.

antonyms handy, insubstantial, small.

bulldoze *v.* browbeat, buffalo, bully, clear, coerce, cow, demolish, drive, flatten, force, hector, intimidate, knock down, level, propel, push, push through, raze, shove, thrust.

bulletin *n.* announcement, communication, communiqué, dispatch, dope, message, newsflash, notification, report, sitrep, statement.

bully *n.* bouncer, browbeater, bucko, bully-boy, bullyrook, coercionist, harasser, intimidator, killcrow, oppressor, persecutor, rowdy, ruffian, termagant, tormentor, tough, tyrant.

v. bluster, browbeat, bulldoze, bullyrag, coerce, cow, domineer, haze, hector, intimidate, oppress, overbear, persecute, push around, swagger, terrorize, tyrannize.

antonyms coax, persuade.

bulwark *n.* bastion, buffer, buttress, defense, embankment, fortification, guard, mainstay, outwork, partition, rampart, redoubt, safeguard, security, support.

bumbling *adj.* awkward, blundering, botching, bungling, clumsy, footling, foozling, incompetent, inefficient, inept, lumbering, maladroit, muddled, stumbling.

antonyms competent, efficient.

bump *v.* bang, bounce, budge, collide (with), crash, dislodge, displace, hit, jar, jerk, jolt, jostle, jounce, knock, move, rattle, remove, shake, shift, slam, strike.

n. bang, blow, bulge, collision, contusion, crash, hit, hump, impact, jar, jolt, knob, knock, knot, lump, node, nodule, protuberance, rap, shock, smash, swelling, thud, thump.

bumptious *adj.* arrogant, boastful, brash, cocky, conceited, egotistic, forward, full of oneself, impudent, overbearing, over-confident, pompous, presumptuous, pushy, self-assertive, self-important, showy, swaggering, vainglorious, vaunting.

antonyms humble, modest.

bumpy *adj.* bouncy, choppy, irregular, jarring, jerky, jolting, jolty, knobbly, knobby, lumpy, rough, rutted, uneven.

antonym smooth.

bunch *n.* assortment, band, batch, bouquet, bundle, clump, cluster, collection, crew, crowd, fascicle, fascicule, flock, gang, gathering, group-knot, heap, lot,

mass, mob, multitude, number, parcel, party, pile, quantity, sheaf, spray, stack, swarm, team, troop, tuft.

v. assemble, bundle, cluster, collect, congregate, crowd, flock, group, herd, huddle, mass, pack.

antonyms scatter, spread out.

bundle *n.* accumulation, assortment, bag, bale, batch, box, bunch, carton, collection, consignment, crate, drum, fascicle, fascicule, group, heap, mass, Matilda, pack, package, packet, pallet, parcel, pile, quantity, roll, shock, shook, stack, stook, swag, truss.

v. bale, bind, fasten, pack, palletize, tie, truss, wrap.

bungle *v.* blunder, bodge, boob, botch, bumble, cock up, duff, flub, footle, foozle, foul up, fudge, goof, louse up, mar, mess up, miscalculate, mismanage, muff, mull, ruin, screw up, spoil.

n. blunder, boob, boo-boo, botch-up, cock-up, foul-up, mull.

buoyant *adj.* afloat, animated, blithe, bouncy, breezy, bright, bullish, carefree, cheerful, debonair, floatable, floating, happy, jaunty, joyful, light, light-hearted, lively, peppy, rising, sprightly, sunny, weightless.

antonym depressed.

burden *n.* affliction, anxiety, bear, care, cargo, clog, dead weight, encumbrance, grievance, load, millstone, obligation, obstruction, onus, responsibility, sorrow, strain, stress, trial, trouble, weight, worry.

v. bother, encumber, handicap, lade, lie hard on, lie heavy on, load, oppress, overload, overwhelm, strain, tax, worry.

antonyms disburden, lighten, relieve.

burdensome *adj.* crushing, difficult, distressing, exacting, heavy, irksome, onerous, oppressive, taxing, troublesome, trying, wearisome, weighty.

antonyms easy, light.

bureau *n.* agency, branch, counter, department, desk, division, office, service.

bureaucrat *n.* administrator, apparatchik, bureaucratist, chinovnik, civil servant, functionary, mandarin, minister, office-holder, officer, official.

burglar *n.* cat-burglar, cracksman, house-breaker, picklock, pilferer, robber, thief, yegg.

burial *n.* burying, entombment, exequies, funeral, inhumation, interment, obsequies, sepulcher, sepulture.

burly *adj.* athletic, beefy, big, brawny, bulky, heavy, hefty, hulking, husky, muscular, powerful, stocky, stout, strapping, strong, sturdy, thickset, well-built.

antonyms puny, slim, small, thin.

burn *v.* bite, blaze, brand, calcine, cauterize, char, combust, conflagrate, consume, corrode, deflagrate, desire, expend, flame, flare, flash, flicker, fume, glow, hurt, ignite, incinerate, kindle, light, oxidize, pain, parch, scorch, seethe, shrivel, simmer, singe, smart, smoke, smolder, sting, tingle, toast, use, wither, yearn.

burnish *v.* brighten, buff, furbish, glaze, polish, polish up, rub, shine.

antonym tarnish.

n. gloss, luster, patina, polish, sheen, shine.

burrow *n.* den, earth, hole, lair, retreat, set(t), shelter, tunnel, warren.

v. delve, dig, earth, excavate, mine, tunnel, undermine.

burst *v.* barge, blow up, break, crack, dehisce, disintegrate, erupt, explode, fragment, gush, puncture, run, rupture, rush, shatter, shiver, split, spout, tear.

n. bang, blast, blasting, blow-out, blow-up, breach,

break, crack, discharge, eruption, explosion, fit, gallop, gush, gust, outbreak, outburst, outpouring, rupture, rush, spate, split, spurt, surge, torrent.

adj. broken, flat, kaput, punctured, rent, ruptured, split, torn.

bury *v.* absorb, conceal, cover, embed, enclose, engage, engross, engulf, enshroud, entomb, hide, immerse, implant, inearth, inhume, inter, interest, lay to rest, occupy, secrete, sepulcher, shroud, sink, submerge.

antonyms disinter, uncover.

business *n.* affair, assignment, bargaining, calling, career, commerce, company, concern, corporation, craft, dealings, duty, employment, enterprise, establishment, firm, function, industry, issue, job, line, line of country, manufacturing, matter, merchandising, métier, occupation, organization, palaver, point, problem, profession, pursuit, question, responsibility, selling, subject, task, topic, trade, trading, transaction(s), venture, vocation, work.

bustle *v.* dash, flutter, fuss, hasten, hurry, rush, scamper, scramble, scurry, scuttle, stir, tear.

n. activity, ado, agitation, commotion, excitement, flurry, fuss, haste, hurly-burly, hurry, palaver, pother, stir, to-do, toing and froing, tumult.

bustling *adj.* active, astir, busy, buzzing, crowded, energetic, eventful, full, humming, lively, restless, rushing, stirring, swarming, teeming, thronged.

antonym quiet.

busy *adj.* active, assiduous, brisk, diligent, eident, employed, energetic, engaged, engrossed, exacting, full, fussy, hectic, industrious, inquisitive, interfering, lively, meddlesome, meddling, nosy, occupied, officious, persevering, prying, restless, slaving, stirabout, stirring, strenuous, tireless, tiring, troublesome, unleisured, versant, working.

antonyms idle, quiet.

v. absorb, bother, concern, employ, engage, engross, immerse, interest, occupy.

busybody *n.* eavesdropper, gossip, intriguer, intruder, meddler, nosey parker, pantopragmatic, pry, scandalmonger, snoop, snooper, troublemaker.

butcher *n.* destroyer, killcow, killer, murderer, slaughterer, slayer.

v. assassinate, botch, carve, clean, cut, destroy, dress, exterminate, joint, kill, liquidate, massacre, mutilate, prepare, ruin, slaughter, slay, spoil, wreck.

butt[1] *n.* base, end, foot, haft, handle, hilt, shaft, shank, stock, stub, tail, tip.

butt[2] *n.* dupe, laughing-stock, mark, object, point, subject, target, victim.

butt[3] *v., n.* buck, buffet, bump, bunt, hit, jab, knock, poke, prod, punch, push, ram, shove, thrust.

buttocks *n.* ass, backside, beam end, behind, bottom, breach, bum, cheeks, derrière, fanny, haunches, hinder-end, hinderlin(g)s, hindquarters, natch, nates, posterior, prat, rear, rump, seat, tush.

buttress *n.* abutment, brace, mainstay, pier, prop, reinforcement, shore, stanchion, stay, strut, support.

v. bolster up, brace, hold up, prop up, reinforce, shore up, strengthen, support, sustain, uphold.

antonyms weaken.

buxom *adj.* ample, bosomy, busty, chesty, comely, debonair, hearty, jocund, jolly, lively, lusty, merry, plump, robust, voluptuous, well-rounded, winsome.

antonyms petite, slim, small.

buy *v.* acquire, bribe, corrupt, fix, get, obtain, procure, purchase, square, suborn.

antonym sell.

n. acquisition, bargain, deal, purchase.

buzz *n.* bombilation, bombination, buzzing, drone, gossip, hearsay, hiss, hum, murmur, news, purr, report, ring, ringing, rumor, scandal, susurration, susurrus, whir(r), whisper, whizz.

v. bombilate, bombinate, drone, hum, murmur, reverberate, ring, susurrate, whir(r), whisper, whizz.

by *prep.* along, beside, near, next to, over, past, through, via.

adv. aside, at hand, away, beyond, close, handy, near, past.

bygone *adj.* ancient, antiquated, departed, erstwhile, forepast, forgotten, former, lost, olden, past, previous.

antonyms modern, recent.

n. antique, grievance, oldie.

bypass *v.* avoid, circumvent, ignore, neglect, outflank.

n. detour, ring road.

by-product *n.* after-effect, consequence, epiphenomenon, fall-out, repercussion, result, side-effect.

bystander *n.* eye-witness, looker-on, observer, onlooker, passer-by, spectator, watcher, witness.

C

cab *n.* hack, minicab, taxi, taxicab, vettura.

cabin *n.* berth, bothy, chalet, compartment, cot, cot-house, cottage, crib, deck-house, hovel, hut, lodge, quarters, room, shack, shanty, shed.

cabinet *n.* almirah, case, chiffonier, closet, commode, cupboard, dresser, escritoire, locker.

cable *n.* chain, cord, hawser, line, mooring, rope.

cache *n.* accumulation, fund, garner, hoard, repository, reserve, stockpile, store, storehouse, supply, treasure-store.

v. bury, conceal, hide, secrete, stash, store, stow.

cad *n.* blackguard, bounder, caitiff, churl, cur, dastard, heel, knave, oik, poltroon, rat, rotter, skunk, swine, worm.

antonym gentleman.

café *n.* cafeteria, coffee bar, coffee shop, estaminet, greasy spoon, restaurant, snack bar, tea-room.

cag(e)y *adj.* careful, chary, circumspect, discreet, guarded, non-committal, secretive, shrewd, wary, wily.

antonyms frank, indiscreet, open.

calamity *n.* adversity, affliction, cataclysm, catastrophe, desolation, disaster, distress, downfall, misadventure, mischance, misfortune, mishap, reverse, ruin, scourge, tragedy, trial, tribulation, woe, wretchedness.

antonyms blessing, godsend.

calculate *v.* aim, cipher, compute, consider, count, determine, enumerate, estimate, figure, gauge, intend, judge, plan, rate, reckon, value, weigh, work out.

calculating *adj.* canny, cautious, contriving, crafty, cunning, designing, devious, Machiavellian, manipulative, politic, scheming, sharp, shrewd, sly.

antonyms artless, naïve, open.

calculation *n.* answer, caution, ciphering, circumspection, computation, deliberation, estimate, estimation, figuring, forecast, foresight, forethought, judgment, planning, precaution, reckoning, result.

call v. announce, appoint, arouse, assemble, awaken, bid, christen, collect, consider, contact, convene, convoke, cry, declare, decree, denominate, designate, dub, elect, entitle, estimate, gather, hail, halloo, invite, judge, label, muster, name, ordain, order, phone, proclaim, rally, regard, rouse, shout, style, summon, telephone, term, think, waken, yell.

n. announcement, appeal, cause, claim, command, cry, demand, excuse, grounds, hail, invitation, justification, need, notice, occasion, order, plea, reason, request, right, ring, scream, shout, signal, summons, supplication, urge, visit, whoop, yell.

calling n. business, career, employment, field, job, line, line of country, métier, mission, occupation, profession, province, pursuit, trade, vocation, work.

callous adj. case-hardened, cold, hard-bitten, hard-boiled, hardened, hard-hearted, heartless, indifferent, indurated, insensate, insensible, insensitive, inured, obdurate, soulless, thick-skinned, uncaring, unfeeling, unresponsive, unsouled, unsusceptible, unsympathetic.
antonyms kind, sensitive, sympathetic.

calm adj. balmy, collected, composed, cool, dispassionate, equable, halcyon, impassive, imperturbable, laid back, mild, pacific, passionless, peaceful, placid, quiet, relaxed, restful, sedate, self-collected, self-possessed, serene, smooth, still, stilly, tranquil, unapprehensive, unclouded, undisturbed, unemotional, uneventful, unexcitable, unexcited, unflappable, unflustered, unmoved, unperturbed, unruffled, untroubled, windless.
antonyms excitable, rough, stormy, wild, worried.
v. compose, hush, mollify, pacify, placate, quieten, relax, soothe.
antonyms excite, irritate, worry.
n. calmness, dispassion, hush, peace, peacefulness, quiet, repose, serenity, stillness.
antonyms restlessness, storminess.

campaign n. attack, crusade, drive, excursion, expedition, jihad, movement, offensive, operation, promotion, push.
v. advocate, attack, crusade, fight, promote, push.

can n. canister, cannikin, container, jar, jerrycan, pail, receptacle, tin.

canal n. waterway, zanja.

cancel v. abolish, abort, abrogate, adeem, annul, compensate, counterbalance, countermand, delete, efface, eliminate, erase, expunge, neutralize, nullify, obliterate, offset, quash, redeem, repeal, repudiate, rescind, revoke, scrub, strike.

candid adj. blunt, clear, fair, forthright, frank, free, guileless, ingenuous, just, open, outspoken, plain, shining, sincere, straightforward, truthful, unbiased, uncontrived, unequivocal, unposed, unprejudiced.
antonyms cagey, devious, evasive.

candidate n. applicant, aspirant, claimant, competitor, contender, contestant, doctorand, entrant, nominee, possibility, pretendant, pretender, runner, solicitant, suitor.

candor n. artlessness, directness, fairness, forthrightness, franchise, frankness, guilelessness, honesty, ingenuousness, naïvety, openness, outspokenness, plain-dealing, simplicity, sincerity, straightforwardness, truthfulness, unequivocalness.
antonyms cageyness, deviousness, evasiveness.

canny adj. acute, artful, astute, careful, cautious, circumspect, clever, comfortable, gentle, harmless, innocent, judicious, knowing, lucky, perspicacious, prudent, sagacious, sharp, shrewd, skilful, sly, subtle, wise, worldly-wise.
antonyms foolish, imprudent.

canopy n. awning, baldachin, covering, dais, shade, sunshade, tabernacle, tester, umbrella.

cant[1] n. argot, humbug, hypocrisy, insincerity, jargon, lingo, pretentiousness, sanctimoniousness, slang, thieves' Latin, vernacular.

cant[2] n. angle, bevel, incline, jerk, rise, slant, slope, tilt, toss.

cantankerous adj. bad-tempered, captious, carnaptious, choleric, contrary, crabbed, crabby, cranky, crotchety, crusty, difficult, disagreeable, feisty, grouchy, grumpy, ill-humored, ill-natured, irascible, irritable, peevish, perverse, piggish, quarrelsome, testy.
antonyms good-natured, pleasant.

canyon n. box-canyon, cañon, coulée, gorge, gulch, gully, ravine.

cap v. beat, better, complete, cover, crown, eclipse, exceed, excel, finish, outdo, outstrip, surpass, top, transcend.
n. beret, bonnet, chapka, cowl, fez, glengarry, hat, shako, skullcap, yarmulka.

capability n. ability, capacity, competence, facility, faculty, means, potential, potentiality, power, proficiency, qualification, skill, talent.

capable adj. able, accomplished, adept, adequate, apt, clever, competent, disposed, efficient, experienced, fitted, gifted, intelligent, liable, masterly, predisposed, proficient, qualified, skilful, suited, susceptible, talented.
antonyms incapable, incompetent, useless.

capacity n. ability, amplitude, appointment, aptitude, aptness, brains, caliber, capability, cleverness, compass, competence, competency, dimensions, efficiency, extent, facility, faculty, forte, function, genius, gift, intelligence, magnitude, office, position, post, power, province, range, readiness, role, room, scope, service, size, space, sphere, strength, volume.

cape[1] n. foreland, head, headland, ness, peninsula, point, promontory, tongue.

cape[2] n. cloak, coat, cope, mantle, pelerine, pelisse, poncho, robe, shawl, wrap.

caper v. bounce, bound, capriole, cavort, dance, frisk, frolic, gambol, hop, jump, leap, romp, skip, spring.
n. affair, antic, business, capriole, dido, escapade, gambado, gambol, high jinks, hop, jape, jest, jump, lark, leap, mischief, prank, revel, sport, stunt.

capital[1] adj. cardinal, central, chief, controlling, essential, excellent, fine, first, first-rate, foremost, great, important, leading, main, major, overruling, paramount, pre-eminent, primary, prime, principal, splendid, superb, upper-case.
antonyms minor, sad, unfortunate.

capital[2] n. assets, cash, finance, finances, financing, fonds, funds, investment(s), means, money, principal, property, resources, stock, wealth, wherewithal.

capricious adj. changeable, crotchety, erratic, fanciful, fickle, fitful, freakish, humorous, impulsive, inconstant, mercurial, odd, queer, quirky, uncertain, unpredictable, variable, wayward, whimsical.
antonyms sensible, steady.

captain *n.* boss, chief, chieftain, commander, head, leader, master, officer, patron, pilot, skip, skipper.

captivate *v.* allure, attract, beguile, besot, bewitch, charm, dazzle, enamor, enchain, enchant, enrapture, enslave, ensnare, enthrall, entrance, fascinate, hypnotize, infatuate, lure, mesmerize, seduce, win.

antonyms appal, repel.

captive *n.* convict, detainee, hostage, internee, prisoner, slave.

adj. caged, confined, enchained, enslaved, ensnared, imprisoned, incarcerated, restricted, secure, subjugated.

antonym free.

captivity *n.* bondage, confinement, custody, detention, durance, duress, enchainment, enthralment, imprisonment, incarceration, internment, restraint, servitude, slavery, thraldom, vassalage.

antonym freedom.

capture *v.* apprehend, arrest, bag, catch, collar, cop, feel someone's collar, lift, nab, secure, seize, snaffle, take.

n. apprehension, arrest, catch, imprisonment, seizure, taking, trapping.

car *n.* auto, automobile, caboose, diner, freight car, handcar, Pullman, sleeper, smoker, streetcar.

carcass *n.* body, cadaver, corpse, framework, hulk, relics, remains, shell, skeleton, stiff.

cardinal *adj.* capital, central, chief, essential, first, foremost, fundamental, greatest, highest, important, key, leading, main, paramount, pre-eminent, primary, prime, principal.

care *n.* affliction, anxiety, attention, burden, carefulness, caution, charge, circumspection, concern, consideration, control, custody, direction, disquiet, forethought, guardianship, hardship, heed, interest, keeping, leading-strings, management, meticulousness, ministration, pains, perplexity, pressure, protection, prudence, regard, responsibility, solicitude, stress, supervision, tribulation, trouble, vexation, vigilance, ward, watchfulness, woe, worry.

antonyms carelessness, inattention, thoughtlessness.

career *n.* calling, course, employment, job, life-work, livelihood, occupation, passage, path, procedure, progress, pursuit, race, vocation, walk.

v. bolt, dash, gallop, hurtle, race, run, rush, shoot, speed, tear.

carefree *adj.* airy, blithe, breezy, buoyant, careless, cheerful, cheery, easy-going, happy, happy-go-lucky, insouciant, jaunty, laid-back, light-hearted, lightsome, radiant, sunny, untroubled, unworried.

antonyms anxious, worried.

careful *adj.* accurate, alert, attentive, cautious, chary, circumspect, concerned, conscientious, discreet, fastidious, heedful, judicious, meticulous, mindful, painstaking, particular, precise, protective, prudent, punctilious, scrupulous, softly-softly, solicitous, thoughtful, thrifty, vigilant, wary, watchful.

antonyms careless, inattentive, thoughtless.

careless *adj.* absent-minded, casual, cursory, derelict, forgetful, heedless, hit-or-miss, inaccurate, incautious, inconsiderate, indiscreet, irresponsible, lackadaisical, messy, neglectful, negligent, nonchalant, offhand, perfunctory, regardless, remiss, slap-dash, slipshod, sloppy, thoughtless, uncaring, unconcerned, unguarded, unmindful, unstudied, untenty, unthinking.

antonyms accurate, careful, meticulous, thoughtful.

caress *v.* canoodle, cuddle, embrace, fondle, hug, kiss, lallygag (lollygag), nuzzle, paw, pet, rub, stroke, touch.

n. cuddle, embrace, fondle, hug, kiss, pat, stroke.

cargo *n.* baggage, consignment, contents, freight, goods, haul, lading, load, merchandise, pay-load, shipment, tonnage, ware.

caricature *n.* burlesque, cartoon, distortion, farce, lampoon, mimicry, parody, Pasquil, Pasquin, pasquinade, representation, satire, send-up, take-off, travesty.

v. burlesque, distort, lampoon, mimic, mock, parody, pasquinade, ridicule, satirize, send up, take off.

carnage *n.* blood-bath, bloodshed, butchery, havoc, holocaust, massacre, murder, shambles, slaughter.

carnal *adj.* animal, bodily, corporeal, earthly, erotic, fleshly, human, impure, lascivious, lecherous, lewd, libidinous, licentious, lustful, mundane, natural, physical, profane, prurient, salacious, secular, sensual, sensuous, sexual, sublunary, temporal, unchaste, unregenerate, unspiritual, voluptuous, wanton, worldly.

antonyms chaste, pure, spiritual.

carnival *n.* celebration, fair, Fasching, festival, fête, fiesta, gala, holiday, jamboree, jubilee, Mardi Gras, merrymaking, revelry, wassail, wassail-bout, wassailry.

carol *n.* canticle, canzonet, chorus, ditty, hymn, lay, noel, song, strain, wassail.

carp *v.* cavil, censure, complain, criticize, hypercriticize, knock, nag, quibble, reproach, ultracrepidate.

antonym praise.

carpet *n.* Axminster, kali, mat, Navaho, Persian, rug, Wilton.

carping *adj.* biting, bitter, captious, caviling, critical, fault-finding, grouchy, hypercritical, nagging, nit-picking, picky, reproachful, Zoilean.

n. censure, complaints, criticism, disparagement, knocking, reproofs, Zoilism.

antonyms compliments, praise.

carriage *n.* air, bearing, behavior, cab, carrying, chaise, coach, comportment, conduct, conveyance, conveying, delivery, demeanor, deportment, four-wheeler, freight, gait, manner, mien, posture, presence, transport, transportation, vehicle, vettura, voiture, wagon, wagonette.

carry *v.* accomplish, bear, bring, broadcast, capture, chair, communicate, conduct, convey, display, disseminate, drive, effect, fetch, gain, give, haul, hip, impel, influence, lift, lug, maintain, motivate, move, offer, publish, relay, release, secure, shoulder, spur, stand, stock, suffer, support, sustain, take, tote, transfer, transmit, transport, underpin, uphold, urge, win.

carve *v.* chip, chisel, cut, divide, engrave, etch, fashion, form, grave, hack, hew, incise, indent, make, mold, sculp(t), sculpture, slash, slice, tool, whittle.

case¹ *n.* box, cabinet, canister, capsule, carton, cartridge, casing, casket, chest, compact, container, cover, covering, crate, envelope, étui, folder, holder, integument, jacket, receptacle, sheath, shell, showcase, suitcase, tray, trunk, wrapper, wrapping.

v. encase, enclose, skin.

case² *n.* argument, circumstances, condition, context, contingency, dilemma, event, example, illustration, instance, occasion, occurrence, plight, point, position, predicament, situation, specimen, state, thesis.

v. investigate, reconnoiter.

case³ *n.* action, argument, cause, dispute, lawsuit, proceedings, process, suit, trial.

cash *n.* bank-notes, bread, bucks, bullion, change, coin, coinage, currency, dough, funds, hard currency, hard money, money, notes, payment, readies, ready, ready money, resources, specie, wherewithal.

v. encash, liquidate, realize.

casserole *n.* pot-au-feu, stew-pan.

cast[1] *v.* abandon, add, allot, appoint, assign, bestow, calculate, categorize, choose, chuck, compute, deposit, diffuse, distribute, drive, drop, emit, figure, fling, forecast, form, found, give, hurl, impel, launch, lob, model, mold, name, pick, pitch, project, radiate, reckon, reject, scatter, select, set, shape, shed, shy, sling, spread, throw, thrust, toss, total.

n. air, appearance, complexion, demeanor, fling, form, lob, look, manner, mien, quality, semblance, shade, stamp, style, throw, thrust, tinge, tone, toss, turn.

cast[2] *n.* actors, artistes, characters, company, dramatis personae, entertainers, performers, players, troupe.

caste *n.* class, degree, estate, grade, lineage, order, position, race, rank, species, station, status, stratum.

castle *n.* casbah (kasba, kasbah), château, citadel, donjon, fastness, fortress, keep, mansion, motte and bailey, palace, peel, schloss, stronghold, tower.

casual *adj.* accidental, apathetic, blasé, chance, contingent, cursory, fortuitous, incidental, indifferent, informal, insouciant, irregular, lackadaisical, negligent, nonchalant, occasional, offhand, perfunctory, random, relaxed, serendipitous, stray, unceremonious, uncertain, unconcerned, unexpected, unforeseen, unintentional, unpremeditated.

antonyms deliberate, painstaking, planned.

casualty *n.* death, injured, injury, loss, sufferer, victim, wounded.

catalog *n.* directory, gazetteer, index, inventory, list, litany, record, register, roll, roster, schedule, table.

v. accession, alphabetize, classify, codify, file, index, inventory, list, record, register.

catastrophe *n.* adversity, affliction, blow, calamity, cataclysm, conclusion, culmination, curtain, debacle (débâcle), dénouement, devastation, disaster, end, failure, fiasco, finale, ill, mischance, misfortune, mishap, reverse, ruin, termination, tragedy, trial, trouble, upheaval, upshot, winding-up.

catch *v.* apprehend, arrest, benet, bewitch, captivate, capture, charm, clutch, contract, cop, delight, detect, develop, discern, discover, enchant, enrapture, ensnare, entangle, entrap, expose, fascinate, feel, follow, grab, grasp, grip, hear, incur, nab, nail, perceive, recognize, seize, sense, snare, snatch, surprise, take, twig, unmask.

antonyms drop, free, miss.

n. bolt, clasp, clip, detent, disadvantage, drawback, fastener, hasp, hitch, hook, latch, obstacle, parti, snag, sneck, snib, trap, trick.

catching *adj.* attractive, captivating, charming, communicable, contagious, enchanting, fascinating, fetching, infectious, infective, taking, transferable, transmissible, transmittable, winning, winsome.

antonyms boring, ugly, unattractive.

catchy *adj.* attractive, captivating, confusing, deceptive, haunting, memorable, popular.

antonyms boring, dull.

category *n.* chapter, class, classification, department, division, grade, grouping, head, heading, list, order, rank, section, sort, type.

cater *v.* furnish, humor, indulge, outfit, pander, provide, provision, purvey, supply, victual.

cause *n.* account, agency, agent, aim, attempt, basis, beginning, belief, causation, consideration, conviction, creator, end, enterprise, genesis, grounds, ideal, impulse, incentive, inducement, mainspring, maker, motivation, motive, movement, object, origin, originator, producer, purpose, reason, root, source, spring, stimulus, undertaking.

antonyms effect, result.

v. begin, compel, create, effect, engender, generate, give rise to, incite, induce, motivate, occasion, precipitate, produce, provoke, result in.

caustic *adj.* acidulous, acrid, acrimonious, astringent, biting, bitter, burning, corroding, corrosive, cutting, escharotic, keen, mordant, pungent, sarcastic, scathing, severe, stinging, trenchant, virulent, waspish.

antonyms mild, soothing.

caution *n.* admonition, advice, alertness, care, carefulness, circumspection, counsel, deliberation, discretion, forethought, heed, heedfulness, injunction, prudence, via trita, via tuta, vigilance, wariness, warning, watchfulness.

v. admonish, advise, urge, warn.

cautious *adj.* alert, cagey, careful, chary, circumspect, discreet, guarded, heedful, judicious, politic, prudent, scrupulous, softly-softly, tentative, unadventurous, vigilant, wary, watchful.

antonyms heedless, imprudent, incautious.

cavalcade *n.* array, march-past, parade, procession, retinue, spectacle, train, troop.

cavalier *n.* attendant, beau, blade, chevalier, equestrian, escort, gallant, gentleman, horseman, knight, partner, royalist.

adj. arrogant, cavalierish, condescending, curt, disdainful, free-and-easy, gay, haughty, insolent, lofty, lordly, misproud, off-hand, scornful, supercilious, swaggering.

cave *n.* antre, cavern, cavity, den, grotto, hole, hollow, mattamore, pothole.

cavity *n.* antrum, belly, caries, crater, dent, gap, hole, hollow, pit, pot-hole, sinus, vacuole, ventricle, well, womb.

cavort *v.* caper, caracole, dance, frisk, frolic, gambol, hop, prance, romp, skip, sport.

cease *v.* call a halt, call it a day, conclude, culminate, desist, die, discontinue, end, fail, finish, halt, pack in, poop out, refrain, stay, stop, terminate.

antonyms begin, start.

cede *v.* abandon, abdicate, allow, concede, convey, give up, grant, relinquish, renounce, resign, surrender, transfer, yield.

celebrate *v.* bless, commemorate, commend, emblazon, eulogize, exalt, extol, glorify, honor, keep, laud, live it up, observe, perform, praise, proclaim, publicize, rejoice, reverence, solemnize, toast, wassail, whoop it up.

celebrated *adj.* acclaimed, big, distingué, distinguished, eminent, exalted, famed, famous, glorious, illustrious, lionized, notable, outstanding, popular, pre-eminent, prominent, renowned, revered, well-known.

antonyms obscure, unknown.

celebrity *n.* big name, big shot, bigwig, dignitary, distinction, éclat, eminence, fame, glory, honor, lion, luminary, name, notability, personage, personality, popularity, pre-eminence, prestige, prominence, renown, reputation, repute, star, stardom, superstar, VIP.

antonyms nobody, obscurity.

celestial *adj.* angelic, astral, divine, elysian, empyrean, eternal, ethereal, godlike, heavenly, immortal, paradisaic(al), seraphic, spiritual, starry, sublime, supernatural, transcendental.

antonyms earthly, mundane.

cement *v.* attach, bind, bond, cohere, combine, fix together, glue, gum, join, plaster, seal, solder, stick, unite, weld.

n. adhesive, concrete, glue, gum, mortar, paste, plaster, sealant.

censure *n.* admonishment, admonition, blame, castigation, condemnation, criticism, disapproval, obloquy, rebuke, remonstrance, reprehension, reprimand, reproach, reprobation, reproof, stricture, telling-off, vituperation.

antonyms approval, compliments, praise.

v. abuse, admonish, animadvert, berate, blame, castigate, chide, condemn, criticize, decry, denounce, jump on, rebuke, reprehend, reprimand, reproach, reprobate, reprove, scold, slam, tell off, upbraid.

antonyms approve, compliment, praise.

center *n.* bull's-eye, core, crux, focus, heart, hub, Mecca, mid, middle, mid-point, nave, nucleus, omphalos, pivot.

antonyms edge, outskirts, periphery.

v. cluster, concentrate, converge, focus, gravitate, hinge, pivot, revolve.

central *adj.* chief, essential, focal, fundamental, important, inner, interior, key, main, mean, median, mid, middle, pivotal, primary, principal, vital.

antonyms minor, peripheral.

ceremonious *adj.* civil, courteous, courtly, deferential, dignified, exact, formal, grand, polite, pompous, precise, punctilious, ritual, solemn, starchy, stately, stiff.

antonyms informal, relaxed, unceremonious.

ceremony *n.* celebration, ceremonial, commemoration, decorum, etiquette, event, form, formality, function, niceties, observance, parade, pomp, propriety, protocol, rite, ritual, service, show, solemnities.

certain *adj.* ascertained, assured, bound, conclusive, confident, constant, convinced, convincing, decided, definite, dependable, destined, determinate, established, express, fated, fixed, incontrovertible, individual, indubitable, ineluctable, inescapable, inevitable, inexorable, irrefutable, known, one, particular, plain, positive, precise, regular, reliable, resolved, satisfied, settled, some, special, specific, stable, steady, sure, true, trustworthy, undeniable, undoubted, unequivocal, unfailing, unmistakable, unquestionable, valid.

antonyms doubtful, hesitant, uncertain, unsure.

certainly *adv.* doubtlessly, naturally, of course, questionless.

certainty *n.* assurance, authoritativeness, certitude, confidence, conviction, fact, faith, indubitableness, inevitability, nap, plerophoria, plerophory, positiveness, reality, sure thing, sureness, surety, trust, truth, validity.

antonyms doubt, hesitation, uncertainty.

certificate *n.* attestation, authorization, award, credentials, diploma, document, endorsement, guarantee,

license, pass, qualification, testimonial, validation, voucher, warrant.

certify *v.* ascertain, assure, attest, authenticate, authorize, aver, avow, confirm, corroborate, declare, endorse, evidence, guarantee, notify, show, testify, validate, verify, vouch, witness.

certitude *n.* assurance, certainty, confidence, conviction, plerophoria, plerophory.

antonym doubt.

cessation *n.* abeyance, arrest, arresting, break, ceasing, desistance, discontinuance, discontinuation, discontinuing, end, ending, halt, halting, hiatus, intermission, interruption, interval, let-up, pause, recess, remission, respite, rest, standstill, stay, stoppage, stopping, suspension, termination.

antonym commencement.

chafe *v.* abrade, anger, annoy, enrage, exasperate, fret, fume, gall, get, grate, heat, incense, inflame, irritate, offend, provoke, rage, rasp, rub, scrape, scratch, vex, wear, worry.

chagrin *n.* annoyance, discomfiture, discomposure, displeasure, disquiet, dissatisfaction, embarrassment, exasperation, fretfulness, humiliation, indignation, irritation, mortification, peevishness, spleen, vexation.

antonyms delight, pleasure.

v. annoy, displease, disquiet, dissatisfy, embarrass, exasperate, humiliate, irk, irritate, mortify, peeve, vex.

chain *n.* bond, catena, concatenation, coupling, fetter, fob, link, manacle, progression, restraint, sequence, series, set, shackle, string, succession, train, union, vinculum.

v. bind, confine, enslave, fasten, fetter, gyve, handcuff, manacle, restrain, secure, shackle, tether, trammel.

antonyms free, release.

chairman *n.* chair, chairperson, chairwoman, convenor, director, master of ceremonies, MC, president, presider, speaker, spokesman, toastmaster.

challenge *v.* accost, beard, brave, confront, dare, defy, demand, dispute, impugn, provoke, query, question, stimulate, summon, tax, test, throw down the gauntlet, try.

n. confrontation, dare, defiance, gauntlet, hurdle, interrogation, obstacle, poser, provocation, question, test, trial, ultimatum.

chamber *n.* apartment, assembly, bed-chamber, bedroom, boudoir, camera, cavity, closet, compartment, council, cubicle, enclosure, hall, legislature, parliament, room, vault.

chance *n.* accident, act of God, coincidence, contingency, destiny, fate, fortuity, fortune, gamble, happenstance, hazard, jeopardy, liability, likelihood, luck, misfortune, occasion, odds, opening, opportunity, peril, possibility, probability, prospect, providence, risk, speculation, time, uncertainty, venture.

antonyms certainty, law, necessity.

v. befall, gamble, happen, hazard, occur, risk, stake, transpire, try, venture, wager.

adj. accidental, casual, contingent, fortuitous, inadvertent, incidental, random, serendipitous, unforeseeable, unforeseen, unintended, unintentional, unlooked-for.

antonyms certain, deliberate, intentional.

change *v.* alter, alternate, barter, convert, denature, displace, diversify, exchange, fluctuate, interchange, metamorphose, moderate, modify, mutate, reform, remodel, remove, reorganize, replace, restyle, shift, substitute, swap, take liberties with, trade, transfigure, transform, transmit, transmute, transpose, vacillate, vary, veer.

n. alteration, break, chop, conversion, difference, diversion, exchange, innovation, interchange, metamorphosis, metanoia, modification, mutation, novelty, permutation, revolution, satisfaction, sea-change, shift, substitution, trade, transformation, transition, transmutation, transposition, upheaval, variation, variety, vicissitude.

changeable *adj.* capricious, chameleonic, changeful, erratic, fickle, fitful, fluid, inconstant, irregular, kaleidoscopic, labile, mercurial, mobile, mutable, protean, shifting, uncertain, unpredictable, unreliable, unsettled, unstable, unsteady, vacillating, variable, vicissitudinous, volatile, wavering, windy.
antonyms constant, reliable, unchangeable.

chaos *n.* anarchy, bedlam, confusion, disorder, disorganization, entropy, lawlessness, pandemonium, snafu, tohu bohu, tumult, unreason.
antonym order.

chaotic *adj.* anarchic, confused, deranged, disordered, disorganized, lawless, purposeless, rampageous, riotous, shambolic, snafu, topsy-turvy, tumultous, tumultuary, uncontrolled.
antonyms organized, purposive.

character[1] *n.* attributes, bent, caliber, cast, complexion, constitution, disposition, feature, honor, individuality, integrity, kidney, make-up, nature, peculiarity, personality, physiognomy, position, quality, rank, rectitude, reputation, stamp, status, strength, temper, temperament, type, uprightness.

character[2] *n.* card, customer, eccentric, fellow, guy, individual, joker, oddball, oddity, original, part, person, persona, portrayal, role, sort, type.

character[3] *n.* cipher, device, emblem, figure, hieroglyph, ideogram, ideograph, letter, logo, mark, rune, sign, symbol, type.

characteristic *adj.* discriminative, distinctive, distinguishing, idiosyncratic, individual, peculiar, representative, singular, special, specific, symbolic, symptomatic, typical, vintage.
antonyms uncharacteristic, untypical.
n. attribute, faculty, feature, hallmark, idiosyncrasy, lineament, mannerism, mark, peculiarity, property, quality, symptom, thing, trait.

charitable *adj.* accommodating, beneficent, benevolent, benign, benignant, bountiful, broad-minded, clement, compassionate, considerate, eleemosynary, favorable, forgiving, generous, gracious, humane, indulgent, kind, kindly, lavish, lenient, liberal, magnanimous, mild, philanthropic, sympathetic, tolerant, understanding.
antonyms uncharitable, unforgiving.

charity *n.* affection, agape, alms-giving, altruism, assistance, benefaction, beneficence, benevolence, benignity, benignness, bountifulness, bounty, clemency, compassion, endowment, fund, generosity, gift, goodness, hand-out, humanity, indulgence, love, philanthropy, relief, tender-heartedness.

charm *v.* allure, attract, becharm, beguile, bewitch, cajole, captivate, delight, enamor, enchant, enrapture, entrance, fascinate, mesmerize, please, win.
n. abraxas, allure, allurement, amulet, appeal, attraction, attractiveness, desirability, enchantment, fasci-

nation, fetish, grisgris, idol, ju-ju, magic, magnetism, medicine, obeah, obi, phylactery, porte-bonheur, sorcery, spell, talisman, trinket, weird.

charming *adj.* appealing, attractive, bewitching, captivating, delectable, delightful, engaging, eye-catching, fetching, honeyed, irresistible, lovely, pleasant, pleasing, seductive, sweet, winning, winsome.
antonyms ugly, unattractive.

chart *n.* abac, alignment chart, blueprint, diagram, graph, map, nomograph, plan, table, tabulation.
v. delineate, draft, draw, graph, map out, mark, outline, place, plot, shape, sketch.

charter *n.* accreditation, authorization, bond, concession, contract, deed, document, franchise, indenture, license, permit, prerogative, privilege, right.
v. authorize, commission, employ, engage, hire, lease, rent, sanction.

chase *v.* course, drive, expel, follow, hunt, hurry, pursue, rush, track.
n. coursing, hunt, hunting, pursuit, race, run, rush, venery.

chasm *n.* abysm, abyss, breach, canyon, cavity, cleft, crater, crevasse, fissure, gap, gorge, gulf, hiatus, hollow, opening, ravine, rent, rift, split, void.

chaste *adj.* austere, decent, decorous, elegant, immaculate, incorrupt, innocent, maidenly, modest, moral, neat, pure, refined, restrained, simple, unaffected, undefiled, unsullied, unvulgar, vestal, virginal, virginly, virtuous, wholesome.
antonyms indecorous, lewd.

chasten *v.* admonish, afflict, castigate, chastise, correct, cow, curb, discipline, humble, humiliate, repress, reprove, soften, subdue, tame.

chastise *v.* beat, berate, castigate, censure, correct, discipline, flog, flyte, lash, punish, reprove, scold, scourge, smack, spank, upbraid, whip.

chat *n.* chatter, chinwag, confab, coze, crack, gossip, heart-to-heart, natter, rap, talk, tête-à-tête, visit.
v. chatter, chew the fat, crack, gossip, jaw, natter, rabbit (on), talk, visit, yackety-yak.

chatter *n.* babble, blather, blether, chat, gab, gabfest, gossip, jabber, prate, prattle, prattlement, tattle, tongue-work, twaddle.
v. babble, blab, blather, blether, chat, clack, clatter, gab, gossip, jabber, prate, prattle, prittle-prattle, talk like a pen-gun, tattle, twaddle, yackety-yak.

cheap *adj.* à bon marché, bargain, base, budget, common, contemptible, cut-price, despicable, dirt-cheap, dog-cheap, economical, economy, inexpensive, inferior, jitney, keen, knock-down, low, low-cost, low-priced, mean, paltry, poor, reasonable, reduced, sale, scurvy, second-rate, shoddy, sordid, tatty, tawdry, uncostly, vulgar, worthless.
antonyms costly, excellent, noble, superior.

cheat *v.* baffle, bam, bamboozle, beguile, bilk, check, chisel, chouse, cog, con, cozen, deceive, defeat, defraud, deprive, diddle, do, double-cross, dupe, finagle, fleece, fob, foil, fool, frustrate, fudge, grift, gudgeon, gull, gyp, hand (someone) a lemon, hoax, hocus, hoodwink, mislead, prevent, queer, rip off, screw, short-change, skin, smouch, swindle, thwart, touch, trick, trim, victimize.
n. artifice, bilker, charlatan, cheater, chouse, cogger, con man, cozener, deceit, deceiver, deception, dodger, double-crosser, extortioner, fraud, grifter, impostor,

imposture, knave, picaroon, rip-off, rogue, shark, sharp, sharper, short-changer, snap, swindle, swindler, trickery, trickster, welsher.

check¹ v. compare, confirm, examine, give the once-over, inspect, investigate, monitor, note, probe, research, scrutinize, study, test, verify.
n. audit, examination, inspection, investigation, research, scrutiny, tab, test.

check² v. arrest, bar, blame, bridle, chide, control, curb, damp, delay, halt, hinder, impede, inhibit, limit, obstruct, pause, rebuke, repress, reprimand, reprove, restrain, retard, scold, stop, thwart.
n. blow, constraint, control, curb, damp, damper, disappointment, frustration, hindrance, impediment, inhibition, limitation, obstruction, rejection, restraint, reverse, setback, stoppage.

check³ n. bill, counterfoil, token.

cheek¹ n. audacity, brass, brass neck, brazenness, brazenry, disrespect, effrontery, face, gall, impertinence, impudence, insolence, nerve, sauce, temerity.

cheek² n. buttock, face, gena, jowl.

cheer v. acclaim, animate, applaud, brighten, clap, comfort, console, elate, elevate, encheer, encourage, enhearten, enliven, exhilarate, gladden, hail, hearten, hurrah, incite, inspirit, solace, uplift, warm.
antonyms boo, dishearten, jeer.
n. acclamation, animation, applause, bravo, buoyancy, cheerfulness, comfort, gaiety, gladness, glee, hoorah, hopefulness, hurrah, joy, liveliness, merriment, merry-making, mirth, optimism, ovation, plaudits, solace.

cheerful adj. animated, blithe, bobbish, bright, bucked, buoyant, canty, cheery, chipper, chirpy, chirrupy, contented, enlivening, enthusiastic, eupeptic, gay, gaysome, genial, glad, gladsome, happy, hearty, jaunty, jolly, jovial, joyful, joyous, light-hearted, lightsome, light-spirited, merry, optimistic, perky, pleasant, sparkling, sprightly, sunny, upbeat, winsome.
antonym sad.

cherish v. comfort, cosset, encourage, entertain, foster, harbor, make much of, nourish, nurse, nurture, prize, shelter, support, sustain, tender, treasure, value.

chest n. ark, box, case, casket, coffer, crate, kist, strongbox, trunk.

chew v. champ, crunch, gnaw, grind, manducate, masticate, munch.

chic adj. à la mode, chichi, elegant, fashionable, modish, smart, stylish, trendy.
antonyms out-moded, unfashionable.

chide v. admonish, berate, blame, censure, check, criticize, lecture, objurgate, rate, rebuke, reprehend, reprimand, reproach, reprove, scold, tell off, upbraid.
antonym praise.

chief adj. capital, cardinal, central, especial, essential, foremost, grand, highest, key, leading, main, outstanding, paramount, predominant, pre-eminent, premier, prevailing, primal, primary, prime, principal, superior, supreme, uppermost, vital.
antonyms junior, minor, unimportant.
n. boss, captain, chieftain, cock of the loft, commander, coryphaeus, director, duke, governor, head, kaid, kingpin, leader, lord, manager, master, paramount, paramount chief, principal, ringleader, ruler, superintendent, superior, supremo, suzerain.

chiefly adv. especially, essentially, for the most part,

generally, mainly, mostly, predominantly, primarily, principally, usually.

childish adj. boyish, foolish, frivolous, girlish, hypocoristic, hypocoristical, immature, infantile, juvenile, puerile, silly, simple, trifling, weak, young.
antonyms adult, sensible.

chill adj. aloof, biting, bleak, chilly, cold, cool, depressing, distant, freezing, frigid, hostile, parky, raw, sharp, stony, unfriendly, unresponsive, unwelcoming, wintry.
antonyms friendly, warm.
v. congeal, cool, dampen, depress, discourage, dishearten, dismay, freeze, frighten, refrigerate, terrify.
n. bite, cold, coldness, coolness, coolth, crispness, frigidity, nip, rawness, sharpness.

chilly adj. aloof, blowy, breezy, brisk, cold, cool, crisp, draughty, fresh, frigid, hostile, nippy, parky, penetrating, sharp, stony, unfriendly, unresponsive, unsympathetic, unwelcoming.
antonyms friendly, warm.

chirp v., n. cheep, chirrup, peep, pipe, tweet, twitter, warble, whistle.

chivalrous adj. bold, brave, chivalric, courageous, courteous, courtly, gallant, gentlemanly, Grandisonian, heroic, honorable, knightly, polite, true, valiant.
antonyms cowardly, ungallant.

chivalry n. boldness, bravery, courage, courtesy, courtliness, gallantry, gentlemanliness, knight-errantry, knighthood, politeness.

choice n. alternative, choosing, decision, dilemma, discrimination, election, espousal, opting, option, pick, preference, say, selection, variety.
adj. best, dainty, elect, élite, excellent, exclusive, exquisite, hand-picked, nice, plum, precious, prime, prize, rare, select, special, superior, uncommon, unusual, valuable.
antonym inferior.

choke v. asphyxiate, bar, block, clog, close, congest, constrict, dam, gag, obstruct, occlude, overpower, reach, retch, smother, stifle, stop, strangle, suffocate, suppress, throttle.

choose v. adopt, cull, designate, desire, elect, espouse, fix on, opt for, pick, plump for, predestine, prefer, see fit, select, settle on, single out, take, vote for, wish.

chop v. cleave, cut, divide, fell, hack, hew, lop, sever, shear, slash, slice, truncate.

chore n. burden, duty, errand, fag, job, stint, task, trouble.

chronic adj. appalling, atrocious, awful, confirmed, deep-rooted, deep-seated, dreadful, habitual, incessant, incurable, ineradicable, ingrained, inveterate, persistent, terrible.
antonym temporary.

chronicle n. account, annals, chanson de geste, diary, epic, gest(e), history, journal, narrative, record, register, saga, story.
v. enter, list, narrate, record, recount, register, relate, report, tell, write down.

chuckle v. chortle, crow, exult, giggle, laugh, snigger, snort, titter.

chummy adj. affectionate, close, friendly, intimate, matey, pally, sociable, thick.

chunk n. block, chuck, dod, dollop, hunk, lump, mass, piece, portion, slab, wad, wodge.

chunky adj. beefy, brawny, dumpy, fat, square, stocky, stubby, thick, thickset.

antonym slim.

cinema *n.* big screen, filmhouse, flicks, movies, picture-house, picture-palace.

circle *n.* area, assembly, band, bounds, circuit, circumference, class, clique, club, coil, company, compass, cordon, coterie, crowd, cycle, disc, domain, enclosure, fellowship, field, fraternity, globe, group, gyre, lap, loop, orb, orbit, perimeter, periphery, province, range, realm, region, revolution, ring, round, roundance, roundel, roundlet, rundle, scene, school, set, society, sphere, turn.

v. belt, circumambulate, circumnavigate, circumscribe, coil, compass, curl, curve, encircle, enclose, encompass, envelop, gird, girdle, hem in, loop, pivot, revolve, ring, rotate, surround, tour, whirl.

circuit *n.* ambit, area, boundary, bounds, circumference, compass, course, district, eyre, journey, limit, orbit, perambulation, range, region, revolution, round, route, tour, track, tract.

circuitous *adj.* ambagious, anfractuous, cagey, devious, indirect, labyrinthine, meandering, oblique, periphrastic, rambling, roundabout, tortuous, winding.

antonyms direct, straight.

circular *adj.* annular, discoid(al), disc-shaped, hoop-shaped, ring-shaped, round.

n. advert, announcement, handbill, leaflet, letter, notice, pamphlet.

circumference *n.* border, boundary, bounds, circuit, edge, extremity, fringe, limits, margin, outline, perimeter, periphery, rim, verge.

circumspection *n.* canniness, care, caution, chariness, deliberation, discretion, guardedness, prudence, wariness.

circumstance *n.* accident, condition, contingency, detail, element, event, fact, factor, happening, happenstance, incident, item, occurrence, particular, position, respect, situation.

circumstances *n.* conditions, galère, lifestyle, means, position, resources, situation, state, state of affairs, station, status, times.

cite *v.* accite, adduce, advance, call, enumerate, evidence, extract, mention, name, quote, specify, subpoena, summon.

citizen *n.* burgess, burgher, city-dweller, denizen, dweller, freeman, inhabitant, oppidan, ratepayer, resident, subject, townsman, urbanite.

city *n.* conurbation, megalopolis, metropolis, municipality, town.

civil *adj.* accommodating, affable, civic, civilized, complaisant, courteous, courtly, domestic, home, interior, internal, internecine, lay, municipal, obliging, polished, polite, political, refined, secular, temporal, urbane, well-bred, well-mannered.

antonym uncivil.

civilization *n.* advancement, cultivation, culture, development, education, enlightenment, kultur, progress, refinement, sophistication, urbanity.

antonyms barbarity, primitiveness.

civilize *v.* ameliorate, cultivate, educate, enlighten, humanize, improve, meliorate, perfect, polish, refine, sophisticate, tame.

claim *v.* affirm, allege, arrogate, ask, assert, challenge, collect, demand, exact, hold, insist, maintain, need, profess, request, require, state, take, uphold.

n. affirmation, allegation, application, assertion, call,

demand, insistence, petition, pretension, privilege, protestation, request, requirement, right, title.

clamor *n.* agitation, babel, blare, brouhaha, commotion, complaint, din, exclamation, hubbub, hue, hullabaloo, katzenjammer, noise, outcry, racket, shout, shouting, uproar, vociferation.

antonym silence.

clan *n.* band, brotherhood, clique, confraternity, coterie, faction, family, fraternity, gens, group, house, phratry, race, sect, sept, set, society, sodality, tribe.

clandestine *adj.* backroom, behind-door, cloak-and-dagger, closet, concealed, covert, fraudulent, furtive, hidden, private, secret, sly, sneaky, stealthy, subreptitious, surreptitious, underground, underhand, under-the-counter.

antonym open.

clarify *v.* cleanse, define, elucidate, explain, gloss, illuminate, purify, refine, resolve, shed/throw light on, simplify.

antonym obscure.

clash *v.* bang, clang, clank, clatter, conflict, crash, disagree, feud, fight, grapple, jangle, jar, quarrel, rattle, war, wrangle.

n. brush, clank, clatter, collision, conflict, confrontation, disagreement, fight, jangle, jar, noise, showdown.

clasp *n.* agraffe, brooch, buckle, catch, clip, embrace, fastener, fastening, grasp, grip, hasp, hold, hook, hug, pin, snap, tach(e).

v. attach, clutch, concatenate, connect, embrace, enclasp, enfold, fasten, grapple, grasp, grip, hold, hug, press, seize, squeeze.

class[1] *n.* caliber, caste, category, classification, collection, denomination, department, description, division, genre, genus, grade, group, grouping, ilk, kidney, kind, kingdom, league, order, phylum, quality, rank, section, set, sort, species, sphere, status, style, taxon, type, value.

v. assort, brand, categorize, classify, codify, designate, grade, group, rank, rate.

class[2] *n.* course, lecture, seminar, teach-in, tutorial.

classic *adj.* abiding, ageless, archetypal, Augustan, best, characteristic, chaste, consummate, deathless, definitive, enduring, established, excellent, exemplary, finest, first-rate, ideal, immortal, lasting, master, masterly, model, paradigmatic, quintessential, refined, regular, restrained, standard, time-honored, traditional, typical, undying, usual.

antonym second-rate.

n. chef d'oeuvre, exemplar, masterpiece, masterwork, model, paradigm, pièce de résistance, prototype, standard.

classification *n.* analysis, arrangement, cataloging, categorization, codification, digestion, grading, pigeon-holing, sorting, taxis, taxonomy.

classify *v.* arrange, assort, catalog, categorize, codify, digest, dispose, distribute, file, grade, pigeon-hole, rank, sort, systematize, tabulate.

clause *n.* article, chapter, condition, demand, heading, item, paragraph, part, passage, point, provision, proviso, section, specification, stipulation, subsection.

claw *n.* griff(e), gripper, nail, nipper, pincer, pounce, talon, tentacle, unguis.

v. dig, graze, lacerate, mangle, maul, rip, scrabble, scrape, scratch, tear.

clean *adj.* antiseptic, chaste, clarified, complete, conclusive, decent, decisive, decontaminated, delicate, elegant, entire, exemplary, faultless, final, flawless, fresh, good, graceful, guiltless, honest, honorable, hygienic, immaculate, innocent, laundered, moral, natural, neat, perfect, pure, purified, respectable, sanitary, simple, spotless, sterile, sterilized, thorough, tidy, total, trim, unblemished, unadulterated, uncluttered, uncontaminated, undefiled, unimpaired, unpolluted, unsoiled, unspotted, unstained, unsullied, upright, virtuous, washed, whole.
antonyms dirty, indecent, polluted, unsterile.
v. bath, cleanse, deodorize, deterge, disinfect, dust, launder, lave, mop, purge, purify, rinse, sanitize, scour, scrub, sponge, swab, sweep, vacuum, wash.
antonyms defile, dirty.

clean up sanitize, tidy, wash.

cleanse *v.* absolve, absterge, catharize, clean, clear, deterge, detoxicate, detoxify, lustrate, purge, purify, rinse, scavenge, scour, scrub, wash.
antonyms defile, dirty.

clear *adj.* apparent, audible, bright, certain, clean, cloudless, coherent, comprehensible, conspicuous, convinced, crystalline, decided, definite, diaphanous, disengaged, distinct, eidetic, empty, evident, explicit, express, fair, fine, free, glassy, guiltless, halcyon, hyaline, immaculate, incontrovertible, innocent, intelligible, light, limpid, lucid, luculent, luminous, manifest, obvious, open, palpable, patent, pellucid, perceptible, perspicuous, plain, positive, pronounced, pure, recognizable, resolved, satisfied, see-through, serene, sharp, shining, smooth, stainless, sunny, sure, translucent, transparent, unambiguous, unblemished, unclouded, undefiled, undimmed, undulled, unequivocal, unhampered, unhindered, unimpeded, unlimited, unmistakable, unobstructed, unquestionable, untarnished, untroubled, well-defined.
antonyms cloudy, fuzzy, guilty, vague.
v. absolve, acquire, acquit, brighten, clarify, clean, cleanse, decode, decongest, deoppilate, disengage, disentangle, earn, emancipate, erase, excuse, exonerate, extricate, fix, free, gain, jump, justify, leap, liberate, lighten, loosen, make, miss, open, pass over, purify, reap, refine, rid, secure, strip, tidy, unblock, unclog, uncloud, unload, unpack, unscramble, vault, vindicate, wipe.
antonyms block, condemn, defile, dirty.

clearly *adv.* distinctly, evidently, incontestably, incontrovertibly, manifestly, markedly, obviously, openly, plainly, undeniably, undoubtedly.
antonyms indistinctly, vaguely.

clemency *n.* compassion, forbearance, forgiveness, generosity, humanity, indulgence, kindness, lenience, leniency, lenity, magnanimity, mercifulness, mercy, mildness, moderation, soft-heartedness, tenderness.
antonyms harshness, ruthlessness.

clerical *adj.* ecclesiastical, pastoral, priestly, sacerdotal.

clerk *n.* account-keeper, assistant, copyist, official, pen-driver, pen-pusher, protocolist, quill-driver, quillman, receptionist, shop-assistant, writer.

clever *adj.* able, adroit, apt, astute, brainy, bright, canny, capable, cunning, deep, dexterous, discerning, elegant, expert, gifted, gleg, good-natured, habile, ingenious, intelligent, inventive, keen, knowing, knowledgeable, quick, quick-witted, rational, resourceful, sagacious, sensible, shrewd, skilful, smart, talented, witty.
antonyms foolish, naïve, senseless.

clever dick smart alec, smart-ass, smartypants, wiseling, witling, wit-monger.

cleverness *n.* ability, adroitness, astuteness, brains, brightness, canniness, cunning, dexterity, flair, gift, gumption, ingenuity, intelligence, nous, quickness, resourcefulness, sagacity, sense, sharpness, shrewdness, smartness, talent, wit.
antonyms foolishness, naïvety, senselessness.

client *n.* applicant, buyer, consumer, customer, dependant, habitué, patient, patron, protégé, shopper.

cliff *n.* bluff, crag, escarpment, face, overhang, precipice, rock-face, scar, scarp.

climate *n.* ambience, atmosphere, clime, country, disposition, feeling, milieu, mood, region, setting, temper, temperature, tendency, trend, weather.

climax *n.* acme, apogee, culmination, head, height, high point, highlight, orgasm, peak, summit, top, zenith.
antonyms bathos, low point, nadir.

climb *v.* ascend, clamber, mount, rise, scale, shin up, soar, swarm (up), top.

clip^1 *v.* crop, curtail, cut, dock, pare, poll, pollard, prune, shear, shorten, snip, trim.

clip^2 *v.* box, clobber, clout, cuff, hit, knock, punch, skelp, slap, smack, sock, thump, wallop, whack.
n. blow, box, clout, cuff, hit, knock, punch, skelp, slap, smack, sock, thump, wallop, whack.

clip^3 *n.* gallop, lick, rate, speed.

clip^4 *v.* attach, fasten, fix, hold, pin, staple.

cloak *n.* blind, cape, coat, cover, front, mantle, mask, pretext, shield, wrap.
v. camouflage, conceal, cover, disguise, hide, mask, obscure, screen, veil.

clog *v.* ball, block, burden, congest, dam up, gaum, hamper, hinder, impede, jam, obstruct, occlude, shackle, stop up, stuff.
antonym unblock.
n. burden, dead-weight, drag, encumbrance, hindrance, impediment, obstruction.

cloistered *adj.* cloistral, confined, enclosed, hermitic, insulated, protected, reclusive, restricted, secluded, sequestered, sheltered, shielded, withdrawn.
antonyms open, urbane.

close^1 *v.* bar, block, cease, choke, clog, cloture, complete, conclude, confine, connect, cork, couple, culminate, discontinue, end, fill, finish, fuse, grapple, join, lock, mothball, obstruct, plug, seal, secure, shut, stop, terminate, unite, wind up.
n. cadence, cessation, completion, conclusion, culmination, denouement, end, ending, finale, finish, junction, pause, stop, termination, wind-up.

close^2 *adj.* accurate, adjacent, adjoining, airless, alert, approaching, approximative, assiduous, at hand, attached, attentive, careful, compact, concentrated, confidential, confined, congested, conscientious, cramped, cropped, crowded, dear, dense, detailed, devoted, dogged, earnest, exact, faithful, familiar, fixed, frowsty, fuggy, handy, hard by, heavy, hidden, humid, illiberal, imminent, impending, impenetrable, inseparable, intense, intent, intimate, jam-packed, keen, literal, loving, mean, mingy, minute, miserly, muggy, narrow, near, near-by, neighboring, niggardly, nigh, oppressive, packed, painstaking, parsimonious, penurious, precise, private, reserved, reticent, retired, rigorous, searching, secluded, secret, secretive, short, solid, stale, stifling, stingy, strict, stuffy, suffocating, sweltering, taciturn, thick, thorough, tight, tight-fisted, uncommunicative, unforthcoming, ungenerous, unventilated.

antonyms careless, cool, far, unfriendly.

cloth *n.* dish-cloth, duster, fabric, face-cloth, material, rag, stuff, textiles, tissue, towel.

clothe *v.* accouter, apparel, array, attire, bedizen, caparison, cover, deck, drape, dress, enclothe, endow, enwarp, equip, garb, habilitate, habit, invest, outfit, rig, robe, swathe, vest.

antonyms unclothe, undress.

clothes *n.* apparel, attire, clobber, clothing, costume, dress, duds, ensemble, garb, garments, garmenture, gear, get-up, habiliments, habit(s), outfit, raiment, rig-out, threads, toggery, togs, vestiture, vestments, vesture, wardrobe, wear, weeds.

cloud *n.* billow, crowd, darkness, flock, fog, gloom, haze, horde, host, mist, multitude, murk, nebula, nebulosity, obscurity, shower, swarm, throng, vapor, water-dog, weft, woolpack.

v. becloud, confuse, darken, defame, dim, disorient, distort, dull, eclipse, impair, muddle, obfuscate, obscure, overcast, overshadow, shade, shadow, stain, veil.

antonym clear.

cloudy *adj.* blurred, blurry, confused, dark, dim, dismal, dull, emulsified, hazy, indistinct, leaden, lightless, lowering, muddy, murky, nebulous, nubilous, obscure, opaque, overcast, somber, sullen, sunless.

antonyms clear, sunny.

club¹ *n.* bat, bludgeon, cosh, cudgel, mace, mere, stick, truncheon, waddy.

v. bash, baste, batter, beat, bludgeon, clobber, clout, cosh, hammer, hit, pummel, strike.

club² *n.* association, bunch, circle, clique, combination, company, fraternity, group, guild, lodge, order, set, society, sodality, union.

clue *n.* clavis, evidence, hint, idea, indication, inkling, intimation, lead, notion, pointer, sign, suggestion, suspicion, tip, tip-off, trace.

clumsy *adj.* awkward, blundering, bumbling, bungling, cack-handed, chuckle, clumping, crude, gauche, gawky, ham-fisted, ham-handed, heavy, hulking, ill-made, inept, inexpert, lubber, lubberly, lumbering, maladroit, ponderous, rough, shapeless, squab, unco-ordinated, uncouth, ungainly, ungraceful, unhandy, unskilful, unwieldy.

antonym graceful.

cluster *n.* assemblage, batch, bunch, clump, collection, gathering, glomeration, group, knot, mass.

v. assemble, bunch, collect, flock, gather, group.

clutch *v.* catch, clasp, embrace, fasten, grab, grapple, grasp, grip, hang on to, seize, snatch.

coalition *n.* affiliation, alliance, amalgam, amalgamation, association, bloc, coadunation, combination, compact, confederacy, confederation, conjunction, federation, fusion, integration, league, merger, union.

coarse *adj.* bawdy, blowzy, boorish, brutish, coarse-grained, crude, earthly, foul-mouthed, homespun, immodest, impolite, improper, impure, indelicate, inelegant, loutish, mean, offensive, Rabelaisian, ribald, rough, rude, smutty, Sotadic, uncivil, unfinished, unpolished, unprocessed, unpurified, unrefined, vulgar.

antonyms fine, polite, refined, sophisticated.

coast *n.* coastline, littoral, seaboard, seaside, shore.

v. cruise, drift, free-wheel, glide, sail.

coax *v.* allure, beguile, cajole, decoy, entice, flatter, inveigle, persuade, soft-soap, sweet-talk, wheedle, whilly, whillywha(w), wile.

antonym force.

coddle *v.* baby, cocker, cosset, humor, indulge, mollycoddle, nurse, pamper, pet, spoil.

code *n.* canon, cipher, convention, cryptograph, custom, ethics, etiquette, manners, maxim, regulations, rules, system.

v. encipher, encode.

coerce *v.* bludgeon, browbeat, bulldoze, bully, compel, constrain, dragoon, drive, drum, force, intimidate, press-gang, pressurize.

antonyms coax, persuade.

coercion *n.* browbeating, bullying, compulsion, constraint, direct action, duress, force, intimidation, pressure, threats.

antonym persuasion.

cognizance *n.* acknowledgment, apprehension, cognition, knowledge, notice, perception, percipience, recognition, regard.

antonym unawareness.

cognizant *adj.* acquainted, aware, conscious, conversant, familiar, informed, knowledgeable, versed, witting.

antonym unaware.

coherent *adj.* articulate, comprehensible, consistent, intelligible, logical, lucid, meaningful, orderly, organized, rational, reasoned, sensible, systematic.

coincide *v.* accord, agree, co-exist, concur, correspond, harmonize, match, square, tally.

coincidence *n.* accident, chance, concomitance, concurrence, conjunction, correlation, correspondence, eventuality, fluke, fortuity, luck, synchronism.

coincidental *adj.* accident, casual, chance, coincident, concomitant, concurrent, fluky, fortuitous, lucky, simultaneous, synchronous, unintentional, unplanned.

antonyms deliberate, planned.

cold *adj.* agued, algid, aloof, apathetic, arctic, benumbed, biting, bitter, bleak, brumal, chill, chilled, chilly, cold-blooded, cool, dead, distant, freezing, frigid, frosty, frozen, gelid, glacial, icy, inclement, indifferent, inhospitable, lukewarm, numbed, parky, passionless, phlegmatic, raw, reserved, shivery, spiritless, stand-offish, stony, undemonstrative, unfeeling, unfriendly, unheated, unmoved, unresponsive, unsympathetic, wintry.

antonyms friendly, warm.

n. catarrh, chill, chilliness, coldness, frigidity, frostiness, hypothermia, iciness, inclemency.

antonyms friendliness, warmth.

cold fish iceberg.

collapse *v.* crumple, fail, faint, fall, fold, founder, peg out, sink, subside.

n. breakdown, cave-in, crash, debacle (débâcle), detumescence, disintegration, downfall, exhaustion, failure, faint, flop, subsidence.

colleague *n.* aide, aider, ally, assistant, associate, auxiliary, bedfellow, coadjutor, collaborator, companion, comrade, confederate, confrère, helper, partner, teammate, workmate.

collect v. accumulate, acquire, aggregate, amass, assemble, cluster, congregate, convene, converge, forgather, gather, gather together, heap, hoard, muster, obtain, raise, rally, save, secure, stockpile, uplift.

collected adj. assembled, calm, composed, confident, cool, efficient, gathered, imperturbable, placid, poised, self-possessed, serene, together, unperturbed, unruffled.

antonyms disorganized, dithery, worried.

collection n. accumulation, anthology, assemblage, assembly, assortment, caboodle, cluster, company, compilation, congeries, conglomerate, conglomeration, congregation, convocation, crowd, festschrift, gathering, group, harvesting, heap, hoard, ingathering, inning, jingbang, job-lot, mass, pile, set, spicilege, stockpile, store, whip-round.

collective adj. aggregate, combined, common, composite, concerted, congregated, co-operative, corporate, cumulative, joint, shared, unified, united.

n. aggregate, assemblage, corporation, gathering, group.

collision n. accident, bump, clash, clashing, conflict, confrontation, crash, encounter, impact, opposition, pile-up, prang, rencounter, skirmish, smash.

collusion n. artifice, cahoots, coactivity, complicity, connivance, conspiracy, craft, deceit, fraudulent, intrigue.

color[1] n. animation, appearance, bloom, blush, brilliance, chroma, colorant, coloration, complexion, disguise, dye, façade, flush, glow, guise, hue, liveliness, paint, pigment, pigmentation, plausibility, pretense, pretext, race, reason, rosiness, ruddiness, semblance, shade, timbre, tincture, tinge, tint, variety, vividness, wash, water-color.

v. blush, burn, colorwash, disguise, distort, dye, embroider, encolor, exaggerate, falsify, flush, misrepresent, paint, pervert, prejudice, redden, slant, stain, strain, taint, tinge, tint.

color[2] n. colors, ensign, flag, standard.

color-blind adj. dichromatic.

colorful adj. bright, brilliant, distinctive, graphic, intense, interesting, jazzy, kaleidoscopic, lively, motley, multicolored, parti-colored, picturesque, psychedelic, rich, stimulating, unusual, variegated, vibrant, vivid.

antonyms colorless, drab, plain.

coma n. catalepsy, drowsiness, hypnosis, insensibility, lethargy, oblivion, somnolence, sopor, stupor, torpor, trance, unconsciousness.

combat n. action, battle, bout, clash, conflict, contest, duel, encounter, engagement, fight, hostilities, j(i)ujitsu, judo, karate, kendo, kung fu, skirmish, struggle, war, warfare.

v. battle, contend, contest, defy, engage, fight, oppose, resist, strive, struggle, withstand.

combination n. alliance, amalgam, amalgamation, association, blend, cabal, cartel, coalescence, coalition, combine, composite, composition, compound, confederacy, confederation, conjunction, connection, consortium, conspiracy, federation, meld, merger, mix, mixture, syndicate, unification, union.

combine v. amalgamate, associate, bind, blend, bond, coadunate, compound, conjoin, connect, cooperate, fuse, incorporate, integrate, join, link, marry, meld, merge, mix, peace, pool, sythesize, unify, unite.

antonym separate.

come v. advance, appear, approach, arrive, attain, become, draw near, ejaculate, enter, happen, materialize, move, near, occur, originate, reach.

antonyms depart, go, leave.

comedian n. card, clown, comic, droll, funny man, gagster, humorist, jester, joker, jokesmith, laugh, wag, wit.

comely adj. attractive, beautiful, becoming, blooming, bonny, buxom, callipygian, callipygous, decent, decorous, fair, fit, fitting, gainly, good-looking, graceful, handsome, lovely, pleasing, pretty, proper, pulchritudinous, seemly, suitable, wholesome, winsome.

come-uppance n. chastening, deserts, dues, merit, punishment, rebuke, recompense, requital, retribution.

comfort v. alleviate, assuage, cheer, console, ease, encheer, encourage, enliven, gladden, hearten, inspirit, invigorate, reassure, refresh, relieve, solace, soothe, strengthen.

n. aid, alleviation, cheer, compensation, consolation, cosiness, ease, easy street, encouragement, enjoyment, help, luxury, opulence, relief, satisfaction, snugness, succor, support, well-being.

antonyms distress, torment.

comfortable adj. adequate, affluent, agreeable, ample, canny, commodious, contented, convenient, cosy, delightful, easy, enjoyable, gemütlich, gratified, happy, homely, loose, loose-fitting, pleasant, prosperous, relaxed, relaxing, restful, roomy, serene, snug, well-off, well-to-do.

antonyms poor, uncomfortable.

comical adj. absurd, amusing, comic, diverting, droll, entertaining, farcical, funny, hilarious, humorous, laughable, ludicrous, priceless, ridiculous, risible, side-splitting, silly, whimsical.

antonyms sad, unamusing.

command v. bid, charge, compel, control, demand, direct, dominate, enjoin, govern, head, lead, manage, order, reign over, require, rule, supervise, sway.

n. authority, behest, bidding, charge, commandment, control, decree, dictation, diktat, direction, directive, domination, dominion, edict, fiat, government, grasp, injunction, instruction, management, mandate, mastery, order, power, precept, requirement, rule, supervision, sway, ukase, ultimatum.

commandeer v. appropriate, confiscate, expropriate, hijack, requisition, seize, sequester, sequestrate, usurp.

commanding adj. advantageous, assertive, authoritative, autocratic, compelling, controlling, decisive, dominant, dominating, forceful, imposing, impressive, peremptory, superior.

commando n. fedayee, Green Beret, soldier.

commence v. begin, embark on, inaugurate, initiate, open, originate, start.

antonyms cease, finish.

commend v. acclaim, applaud, approve, commit, compliment, confide, consign, deliver, entrust, eulogize, extol, praise, recommend, yield.

antonym criticize.

commendable adj. admirable, creditable, deserving, estimable, excellent, exemplary, laudable, meritorious, noble, praiseworthy, worthy.

antonyms blameworthy, poor.

commendation n. acclaim, acclamation, accolade, applause, approbation, approval, credit, encomium, encouragement, panegyric, praise, recommendation.

antonyms blame, criticism.

commensurate *adj.* acceptable, adequate, appropriate, co-extensive, comparable, compatible, consistent, corresponding, due, equivalent, fitting, just, meet, proportionate, sufficient.
antonym inappropriate.

comment *v.* animadvert, annotate, criticize, descant, elucidate, explain, gloss, interpose, interpret, mention, note, observe, opine, remark, say.
n. animadversion, annotation, commentary, criticism, elucidation, explanation, exposition, footnote, illustration, marginal note, marginalia, note, observation, remark, statement.

commerce *n.* business, communication, dealing(s), exchange, intercourse, merchandising, relations, trade, traffic.

commission *n.* allowance, appointment, authority, board, brokerage, brok(er)age, charge, committee, compensation, cut, delegation, deputation, duty, employment, errand, fee, function, mandate, mission, percentage, rake-off, representative, task, trust, warrant.
v. appoint, ask for, authorize, contract, delegate, depute, empower, engage, nominate, order, request, select, send.

commit *v.* align, bind, commend, compromise, confide, confine, consign, deliver, deposit, do, enact, endanger, engage, entrust, execute, give, imprison, involve, obligate, perform, perpetrate, pledge.

commitment *n.* adherence, assurance, dedication, devotion, duty, engagement, guarantee, involvement, liability, loyalty, obligation, pledge, promise, responsibility, tie, undertaking, vow, word.

committee *n.* advisory group, board, cabinet, commission, council, jury, panel, table, task force, think-tank, working party.

commodious *adj.* ample, capacious, comfortable, expansive, extensive, large, loose, roomy, spacious.
antonym cramped.

commodities *n.* goods, merchandise, output, produce, products, stock, things, wares.

common *adj.* accepted, average, coarse, collective, commonplace, communal, conventional, customary, daily, everyday, familiar, flat, frequent, general, habitual, hackneyed, humdrum, inferior, low, mutual, obscure, ordinary, pedestrian, plain, plebby, plebeian, popular, prevailing, prevalent, public, regular, routine, run-of-the-mill, simple, social, stale, standard, stock, trite, tritical, undistinguished, unexceptional, universal, usual, vulgar, widespread, workaday.
antonyms noteworthy, uncommon.

commonplace *adj.* common, customary, everyday, humdrum, obvious, ordinary, pedestrian, quotidian, stale, threadbare, trite, uninteresting, widespread, worn out.
antonyms exceptional, rare.
n. banality, cliché, platitude, truism.

common-sense *adj.* astute, common-sensical, down-to-earth, hard-headed, judicious, level-headed, matter-of-fact, practical, pragmatical, realistic, reasonable, sane, sensible, shrewd, sound.
antonym foolish.

commotion *n.* ado, agitation, ballyhoo, bobbery, brouhaha, burst-up, bustle, bust-up, carfuffle, disorder, disturbance, excitement, ferment, fracas, furore, fuss, hubbub, hullabaloo, hurly-burly, perturbation, pother, pudder, racket, riot, rumpus, to-do, toss, tumult, turmoil, uproar.

communicable *adj.* catching, contagious, conveyable, impartible, infectious, infective, spreadable, transferable, transmittable.

communicate *v.* acquaint, announce, bestow, connect, contact, convey, correspond, declare, diffuse, disclose, disseminate, divulge, impart, inform, intimate, notify, proclaim, promulgate, publish, report, reveal, signify, spread, transmit, unfold.

communication *n.* announcement, bulletin, communiqué, connection, contact, conversation, converse, correspondence, disclosure, dispatch, dissemination, information, intelligence, intercourse, intimation, message, news, promulgation, report, statement, transmission, word.

communicative *adj.* candid, chatty, conversable, conversational, expansive, extrovert, forthcoming, frank, free, friendly, informative, loquacious, open, outgoing, sociable, talkative, unreserved, voluble.
antonym reticent.

communion *n.* accord, affinity, agreement, closeness, communing, concord, converse, empathy, Eucharist, fellow-feeling, fellowship, harmony, Holy Communion, housel, intercourse, Lord's Supper, Mass, participation, rapport, Sacrament, sympathy, togetherness, unity.

community *n.* affinity, agreement, association, body politic, brotherhood, coincidence, colony, commonness, commonwealth, company, concurrence, confraternity, confrèrie, correspondence, district, fellowship, fraternity, identity, kibbutz, kindredness, likeness, locality, nest, people, populace, population, public, residents, sameness, similarity, society, state.

compact[1] *adj.* brief, close, compendious, compressed, concise, condensed, dense, firm, impenetrable, solid, stocky, succinct, thick, well-knit.
antonyms diffuse, rambling, rangy.
v. compress, condense, consolidate, cram, flatten, ram, squeeze, tamp.

compact[2] *n.* agreement, alliance, arrangement, bargain, bond, concordat, contract, covenant, deal, entente, pact, settlement, treaty, understanding.

companion *n.* accomplice, aide, ally, assistant, associate, attendant, attender, buddy, chaperon, cohort, colleague, compeer, complement, comrade, confederate, confidant, confidante, consort, counterpart, crony, duenna, escort, fellow, follower, friend, intimate, mate, partner, satellite, shadow, squire, twin.

companionship *n.* camaraderie, companionhood, company, comradeship, confraternity, consociation, conviviality, esprit de corps, fellowship, fraternity, friendship, rapport, support, sympathy, togetherness.

company[1] *n.* assemblage, assembly, association, band, body, business, cartel, circle, collection, community, concern, concourse, consociation, consortium, convention, corporation, coterie, crew, crowd, ensemble, establishment, firm, fraternity, gathering, group, house, league, line, partnership, party, set, set-out, syndicate, throng, troop, troupe.

company[2] *n.* attendance, callers, companionhood, companionship, fellowship, guests, party, presence, society, support, visitors.

comparable *adj.* akin, alike, analogous, cognate, commensurate, correspondent, corresponding, equal, equivalent, kindred, parallel, proportionate, related, similar, tantamount.

antonym unlike.

compare *v.* balance, collate, confront, contrast, correlate, emulate, equal, equate, juxtapose, liken, match, parallel, resemble, similize, vie, weigh.

comparison *n.* analogy, collation, comparability, contrast, correlation, distinction, juxtaposition, likeness, parallel, parallelism, resemblance, similarity, similitude.

compartment *n.* alcove, area, bay, berth, booth, box, carrel, carriage, category, cell, chamber, cubby-hole, cubicle, department, division, locker, niche, pigeonhole, section, stall, subdivision.

compassion *n.* charity, clemency, commiseration, concern, condolence, fellow-feeling, heart, humanity, kindness, loving-kindness, mercy, pity, ruth, sorrow, sympathy, tenderness, understanding, weltschmerz, yearning.

antonym indifference.

compassionate *adj.* benevolent, caring, charitable, clement, humane, humanitarian, indulgent, kind-hearted, kindly, lenient, merciful, piteous, pitying, supportive, sympathetic, tender, tender-hearted, understanding, warm-hearted.

antonym indifferent.

compatibility *n.* accord, affinity, agreement, amity, concord, congeniality, consistency, consonance, correspondence, empathy, fellowship, harmony, like-mindedness, rapport, reconcilability, sympathy, understanding, unity.

antonyms antagonism, antipathy, incompatibility.

compatible *adj.* accordant, adaptable, agreeable, conformable, congenial, congruent, congruous, consistent, consonant, harmonious, kindred, like-minded, reconcilable, suitable, sympathetic.

antonyms antagonistic, antipathetic, incompatible.

compel *v.* browbeat, bulldoze, bully, coact, coerce, constrain, dragoon, drive, enforce, exact, force, hustle, impel, make, necessitate, obligate, oblige, press-gang, pressurize, strongarm, urge.

compensate *v.* atone, balance, cancel, counteract, counterbalance, countervail, expiate, guerdon, indemnify, offset, recompense, recover, recuperate, redeem, redress, refund, reimburse, remunerate, repay, requite, restore, reward, satisfy.

compensation *n.* amends, atonement, comfort, consolation, damages, guerdon, indemnification, indemnity, payment, quittance, recompense, redress, refund, reimbursement, remuneration, reparation, repayment, requital, restitution, restoration, return, reward, satisfaction, solatium.

compete *v.* battle, challenge, contend, contest, duel, emulate, fight, oppose, rival, strive, struggle, tussle, vie.

competence *n.* ability, adequacy, appropriateness, aptitude, capability, capacity, competency, experience, expertise, facility, fitness, proficiency, skill, suitability, technique.

antonym incompetence.

competent *adj.* able, adapted, adequate, appropriate, belonging, capable, clever, efficient, endowed, equal, fit, legitimate, masterly, pertinent, proficient, qualified, satisfactory, strong, sufficient, suitable, trained, well-qualified.

antonym incompetent.

competition *n.* challenge, challengers, championship, combativeness, competitiveness, competitors, contention, contest, corrivalry, cup, emulation, event, field, match, opposition, quiz, race, rivalry, rivals, series, strife, struggle, tournament, tourney, trial.

competitor *n.* adversary, agonist, antagonist, challenger, competition, contender, contestant, corrival, emulator, entrant, opponent, opposition, rival.

complain *v.* beef, belly-ache, bemoan, bewail, bind, bitch, bleat, carp, deplore, fuss, girn, grieve, gripe, groan, grouse, growl, grumble, kvetch, lament, moan, squeal, whine, whinge.

complaint¹ *n.* accusation, annoyance, beef, belly-ache, bitch, bleat, censure, charge, criticism, dissatisfaction, fault-finding, girn, gravamen, grievance, gripe, grouse, grumble, lament, moan, nit-picking, plaint, querimony, remonstrance, squawk, stricture, wail, whinge, winge.

complaint² *n.* affliction, ailment, disease, disorder, illness, indisposition, malady, malaise, sickness, trouble, upset.

complement *n.* aggregate, capacity, companion, completion, consummation, counterpart, entirety, fellow, quota, sum, supplement, total, totality, wholeness.

complete *adj.* absolute, accomplished, achieved, all, concluded, consummate, ended, entire, equipped, faultless, finished, full, intact, integral, integrate, out-and-out, perfect, plenary, root-and-branch, self-contained, thorough, thoroughgoing, thorough-paced, total, unabbreviated, unabridged, unbroken, uncut, undivided, unedited, unexpurgated, unimpaired, utter, whole, whole-hog.

antonyms imperfect, incomplete.

v. accomplish, achieve, cap, clinch, close, conclude, consummate, crown, discharge, do, effect, end, execute, finalize, finish, fulfil, perfect, perform, realize, settle, terminate, wind up.

completion *n.* accomplishment, achievement, attainment, close, conclusion, consummation, crowning, culmination, discharge, end, expiration, finalization, finish, fruition, fulfilment, perfection, plenitude, realization, settlement, telos, termination.

complex *adj.* ambagious, Byzantine, circuitous, complicated, composite, compound, compounded, convoluted, Daedalian, devious, diverse, elaborate, heterogeneous, intricate, involved, knotty, labyrinthine, manifold, mingled, mixed, multifarious, multipartite, multiple, plexiform, polymerous, ramified, tangled, tortuous.

antonym simple.

n. aggregate, composite, establishment, fixation, hang-up, idée fixe, institute, network, obsession, organization, phobia, preoccupation, scheme, structure, syndrome, synthesis, system.

complexion *n.* appearance, aspect, cast, character, color, coloring, composition, countenance, disposition, guise, hue, kind, light, look, make-up, nature, pigmentation, rud, skin, stamp, temperament, type.

compliant *adj.* accommodating, acquiescent, agreeable, amenable, biddable, complaisant, conformable, deferential, docile, obedient, obliging, passive, submissive, tractable, yielding.

antonyms disobedient, intractable.

complicated *adj.* ambivalent, baroque, Byzantine, com-

plex, convoluted, devious, difficult, elaborate, entangled, intricate, involved, labyrinthine, perplexing, problematic, puzzling, rigmarole, tangled, tortuous, troublesome.
antonyms easy, simple.

compliment *n.* accolade, admiration, bouquet, commendation, congratulations, courtesy, douceur, encomium, eulogy, favor, felicitation, flattery, honor, plaudit, praise, tribute.
antonyms criticism, insult.
v. admire, applaud, commend, congratulate, eulogize, extol, felicitate, flatter, laud, praise, salute.
antonyms condemn, insult.

complimentary *adj.* admiring, appreciative, approving, commendatory, congratulatory, courtesy, encomiastic, eulogistic, favorable, flattering, free, gratis, honorary, laudatory, panegyrical.
antonyms critical, insulting, unflattering.

comply *v.* accede, accommodate, accord, acquiesce, agree, assent, conform, consent, defer, discharge, fall in, follow, fulfil, obey, oblige, observe, perform, respect, satisfy, submit, yield.
antonyms disobey, resist.

component *n.* bit, constituent, element, factor, ingredient, item, part, piece, spare part, unit.

comport *v.* acquit, act, bear, behave, carry, conduct, demean, deport, perform.

compose *v.* adjust, arrange, build, calm, collect, compound, comprise, constitute, construct, contrive, control, create, devise, fashion, form, frame, govern, imagine, indite, invent, make, meditate the muse, pacify, produce, quell, quiet, recollect, reconcile, regulate, resolve, settle, soothe, still, structure, tranquilize, write.

composed *adj.* calm, collected, complacent, confident, cool, imperturbable, level-headed, placid, poised, relaxed, self-possessed, serene, together, tranquil, unflappable, unruffled, unworried.
antonym agitated.

composer *n.* arranger, author, bard, creator, maker, originator, poet, songsmith, songwriter, tunesmith, writer.

composition *n.* arrangement, balance, combination, compilation, compromise, concord, confection, configuration, congruity, consonance, constitution, creation, design, essay, exaration, exercise, form, formation, formulation, harmony, invention, lay-out, lucubration, make-up, making, mixture, opus, organization, piece, placing, production, proportion, structure, study, symmetry, work, writing.

composure *n.* aplomb, assurance, calm, calmness, confidence, cool, coolness, dignity, dispassion, ease, equanimity, impassivity, imperturbability, placidity, poise, sang-froid, savoir-faire, sedateness, self-assurance, self-possession, serenity, tranquility.
antonym discomposure.

compound *v.* aggravate, alloy, amalgamate, augment, blend, coalesce, combine, complicate, compose, concoct, exacerbate, fuse, heighten, increase, intensify, intermingle, magnify, mingle, mix, synthesize, unite, worsen.
n. alloy, amalgam, amalgamation, blend, combination, composite, composition, confection, conglomerate, conglomeration, fusion, medley, mixture, synthesis.

adj. complex, complicated, composite, conglomerate, intricate, mixed, multiple.

comprehend *v.* appreciate, apprehend, assimilate, compass, comprise, conceive, cover, discern, embrace, encompass, fathom, grasp, include, know, penetrate, perceive, see, see daylight, tumble to, twig, understand.
antonym misunderstand.

comprehension *n.* appreciation, apprehension, capacity, conception, discernment, grasp, intellection, intelligence, intension, judgment, knowledge, perception, realization, sense, understanding.
antonym incomprehension.

comprehensive *adj.* across-the-board, all-embracing, all-inclusive, blanket, broad, catholic, compendious, complete, encyclopedic, exhaustive, extensive, full, general, inclusive, omnibus, sweeping, thorough, wide.
antonyms incomplete, selective.

compress *v.* abbreviate, astrict, astringe, compact, concentrate, condense, constrict, contract, cram, crowd, crush, flatten, impact, jam, précis, press, shorten, squash, squeeze, stuff, summarize, synopsize, telescope, wedge.
antonyms diffuse, expand, separate.

comprise *v.* comprehend, consist of, contain, cover, embody, embrace, encompass, include, incorporate, involve, subsume.

compromise[1] *v.* adapt, adjust, agree, arbitrate, bargain, concede, make concessions, negotiate, retire, retreat, settle.
antonyms differ, quarrel.
n. accommodation, accord, adjustment, agreement, bargain, concession, co-operation, settlement, trade-off, via media.
antonyms disagreement, intransigence.

compulsion *n.* coercion, constraint, demand, distress, drive, duress, exigency, force, impulse, necessity, need, obligation, obsession, preoccupation, pressure, urge, urgency.
antonyms freedom, liberty.

compulsory *adj.* binding, de rigueur, forced, imperative, mandatory, obligatory, required, requisite, stipulated, stipulatory.
antonyms optional, voluntary.

compute *v.* assess, calculate, count, enumerate, estimate, evaluate, figure, measure, rate, reckon, sum, tally, total.

computer *n.* adding machine, analog computer, calculator, data processor, digital computer, mainframe, processor, word processor.

comrade *n.* Achates, ally, associate, brother, buddy, bully-rook, butty, china, cobber, colleague, companion, compatriot, compeer, confederate, co-worker, crony, fellow, frater, friend, mate, pal, partner, sidekick.

con *v.* bamboozle, beguile, bilk, bluff, bunko, cheat, cozen, deceive, defraud, double-cross, dupe, fiddle, grift, gull, hoax, hoodwink, humbug, inveigle, mislead, racket, rip off, rook, swindle, trick.
n. bluff, deception, fraud, grift, kidology, scam, swindle, trick.

conceal *v.* bury, camouflage, cloak, cover, disguise, dissemble, hide, keep dark, mask, obscure, screen, secrete, shelter, sink, smother, submerge, suppress, veil.

antonym reveal.

concede *v.* accept, acknowledge, admit, allow, cede, confess, forfeit, grant, own, recognize, relinquish, sacrifice, surrender, yield.

antonyms deny, dispute.

conceit[1] *n.* arrogance, assumption, cockiness, complacency, conceitedness, egotism, narcissism, pride, self-assumption, self-conceit, self-importance, self-love, self-pride, self-satisfaction, swagger, vainglory, vainness, vanity.

antonyms diffidence, modesty.

conceit[2] *n.* belief, caprice, concetto, fancy, fantasy, freak, humor, idea, image, imagination, impulse, jeu d'esprit, judgment, notion, opinion, quip, quirk, thought, vagary, whim, whimsy, wit.

conceited *adj.* arrogant, assuming, bigheaded, cocky, complacent, egotistical, highty-tighty, hoity-toity, immodest, narcissistic, overweening, self-important, self-satisfied, stuck-up, swell-headed, swollen-headed, toffee-nose(d), uppist, uppity, vain, vainglorious, windy.

antonyms diffident, modest.

conceive *v.* appreciate, apprehend, believe, comprehend, contrive, create, design, develop, devise, envisage, fancy, form, formulate, germinate, grasp, ideate, imagine, invent, originate, produce, project, purpose, realize, suppose, think, understand, visualize.

concentrate *v.* absorb, accumulate, attend, attract, center, cluster, collect, condense, congregate, converge, crowd, draw, engross, focus, foregather, gather, huddle, intensify.

antonyms disperse, distract, separate.

n. apozem, decoction, decocture, distillate, distillation, elixir, essence, extract, juice, quintessence.

concentrated *adj.* all-out, compact, condensed, deep, dense, evaporated, hard, intense, intensive, reduced, rich, thickened, undiluted.

antonyms desultory, diffuse, diluted.

concept *n.* abstraction, conception, conceptualization, construct, hyphothesis, idea, image, impression, invention, notion, pattern, picture, plan, theory, type, view, visualization.

conception *n.* appreciation, apprehension, beginning, birth, clue, comprehension, concept, design, envisagement, fertilization, formation, germination, idea, image, impregnation, impression, inauguration, inception, initiation, inkling, insemination, invention, knowledge, launching, notion, origin, outset, perception, picture, plan, understanding, visualization.

concern *v.* affect, bother, disquiet, distress, disturb, interest, involve, pertain to, perturb, refer to, regard, relate to, touch, trouble, upset, worry.

n. affair, anxiety, apprehension, attention, bearing, burden, business, care, charge, company, consideration, corporation, disquiet, disquietude, distress, enterprise, establishment, field, firm, heed, house, importance, interest, involvement, job, matter, mission, occupation, organization, perturbation, reference, relation, relevance, responsibility, solicitude, stake, task, transaction, unease, uneasiness, worry.

antonym unconcern.

concerning *prep.* about, anent, apropos of, as regards, germane to, in regard to, in the matter of, re, regarding, relating to, relevant to, respecting, touching, with reference to, with regard to.

concerted *adj.* collaborative, collective, combined, co-ordinated, joint, organized, planned, prearranged, shared, united.

antonyms disorganized, separate, unco-ordinated.

concession *n.* acknowledgment, adjustment, admission, allowance, assent, boon, compromise, exception, favor, grant, indulgence, permit, privilege, relaxation, sacrifice, surrender, yielding.

concise *adj.* abbreviated, abridged, aphoristic, brief, compact, compendious, compressed, condensed, epigrammatic, gnomic, laconic, pithy, short, succinct, summary, synoptic, terse, thumbnail.

antonyms diffuse, expansive.

conclude *v.* accomplish, assume, cease, clinch, close, complete, consummate, culminate, decide, deduce, determine, effect, end, establish, finish, fix, gather, infer, judge, opine, reckon, resolve, settle, suppose, surmise, terminate.

concluding *adj.* closing, epilogic, epilogistic, final, last, perorating, terminal, ultimate.

antonym introductory.

conclusion *n.* answer, assumption, clincher, close, come-off, completion, consequence, consummation, conviction, culmination, decision, deduction, end, explicit, finale, fine, finis, finish, illation, inference, issue, judgment, opinion, outcome, resolution, result, settlement, solution, termination, upshot, verdict.

conclusive *adj.* clear, clinching, convincing, decisive, definite, definitive, final, incontrovertible, irrefragable, irrefutable, manifest, ultimate, unanswerable, unappealable, unarguable, undeniable.

antonym inconclusive.

concord *n.* accord, agreement, amicability, amity, brotherliness, compact, concert, concordat, consensus, consonance, convention, diapason, entente, friendship, harmony, peace, protocol, rapport, treaty, unanimity, unison.

antonym discord.

concrete *adj.* actual, calcified, compact, compressed, conglomerated, consolidated, definite, explicit, factual, firm, material, perceptible, petrified, physical, real, seeable, sensible, solid, solidified, specific, substantial, tactile, tangible, touchable, visible.

antonym abstract.

concur *v.* accede, accord, acquiesce, agree, approve, assent, coincide, combine, comply, consent, co-operate, harmonize, join, meet, unite.

antonym disagree.

condemn *v.* ban, blame, castigate, censure, convict, damn, decry, denounce, disapprove, disparage, doom, pan, proscribe, reprehend, reproach, reprobate, reprove, revile, sentence, slam, slate, upbraid.

antonyms approve, praise.

condense *v.* abbreviate, abridge, capsulize, coagulate, compact, compress, concentrate, contract, crystallize, curtail, decoct, distil, encapsulate, epitomize, evaporate, inspissate, precipitate, précis, reduce, shorten, solidify, summarize, synopsize, thicken.

antonyms dilute, expand.

condition *n.* ailment, arrangement, article, case, caste, circumstances, class, complaint, defect, demand, diathesis, disease, disorder, estate, fettle, fitness, grade, health, infirmity, kilter, level, liability, limitation, malady, modification, nick, obligation, order, plight, position, predicament, prerequisite, problem, provision, proviso, qualification, rank, requirement, requisite, restriction, rule, shape, situation, state, status, stipulation, stratum, terms, trim, understanding, weakness.

v. accustom, adapt, adjust, attune, determine, educate, equip, groom, habituate, hone, indoctrinate, inure, limit, prepare, prime, ready, restrict, season, temper, train, tune.

conditional *adj.* contingent, dependent, limited, provisional, qualified, relative, restricted, tied.
antonym unconditional.

condolence *n.* commiseration, compassion, condolences, consolation, pity, support, sympathy.
antonym congratulation.

conduct *n.* actions, administration, attitude, bearing, behavior, carriage, comportment, control, co-ordination, demeanor, deportment, direction, discharge, escort, guidance, guide, leadership, management, manners, mien, orchestration, organization, running, supervision, ways.

v. accompany, acquit, act, administer, attend, bear, behave, carry, chair, comport, control, convey, demean, deport, direct, escort, govern, guide, handle, lead, manage, orchestrate, organize, pilot, regulate, run, solicit, steer, supervise, transact, usher.

confederate *adj.* allied, associated, combined, federal, federated.
n. abettor, accessory, accomplice, ally, assistant, associate, collaborator, colleague, conspirator, friend, leaguer, partner, practisant, supporter.
v. ally, amalgamate, associate, bind, combine, federate, join, merge, unite, weld.

confer *v.* accord, award, bestow, consult, converse, deliberate, discourse, discuss, give, grant, impart, lay heads together, lend, parley, powwow, present, talk, vouchsafe.

confess *v.* acknowledge, admit, affirm, agnize, allow, assert, attest, aver, betray, concede, confide, confirm, declare, disclose, divulge, evince, expose, grant, manifest, own, own up, profess, prove, recognize, reveal, show.
antonyms conceal, deny.

confession *n.* acknowledgment, admission, affirmation, assertion, attestation, averment, avowal, confidences, confiteor, declaration, disclosure, divulgence, exposé, exposure, profession, revelation, unbosoming, unburdening, verbal.
antonyms concealment, denial.

confidence *n.* aplomb, assurance, belief, boldness, calmness, communication, composure, confession, coolness, courage, credence, dependence, disclosure, divulgence, faith, firmness, nerve, reliance, savoir-faire, secret, self-assurance, self-confidence, self-possession, self-reliance, trust.
antonyms diffidence, distrust.

confident *adj.* assured, bold, certain, composed, convinced, cool, dauntless, fearless, persuaded, positive, sanguine, satisfied, secure, self-assured, self-confident, self-possessed, self-reliant, sure, unabashed, unbashful, unselfconscious.
antonyms diffident, sceptical.

confidential *adj.* classified, close, closed, faithful, familiar, hush-hush, in camera, intimate, private, privy, secret, tête-à-tête, trusted, trustworthy, trusty.
antonyms common, public.

confine *v.* bind, bound, cage, chamber, circumscribe, constrain, cramp, crib, emmew, enclose, immew, immure, imprison, incarcerate, inhibit, intern, keep, keep prisoner, limit, mew, repress, restrain, restrict, shackle, shut up, thirl, trammel.
antonym free.

confirm *v.* approve, assure, attest, authenticate, back, buttress, clinch, corroborate, endorse, establish, evidence, fix, fortify, homologate, prove, ratify, reinforce, sanction, settle, strengthen, substantiate, support, validate, verify, witness to.
antonym deny.

confirmation *n.* acceptance, agreement, approval, assent, attestation, authentication, backing, clincher, corroboration, endorsement, evidence, proof, ratification, sanction, substantiation, support, testimony, validation, verification, witness.
antonym denial.

confirmed *adj.* authenticated, chronic, committed, corroborated, deep-dyed, dyed-in-the-wool, entrenched, established, habitual, hardened, incorrigible, incurable, ingrained, inured, inveterate, irredeemable, long-established, long-standing, proved, proven, rooted, seasoned, substantiated, unredeemed.
antonyms uncommitted, unconfirmed.

conflict *n.* agony, ambivalence, antagonism, antipathy, Armageddon, battle, brawl, clash, collision, combat, confrontation, contention, contest, difference, disagreement, discord, dissension, encounter, engagement, feud, fight, fracas, friction, hostility, interference, opposition, quarrel, set-to, skirmish, strife, turmoil, unrest, variance, war, warfare.
antonyms agreement, concord.

v. battle, clash, collide, combat, contend, contest, contradict, differ, disagree, fight, interfere, oppose, strive, struggle, war, wrangle.
antonym agree.

conform *v.* accommodate, accord, adapt, adjust, agree, assimilate, comply, correspond, follow, harmonize, match, obey, quadrate, square, suit, tally, yield.
antonym differ.

conformity *n.* affinity, agreement, allegiance, Babbitry, compliance, congruity, consonance, conventionalism, conventionality, correspondence, Gleichschaltung, harmony, likeness, observance, orthodoxy, resemblance, similarity, traditionalism.
antonyms difference, nonconformity.

comfound *v.* abash, amaze, astonish, astound, baffle, bamboozle, bewilder, confuse, contradict, demolish, destroy, discombobulate, dismay, dumbfound, flabbergast, mystify, nonplus, overthrow, overwhelm, perplex, ruin, startle, stupefy, surprise, thwart, unshape, upset.

confront *v.* accost, address, appose, beard, brave, challenge, defy, encounter, face, front, oppose.
antonym evade.

confuse *v.* abash, addle, baffle, befuddle, bemuse, bewilder, buffalo, burble, confound, darken, demoralize, disarrange, discomfit, discompose, disconcert, discountenance, disorder, disorient, disorientate, embarrass, embrangle, flummox, fluster, intermingle, involve, jumble, maze, mingle, mistake, mix up, mortify, muddle, mystify, nonplus, obscure, perplex, puzzle, rattle, shame, tangle, tie in knots, upset.
antonyms clarify, enlighten, reassure.

confused *adj.* addle-brained, addle(d), addle-headed, addle-pated, baffled, bewildered, bushed, chaotic, dazed, désorienté, disarranged, discombobulated, disordered, disorderly, disorganized, disorientated, distracted, embarrassed, flummoxed, fuddled, higgledy-piggledy, jumbled, maffled, mistaken, misunderstood, muddled, muddle-headed, muzzy, nonplused, perplexed, puzzled, puzzle-headed, streaked, topsy-turvy, tosticated, untidy, upset.
antonym clear.

confusion *n.* abashment, Babel, befuddlement, bemusement, bewilderment, bustle, chagrin, chaos, clutter, combustion, commotion, demoralization, disarrangement, discomfiture, disorder, disorganization, disorientation, distraction, égarement, embarrassment, embroglio, embroilment, fluster, foul-up, hotchpotch, hubble-bubble, hugger-mugger, imbroglio, jumble, mess, mix-up, muddle, mystification, overthrow, palaver, perdition, perplexity, perturbation, pie, puzzlement, screw-up, shambles, shame, tangle, tizz(y), topsyturviness, topsyturvy, topsyturvydom, toss, turmoil, untidiness, upheaval, welter.
antonyms clarity, composure, order.

congratulate *v.* compliment, felicitate, gratulate.
antonym commiserate.

congregate *v.* accumulate, assemble, bunch, clump, cluster, collect, concentrate, conglomerate, convene, converge, convoke, crowd, flock, foregather, gather, mass, meet, muster, rally, rendezvous, throng.
antonyms dismiss, disperse.

congress *n.* assembly, conclave, conference, convention, convocation, council, diet, forum, legislature, meeting, parliament, synod.

congruity *n.* agreement, coincidence, compatibility, concinnity, concurrence, conformity, congruence, congruousness, consistency, correspondence, harmony, identity, match, parallelism.
antonym incongruity.

conjecture *v.* assume, estimate, extrapolate, fancy, guess, hypothesize, imagine, infer, opine, reckon, speculate, suppose, surmise, suspect, theorize.
n. assumption, conclusion, estimate, extrapolation, fancy, guess, guesstimate, guesswork, hypothesis, inference, notion, opinion, presumption, projection, speculation, supposition, surmise, theorizing, theory.

conjunction *n.* amalgamation, association, coincidence, combination, concurrence, juxtaposition, syzygy, unification, union, unition.

connect *v.* affix, ally, associate, cohere, combine, compaginate, concatenate, couple, enlink, fasten, join, link, relate, unite.
antonym disconnect.

connection *n.* acquaintance, affinity, alliance, ally, arthrosis, associate, association, attachment, bond, catenation, coherence, commerce, communication, compagination, conjunction, contact, context, correlation, correspondence, coupling, fastening, friend, hook-up, intercourse, interrelation, intimacy, junction, kin, kindred, kinsman, kith, link, marriage, reference, relation, relationship, relative, relevance, sponsor, tie, tie-in, union.
antonym disconnection.

conquer *v.* acquire, annex, beat, best, checkmate, crush, defeat, discomfit, get the better of, humble, master, obtain, occupy, overcome, overpower, overrun, overthrow, prevail, quell, rout, seize, subdue, subjugate, succeed, surmount, triumph, vanquish, win, worst.
antonyms surrender, yield.

conquest *n.* acquisition, annexation, appropriation, captivation, coup, defeat, discomfiture, enchantment, enthralment, enticement, invasion, inveiglement, mastery, occupation, overthrow, rout, seduction, subjection, subjugation, takeover, triumph, vanquishment, victory.

conscientious *adj.* careful, diligent, exact, faithful, hard-working, high-minded, high-principled, honest, honorable, incorruptible, just, meticulous, moral, painstaking, particular, punctilious, responsible, scrupulous, solicitous, straightforward, strict, thorough, upright.
antonyms careless, irresponsible.

conscious *adj.* alert, alive, awake, aware, calculated, cognizant, deliberate, heedful, intentional, knowing, mindful, percipient, premeditated, rational, reasoning, reflective, regardful, responsible, responsive, self-conscious, sensible, sentient, studied, wilful, witting.
antonym unconscious.

consecrate *v.* beatify, dedicate, devote, exalt, hallow, ordain, revere, sanctify, venerate.

consecutive *adj.* chronological, continuous, following, running, sequential, seriatim, succeeding, successive, unbroken, uninterrupted.
antonym discontinuous.

consent *v.* accede, acquiesce, admit, agree, allow, approve, assent, comply, concede, concur, grant, homologate, permit, yield.
antonyms oppose, refuse.
n. accordance, acquiescence, agreement, approval, assent, compliance, concession, concurrence, consentience, go-ahead, green light, permission, sanction.
antonyms opposition, refusal.

consequence *n.* account, concern, distinction, effect, eminence, end, event, fall-out, import, importance, interest, issue, moment, notability, note, outcome, portent, rank, repercussion, repute, result, side effect, significance, standing, status, upshot, value, weight.
antonym cause.

consequential *adj.* arrogant, bumptious, conceited, consequent, eventful, far-reaching, grave, important, impressive, indirect, inflated, momentous, noteworthy, pompous, pretentious, resultant, self-important, serious, significant, supercilious, vainglorious, weighty.
antonyms inconsequential, unimportant.

consequently *adv.* accordingly, consequentially, ergo, hence, inferentially, necessarily, subsequently, therefore, thus.

conservative *adj.* cautious, conventional, die-hard, establishmentarian, guarded, hidebound, middle-of-the-road, moderate, quiet, reactionary, right-wing, sober, Tory, traditional, unexaggerated, unprogressive, verkrampte.
antonyms left-wing, radical.
n. diehard, moderate, moss-back, reactionary, right-winger, stick-in-the-mud, Tory, traditionalist.
antonyms left-winger, radical.

conserve *v.* guard, hoard, husband, keep, maintain, nurse, preserve, protect, save.
antonyms squander, use, waste.

consider *v.* believe, bethink, cogitate, consult, contemplate, count, deem, deliberate, discuss, examine, judge, meditate, mull over, muse, perpend, ponder, rate,

reflect, regard, remember, respect, revolve, ruminate, study, think, weigh.
antonym ignore.

considerable *adj.* abundant, ample, appreciable, big, comfortable, distinguished, goodly, great, important, influential, large, marked, much, noteworthy, noticeable, plentiful, reasonable, renowned, significant, sizable, substantial, tidy, tolerable, venerable.
antonyms insignificant, slight.

considerate *adj.* attentive, charitable, circumspect, concerned, discreet, forbearing, gracious, kind, kindly, mindful, obliging, patient, solicitous, tactful, thoughtful, unselfish.
antonyms selfish, thoughtless.

consideration *n.* analysis, attention, cogitation, concern, considerateness, contemplation, deliberation, discussion, examination, factor, fee, friendliness, issue, kindliness, kindness, meditation, payment, perquisite, point, recompense, reflection, regard, remuneration, respect, review, reward, rumination, scrutiny, solicitude, study, tact, thought, thoughtfulness, tip.
antonyms disdain, disregard.

consistent *adj.* accordant, agreeing, coherent, compatible, congruous, consonant, constant, dependable, harmonious, logical, of a piece, persistent, regular, steady, unchanging, undeviating, unfailing, uniform.
antonyms erratic, inconsistent.

consolation *n.* aid, alleviation, assuagement, cheer, comfort, ease, easement, encouragement, help, relief, solace, succor, support.
antonym discouragement.

console *v.* assuage, calm, cheer, comfort, encourage, hearten, solace, soothe.
antonyms agitate, upset.

consolidate *v.* affiliate, amalgamate, cement, combine, compact, condense, confederate, conjoin, federate, fortify, fuse, harden, join, reinforce, secure, solidify, stabilize, strengthen, thicken, unify, unite.

consort *n.* associate, companion, fellow, helpmate, helpmeet, husband, partner, spouse, wife.
v. accord, agree, associate, correspond, fraternize, harmonize, jibe, mingle, mix, square, tally.

conspicuous *adj.* apparent, blatant, clear, discernible, evident, flagrant, flashy, garish, glaring, kenspeck(le), manifest, noticeable, obvious, patent, perceptible, remarked, showy, visible.
antonym inconspicuous.

conspiracy *n.* cabal, collusion, complot, confederacy, fix, frame-up, intrigue, league, machination, plot, scheme, treason.

conspire *v.* cabal, collude, combine, complot, concur, conduce, confederate, contribute, contrive, co-operate, devise, hatch, intrigue, machinate, maneuver, plot, scheme, tend, treason.

constancy *n.* determination, devotion, faithfulness, fidelity, firmness, fixedness, loyalty, permanence, perseverance, regularity, resolution, stability, steadfastness, steadiness, tenacity, uniformity.
antonyms inconstancy, irregularity.

constant *adj.* attached, ceaseless, changeless, continual, continuous, dependable, determined, devoted, dogged, endless, eternal, even, everlasting, faithful, firm, fixed, habitual, immutable, incessant, interminable, invariable, loyal, never-ending, non-stop, permanent, perpetual, persevering, persistent, regular, relentless,

resolute, stable, staunch, steadfast, steady, sustained, tried-and-true, true, trustworthy, trusty, unalterable, unbroken, unchangeable, unfailing, unflagging, uniform, uninterrupted, unrelenting, unremitting, unshaken, unvarying, unwavering.
antonyms fickle, fitful, irregular, occasional, variable.

constantly *adv.* always, continually, continuously, endlessly, everlastingly, incessantly, interminably, invariably, non-stop, perpetually, relentlessly, steadfastly, uniformly.
antonym occasionally.

consternation *n.* alarm, amazement, anxiety, awe, bewilderment, confusion, dismay, disquietude, distress, dread, fear, fright, horror, panic, perturbation, shock, terror, trepidation.
antonym composure.

constitute *v.* appoint, authorize, commission, compose, comprise, create, delegate, depute, empower, enact, establish, fix, form, found, inaugurate, make, name, nominate, ordain.

constitution *n.* build, character, composition, configuration, construction, disposition, establishment, form, formation, habit, health, make-up, nature, organization, physique, structure, temper, temperament.

constrain *v.* bind, bulldoze, chain, check, coerce, compel, confine, constrict, curb, drive, force, impel, necessitate, oblige, pressure, pressurize, railroad, restrain, urge.

construct *v.* assemble, build, compose, create, design, elevate, engineer, erect, establish, fabricate, fashion, form, formulate, found, frame, knock together, make, manufacture, model, organize, raise, shape.
antonyms demolish, destroy.

construction *n.* assembly, building, composition, constitution, creation, edifice, erection, fabric, fabrication, figure, form, formation, model, organization, shape, structure.
antonym destruction.

constructive *adj.* advantageous, beneficial, helpful, positive, practical, productive, useful, valuable.
antonyms destructive, negative, unhelpful.

construe *v.* analyze, decipher, deduce, explain, expound, infer, interpret, parse, read, render, take, translate.

consult *v.* ask, commune, confer, consider, debate, deliberate, interrogate, parley, powwow, question, regard, respect.

consume *v.* absorb, annihilate, decay, demolish, deplete, destroy, devastate, devour, discuss, dissipate, drain, eat, employ, engulf, envelop, exhaust, expend, gobble, guzzle, lessen, ravage, spend, squander, swallow, use (up), utilize, vanish, waste, wear out.

consumer *n.* buyer, customer, end-user, purchaser, shopper, user.

consummate *v.* accomplish, achieve, cap, compass, complete, conclude, crown, effectuate, end, finish, fulfil, perfect, perform, terminate.
adj. absolute, accomplished, complete, conspicuous, distinguished, finished, matchless, perfect, polished, practised, skilled, superb, superior, supreme, total, transcendent, ultimate, unqualified, utter.
antonym imperfect.

consummation *n.* achievement, actualization, completion, culmination, end, fulfilment, perfection, realization, termination.

contact *n.* acquaintance, approximation, association, communication, connection, contiguity, contingence, impact, junction, juxtaposition, meeting, tangency, touch, union.

v. approach, call, get hold of, notify, phone, reach, ring.

contagious *adj.* catching, communicable, epidemic, epizootic, infectious, pestiferous, pestilential, spreading, transmissible, zymotic.

contain *v.* accommodate, check, comprehend, comprise, control, curb, embody, embrace, enclose, entomb, hold, include, incorporate, involve, limit, repress, restrain, seat, stifle.

antonym exclude.

contaminate *v.* adulterate, befoul, besmirch, corrupt, debase, defile, deprave, infect, pollute, soil, stain, sully, taint, tarnish, vitiate.

antonym purify.

contemplate *v.* behold, cerebrate, consider, deliberate, design, envisage, examine, expect, eye, foresee, inspect, intend, mean, meditate, mull over, observe, plan, ponder, propose, reflect on, regard, ruminate, scrutinize, study, survey, view.

contemplative *adj.* cerebral, intent, introspective, meditative, musing, pensive, rapt, reflective, ruminative, thoughtful.

antonyms impulsive, thoughtless.

contemporary *adj.* à la mode, coetaneous, coeval, co-existent, co-existing, concurrent, contemporaneous, conterminous, coterminous, current, latest, modern, newfangled, present, present-day, recent, synchronous, ultra-modern, up-to-date, up-to-the-minute, with it.

antonyms preceding, succeeding.

contempt *n.* condescension, contemptuousness, contumely, derision, despite, detestation, disdain, disgrace, dishonor, disregard, disrespect, humiliation, loathing, mockery, neglect, scorn, shame, slight.

antonyms admiration, regard.

contemptible *adj.* abject, base, cheap, degenerate, despicable, detestable, ignominious, loathsome, low, low-down, mean, paltry, pitiful, scurvy, shabby, shameful, vile, worthless, wretched.

antonyms admirable, honorable.

contemptuous *adj.* arrogant, cavalier, condescending, contumacious, contumelious, cynical, derisive, disdainful, haughty, high and mighty, insolent, insulting, scornful, sneering, supercilious, tossy, withering.

antonyms humble, polite, respectful.

contend *v.* affirm, allege, argue, assert, aver, avow, clash, compete, contest, cope, debate, declare, dispute, emulate, grapple, hold, jostle, litigate, maintain, skirmish, strive, struggle, vie, wrestle.

content[1] *v.* appease, delight, gladden, gratify, humor, indulge, mollify, pacify, placate, please, reconcile, satisfy, suffice.

antonym displease.

n. comfort, contentment, delight, ease, gratification, happiness, peace, pleasure, satisfaction.

antonym discontent.

adj. agreeable, comfortable, contented, fulfilled, pleased, satisfied, untroubled.

antonym dissatisfied.

content[2] *n.* burden, capacity, essence, gist, ideas, load, matter, meaning, measure, significance, size, subject matter, substance, text, thoughts, volume.

contented *adj.* cheerful, comfortable, complacent, content, glad, gratified, happy, placid, pleased, relaxed, satisfied, serene, thankful.

antonym discontented.

contention *n.* affirmation, allegation, argument, assertion, asseveration, belief, claim, competition, contest, controversy, debate, declaration, discord, dispute, dissension, enmity, feuding, ground, hostility, idea, opinion, position, profession, rivalry, stand, strife, struggle, thesis, view, wrangling.

contentment *n.* comfort, complacency, content, contentedness, ease, equanimity, fulfilment, gladness, gratification, happiness, peace, peacefulness, placidity, pleasure, repletion, satisfaction, serenity.

antonym dissatisfaction.

contest *n.* affray, altercation, battle, combat, competition, concours, conflict, controversy, debate, discord, dispute, encounter, fight, game, match, olympiad, set-to, shock, struggle, tournament, trial.

v. argue against, challenge, compete, contend, debate, deny, dispute, doubt, fight, litigate, oppose, question, refute, strive, vie.

continence *n.* abstemiousness, abstinence, asceticism, celibacy, chastity, moderation, self-control, self-restraint, sobriety, temperance.

antonym incontinence.

contingency *n.* accident, arbitrariness, chance, emergency, event, eventuality, fortuity, happening, incident, juncture, possibility, randomness, uncertainty.

contingent *n.* batch, body, bunch, company, complement, deputation, detachment, group, mission, quota, section, set.

continual *adj.* ceaseless, constant, continuous, endless, eternal, everlasting, frequent, incessant, interminable, oft-repeated, perpetual, recurrent, regular, repeated, repetitive, unbroken, unceasing, uninterrupted, unremitting.

antonyms intermittent, occasional, temporary.

continue *v.* abide, aby(e), adjourn, carry on, endure, extend, go on, last, lengthen, maintain, persevere, persist, proceed, project, prolong, pursue, reach, recommence, remain, rest, resume, stay, stick at, survive, sustain.

antonyms discontinue, stop.

continuous *adj.* connected, consecutive, constant, continued, extended, non-stop, prolonged, unbroken, unceasing, undivided, uninterrupted.

antonyms discontinuous, intermittent, sporadic.

contract *v.* abbreviate, abridge, acquire, agree, arrange, bargain, catch, clinch, close, compress, condense, confine, constrict, constringe, covenant, curtail, develop, dwindle, engage, epitomize, incur, lessen, narrow, negotiate, pledge, purse, reduce, shrink, shrivel, stipulate, tighten, wither, wrinkle.

antonyms enlarge, expand, lengthen.

n. agreement, arrangement, bargain, bond, commission, commitment, compact, concordat, convention, covenant, deal, engagement, handfast, instrument, pact, settlement, stipulation, transaction, treaty, understanding.

contraction *n.* abbreviation, astringency, compression, constriction, diminution, elision, narrowing, reduction, retrenchment, shortening, shrinkage, shriveling, tensing, tightening.

antonyms expansion, growth.

contradict v. belie, challenge, contravene, controvert, counter, counteract, deny, disaffirm, dispute, gainsay, impugn, negate, oppose.
antonyms agree, confirm, corroborate.

contradictory adj. antagonistic, antithetical, conflicting, contrary, discrepant, dissident, double-mouthed, incompatible, inconsistent, irreconcilable, opposed, opposite, paradoxical, repugnant, unreconciled.
antonym consistent.

contrary adj. adverse, antagonistic, arsy-versy, awkward, balky, cantankerous, clashing, contradictory, counter, cross-grained, cussed, difficult, discordant, disobliging, froward, hostile, inconsistent, inimical, intractable, intractible, obstinate, opposed, opposite, paradoxical, perverse, stroppy, thrawn, unaccommodating, wayward, wilful.
antonyms like, obliging, similar.
n. antithesis, converse, opposite, reverse.

contrast n. comparison, contraposition, contrariety, counter-view, difference, differentiation, disparity, dissimilarity, distinction, divergence, foil, opposition, set-off.
antonym similarity.
v. compare, differ, differentiate, discriminate, distinguish, oppose, set off.

contribute v. add, afford, bestow, conduce, dob in, donate, furnish, give, help, kick in, lead, provide, subscribe, supply, tend.
antonyms subtract, withhold.

contribution n. addition, bestowal, donation, gift, grant, gratuity, handout, input, offering, subscription.

contrive v. arrange, compass, concoct, construct, create, design, devise, effect, engineer, excogitate, fabricate, frame, improvise, invent, manage, maneuver, plan, plot, scheme, wangle.

control v. boss, bridle, check, command, conduct, confine, constrain, contain, curb, determine, direct, dominate, govern, lead, limit, manage, manipulate, master, monitor, oversee, pilot, regiment, regulate, repress, restrain, rule, run, stage-manage, steer, subdue, superintend, supervise, suppress, verify.
n. authority, brake, charge, check, clutches, command, curb, direction, dirigism(e), discipline, governance, government, guidance, jurisdiction, leading-strings, leash, limitation, management, mastery, oversight, regulation, rule, superintendence, supervision, supremacy.

controversy n. altercation, argument, contention, debate, disagreement, discussion, dispute, dissension, polemic, quarrel, squabble, strife, war of words, wrangle, wrangling.
antonyms accord, agreement.

convenience n. accessibility, accommodation, advantage, amenity, appliance, appropriateness, availability, benefit, chance, comfort, ease, enjoyment, facility, fitness, handiness, help, leisure, opportuneness, opportunity, satisfaction, service, serviceability, suitability, timeliness, use, usefulness, utility.

convenient adj. accessible, adapted, advantageous, appropriate, at hand, available, beneficial, commodious, fit, fitted, handy, helpful, labor-saving, nearby, opportune, seasonable, serviceable, suitable, suited, timely, useful, utile, well-timed.
antonyms awkward, inconvenient.

convention n. agreement, assembly, bargain, code, compact, conclave, concordat, conference, congress, contract, convocation, council, custom, delegates, etiquette, formality, matter of form, meeting, pact, practice, propriety, protocol, representatives, stipulation, synod, tradition, treaty, understanding, usage.

conventional adj. accepted, arbitrary, bourgeois, common, commonplace, copybook, correct, customary, decorous, expected, formal, habitual, hackneyed, hidebound, iconic, nomic, normal, ordinary, orthodox, pedestrian, prevailing, prevalent, proper, prosaic, regular, ritual, routine, run-of-the-mill, standard, stereotyped, straight, stylized, traditional, unoriginal, uptight, usual, wonted.
antonyms exotic, unconventional, unusual.

conversant with acquainted with, apprised of, au fait with, experienced in, familiar with, informed about, knowledgeable about, practiced in, proficient in, skilled in, versant with, versed in.
antonym ignorant of.

conversation n. chat, chinwag, chitchat, colloquy, communication, communion, confab, confabulation, conference, converse, dialogue, discourse, discussion, exchange, gossip, intercourse, interlocution, powwow, talk, tête-à-tête.

converse[1] v. chat, colloquize, commune, confabulate, confer, discourse, talk.

converse[2] n. antithesis, contrary, counterpart, obverse, opposite, reverse.
adj. antipodal, antipodean, contrary, counter, opposite, reverse, reversed, transposed.

conversion n. adaptation, alteration, change, metamorphosis, metania, modification, permutation, proselytization, rebirth, reconstruction, reformation, regeneration, remodeling, reorganization, transfiguration, transformation, transmogrification, transmutation.

convert v. adapt, alter, apply, appropriate, baptize, change, convince, interchange, metamorphose, modify, permute, proselytize, reform, regenerate, remodel, reorganize, restyle, revise, save, transform, transmogrify, transmute, transpose, turn.
n. catechumen, disciple, neophyte, proselyte, vert.

convey v. bear, bequeath, bring, carry, cede, communicate, conduct, deliver, demise, devolve, disclose, fetch, forward, grant, guide, impart, lease, move, relate, reveal, send, steal, support, tell, transfer, transmit, transport, waft, will.

conveyance n. carriage, movement, shipment, transfer, transference, transmission, transport, transportation, tran(s)shipment, vehicle, wagonage.

convict v. attaint, condemn, imprison, sentence.
n. con, criminal, culprit, felon, forçat, jail-bird, lag, malefactor, prisoner.

conviction n. assurance, belief, certainty, certitude, confidence, convincement, creed, earnestness, faith, fervor, firmness, opinion, persuasion, plerophory, principle, reliance, tenet, view.

convince v. assure, confirm, persuade, reassure, satisfy, sway, win over.

convivial adj. back-slapping, cheerful, festive, friendly, fun-loving, gay, genial, hearty, hilarious, jolly, jovial, lively, merry, mirthful, sociable.
antonym taciturn.

convoy n. attendance, attendant, escort, fleet, guard, protection, train.

cool adj. aloof, apathetic, audacious, bold, brazen, calm, cheeky, chilled, chilling, chilly, coldish, collected, composed, cosmopolitan, dégagé, deliberate, dispassionate, distant, down-beat, elegant, frigid, impertinent, imperturbable, impudent, incurious, indifferent, laid-back, level-headed, lukewarm, nippy, offhand, placid, pleasant, presumptuous, quiet, refreshing, relaxed, reserved, satisfying, self-controlled, self-possessed, serene, shameless, sophisticated, stand-offish, together, uncommunicative, unconcerned, unemotional, unenthusiastic, unexcited, unfriendly, unheated, uninterested, unresponsive, unruffled, unwelcoming, urbane.

antonyms excited, friendly, hot, warm.

v. abate, allay, assuage, calm, chill, dampen, defuse, fan, freeze, lessen, moderate, quiet, refrigerate, temper.

antonyms excite, heat, warm.

n. calmness, collectedness, composure, control, poise, sangfroid, self-control, self-discipline, self-possession, temper.

co-operate *v.* abet, aid, assist, collaborate, combine, concur, conduce, conspire, contribute, co-ordinate, help, play along, play ball.

co-ordinate *v.* codify, correlate, grade, graduate, harmonize, integrate, match, mesh, organize, relate, synchronize, systematize, tabulate.

adj. coequal, correlative, correspondent, equal, equipotent, equivalent, parallel, reciprocal.

copious *adj.* abundant, ample, bounteous, bountiful, extensive, exuberant, full, generous, great, huge, inexhaustible, lavish, liberal, luxuriant, overflowing, plenteous, plentiful, profuse, rich, superabundant.

antonyms meager, scarce.

copy *n.* apograph, archetype, autotype, borrowing, calque, carbon copy, counterfeit, crib, duplicate, ectype, engrossment, exemplar, facsimile, flimsy, forgery, image, imitation, likeness, loan translation, loanword, model, Ozalid®, pattern, photocopy, Photostat®, plagiarization, print, replica, replication, representation, reproduction, tracing, transcript, transcription, Xerox®.

antonym original.

v. ape, borrow, counterfeit, crib, duplicate, echo, emulate, engross, exemplify, extract, facsimile, follow, imitate, mimic, mirror, parrot, personate, photocopy, Photostat®, plagiarize, repeat, replicate, reproduce, simulate, transcribe, Xerox®.

cordial *adj.* affable, affectionate, agreeable, cheerful, earnest, friendly, genial, heartfelt, hearty, invigorating, pleasant, restorative, sociable, stimulating, warm, warm-hearted, welcoming, whole-hearted.

antonyms aloof, cool, hostile.

core *n.* center, crux, essence, germ, gist, heart, kernel, nitty-gritty, nub, nucleus, pith.

antonyms exterior, perimeter, surface.

corporation[1] *n.* association, authorities, body, combine, conglomerate, council, society.

corporation[2] *n.* beer belly, paunch, pod, pot, pot-belly, spare tire.

corpse *n.* body, cadaver, carcass, deader, remains, skeleton, stiff.

corpulent *adj.* adipose, beefy, bulky, burly, fat, fattish, fleshy, large, lusty, obese, overweight, plump, poddy, podgy, portly, pot-bellied, pudgy, roly-poly, rotund, stout, tubby, well-padded.

antonym thin.

correct *v.* adjust, admonish, amend, blue-pencil, chasten, chastise, chide, counterbalance, cure, debug, discipline, emend, emendate, improve, punish, rectify, redress, reform, regulate, remedy, reprimand, reprove, right.

adj. acceptable, accurate, appropriate, comme il faut, diplomatic, equitable, exact, faultless, fitting, flawless, jake, just, OK, precise, proper, regular, right, seemly, standard, strict, true, well-formed, word-perfect.

antonyms inaccurate, incorrect, wrong.

correction *n.* adjustment, admonition, alteration, amendment, castigation, chastisement, discipline, emendation, improvement, modification, punishment, rectification, reformation, reproof, righting.

correlation *n.* alternation, correspondence, equivalence, interaction, interchange, interdependence, interrelationship, link, reciprocity, relationship.

correspond *v.* accord, agree, answer, coincide, communicate, complement, concur, conform, correlate, dovetail, fit, harmonize, match, square, tally, write.

correspondent *n.* contributor, journalist, penpal, reporter, writer.

adj. analogous, comparable, equivalent, like, matching, parallel, reciprocal, similar.

corridor *n.* aisle, ambulatory, foyer, hallway, lobby, passage, passageway, vestibule.

corrode *v.* canker, consume, corrupt, crumble, deteriorate, disintegrate, eat away, erode, fret, impair, oxidize, rust, waste, wear away.

corrupt *adj.* abandoned, adulterate(d), altered, bent, bribed, contaminated, crooked, debased, decayed, defiled, degenerate, demoralized, depraved, dishonest, dishonored, dissolute, distorted, doctored, falsified, fraudulent, infected, polluted, profligate, putrescent, putrid, rotten, shady, tainted, unethical, unprincipled, unscrupulous, venal, vicious.

antonyms honest, trustworthy, upright.

v. adulterate, barbarize, bribe, canker, contaminate, debase, debauch, defile, demoralize, deprave, doctor, empoison, entice, fix, infect, lure, pervert, putrefy, seduce, spoil, square, suborn, subvert, taint, vitiate.

antonym purify.

corruption *n.* adulteration, baseness, bribery, bribing, crookedness, debasement, decadence, decay, defilement, degeneration, degradation, demoralization, depravity, dishonesty, distortion, doctoring, evil, extortion, falsification, fiddling, foulness, fraud, fraudulence, fraudulency, graft, immorality, impurity, infection, iniquity, jobbery, leprosy, malversation, perversion, pollution, profiteering, profligacy, putrefaction, putrescence, rot, rottenness, shadiness, sinfulness, turpitude, ulcer, unscrupulousness, venality, vice, viciousness, virus, wickedness.

antonyms honesty, purification.

cost *n.* amount, charge, damage, deprivation, detriment, disbursement, expenditure, expense, figure, harm, hurt, injury, loss, outlay, payment, penalty, price, rate, sacrifice, worth.

costly *adj.* catastrophic, damaging, dear, deleterious, disastrous, excessive, exorbitant, expensive, extortionate, gorgeous, harmful, highly-priced, lavish, loss-making, luxurious, opulent, precious, priceless, pricy, rich, ruinous, sacrificial, splendid, steep, sumptuous, valuable.

antonyms cheap, inexpensive.

costume *n.* apparel, attire, clothing, dress, ensemble, garb, get-up, livery, outfit, raiment, robes, uniform, vestment.

cough *n.* bark, hack, tussis.

v. bark, hack, harrumph, hawk, hem, hoast.

council *n.* assembly, board, cabinet, chamber, committee, conclave, conference, congress, consistory, consult, convention, convocation, diet, divan, ministry, panchayat, panel, parliament, soviet, syndicate, synod, volost.

counsel *n.* admonition, advice, advocate, attorney, barrister, caution, consideration, consultation, deliberation, direction, forethought, guidance, information, lawyer, plan, purpose, recommendation, solicitor, suggestion, warning.

v. admonish, advise, advocate, caution, direct, exhort, guide, instruct, recommend, suggest, urge, warn.

count *v.* add, ascribe, calculate, check, compute, consider, deem, enumerate, esteem, estimate, hold, impute, include, judge, list, matter, number, rate, reckon, regard, score, signify, tally, tell, think, tot up, total, weigh.

n. addition, calculation, computation, enumeration, numbering, poll, reckoning, sum, tally, total.

countenance *n.* acquiescence, aid, air, appearance, approval, aspect, assistance, backing, demeanor, endorsement, expression, face, favor, features, help, look, mien, physiognomy, sanction, support, visage.

v. abet, acquiesce, agree to, aid, approve, back, brook, champion, condone, encourage, endorse, endure, help, sanction, support, tolerate.

counteract *v.* act against, annul, check, contravene, counterbalance, countervail, cross, defeat, foil, frustrate, hinder, invalidate, negate, neutralize, offset, oppose, resist, thwart, undo.

antonyms assist, support.

counterfeit *v.* copy, fabricate, fake, feign, forge, imitate, impersonate, phony, pretend, sham, simulate.

adj. bogus, copied, ersatz, faked, false, feigned, forged, fraudulent, imitation, phony, postiche, pretend(ed), pseud, pseudo, sham, simular, simulated, simulate(d), spurious, supposititious.

antonym genuine.

n. copy, fake, forgery, fraud, imitant, imitation, phantasm(a), phony, reproduction, sham.

country *n.* backwoods, boondocks, citizenry, citizens, clime, commonwealth, community, countryside, electors, farmland, fatherland, green belt, homeland, inhabitants, kingdom, land, motherland, nation, nationality, outback, outdoors, part, people, populace, provinces, public, realm, region, society, sovereign state, state, sticks, terrain, territory, voters.

adj. agrarian, agrestic, arcadian, bucolic, georgic, landed, pastoral, provincial, rude, rural, rustic.

antonyms oppidan, urban.

couple *n.* brace, Darby and Joan, duo, dyad, pair, span, team, twain, twosome, yoke.

v. accompany, buckle, clasp, conjoin, connect, copulate, fornicate, hitch, join, link, marry, pair, unite, wed, yoke.

courage *n.* boldness, bottle, bravery, daring, dauntlessness, fearlessness, firmness, fortitude, gallantry, grit, guts, hardihood, heroism, mettle, nerve, pluck, resolution, spirit, spunk, stomach, valor.

antonym cowardice.

courageous *adj.* audacious, bold, brave, daring, dauntless, dreadless, fearless, gallant, gutsy, hardy, heroic, high-hearted, indomitable, intrepid, lion-hearted, plucky, resolute, stout-hearted, valiant, valorous.

antonym cowardly.

course *n.* advance, advancement, channel, circuit, circus, classes, continuity, current, curriculum, development, diadrom, direction, duration, flight-path, flow, furtherance, hippodrome, lap, lapse, lectures, line, march, method, mode, movement, orbit, order, passage, passing, path, piste, plan, policy, procedure, program, progress, progression, race, race-course, race-track, raik, regimen, road, round, route, schedule, sequence, series, studies, succession, sweep, syllabus, tack, term, time, track, trail, trajectory, unfolding, vector, voyage, way, wheel.

v. chase, dash, flow, follow, gush, hunt, move, pour, pursue, race, run, scud, scurry, speed, stream, surge, tumble.

courteous *adj.* affable, attentive, ceremonious, civil, considerate, courtly, debonair, elegant, gallant, gracious, mannerly, obliging, polished, polite, refined, respectful, urbane, well-bred, well-mannered.

antonyms discourteous, rude.

courtesy *n.* affability, attention, benevolence, breeding, civility, comity, consent, consideration, courteousness, courtliness, elegance, favor, gallantness, gallantry, generosity, gentilesse, graciousness, indulgence, kindness, manners, polish, politeness, urbanity.

antonyms discourtesy, rudeness.

covenant *n.* arrangement, bargain, bond, commitment, compact, concordat, contract, convention, deed, engagement, pact, pledge, promise, stipulation, treaty, trust, undertaking.

v. agree, bargain, contract, engage, pledge, promise, stipulate, undertake.

cover *v.* balance, camouflage, canopy, clad, cloak, clothe, coat, compensate, comprehend, comprise, conceal, consider, contain, counterbalance, curtain, daub, defend, describe, detail, disguise, dress, eclipse, embody, embrace, encase, encompass, enshroud, envelop, examine, guard, hide, hood, house, include, incorporate, insure, invest, investigate, involve, layer, mantle, mask, narrate, obscure, offset, overlay, overspread, protect, recount, reinforce, relate, report, screen, secrete, shade, sheathe, shelter, shield, shroud, suffuse, survey, veil.

n. bedspread, binding, camouflage, canopy, cap, case, cloak, clothing, coating, compensation, concealment, confederate, covering, cover-up, defence, disguise, dress, envelope, façade, front, guard, indemnity, insurance, jacket, lid, mask, payment, pretense, pretext, protection, refuge, reimbursement, sanctuary, screen, sheath, shelter, shield, smoke, spread, top, undergrowth, veil, woods, wrapper.

covert *adj.* clandestine, concealed, disguised, dissembled, hidden, private, secret, sneaky, stealthy, subreptitious, surreptitious, ulterior, under the table, underhand, unsuspected, veiled.

antonym open.

covetous *adj.* acquisitive, avaricious, close-fisted, envious, grasping, greedy, insatiable, jealous, mercenary, rapacious, thirsting, yearning.

antonyms generous, temperate.

coward *n.* caitiff, chicken, craven, dastard, faint-heart, funk, hilding, nithing, poltroon, recreant, renegade, scaredy-cat, skulker, sneak, yellow-belly, yellow-dog.
antonym hero.

cowardice *n.* faint-heartedness, fear, funk, gutlessness, pusillanimity, spinelessness.
antonyms courage, valor.

cowardly *adj.* base, caitiff, chicken, chicken-hearted, chicken-livered, craven, dastard(ly), faint-hearted, fearful, gutless, hilding, lily-livered, nesh, nithing, pusillanimous, recreant, scared, shrinking, soft, spineless, timorous, unheroic, weak, weak-kneed, white-livered, yellow, yellow-bellied.
antonym courageous.

cower *v.* cringe, crouch, flinch, grovel, quail, ruck, shake, shiver, shrink, skulk, tremble.

coy *adj.* arch, backward, bashful, coquettish, demure, diffident, evasive, flirtatious, kittenish, maidenly, modest, prudish, reserved, retiring, self-effacing, shrinking, shy, skittish, timid, virginal.
antonyms forward, impudent, sober.

crack *v.* break, buffet, burst, chap, chip, chop, cleave, clip, clout, collapse, crackle, crash, craze, cuff, decipher, detonate, explode, fathom, fracture, pop, ring, rive, slap, snap, solve, splinter, split, succumb, thump, wallop, whack, yield.
n. attempt, blow, breach, break, buffet, burst, chap, chink, chip, clap, cleft, clip, clout, cranny, crash, craze, crevasse, crevice, cuff, dig, expert, explosion, fent, fissure, flaw, fracture, gag, gap, go, insult, interstice, jibe, joke, moment, opportunity, pop, quip, report, rift, slap, smack, snap, stab, thump, try, wallop, whack, wisecrack, witticism.
adj. ace, choice, élite, excellent, first-class, first-rate, hand-picked, superior, top-notch.

craft *n.* ability, aircraft, aptitude, art, artfulness, artifice, artistry, barque, boat, business, calling, cleverness, contrivance, craftiness, cunning, deceit, dexterity, duplicity, employment, expertise, expertness, guile, handicraft, handiwork, ingenuity, knack, know-how, line, occupation, plane, pursuit, ruse, scheme, ship, shrewdness, skill, spacecraft, spaceship, stratagem, subterfuge, subtlety, technique, trade, trickery, vessel, vocation, wiles, work, workmanship.
antonyms naïvety, openness.

craftiness *n.* artfulness, astuteness, canniness, cunning, deceit, deviousness, double-dealing, duplicity, foxiness, guile, shrewdness, slyness, subtlety, trickiness, underhandedness, vulpinism, wiliness.
antonyms naïvety, openness.

crafty *adj.* artful, astute, calculating, canny, cunning, deceitful, designing, devious, duplicitous, foxy, fraudulent, guileful, insidious, knowing, machiavellian, scheming, sharp, shrewd, sly, subtle, tricksy, tricky, versute, vulpine, wily.
antonyms naïve, open.

craggy *adj.* broken, brusque, cragged, jagged, jaggy, precipitous, rocky, rough, rugged, stony, surly, uneven.
antonyms pleasant, smooth.

crank *n.* eccentric, loony, madman, nutter.

cranky *adj.* bizarre, capricious, crabbed, cross, crotchety, dotty, eccentric, erratic, freakish, freaky, funny, idiosyncratic, irritable, odd, peculiar, prickly, queer, quirky, strange, surly, viewy, wacky.

antonyms normal, placid, sensible.

crash *n.* accident, bang, bankruptcy, boom, bump, clang, clash, clatter, clattering, collapse, collision, debacle (débâcle), depression, din, downfall, failure, fragor, jar, jolt, pile-up, prang, racket, ruin, smash, smashing, smash-up, thud, thump, thunder, wreck.
v. bang, break, bump, collapse, collide, dash, disintegrate, fail, fall, fold (up), fracture, fragment, go bust, go under, hurtle, lurch, overbalance, pitch, plunge, prang, shatter, shiver, smash, splinter, sprawl, topple.
adj. concentrated, emergency, immediate, intensive, round-the-clock, telescoped, urgent.

crave *v.* ask, beg, beseech, desire, entreat, fancy, hanker after, hunger after, implore, long for, need, petition, pine for, require, seek, solicit, supplicate, thirst for, want, yearn for, yen for.
antonyms dislike, spurn.

craving *n.* appetence, appetency, appetite, cacoethes, desire, hankering, hunger, longing, lust, thirst, urge, yearning, yen.
antonyms dislike, distaste.

crazy *adj.* absurd, ardent, bananas, barmy, bats, batty, berserk, bird-brained, bizarre, bonkers, cockeyed, cracked, crazed, cuckoo, daffy, daft, delirious, demented, deranged, derisory, devoted, dippy, eager, eccentric, enamored, enthusiastic, fanatical, fantastic, fatuous, foolhardy, foolish, fruity, half-baked, hysterical, idiotic, ill-conceived, impracticable, imprudent, inane, inappropriate, infatuated, insane, irresponsible, ludicrous, lunatic, mad, maniacal, mental, nonsensical, nuts, nutty, odd, off one's rocker, outrageous, passionate, peculiar, pixil(l)ated, potty, preposterous, puerile, quixotic, ridiculous, scatty, senseless, short-sighted, silly, smitten, strange, touched, unbalanced, unhinged, unrealistic, unwise, unworkable, up the pole, wacky, weird, wild, zany, zealous.
antonyms sane, sensible.

creak *v.* grate, grind, groan, rasp, scrape, scratch, screak, screech, squeak, squeal.

create *v.* appoint, beget, cause, coin, compose, concoct, constitute, design, develop, devise, engender, establish, form, formulate, found, generate, hatch, initiate, install, institute, invent, invest, make, occasion, originate, produce, set up, sire, spawn.
antonym destroy.

creative *adj.* adept, artistic, clever, fertile, gifted, imaginative, ingenious, inspired, inventive, original, productive, resourceful, stimulating, talented, visionary.
antonym unimaginative.

credence *n.* belief, confidence, credit, dependence, faith, reliance, support, trust.
antonym distrust.

credible *adj.* believable, conceivable, convincing, dependable, honest, imaginable, likely, persuasive, plausible, possible, probable, reasonable, reliable, sincere, supposable, tenable, thinkable, trustworthy, trusty.
antonyms implausible, unreliable.

credit *n.* acclaim, acknowledgment, approval, belief, character, clout, commendation, confidence, credence, distinction, esteem, estimation, faith, fame, glory, honor, influence, kudos, merit, position, praise, prestige, recognition, regard, reliance, reputation, repute, standing, status, thanks, tribute, trust.

antonym discredit.

v. accept, believe, buy, subscribe to, swallow, trust.
antonym disbelieve.

creditable *adj.* admirable, commendable, deserving, estimable, excellent, exemplary, good, honorable, laudable, meritorious, praiseworthy, reputable, respectable, sterling, worthy.
antonyms blameworthy, shameful.

credulous *adj.* dupable, green, gullible, naïve, trusting, uncritical, unsuspecting, unsuspicious, wide-eyed.
antonym skeptical.

creed *n.* articles, belief, canon, catechism, confession, credo, doctrine, dogma, faith, persuasion, principles, tenets.

creek *n.* bay, bight, brook, cove, fiord, firth, frith, inlet, rivulet, stream, streamlet, tributary, voe, watercourse.

creepy *adj.* awful, direful, disturbing, eerie, frightening, ghoulish, gruesome, hair-raising, horrible, macabre, menacing, nightmarish, ominous, scary, sinister, spookish, spooky, terrifying, threatening, unearthly, unpleasant, weird.
antonyms normal, pleasant.

crime *n.* atrocity, corruption, delinquency, fault, felony, flagitiousness, guilt, illegality, iniquity, law-breaking, malefaction, malfeasance, misconduct, misdeed, misdemeanor, offense, outrage, sin, transgression, trespass, unrighteousness, vice, villainy, violation, wickedness, wrong, wrong-doing.

criminal *n.* con, convict, crook, culprit, delinquent, evildoer, felon, infractor, jail-bird, law-breaker, malefactor, offender, sinner, transgressor.
adj. bent, corrupt, crooked, culpable, deplorable, felonious, flagitious, foolish, illegal, immoral, indictable, iniquitous, lawless, malfeasant, nefarious, peccant, preposterous, ridiculous, scandalous, senseless, unlawful, unrighteous, vicious, villainous, wicked, wrong.
antonyms honest, upright.

cripple *v.* cramp, damage, debilitate, destroy, disable, enfeeble, halt, hamstring, impair, incapacitate, lame, maim, mutilate, paralyze, ruin, sabotage, spoil, vitiate, weaken.

crippled *adj.* deformed, disabled, enfeebled, handicapped, incapacitated, invalid, lame, paralyzed.

crisis *n.* calamity, catastrophe, climacteric, climax, confrontation, conjuncture, crunch, crux, culmination, difficulty, dilemma, disaster, emergency, exigency, extremity, height, impasse, mess, pinch, plight, predicament, quandary, strait, trouble.

crisp *adj.* bracing, brief, brisk, brittle, brusque, clear, crispy, crumbly, crunchy, decisive, firm, forthright, fresh, incisive, invigorating, neat, orderly, pithy, refreshing, short, smart, snappy, spruce, succinct, tart, terse, tidy, vigorous.
antonyms flabby, limp, vague.

criterion *n.* bench-mark, canon, gauge, measure, norm, precedent, principle, proof, rule, shibboleth, standard, test, touchstone, yardstick.

critic *n.* analyst, animadverter, arbiter, Aristarch, attacker, authority, carper, caviler, censor, censurer, commentator, connoisseur, detractor, expert, expositor, fault-finder, feuilletonist, judge, knocker, Momus, pundit, reviewer, reviler, vilifier, Zoilist.

critical *adj.* accurate, all-important, analytical, captious, carping, caviling, censorious, climacteric, crucial, dangerous, deciding, decisive, derogatory, diagnostic, disapproving, discerning, discriminating, disparaging, fastidious, fault-finding, grave, hairy, high-priority, judicious, momentous, nagging, niggling, nit-picking, penetrating, perceptive, perilous, pivotal, precarious, precise, pressing, psychological, risky, serious, sharp-tongued, uncomplimentary, urgent, vital, Zoilean.
antonyms uncritical, unimportant.

criticize *v.* analyze, animadvert, appraise, assess, badmouth, blame, carp, censure, condemn, crab, decry, disparage, evaluate, excoriate, judge, knock, pan, review, roast, scarify, slag, slam, slash, slate, snipe.
antonym praise.

critique *n.* analysis, appraisal, assessment, commentary, essay, evaluation, examination, review.

crony *n.* accomplice, ally, associate, buddy, china, chum, colleague, companion, comrade, follower, friend, henchman, mate, pal, sidekick.

crooked¹ *adj.* bent, corrupt, crafty, criminal, deceitful, discreditable, dishonest, dishonorable, dubious, fraudulent, illegal, knavish, nefarious, questionable, shady, shifty, treacherous, underhand, unethical, unlawful, unprincipled, unscrupulous.
antonym honest.

crooked² *adj.* anfractuous, angled, askew, asymmetric, awry, bent, bowed, crank, cranky, crippled, crump, curved, deformed, deviating, disfigured, distorted, hooked, irregular, lopsided, meandering, misshapen, off-center, skew-whiff, slanted, slanting, squint, tilted, tortuous, twisted, twisting, uneven, warped, winding, zigzag.
antonym straight.

crop¹ *n.* fruits, gathering, growth, harvest, ingathering, produce, vintage, yield.
v. browse, clip, collect, curtail, cut, garner, gather, graze, harvest, lop, mow, nibble, pare, pick, prune, reap, reduce, shear, shingle, shorten, snip, top, trim, yield.

crop² *n.* craw, gizzard, gullet, maw, oesophagus, throat.

cross *adj.* adverse, angry, annoyed, cantankerous, captious, churlish, contrary, cranky, crosswise, crotchety, crusty, disagreeable, displeased, fractious, fretful, grouchy, grumpy, hybrid, ill-humored, ill-tempered, impatient, interchanged, intersecting, irascible, irritable, oblique, opposed, opposing, opposite, peeved, peevish, pettish, petulant, querulous, reciprocal, shirty, short, snappish, snappy, splenetic, sullen, surly, testy, transverse, unfavorable, vexed, waspish.
antonyms calm, placid, pleasant.
v. annoy, bestride, blend, block, bridge, cancel, crisscross, crossbreed, cross-fertilize, cross-pollinate, decussate, deny, foil, ford, frustrate, hinder, hybridize, impede, interbreed, intercross, interfere, intersect, intertwine, lace, meet, mix, mongrelize, obstruct, oppose, resist, span, thwart, traverse, zigzag.
n. affliction, amalgam, blend, burden, combination, crossbreed, crossing, crossroads, crucifix, cur, grief, holy-rood, hybrid, hybridization, intersection, load, misery, misfortune, mixture, mongrel, rood, trial, tribulation, trouble, woe, worry.

crouch *v.* bend, bow, cower, cringe, duck, hunch, kneel, ruck, squat, stoop.

crow *v.* bluster, boast, brag, exult, flourish, gloat, prate, rejoice, triumph, vaunt.

crowd *n.* army, assembly, attendance, audience, boodle, bunch, caboodle, circle, clique, company, concourse, flock, gate, group, herd, hoi polloi, horde, host, house, lot, many-headed beast/monster, mass, masses, mob, multitude, pack, people, populace, press, proletariat, public, rabble, riff-raff, set, spectators, squash, swarm, the many, throng, troupe.

v. bundle, cluster, compress, congest, congregate, cram, elbow, flock, for(e)gather, gather, huddle, jostle, mass, muster, pack, pile, press, push, shove, squeeze, stream, surge, swarm, throng.

crown *n.* acme, apex, bays, chaplet, circlet, coronal, coronet, crest, diadem, distinction, forehead, garland, head, honor, kudos, laurel wreath, laurels, monarch, monarchy, pate, perfection, pinnacle, prize, royalty, ruler, skull, sovereign, sovereignty, summit, tiara, tip, top, trophy, ultimate, zenith.

v. adorn, biff, box, cap, clout, complete, consummate, cuff, dignify, festoon, finish, fulfil, honor, instal, perfect, punch, reward, surmount, terminate, top.

crude *adj.* amateurish, blue, boorish, clumsy, coarse, crass, dirty, earthy, gross, half-baked, immature, inartistic, indecent, lewd, makeshift, natural, obscene, outline, primitive, raw, rough, rough-hewn, rude, rudimentary, sketchy, smutty, tactless, tasteless, uncouth, undeveloped, undigested, unfinished, unformed, unpolished, unprepared, unprocessed, unrefined, unsubtle, vulgar.

antonyms finished, polite, refined, tasteful.

cruel *adj.* atrocious, barbarous, bitter, bloodthirsty, brutal, brutish, butcherly, callous, cold-blooded, cutting, depraved, excruciating, fell, ferocious, fierce, flinty, grim, hard, hard-hearted, harsh, heartless, heathenish, hellish, immane, implacable, inclement, inexorable, inhuman, inhumane, malevolent, marble-breasted, merciless, murderous, painful, pitiless, poignant, ravening, raw, relentless, remorseless, ruthless, sadistic, sanguinary, savage, severe, spiteful, stony-hearted, unfeeling, ungentle, unkind, unmerciful, unnatural, unrelenting, vengeful, vicious.

antonyms compassionate, kind, merciful.

cruelty *n.* barbarity, bestiality, bloodthirstiness, brutality, brutishness, callousness, depravity, ferocity, fiendishness, hard-heartedness, harshness, heartlessness, immanity, inhumanity, mercilessness, murderousness, ruthlessness, sadism, savagery, severity, spite, spitefulness, tyranny, ungentleness, venom, viciousness.

antonyms compassion, kindness, mercy.

crumb *n.* atom, bit, grain, iota, jot, mite, morsel, particle, scrap, shred, sliver, snippet, soupçon, speck.

crunch *v.* champ, chomp, grind, masticate, munch, scranch.

n. crisis, crux, emergency, pinch, test.

crush *v.* abash, break, browbeat, bruise, chagrin, champ, comminute, compress, conquer, contuse, crease, crumble, crumple, crunch, embrace, enfold, extinguish, hug, humiliate, mash, mortify, overcome, overpower, overwhelm, pound, press, pulverize, quash, quell, rumple, shame, smash, squabash, squeeze, squelch, steam-roller, subdue, vanquish, wrinkle.

n. check, crowd, huddle, jam.

cry *v.* advertise, announce, bark, bawl, beg, bellow, beseech, bewail, blubber, boo-hoo, broadcast, bruit, call, caterwaul, clamor, ejaculate, entreat, exclaim, greet, hail, halloo, hawk, holler, howl, implore, keen, lament, mewl, miaow, miaul, noise, plead, pray, pro-

claim, promulgate, pule, roar, scream, screech, shout, shriek, snivel, sob, squall, squeal, trumpet, vociferate, wail, weep, whimper, whine, whinge, whoop, yell, yowl.

n. announcement, appeal, battle-cry, bawl(ing), bellow, blubber(ing), call, caterwaul, caterwaul(ing), ejaculation, entreaty, exclamation, greet, holler, hoot, howl, keening, lament, lamentation, miaow, miaul, outcry, petition, plaint, plea, prayer, proclamation, report, roar, rumor, scream, screech, shriek, slogan, snivel(ing), sob(bing), sorrowing, squall, squawk, squeal, supplication, utterance, wail(ing), watch-word, weep(-ing), whoop, yell, yelp, yoo-hoo.

cryptic *adj.* abstruse, ambiguous, aprocryphal, arcane, bizarre, cabbalistic, dark, Delphic, enigmatic, equivocal, esoteric, hidden, mysterious, obscure, occult, oracular, perplexing, puzzling, recondite, secret, strange, vague, veiled.

antonyms clear, obvious, straightforward.

cuddly *adj.* buxom, cosy, cuddlesome, curvaceous, huggable, lovable, plump, soft, warm.

cull *v.* amass, choose, collect, decimate, destroy, gather, glean, kill, pick, pick out, pluck, select, sift, thin, winnow.

culpable *adj.* answerable, blamable, blameworthy, censurable, guilty, liable, offending, peccant, reprehensible, sinful, to blame, wrong.

antonyms blameless, innocent.

culprit *n.* criminal, delinquent, evil-doer, felon, guilty party, law-breaker, malefactor, miscreant, offender, rascal, sinner, transgressor, wrong-doer.

cultivate *v.* aid, ameliorate, better, cherish, civilize, court, develop, discipline, elevate, encourage, enrich, farm, fertilize, forward, foster, further, harvest, help, improve, patronize, plant, plow, polish, prepare, promote, pursue, refine, school, support, tend, till, train, work.

antonym neglect.

cultivation *n.* advancement, advocacy, agronomy, breeding, civilization, civility, culture, development, discernment, discrimination, education, encouragement, enhancement, enlightenment, farming, fostering, furtherance, gardening, gentility, help, husbandry, learning, letters, manners, nurture, patronage, planting, plowing, polish, promotion, pursuit, refinement, schooling, study, support, taste, tillage, tilling, tilth, working.

cultural *adj.* aesthetic, artistic, arty, broadening, civilizing, developmental, edifying, educational, educative, elevating, enlightening, enriching, humane, humanizing, liberal.

culture *n.* accomplishment, aestheticism, agriculture, agronomy, art, breeding, civilization, cultivation, customs, education, elevation, enlightenment, erudition, farming, gentility, husbandry, improvement, Kultur, lifestyle, mores, polish, politeness, refinement, society, taste, the arts, urbanity.

cultured *adj.* accomplished, advanced, aesthetic, arty, civilized, educated, enlightened, erudite, genteel, highbrow, knowledgeable, polished, refined, scholarly, urbane, versed, well-bred, well-informed, well-read.

antonyms ignorant, uncultured.

cumbersome *adj.* awkward, bulky, burdensome, clumsy, cumbrous, embarrassing, heavy, hefty, incommodious, inconvenient, onerous, oppressive, ponderous, unmanageable, unwieldy, weighty.

antonyms convenient, manageable.

cunning *adj.* adroit, arch, artful, astute, canny, crafty, deep, deft, devious, dexterous, foxy, guileful, imaginative, ingenious, knowing, leery, Machiavellian, rusé, sharp, shifty, shrewd, skilful, sneaky, subtle, tricky, vulpine, wily.

antonyms gullible, naïve.

n. ability, adroitness, art, artfulness, artifice, astuteness, cleverness, craftiness, deceitfulness, deftness, deviousness, dexterity, finesse, foxiness, guile, ingenuity, policy, shrewdness, skill, slyness, subtlety, trickery, vulpinism, wiliness.

antonyms openness, simplicity.

curb *v.* bit, bridle, check, constrain, contain, control, hamper, hinder, hobble, impede, inhibit, moderate, muzzle, repress, restrain, restrict, retard, subdue, suppress.

antonyms encourage, foster, goad.

n. brake, bridle, check, control, deterrent, hamper, hobble, limitation, rein, restraint.

cure[1] *v.* alleviate, correct, ease, heal, help, mend, rehabilitate, relieve, remedy, restore.

n. alleviation, antidote, corrective, detoxicant, febrifuge, healing, medicine, panacea, panpharmacon, recovery, remedy, restorative, specific, treatment, vulnerary.

cure[2] *v.* brine, dry, kipper, pickle, preserve, salt, smoke.

curiosity *n.* bibelot, bygone, celebrity, curio, freak, inquisitiveness, interest, knick-knack, marvel, nosiness, novelty, object of virtu, objet d'art, objet de vertu, oddity, phenomenon, prying, rarity, sight, snooping, spectacle, trinket, wonder.

curious *adj.* bizarre, enquiring, exotic, extraordinary, funny, inquisitive, interested, marvelous, meddling, mysterious, nosy, novel, odd, peculiar, peeping, peering, prying, puzzled, puzzling, quaint, queer, questioning, rare, searching, singular, snoopy, strange, unconventional, unexpected, unique, unorthodox, unusual, wonderful.

antonyms incurious, indifferent, normal, ordinary, uninterested.

current *adj.* accepted, circulating, common, contemporary, customary, extant, fashionable, general, on-going, popular, present, present-day, prevailing, prevalent, reigning, rife, trendy, up-to-date, up-to-the-minute, widespread.

antonyms antiquated, old-fashioned.

n. atmosphere, course, draft, drift, feeling, flow, inclination, jet, juice, mood, progression, river, stream, tendency, thermal, tide, trend, undercurrent.

curse *n.* affliction, anathema, ban, bane, blasphemy, burden, calamity, cross, damn, denunciation, disaster, evil, excommunication, execration, expletive, imprecation, jinx, malediction, malison, misfortune, oath, obscenity, ordeal, plague, scourge, swearing, swearword, torment, tribulation, trouble, vexation, woe.

antonyms advantage, blessing.

v. accurse, afflict, anathematize, blaspheme, blight, blind, blow, burden, cuss, damn, destroy, doom, excommunicate, execrate, fulminate, imprecate, plague, scourge, swear, torment, trouble, vex.

antonym bless.

cursory *adj.* brief, careless, casual, desultory, fleeting,

hasty, hurried, offhand, passing, perfunctory, quick, rapid, slap-dash, slight, summary, superficial.

antonyms painstaking, thorough.

curt *adj.* abrupt, blunt, brief, brusque, concise, gruff, laconic, offhand, pithy, rude, sharp, short, short-spoken, snappish, succinct, summary, tart, terse, unceremonious, uncivil, ungracious.

antonym voluble.

curtail *v.* abbreviate, abridge, circumscribe, contract, cut, decrease, dock, lessen, lop, pare, prune, reduce, restrict, retrench, shorten, trim, truncate.

antonyms extend, lengthen, prolong.

curtain *v.* conceal, drape, hide, screen, shield, shroud, shutter, veil.

n. arras, backdrop, drapery, hanging, portière, tab, tapestry, vitrage.

curve *v.* arc, arch, bend, bow, coil, hook, incurvate, incurve, inflect, spiral, swerve, turn, twist, wind.

n. arc, bend, camber, curvature, half-moon, incurvation, incurvature, inflexure, loop, trajectory, turn.

cushion *n.* bean-bag, bolster, buffer, hassock, headrest, pad, pillion, pillow, shock absorber, squab.

v. allay, bolster, buttress, cradle, dampen, deaden, lessen, mitigate, muffle, pillow, protect, soften, stifle, support, suppress.

custodian *n.* caretaker, castellan, chatelaine, claviger, conservator, curator, guardian, keeper, overseer, protector, superintendent, warden, warder, watch-dog, watchman.

custody *n.* aegis, arrest, auspices, care, charge, confinement, custodianship, detention, durance, duress, guardianship, holding, imprisonment, incarceration, keeping, observation, possession, preservation, protection, retention, safe-keeping, supervision, trusteeship, tutelage, ward, wardship, watch.

custom *n.* consuetude, convention, customers, etiquette, fashion, form, formality, habit, habitude, manner, mode, observance, observation, patronage, policy, practice, praxis, procedure, ritual, routine, rule, style, thew, trade, tradition, usage, use, way, wont.

customary *adj.* accepted, accustomed, acknowledged, common, confirmed, conventional, established, everyday, familiar, fashionable, favorite, general, habitual, nomic, normal, ordinary, popular, prevailing, regular, routine, traditional, usual, wonted.

antonyms occasional, rare, unusual.

customer *n.* buyer, client, consumer, habitué, patron, prospect, punter, purchaser, regular, shopper, vendee.

cut *v.* abbreviate, abridge, avoid, bisect, carve, castrate, chip, chisel, chop, cleave, clip, cold-shoulder, condense, contract, cross, curtail, decrease, delete, dissect, divide, dock, edit, engrave, excise, fashion, fell, form, gash, gather, gride, grieve, hack, harvest, hew, hurt, ignore, incise, insult, interrupt, intersect, lacerate, lop, lower, mow, nick, notch, pain, pare, part, penetrate, pierce, précis, prune, rationalize, reap, reduce, saw, scissor, score, sculpt, sculpture, segment, sever, shape, share, shave, shorten, slash, slice, slight, slim, slit, sned, snub, split, spurn, sting, sunder, trim, truncate, whittle, wound.

n. abscission, blow, chop, configuration, cutback, decrease, decrement, diminution, division, economy, fall, fashion, form, gash, graze, groove, incision, incisure, insection, kickback, laceration, look, lowering, mode, nick, percentage, piece, portion, race, rake-off, reduction, rent, rip, saving, section, shape, share, slash, slice, slit, snick, stroke, style, wound.

cut back check, crop, curb, decrease, economize, lessen, lop, lower, prune, reduce, retrench, slash, trim.

cut in interjaculate, interject, interpose, interrupt, intervene, intrude.

cut off abscind, block, disconnect, discontinue, disinherit, disown, end, excide, excise, exscind, halt, intercept, interclude, interrupt, intersect, isolate, obstruct, prescind, renounce, separate, sever, stop, suspend.

cut short abbreviate, abort, arrest, check, crop, curtail, dock, halt, interrupt, postpone, prune, reduce, stop, terminate.

antonym prolong.

cut-throat *n.* assassin, bravo, butcher, executioner, hatchet man, hit-man, homicide, killer, liquidator, murderer, slayer, thug.

adj. barbarous, bloodthirsty, bloody, brutal, competitive, cruel, dog-eat-dog, ferine, ferocious, fierce, homicidal, murderous, relentless, ruthless, savage, thuggish, unprincipled, vicious, violent.

cutting *adj.* acid, acrimonious, barbed, biting, bitter, caustic, chill, hurtful, incisive, keen, malicious, mordant, numbing, penetrating, piercing, pointed, raw, sarcastic, sardonic, scathing, severe, sharp, stinging, trenchant, wounding.

n. bit, cleavage, clipping, piece, scion, scission, slice.

cynical *adj.* contemptuous, derisive, distrustful, ironic, mephistophelian, mephistophilic, misanthropic(al), mocking, mordant, pessimistic, sarcastic, sardonic, sceptical, scoffing, scornful, sharp-tongued, sneering.

D

dab[1] *v.* blot, daub, pat, stipple, swab, tap, touch, wipe.

n. bit, dollop, drop, fingerprint, fleck, flick, pat, peck, smear, smidgen, smudge, speck, spot, stroke, tap, touch, trace.

dab[2] ace, adept, dab hand, dabster, expert, pastmaster, wizard.

dabble *v.* dally, dip, fiddle, guddle, moisten, paddle, potter, spatter, splash, sprinkle, tinker, toy, trifle, wet.

daft *adj.* absurd, asinine, berserk, besotted, crackers, crazy, daffy, delirious, demented, deranged, dop(e)y, doting, dotty, foolish, giddy, hysterical, idiotic, inane, infatuated, insane, lunatic, mad, mental, nuts, nutty, potty, scatty, screwy, silly, simple, stupid, touched, unhinged, witless.

antonyms bright, sane.

daily *adj.* circadian, common, commonplace, customary, day-to-day, diurnal, everyday, normal, ordinary, quotidian, regular, routine.

dainty *adj.* charming, choice, choos(e)y, delectable, delicate, delicious, dinky, elegant, exquisite, fastidious, fine, finical, finicking, finicky, friand(e), fussy, genty, graceful, lickerish, liquorish, meticulous, mignon(ne), mincing, minikin, neat, nice, palatable, particular, petite, pretty, refined, savory, scrupulous, tasty, tender, toothsome.

antonyms clumsy, gross.

n. bonbon, bonne-bouche, delicacy, fancy, sweetmeat, tidbit.

dally *v.* canoodle, dawdle, delay, dilly-dally, fiddle-

faddle, flirt, frivol, linger, loiter, play, procrastinate, sport, tamper, tarry, toy, trifle.

antonyms hasten, hurry.

dam *n.* an(n)icut, barrage, barrier, blockage, embankment, hindrance, obstruction, wall.

v. barricade, block, check, choke, confine, obstruct, restrict, stanch, staunch, stem.

damage *n.* destruction, detriment, devastation, disprofit, harm, hurt, impairment, injury, loss, mischief, mutilation, scathe, suffering.

antonym repair.

v. deface, harm, hurt, impair, incapacitate, injure, mar, mutilate, play havoc with, play hell with, ruin, spoil, tamper with, weaken, wreck.

antonyms fix, repair.

dame *n.* baroness, broad, dowager, female, lady, matron, noblewoman, peeress, woman.

damn *v.* abuse, anathematize, blaspheme, blast, castigate, censure, condemn, criticize, curse, dang, darn, dash, denounce, denunciate, doom, excoriate, execrate, imprecate, pan, revile, sentence, slam, slate, swear.

antonym bless.

n. brass farthing, darn, dash, hoot, iota, jot, monkey's, tinker's cuss, two hoots, whit.

damnable *adj.* abominable, accursed, atrocious, culpable, cursed, despicable, detestable, execrable, hateful, horrible, iniquitous, offensive, sinful, wicked.

antonyms admirable, praiseworthy.

damp *n.* clamminess, dampness, dankness, dew, drizzle, fog, humidity, mist, moisture, muzziness, vapor, wet.

antonym dryness.

adj. clammy, dank, dewy, dripping, drizzly, humid, misty, moist, muggish, muggy, sodden, soggy, sopping, vaporous, vaporish, vapory, wet.

antonyms arid, dry.

v. allay, bedew, check, chill, cool, curb, dampen, dash, deaden, deject, depress, diminish, discourage, dispirit, dull, inhibit, moderate, moisten, restrain, stifle, wet.

antonym dry.

dampen *v.* bedew, besprinkle, check, dash, deaden, decrease, depress, deter, diminish, dishearten, dismay, dull, lessen, moderate, moisten, muffle, reduce, restrain, smother, spray, stifle, wet.

antonyms dry, encourage.

dance *v.* caper, frolic, gambol, hoof it, hop, jig, juke, kantikoy, prance, rock, skip, spin, stomp, sway, swing, tread a measure, whirl.

n. bal masqué, bal paré, ball, hop, kantikoy, kick-up, knees-up, prom, shindig, social.

danger *n.* endangerment, hazard, insecurity, jeopardy, liability, menace, peril, precariousness, risk, threat, trouble, venture, vulnerability.

antonyms safety, security.

dangerous *adj.* alarming, breakneck, chancy, critical, daring, exposed, grave, hairy, harmful, hazardous, insecure, menacing, nasty, parlous, perilous, precarious, reckless, risky, serious, severe, threatening, tickly, treacherous, ugly, unsafe, vulnerable.

antonyms harmless, safe, secure.

dangle *v.* droop, flap, flaunt, flourish, hang, lure, sway, swing, tantalize, tempt, trail, wave.

dank *adj.* chilly, clammy, damp, dewy, dripping, moist, rheumy, slimy, soggy.

antonym dry.

dapper *adj.* active, brisk, chic, dainty, natty, neat,

nimble, smart, spiffy, spruce, spry, stylish, trig, trim, well-dressed, well-groomed.

antonyms dishevelled, dowdy, scruffy, shabby, sloppy.

dappled *adj.* bespeckled, brindled, checkered, dotted, flecked, freckled, mottled, piebald, pied, speckled, spotted, stippled, variegated.

dare *v.* adventure, brave, challenge, defy, endanger, gamble, goad, have the gall, hazard, presume, provoke, risk, stake, taunt, venture.

n. challenge, gauntlet, provocation, taunt.

daredevil *n.* adventurer, desperado, exhibitionist, Hotspur, madcap, stuntman.

antonym coward.

adj. adventurous, audacious, bold, daring, death-defying, fearless, madcap, rash, reckless.

antonyms cautious, prudent, timid.

daring *adj.* adventurous, audacious, bold, brave, brazen, dauntless, fearless, game, impulsive, intrepid, plucky, rash, reckless, valiant, venturesome.

antonyms afraid, timid.

n. audacity, boldness, bottle, bravery, bravura, courage, defiance, derring-do, fearlessness, gall, grit, guts, intrepidity, nerve, pluck, prowess, rashness, spirit, spunk, temerity.

antonyms cowardice, timidity.

dark *adj.* abstruse, angry, aphotic, arcane, atrocious, benighted, black, bleak, brunette, caliginous, cheerless, cloudy, concealed, cryptic, damnable, darkling, dark-skinned, darksome, deep, dim, dingy, dismal, doleful, dour, drab, dusky, ebony, enigmatic, evil, forbidding, foul, frowning, gloomy, glowering, glum, grim, hellish, hidden, horrible, ignorant, indistinct, infamous, infernal, joyless, lightless, melanic, melanous, midnight, mirk, mirky, morbid, morose, mournful, murk, murky, mysterious, mystic, nefarious, obscure, occult, ominous, overcast, pitch-black, pitchy, puzzling, recondite, sable, satanic, scowling, secret, shadowy, shady, sinful, sinister, somber, sulky, sullen, sunless, swarthy, tenebr(i)ous, threatening, uncultivated, unenlightened, unillumed, unilluminated, unlettered, unlit, vile, wicked.

antonyms bright, happy, light, lucid.

n. concealment, darkness, dimness, dusk, evening, gloom, ignorance, mirk, mirkiness, murk, murkiness, night, nightfall, night-time, obscurity, secrecy, twilight, yin.

antonyms brightness, light.

darling *n.* acushla, apple of one's eye, asthore, beloved, blue-eyed boy, dear, dearest, fair-haired boy, favorite, jo(e), lady-love, love, lovey, machree, mavourneen, minikin, pet, poppet, sweetheart, true-love.

adj. adored, beloved, cherished, dear, precious, treasured, white-headed.

dart *v.* bound, cast, dartle, dash, flash, fling, flit, fly, hurl, launch, propel, race, run, rush, scoot, send, shoot, sling, spring, sprint, start, tear, throw, whistle, whizz.

n. arrow, barb, bolt, flight, shaft.

dash[1] *v.* abash, blight, break, cast, chagrin, confound, crash, dampen, destroy, ding, disappoint, discomfort, discourage, fling, foil, frustrate, hurl, ruin, shatter, shiver, slam, sling, smash, splinter, spoil, throw, thwart.

n. bit, bravura, brio, da(u)d, drop, élan, flair, flavor, flourish, hint, little, panache, pinch, smack, soupçon,

spirit, sprinkling, style, suggestion, tinge, touch, verve, vigor, vivacity.

dash[2] *v.* be off like a shot, bolt, bound, dart, dartle, fly, haste(n), hurry, race, run, rush, speed, spring, sprint, tear.

n. bolt, dart, race, run, rush, sprint, spurt.

dashing *adj.* bold, dapper, daring, dazzling, debonair, doggy, elegant, exuberant, flamboyant, gallant, impressive, jaunty, lively, plucky, showy, smart, spirited, sporty, stylish, swashbuckling, swish.

antonym drab.

dastardly *adj.* base, caitiff, contemptible, cowardly, craven, despicable, faint-hearted, lily-livered, low, mean, niddering, pusillanimous, recreant, sneaking, sneaky, spiritless, timorous, underhand, vile.

antonyms heroic, noble.

data *n.* details, documents, dope, facts, figures, info, information, input, materials, statistics.

date[1] *n.* age, epoch, era, period, point, point in time, stage, time.

date[2] *n.* appointment, assignation, engagement, escort, friend, meeting, partner, rendezvous, steady, tryst.

dated *adj.* antiquated, archaic, démodé, obsolescent, obsolete, old hat, old-fashioned, out, outdated, outmoded, out-of-date, passé, superseded, unfashionable.

antonyms fashionable, up-to-the-minute.

daub *v.* begrime, besmear, blur, coat, cover, dedaub, deface, dirty, gaum, grime, paint, plaster, smear, smirch, smudge, spatter, splatter, stain, sully.

n. blot, blotch, smear, splash, splodge, splotch, spot, stain.

daunt *v.* alarm, appal, cow, deter, discourage, dishearten, dismay, dispirit, frighten, intimidate, overawe, put off, scare, shake, subdue, terrify, unnerve.

antonyms encourage, hearten.

dauntless *adj.* bold, brave, courageous, daring, doughty, fearless, gallant, game, heroic, indomitable, intrepid, lion-hearted, plucky, resolute, stout-hearted, undaunted, unflinching, valiant, valorous.

antonyms discouraged, disheartened.

dawn *n.* advent, aurora, beginning, birth, cockcrow(ing), dawning, daybreak, daylight, day-peep, dayspring, emergence, genesis, inception, morning, onset, origin, outset, peep of day, rise, start, sunrise, sun-up.

antonyms dusk, sundown, sunset.

v. appear, begin, break, brighten, develop, emerge, gleam, glimmer, hit, initiate, lighten, occur, open, originate, register, rise, strike, unfold.

daydream *n.* castles in Spain, castles in the air, dream, dwa(l)m, fantasy, figment, fond hope, imagining, musing, phantasm, pipe dream, reverie, star-gazing, vision, wish, wool-gathering.

v. dream, fancy, fantasize, hallucinate, imagine, muse, stargaze.

daze *v.* amaze, astonish, astound, befog, benumb, bewilder, blind, confuse, dazzle, dumbfound, flabbergast, numb, paralyze, perplex, shock, stagger, startle, stun, stupefy, surprise.

n. bewilderment, confusion, distraction, dwa(l)m, shock, stupor, trance.

dazzle *v.* amaze, astonish, awe, bedazzle, blind, blur, confuse, daze, fascinate, hypnotize, impress, overawe, overpower, overwhelm, scintillate, sparkle, stupefy.

dead[1] *adj.* ad patres, apathetic, barren, boring, breath-

less, callous, cold, dead-and-alive, dead-beat, deceased, defunct, departed, dull, exhausted, extinct, flat, frigid, glassy, glazed, gone, inactive, inanimate, indifferent, inert, inoperative, insipid, late, lifeless, lukewarm, napoo, numb, obsolete, paralyzed, perished, spent, spiritless, stagnant, stale, sterile, stiff, still, tasteless, tired, torpid, unemployed, uninteresting, unprofitable, unresponsive, useless, vapid, wooden, worn out.
antonyms active, alive, animated.

dead² *adj.* absolute, complete, downright, entire, outright, perfect, thorough, total, unqualified, utter.
adv. absolutely, completely, entirely, exactly, perfectly, quite, totally.

deaden *v.* abate, allay, alleviate, anesthetize, benumb, blunt, check, cushion, damp, dampen, desensitize, diminish, dull, hush, impair, lessen, muffle, mute, numb, obtund, paralyze, quieten, reduce, smother, stifle, suppress, weaken.
antonym enliven.

deadlock *n.* halt, impasse, stalemate, standstill.

deadly *adj.* accurate, ashen, baleful, baneful, boring, cruel, dangerous, death-dealing, deathful, deathlike, deathly, destructive, devastating, dull, effective, exact, fatal, feral, funest, ghastly, ghostly, grim, implacable, lethal, malignant, monotonous, mortal, noxious, pallid, pernicious, pestilent, poisonous, precise, ruthless, savage, sure, tedious, thanatoid, true, unerring, unfailing, uninteresting, unrelenting, venomous, wearisome, white.
antonyms harmless, healthy.

deaf *adj.* hard of hearing, heedless, indifferent, oblivious, stone-deaf, unconcerned, unmindful, unmoved.
antonyms aware, conscious.

deafening *adj.* booming, dinning, ear-piercing, ear-splitting, fortissimo, piercing, resounding, ringing, roaring, thunderous.
antonyms pianissimo, quiet.

deal *v.* allot, apportion, assign, bargain, bestow, dispense, distribute, divide, dole out, give, mete out, negotiate, reward, sell, share, stock, trade, traffic, treat.
n. agreement, amount, arrangement, bargain, buy, contract, degree, distribution, extent, hand, pact, portion, quantity, round, share, transaction, understanding.

dear *adj.* beloved, cherished, close, costly, darling, esteemed, expensive, familiar, favorite, high-priced, intimate, loved, overpriced, precious, pric(e)y, prized, respected, treasured, valued.
antonyms cheap, hateful.
n. angel, beloved, darling, dearie, deary, loved one, precious, treasure.

dearth *n.* absence, barrenness, deficiency, exiguousness, famine, inadequacy, insufficiency, lack, need, paucity, poverty, scantiness, scarcity, shortage, sparseness, sparsity, want.
antonyms abundance, excess.

death *n.* annihilation, bane, bereavement, cessation, curtains, decease, demise, departure, destruction, dissolution, dormition, downfall, dying, end, eradication, exit, expiration, extermination, extinction, fatality, finish, grave, loss, obliteration, passing, quietus, release, ruin, ruination, undoing.
antonyms birth, life.

debase *v.* abase, adulterate, allay, bastardize, cheapen, contaminate, corrupt, defile, degrade, demean, depreciate, devalue, diminish, disgrace, dishonor,

embase, humble, humiliate, impair, lower, pollute, reduce, shame, taint, vitiate.
antonyms elevate, upgrade.

debate *v.* argue, cogitate, consider, contend, contest, controvert, deliberate, discuss, dispute, logicize, meditate on, mull over, ponder, question, reflect, revolve, ruminate, weigh, wrangle.
antonym agree.
n. altercation, argument, cogitation, consideration, contention, controversy, deliberation, discussion, disputation, dispute, meditation, polemic, quodlibet, reflection.
antonym agreement.

debauched *adj.* abandoned, corrupt, corrupted, debased, degenerate, degraded, depraved, dissipated, dissolute, immoral, intemperate, lewd, licentious, perverted, profligate, raddled, rakehell, rakehelly, wanton.
antonyms decent, pure, virtuous.

debonair *adj.* affable, breezy, buoyant, charming, cheerful, courteous, dashing, elegant, gay, jaunty, lighthearted, refined, smooth, sprightly, suave, urbane, well-bred.

debris *n.* bits, brash, detritus, drift, dross, duff, eluvium, exuviae, fragments, litter, moraine, pieces, remains, rubbish, rubble, ruins, sweepings, trash, waste, wreck, wreckage.

debt *n.* arrears, bill, claim, commitment, debit, due, duty, indebtedness, liability, obligation, score, sin.
antonyms asset, credit.

decay *v.* atrophy, canker, corrode, crumble, decline, decompose, decompound, degenerate, deteriorate, disintegrate, dissolve, dote, dwindle, mortify, molder, perish, putrefy, rot, shrivel, sink, spoil, wane, waste away, wear away, wither.
antonyms flourish, grow, ripen.
n. atrophy, caries, collapse, consenescence, decadence, decline, decomposition, decrepitness, decrepitude, degeneracy, degeneration, deterioration, disintegration, dying, fading, failing, gangrene, labefactation, labefaction, mortification, perishing, putrefaction, putrescence, putridity, putridness, rot, rotting, wasting, withering.

deceased *adj.* dead, defunct, departed, expired, extinct, finished, former, gone, late, lifeless, lost.
n. dead, decedent, departed.

deceit *n.* abuse, artifice, blind, cheat, cheating, chicanery, con, cozenage, craftiness, cunning, deceitfulness, deception, dissimulation, double-dealing, duplicity, fake, feint, fraud, fraudulence, guile, hypocrisy, imposition, imposture, misrepresentation, pretense, ruse, sham, shift, slyness, stratagem, subterfuge, swindle, treachery, trick, trickery, underhandedness, wile..
antonyms honesty, openness.

deceitful *adj.* collusive, counterfeit, crafty, deceiving, deceptive, designing, dishonest, disingenuous, double-dealing, duplicitous, elusory, fallacious, false, fraudulent, guileful, hypocritical, illusory, insincere, knavish, prestigious, Punic, rusé, sneaky, treacherous, tricky, two-faced, underhand, untrustworthy.
antonyms honest, open, trustworthy.

deceive *v.* abuse, bamboozle, befool, beguile, betray, camouflage, cheat, cog, con, cozen, delude, diddle, disappoint, dissemble, dissimulate, double-cross, dupe, ensnare, entrap, flam, fool, gag, gammon, gull, have on, hoax, hoodwink, impose upon, lead on, mislead, outwit, seel, swindle, take for a ride, take in, trick, two-time.

antonym enlighten.

decency *n.* appropriateness, civility, correctness, courtesy, decorum, etiquette, fitness, good form, good manners, helpfulness, modesty, propriety, respectability, seemliness, thoughtfulness.

antonyms discourtesy, indecency.

decent *adj.* acceptable, accommodating, adequate, ample, appropriate, average, becoming, befitting, chaste, comely, comme il faut, competent, courteous, decorous, delicate, fair, fit, fitting, friendly, generous, gracious, gradely, helpful, kind, modest, nice, obliging, passable, polite, presentable, proper, pure, reasonable, respectable, satisfactory, seemly, sufficient, suitable, thoughtful, tolerable.

antonyms disobliging, indecent, poor.

deception *n.* artifice, bluff, cheat, conning, craftiness, cunning, deceitfulness, deceit, deceptiveness, decoy, defraudation, defraudment, dissembling, dissimulation, duplicity, false-pretences, feint, flim-flam, fraud, fraudulence, guile, gullery, hoax, hype, hypocrisy, illusion, imposition, imposture, insincerity, legerdemain, leg-pull, lie, ruse, sell, sham, snare, stratagem, subterfuge, take-in, treachery, trick, trickery, wile.

antonyms artlessness, openness.

deceptive *adj.* ambiguous, catchy, delusive, delusory, dishonest, elusory, fake, fallacious, false, fraudulent, illusive, illusory, misleading, mock, specious, spurious, unreliable.

antonyms artless, genuine, open.

decide *v.* adjudge, adjudicate, choose, conclude, decree, determine, dijudicate, elect, end, fix, judge, opt, purpose, reach a decision, resolve, settle.

decipher *v.* construe, crack, decode, decrypt, deduce, explain, figure out, interpret, make out, read, solve, transliterate, uncipher, understand, unfold, unravel, unscramble.

antonym encode.

decision *n.* arbitrament, arbitration, arrêt, conclusion, decisiveness, determination, fetwa, finding, firmness, judgment, outcome, parti, purpose, purposefulness, resoluteness, resolution, resolve, result, ruling, settlement, verdict.

decisive *adj.* absolute, conclusive, critical, crucial, crunch, decided, definite, definitive, determinate, determined, fateful, final, firm, forceful, forthright, incisive, influential, momentous, positive, resolute, significant, strong-minded, supreme, trenchant.

antonyms indecisive, insignificant.

declaration *n.* acknowledgment, affirmation, announcement, assertion, asseveration, attestation, averment, avouchment, avowal, deposition, disclosure, edict, manifesto, notification, proclamation, profession, promulgation, pronouncement, pronunciamento, protestation, revelation, statement, testimony.

declare *v.* affirm, announce, assert, attest, aver, avouch, avow, certify, claim, confess, confirm, convey, disclose, maintain, manifest, nuncupate, proclaim, profess, pronounce, reveal, show, state, swear, testify, validate, witness.

decline[1] *v.* avoid, balk, decay, decrease, degenerate, deny, deteriorate, deviate, diminish, droop, dwindle, ebb, fade, fail, fall, fall off, flag, forgo, languish, lessen,

pine, refuse, reject, shrink, sink, turn down, wane, weaken, worsen.

n. abatement, consumption, decay, declension, decrepitude, degeneration, deterioration, deviation, diminution, downturn, dwindling, enfeeblement, failing, falling-off, lessening, paracme, phthisis, recession, senility, slump, tuberculosis, weakening, worsening.

decline[2] *v.* descend, dip, sink, slant, slope.

n. brae, declination, declivity, descent, deviation, dip, divergence, hill, incline, obliqueness, obliquity, slope.

decompose *v.* analyze, atomize, break down, break up, crumble, decay, decompound, degrade, disintegrate, dissolve, distil, fall apart, fester, fractionate, putrefy, rot, separate, spoil.

antonyms combine, unite.

decorate[1] *v.* adorn, beautify, bedeck, color, deck, do up, embellish, enrich, furbish, grace, impearl, miniate, ornament, paint, paper, prettify, renovate, tart up, trick out, trim, wallpaper.

decorate[2] *v.* bemedal, cite, crown, garland, honor.

decoration[1] *n.* adornment, arabesque, bauble, beautification, curlicue, elaboration, embellishment, enrichment, falderal, flounce, flourish, frill, frou-frou, furbelow, garnish, ornament, ornamentation, pass(e)ment, passementerie, scroll, spangle, trimming, trinket.

decoration[2] *n.* award, badge, colors, crown, emblem, garland, garter, laurel, laurel-wreath, medal, order, ribbon, star.

decoy *n.* attraction, bait, ensnarement, enticement, inducement, lure, pretence, roper(-in), trap.

v. allure, attract, bait, beguile, deceive, draw, ensnare, entice, entrap, inveigle, lead, lure, seduce, tempt.

decrease *v.* abate, ablate, contract, curtail, cut down, decline, diminish, drop, dwindle, ease, fall off, lessen, lower, peter out, reduce, shrink, slacken, slim, subside, taper, wane.

antonym increase.

n. abatement, ablation, contraction, cutback, decline, decrement, degression, diminution, downturn, dwindling, ebb, falling-off, lessening, loss, reduction, shrinkage, step-down, subsidence.

antonym increase.

decree *n.* act, command, decretal, dictum, edict, enactment, firman, hatti-sherif, indiction, interlocution, interlocutor, law, mandate, order, ordinance, precept, proclamation, regulation, ruling, statute, ukase.

v. command, decide, determine, dictate, enact, lay down, ordain, order, prescribe, proclaim, pronounce, rescript, rule.

decrepit *adj.* aged, antiquated, battered, broken-backed, broken-down, crippled, debilitated, deteriorated, dilapidated, doddering, doddery, feeble, frail, incapacitated, infirm, ramshackle, rickety, run-down, superannuated, tumble-down, warby, wasted, weak, worn-out.

antonyms fit, well-cared-for, youthful.

decry *v.* abuse, belittle, blame, censure, condemn, criticize, cry down, declaim against, denounce, depreciate, derogate, detract, devalue, discredit, disparage, inveigh against, rail against, run down, traduce, underestimate, underrate, undervalue.

antonyms praise, value.

dedicate *v.* address, assign, bless, commit, consecrate, devote, give over to, hallow, inscribe, offer, pledge, present, sacrifice, sanctify, set apart, surrender.

dedicated *adj.* committed, devoted, enthusiastic, given

over to, purposeful, single-hearted, single-minded, sworn, whole-hearted, zealous.
antonyms apathetic, uncommitted.

deduct *v.* decrease by, knock off, reduce by, remove, subduct, subtract, take away, withdraw.
antonym add.

deed[1] *n.* achievement, act, action, exploit, fact, factum, feat, gest(e), performance, reality, truth.

deed[2] *n.* contract, document, indenture, instrument, record, title, transaction.

deem *v.* account, adjudge, believe, conceive, consider, esteem, estimate, hold, imagine, judge, reckon, regard, suppose, think.

deep *adj.* absorbed, abstract, abstruse, abyssal, acute, arcane, artful, astute, bass, booming, bottomless, broad, canny, cryptic, cunning, dark, designing, devious, discerning, engrossed, esoteric, extreme, far, fathomless, full-toned, grave, great, hidden, immersed, insidious, intense, knowing, learned, lost, low, low-pitched, mysterious, obscure, penetrating, preoccupied, profound, rapt, recondite, resonant, rich, sagacious, scheming, secret, shrewd, sonorous, strong, unfathomable, unfathomed, unplumbed, unsoundable, unsounded, vivid, wide, wise, yawning.
antonyms open, shallow.
n. briny, drink, high seas, main, ocean, sea.

deface *v.* blemish, damage, deform, destroy, disfeature, disfigure, impair, injure, mar, mutilate, obliterate, spoil, sully, tarnish, vandalize.
antonym repair.

defamation *n.* aspersion, calumny, denigration, derogation, disparagement, innuendo, libel, mud-slinging, obloquy, opprobrium, scandal, slander, slur, smear, traducement, vilification.
antonym praise.

default *n.* absence, defalcation, defect, deficiency, dereliction, failure, fault, lack, lapse, neglect, non-payment, omission, want.
v. backslide, bilk, defraud, dodge, evade, fail, levant, neglect, rat, swindle, welsh.

defeat *v.* baffle, balk, beat, best, checkmate, clobber, confound, conquer, counteract, crush, disappoint, discomfit, down, foil, frustrate, get the better of, outbargain, overpower, overthrow, overwhelm, psych out, quell, repulse, rout, ruin, stump, subdue, subjugate, tank, thump, thwart, trounce, vanquish, vote down, whop.
n. beating, conquest, débâcle, disappointment, discomfiture, failure, frustration, overthrow, rebuff, repulse, reverse, rout, setback, thwarting, trouncing, vanquishment, Waterloo.

defect *n.* absence, blemish, bug, default, deficiency, error, failing, fault, flaw, frailty, hamartia, imperfection, inadequacy, lack, mistake, shortcoming, spot, taint, want, weakness.
v. apostatize, break faith, desert, rebel, renegue, revolt, tergiversate.

defective *adj.* abnormal, broken, deficient, faulty, flawed, imperfect, inadequate, incomplete, insufficient, kaput, out of order, retarded, scant, short, subnormal.
antonyms normal, operative.

defend *n.* assert, bulwark, champion, contest, cover, endorse, espouse, fortify, guard, justify, maintain, plead, preserve, protect, safeguard, screen, secure,

shelter, shield, speak up for, stand by, stand up for, support, sustain, uphold, vindicate, watch over.
antonym attack.

defensive *adj.* apologetic, aposematic, averting, cautious, defending, opposing, protective, safeguarding, self-justifying, wary, watchful, withstanding.
antonym bold.

defer[1] *v.* adjourn, delay, hold over, postpone, procrastinate, prorogue, protract, put off, put on ice, shelve, suspend, waive.

defer[2] *v.* accede, bow, capitulate, comply, give way, kowtow, respect, submit, yield.

deference *n.* acquiescence, attention, capitulation, civility, complaisance, compliance, consideration, courtesy, esteem, homage, honor, morigeration, obedience, obeisance, obsequiousness, politeness, regard, respect, reverence, submission, submissiveness, thoughtfulness, veneration, yielding.

defiant *adj.* aggressive, audacious, bold, challenging, contumacious, daring, disobedient, insolent, insubordinate, intransigent, mutinous, obstinate, provocative, rebellious, recalcitrant, refractory, truculent, uncooperative.
antonyms acquiescent, submissive.

deficient *adj.* defectible, defective, exiguous, faulty, flawed, impaired, imperfect, inadequate, incomplete, inferior, insufficient, lacking, meager, scanty, scarce, short, skimpy, unsatisfactory, wanting, weak.
antonyms excessive, superfluous.

defile[1] *v.* abuse, befoul, besmirch, contaminate, corrupt, debase, deflower, defoul, degrade, desecrate, dirty, disgrace, dishonor, inquinate, make foul, molest, pollute, profane, rape, ravish, seduce, smear, soil, stain, sully, taint, tarnish, violate, vitiate.
antonym cleanse.

defile[2] *n.* gorge, gulch, gully, pass, passage, ravine.

define *v.* bound, characterize, circumscribe, delimit, delimitate, delineate, demarcate, describe, designate, detail, determine, explain, expound, interpret, limit, mark out, outline, specify, spell out.

definite *adj.* assured, certain, clear, clear-cut, decided, determined, exact, explicit, express, fixed, guaranteed, marked, obvious, particular, positive, precise, settled, specific, substantive, sure.
antonyms indefinite, vague.

definitely *adv.* absolutely, beyond doubt, categorically, certainly, clearly, decidedly, doubtless, doubtlessly, easily, finally, indeed, indubitably, obviously, plainly, positively, surely, undeniably, unequivocally, unmistakably, unquestionably, without doubt, without fail.

definition[1] *n.* clarification, delimitation, delineation, demarcation, description, determination, elucidation, explanation, exposition, interpretation, outlining, settling.

definition[2] *n.* clarity, clearness, contrast, distinctness, focus, precision, sharpness.

deft *adj.* able, adept, adroit, agile, clever, dexterous, expert, feat, habile, handy, neat, nifty, nimble, proficient, skilful.
antonym clumsy.

defunct *adj.* dead, deceased, departed, expired, extinct, gone, inoperative, invalid, kaput, non-existent, obsolete, passé.
antonyms alive, live, operative.

defy *v.* baffle, beard, beat, brave, challenge, confront,

contemn, dare, defeat, despise, disregard, elude, face, flout, foil, frustrate, outdare, provoke, repel, repulse, resist, scorn, slight, spurn, thwart, withstand.
antonyms flinch, quail, yield.

degenerate *adj.* base, corrupt, debased, debauched, decadent, degenerated, degraded, depraved, deteriorated, dissolute, effete, fallen, immoral, low, mean, perverted.
antonyms upright, virtuous.
v. age, decay, decline, decrease, deteriorate, fall off, lapse, regress, retrogress, rot, sink, slip, worsen.
antonym improve.

degrade *v.* abase, adulterate, break, brutalize, cashier, cheapen, corrupt, debase, declass, demean, demote, depose, deprive, deteriorate, discredit, disennoble, disgrace, disgrade, dishonor, disrank, disrate, downgrade, embase, humble, humiliate, impair, injure, lower, pervert, shame, unfrock, ungown, vitiate, weaken.
antonyms enhance, improve.

degree *n.* caliber, class, division, doctorate, extent, gradation, grade, intensity, interval, level, limit, mark, masterate, measure, notch, order, point, position, proportion, quality, quantity, range, rank, rate, ratio, run, scale, scope, severity, stage, standard, standing, station, status, step, unit.

deign *v.* condescend, consent, demean oneself, lower oneself, stoop, vouchsafe.

dejected *adj.* abattu, alamort, blue, cast down, crestfallen, depressed, despondent, disconsolate, disheartened, dismal, doleful, down, downcast, downhearted, gloomy, glum, jaw-fallen, low, low-spirited, melancholy, miserable, morose, sad, spiritless, woebegone, wretched.
antonyms bright, happy, high-spirited.

delectable *adj.* adorable, agreeable, ambrosial, ambrosian, appetizing, charming, dainty, delicious, delightful, enjoyable, enticing, flavorsome, gratifying, inviting, luscious, lush, palatable, pleasant, pleasurable, satisfying, scrumptious, tasty, toothsome, yummy.
antonyms horrid, unpleasant.

delegate *n.* agent, ambassador, commissioner, deputy, envoy, legate, messenger, nuncio, representative.
v. accredit, appoint, assign, authorize, charge, commission, consign, depute, designate, devolve, empower, entrust, give, hand over, mandate, name, nominate, pass on, relegate, transfer.

delete *v.* blot out, blue-pencil, cancel, cross out, dele, edit, edit out, efface, erase, expunge, obliterate, remove, rub out, strike, strike out.
antonym add in.

deleterious *adj.* bad, damaging, destructive, detrimental, harmful, hurtful, injurious, noxious, pernicious, prejudicial, ruinous.
antonyms enhancing, helpful.

deliberate *v.* cogitate, consider, consult, debate, discuss, meditate, mull over, ponder, reflect, ruminate, think, weigh.
adj. advised, calculated, careful, cautious, circumspect, conscious, considered, designed, heedful, intentional, measured, methodical, planned, ponderous, prearranged, premeditated, prudent, purposeful, slow, studied, thoughtful, unhurried, volitive, voulu, wary, wilful, willed, witting.
antonyms chance, unintentional.

delicate *adj.* accurate, ailing, careful, choice, considerate, critical, dainty, debilitated, deft, delicious, detailed, diaphanous, difficult, diplomatic, discreet, discriminating, eggshell, elegant, elfin, exquisite, faint, fastidious, fine, flimsy, fragile, frail, friand(e), gauzy, graceful, hazardous, kid-glove, minikin, minute, muted, pastel, precarious, precise, prudish, pure, refined, risky, savory, scrupulous, sensible, sensitive, sickly, skilled, slender, slight, soft, softly-softly, squeamish, sticky, subdued, subtle, tactful, tender, ticklish, touchy, weak.
antonyms harsh, imprecise, strong.

delicious *adj.* agreeable, ambrosial, ambrosian, appetizing, charming, choice, dainty, delectable, delightful, enjoyable, entertaining, exquisite, flavorsome, goluptious, luscious, mouthwatering, nectareous, palatable, pleasant, pleasing, savory, scrummy, scrumptious, tasty, toothsome, yummy.
antonym unpleasant.

delight *n.* bliss, ecstasy, enjoyment, felicity, gladness, gratification, happiness, heaven, joy, jubilation, pleasure, rapture, transport.
antonyms dismay, displeasure.
v. amuse, charm, cheer, divert, enchant, gladden, gratify, please, ravish, rejoice, satisfy, thrill, tickle.
antonyms dismay, displease.

delightful *adj.* agreeable, amusing, captivating, charming, congenial, delectable, delightsome, enchanting, engaging, enjoyable, entertaining, fascinating, fetching, gratifying, heavenly, pleasant, pleasing, pleasurable, rapturous, ravishing, scrummy, scrumptious, sweet, thrilling, wizard.
antonym horrible.

delirious *adj.* bacchic, beside oneself, corybantic, crazy, demented, deranged, ecstatic, excited, frantic, frenzied, hysterical, incoherent, insane, light-headed, mad, maenadic, raving, unhinged, wild.
antonym sane.

deliver *v.* acquit, administer, aim, announce, bear, bring, carry, cart, cede, commit, convey, deal, declare, direct, discharge, dispense, distribute, emancipate, feed, free, give, give forth, give up, grant, hand over, inflict, launch, liberate, loose, make over, pass, present, proclaim, pronounce, publish, ransom, read, redeem, release, relinquish, rescue, resign, save, strike, supply, surrender, throw, transfer, transport, turn over, utter, yield.

deluge *n.* avalanche, barrage, cataclysm, downpour, flood, hail, inundation, rush, spate, torrent.
v. bury, douse, drench, drown, engulf, flood, inundate, overload, overrun, overwhelm, soak, submerge, swamp.

delusion *n.* deception, error, fallacy, fancy, fata Morgana, hallucination, illusion, mirage, misapprehension, misbelief, misconception, mistake, phantasm.

demand *v.* ask, call for, challenge, claim, exact, expect, inquire, insist on, interrogate, involve, necessitate, need, order, question, request, require, take, want.
antonyms cede, supply.
n. bidding, call, charge, claim, desire, inquiry, interrogation, necessity, need, order, question, request, requirement, requisition, want.
antonym supply.

demean *v.* abase, condescend, debase, degrade, deign, descend, humble, lower, stoop.

antonym enhance.

demeanor *n.* air, bearing, behavior, carriage, comportment, conduct, deportment, manner, mien, port.

demented *adj.* crazed, crazy, deranged, distracted, distraught, dotty, foolish, frenzied, idiotic, insane, lunatic, mad, maenadic, maniacal, manic, non compos mentis, nutty, unbalanced, unhinged.

antonym sane.

demolish *v.* annihilate, bulldoze, consume, defeat, destroy, devour, dilapidate, dismantle, down, eat, flatten, gobble, gulp, guzzle, knock down, level, overthrow, overturn, pull down, pulverize, raze, ruin, tear down, unbuild, undo, wreck.

antonym build up.

demolition *n.* bulldozing, destruction, dismantling, leveling, razing, wrecking.

demon[1] *n.* afrit, daemon, daimon, devil, evil spirit, fallen angel, fiend, genius, goblin, guardian spirit, incubus, monster, numen, rakshas, rakshasa, succubus, villain, warlock.

demon[2] *n.* ace, addict, dab hand, fanatic, fiend, master, pastmaster, wizard.

demonstrate[1] *v.* describe, display, establish, evidence, evince, exhibit, explain, expound, illustrate, indicate, manifest, prove, show, substantiate, teach, testify to.

demonstrate[2] *v.* march, parade, picket, protest, rally, sit in.

demonstration[1] *n.* affirmation, confirmation, deixis, description, display, evidence, exhibition, explanation, exposition, expression, illustration, manifestation, presentation, proof, substantiation, test, testimony, trial, validation.

demonstration[2] *v.* demo, march, parade, picket, protest, rally, sit-in, work-in.

demur *v.* balk, cavil, disagree, dispute, dissent, doubt, hesitate, object, pause, protest, refuse, take exception, waver.

n. arrière pensée, compunction, demurral, demurrer, dissent, hesitation, misgiving, objection, protest, qualm, reservation, scruple.

demure *adj.* coy, decorous, diffident, grave, maidenly, modest, priggish, prim, prissy, prudish, reserved, reticent, retiring, sedate, shy, sober, staid, strait-laced.

antonym forward.

den *n.* cave, cavern, cloister, cubby-hole, earth, haunt, hide-away, hide-out, hole, lair, retreat, sanctuary, sanctum, set(t), shelter, study.

denial *n.* abjuration, abnegation, contradiction, denegation, disaffirmance, disaffirmation, disavowal, disclaimer, dismissal, dissent, gainsay, negation, prohibition, rebuff, refusal, rejection, renunciation, repudiation, repulse, retraction, veto.

denounce *v.* accuse, anathematize, arraign, assail, attack, brand, castigate, censure, condemn, declaim against, decry, denunciate, fulminate, hereticate, impugn, inveigh against, proscribe, revile, stigmatize, vilify, vilipend.

antonym praise.

dense *adj.* blockish, close, close-knit, compact, compressed, condensed, crass, crowded, dull, heavy, impenetrable, jam-packed, obtuse, opaque, packed, slow, slow-witted, solid, stolid, stupid, substantial, thick, thickset, thick-witted.

antonyms clever, sparse.

dent *n.* bang, chip, concavity, crater, depression, dimple, dint, dip, dunt, hollow, impression, indentation, pit.

v. depress, dint, gouge, indent, push in.

deny *v.* abjure, begrudge, contradict, decline, disaffirm, disagree with, disallow, disavow, discard, disclaim, disown, disprove, forbid, gainsay, negative, oppose, rebuff, recant, refuse, refute, reject, renounce, repudiate, revoke, traverse, turn down, veto, withhold.

antonyms admit, allow.

depart *v.* absent oneself, decamp, deviate, differ, digress, disappear, diverge, escape, exit, go, leave, levant, make off, migrate, mizzle, quit, remove, retire, retreat, set forth, stray, swerve, take one's leave, toddle, vanish, vary, veer, withdraw.

antonyms arrive, keep to.

departure *n.* abandonment, branching, branching out, change, decession, deviation, difference, digression, divergence, exit, exodus, going, innovation, leavetaking, leaving, lucky, novelty, removal, retirement, shift, variation, veering, withdrawal.

antonym arrival.

depend on anticipate, bank on, build upon, calculate on, count on, expect, hang on, hinge on, lean on, reckon on, rely upon, rest on, revolve around, trust in, turn to.

dependable *adj.* certain, conscientious, faithful, gilt-edged, honest, reliable, responsible, steady, sure, trustworthy, trusty, unfailing.

antonyms undependable, unreliable.

dependent *adj.* adjective, conditional, contingent, defenceless, depending, determined by, feudal, helpless, immature, liable to, relative, reliant, relying on, subject, subject to, subordinate, tributary, vulnerable, weak.

antonym independent.

depict *v.* caricature, characterize, delineate, describe, detail, draw, illustrate, limn, narrate, outline, paint, picture, portray, render, reproduce, sculpt, sketch, trace.

deplore *v.* abhor, bemoan, bewail, censure, condemn, denounce, deprecate, grieve for, lament, mourn, regret, repent of, rue.

antonym praise.

deport[1] *v.* banish, exile, expatriate, expel, extradite, ostracize, oust.

deport[2] *v.* acquit, act, bear, behave, carry, comport, conduct, hold, manage.

deportment *n.* air, appearance, aspect, bearing, behavior, carriage, cast, comportment, conduct, demeanor, etiquette, manner, mien, pose, posture, stance.

deposit[1] *v.* drop, dump, lay, locate, park, place, precipitate, put, settle, sit.

n. accumulation, alluvium, deposition, dregs, hypostasis, lees, precipitate, sediment, silt.

deposit[2] *v.* amass, bank, consign, depone, entrust, file, hoard, lodge, reposit, save, store.

n. bailment, down payment, instalment, money, part payment, pledge, retainer, security, stake, warranty.

depreciate *v.* belittle, decrease, decry, deflate, denigrate, deride, derogate, detract, devaluate, devalue, disparage, downgrade, drop, fall, lessen, lower, minimize, misprize, reduce, ridicule, scorn, slump, traduce, underestimate, underrate, undervalue.

antonyms appreciate, overrate, praise.

depress *v.* burden, cheapen, chill, damp, daunt, debili-

tate, deject, depreciate, devaluate, devalue, devitalize, diminish, discourage, dishearten, dispirit, downgrade, drain, enervate, engloom, exhaust, flatten, hip, impair, lessen, level, lower, oppress, overburden, press, reduce, sadden, sap, squash, tire, undermine, upset, weaken, weary.
antonym cheer.

depression¹ *n.* blues, cafard, decline, dejection, demission, despair, despondency, doldrums, dolefulness, downheartedness, dullness, dumps, examination, gloominess, glumness, hard times, heart-heaviness, hopelessness, inactivity, low spirits, lowness, mal du siècle, megrims, melancholia, melancholy, panophobia, recession, sadness, slump, stagnation, vapors.
antonyms cheerfulness, prosperity.

depression² *n.* basin, bowl, cavity, concavity, dent, dimple, dint, dip, dish, excavation, fossa, fossula, fovea, foveola, hollow, hollowness, impression, indentation, pit, sag, sink, umbilicus, valley.
antonyms convexity, prominence, protuberance.

deprive *v.* amerce, bereave, denude, deny, despoil, dispossess, divest, expropriate, mulct, rob, starve, strip.
antonym bestow.

deputation *n.* appointment, assignment, commission, delegates, delegation, deputies, deputing, designation, embassy, legation, mission, nomination, representatives.

derelict *adj.* abandoned, deserted, desolate, dilapidated, discarded, forlorn, forsaken, neglected, ruined.
n. dosser, down-and-out, drifter, hobo, outcast, toe-rag, tramp, vagrant, wastrel.

dereliction *n.* abandonment, abdication, apostasy, betrayal, delinquency, desertion, evasion, failure, faithlessness, fault, forsaking, neglect, negligence, relinquishment, remissness, renegation, renunciation.
antonyms devotion, faithfulness, fulfilment.

derision *n.* contempt, contumely, dicacity, disdain, disparagement, disrespect, insult, irrision, laughter, mockery, raillery, ridicule, satire, scoffing, scorn, sneering.
antonym praise.

derivation *n.* acquisition, ancestry, basis, beginning, deduction, descent, etymology, extraction, foundation, genealogy, inference, origin, root, source.

derive *v.* acquire, arise, borrow, collect, crib, deduce, descend, develop, draw, elicit, emanate, extract, flow, follow, gain, gather, get, glean, grow, infer, issue, obtain, originate, proceed, procure, receive, spring, stem, trace.

descend *v.* alight, arrive, assail, assault, attack, condescend, degenerate, dégringoler, deign, derive, deteriorate, develop, dip, dismount, drop, fall, gravitate, incline, invade, issue, leap, originate, plummet, plunge, pounce, proceed, raid, sink, slant, slope, spring, stem, stoop, subside, swoop, tumble.

descendants *n.* children, epigones, epigoni, epigons, family, issue, line, lineage, offspring, posterity, progeny, race, scions, seed, sons and daughters, successors.

describe *v.* characterize, define, delineate, depict, detail, draw, enlarge on, explain, express, illustrate, mark out, narrate, outline, portray, present, recount, relate, report, sketch, specify, tell, trace.

description *n.* account, brand, breed, category, characterization, class, delineation, depiction, detail, expla-

nation, exposition, genre, genus, hypotyposis, ilk, kidney, kind, narration, narrative, order, outline, portrayal, presentation, report, representation, sketch, sort, species, specification, type, variety, word-painting, word-picture.

desecration *n.* blasphemy, debasement, defilement, dishonoring, impiety, insult, invasion, pollution, profanation, sacrilege, violation.

desert¹ *n.* solitude, vacuum, vast, void, waste, wasteland, wilderness, wilds.
adj. arid, bare, barren, desolate, droughty, dry, eremic, infertile, lonely, solitary, sterile, uncultivated, uninhabited, unproductive, untilled, waste, waterless, wild.

desert² *v.* abandon, abscond, apostatize, backslide, betray, decamp, deceive, defect, forsake, give up, jilt, leave, leave in the lurch, maroon, quit, rat on, relinquish, renege, renounce, resign, strand, tergiversate, vacate.

desert³ *n.* come-uppance, demerit, deserts, due, guerdon, meed, merit, payment, recompense, remuneration, requital, retribution, return, reward, right, virtue, worth.

deserter *n.* absconder, apostate, backslider, betrayer, defector, delinquent, escapee, fugitive, rat, renegade, runaway, traitor, truant.

deserve *v.* ask for, earn, gain, incur, justify, merit, procure, rate, warrant, win.

design *n.* aim, arrangement, blueprint, composition, configuration, conformation, conspiracy, construction, contrivance, delineation, draft, drawing, end, enterprise, exemplar, figure, form, goal, guide, intent, intention, intrigue, machination, maneuver, meaning, model, motif, object, objective, organization, outline, pattern, plan, plot, project, prototype, purpose, schema, scheme, shape, sketch, structure, style, target, undertaking.
v. aim, conceive, construct, contrive, create, delineate, describe, destine, develop, devise, draft, draw, draw up, fabricate, fashion, form, intend, invent, make, mean, model, originate, outline, plan, project, propose, purpose, scheme, shape, sketch, structure, tailor, trace.

designate *v.* allot, appoint, assign, bill, call, characterize, choose, christen, code-name, deem, define, delegate, denominate, denote, depute, describe, docket, dub, earmark, entitle, indicate, label, name, nickname, nominate, select, show, specify, stipulate, style, term, ticket, title.

desirable *adj.* adorable, advantageous, advisable, agreeable, alluring, appetible, appropriate, attractive, beneficial, captivating, covetable, eligible, enviable, expedient, fascinating, fetching, good, nubile, pleasing, plummy, preferable, profitable, seductive, sensible, sexy, tempting, worthwhile.
antonyms undesirable.

desire *v.* ask, aspire to, beg, covet, crave, desiderate, entreat, fancy, hanker after, hunger for, importune, lack, long for, need, petition, request, solicit, want, wish for, yearn for.
n. appeal, appetence, appetency, appetite, ardor, aspiration, besoin, concupiscence, covetousness, craving, cupidity, desideration, entreaty, greed, hankering, hot pants, importunity, kama, kamadeva, lasciviousness, lechery, libido, longing, lust, lustfulness, month's mind, need, passion, petition, request, solicitation, supplication, velleity, want, wish, yearning, yen.

desist v. abstain, break off, cease, come to a halt, discontinue, end, forbear, give over, give up, halt, leave off, pause, peter out, refrain, remit, stop, suspend.
antonyms continue, resume.

desolate adj. abandoned, arid, bare, barren, benighted, bereft, bleak, cheerless, comfortless, companionless, dejected, depopulated, depressed, depressing, desert, desolated, despondent, disconsolate, disheartened, dismal, dismayed, distressed, downcast, dreary, forlorn, forsaken, gloomy, god-forsaken, grieved, inconsolable, lonely, melancholy, miserable, ravaged, ruined, solitary, unfrequented, uninhabited, unpopulous, unsolaced, waste, wild, wretched.
antonym cheerful.
v. denude, depopulate, despoil, destroy, devastate, lay waste, pillage, plunder, ravage, ruin, spoil, waste, wreck.

despair v. capitulate, collapse, crumple, despond, give in, give up, lose heart, lose hope, quit, surrender.
antonym hope.
n. anguish, dejection, depression, desperation, despond, despondency, emptiness, gloom, hopelessness, inconsolableness, melancholy, misery, ordeal, pain, resourcelessness, sorrow, trial, tribulation, wretchedness.
antonyms cheerfulness, resilience.

desperado n. bandit, brigand, cateran, criminal, cutthroat, dacoit, gangster, gunman, heavy, hood, hoodlum, law-breaker, mugger, outlaw, ruffian, thug.

desperate adj. grave, abandoned, acute, audacious, critical, dangerous, daring, despairing, despondent, determined, dire, do-or-die, drastic, extreme, foolhardy, forlorn, frantic, frenzied, furious, great, hasty, hazardous, headlong, headstrong, hopeless, impetuous, inconsolable, irremediable, irretrievable, madcap, precipitate, rash, reckless, risky, serious, severe, temerarious, urgent, violent, wild, wretched.

despicable adj. abhorrent, abject, base, cheap, contemptible, degrading, detestable, disgraceful, disgusting, disreputable, hateful, ignoble, ignominious, infamous, low, mean, reprehensible, reprobate, scurvy, shameful, sordid, unprincipled, vile, worthless, wretched.
antonyms laudable, noble.

despise v. abhor, condemn, deplore, deride, detest, disdain, dislike, disregard, ignore, loathe, misprize, revile, scorn, slight, spurn, undervalue, vilipend.
antonyms appreciate, prize.

despite prep. against, defying, heedless of, in spite of, in the face of, in the teeth of, notwithstanding, regardless of, undeterred by.

despoil v. bereave, denude, depredate, deprive, destroy, devastate, disgarnish, dispossess, divest, loot, maraud, pillage, plunder, ransack, ravage, rifle, rob, spoliate, strip, vandalize, wreck.
antonyms adorn, enrich.

despondent adj. blue, broken-hearted, dejected, depressed, despairing, disconsolate, discouraged, disheartened, dispirited, doleful, down, downcast, downhearted, gloomy, glum, hopeless, inconsolable, low, low-spirited, melancholy, miserable, morose, mournful, overwhelmed, sad, sorrowful, woebegone, wretched.
antonyms cheerful, hopeful.

despot n. absolutist, autocrat, boss, dictator, monocrat, oppressor, tyrant.
antonyms democrat, egalitarian, liberal.

despotic adj. absolute, absolutist, arbitrary, arrogant, authoritarian, autocratic, bossy, dictatorial, domineering, imperious, monocratic, oppressive, overbearing, peremptory, tyrannical.
antonyms democratic, egalitarian, liberal, tolerant.

destiny n. cup, doom, fate, fortune, joss, karma, kismet, lot, Moira, portion, predestiny, weird.

destitute adj. bankrupt, beggared, bereft, deficient, depleted, deprived, devoid of, distressed, down and out, impecunious, impoverished, indigent, innocent of, insolvent, lacking, necessitous, needy, penniless, penurious, poor, poverty-stricken, skint, strapped, wanting.
antonyms prosperous, wealthy.

destroy v. annihilate, banjax, break, canker, crush, demolish, destruct, devastate, dismantle, dispatch, eliminate, eradicate, extinguish, extirpate, gut, kill, level, nullify, overthrow, ravage, raze, ruin, sabotage, scuttle, shatter, slay, slight, smash, stonker, thwart, torpedo, undermine, undo, unshape, vaporize, waste, wreck, zap.
antonym create.

destruction n. annihilation, bane, confutation, crushing, defeat, demolition, depopulation, desolation, devastation, downfall, elimination, end, eradication, estrepement, extermination, extinction, extirpation, havoc, liquidation, massacre, nullification, overthrow, ravagement, ruin, ruination, shattering, slaughter, undoing, wastage, wrack, wreckage.
antonym creation.

destructive adj. adverse, antagonistic, baleful, baneful, calamitous, cataclysmic, catastrophic, contrary, damaging, deadly, deathful, deleterious, derogatory, detrimental, devastating, disastrous, discouraging, disparaging, disruptive, fatal, harmful, hostile, hurtful, injurious, invalidating, lethal, malignant, mischievous, negative, noxious, nullifying, pernicious, pestful, pestiferous, pestilent, pestilential, ruinous, slaughterous, subversive, undermining, vexatious, vicious.
antonyms creative, positive, productive.

detach v. abstract, alienate, cut off, deglutinate, disconnect, disengage, disentangle, disjoin, dissociate, disunite, divide, estrange, free, isolate, loosen, remove, segregate, separate, sever, uncouple, undo, unfasten, unfix, unhitch.
antonym attach.

detail n. aspect, attribute, complexity, complication, component, count, elaborateness, elaboration, element, fact, factor, feature, ingredient, intricacy, item, meticulousness, nicety, particular, particularity, point, refinement, respect, specific, specificity, technicality, thoroughness, triviality.
v. allocate, appoint, assign, catalog, charge, commission, delegate, delineate, depict, depute, describe, detach, enarrate, enumerate, individualize, itemize, list, narrate, overname, particularize, portray, recount, rehearse, relate, send, specify.

detain v. arrest, buttonhole, check, confine, delay, hinder, hold, hold up, impede, intern, keep, prevent, restrain, retard, slow, stay, stop.
antonym release.

detect v. ascertain, catch, descry, discern, disclose, discover, distinguish, espy, expose, find, identify, note, notice, observe, perceive, recognize, reveal, scent, sight, spot, spy, track down, uncover, unmask.

deterioration n. atrophy, corrosion, debasement, decline, degeneration, degradation, dégringolade, depreciation, descent, dilapidation, disintegration, downturn, drop, failing, fall, falling-off, lapse, pejoration, retrogression, slump, tabes, tabescence, vitiation, wastage, worsening.

antonym improvement.

determination n. backbone, conclusion, constancy, conviction, decision, dedication, doggedness, drive, firmness, fortitude, indomitability, insistence, intention, judgment, obstinacy, perseverance, persistence, pertinacity, purpose, resoluteness, resolution, resolve, result, settlement, single-mindedness, solution, steadfastness, stubbornness, tenacity, verdict, will, willpower.

antonym irresolution.

determine v. affect, arbitrate, ascertain, certify, check, choose, conclude, control, decide, detect, dictate, direct, discover, elect, end, establish, finish, fix, govern, guide, identify, impel, impose, incline, induce, influence, intend, lead, learn, modify, ordain, point, purpose, regulate, resolve, rule, settle, shape, terminate, undertake, verify.

detest v. abhor, abominate, deplore, despise, dislike, execrate, hate, loathe, recoil from.

antonym adore.

detour n. bypass, bypath, byroad, byway, circumbendibus, deviation, digression, diversion, excursus.

detriment n. damage, disadvantage, disservice, evil, harm, hurt, ill, impairment, injury, loss, mischief, prejudice.

antonym advantage.

detrimental adj. adverse, baleful, damaging, deleterious, destructive, disadvantageous, harmful, hurtful, inimical, injurious, mischievous, noxious, pernicious, prejudicial, unfavorable, untoward.

antonym advantageous.

develop v. acquire, advance, amplify, augment, begin, bloom, blossom, branch out, breed, broaden, commence, contract, cultivate, dilate, diversify, elaborate, engender, enlarge, ensue, establish, evolve, expand, flourish, follow, form, foster, generate, grow, happen, invent, make headway, mature, move on, originate, pick up, progress, promote, prosper, result, ripen, sprout, start, unfold.

development n. advance, advancement, blooming, blossoming, change, circumstance, detail, elaboration, event, evolution, expansion, extension, furtherance, growth, happening, improvement, incident, increase, issue, maturation, maturity, occurrence, outcome, phenomenon, phylogenesis, phylogeny, progress, progression, promotion, refinement, result, ripening, situation, spread, unfolding, unraveling, upbuilding, upshot.

deviate v. aberrate, depart, differ, digress, divagate, diverge, drift, err, go astray, go off the rails, part, stray, swerve, turn, turn aside, vary, veer, wander, yaw.

device n. apparatus, appliance, artifice, badge, blazon, colophon, contraption, contrivance, crest, design, dodge, emblem, episemon, expedient, figure, gadget, gambit, gimmick, gismo, implement, improvisation, insignia, instrument, invention, logo, machination, maneuver, motif, motto, plan, plot, ploy, project, ruse, scheme, shield, shift, stratagem, strategy, stunt, symbol, tactic, token, tool, trick, utensil, wile.

devilish adj. accursed, black-hearted, damnable, demoniac, demoniacal, diabolic, diabolical, execrable, fiendish, hellish, impious, infernal, iniquitous, mischievous, monstrous, nefarious, satanic, wicked.

devious adj. calculating, circuitous, confusing, crooked, cunning, deceitful, deviating, dishonest, disingenuous, double-dealing, erratic, evasive, excursive, indirect, insidious, insincere, misleading, rambling, roundabout, scheming, slippery, sly, subtle, surreptitious, tortuous, treacherous, tricky, underhand, wandering, wily, winding.

antonyms artless, candid, straightforward.

devise v. arrange, compass, compose, conceive, concoct, construct, contrive, design, excogitate, forge, form, formulate, frame, imagine, invent, plan, plot, prepare, project, scheme, shape.

devote v. allocate, allot, apply, appropriate, assign, commit, consecrate, dedicate, enshrine, give, oneself, pledge, reserve, sacrifice, set apart, set aside, surrender.

devoted adj. ardent, attentive, caring, committed, concerned, constant, dedicated, devout, faithful, fond, loving, loyal, staunch, steadfast, tireless, true, unremitting, unswerving.

antonyms inconstant, indifferent, negligent.

devotion n. adherence, adoration, affection, allegiance, ardor, assiduity, attachment, commitment, consecration, constancy, dedication, devoutness, earnestness, faith, faithfulness, fervor, fidelity, fondness, godliness, holiness, indefatigability, love, loyalty, partiality, passion, piety, prayer, regard, religiousness, reverence, sanctity, sedulousness, spirituality, steadfastness, support, worship, zeal.

antonyms inconstancy, negligence.

devour v. absorb, annihilate, bolt, consume, cram, destroy, dispatch, down, eat, engulf, feast on, feast one's eyes on, gluttonize, gobble, gorge, gormandize, gulp, guzzle, polish off, ravage, relish, revel in, spend, stuff, swallow, waste, wolf.

devout adj. ardent, constant, deep, devoted, earnest, faithful, fervent, genuine, godly, heartfelt, holy, intense, orthodox, passionate, pious, prayerful, profound, pure, religious, reverent, saintly, serious, sincere, staunch, steadfast, unswerving, whole-hearted, zealous.

antonyms insincere, uncommitted.

dexterity n. ability, address, adroitness, agility, aptitude, art, artistry, cleverness, cunning, deftness, effortlessness, expertise, expertness, facility, finesse, handiness, ingenuity, knack, legerdemain, mastery, neatness, nimbleness, proficiency, readiness, skilfulness, skill, smoothness, tact, touch.

antonyms clumsiness, ineptitude.

dexterous adj. able, active, acute, adept, adroit, agile, apt, clever, cunning, deft, expert, facile, feat, habile, handy, ingenious, light-handed, masterly, neat, neat-handed, nifty, nimble, nimble-fingered, nippy, proficient, prompt, quick, skilful.

antonyms clumsy, inept.

dialect n. accent, diction, Doric, idiom, jargon, language, lingo, localism, patois, pronunciation, provincialism, regionalism, speech, tongue, vernacular.

dialogue n. causerie, colloquy, communication, confabulation, conference, conversation, converse, debate, discourse, discussion, duologue, exchange, interchange, interlocution, lines, script, stichomythia, table talk, talk.

diary *n.* appointment book, chronicle, commonplace book, day-book, diurnal, engagement book, journal, journal intime, logbook, year-book.

diatribe *n.* abuse, attack, castigation, criticism, denunciation, flyting, harangue, insult, invective, onslaught, philippic, reviling, stricture, tirade, upbraiding, vituperation.

antonyms bouquet, encomium, praise.

dictate *v.* announce, command, decree, direct, enjoin, impose, instruct, ordain, order, prescribe, pronounce, rule, say, speak, transmit, utter.

n. behest, bidding, code, command, decree, dictation, dictum, direction, edict, fiat, injunction, law, mandate, order, ordinance, precept, principle, requirement, ruling, statute, ultimatum, word.

dictator *n.* autarch, autocrat, Big Brother, boss, despot, supremo, tyrant.

die *v.* breathe one's last, croak, decay, decease, decline, depart, desire, disappear, dwindle, ebb, end, expire, fade, finish, fizzle out, gangrene, go over to the majority, go to one's (long) account, hunger, kick in, kick it, kick the bucket, languish, lapse, long for, pass, pass away, pass over, peg out, perish, peter out, pine for, pop off, run down, sink, slip the cable, snuff it, starve, stop, subside, succumb, suffer, vanish, wane, wilt, wither, yearn.

difference *n.* alteration, argument, balance, change, clash, conflict, contention, contrariety, contrast, contretemps, controversy, debate, deviation, differentia, differentiation, difformity, disagreement, discordance, discrepancy, discreteness, disparateness, disparity, dispute, dissimilarity, distinction, distinctness, divergence, diversity, exception, idiosyncrasy, jizz, particularity, peculiarity, quarrel, remainder, rest, set-to, singularity, strife, tiff, unlikeness, variation, variety, wrangle.

antonyms agreement, conformity, uniformity.

different *adj.* altered, anomalous, assorted, at odds, at variance, atypical, bizarre, changed, clashing, contrasting, deviating, discrepant, discrete, disparate, dissimilar, distinct, distinctive, divergent, divers, diverse, eccentric, extraordinary, inconsistent, individual, manifold, many, miscellaneous, multifarious, numerous, opposed, original, other, peculiar, rare, separate, several, singular, special, strange, sundry, unalike, uncommon, unconventional, unique, unlike, unusual, varied, various.

antonyms conventional, normal, same, similar, uniform.

differentiate *v.* adapt, alter, change, contrast, convert, demarcate, discern, discriminate, distinguish, individualize, mark off, modify, particularize, separate, tell apart, transform.

antonyms assimilate, associate, confuse, link.

difficult *adj.* abstract, abstruse, arduous, Augean, baffling, burdensome, captious, complex, complicated, dark, delicate, demanding, difficile, disruptive, enigmatical, fastidious, formidable, fractious, fussy, Gordian, grim, hard, herculean, iffy, intractable, intricate, involved, knotty, laborious, obscure, obstinate, obstreperous, onerous, painful, perplexing, perverse, problematic, problematical, recalcitrant, refractory,

rigid, steep, sticky, stiff, straitened, strenuous, stubborn, thorny, ticklish, tiresome, toilsome, tough, troublesome, trying, unamenable, unco-operative, unmanageable, uphill, wearisome.

antonyms easy, straightforward.

difficulty *n.* a bad patch, arduousness, awkwardness, block, complication, dilemma, distress, embarrassment, fix, hang-up, hardship, hiccup, hindrance, hole, hurdle, impediment, jam, labor, laboriousness, mess, nineholes, objection, obstacle, opposition, pain, painfulness, perplexity, pickle, pinch, pitfall, plight, predicament, problem, protest, quandary, scruple, spot, strain, strait, straits, strenuousness, stumbling-block, trial, tribulation, trouble, vexata quaestio, vexed question.

antonyms advantage, ease.

diffidence *n.* abashment, backwardness, bashfulness, constraint, doubt, fear, hesitancy, hesitation, humility, inhibition, insecurity, meekness, modesty, reluctance, reserve, self-consciousness, self-distrust, self-doubt, self-effacement, shamefacedness, shamefast, sheepishness, shyness, tentativeness, timidity, timidness, timorousness, unassertiveness.

antonym confidence.

diffuse *adj.* ambagious, circuitous, circumlocutory, copious, diffused, digressive, disconnected, discursive, dispersed, long-winded, loose, maundering, meandering, prolix, rambling, scattered, unconcentrated, unco-ordinated, vague, verbose, waffling, wordy.

antonyms concentrated, succinct.

v. circulate, dispense, disperse, disseminate, dissipate, distribute, propagate, scatter, spread, winnow.

antonyms concentrate, suppress.

dig[1] *v.* burrow, delve, drive, excavate, go into, gouge, graft, grub, hoe, howk, investigate, jab, mine, penetrate, pierce, poke, probe, prod, punch, quarry, research, scoop, search, spit, thrust, till, tunnel.

n. aspersion, barb, crack, cut, gibe, insinuation, insult, jab, jeer, poke, prod, punch, quip, sneer, taunt, thrust, wisecrack.

antonym compliment.

dig[2] *v.* adore, appreciate, be into, enjoy, fancy, follow, get a kick out of, get off on, go a bundle on, go for, go overboard about, groove, have the hots for, like, love, understand, warm to.

antonym hate.

digest *v.* abridge, absorb, arrange, assimilate, classify, codify, compress, condense, consider, contemplate, dispose, dissolve, grasp, incorporate, ingest, macerate, master, meditate, methodize, ponder, process, reduce, shorten, stomach, study, summarize, systematize, tabulate, take in, understand.

n. abbreviation, abridgment, abstract, compendium, compression, condensation, epitome, précis, reduction, résumé, summary, synopsis.

dignified *adj.* august, decorous, distinguished, exalted, formal, grave, honorable, imposing, impressive, lofty, lordly, majestic, noble, oro(ro)tund, reserved, solemn, stately, upright.

antonym undignified.

dignify *v.* adorn, advance, aggrandize, apotheosize, distinguish, elevate, ennoble, exalt, glorify, honor, promote, raise.

antonyms degrade, demean.

dignity *n.* amour-propre, courtliness, decorum, elevation, eminence, excellence, glory, grandeur, gravitas, gravity, greatness, hauteur, honor, importance, loftiness, majesty, nobility, nobleness, pride, propriety, rank, respectability, self-esteem, self-importance, self-possession, self-regard, self-respect, solemnity, standing, stateliness, station, status.

digress v. depart, deviate, divagate, diverge, drift, excurse, expatiate, go off at a tangent, ramble, stray, wander.

dilate v. amplify, broaden, descant, detail, develop, distend, dwell on, elaborate, enlarge, expand, expatiate, expound, extend, increase, puff out, spin out, stretch, swell, widen.

antonyms abbreviate, constrict, curtail.

dilemma n. bind, corner, difficulty, embarrassment, fix, jam, mess, perplexity, pickle, pinch, plight, predicament, problem, puzzle, quandary, spot, strait.

diligent adj. active, assiduous, attentive, busy, careful, conscientious, constant, dogged, earnest, hard-working, indefatigable, industrious, laborious, painstaking, persevering, persistent, pertinacious, sedulous, studious, tireless.

antonyms dilatory, lazy.

dim adj. bleary, blurred, caliginous, cloudy, confused, dark, darkish, dense, depressing, dingy, discouraging, dull, dumb, dusky, faint, feeble, foggy, fuzzy, gloomy, gray, hazy, ill-defined, imperfect, indistinct, intangible, lackluster, misty, muted, obscure, obscured, obtuse, opaque, overcast, pale, remote, shadowy, slow, somber, stupid, sullied, tarnished, tenebrious, thick, unclear, unfavorable, unilluminated, unpromising, vague, weak.

antonyms bright, distinct.

v. becloud, bedim, blear, blur, cloud, darken, dull, fade, lower, obscure, tarnish.

antonyms brighten, illuminate.

dimension(s) n. amplitude, bulk, capacity, extent, greatness, importance, largeness, magnitude, measure, range, scale, scope, size.

diminish v. abate, bate, belittle, cheapen, contract, curtail, cut, deactivate, decline, decrease, demean, depreciate, devalue, dwindle, ebb, fade, lessen, lower, minify, peter out, recede, reduce, retrench, shrink, shrivel, sink, slacken, subside, taper off, wane, weaken.

antonyms enhance, enlarge, increase.

diminutive adj. bantam, dinky, Lilliputian, little, midget, mini, miniature, minute, petite, pint-size(d), pocket(-sized), pygmy, small, tiny, undersized, wee.

antonyms big, great, huge, large.

n. hypocorisma, pet-name.

din n. babble, chirm, clamor, clangor, clash, clatter, commotion, crash, hubbub, hullabaloo, noise, outcry, pandemonium, racket, randan, row, shout, uproar.

antonyms calm, quiet.

dine v. banquet, break bread, eat, feast, feed, lunch, sup.

dingy adj. bedimmed, colorless, dark, dim, dirty, discolored, drab, dreary, dull, dusky, faded, fuscous, gloomy, grimy, murky, obscure, run-down, seedy, shabby, soiled, somber, tacky, worn.

antonyms bright, clean.

dip v. bathe, decline, descend, disappear, dook, dop, douse, droop, drop, duck, dunk, fade, fall, immerse,

ladle, lower, plunge, rinse, sag, scoop, set, sink, slope, slump, souse, spoon, subside, tilt.

n. basin, bathe, concavity, concoction, decline, depression, dilution, dive, dook, douche, drenching, ducking, fall, hole, hollow, immersion, incline, infusion, lowering, mixture, plunge, preparation, sag, slip, slope, slump, soaking, solution, suspension, swim.

diplomacy n. artfulness, craft, delicacy, discretion, finesse, maneuvering, savoir-faire, skill, statecraft, statesmanship, subtlety, tact, tactfulness.

diplomatic adj. discreet, judicious, polite, politic, prudent, sagacious, sensitive, subtle, tactful.

antonyms rude, tactless, thoughtless.

dire adj. alarming, appalling, awful, calamitous, cataclysmic, catastrophic, critical, crucial, cruel, crying, desperate, disastrous, dismal, distressing, drastic, dreadful, exigent, extreme, fearful, gloomy, grave, grim, horrible, horrid, ominous, portentous, pressing, ruinous, terrible, urgent, woeful.

direct[1] v. address, administer, advise, aim, bid, case, charge, command, conduct, control, dictate, dispose, enjoin, fix, focus, govern, guide, handle, indicate, instruct, intend, label, lead, level, mail, manage, mastermind, mean, order, oversee, point, regulate, route, rule, run, send, show, stage-manage, superintend, superscribe, supervise, train, turn.

direct[2] adj. absolute, blunt, candid, categorical, downright, explicit, express, face-to-face, first-hand, frank, head-on, honest, immediate, man-to-man, matter-of-fact, non-stop, open, outright, outspoken, personal, plain, plain-spoken, point-blank, shortest, sincere, straight, straightforward, through, unambiguous, unbroken, undeviating, unequivocal, uninterrupted.

antonyms crooked, devious, indirect.

direction n. address, administration, aim, approach, bearing, bent, bias, charge, command, control, course, current, drift, end, government, guidance, label, leadership, line, management, mark, order, orientation, oversight, path, proclivity, purpose, road, route, superintendence, superscription, supervision, tack, tendency, tenor, track, trend, way.

directions n. briefing, guidance, guidelines, indication, instructions, orders, plan, recipe, recommendations, regulations.

directly adv. bluntly, candidly, dead, due, exactly, face-to-face, forthwith, frankly, honestly, immediately, instantaneously, instantly, openly, personally, plainly, point-blank, precisely, presently, promptly, pronto, quickly, right away, soon, speedily, straight, straightaway, straightforwardly, truthfully, unequivocally, unerringly, unswervingly.

antonym indirectly.

dirt n. clay, crud, dust, earth, excrement, filth, grime, impurity, indecency, loam, mire, muck, mud, obscenity, ordure, pornography, slime, smudge, smut, smutch, soil, sordor, stain, tarnish, vomit, yuck.

antonyms cleanliness, cleanness.

dirty adj. angry, base, beggarly, begrimed, bitter, blue, clouded, contemptible, corrupt, cowardly, crooked, cruddy, dark, despicable, dishonest, dull, filthy, foul, fraudulent, grimy, grubby, ignominious, illegal, indecent, low, low-down, maculate, manky, mean, messy, miry, mucky, muddy, nasty, obscene, off-color, piggish, polluted, pornographic, risqué, salacious, scruffy, scurvy, shabby, sluttish, smutty, soiled, sordid, squalid, sullied, treacherous, unclean, unfair, unscrupulous, unsporting, unsterile, unswept, vile, vulgar, yucky.

antonyms clean, spotless.

v. bedaub, begrime, besmear, besmirch, besmut, bespatter, blacken, defile, foul, mess up, muddy, pollute, smear, smirch, smudge, soil, soss, spoil, stain, sully.

antonyms clean, cleanse.

disability *n.* affliction, ailment, complaint, crippledom, defect, disablement, disorder, disqualification, handicap, impairment, impotency, inability, incapacitation, incapacity, incompetency, infirmity, malady, unfitness, weakness.

disable *v.* cripple, damage, debilitate, disenable, disqualify, enfeeble, hamstring, handicap, immobilize, impair, incapacitate, invalidate, lame, paralyze, prostrate, unfit, unman, weaken.

disabled *adj.* bedridden, crippled, handicapped, hors de combat, immobilized, incapacitated, infirm, lame, maimed, mangled, mutilated, paralyzed, weak, weakened, wrecked.

antonyms able, able-bodied.

disadvantage *n.* burden, damage, debit, detriment, disservice, drawback, flaw, fly in the ointment, handicap, hardship, harm, hindrance, hurt, impediment, inconvenience, injury, liability, loss, minus, nuisance, prejudice, privation, snag, trouble, unfavorableness, weakness.

antonyms advantage, benefit.

v. hamper, handicap, hinder, inconvenience, wrongfoot.

antonyms aid, help.

disagree *v.* altercate, argue, bicker, bother, clash, conflict, contend, contest, contradict, counter, depart, deviate, differ, discomfort, dissent, distress, diverge, fall out, hurt, nauseate, object, oppose, quarrel, run counter to, sicken, spat, squabble, take issue with, tiff, trouble, upset, vary, wrangle.

antonym agree.

disagreement *n.* altercation, argument, clash, conflict, debate, difference, discord, discrepancy, disparity, dispute, dissent, dissimilarity, dissimilitude, divergence, diversity, division, falling-out, incompatibility, incongruity, misunderstanding, quarrel, squabble, strife, tiff, unlikeness, variance, wrangle.

antonym agreement.

disappear *v.* cease, dematerialize, depart, dissolve, ebb, end, escape, evanesce, evaporate, expire, fade, flee, fly, go, pass, perish, recede, retire, scarper, vamoose, vanish, wane, withdraw.

antonym appear.

disappoint *v.* baffle, balk, chagrin, dash, deceive, defeat, delude, disconcert, disenchant, disgruntle, dishearten, disillusion, dismay, dissatisfy, fail, foil, frustrate, hamper, hinder, let down, miff, sadden, thwart, vex.

antonyms delight, please, satisfy.

disappointment[1] *n.* bafflement, chagrin, discontent, discouragement, disenchantment, disillusionment, displeasure, dissatisfaction, distress, failure, frustration, mortification, regret.

antonyms delight, pleasure, satisfaction.

disappointment[2] *n.* blow, calamity, comedown, disaster, drop, failure, fiasco, frost, lemon, let-down, misfortune, setback, swiz, swizzle.

antonyms boost, success.

disapprove of blame, censure, condemn, denounce, deplore, deprecate, disallow, discountenance, dislike, disparage, object to, reject, spurn, take exception to.

antonym approve of.

disarm[1] *v.* deactivate, demilitarize, demobilize, disable, disband, unarm, unweapon.

antonym arm.

disarm[2] appease, conciliate, modify, persuade, win over.

disaster *n.* accident, act of God, blow, calamity, cataclysm, catastrophe, curtains, debacle, misadventure, mischance, misfortune, mishap, reverse, ruin, ruination, stroke, tragedy, trouble.

antonyms success, triumph.

disband *v.* break up, demobilize, dismiss, disperse, dissolve, part company, retire, scatter, separate.

antonyms assemble, band, combine.

disbelief *n.* distrust, doubt, dubiety, incredulity, mistrust, rejection, scepticism, suspicion, unbelief.

antonym belief.

discard *v.* abandon, cashier, cast aside, dispense with, dispose of, ditch, drop, dump, jettison, leave off, reject, relinquish, remove, repudiate, scrap, shed.

antonyms adopt, embrace, espouse.

discern *v.* ascertain, behold, descry, detect, determine, differentiate, discover, discriminate, distinguish, espy, judge, make out, notice, observe, perceive, recognize, see, wot.

discernment *n.* acumen, acuteness, ascertainment, astuteness, awareness, clear-sightedness, cleverness, discrimination, ingenuity, insight, intelligence, judgment, keenness, penetration, perception, perceptiveness, percipience, perspicacity, sagacity, sharpness, understanding, wisdom.

discharge *v.* absolve, accomplish, acquit, carry out, cashier, clear, detonate, disburden, discard, disembogue, dismiss, dispense, drum out, effectuate, egest, eject, emit, empty, excrete, execute, exonerate, expel, explode, exude, fire, free, fulfil, give off, gush, honor, leak, let off, liberate, meet, offload, ooze, oust, pardon, pay, perform, release, relieve, remove, sack, satisfy, set off, settle, shoot, unburden, unload, vent, void, volley.

antonyms employ, engage, hire.

n. accomplishment, achievement, acquittal, acquittance, blast, burst, clearance, congé, defluxion, demobilization, detonation, disburdening, discharging, dismissal, effluent, ejecta, ejectamenta, ejection, emission, emptying, excretion, execution, exoneration, explosion, firing, flight, flow, flux, fluxion, fulfilment, fusillade, gleet, glit, liberation, mittimus, observance, ooze, pardon, payment, performance, pus, quietus, quittance, release, remittance, report, salvo, satisfaction, secretion, seepage, settlement, shot, suppuration, the boot, the sack, unburdening, unloading, vent, voidance, voiding, volley, whiff.

disciple *n.* acolyte, adherent, apostle, believer, catechumen, chela, convert, devotee, follower, learner, partisan, proselyte, pupil, student, supporter, votary.

discipline *n.* castigation, chastisement, conduct, control, correction, course, curriculum, drill, exercise, martinetism, method, orderliness, practice, punishment, regimen, regulation, restraint, self-control, specialty, strictness, subject, training.

antonyms carelessness, negligence.

v. break in, castigate, chasten, chastise, check, control, correct, drill, educate, exercise, form, govern, habituate, instruct, inure, penalize, prepare, punish, regulate, reprimand, reprove, restrain, toughen, train.

disclaim v. abandon, abjure, abnegate, decline, deny, disacknowledge, disaffirm, disallow, disavow, disown, forswear, reject, renounce, repudiate.

antonyms accept, acknowledge, claim.

disclose v. broadcast, communicate, confess, discover, divulge, exhibit, expose, impart, lay, lay bare, leak, let slip, propale, publish, relate, reveal, show, tell, unbare, unbosom, unburden, uncover, unfold, unveil, utter.

antonyms conceal, hide.

discomfit v. abash, baffle, balk, beat, checkmate, confound, confuse, defeat, demoralize, discompose, disconcert, embarrass, faze, flurry, fluster, foil, frustrate, humble, humiliate, outwit, overcome, perplex, perturb, rattle, ruffle, thwart, trump, unsettle, vanquish, worry, worst.

discomfort n. ache, annoyance, disquiet, distress, hardship, hurt, inquietude, irritant, irritation, malaise, trouble, uneasiness, unpleasantness, unpleasantry, vexation.

antonyms comfort, ease.

disconcerted adj. annoyed, bewildered, confused, discombobulated, discomfited, distracted, disturbed, embarrassed, fazed, flurried, flustered, mixed-up, nonplused, perturbed, rattled, ruffled, taken aback, thrown, troubled, unsettled, upset.

disconnect v. cut off, detach, disengage, divide, part, separate, sever, uncouple, ungear, unhitch, unhook, unlink, unplug, unyoke.

antonyms attach, connect, engage.

disconsolate adj. crushed, dejected, desolate, despairing, dispirited, forlorn, gloomy, grief-stricken, heartbroken, heavy-hearted, hopeless, inconsolable, melancholy, miserable, sad, unhappy, unsolaced, woeful, wretched.

antonyms cheerful, cheery.

discontent n. discontentment, displeasure, disquiet, dissatisfaction, envy, fretfulness, impatience, regret, restlessness, uneasiness, unhappiness, unrest, vexation.

antonym content.

discontinue v. abandon, break off, cancel, cease, drop, end, finish, halt, interrupt, pause, quit, stop, suspend, terminate.

antonym continue.

discord n. cacophony, clashing, conflict, contention, difference, din, disagreement, discordance, disharmony, dispute, dissension, dissonance, disunity, division, friction, harshness, incompatibility, jangle, jarring, opposition, racket, rupture, split, strife, tumult, variance, wrangling.

antonyms agreement, concord, harmony.

discourage v. abash, awe, check, chill, cow, curb, damp, dampen, dash, daunt, deject, demoralize, deprecate, depress, deter, discountenance, disfavor, dishearten, dismay, dispirit, dissuade, frighten, hinder, inhibit, intimidate, overawe, prevent, put off, restrain, scare, unman, unnerve.

antonyms encourage, favor, hearten, inspire.

discourteous adj. abrupt, bad-mannered, boorish, brusque, curt, disrespectful, ill-bred, ill-mannered, impolite, insolent, offhand, rude, slighting, unceremonious, uncivil, uncourteous, ungracious, unmannerly.

antonyms courteous, polite, respectful.

discover v. ascertain, conceive, contrive, descry, design, detect, determine, devise, dig up, discern, disclose, espy, find, invent, learn, light on, locate, notice, originate, perceive, pioneer, realize, recognize, reveal, see, spot, suss out, uncover, unearth.

antonyms conceal, hide.

discredit v. blame, censure, challenge, defame, degrade, deny, disbelieve, discount, disgrace, dishonor, disparage, dispute, distrust, doubt, explode, mistrust, question, reproach, slander, slur, smear, vilify.

antonyms believe, credit.

n. aspersion, blame, censure, disgrace, dishonor, disrepute, distrust, doubt, ignominy, ill-repute, imputation, mistrust, odium, opprobium, question, reproach, scandal, shame, skepticism, slur, smear, stigma, suspicion.

antonym credit.

discreet adj. careful, cautious, circumspect, considerate, delicate, diplomatic, discerning, guarded, judicious, politic, prudent, reserved, sagacious, sensible, softly-softly, tactful, wary.

antonyms careless, indiscreet, tactless.

discrepancy n. conflict, contrariety, difference, disagreement, discordance, disparity, dissimilarity, dissonance, divergence, imparity, incongruity, inconsistency, inequality, variance, variation.

discretion n. acumen, care, carefulness, caution, choice, circumspection, consideration, diplomacy, discernment, disposition, heedfulness, inclination, judgment, judiciousness, liking, maturity, mind, option, pleasure, predilection, preference, prudence, responsibility, sagacity, tact, volition, wariness, will, wisdom, wish.

antonym indiscretion.

discriminating adj. acute, astute, critical, cultivated, discerning, discriminant, fastidious, nasute, particular, perceptive, selective, sensitive, tasteful.

discrimination[1] n. bias, bigotry, favoritism, inequity, intolerance, Jim Crow, prejudice, unfairness.

discrimination[2] n. acumen, acuteness, discernment, insight, judgment, keenness, penetration, perception, percipience, refinement, sagacity, subtlety, taste.

discuss v. argue, confer, consider, consult, converse, debate, deliberate, examine, lay heads together, rap.

discussion n. analysis, argument, colloquium, colloquy, confabulation, conference, consideration, consultation, conversation, debate, deliberation, dialogue, discourse, examination, exchange, gabfest, moot, quodlibet, rap, review, scrutiny, seminar, symposium, talkfest.

disdain v. belittle, contemn, deride, despise, disavow, disregard, misprize, pooh-pooh, rebuff, reject, scorn, slight, sneer at, spurn, undervalue.

antonyms admire, respect.

n. arrogance, contempt, contumely, deprecation, derision, dislike, haughtiness, hauteur, imperiousness, indifference, scorn, sneering, snobbishness, superciliousness.

antonyms admiration, respect.

disdainful adj. aloof, arrogant, contemptuous, derisive, haughty, hoity-toity, imperious, insolent, proud, scornful, sneering, supercilious, superior, uppish.

antonyms admiring, respectful.

disease n. affection, affliction, ailment, blight, cancer, canker, complaint, condition, contagion, contamination, disorder, distemper, epidemic, epizootic, idiopathy, ill-health, illness, indisposition, infection,

infirmity, malady, malaise, murrain, pest, plague, sickness, upset.
antonym health.

disentangle *v.* clarify, debarrass, detach, disconnect, disembarrass, disengage, disentwine, disinvolve, extricate, free, loose, ravel out, resolve, separate, sever, simplify, unfold, unravel, unsnarl, untangle, untwine, untwist.
antonym entangle.

disfigured *adj.* damaged, defaced, deformed, flawed, ruined, scarred, spoilt, ugly.
antonym adorned.

disgrace *n.* aspersion, attaint, baseness, blemish, blot, contempt, defamation, degradation, discredit, disesteem, disfavor, dishonor, disrepute, dog-house, ignominy, infamy, obloquy, odium, opprobrium, reproach, scandal, shame, slur, stain, stigma.
antonyms esteem, honor, respect.
v. abase, attaint, defame, degrade, discredit, disfavor, dishonor, disparage, humiliate, reproach, scandalize, shame, slur, stain, stigmatize, sully, taint.
antonyms honor, respect.

disgraceful *adj.* appalling, blameworthy, contemptible, degrading, detestable, discreditable, dishonorable, disreputable, dreadful, ignominious, infamous, low, mean, opprobrious, scandalous, shameful, shocking, unworthy.
antonyms honorable, respectable.

disguise *v.* camouflage, cloak, conceal, cover, deceive, dissemble, dissimulate, dress up, explain away, fake, falsify, fudge, hide, mask, misrepresent, screen, secrete, shroud, veil.
antonyms expose, reveal, uncover.
n. camouflage, cloak, concealment, costume, cover, coverture, deception, dissimulation, façade, front, get-up, mask, masquerade, pretence, screen, semblance, travesty, trickery, veil, veneer, visor.

disgust *v.* displease, nauseate, offend, outrage, put off, repel, revolt, scandalize, scunner, sicken.
antonyms delight, gratify, tempt.
n. abhorrence, abomination, antipathy, aversion, detestation, dislike, disrelish, distaste, hatefulness, hatred, loathing, nausea, odium, repugnance, repulsion, revulsion.
antonyms admiration, liking.

disgusting *adj.* abominable, detestable, distasteful, foul, gross, hateful, loathsome, nasty, nauseating, nauseous, objectionable, obnoxious, obscene, odious, offensive, repellent, repugnant, revolting, shameless, sickening, sick-making, stinking, ugsome, unappetizing, vile, vulgar.
antonyms attractive, delightful, pleasant.

dish[1] *n.* bowl, fare, food, plate, platter, porringer, ramekin, recipe, salver, trencher.
dish[2] *v.* finish, ruin, spoil, torpedo, wreck.

dishearten *v.* cast down, crush, damp, dampen, dash, daunt, deject, depress, deter, discourage, dismay, dispirit, frighten, weary.

disheartened *adj.* crestfallen, crushed, daunted, dejected, depressed, disappointed, discouraged, dismayed, dispirited, downcast, downhearted, frightened, weary.
antonyms encouraged, heartened.

disheveled *adj.* bedraggled, blowsy, disarranged, disordered, frowsy, messy, mussy, ruffled, rumpled, slovenly, tousled, uncombed, unkempt, untidy.

antonyms neat, spruce, tidy.

dishonest *adj.* bent, cheating, corrupt, crafty, crooked, deceitful, deceiving, deceptive, designing, disreputable, double-dealing, false, fraudulent, guileful, immoral, knavish, lying, mendacious, perfidious, shady, snide, swindling, treacherous, unethical, unfair, unprincipled, unscrupulous, untrustworthy, untruthful, wrongful.
antonyms fair, honest, scrupulous, trustworthy.

dishonor *v.* abase, blacken, corrupt, debase, debauch, defame, defile, deflower, degrade, demean, discredit, disgrace, disparage, pollute, rape, ravish, seduce, shame, sully.
antonym honor.
n. abasement, abuse, affront, aspersion, degradation, discourtesy, discredit, disfavor, disgrace, disrepute, ignominy, imputation, indignity, infamy, insult, obloquy, odium, offence, opprobrium, outrage, reproach, scandal, shame, slight, slur.
antonym honor.

disinclined *adj.* antipathetic, averse, hesitant, indisposed, loath, opposed, reluctant, resistant, undisposed, unenthusiastic, unwilling.
antonyms inclined, willing.

disingenuous *adj.* artful, cunning, deceitful, designing, devious, dishonest, duplicitous, guileful, insidious, insincere, shifty, two-faced, uncandid, wily.
antonyms artless, frank, ingenuous, naive.

disintegrate *v.* break up, crumble, decompose, disunite, fall apart, molder, rot, separate, shatter, splinter.
antonyms combine, merge, unite.

disinterested *adj.* candid, detached, dispassionate, equitable, even-handed, impartial, impersonal, neutral, open-minded, unbiased, uninvolved, unprejudiced, unselfish.
antonyms biased, concerned, interested, prejudiced.

dislike *n.* animosity, animus, antagonism, antipathy, aversion, detestation, disapprobation, disapproval, disgust, disinclination, displeasure, disrelish, distaste, dyspathy, enmity, hatred, hostility, loathing, repugnance.
antonyms attachment, liking, predilection.
v. abhor, abominate, despise, detest, disapprove, disfavor, disrelish, hate, keck, loathe, scorn, shun.
antonyms favor, like, prefer.

disloyal *adj.* apostate, disaffected, faithless, false, perfidious, seditious, subversive, traitorous, treacherous, treasonable, two-faced, unfaithful, unleal, unpatriotic, untrustworthy, unwifely.
antonym loyal.

dismal *adj.* black, bleak, burdan, cheerless, dark, depressing, despondent, discouraging, doleful, dolorous, dowie, dreary, dreich, forlorn, funereal, ghostful, gloomy, gruesome, hopeless, incompetent, inept, lac(h)rymose, lonesome, long-faced, long-visaged, lowering, low-spirited, lugubrious, melancholy, poor, sad, sepulchral, somber, sorrowful, stupid, thick, useless.
antonyms bright, cheerful.

dismantle *v.* demolish, demount, disassemble, dismount, raze, strike, strip, unrig.
antonym assemble.

dismay *v.* affright, alarm, appal, consternate, daunt, depress, disappoint, disconcert, discourage, dishearten, disillusion, dispirit, distress, frighten, horrify, paralyze, put off, scare, terrify, unnerve, unsettle.

antonym encourage.

n. agitation, alarm, anxiety, apprehension, consternation, disappointment, distress, dread, fear, fright, funk, horror, panic, terror, trepidation, upset.

antonyms boldness, encouragement.

dismiss *v.* ax, banish, bounce, bowler-hat, cashier, chassé, chuck, disband, discharge, discount, dispel, disperse, disregard, dissolve, drop, fire, free, give (someone) the push, lay off, let go, oust, pooh-pooh, reject, release, relegate, remove, repudiate, sack, send packing, set aside, shelve, spurn.

antonyms accept, appoint.

disobedient *adj.* contrary, contumacious, defiant, disorderly, froward, insubordinate, intractable, mischievous, naughty, obstreperous, refractory, unruly, wayward, wilful.

antonym obedient.

disobey *v.* contravene, defy, disregard, flout, ignore, infringe, overstep, rebel, resist, transgress, violate.

antonym obey.

disorder *n.* affliction, ailment, brawl, chaos, clamor, clutter, commotion, complaint, confusion, derangement, disarray, disease, disorderliness, disorganization, disturbance, fight, fracas, hubbub, hullabaloo, illness, indisposition, irregularity, jumble, malady, mess, misarrangement, misarray, misorder, misrule, muddle, muss(e), mussiness, quarrel, riot, rumpus, shambles, sickness, tumult, untidiness, uproar.

antonym order.

v. clutter, confound, confuse, derange, disarrange, discompose, disorganize, disrank, disturb, jumble, mess up, misorder, mix up, muddle, scatter, unsettle, upset.

antonyms arrange, organize.

disorganization *n.* chaos, confusion, derangement, disarray, disjointedness, dislocation, disorder, disruption, incoherence, unconnectedness.

antonyms order, tidiness.

disorganized *adj.* chaotic, confused, disordered, haphazard, jumbled, muddled, shambolic, shuffled, topsyturvy, unmethodical, unorganized, unregulated, unsifted, unsorted, unstructured, unsystematic, unsystematized.

antonyms organized, tidy.

disown *v.* abandon, abnegate, cast off, deny, disacknowledge, disallow, disavow, disclaim, reject, renounce, repudiate, unget.

antonym accept.

disparage *v.* belittle, criticize, decry, defame, degrade, denigrate, deprecate, depreciate, deride, derogate, detract from, discredit, disdain, dishonor, dismiss, disvalue, malign, minimize, ridicule, run down, scorn, slander, traduce, underestimate, underrate, undervalue, vilify, vilipend.

antonym praise.

disparagement *n.* aspersion, belittlement, condemnation, contempt, contumely, criticism, debasement, decrial, decrying, degradation, denunciation, deprecation, depreciation, derision, derogation, detraction, discredit, disdain, ridicule, scorn, slander, underestimation, vilification.

antonym praise.

dispassionate *adj.* calm, candid, collected, composed, cool, detached, disinterested, fair, impartial, impersonal, imperturbable, indifferent, moderate, neutral, objective, quiet, serene, sober, temperate, unbiased,

unemotional, unexcitable, unexcited, uninvolved, unmoved, unprejudiced, unruffled.

antonyms biased, emotional.

dispatch[1], **despatch** *v.* accelerate, conclude, discharge, dismiss, dispose of, expedite, finish, hasten, hurry, perform, quicken, settle.

antonym impede.

n. alacrity, celerity, dépêche, expedition, haste, precipitateness, promptitude, promptness, quickness, rapidity, speed, swiftness.

antonym slowness.

dispatch[2], **despatch** *v.* consign, express, forward, remit, send, transmit.

n. account, bulletin, communication, communiqué, document, instruction, item, letter, message, missive, news, piece, report, story.

dispatch[3], **despatch** *v.* assassinate, bump off, execute, kill, murder, rub out, slaughter, slay, waste.

dispel *v.* allay, banish, discuss, dismiss, disperse, dissipate, drive off, eliminate, expel, melt away, resolve, rout, scatter.

antonym give rise to.

dispense *v.* administer, allocate, allot, apply, apportion, assign, deal out, direct, disburse, discharge, distribute, dole out, enforce, except, excuse, execute, exempt, exonerate, implement, let off, measure, mete out, mix, operate, prepare, release, relieve, reprieve, share, supply, undertake.

disperse *v.* broadcast, circulate, diffuse, disappear, disband, dismiss, dispel, disseminate, dissipate, dissolve, distribute, drive off, evanesce, melt away, rout, scatter, separate, spread, strew, vanish.

antonym gather.

dispirited *adj.* brassed off, browned off, cast down, crestfallen, dejected, depressed, despondent, discouraged, disheartened, down, downcast, fed up, gloomy, glum, low, morose, sad.

antonym encouraged.

displace *v.* cashier, crowd out, depose, derange, disarrange, discard, discharge, dislocate, dislodge, dismiss, dispossess, disturb, eject, evict, fire, luxate, misplace, move, oust, remove, replace, sack, shift, succeed, supersede, supplant, transpose, unsettle.

display *v.* betray, blazon, boast, demonstrate, disclose, evidence, evince, exhibit, expand, expose, extend, flash, flaunt, flourish, manifest, model, parade, present, reveal, show, show off, showcase, splash, sport, unfold, unfurl, unveil, vaunt, wear.

antonym hide.

n. array, demonstration, étalage, exhibition, exposition, exposure, flourish, manifestation, ostentation, pageant, parade, pomp, presentation, revelation, show, spectacle, splurge.

displeasure *n.* anger, annoyance, disapprobation, disapproval, discontent, disfavor, disgruntlement, dudgeon, huff, indignation, irritation, offense, pique, resentment, vexation, wrath.

antonyms gratification, pleasure.

disposal *n.* arrangement, array, assignment, authority, bequest, bestowal, clearance, conduct, consignment, control, conveyance, determination, direction, discarding, discretion, dispensation, disposition, distribution, dumping, ejection, gift, government, jettisoning, management, ordering, position, regulation, relinquishment, removal, responsibility, riddance, scrapping, settlement, transfer.

antonym provision.

dispose *v.* actuate, adapt, adjust, align, arrange, array, bias, condition, determine, dispone, distribute, fix, group, incline, induce, influence, lay, lead, marshal, motivate, move, order, place, position, predispose, prompt, put, range, rank, regulate, set, settle, situate, stand, tempt.

disposition *n.* adjustment, arrangement, bent, bias, character, classification, constitution, control, direction, disposal, distribution, grain, grouping, habit, inclination, kidney, leaning, make-up, management, nature, ordering, organization, placement, predisposition, proclivity, proneness, propensity, readiness, regulation, spirit, temper, temperament, tendency, velleity.

dispossess *v.* deprive, dislodge, disseize, divest, eject, evict, expel, oust, rob, strip, unhouse.

antonyms give, provide.

disprove *v.* answer, confute, contradict, controvert, discredit, explode, expose, invalidate, negate, rebut, refute.

antonym prove.

dispute *v.* altercate, argue, brawl, challenge, clash, contend, contest, contradict, controvert, debate, deny, discuss, doubt, gainsay, impugn, litigate, moot, oppugn, quarrel, question, spar, squabble, traverse, wrangle.

antonym agree.

n. altercation, argument, brawl, conflict, contention, controversy, debate, disagreement, discord, discussion, dissension, disturbance, feud, friction, quarrel, spar, squabble, strife, wrangle.

antonym agreement.

disqualify *v.* debar, disable, disauthorize, disentitle, dishabilitate, disprivilege, incapacitate, invalidate, preclude, prohibit, rule out, unfit.

antonyms accept, allow.

disregard *v.* brush aside, cold-shoulder, contemn, despise, discount, disdain, disobey, disparage, ignore, laugh off, make light of, neglect, overlook, pass over, pooh-pooh, slight, snub, turn a blind eye to.

antonyms note, pay attention to.

n. brush-off, contempt, disdain, disesteem, disrespect, heedlessness, ignoring, inattention, indifference, neglect, negligence, oversight, slight.

antonym attention.

disrepair *n.* collapse, decay, deterioration, dilapidation, ruin, ruination, shabbiness, unrepair.

antonyms good repair, restoration.

disreputable *adj.* base, contemptible, derogatory, discreditable, disgraceful, dishonorable, disorderly, disrespectable, ignominious, infamous, louche, low, mean, notorious, opprobrious, scandalous, seedy, shady, shameful, shocking, unprincipled.

antonyms decent, honorable.

disrespectful *adj.* bad-tempered, cheeky, contemptuous, discourteous, impertinent, impolite, impudent, insolent, insulting, irreverent, rude, uncivil, unmannerly.

antonym respectful.

dissect *v.* analyze, anatomize, break down, dismember, examine, explore, inspect, investigate, pore over, scrutinize, study.

disseminate *v.* broadcast, circulate, diffuse, disperse, dissipate, distribute, evangelize, proclaim, promulgate, propagate, publicize, publish, scatter, sow, spread.

dissent *v.* decline, differ, disagree, disconsent, object, protest, quibble, refuse.

antonyms agree, consent.

n. difference, disagreement, discord, dissension, dissidence, nonconformity, objection, opposition, quibble, refusal, resistance.

antonym agreement.

dissertation *n.* critique, discourse, disquisition, essay, exposition, monograph, paper, prolegomena, propaedeutic, thesis, treatise.

dissident *adj.* differing, disagreeing, discordant, dissentient, dissenting, heterodox, nonconformist, recusant, schismatic.

antonyms acquiescent, agreeing.

n. agitator, dissenter, protestor, rebel, recusant, refus(e)nik, schismatic.

antonym assenter.

dissimilar *adj.* different, disparate, divergent, diverse, heterogeneous, incompatible, mismatched, unlike, unrelated, various.

antonyms compatible, similar.

dissimulation *n.* act, affectation, concealment, deceit, deception, dissembling, double-dealing, duplicity, feigning, hypocrisy, play-acting, pretence, sham, wile.

antonym openness.

dissipate *v.* burn up, consume, deplete, disappear, dispel, disperse, dissolve, evaporate, expend, fritter away, lavish, rig, scatter, spend, squander, vanish, wanton, waste.

antonym accumulate.

dissolute *adj.* abandoned, corrupt, debauched, degenerate, depraved, dissipated, immoral, lax, lewd, libertine, licentious, loose, profligate, rakehell, rakehelly, rakish, unrestrained, vicious, wanton, wide, wild.

antonym virtuous.

dissolve *v.* break up, crumble, decompose, deliquesce, destroy, diffuse, disappear, discontinue, disintegrate, dismiss, disorganize, disperse, dissipate, disunite, divorce, dwindle, end, evanesce, evaporate, fade, flux, fuse, liquefy, loose, melt, overthrow, perish, ruin, separate, sever, soften, suspend, terminate, thaw, vanish, wind up.

dissuade *v.* dehort, deter, discourage, disincline, divert, expostulate, put off, remonstrate, warn.

antonym persuade.

distant *adj.* abroad, afar, aloof, apart, ceremonious, cold, cool, disparate, dispersed, distinct, faint, far, faraway, far-flung, far-off, formal, haughty, indirect, indistinct, isolated, obscure, outlying, out-of-the-way, remote, removed, reserved, restrained, reticent, scattered, separate, slight, stand-offish, stiff, unapproachable, uncertain, unfriendly, withdrawn.

antonyms close, friendly.

distasteful *adj.* abhorrent, aversive, disagreeable, displeasing, dissatisfying, loathsome, nasty, nauseous, objectionable, obnoxious, offensive, repugnant, repulsive, undesirable, uninviting, unpalatable, unpleasant, unsavory.

antonym pleasing.

distend *v.* balloon, bloat, bulge, dilate, enlarge, expand, fill out, increase, inflate, intumesce, puff, stretch, swell, widen.

antonym deflate.

distinct *adj.* apparent, clear, clear-cut, decided, definite, detached, different, discrete, dissimilar, evident, individual, lucid, manifest, marked, noticeable, obvious, palpable, patent, plain, recognizable, separate, several, sharp, unambiguous, unconnected, unmistakable, well-defined.
antonyms fuzzy, hazy, indistinct.

distinction[1] *n.* characteristic, contradistinction, contrast, difference, differential, differentiation, diorism, discernment, discrimination, dissimilarity, distinctiveness, division, feature, individuality, mark, nuance, particularity, peculiarity, penetration, perception, quality, separation.

distinction[2] *n.* account, celebrity, consequence, credit, eminence, excellence, fame, glory, greatness, honor, importance, merit, name, note, prestige, prominence, quality, rank, renown, reputation, repute, significance, superiority, worth.
antonym insignificance.

distinctive *adj.* characteristic, different, discriminative, discriminatory, distinguishing, extraordinary, idiosyncratic, individual, inimitable, original, peculiar, singular, special, typical, uncommon, unique.
antonym common.

distinguish *v.* ascertain, categorize, celebrate, characterize, classify, decide, determine, differentiate, dignify, discern, discriminate, honor, immortalize, individualize, judge, know, make out, mark, perceive, pick out, recognize, see, separate, signalize, tell, tell apart.

distinguished *adj.* acclaimed, celebrated, conspicuous, distingué, eminent, eximious, extraordinary, famed, famous, illustrious, marked, nameworthy, notable, noted, outstanding, renowned, signal, striking, well-known.
antonyms insignificant, ordinary.

distort *v.* bend, bias, buckle, color, contort, deform, disfigure, falsify, garble, miscolor, misrepresent, misshape, pervert, skew, slant, torture, twist, warp, wrench, wrest, wring.

distract *v.* agitate, amuse, beguile, bewilder, confound, confuse, derange, discompose, disconcert, disturb, divert, engross, entertain, faze, harass, madden, occupy, perplex, puzzle, sidetrack, torment, trouble.

distracted *adj.* agitated, bemused, bewildered, confounded, confused, crazy, deranged, distraught, éperdu(e), flustered, frantic, frenzied, grief-stricken, harassed, hassled, insane, mad, maddened, overwrought, perplexed, puzzled, raving, troubled, wild, worked up, wrought up.
antonyms calm, untroubled.

distraction *n.* aberration, abstraction, agitation, alienation, amusement, beguilement, bewilderment, commotion, confusion, delirium, derangement, desperation, discord, disorder, disturbance, diversion, divertissement, entertainment, frenzy, hallucination, harassment, incoherence, insanity, interference, interruption, mania, pastime, recreation.

distress *n.* adversity, affliction, agony, anguish, anxiety, calamity, depravation, desolation, destitution, difficulties, discomfort, grief, hardship, heartache, indigence, katzenjammer, misery, misfortune, need, pain, pauperism, poverty, privation, sadness, sorrow, strait(s), suffering, torment, torture, trial, trouble, woe, worry, wretchedness.
antonyms comfort, ease, security.

v. afflict, agonize, bother, constrain, cut up, disturb, grieve, harass, harrow, pain, perplex, sadden, straiten, torment, trouble, upset, worry, wound.
antonyms assist, comfort.

distribute *v.* administer, allocate, allot, apportion, arrange, assign, assort, bestow, carve up, categorize, circulate, class, classify, convey, deal, deliver, diffuse, dish out, dispense, disperse, dispose, disseminate, divide, dole, file, give, group, hand out, mete, scatter, share, spread, strew.
antonyms collect, gather in.

district *n.* area, canton, cantred, cantret, community, gau, hundred, locale, locality, neighborhood, parish, precinct, quarter, region, sector, vicinity, ward.

distrust *v.* disbelieve, discredit, doubt, misbelieve, miscredit, misdeem, mistrust, question, suspect.
antonym trust.

n. disbelief, doubt, misfaith, misgiving, mistrust, qualm, question, skepticism, suspicion, untrust, wariness.
antonym trust.

disturb *v.* affray, agitate, alarm, annoy, bother, concuss, confound, confuse, derange, disarrange, discompose, disorder, disorganize, disrupt, distract, distress, excite, fluster, harass, interrupt, muddle, perturb, pester, rouse, ruffle, shake, startle, trouble, unsettle, upset, worry.
antonyms calm, quiet, reassure.

disturbance *n.* agitation, annoyance, bother, brawl, breeze, broil, burst-up, bust-up, commotion, confusion, derangement, disorder, distraction, fracas, fray, hindrance, hubbub, interruption, intrusion, katzenjammer, kick-up, misarrangement, molestation, muss(e), perturbation, riot, ruckus, ruction, shake-up, stour, stramash, tumult, turmoil, unrest, upheaval, uproar, upset, upturn.
antonyms peace, quiet.

disturbed *adj.* agitated, anxious, apprehensive, bothered, concerned, confused, discomposed, disordered, disquieted, flustered, maladjusted, neurotic, troubled, unbalanced, uneasy, unrestful, upset, worried.
antonyms calm, sane.

disuse *n.* abandonment, decay, desuetude, discontinuance, disusage, idleness, neglect.
antonym use.

diverge *v.* bifurcate, branch, conflict, depart, deviate, differ, digress, disagree, dissent, divaricate, divide, fork, part, radiate, separate, split, spread, stray, vary, wander.
antonyms agree, come together, join.

diverse *adj.* assorted, different, differing, discrete, disparate, dissimilar, distinct, divergent, diversified, heterogeneous, manifold, many, miscellaneous, multifarious, multiform, numerous, separate, several, some, sundry, unlike, varied, various, varying.
antonym identical.

diversify *v.* alter, assort, branch out, change, expand, mix, spread out, variegate, vary.

diversion *n.* alteration, amusement, beguilement, change, deflection, delight, departure, detour, deviation, digression, disportment, distraction, divertissement, enjoyment, entertainment, game, gratification, pastime, play, pleasure, recreation, relaxation, sport, variation.

divert *v.* amuse, avert, beguile, deflect, delight, detract,

distract, entertain, gratify, hive off, recreate, redirect, regale, side-track, switch, tickle.
antonyms direct, irritate.

divide *v.* alienate, allocate, allot, apportion, arrange, bisect, break up, categorize, classify, cleave, cut, deal out, detach, disconnect, dispense, distribute, disunite, divvy, estrange, grade, group, part, partition, portion, segment, segregate, separate, sever, share, shear, sort, split, subdivide, sunder.
antonyms collect, gather, join.

divide out allocate, allot, apportion, dole out, measure out, morsel, parcel out, share, share out.

divine *adj.* angelic, beatific, beautiful, blissful, celestial, consecrated, exalted, excellent, glorious, godlike, heavenly, holy, marvelous, mystical, perfect, rapturous, religious, sacred, sanctified, spiritual, splendid, superhuman, superlative, supernatural, supreme, transcendent, transcendental, transmundane, wonderful.
n. churchman, clergyman, cleric, ecclesiastic, minister, parson, pastor, prelate, priest, reverend.
v. apprehend, conjecture, deduce, foretell, guess, hariolate, haruspicate, infer, intuit, perceive, prognosticate, suppose, surmise, suspect, understand.

division *n.* allotment, apportionment, bisection, border, boundary, branch, breach, category, class, compartment, cutting, demarcation, department, detaching, dichotomy, disagreement, discord, distribution, disunion, divide, divider, dividing, estrangement, feud, group, head, part, partition, portion, rupture, schism, scission, section, sector, segment, separation, sept, sharing, side, split, splitting, stream, variance, wapentake, ward, watershed, wing.
antonyms agreement, multiplication, unification.

divorce *n.* annulment, breach, break, break-up, decree nisi, diffarreation, dissolution, disunion, rupture, separation, severance, split-up.
v. annul, cancel, disconnect, dissever, dissociate, dissolve, disunite, divide, part, separate, sever, split up, sunder.
antonyms marry, unify.

divulge *v.* betray, broadcast, communicate, confess, declare, disclose, evulgate, exhibit, expose, impart, leak, let slip, proclaim, promulgate, publish, reveal, spill, tell, uncover.

dizzy *adj.* befuddled, bemused, bewildered, capricious, confused, dazed, dazzled, faint, fickle, flighty, foolish, frivolous, giddy, light-headed, lofty, muddled, reeling, scatter-brained, shaky, staggering, steep, swimming, vertiginous, wobbly, woozy.

do *v.* accomplish, achieve, act, adapt, answer, arrange, behave, carry out, cause, cheat, complete, con, conclude, cover, cozen, create, deceive, decipher, decode, defraud, discharge, dupe, effect, end, execute, explore, fare, fix, fleece, give, hoax, implement, make, manage, organize, pass muster, perform, prepare, present, proceed, produce, put on, render, resolve, satisfy, serve, solve, suffice, suit, swindle, tour, transact, translate, transpose, travel, trick, undertake, visit, work, work out.
n. affair, event, function, gathering, occasion, party.

docile *adj.* amenable, biddable, complaisant, compliant, ductile, manageable, obedient, obliging, pliable, pliant, submissive, teachable, tractable, unmurmuring, unprotesting, unquestioning.
antonyms truculent, unco-operative.

dock[1] *n.* boat-yard, harbor, marina, pier, quay, waterfront, wharf.
v. anchor, berth, drop anchor, join up, land, link up, moor, put in, rendezvous, tie up, unite.

dock[2] *v.* clip, crop, curtail, cut, decaudate, decrease, deduct, diminish, lessen, reduce, shorten, subtract, truncate, withhold.

doctor *n.* clinician, doctoress, doctress, general practitioner, GP, hakim, internist, leech, medic, medical officer, medical practitioner, medicaster, medico, physician, pill(s).
v. adulterate, alter, botch, change, cobble, cook, cut, dilute, disguise, falsify, fix, fudge, hocus, load, medicate, mend, misrepresent, patch, pervert, repair, spike, tamper with, treat.

doctrine *n.* belief, canon, concept, conviction, creed, dogma, ism, opinion, precept, principle, teaching, tenet.

document *n.* certificate, chirograph, deed, form, instrument, paper, parchment, record, report.
v. authenticate, back, certify, cite, corroborate, detail, enumerate, instance, list, particularize, prove, substantiate, support, validate, verify.

dodge *v.* avoid, dart, deceive, duck, elude, equivocate, evade, fend off, fudge, hedge, parry, shift, shirk, shuffle, side-step, skive, swerve, swing the lead, trick.
n. chicane, contrivance, device, feint, machination, maneuver, ploy, ruse, scheme, stratagem, subterfuge, trick, wheeze, wile.

dogged *adj.* determined, firm, indefatigable, indomitable, obstinate, persevering, persistent, pertinacious, relentless, resolute, single-minded, staunch, steadfast, steady, stubborn, tenacious, unflagging, unshakable, unyielding.
antonym irresolute.

dogma *n.* article, article of faith, belief, conviction, credendum, credo, creed, doctrine, opinion, precept, principle, teaching, tenet.

dogmatic *adj.* affirmative, arbitrary, assertive, authoritative, canonical, categorical, dictatorial, didactic, doctrinaire, doctrinal, downright, emphatic, ex cathedra, high-dried, imperious, magisterial, obdurate, opinionated, oracular, overbearing, peremptory, pontific(al), positive.

doings *n.* actions, activities, acts, adventures, affairs, concerns, dealings, deeds, events, exploits, goings-on, handiwork, happenings, proceedings, transactions.

dole *n.* allocation, allotment, allowance, alms, apportionment, benefit, dispensation, dispersal, distribution, division, donation, gift, grant, gratuity, issuance, modicum, parcel, pittance, portion, quota, share.

doleful *adj.* blue, cheerless, depressing, dismal, distressing, dolorous, dreary, forlorn, funereal, gloomy, lugubrious, melancholy, mournful, painful, pathetic, pitiful, rueful, sad, somber, sorrowful, woebegone, woeful, wretched.
antonym cheerful.

dolt *n.* ass, beetlebrain, beetlehead, besom-head, blockhead, bonehead, booby, boodle, bufflehead, bull-calf, calf, chump, clod, clodhopper, clodpate, clodpoll, clot, clunk, dimwit, dope, dullard, dunce, fool, galoot, halfwit, idiot, ignoramus, leather-head, loggerhead, loghead, lurdan(e), lurden, mutt, mutton-head, nitwit, nutcase, palooka, sheep's-head, simpleton, turnip.

domain *n.* area, authority, bailiwick, business, concern, demesne, department, discipline, dominion, empire, estate, field, jurisdiction, kingdom, lands, orbit, pidgin, policies, power, province, realm, region, scope, specialty, sphere, sway, territory.

domestic *adj.* autochthonic, domal, domesticated, domiciliary, family, home, home-bred, home-loving, homely, house, household, house-trained, housewifely, indigenous, internal, native, pet, private, stay-at-home, tame, trained.

n. au pair, char, charwoman, daily, daily help, help, maid, scullery maid, servant, slavey, woman.

domesticate *v.* acclimatize, accustom, break, domesticize, familiarize, habituate, house-train, naturalize, tame, train.

domicile *n.* abode, dwelling, habitation, home, house, lodging(s), mansion, quarters, residence, residency, settlement.

dominate *v.* bestride, control, direct, domineer, dwarf, eclipse, govern, have the whip hand, keep under one's thumb, lead, master, monopolize, outshine, overbear, overgang, overlook, overrule, overshadow, predominate, prevail, rule, tyrannize.

domination *n.* ascendancy, authority, command, control, despotism, dictatorship, hegemony, influence, leadership, mastery, oppression, power, repression, rule, subjection, subordination, superiority, suppression, supremacy, sway, tyranny.

domineering *adj.* arrogant, authoritarian, autocratic, bossy, coercive, despotic, dictatorial, harsh, high-handed, imperious, iron-handed, magisterial, masterful, oppressive, overbearing, severe, tyrannical.

antonyms meek, obsequious, servile.

don *v.* affect, assume, clothe oneself in, dress in, get into, put on.

antonym doff.

donate *v.* bequeath, bestow, chip in, confer, contribute, cough up, fork out, gift, give, impart, present, proffer, subscribe.

donation *n.* alms, benefaction, boon, conferment, contribution, gift, grant, gratuity, largess(e), offering, present, presentation, subscription.

done *adj.* acceptable, accomplished, advised, agreed, completed, concluded, consummated, conventional, cooked, cooked to a turn, de rigueur, depleted, drained, ended, executed, exhausted, fatigued, finished, OK, over, perfected, proper, ready, realized, settled, spent, terminated, through, used up.

doom *n.* Armageddon, catastrophe, condemnation, death, death-knell, decision, decree, destiny, destruction, Doomsday, downfall, fate, fortune, judgment, Judgment Day, karma, kismet, lot, portion, ruin, sentence, the Last Judgment, the last trump, verdict.

v. condemn, consign, damn, decree, destine, foredoom, foreordain, judge, predestine, preordain, sentence, threaten.

doomed *adj.* accursed, bedeviled, bewitched, condemned, cursed, fated, fey, hopeless, ill-fated, ill-omened, ill-starred, luckless, star-crossed.

dormant *adj.* asleep, comatose, fallow, hibernating, inactive, inert, inoperative, latent, latescent, quiescent, sleeping, sluggish, slumbering, suspended, torpid, undeveloped, unrealized.

antonyms active.

dose *n.* dosage, draught, drench, hit, measure, portion, potion, prescription, quantity, shot, slug.

v. administer, dispense, drench, medicate, treat.

doting *adj.* adoring, devoted, fond, foolish, indulgent, lovesick, soft.

double *adj.* bifarious, bifold, binate, coupled, diploid, doubled, dual, duple, duplex, duplicate, paired, twice, twin, twofold.

v. duplicate, enlarge, fold, geminate, grow, increase, magnify, multiply, repeat.

n. clone, copy, counterpart, dead ringer, dead spit, Doppelgänger, duplicate, fellow, image, impersonator, lookalike, mate, replica, ringer, spitting image, twin.

double-cross *v.* betray, cheat, con, cozen, defraud, hoodwink, mislead, swindle, trick, two-time.

double-dealer *n.* betrayer, cheat, con man, cozener, deceiver, dissembler, double-crosser, fraud, hypocrite, Machiavellian, rogue, swindler, traitor, two-timer.

doubt *v.* be dubious, be uncertain, demur, discredit, distrust, dubitate, fear, fluctuate, hesitate, misgive, mistrust, query, question, scruple, suspect, vacillate, waver.

antonyms believe, trust.

n. ambiguity, apprehension, arrière pensée, confusion, difficulty, dilemma, disquiet, distrust, dubiety, fear, hesitancy, hesitation, incredulity, indecision, irresolution, misgiving, mistrust, perplexity, problem, qualm, quandary, reservation, skepticism, suspense, suspicion, uncertainty, vacillation.

antonyms belief, certainty, confidence, trust.

doubtful *adj.* ambiguous, debatable, disreputable, distrustful, dubious, dubitable, equivocal, hazardous, hesitant, hesitating, inconclusive, indefinite, indeterminate, irresolute, litigious, obscure, perplexed, precarious, problematic, problematical, questionable, sceptical, shady, suspect, suspicious, tentative, uncertain, unclear, unconfirmed, unconvinced, undecided, unresolved, unsettled, unsure, vacillating, vague, wavering.

antonyms certain, definite.

doubtless *adv.* apparently, assuredly, certainly, clearly, indisputably, most likely, of course, ostensibly, out of question, precisely, presumably, probably, questionless, seemingly, supposedly, surely, truly, undoubtedly, unquestionably, without doubt.

doughty *adj.* able, bold, brave, courageous, daring, dauntless, fearless, gallant, game, hardy, heroic, intrepid, redoubtable, resolute, stout-hearted, strong, valiant, valorous.

antonyms cowardly, weak.

douse, dowse *v.* blow out, dip, drench, duck, dunk, extinguish, immerge, immerse, plunge, put out, saturate, smother, snuff, soak, souse, steep, submerge.

dowdy *adj.* dingy, drab, frowzy, frumpish, frumpy, ill-dressed, old-fashioned, scrubby, shabby, slovenly, tacky, tatty, unfashionable, unmodish, unsmart.

antonyms dressy, smart, spruce.

downcast *adj.* cheerless, chopfallen, crestfallen, daunted, dejected, depressed, despondent, disappointed, disconsolate, discouraged, disheartened, dismayed, dispirited, down, miserable, sad, unhappy.

antonyms cheerful, elated, happy.

downfall *n.* breakdown, cloudburst, collapse, comedown, come-uppance, debacle, deluge, descent, destruction, disgrace, downpour, failure, fall, humiliation, overthrow, rainstorm, ruin, undoing, Waterloo.

downgrade *v.* belittle, decry, degrade, demote, denigrate, detract from, disparage, humble, lower, reduce in rank, run down.

antonyms improve, upgrade.

downhearted *adj.* blue, chopfallen, crestfallen, dejected, depressed, despondent, discouraged, disheartened, dismayed, dispirited, downcast, gloomy, glum, jaw-fallen, low-spirited, sad, sorrowful, unhappy.

antonyms cheerful, enthusiastic, happy.

downpour *n.* cloudburst, deluge, downcome, flood, inundation, rainstorm, torrent, water-spout.

downright *adj.* absolute, blatant, blunt, candid, categorical, clear, complete, explicit, forthright, frank, honest, open, out-and-out, outright, outspoken, plain, positive, simple, sincere, straightforward, thoroughgoing, total, undisguised, unequivocal, unqualified, utter, wholesale.

dowry *n.* dot, dower, endowment, faculty, gift, inheritance, legacy, portion, provision, share, talent, wedding-dower.

drab *adj.* cheerless, colorless, dingy, dismal, dreary, dull, dun-colored, flat, gloomy, gray, lackluster, mousy, shabby, somber, uninspired, vapid.

antonym bright.

draft[1] *v.* compose, delineate, design, draw, draw up, formulate, outline, plan, sketch.

n. abstract, delineation, ébauche, outline, plan, protocol, rough, sketch, version.

draft[2] *n.* bill, check, order, postal order.

draft[3] *n.* cup, current, dose, dragging, drawing, drench, drink, flow, haulage, influx, movement, portion, potation, puff, pulling, quantity, traction.

drag *v.* crawl, creep, dawdle, draggle, draw, hale, harl, haul, inch, lag, linger, loiter, lug, pull, schlep, shamble, shuffle, straggle, sweep, tow, trail, tug, yank.

n. annoyance, bore, bother, brake, drogue, nuisance, pain, pest, pill.

drain *v.* bleed, consume, deplete, discharge, dissipate, down, draw off, drink up, dry, effuse, empty, emulge, evacuate, exhaust, exude, finish, flow out, lade, leak, milk, ooze, quaff, remove, sap, seep, strain, swallow, tap, tax, trickle, use up, weary, withdraw.

antonym fill.

n. channel, conduit, culvert, depletion, ditch, drag, duct, exhaustion, expenditure, grip, outlet, pipe, reduction, sap, sewer, sink, sough, stank, strain, trench, watercourse, withdrawal.

drama *n.* acting, crisis, dramatics, dramatization, dramaturgy, excitement, histrionics, kabuki, kathakali, melodrama, play, scene, show, spectacle, stage-craft, theater, theatricals, Thespian art, turmoil.

dramatist *n.* comedian, dramaturge, dramaturgist, playwright, play-writer, screen-writer, scriptwriter, tragedian.

drape *v.* adorn, array, cloak, cover, dangle, droop, drop, enrap, fold, hang, suspend, swathe, vest, wrap.

drastic *adj.* desperate, dire, draconian, extreme, far-reaching, forceful, harsh, heroic, radical, severe, strong.

antonym mild.

draw[1] *v.* allure, attenuate, attract, borrow, breathe in, bring forth, choose, deduce, delineate, depict, derive, design, drag, drain, elicit, elongate, engage, entice, entrain, evoke, extend, extort, extract, get, haul, induce, infer, influence, inhale, inspire, invite, lengthen, make, map out, mark out, outline, paint, pencil,

persuade, pick, portray, puff, pull, respire, select, sketch, stretch, suck, take, tow, trace, tug, unsheathe.

antonyms propel, push.

n. appeal, attraction, bait, enticement, interest, lure, pull.

draw[2] *v.* be equal, be even, be neck and neck, dead-heat, tie.

n. dead-heat, deadlock, impasse, stalemate, tie.

drawback *n.* block, defect, deficiency, désagrément, detriment, difficulty, disability, disadvantage, fault, flaw, fly in the ointment, handicap, hindrance, hitch, impediment, imperfection, nuisance, obstacle, pullback, snag, stumbling, trouble.

antonym advantage.

drawing *n.* cartoon, delineation, depiction, graphic, illustration, outline, picture, portrait, portrayal, representation, sketch, study.

drawn *adj.* fatigued, fraught, haggard, harassed, harrowed, hassled, pinched, sapped, strained, stressed, taut, tense, tired, worn.

dread *v.* cringe at, fear, flinch, quail, shrink from, shudder, shy, tremble.

n. alarm, apprehension, aversion, awe, dismay, disquiet, fear, fright, funk, heebie-jeebies, horror, misgiving, terror, trepidation, worry.

antonyms confidence, security.

adj. alarming, awe-inspiring, awful, dire, dreaded, dreadful, frightening, frightful, ghastly, grisly, gruesome, horrible, terrible, terrifying.

dreadful *adj.* alarming, appalling, awful, dire, distressing, fearful, formidable, frightful, ghastly, grievous, grisly, gruesome, harrowing, hideous, horrendous, horrible, monstrous, shocking, terrible, tragic, tremendous.

antonym comforting.

dream *n.* ambition, aspiration, beauty, castle in Spain, castle in the air, daydream, delight, delusion, design, desire, fantasy, goal, hallucination, hope, illusion, imagination, joy, marvel, notion, phantasm, pipedream, pleasure, reverie, speculation, trance, treasure, vagary, vision, wish.

v. conjure, daydream, envisage, fancy, fantasize, hallucinate, imagine, muse, star-gaze, think, visualize.

dreamer *n.* daydreamer, Don Quixote, fantasist, fantasizer, fantast, idealist, John o'dreams, Johnny-head-in-the-air, romancer, star-gazer, theorizer, utopian, visionary, Walter Mitty, wool-gatherer.

antonyms pragmatist, realist.

dreary *adj.* bleak, boring, cheerless, colorless, comfortless, commonplace, depressing, dismal, doleful, downcast, drab, drear, dreich, dull, forlorn, gloomy, glum, humdrum, joyless, lifeless, lonely, lonesome, melancholy, monotonous, mournful, routine, sad, solitary, somber, sorrowful, tedious, trite, uneventful, uninteresting, wearisome, wretched.

antonyms bright, interesting.

dregs *n.* canaille, deposit, draff, dross, excrement, faeces, fag-end, fecula, grounds, lags, lees, left-overs, mother, outcasts, rabble, residue, residuum, riff-raff, scourings, scum, sediment, tailings, trash, waste.

drench *v.* douse, drouk, drown, duck, flood, imbrue, imbue, immerse, inundate, saturate, soak, souse, steep, wet.

dress *n.* apparel, attire, caparison, clothes, clothing, costume, ensemble, frock, garb, garment, garments, gear, get-up, gown, guise, habiliments, habit, outfit, raiment, rig-out, robe, suit, togs, vestment.

v. accouter, adjust, adorn, align, apparel, arrange, array, attire, bandage, bedeck, bedizen, betrim, bind up, boun, busk, caparison, change, clothe, deck, decorate, dispose, don, drape, embellish, fit, furbish, garb, garnish, groom, habilitate, habit, ornament, plaster, prepare, put on, rig, robe, set, straighten, tend, treat, trim.

antonyms disrobe, strip, undress.

dressing *n.* bandage, compress, emplastron, emplastrum, ligature, pad, plaster, pledget, poultice, spica, tourniquet.

dressy *adj.* classy, elaborate, elegant, formal, natty, ornate, ritzy, smart, stylish, swanky, swish.

antonyms dowdy, scruffy.

dribble *v.* drip, drivel, drool, drop, leak, ooze, run, saliva, seep, slaver, slobber, sprinkle, trickle.

n. drip, droplet, gobbet, leak, seepage, sprinkling, trickle.

drift *v.* accumulate, amass, coast, drive, float, freewheel, gather, meander, pile up, stray, waft, wander.

n. accumulation, aim, bank, course, current, design, direction, dune, flow, gist, heap, implication, import, impulse, intention, mass, meaning, mound, movement, object, pile, purport, ridge, rush, scope, significance, sweep, tendency, tenor, thrust, trend.

drifter *n.* beachcomber, hobo, intinerant, rolling stone, rover, swagman, tramp, vagabond, vagrant, wanderer.

drill[1] *v.* coach, discipline, exercise, instruct, practice, rehearse, teach, train, tutor.

n. coaching, discipline, exercise, instruction, practice, preparation, repetition, training, tuition.

drill[2] *v.* bore, penetrate, perforate, pierce, puncture, transpierce.

n. awl, bit, borer, gimlet.

drink *v.* absorb, bib, booze, carouse, down, drain, dram, gulp, guzzle, hit the bottle, imbibe, indulge, knock back, liquefy, liquor up, partake of, quaff, revel, sip, suck, sup, swallow, swig, swill, tank up, tipple, tope, toss off, wassail, water.

n. alcohol, ambrosia, beverage, bev(v)y, booze, deochan-doris, dose, dram, draught, glass, gulp, hooch, liquid, liquor, noggin, plonk, potion, refreshment, sensation, sip, slug, snifter, snort, spirits, stiffener, suck, swallow, swig, swizzle, taste, the bottle, tickler, tiff, tipple, toss, tot.

drip *v.* dribble, drizzle, drop, exude, filter, plop, splash, sprinkle, trickle, weep.

n. dribble, dripping, drop, leak, milk-sop, ninny, softy, stillicide, trickle, weakling, weed, wet.

drive *v.* actuate, bear, coerce, compel, constrain, dash, dig, direct, force, goad, guide, hammer, handle, harass, herd, hurl, impel, manage, motivate, motor, oblige, operate, overburden, overwork, plunge, press, prod, propel, push, ram, ride, rush, send, sink, spur, stab, steer, task, tax, thrust, travel, urge.

n. action, advance, ambition, appeal, campaign, crusade, determination, effort, energy, enterprise, excursion, get-up-and-go, hurl, initiative, jaunt, journey, motivation, outing, pressure, push, ride, run, spin, surge, trip, turn, vigor, vim, zip.

drivel *n.* blathering, bunkum, eyewash, gibberish, gobbledegook, guff, gush, jive, mumbo-jumbo, nonsense, slush, stultiloquy, twaddle, waffle.

driver *n.* cabbie, cabman, charioteer, chauffeur, coachman, Jehu, motorist, trucker, vetturino, voiturier, wagoner.

droll *adj.* amusing, clownish, comic, comical, diverting, eccentric, entertaining, farcical, funny, humorous, jocular, laughable, ludicrous, pawky, quaint, ridiculous, risible, waggish, whimsical, witty.

drone *v.* bombilate, bombinate, buzz, chant, drawl, hum, intone, purr, thrum, vibrate, whirr.

n. buzz, chant, hum, murmuring, purr, thrum, vibration, whirr, whirring.

drool *v.* dote, dribble, drivel, enthuse, fondle, gloat, gush, rave, salivate, slaver, slobber, water at the mouth.

droop *v.* bend, dangle, decline, despond, diminish, drop, fade, faint, fall down, falter, flag, hang (down) sag, languish, lose heart, sink, slouch, slump, stoop, wilt, wither.

antonyms rise, straighten.

drop *n.* abyss, bead, bubble, chasm, cut, dab, dash, decline, declivity, decrease, descent, deterioration, downturn, drib, driblet, drip, droplet, fall, falling-off, glob, globule, globulet, goutte, gutta, lowering, mouthful, nip, pearl, pinch, plunge, precipice, reduction, shot, sip, slope, slump, spot, taste, tear, tot, trace, trickle.

v. abandon, cease, chuck, decline, depress, descend, desert, diminish, discontinue, disown, dive, dribble, drip, droop, fall, forsake, give up, jilt, kick, leave, lower, plummet, plunge, quit, reject, relinquish, remit, renounce, repudiate, sink, stop, terminate, throw over, trickle, tumble.

antonyms mount, rise.

drop-out *n.* Bohemian, deviant, dissenter, dissentient, hippie, loner, malcontent, non-conformist, rebel, renegade.

droppings *n.* dung, egesta, excrement, excreta, faeces, fumet, guano, manure, ordure, spraint, stools.

dross *n.* crust, debris, dregs, impurity, lees, recrement, refuse, remains, rubbish, scoria, scum, trash, waste.

drove *n.* collection, company, crowd, drift, flock, gathering, herd, horde, mob, multitude, press, swarm, throng.

drown *v.* deaden, deluge, drench, engulf, extinguish, flood, go under, immerse, inundate, muffle, obliterate, overcome, overpower, overwhelm, silence, sink, stifle, submerge, swallow up, swamp, wipe out.

drowsiness *n.* dopeyness, doziness, grogginess, lethargy, narcosis, oscitancy, sleepiness, sluggishness, somnolence, torpor.

drowsy *adj.* comatose, dazed, dopey, dozy, dreamy, drugged, heavy, lethargic, lulling, nodding, restful, sleepy, somniculous, somnolent, soothing, soporific, tired, torpid.

antonyms alert, awake.

drubbing *n.* beating, clobbering, defeat, flogging, hammering, licking, pounding, pummeling, thrashing, trouncing, walloping, whipping, whitewash.

drudge *n.* afterguard, devil, dogsbody, factotum, galley-slave, hack, jackal, lackey, maid-of-all-work, man-of-all-work, menial, scullion, servant, skivvy, slave, toiler, worker.

v. beaver, droil, grind, labor, moil, plod, plug away, slave, toil, work.

antonyms idle, laze.

drudgery n. chore, collar-work, donkey-work, drudgism, fag, faggery, grind, hack-work, labor, labor improbus, skivvying, slavery, slog, sweat, sweated labor, toil.

drug n. depressant, dope, kef, medicament, medication, medicine, Mickey, Mickey Finn, narcotic, opiate, physic, poison, potion, remedy, stimulant.

v. anesthetize, deaden, dope, dose, drench, knock out, load, medicate, numb, poison, stupefy, treat.

drug-addict n. acid head, dope-fiend, head, hop-head, hype, junkie, tripper.

drugged adj. comatose, doped, dopey, high, looped, spaced out, stoned, stupefied, tripping, turned on, zonked.

druggist n. apothecary, chemist, pharmacologist.

drunk adj. a peg too low, a sheet (three sheets) in the wind, bevvied, blind, blotto, bonkers, bottled, canned, cockeyed, corked, corny, drunken, fou, fuddled, half-seas-over, in liquor, inebriate, inebriated, intoxicated, legless, liquored, lit up, loaded, lushy, maggoty, maudlin, merry, moony, moppy, mops and brooms, mortal, muddled, nappy, obfuscated, paralytic, pickled, pie-eyed, pissed, pixilated, plastered, shickered, sloshed, soaked, sottish, soused, sow-drunk, sozzled, stewed, stoned, stotious, tanked up, temulent, tiddly, tight, tipsy, up the pole, well-oiled, wet.

antonym sober.

n. boozer, drunkard, inebriate, lush, soak, sot, toper, wino.

drunkard n. alcoholic, bacchant, carouser, dipsomaniac, drinker, drunk, lush, soak, sot, souse, sponge, tippler, toper, tosspot, wino.

dry adj. arid, barren, boring, cutting, cynical, deadpan, dehydrated, desiccated, dreary, dried up, droll, droughty, drouthy, dull, juiceless, keen, low-key, moistureless, monotonous, parched, pawky, plain, sapless, sarcastic, sec, secco, sharp, sly, tedious, thirsty, tiresome, torrid, uninteresting, waterless, withered, xeric.

antonyms interesting, sweet, wet.

v. dehumidify, dehydrate, drain, exsiccate, harden, mummify, parch, sear, shrivel, welt, wilt, wither, wizen.

antonyms soak, wet.

dub[1] v. bestow, call, christen, confer, denominate, designate, entitle, knight, label, name, nickname, style, tag, term.

dubious adj. ambiguous, debatable, doubtful, equivocal, fishy, hesitant, iffy, indefinite, indeterminate, obscure, problematical, questionable, shady, skeptical, speculative, suspect, suspicious, uncertain, unclear, unconvinced, undecided, undependable, unreliable, unsettled, unsure, untrustworthy, wavering.

antonyms certain, reliable, trustworthy.

duck[1] v. avoid, bend, bob, bow, crouch, dodge, drop, escape, evade, lower, shirk, shun, sidestep, squat, stoop.

duck[2] v. dip, dive, dook, douse, dunk, immerse, plunge, souse, submerge, wet.

duct n. blood, canal, channel, conduit, fistula, funnel, passage, pipe, tube, vas, vessel.

due adj. adequate, ample, appropriate, becoming, bounden, deserved, enough, expected, fit, fitting, in arrears, just, justified, mature, merited, obligatory, outstanding, owed, owing, payable, plenty of, proper, requisite, returnable, right, rightful, scheduled, sufficient, suitable, unpaid, well-earned.

n. birthright, come-uppance, deserts, merits, prerogative, privilege, right(s).

adv. dead, direct, directly, exactly, precisely, straight.

duel n. affair of honor, clash, competition, contest, duello, encounter, engagement, fight, monomachia, monomachy, rivalry, single combat, struggle.

v. battle, clash, compete, contend, contest, fight, rival, struggle, vie.

dues n. charge(s), contribution, fee, levy, subscription.

duffer n. blunderer, bonehead, booby, bungler, clod, clot, dolt, galoot, lubber, lummox, muff, oaf.

dull adj. apathetic, blank, blockish, blunt, blunted, Boeotian, boring, bovine, callous, cloudy, commonplace, corny, dead, dead-and-alive, dense, depressed, dim, dimwitted, dismal, doltish, drab, dreary, dry, dulled, edgeless, empty, faded, featureless, feeble, flat, gloomy, heavy, humdrum, inactive, indifferent, indistinct, insensible, insensitive, insipid, lackluster, leaden, lifeless, listless, monotonous, mopish, muffled, mumpish, murky, muted, opaque, overcast, passionless, pedestrian, plain, prosaic, run-of-the-mill, slack, sleepy, slow, sluggish, somber, stodgy, stolid, stultifying, stupid, subdued, subfusc, sullen, sunless, tame, tedious, thick, tiresome, toneless, torpid, turbid, uneventful, unexciting, unfunny, ungifted, unidea'd, unimaginative, unintelligent, uninteresting, unlively, unresponsive, unsharpened, unsunny, unsympathetic, untalented, vacuous, vapid.

antonyms alert, bright, clear, exciting, sharp.

v. allay, alleviate, assuage, blunt, cloud, dampen, darken, deject, depress, dim, discourage, disedge, dishearten, dispirit, fade, hebetate, lessen, mitigate, moderate, muffle, obscure, obtund, opiate, palliate, paralyze, rebate, relieve, sadden, soften, stain, stupefy, subdue, sully, tarnish.

antonyms brighten, sharpen, stimulate.

dullard n. blockhead, bonehead, chump, clod, clot, dimwit, dolt, dope, dummy, dunce, dunderhead, flat tire, idiot, ignoramus, imbecile, moron, nitwit, noodle, numskull, oaf, simpleton, vegetable.

antonym brain.

dumb adj. aphonic, aphonous, dense, dimwitted, dull, foolish, inarticulate, mum, mute, silent, soundless, speechless, stupid, thick, tongue-tied, unintelligent, voiceless, wordless.

antonym intelligent.

dum(b)founded adj. amazed, astonished, astounded, bewildered, bowled over, breathless, confounded, confused, dumb, flabbergasted, floored, knocked sideways, nonplused, overcome, overwhelmed, paralyzed, speechless, staggered, startled, stunned, taken aback, thrown, thunderstruck.

dump v. deposit, discharge, dispose of, ditch, drop, empty out, get rid of, jettison, let fall, offload, park, scrap, throw away, throw down, tip, unload.

n. coup, hole, hovel, joint, junk-yard, landhill, mess, midden, pigsty, rubbish-heap, rubbish-tip, shack, shanty, slum, tip.

dunce n. ass, blockhead, bonehead, dimwit, dolt, donkey, duffer, dullard, dunderhead, goose, half-wit, ignoramus, loggerhead, log-head, loon, moron, nincompoop, numskull, simpleton.

antonyms brain, intellectual.

dungeon *n.* cage, cell, donjon, lock-up, oubliette, pit, prison, vault.

dupe *n.* cat's-paw, fall guy, flat, geck, gull, instrument, mug, pawn, pigeon, puppet, push-over, sap, simpleton, sitter, soft mark, stooge, sucker, tool, victim.

v. bamboozle, beguile, cheat, con, cozen, deceive, defraud, delude, gammon, grift, gudgeon, gull, hoax, hoodwink, humbug, outwit, overreach, pigeon, rip off, swindle, trick.

duplicate *adj.* corresponding, geminate, identical, matched, matching, twin, twofold.

n. carbon copy, copy, facsimile, match, photocopy, Photostat®, replica, reproduction, Xerox®.

v. clone, copy, ditto, double, echo, geminate, photocopy, Photostat®, repeat, replicate, reproduce, Xerox®.

duplicity *n.* artifice, chicanery, deceit, deception, dishonesty, dissimulation, double-dealing, falsehood, fraud, guile, hypocrisy, mendacity, perfidy, treachery.

durability *n.* constancy, durableness, endurance, imperishability, lastingness, longevity, permanence, persistence, stability, strength.

antonyms fragility, impermanence, weakness.

durable *adj.* abiding, constant, dependable, enduring, fast, firm, fixed, hard-wearing, lasting, long-lasting, perdurable, permanent, persistent, reliable, resistant, sound, stable, strong, sturdy, substantial, tough, unfading.

antonyms fragile, impermanent, perishable, weak.

duration *n.* continuance, continuation, extent, fullness, length, period, perpetuation, prolongation, span, spell, stretch, term-time.

antonym shortening.

duress *n.* bullying, captivity, coaction, coercion, compulsion, confinement, constraint, force, hardship, imprisonment, incarceration, pressure, restraint, threat.

dusky *adj.* caliginous, cloudy, crepuscular, dark, dark-hued, darkish, dim, fuliginous, gloomy, murky, obscure, overcast, sable, shadowy, shady, sooty, subfusc, swarthy, tenebr(i)ous, twilight, twilit, umbrose, veiled.

antonyms bright, light, white.

dusty *adj.* chalky, crumbly, dirty, filthy, friable, granular, grubby, powdery, pulverous, sandy, sooty, unswept.

antonyms clean, hard, polished, solid.

dutiful *adj.* acquiescent, complaisant, compliant, conscientious, deferential, devoted, docile, duteous, filial, obedient, punctilious, regardful, respectful, reverential, submissive.

duty *n.* allegiance, assignment, business, calling, charge, chore, customs, debt, deference, devoir, due, engagement, excise, function, impost, job, levy, loyalty, mission, obedience, obligation, office, onus, province, respect, responsibility, reverence, role, service, tariff, task, tax, toll, work.

dwarf *n.* droich, durgan, elf, gnome, goblin, homuncle, homuncule, homunculus, hop-o'-my-thumb, Lilliputian, manikin, midget, pygmy, Tom Thumb.

adj. baby, bonsai, diminutive, dwarfed, dwarfish, Lilliputian, mini, miniature, petite, pint-size(d), pocket, small, tiny, undersized.

antonym large.

v. check, dim, diminish, dominate, lower, minimize, overshadow, retard, stunt.

dwell *v.* abide, bide, hang out, inhabit, live, lodge, people, populate, quarter, remain, reside, rest, settle, sojourn, stay, stop, tenant.

dwelling *n.* abode, domicile, dwelling-house, establishment, habitation, home, house, lodge, lodging, quarters, residence, tent, tepee.

dwindle *v.* abate, contract, decay, decline, decrease, die, die out, diminish, disappear, ebb, fade, fall, lessen, peter out, pine, shrink, shrivel, sink, subside, tail off, taper off, vanish, wane, waste away, weaken, wither.

antonym increase.

dying *adj.* at death's door, declining, disappearing, ebbing, expiring, fading, failing, final, going, in articulo mortis, in extremis, moribund, mortal, not long for this world, obsolescent, passing, perishing, sinking, vanishing.

antonyms coming, reviving.

dynamic *adj.* active, driving, electric, energetic, forceful, go-ahead, go-getting, high-powered, lively, powerful, self-starting, spirited, vigorous, vital, zippy.

antonyms apathetic, inactive, slow.

E

eager *adj.* agog, anxious, ardent, athirst, avid, desirous, earnest, empressé, enthusiastic, fervent, fervid, fervorous, freck, greedy, gung-ho, hot, hungry, impatient, intent, keen, longing, perfervid, raring, unshrinking, vehement, yearning, zealous.

antonyms apathetic, unenthusiastic.

early *adj.* advanced, forward, matutinal, matutine, prehistoric, premature, primeval, primitive, primordial, undeveloped, untimely, young.

adv. ahead of time, beforehand, betimes, in advance, in good time, prematurely, too soon.

antonym late.

earmark *v.* allocate, designate, keep back, label, put aside, reserve, set aside, tag.

earn *v.* acquire, attain, bring in, collect, deserve, draw, gain, get, gross, make, merit, net, obtain, procure, rate, realize, reap, receive, warrant, win.

antonyms lose, spend.

earnest *adj.* ardent, close, constant, determined, devoted, eager, enthusiastic, fervent, fervid, firm, fixed, grave, heartfelt, impassioned, intent, keen, passionate, purposeful, resolute, resolved, serious, sincere, solemn, stable, staid, steady, thoughtful, urgent, vehement, warm, zealous.

antonyms apathetic, flippant, unenthusiastic.

n. assurance, deposit, determination, down payment, guarantee, pledge, promise, resolution, security, seriousness, sincerity, token, truth.

earnings *n.* emoluments, gain, income, pay, proceeds, profits, receipts, remuneration, return, revenue, reward, salary, stipend, takings, wages.

antonyms expenses, outgoings.

earth[1] *n.* geosphere, globe, middle-earth, middle-world, Midgard, orb, planet, sphere, world.

earth[2] *n.* clay, clod, dirt, ground, humus, land, loam, mold, sod, soil, topsoil.

earthly *adj.* base, carnal, conceivable, earthern, feasible,

fleshly, gross, human, imaginable, likely, low, material, materialistic, mortal, mundane, physical, possible, practical, profane, secular, sensual, slight, slightest, sordid, sublunar, sublunary, tellurian, telluric, temporal, terrene, terrestrial, vile, worldly.
antonyms heavenly, spiritual.

earthy *adj.* bawdy, blue, coarse, crude, down-to-earth, homely, indecorous, lusty, natural, raunchy, ribald, robust, rough, simple, uninhibited, unrefined, unsophisticated, vulgar.
antonyms cultured, refined.

ease *n.* affluence, aplomb, calmness, comfort, composure, content, contentment, deftness, dexterity, easiness, effortlessness, enjoyment, facileness, facility, flexibility, freedom, happiness, informality, insouciance, leisure, liberty, naturalness, nonchalance, peace, peace of mind, poise, quiet, quietude, readiness, relaxation, repose, rest, restfulness, serenity, simplicity, solace, tranquility, unaffectedness, unconstraint, unreservedness.
antonyms difficulty, discomfort.

v. abate, aid, allay, appease, assist, assuage, calm, comfort, disburden, edge, expedite, facilitate, forward, further, guide, inch, lessen, lighten, maneuver, mitigate, moderate, mollify, pacify, palliate, quiet, relax, relent, relieve, simplify, slacken, slide, slip, smooth, solace, soothe, speed up, squeeze, steer, still, tranquilize.
antonyms hinder, retard, torment.

easily[1] *adv.* comfortably, effortlessly, facilely, readily, simply, smoothly, standing on one's head, with one arm tied behind one's back.
antonym laboriously.

easily[2] *adv.* absolutely, by far, certainly, clearly, definitely, doubtlessly, far and away, indisputably, indubitably, plainly, probably, simply, surely, undeniably, undoubtedly, unequivocally, unquestionably, well.

easy *adj.* a doddle, a piece of cake, a pushover, accommodating, affable, amenable, biddable, calm, carefree, casual, child's play, clear, comfortable, compliant, contented, cushy, docile, easeful, easy-going, effortless, facile, flexible, friendly, gentle, graceful, gracious, gullible, idiot-proof, indulgent, informal, leisurely, lenient, liberal, light, manageable, mild, moderate, natural, no bother, open, painless, peaceful, permissive, pleasant, pliant, quiet, relaxed, satisfied, serene, simple, smooth, soft, straightforward, submissive, suggestible, susceptible, temperate, tolerant, tractable, tranquil, trusting, unaffected, unburdensome, unceremonious, uncomplicated, unconstrained, undemanding, undisturbed, unexacting, unforced, unhurried, unlabored, unoppressive, unpretentious, untroubled, unworried, well-to-do, yielding.
antonyms demanding, difficult, fast, impossible, intolerant.

easy-going *adj.* amenable, calm, carefree, casual, complacent, easy, easy-osy, even-tempered, flexible, happy-go-lucky, indulgent, insouciant, laid-back, lenient, liberal, mild, moderate, nonchalant, permissive, placid, relaxed, serene, tolerant, unconcerned, uncritical, undemanding, unhurried, unworried.
antonyms fussy, intolerant.

eat *v.* banquet, break bread, chew, chop, consume, corrode, crumble, decay, devour, dine, dissolve, erode,

feed, grub, ingest, knock back, manducate, munch, pig, rot, scoff, swallow, wear away.

eavesdrop *v.* bug, earwig, listen in, monitor, overhear, snoop, spy, tap.

eavesdropper *n.* listener, monitor, snoop, snooper, spy.

ebb *v.* abate, decay, decline, decrease, degenerate, deteriorate, diminish, drop, dwindle, fade away, fall away, fall back, flag, flow back, go out, lessen, peter out, recede, reflow, retire, retreat, retrocede, shrink, sink, slacken, subside, wane, weaken, withdraw.
antonyms increase, rise.

n. decay, decline, decrease, degeneration, deterioration, diminution, drop, dwindling, ebb tide, flagging, lessening, low tide, low water, reflow, refluence, reflux, regression, retreat, retrocession, shrinkage, sinking, slackening, subsidence, wane, waning, weakening, withdrawal.
antonyms flow, increase, rising.

ebullient *adj.* boiling, breezy, bright, bubbling, buoyant, chirpy, effervescent, effusive, elated, enthusiastic, excited, exhilarated, exuberant, foaming, frothing, frothy, gushing, irrepressible, seething, vivacious, zestful.
antonyms apathetic, dull, lifeless.

eccentric *adj.* aberrant, abnormal, anomalous, bizarre, capricious, dotty, erratic, fey, freakish, fruity, idiosyncratic, irregular, nuts, nutty, odd, offbeat, outlandish, peculiar, queer, quirky, screwball, screwy, singular, spac(e)y, strange, uncommon, unconventional, way-out, weird, whimsical.
antonyms normal, sane.

n. case, character, crank, freak, fruit-cake, nonconformist, nut, nutter, oddball, oddity, queer fish, screwball, weirdie, weirdo.

eccentricity *n.* aberration, abnormality, anomaly, bizarreness, bizarrerie, caprice, capriciousness, foible, freakishness, idiosyncrasy, irregularity, nonconformity, oddity, outlandishness, peculiarity, queerness, quirk, singularity, strangeness, unconventionality, waywardness, weirdness, whimsicality.
antonyms normalcy, normality, ordinariness.

ecclesiastic(al) *adj.* church, churchly, churchy, clerical, divine, holy, pastoral, priestly, religious, spiritual, templar.

echelon *n.* degree, grade, level, place, position, rank, status, step, tier.

echo *v.* ape, copy, echoize, imitate, mimic, mirror, parallel, parrot, recall, reflect, reiterate, repeat, reproduce, resemble, resound, reverberate, ring, second.
n. allusion, answer, copy, evocation, hint, image, imitation, intimation, memory, mirror image, parallel, reflection, reiteration, reminder, repetition, reproduction, reverberation, suggestion, sympathy, trace.

eclectic *adj.* all-embracing, broad, catholic, comprehensive, dilettantish, diverse, diversified, general, heterogeneous, liberal, many-sided, multifarious, selective, varied, wide-ranging.
antonyms narrow, one-sided.

eclipse *v.* blot out, cloud, darken, dim, dwarf, exceed, excel, extinguish, obscure, outdo, outshine, overshadow, shroud, surpass, transcend, veil.
n. darkening, decline, deliquium, diminution, dimming, extinction, failure, fall, loss, obscuration, occultation, overshadowing, shading.

economical *adj.* careful, cheap, cost-effective, economic,

economizing, efficient, fair, frugal, inexpensive, labor-saving, low, low-priced, modest, prudent, reasonable, saving, scrimping, sparing, thrifty, time-saving.
antonyms expensive, uneconomical.

economize *v.* cut back, cut corners, husband, retrench, save, scrimp, tighten one's belt.
antonym squander.

economy *n.* frugality, frugalness, husbandry, parsimony, providence, prudence, restraint, retrenchment, saving, scrimping, sparingness, thrift, thriftiness.
antonym improvidence.

ecstasy *n.* bliss, delight, ecstasis, elation, enthusiasm, euphoria, exaltation, fervor, frenzy, joy, rapture, ravishment, rhapsody, seventh heaven, sublimation, trance, transport.
antonym torment.

ecstatic *adj.* blissful, delirious, elated, enraptured, enthusiastic, entranced, euphoric, exultant, fervent, frenzied, joyful, joyous, on cloud nine, over the moon, overjoyed, rapturous, rhapsodic, transported.
antonym downcast.

edge *n.* acuteness, advantage, animation, arris, ascendancy, bezel, bite, border, bound, boundary, brim, brink, cantle, contour, dominance, effectiveness, force, fringe, incisiveness, interest, keenness, lead, limit, line, lip, margin, outline, perimeter, periphery, point, pungency, rim, sharpness, side, sting, superiority, threshold, upper hand, urgency, verge, zest.
v. bind, border, creep, drib, ease, fringe, gravitate, hem, hone, inch, rim, shape, sharpen, sidle, steal, strop, trim, verge, whet, work, worm.

edgy *adj.* anxious, ill at ease, irascible, irritable, keyed-up, nervous, on edge, prickly, restive, tense, testy, touchy.
antonym calm.

edict *n.* act, command, decree, dictate, dictum, enactment, fiat, injunction, law, mandate, manifesto, order, ordinance, proclamation, pronouncement, pronunciamento, regulation, rescript, ruling, statute, ukase.

edifice *n.* building, construction, erection, structure.

edit *v.* adapt, annotate, assemble, blue-pencil, bowdlerize, censor, check, compose, condense, correct, emend, polish, rearrange, redact, reorder, rephrase, revise, rewrite, select.

educate *v.* catechize, civilize, coach, cultivate, develop, discipline, drill, edify, exercise, improve, indoctrinate, inform, instruct, learn, mature, rear, school, teach, train, tutor.

education *n.* breeding, civilization, coaching, cultivation, culture, development, discipline, drilling, edification, enlightenment, erudition, guidance, improvement, indoctrination, instruction, knowledge, nurture, scholarship, schooling, teaching, training, tuition, tutelage, tutoring.

eerie *adj.* awesome, chilling, creepy, eldritch, fearful, frightening, ghastly, ghostly, mysterious, scary, spectral, spine-chilling, spooky, strange, uncanny, unearthly, unnatural, weird.
antonyms natural, ordinary.

efface *v.* annihilate, blank out, blot out, blue-pencil, cancel, cross out, delete, destroy, dim, eliminate, eradicate, erase, excise, expunge, extirpate, humble, lower, obliterate, raze, remove, rub out, wipe out, withdraw.

effect *n.* action, aftermath, clout, conclusion, consequence, drift, éclat, effectiveness, efficacy, efficiency,

enforcement, essence, event, execution, fact, force, fruit, impact, implementation, import, impression, influence, issue, meaning, operation, outcome, power, purport, purpose, reality, result, sense, significance, strength, tenor, upshot, use, validity, vigor, weight, work.
v. accomplish, achieve, actuate, cause, complete, consummate, create, effectuate, execute, fulfil, initiate, make, perform, produce, wreak.

effective *adj.* able, active, adequate, capable, cogent, compelling, competent, convincing, current, effectual, efficacious, efficient, emphatic, energetic, forceful, forcible, implemental, impressive, moving, operative, perficient, persuasive, potent, powerful, productive, real, serviceable, striking, telling, useful.
antonyms ineffective, useless.

efficiency *n.* ability, adeptness, capability, competence, competency, economy, effectiveness, efficacy, mastery, power, productivity, proficiency, readiness, skilfulness, skill.
antonym inefficiency.

efficient *adj.* able, adept, businesslike, capable, competent, economic, effective, effectual, powerful, productive, proficient, ready, skilful, streamlined, well-conducted, well-ordered, well-organized, well-regulated, workmanlike.
antonym inefficient.

effort *n.* accomplishment, achievement, application, attempt, conatus, creation, deed, endeavor, energy, essay, exertion, feat, force, go, job, labor, molimen, nisus, pains, power, production, shot, stab, strain, stress, stretch, striving, struggle, toil, travail, trouble, try, work.

effortless *adj.* easy, facile, painless, simple, smooth, uncomplicated, undemanding, unlabored.
antonym difficult.

egg on coax, encourage, exhort, goad, incite, prick, prod, prompt, push, spur, stimulate, urge, wheedle.
antonym discourage.

egghead *n.* brain, Einstein, genius, headpiece, intellect, intellectual, scholar.

egoism *n.* amour-propre, egocentricity, egomania, egotism, narcissism, self-absorption, self-centeredness, self-importance, self-interest, selfishness, self-love, self-regard, self-seeking.
antonym altruism.

eject *v.* banish, belch, boot out, bounce, deport, discharge, disgorge, dislodge, dismiss, dispossess, drive out, emit, evacuate, evict, exile, expel, fire, kick out, oust, remove, sack, spew, spout, throw out, turn out, unhouse, vomit.

elaborate *adj.* careful, complex, complicated, daedal(ic), decorated, dedal(ian), detailed, exact, extravagant, fancy, fussy, intricate, involved, labored, minute, ornamental, ornate, ostentatious, painstaking, perfected, precise, showy, skilful, studied, thorough.
antonyms plain, simple.
v. amplify, complicate, decorate, detail, develop, devise, embellish, enhance, enlarge, expand, expatiate, explain, flesh out, garnish, improve, ornament, polish, refine.
antonyms précis, simplify.

elapse *v.* go by, lapse, pass, slip away.

elastic *adj.* accommodating, adaptable, adjustable, bouncy, buoyant, complaisant, compliant, distensible, ductile, flexible, irrepressible, plastic, pliable, pliant, resilient, rubbery, springy, stretchable, stretchy, supple, tolerant, variable, yielding.

antonym rigid.

elated *adj.* animated, blissful, cheered, delighted, ecstatic, euphoric, excited, exhilarated, exultant, gleeful, joyful, joyous, jubilant, on the high ropes, over the moon, overjoyed, pleased, proud, roused.

antonym downcast.

elder *adj.* aîné(e), ancient, eigne, first-born, older, senior.

antonym younger.

n. deacon, presbyter, senior.

elderly *adj.* aged, aging, badgerly, hoary, old, senile.

antonyms young, youthful.

elect *v.* adopt, appoint, choose, designate, determine, opt for, pick, prefer, select, vote.

adj. choice, chosen, designate, designated, elite, handpicked, picked, preferred, presumptive, prospective, select, selected, to be.

electrify *v.* amaze, animate, astonish, astound, excite, fire, galvanize, invigorate, jolt, rouse, shock, stagger, startle, stimulate, stir, stun, thrill.

antonym bore.

elegant *adj.* à la mode, appropriate, apt, artistic, beautiful, chic, choice, clever, comely, concinnous, courtly, cultivated, debonair, delicate, effective, exquisite, fashionable, fine, genteel, graceful, handsome, ingenious, luxurious, modish, neat, nice, polished, refined, simple, smooth, stylish, sumptuous, tasteful.

antonym inelegant.

elementary *adj.* basic, clear, easy, elemental, facile, fundamental, initial, introductory, original, plain, primary, principal, rudimentary, simple, straightforward, uncomplicated.

antonyms advanced, complex.

elevate *v.* advance, aggrandize, animate, augment, boost, brighten, buoy up, cheer, elate, exalt, excite, exhilarate, hearten, heighten, hoist, increase, intensify, lift, magnify, prefer, promote, raise, rouse, sublimate, swell, upgrade, uplift, upraise.

antonyms lessen, lower.

elfin *adj.* arch, charming, delicate, elfish, elflike, elvish, frolicsome, impish, mischievous, petite, playful, puckish, small, sprightly.

elicit *v.* cause, derive, draw out, educe, evoke, evolve, exact, extort, extract, fish, mole out, obtain, wrest, wring.

eligible *adj.* acceptable, appropriate, available, desirable, fit, proper, qualified, suitable, suited, worthy.

antonym ineligible.

eliminate *v.* annihilate, bump off, cut out, delete, dispense with, dispose of, disregard, do away with, drop, eject, eradicate, exclude, expel, expunge, exterminate, extinguish, get rid of, ignore, kill, knock out, liquidate, murder, omit, reject, remove, rub out, slay, stamp out, take out, terminate, waste.

antonym accept.

elite *n.* aristocracy, best, cream, crème de la crème, elect, establishment, flower, gentry, high society, meritocracy, nobility, pick.

adj. aristocratic, best, choice, crack, exclusive, first-class, noble, pick, selected, top, top-class, upper-class.

antonyms ordinary, run-of-the-mill.

elongated *adj.* extended, lengthened, long, prolonged, protracted, stretched.

elope *v.* abscond, bolt, decamp, disappear, do a bunk, escape, leave, run away, run off, slip away, steal away.

eloquent *adj.* articulate, Demosthenic, expressive, fluent, forceful, graceful, honeyed, meaningful, moving, persuasive, plausible, pregnant, revealing, silver-tongued, stirring, suggestive, telling, vivid, vocal, voluble, well-expressed.

antonyms inarticulate, tongue-tied.

elude *v.* avoid, baffle, beat, circumvent, confound, dodge, duck, escape, evade, flee, foil, frustrate, outrun, puzzle, shirk, shun, stump, thwart.

emaciated *adj.* atrophied, attenuate, attenuated, cadaverous, gaunt, haggard, lank, lean, meager, pinched, scrawny, skeletal, tabefied, tabescent, thin, wasted.

antonyms plump, well-fed.

emancipate *v.* deliver, discharge, disencumber, disenthral, enfranchise, free, liberate, manumit, release, set free, unbind, unchain, unfetter, unshackle.

antonym enslave.

embankment *n.* bund, causeway, causey, defenses, earthwork, levee, rampart.

embargo *n.* ban, bar, barrier, blockage, check, hindrance, impediment, interdict, interdiction, prohibition, proscription, restraint, restriction, seizure, stoppage.

v. ban, bar, block, check, embar, impede, interdict, prohibit, proscribe, restrict, seize, stop.

antonym allow.

embark *v.* board ship, emplane, entrain, take ship.

antonym disembark.

embarrass *v.* abash, chagrin, confuse, discomfit, discomfort, discompose, disconcert, discountenance, distress, fluster, mortify, shame, show up.

embassy *n.* consulate, delegation, deputation, embassade, embassage, legation, mission.

embed *v.* fix, imbed, implant, insert, plant, root, set, sink.

embellish *v.* adorn, beautify, bedeck, deck, decorate, dress up, elaborate, embroider, enhance, enrich, exaggerate, festoon, garnish, gild, grace, ornament, trim, varnish.

antonyms denude, simplify.

embezzle *v.* abstract, appropriate, defalcate, filch, misapply, misappropriate, misuse, peculate, pilfer, pinch, purloin, steal, sting.

embitter *v.* acerbate, aggravate, alienate, anger, disaffect, disillusion, empoison, envenom, exacerbate, exasperate, poison, sour, worsen.

antonym pacify.

emblem *n.* badge, crest, device, figure, ichthys, image, insignia, mark, representation, sigil, sign, symbol, token, type.

embody *v.* codify, collect, combine, comprehend, comprise, concentrate, concretize, consolidate, contain, encarnalize, exemplify, express, incarnate, include, incorporate, integrate, manifest, organize, personify, realize, reify, represent, stand for, symbolize, systematize, typify.

embrace *v.* accept, canoodle, clasp, complect, comprehend, comprise, contain, cover, cuddle, dally, embody, embosom, encircle, enclose, encompass, enfold, enlace, espouse, grab, grasp, halse, hold, hug, inarm, include, incorporate, involve, neck, receive, seize, snog, squeeze, subsume, take up, welcome.

n. accolade, clasp, clinch, cuddle, hug, squeeze.

embroidery *n.* fancywork, needle-point, needlework, sewing, tapestry, tatting.

embroil *v.* confound, confuse, distract, disturb, encumber, enmesh, ensnare, entangle, implicate, incriminate, involve, mire, mix up, muddle, perplex, trouble.

emerge *v.* appear, arise, crop up, debouch, develop, eclose, emanate, issue, materialize, proceed, rise, surface, transpire, turn up.

antonyms disappear, fade.

emergency *n.* crisis, crunch, danger, difficulty, exigency, extremity, necessity, pass, pinch, plight, predicament, quandary, scrape, strait.

adj. alternative, back-up, extra, fall-back, reserve, spare, substitute.

eminent *adj.* august, celebrated, conspicuous, distinguished, elevated, esteemed, exalted, famous, grand, great, high, high-ranking, illustrious, important, notable, noted, noteworthy, outstanding, paramount, pre-eminent, prestigious, prominent, renowned, reputable, respected, revered, signal, superior, well-known.

antonyms unimportant, unknown.

emissary *n.* agent, ambassador, courier, delegate, deputy, envoy, herald, legate, messenger, nuncio, plenipotentiary, representative, scout, spy.

emit *v.* diffuse, discharge, eject, emanate, exhale, exude, give off, give out, issue, radiate, shed, vent.

antonym absorb.

emotion *n.* affect, agitation, ardor, excitement, feeling, fervor, passion, perturbation, reaction, sensation, sentiment, vehemence, warmth.

emotional *adj.* affecting, ardent, demonstrative, emotive, enthusiastic, excitable, exciting, feeling, fervent, fervid, fiery, heart-warming, heated, hot-blooded, impassioned, moved, moving, overcharged, passionate, pathetic, poignant, responsive, roused, sensitive, sentimental, stirred, stirring, susceptible, tear-jerking, temperamental, tempestuous, tender, thrilling, touching, volcanic, warm, zealous.

antonyms calm, cold, detached, emotionless, unemotional.

emphasis *n.* accent, accentuation, attention, force, import, importance, impressiveness, insistence, intensity, mark, moment, positiveness, power, pre-eminence, priority, prominence, significance, strength, stress, underscoring, urgency, weight.

emphatic *adj.* absolute, categorical, certain, decided, definite, direct, distinct, earnest, energetic, forceful, forcible, graphic, important, impressive, insistent, marked, momentous, positive, powerful, pronounced, punctuated, resounding, significant, striking, strong, telling, trenchant, unequivocal, unmistakable, vigorous, vivid.

antonyms quiet, understated, unemphatic.

employ *v.* apply, apprentice, bring to bear, commission, engage, enlist, exercise, exert, fill, hire, indent(ure), occupy, ply, retain, spend, take on, take up, use, utilize.

n. employment, hire, pay, service.

employee *n.* hand, job-holder, member of staff, staffer, wage-earner, worker, workman.

employer *n.* boss, business, company, establishment, firm, gaffer, organization, outfit, owner, padrone,

patron, proprietor, taskmaster, workmaster, workmistress.

employment *n.* application, avocation, business, calling, craft, employ, engagement, enlistment, errand, exercise, exercitation, exertion, hire, job, line, métier, occupation, profession, pursuit, service, trade, use, utilization, vocation, work.

antonym unemployment.

empower *v.* accredit, allow, authorize, commission, delegate, enable, enfranchise, entitle, license, permit, qualify, sanction, warrant.

empty *adj.* absent, aimless, banal, bare, blank, bootless, cheap, clear, deserted, desolate, destitute, expressionless, famished, frivolous, fruitless, futile, hollow, hungry, idle, inane, ineffective, insincere, insubstantial, meaningless, purposeless, ravenous, senseless, silly, starving, superficial, trivial, unfed, unfilled, unfrequented, unfurnished, uninhabited, unintelligent, unoccupied, unreal, unsatisfactory, unsubstantial, untenanted, vacant, vacuous, vain, valueless, viduous, void, waste, worthless.

antonyms filled, full, replete.

v. clear, consume, deplete, discharge, drain, dump, evacuate, exhaust, gut, lade, pour out, unburden, unload, vacate, void.

antonym fill.

emulate *v.* challenge, compete with, contend with, copy, echo, follow, imitate, match, mimic, rival, vie with.

enable *v.* accredit, allow, authorize, capacitate, commission, empower, endue, equip, facilitate, fit, license, permit, prepare, qualify, sanction, warrant.

antonyms inhibit, prevent.

enact *v.* act (out), authorize, command, decree, depict, establish, impersonate, legislate, ordain, order, pass, perform, personate, play, portray, proclaim, ratify, represent, sanction.

antonym repeal.

enchant *v.* becharm, beguile, bewitch, captivate, charm, delight, enamor, enrapture, enravish, ensorcell, enthral, fascinate, hypnotize, mesmerize, spellbind.

antonyms bore, disenchant.

encircle *v.* begird, circle, circumscribe, compass, enclose, encompass, enfold, engird, engirdle, enlace, enring, envelop, environ, enwreathe, gird, girdle, hem in, ring, surround.

enclose *v.* bound, circumscribe, compass, comprehend, confine, contain, cover, embale, embosom, embrace, encase, encircle, encompass, enlock, environ, fence, hedge, hem in, hold, inclose, include, incorporate, insert, pen, shut in, wall in, wrap.

encompass *v.* admit, begird, bring about, cause, circle, circumscribe, comprehend, comprise, contain, contrive, cover, devise, effect, embody, embrace, encircle, enclose, envelop, environ, girdle, hem in, hold, include, incorporate, involve, manage, ring, subsume, surround.

encounter *v.* chance upon, clash with, combat, come upon, confront, contend, cross swords with, engage, experience, face, fight, grapple with, happen on, meet, rencontre, rencounter, run across, run into, strive, struggle.

n. action, battle, brush, clash, collision, combat, conflict, confrontation, contest, dispute, engagement, fight, meeting, rencontre, rencounter, run-in, set-to, skirmish.

encourage v. abet, advance, advocate, aid, animate, boost, buoy up, cheer, comfort, console, egg on, embolden, embrave, favor, forward, foster, further, hearten, help, incite, inspire, inspirit, promote, rally, reassure, rouse, second, spirit, spur, stimulate, strengthen, succor, support, urge.

antonyms depress, discourage, dissuade.

encroach v. appropriate, arrogate, impinge, infringe, intrude, invade, make inroads, muscle in, obtrude, overstep, trench, trespass, usurp.

encumber v. burden, clog, cramp, cumber, embarrass, hamper, handicap, hinder, impede, incommode, inconvenience, lumber, obstruct, oppress, overload, retard, saddle, slow down, trammel, weigh down.

end n. aim, annihilation, aspiration, attainment, bit, bound, boundary, butt, cessation, close, closure, completion, conclusion, consequence, consummation, culmination, curtain, death, demise, dénouement, design, destruction, dissolution, doom, downfall, drift, edge, ending, expiration, expiry, extent, extermination, extinction, extreme, extremity, finale, fine, finis, finish, fragment, goal, intent, intention, issue, left-over, limit, object, objective, outcome, part, pay-off, piece, point, portion, purpose, reason, remainder, remnant, resolution, responsibility, result, ruin, ruination, scrap, share, side, stop, stub, telos, termination, terminus, tip, upshot, wind-up.

antonyms beginning, opening, start.

v. abate, abolish, annihilate, cease, close, complete, conclude, culminate, destroy, dissolve, expire, exterminate, extinguish, fetch up, finish, resolve, ruin, sopite, stop, terminate, wind up.

antonyms begin, start.

endanger v. compromise, expose, hazard, imperil, jeopardize, risk, threaten.

antonyms protect, shelter, shield.

endearing adj. adorable, attractive, captivating, charming, delightful, enchanting, engaging, lovable, sweet, winning, winsome.

endeavor n. aim, attempt, conatus, crack, effort, enterprise, essay, go, nisus, shot, stab, trial, try, undertaking, venture.

v. aim, aspire, attempt, essay, labor, strive, struggle, take pains, try, undertake, venture.

endless adj. boundless, ceaseless, constant, continual, continuous, eternal, everlasting, immortal, incessant, infinite, interminable, interminate, limitless, measureless, monotonous, overlong, perpetual, Sisyphean, termless, unbounded, unbroken, undivided, undying, unending, uninterrupted, unlimited, whole.

endorse v. adopt, advocate, affirm, approve, authorize, back, champion, confirm, countenance, countersign, favor, indorse, ratify, recommend, sanction, sign, subscribe to, superscribe, support, sustain, undersign, vouch for, warrant.

antonyms denounce, disapprove.

endow v. award, bequeath, bestow, confer, donate, dower, endue, enrich, favor, finance, fund, furnish, give, grant, invest, leave, make over, present, provide, settle on, supply, will.

antonym divest.

endowment n. ability, aptitude, attribute, award, benefaction, bequest, bestowal, boon, capability, capacity, donation, dotation, dowry, faculty, flair, fund, genius, gift, grant, income, largesse, legacy, power, presen-

tation, property, provision, qualification, quality, revenue, talent.

endure v. abear, abide, aby(e), allow, bear, brave, brook, continue, cope with, countenance, digest, experience, go through, hold, last, live, perdure, permit, persist, prevail, put up with, remain, stand, stay, stick, stomach, submit to, suffer, support, survive, sustain, swallow, thole, tolerate, undergo, weather, withstand.

antonyms cease, end.

enemy n. adversary, antagonist, competitor, foe, foeman, opponent, opposer, Philistine, rival, the opposition.

antonyms ally, friend.

energy n. activity, animation, ardor, brio, drive, efficiency, élan, exertion, fire, force, forcefulness, get-up-and-go, intensity, inworking, jism, juice, life, liveliness, pluck, power, spirit, stamina, steam, strength, strenuousness, verve, vigor, vim, vitality, vivacity, vroom, zeal, zest, zip.

antonyms inertia, lethargy, weakness.

enervate v. debilitate, deplete, devitalize, enfeeble, exhaust, fatigue, incapacitate, paralyze, prostrate, sap, tire, unman, unnerve, weaken, wear out.

antonyms activate, energize.

enfold v. clasp, embrace, encircle, enclose, encompass, envelop, enwrap, fold, hold, hug, shroud, swathe, wimple, wrap (up).

enforce v. administer, apply, carry out, coact, coerce, compel, constrain, discharge, exact, execute, implement, impose, insist on, oblige, prosecute, reinforce, require, urge.

engage v. absorb, activate, affiance, agree, allure, apply, appoint, arrest, assail, attach, attack, attract, bespeak, betroth, bind, book, busy, captivate, catch, charm, charter, combat, commission, commit, contract, covenant, draw, embark, employ, enamor, enchant, encounter, energize, engross, enlist, enrol, enter, fascinate, fit, fix, gain, grip, guarantee, hire, interact, interconnect, interlock, involve, join, lease, meet, mesh, obligate, oblige, occupy, operate, partake, participate, pledge, practice, prearrange, preoccupy, promise, rent, reserve, retain, secure, take on, tie up, undertake, vouch, vow, win.

antonyms discharge, disengage, dismiss.

engaged adj. absorbed, affianced, betrothed, busy, committed, employed, engrossed, immersed, involved, occupied, pledged, preoccupied, promised, spoken for, tied up, unavailable.

engaging adj. agreeable, appealing, attractive, beguiling, captivating, charming, enchanting, fascinating, fetching, likable, lovable, pleasant, pleasing, prepossessing, winning, winsome.

antonyms boring, loathsome.

engender v. beget, breed, bring about, cause, create, encourage, excite, father, foment, generate, give rise to, hatch, incite, induce, instigate, lead to, make, nurture, occasion, precipitate, procreate, produce, propagate, provoke, sire, spawn.

engineer n. architect, contriver, designer, deviser, driver, inventor, operator, originator, planner.

v. cause, concoct, contrive, control, create, devise, effect, encompass, finagle, machinate, manage, maneuver, manipulate, mastermind, originate, plan, plot, scheme, wangle.

engrave v. blaze, carve, chase, chisel, cut, embed, enchase, etch, fix, grave, impress, imprint, infix, ingrain, inscribe, lodge, mark, print.

engross v. absorb, arrest, corner, engage, engulf, fixate, hold, immerse, involve, monopolize, occupy, preoccupy, rivet.

engulf v. absorb, bury, consume, deluge, drown, encompass, engross, envelop, flood, immerse, ingulf, inundate, overrun, overwhelm, plunge, submerge, swallow up, swamp.

enhance v. amplify, augment, boost, complement, elevate, embellish, escalate, exalt, heighten, improve, increase, intensify, lift, magnify, raise, reinforce, strengthen, swell.
antonyms decrease, minimize.

enigma n. brain-teaser, conundrum, mystery, poser, problem, puzzle, riddle.

enigmatic adj. ambiguous, cryptic, Delphic, doubtful, enigmatical, equivocal, impenetrable, incomprehensible, indecipherable, inexplicable, inscrutable, mysterious, obscure, perplexing, puzzling, recondite, riddling, strange, uncertain, unfathomable, unintelligible.
antonyms simple, straightforward.

enjoy v. appreciate, delight in, dig, experience, have, like, make a meal of, own, possess, rejoice in, relish, revel in, savor, take pleasure in, use.
antonyms abhor, detest.

enjoyment n. advantage, amusement, benefit, comfort, delectation, delight, diversion, ease, entertainment, exercise, fun, gaiety, gladness, gratification, gusto, happiness, indulgence, jollity, joy, ownership, pleasure, possession, recreation, relish, satisfaction, use, zest.
antonyms displeasure, dissatisfaction.

enlarge v. add to, amplify, augment, blow up, broaden, descant, develop, diffuse, dilate, distend, elaborate, elongate, expand, expatiate, extend, greaten, grow, heighten, increase, inflate, intumesce, jumboize, lengthen, magnify, multiply, stretch, swell, wax, widen.
antonyms decrease, diminish, shrink.

enlighten v. advise, apprise, civilize, counsel, edify, educate, illuminate, indoctrinate, inform, instruct, teach, undeceive.
antonyms confuse, puzzle.

enlist v. conscript, employ, engage, enrol, enter, gather, join (up), muster, obtain, procure, recruit, register, secure, sign up, volunteer.

enliven v. animate, brighten, buoy up, cheer (up), excite, exhilarate, fire, gladden, hearten, inspire, inspirit, invigorate, kindle, liven (up), pep up, perk up, quicken, rouse, spark, stimulate, vitalize, vivify, wake up.
antonyms subdue.

enmity n. acrimony, animosity, animus, antagonism, antipathy, aversion, bad blood, bitterness, feud, hate, hatred, hostility, ill-will, invidiousness, malevolence, malice, malignity, rancor, spite, venom.
antonyms amity, friendship.

enormity n. abomination, atrociousness, atrocity, crime, depravity, disgrace, evil, evilness, flagitiousness, heinousness, horror, iniquity, monstrosity, monstrousness, nefariousness, outrage, outrageousness, turpitude, viciousness, vileness, villainy, wickedness.
antonyms triviality, unimportance.

enormous adj. abominable, astronomic(al), atrocious, Brobdingnagian, colossal, cyclopean, depraved, disgraceful, evil, excessive, gargantuan, gigantic, gross, heinous, herculean, huge, hulking, immense, jumbo, leviathan, mammoth, massive, monstrous, mountainous, nefarious, odious, outrageous, prodigious, titanic, tremendous, vast, vasty, vicious, vile, villainous, wicked.
antonyms small, tiny.

enough adj. abundant, adequate, ample, enow, plenty, sufficient.
n. abundance, adequacy, plenitude, plenty, repletion, sufficiency.
adv. abundantly, adequately, amply, aplenty, enow, fairly, moderately, passably, reasonably, satisfactorily, sufficiently, tolerably.

enquiry, inquiry n. examination, exploration, inquest, inspection, investigation, probe, query, quest, question, research, scrutiny, search, study, survey.

enrage v. acerbate, aggravate, anger, exasperate, incense, incite, inflame, infuriate, irritate, madden, make someone's hackles rise, provoke.
antonyms calm, placate, soothe.

enrich v. adorn, aggrandize, ameliorate, augment, cultivate, decorate, develop, embellish, endow, enhance, fortify, grace, improve, ornament, prosper, refine, supplement.
antonym impoverish.

enrol(l) v. accept, admit, chronicle, empanel, engage, enlist, enregister, inscribe, join up, list, matriculate, note, record, recruit, register, sign on, sign up, take on.
antonyms leave, reject.

enshrine v. apotheosize, cherish, consecrate, dedicate, embalm, exalt, hallow, idolize, preserve, revere, sanctify, treasure.

ensign n. badge, banner, colors, flag, gonfalon, jack, oriflamme, pennant, pennon, standard, streamer.

enslave v. bind, conquer, dominate, enchain, enthrall, overcome, subject, subjugate, yoke.
antonyms emancipate, free.

ensue v. arise, attend, befall, derive, eventuate, flow, follow, happen, issue, proceed, result, stem, succeed, supervene, turn out, turn up.
antonym precede.

ensure v. certify, clinch, confirm, effect, guarantee, guard, insure, protect, safeguard, secure, warrant.

entangle v. ball, bewilder, catch, complicate, compromise, confuse, embroil, enlace, enmesh, ensnare, entoil, entrap, foul, implicate, involve, jumble, knot, mat, mix up, muddle, perplex, puzzle, ravel, snag, snare, snarl, tangle, trammel, trap, twist.
antonym disentangle.

entanglement n. complication, confusion, difficulty, embarrassment, ensnarement, entoilment, entrapment, imbroglio, involvement, jumble, knot, liaison, mesh, mess, mix-up, muddle, predicament, snare, snarl-up, tangle, tie, toils, trap.
antonym disentanglement.

enter v. arrive, begin, board, commence, embark upon, enlist, enrol, inscribe, insert, introduce, join, list, log, note, offer, participate, participate in, penetrate, pierce, present, proffer, record, register, set about, set down, sign up, start, submit, take down, take up, tender.
antonyms delete, issue, leave.

enterprise n. activity, adventure, adventurousness, alertness, audacity, boldness, business, company, concern,

daring, dash, drive, eagerness, effort, emprise, endeavor, energy, enthusiasm, essay, establishment, firm,
get-up-and-go, gumption, imagination, initiative, operation, plan, program, project, push, readiness,
resource, resourcefulness, spirit, undertaking, venture,
vigor, zeal.
antonyms apathy, inertia.

enterprising *adj.* active, adventurous, alert, ambitious,
aspiring, audacious, bold, daring, dashing, eager, energetic, enthusiastic, go-ahead, imaginative, intrepid,
keen, pushful, ready, resourceful, self-reliant, spirited,
stirring, up-and-coming, venturesome, vigorous,
zealous.
antonyms lethargic, unadventurous.

entertain *v.* accommodate, accourt, amuse, charm,
cheer, cherish, conceive, consider, contemplate, countenance, delight, divert, fête, foster, harbor, hold,
imagine, lodge, maintain, occupy, please, ponder, put
up, recreate, regale, support, treat.
antonyms bore, reject.

enthral(l) *v.* beguile, captivate, charm, enchant, enrapture, enravish, entrance, fascinate, grip, hypnotize,
intrigue, mesmerize, rivet, spellbind, thrill.
antonyms bore, weary.

enthusiasm *n.* ardor, avidity, craze, devotion, eagerness,
earnestness, empressement, entraînement, estro,
excitement, fad, fervor, frenzy, hobby, hobby-horse,
interest, keenness, mania, oomph, passion, rage, relish,
spirit, vehemence, warmth, zeal, zest.
antonym apathy.

enthusiastic *adj.* ardent, avid, devoted, eager, earnest,
ebullient, empressé, excited, exuberant, fervent,
fervid, forceful, gung-ho, hearty, keen, keen as mustard, lively, passionate, spirited, unstinting, vehement,
vigorous, warm, whole-hearted, zealous.
antonyms apathetic, reluctant, unenthusiastic.

entice *v.* allure, attract, beguile, blandish, cajole, coax,
decoy, draw, induce, inveigle, lead on, lure, persuade,
prevail on, seduce, sweet-talk, tempt, wheedle.

entire *adj.* absolute, all-in, complete, continuous, full,
intact, integrated, outright, perfect, sound, thorough,
total, unabridged, unbroken, uncut, undamaged, undiminished, undivided, unified, unmarked, unmarred,
unmitigated, unreserved, unrestricted, whole.
antonyms impaired, incomplete, partial.

entirely *adv.* absolutely, altogether, completely, every
inch, exclusively, fully, hook line and sinker, in toto,
lock stock and barrel, only, perfectly, solely,
thoroughly, totally, unreservedly, utterly, wholly,
without exception, without reservation.
antonym partially.

entitle *v.* accredit, allow, authorize, call, christen,
denominate, designate, dub, empower, enable, enfranchise, label, license, name, permit, style, term, title,
warrant.

entourage *n.* associates, attendants, claque, companions,
company, cortège, coterie, court, escort, followers, following, retainers, retinue, staff, suite, train.

entrance¹ *n.* access, admission, admittance, appearance,
arrival, atrium, avenue, beginning, commencement,
debut, door, doorway, entrée, entry, gate, ingress,
initiation, inlet, introduction, opening, outset, passage,
portal, start.
antonyms departure, exit.

entrance² *v.* bewitch, captivate, charm, delight,

enchant, enrapture, enravish, enthrall, fascinate, gladden, hypnotize, magnetize, mesmerize, ravish,
spellbind, transport.
antonyms bore, repel.

entreat *v.* appeal to, ask, beg, beseech, conjure, crave,
enjoin, exhort, flagitate, implore, importune, invoke,
petition, plead with, pray, request, sue, supplicate.

entreaty *n.* appeal, entreatment, exhortation, importunity, invocation, petition, plea, prayer, request, solicitation, suing, suit, supplication.

entrust *v.* assign, authorize, charge, commend, commit,
confide, consign, delegate, deliver, depute, invest,
trust, turn over.

enumerate *v.* calculate, cite, count, detail, itemize, list,
mention, name, number, quote, recapitulate, recite,
reckon, recount, rehearse, relate, specify, spell out,
tell.

enunciate *v.* articulate, broadcast, declare, enounce,
proclaim, promulgate, pronounce, propound, publish,
say, sound, speak, state, utter, vocalize, voice.

envelop *v.* blanket, cloak, conceal, cover, embrace,
encase, encircle, enclose, encompass, enfold, engulf,
enshroud, enwrap, enwreathe, hide, obscure, sheathe,
shroud, surround, swaddle, swathe, veil, wrap.

environment *n.* ambience, atmosphere, background,
conditions, context, domain, element, entourage, habitat, locale, medium, milieu, scene, setting, situation,
surroundings, territory.

envisage *v.* anticipate, conceive of, conceptualize, contemplate, envision, fancy, foresee, ideate, image,
imagine, picture, preconceive, predict, see, visualize.

envoy *n.* agent, ambassador, courier, delegate, deputy,
diplomat, elchi, emissary, intermediary, legate, messenger, minister, nuncio, plenipotentiary, representative.

envy *n.* covetousness, cupidity, dissatisfaction, envious-
ness, grudge, hatred, ill-will, jealousy, malice, malignity, resentfulness, resentment, spite.
v. begrudge, covet, crave, grudge, resent.

epicure *n.* arbiter elegantiae, bon vivant, bon viveur,
connoisseur, epicurean, gastronome, glutton, gourmand, gourmet, hedonist, sensualist, sybarite, voluptuary.

epidemic *adj.* epizootic, general, pandemic, prevailing,
prevalent, rampant, rife, sweeping, wide-ranging,
widespread.
n. growth, outbreak, pandemic, plague, rash, spread,
upsurge, wave.

episode *n.* adventure, affaire, business, chapter, circumstance, event, experience, happening, incident, instalment, matter, occasion, occurrence, part, passage,
scene, section.

epitomize *v.* abbreviate, abridge, abstract, compress,
condense, contract, curtail, cut, embody, encapsulate,
exemplify, illustrate, incarnate, personify, précis,
reduce, represent, shorten, summarize, symbolize,
typify.
antonyms elaborate, expand.

epoch *n.* age, date, epocha, era, period, time.

equal *adj.* able, adequate, alike, balanced, capable, commensurate, competent, corresponding, egalitarian,
equable, equivalent, even, even-handed, evenly-balanced, evenly-matched, evenly-proportioned, fair, fifty-
fifty, fit, identical, impartial, just, level-pegging, like,
matched, proportionate, ready, regular, sufficient, suit-

able, symmetrical, tantamount, the same, unbiased, uniform, unvarying, up to.

antonyms different, inequitable, unequal.

n. brother, coequal, compeer, counterpart, equivalent, fellow, match, mate, parallel, peer, rival, twin.

v. balance, commeasure, correspond to, equalize, equate, even, level, match, parallel, rival, square with, tally with.

equanimity *n.* aplomb, calm, calmness, composure, coolness, equability, equableness, imperturbability, levelheadedness, peace, phlegm, placidity, poise, presence of mind, sang-froid, self-possession, serenity, steadiness, tranquility.

antonyms alarm, anxiety, discomposure.

equilibrium *n.* balance, calm, calmness, collectedness, composure, cool, coolness, counterpoise, equanimity, equipoise, equiponderance, evenness, poise, rest, self-possession, serenity, stability, steadiness, symmetry.

antonym imbalance.

equip *v.* accouter, arm, array, attire, bedight, deck out, dight, dress, endow, fit out, fit up, furnish, habilitate, kit out, outfit, prepare, provide, rig, stock, supply.

equipment *n.* accessories, accouterments, apparatus, appurtenances, baggage, equipage, furnishings, furniture, gear, graith, impedimenta, implements, material, matériel, muniments, outfit, paraphernalia, rig-out, stuff, supplies, tackle, things, tools, traps.

equitable *adj.* disinterested, dispassionate, due, ethical, even-handed, fair, fair-and-square, honest, impartial, just, legitimate, objective, proper, proportionate, reasonable, right, rightful, square, unbiased, unprejudiced.

antonyms inequitable, unfair.

equity *n.* disinterestedness, equality, equitableness, even-handedness, fair play, fair-mindedness, fairness, honesty, impartiality, integrity, justice, justness, objectivity, reasonableness, rectitude, righteousness, uprightness.

antonym inequity.

equivalent *adj.* alike, commensurate, comparable, convertible, correlative, correspondent, corresponding, equal, equipollent, equipotent, even, homologous, homotypal, homotypic, interchangeable, same, similar, substitutable, synonymous, tantamount, twin.

antonyms dissimilar, unlike.

n. correlative, correspondent, counterpart, equal, homologue, homotype, match, opposite number, parallel, peer, twin.

equivocal *adj.* ambiguous, ambivalent, casuistical, confusing, Delphic, doubtful, dubious, evasive, indefinite, indeterminate, misleading, oblique, obscure, oracular, questionable, suspicious, uncertain, vague.

antonyms clear, unequivocal.

equivocate *v.* dodge, evade, fence, fudge, hedge, mislead, palter, parry, prevaricate, pussyfoot, quibble, shift, shuffle, sidestep, tergiversate, weasel.

era *n.* age, century, cycle, date, day, days, eon, epoch, generation, period, stage, time.

eradicate *v.* abolish, annihilate, deracinate, destroy, efface, eliminate, erase, expunge, exterminate, extinguish, extirpate, get rid of, obliterate, raze, remove, root out, stamp out, suppress, unroot, uproot, weed out.

erase *v.* blot out, cancel, cleanse, delete, efface, elimin-

ate, eradicate, expunge, get rid of, obliterate, remove, rub out.

erect *adj.* elevated, engorged, firm, hard, perpendicular, pricked, raised, rigid, standing, stiff, straight, taut, tense, tumescent, upright, upstanding, vertical.

antonyms limp, relaxed.

v. assemble, build, constitute, construct, create, elevate, establish, fabricate, form, found, initiate, institute, lift, mount, organize, pitch, put up, raise, rear, set up.

erection *n.* assembly, building, construction, creation, edifice, elevation, establishment, fabrication, manufacture, pile, raising, rigidity, stiffness, structure, tumescence.

erode *v.* abrade, consume, corrade, corrode, denude, destroy, deteriorate, disintegrate, eat away, grind down, spoil, wear away, wear down.

erotic *adj.* amatorial, amatorious, amatory, amorous, aphrodisiac, carnal, concupiscent, erogenic, erogenous, erotogenic, erotogenous, libidinous, lustful, rousing, seductive, sensual, sexy, stimulating, suggestive, titillating, venereal, voluptuous.

err *v.* blunder, deviate, fail, go astray, lapse, misapprehend, misbehave, miscalculate, misjudge, mistake, misunderstand, offend, sin, slip up, stray, stumble, transgress, trespass, trip up, wander.

errand *n.* assignment, charge, commission, duty, job, message, mission, task.

errant *adj.* aberrant, deviant, erring, itinerant, journeying, loose, nomadic, offending, peccant, peripatetic, rambling, roaming, roving, sinful, sinning, stray, straying, vagrant, wandering, wayward, wrong.

erratic *adj.* aberrant, abnormal, capricious, changeable, desultory, directionless, eccentric, fitful, fluctuating, inconsistent, inconstant, irregular, meandering, planetary, shifting, unpredictable, unreliable, unstable, variable, wandering, wayward.

antonyms consistent, reliable, stable, straight.

erroneous *adj.* amiss, fallacious, false, faulty, flawed, illogical, inaccurate, incorrect, inexact, invalid, mistaken, specious, spurious, unfounded, unsound, untrue, wrong.

antonym correct.

error *n.* barbarism, bêtise, bish, bloomer, blunder, boner, boob, corrigendum, delinquency, delusion, deviation, erratum, fallacy, fault, faux pas, flaw, gaucherie, howler, ignorance, ignoratio elenchi, illusion, inaccuracy, inexactitude, lapse, lapsus calami, lapsus linguae, lapsus memoriae, literal, malapropism, misapprehension, miscalculation, misconception, miscopy, miscorrection, misdeed, misprint, mistake, misunderstanding, mumpsimus, offence, omission, oversight, overslip, sin, slip, slip-up, solecism, transgression, trespass, wrong, wrongdoing.

erudite *adj.* academic, cultivated, cultured, educated, highbrow, knowledgeable, learned, lettered, literate, profound, recondite, scholarly, scholastic, well-educated, well-read, wise.

antonym unlettered.

erupt *v.* belch, break, break out, burst, discharge, eruct, eructate, explode, flare, gush, rift, spew, spout, vent, vomit.

escalate *v.* accelerate, amplify, ascend, climb, enlarge, expand, extend, grow, heighten, increase, intensify, magnify, mount, raise, rise, spiral, step up.

antonym diminish.

antonym inevitable.

escapade *n.* adventure, antic, caper, doing, escapado, exploit, fling, fredaine, gest, lark, prank, romp, scrape, spree, stunt, trick.

escape *v.* abscond, avoid, baffle, bolt, break free, break loose, break off, break out, circumvent, decamp, discharge, do a bunk, dodge, drain, duck, elude, emanate, evade, flee, flit, flow, fly, foil, get away, gush, issue, leak, ooze, pass, pour forth, scape, scarper, seep, shake off, shun, skedaddle, skip, slip, slip away, spurt, take it on the run, take to one's heels, trickle, vamoose.
n. abscondence, avoidance, bolt, break, break-out, circumvention, decampment, discharge, distraction, diversion, drain, effluence, effluent, efflux, effluxion, elusion, emanation, emission, escapism, evasion, flight, flit, getaway, gush, jail-break, leak, leakage, meuse, out, outflow, outlet, outpour, pastime, recreation, relaxation, relief, safety-valve, seepage, spurt, vent.

escort *n.* aide, attendant, beau, bodyguard, chaperon, cicisbeo, companion, company, convoy, cortège, entourage, gigolo, guard, guardian, guide, partner, pilot, procession, protection, protector, retinue, safeguard, squire, suite, train.
v. accompany, chaperon, chum, company, conduct, convoy, guard, guide, lead, partner, protect, shepherd, squire, usher.

especially *adv.* chiefly, conspicuously, eminently, exceedingly, exceptionally, exclusively, expressly, extraordinarily, mainly, markedly, notably, noticeably, outstandingly, particularly, passing, peculiarly, pre-eminently, principally, remarkably, signally, singularly, specially, specifically, strikingly, supremely, uncommonly, uniquely, unusually, very.

espousal *n.* adoption, advocacy, affiance, alliance, backing, betrothal, betrothing, bridal, championing, championship, defence, embracing, engagement, espousing, maintenance, marriage, matrimony, nuptials, plighting, spousal, support, wedding.

essay[1] *n.* article, assignment, commentary, composition, critique, discourse, disquisition, dissertation, essayette, leader, paper, piece, review, thesis, tract, treatise.

essay[2] *n.* attempt, bash, bid, crack, effort, endeavor, exertion, experiment, go, shot, stab, struggle, test, trial, try, undertaking, venture, whack, whirl.
v. attempt, endeavor, go for, have a bash, have a crack, have a go, have a stab, strain, strive, struggle, tackle, take on, test, try, undertake.

essence *n.* alma, attar, attributes, being, center, character, characteristics, concentrate, core, crux, decoction, decocture, distillate, elixir, ens, entity, esse, extract, fragrance, haecceity, heart, hypostasis, inscape, kernel, life, lifeblood, marrow, meaning, nature, perfume, pith, principle, properties, qualities, quality, quiddit, quiddity, quintessence, scent, significance, soul, spirit, spirits, substance, tincture, virtuality, whatness.

essential[1] *adj.* absolute, basic, cardinal, characteristic, complete, constituent, constitutional, constitutive, crucial, definitive, elemental, elementary, formal, fundamental, ideal, important, indispensable, inherent, innate, intrinsic, key, main, necessary, needed, perfect, principal, quintessential, required, requisite, typical, vital.
antonym inessential.
n. basic, fundamental, must, necessary, necessity, pre-

requisite, principle, qualification, quality, requirement, requisite, rudiment, sine qua non.
antonym inessential.

essential[2] *adj.* concentrated, decocted, distilled, ethereal, extracted, pure, purified, rectified, refined, volatile.

establish *v.* affirm, attest to, authenticate, authorize, base, certify, confirm, constitute, corroborate, create, decree, demonstrate, enact, ensconce, entrench, fix, form, found, ground, implant, inaugurate, install, institute, introduce, invent, lodge, ordain, organize, plant, prove, radicate, ratify, root, sanction, seat, secure, set up, settle, show, start, station, substantiate, validate, verify.

esteem *v.* account, adjudge, admire, believe, calculate, cherish, consider, count, deem, estimate, hold, honor, include, judge, like, love, prize, rate, reckon, regard, regard highly, respect, revere, reverence, think, treasure, value, venerate, view.
n. account, admiration, consideration, count, credit, estimation, good opinion, honor, judgment, love, reckoning, regard, respect, reverence, veneration.

estimate *v.* appraise, approximate, assess, believe, calculate, compute, conjecture, consider, count, evaluate, gauge, guess, judge, number, opine, rank, rate, reckon, surmise, think, value.
n. appraisal, appraisement, approximation, assessment, belief, computation, conceit, conception, conjecture, estimation, evaluation, guess, guesstimate, judgment, opinion, reckoning, surmise, valuation.

estimation *n.* account, admiration, appraisal, appreciation, assessment, belief, calculation, computation, conception, consideration, credit, esteem, estimate, evaluation, good opinion, honor, judgment, opinion, rating, reckoning, regard, respect, reverence, veneration, view.

etch *v.* bite, burn, carve, corrode, cut, dig, engrave, furrow, grave, groove, hatch, impress, imprint, incise, ingrain, inscribe, stamp.

eternal *adj.* abiding, ceaseless, changeless, constant, deathless, durable, endless, enduring, eonian, eterne, everlasting, eviternal, illimitable, immortal, immutable, imperishable, incessant, indestructible, infinite, interminable, lasting, limitless, never-ending, perennial, permanent, perpetual, sempiternal, timeless, unbegotten, unceasing, unchanging, undying, unending, unextinguishable, unremitting.
antonyms changeable, ephemeral, temporary.

ethical *adj.* commendable, conscientious, correct, decent, fair, fitting, good, honest, honorable, just, meet, moral, noble, principled, proper, right, righteous, seemly, upright, virtuous.
antonym unethical.

etiquette *n.* ceremony, civility, code, convention, conventionalities, correctness, courtesy, customs, decency, decorum, formalities, manners, politeness, politesse, propriety, protocol, rules, seemliness, usage, use.

eulogy *n.* acclaim, acclamation, accolade, applause, commendation, compliment, encomium, exaltation, glorification, laud, laudation, laudatory, paean, panegyric, plaudit, praise, tribute.
antonym condemnation.

euphemism *n.* evasion, fig-leaf, genteelism, hypocorism, hypocorisma, polite term, politeness, substitution, understatement.

euphoria n. bliss, buoyancy, cheerfulness, cloud nine, ecstasy, elation, enthusiasm, euphory, exaltation, exhilaration, exultation, glee, high, high spirits, intoxication, joy, joyousness, jubilation, rapture, transport.
antonym depression.

evacuate[1] v. abandon, clear, clear out, decamp, depart, desert, forsake, leave, quit, relinquish, remove, retire from, vacate, withdraw.

evacuate[2] v. defecate, discharge, eject, eliminate, empty, excrete, expel, purge, void.

evade v. avert, avoid, balk, blink, chicken out of, circumvent, cop out, decline, dodge, duck, elude, equivocate, escape, fence, fend off, fudge, hedge, parry, prevaricate, quibble, scrimshank, shirk, shun, sidestep, skive, steer clear of, temporize.
antonym face.

evaluate v. appraise, assay, assess, calculate, compute, estimate, gauge, judge, rank, rate, reckon, size up, value, weigh.

evaporate v. condense, dehydrate, dematerialize, desiccate, disappear, dispel, disperse, dissipate, dissolve, distil, dry, evanesce, exhale, fade, melt (away), vanish, vaporize, vapor.

evasive adj. ambiguous, cag(e)y, casuistic, casuistical, cunning, deceitful, deceptive, devious, disingenuous, dissembling, elusive, elusory, equivocating, indirect, misleading, oblique, prevaricating, secretive, shifty, shuffling, slippery, sophistical, tricky, unforthcoming, vacillating.
antonyms direct, frank.

even adj. abreast, alongside, balanced, calm, coequal, commensurate, comparable, complanate, composed, constant, cool, disinterested, dispassionate, drawn, equable, equal, equalized, equanimous, equitable, even-tempered, fair, fair and square, fifty-fifty, flat, fluent, flush, horizontal, identical, impartial, impassive, imperturbable, just, level, level-pegging, like, matching, metrical, monotonous, neck and neck, on a par, parallel, peaceful, placid, plane, plumb, proportionate, quits, regular, rhythmical, serene, side by side, similar, smooth, square, stable, steady, straight, symmetrical, tied, tranquil, true, unbiased, unbroken, undisturbed, unexcitable, unexcited, uniform, uninterrupted, unprejudiced, unruffled, unvarying, unwavering, well-balanced.
antonyms unequal, uneven.
adv. all the more, also, although, as well, at all, directly, exactly, hardly, including, just, much, scarcely, so much as, still, yet.
v. align, balance, equal, equalize, flatten, flush, level, match, regularize, regulate, smooth, square, stabilize, steady, straighten.

evening n. crepuscule, dusk, eve, even, eventide, forenight, gloaming, Hesper, Hesperus, nightfall, sundown, sunset, twilight, vesper.
adj. crepuscular, twilight, vesperal, vespertinal, vespertine.

event n. adventure, affair, bout, business, case, circumstance, competition, conclusion, consequence, contest, effect, end, engagement, episode, eventuality, experience, fact, game, happening, incident, issue, match, matter, milestone, occasion, occurrence, outcome, possibility, result, termination, tournament, upshot.

even-tempered adj. calm, composed, cool, cool-headed, equable, equanimous, impassive, imperturbable, level-headed, peaceable, peaceful, placid, serene, stable, steady, tranquil, unexcitable, unfussed, unruffled.
antonym excitable.

eventual adj. concluding, consequent, ensuing, final, future, impending, last, later, overall, planned, projected, prospective, resulting, subsequent, ultimate.

eventually adv. after all, at last, at length, finally, in one's own good time, sooner or later, subsequently, ultimately.

ever adv. always, at all, at all times, at any time, ceaselessly, constantly, continually, endlessly, eternally, everlastingly, evermore, for ever, in any case, in any circumstances, incessantly, on any account, perpetually, unceasingly, unendingly.

everlasting adj. abiding, boring, ceaseless, changeless, constant, continual, continuous, deathless, durable, endless, enduring, eternal, immarcescible, immortal, imperishable, incessant, indestructible, infinite, interminable, lasting, monotonous, never-ending, perdurable, permanent, perpetual, relentless, tedious, timeless, unceasing, unchanging, undying, unfading, uninterrupted, unremitting.
antonyms temporary, transient.

evermore adv. always, eternally, ever, ever after, for aye, for ever, for ever and a day, for ever and ever, henceforth, hereafter, in perpetuum, in saecula saeculorum, till doomsday, to the end of time, unceasingly.

everyday adj. accustomed, banal, boring, circadian, common, common-or-garden, commonplace, conventional, customary, daily, diurnal, dull, familiar, frequent, habitual, informal, monotonous, mundane, normal, ordinary, plain, prosaic, quotidian, regular, routine, run-of-the-mill, simple, stock, unexceptional, unimaginative, usual, wonted, workaday.
antonyms exceptional, special.

evict v. boot out, cast out, chuck out, defenestrate, dislodge, dispossess, disseize, eject, expel, expropriate, give the bum's rush, kick out, oust, put out, remove, show the door, turf out.

evidence n. affirmation, attestation, betrayal, confirmation, corroboration, data, declaration, demonstration, deposition, documentation, grounds, hint, indication, manifestation, mark, pledge, proof, sign, substantiation, suggestion, testimony, token, voucher, witness.
v. affirm, attest, betray, confirm, demonstrate, denote, display, establish, evince, exhibit, indicate, manifest, prove, reveal, show, signify, testify to, witness.

evident adj. apparent, clear, clear-cut, confessed, conspicuous, detectable, discernible, distinct, incontestable, incontrovertible, indisputable, manifest, noticeable, obvious, ostensible, palpable, patent, perceptible, plain, tangible, undeniable, unmistakable, visible.
antonym uncertain.

evil adj. adverse, bad, baleful, baneful, base, blackguardly, black-hearted, calamitous, catastrophic, corrupt, cruel, deadly, deleterious, depraved, destructive, detrimental, devilish, dire, disastrous, facinorous, flagitious, foul, ghastly, grim, harmful, heinous, hurtful, immoral, inauspicious, inimical, iniquitous, injurious, knavish, malefactory, malefic, maleficent, malevolent, malicious, malignant, mephitic, mischievous, miscreant, nefarious, nefast, nocuous, noisome, noxious, offensive, painful, perfidious, pernicious, pestiferous, pestilential, poisonous, putrid, reprobate, ruinous, sinful, sorrowful, ugly, unfortunate, unlucky, unpleasant, unspeakable, vicious, vile, villainous, wicked, woeful, wrong.

n. adversity, affliction, amiss, badness, bane, baseness, blow, calamity, catastrophe, corruption, curse, demonry, depravity, disaster, distress, facinorousness, flagitiousness, foulness, harm, heinousness, hurt, hydra, ill, immorality, impiety, improbity, iniquity, injury, knavery, maleficence, malignity, mischief, misery, misfortune, pain, perfidy, ruin, sin, sinfulness, sorrow, suffering, turpitude, ulcer, vice, viciousness, villainy, wickedness, woe, wrong, wrong-doing.

evoke *v.* activate, actuate, arouse, awaken, call, call forth, call up, conjure up, educe, elicit, excite, induce, invoke, produce, provoke, raise, recall, rekindle, stimulate, stir, summon, summon up.

antonyms quell, suppress.

evolve *v.* derive, descend, develop, disclose, elaborate, emerge, enlarge, expand, grow, increase, mature, progress, result, unravel.

exact *adj.* accurate, blow-by-blow, careful, close, correct, definite, detailed, explicit, express, factual, faithful, faultless, finical, finicky, flawless, identical, letter-perfect, literal, methodical, meticulous, nice, orderly, painstaking, particular, perfectionist, perjink, precise, punctilious, right, rigorous, scrupulous, severe, specific, square, strict, true, unambiguous, unequivocal, unerring, veracious, very, word-perfect.

antonym inexact.

v. bleed, claim, command, compel, demand, extort, extract, force, impose, insist on, milk, require, requisition, squeeze, wrest, wring.

exactly *adv.* absolutely, accurately, bang, carefully, correctly, dead, definitely, explicitly, expressly, faithfully, faultlessly, just, literally, literatim, methodically, particularly, plumb, precisely, punctiliously, quite, rigorously, scrupulously, severely, specifically, strictly, to the letter, truly, truthfully, unambiguously, unequivocally, unerringly, veraciously, verbatim.

interj. absolutely, agreed, certainly, indeed, just so, of course, precisely, quite, right, true.

exaggerate *v.* amplify, bounce, caricature, distend, embellish, embroider, emphasize, enlarge, exalt, hyperbolize, inflate, magnify, overdo, overdraw, over-emphasize, overestimate, oversell, overstate, pile it on.

antonyms belittle, understate.

exalt *v.* acclaim, advance, aggrandize, animate, apotheosize, applaud, arouse, bless, crown, deify, delight, dignify, elate, electrify, elevate, enliven, ennoble, enthrone, excite, exhilarate, extol, fire, glorify, heighten, honor, idolize, inspire, inspirit, laud, magnify, praise, promote, raise, revere, reverence, stimulate, sublimize, thrill, upgrade, uplift, venerate, worship.

antonym debase.

examination *n.* analysis, appraisal, assay, audit, catechism, check, check-up, critique, cross-examination, cross-questioning, docimasy, exam, exploration, inquiry, inquisition, inspection, interrogation, investigation, observation, once-over, perusal, probe, questioning, quiz, research, review, scan, scrutinization, scrutiny, search, sift, study, survey, test, trial, visitation, viva.

examine *v.* analyze, appraise, assay, audit, case, catechize, check (out), consider, cross-examine, cross-ques-

tion, explore, grill, inquire, inspect, interrogate, investigate, jerque, peruse, ponder, pore over, probe, question, quiz, review, scan, scrutinize, sift, study, survey, sus out, test, vet, visit, weigh.

example *n.* admonition, archetype, case, case in point, caution, citation, ensample, exemplar, exemplification, exemplum, ideal, illustration, instance, lesson, mirror, model, occurrence, paradigm, paragon, parallel, pattern, praxis, precedent, prototype, sample, specimen, standard, type, warning.

exasperate *v.* aggravate, anger, annoy, bug, enrage, exacerbate, excite, exulcerate, gall, get, get in someone's hair, get on someone's nerves, get on someone's wick, get to, goad, incense, inflame, infuriate, irk, irritate, madden, needle, nettle, peeve, pique, plague, provoke, rankle, rile, rouse, vex.

antonyms calm, soothe.

excavate *v.* burrow, cut, delve, dig, dig out, dig up, disinter, drive, exhume, gouge, hollow, mine, quarry, sap, scoop, stope, trench, tunnel, uncover, undermine, unearth.

exceed *v.* beat, better, cap, contravene, eclipse, excel, outdistance, outdo, outreach, outrival, outrun, outshine, outstrip, overdo, overstep, overtake, pass, surmount, surpass, take liberties with, top, transcend, transgress.

exceedingly *adv.* amazingly, astonishingly, enormously, especially, exceeding, exceptionally, excessively, extraordinarily, extremely, greatly, highly, hugely, inordinately, passing, superlatively, surpassingly, unprecedentedly, unusually, vastly, very.

excel *v.* beat, better, cap, eclipse, exceed, outclass, outdo, outperform, outrank, outrival, outshine, outstrip, overshadow, pass, predominate, shine, stand out, surmount, surpass, top, transcend, trump.

excellence *n.* distinction, eminence, fineness, goodness, greatness, merit, perfection, pre-eminence, purity, quality, superiority, supremacy, transcendence, virtue, water, worth.

antonym inferiority.

excellent *adj.* A1, admirable, beaut, bosker, boss, brave, bully, capital, champion, choice, commendable, copacetic, corking, crack, cracking, distinguished, estimable, exemplary, eximious, exquisite, fine, first-class, first-rate, good, great, hot stuff, laudable, meritorious, nonpareil, noble, noted, noteworthy, outstanding, peerless, prime, remarkable, ripping, select, splendid, sterling, stunning, superb, supereminent, superior, superlative, surpassing, tipping, tiptop, top-flight, top-notch, topping, unequaled, unexceptionable, up to dick, way-out, wonderful, worthy.

antonym inferior.

except *prep.* apart from, bar, barring, besides, but, except for, excepting, excluding, exclusive of, leaving out, less, minus, not counting, omitting, other than, save, saving.

v. ban, bar, debar, disallow, eliminate, exclude, leave out, omit, pass over, reject, rule out.

exception *n.* abnormality, anomaly, curiosity, debarment, departure, deviation, disallowment, eccentricity, excepting, exclusion, exemption, freak, inconsistency, irregularity, oddity, omission, peculiarity, prodigy, quirk, rarity, rejection, special case.

exceptional *adj.* aberrant, abnormal, anomalous, atypical, curious, deviant, eccentric, excellent, extraordinary, freakish, inconsistent, irregular, marvelous, notable, noteworthy, odd, outstanding, peculiar, phenomenal, prodigious, quirky, rare, remarkable, singular, special, strange, superior, superlative, uncommon, unconventional, unequaled, unexpected, unusual.

antonyms mediocre, unexceptional.

excerpt *n.* citation, extract, fragment, gobbet, part, passage, pericope, portion, quotation, quote, scrap, section, selection.

v. borrow, cite, crib, cull, extract, lift, mine, quarry, quote, select.

excess *n.* debauchery, diarrhoea, dissipation, dissoluteness, excesses, exorbitance, extravagance, glut, gluttony, immoderateness, immoderation, intemperance, left-overism, libertinism, licentiousness, overabundance, overdose, overflow, overflush, overindulgence, overkill, overload, plethora, prodigality, remainder, superabundance, superfluity, surfeit, surplus, unrestraint.

antonym dearth.

adj. additional, extra, left-over, redundant, remaining, residual, spare, superfluous, supernumerary, surplus.

exchange *v.* bandy, bargain, barter, change, commute, convert, interchange, reciprocate, replace, substitute, swap, switch, toss about, trade, truck.

n. bargain, barter, bourse, brush, chat, commerce, conversation, converse, conversion, dealing, interchange, intercourse, market, quid pro quo, reciprocity, replacement, substitution, swap, switch, tit for tat, trade, traffic, truck.

excite *v.* activate, actuate, aerate, affect, agitate, animate, arouse, awaken, discompose, disturb, elate, electrify, elicit, engender, evoke, fire, foment, galvanize, generate, ignite, impress, incite, induce, inflame, initiate, inspire, instigate, kindle, motivate, move, provoke, quicken, rouse, stimulate, stir up, suscitate, sway, thrill, titillate, touch, turn on, upset, waken, warm, whet.

antonyms bore, quell.

excitement *n.* action, activity, ado, adventure, agitation, animation, brouhaha, clamor, commotion, deliriousness, delirium, discomposure, eagerness, elation, enthusiasm, excitation, ferment, fever, flurry, furore, fuss, heat, hubbub, hue and cry, hurly-burly, kerfuffle, kicks, passion, perturbation, restlessness, stimulation, stimulus, tew, thrill, titillation, tumult, unrest, urge.

antonyms apathy, calm.

exclaim *v.* blurt, call, cry, declare, ejaculate, interject, proclaim, shout, utter, vociferate.

exclamation *n.* call, cry, ecphonesis, ejaculation, expletive, interjection, outcry, shout, utterance, vociferation.

exclude *v.* anathematize, ban, bar, blackball, blacklist, bounce, boycott, debar, disallow, eject, eliminate, embargo, evict, except, excommunicate, expel, forbid, ignore, include out, interclude, interdict, keep out, leave out, omit, ostracize, oust, preclude, prohibit, proscribe, refuse, reject, remove, repudiate, rule out, shut out, veto.

antonyms admit, allow, include.

exclusion *n.* ban, bar, boycott, debarment, disfellowship, ejection, elimination, embargo, eviction, exception, expulsion, forbiddal, forbiddance, interdict, nonadmission, omission, ostracization, preclusion, prohib-

ition, proscription, refusal, rejection, removal, repudiation, veto.

antonyms admittance, allowance, inclusion.

exclusive *adj.* absolute, arrogant, chic, choice, clannish, classy, cliquey, cliquish, closed, complete, confined, discriminative, elegant, entire, esoteric, exclusory, fashionable, full, limited, luxurious, monopolistic, narrow, only, peculiar, posh, private, restricted, restrictive, select, selective, selfish, single, snobbish, sole, total, undivided, unique, unshared, whole.

excruciating *adj.* acute, agonizing, atrocious, bitter, burning, exquisite, extreme, harrowing, insufferable, intense, intolerable, painful, piercing, racking, savage, searing, severe, sharp, tormenting, torturing, torturous, unbearable, unendurable.

excursion *n.* airing, breather, day trip, detour, deviation, digression, divagation, ecbole, episode, excursus, expedition, jaunt, journey, outing, ramble, ride, sashay, tour, trip, walk, wandering, wayzgoose.

excuse *v.* absolve, acquit, apologize for, condone, defend, discharge, exculpate, exempt, exonerate, explain, extenuate, forgive, free, ignore, indulge, justify, let off, liberate, mitigate, overlook, palliate, pardon, release, relieve, sanction, spare, tolerate, vindicate, warrant, wink at.

n. alibi, apology, cop-out, defence, disguise, evasion, exculpation, exoneration, expedient, explanation, extenuation, grounds, justification, makeshift, mitigation, mockery, palliation, parody, plea, pretense, pretext, put-off, reason, semblance, shift, substitute, subterfuge, travesty, vindication.

execrate *v.* abhor, abominate, anathematize, blast, condemn, curse, damn, denounce, denunciate, deplore, despise, detest, excoriate, fulminate, hate, imprecate, inveigh against, loathe, revile, vilify.

antonyms commend, praise.

execute[1] *v.* behead, burn, crucify, decapitate, decollate, electrocute, guillotine, hang, kill, liquidate, put to death, shoot.

execute[2] *v.* accomplish, achieve, administer, complete, consummate, deliver, discharge, dispatch, do, effect, effectuate, enact, enforce, expedite, finish, fulfil, implement, perform, prosecute, realize, render, seal, serve, sign, validate.

executive *n.* administration, administrator, controller, director, directorate, directors, government, hierarchy, leadership, management, manager, official, organizer.

adj. administrative, controlling, decision-making, directing, directorial, governing, gubernatorial, guiding, leading, managerial, organizational, organizing, regulating, supervisory.

exemplify *v.* demonstrate, depict, display, embody, ensample, epitomize, evidence, example, exhibit, illustrate, instance, manifest, represent, show, typify.

exempt *v.* absolve, discharge, dismiss, except, excuse, exonerate, free, let off, liberate, make an exception of, release, relieve, spare.

adj. absolved, clear, discharged, excepted, excluded, excused, favored, free, immune, liberated, released, spared.

antonym liable.

exercise *v.* afflict, agitate, annoy, apply, burden, discharge, discipline, distress, disturb, drill, employ, enjoy, exert, habituate, inure, occupy, operate, pain, perturb, practice, preoccupy, train, trouble, try, upset, use, utilize, vex, wield, work out, worry.

n. accomplishment, action, activity, aerobics, application, assignment, daily dozen, discharge, discipline, drill, drilling, effort, employment, enjoyment, exercitation, exertion, fulfilment, implementation, krieg(s)-spiel, labor, lesson, operation, physical jerks, practice, problem, schooling, school-work, task, toil, training, use, utilization, war-game, work, work-out.

exertion *n.* action, application, assiduity, attempt, diligence, effort, employment, endeavor, exercise, industry, labor, operation, pains, perseverance, sedulousness, strain, stretch, struggle, toil, travail, trial, use, utilization, work.
antonyms idleness, rest.

exhale *v.* breathe (out), discharge, eject, emanate, emit, evaporate, expel, expire, give off, issue, respire, steam.
antonym inhale.

exhaust *v.* bankrupt, beggar, consume, cripple, debilitate, deplete, disable, dissipate, drain, dry, empty, enervate, enfeeble, expend, fatigue, finish, impoverish, overtax, overtire, overwork, prostrate, run through, sap, spend, squander, strain, tax, tire (out), use up, void, waste, weaken, wear out, weary.
antonym refresh.

n. discharge, eduction, effluvium, emanation, emission, exhalation, fumes.

exhaustive *adj.* all-embracing, all-inclusive, all-out, complete, comprehensive, definitive, detailed, encyclopedic, expansive, extensive, far-reaching, full, full-scale, in-depth, intensive, sweeping, thorough, thoroughgoing, total.
antonym incomplete.

exhibit *v.* air, demonstrate, disclose, display, evidence, evince, expose, express, flaunt, indicate, manifest, offer, parade, present, reveal, show, showcase, sport.
antonym hide.

n. display, exhibition, illustration, model, show.

exhilarate *v.* animate, cheer, delight, elate, energize, enhearten, enliven, exalt, excite, gladden, hearten, inspirit, invigorate, lift, stimulate, thrill, vitalize.
antonyms bore, discourage.

exhort *v.* admonish, advise, beseech, bid, call upon, caution, counsel, encourage, enjoin, entreat, goad, implore, incite, inflame, inspire, instigate, persuade, press, spur, urge, warn.

exigent *adj.* acute, arduous, constraining, critical, crucial, demanding, difficult, exacting, exhausting, hard, harsh, imperative, importunate, insistent, necessary, needful, pressing, rigorous, severe, stiff, strict, stringent, taxing, tough, urgent.
antonym mild.

exile *n.* banishment, deportation, deportee, émigré, exilement, expatriate, expatriation, expulsion, galut(h), ostracism, outcast, proscription, refugee, separation.

v. banish, deport, drive out, expatriate, expel, ostracize, oust, proscribe.

exist *v.* abide, be, be available, be extant, breathe, continue, endure, happen, have one's being, last, live, obtain, occur, prevail, remain, stand, subsist, survive.

exit *n.* adieu, aperture, congé, departure, door, doorway, egress, evacuation, exodus, farewell, gate, going, leave-taking, outlet, retirement, retreat, vent, way out, withdrawal.
antonym entrance.

v. arrive, depart, enter, issue, leave, retire, retreat, take one's leave, withdraw.

exodus *n.* departure, evacuation, exit, flight, hegira, leaving, long march, migration, retirement, retreat, withdrawal.

exonerate *v.* absolve, acquit, clear, discharge, disculpate, dismiss, except, exculpate, excuse, exempt, free, justify, let off, liberate, pardon, release, relieve, vindicate.
antonym incriminate.

exorbitant *adj.* enormous, excessive, extortionate, extravagant, extreme, immoderate, inordinate, monstrous, outrageous, preposterous, unconscionable, undue, unreasonable, unwarranted.
antonyms fair, reasonable.

exorcism *n.* adjuration, deliverance, expulsion, exsufflation, purification.

exotic *adj.* alien, bizarre, colorful, curious, different, external, extraneous, extraordinary, extrinsic, fascinating, foreign, foreign-looking, glamorous, imported, introduced, mysterious, naturalized, outlandish, outré, peculiar, recherché, strange, striking, unfamiliar, unusual.
antonym ordinary.

expand *v.* amplify, augment, bloat, blow up, branch out, broaden, develop, diffuse, dilate, dispread, distend, diversify, elaborate, embellish, enlarge, expatiate, expound, extend, fatten, fill out, flesh out, grow, heighten, increase, inflate, lengthen, magnify, multiply, open, outspread, prolong, protract, snowball, spread, stretch, swell, thicken, unfold, unfurl, unravel, unroll, wax, widen.
antonyms contract, précis.

expansive *adj.* affable, all-embracing, broad, communicative, comprehensive, dilating, distending, easy, effusive, elastic, expanding, expatiative, expatiatory, extendable, extensive, far-reaching, free, friendly, garrulous, genial, inclusive, loquacious, open, outgoing, sociable, stretching, stretchy, swelling, talkative, thorough, unreserved, voluminous, warm, wide, wide-ranging, widespread.
antonyms cold, reserved.

expect *v.* anticipate, assume, await, bank on, bargain for, believe, calculate, conjecture, contemplate, count on, demand, envisage, forecast, foresee, hope for, imagine, insist on, look for, look forward to, predict, presume, project, reckon, rely on, require, suppose, surmise, think, trust, want, wish.

expectant *adj.* agog, anticipating, anxious, apprehensive, awaiting, curious, eager, enceinte, expecting, gravid, hopeful, in suspense, pregnant, ready, watchful.

expecting *adj.* enceinte, expectant, gravid, in the club, in the family way, pregnant, with child.

expedient *adj.* advantageous, advisable, appropriate, beneficial, convenient, desirable, effective, fit, helpful, judicious, meet, opportune, politic, practical, pragmatic, profitable, proper, prudent, serviceable, suitable, useful, utilitarian, worthwhile.
antonym inexpedient.

n. contrivance, device, dodge, makeshift, maneuver, means, measure, method, resort, resource, ruse, scheme, shift, stop-gap, stratagem, substitute.

expedition[1] *n.* company, crusade, enterprise, excursion, exploration, explorers, hike, journey, mission, pilgrimage, quest, raid, ramble, safari, sail, team, tour, travelers, trek, trip, undertaking, voyage, voyagers.

expedition² *n.* alacrity, briskness, celerity, dispatch, expeditiousness, haste, hurry, immediacy, promptness, quickness, rapidity, readiness, speed, swiftness.
antonym delay.

expel *v.* ban, banish, bar, belch, blackball, cast out, disbar, discharge, dislodge, dismiss, drive out, drum out, egest, eject, evict, exclude, exile, expatriate, hoof out, oust, proscribe, remove, send packing, spew, throw out, turf out.
antonym admit.

expend *v.* consume, disburse, dissipate, employ, exhaust, fork out, pay, shell out, spend, use, use up.
antonym save.

expense *n.* charge, consumption, cost, damage, disbursement, expenditure, loss, outlay, output, payment, sacrifice, spending, toll, use.

expensive *adj.* costly, dear, excessive, exorbitant, extortionate, extravagant, high-priced, inordinate, lavish, overpriced, rich, steep, stiff.
antonyms cheap, inexpensive.

experience *n.* adventure, affair, assay, contact, doing, encounter, episode, event, evidence, exposure, familiarity, happening, incident, involvement, know-how, knowledge, observation, occurrence, ordeal, participation, practice, proof, taste, test, training, trial, understanding.
antonym inexperience.
v. apprehend, behold, empathize, encounter, endure, face, feel, have, know, meet, observe, perceive, sample, sense, suffer, sustain, taste, try, undergo.

experienced *adj.* accomplished, adept, capable, competent, expert, familiar, knowing, knowledgeable, master, mature, practiced, professional, qualified, schooled, seasoned, skilful, sophisticated,- tested, trained, travailed, traveled, tried, veteran, well-versed, wise, worldly, worldly-wise.
antonym inexperienced.

experiment *n.* assay, attempt, ballon d'essai, examination, experimentation, heurism, investigation, procedure, proof, research, test, trial, trial and error, trial run, venture.
v. assay, examine, investigate, research, sample, test, try, verify.

expert *n.* ace, adept, authority, boffin, connoisseur, dab hand, dabster, deacon, dean, maestro, master, pastmaster, pro, professional, specialist, virtuoso, wizard.
adj. able, adept, adroit, apt, clever, crack, deft, dexterous, experienced, facile, handy, knowledgeable, master, masterly, practiced, professional, proficient, qualified, skilful, skilled, trained, virtuoso.
antonym novice.

expire *v.* cease, close, conclude, decease, depart, die, discontinue, emit, end, exhale, finish, lapse, perish, run out, stop, terminate.
antonyms begin, continue.

explain *v.* account for, clarify, clear up, construe, decipher, decode, define, demonstrate, describe, disclose, elucidate, enucleate, excuse, explicate, expound, gloss, gloze, illustrate, interpret, justify, resolve, simplify, solve, spell out, teach, translate, unfold, unravel, untangle.
antonyms obfuscate, obscure.

explanation *n.* account, answer, cause, clarification,

definition, demonstration, description, éclaircissement, elucidation, enucleation, excuse, exegesis, explication, exposition, gloss, illustration, interpretation, justification, legend, meaning, mitigation, motive, reason, resolution, sense, significance, solution, vindication, voice-over.

explicit *adj.* absolute, accurate, categorical, certain, clear, declared, definite, detailed, direct, distinct, exact, express, frank, open, outspoken, patent, plain, positive, precise, specific, stated, straightforward, unambiguous, unequivocal, unqualified, unreserved.
antonyms inexplicit, vague.

exploit *n.* accomplishment, achievement, adventure, attainment, deed, feat, gest(e), stunt.
v. abuse, bleed, capitalize on, cash in on, fleece, impose on, make capital out of, manipulate, milk, misuse, profit by, rip off, skin, soak, take advantage of, turn to account, use, utilize.

explore *v.* analyze, case, examine, inspect, investigate, probe, prospect, reconnoiter, research, scout, scrutinize, search, survey, tour, travel, traverse.

explosion *n.* bang, blast, burst, clap, crack, debunking, detonation, discharge, discrediting, eruption, fit, outbreak, outburst, paroxysm, refutation, report.

explosive *adj.* charged, dangerous, fiery, hazardous, overwrought, perilous, stormy, tense, touchy, ugly, unstable, vehement, violent, volatile, volcanic.
antonym calm.
n. cordite, dynamite, gelignite, gun-powder, jelly, lyddite, melinite, nitroglycerine, TNT.

exponent *n.* advocate, backer, champion, commentator, defender, demonstrator, elucidator, example, executant, exegetist, exemplar, expositor, expounder, illustration, illustrator, indication, interpreter, model, performer, player, presenter, promoter, propagandist, proponent, representative, sample, specimen, spokesman, spokeswoman, supporter, type, upholder.

expose *v.* air, betray, bring to light, denounce, detect, disclose, display, divulge, endanger, exhibit, hazard, imperil, jeopardize, manifest, present, reveal, risk, show, uncover, unearth, unmask, unveil, wash one's dirty linen in public.
antonym cover.

exposition *n.* account, commentary, critique, demonstration, description, discourse, display, elucidation, exegesis, exhibition, explanation, explication, expo, fair, illustration, interpretation, monograph, paper, presentation, show, study, thesis.

expound *v.* describe, elucidate, explain, explicate, illustrate, interpet, preach, sermonize, set forth, spell out, unfold.

express *v.* articulate, assert, asseverate, bespeak, communicate, conceive, convey, couch, declare, denote, depict, designate, disclose, divulge, embody, enunciate, evince, exhibit, extract, force out, formulate, formulize, indicate, intimate, manifest, phrase, pronounce, put, put across, represent, reveal, say, show, signify, speak, stand for, state, symbolize, tell, testify, utter, verbalize, voice, word.
adj. accurate, categorical, certain, clear, clear-cut, definite, direct, distinct, especial, exact, explicit, fast, high-speed, manifest, non-stop, outright, particular, plain, pointed, precise, quick, rapid, singular, special, speedy, stated, swift, unambiguous, unqualified.
antonym vague.

expression *n.* air, announcement, appearance, aspect, assertion, asseveration, communication, countenance, declaration, delivery, demonstration, diction, embodiment, emphasis, enunciation, execution, exhibition, face, idiom, indication, intonation, language, locution, look, manifestation, mention, mien, phrase, phraseology, phrasing, pronouncement, reflex, remark, representation, set phrase, show, sign, speaking, speech, statement, style, symbol, term, token, turn of phrase, utterance, verbalism, verbalization, voicing, word, wording.

expressive *adj.* allusive, demonstrative, eloquent, emphatic, energetic, forcible, indicative, informative, lively, meaningful, mobile, moving, poignant, pointed, pregnant, representative, revealing, significant, striking, strong, suggestive, sympathetic, telling, thoughtful, vivid.
antonyms expressionless, poker-faced.

expressly *adv.* absolutely, categorically, clearly, decidedly, definitely, distinctly, especially, exactly, explicitly, intentionally, manifestly, on purpose, outright, particularly, plainly, pointedly, positively, precisely, purposely, specially, specifically, unambiguously, unequivocally.

expulsion *n.* banishment, debarment, disbarment, discharge, dislodgment, dislodging, dismissal, ejection, ejectment, eviction, exclusion, exile, expatriation, extrusion, proscription, removal.

expunge *v.* abolish, annihilate, annul, blot out, cancel, delete, destroy, efface, eradicate, erase, exterminate, extinguish, extirpate, obliterate, raze, remove, uncreate, unmake, wipe out.

expurgate *v.* blue-pencil, bowdlerize, censor, clean up, cut, emend, purge, purify, sanitize.

exquisite *adj.* acute, admirable, alembicated, appreciative, attractive, beautiful, charming, choice, comely, consummate, cultivated, dainty, delicate, delicious, discerning, discriminating, elegant, excellent, excruciating, fastidious, fine, flawless, impeccable, incomparable, intense, keen, lovely, matchless, meticulous, outstanding, peerless, perfect, piercing, pleasing, poignant, polished, precious, rare, refined, select, selective, sensitive, sharp, splendid, striking, superb, superlative, too-too.
antonyms flawed, imperfect, poor, ugly.

extant *adj.* alive, existent, existing, in existence, living, remaining, subsistent, subsisting, surviving.
antonyms dead, extinct, non-existent.

extemporary *adj.* ad-lib, expedient, extemporaneous, extempore, free, impromptu, improvisatory, improvised, jazz, made-up, makeshift, offhand, off-the-cuff, on-the-spot, spontaneous, temporary, unplanned, unpremeditated, unprepared, unrehearsed.
antonym planned.

extemporize *v.* ad-lib, autoschediaze, improvise, make up, play by ear.

extend *v.* advance, amplify, attain, augment, bestow, broaden, confer, continue, develop, dilate, drag out, draw out, elongate, enhance, enlarge, expand, give, grant, hold out, impart, increase, last, lengthen, offer, present, proffer, prolong, protract, pull out, reach, spin out, spread, stretch, supplement, take, uncoil, unfold, unfurl, unroll, widen, yield.
antonym shorten.

extension *n.* accretion, addendum, addition, adjunct,

amplification, annexe, appendage, appendix, augmentation, branch, broadening, continuation, delay, development, dilatation, distension, el, elongation, enhancement, enlargement, expansion, extent, increase, lengthening, postponement, prolongation, protraction, spread, stretching, supplement, widening, wing.

extensive *adj.* all-inclusive, broad, capacious, commodious, comprehensive, expanded, expansive, extended, far-flung, far-reaching, general, great, huge, large, large-scale, lengthy, long, pervasive, prevalent, protracted, roomy, spacious, sweeping, thorough, thoroughgoing, universal, unrestricted, vast, voluminous, wholesale, wide, widespread.
antonyms narrow, restricted.

extent *n.* amount, amplitude, area, bounds, breadth, bulk, compass, degree, dimension(s), duration, expanse, expansion, length, magnitude, measure, play, proportions, quantity, range, reach, scope, size, sphere, spread, stretch, sweep, term, time, volume, width.

extenuating *adj.* exculpatory, extenuative, extenuatory, justifying, mitigating, moderating, palliative, qualifying.

exterior *n.* appearance, aspect, coating, covering, externals, façade, face, finish, outside, shell, skin, superficies, surface.
antonym interior.
adj. alien, exotic, external, extraneous, extrinsic, foreign, outer, outermost, outside, outward, peripheral, superficial, surface, surrounding.
antonym interior.

exterminate *v.* abolish, annihilate, deracinate, destroy, eliminate, eradicate, extirpate, massacre, wipe out.

external *adj.* alien, apparent, exoteric, exotic, exterior, extern, externe, extramural, extraneous, extrinsic, foreign, independent, outer, outermost, outside, outward, superficial, surface, visible.
antonym internal.

extinct *adj.* abolished, dead, defunct, doused, ended, exterminated, extinguished, gone, inactive, lost, obsolete, out, quenched, terminated, vanished, void.
antonyms extant, living.

extinction *n.* abolition, annihilation, death, destruction, eradication, excision, extermination, extinguishment, extirpation, obliteration, oblivion, quietus.

extinguish *v.* abolish, annihilate, destroy, douse, dout, eliminate, end, eradicate, erase, expunge, exterminate, extirpate, kill, obscure, put out, quench, remove, slake, smother, snuff out, stifle, suppress.

extol *v.* acclaim, applaud, celebrate, commend, cry up, eulogize, exalt, glorify, laud, magnify, panegyrize, praise, puff.
antonyms blame, denigrate.

extort *v.* blackmail, bleed, bully, coerce, exact, extract, force, milk, squeeze, wrest, wring.

extra *adj.* accessory, added, additional, ancillary, auxiliary, excess, extraneous, for good measure, fresh, further, gash, inessential, leftover, more, needless, new, other, redundant, reserve, spare, supererogatory, superfluous, supernumerary, supplemental, supplementary, surplus, unnecessary, unneeded, unused.
antonym integral.
n. accessory, addendum, addition, adjunct, affix, appendage, appurtenance, attachment, bonus, comp-

lement, extension, lagniappe, plus(s)age, supernumerary, supplement.

adv. especially, exceptionally, extraordinarily, extremely, particularly, remarkably, uncommonly, unusually.

extract *v.* abstract, choose, cite, cull, decoct, deduce, derive, develop, distil, draw, draw out, educe, elicit, enucleate, evoke, evolve, evulse, exact, express, extirpate, gather, get, glean, obtain, quote, reap, remove, select, uproot, withdraw, wrest, wring.

antonym insert.

n. abstract, apozem, citation, clip, clipping, concentrate, cutting, decoction, decocture, distillate, distillation, essence, excerpt, juice, passage, quotation, selection.

extraordinary *adj.* amazing, bizarre, curious, exceptional, fantastic, marvelous, notable, noteworthy, odd, outstanding, particular, peculiar, phenomenal, rare, remarkable, significant, singular, special, strange, striking, surprising, uncommon, uncontemplated, unfamiliar, unheard-of, unimaginable, unique, unprecedented, unusual, unwonted, weird, wonderful.

antonyms commonplace, ordinary.

extravagant *adj.* absurd, costly, exaggerated, excessive, exorbitant, expensive, extortionate, fanciful, fancy, fantastic, flamboyant, flashy, foolish, garish, gaudy, grandiose, hyperbolic, hyperbolical, immoderate, improvident, imprudent, inordinate, lavish, ornate, ostentatious, outrageous, outré, overpriced, preposterous, pretentious, prodigal, profligate, reckless, showy, spendthrift, steep, thriftless, unreasonable, unrestrained, unthrifty, wasteful, wild.

antonyms moderate, thrifty.

extreme *adj.* acute, deep-dyed, dire, double-dyed, downright, Draconian, drastic, egregious, exaggerated, exceptional, excessive, exquisite, extraordinary, extravagant, fanatical, faraway, far-off, farthest, final, great, greatest, harsh, high, highest, immoderate, inordinate, intemperate, intense, last, maximum, out-and-out, outermost, outrageous, radical, red-hot, remarkable, remotest, rigid, severe, sheer, stern, strict, supreme, terminal, ultimate, ultra, unbending, uncommon, uncompromising, unconventional, unreasonable, unusual, utmost, utter, uttermost, worst, zealous.

antonyms mild, moderate.

n. acme, apex, apogee, boundary, climax, consummation, depth, edge, end, excess, extremity, height, limit, maximum, minimum, nadir, peak, pinnacle, pole, termination, top, ultimate, utmost, zenith.

extremism *n.* fanaticism, radicalism, terrorism, ultraism, zeal, zealotism, zealotry.

antonym moderation.

extricate *v.* clear, deliver, disembarrass, disembrangle, disembroil, disengage, disentangle, disintricate, free, liberate, release, relieve, remove, rescue, withdraw.

antonym involve.

exuberant *adj.* abundant, animated, baroque, buoyant, cheerful, copious, eager, ebullient, effervescent, effusive, elated, energetic, enthusiastic, exaggerated, excessive, excited, exhilarated, fulsome, high-spirited, lavish, lively, lush, luxuriant, overdone, overflowing, plenteous, plentiful, prodigal, profuse, rambunctious, rank, rich, sparkling, spirited, sprightly, superabundant, superfluous, teeming, vigorous, vivacious, zestful.

antonyms apathetic, lifeless, scant.

exult *v.* boast, brag, celebrate, crow, delight, gloat, glory, jubilate, rejoice, relish, revel, taunt, triumph.

eye *n.* appreciation, belief, discernment, discrimination, eyeball, glim, judgment, keeker, mind, opinion, optic, orb, peeper, perception, recognition, taste, viewpoint.

v. contemplate, examine, eye up, gaze at, glance at, inspect, leer at, look at, make eyes at, observe, ogle, peruse, regard, scan, scrutinize, stare at, study, survey, view, watch.

F

fable *n.* allegory, apologue, fabliau, fabrication, fairy story, falsehood, fantasy, fib, fiction, figment, invention, legend, lie, Märchen, myth, narrative, old wives' tale, parable, romance, saga, story, tale, tall story, untruth, yarn.

fabled *adj.* fabulous, famed, famous, feigned, fictional, legendary, mythical, renowned, storied.

antonym unknown.

fabric *n.* cloth, constitution, construction, foundations, framework, infrastructure, make-up, material, organization, structure, stuff, textile, texture, web.

fabricate *v.* assemble, build, coin, concoct, construct, create, devise, erect, fake, falsify, fashion, feign, forge, form, frame, invent, make, manufacture, shape, trump up.

fabrication *n.* assemblage, assembly, building, cock-and-bull story, concoction, construction, erection, fable, fairy story, fake, falsehood, fiction, figment, forgery, frame-up, invention, lie, manufacture, myth, production, story, untruth.

antonym truth.

fabulous *adj.* amazing, apocryphal, astounding, breathtaking, fabled, false, fantastic, feigned, fictitious, imaginary, immense, inconceivable, incredible, invented, legendary, marvelous, mythical, phenomenal, renowned, spectacular, superb, unbelievable, unreal, wonderful.

antonyms moderate, real, small.

façade *n.* appearance, cloak, cover, disguise, exterior, face, front, frontage, guise, mask, pretense, semblance, show, veil, veneer.

face *n.* air, appearance, aspect, assurance, audacity, authority, boatrace, boldness, brass neck, cheek, confidence, countenance, cover, dial, dignity, disguise, display, effrontery, expression, exterior, façade, facet, favor, features, front, frown, gall, grimace, honor, image, impudence, kisser, lineaments, look, mask, metope, moue, mug, nerve, outside, phiz, phizog, physiognomy, pout, prestige, presumption, pretence, reputation, sauce, scowl, self-respect, semblance, show, side, smirk, snoot, standing, status, surface, visage.

v. clad, coat, confront, cope with, cover, deal with, defy, dress, encounter, experience, finish, front, give on to, level, line, meet, oppose, overlay, overlook, sheathe, surface, tackle, veneer.

facet *n.* angle, aspect, characteristic, face, feature, part, phase, plane, point, side, slant, surface.

facetious *adj.* amusing, comical, droll, facete, flippant, frivolous, funny, humorous, jesting, jocose, jocular, facile 107 fair

merry, playful, pleasant, tongue-in-cheek, unserious, waggish, witty.
antonym serious.

facile *adj.* adept, adroit, complaisant, cursory, dexterous, easy, effortless, fluent, glib, hasty, light, plausible, proficient, quick, ready, shallow, simple, skilful, slick, smooth, superficial, uncomplicated, yielding.
antonyms clumsy, implausible, profound.

facilitate *v.* assist, ease, expedite, forward, further, grease, help, promote, speed up.

facilities *n.* amenity, appliance, convenience, equipment, means, mod cons, opportunity, prerequisites, resource.

facility *n.* ability, adeptness, adroitness, bent, dexterity, ease, efficiency, effortlessness, expertness, fluency, gift, knack, proficiency, quickness, readiness, skilfulness, skill, smoothness, talent, turn.

facsimile *n.* carbon, carbon copy, copy, duplicate, image, mimeograph, photocopy, Photostat®, print, replica, repro, reproduction, transcript, Xerox®.

fact *n.* act, actuality, certainty, circumstance, datum, deed, detail, event, fait accompli, feature, gospel, happening, incident, item, occurrence, particular, point, reality, specific, truth.

faction[1] *n.* band, bloc, cabal, cadre, camp, caucus, clique, coalition, combination, confederacy, contingent, coterie, crowd, division, gang, ginger group, group, junta, lobby, minority, party, pressure group, ring, section, sector, set, splinter group, splinter party, troop.

faction[2] *n.* conflict, disagreement, discord, disharmony, dissension, disunity, division, divisiveness, fighting, friction, infighting, quarreling, rebellion, sedition, strife, tumult, turbulence.
antonyms agreement, peace.

factitious *adj.* affected, artificial, assumed, contrived, counterfeit, engineered, fabricated, fake, false, imitation, insincere, made-up, manufactured, mock, phony, pinchbeck, pretended, put-on, sham, simulated, spurious, supposititious, synthetic, unnatural, unreal.
antonym genuine.

factor *n.* agent, aspect, cause, circumstance, component, consideration, deputy, determinant, element, estate manager, influence, item, joker, middleman, parameter, part, point, reeve, steward, thing, unknown quantity.

factory *n.* hacienda, manufactory, mill, plant, shop, shop-floor, works.

factual *adj.* accurate, authentic, circumstantial, close, correct, credible, detailed, exact, faithful, genuine, literal, objective, precise, real, straight, sure, true, unadorned, unbiased, veritable.
antonym false.

faculty[1] *n.* academics, department, discipline, lecturers, profession, school, staff.

faculty[2] *n.* ability, adroitness, aptitude, bent, brainpower, capability, capacity, cleverness, dexterity, facility, gift, knack, power, propensity, readiness, skill, talent, turn.

faculty[3] *n.* authorization, authority, license, prerogative, privilege, right.

fad *n.* affectation, craze, crotchet, fancy, fashion, mania, mode, rage, trend, vogue, whim.

fade *v.* blanch, bleach, blench, decline, die, dim, diminish, disappear, discolor, disperse, dissolve, droop, dull, dwindle, ebb, etiolate, evanesce, fail, fall, flag, languish, pale, perish, shrivel, vanish, wane, wilt, wither, yellow.

fagged *adj.* all in, beat, exhausted, fatigued, jaded, jiggered, knackered, on one's last legs, wasted, weary, worn out, zonked.
antonym refreshed.

fail *v.* abandon, cease, come to grief, conk out, crack up, crash, cut out, decline, desert, die, disappoint, droop, dwindle, fade, fall, flop, flub, flunk, fold, forget, forsake, founder, fudge, give out, give up, go bankrupt, go bust, go to the wall, go under, gutter, languish, lay an egg, let down, miscarry, misfire, miss, miss one's trip, neglect, omit, peter out, plow, sink, smash, underachieve, underperform, wane, weaken.
antonyms gain, improve, prosper, succeed.

failing *n.* blemish, blind spot, decay, decline, defect, deficiency, deterioration, drawback, error, failure, fault, flaw, foible, frailty, hamartia, imperfection, lapse, miscarriage, misfortune, peccadillo, shortcoming, weakness.
antonyms advantage, strength.
adj. collapsing, decaying, declining, deteriorating, drooping, dwindling, dying, flagging, languishing, moribund, waning, weak, weakening.
antonyms thriving, vigorous.
prep. in default of, in the absence of, lacking, wanting, without.

failure *n.* abortion, also-ran, bankruptcy, breakdown, bummer, collapse, crash, cropper, damp squib, dead duck, decay, decline, default, defeat, deficiency, dereliction, deterioration, disappointment, downfall, dud, failing, fiasco, flivver, flop, folding, frost, frustration, goner, incompetent, insolvency, loser, loss, miscarriage, neglect, negligence, no-hoper, non-performance, omission, remissness, ruin, shortcoming, slip-up, stoppage, turkey, unsuccess, wash-out, wreck.
antonym success.

faint *adj.* bleached, delicate, dim, distant, dizzy, drooping, dull, enervated, exhausted, faded, faltering, fatigued, feeble, feint, giddy, hazy, hushed, ill-defined, indistinct, languid, lethargic, light, light-headed, low, muffled, muted, muzzy, remote, slight, soft, subdued, thin, unenthusiastic, vague, vertiginous, weak, whispered, woozy.
antonyms clear, strong.
v. black out, collapse, droop, drop, flag, flake out, keel over, pass out, swoon.
n. blackout, collapse, deliquium, swoon, syncope, unconsciousness.

fair[1] *adj.* adequate, all right, average, beauteous, beautiful, bonny, bright, clean, clear, clement, cloudless, comely, decent, disinterested, dispassionate, dry, equal, equitable, even-handed, favorable, fine, handsome, honest, honorable, impartial, just, lawful, legitimate, lovely, mediocre, middling, moderate, not bad, objective, OK, on the level, passable, pretty, proper, reasonable, respectable, satisfactory, so-so, square, sunny, sunshiny, tolerable, trustworthy, unbiased, unclouded, unprejudiced, upright, well-favored.
antonyms cloudy, inclement, poor, unfair.

fair[2] *adj.* blond(e), fair-haired, fair-headed, flaxen, light, tow-headed.
antonym dark.

fair³ *n.* bang, bazaar, carnival, expo, exposition, festival, fête, gaff, gala, kermis, market, show.

fairly *adv.* absolutely, adequately, deservedly, equitably, ex aequo, fully, honestly, impartially, justly, moderately, objectively, plainly, positively, pretty, properly, quite, rather, really, reasonably, somewhat, tolerably, unbiasedly, veritably.
antonym unfairly.

fairness *n.* decency, disinterestedness, equitableness, equity, impartiality, justice, legitimacy, legitimateness, rightfulness, rightness, unbiasedness, uprightness.
antonym unfairness.

fairy *n.* brownie, buggane, elf, fay, fée, hob, hobgoblin, leprechaun, Mab, peri, pisky, pixie, Robin Goodfellow, rusalka, sprite.

faith *n.* allegiance, assurance, belief, church, communion, confidence, constancy, conviction, credence, credit, creed, denomination, dependence, dogma, faithfulness, fealty, fidelity, honesty, honor, loyalty, persuasion, pledge, promise, reliance, religion, sincerity, trust, truth, truthfulness, uberrima fides, vow, word, word of honor.
antonyms mistrust, treachery, unfaithfulness.

faithful *adj.* accurate, attached, card-carrying, close, constant, convinced, dependable, devoted, exact, just, leal, loyal, precise, reliable, soothfast, soothful, staunch, steadfast, strict, true, true-blue, true-hearted, trusty, truthful, unswerving, unwavering.
antonyms disloyal, inaccurate, treacherous.
n. adherents, believers, brethren, communicants, congregation, followers, supporters.

faithless *adj.* adulterous, delusive, disloyal, doubting, false, false-hearted, fickle, inconstant, perfidious, punic, recreant, traitorous, treacherous, unbelieving, unfaithful, unreliable, untrue, untrustworthy, untruthful.
antonyms believing, faithful.

fake *v.* affect, assume, copy, counterfeit, fabricate, feign, forge, phony, pretend, put on, sham, simulate.
n. charlatan, copy, forgery, fraud, hoax, imitant, imitation, impostor, mountebank, phony, reproduction, sham, simulation.
adj. affected, artificial, assumed, bastard, bogus, counterfeit, ersatz, false, forged, hyped up, imitation, mock, phony, pinchbeck, pretended, pseudo, reproduction, sham, simulated, spurious.
antonym genuine.

fall *v.* abate, backslide, become, befall, capitulate, cascade, chance, collapse, come about, come to pass, crash, decline, decrease, depreciate, descend, die, diminish, dive, drop, drop down, dwindle, ebb, err, fall away, fall off, fall out, flag, give in, give up, give way, go a purler, go astray, go down, happen, incline, keel over, lapse, lessen, measure one's length, meet one's end, nose-dive, occur, offend, perish, pitch, plummet, plunge, push, resign, settle, sin, sink, slope, slump, souse, stumble, subside, succumb, surrender, take place, topple, transgress, trespass, trip, trip over, tumble, yield, yield to temptation.
antonym rise.
n. capitulation, collapse, cropper, cut, death, decline, declivity, decrease, defeat, degradation, descent, destruction, diminution, dip, dive, downfall, downgrade, drop, dwindling, failure, incline, lapse, lessening, lowering, nose-dive, overthrow, plummet, plunge,

pusher, reduction, resignation, ruin, sin, slant, slip, slope, slump, souse, spill, surrender, transgression, tumble, voluntary.
antonym rise.

fallacious *adj.* casuistical, deceptive, delusive, delusory, erroneous, false, fictitious, illogical, illusory, incorrect, misleading, mistaken, sophistic, sophistical, spurious, untrue, wrong.
antonyms correct, true.

fallacy *n.* casuistry, deceit, deception, deceptiveness, delusion, error, falsehood, faultiness, flaw, illusion, inconsistency, misapprehension, misconception, mistake, sophism, sophistry, untruth.
antonym truth.

fallow *adj.* dormant, idle, inactive, inert, resting, uncultivated, undeveloped, unplanted, unsown, untilled, unused.

false *adj.* artificial, bastard, bogus, concocted, counterfeit, deceitful, deceiving, deceptive, delusive, dishonest, dishonorable, disloyal, double-dealing, double-faced, duplicitous, erroneous, ersatz, faithless, fake, fallacious, false-hearted, faulty, feigned, fictitious, forged, fraudulent, hypocritical, illusive, imitation, improper, inaccurate, incorrect, inexact, invalid, lying, mendacious, misleading, mistaken, mock, perfidious, postiche, pretended, pseud, pseudo, sham, simulated, spurious, synthetic, treacherous, treasonable, trumped-up, truthless, two-faced, unfaithful, unfounded, unreal, unreliable, unsound, untrue, untrustworthy, untruthful, wrong.
antonyms honest, reliable, true.

falsehood *n.* deceit, deception, dishonesty, dissimulation, fable, fabrication, fib, fiction, inexactitude, inveracity, lie, mendacity, misstatement, perjury, prevarication, pseudery, story, unfact, untruth, untruthfulness.
antonyms truth, truthfulness.

falsify *v.* adulterate, alter, belie, cook, counterfeit, distort, doctor, fake, forge, garble, misrepresent, misstate, pervert, sophisticate, take liberties with, tamper with.

falter *v.* break, fail, flag, flinch, halt, hem and haw, hesitate, shake, stammer, stumble, stutter, totter, tremble, vacillate, waver.

fame *n.* celebrity, credit, eminence, esteem, glory, honor, illustriousness, kudos, name, prominence, renown, reputation, repute, stardom.

famed *adj.* acclaimed, celebrated, famous, noted, recognized, renowned, well-known, widely-known.
antonym unknown.

familiar *adj.* abreast, accustomed, acquainted, amicable, au courant, au fait, aware, bold, chummy, close, common, common-or-garden, confidential, conscious, conventional, conversant, cordial, customary, disrespectful, domestic, easy, everyday, forward, free, free-and-easy, frequent, friendly, household, impudent, informal, intimate, intrusive, knowledgeable, mundane, near, open, ordinary, overfree, presuming, presumptuous, private, recognizable, relaxed, repeated, routine, stock, unceremonious, unconstrained, unreserved, versed, well-known.
antonyms formal, reserved, unfamiliar, unversed.

familiarity *n.* acquaintance, acquaintanceship, awareness, boldness, cheek, closeness, conversance, disrespect, ease, experience, fellowship, forwardness, freedom, friendliness, grasp, impertinence, impudence,

informality, intimacy, liberties, liberty, license, naturalness, openness, presumption, sociability, unceremoniousness, understanding.
antonyms formality, reservation, unfamiliarity.
familiarize v. acclimatize, accustom, brief, coach, habituate, instruct, inure, prime, school, season, train.
family n. ancestors, ancestry, birth, blood, brood, children, clan, class, classification, descendants, descent, dynasty, extraction, folk, forebears, forefathers, genealogy, genre, group, house, household, issue, kin, kind, kindred, kinsmen, kith and kin, line, lineage, ménage, network, offspring, parentage, pedigree, people, progeny, quiverful, race, relations, relatives, sept, stemma, stirps, strain, subdivision, system, tribe.
family tree ancestry, extraction, genealogy, line, lineage, pedigree, stemma, stirps.
famine n. dearth, destitution, hunger, scarcity, starvation, want.
antonym plenty.
famous adj. acclaimed, celebrated, conspicuous, distinguished, eminent, excellent, famed, far-famed, glorious, great, honored, illustrious, legendary, lionized, notable, noted, prominent, remarkable, renowned, signal, well-known.
antonym unknown.
fan[1] v. aggravate, agitate, air-condition, air-cool, arouse, blow, cool, enkindle, excite, impassion, increase, provoke, refresh, rouse, stimulate, stir up, ventilate, whip up, winnow, work up.
n. air-conditioner, blower, extractor fan, flabellum, propeller, punkah, vane, ventilator.
fan[2] n. adherent, admirer, aficionado, buff, devotee, enthusiast, fiend, follower, freak, groupie, lover, rooter, supporter, zealot.
fanatic n. activist, addict, bigot, demoniac, devotee, energumen, enthusiast, extremist, fiend, freak, militant, visionary, zealot.
fancy v. be attracted to, believe, conceive, conjecture, crave, desire, dream of, favor, go for, guess, hanker after, have an eye for, imagine, infer, like, long for, lust after, picture, prefer, reckon, relish, suppose, surmise, take a liking to, take to, think, think likely, whim, wish for, yearn for, yen for.
antonym dislike.
n. caprice, chim(a)era, conception, daydream, delusion, desire, dream, fantasy, fondness, hankering, humor, idea, image, imagination, impression, impulse, inclination, liking, nightmare, notion, partiality, penchant, phantasm, predilection, preference, relish, thought, urge, vapor, velleity, vision, whim.
antonyms dislike, fact, reality.
adj. baroque, capricious, chimerical, decorated, decorative, delusive, elaborate, elegant, embellished, extravagant, fanciful, fantastic, far-fetched, illusory, ornamented, ornate, rococo, whimsical.
antonym plain.
fantastic adj. absurd, ambitious, capricious, chimerical, comical, eccentric, enormous, excellent, exotic, extravagant, extreme, fanciful, fantasque, far-fetched, first-rate, freakish, grandiose, great, grotesque, illusory, imaginative, implausible, incredible, irrational, ludicrous, mad, marvelous, odd, out of this world, outlandish, outré, overwhelming, peculiar, phantasmagorical, preposterous, quaint, queer, ridiculous, rococo, sensational, severe, strange, superb,

tremendous, unlikely, unreal, unrealistic, visionary, weird, whimsical, wild, wonderful.
antonyms ordinary, plain, poor.
fantasy n. apparition, caprice, creativity, daydream, delusion, dream, dreamery, fancy, fantasia, fantasque, flight of fancy, hallucination, illusion, imagination, invention, mirage, nightmare, originality, phantasy, pipe-dream, reverie, vision, whimsy.
antonym reality.
far adv. a good way, a long way, afar, considerably, decidedly, deep, extremely, greatly, incomparably, miles, much.
antonym near.
adj. distal, distant, faraway, far-flung, far-off, far-removed, further, god-forsaken, long, opposite, other, outlying, out-of-the-way, remote, removed.
antonyms close, nearby.
fare[1] n. charge, cost, fee, passage, passenger, pick-up, price, traveler.
fare[2] n. board, commons, diet, eatables, food, meals, menu, provisions, rations, sustenance, table, victuals.
fare[3] v. be, do, get along, get on, go, go on, happen, make out, manage, proceed, prosper, turn out.
farewell n. adieu, departure, good-bye, leave-taking, parting, send-off, valediction.
antonym hello.
adj. final, parting, valedictory.
interj. aloha, bye-bye, cheers, ciao, good-bye.
farm n. acreage, acres, bowery, croft, farmstead, grange, holding, homestead, kolkhoz, land, mains, plantation, ranch, smallholding, station.
v. cultivate, operate, plant, till, work the land.
fascinate v. absorb, allure, beguile, bewitch, captivate, charm, delight, enchant, engross, enrapture, enravish, enthrall, entrance, hypnotize, infatuate, intrigue, mesmerize, rivet, spellbind, transfix.
antonym bore.
fashion n. appearance, attitude, beau monde, configuration, convention, craze, custom, cut, demeanor, dernier cri, description, fad, figure, form, guise, haut ton, haute couture, high society, jet set, kind, latest, line, look, make, manner, method, mode, model, mold, pattern, rage, shape, sort, style, trend, type, usage, vogue, way.
v. accommodate, adapt, adjust, alter, construct, contrive, create, design, fit, forge, form, make, manufacture, mold, shape, suit, tailor, work.
fashionable adj. à la mode, alamode, all the rage, chic, chichi, contemporary, current, customary, funky, genteel, in, in vogue, latest, modern, modish, popular, prevailing, smart, snazzy, stylish, swagger, tippy, tony, tonish, trendsetting, trendy, up-to-date, up-to-the-minute, usual, with it.
antonym unfashionable.
fast[1] adj. accelerated, brisk, fleet, flying, hasty, hurried, mercurial, nippy, quick, rapid, spanking, speedy, swift, winged.
antonym slow.
adv. apace, hastily, hell for leather, hurriedly, like a flash, like a shot, posthaste, presto, quickly, rapidly, speedily, swiftly, ventre à terre.
antonym slowly.
fast[2] adj. close, constant, fastened, firm, fixed, fortified, immovable, impregnable, lasting, loyal, permanent,

secure, sound, staunch, steadfast, tight, unflinching, unwavering.

antonyms impermanent, loose.

adv. close, deeply, firmly, fixedly, near, rigidly, securely, soundly, sound(ly), tightly, unflinchingly.

antonym loosely.

fast³ *adj.* dissipated, dissolute, extravagant, immoral, intemperate, licentious, loose, profligate, promiscuous, rakehell, rakehelly, rakish, reckless, self-indulgent, wanton, whorish, wild.

antonyms chaste, moral.

fast⁴ *v.* abstain, bant, diet, go hungry, starve.

n. abstinence, diet, fasting, starvation, xerophagy.

antonyms gluttony, self-indulgence.

fasten *v.* affix, aim, anchor, attach, belay, bend, bind, bolt, chain, clamp, concentrate, connect, direct, fix, focus, grip, infibulate, join, lace, link, lock, nail, rivet, seal, secure, spar, tie, unite.

antonym unfasten.

fastidious *adj.* choosy, critical, dainty, difficult, discriminating, finical, finicky, fussy, hypercritical, meticulous, overnice, particular, pernickety, picky, precise, punctilious, squeamish.

antonym undemanding.

fat *adj.* abdominous, adipose, affluent, beefy, blowzy, corpulent, cushy, elephantine, fatling, fatty, fertile, fleshed, fleshy, flourishing, fozy, fruitful, greasy, gross, heavy, jammy, lucrative, lush, obese, oily, oleaginous, overweight, paunchy, pinguid, plump, poddy, podgy, portly, pot-bellied, productive, profitable, prosperous, pudgy, remunerative, rich, roly-poly, rotund, round, solid, squab, stout, suety, thriving, tubbish, tubby, well-upholstered.

antonyms thin, unproductive.

n. adipose tissue, blubber, brown fat, cellulite, corpulence, degras, embonpoint, fatness, flab, obesity, overweight, paunch, pot (belly), speck.

fatal *adj.* baleful, baneful, calamitous, catastrophic, deadly, destructive, disastrous, final, incurable, killing, lethal, malignant, mortal, mortiferous, mortific, pernicious, ruinous, terminal, vital.

antonym harmless.

fatality *n.* casualty, deadliness, death, disaster, lethalness, loss, mortality, unavoidability.

fate *n.* chance, cup, death, destiny, destruction, divine will, doom, downfall, end, fortune, future, horoscope, issue, joss, karma, kismet, lot, Moira, nemesis, outcome, portion, predestination, predestiny, providence, ruin, stars, upshot, weird.

father *n.* abbé, ancestor, architect, author, begetter, confessor, creator, curé, dad, daddy, elder, forebear, forefather, founder, generant, genitor, governor, inventor, leader, maker, old boy, old man, originator, pa, padre, papa, pappy, parent, pastor, pater, paterfamilias, patriarch, patron, pop, poppa, pops, predecessor, priest, prime mover, procreator, progenitor, senator, sire.

v. beget, conceive, create, dream up, engender, establish, found, get, institute, invent, originate, procreate, produce, sire.

fatherland *n.* home, homeland, mother-country, motherland, native land, old country.

fatherly *adj.* affectionate, avuncular, benevolent, benign, forbearing, indulgent, kind, kindly, paternal, patriarchal, protective, supportive, tender.

antonyms cold, harsh, unkind.

fathom *v.* comprehend, deduce, divine, estimate, gauge, get to the bottom of, grasp, interpret, measure, penetrate, plumb, plummet, probe, see, sound, understand, work out.

fatigue *v.* do in, drain, exhaust, fag, jade, knacker, overtire, shatter, tire, weaken, wear out, weary, whack.

antonym refresh.

n. debility, decay, degeneration, ennui, failure, heaviness, languor, lethargy, listlessness, overtiredness, tiredness.

antonyms energy, freshness.

fault *n.* accountability, blemish, blunder, boner, boob, booboo, culpability, defect, deficiency, delict, delinquency, demerit, dislocation, drawback, error, failing, flaw, frailty, goof, hamartia, imperfection, inaccuracy, indiscretion, infirmity, lack, lapse, liability, misconduct, misdeed, misdemeanor, mistake, negligence, offense, omission, oversight, peccadillo, responsibility, shortcoming, sin, slip, slip-up, snag, solecism, transgression, trespass, weakness, wrong.

antonyms advantage, strength.

v. blame, call to account, censure, criticize, find fault with, impugn, pick a hole in someone's coat, pick at, pick holes in.

antonym praise.

faulty *adj.* bad, blemished, broken, casuistic, damaged, defective, erroneous, fallacious, flawed, illogical, impaired, imperfect, imprecise, inaccurate, incorrect, invalid, malfunctioning, out of order, specious, unsound, weak, wrong.

favor *n.* acceptance, approbation, approval, backing, badge, benefit, bias, boon, championship, courtesy, decoration, esteem, favoritism, friendliness, gift, good turn, goodwill, grace, indulgence, keepsake, kindness, knot, love-token, memento, obligement, partiality, patronage, present, regard, rosette, service, smile, souvenir, support, token.

antonym disfavor.

v. abet, accommodate, advance, advocate, aid, approve, assist, back, befriend, champion, choose, commend, countenance, ease, encourage, esteem, extenuate, facilitate, fancy, have in one's good books, help, indulge, like, oblige, opt for, pamper, patronize, prefer, promote, resemble, spare, spoil, succor, support, take after, take kindly to, value.

antonyms disfavor, hinder, thwart.

favorite *adj.* best-loved, choice, dearest, esteemed, favored, pet, preferred.

antonyms hated, unfavorite.

n. beloved, blue-eyed boy, choice, darling, dear, form horse, idol, pet, pick, preference, teacher's pet, the apple of one's eye, whitehead, whiteheaded boy.

antonym pet hate.

favoritism *n.* bias, biasedness, injustice, jobs for the boys, nepotism, old school tie, one-sidedness, partiality, partisanship, preference, preferential treatment.

antonym impartiality.

fear *n.* agitation, alarm, anxiety, apprehension, apprehensiveness, awe, bogey, bugbear, concern, consternation, cravenness, danger, dismay, disquietude, distress, doubt, dread, foreboding(s), fright, funk, heartquake, horror, likelihood, misgiving(s), nightmare, panic, phobia, phobism, qualms, reverence, risk, solicitude, specter, suspicion, terror, timidity, tremors, trepidation, unease, uneasiness, veneration, wonder, worry.

antonyms courage, fortitude.

v. anticipate, apprehend, dread, expect, foresee, respect, reverence, shudder at, suspect, take fright, tremble, venerate, worry.

fearless *adj.* aweless, bold, brave, confident, courageous, daring, dauntless, doughty, gallant, game, gutsy, heroic, impavid, indomitable, intrepid, lion-hearted, plucky, unabashed, unafraid, unapprehensive, unblenching, unblinking, undaunted, unflinching, valiant, valorous.

antonyms afraid, timid.

feast *n.* banquet, barbecue, beanfeast, beano, binge, blow-out, carousal, carouse, celebration, delight, dinner, enjoyment, entertainment, epulation, festival, fête, gala day, gaudy, gratification, holiday, holy day, jollification, junket, pig, pleasure, repast, revels, saint's day, spread, treat.

v. delight, eat one's fill, entertain, gladden, gorge, gormandize, gratify, indulge, overindulge, regale, rejoice, stuff, stuff one's face, thrill, treat, wine and dine.

feat *n.* accomplishment, achievement, act, attainment, deed, exploit, gest(e), performance.

feature *n.* article, aspect, attraction, attribute, character, characteristic, column, comment, draw, facet, factor, hallmark, highlight, innovation, item, lineament, mark, peculiarity, piece, point, property, quality, report, special, specialty, story, trait.

v. accentuate, emphasize, headline, highlight, play up, present, promote, push, recommend, show, spotlight, star.

fee *n.* account, bill, charge, compensation, emolument, hire, honorarium, pay, payment, recompense, remuneration, retainer, terms, toll.

feeble *adj.* debilitated, delicate, doddering, effete, enervated, enfeebled, exhausted, failing, faint, flat, flimsy, forceless, frail, fushionless, inadequate, incompetent, indecisive, ineffective, ineffectual, inefficient, inform, insignificant, insufficient, lame, languid, paltry, poor, powerless, puny, shilpit, sickly, silly, slight, tame, thin, unconvincing, vacillating, weak, weakened, weakly.

antonyms strong, worthy.

feed *v.* augment, bolster, cater for, dine, eat, encourage, fare, foster, fuel, graze, grub, nourish, nurture, pasture, provide for, provision, strengthen, subsist, supply, sustain, victual.

n. banquet, feast, fodder, food, forage, meal, nosh, pasturage, pasture, provender, repast, silage, spread, tuck-in, victuals.

feed in inject, input, key in, supply.

feed on consume, devour, eat, exist on, live on, partake of.

feel *v.* appear, believe, caress, consider, deem, empathize, endure, enjoy, experience, explore, finger, fondle, fumble, go through, grope, handle, have, have a hunch, hold, intuit, judge, know, manipulate, maul, notice, observe, paw, perceive, reckon, resemble, seem, sense, sound, stroke, suffer, take to heart, test, think, touch, try, undergo.

n. bent, feeling, finish, gift, impression, knack, quality, sense, surface, texture, touch, vibes.

feeling *n.* (a)esthesia, (a)esthesis, affection, air, ambience, appreciation, apprehension, ardor, atmosphere,

aura, compassion, concern, consciousness, emotion, empathy, Empfindung, feel, fervor, fondness, heat, hunch, idea, impression, inclination, inkling, instinct, intensity, mood, notion, opinion, passion, perception, pity, point of view, presentiment, quality, sensation, sense, sensibility, sensitivity, sentiment, sentimentality, suspicion, sympathy, touch, understanding, vibes, vibrations, view, warmth.

fellowship *n.* amity, association, brotherhood, camaraderie, club, communion, companionability, companionableness, companionship, endowment, familiarity, fraternization, fraternity, guild, intercourse, intimacy, kindliness, league, order, sisterhood, sociability, society, sodality.

feminine *adj.* delicate, effeminate, effete, gentle, girlish, graceful, ladylike, modest, petticoat, sissy, soft, tender, unmanly, unmasculine, weak, womanish, womanly.

antonym masculine.

ferocious *adj.* barbaric, barbarous, bloodthirsty, bloody, brutal, brutish, catamountain, cruel, fearsome, feral, fiendish, fierce, homicidal, inhuman, merciless, murderous, pitiless, predatory, rapacious, ravening, relentless, ruthless, sadistic, sanguinary, savage, truculent, vicious, violent, wild.

antonyms gentle, mild.

fertile *adj.* abundant, fat, fecund, feracious, flowering, fructiferous, fructuous, frugiferous, fruit-bearing, fruitful, generative, lush, luxuriant, plenteous, plentiful, potent, productive, prolific, rich, teeming, uberous, virile, yielding.

antonyms arid, barren.

festival *n.* anniversary, carnival, celebration, commemoration, eisteddfod, entertainment, feast, festa, festivities, fête, field day, fiesta, gala, holiday, holy day, jubilee, junketing, merry-make, merrymaking, merrynight, mod, puja, saint's day, treat.

festive *adj.* carnival, celebratory, cheery, Christmassy, convivial, cordial, en fête, festal, festivous, gala, gay, gleeful, happy, hearty, holiday, jolly, jovial, joyful, joyous, jubilant, merry, mirthful, rollicking, sportive, uproarious.

antonyms gloomy, sober, somber.

fetch *v.* be good for, bring, bring in, carry, conduct, convey, deliver, draw, earn, elicit, escort, evoke, get, go for, lead, make, obtain, produce, realize, retrieve, sell for, transport, uplift, utter, yield.

fetching *adj.* alluring, attractive, beguiling, captivating, charming, cute, disarming, enchanting, enticing, fascinating, pretty, sweet, taking, winning, winsome.

antonym repellent.

feud *n.* animosity, antagonism, argument, bad blood, bickering, bitterness, conflict, contention, disagreement, discord, dispute, dissension, enmity, estrangement, faction, feuding, grudge, hostility, ill will, quarrel, rivalry, row, strife, variance, vendetta.

antonyms agreement, peace.

v. altercate, argue, be at odds, bicker, brawl, clash, contend, dispute, duel, fight, quarrel, row, squabble, war, wrangle.

antonym agree.

fever *n.* agitation, calenture, delirium, ecstasy, excitement, febricity, febricula, febricule, ferment, fervor, feverishness, flush, frenzy, heat, intensity, passion, pyrexia, restlessness, temperature, turmoil, unrest.

fiber *n.* backbone, bast, caliber, character, courage,

determination, essence, fibril, filament, filasse, funicle, grit, guts, nature, nerve, pile, pluck, quality, resolution, sinew, spirit, stamina, staple, strand, strength, substance, temperament, tenacity, tendril, texture, thread, toughness.

fickle *adj.* capricious, changeable, disloyal, dizzy, erratic, faithless, fitful, flighty, fluctuating, inconstant, irresolute, mercurial, mutable, quicksilver, treacherous, unfaithful, unpredictable, unreliable, unstable, unsteady, vacillating, variable, volage, volageous, volatile, wind-changing.

antonym constant.

fiction *n.* canard, cock-and-bull story, concoction, fable, fabrication, falsehood, fancy, fantasy, feuilleton, fib, figment, imagination, improvisation, invention, legend, lie, myth, novel, parable, romance, story, story-telling, tale, tall story, untruth, whopper, yarn.

antonym truth.

fictitious *adj.* aprocryphal, artificial, assumed, bogus, counterfeit, fabricated, false, fanciful, feigned, fictive, fraudulent, imaginary, imagined, improvised, invented, made-up, make-believe, mythical, non-existent, spurious, supposed, suppositional, supposititious, unreal, untrue.

antonyms genuine, real.

fidelity *n.* accuracy, adherence, allegiance, authenticity, closeness, constancy, correspondence, dedication, dependability, devotedness, devotion, dutifulness, exactitude, exactness, faith, faithfulness, fealty, incorruptibility, integrity, loyalty, loyalty, preciseness, precision, reliability, scrupulousness, staunchness, steadfastness, true-heartedness, trustworthiness.

antonyms inaccuracy, inconstancy, treachery.

fidget *v.* bustle, chafe, fiddle, fidge, fike, fret, jerk, jiggle, jitter, jump, mess about, play around, squirm, toy, twitch, worry.

n. agitation, anxiety, creeps, discomposure, edginess, fidgetiness, fidgets, heebie-jeebies, jimjams, jitteriness, jitters, jumpiness, nerves, nerviness, nervousness, restlessness, shakes, twitchiness, unease, uneasiness, willies.

fierce *adj.* baleful, barbarous, blustery, boisterous, brutal, cruel, cut-throat, dangerous, fearsome, fell, feral, ferocious, fiery, frightening, furious, grim, howling, intense, keen, menacing, merciless, murderous, passionate, powerful, raging, relentless, savage, stern, stormy, strong, tempestuous, threatening, truculent, tumultuous, uncontrollable, unrelenting, untamed, vicious, violent, wild.

antonyms calm, gentle, kind.

fiercely *adv.* ardently, bitterly, fanatically, ferociously, furiously, implacably, intensely, keenly, menacingly, mercilessly, murderously, passionately, relentlessly, savagely, sternly, tempestuously, tigerishly, tooth and nail, viciously, violently, wildly, zealously.

antonyms gently, kindly.

fight *v.* altercate, argue, assault, battle, bear arms against, bicker, box, brawl, clash, close, combat, conduct, conflict, contend, contest, cross swords, defy, dispute, do battle, engage, exchange blows, fence, feud, grapple, joust, lock horns, measure strength, measure swords, mell, mix it, oppose, prosecute, quarrel, resist, scrap, scuffle, skirmish, spar, squabble, stand up to, strive, struggle, take the field, tilt, tussle, wage, wage war, war, withstand, wrangle, wrestle.

n. action, affray, altercation, argument, barney, battle, belligerence, bicker, bout, brawl, brush, clash, combat, conflict, contest, courage, dispute, dissension, dogfight, duel, encounter, engagement, fisticuffs, fracas, fray, free-for-all, gameness, hostilities, joust, luctation, mêlée, mettle, militancy, monomachy, passage of arms, pluck, pugnacity, quarrel, rammy, resilience, resistance, riot, row, ruck, rumble, scrap, scuffle, set-to, skirmish, spirit, strength, struggle, tenacity, tussle, war.

fighter *n.* adventurer, antagonist, battler, belligerent, boxer, brave, bruiser, champion, combatant, contender, contestant, disputant, fighting man, filibuster, free lance, gladiator, man-at-arms, mercenary, militant, prize-fighter, pugilist, soldier, soldier of fortune, swordsman, trouper, warrior, wrestler.

figment *n.* concoction, creation, deception, delusion, fable, fabrication, falsehood, fancy, fiction, illusion, improvisation, invention, mare's nest, production, work.

figure *n.* amount, body, build, celebrity, character, chassis, cipher, configuration, conformation, cost, depiction, design, device, diagram, digit, dignitary, drawing, embellishment, emblem, form, frame, illustration, image, leader, motif, notability, notable, number, numeral, outline, pattern, personage, personality, physique, presence, price, proportions, representation, shadow, shape, sign, silhouette, sketch, somebody, sum, symbol, torso, total, trope, value.

v. act, add, appear, believe, calculate, compute, count, estimate, feature, guess, judge, opine, reckon, sum, surmise, tally, think, tot up, work out.

file[1] *v.* abrade, burnish, furbish, grate, hone, pare, plane, polish, rasp, refine, rub (down), sand, scour, scrape, shape, shave, smooth, trim, whet.

file[2] *n.* binder, cabinet, case, date, documents, dossier, folder, information, portfolio, record.

v. capture, document, enter, memorize, pigeonhole, process, record, register, slot in, store.

file[3] *n.* column, cortège, line, list, procession, queue, row, stream, string, trail, train.

v. defile, march, parade, stream, trail, troop.

fill *v.* assign, block, bung, charge, clog, close, congest, cork, cram, crowd, discharge, drench, engage, englut, engorge, execute, fulfil, furnish, glut, gorge, hold, imbue, impregnate, inflate, load, occupy, officiate, overspread, pack, perform, permeate, pervade, plug, replenish, sate, satiate, satisfy, saturate, seal, soak, stock, stop, stuff, suffuse, supply, surfeit, swell, take up.

antonyms clear, empty.

n. abundance, ample, enough, plenty, sufficiency, sufficient.

fillip *n.* boost, flick, goad, impetus, incentive, prod, push, shove, spice, spur, stimulus, zest.

antonym damper.

filter *v.* clarify, dribble, escape, exude, filtrate, leach, leak, ooze, penetrate, percolate, purify, refine, screen, seep, sieve, sift, strain, transpire, transude, trickle, well.

n. colander, gauze, membrane, mesh, riddle, sieve, sifter, strainer.

filth *n.* bilge, carrion, coarseness, colluvies, contamination, coprolalia, coprophilia, corruption, crud, defilement, dirt, dirty-mindedness, dung, excrement, excreta, faex, feces, filthiness, foulness, garbage, grime, grossness, gunge, impurity, indecency, muck, nastiness, obscenity, ordure, pollution, pornography, putrefaction, putrescence, refuse, scatology, sewage, slime, sludge, smut, smuttiness, soil, sordes, sordidness, squalor, sullage, uncleanness, vileness, vulgarity.

antonyms cleanliness, decency, purity.

filthy *adj.* Augean, base, bawdy, begrimed, black, blackened, blue, coarse, contemptible, coprolaliac, coprophilous, corrupt, depraved, despicable, dirty, dirtyminded, fecal, feculent, foul, foul-mouthed, grimy, gross, grubby, impure, indecent, lavatorial, lewd, licentious, low, mean, miry, mucky, muddy, nasty, nasty-minded, obscene, offensive, polluted, pornographic, putrid, scatological, scurrilous, slimy, smoky, smutty, sooty, sordid, squalid, suggestive, swinish, unclean, unwashed, vicious, vile, vulgar.

antonyms clean, decent, inoffensive, pure.

final *adj.* absolute, clinching, closing, concluding, conclusive, conclusory, decided, decisive, definite, definitive, desinent, desinential, determinate, dying, eleventh-hour, end, eventual, finished, incontrovertible, irrefragable, irrefutable, irrevocable, last, last-minute, latest, settled, terminal, terminating, ultimate, undeniable.

finalize *v.* agree, clinch, complete, conclude, decide, dispose of, finish, get signed and sealed, get taped, resolve, round off, seal, settle, sew up, tie up, work out, wrap up.

finally *adv.* absolutely, at last, at length, completely, conclusively, convincingly, decisively, definitely, eventually, for ever, for good, for good and all, in conclusion, in the end, inescapably, inexorably, irreversibly, irrevocably, lastly, once and for all, permanently, ultimately.

find *v.* achieve, acquire, ascertain, attain, bring, catch, chance on, come across, consider, contribute, cough up, descry, detect, discover, earn, encounter, espy, experience, expose, ferret out, furnish, gain, get, hit on, judge, learn, light on, locate, meet, note, notice, observe, obtain, perceive, procure, provide, reach, realize, recognize, recover, rediscover, regain, remark, repossess, retrieve, spot, stumble on, supply, think, track down, turn up, uncover, unearth, win.

n. acquisition, asset, bargain, catch, coup, discovery, good buy, unconsidered trifle.

fine¹ *adj.* abstruse, acceptable, acute, admirable, agreeable, all right, attractive, balmy, beau, beaut, beautiful, bonny, brave, braw, bright, brilliant, choice, clear, clement, cloudless, convenient, critical, cutting, dainty, dandy, delicate, diaphanous, discriminating, dry, elegant, elusive, excellent, exceptional, expensive, exquisite, fair, fastidious, fine-drawn, first-class, first-rate, flimsy, four-square, fragile, gauzy, good, good-looking, goodly, gorgeous, gossamer, great, hair-splitting, handsome, honed, hunky-dory, impressive, intelligent, jake, keen, light, lovely, magnificent, masterly, minute, nice, OK, ornate, outstanding, pleasant, polished, powdery, precise, pure, quick, rare, refined, robust, satisfactory, select, sensitive, sharp, sheer, showy, skilful, skilled, slender, small, smart, solid, splendid, sterling, strong, sturdy, stylish, sublime, subtle, suitable, sunny, superior, supreme, tasteful, tenuous, thin, tickety-boo, unalloyed, virtuoso, well-favored, wiredrawn.

fine² *v.* amerce, mulct, penalize, punish, sting.

n. amercement, amerciament, damages, forfeit, forfeiture, mulct, penalty, punishment.

finesse *n.* address, adeptness, adroitness, artfulness, artifice, cleverness, craft, deftness, delicacy, diplomacy, discretion, elegance, expertise, gracefulness, know-how, neatness, polish, quickness, refinement, savoir-faire, skill, sophistication, subtlety, tact.

v. bluff, evade, manipulate, maneuver, trick.

finicky *adj.* choosy, critical, dainty, delicate, difficult, fastidious, finical, finicking, fussy, hypercritical, meticulous, nice, nit-picking, overnice, particular, pernickety, scrupulous, squeamish, tricky.

antonyms easy, easy-going.

finish *v.* accomplish, achieve, annihilate, best, buff, burnish, cease, close, coat, complete, conclude, consume, consummate, culminate, deal with, defeat, destroy, devour, discharge, dispatch, dispose of, do, drain, drink, eat, elaborate, empty, encompass, end, execute, exhaust, expend, exterminate, face, finalize, fulfil, get rid of, gild, hone, kill, lacquer, overcome, overpower, overthrow, perfect, polish, put an end to, put the last hand to, refine, round off, rout, ruin, settle, smooth, smooth off, sophisticate, spend, stain, stop, terminate, texture, use (up), veneer, wax, wind up, worst, zap.

n. annihilation, appearance, bankruptcy, burnish, cessation, close, closing, completion, conclusion, coup de grâce, culmination, cultivation, culture, curtain, curtains, death, defeat, dénouement, elaboration, end, end of the road, ending, finale, gloss, grain, liquidation, luster, patina, perfection, polish, refinement, ruin, shine, smoothness, sophistication, surface, termination, texture, wind-up.

fire *n.* animation, ardor, bale-fire, barrage, blaze, bombardment, bonfire, brio, broadside, burning, cannonade, combustion, conflagration, dash, eagerness, earnestness, élan, enthusiasm, excitement, feeling, fervency, fervidity, fervidness, fervor, feu de joie, fierceness, flak, flames, force, fusillade, hail, heat, impetuosity, inferno, intensity, life, light, luster, passion, radiance, salvo, scintillation, shelling, sniping, sparkle, spirit, splendor, verve, vigor, virtuosity, vivacity, volley, warmth, zeal.

v. activate, animate, arouse, boot out, cashier, depose, detonate, discharge, dismiss, eject, electrify, enkindle, enliven, excite, explode, galvanize, give marching orders, give the bum's rush, hurl, ignite, impassion, incite, inflame, inspire, inspirit, kindle, launch, let off, light, loose, put a match to, quicken, rouse, sack, send off, set alight, set fire to, set off, set on fire, shell, shoot, show the door, stimulate, stir, touch off, trigger off, whet.

firm¹ *adj.* abiding, adamant, anchored, balanced, braced, cast-iron, cemented, changeless, committed, compact, compressed, concentrated, congealed, constant, convinced, crisp, definite, dense, dependable, determined, dogged, durable, embedded, enduring, established, fast, fastened, fixed, grounded, hard, hardened, immovable, impregnable, indurate, inelastic, inflexible, iron-hearted, jelled, jellified, motionless, obdurate, reliable, resolute, resolved, rigid, robust, secure, secured, set, settled, solid, solidified, stable, stationary, staunch, steadfast, steady, stiff, strict, strong, sturdy, substantial, sure, taut, tight, true, unalterable, unassailable, unbending, unchanging, undeviating, unfaltering, unflinching, unmoved, unmoving, unshakable, unshakeable, unshaken, unshifting, unswerving, unwavering, unyielding, well-knit.

antonyms infirm, soft, unsound.

firm² *n.* association, business, company, concern, conglomerate, corporation, enterprise, establishment, house, institution, organization, outfit, partnership, set-up, syndicate.

first *adj.* basic, cardinal, chief, earliest, eldest, elementary, embryonic, foremost, fundamental, head, highest, initial, introductory, key, leading, maiden, main, oldest, opening, original, paramount, predominant, pre-eminent, premier, primal, primary, prime, primeval, primitive, primordial, principal, prior, pristine, rudimentary, ruling, senior, sovereign, uppermost.

adv. at the outset, before all else, beforehand, early on, firstly, in preference, in the beginning, initially, originally, primarily, rather, sooner, to begin with, to start with.

fishy *adj.* doubtful, dubious, fish-like, funny, glassy, implausible, improbable, irregular, odd, piscatorial, piscatory, pisciform, piscine, queer, questionable, rummy, shady, suspect, suspicious, unlikely, vacant.

antonyms honest, legitimate.

fissile *adj.* cleavable, divisible, easily split, fissionable, fissive, flaky, scissile, separable, severable.

fission *n.* breaking, cleavage, division, parting, rending, rupture, scission, scission, severance, splitting.

fit¹ *adj.* able, able-bodied, adapted, adequate, apposite, appropriate, apt, becoming, blooming, capable, commensurate, competent, condign, convenient, correct, deserving, due, eligible, equipped, expedient, fit as a fiddle, fitted, fitting, hale, hale and hearty, healthy, in fine fettle, in good form, in good nick, in good shape, in good trim, in the pink, meet, prepared, proper, qualified, ready, right, robust, satisfactory, seemly, sound, strapping, strong, sturdy, suitable, suited, trained, trim, well, well-suited, worthy.

antonym unfit.

v. accommodate, accord, adapt, adjust, agree, alter, arrange, assimilate, belong, change, concur, conform, correspond, dispose, dovetail, fashion, fay, figure, follow, gee, go, harmonize, interlock, join, match, meet, modify, place, position, reconcile, shape, suit, tally.

fit² *n.* access, attack, bout, burst, caprice, convulsion, eruption, exies, explosion, fancy, humor, mood, outbreak, outburst, paroxysm, seizure, spasm, spell, storm, surge, whim.

fitful *adj.* broken, desultory, disturbed, erratic, fluctuating, haphazard, intermittent, irregular, occasional, spasmodic, sporadic, uneven, unstable, unsteady, variable.

antonyms regular, steady.

fitting *adj.* apposite, appropriate, apt, becoming, comme il faut, condign, correct, decent, decorous, deserved, desirable, harmonious, meet, merited, proper, right, seasonable, seemly, suitable.

antonym unsuitable.

n. accessory, attachment, component, connection, fitment, fixture, part, piece, unit.

fix¹ *v.* adjust, agree on, anchor, appoint, arrange, arrive at, attach, bind, cement, conclude, confirm, congeal, connect, consolidate, correct, couple, decide, define, determine, direct, embed, establish, fasten, fiddle,

finalize, firm, focus, freeze, glue, harden, implant, inculcate, influence, install, irradicate, limit, link, locate, make, manipulate, maneuver, mend, nail, name, ordain, pin, place, plant, point, position, prearrange, preordain, produce, regulate, repair, resolve, restore, rigidify, rigidize, rivet, root, seal, seat, secure, see to, set, settle, solidify, sort, sort out, specify, stabilize, stick, stiffen, straighten, swing, thicken, tidy, tie.

n. corner, difficulty, dilemma, embarrassment, hole, jam, mess, muddle, nineholes, pickle, plight, predicament, quagmire, quandary, scrape, spot.

fix² *n.* dose, hit, injection, jag, score, shot, slug.

fixation *n.* complex, compulsion, fetish, hang-up, idée fixe, infatuation, mania, monomania, obsession, preoccupation, thing.

flabbergasted *adj.* amazed, astonished, astounded, bowled over, confounded, dazed, disconcerted, dumbfounded, nonplused, overcome, overwhelmed, speechless, staggered, stunned, stupefied.

flagrant *adj.* arrant, atrocious, audacious, barefaced, blatant, bold, brazen, conspicuous, crying, egregious, enormous, flagitious, flaunting, glaring, heinous, immodest, infamous, notorious, open, ostentatious, outrageous, overt, rank, scandalous, shameless, unashamed, undisguised.

antonyms covert, secret.

flair *n.* ability, accomplishment, acumen, aptitude, chic, dash, discernment, elegance, facility, faculty, feel, genius, gift, knack, mastery, nose, panache, skill, style, stylishness, talent, taste.

antonym ineptitude.

flamboyant *adj.* baroque, brilliant, colorful, dashing, dazzling, elaborate, exciting, extravagant, flashy, florid, gaudy, glamorous, jaunty, ornate, ostentatious, rich, showy, striking, stylish, swashbuckling, theatrical.

antonyms modest, restrained.

flame *v.* beam, blaze, burn, flare, flash, glare, glow, radiate, shine.

n. affection, ardor, beau, blaze, brightness, enthusiasm, fervency, fervor, fire, flake, flammule, heartthrob, intensity, keenness, light, lover, passion, radiance, sweetheart, warmth, zeal.

flash *v.* blaze, bolt, brandish, coruscate, dart, dash, display, exhibit, expose, flare, flaunt, flicker, flourish, fly, fulgurate, fulminate, glare, gleam, glint, glisten, glitter, light, race, scintillate, shimmer, shoot, show, sparkle, speed, sprint, streak, sweep, twinkle, whistle.

n. blaze, bluette, burst, coruscation, dazzle, demonstration, display, flare, flaught, flicker, fulguration, gleam, hint, instant, jiff, jiffy, manifestation, moment, outburst, ray, scintillation, second, shaft, shake, shimmer, show, sign, spark, sparkle, split second, streak, touch, trice, twinkle, twinkling.

flashy *adj.* bold, brassy, cheap, flamboyant, flash, garish, gaudy, glamorous, glittery, glitzy, jazzy, loud, meretricious, obtrusive, ostentatious, raffish, rakish, ritzy, showy, snazzy, tacky, tasteless, tawdry, tig(e)rish, tinselly, vulgar.

antonyms plain, simple, tasteful.

flat¹ *adj.* even, horizontal, lamellar, lamelliform, level, leveled, low, outstretched, planar, plane, prone, prostrate, reclining, recumbent, smooth, spread-eagled, supine, unbroken, uniform.

n. lowland, marsh, morass, moss, mud flat, plain, shallow, shoal, strand, swamp.

flat[2] *adj.* bored, boring, burst, collapsed, dead, deflated, depressed, dull, empty, flavorless, insipid, jejune, lackluster, lifeless, monotonous, pointless, prosaic, punctured, spiritless, stale, tedious, uninteresting, unpalatable, vapid, watery, weak.

flat[3] *adj.* absolute, categorical, direct, downright, explicit, final, fixed, out-and-out, peremptory, plain, point-blank, positive, straight, total, uncompromising, unconditional, unequivocal, unqualified.
antonym equivocal.
adv. absolutely, categorically, completely, entirely, exactly, point-blank, precisely, totally, utterly.

flat[4] *n.* apartment, bed-sit, bed-sitter, maison(n)ette, pad, penthouse, pied-à-terre, rooms, tenement.

flatly *adv.* absolutely, categorically, completely, peremptorily, point-blank, positively, uncompromisingly, unconditionally, unhesitatingly.

flattery *n.* adulation, backscratching, blandishment, blarney, bootlicking, butter, cajolement, cajolery, eulogy, fawning, flannel, flapdoodle, fleechment, fulsomeness, ingratiation, obsequiousness, servility, soap, soft sawder, soft soap, sugar, sweet talk, sycophancy, sycophantism, taffy, toadyism, unctuousness.
antonym criticism.

flaunt *v.* air, boast, brandish, dangle, display, disport, exhibit, flash, flourish, parade, show off, sport, vaunt, wield.

flavor *n.* aroma, aspect, character, essence, extract, feel, feeling, flavoring, hint, odor, piquancy, property, quality, relish, sapidity, savor, savoriness, seasoning, smack, soupçon, stamp, style, suggestion, tang, taste, tastiness, tinge, tone, touch, zest, zing.
v. contaminate, ginger up, imbue, infuse, lace, leaven, season, spice, taint.

flaw *n.* blemish, breach, break, cleft, crack, craze, crevice, defect, disfigurement, failing, fallacy, fault, fissure, fracture, hamartia, imperfection, lapse, macula, mark, mistake, rent, rift, shortcoming, slip, speck, split, spot, tear, weakness, wreath.

flee *v.* abscond, avoid, beat a hasty retreat, bolt, bunk (off), cut and run, decamp, depart, escape, fly, get away, leave, make off, make oneself scarce, scarper, scram, shun, skedaddle, split, take flight, take it on the lam, take off, take to one's heels, vamoose, vanish, withdraw.
antonyms stand, stay.

fleece *v.* bilk, bleed, cheat, clip, con, defraud, diddle, mulct, overcharge, plunder, rifle, rip off, rob, rook, shear, skin, soak, squeeze, steal, sting, swindle.

fleet[1] *n.* argosy, armada, escadrille, flota, flotilla, navy, squadron, task force.

fleet[2] *adj.* expeditious, fast, flying, light-footed, mercurial, meteoric, nimble, quick, rapid, speedy, swift, velocipede, winged.
antonym slow.

fleeting *adj.* brief, disappearing, ephemeral, evanescent, flitting, flying, fugacious, fugitive, impermanent, momentary, passing, short, short-lived, temporary, transient, transitory, vanishing.
antonym lasting.

fleshy *adj.* ample, beefy, brawny, carneous, carnose, chubby, chunky, corpulent, fat, flabby, hefty, meaty, obese, overweight, paunchy, plump, podgy, portly, rotund, stout, tubby, well-padded.
antonym thin.

flexible *adj.* accommodating, adaptable, adjustable, agreeable, amenable, bendable, biddable, complaisant, compliant, discretionary, docile, double-jointed, ductile, elastic, flexile, gentle, limber, lissome, lithe, loose-limbed, manageable, mobile, moldable, open, plastic, pliable, pliant, responsive, springy, stretchy, supple, tensile, tractable, variable, whippy, willowy, withy, yielding.
antonym inflexible.

flighty *adj.* bird-brained, bird-witted, capricious, changeable, dizzy, fickle, frivolous, giddy, hare-brained, impetuous, impulsive, inconstant, irresponsible, light-headed, mercurial, rattle-brained, rattle-headed, rattle-pated, scatterbrained, silly, skittish, thoughtless, unbalanced, unstable, unsteady, volage, volageous, volatile, whisky-frisky, wild.
antonym steady.

flimsy *adj.* cardboard, chiffon, cobwebby, delicate, diaphanous, ethereal, feeble, fragile, frail, frivolous, gauzy, gimcrack, gossamer, implausible, inadequate, insubstantial, light, makeshift, meager, poor, rickety, shaky, shallow, sheer, slight, superficial, thin, transparent, trivial, unconvincing, unsatisfactory, unsubstantial, vaporous, weak.
antonym sturdy.

fling *v.* bung, cant, cast, catapult, chuck, heave, hurl, jerk, let fly, lob, pitch, precipitate, propel, send, shoot, shy, sling, slug, souse, throw, toss.
n. attempt, bash, binge, cast, crack, gamble, go, heave, indulgence, lob, pitch, shot, spree, stab, throw, toss, trial, try, turn, venture, whirl.

flippant *adj.* brash, cheeky, cocky, disrespectful, flip, frivolous, glib, impertinent, impudent, irreverent, malapert, nonchalant, offhand, pert, pococurante, rude, saucy, superficial, unserious.
antonym earnest.

flit *v.* beat, bob, dance, dart, elapse, flash, fleet, flutter, fly, pass, skim, slip, speed, volitate, whisk, wing.

flock *v.* bunch, cluster, collect, congregate, converge, crowd, gather, gravitate, group, herd, huddle, mass, swarm, throng, troop.
n. assembly, bevy, collection, colony, company, congregation, convoy, crowd, drove, flight, gaggle, gathering, group, herd, horde, host, mass, multitude, pack, shoal, skein, swarm, throng.

flog *v.* beat, birch, breech, chastise, drive, drub, flagellate, flay, hide, knout, k(o)urbash, larrup, lash, overexert, overtax, overwork, punish, push, scourge, strain, swish, tat, tax, thrash, trounce, vapulate, verberate, welt, whack, whale, whang, whip, whop.

flood *v.* bog down, brim, choke, deluge, drench, drown, engulf, fill, flow, glut, gush, immerse, inundate, overflow, oversupply, overwhelm, pour, rush, saturate, soak, submerge, surge, swamp, swarm, sweep.
n. abundance, alluvion, bore, cataclysm, debacle, deluge, diluvion, diluvium, downpour, eagre, flash flood, flow, freshet, glut, inundation, multitude, outpouring, overflow, plethora, profusion, rush, spate, stream, superfluity, tide, torrent.
antonyms dearth, drought, trickle.

florid *adj.* baroque, blowzy, bombastic, busy, coloratura, elaborate, embellished, euphuistic, figurative, flamboyant, flourishy, flowery, flushed, fussy, grandiloquent, high-colored, high-falutin(g), high-flown, melismatic, ornate, overelaborate, purple, raddled, red, rococo, rubicund, ruddy.

antonyms pale, plain.

flourish¹ *v.* advance, bloom, blossom, boom, burgeon, develop, do well, flower, get on, grow, increase, mushroom, progress, prosper, succeed, thrive, wax.

antonyms fail, languish.

flourish² *v.* brandish, display, flaunt, flutter, parade, shake, sweep, swing, swish, twirl, vaunt, wag, wave, wield.

n. arabesque, brandishing, ceremony, curlicue, dash, decoration, display, élan, embellishment, fanfare, ornament, ornamentation, panache, parade, paraph, pizzazz, plume, shaking, show, sweep, twirling, wave.

flout *v.* affront, contemn, defy, deride, disregard, insult, jeer at, mock, outrage, reject, ridicule, scoff at, scorn, scout, spurn, taunt.

antonym respect.

flow *v.* arise, bubble, cascade, circulate, course, deluge, derive, distil, drift, emanate, emerge, flood, glide, gush, inundate, issue, move, originate, overflow, pour, proceed, purl, result, ripple, roll, run, rush, slide, slip, spew, spill, spring, spurt, squirt, stream, surge, sweep, swirl, teem, well, whirl.

n. abundance, cascade, course, current, deluge, drift, effluence, efflux, effusion, emanation, flood, flowage, flux, fluxion, gush, outflow, outpouring, plenty, plethora, spate, spurt, stream, succession, tide, train, wash.

fluctuate *v.* alter, alternate, change, ebb and flow, float, hesitate, oscillate, pendulate, rise and fall, seesaw, shift, shuffle, sway, swing, undulate, vacillate, vary, veer, waver.

fluent *adj.* articulate, easy, effortless, eloquent, facile, flowing, fluid, glib, mellifluous, natural, ready, smooth, smooth-talking, voluble, well-versed.

antonym tongue-tied.

fluff *n.* down, dust, dustball, floccus, flosh, floss, flue, fug, fuzz, lint, nap, oose, pile.

v. balls up, botch, bungle, cock up, fumble, mess up, muddle, muff, screw up, spoil.

antonym bring off.

fluid *adj.* adaptable, adjustable, aqueous, changeable, diffluent, easy, elegant, feline, flexible, floating, flowing, fluctuating, fluent, fluidal, fluidic, graceful, inconstant, indefinite, liquefied, liquid, melted, mercurial, mobile, molten, mutable, protean, running, runny, shifting, sinuous, smooth, unstable, watery.

antonyms solid, stable.

n. humor, juice, liquid, liquor, sanies, sap, solution.

fluke *n.* accident, blessing, break, chance, coincidence, fortuity, freak, lucky break, quirk, serendipity, stroke, windfall.

flummoxed *adj.* at a loss, at sea, baffled, befuddled, bewildered, confounded, confused, foxed, mystified, nonplused, perplexed, puzzled, stumped, stymied.

flush¹ *v.* blush, burn, color, crimson, flame, glow, go red, mantle, redden, rouge, suffuse.

antonym pale.

n. bloom, blush, color, freshness, glow, redness, rosiness, rud, vigor.

flush² *v.* cleanse, douche, drench, eject, empty, evacuate, expel, hose, rinse, swab, syringe, wash.

adj. abundant, affluent, full, generous, in funds, lavish, liberal, moneyed, overflowing, prodigal, prosperous, rich, rolling, wealthy, well-heeled, well-off, well-supplied, well-to-do.

flush³ *adj.* even, flat, level, plane, smooth, square, true.

flush⁴ *v.* discover, disturb, drive out, force out, rouse, run to earth, start, uncover.

fluster *v.* abash, agitate, bother, bustle, confound, confuse, discombobulate, disconcert, discountenance, disturb, embarrass, excite, faze, flurry, hassle, heat, hurry, perturb, pother, pudder, rattle, ruffle, unnerve, unsettle, upset.

antonym calm.

n. agitation, bustle, commotion, discomposure, distraction, disturbance, dither, embarrassment, faze, flap, flurry, flutter, furore, kerfuffle, perturbation, ruffle, state, tizzy, turmoil.

antonym calm.

fly¹ *v.* abscond, aviate, avoid, bolt, career, clear out, dart, dash, decamp, disappear, display, elapse, escape, flap, flee, flit, float, flutter, get away, glide, hare, hasten, hasten away, hedge-hop, hightail it, hoist, hover, hurry, light out, mount, operate, pass, pilot, race, raise, retreat, roll by, run, run for it, rush, sail, scamper, scarper, scoot, shoot, show, shun, skim, soar, speed, sprint, take flight, take off, take to one's heels, take wing, tear, vamoose, volitate, wave, whisk, whiz, wing, zoom.

fly² *adj.* alert, artful, astute, canny, careful, cunning, knowing, nobody's fool, on the ball, prudent, sagacious, sharp, shrewd, smart, wide-awake.

foam *n.* barm, bubbles, effervescence, foaminess, froth, frothiness, head, lather, scum, spume, spumescence, suds.

v. boil, bubble, effervesce, fizz, froth, lather, spume.

foe *n.* adversary, antagonist, enemy, foeman, ill-wisher, opponent, rival.

antonym friend.

fog *n.* bewilderment, blanket, blindness, brume, confusion, daze, gloom, haze, London particular, miasma, mist, muddle, murk, murkiness, obscurity, peasouper, perplexity, puzzlement, smog, stupor, trance, vagueness.

v. becloud, bedim, befuddle, bewilder, blanket, blind, cloud, confuse, darken, daze, dim, dull, mist, muddle, obfuscate, obscure, perplex, shroud, steam up, stupefy.

foible *n.* crotchet, defect, eccentricity, failing, fault, habit, idiosyncrasy, imperfection, infirmity, oddity, oddness, peculiarity, quirk, shortcoming, strangeness, weakness.

foist *v.* fob off, force, get rid of, impose, insert, insinuate, interpolate, introduce, palm off, pass off, thrust, unload, wish on.

fold *v.* bend, clasp, close, collapse, crash, crease, crimp, crumple, dog-ear, double, embrace, enclose, enfold, entwine, envelop, fail, fake, gather, go bust, hug, intertwine, overlap, pleat, ply, shut down, tuck, wrap, wrap up.

n. bend, corrugation, crease, crimp, duplicature, furrow, knife-edge, layer, overlap, pleat, ply, turn, wimple, wrinkle.

follow *v.* accompany, accord, act according to, appreciate, arise, attend, catch, catch on, chase, come after, come next, comply, comprehend, conform, cultivate, dangle, develop, dog, emanate, ensue, escort, fathom, get, get the picture, grasp, haunt, heed, hound, hunt, imitate, keep abreast of, live up to, mind, note, obey, observe, pursue, realize, regard, result, second, see, shadow, stag, stalk, succeed, supersede, supervene, supplant, support, tag along, tail, track, trail, twig, understand, watch.

antonyms desert, precede.

follower *n.* acolyte, adherent, admirer, Anthony, apostle, attendant, backer, believer, buff, cohort, companion, convert, devotee, disciple, emulator, fan, fancier, freak, galloglass, habitué, hanger-on, heeler, helper, henchman, imitator, lackey, minion, partisan, poodle-dog, poursuivant, pupil, representative, retainer, running dog, servitor, sidekick, supporter, tantony, votary, worshipper.

antonyms leader, opponent.

following *adj.* coming, consecutive, consequent, consequential, ensuing, later, next, resulting, sequent, subsequent, succeeding, successive.

n. audience, backing, circle, claque, clientèle, coterie, entourage, fans, followers, patronage, public, retinue, suite, support, supporters, train.

folly[1] *n.* absurdity, craziness, daftness, fatuity, foolishness, idiocy, illogicality, imbecility, imprudence, indiscretion, insanity, irrationality, irresponsibility, lunacy, madness, moonraking, moria, nonsense, preposterousness, rashness, recklessness, senselessness, silliness, stupidity, unreason, unwisdom.

antonym prudence.

folly[2] *n.* belvedere, gazebo, monument, tower, whim.

fond *adj.* absurd, adoring, affectionate, amorous, caring, credulous, deluded, devoted, doting, empty, foolish, indiscreet, indulgent, loving, naive, over-optimistic, sanguine, tender, uxorious, vain, warm.

antonyms hostile, realistic.

fondness *n.* affection, attachment, devotion, engouement, enthusiasm, fancy, inclination, kindness, leaning, liking, love, partiality, penchant, predilection, preference, soft spot, susceptibility, taste, tenderness, weakness.

antonym aversion.

food *n.* aliment, ambrosia, board, bread, cheer, chow, comestibles, commons, cooking, cuisine, diet, eatables, eats, edibles, fare, feed, fodder, foodstuffs, forage, grub, larder, meat, menu, nosh, nourishment, nouriture, nutriment, nutrition, pabulum, pap, prog, provand, provend, provender, proviant, provisions, rations, refreshment, scoff, scran, stores, subsistence, sustenance, table, tack, tommy, tuck, tucker, viands, victuals, vittles, vivers.

fool *n.* ass, bécasse, berk, besom-head, bête, bird-brain, blockhead, bonehead, boodle, buffethead, buffoon, burk, butt, capocchia, Charlie, chump, clodpate, clot, clown, cluck, comic, coxcomb, cuckoo, daftie, daw, dawcock, dimwit, dizzard, Dogberry, dolt, dope, dottle, droll, drongo, dumb-bell, dumb-cluck, dumbo, dunce, dunderhead, dunderpate, dupe, easy mark, fall guy, fathead, fon, galah, gaupus, git, goon, goop, goose, greenhorn, gudgeon, gull, halfwit, harlequin, idiot, ignoramus, illiterate, imbecile, jackass, Jack-fool, jerk, jester, jobernowl, josh, joskin, leather-head, loggerhead, log-head, loon, madhaun, merry-andrew, mooncalf, moron, motley, mug, nig-nog, nincompoop, ninny, nit, nitwit, nong, noodle, numskull, pierrot, pot-head, prat, prick, punchinello, sap, saphead, sawney, schmo, schmuck, silly, silly-billy, simpleton, soft, soft-head, softie, softy, stooge, stupe, stupid,

sucker, tomfool, Tom-noddy, turnip, twerp, twit, wally, want-wit, wimp, witling, wooden-head, yap, zany, zombie.

v. act dido, act the fool, act up, bamboozle, be silly, beguile, bluff, cavort, cheat, clown, con, cozen, cut capers, daff, deceive, delude, diddle, dupe, feign, fiddle, fon, frolic, gull, have on, hoax, hoodwink, horse around, jest, joke, kid, lark, meddle, mess, mess about, mislead, monkey, play, play the fool, play the goat, play up, pretend, put one over on, string, string along, swindle, take in, tamper, tease, toy, trick, trifle.

foolish *adj.* absurd, brainless, cockle-brained, crazy, daft, desipient, doited, dotish, dotish, dottled, dunderheaded, étourdi(e), fatuous, glaikit, gudgeon, half-baked, half-witted, hare-brained, idiotic, idle-headed, ill-advised, illaudable, ill-considered, ill-judged, imbecile, imbecilic, imprudent, incautious, indiscreet, inept, injudicious, insipient, lean-witted, ludicrous, mad, moronic, nonsensical, potty, ridiculous, senseless, short-sighted, silly, simple, simple-minded, sottish, stupid, tomfool, unintelligent, unreasonable, unwise, weak, wet, witless.

antonym wise.

footing *n.* base, basis, condition, conditions, establishment, foot-hold, foundation, grade, ground, groundwork, installation, position, purchase, rank, relations, relationship, settlement, standing, state, status, terms.

footnotes *n.* annotations, apparatus criticus, commentary, marginalia, notes, scholia.

footprint *n.* footmark, spoor, trace, track, trail, vestige.

footstep *n.* footfall, plod, step, tramp, tread, trudge.

fop *n.* beau, coxcomb, dandy, dude, exquisite, Jack-a-dandy, Jessie, macaroni, muscadin, musk-cat, pansy, peacock, petit maître, popinjay, spark, swell.

forbearance *n.* abstinence, avoidance, clemency, endurance, indulgence, leniency, lenity, longanimity, long-suffering, mildness, moderation, patience, refraining, resignation, restraint, self-control, sufferance, temperance, tolerance, toleration.

antonym intolerance.

forbid *v.* ban, block, contraindicate, debar, deny, disallow, exclude, hinder, inhibit, interdict, outlaw, preclude, prevent, prohibit, proscribe, refuse, rule out, veto.

antonym allow.

forbidding *adj.* abhorrent, awesome, daunting, formidable, frightening, gaunt, grim, hostile, inhospitable, menacing, off-putting, ominous, repellent, repulsive, sinister, threatening, unapproachable, unfriendly.

antonyms approachable, congenial.

force[1] *n.* aggression, arm-twisting, beef, big stick, bite, coercion, cogency, compulsion, constraint, drive, duress, dynamism, effect, effectiveness, efficacy, emphasis, energy, enforcement, fierceness, foison, forcefulness, fushion, impact, impetus, impulse, incentive, influence, intensity, jism, life, mailed fist, might, momentum, motivation, muscle, persistence, persuasiveness, potency, power, pressure, punch, shock, steam, stimulus, strength, stress, validity, vehemence, vigor, violence, vis, vitality, weight.

v. bulldoze, coerce, compel, constrain, drag, drive, exact, extort, impel, impose, lean on, make, necessitate, obligate, oblige, press, press-gang, pressure, pressurize, prize, propel, push, strong-arm, thrust, urge, wrench, wrest, wring.

force² *n.* army, battalion, body, corps, detachment, detail, division, effective, enomoty, host, legion, patrol, phalanx, regiment, squad, squadron, troop, unit, Wehrmacht.

forceful *adj.* cogent, compelling, convincing, domineering, drastic, dynamic, effective, emphatic, energetic, persuasive, pithy, potent, powerful, strong, telling, urgent, vigorous, weighty.
antonym feeble.

forcible *adj.* active, aggressive, coercive, cogent, compelling, compulsory, drastic, effective, efficient, energetic, forceful, impressive, mighty, pithy, potent, powerful, strong, telling, urgent, vehement, violent, weighty.
antonym feeble.

forebear *n.* ancestor, antecedent, antecessor, father, forefather, forerunner, predecessor, primogenitor, progenitor.
antonym descendant.

foreboding *n.* anticipation, anxiety, apprehension, apprehensiveness, augury, boding, chill, dread, fear, foreshadowing, foretoken, hoodoo, intuition, misgiving, omen, portent, prediction, prefigurement, premonition, presage, presentiment, prodrome, prodromus, prognostication, sign, token, warning, worry.

forecast *v.* augur, bode, calculate, conjecture, divine, estimate, expect, foresee, foretell, plan, predict, prognosticate, prophesy.
n. augury, conjecture, foresight, forethought, guess, guesstimate, outlook, planning, prediction, prognosis, prognostication, projection, prophecy.

foregoing *adj.* above, aforementioned, antecedent, anterior, earlier, former, preceding, previous, prior, prodromal, prodromic.

foreign *adj.* adventitious, adventive, alien, borrowed, distant, exotic, external, extraneous, extrinsic, fremd, imported, incongruous, irrelevant, outlandish, outside, overseas, remote, strange, tramontane, unassimilable, uncharacteristic, unfamiliar, unknown, unnative, unrelated.
antonym native.

foreigner *n.* alien, Ausländer, barbarian, dago, étranger, étrangère, immigrant, incomer, metic, newcomer, outlander, stranger, uitlander, wog, wop.
antonym native.

foreman *n.* charge-hand, charge-man, gaffer, ganger, gangsman, overman, overseer, oversman, steward, straw boss, supervisor.

foremost *adj.* cardinal, central, chief, first, front, headmost, highest, inaugural, initial, leading, main, paramount, pre-eminent, primary, prime, principal, salient, supreme, uppermost.

forerunner *n.* ancestor, announcer, antecedent, antecessor, envoy, forebear, foregoer, foretoken, harbinger, herald, indication, omen, portent, precursor, predecessor, premonition, prodrome, prodromus, progenitor, prognostic, prototype, sign, token, vaunt-courier.
antonyms aftermath, result.

foreshadow *v.* adumbrate, anticipate, augur, betoken, bode, forebode, forepoint, foreshow, foresignify, foretoken, imply, import, indicate, omen, portend, predict, prefigure, presage, promise, prophesy, signal.

foresight *n.* anticipation, care, caution, circumspection, far-sightedness, forethought, perspicacity, precaution, preparedness, prescience, prevision, providence, provision, prudence, readiness, vision.

antonym improvidence.

forestall *v.* anticipate, avert, balk, circumvent, frustrate, head off, hinder, intercept, obstruct, obviate, parry, preclude, pre-empt, prevent, thwart, ward off.
antonyms encourage, facilitate.

foretell *v.* adumbrate, augur, bode, forebode, forecast, foresay, foreshadow, foreshow, forespeak, forewarn, portend, predict, presage, presignify, prognosticate, prophesy, signify, soothsay, vaticinate.

forever *adv.* always, ceaselessly, constantly, continually, endlessly, eternally, everlastingly, evermore, for all time, for good and all, for keeps, in perpetuity, in saecula saeculorum, incessantly, interminably, permanently, perpetually, persistently, till the cows come home, till the end of time, unremittingly, world without end.

forewarn *v.* admonish, advise, alert, apprize, caution, dissuade, previse, tip off.

forfeit *n.* amercement, damages, escheat, fine, forfeiture, loss, mulct, penalization, penalty, surrender.
v. abandon, forgo, give up, lose, relinquish, renounce, sacrifice, surrender.

forge¹ *v.* beat out, cast, coin, construct, contrive, copy, counterfeit, create, devise, fabricate, fake, falsify, fashion, feign, form, frame, hammer out, imitate, invent, make, mold, shape, simulate, work.

forge² *v.* advance, gain ground, improve, make great strides, make headway, press on, proceed, progress, push on.

forget *v.* consign to oblivion, discount, dismiss, disregard, fail, ignore, lose sight of, misremember, neglect, omit, overlook, think no more of, unlearn.
antonym remember.

forgetful *adj.* absent-minded, amnesiac, amnesic, careless, dreamy, heedless, inattentive, lax, neglectful, negligent, oblivious, unmindful, unretentive.
antonyms attentive, heedful.

forgive *v.* absolve, acquit, condone, exculpate, excuse, exonerate, let off, overlook, pardon, remit, shrive.
antonym censure.

forgiving *adj.* clement, compassionate, forbearing, humane, indulgent, lenient, magnanimous, merciful, mild, remissive, soft-hearted, sparing, tolerant.
antonym censorious.

forgo, forego *v.* abandon, abjure, abstain from, cede, do without, eschew, forfeit, give up, pass up, refrain from, relinquish, renounce, resign, sacrifice, surrender, waive, yield.
antonyms claim, indulge in, insist on.

forgotten *adj.* blotted out, buried, bygone, disregarded, ignored, irrecoverable, irretrievable, lost, neglected, obliterated, omitted, out of mind, overlooked, past, past recall, past recollection, unrecalled, unremembered, unretrieved.
antonym remembered.

forlorn *adj.* abandoned, abject, bereft, cheerless, comfortless, deserted, desolate, desperate, destitute, disconsolate, forgotten, forsaken, friendless, helpless, homeless, hopeless, lonely, lost, miserable, pathetic, piteous, pitiable, pitiful, unhappy, woebegone, woeful, wretched.
antonym hopeful.

form *v.* accumulate, acquire, appear, arrange, assemble, bring up, build, combine, compose, comprise, concoct, constitute, construct, contract, contrive, create, crystallize, cultivate, design, develop, devise, discipline, dispose, draw up, educate, establish, evolve, fabricate, fashion, forge, formulate, found, frame, group, grow, hatch, instruct, invent, make, make up, manufacture, materialize, model, mold, organize, pattern, plan, produce, put together, rear, rise, school, serve as, settle, shape, take shape, teach, train.

n. anatomy, appearance, application, arrangement, behavior, being, body, build, cast, ceremony, character, class, condition, configuration, construction, convention, custom, cut, description, design, document, etiquette, fashion, fettle, figure, fitness, formality, format, formation, frame, framework, genre, Gestalt, grade, guise, harmony, health, kind, manifestation, manner, manners, matrix, method, mode, model, mold, nature, nick, order, orderliness, organization, outline, pattern, person, physique, plan, practice, procedure, proportion, protocol, questionnaire, rank, ritual, rule, schedule, semblance, shape, sheet, silhouette, sort, species, spirits, stamp, structure, style, symmetry, system, trim, type, variety, way.

formal *adj.* academic, aloof, approved, ceremonial, ceremonious, conventional, correct, exact, explicit, express, fixed, full-dress, impersonal, lawful, legal, methodical, nominal, official, perfunctory, precise, prescribed, prim, punctilious, recognized, regular, reserved, rigid, ritualistic, set, solemn, starch, starched, starchy, stiff, stiff-necked, stilted, strict, unbending.
antonym informal.

formality *n.* ceremoniousness, ceremony, convenance, convention, conventionality, correctness, custom, decorum, etiquette, form, formalism, gesture, matter of form, politeness, politesse, procedure, propriety, protocol, punctilio, red tape, rite, ritual.
antonym informality.

former *adj.* above, aforementioned, aforesaid, ancient, antecedent, anterior, bygone, departed, earlier, erstwhile, ex-, first mentioned, foregoing, late, long ago, of yore, old, old-time, one-time, past, preceding, preexistent, previous, prior, pristine, quondam, sometime, umwhile, whilom.
antonyms current, future, later, present, prospective, subsequent.

formidable *adj.* alarming, appalling, arduous, awesome, challenging, colossal, dangerous, daunting, difficult, dismaying, dreadful, enormous, fearful, frightening, frightful, great, horrible, huge, impressive, indomitable, intimidating, leviathan, mammoth, menacing, mighty, onerous, overwhelming, powerful, puissant, redoubtable, shocking, staggering, terrific, terrifying, threatening, toilsome, tremendous.
antonyms easy, genial.

forsake *v.* abandon, abdicate, cast off, desert, discard, disown, forgo, forswear, give up, jettison, jilt, leave, leave in the lurch, quit, reject, relinquish, renounce, repudiate, surrender, throw over, turn one's back on, vacate, yield.
antonyms resume, revert to.

forte *n.* aptitude, bent, gift, long suit, métier, skill, specialty, strength, strong point, talent.
antonyms inadequacy, weak point.

forthcoming[1] *adj.* accessible, approaching, at hand, available, coming, expected, future, imminent, impending, obtainable, projected, prospective, ready.

forthcoming[2] *adj.* chatty, communicative, conversational, expansive, frank, free, informative, loquacious, open, sociable, talkative, unreserved.
antonyms bygone, distant, lacking, reserved.

forthright *adj.* above-board, blunt, bold, candid, direct, four-square, frank, open, outspoken, plain-speaking, plain-spoken, straightforward, straight-from-the-shoulder, trenchant, unequivocal.
antonyms devious, tactful.

forthwith *adv.* at once, directly, eftsoons, immediately, incontinent, instanter, instantly, posthaste, pronto, quickly, right away, straightaway, tout de suite, without delay.

fortify *v.* boost, brace, bulwark, buttress, cheer, confirm, embattle, embolden, encourage, entrench, garrison, hearten, invigorate, lace, load, mix, munify, protect, reassure, reinforce, secure, shore up, spike, steel, stiffen, strengthen, support, sustain.
antonyms dilute, weaken.

fortuitous *adj.* accidental, adventitious, arbitrary, casual, chance, coincidental, contingent, felicitous, fluky, fortunate, happy, incidental, lucky, providential, random, serendipitous, unexpected, unforeseen, unintentional, unplanned.
antonym intentional.

fortunate *adj.* advantageous, auspicious, blessed, bright, convenient, encouraging, favorable, favored, felicitous, fortuitous, golden, happy, helpful, lucky, opportune, profitable, promising, propitious, prosperous, providential, rosy, serendipitous, successful, timely, well-off, well-timed.
antonym unfortunate.

fortune[1] *n.* affluence, assets, bomb, bundle, estate, income, king's ransom, means, mint, opulence, packet, pile, possessions, property, prosperity, riches, treasure, wealth.

fortune[2] *n.* accident, adventures, chance, circumstances, contingency, cup, destiny, doom, expectation, experience, fate, fortuity, hap, happenstance, hazard, history, kismet, life, lot, luck, portion, providence, star, success, weird.

fortune-telling *n.* augury, chiromancy, crystal-gazing, divination, dukkeripen, palmistry, prediction, prognostication, prophecy, second sight.

forward[1] *adj.* advance, advanced, early, enterprising, first, fore, foremost, forward-looking, front, go-ahead, head, leading, onward, precocious, premature, progressive, well-advanced, well-developed.
antonym retrograde.
adv. ahead, en avant, forth, forwards, into view, on, onward, out, outward, to light, to the fore, to the surface.
antonym backward.
v. accelerate, advance, aid, assist, back, dispatch, encourage, expedite, facilitate, favor, foster, freight, further, hasten, help, hurry, post, promote, route, send, send on, ship, speed, support, transmit.
antonyms impede, obstruct.

forward[2] *adj.* assertive, assuming, audacious, bare-faced, bold, brash, brass-necked, brazen, brazen-faced, cheeky, confident, familiar, fresh, impertinent, impudent, malapert, officious, overweening, pert, presuming, presumptuous, pushy.
antonym diffident.

fossilized *adj.* anachronistic, antediluvian, antiquated, archaic, archaistic, dead, démodé, extinct, exuvial, inflexible, obsolete, old-fashioned, old-fog(e)yish, ossified, out of date, outmoded, passé, petrified, prehistoric, stony, superannuated.

antonym up-to-date.

foul *adj.* abhorrent, abominable, abusive, bad, base, blasphemous, blue, blustery, choked, coarse, contaminated, crooked, despicable, detestable, dirty, disagreeable, disfigured, disgraceful, disgusting, dishonest, dishonorable, entangled, fetid, filthy, foggy, foul-mouthed, fraudulent, gross, hateful, heinous, impure, indecent, inequitable, infamous, iniquitous, lewd, loathsome, low, malodorous, mephitic, murky, nasty, nauseating, nefarious, noisome, notorious, obscene, offensive, polluted, profane, putrid, rainy, rank, repulsive, revolting, rotten, rough, scandalous, scatological, scurrilous, shady, shameful, smutty, squalid, stinking, stormy, sullied, tainted, unclean, underhand, unfair, unfavorable, unjust, unsportsmanlike, untidy, vicious, vile, virose, vulgar, wet, wicked, wild.

antonyms clean, fair, pure, worthy.

v. befoul, begrime, besmear, besmirch, block, catch, choke, clog, contaminate, defile, dirty, ensnare, entangle, foul up, jam, pollute, smear, snarl, soil, stain, sully, taint, twist.

antonyms clean, clear, disentangle.

found *v.* base, bottom, build, constitute, construct, create, endow, erect, establish, fix, ground, inaugurate, initiate, institute, organize, originate, plant, raise, rest, root, set up, settle, start, sustain.

foundation *n.* base, basis, bedrock, bottom, endowment, establishment, fond, footing, ground, groundwork, inauguration, institution, organization, setting up, settlement, substance, substratum, substructure, underpinning.

foxy *adj.* artful, astute, canny, crafty, cunning, devious, fly, guileful, knowing, sharp, shrewd, sly, tricky, vulpine, wily.

antonyms naïve, open.

fractious *adj.* awkward, captious, choleric, crabbed, crabby, cross, crotchety, fretful, froward, grouchy, irritable, peevish, pettish, petulant, quarrelsome, querulous, recalcitrant, refractory, testy, touchy, unruly.

antonyms complaisant, placid.

fracture *n.* breach, break, cleft, crack, fissure, gap, opening, rent, rift, rupture, schism, scission, split.

v. break, crack, rupture, splinter, split.

antonym join.

fragile *adj.* breakable, brittle, dainty, delicate, feeble, fine, flimsy, frail, frangible, infirm, insubstantial, shattery, slight, weak.

antonyms durable, robust, tough.

fragment *n.* bit, cantlet, chip, flinder, fraction, frazzle, fritter, morceau, morsel, ort, part, particle, piece, portion, remnant, scrap, shard, shatter, sheave, shiver, shred, sliver.

v. break, break up, come apart, come to pieces, crumble, disintegrate, disunite, divide, fractionalize, fritter, shatter, shiver, splinter, split, split up.

antonyms hold together, join.

fragrance *n.* aroma, balm, balminess, bouquet, fragrancy, odor, perfume, redolence, scent, smell.

fragrant *adj.* aromatic, balmy, balsamy, odoriferous, odorous, perfumed, redolent, suaveolent, sweet, sweet-scented, sweet-smelling.

antonyms smelly, unscented.

frail *adj.* breakable, brittle, decrepit, delicate, feeble, flimsy, fragile, frangible, infirm, insubstantial, puny, slight, tender, unchaste, unsound, vulnerable, weak.

antonyms firm, robust, strong, tough.

frame *v.* assemble, block out, build, case, compose, conceive, concoct, constitute, construct, contrive, cook up, devise, draft, draw up, enclose, enframe, fabricate, fashion, forge, form, formulate, hatch, institute, invent, make, manufacture, map out, model, mold, mount, plan, put together, redact, set up, shape, sketch, surround, trap, victimize.

n. anatomy, body, bodyshell, bodywork, build, carcass, casing, chassis, construction, fabric, flake, form, framework, monture, morphology, mount, mounting, physique, scaffolding, scheme, setting, shell, skeleton, structure, system.

frank *adj.* artless, blunt, candid, direct, downright, forthright, four-square, free, honest, ingenuous, open, outright, outspoken, plain, plain-spoken, simple-hearted, sincere, straight, straightforward, transparent, truthful, unconcealed, undisguised, unreserved, unrestricted.

frantic *adj.* berserk, beside oneself, desperate, distracted, distraught, fraught, frenetic, frenzied, furious, hairless, hectic, mad, overwrought, raging, raving, wild.

antonym calm.

fraternize *v.* affiliate, associate, concur, consort, cooperate, forgather, hobnob, mingle, mix, socialize, sympathize, unite.

antonyms ignore, shun.

fraud[1] *n.* artifice, cheat, chicane, chicanery, craft, deceit, deception, double-dealing, duplicity, fake, forgery, guile, hoax, humbug, imposture, sham, sharp practice, spuriousness, swindling, swiz, swizzle, take-in, treachery, trickery.

fraud[2] *n.* bluffer, charlatan, cheat, counterfeit, double-dealer, hoaxer, impostor, malingerer, mountebank, phony, pretender, pseud, quack, swindler.

fraudulent *adj.* bogus, counterfeit, crafty, criminal, crooked, deceitful, deceptive, dishonest, double-dealing, duplicitous, false, knavish, phony, sham, specious, spurious, swindling, treacherous.

antonyms genuine, honest.

fray *n.* affray, bagarre, barney, battle, brawl, broil, clash, combat, conflict, disturbance, Donnybrook, dust-up, fight, free-for-all, mêlée, quarrel, rammy, riot, row, ruckus, ruction, rumble, rumpus, scuffle, set-to, shindy.

freak[1] *n.* aberration, abnormality, abortion, anomaly, caprice, crotchet, fad, fancy, folly, grotesque, humor, irregularity, lusus naturae, malformation, misgrowth, monster, monstrosity, mutant, oddity, queer fish, quirk, rara avis, sport, teratism, turn, twist, vagary, weirdie, weirdo, whim, whimsy.

adj. aberrant, abnormal, atypical, bizarre, capricious, erratic, exceptional, fluky, fortuitous, odd, queer, surprise, unaccountable, unexpected, unforeseen, unparalleled, unpredictable, unpredicted, unusual.

antonyms common, expected.

freak[2] *n.* addict, aficionado, buff, devotee, enthusiast, fan, fanatic, fiend, monomaniac, nut, votary.

freckle *n.* fernitickle, heatspot, lentigo.

free *adj.* able, allowed, at large, at leisure, at liberty,

autarchic, autonomous, available, bounteous, bountiful, buckshee, casual, charitable, clear, complimentary, cost-free, dégagé, democratic, disengaged, eager, easy, emancipated, empty, extra, familiar, footloose, forward, frank, free and easy, free of charge, generous, gratis, hospitable, idle, independent, informal, laidback, lavish, lax, leisured, liberal, liberated, loose, munificent, natural, off the hook, on the house, on the loose, open, open-handed, permitted, prodigal, relaxed, self-governing, self-ruling, solute, sovereign, spare, spontaneous, unattached, unbidden, unbowed, unceremonious, uncommitted, unconstrained, unemployed, unencumbered, unengaged, unfettered, unforced, unhampered, unhindered, unimpeded, uninhabited, uninhibited, unobstructed, unoccupied, unpaid, unpent, unpreoccupied, unregimented, unregulated, unrestrained, unrestricted, unsparing, unstinting, untrammeled, unused, vacant, willing, without charge.
antonyms attached, confined, costly, formal, mean, niggardly, restricted, tied.
adv. abundantly, copiously, for free, for love, for nothing, freely, gratis, idly, loosely, without charge.
antonym meanly.
v. absolve, affranchise, clear, debarrass, declassify, decolonize, decontrol, deliver, disburden, discage, discharge, disembarrass, disembrangle, disenchain, disengage, disenslave, disentangle, disenthral, disimprison, disprison, emancipate, exempt, extricate, let go, liberate, loose, manumit, ransom, release, relieve, rescue, rid, set free, turn loose, unbind, unburden, uncage, unchain, undo, unfetter, unhand, unleash, unlock, unloose, unmanacle, unmew, unpen, unshackle, unstick, untether, untie, unyoke.
antonyms confine, enslave, imprison.
freedom *n.* abandon, ability, affranchisement, autonomy, boldness, brazenness, candor, carte-blanche, deliverance, directness, discretion, disrespect, ease, elbow-room, emancipation, exemption, facility, familiarity, flexibility, forwardness, frankness, free rein, home rule, immunity, impertinence, impunity, independence, informality, ingenuousness, lack of restraint or reserve, latitude, laxity, leeway, liberty, Liberty Hall, license, manumission, openness, opportunity, overfamiliarity, play, power, presumption, privilege, range, release, scope, self-government, uhuru, unconstraint.
antonyms confinement, reserve, restriction.
freely *adv.* abundantly, amply, bountifully, candidly, cleanly, copiously, easily, extravagantly, frankly, generously, lavishly, liberally, loosely, of one's own accord, open-handedly, openly, plainly, readily, smoothly, spontaneously, sponte sua, unchallenged, unreservedly, unstintingly, voluntarily, willingly.
antonyms evasively, meanly, roughly, under duress.
freight *n.* bulk, burden, cargo, carriage, charge, consignment, contents, conveyance, fee, goods, haul, lading, load, merchandise, pay-load, shipment, tonnage, transportation.
frenzy *n.* aberration, agitation, bout, burst, convulsion, delirium, derangement, distraction, estrus, fit, fury, hysteria, insanity, lunacy, madness, mania, must, outburst, paroxysm, passion, rage, seizure, spasm, transport, turmoil.
antonyms calm, placidness.
frequent[1] *adj.* common, commonplace, constant, contin-

ual, customary, everyday, familiar, habitual, incessant, numerous, persistent, recurrent, recurring, regular, reiterated, repeated, usual.
antonym infrequent.
frequent[2] *v.* associate with, attend, crowd, hang about, hang out at, haunt, haunt about, patronize, resort, visit.
fresh *adj.* added, additional, alert, artless, auxiliary, blooming, bold, bouncing, bracing, brazen, bright, brisk, callow, cheeky, chipper, clean, clear, cool, crisp, crude, dewy, different, disrespectful, energetic, extra, fair, familiar, flip, florid, forward, further, glowing, green, hardy, healthy, impudent, inexperienced, innovative, insolent, inventive, invigorated, invigorating, keen, latest, lively, malapert, modern, modernistic, more, natural, new, new-fangled, novel, original, other, pert, presumptuous, pure, raw, recent, refreshed, refreshing, renewed, rested, restored, revived, rosy, ruddy, saucy, span, spanking, sparkling, spick, sprightly, spry, stiff, supplementary, sweet, unblown, unconventional, uncultivated, undimmed, unhackneyed, unjaded, unjaundiced, unpolluted, unsoured, unspoilt, untrained, untried, unusual, unwarped, unwearied, up-to-date, verdant, vernal, vigorous, virescent, vital, vivid, warm, wholesome, young, youthful.
antonyms experienced, faded, old hat, polite, stale, tired.
fret *v.* abrade, agitate, agonize, annoy, bother, brood, chafe, chagrin, corrode, distress, disturb, eat into, erode, fray, gall, goad, grieve, harass, irk, irritate, nag, nettle, peeve, pique, provoke, rankle, repine, rile, ripple, rub, ruffle, torment, trouble, vex, wear, wear away, worry.
antonym calm.
fretful *adj.* cantankerous, captious, complaining, cross, crotchety, edgy, fractious, irritable, peevish, petulant, querulous, short-tempered, snappish, snappy, splenetic, testy, thrawn, touchy, uneasy.
antonym calm.
friction *n.* abrasion, animosity, antagonism, attrition, bad blood, bad feeling, bickering, chafing, conflict, contention, disagreement, discontent, discord, disharmony, dispute, dissension, erosion, fretting, grating, hostility, ill-feeling, incompatibility, irritation, limitation, opposition, quarreling, rasping, resentment, resistance, rivalry, rubbing, scraping, wearing away, wrangling, xerotripsis.
friend *n.* Achates, adherent, advocate, ally, alter ego, associate, backer, benefactor, boon companion, bosom friend, buddy, china, chum, cobber, companion, comrade, confidant, crony, familiar, gossip, intimate, mate, paisano, pal, partisan, partner, patron, playmate, sidekick, soul mate, supporter, well-wisher.
antonym enemy.
friendly *adj.* affable, affectionate, amiable, amicable, approachable, attached, attentive, auspicious, beneficial, benevolent, benign, chummy, close, clubby, companionable, comradely, conciliatory, confiding, convivial, cordial, familiar, Favonian, favorable, fond, fraternal, gemütlich, genial, good, helpful, intimate, kind, kindly, maty, neighborly, outgoing, palsy-walsy, peaceable, propitious, receptive, sociable, sympathetic, thick, welcoming, well-disposed.
antonyms cold, unsociable.

friendship *n.* affection, affinity, alliance, amity, attachment, benevolence, closeness, concord, familiarity, fellowship, fondness, friendliness, goodwill, harmony, intimacy, love, neighborliness, rapport, regard.
antonym enmity.

fright *n.* alarm, apprehension, consternation, dismay, dread, eyesore, fear, fleg, funk, horror, mess, monstrosity, panic, quaking, scare, scarecrow, shock, sight, spectacle, sweat, terror, the shivers, trepidation.

frighten *v.* affray, affright, affrighten, alarm, appal, cow, daunt, dismay, fleg, intimidate, petrify, scare, scare stiff, shock, spook, startle, terrify, terrorize, unman, unnerve.
antonyms calm, reassure.

frigid *adj.* aloof, arctic, austere, brumous, chill, chilly, cold, cold-hearted, cool, forbidding, formal, frore, frost-bound, frosty, frozen, gelid, glacial, icy, lifeless, passionless, passive, repellent, rigid, stand-offish, stiff, unanimated, unapproachable, unbending, unfeeling, unloving, unresponsive, wintry.
antonyms responsive, warm.

fringe *n.* borderline, edge, fimbriation, frisette, limits, march, marches, margin, outskirts, perimeter, periphery.
adj. alternative, unconventional, unofficial, unorthodox.
v. border, edge, enclose, fimbriate, skirt, surround, trim.

frisky *adj.* bouncy, buckish, coltish, frolicsome, gamesome, high-spirited, kittenish, lively, playful, rollicking, romping, skittish, spirited, sportive.
antonym quiet.

frolic *v.* caper, cavort, cut capers, frisk, gambol, gammock, lark, make merry, play, rollick, romp, skylark, sport, wanton.
n. amusement, antic, drollery, escapade, fun, gaiety, gambado, gambol, game, gammock, gilravage, high jinks, lark, merriment, prank, razzle-dazzle, revel, rig, romp, skylarking, sport, spree.

front *n.* air, anterior, appearance, aspect, bearing, beginning, blind, countenance, cover, cover-up, demeanor, disguise, expression, exterior, façade, face, facing, fore, forefront, foreground, forepart, front line, frontage, head, lead, manner, mask, metope, mien, obverse, pretence, pretext, show, top, van, vanguard.
antonym back.
adj. anterior, anticous, first, fore, foremost, head, lead, leading.
antonyms back, last, least, posterior.
v. confront, face, look over, meet, oppose, overlook.

frontier *n.* borderland, borderline, bound, boundary, bourn(e), confines, edge, limit, march, marches, perimeter, verge.
adj. backwoods, limitrophe, outlying, pioneering.

frown *v.* glare, glower, grimace, lower, scowl.
n. dirty look, glare, glower, grimace, moue, scowl.

frugal *adj.* abstemious, careful, cheese-paring, economical, meager, niggardly, parsimonious, penny-wise, provident, prudent, saving, sparing, Spartan, thrifty, ungenerous.
antonym wasteful.

fruitful *adj.* abundant, advantageous, beneficial, copious, effective, fecund, feracious, fertile, flush, fructiferous, fructuous, gainful, plenteous, plentiful, productive, profitable, profuse, prolific, rewarding, rich, spawning, successful, teeming, uberous, useful, well-spent, worthwhile.
antonyms barren, fruitless.

fruitfulness *n.* fecundity, feracity, fertility, productiveness, profitability, uberty, usefulness.
antonym fruitlessness.

fruitless *adj.* abortive, barren, bootless, futile, hopeless, idle, ineffectual, pointless, profitless, unavailing, unfruitful, unproductive, unprofitable, unsuccessful, useless, vain.
antonyms fruitful, successful.

frustrate *v.* baffle, balk, block, bugger, check, circumvent, confront, counter, countermine, crab, defeat, depress, disappoint, discourage, dishearten, foil, forestall, inhibit, neutralize, nullify, scotch, spike, stymie, thwart.
antonyms fulfil, further, promote.

fuddled *adj.* bemused, confused, drunk, groggy, hazy, inebriated, intoxicated, muddled, mused, muzzy, sozzled, stupefied, tipsy, woozy.
antonyms clear, sober.

fuel *n.* ammunition, eilding, encouragement, fodder, food, incitement, material, means, nourishment, provocation.
v. charge, encourage, fan, feed, fire, incite, inflame, nourish, stoke up, sustain.
antonyms damp down, discourage.

fugitive *n.* deserter, escapee, refugee, runagate, runaway.
adj. brief, elusive, ephemeral, evanescent, fleeing, fleeting, flitting, flying, fugacious, intangible, momentary, passing, short, short-lived, temporary, transient, transitory, unstable.
antonym permanent.

fulfill *v.* accomplish, achieve, answer, carry out, complete, comply with, conclude, conform to, consummate, discharge, effect, effectuate, execute, fill, finish, implement, keep, meet, obey, observe, perfect, perform, realize, satisfy.
antonyms break, defect, fail, frustrate.

full *adj.* abundant, adequate, all-inclusive, ample, baggy, brimful, brimming, broad, buxom, capacious, chock-a-block, chock-full, clear, complete, comprehensive, copious, crammed, crowded, curvaceous, deep, detailed, distinct, entire, exhaustive, extensive, filled, generous, gorged, intact, jammed, large, loaded, loud, maximum, occupied, orotund, packed, plenary, plenteous, plentiful, plump, replete, resonant, rich, rounded, sated, satiated, satisfied, saturated, stocked, sufficient, taken, thorough, unabbreviated, unabridged, uncut, unedited, unexpurgated, voluminous, voluptuous.
antonyms empty, incomplete.

full-blooded *adj.* gutsy, hearty, lusty, mettlesome, red-blooded, thoroughbred, vigorous, virile, whole-hearted.

full-grown *adj.* adult, developed, full-aged, full-blown, full-scale, grown-up, marriageable, mature, nubile, of age, ripe.
antonyms undeveloped, young.

fullness *n.* abundance, adequateness, ampleness, broadness, clearness, completeness, comprehensiveness, copiousness, curvaceousness, dilation, distension, enlargement, entirety, extensiveness, fill, glut, loudness, orotundity, plenitude, plenty, pleroma, profusion, repletion, resonance, richness, roundness, satiety, saturation, strength, sufficiency, swelling, totality, tumescence, vastness, voluptuousness, wealth, wholeness.

antonyms emptiness, incompleteness.

full-scale *adj.* all-encompassing, all-out, comprehensive, exhaustive, extensive, full-dress, in-depth, intensive, major, proper, sweeping, thorough, thoroughgoing, wide-ranging.

antonym partial.

fulminate *v.* animadvert, criticize, curse, denounce, detonate, fume, inveigh, protest, rage, rail, thunder, vilipend, vituperate.

antonym praise.

fulsome *adj.* adulatory, cloying, effusive, excessive, extravagant, fawning, gross, immoderate, ingratiating, inordinate, insincere, nauseating, nauseous, offensive, overdone, rank, saccharine, sickening, smarmy, sycophantic, unctuous.

antonym sincere.

fume *v.* boil, chafe, fizz, get steamed up, give off, rage, rant, rave, reek, seethe, smoke, smolder, storm.

fun *n.* amusement, buffoonery, cheer, clowning, distraction, diversion, enjoyment, entertainment, foolery, frolic, gaiety, game, gammock, high jinks, horseplay, jesting, jocularity, joking, jollification, jollity, joy, junketing, merriment, merrymaking, mirth, nonsense, play, playfulness, pleasure, recreation, romp, skylarking, sport, teasing, tomfoolery, treat, waggery, whoopee.

function[1] *n.* activity, business, capacity, charge, concern, duty, employment, exercise, faculty, job, mission, occupation, office, operation, part, post, province, purpose, raison d'être, responsibility, role, situation, task.

v. act, be in running order, behave, do duty, functionate, go, officiate, operate, perform, run, serve, work.

function[2] *n.* affair, dinner, do, gathering, junket, luncheon, party, reception, shindig.

fundamental *adj.* axiomatic, basal, basic, basilar, cardinal, central, constitutional, crucial, elementary, essential, first, important, indispensable, integral, intrinsic, key, keynote, necessary, organic, primal, primary, prime, principal, rudimentary, underlying, vital.

antonym advanced.

n. axiom, basic, cornerstone, essential, first principle, law, principle, rudiment, rule, sine qua non.

funereal *adj.* dark, deathlike, depressing, dirgelike, dismal, dreary, exequial, feral, funebral, funebrial, gloomy, grave, lamenting, lugubrious, mournful, sad, sepulchral, solemn, somber, woeful.

antonyms happy, lively.

funny *adj.* a card, a caution, a scream, absurd, amusing, comic, comical, curious, diverting, droll, dubious, entertaining, facetious, farcical, funny ha-ha, funny peculiar, hilarious, humorous, jocose, jocular, jolly, killing, laughable, ludicrous, mirth-provoking, mysterious, odd, peculiar, perplexing, puzzling, queer, remarkable, rich, ridiculous, riotous, risible, side-splitting, silly, slapstick, strange, suspicious, unusual, waggish, weird, witty.

antonyms sad, solemn, unamusing, unfunny.

furious *adj.* acharné, agitated, angry, boiling, boisterous, enraged, fierce, fizzing, frantic, frenzied, fuming, furibund, impetuous, incensed, infuriated, intense, livid,

mad, maddened, maenadic, raging, savage, stormy, tempestuous, tumultuous, turbulent, up in arms, vehement, violent, waxy, wild, wrathful, wroth.

antonyms calm, pleased.

furnish *v.* afford, appoint, bedight, bestow, decorate, endow, equip, fit out, fit up, give, grant, offer, outfit, present, provide, provision, reveal, rig, stake, stock, store, suit, supply.

antonym divest.

furore *n.* commotion, craze, disturbance, enthusiasm, excitement, flap, frenzy, fury, fuss, hullabaloo, mania, outburst, outcry, rage, stir, to-do, tumult, uproar.

antonym calm.

furtherance *n.* advancement, advancing, advocacy, backing, boosting, carrying-out, championship, promoting, promotion, prosecution, pursuit.

furthermore *adv.* additionally, also, as well, besides, further, in addition, into the bargain, likewise, moreover, not to mention, to boot, too, what's more.

furtive *adj.* back-door, backstairs, clandestine, cloaked, conspiratorial, covert, hidden, secret, secretive, skulking, slinking, sly, sneaking, sneaky, stealthy, surreptitious, underhand.

antonym open.

fury[1] *n.* anger, desperation, ferocity, fierceness, force, frenzy, impetuosity, intensity, ire, madness, passion, power, rage, savagery, severity, tempestuousness, turbulence, vehemence, violence, wax, wrath.

antonym calm.

fury[2] *n.* bacchante, hag, harridan, hell-cat, shrew, spitfire, termagant, virago, vixen.

fuss *n.* ado, agitation, bother, brouhaha, bustle, coil, commotion, confusion, difficulty, display, doodah, excitement, fantigue, fash, fidget, fikery, flap, flurry, fluster, flutter, furore, hassle, hoo-ha, hurry, kerfuffle, objection, palaver, pother, pudder, row, squabble, stew, stir, to-do, trouble, unrest, upset, worry.

antonym calm.

v. bustle, chafe, complain, emote, fash, fidget, flap, fret, fume, niggle, pother, pudder, take pains, worry.

futile *adj.* abortive, barren, bootless, empty, forlorn, fruitless, hollow, idle, ineffectual, nugatory, otiose, pointless, profitless, Sisyphean, sterile, trifling, trivial, unavailing, unimportant, unproductive, unprofitable, unsuccessful, useless, vain, valueless, worthless.

antonyms fruitful, profitable.

futility *n.* aimlessness, bootlessness, emptiness, fruitlessness, hollowness, idleness, ineffectiveness, otioseness, pointlessness, triviality, unimportance, uselessness, vanity.

antonyms fruitfulness, profitability.

future *n.* expectation, futurition, futurity, hereafter, outlook, prospects.

antonym past.

adj. approaching, coming, designate, destined, eventual, expected, fated, forthcoming, impending, in the offing, later, prospective, rising, subsequent, to be, to come, ultimate, unborn.

antonym past.

fuzzy *adj.* bleary, blurred, blurry, distanceless, distorted, downy, faint, fluffy, frizzy, hazy, ill-defined, indistinct, linty, muffled, napped, shadowy, unclear, unfocused, vague, woolly.

antonyms base, distinct.

G

gab v. babble, blabber, blather, blether, buzz, chatter, drivel, gossip, jabber, jaw, prattle, talk, tattle, yabber, yak, yatter.

n. blab, blarney, blethering, blethers, chat, chatter, chitchat, conversation, drivel, gossip, loquacity, palaver, prattle, prattling, small talk, tête-à-tête, tittle-tattle, tongue-wagging, yabber, yackety-yak, yak, yatter.

gabble v. babble, blab, blabber, blether, cackle, chatter, gaggle, gibber, gush, jabber, prattle, rattle, splutter, spout, sputter, yabber, yatter.

n. babble, blabber, blethering, cackling, chatter, drivel, gibberish, jargon, nonsense, prattle, twaddle, waffle, yabber, yatter.

gad about dot about, gallivant, ramble, range, roam, rove, run around, stray, traipse, wander.

gadabout n. gallivanter, pleasure-seeker, rambler, rover, runabout, stravaiger, wanderer.

gadget n. appliance, contraption, contrivance, device, doodad, gimmick, gismo, gizmo, invention, jiggumbob, jigjam, jigmaree, novelty, thing, thingumajig, tool, widget.

gaffer n. boss, foreman, ganger, manager, overman, overseer, superintendent, supervisor.

gag[1] v. choke, choke up, curb, disgorge, gasp, heave, muffle, muzzle, puke, quiet, retch, silence, spew, stifle, still, stop up, suppress, throttle, throw up, vomit.

gag[2] n. funny, hoax, jest, joke, one-liner, pun, quip, wisecrack, witticism.

gaiety n. animation, blitheness, blithesomeness, brightness, brilliance, celebration, cheerfulness, color, colorfulness, conviviality, effervescence, elation, exhilaration, festivity, fun, galliardize, gaudiness, glee, glitter, good humor, high spirits, hilarity, joie de vivre, jollification, jollity, joviality, joyousness, light-heartedness, liveliness, merriment, merrymaking, mirth, revelry, revels, show, showiness, sparkle, sprightliness, vivacity.

antonyms drabness, dreariness, sadness.

gain v. achieve, acquire, advance, arrive at, attain, avail, bag, bring in, capture, clear, collect, come to, earn, enlist, gather, get, get to, glean, harvest, impetrate, improve, increase, make, net, obtain, pick up, procure, produce, profit, progress, reach, realize, reap, secure, win, win over, yield.

antonym lose.

n. accretion, achievement, acquisition, advance, advancement, advantage, attainment, benefit, bunce, dividend, earnings, emolument, growth, headway, improvement, income, increase, increment, lucre, proceeds, produce, profit, progress, pudding, return, rise, winnings, yield.

antonyms loss, losses.

gainful adj. advantageous, beneficial, feracious, fructuous, fruitful, lucrative, moneymaking, paying, productive, profitable, remunerative, rewarding, useful, worthwhile.

antonym useless.

gainsay v. contradict, contravene, controvert, deny, disaffirm, disagree with, dispute, nay-say.

antonym agree.

gait n. bearing, carriage, manner, pace, step, stride, tread, walk.

gala n. carnival, celebration, festival, festivity, fête, glorification, jamboree, jubilee, Mardi Gras, pageant, party, procession.

gale n. blast, burst, cyclone, eruption, explosion, fit, howl, hurricane, outbreak, outburst, peal, ripsnorter, shout, shriek, squall, storm, tempest, tornado, typhoon.

gall[1] n. acrimony, animosity, animus, antipathy, assurance, bad blood, bile, bitterness, brass, brass neck, brazenness, cheek, effrontery, enmity, hostility, impertinence, impudence, insolence, malevolence, malice, malignity, neck, nerve, presumption, presumptuousness, rancor, sauciness, sourness, spite, spleen, venom, virulence.

antonyms friendliness, modesty, reserve.

gall[2] v. abrade, aggravate, annoy, bark, bother, chafe, exasperate, excoriate, fret, get, get to, graze, harass, hurt, irk, irritate, nag, nettle, peeve, pester, plague, provoke, rankle, rile, rub raw, ruffle, scrape, skin, vex.

gallant adj. attentive, august, bold, brave, chivalrous, courageous, courteous, courtly, daring, dashing, dauntless, dignified, doughty, elegant, fearless, game, gentlemanly, glorious, gracious, grand, heroic, high-spirited, honorable, imposing, indomitable, intrepid, lion-hearted, lofty, magnanimous, magnificent, manful, manly, mettlesome, noble, plucky, polite, splendid, stately, valiant, valorous.

antonyms cowardly, craven, ungentlemanly.

n. admirer, adventurer, beau, blade, boyfriend, buck, cavalier, champion, cicisbeo, dandy, daredevil, escort, fop, hero, knight, ladies' man, lady-killer, lover, paramour, suitor, wooer.

gallantry n. attention, attentiveness, audacity, boldness, bravery, chivalry, courage, courageousness, courteousness, courtesy, courtliness, daring, dauntlessness, derring-do, elegance, fearlessness, gentlemanliness, graciousness, heroism, intrepidity, manliness, mettle, nerve, nobility, pluck, politeness, politesse, prowess, spirit, valiance, valor.

antonyms cowardice, ungentlemanliness.

gallery n. arcade, art-gallery, balcony, circle, gods, grandstand, loggia, museum, passage, pawn, spectators, walk.

galling adj. aggravating, annoying, bitter, bothersome, exasperating, harassing, humiliating, infuriating, irksome, irritating, nettling, plaguing, provoking, rankling, vexatious, vexing.

antonym pleasing.

galore adv. aplenty, everywhere, heaps of, in abundance, in numbers, in profusion, lots of, millions of, stacks of, to spare, tons of.

antonym scarce.

gamble v. back, bet, chance, gaff, game, have a flutter, hazard, play, punt, risk, speculate, stake, stick one's neck out, take a chance, try one's luck, venture, wager.

n. bet, chance, flutter, leap in the dark, lottery, punt, risk, speculation, uncertainty, venture, wager.

gambol v. bounce, bound, caper, cavort, curvet, cut a caper, frisk, frolic, hop, jump, prance, rollick, skip.

n. antic, bound, caper, frisk, frolic, gambado, hop, jump, prance, skip, spring.

game[1] n. adventure, amusement, business, competition, contest, design, device, distraction, diversion, enterprise, entertainment, event, frolic, fun, jest, joke, lark, line, main, match, meeting, merriment, merry-making, occupation, pastime, plan, play, plot, ploy, proceeding, recreation, romp, round, scheme, sport, stratagem, strategy, tactic, tournament, trick, undertaking.

game² *n.* animals, bag, flesh, game-birds, meat, prey, quarry, spoils.

game³ *adj.* bold, brave, courageous, dauntless, desirous, disposed, dogged, eager, fearless, gallant, gamy, heroic, inclined, interested, intrepid, persevering, persistent, plucky, prepared, ready, resolute, spirited, spunky, unflinching, valiant, valorous, willing.
antonyms cowardly, unwilling.

game⁴ *adj.* bad, crippled, deformed, disabled, gammy, gouty, hobbling, incapacitated, injured, lame, maimed.

gamut *n.* area, catalog, compass, field, range, scale, scope, series, spectrum, sweep.

gang *n.* band, circle, clique, club, coffle, company, core, coterie, crew, crowd, group, herd, horde, lot, mob, pack, party, ring, set, shift, squad, team, troupe.

gangling *adj.* angular, awkward, bony, gangly, gauche, gawky, lanky, loose-jointed, rangy, raw-boned, skinny, spindly, tall, ungainly.

gangster *n.* bandit, brigand, crook, desperado, heavy, hood, hoodlum, mobster, racketeer, robber, rough, ruffian, thug, tough.

gap *n.* blank, breach, break, chink, cleft, crack, cranny, crevice, diastema, difference, disagreement, discontinuity, disparateness, disparity, divergence, divide, hiatus, hole, inconsistency, interlude, intermission, interruption, interspace, interstice, interval, lacuna, lull, opening, pause, recess, rent, rift, space, vacuity, void.

gape *v.* crack, dehisce, gawk, gawp, goggle, open, split, stare, wonder, yawn.

garb *n.* accouterments, apparel, appearance, array, aspect, attire, clothes, clothing, costume, covering, cut, dress, fashion, garment, gear, guise, habiliment, habit, look, mode, outfit, raiment, robes, style, uniform, vestments, wear.
v. apparel, array, attire, clothe, cover, dress, habilitate, rig out, robe.

garbage *n.* bits and pieces, debris, detritus, dross, filth, gash, junk, litter, muck, odds and ends, offal, refuse, rubbish, scourings, scraps, slops, sweepings, swill, trash, waste.

garble *v.* confuse, corrupt, distort, doctor, edit, falsify, jumble, misinterpret, misquote, misreport, misrepresent, misstate, mistranslate, mix up, muddle, mutilate, pervert, slant, tamper with, twist.
antonym decipher.

gargantuan *adj.* big, Brobdingnag(ian), colossal, elephantine, enormous, giant, gigantic, huge, immense, large, leviathan, mammoth, massive, monstrous, monumental, mountainous, prodigious, titanic, towering, tremendous, vast.
antonym small.

garments *n.* apparel, array, attire, clothes, clothing, costume, dress, duds, garb, gear, get-up, habiliment, habit, outfit, raiment, robes, togs, uniform, vestments, wear.

garnish *v.* adorn, beautify, bedeck, deck, decorate, embellish, enhance, furnish, grace, ornament, set off, trim.
antonym divest.

n. adornment, decoration, embellishment, enhancement, garnishment, garnishry, garniture, ornament, ornamentation, relish, trim, trimming.

garrulous *adj.* babbling, chattering, chatty, diffuse, effusive, gabby, gassy, glib, gossiping, gushing, long-winded, loquacious, mouthy, prating, prattling, prolix, prosy, talkative, verbose, voluble, windy, wordy, yabbering.
antonyms taciturn, terse.

gash *v.* cleave, cut, gouge, incise, lacerate, nick, notch, rend, score, slash, slit, split, tear, wound.
n. cleft, cut, gouge, incision, laceration, nick, notch, rent, score, slash, slit, split, tear, wound.

gasp *v.* blow, breathe, choke, ejaculate, gulp, pant, puff, utter.
n. blow, breath, ejaculation, exclamation, gulp, pant, puff.

gather *v.* accumulate, amass, assemble, assume, build, clasp, collect, conclude, congregate, convene, crop, cull, deduce, deepen, draw, embrace, enfold, enlarge, expand, flock, fold, foregather, garner, glean, group, grow, harvest, heap, hear, heighten, hoard, hold, hug, increase, infer, intensify, learn, make, marshal, mass, muster, pick, pile up, pleat, pluck, pucker, rake up, reap, rise, round up, ruche, ruffle, select, shirr, stockpile, surmise, swell, thicken, tuck, understand, wax.
antonyms dissipate, scatter.

gathering *n.* accumulation, acquisition, aggregate, assemblage, assembly, collection, company, concentration, conclave, concourse, congregation, congress, convention, convocation, crowd, fest, flock, gain, galère, get-together, group, heap, hoard, jamboree, kgotla, knot, mass, meeting, moot, muster, omnium-gatherum, party, pile, procurement, rally, round-up, rout, stock, stockpile, throng, turn-out.
antonym scattering.

gaudy *adj.* bright, brilliant, chintzy, flash, flashy, florid, garish, gay, glaring, glitzy, loud, meretricious, ostentatious, raffish, showy, tasteless, tawdry, tinsel(ly), vulgar.
antonyms drab, plain, quiet.

gaunt *adj.* angular, attenuated, bare, bleak, bony, cadaverous, desolate, dismal, dreary, emaciated, forbidding, forlorn, grim, haggard, hagged, harsh, hollow-eyed, lank, lean, meager, pinched, rawboned, scraggy, scrawny, skeletal, skinny, spare, thin, wasted.
antonyms hale, plump.

gay¹ *adj.* animated, blithe, boon, bright, brilliant, carefree, cavalier, cheerful, colorful, convivial, debonair, festive, flamboyant, flashy, fresh, frivolous, frolicsome, fun-loving, gamesome, garish, gaudy, glad, gleeful, happy, hilarious, insouciant, jolly, jovial, joyful, joyous, lifesome, light-hearted, lightsome, lively, merry, playful, pleasure-seeking, rakish, riant, rich, rollicking, rorty, showy, sparkish, sparkling, sportive, sunny, tit(t)upy, vivacious, vivid, waggish.
antonyms gloomy, sad.

gay² *adj.* bent, dikey, homosexual, lesbian, queer.
antonyms heterosexual, straight.
n. dike, homo, homosexual, lesbian, poof, queer, sapphist.
antonym heterosexual.

gaze *v.* contemplate, gape, gaup, gawp, look, ogle, regard, stare, view, watch.
n. gaup, gawp, look, stare.

gear *n.* accessories, accouterments, affair, apparatus, apparel, armor, array, attire, baggage, belongings, business, clothes, clothing, cog, costume, doings, dress, effects, equipment, garb, garments, gearing, get-up, habit, harness, instruments, kit, luggage, machinery, matter, mechanism, outfit, paraphernalia, possessions, rigging, rig-out, stuff, supplies, tackle, things, togs, tools, trappings, traps, wear, works.

v. adapt, adjust, equip, fit, harness, rig, suit, tailor.

gel *v.* coagulate, congeal, crystallize, finalize, form, gee, gel, gelatinate, gelatinize, harden, jelly, materialize, set, solidify, take form, take shape, thicken.

antonym disintegrate.

gem *n.* angel, bijou, brick, flower, honey, jewel, masterpiece, pearl, pick, pièce de résistance, precious stone, prize, stone, treasure.

general *adj.* accepted, accustomed, across-the-board, all-inclusive, approximate, blanket, broad, catholic, collective, common, comprehensive, conventional, customary, ecumenic, ecumenical, encyclopedic, everyday, extensive, generic, habitual, ill-defined, imprecise, inaccurate, indefinite, indiscriminate, inexact, loose, miscellaneous, normal, ordinary, panoramic, popular, prevailing, prevalent, public, regular, sweeping, total, typical, universal, unspecific, usual, vague, widespread.

antonyms limited, novel, particular.

n. chief, c-in-c, commander, commander in chief, generalissimo, hetman, leader, marshal, officer.

generally *adv.* approximately, as a rule, broadly, by and large, characteristically, chiefly, commonly, conventionally, customarily, extensively, for the most part, habitually, in the main, largely, mainly, mostly, normally, on average, on the whole, ordinarily, popularly, predominantly, principally, publicly, regularly, typically, universally, usually, widely.

antonym rarely.

generate *v.* beget, breed, bring about, cause, create, engender, father, form, gender, give rise to, initiate, make, originate, procreate, produce, propagate, spawn, whip up.

antonym prevent.

generation *n.* age, age group, begetting, breed, breeding, creation, crop, day, days, engendering, engenderment, engend(r)ure, epoch, era, formation, generating, genesis, geniture, origination, period, procreation, production, progeniture, propagation, reproduction, time, times.

generosity *n.* beneficence, benevolence, big-heartedness, bounteousness, bounty, charity, goodness, high-mindedness, kindness, large-heartedness, liberality, magnanimity, munificence, nobleness, open-handedness, softheartedness, unselfishness, unsparingness.

antonyms meanness, selfishness.

generous *adj.* abundant, ample, beneficent, benevolent, big-hearted, bounteous, bountiful, charitable, copious, disinterested, free, full, good, high-minded, hospitable, kind, large-hearted, large-minded, lavish, liberal, lofty, magnanimous, munificent, noble, open-handed, overflowing, plentiful, princely, rich, soft-boiled, softhearted, ungrudging, unreproachful, unresentful, unselfish, unsparing, unstinted, unstinting.

antonyms mean, selfish.

genesis *n.* beginning, birth, commencement, creation, dawn, engendering, formation, foundation, founding, generation, inception, initiation, origin, outset, propagation, root, source, start.

antonym end.

genius[1] *n.* adept, brain, expert, intellect, maestro, master, master-hand, mastermind, pastmaster, virtuoso.

genius[2] *n.* ability, aptitude, bent, brightness, brilliance, capacity, endowment, faculty, flair, gift, inclination, intellect, knack, propensity, talent, turn.

genius[3] *n.* daemon, double, genie, ka, spirit.

genre *n.* brand, category, character, class, fashion, genus, group, kind, race, school, sort, species, strain, style, type, variety.

genteel *adj.* aristocratic, civil, courteous, courtly, cultivated, cultured, elegant, fashionable, formal, gentlemanly, graceful, ladylike, mannerly, polished, polite, refined, respectable, stylish, urbane, well-bred, well-mannered.

antonyms crude, rough, unpolished.

gentle *adj.* amiable, aristocratic, balmy, benign, biddable, bland, broken, calm, canny, clement, compassionate, courteous, cultured, docile, easy, elegant, genteel, gentlemanlike, gentlemanly, gradual, high-born, humane, imperceptible, kind, kindly, ladylike, lamb-like, lenient, light, low, maidenly, manageable, meek, merciful, mild, moderate, muted, noble, pacific, peaceful, placid, polished, polite, quiet, refined, serene, slight, slow, smooth, soft, soothing, sweet, sweet-tempered, tame, temperate, tender, tractable, tranquil, untroubled, upper-class, well-born, well-bred.

antonyms crude, rough, unkind, unpolished.

genuine *adj.* actual, artless, authentic, bona fide, candid, earnest, frank, heartfelt, honest, kosher, legitimate, natural, original, pukka, pure, real, simon-pure, sincere, sound, sterling, sure-enough, true, unadulterate(d), unaffected, unalloyed, unfeigned, unsophisticated, veritable.

antonyms artificial, insincere.

genus *n.* breed, category, class, division, genre, group, kind, order, race, set, sort, species, taxon, type.

germ *n.* bacterium, beginning, bud, bug, cause, egg, embryo, microbe, micro-organism, nucleus, origin, ovule, ovum, root, rudiment, seed, source, spark, spore, sprout, virus, zyme.

germinate *v.* bud, develop, generate, grow, originate, pullulate, root, shoot, sprout, swell, vegetate.

gesture *n.* act, action, gesticulation, indication, motion, sign, signal, wave.

v. gesticulate, indicate, motion, point, sign, signal, wave.

get *v.* achieve, acquire, affect, annoy, arouse, arrange, arrest, arrive, attain, baffle, bag, become, bother, bring, bug, capture, catch, coax, collar, come, come by, come down with, communicate with, comprehend, confound, contact, contract, contrive, convince, earn, excite, fathom, fetch, fix, follow, gain, glean, grab, grow, hear, impetrate, impress, induce, influence, inherit, irk, irritate, make, make it, manage, move, mystify, net, nonplus, notice, obtain, perceive, perplex, persuade, pick up, pique, prevail upon, procure, puzzle, reach, realize, reap, receive, secure, see, seize, stimulate, stir, stump, succeed, sway, take, touch, trap, turn, twig, understand, upset, vex, wangle, wax, wheedle, win.

antonyms lose, misunderstand, pacify.

ghastly *adj.* ashen, cadaverous, deathlike, deathly, dreadful, frightful, ghostly, grim, grisly, gruesome, hideous, horrendous, horrible, horrid, livid, loathsome, lurid, pale, pallid, repellent, shocking, spectral, terrible, terrifying, wan.
antonym delightful.

ghost *n.* apparition, astral body, duppy, eidolon, fetch, glimmer, gytrash, hint, jumby, larva, lemur, manes, phantasm, phantom, possibility, revenant, semblance, shade, shadow, simulacrum, soul, specter, spirit, spook, suggestion, trace, umbra, visitant, white-lady.

ghoulish *adj.* grisly, gruesome, macabre, morbid, revolting, sick, unhealthy, unwholesome.

giant *n.* behemoth, colossus, Goliath, Hercules, jotun, leviathan, monster, Patagonian, titan.
adj. Atlantean, Babylonian, Brobdingnag(ian), colossal, cyclopean, elephantine, enormous, gargantuan, gigantean, gigantesque, gigantic, huge, immense, jumble, king-size, large, leviathan, mammoth, monstrous, Patagonian, prodigious, rounceval, titanic, vast.

giddy *adj.* capricious, careless, changeable, changeful, dizzy, dizzying, erratic, faint, fickle, flighty, frivolous, heedless, impulsive, inconstant, irresolute, irresponsible, light-headed, reckless, reeling, scatterbrained, scatty, silly, thoughtless, unbalanced, unstable, unsteady, vacillating, vertiginous, volage, volageous, volatile, wild.
antonyms sensible, sober.

gift *n.* ability, aptitude, attribute, benefaction, beneficence, bent, bequest, bonus, boon, bounty, cadeau, capability, capacity, contribution, cumshaw, deodate, dolly, donary, donation, donative, douceur, earnest, endowment, faculty, flair, foy, freebie, genius, grant, gratuity, knack, largess(e), legacy, manna, offering, power, present, sop, talent, turn, xenium.

gigantic *adj.* Atlantean, Babylonian, Brobdingnag(ian), colossal, cyclopean, elephantine, enormous, gargantuan, giant, herculean, huge, immense, leviathan, mammoth, monstrous, Patagonian, prodigious, rounceval, stupendous, titanic, tremendous, vast.
antonym small.

giggle *v.* chortle, chuckle, laugh, snigger, tee-hee, titter.
n. chortle, chuckle, fou rire, laugh, snigger, tee-hee, titter.

gild *v.* adorn, array, beautify, bedeck, brighten, coat, deck, dress up, embellish, embroider, enhance, enrich, festoon, garnish, grace, ornament, paint, trim.

gingerly *adv.* carefully, cautiously, charily, circumspectly, daintily, delicately, fastidiously, gently, hesitantly, reluctantly, squeamishly, suspiciously, timidly, warily.
antonyms carelessly, roughly.

gird *v.* belt, bind, blockade, brace, encircle, enclose, encompass, enfold, engird, environ, enzone, fortify, girdle, hem in, pen, prepare, ready, ring, steel, surround.

girdle *n.* band, belt, ceinture, cestus, cincture, cingulum, corset, cummerbund, fillet, sash, waistband, zona, zone, zonule.
v. bind, bound, encircle, enclose, encompass, engird, environ, enzone, gird, gird round, go round, hem, ring, surround.

girl *n.* backfisch, bird, chick, chicken, chit, colleen, damsel, daughter, demoiselle, filly, fizgig, flapper, flibbertigibbet, floosie, fluff, fräulein, gal, giglet, girl-

friend, gouge, grisette, judy, lass, lassie, maid, maiden, miss, moppet, peach, piece, popsy(-wopsy), quean, quine, sheila, sweetheart, wench.

girth *n.* band, belly-band, bulk, circumference, measure, saddle-band, size, strap.

gist *n.* core, direction, drift, essence, force, idea, import, marrow, matter, meaning, nub, pith, point, quintessence, sense, significance, substance.

give *v.* accord, administer, admit, allow, announce, award, bend, bestow, break, cause, cede, collapse, commit, communicate, concede, confer, consign, contribute, deliver, demonstrate, devote, display, do, donate, emit, engender, entrust, evidence, fall, furnish, grant, hand, hand over, impart, indicate, issue, lead, lend, make, make over, manifest, notify, occasion, offer, pay, perform, permit, present, produce, proffer, pronounce, provide, publish, recede, relinquish, render, retire, set forth, show, sink, state, supply, surrender, transmit, utter, vouchsafe, yield.
antonyms hold out, take, withstand.

given *adj.* addicted, admitted, agreed, apt, bestowed, disposed, granted, inclined, liable, likely, prone, specified.

glacial *adj.* antagonistic, arctic, biting, bitter, brumous, chill, chilly, cold, freezing, frigid, frore, frosty, frozen, gelid, hostile, icy, inimical, piercing, polar, raw, Siberian, stiff, unfriendly, wintry.
antonym warm.

glad *adj.* animated, blithe, blithesome, bright, cheerful, cheering, cheery, chuffed, contented, delighted, delightful, felicitous, gay, gleeful, gratified, gratifying, happy, jocund, jovial, joyful, joyous, merry, over the moon, overjoyed, pleasant, pleased, pleasing, willing.
antonym sad.

gladness *n.* animation, blitheness, blithesomeness, brightness, cheerfulness, delight, felicity, gaiety, glee, happiness, high spirits, hilarity, jollity, joy, joyousness, mirth, pleasure.
antonym sadness.

glamor *n.* allure, appeal, attraction, beauty, bewitchment, charm, enchantment, fascination, magic, magnetism, prestige, ravishment, witchery.

glamorous *adj.* alluring, attractive, beautiful, bewitching, captivating, charming, classy, dazzling, elegant, enchanting, entrancing, exciting, fascinating, glittering, glossy, gorgeous, lovely, prestigious, smart.
antonyms boring, drab, plain.

glance[1] *v.* browse, dip, flip, gaze, glimpse, leaf, look, peek, peep, riffle, scan, skim, thumb, touch on, view.
n. allusion, coup d'oeil, dekko, gander, glimpse, look, mention, once over, peek, peep, reference, squint, view.

glance[2] *v.* bounce, brush, cannon, carom, coruscate, flash, gleam, glimmer, glint, glisten, glister, glitter, graze, rebound, reflect, ricochet, shimmer, shine, skim, twinkle.

glare *v.* blaze, coruscate, dazzle, flame, flare, frown, glower, look daggers, lower, scowl, shine.
n. black look, blaze, brilliance, dazzle, dirty look, flame, flare, flashiness, floridness, frown, gaudiness, glow, glower, light, look, loudness, lower, scowl, showiness, stare, tawdriness.

glaring *adj.* audacious, blatant, blazing, bright, conspicuous, dazzling, dreadful, egregious, flagrant, flashy, florid, garish, glowing, gross, horrendous, loud, manifest, obvious, open, outrageous, outstanding, overt, patent, rank, terrible, unconcealed, visible.

antonyms dull, hidden, minor.

glass *n.* beaker, crystal, goblet, lens, looking-glass, magnifying glass, pane, pocket-lens, roemer, rummer, schooner, tumbler, vitrics, window.

glassy *adj.* blank, clear, cold, dazed, dull, empty, expressionless, fixed, glasslike, glazed, glazy, glossy, hyaline, icy, lifeless, shiny, slick, slippery, smooth, transparent, vacant, vitreous, vitriform.

glaze *v.* burnish, coat, crystallize, enamel, furbish, gloss, lacquer, polish, varnish.

n. coat, enamel, finish, gloss, lacquer, luster, patina, polish, shine, varnish.

gleam *n.* beam, brightness, brilliance, coruscation, flash, flicker, glimmer, glint, gloss, glow, hint, inkling, luster, ray, sheen, shimmer, sparkle, splendor, suggestion, trace.

v. coruscate, flare, flash, glance, glimmer, glint, glisten, glister, glitter, glow, scintillate, shimmer, shine, sparkle.

glean *v.* accumulate, amass, collect, cull, find out, garner, gather, harvest, learn, pick (up), reap, select.

glee *n.* cheerfulness, delight, elation, exhilaration, exuberance, exultation, fun, gaiety, gladness, gratification, hilarity, jocularity, jollity, joviality, joy, joyfulness, joyousness, liveliness, merriment, mirth, pleasure, sprightliness, triumph, verve.

gleeful *adj.* beside oneself, cheerful, cock-a-hoop, delighted, elated, exuberant, exultant, gay, gleesome, gratified, happy, jovial, joyful, joyous, jubilant, merry, mirthful, over the moon, overjoyed, pleased, triumphant.

antonym sad.

glib *adj.* artful, easy, facile, fast-talking, fluent, garrulous, insincere, logodaedalic, plausible, quick, ready, slick, slippery, smooth, smooth-spoken, smooth-tongued, suave, talkative, voluble.

antonyms implausible, tongue-tied.

glide *v.* coast, drift, float, flow, fly, glissade, roll, run, sail, skate, skim, slide, slip, soar, volplane.

glimmer *v.* blink, flicker, gleam, glint, glisten, glitter, glow, shimmer, shine, sparkle, twinkle.

n. blink, flicker, gleam, glimmering, glint, glow, grain, hint, inkling, ray, shimmer, sparkle, suggestion, trace, twinkle.

glimpse *n.* glance, gliff, glim, glisk, look, peek, peep, sight, sighting, squint.

v. descry, espy, sight, spot, spy, view.

glint *v.* flash, gleam, glimmer, glitter, reflect, shine, sparkle, twinkle.

n. flash, gleam, glimmer, glimmering, glitter, shine, sparkle, twinkle, twinkling.

glisten *v.* coruscate, flash, glance, glare, gleam, glimmer, glint, glister, glitter, scintillate, shimmer, shine, sparkle, twinkle.

glitter *v.* coruscate, flare, flash, glare, gleam, glimmer, glint, glisten, scintillate, shimmer, shine, spangle, sparkle, twinkle.

n. beam, brightness, brilliance, clinquant, display, flash, gaudiness, glamor, glare, gleam, luster, pageantry, radiance, scintillation, sheen, shimmer, shine, show, showiness, sparkle, splendor, tinsel.

gloat *v.* crow, exult, eye, glory, ogle, rejoice, relish, revel in, rub it in, triumph, vaunt.

global *adj.* all-encompassing, all-inclusive, all-out, comprehensive, encyclopedic, exhaustive, general, globular, international, pandemic, planetary, spherical, thorough, total, unbounded, universal, unlimited, world, world-wide.

antonyms limited, parochial.

globe *n.* ball, earth, orb, planet, round, roundure, sphere, world.

gloom *n.* blackness, blues, cloud, cloudiness, damp, dark, darkness, dejection, depression, desolation, despair, despondency, dimness, downheartedness, dullness, dusk, duskiness, gloominess, glumness, low spirits, melancholy, misery, murk, murkiness, obscurity, sadness, shade, shadow, sorrow, twilight, unhappiness, woe.

antonym brightness.

gloomy *adj.* bad, black, blue, chapfallen, cheerless, comfortless, crepuscular, crestfallen, dark, darksome, dejected, delightless, depressing, despondent, dim, disheartening, dismal, dispirited, dispiriting, down, down in the dumps, down in the mouth, down-beat, downcast, downhearted, dreary, dreich, dull, dusky, gloomful, glum, joyless, long-faced, long-visaged, low-spirited, melancholy, mirk(y), miserable, moody, morose, murk(y), obscure, overcast, pessimistic, sad, saddening, saturnine, sepulchral, shadowy, somber, Stygian, sullen, tenebrous.

antonym bright.

glorify *v.* adore, adorn, aggrandize, apotheosize, augment, beatify, bless, canonize, celebrate, deify, dignify, elevate, enhance, ennoble, enshrine, eulogize, exalt, extol, honor, hymn, idolize, illuminate, immortalize, laud, lift up, magnify, panegyrize, praise, raise, revere, sanctify, venerate, worship.

antonyms denounce, vilify.

glorious *adj.* beautiful, bright, brilliant, celebrated, dazzling, delightful, distinguished, divine, drunk, effulgent, elated, elevated, eminent, enjoyable, excellent, famed, famous, fine, gorgeous, grand, great, heavenly, honored, illustrious, intoxicated, magnificent, majestic, marvelous, noble, noted, pleasurable, radiant, renowned, resplendent, shining, splendid, sublime, superb, tipsy, triumphant, wonderful.

antonyms dreadful, inglorious, plain, unknown.

glory *n.* adoration, beauty, benediction, blessing, brightness, brilliance, celebrity, dignity, distinction, effulgence, eminence, exaltation, fame, gloire, gloria, gorgeousness, grandeur, gratitude, greatness, heaven, homage, honor, illustriousness, immortality, kudos, laudation, luster, magnificence, majesty, nobility, pageantry, pomp, praise, prestige, radiance, renown, resplendence, richness, splendor, sublimity, thanksgiving, triumph, veneration, worship.

antonyms blame, restraint.

v. boast, crow, delight, exult, gloat, pride oneself, rejoice, relish, revel, triumph.

gloss[1] *n.* appearance, brightness, brilliance, burnish, façade, front, gleam, luster, mask, polish, semblance, sheen, shine, show, surface, varnish, veneer, window-dressing.

gloss[2] *n.* annotation, comment, commentary, elucidation, explanation, footnote, interpretation, note, postillation, scholion, scholium, translation.

v. annotate, comment, construe, elucidate, explain, interpret, postil, postillate, translate.

glossary *n.* dictionary, idioticon, lexicon, phrase-book, vocabulary, word-book, word-list.

glossy *adj.* bright, brilliant, burnished, enameled, glacé, glassy, glazed, lustrous, polished, sheeny, shining, shiny, silken, silky, sleek, smooth.

antonym mat(t).

glow *n.* ardor, bloom, blush, brightness, brilliance, burning, earnestness, effulgence, enthusiasm, excitement, fervor, flush, gleam, glimmer, gusto, impetuosity, incandescence, intensity, lambency, light, luminosity, passion, phosphorescence, radiance, reddening, redness, rosiness, splendor, vehemence, vividness, warmth.

v. blush, brighten, burn, color, fill, flush, gleam, glimmer, glowing, radiate, redden, shine, smolder, thrill, tingle.

glower *v.* frown, glare, look daggers, lower, scowl.

n. black look, dirty look, frown, glare, look, lower, scowl, stare.

glowing *adj.* adulatory, aglow, beaming, bright, complimentary, ecstatic, enthusiastic, eulogistic, flaming, florid, flushed, gleamy, lambent, laudatory, luminous, panegyrical, rave, red, rhapsodic, rich, ruddy, suffused, vibrant, vivid, warm.

antonyms dull, restrained.

glue *n.* adhesive, cement, fish-glue, gum, isinglass, mucilage, paste, size.

v. affix, agglutinate, cement, fix, gum, paste, seal, stick.

glum *adj.* chapfallen, churlish, crabbed, crestfallen, dejected, doleful, down, gloomy, glumpish, glumpy, gruff, grumpy, ill-humored, low, moody, morose, pessimistic, saturnine, sour, sulky, sullen, surly.

antonyms ecstatic, happy.

glut *n.* excess, overabundance, oversupply, pleroma, saturation, superabundance, superfluity, surfeit, surplus.

antonyms lack, scarcity.

v. choke, clog, cram, deluge, englut, fill, flesh, flood, gorge, inundate, overfeed, overload, oversupply, sate, satiate, saturate, stuff.

glutton *n.* cormorant, free-liver, gannet, gobbler, gorger, gormandizer, gourmand, guzzler, hog, omnivore, pig, trencherman, whale.

antonym ascetic.

gluttony *n.* edacity, esurience, gormandize, gormandizing, gormandism, greed, greediness, gulosity, insatiability, omnivorousness, piggishness, rapaciousness, rapacity, voraciousness, voracity.

antonyms abstinence, asceticism.

gnarled *adj.* contorted, distorted, gnarly, gnarred, knarred, knotted, knotty, knurled, leathery, rough, rugged, twisted, weather-beaten, wrinkled.

gnaw *v.* bite, chew, consume, devour, distress, eat, erode, fret, harry, haunt, munch, nag, nibble, niggle, plague, prey, trouble, wear, worry.

go *v.* accord, advance, agree, avail, beat it, blend, chime, complement, concur, conduce, connect, contribute, correspond, decamp, decease, depart, develop, die, disappear, elapse, eventuate, expire, extend, fare, fit, flow, function, gee, happen, harmonize, incline, jib, journey, lapse, lead, lead to, leave, levant, make for, match, mosey, move, naff off, nip, operate, pass, pass away, perform, perish, proceed, progress, rate, reach, repair, result, retreat, roll, run, sally, scram, serve, shift, shove off, slip, span, spread, stretch, suit, take one's leave, tend, travel, trot, vanish, wag, walk, wend, withdraw, work.

n. animation, attempt, bid, crack, drive, dynamism, effort, energy, essay, force, get-up-and-go, life, oomph, pep, shot, spirit, stab, try, turn, verve, vigor, vim, vitality, vivacity, whack, whirl, zest.

goad *n.* fillip, impetus, incentive, incitement, irritation, jab, motivation, poke, pressure, prod, push, spur, stimulation, stimulus, thrust, urge.

v. annoy, arouse, badger, bullyrag, chivvy, drive, egg on, exasperate, exhort, harass, hassle, hector, hound, impel, incite, infuriate, instigate, irritate, lash, madden, nag, needle, persecute, prick, prod, prompt, propel, push, spur, stimulate, sting, urge, vex, worry.

go-ahead *n.* agreement, assent, authorization, clearance, consent, fiat, green light, leave, OK, permission, sanction.

antonyms ban, embargo, moratorium, veto.

adj. ambitious, avant-garde, enterprising, goey, go-getting, pioneering, progressive, up-and-coming.

antonyms sluggish, unenterprising.

goal *n.* aim, ambition, aspiration, bourn(e), design, destination, destiny, end, grail, intention, limit, mark, object, objective, purpose, target.

gobble *v.* bolt, consume, cram, devour, gorge, gulp, guttle, guzzle, hog, put away, shovel, slabber, stuff, swallow, wire into, wolf.

go-between *n.* agent, broker, contact, dealer, factor, informer, intermediary, internuncio, liaison, mediator, medium, messenger, middleman, ombudsman, pander, pimp, procuress.

goblet *n.* balloon glass, brandy-glass, chalice, drinking-cup, hanap, Paris goblet, quaich, rummer, tass, wine-glass.

goblin *n.* barghest, bogey, bogle, brownie, bugbear, demon, esprit follet, fiend, gremlin, hobgoblin, imp, kelpie, kobold, lubber fiend, nis, nix, nixie, red-cap, red-cowl, spirit, sprite.

God, god *n.* Allah, avatar, Brahma, deity, divinity, genius, Godhead, Holy One, idol, Jah, Jehovah, joss, Jove, kami, lar, Lord, Lord God, monad, Mumbo-jumbo, numen, penates, power, Providence, spirit, the Almighty, the Creator, tutelar, tutelary, Yahweh, Zeus.

godlike *adj.* celestial, deiform, divine, exalted, heavenly, saintly, sublime, superhuman, theomorphic, transcendent.

godly *adj.* blameless, devout, god-fearing, good, holy, innocent, pious, pure, religious, righteous, saintly, virtuous.

antonyms godless, impious.

golden *adj.* advantageous, aureate, auric, auspicious, best, blissful, blond(e), bright, brilliant, delightful, excellent, fair, favorable, favored, flaxen, flourishing, glorious, happy, inaurate, invaluable, joyful, lustrous, opportune, precious, priceless, promising, propitious, prosperous, resplendent, rich, rosy, shining, successful, timely, valuable, xanthous, yellow.

gone *adj.* absent, astray, away, broken, bygone, closed, concluded, consumed, dead, deceased, defunct, departed, disappeared, done, elapsed, ended, extinct, finished, kaput, lacking, lost, missed, missing, over, over and done with, past, pregnant, spent, used, vanished, wanting.

good *adj.* able, acceptable, accomplished, adept, adequate, admirable, adroit, advantageous, agreeable, altruistic, amiable, ample, appropriate, approved, approving, auspicious, authentic, balmy, beneficent, beneficial, benevolent, benign, bona fide, bonzer, boshta, bosker, bright, brotherly, budgeree, buoyant, calm, capable, capital, charitable, cheerful, choice, clear, clever, cloudless, commendable, competent, complete, congenial, considerate, convenient, convivial, correct, decorous, dependable, deserving, dexterous, dutiful, eatable, efficient, enjoyable, entire, estimable, ethical, excellent, exemplary, expert, extensive, fair, favorable, fine, first-class, first-rate, fit, fitting, friendly, full, genuine, gracious, gratifying, great, happy, healthy, helpful, honest, honorable, humane, kind, kindly, large, legitimate, long, loyal, mannerly, merciful, meritorious, mild, moral, nice, noble, nourishing, nutritious, obedient, obliging, opportune, orderly, pious, pleasant, pleasing, pleasurable, polite, positive, praiseworthy, precious, presentable, professional, proficient, profitable, proper, propitious, rattling, real, reliable, right, righteous, safe, salubrious, salutary, satisfactory, satisfying, seemly, serviceable, sizeable, skilful, skilled, solid, sound, special, splendid, substantial, sufficient, suitable, sunny, super, superior, sustaining, talented, tested, thorough, tranquil, true, trustworthy, uncorrupted, untainted, upright, useful, valid, valuable, virtuous, well-behaved, well-disposed, well-mannered, whole, wholesome, worthwhile, worthy.

n. advantage, avail, behalf, behoof, benefit, boon, convenience, excellence, gain, goodness, interest, merit, morality, probity, profit, rectitude, right, righteousness, service, uprightness, use, usefulness, virtue, weal, welfare, well-being, worth, worthiness.

good-bye *n.*, *interj.* adieu, adiós, arrivederci, au revoir, auf Wiedersehen, chin-chin, ciao, farewell, leave-taking, parting, valediction, valedictory.

good-humored *adj.* affable, amiable, approachable, blithe, cheerful, congenial, expansive, genial, good-tempered, happy, jocund, jovial, pleasant.

antonym ill-humored.

good-looking *adj.* attractive, beautiful, bonny, comely, easy on the eye, fair, handsome, personable, presentable, pretty, well-favored, well-looking, well-proportioned, well-set-up.

antonyms ill-favored, plain, ugly.

good-natured *adj.* agreeable, amenable, approachable, benevolent, broad-minded, friendly, gentle, good-hearted, helpful, kind, kind-hearted, kindly, neighborly, open-minded, sympathetic, tolerant, warm-hearted.

antonym ill-natured.

goodness *n.* advantage, altruism, beneficence, benefit, benevolence, condescension, excellence, fairness, friendliness, generosity, goodwill, graciousness, honesty, honor, humaneness, humanity, integrity, justness, kindliness, kindness, mercy, merit, morality, nourishment, nutrition, piety, probity, quality, rectitude, righteousness, salubriousness, superiority, unselfishness, uprightness, value, virtue, wholesomeness, worth.

antonyms badness, inferiority, wickedness.

goods *n.* appurtenances, bags and baggage, belongings, chattels, commodities, effects, furnishings, furniture, gear, merchandise, movables, paraphernalia, plenishing, possessions, property, stock, stuff, traps, vendibles, wares.

goodwill *n.* altruism, amity, benevolence, compassion, earnestness, favor, friendliness, friendship, generosity, heartiness, kindliness, loving-kindness, sincerity, sympathy, zeal.

antonym ill-will.

gooseflesh *n.* creeps, duck bumps, formication, goose bumps, goose-pimples, grue, heebie-jeebies, horripilation, horrors, shivers, shudders.

gore¹ *n.* blood, bloodiness, bloodshed, butchery, carnage, cruor, grume, slaughter.

gore² *v.* impale, penetrate, pierce, rend, spear, spit, stab, stick, transfix, wound.

n. flare, gair, godet, gusset.

gorge¹ *n.* abyss, barranca, canyon, chasm, cleft, clough, defile, fissure, gap, gulch, gully, pass, ravine.

gorge² *v.* bolt, cram, devour, feed, fill, fill one's face, glut, gluttonize, gobble, gormandize, gulp, guzzle, hog, make a pig of oneself, overeat, sate, satiate, stuff, surfeit, swallow, wolf.

antonym abstain.

gorgeous *adj.* attractive, beautiful, bright, brilliant, dazzling, delightful, elegant, enjoyable, exquisite, fine, flamboyant, glamorous, glittering, glorious, good, good-looking, grand, lovely, luxuriant, luxurious, magnificent, opulent, pleasing, ravishing, resplendent, rich, showy, splendid, splendiferous, stunning, sumptuous, superb.

antonyms dull, plain, seedy.

gory *adj.* blood-soaked, bloodstained, bloodthirsty, bloody, brutal, ensanguined, murderous, sanguinary, sanguineous, sanguinolent, savage.

gossamer *adj.* airy, cobwebby, delicate, diaphanous, fine, flimsy, gauzy, insubstantial, light, sheer, shimmering, silky, thin, translucent, transparent.

antonyms heavy, opaque, thick.

gossip¹ *n.* blether, bush telegraph, causerie, chinwag, chitchat, clash, clish-clash, clishmaclaver, gup, hearsay, idle talk, jaw, newsmongering, prattle, report, rumor, scandal, schmooze, small talk, tittle-tattle, yackety-yak.

gossip² *n.* babbler, blatherskite, blether, bletherskate, busybody, chatterbox, chatterer, gossip-monger, newsmonger, nosy parker, prattler, quidnunc, rumorer, scandalmonger, tabby, talebearer, tattler, telltale, whisperer.

v. blather, blether, bruit, chat, clash, gabble, jaw, prattle, rumor, tattle, tell tales, whisper.

gouge *v.* chisel, claw, cut, dig, extract, force, gash, grave, groove, hack, hollow, incise, scoop, score, scratch, slash.

n. cut, furrow, gash, groove, hack, hollow, incision, notch, scoop, score, scratch, slash, trench.

gourmand *n.* cormorant, free-liver, gannet, glutton, gorger, gormandizer, guzzler, hog, omnivore, pig, trencherman, whale.

antonym ascetic.

gourmet *n.* arbiter elegantiae, arbiter elegantiarum, bon vivant, bon viveur, connoisseur, dainty eater, epicure, epicurean, gastronome, gastronomer, gastrosoph, gastrosopher.

antonym omnivore.

govern *v.* administer, allay, bridle, check, command, conduct, contain, control, curb, decide, determine, direct, discipline, guide, influence, inhibit, lead, manage, master, order, oversee, pilot, preside, quell, regulate, reign, restrain, rule, steer, subdue, superintend, supervise, sway, tame, underlie.

government n. administration, authority, charge, command, conduct, control, direction, domination, dominion, Establishment, executive, governance, guidance, kingcraft, law, management, ministry, polity, powers-that-be, raj, régime, regimen, regulation, restraint, rule, sovereignty, state, statecraft, superintendence, supervision, surveillance, sway.

governor n. adelantado, administrator, alcalde, alderman, boss, chief, commander, commissioner, comptroller, controller, corrector, director, executive, gubernator, hakim, head, leader, manager, naik, overseer, ruler, superintendent, supervisor, vali.

gown n. costume, creation, dress, dressing-gown, frock, garb, garment, habit, kirtle, négligé, robe.

grab v. affect, annex, appropriate, bag, capture, catch, catch hold of, clutch, collar, commandeer, grasp, grip, impress, latch on to, nab, pluck, ramp, rap, seize, snap up, snatch, strike, usurp.

grace[1] n. attractiveness, beauty, benefaction, beneficence, benevolence, benignity, benison, breeding, charity, charm, clemency, comeliness, compassion, compassionateness, consideration, courtesy, cultivation, decency, decorum, deftness, ease, elegance, eloquence, etiquette, favor, finesse, fluency, forgiveness, generosity, goodness, goodwill, gracefulness, graciousness, indulgence, kindliness, kindness, leniency, lenity, love, loveliness, mannerliness, manners, mercifulness, mercy, merit, pardon, pleasantness, poise, polish, propriety, quarter, refinement, reprieve, shapeliness, tact, tastefulness, unction, virtue.

v. adorn, beautify, bedeck, deck, decorate, dignify, distinguish, dress, elevate, embellish, enhance, enrich, favor, garnish, glorify, honor, ornament, prettify, set off, trim.

antonyms deface, detract from, spoil.

grace[2] n. benediction, benedictus, blessing, consecration, prayer, thanks, thanksgiving.

graceful adj. agile, balletic, beautiful, becoming, charming, comely, deft, easy, elegant, facile, feat, feline, fine, flowing, fluid, gainly, genty, gracile, lightsome, natural, pleasing, pliant, slender, smooth, suave, supple, tasteful, willowish, willowy.

antonym graceless.

gracious adj. accommodating, affable, affluent, amenable, amiable, beneficent, benevolent, benign, benignant, charitable, chivalrous, civil, compassionate, complaisant, condescending, considerate, cordial, courteous, courtly, elegant, friendly, grand, hospitable, indulgent, kind, kindly, lenient, loving, luxurious, merciful, mild, obliging, pleasant, pleasing, polite, refined, sweet, well-mannered.

antonym ungracious.

grade n. acclivity, bank, brand, category, class, condition, dan, declivity, degree, downgrade, echelon, gradation, gradient, group, hill, incline, level, mark, notch, order, place, position, quality, rank, rise, rung, size, slope, stage, station, step, upgrade.

v. arrange, blend, brand, categorize, class, classify, docket, evaluate, group, label, mark, order, pigeonhole, range, rank, rate, shade, size, sort, type, value.

gradual adj. cautious, continuous, deliberate, even, gentle, graduated, leisurely, measured, moderate, piecemeal, progressive, regular, slow, steady, step-by-step, successive, unhurried.

antonyms precipitate, sudden.

graduate[1] v. arrange, calibrate, classify, grade, group, make the grade, mark off, measure out, order, pass, proportion, qualify, range, rank, regulate, sort.

graduate[2] n. alumna, alumnus, bachelor, diplomate, diplômé, diplômée, doctor, fellow, graduand, licentiate, literate, master, member.

graft n. bud, engraft, engraftation, engraftment, heteroplasty, imp, implant, implantation, insert, scion, shoot, splice, sprout, transplant.

v. engraft, implant, insert, join, splice, transplant.

grain n. atom, bit, cereals, corn, crumb, doit, fiber, fragment, granule, grist, grits, iota, jot, kernel, marking, mite, modicum, molecule, morsel, mote, nap, ounce, panic, particle, pattern, piece, scintilla, scrap, scruple, seed, smidgeon, spark, speck, surface, suspicion, texture, trace, weave, whit.

grand adj. A1, admirable, affluent, ambitious, august, chief, condescending, dignified, elevated, eminent, exalted, excellent, fine, first-class, first-rate, glorious, gracious, grandiose, great, haughty, head, highest, illustrious, imperious, imposing, impressive, large, leading, lofty, lordly, luxurious, magnificent, main, majestic, marvelous, monumental, noble, opulent, ostentatious, outstanding, palatial, patronizing, pompous, pre-eminent, pretentious, princely, principal, regal, senior, smashing, splendid, stately, striking, sublime, sumptuous, super, superb, supreme, wonderful.

grandeur n. augustness, dignity, graciousness, gravitas, greatness, hauteur, imperiousness, importance, loftiness, magnificence, majesty, morgue, nobility, pomp, splendor, state, stateliness, sublimity.

antonyms humbleness, lowliness, simplicity.

grandiose adj. affected, ambitious, bombastic, euphuistic, extravagant, flamboyant, grand, high-flown, imposing, impressive, lofty, magnificent, majestic, monumental, ostentatious, pompous, ponderous, pretentious, showy, stately, Wagnerian, weighty.

antonym unpretentious.

grant v. accede to, accord, acknowledge, admit, agree to, allocate, allot, allow, apportion, assign, award, bestow, cede, concede, confer, consent to, convey, deign, dispense, donate, give, impart, permit, present, provide, transfer, transmit, vouchsafe, yield.

antonyms deny, refuse.

n. accord, admission, allocation, allotment, allowance, annuity, award, benefaction, bequest, boon, bounty, bursary, concession, donation, endowment, gift, honorarium, present, scholarship, subsidy, subvention.

granular adj. crumbly, grainy, granulase, granulated, granulous, gravelly, gritty, murly, rough, sabulose, sabulous, sandy.

graphic adj. blow-by-blow, clear, cogent, delineated, delineative, descriptive, detailed, diagrammatic, drawn, explicit, expressive, forcible, illustrative, lively, lucid, pictorial, picturesque, representational, seen, specific, striking, telling, visible, visual, vivid.

antonyms impressionistic, vague.

grapple v. attack, battle, catch, clash, clasp, clinch, close, clutch, combat, come to grips, confront, contend, cope, deal with, encounter, engage, face, fasten, fight, grab, grasp, grip, gripe, hold, hug, lay hold, make fast, seize, snatch, struggle, tackle, tussle, wrestle.

antonyms avoid, evade.

grasping *adj.* acquisitive, avaricious, close-fisted, covetous, greedy, mean, mercenary, miserly, niggardly, parsimonious, penny-pinching, rapacious, selfish, stingy, tight-fisted, usurious.

antonym generous.

grass² *n.* ganja, hash, hay, hemp, joint, marijuana, pot, reefer.

grate *v.* aggravate, annoy, chafe, comminute, creak, exasperate, fret, gall, get on one's nerves, granulate, gride, grind, irk, irritate, jar, mince, nettle, peeve, pulverize, rankle, rasp, rub, scrape, scratch, set one's teeth on edge, shred, triturate, vex.

grateful *adj.* appreciative, aware, beholden, indebted, mindful, obligated, obliged, sensible, thankful.

antonym ungrateful.

gratify *v.* appease, cater to, content, delight, favor, fulfil, gladden, humor, indulge, pander to, please, pleasure, recompense, requite, satisfy, thrill.

antonyms frustrate, thwart.

grating¹ *adj.* annoying, cacophonous, disagreeable, discordant, displeasing, grinding, harsh, horrisonant, irksome, irritating, jarring, rasping, raucous, scraping, squeaky, strident, unharmonious, unmelodious, unpleasant, vexatious.

antonyms harmonious, pleasing.

grating² *n.* grid, grill, grille, hack, heck, lattice, latticework, treillage, treille, trellis, trelliswork.

gratitude *n.* acknowledgment, appreciation, awareness, gratefulness, indebtedness, mindfulness, obligation, recognition, thankfulness, thanks.

antonym ingratitude.

gratuity *n.* baksheesh, beer-money, benefaction, bonus, boon, bounty, dash, donation, donative, douceur, drink-money, gift, lagniappe, largess, perquisite, pourboire, present, recompense, reward, tip, Trinkgeld.

grave¹ *n.* barrow, burial-place, burying-place, cairn, cist, crypt, long home, mausoleum, pit, sepulcher, tomb, vault.

grave² *adj.* acute, Catonian, critical, crucial, dangerous, depressing, dignified, disquieting, dour, dull, earnest, exigent, gloomy, grim, grim-faced, hazardous, heavy, important, leaden, long-faced, momentous, muted, perilous, ponderous, preoccupied, pressing, quiet, reserved, restrained, sad, sage, saturnine, sedate, serious, severe, significant, sober, solemn, somber, staid, subdued, thoughtful, threatening, unsmiling, urgent, vital, weighty.

antonyms cheerful, light, slight, trivial.

gravel *n.* chesil, grail, hogging, shingle.

gravitate *v.* descend, drop, fall, head for, incline, lean, move, precipitate, settle, sink, tend.

gravity *n.* acuteness, consequence, demureness, dignity, earnestness, exigency, gloom, gravitas, grimness, hazardousness, importance, magnitude, moment, momentousness, perilousness, ponderousness, reserve, restraint, sedateness, seriousness, severity, significance, sobriety, solemnity, somberness, thoughtfulness, urgency, weightiness.

antonyms gaiety, levity, triviality.

gray *adj.* aged, ancient, anonymous, ashen, bloodless, characterless, cheerless, cloudy, colorless, dark, depressing, dim, dismal, drab, dreary, dull, elderly,

experienced, glaucous, gloomy, grège, greige, griseous, grizzle, grizzled, hoar, hoary, indistinct, leaden, liard, livid, mature, murksome, murky, neutral, old, overcast, pale, pallid, sunless, uncertain, unclear, unidentifiable, venerable, wan.

graze¹ *v.* batten, browse, crop, feed, fodder, pasture.

graze² *v.* abrade, bark, brush, chafe, gride, rub, scart, score, scotch, scrape, scratch, shave, skim, skin, touch.

n. abrasion, score, scrape, scratch.

grease *n.* dope, dripping, fat, gunge, lard, oil, ointment, sebum, tallow, unction, unguent, wax.

greasy *adj.* fatty, fawning, glib, groveling, ingratiating, lardy, oily, oleaginous, sebaceous, slick, slimy, slippery, smarmy, smeary, smooth, sycophantic, tallowy, toadying, unctuous, waxy.

great *adj.* able, ace, active, adept, admirable, adroit, august, big, bulky, capital, celebrated, chief, colossal, consequential, considerable, crack, critical, crucial, decided, devoted, dignified, distinguished, eminent, enormous, enthusiastic, exalted, excellent, excessive, expert, extended, extensive, extravagant, extreme, fab, fabulous, famed, famous, fantastic, fine, finished, first-rate, generous, gigantic, glorious, good, grand, grave, great-hearted, grievous, heavy, heroic, high, high-minded, huge, idealistic, illustrious, immense, important, impressive, inordinate, invaluable, jake, keen, large, leading, lengthy, lofty, long, magnanimous, main, major, mammoth, manifold, marked, marvelous, massive, masterly, momentous, multitudinous, munificent, noble, nonpareil, notable, noteworthy, noticeable, outstanding, paramount, ponderous, precious, pre-eminent, priceless, primary, princely, principal, prodigious, proficient, prolific, prolonged, prominent, pronounced, protracted, remarkable, renowned, senior, serious, significant, skilful, skilled, strong, stupendous, sublime, superb, superior, superlative, swingeing, talented, terrific, tremendous, valuable, vast, virtuoso, voluminous, weighty, wonderful, zealous.

antonyms insignificant, pusillanimous, small, unimportant.

greed *n.* acquisitiveness, anxiety, avidity, covetousness, craving, cupidity, desire, eagerness, edacity, esurience, esuriency, gluttony, gormandizing, gormandism, gourmandize, greediness, gulosity, hunger, insatiability, insatiableness, itchy palm, land-hunger, longing, plutolatry, rapacity, ravenousness, selfishness, voraciousness, voracity.

antonym abstemiousness.

greedy *adj.* acquisitive, anxious, avaricious, avid, covetous, craving, curious, desirous, eager, edacious, esurient, gare, gluttonish, gluttonous, gormandizing, grasping, gripple, gutsy, hoggery, hoggish, hungry, impatient, insatiable, itchy-palmed, land-grabbing, piggish, rapacious, ravenous, selfish, ventripotent, voracious.

antonym abstemious.

green *adj.* blooming, budding, callow, covetous, credulous, emerald, envious, flourishing, fresh, glaucous, grassy, grudging, gullible, ignorant, ill, immature, inexperienced, inexpert, ingenuous, innocent, jealous, leafy, naive, nauseous, new, pale, pliable, raw, recent, resentful, sick, starry-eyed, supple, tender, unhealthy, unpracticed, unripe, unseasoned, unsophisticated, untrained, untried, unversed, verdant, verdurous, vert, virescent, virid, viridescent, vitreous, wan, wet behind the ears, young.

n. common, grass, greensward, lawn, sward, turf.

reenhorn *n.* apprentice, beginner, catechumen, fledgling, ignoramus, ingénue, initiate, Johnnie raw, learner, naïf, neophyte, newcomer, novice, novitiate, recruit, rookie, simpleton, tenderfoot, tyro.

antonyms old hand, veteran.

reenhouse *n.* conservatory, glasshouse, hothouse, nursery, pavilion, vinery.

reet *v.* accost, acknowledge, address, compliment, hail, hallo, halloo, meet, receive, salute, wave to, welcome.

antonym ignore.

regarious *adj.* affable, chummy, companionable, convivial, cordial, extrovert, friendly, outgoing, pally, sociable, social, warm.

antonym unsociable.

grief *n.* ache, affliction, agony, anguish, bereavement, blow, burden, dejection, desiderium, desolation, distress, dole, grievance, heartache, heartbreak, lamentation, misery, mournfulness, mourning, pain, regret, remorse, sadness, sorrow, suffering, tragedy, trial, tribulation, trouble, woe.

antonym happiness.

grief-stricken *adj.* afflicted, agonized, broken, brokenhearted, crushed, dejection, desiderium, desolation, dressolate, distracted, grieving, heartbroken, inconsolable, mourning, overcome, overwhelmed, sad, sorrowful, sorrowing, stricken, unhappy, woebegone, wretched.

antonym overjoyed.

grievance *n.* affliction, beef, bitch, charge, complaint, damage, distress, gravamen, grief, gripe, grouse, hardship, injury, injustice, moan, peeve, resentment, sorrow, trial, tribulation, trouble, unhappiness, wrong.

grieve *v.* ache, afflict, agonize, bemoan, bewail, complain, crush, cut to the quick, deplore, distress, disturb, eat one's heart out, harrow, hurt, injure, lament, mourn, pain, regret, rue, sadden, sorrow, suffer, upset, wail, weep, wound.

grieved *adj.* abashed, affronted, ashamed, desolated, displeased, distressed, horrified, hurt, injured, offended, pained, sad, saddened, shocked, sorry, upset, wounded.

grievous *adj.* appalling, atrocious, burdensome, calamitous, damaging, deplorable, devastating, distressing, dreadful, flagrant, glaring, grave, harmful, heart-rending, heavy, heinous, hurtful, injurious, intolerable, lamentable, monstrous, mournful, offensive, oppressive, outrageous, overwhelming, painful, pitiful, plightful, severe, shameful, shocking, sorrowful, tragic, unbearable, wounding.

grim *adj.* adamant, cruel, doom-laden, dour, fearsome, ferocious, fierce, forbidding, formidable, frightening, frightful, ghastly, grisly, gruesome, harsh, hideous, horrible, horrid, implacable, merciless, morose, relentless, repellent, resolute, ruthless, severe, shocking, sinister, stern, sullen, surly, terrible, unpleasant, unrelenting, unwelcome, unyielding.

antonyms benign, congenial, pleasant.

grimace *n.* face, fit of the face, frown, moue, mouth, pout, scowl, smirk, sneer, wry face.

v. fleer, frown, girn, make a face, mop, mop and mow, mouth, mow, mug, pout, scowl, smirk, sneer.

grimy *adj.* begrimed, besmeared, besmirched, contaminated, dirty, filthy, foul, grubby, murky, reechy, smudgy, smutty, soiled, sooty, squalid.

antonyms clean, pure.

grind *v.* abrade, beaver, bray, comminute, crush, drudge, file, gnash, granulate, grate, grit, kibble, labor, levigate, lucubrate, mill, polish, pound, powder, pulverize, sand, scrape, sharpen, slave, smooth, sweat, swot, toil, triturate, whet.

n. chore, drudgery, exertion, grindstone, labor, round, routine, slavery, sweat, task, toil.

grip *n.* acquaintance, clasp, clutches, comprehension, control, domination, embrace, grasp, handclasp, hold, influence, keeping, mastery, perception, possession, power, purchase, sway, tenure, understanding.

v. absorb, catch, clasp, clutch, compel, divert, engross, enthrall, entrance, fascinate, grasp, hold, involve, latch on to, mesmerize, rivet, seize, spellbind, thrill, vice.

gripe *v.* beef, bellyache, bitch, carp, complain, groan, grouch, grouse, grumble, moan, nag, whine, whinge.

n. ache, aching, affliction, beef, bitch, colic, collywobbles, complaint, cramps, distress, grievance, griping, groan, grouch, grouse, grumble, moan, objection, pain, pang, pinching, spasm, stomach-ache, twinge.

grit[1] *n.* chesil, dust, grail, gravel, hogging, pebbles, sand, shingle, swarf.

v. clench, gnash, grate, grind, lock.

grit[2] backbone, bottle, bravery, courage, determination, doggedness, foison, fortitude, fushion, gameness, guts, hardihood, mettle, nerve, perseverance, pluck, resolution, spine, spirit, spunk, stamina, staying power, tenacity, toughness.

groan *n.* complaint, cry, moan, objection, outcry, protest, sigh, wail.

antonym cheer.

v. complain, cry, lament, moan, object, protest, sigh, wail.

antonym cheer.

groggy *adj.* befuddled, confused, dazed, dizzy, dopey, faint, fuddled, knocked-up, muzzy, punch-drunk, reeling, shaky, stunned, stupefied, unsteady, weak, wobbly, woozy.

antonym lucid.

groom *v.* brush, clean, coach, curry, dress, drill, educate, neaten, nurture, preen, prepare, prime, primp, prink, ready, school, smarten, spruce up, tart up, tend, tidy, titivate, train, turn out, tutor.

groove *n.* canal, cannelure, chamfer, channel, chase, cut, cutting, flute, furrow, gutter, hollow, indentation, kerf, rabbet, rebate, rigol, rut, score, scrobe, sulcus, trench, vallecula.

antonym ridge.

grope *v.* cast about, feel, feel about, feel up, finger, fish, flounder, fumble, goose, grabble, probe, scrabble, search.

gross[1] *adj.* apparent, arrant, bawdy, bestial, big, blatant, blue, boorish, broad, brutish, bulky, callous, coarse, colossal, corpulent, crass, crude, cumbersome, dense, downright, dull, earthy, egregious, fat, flagrant, foul, glaring, great, grievous, heavy, heinous, huge, hulking, ignorant, immense, imperceptive, improper, impure, indecent, indelicate, insensitive, large, lewd, low, lumpish, manifest, massive, obese, obscene, obtuse, obvious, offensive, outrageous, outright, overweight, plain, rank, ribald, rude, sensual, serious, shameful, shameless, sheer, shocking, slow, sluggish, smutty,

tasteless, thick, uncivil, uncouth, uncultured, undiscriminating, undisguised, unfeeling, unmitigated, unseemly, unsophisticated, unwieldy, utter, vulgar.
antonyms delicate, fine, seemly, slight.

gross² *n.* aggregate, bulk, entirety, sum, total, totality, whole.
adj. aggregate, all-inclusive, complete, entire, inclusive, total, whole.
v. accumulate, aggregate, bring, earn, make, rake in, take, total.

grotesque *adj.* absurd, antic, bizarre, deformed, distorted, extravagant, fanciful, fantastic, freakish, gruesome, hideous, incongruous, laughable, ludicrous, macabre, malformed, misshapen, monstrous, odd, outlandish, preposterous, ridiculous, rococo, strange, ugly, unnatural, unsightly, weird.
n. bizarrerie, extravaganza, fantastic figure, gargoyle, gobbo, grotesquerie, manikin.

grotto *n.* catacomb, cave, cavern, chamber, dene-hole, grot, souterrain, subterranean (chamber), subterrene, underground chamber.

grouch *v.* beef, bellyache, bitch, carp, complain, find fault, gripe, grouse, grumble, moan, whine, whinge.
antonym acquiesce.
n. belly-acher, churl, complainer, complaint, crab, crosspatch, crotcheteer, curmudgeon, fault-finder, grievance, gripe, grouse, grouser, grumble, grumbler, malcontent, moan, moaner, murmer, murmurer, mutterer, objection, whiner, whinge, whinger.

grouchy *adj.* bad-tempered, cantankerous, captious, churlish, complaining, cross, crotchety, discontented, dissatisfied, grumbling, grumpy, ill-tempered, irascible, irritable, mutinous, peevish, petulant, querulous, sulky, surly, testy, truculent.
antonym contented.

ground *n.* arena, background, ball-park, bottom, clay, clod, deck, dirt, dry land, dust, earth, field, foundation, land, loam, mold, park, pitch, sod, soil, solum, stadium, surface, terra firma, terrain, turf.
v. acquaint with, base, build up, coach, drill, establish, familiarize with, fix, found, inform, initiate, instruct, introduce, prepare, set, settle, teach, train, tutor.

groundless *adj.* absurd, baseless, chimerical, empty, false, gratuitous, idle, illusory, imaginary, irrational, unauthorized, uncalled-for, unfounded, unjustified, unproven, unprovoked, unreasonable, unsubstantiated, unsupported, unwarranted.
antonyms justified, reasonable.

grounds¹ *n.* acres, area, country, district, domain, estate, fields, gardens, habitat, holding, land, park, property, realm, surroundings, terrain, territory, tract.

grounds² *n.* account, argument, base, basis, call, cause, excuse, factor, foundation, inducement, justification, motive, occasion, premise, pretext, principle, rationale, reason, score, vindication.

grounds³ *n.* deposit, dregs, grouts, lees, precipitate, precipitation, sediment, settlings.

groundwork *n.* base, basis, cornerstone, essentials, footing, foundation, fundamentals, homework, preliminaries, preparation, research, spadework, underpinnings.

group *n.* accumulation, aggregation, assemblage, association, band, batch, bracket, bunch, category, caucus, circle, class, classification, classis, clique, clump, cluster, clutch, cohort, collection, collective, combination, company, conclave, conglomeration, congregation, constellation, core, coterie, covey, crowd, detachment, faction, formation, front, galère, gang, gathering, Gemeinschaft, genus, grouping, knot, lot, nexus, organization, pack, parti, party, pop-group, set, shower, species, squad, squadron, team, troop.
v. arrange, assemble, associate, assort, band, bracket, categorize, class, classify, cluster, collect, congregate, consort, deploy, dispose, fraternize, gather, get together, link, marshal, mass, order, organize, range, sort.

grouse *v.* beef, belly-ache, bitch, carp, complain, find fault, fret, fuss, gripe, grouch, grumble, moan, mutter, whine, whinge.
antonym acquiesce.
n. belly-ache, complaint, grievance, gripe, grouch, grumble, moan, murmur, mutter, objection, peeve, whine, whinge.

grovel *v.* abase oneself, backscratch, bootlick, cower, crawl, creep, cringe, crouch, defer, demean oneself, fawn, flatter, kowtow, sneak, sycophantize, toady.

groveling *adj.* backscratching, bootlicking, fawning, flattering, ingratiating, obsequious, sycophantic, wormy.
antonyms outspoken, straightforward.

grow *v.* advance, arise, augment, become, branch out, breed, broaden, burgeon, cultivate, develop, diversify, enlarge, evolve, expand, extend, farm, flourish, flower, germinate, get, heighten, improve, increase, issue, mature, multiply, nurture, originate, produce, progress, proliferate, propagate, prosper, raise, ripen, rise, shoot, spread, spring, sprout, stem, stretch, succeed, swell, thicken, thrive, turn, vegetate, wax, widen.
antonyms decrease, fail, halt.

grown-up *adj.* adult, full-grown, fully-fledged, fully-grown, mature, of age.
antonyms childish, immature.
n. adult, gentleman, lady, man, woman.
antonym child.

growth *n.* accrescence, accretion, advance, advancement, aggrandizement, augmentation, auxesis, broadening, change, crop, cultivation, development, diversification, enlargement, evolution, excrement, excrescence, expansion, extension, flowering, gall, germination, growing, heightening, improvement, increase, intumescence, lump, maturation, multiplication, outgrowth, produce, production, progress, proliferation, prosperity, protuberance, ripening, rise, shooting, sprouting, stretching, success, swelling, thickening, transformation, tumor, vegetation, waxing, widening.
antonyms decrease, failure, stagnation, stoppage.

grub¹ *v.* burrow, delve, dig, explore, ferret, forage, grout, hunt, investigate, nose, probe, pull up, root, rootle, rummage, scour, uproot.
n. caterpillar, chrysalis, larva, maggot, nymph, pupa, worm.

grub² *n.* chow, commons, eats, edibles, fodder, food, nosh, provisions, rations, scoff, sustenance, victuals.

grubby *adj.* crummy, dirty, filthy, fly-blown, frowzy, grimy, manky, mean, messy, mucky, scruffy, seedy, shabby, slovenly, smutty, soiled, sordid, squalid, unkempt, untidy, unwashed.
antonyms clean, smart.

grudge *n.* animosity, animus, antagonism, antipathy, aversion, bitterness, dislike, enmity, envy, grievance, hard feelings, hate, ill-will, jealousy, malevolence, malice, pique, rancor, resentment, spite.

antonyms favor, regard.

v. begrudge, covet, dislike, envy, mind, niggard, object to, regret, repine, resent, stint, take exception to.
antonyms applaud, approve.

grueling *adj.* arduous, backbreaking, brutal, crushing, demanding, difficult, exhausting, fatiguing, fierce, grinding, hard, hard-going, harsh, laborious, punishing, severe, stern, stiff, strenuous, taxing, tiring, tough, trying, uphill, wearing, wearying.
antonym easy.

gruesome *adj.* abominable, awful, chilling, eldritch, fearful, fearsome, ghastly, grim, grisly, grooly, hideous, horrible, horrid, horrific, horrifying, loathsome, macabre, monstrous, repellent, repugnant, repulsive, shocking, sick, spine-chilling, terrible, weird.
antonyms charming, congenial.

gruff *adj.* abrupt, bad-tempered, bearish, blunt, brusque, churlish, crabbed, croaking, crusty, curt, discourteous, gravelly, grouchy, grumpy, guttural, harsh, hoarse, husky, ill-humored, ill-natured, impolite, low, rasping, rough, rude, sour, sullen, surly, throaty, uncivil, ungracious, unmannerly.
antonyms clear, courteous, sweet.

grumble *v.* beef, bellyache, bitch, bleat, carp, chunter, complain, croak, find fault, gripe, grouch, grouse, growl, gurgle, moan, murmur, mutter, nark, repine, roar, rumble, whine.
antonym acquiesce.

n. beef, bitch, bleat, complaint, grievance, gripe, grouch, grouse, growl, gurgle, moan, murmur, muttering, objection, roar, rumble, whinge.

grumpy *adj.* bad-tempered, cantankerous, churlish, crabbed, cross, crotchety, discontented, grouchy, grumbling, ill-tempered, irritable, mutinous, peevish, petulant, querulous, sulky, sullen, surly, testy, truculent.
antonyms civil, contented.

guarantee *n.* assurance, attestation, bond, certainty, collateral, covenant, earnest, endorsement, guaranty, insurance, oath, pledge, promise, security, surety, testimonial, undertaking, voucher, warranty, word, word of honor.

v. answer for, assure, avouch, certify, ensure, insure, maintain, make certain, make sure of, pledge, promise, protect, secure, swear, underwrite, vouch for, warrant.

guarantor *n.* angel, backer, bailsman, bondsman, covenanter, guarantee, referee, sponsor, supporter, surety, underwriter, voucher, warrantor.

guard *v.* be on the qui vive, be on the watch, beware, conserve, cover, defend, escort, keep, look out, mind, oversee, patrol, police, preserve, protect, safeguard, save, screen, secure, sentinel, shelter, shield, supervise, tend, ward, watch.

n. attention, backstop, barrier, buffer, bulwark, bumper, care, caution, convoy, custodian, defense, defender, escort, guarantee, heed, lookout, minder, pad, patrol, picket, precaution, protection, protector, rampart, safeguard, screen, security, sentinel, sentry, shield, vigilance, wall, warder, wariness, watch, watchfulness, watchman.

guarded *adj.* cagey, careful, cautious, circumspect, discreet, disingenuous, non-committal, prudent, reserved, restrained, reticent, secretive, suspicious, uncommunicative, unforthcoming, wary, watchful.
antonyms frank, whole-hearted.

guardian *n.* attendant, champion, conservator, curator, custodian, defender, depositary, depository, escort, fiduciary, guard, keeper, minder, preserver, protector, trustee, warden, warder.

guess *v.* assume, believe, conjecture, dare say, deem, divine, estimate, fancy, fathom, feel, guesstimate, hazard, hypothesize, imagine, intuit, judge, opine, penetrate, predict, reckon, solve, speculate, suppose, surmise, suspect, think, work out.

n. assumption, belief, conjecture, fancy, feeling, guesstimate, hypothesis, intuition, judgment, notion, opinion, prediction, reckoning, shot (in the dark), speculation, supposition, surmise, suspicion, theory.

guest *n.* boarder, caller, company, freeloader, habitué, lodger, parasite, regular, roomer, visitant, visitor.

guide *v.* accompany, advise, attend, command, conduct, control, convoy, counsel, direct, educate, escort, govern, handle, head, influence, instruct, lead, manage, maneuver, oversee, pilot, point, regulate, rule, shape, shepherd, steer, superintend, supervise, sway, teach, train, usher, vector.

n. ABC, adviser, attendant, beacon, catalog, chaperon, cicerone, clue, companion, conductor, controller, counselor, courier, criterion, director, directory, dragoman, escort, example, exemplar, guide-book, guideline, handbook, ideal, index, indication, informant, inspiration, instructions, key, landmark, leader, lodestar, manual, mark, marker, master, mentor, model, monitor, paradigm, pilot, pointer, praxis, sign, signal, signpost, standard, steersman, teacher, template, usher, vade-mecum.

guild *n.* association, brotherhood, chapel, club, company, corporation, fellowship, fraternity, incorporation, league, lodge, order, organization, society, union.

guile *n.* art, artfulness, artifice, cleverness, craft, craftiness, cunning, deceit, deception, deviousness, disingenuity, duplicity, gamesmanship, knavery, ruse, slyness, treachery, trickery, trickiness, wiliness.
antonyms artlessness, guilelessness.

guileless *adj.* artless, candid, direct, frank, genuine, honest, ingenuous, innocent, naïve, natural, open, simple, sincere, straightforward, transparent, trusting, truthful, unreserved, unsophisticated, unworldly.
antonyms artful, guileful.

guilt *n.* blamability, blame, blameworthiness, compunction, conscience, contrition, criminality, culpability, delinquency, disgrace, dishonor, guiltiness, guilty conscience, infamy, iniquity, mens rea, regret, remorse, responsibility, self-condemnation, self-reproach, self-reproof, shame, sinfulness, stigma, wickedness, wrong.
antonyms innocence, shamelessness.

guilty *adj.* ashamed, blamable, blameworthy, compunctious, conscience-stricken, contrite, convicted, criminal, culpable, delinquent, errant, erring, evil, felonious, guilt-ridden, hangdog, illicit, iniquitous, nefarious, nocent, offending, penitent, regretful, remorseful, repentant, reprehensible, responsible, rueful, shamefaced, sheepish, sinful, sorry, wicked, wrong.
antonyms guiltless, innocent.

guise *n.* air, appearance, aspect, behavior, custom, demeanor, disguise, dress, façade, face, fashion, features, form, front, likeness, manner, mask, mode, pretense, semblance, shape, show.

gulf *n.* abyss, basin, bay, bight, breach, chasm, cleft, gap, gorge, opening, rent, rift, separation, split, void, whirlpool.

gullible *adj.* born yesterday, credulous, foolish, glaikit, green, innocent, naïve, trusting, unsuspecting, verdant.
antonym astute.

gully *n.* channel, ditch, donga, geo, gio, gulch, gutter, ravine, watercourse.

gulp *v.* bolt, choke, devour, gasp, gobble, gollop, gormandize, guzzle, knock back, quaff, stifle, stuff, swallow, swig, swill, toss off, wolf.
antonyms nibble, sip.
n. draft, mouthful, slug, swallow, swig.

gun *n.* equalizer, gat, heater, peacemaker, persuader, piece, pistol, shooter, shooting-iron, tool.

gush *v.* babble, blather, burst, cascade, chatter, drivel, effuse, enthuse, flood, flow, jabber, jet, pour, run, rush, spout, spurt, stream, yatter.
n. babble, burst, cascade, chatter, ebullition, effusion, eruption, exuberance, flood, flow, jet, outburst, outflow, rush, spout, spurt, stream, tide, torrent.

gust *n.* blast, blow, breeze, burst, flaught, flaw, flurry, gale, puff, rush, squall, williwaw.
v. blast, blow, bluster, breeze, puff, squall.

gutter *n.* channel, conduit, ditch, drain, duct, grip, kennel, pipe, rigol(l), sluice, trench, trough, tube.

gypsy *n.* Bohemian, diddicoy, faw, gipsy, gitana, gitano, nomad, rambler, roamer, Romany, rover, tink, tinker, traveler, tsigane, tzigany, vagabond, vagrant, wanderer, Zigeuner, Zincalo, Zingaro.

H

habit[1] *n.* accustomedness, addiction, assuetude, bent, constitution, convention, custom, dependence, diathesis, disposition, fixation, frame of mind, habitude, inclination, make-up, manner, mannerism, mode, mores, nature, obsession, practice, proclivity, propensity, quirk, routine, rule, second nature, tendency, usage, vice, way, weakness, wont.

habit[2] *n.* apparel, attire, clothes, clothing, dress, garb, garment, habiliment.

habitation *n.* abode, cottage, domicile, dwelling, dwelling-place, home, house, hut, inhabitance, inhabitancy, inhabitation, living quarters, lodging, mansion, occupancy, occupation, quarters, residence, tenancy.

habitual *adj.* accustomed, chronic, common, confirmed, constant, customary, established, familiar, fixed, frequent, hardened, ingrained, inveterate, natural, normal, ordinary, persistent, recurrent, regular, routine, standard, traditional, usual, wonted.
antonym occasional.

habituate *v.* acclimatize, accustom, break in, condition, discipline, familiarize, harden, inure, school, season, tame, train.

hack[1] *v.* bark, chop, cough, cut, gash, haggle, hew, kick, lacerate, mangle, mutilate, notch, rasp, slash.
n. bark, chop, cough, cut, gash, notch, rasp, slash.

hack[2] *adj.* banal, hackneyed, mediocre, pedestrian, poor, stereotyped, tired, undistinguished, uninspired, unoriginal.

n. crock, drudge, horse, jade, journalist, nag, paperstainer, penny-a-liner, scribbler, slave.

hackneyed *adj.* banal, clichéd, common, commonplace, corny, hack, hand-me-down, overworked, pedestrian, percoct, played-out, run-of-the-mill, second-hand, stale, stereotyped, stock, threadbare, time-worn, tired, trite, unoriginal, worn-out.
antonyms arresting, new.

hag *n.* battle-ax, beldame, crone, fury, harpy, harridan, ogress, shrew, termagant, virago, vixen, witch.

haggard *adj.* cadaverous, careworn, drawn, emaciated, gaunt, ghastly, hagged, hollow-eyed, pinched, shrunken, thin, wan, wasted, wrinkled.
antonym hale.

haggle *v.* bargain, barter, bicker, cavil, chaffer, dicker, dispute, higgle, palter, quarrel, squabble, wrangle.

hail[1] *n.* barrage, bombardment, rain, shower, storm, torrent, volley.
v. assail, barrage, batter, bombard, pelt, rain, shower, storm, volley.

hail[2] *v.* acclaim, accost, acknowledge, address, applaud, call, cheer, exalt, flag down, glorify, greet, halloo, honor, salute, shout, signal to, wave, welcome.
n. call, cry, halloo, holla, shout.

hair-do *n.* coiffure, cut, haircut, hairstyle, perm, set, style.

hairdresser *n.* barber, coiffeur, coiffeuse, friseur, hairstylist, stylist.

hairless *adj.* bald, bald-headed, beardless, clean-shaven, depilated, desperate, frantic, glabrate, glabrous, shorn, tonsured.
antonym hairy.

hair-raising *adj.* alarming, bloodcurdling, breathtaking, creepy, eerie, exciting, frightening, ghastly, ghostly, horrifying, petrifying, scary, shocking, spine-chilling, startling, terrifying, thrilling.
antonym calming.

hairy *adj.* bearded, bewhiskered, bushy, crinigerous, crinite, crinose, dangerous, dicey, difficult, fleecy, furry, hazardous, hirsute, hispid, lanuginose, lanuginous, perilous, pilose, pilous, risky, scaring, shaggy, stubbly, tricky, villose, villous, woolly.
antonyms bald, clean-shaven.

hale *adj.* able-bodied, athletic, blooming, fit, flourishing, healthy, hearty, in fine fettle, in the pink, robust, sound, strong, vigorous, well, youthful.
antonym ill.

half-baked *adj.* brainless, crazy, foolish, harebrained, ill-conceived, ill-judged, impractical, senseless, short-sighted, silly, stupid, unplanned.
antonym sensible.

half-hearted *adj.* apathetic, cool, indifferent, lackadaisical, lackluster, listless, lukewarm, neutral, passive, perfunctory, uninterested.
antonym enthusiastic.

half-wit *n.* cretin, dimwit, dolt, dullard, dunce, dunderhead, fool, gaupus, idiot, imbecile, moron, nitwit, nut, simpleton, underwit, witling.
antonym brain.

hall *n.* assembly-room, auditorium, aula, basilica, chamber, concert-hall, concourse, corridor, entrance-hall, entry, foyer, hallway, lobby, salon, saloon, vestibule.

hallowed *adj.* age-old, beatified, blessed, consecrated, dedicated, established, holy, honored, inviolable, revered, sacred, sacrosanct, sanctified.

hallucination *n.* aberration, apparition, delusion, dream, fantasy, figment, illusion, mirage, phantasmagoria, pink elephants, vision.

halt *v.* arrest, block, break off, call it a day, cease, check, curb, desist, draw up, end, impede, obstruct, pack it in, quit, rest, stem, stop, terminate, wait.
antonyms assist, continue, start.
n. arrest, break, close, end, étape, impasse, interruption, pause, stand, standstill, stop, stoppage, termination, way point.
antonyms continuation, start.

halting *adj.* awkward, broken, faltering, hesitant, imperfect, labored, stammering, stumbling, stuttering, uncertain.
antonym fluent.

hammer *v.* bang, beat, clobber, defeat, din, dolly, drive, drive home, drub, drum, form, grind, hit, impress upon, instruct, knock, make, malleate, pan, repeat, shape, slate, thrash, trounce, worst.
n. beetle, gavel, madge, mall, mallet, maul, monkey.

hamper *v.* bind, cramp, cumber, curb, curtail, distort, embarrass, encumber, entangle, fetter, frustrate, hamshackle, hamstring, handicap, hinder, hobble, hold up, impede, interfere with, obstruct, pinch, prevent, restrain, restrict, shackle, slow down, tangle, thwart, trammel.
antonyms aid, expedite.

hamstring *adj.* balked, crippled, disabled, foiled, frustrated, handicapped, helpless, hors de combat, incapacitated, paralyzed, stymied.

hand[1] *n.* ability, agency, aid, applause, art, artistry, assistance, calligraphy, cheirography, clap, daddle, direction, fist, flipper, handwriting, help, influence, mitt, ovation, palm, part, participation, paw, penmanship, pud, puddy, script, share, skill, support.
v. aid, assist, conduct, convey, deliver, give, guide, help, lead, offer, pass, present, provide, transmit, yield.

hand[2] *n.* artificer, artisan, craftsman, employee, farmhand, hired man, hireling, laborer, operative, orra man, redneck, worker, workman.

handicap *n.* barrier, block, defect, disability, disadvantage, drawback, encumbrance, hindrance, impairment, impediment, impost, limitation, millstone, obstacle, odds, penalty, restriction, shortcoming, stumblingblock.
antonyms assistance, benefit.
v. burden, disadvantage, encumber, hamper, hamstring, hinder, impede, limit, restrict, retard.
antonyms assist, further.

handiness *n.* accessibility, adroitness, aptitude, availability, cleverness, closeness, convenience, deftness, dexterity, efficiency, expertise, knack, practicality, proficiency, proximity, skill, usefulness, workability.
antonym clumsiness.

handkerchief *n.* fogle, handkercher, hanky, monteith, mouchoir, nose-rag, romal, rumal, sudary, wipe.

handle *n.* ear, grip, haft, handfast, handgrip, heft, helve, hilt, knob, lug, stock, wythe.
v. administer, carry, conduct, control, cope with, deal in, deal with, direct, discourse, discuss, feel, finger, fondle, grasp, guide, hold, manage, manipulate, maneuver, market, maul, operate, paw, pick up, poke,

sell, steer, stock, supervise, touch, trade, traffic in, treat, use, wield.

hand-out[1] *n.* alms, charity, dole, freebie, issue, largess(e), share, share-out.

hand-out[2] *n.* bulletin, circular, free sample, leaflet, literature, press release, statement.

handsome *adj.* abundant, admirable, ample, attractive, beau, becoming, bountiful, braw, comely, considerable, elegant, feat(e)ous, featuous, featurely, fine, generous, good-looking, graceful, gracious, large, liberal, magnanimous, majestic, personable, plentiful, seemly, sizeable, stately, well-favored, well-looking, well-proportioned, well-set-up.
antonyms mean, stingy, ugly.

handy *adj.* accessible, adept, adroit, at hand, available, clever, close, convenient, deft, dexterous, expert, helpful, manageable, near, nearby, neat, nimble, practical, proficient, ready, serviceable, skilful, skilled, useful.
antonyms clumsy, inconvenient, unwieldy.

hang *v.* adhere, attach, bow, cling, cover, dangle, deck, decorate, depend, drape, drift, droop, drop, execute, fasten, fix, float, furnish, gibbet, hold, hover, incline, lean, loll, lower, remain, rest, sag, stick, string up, suspend, suspercollate, swing, trail, weep.

hanker for/after covet, crave, desire, hunger for, itch for, long for, lust after, pine for, thirst for, want, wish, yearn for, yen for.
antonym dislike.

haphazard *adj.* accidental, aimless, arbitrary, careless, casual, chance, disorderly, disorganized, flukey, hit-or-miss, indiscriminate, promiscuous, random, slapdash, slipshod, unmethodical, unsystematic.
antonyms deliberate, planned.

hapless *adj.* cursed, ill-fated, ill-starred, jinxed, luckless, miserable, star-crossed, unfortunate, unhappy, unlucky, wretched.
antonym lucky.

happen *v.* appear, arise, befall, chance, come about, crop up, develop, ensue, eventuate, fall out, follow, materialize, occur, result, supervene, take place, transpire, turn out.

happening *n.* accident, adventure, affair, case, chance, circumstance, episode, event, experience, incident, occasion, occurrence, phenomenon, proceeding, scene.

happiness *n.* beatitude, blessedness, bliss, cheer, cheerfulness, cheeriness, chirpiness, contentment, delight, ecstasy, elation, enjoyment, exuberance, felicity, gaiety, gladness, high spirits, joy, joyfulness, jubilation, light-heartedness, merriment, pleasure, satisfaction, well-being.
antonym unhappiness.

happy *adj.* advantageous, appropriate, apt, auspicious, befitting, blessed, blest, blissful, blithe, chance, cheerful, content, contented, convenient, delighted, ecstatic, elated, enviable, favorable, felicitous, fit, fitting, fortunate, glad, gratified, gruntled, idyllic, jolly, joyful, joyous, jubilant, lucky, merry, opportune, over the moon, overjoyed, pleased, promising, propitious, satisfactory, Saturnian, seasonable, starry-eyed, successful, sunny, thrilled, timely, well-timed.
antonym unhappy.

happy-go-lucky *adj.* blithe, carefree, casual, cheerful, devil-may-care, easy-going, heedless, improvident, insouciant, irresponsible, light-hearted, nonchalant, reckless, unconcerned, untroubled, unworried.

antonyms anxious, wary.

harangue *n.* address, declamation, diatribe, discourse, exhortation, homily, lecture, oration, paternoster, peroration, philippic, sermon, speech, spiel, tirade.

v. address, declaim, descant, exhort, hold forth, lecture, monolog(u)ize, orate, perorate, preach, rant, rhetorize, sermonize, spout.

harass *v.* annoy, badger, bait, beleaguer, bother, chivvy, distress, disturb, exasperate, exhaust, fatigue, harry, hassle, hound, perplex, persecute, pester, plague, tease, tire, torment, trash, trouble, vex, wear out, weary, worry.

antonym assist.

harbinger *n.* avant-courier, forerunner, foretoken, herald, indication, messenger, omen, portent, precursor, presage, sign, warning.

harbor *n.* anchorage, asylum, covert, destination, haven, marina, port, refuge, roadstead, sanctuary, sanctum, security, shelter.

v. believe, cherish, cling to, conceal, entertain, foster, hide, hold, imagine, lodge, maintain, nurse, nurture, protect, retain, secrete, shelter, shield.

hard *adj.* acrimonious, actual, adamantine, alcoholic, angry, antagonistic, arduous, backbreaking, baffling, bare, bitter, burdensome, calamitous, callous, castiron, cold, compact, complex, complicated, cruel, crusty, dark, definite, dense, difficult, disagreeable, disastrous, distressing, driving, exacting, exhausting, fatiguing, fierce, firm, flinty, forceful, formidable, grievous, grim, habit-forming, hard-hearted, harsh, heavy, Herculean, hostile, impenetrable, implacable, indisputable, inflexible, intolerable, intricate, involved, irony, knotty, laborious, marbly, obdurate, painful, perplexing, pitiless, plain, powerful, puzzling, rancorous, resentful, rigid, rigorous, ruthless, sclerous, severe, shrewd, solid, stern, stiff, stony, strenuous, strict, strong, stubborn, tangled, thorny, toilsome, tough, undeniable, unfathomable, unfeeling, ungentle, unjust, unkind, unpleasant, unrelenting, unsparing, unsympathetic, unvarnished, unyielding, uphill, verified, violent, wearying.

antonyms harmless, kind, mild, non-alcoholic, pleasant, pleasing, soft, yielding.

adv. agonizingly, assiduously, badly, bitterly, close, completely, determinedly, diligently, distressingly, doggedly, earnestly, energetically, fiercely, forcefully, forcibly, fully, hardly, harshly, heavily, industriously, intensely, intently, keenly, laboriously, near, painfully, persistently, powerfully, rancorously, reluctantly, resentfully, roughly, severely, sharply, slowly, sorely, steadily, strenuously, strongly, uneasily, untiringly, vigorously, violently, with difficulty.

antonyms gently, mildly, moderately, unenthusiastically.

harden *v.* accustom, anneal, bake, brace, brutalize, buttress, cake, case-harden, concrete, fortify, freeze, gird, habituate, indurate, inure, nerve, reinforce, sclerose, season, set, solidify, steel, stiffen, strengthen, toughen, train.

antonym soften.

hard-headed *adj.* astute, clear-thinking, cool, hard-boiled, level-headed, practical, pragmatic, realistic, sensible, shrewd, tough, unsentimental.

antonym unrealistic.

hard-hearted *adj.* callous, cold, cruel, hard, heartless,

indifferent, inhuman, insensitive, intolerant, iron-hearted, marble-breasted, marble-hearted, merciless, pitiless, stony, uncaring, uncompassionate, unfeeling, unkind, unsympathetic.

antonyms kind, merciful.

hardly *adv.* barely, by no means, faintly, harshly, infrequently, just, no way, not at all, not quite, only, only just, roughly, scarcely, severely, with difficulty.

antonyms easily, very.

hardship *n.* adversity, affliction, austerity, burden, calamity, destitution, difficulty, fatigue, grievance, labor, misery, misfortune, need, oppression, persecution, privation, strait, suffering, toil, torment, trial, tribulation, trouble, want.

antonym ease.

hardy *adj.* audacious, bold, brave, brazen, courageous, daring, firm, fit, foolhardy, hale, headstrong, healthy, hearty, heroic, impudent, intrepid, lusty, manly, plucky, rash, reckless, resolute, robust, rugged, sound, Spartan, stalwart, stout, stout-hearted, strong, sturdy, tough, valiant, valorous, vigorous.

antonyms unhealthy, weak.

harm *n.* abuse, damage, detriment, disservice, evil, hurt, ill, immorality, impairment, iniquity, injury, loss, mischief, misfortune, scathe, sin, sinfulness, vice, wickedness, wrong.

antonyms benefit, service.

v. abuse, blemish, damage, hurt, ill-treat, ill-use, impair, injure, maltreat, mar, molest, ruin, scathe, spoil, wound.

antonyms benefit, improve.

harmful *adj.* baleful, baneful, damaging, deleterious, destructive, detrimental, disadvantageous, evil, hurtful, injurious, noxious, pernicious, pestful, pestiferous, pestilent, scatheful.

antonym harmless.

harmless *adj.* gentle, innocent, innocuous, innoxious, inoffensive, non-toxic, safe, scatheless, unharmed, uninjured, unobjectionable, unscathed.

antonym harmful.

harmonious *adj.* according, agreeable, amicable, compatible, concinnous, concordant, congenial, congruous, consonant, consonous, co-ordinated, cordial, correspondent, dulcet, euharmonic, euphonic, euphonious, eurhythmic, friendly, harmonic, harmonizing, matching, mellifluous, melodious, musical, sweet-sounding, sympathetic, symphonious, tuneful.

antonym inharmonious.

harmony *n.* accord, agreement, amicability, amity, balance, chime, compatibility, concinnity, concord, conformity, congruity, consensus, consistency, consonance, co-operation, co-ordination, correspondence, correspondency, diapason, euphony, eurhythmy, fitness, friendship, goodwill, like-mindedness, melodiousness, melody, parallelism, peace, rapport, suitability, symmetry, sympathy, tune, tunefulness, unanimity, understanding, unity.

antonym discord.

harness *n.* equipment, gear, reins, straps, tack, tackle, trappings.

v. apply, channel, control, couple, employ, exploit, make use of, mobilize, saddle, turn to account, use, utilize, yoke.

harry *v.* annoy, badger, bedevil, chivvy, depredate, despoil, devastate, disturb, fret, harass, hassle, maraud, molest, persecute, pester, pillage, plague, plunder, raid, ravage, rob, sack, tease, torment, trouble, vex, worry.

antonyms aid, calm.

harsh *adj.* abrasive, abusive, austere, bitter, bleak, brutal, coarse, comfortless, croaking, crude, cruel, discordant, dissonant, dour, Draconian, glaring, grating, grim, guttural, hard, jarring, pitiless, punitive, rasping, raucous, relentless, rough, ruthless, scabrous, severe, sharp, Spartan, stark, stern, strident, stringent, unfeeling, ungentle, unkind, unmelodious, unpleasant, unrelenting.

antonyms mild, smooth, soft.

harvest *n.* collection, consequence, crop, effect, fruition, harvesting, harvest-time, hockey, ingathering, inning, produce, product, reaping, result, return, vendage, yield.

v. accumulate, acquire, amass, collect, garner, gather, mow, pick, pluck, reap.

haste *n.* alacrity, briskness, bustle, celerity, dispatch, expedition, fleetness, hastiness, hurry, hustle, impetuosity, nimbleness, precipitance, precipitancy, precipitateness, precipitation, promptitude, quickness, rapidity, rapidness, rashness, recklessness, rush, speed, swiftness, urgency, velocity.

antonyms care, deliberation, slowness.

hasten *v.* accelerate, advance, bolt, dash, dispatch, expedite, fly, gallop, goad, haste, have it on one's toes, hightail it, hurry, make haste, precipitate, press, quicken, race, run, rush, scurry, scuttle, speed, speed up, sprint, step on it, step up, tear, trot, urge.

antonym dawdle.

hasty *adj.* brief, brisk, brusque, cursory, eager, excited, expeditious, fast, fiery, fleet, fleeting, foolhardy, headlong, heedless, hot-headed, hot-tempered, hurried, impatient, impetuous, impulsive, indiscreet, irascible, irritable, passing, passionate, perfunctory, precipitant, precipitate, prompt, quick-tempered, rapid, rash, reckless, rushed, short, snappy, speedy, subitaneous, superficial, swift, thoughtless, urgent.

antonyms careful, deliberate, placid, slow.

hat *n.* beret, biretta, boater, bonnet, bowler, cap, lid, night-cap, poke-bonnet, skull-cap, sombrero, sou'wester, top-hat, trilby, yarmulka.

hatch *v.* breed, brood, conceive, concoct, contrive, cook up, design, develop, devise, dream up, incubate, originate, plan, plot, project, scheme, think up.

hate *v.* abhor, abominate, despise, detest, dislike, execrate, loathe, spite.

antonym like.

n. abhorrence, abomination, animosity, animus, antagonism, antipathy, averseness, aversion, detestation, dislike, enmity, execration, hatred, hostility, loathing, odium, odium theologicum.

antonym like.

hateful *adj.* abhorrent, abominable, damnable, despicable, detestable, disgusting, execrable, forbidding, foul, hateworthy, heinous, horrible, loathsome, obnoxious, odious, offensive, repellent, repugnant, repulsive, revolting, vile.

antonym pleasing.

hatred *n.* abomination, animosity, animus, antagonism, antipathy, aversion, despite, detestation, dislike, enmity, execration, hate, ill-will, misandry, misanthropy, odium, repugnance, revulsion.

antonym like.

haughtiness *n.* airs, aloofness, arrogance, conceit, contempt, contemptuousness, disdain, hauteur, insolence, loftiness, pomposity, pride, snobbishness, snootiness, superciliousness.

antonyms friendliness, humility.

haughty *adj.* arrogant, assuming, cavalier, conceited, contemptuous, disdainful, fastuous, high, high and mighty, highty-tighty, hoity-toity, imperious, lofty, overweening, proud, scornful, snobbish, snooty, stiff-necked, stomachful, stuck-up, supercilious, superior, uppish.

antonyms friendly, humble.

haul *v.* bouse, carry, cart, convey, drag, draw, hale, heave, hump, lug, move, pull, tow, trail, transport, trice, tug.

n. booty, bunce, catch, drag, find, gain, harvest, heave, loot, pull, spoils, swag, takings, tug, yield.

have *v.* accept, acquire, allow, bear, beget, cheat, comprehend, comprise, consider, contain, deceive, deliver, dupe, embody, endure, enjoy, entertain, experience, feel, fool, gain, get, give birth to, hold, include, keep, obtain, occupy, outwit, own, permit, possess, procure, produce, put up with, receive, retain, secure, suffer, sustain, swindle, take, tolerate, trick, undergo.

havoc *n.* carnage, chaos, confusion, damage, depopulation, desolation, despoliation, destruction, devastation, disorder, disruption, mayhem, rack and ruin, ravages, ruin, shambles, slaughter, waste, wreck.

hazard *n.* accident, chance, coincidence, danger, death-trap, endangerment, fluke, imperilment, jeopardy, luck, mischance, misfortune, mishap, peril, risk, threat.

antonym safety.

v. advance, attempt, chance, conjecture, dare, endanger, expose, gamble, imperil, jeopardize, offer, presume, proffer, risk, speculate, stake, submit, suggest, suppose, threaten, venture, volunteer.

hazardous *adj.* chancy, dangerous, dicey, difficult, fraught, hairy, haphazard, insecure, perilous, precarious, risky, thorny, ticklish, uncertain, unpredictable, unsafe.

antonyms safe, secure.

hazy *adj.* blurry, clouded, cloudy, dim, distanceless, dull, faint, foggy, fuzzy, ill-defined, indefinite, indistinct, loose, milky, misty, muddled, muzzy, nebulous, obscure, overcast, smoky, uncertain, unclear, vague, veiled.

antonyms clear, definite.

head *n.* ability, apex, aptitude, bean, beginning, bonce, boss, brain, brains, branch, capacity, cape, captain, caput, category, chief, chieftain, chump, class, climax, commander, commencement, conclusion, conk, cop, cranium, crest, crisis, crown, culmination, department, director, division, end, faculty, flair, fore, forefront, foreland, front, godfather, head teacher, heading, headland, headmaster, headmistress, height, intellect, intelligence, knowledge box, leader, manager, master, mastermind, mentality, mind, nab, napper, nob, noddle, nut, origin, pate, peak, pitch, point, principal, promontory, rise, sconce, section, skull, source, start, subject, summit, super, superintendent, supervisor, talent, tête, thought, tip, top, topic, topknot, turning-point, understanding, upperworks, van, vanguard, vertex.

antonyms foot, subordinate, tail.

adj. arch, chief, dominant, first, foremost, front, highest, leading, main, pre-eminent, premier, prime, principal, supreme, top, topmost.

v. aim, cap, command, control, crown, direct, govern, guide, lead, make a beeline, make for, manage, oversee, point, precede, rule, run, steer, superintend, supervise, top, turn.

headstrong *adj.* bull-headed, contrary, foolhardy, fractious, froward, heedless, imprudent, impulsive, intractable, mulish, obstinate, perverse, pig-headed, rash, reckless, self-willed, stubborn, ungovernable, unruly, wilful.

antonyms biddable, docile, obedient.

headway *n.* advance, improvement, inroad(s), progress, progression, way.

heady *adj.* exciting, exhilarating, hasty, impetuous, impulsive, inconsiderate, inebriant, intoxicating, overpowering, potent, precipitate, rash, reckless, spirituous, stimulating, strong, thoughtless, thrilling.

heal *v.* alleviate, ameliorate, balsam, compose, conciliate, cure, harmonize, mend, patch up, physic, reconcile, regenerate, remedy, restore, salve, settle, soothe, treat.

healthy *adj.* active, beneficial, blooming, bracing, fine, fit, flourishing, good, hale (and hearty), hardy, healthful, health-giving, hearty, hygienic, in fine feather, in fine fettle, in fine form, in good condition, in good shape, in the pink, invigorating, nourishing, nutritious, physically fit, robust, salubrious, salutary, salutiferous, sound, strong, sturdy, vigorous, well, wholesome.

antonyms diseased, ill, infirm, sick, unhealthy.

heap *n.* accumulation, acervation, aggregation, bing, clamp, cock, collection, cumulus, hoard, lot, mass, mound, mountain, pile, ruck, stack, stockpile, store.

v. accumulate, amass, assign, augment, bank, bestow, build, burden, collect, confer, gather, hoard, increase, lavish, load, mound, pile, shower, stack, stockpile, store.

hear *v.* acknowledge, ascertain, attend, catch, discover, eavesdrop, examine, find, gather, hark, hearken, heed, investigate, judge, learn, listen, overhear, pick up, try, understand.

heart *n.* affection, benevolence, boldness, bravery, center, character, compassion, concern, core, courage, crux, disposition, emotion, essence, feeling, fortitude, guts, hub, humanity, inclination, kernel, love, marrow, mettle, middle, mind, nature, nerve, nerve center, nub, nucleus, pith, pity, pluck, purpose, quintessence, resolution, root, sentiment, soul, spirit, spunk, sympathy, temperament, tenderness, ticker, understanding, will.

heart and soul absolutely, completely, devotedly, eagerly, entirely, gladly, heartily, unreservedly, wholeheartedly.

heartache *n.* affliction, agony, anguish, bitterness, dejection, despair, despondency, distress, grief, heartbreak, heart-sickness, pain, remorse, sorrow, suffering, torment, torture.

heartbroken *adj.* broken-hearted, crestfallen, crushed, dejected, desolate, despondent, disappointed, disconsolate, disheartened, dispirited, down, downcast, grieved, heart-sick, miserable, woebegone.

antonyms delighted, elated.

hearten *v.* animate, assure, buck up, buoy up, cheer, comfort, console, embolden, encourage, gladden,

incite, inspire, inspirit, pep up, reassure, revivify, rouse, stimulate.

antonym dishearten.

heartless *adj.* brutal, callous, cold, cold-blooded, cold-hearted, cruel, hard, hard-hearted, harsh, inhuman, merciless, pitiless, stern, uncaring, unfeeling, unkind.

antonyms considerate, kind, merciful, sympathetic.

heart-rending *adj.* affecting, distressing, harrowing, heartbreaking, moving, pathetic, piteous, pitiful, poignant, sad, tear-jerking, tragic.

hearty *adj.* active, affable, ample, ardent, cordial, doughty, eager, earnest, ebullient, effusive, energetic, enthusiastic, exuberant, filling, friendly, generous, genial, genuine, hale, hardy, healthy, heartfelt, honest, jovial, nourishing, real, robust, sincere, sizeable, solid, sound, square, stalwart, strong, substantial, true, unfeigned, unreserved, vigorous, warm, well, wholehearted.

antonyms cold, emotionless.

heat *n.* agitation, ardor, calefaction, earnestness, excitement, fervor, fever, fieriness, fury, hotness, impetuosity, incandescence, intensity, passion, sizzle, sultriness, swelter, torridity, vehemence, violence, warmness, warmth, zeal.

antonyms cold(ness), coolness.

v. animate, calefy, chafe, excite, flush, glow, impassion, inflame, inspirit, reheat, rouse, stimulate, stir, toast, warm up.

antonyms chill, cool.

heated *adj.* acrimonious, angry, bitter, excited, fierce, fiery, frenzied, furious, impassioned, intense, passionate, perfervid, raging, stormy, tempestuous, vehement, violent.

antonym dispassionate.

heave *v.* billow, breathe, cast, chuck, dilate, drag, elevate, exhale, expand, fling, gag, groan, haul, heft, hitch, hoist, hurl, let fly, lever, lift, palpitate, pant, pitch, puff, pull, raise, retch, rise, send, sigh, sling, sob, spew, surge, suspire, swell, throb, throw, throw up, toss, tug, vomit, yomp.

heaven *n.* bliss, ecstasy, Elysian fields, Elysium, empyrean, enchantment, ether, felicity, fiddler's green, firmament, happiness, happy hunting-ground(s), hereafter, Land of the Leal, next world, nirvana, paradise, rapture, sky, Swarga, transport, utopia, Valhalla, welkin, Zion.

antonym hell.

heavenly *adj.* alluring, ambrosial, angelic, beatific, beautiful, blessed, blest, blissful, celestial, delightful, divine, empyrean, entrancing, exquisite, extra-terrestrial, glorious, godlike, holy, immortal, lovely, paradisaic(al), paradisal, paradisean, paradisial, paradisian, paradisic, rapturous, ravishing, seraphic, sublime, superhuman, supernal, supernatural, Uranian, wonderful.

antonym hellish.

heavy *adj.* abundant, apathetic, boisterous, bulky, burdened, burdensome, clumpy, complex, considerable, copious, crestfallen, deep, dejected, depressed, despondent, difficult, disconsolate, downcast, drowsy, dull, encumbered, excessive, gloomy, grave, grieving, grievous, hard, harsh, hefty, inactive, indolent, inert, intolerable, laborious, laden, large, leaden, listless, loaded, lumping, lumpish, massive, melancholy, onerous, oppressed, oppressive, ponderous, portly, profound,

profuse, rough, sad, serious, severe, slow, sluggish, solemn, sorrowful, squabbish, stodgy, stormy, stupid, tedious, tempestuous, torpid, turbulent, vexatious, violent, wearisome, weighted, weighty, wild, wooden.
antonyms airy, insignificant, light.

heckle *v.* bait, barrack, catcall, disrupt, gibe, interrupt, jeer, pester, shout down, taunt.

heed *n.* animadversion, attention, care, caution, consideration, ear, heedfulness, mind, note, notice, reck, regard, respect, thought, watchfulness.
antonyms inattention, indifference, unconcern.
v. animadvert, attend, consider, follow, listen, mark, mind, note, obey, observe, regard, take notice of.
antonyms disregard, ignore.

heedless *adj.* careless, étourdi(e), foolhardy, imprudent, inattentive, incautious, incurious, inobservant, neglectful, negligent, oblivious, precipitate, rash, reckless, thoughtless, uncaring, unconcerned, unheedful, unheedy, unmindful, unobservant, unthinking.
antonym heedful.

height *n.* acme, altitude, apex, apogee, ceiling, celsitude, climax, crest, crown, culmination, degree, dignity, elevation, eminence, exaltation, extremity, grandeur, highness, hill, limit, loftiness, maximum, mountain, ne plus ultra, peak, pinnacle, prominence, stature, summit, tallness, top, ultimate, utmost, uttermost, vertex, zenith.
antonym depth.

heighten *v.* add to, aggrandize, aggravate, amplify, augment, elevate, enhance, ennoble, exalt, greaten, improve, increase, intensify, magnify, raise, sharpen, strengthen, uplift.
antonyms decrease, diminish.

heinous *adj.* abhorrent, abominable, atrocious, awful, evil, execrable, facinorous, flagrant, grave, hateful, hideous, immitigable, infamous, iniquitous, monstrous, nefarious, odious, outrageous, revolting, shocking, unspeakable, vicious, villainous.

hello *interj.* chin-chin, ciao, hail, hi, hiya, how-do-you-do, howdy, salve, what cheer, wotcher.
antonym good-bye.

help¹ *v.* abet, abstain, aid, alleviate, ameliorate, assist, avoid, back, befriend, bestead, control, co-operate, cure, ease, eschew, facilitate, forbear, heal, hinder, improve, keep from, lend a hand, mitigate, prevent, promote, rally round, refrain from, relieve, remedy, resist, restore, save, second, serve, shun, stand by, succor, support, withstand.
antonym hinder.
n. adjuvant, advice, aid, aidance, assistance, avail, benefit, co-operation, guidance, leg up, service, support, use, utility.
antonym hindrance.

help² *n.* assistant, daily, employee, hand, helper, worker.

helper *n.* abettor, adjutant, aide, aider, ally, assistant, attendant, auxiliary, coadjutor, collaborator, colleague, deputy, girl Friday, helpmate, man Friday, mate, PA, partner, person Friday, right-hand man, Samaritan, second, subsidiary, supporter.

helpful *adj.* accommodating, adjuvant, advantageous, beneficent, beneficial, benevolent, caring, considerate, constructive, co-operative, favorable, fortunate, friendly, furthersome, kind, neighborly, practical, productive, profitable, serviceable, supportive, sympathetic, timely, useful.

antonyms futile, useless, worthless.

helpless *adj.* abandoned, adynamic, aidless, debilitated, defenceless, dependent, destitute, disabled, exposed, feeble, forlorn, friendless, impotent, incapable, incompetent, infirm, paralyzed, powerless, unfit, unprotected, vulnerable, weak.
antonyms competent, enterprising, independent, resourceful, strong.

helter-skelter *adv.* carelessly, confusedly, hastily, headlong, hurriedly, impulsively, pell-mell, rashly, recklessly, wildly.
adj. anyhow, confused, disordered, disorganized, haphazard, higgledy-piggledy, hit-or-miss, jumbled, muddled, random, topsy-turvy, unsystematic.

hem *n.* border, edge, fringe, margin, skirt, trimming.
v. beset, border, circumscribe, confine, edge, enclose, engird, environ, fimbriate, gird, hedge, restrict, skirt, surround.

hemerrhoids *n.* emerods, piles.

hence *adv.* accordingly, ergo, therefore, thus.

herald *n.* courier, crier, forerunner, harbinger, indication, messenger, omen, precursor, sign, signal, token, vaunt-courier.
v. advertise, announce, broadcast, forebode, foretoken, harbinger, indicate, pave the way, portend, precede, presage, proclaim, prognosticate, promise, publicize, publish, show, trumpet, usher in.

herculean *adj.* arduous, athletic, brawny, colossal, daunting, demanding, difficult, enormous, exacting, exhausting, formidable, gigantic, great, grueling, hard, heavy, huge, husky, laborious, large, mammoth, massive, mighty, muscular, onerous, powerful, prodigious, rugged, sinewy, stalwart, strapping, strenuous, strong, sturdy, titanic, toilsome, tough, tremendous.

herd *n.* assemblage, canaille, collection, cowherd, crowd, crush, drove, flock, herdboy, herdsman, horde, mass, mob, multitude, populace, press, rabble, riff-raff, shepherd, swarm, the hoi polloi, the masses, the plebs, throng, vulgus.
v. assemble, associate, collect, congregate, drive, flock, force, gather, goad, guard, guide, huddle, lead, muster, protect, rally, shepherd, spur, watch.

heretic *n.* apostate, dissenter, dissident, free-thinker, nonconformist, renegade, revisionist, schismatic, sectarian, separatist.
antonym conformist.

heritage *n.* bequest, birthright, deserts, due, endowment, estate, history, inheritance, legacy, lot, past, patrimony, portion, record, share, tradition.

hermit *n.* anchoret, anchorite, ascetic, eremite, monk, recluse, solitaire, solitarian, solitary, stylite.

hero *n.* celebrity, champion, conqueror, exemplar, goody, heart-throb, idol, male lead, paragon, protagonist, star, superstar, victor.

heroic *adj.* bold, brave, classic, classical, courageous, daring, dauntless, doughty, elevated, epic, exaggerated, extravagant, fearless, gallant, game, grand, grandiose, gritty, high-flown, Homeric, inflated, intrepid, legendary, lion-hearted, mythological, spunky, stouthearted, undaunted, valiant, valorous.
antonyms cowardly, pusillanimous, timid.

heroism *n.* boldness, bravery, courage, courageousness, daring, derring-do, fearlessness, fortitude, gallantry, gameness, grit, intrepidity, prowess, spirit, valor.
antonyms cowardice, pusillanimity, timidity.

hesitant *adj.* diffident, dilatory, doubtful, half-hearted, halting, hesitating, hesitative, hesitatory, irresolute, reluctant, sceptical, shy, swithering, timid, uncertain, unsure, vacillating, wavering.
antonyms resolute, staunch.

hesitate *v.* balk, be reluctant, be uncertain, be unwilling, boggle, delay, demur, dither, doubt, dubitate, falter, fumble, halt, haver, pause, scruple, shillyshally, shrink from, stammer, stumble, stutter, swither, think twice, vacillate, wait, waver.

hesitation *n.* delay, demurral, doubt, dubiety, faltering, fumbling, hesitancy, indecision, irresolution, misdoubt, misgiving(s), qualm(s), reluctance, scruple(s), second thought(s), stammering, stumbling, stuttering, swithering, uncertainty, unwillingness, vacillation.
antonyms alacrity, assurance, eagerness.

hidden *adj.* abstruse, cabbalistic(al), clandestine, close, concealed, covered, covert, cryptic, dark, de(a)rn, delitescent, doggo, hermetic, hermetical, latent, mysterious, mystic, mystical, obscure, occult, recondite, secret, shrouded, ulterior, unapparent, unseen, veiled.
antonyms open, showing.

hide[1] *v.* abscond, bury, cache, camouflage, cloak, conceal, cover, disguise, earth, eclipse, ensconce, feal, go to ground, go underground, hole up, keep dark, lie low, mask, obscure, occult, screen, secrete, shadow, shelter, shroud, stash, suppress, take cover, tappice, veil, withhold.
antonyms display, reveal, show.

hide[2] *n.* deacon, fell, flaught, nebris, pelt, skin.

hideous *adj.* abominable, appalling, awful, detestable, disgusting, dreadful, frightful, gash, gashful, gashly, ghastly, grim, grisly, grotesque, gruesome, horrendous, horrible, horrid, loathsome, macabre, monstrous, odious, repulsive, revolting, shocking, sickening, terrible, terrifying, ugly, ugsome, unsightly.
antonym beautiful.

high *adj.* acute, altissimo, alto, arch, arrogant, boastful, boisterous, bouncy, bragging, capital, cheerful, chief, consequential, costly, dear, delirious, despotic, distinguished, domineering, elated, elevated, eminent, euphoric, exalted, excessive, excited, exhilarated, exorbitant, expensive, extraordinary, extravagant, extreme, exuberant, freaked out, gamy, grand, grave, great, haughty, high-pitched, important, inebriated, influential, intensified, intoxicated, joyful, lavish, leading, light-hearted, lofty, lordly, luxurious, merry, mountain(s)-high, niffy, orthian, ostentatious, overbearing, penetrating, piercing, piping, pongy, powerful, prominent, proud, rich, ruling, serious, sharp, shrill, significant, soaring, soprano, spaced out, steep, stiff, stoned, strident, strong, superior, tainted, tall, towering, treble, tripping, tumultuous, turbulent, tyrannical, vainglorious, whiffy.
antonyms deep, low, lowly, short.

n. apex, apogee, delirium, ecstasy, euphoria, height, intoxication, level, peak, record, summit, top, trip, zenith.
antonyms low, nadir.

highbrow *n.* aesthete, boffin, Brahmin, brain, egghead, intellectual, long-hair, mandarin, mastermind, savant, scholar.
adj. bookish, brainy, cultivated, cultured, deep, intellectual, long-haired, serious, sophisticated.
antonym lowbrow.

highly *adv.* appreciatively, approvingly, considerably, decidedly, eminently, enthusiastically, exceptionally, extraordinarily, extremely, favorably, greatly, immensely, supremely, tremendously, vastly, very, warmly, well.

high-minded *adj.* elevated, ethical, fair, good, honorable, idealistic, lofty, magnanimous, moral, noble, principled, pure, righteous, scrupulous, upright, virtuous, worthy.
antonyms immoral, unscrupulous.

high-priced *adj.* costly, dear, excessive, exorbitant, expensive, extortionate, high, pricy, steep, stiff, unreasonable.
antonym cheap.

high-spirited *adj.* animated, boisterous, bold, bouncy, daring, dashing, ebullient, effervescent, energetic, exuberant, frolicsome, lively, mettlesome, peppy, sparkling, spirited, spunky, vibrant, vital, vivacious.
antonyms downcast, glum.

highwayman *n.* bandit, bandolero, footpad, knight of the road, land-pirate, rank-rider, robber.

hilarious *adj.* amusing, comical, convivial, entertaining, funny, gay, happy, humorous, hysterical, jolly, jovial, joyful, joyous, killing, merry, mirthful, noisy, rollicking, side-splitting, uproarious.
antonyms grave, serious.

hinder *v.* arrest, check, counteract, debar, delay, deter, embar, encumber, forelay, frustrate, hamper, hamstring, handicap, hold back, hold up, impede, interrupt, obstruct, oppose, prevent, retard, slow down, stop, stymie, thwart, trammel.
antonyms aid, assist, help.

hindrance *n.* bar, barrier, check, demurrage, deterrent, difficulty, drag, drawback, encumbrance, handicap, hitch, impediment, interruption, limitation, obstacle, obstruction, pull-back, remora, restraint, restriction, snag, stoppage, stumbling-block, trammel.
antonyms aid, assistance, help.

hinge *v.* be contingent, center, depend, hang, pivot, rest, revolve around, turn.
n. articulation, condition, foundation, garnet, joint, premise, principle.

hint *n.* advice, allusion, breath, clue, dash, help, implication, indication, inkling, innuendo, insinuation, intimation, mention, pointer, reminder, scintilla, sign, signal, soupçon, speck, subindication, suggestion, suspicion, taste, tinge, tip, tip-off, touch, trace, undertone, whiff, whisper, wrinkle.
v. allude, imply, indicate, inkle, innuendo, insinuate, intimate, mention, prompt, subindicate, suggest, tip off.

hire *v.* appoint, book, charter, commission, employ, engage, lease, let, rent, reserve, retain, sign up, take on.
antonyms dismiss, fire.
n. charge, cost, fare, fee, price, rent, rental, toll.

history *n.* account, annals, antecedents, antiquity, autobiography, biography, chronicle, chronology, days of old, days of yore, genealogy, memoirs, narration, narrative, olden days, recapitulation, recital, record, relation, saga, story, tale, the past.

hit *v.* accomplish, achieve, affect, arrive at, attain, bang, bash, batter, beat, belt, bump, clip, clobber, clock, clonk, clout, collide with, crown, cuff, damage, devastate, flog, frap, fustigate, gain, impinge on, influence, knock, lob, move, overwhelm, prop, punch, reach, secure, slap, slog, slosh, slug, smack, smash, smite, sock, strike, swat, thump, touch, volley, wallop, whack, wham, whap, w(h)op, wipe.

n. blow, bump, clash, clout, collision, cuff, impact, knock, rap, sell-out, sensation, shot, slap, slog, slosh, smack, smash, sock, stroke, success, swipe, triumph, venue, wallop, winner.

hitch *v.* attach, connect, couple, fasten, harness, heave, hike (up), hitch-hike, hoi(c)k, hoist, jerk, join, pull, tether, thumb a lift, tie, tug, unite, yank, yoke.

antonyms unfasten, unhitch.

n. catch, check, delay, difficulty, drawback, hiccup, hindrance, hold-up, impediment, mishap, problem, snag, stick, stoppage, trouble.

hoard *n.* accumulation, cache, fund, heap, mass, pile, profusion, reserve, reservoir, stockpile, store, supply, treasure-trove.

v. accumulate, amass, cache, coffer, collect, deposit, garner, gather, hive, husband, lay up, put by, reposit, save, stash away, stockpile, store, treasure.

antonyms spend, squander, use.

hoarse *adj.* croaky, discordant, grating, gravelly, growling, gruff, guttural, harsh, husky, rasping, raspy, raucous, rough, throaty.

antonyms clear, smooth.

hoax *n.* bam, cheat, cod, con, deception, fast one, fraud, grift, hum, huntiegowk, hunt-the-gowk, imposture, joke, josh, leg-pull, practical joke, prank, put-on, quiz, ruse, spoof, string, swindle, trick.

v. bam, bamboozle, befool, bluff, cod, con, deceive, delude, dupe, fool, gammon, gull, have on, hoodwink, hornswoggle, hum, lead on, pull someone's leg, spoof, string, stuff, swindle, take for a ride, trick.

hobble *v.* clog, dodder, falter, fasten, fetter, halt, hamshackle, hamstring, hirple, limp, restrict, shackle, shamble, shuffle, stagger, stumble, tie, totter.

hobby *n.* avocation, diversion, pastime, pursuit, recreation, relaxation, sideline.

hoist *v.* elevate, erect, heave, jack up, lift, raise, rear, uplift, upraise.

n. crane, davit, elevator, jack, lift, tackle, winch.

hold *v.* accommodate, account, adhere, apply, arrest, assemble, assume, be in force, be the case, bear, believe, bond, brace, call, carry, carry on, celebrate, check, clasp, cleave, clinch, cling, clip, clutch, comprise, conduct, confine, consider, contain, continue, convene, cradle, curb, deem, delay, detain, embrace, endure, enfold, entertain, esteem, exist, grasp, grip, have, hold good, imprison, judge, keep, last, maintain, occupy, operate, own, persevere, persist, possess, preside over, presume, prop, reckon, regard, remain, remain true, remain valid, resist, restrain, retain, run, seat, shoulder, solemnize, stand up, stay, stick, stop, summon, support, suspend, sustain, take, think, view, wear.

n. anchorage, asendancy, authority, clasp, clout, clutch, control, dominance, dominion, foothold, footing, grasp, grip, holt, influence, leverage, mastery, prop, pull, purchase, stay, support, sway, vantage.

hold-up[1] *n.* bottle-neck, delay, difficulty, gridlock, hitch, obstruction, setback, snag, stoppage, (traffic) jam, trouble, wait.

hold-up[2] *n.* heist, robbery, stick-up.

hole *n.* aperture, breach, break, burrow, cave, cavern, cavity, chamber, covert, crack, defect, den, depression, dilemma, dimple, discrepancy, dive, dump, earth, error, excavation, eyelet, fallacy, fault, fissure, fix, flaw, foramen, fovea, gap, hollow, hovel, imbroglio, inconsistency, jam, joint, lair, loophole, mess, nest, opening, orifice, outlet, perforation, pit, pocket, pore, predicament, puncture, quandary, rent, retreat, scoop, scrape, shaft, shelter, slum, split, spot, tangle, tear, tight spot, vent, ventage.

hollow *adj.* artificial, cavernous, concave, coreless, cynical, deaf, deceitful, deceptive, deep, deep-set, depressed, dished, dull, empty, expressionless, faithless, false, famished, flat, fleeting, flimsy, fruitless, futile, gaunt, glenoid(al), hungry, hypocritical, indented, insincere, lantern-jawed, low, meaningless, muffled, muted, pointless, Pyrrhic, ravenous, reverberant, rumbling, sepulchral, specious, starved, sunken, toneless, treacherous, unavailing, unfilled, unreal, unreliable, unsound, useless, vacant, vain, void, weak, worthless.

n. basin, bottom, bowl, cave, cavern, cavity, channel, concave, concavity, coomb, crater, cup, dale, dell, den, dent, depression, dimple, dingle, dint, dish, druse, excavation, fossa, fossula, fovea, foveola, foveole, geode, glen, groove, hole, hope, how(e), indentation, invagination, pit, trough, umbilicus, vacuity, valley, vlei, well, womb.

v. burrow, channel, dent, dig, dint, dish, excavate, furrow, gouge, groove, indent, pit, scoop.

holocaust *n.* annihilation, carnage, conflagration, destruction, devastation, extermination, extinction, flames, genocide, hecatomb, immolation, inferno, mass murder, massacre, pogrom, sacrifice, slaughter.

holy *adj.* blessed, consecrated, dedicated, devout, divine, evangelical, evangelistic, faithful, god-fearing, godly, good, hallowed, perfect, pietistic, pious, pure, religiose, religious, righteous, sacred, sacrosanct, saintly, sanctified, sanctimonious, spiritual, sublime, unctuous, venerable, venerated, virtuous.

antonyms impious, unsanctified, wicked.

homage *n.* acknowledgment, admiration, adoration, adulation, allegiance, awe, deference, devotion, duty, esteem, faithfulness, fealty, fidelity, honor, loyalty, obeisance, praise, recognition, regard, respect, reverence, service, tribute, veneration, worship.

home *n.* abode, almshouse, asylum, birthplace, blighty, clinic, domicile, dwelling, dwelling-place, element, environment, family, fireside, habitat, habitation, haunt, hearth, home ground, home town, homestead, hospice, hospital, house, household, institution, native heath, nest, nursing-home, old people's home, pad, pied-à-terre, range, residence, roof, sanatorium, stamping-ground, territory.

adj. candid, central, direct, domestic, domiciliary, familiar, family, household, incisive, inland, internal, intimate, local, national, native, penetrating, plain, pointed, unanswerable, uncomfortable, wounding.

homely *adj.* comfortable, comfy, congenial, cosy, domestic, easy, everyday, familiar, folksy, friendly, gemütlich, homelike, homespun, hom(e)y, informal, intimate, modest, natural, ordinary, plain, relaxed, simple, snug, unaffected, unassuming, unpretentious, unsophisticated, welcoming.

antonyms formal, unfamiliar.

homesickness n. Heimweh, mal du pays, nostalgia, nostomania.
antonym wanderlust.

homicide n. assassin, assassination, bloodshed, cut-throat, killer, killing, liquidator, manslaughter, murder, murderer, slayer, slaying.

homily n. address, discourse, harangue, heart-to-heart, lecture, postil, preachment, sermon, spiel, talk.

honest adj. above-board, authentic, bona fide, candid, chaste, conscientious, decent, direct, equitable, ethical, fair, fair and square, forthright, four-square, frank, genuine, high-minded, honorable, humble, impartial, ingenuous, jake, just, law-abiding, legitimate, modest, objective, on the level, open, outright, outspoken, plain, plain-hearted, proper, real, reliable, reputable, respectable, scrupulous, seemly, simple, sincere, soothfast, square, straight, straightforward, true, trustworthy, trusty, truthful, undisguised, unequivocal, unfeigned, unreserved, upright, veracious, virtuous, well-gotten, well-won, white.
antonyms covert, devious, dishonest, dishonorable.

honestly adv. by fair means, candidly, cleanly, conscientiously, directly, dispassionately, equitably, ethically, fairly, frankly, honorably, in all sincerity, in good faith, justly, lawfully, legally, legitimately, objectively, on the level, openly, outright, plainly, really, scrupulously, sincerely, straight, straight out, truly, truthfully, undisguisedly, unreservedly, uprightly, verily.
antonyms dishonestly, dishonorably.

honesty n. artlessness, bluntness, candor, equity, even-handedness, explicitness, fairness, faithfulness, fidelity, frankness, genuineness, honor, incorruptibility, integrity, justness, morality, objectivity, openness, outspokenness, plain-heartedness, plainness, plain-speaking, probity, rectitude, reputability, scrupulousness, sincerity, sooth, squareness, straightforwardness, straightness, trustworthiness, truthfulness, unreserve, uprightness, veracity, verity, virtue.
antonyms deviousness, dishonesty.

honor n. acclaim, accolade, acknowledgment, admiration, adoration, chastity, commendation, compliment, credit, decency, deference, dignity, distinction, duty, elevation, esteem, fairness, favor, good name, goodness, homage, honesty, honorableness, honorificabilitudinity, innocence, integrity, kudos, laudation, laurels, loyalty, modesty, morality, pleasure, praise, principles, privilege, probity, purity, rank, recognition, rectitude, regard, renown, reputation, repute, respect, reverence, righteousness, self-respect, tribute, trust, trustworthiness, uprightness, veneration, virginity, virtue, worship.
antonyms disgrace, dishonor, obloquy.
v. accept, acclaim, acknowledge, admire, adore, applaud, appreciate, carry out, cash, celebrate, clear, commemorate, commend, compliment, credit, crown, decorate, dignify, discharge, esteem, exalt, execute, fulfil, glorify, hallow, homage, keep, laud, laureate, lionize, observe, pass, pay, pay homage, perform, praise, prize, remember, respect, revere, reverence, take, value, venerate, worship.
antonyms betray, debase, disgrace, dishonor.

honorable adj. creditable, distinguished, eminent, equitable, estimable, ethical, fair, great, high-minded, honest, illustrious, irreproachable, just, meritorious, moral, noble, prestigious, principled, proper, renowned, reputable, respectable, respected, right, righteous, sincere, straight, true, trustworthy, trusty, unexceptionable, upright, upstanding, venerable, virtuous, worthful, worthy.
antonyms dishonest, dishonorable, unworthy.

honorary adj. complimentary, ex officio, formal, honorific, honoris causa, in name only, nominal, titular, unofficial, unpaid, virtute officii.
antonyms gainful, paid, salaried, waged.

hop v. bound, caper, dance, fly, frisk, hitch, hobble, jump, leap, limp, nip, prance, skip, spring, vault.
n. ball, barn-dance, bounce, bound, crossing, dance, flight, jump, leap, skip, social, spring, step, trip, vault.

hope n. ambition, anticipation, aspiration, assumption, assurance, belief, confidence, conviction, desire, dream, expectancy, expectation, faith, hopefulness, longing, optimism, promise, prospect, wish.
antonyms apathy, despair, pessimism.
v. anticipate, aspire, assume, await, believe, contemplate, desire, expect, foresee, long, reckon on, rely, trust, wish.
antonym despair.

hopeful adj. assured, auspicious, bright, bullish, buoyant, cheerful, confident, encouraging, expectant, favorable, heartening, optimistic, promising, propitious, reassuring, rosy, sanguine.
antonyms despairing, discouraging, pessimistic.
n. great white hope, white hope, wunderkind.

hopeless adj. defeatist, dejected, demoralized, despairing, desperate, despondent, disconsolate, downhearted, foolish, forlorn, futile, helpless, impossible, impracticable, inadequate, incompetent, incorrigible, incurable, ineffectual, irredeemable, irremediable, irreparable, irreversible, lost, madcap, past cure, pessimistic, pointless, poor, reckless, unachievable, unattainable, useless, vain, woebegone, worthless, wretched.
antonyms curable, hopeful, optimistic.

horde n. band, bevy, concourse, crew, crowd, drove, flock, gang, herd, host, mob, multitude, pack, press, swarm, throng, troop.

horizon n. compass, ken, perspective, prospect, purview, range, realm, scope, skyline, sphere, stretch, verge, vista.

horrible adj. abhorrent, abominable, appalling, atrocious, awful, beastly, bloodcurdling, cruel, disagreeable, dreadful, fearful, fearsome, frightful, ghastly, grim, grisly, gruesome, heinous, hideous, horrid, horrific, loathsome, macabre, nasty, repulsive, revolting, shameful, shocking, terrible, terrifying, unkind, unpleasant, weird.
antonyms agreeable, pleasant.

horrid adj. abominable, alarming, appalling, awful, beastly, bloodcurdling, cruel, despicable, disagreeable, disgusting, dreadful, formidable, frightening, hair-raising, harrowing, hateful, hideous, horrible, horrific, mean, nasty, odious, offensive, repulsive, revolting, shocking, terrible, terrifying, unkind, unpleasant.
antonyms agreeable, lovely, pleasant.

horror n. abhorrence, abomination, alarm, antipathy, apprehension, aversion, awe, awfulness, consternation, detestation, disgust, dismay, dread, fear, fright, frightfulness, ghastliness, gooseflesh, goose-pimples, grimness, hatred, hideousness, horripilation, loathing, outrage, panic, repugnance, revulsion, shock, terror.

horseplay *n.* buffoonery, capers, clowning, desipience, fooling, fooling around, fun and games, high jinks, pranks, romping, rough-and-tumble, rough-housing, rough-stuff, rumpus, skylarking.

hospitable *adj.* accessible, amenable, amicable, approachable, bountiful, congenial, convivial, cordial, couthie, friendly, gemütlich, generous, genial, gracious, kind, liberal, liv(e)able, open-minded, receptive, responsive, sociable, tolerant, welcoming.
antonyms hostile, inhospitable.

hospital *n.* clinic, lazaret, lazaretto, leprosarium, leproserie, leprosery, sanatorium.

hospitality *n.* cheer, congeniality, conviviality, cordiality, friendliness, generosity, graciousness, open-handedness, sociability, warmth, welcome.
antonyms hostility, inhospitality.

hostile *adj.* adverse, alien, antagonistic, anti, antipathetic, bellicose, belligerent, contrary, ill-disposed, inhospitable, inimical, malevolent, opposed, opposite, oppugnant, rancorous, unfriendly, ungenial, unkind, unpropitious, unsympathetic, unwelcoming, warlike.
antonyms friendly, sympathetic.

hostility *n.* abhorrence, animosity, animus, antagonism, antipathy, aversion, breach, detestation, disaffection, dislike, enmity, estrangement, hate, hatred, ill-will, malevolence, malice, opposition, resentment, unfriendliness.
antonyms friendliness, sympathy.

hot *adj.* acrid, animated, approved, ardent, biting, blistering, boiling, burning, candent, clever, close, dangerous, eager, excellent, excited, exciting, favored, febrile, fervent, fervid, fevered, feverish, fierce, fiery, flaming, fresh, heated, hotheaded, impetuous, impulsive, in demand, in vogue, incandescent, inflamed, intense, irascible, latest, lustful, near, new, passionate, peppery, perfervid, piping, piquant, popular, pungent, quick, raging, recent, risky, roasting, scalding, scorching, searing, sensual, sharp, sizzling, skilful, sought-after, spicy, steaming, stormy, strong, sultry, sweltering, torrid, touchy, tropical, vehement, violent, voluptuous, warm, zealous.
antonyms calm, cold, mild, moderate.

hotbed *n.* breeding-ground, cradle, den, forcing-house, hive, nest, nidus, nursery, school, seedbed.

hot-blooded *adj.* ardent, bold, eager, excitable, fervent, fiery, heated, high-spirited, homothermous, impetuous, impulsive, lustful, lusty, passionate, perfervid, precipitate, rash, sensual, spirited, temperamental, warm-blooded, wild.
antonyms cool, dispassionate.

hotel *n.* auberge, boarding-house, doss-house, flophouse, Gasthaus, Gasthof, guest-house, hostelry, hydro, hydropathic, inn, motel, pension, pub, public house, tavern.

hotheaded *adj.* daredevil, fiery, foolhardy, hasty, headstrong, hot-tempered, impetuous, impulsive, intemperate, madcap, over-eager, precipitate, quick-tempered, rash, reckless, unruly, volatile.
antonyms calm, cool.

hound *v.* badger, chase, chivvy, drive, dun, goad, harass, harry, hunt (down), impel, importune, persecute, pester, prod, provoke, pursue.

house *n.* abode, ancestry, biggin, blood, building, business, clan, company, concern, domicile, dwelling, dynasty, edifice, establishment, family, family tree, firm, gens, habitation, home, homestead, hostelry, hotel, household, inn, kindred, line, lineage, lodgings, maison, maison(n)ette, ménage, organization, outfit, parliament, partnership, pied-à-terre, public house, race, residence, roof, stem, tavern, tribe.
v. accommodate, bed, billet, board, contain, cover, domicile, domiciliate, harbor, hold, keep, lodge, place, protect, put up, quarter, sheathe, shelter, store, take in.

household *n.* establishment, family, family circle, home, house, ménage, set-up.
adj. common, domestic, domiciliary, established, everyday, familiar, family, home, ordinary, plain, well-known.

householder *n.* franklin, freeholder, goodman, head of the household, home-owner, house-father, landlord, occupant, occupier, owner, property owner, proprietor, resident, tenant.

housing *n.* accommodation, case, casing, container, cover, covering, dwellings, enclosure, habitation, holder, homes, houses, living quarters, matrix, protection, roof, sheath, shelter.

hovel *n.* bothy, but-and-ben, cabin, cot, croft, den, doghole, dump, hole, hut, hutch, shack, shanty, shed.

hover *v.* alternate, dally, dither, drift, falter, flap, float, fluctuate, flutter, fly, hang, hang about, hesitate, impend, linger, loom, menace, oscillate, pause, poise, seesaw, threaten, vacillate, waver.

however *conj.* anyhow, but, even so, howbeit, in spite of that, natheless, nevertheless, nonetheless, notwithstanding, still, though, yet.

howl *n.* bay, bellow, clamor, cry, groan, holler, hoot, outcry, roar, scream, shriek, ululation, wail, yell, yelp, yowl.
v. bellow, cry, holler, hoot, lament, quest, roar, scream, shout, shriek, ululate, wail, waul, weep, yawl, yell, yelp.

hub *n.* axis, center, core, focal point, focus, heart, linchpin, middle, nave, nerve center, pivot.

hubbub *n.* ado, agitation, babel, bedlam, brouhaha, chaos, clamor, coil, confusion, din, disorder, disturbance, hue and cry, hullabaloo, hurly-burly, kerfuffle, noise, palaver, pandemonium, racket, riot, rowdedow, rowdydow, ruckus, ruction, rumpus, tumult, turbulence, uproar, upset.
antonym calm.

huckster *n.* barker, chapman, dealer, haggler, hawker, packman, pedlar, pitcher, salesman, tinker, vendor.

huddle *n.* clump, clutch, conclave, confab, conference, confusion, crowd, discussion, disorder, heap, jumble, knot, mass, meeting, mess, muddle.
v. cluster, conglomerate, congregate, converge, crouch, crowd, cuddle, curl up, flock, gather, gravitate, hunch, nestle, press, ruck, snuggle, throng.
antonym disperse.

hue *n.* aspect, cast, character, color, complexion, dye, light, nuance, shade, tincture, tinge, tint, tone.

huffy *adj.* angry, crabbed, cross, crotchety, crusty, disgruntled, grumpy, hoity-toity, huffish, irritable, miffed, miffy, moody, moping, morose, offended, peevish, pettish, petulant, querulous, resentful, shirty, short, snappy, sulky, surly, testy, touchy, waspish.
antonyms cheery, happy.

hug *v.* cherish, clasp, cling to, cuddle, embrace, enclose, enfold, follow, grip, hold, lock, nurse, retain, skirt, squeeze.

n. clasp, clinch, cuddle, embrace, squeeze.

huge *adj.* Babylonian, Brobdingnagian, bulky, colossal, Cyclopean, enormous, extensive, gargantuan, giant, gigantean, gigantesque, gigantic, great, gross, immense, jumbo, large, leviathan, mammoth, massive, monumental, mountainous, Patagonian, prodigious, rounceval, stupendous, swingeing, thundering, titanic, tremendous, unwieldy, vast, walloping, whacking.

antonyms dainty, tiny.

hulking *adj.* awkward, bulky, cloddish, clodhopping, clumsy, cumbersome, galumphing, gross, hulky, loutish, lubberly, lumbering, lumpish, massive, oafish, overgrown, ponderous, ungainly, unwieldy.

antonyms delicate, small.

hullabaloo *n.* agitation, babel, bedlam, brouhaha, chaos, clamor, commotion, confusion, din, disturbance, furore, fuss, hubbub, hue and cry, hurly-burly, kerfuffle, noise, outcry, pandemonium, panic, racket, ruckus, ruction, rumpus, to-do, tumult, turmoil, uproar.

hum *v.* bombilate, bombinate, bum, bustle, buzz, croon, drone, lilt, move, mumble, murmur, pulsate, pulse, purr, sing, stir, susurrate, throb, thrum, vibrate, whirr, zoom.

n. bombilation, bombination, bustle, busyness, buzz, drone, mumble, murmur, noise, pulsation, pulse, purr, purring, singing, stir, susurration, susurrus, throb, thrum, vibration, whirr.

human *adj.* anthropoid, approachable, compassionate, considerate, fallible, fleshly, forgivable, hominoid, humane, kind, kindly, man-like, mortal, natural, reasonable, susceptible, understandable, understanding, vulnerable.

antonym inhuman.

n. body, child, creature, hominid, homo sapiens, human being, individual, living soul, man, mortal, person, soul, wight, woman.

humane *adj.* beneficent, benevolent, benign, charitable, civilizing, clement, compassionate, forbearing, forgiving, gentle, good, good-natured, human, humanizing, kind, kind-hearted, kindly, lenient, loving, magnanimous, merciful, mild, sympathetic, tender, understanding.

antonym inhumane.

humanitarian *adj.* altruistic, beneficent, benevolent, charitable, compassionate, humane, philanthropic, philanthropical, public-spirited.

n. altruist, benefactor, do-gooder, Good Samaritan, philanthrope, philanthropist.

antonyms egoist, self-seeker.

humanitarianism *n.* beneficence, benevolence, charitableness, charity, compassionateness, do-goodery, generosity, goodwill, humanism, loving-kindness, philanthropy.

antonyms egoism, self-seeking.

humanity *n.* altruism, benevolence, benignity, brotherly love, charity, compassion, everyman, fellow-feeling, flesh, generosity, gentleness, goodwill, Homo sapiens, human nature, human race, humankind, humaneness, kind-heartedness, kindness, loving-kindness, man, mandom, mankind, men, mercy, mortality, people, philanthropy, sympathy, tenderness, tolerance, understanding.

antonym inhumanity.

humble *adj.* common, commonplace, courteous, deferential, demiss, docile, homespun, humdrum, insignificant, low, low-born, lowly, mean, meek, modest, obedient, obliging, obscure, obsequious, ordinary, plebeian, polite, poor, respectful, self-effacing, servile, simple, submissive, subservient, supplicatory, unassertive, unassuming, undistinguished, unimportant, unostentatious, unpretending, unpretentious.

antonyms assertive, important, pretentious, proud.

v. abase, abash, break, bring down, bring low, chagrin, chasten, confound, crush, debase, deflate, degrade, demean, discomfit, discredit, disgrace, humiliate, lower, mortify, reduce, shame, sink, subdue, take down a peg.

antonyms exalt, raise.

humbly *adv.* deferentially, diffidently, docilely, heepishly, meekly, modestly, obsequiously, respectfully, servilely, simply, submissively, subserviently, unassumingly, unpretentiously.

antonyms confidently, defiantly.

humbug *n.* baloney, blague, bluff, bounce, bullshit, bunk, bunkum, cant, charlatan, charlatanry, cheat, claptrap, con, con man, deceit, deception, dodge, eyewash, faker, feint, fraud, fudge, gaff, gammon, hoax, hollowness, hype, hypocrisy, imposition, impostor, imposture, mountebank, nonsense, phony, pretense, pseud, quack, quackery, rubbish, ruse, sham, shenanigans, swindle, swindler, trick, trickery, trickster, wile.

v. bamboozle, befool, beguile, cajole, cheat, cozen, deceive, delude, dupe, fool, gammon, gull, hoax, hoodwink, impose, mislead, swindle, trick.

humdrum *adj.* boring, commonplace, dreary, droning, dull, everyday, humble, monotonous, mundane, ordinary, prosy, repetitious, routine, tedious, tiresome, uneventful, uninteresting, unvaried, wearisome.

antonyms exceptional, unusual.

humid *adj.* clammy, damp, dank, moist, muggy, soggy, steamy, sticky, sultry, vaporous, watery, wet.

antonym dry.

humiliate *v.* abase, abash, bring low, chagrin, chasten, confound, crush, debase, deflate, degrade, discomfit, discredit, disgrace, embarrass, humble, mortify, shame, subdue, undignify.

antonyms boost, dignify, exalt, vindicate.

humiliation *n.* abasement, affront, chagrin, condescension, deflation, degradation, discomfiture, discrediting, disgrace, dishonor, embarrassment, humbling, ignominy, indignity, mortification, put-down, rebuff, resignation, shame, snub.

antonyms gratification, triumph.

humor *n.* amusement, badinage, banter, bent, bias, caprice, choler, comedy, conceit, disposition, drollery, facetiousness, fancy, farce, frame of mind, fun, funniness, gags, jesting, jests, jocoseness, jocosity, jocularity, jokes, joking, ludicrousness, melancholy, mood, phlegm, pleasantries, propensity, quirk, raillery, repartee, spirits, temper, temperament, vagary, vein, whim, wisecracks, wit, witticisms, wittiness.

v. accommodate, appease, coax, comply with, cosset, favor, flatter, go along with, gratify, indulge, mollify, pamper, spoil.

antonym thwart.

humorous *adj.* absurd, amusing, comic, comical, entertaining, facetious, farcical, funny, hilarious, humoristic, jocose, jocular, laughable, ludicrous, merry, play-

ful, pleasant, Rabelaisian, satirical, side-splitting, waggish, whimsical, wisecracking, witty, zany.
antonym humorless.

hunger *n.* appetence, appetency, appetite, craving, desire, emptiness, esurience, esuriency, famine, greediness, hungriness, itch, lust, rapacity, ravenousness, starvation, voracity, yearning, yen, yird-hunger.
antonyms appeasement, satisfaction.

v. ache, crave, desire, hanker, itch, long, lust, pine, starve, thirst, want, wish, yearn.

hungry *adj.* aching, appetitive, athirst, avid, covetous, craving, desirous, eager, empty, esurient, famished, famishing, greedy, hollow, hungerful, keen, lean, longing, peckish, ravenous, sharp-set, starved, starving, underfed, undernourished, voracious, yearning.
antonyms replete, satisfied.

hunt *v.* chase, chevy, course, dog, ferret, forage, gun for, hound, investigate, look for, pursue, rummage, scour, search, seek, stalk, track, trail.

n. battue, chase, chevy, hue and cry, hunting, investigation, pursuit, quest, search, venation.

hurl *v.* cast, catapult, chuck, dash, fire, fling, heave, launch, let fly, pitch, project, propel, send, shy, sling, throw, toss.

hurried *adj.* breakneck, brief, careless, cursory, hasty, headlong, hectic, passing, perfunctory, precipitate, quick, rushed, shallow, short, slapdash, speedy, superficial, swift, unthorough.
antonym leisurely.

hurry *v.* accelerate, belt, bustle, dash, dispatch, expedite, festinate, fly, get a move on, goad, hasten, hightail it, hump, hustle, jump to it, look lively, move, pike, quicken, rush, scoot, scurry, scutter, scuttle, shake a leg, shift, speed up, step on it, step on the gas, urge.
antonyms dally, delay.

n. bustle, celerity, commotion, dispatch, expedition, flurry, haste, precipitance, precipitancy, precipitation, promptitude, quickness, rush, scurry, speed, sweat, urgency.
antonyms calm, leisureliness.

hurt *v.* abuse, ache, afflict, aggrieve, annoy, bruise, burn, damage, disable, distress, grieve, harm, impair, injure, maim, maltreat, mar, pain, sadden, smart, spoil, sting, throb, tingle, torture, upset, wound.

n. abuse, bruise, damage, detriment, disadvantage, discomfort, distress, harm, injury, lesion, loss, mischief, pain, pang, scathe, sore, soreness, suffering, wound, wrong.

adj. aggrieved, annoyed, bruised, crushed, cut, damaged, displeased, grazed, harmed, huffed, injured, maimed, miffed, offended, pained, piqued, rueful, sad, saddened, scarred, scraped, scratched, wounded.

hurtful *adj.* catty, cruel, cutting, damaging, derogatory, destructive, detrimental, disadvantageous, distressing, harmful, humiliating, injurious, malefactory, malefic, maleficent, malicious, malificious, malignant, mean, mischievous, nasty, nocuous, pernicious, pestful, pestiferous, pestilent(ial), pointed, prejudicial, scathing, spiteful, unkind, upsetting, vicious, wounding.
antonyms helpful, kind.

hurtle *v.* bowl, charge, chase, crash, dash, fly, plunge, race, rattle, rush, scoot, scramble, shoot, speed, spin, spurt, tear.

husband[1] *v.* budget, conserve, economize, eke out, hoard, ration, save, save up, store, use sparingly.
antonyms squander, waste.

husband[2] *n.* Benedick, consort, goodman, hubby, man, married man, mate, old man, spouse.

hush *v.* calm, compose, mollify, mute, muzzle, quieten, settle, shush, silence, soothe, still.
antonyms disturb, rouse.

n. calm, calmness, peace, peacefulness, quiet, quietness, repose, serenity, silence, still, stillness, tranquility.
antonyms clamor, uproar.

interj. belt up, euphemeite, favete linguis, hold your tongue, leave it out, not another word, pipe down, quiet, say no more, shush, shut up, ssh, stow it, unberufen, wheesht, whisht.

husk *n.* bark, bract, bran, case, chaff, covering, glume, hull, pod, rind, shell, shuck, tegmen.

husky[1] *adj.* croaking, croaky, gruff, guttural, harsh, hoarse, low, rasping, raucous, rough, roupy, throaty.

husky[2] *adj.* beefy, brawny, burly, hefty, muscular, powerful, rugged, stocky, strapping, strong, sturdy, thickset, tough.

hustle *v.* bustle, crowd, elbow, force, frog-march, haste, hasten, hurry, impel, jog, jostle, pressgang, pressure, push, rush, shove, thrust.

hut *n.* booth, bothan, bothy, cabin, caboose, crib, den, hogan, hovel, kraal, lean-to, shack, shanty, shebang, shed, shelter, shiel, shieling, tilt.

hybrid *n.* amalgam, combination, composite, compound, conglomerate, cross, crossbreed, half-blood, half-breed, heterogeny, mixture, mongrel, mule, pastiche.

adj. bastard, combined, composite, compound, cross, heterogeneous, hybridous, hyphenated, mixed, mongrel, mule, patchwork.
antonyms pure, pure-bred.

hygiene *n.* asepsis, cleanliness, disinfection, hygienics, purity, salubriousness, salubrity, salutariness, sanitariness, sanitation, sterility, wholesomeness.
antonyms filth, insanitariness.

hygienic *adj.* aseptic, clean, cleanly, disinfected, germ-free, healthy, pure, salubrious, salutary, sanitary, sterile, wholesome.
antonym unhygienic.

hyperbole *n.* enlargement, exaggeration, excess, extravagance, magnification, overkill, overplay, overstatement.
antonyms meiosis, understatement.

hypercritical *adj.* captious, carping, caviling, censorious, exceptious, fault-finding, finicky, fussy, hair-splitting, niggling, nit-picking, over-particular, pedantic, pernickety, quibbling, strict, ultracrepidarian, Zoilean.
antonyms tolerant, uncritical.

hypnotic *adj.* compelling, dazzling, fascinating, irresistible, magnetic, mesmeric, mesmerizing, narcotic, opiate, sleep-inducing, somniferous, soothing, soporific, spellbinding.

hypnotize *v.* bewitch, captivate, dazzle, entrance, fascinate, magnetize, mesmerize, spellbind, stupefy.

hypocrisy *n.* cant, deceit, deceitfulness, deception, dissembling, double-talk, duplicity, falsity, imposture, insincerity, lip-service, pharisaicalness, pharisaism, phariseeism, phoneyness, pietism, pretense, quackery, sanctimoniousness, self-righteousness, speciousness, Tartuffism, two-facedness.
antonyms humility, sincerity.

hypocrite n. canter, charlatan, deceiver, dissembler, fraud, Holy Willie, impostor, mountebank, Pharisee, phony, pretender, pseud, pseudo, Tartuffe, whited sepulcher.

hypocritical adj. canting, deceitful, deceptive, dissembling, double-faced, duplicitous, false, fraudulent, hollow, insincere, Pecksniffian, pharisaic(al), phony, pietistic, sanctimonious, self-pious, self-righteous, specious, spurious, Tartuffian, Tartuffish, two-faced.
antonyms genuine, humble, sincere.

hypothesis n. assumption, conjecture, guess, postulate, postulatum, premise, premiss, presumption, proposition, starting-point, supposition, theory, thesis.

hypothetical adj. academic, assumed, conjectural, imaginary, postulated, proposed, putative, speculative, supposed, suppositional, theoretical.
antonyms actual, real.

I

idea n. abstraction, aim, approximation, archetype, belief, clue, conceit, concept, conception, conceptualization, conclusion, conjecture, construct, conviction, design, doctrine, end, essence, estimate, fancy, form, guess, guesstimate, hint, hypothesis, idée fixe, image, import, impression, inkling, intention, interpretation, intimation, judgment, meaning, monomania, notion, object, opinion, pattern, perception, plan, purpose, reason, recept, recommendation, scheme, sense, significance, solution, suggestion, surmise, suspicion, teaching, theory, thought, type, understanding, view, viewpoint, vision.

ideal n. archetype, criterion, dreamboat, epitome, example, exemplar, image, last word, model, ne plus ultra, nonpareil, paradigm, paragon, pattern, perfection, pink of perfection, principle, prototype, standard, type.
adj. abstract, archetypal, best, classic, complete, conceptual, consummate, fanciful, highest, hypothetical, imaginary, impractical, model, optimal, optimum, perfect, quintessential, supreme, theoretical, transcendent, transcendental, unattainable, unreal, Utopian, visionary.

idealistic adj. impracticable, impractical, optimistic, perfectionist, quixotic, romantic, starry-eyed, unrealistic, utopian, visionary.
antonyms pragmatic, realistic.

identify v. catalog, classify, detect, diagnose, distinguish, finger, know, label, make out, name, pick out, pinpoint, place, recognize, single out, specify, spot, tag.

identity n. accord, coincidence, correspondence, empathy, existence, haecceity, individuality, oneness, particularity, personality, quiddity, rapport, sameness, self, selfhood, singularity, unanimity, uniqueness, unity.

ideology n. belief(s), convictions, creed, doctrine(s), dogma, ethic, faith, ideas, metaphysics, philosophy, principles, speculation, tenets, Weltanschauung, world view.

idiom n. colloquialism, expression, idiolect, idiotism, jargon, language, locution, parlance, phrase, regionalism, set phrase, style, talk, turn of phrase, usage, vernacular.

idiot n. ament, ass, blockhead, booby, cretin, cuckoo, dimwit, dolt, dumbbell, dummy, dunderhead, fathead, featherbrain, fool, golem, half-wit, imbecile, mental defective, mooncalf, moron, natural, nidget, nig-nog, nincompoop, nitwit, noodle, saphead, schlep, schmo, schmuck, simpleton, thick, thickhead.

idiotic adj. asinine, crazy, cretinous, daft, dumb, fatheaded, fatuous, foolhardy, foolish, hair-brained, half-witted, harebrained, idiotical, imbecile, imbecilic, inane, insane, loony, lunatic, moronic, nutty, screwy, senseless, simple, stupid, tomfool, unintelligent.
antonyms sane, sensible.

idle adj. abortive, bootless, dead, dormant, dronish, empty, foolish, frivolous, fruitless, futile, good-for-nothing, groundless, inactive, indolent, ineffective, ineffectual, inoperative, jobless, lackadaisical, lazy, mothballed, nugatory, of no avail, otiose, pointless, purposeless, redundant, shiftless, slothful, sluggish, stationary, superficial, torpid, trivial, unavailing, unbusy, unemployed, unproductive, unsuccessful, unused, useless, vain, work-shy, worthless.
antonyms active, effective, purposeful.
v. coast, dally, dawdle, drift, fool, fritter, kill time, lallygag, laze, lie up, loiter, lounge, potter, rest on one's laurels, shirk, skive, slack, take it easy, tick over, vegetate, waste, while.
antonyms act, work.

idol n. beloved, darling, deity, favorite, fetish, god, graven image, hero, icon, image, joss, ju-ju, Mumbo-jumbo, pet, pin-up, superstar.

idolize v. admire, adore, apotheosize, deify, dote on, exalt, glorify, hero-worship, iconize, lionize, love, revere, reverence, venerate, worship.
antonym vilify.

ignoble adj. abject, base, base-born, caddish, common, contemptible, cowardly, craven, dastardly, degenerate, degraded, despicable, disgraceful, dishonorable, heinous, humble, infamous, low, low-born, lowly, mean, petty, plebeian, shabby, shameless, unworthy, vile, vulgar, worthless, wretched.
antonyms honorable, noble.

ignominious adj. abject, crushing, degrading, despicable, discreditable, disgraceful, dishonorable, disreputable, humiliating, indecorous, inglorious, mortifying, scandalous, shameful, sorry, undignified.
antonyms honorable, triumphant.

ignorant adj. as thick as two short planks, benighted, blind, bookless, clueless, crass, dense, green, gross, half-baked, idealess, ill-informed, illiterate, ill-versed, inexperienced, innocent, innumerate, insensitive, know-nothing, naïve, nescient, oblivious, pig-ignorant, stupid, thick, unacquainted, unaware, unconscious, uncultivated, uneducated, unenlightened, unidea'd, uninformed, uninitiated, uninstructed, unknowing, unlearned, unlettered, unread, unscholarly, unschooled, untaught, untrained, untutored, unwitting.
antonyms knowlegeable, wise.

ignore v. blink, cold-shoulder, cut, disregard, neglect, omit, overlook, pass over, pay no attention to, pigeonhole, reject, send to Coventry, set aside, shut one's eyes to, slight, take no notice of, turn a blind eye to, turn a deaf ear to, turn one's back on.

antonym note.

ill[1] *adj.* ailing, dicky, diseased, frail, funny, indisposed, infirm, laid up, not up to snuff, off-color, on the sick list, out of sorts, peelie-wally, poorly, queasy, queer, seedy, sick, under the weather, unhealthy, unwell, valetudinarian.

antonym well.

n. affliction, ailment, complaint, disease, disorder, illness, indisposition, infection, infirmity, malady, malaise, sickness.

ill[2] *adj.* acrimonious, adverse, antagonistic, bad, cantankerous, cross, damaging, deleterious, detrimental, difficult, disturbing, evil, foul, harmful, harsh, hateful, hostile, hurtful, inauspicious, incorrect, inimical, iniquitous, injurious, malevolent, malicious, ominous, reprehensible, ruinous, sinister, sullen, surly, threatening, unfavorable, unfortunate, unfriendly, unhealthy, unkind, unlucky, unpromising, unpropitious, unwholesome, vile, wicked, wrong.

antonyms beneficial, fortunate, good, kind.

n. abuse, affliction, badness, cruelty, damage, depravity, destruction, evil, harm, hurt, ill-usage, injury, malice, mischief, misery, misfortune, pain, sorrow, suffering, trial, tribulation, trouble, unpleasantness, wickedness, woe.

antonym benefit.

adv. amiss, badly, by no means, hard, hardly, inauspiciously, insufficiently, poorly, scantily, scarcely, unfavorably, unluckily, wrongfully.

antonym well.

ill-advised *adj.* daft, foolhardy, foolish, hasty, hazardous, ill-considered, ill-judged, impolitic, imprudent, inappropriate, incautious, indiscreet, injudicious, misguided, overhasty, rash, reckless, short-sighted, thoughtless, unseemly, unwise, wrong-headed.

antonym sensible.

ill-assorted *adj.* discordant, incompatible, incongruous, inharmonious, misallied, mismatched, uncongenial, unsuited.

antonym harmonious.

illegal *adj.* actionable, banned, black-market, contraband, criminal, felonious, forbidden, illicit, outlawed, pirate, prohibited, proscribed, unauthorized, unconstitutional, under-the-counter, unlawful, unlicensed, wrongful, wrongous.

antonym legal.

ill-fated *adj.* blighted, doomed, forlorn, hapless, ill-omened, ill-starred, infaust, luckless, star-crossed, unfortunate, unhappy, unlucky.

antonym lucky.

illiberal *adj.* bigoted, close-fisted, hidebound, intolerant, mean, miserly, narrow-minded, niggardly, parsimonious, petty, prejudiced, reactionary, small-minded, sordid, stingy, tight, tightfisted, uncharitable, ungenerous, verkrampte.

antonym liberal.

illicit *adj.* black, black-market, bootleg, clandestine, contraband, criminal, felonious, forbidden, furtive, guilty, illegal, illegitimate, ill-gotten, immoral, improper, inadmissible, prohibited, unauthorized, unlawful, unlicensed, unsanctioned, wrong.

antonyms legal, licit.

illiterate *adj.* analphabetic, benighted, ignorant, uncultured, uneducated, unlettered, untaught, untutored.

antonym literate.

ill-natured *adj.* bad-tempered, churlish, crabbed, cross, cross-grained, disagreeable, disobliging, malevolent, malicious, malignant, mean, nasty, perverse, petulant, spiteful, sulky, sullen, surly, unfriendly, unkind, unpleasant, vicious, vindictive.

antonym good-natured.

illness *n.* affliction, ailment, attack, complaint, disability, disease, disorder, distemper, dyscrasia, idiopathy, ill-being, ill-health, indisposition, infirmity, malady, malaise, sickness.

antonym health.

illogical *adj.* absurd, fallacious, faulty, illegitimate, inconclusive, inconsistent, incorrect, invalid, irrational, meaningless, senseless, sophistical, specious, spurious, unreasonable, unscientific, unsound.

antonym logical.

ill-tempered *adj.* bad-tempered, choleric, cross, curt, grumpy, ill-humored, ill-natured, impatient, irascible, irritable, sharp, spiteful, testy, tetchy, touchy, vicious, vixenish, vixenly.

antonym good-tempered.

ill-treatment *n.* abuse, damage, harm, ill-use, injury, maltreatment, manhandling, mishandling, mistreatment, misuse, neglect.

antonym care.

illuminate *v.* adorn, beacon, brighten, clarify, clear up, decorate, edify, elucidate, enlighten, explain, illumine, illustrate, instruct, irradiate, light, light up, limn, miniate, ornament.

antonyms darken, deface, divest.

illusion *n.* apparition, chimera, daydream, deception, delusion, error, fallacy, fancy, fantasy, figment, hallucination, ignis fatuus, maya, mirage, misapprehension, misconception, phantasm, semblance, will-o'-the-wisp.

antonym reality.

illusory *adj.* apparent, Barmecidal, beguiling, chimerical, deceitful, deceptive, deluding, delusive, fallacious, false, hallucinatory, illusive, misleading, mistaken, seeming, sham, unreal, unsubstantial, untrue, vain.

antonym real.

illustrate *v.* adorn, clarify, decorate, demonstrate, depict, draw, elucidate, emphasize, exemplify, exhibit, explain, illuminate, instance, interpret, miniate, ornament, picture, show, sketch.

illustration *n.* adornment, analogy, case, case in point, clarification, decoration, delineation, demonstration, drawing, elucidation, example, exemplification, explanation, figure, graphic, half-tone, instance, interpretation, photograph, picture, plate, representation, sketch, specimen.

illustrious *adj.* brilliant, celebrated, distinguished, eminent, exalted, excellent, famed, famous, glorious, great, magnificent, noble, notable, noted, outstanding, prominent, remarkable, renowned, resplendent, signal, splendid.

antonyms inglorious, shameful.

image *n.* appearance, conceit, concept, conception, counterpart, dead ringer, Doppelgänger, double, effigies, effigy, eidolon, eikon, facsimile, figure, icon, idea, idol, impression, likeness, perception, picture, portrait, reflection, replica, representation, semblance, similitude, simulacrum, spit, spitting image, statue, trope.

imaginary *adj.* assumed, Barmecidal, chimerical, dreamlike, fancied, fanciful, fictional, fictitious, hallucinatory, hypothetical, ideal, illusive, illusory, imagined,

insubstantial, invented, legendary, made-up, mythological, non-existent, phantasmal, shadowy, supposed, unreal, unsubstantial, visionary.
antonym real.

imagination *n.* chimera, conception, creativity, enterprise, fancy, idea, ideality, illusion, image, imaginativeness, ingenuity, innovativeness, innovatoriness, insight, inspiration, invention, inventiveness, notion, originality, resourcefulness, supposition, unreality, vision, wit, wittiness.
antonyms reality, unimaginativeness.

imaginative *adj.* clever, creative, dreamy, enterprising, fanciful, fantastic, fertile, ingenious, innovative, inspired, inventive, original, poetical, resourceful, visionary, vivid.
antonym unimaginative.

imagine *v.* apprehend, assume, believe, conceive, conceptualize, conjecture, conjure up, create, deduce, deem, devise, dream up, envisage, envision, fancy, fantasize, frame, gather, guess, ideate, infer, invent, judge, picture, plan, project, realize, scheme, suppose, surmise, suspect, take it, think, think of, think up, visualize.

imbecile *n.* ament, blockhead, bungler, clown, cretin, dolt, dotard, fool, half-wit, idiot, moron, thickhead.
adj. anile, asinine, doltish, fatuous, feeble-minded, foolish, idiotic, imbecilic, inane, ludicrous, moronic, senile, simple, stupid, thick, witless.
antonyms intelligent, sensible.

imbibe *v.* absorb, acquire, assimilate, consume, drink, drink in, gain, gather, gulp, ingest, knock back, lap up, quaff, receive, sink, sip, soak in, soak up, swallow, swig, take in.

imitate *v.* affect, ape, burlesque, caricature, clone, copy, copy-cat, counterfeit, do, duplicate, echo, emulate, follow, follow suit, forge, impersonate, mimic, mirror, mock, monkey, parody, parrot, personate, repeat, reproduce, send up, simulate, spoof, take off, travesty.

imitation *n.* apery, aping, copy, counterfeit, counterfeiting, duplication, echoing, echopraxia, echopraxis, fake, forgery, impersonation, impression, likeness, mimesis, mimicry, mockery, parody, reflection, replica, reproduction, resemblance, sham, simulation, substitution, take-off, travesty.
adj. artificial, dummy, ersatz, man-made, mock, phony, pinchbeck, pseudo, repro, reproduction, sham, simulated, synthetic.
antonym genuine.

immaculate *adj.* blameless, clean, faultless, flawless, guiltless, impeccable, incorrupt, innocent, neat, perfect, pure, scrupulous, sinless, spick-and-span, spotless, spruce, stainless, trim, unblemished, uncontaminated, undefiled, unexceptionable, unpolluted, unsullied, untainted, untarnished, virtuous.
antonyms contaminated, spoiled.

immature *adj.* adolescent, babyish, callow, childish, crude, green, immatured, imperfect, inexperienced, infantile, jejune, juvenile, premature, puerile, raw, under-age, undeveloped, unfinished, unfledged, unformed, unripe, unseasonable, untimely, young.
antonym mature.

immeasurable *adj.* bottomless, boundless, endless, illimitable, immense, immensurable, incalculable, inestimable, inexhaustible, infinite, limitless, measureless,
unbounded, unfathomable, unlimited, unmeasurable, vast.
antonym limited.

immediate *adj.* actual, adjacent, close, contiguous, current, direct, existing, extant, instant, instantaneous, near, nearest, neighboring, next, on hand, present, pressing, primary, prompt, proximate, recent, unhesitating, up-to-date, urgent.
antonym distant.

immediately *adv.* at once, closely, directly, forthwith, incontinent, instantly, lickety-split, nearly, now, off the top of one's head, on the instant, posthaste, promptly, pronto, right away, straight away, straight off, straight way, tout de suite, unhesitatingly, without delay.
antonyms eventually, never.

immense *adj.* Brobdingnag(ian), colossal, cyclopean, elephantine, enormous, extensive, giant, gigantic, great, herculean, huge, illimitable, immeasurable, infinite, interminable, jumbo, large, limitless, mammoth, massive, monstrous, monumental, prodigious, rounceval, stupendous, Titanesque, titanic, tremendous, vast.
antonym minute.

immensity *n.* bulk, enormousness, expanse, extent, greatness, hugeness, infinity, magnitude, massiveness, scope, size, sweep, vastness.
antonym minuteness.

immerse *v.* bathe, demerge, demerse, dip, douse, duck, dunk, plunge, sink, submerge, submerse.

immigrate *v.* come in, migrate, move in, remove, resettle, settle.
antonym emigrate.

imminent *adj.* afoot, approaching, at hand, brewing, close, coming, forthcoming, gathering, impending, in the air, in the offing, looming, menacing, near, nigh, overhanging, threatening.
antonym far-off.

immoderately *adv.* exaggeratedly, excessively, exorbitantly, extravagantly, extremely, inordinately, unduly, unjustifiably, unreasonably, unrestrainedly, wantonly, without measure.
antonym moderately.

immoral *adj.* abandoned, bad, corrupt, debauched, degenerate, depraved, dishonest, dissolute, evil, foul, impure, indecent, iniquitous, lecherous, lewd, licentious, nefarious, obscene, pornographic, profligate, reprobate, sinful, unchaste, unethical, unprincipled, unrighteous, unscrupulous, vicious, vile, wanton, wicked, wrong.
antonym moral.
antonym morality.

immortal *adj.* abiding, ambrosial, constant, deathless, endless, enduring, eternal, everlasting, imperishable, incorruptible, indestructible, lasting, perennial, perpetual, sempiternal, timeless, undying, unfading, unforgettable.
antonym mortal.
n. deity, divinity, genius, god, goddess, great, hero, Olympian.

immortalize *v.* apotheosize, celebrate, commemorate, deify, enshrine, eternalize, eternize, exalt, glorify, hallow, memorialize, perpetuate, solemnize.

immune *adj.* clear, exempt, free, insusceptible, insusceptive, invulnerable, proof, protected, resistant, safe, unaffected, unsusceptible.

antonym susceptible.

immutable *adj*. abiding, changeless, constant, enduring, fixed, inflexible, invariable, lasting, permanent, perpetual, sacrosanct, solid, stable, steadfast, unalterable, unchangeable.

antonym mutable.

impact *n*. aftermath, bang, blow, brunt, bump, burden, collision, concussion, consequences, contact, crash, effect, force, impression, influence, jolt, knock, knock-on effect, meaning, power, repercussions, shock, significance, smash, stroke, thrust, thump, weight.

v. clash, collide, crash, crush, fix, hit, press together, strike, wedge.

impair *v*. blunt, craze, damage, debilitate, decrease, deteriorate, devalue, diminish, enervate, enfeeble, harm, hinder, injure, lessen, mar, reduce, spoil, undermine, vitiate, weaken, worsen.

antonym enhance.

impart *v*. accord, afford, bestow, communicate, confer, contribute, convey, disclose, discover, divulge, give, grant, hand over, lend, make known, offer, pass on, relate, reveal, tell, yield.

impartial *adj*. detached, disinterested, dispassionate, equal, equitable, even-handed, fair, just, neutral, non-discriminating, non-partisan, objective, open-minded, uncommitted, unbiased, unprejudiced.

antonym biased.

impartiality *n*. detachment, disinterest, disinterestedness, dispassion, equality, equity, even-handedness, fairness, neutrality, non-partisanship, objectivity, open-mindedness, unbiasedness.

antonym bias.

impasse *n*. blind alley, cul-de-sac, dead end, deadlock, halt, nonplus, stalemate, stand-off, standstill.

impassioned *adj*. animated, ardent, blazing, enthusiastic, excited, fervent, fervid, fiery, furious, glowing, heated, inflamed, inspired, intense, passionate, rousing, spirited, stirring, vehement, vigorous, violent, vivid, warm.

antonyms apathetic, mild.

impassive *adj*. aloof, apathetic, blockish, callous, calm, composed, cool, dispassionate, emotionless, expressionless, immobile, impassible, imperturbable, indifferent, inscrutable, insensible, insusceptible, laid back, phlegmatic, poker-faced, reserved, serene, stoical, stolid, unconcerned, unemotional, unexcitable, unfeeling, unimpressible, unmoved, unruffled.

antonyms moved, responsive, warm.

impede *v*. bar, block, brake, check, clog, curb, delay, disrupt, hamper, hinder, hobble, hold up, let, obstruct, restrain, retard, slow, stop, thwart, trammel.

antonym aid.

impediment *n*. bar, barrier, block, burr, check, clog, curb, defect, difficulty, encumbrance, hindrance, let, log, obstacle, obstruction, snag, stammer, stumbling-block, stutter.

antonym aid.

impel *v*. actuate, chivvy, compel, constrain, drive, excite, force, goad, incite, induce, influence, inspire, instigate, motivate, move, oblige, poke, power, prod, prompt, propel, push, spur, stimulate, urge.

antonym dissuade.

impending *adj*. approaching, brewing, close, collecting, coming, forthcoming, gathering, hovering, imminent, in store, looming, menacing, near, nearing, threatening.

antonym remote.

impenetrable *adj*. arcane, baffling, cabbalistic, cryptic, dark, dense, enigmatic(al), fathomless, hermetic, hidden, impassable, impermeable, impervious, incomprehensible, indiscernible, inexplicable, inscrutable, inviolable, mysterious, obscure, solid, thick, unfathomable, unintelligible, unpiercable.

antonyms intelligible, penetrable.

imperative *adj*. authoritative, autocratic, bossy, commanding, compulsory, crucial, dictatorial, domineering, essential, exigent, high-handed, imperious, indispensable, insistent, lordly, magisterial, obligatory, peremptory, pressing, tyrannical, tyrannous, urgent, vital.

antonyms humble, optional.

imperceptible *adj*. faint, fine, gradual, impalpable, inapparent, inappreciable, inaudible, inconsensequential, indiscernible, indistinguishable, infinitesimal, insensible, invisible, microscopic, minute, shadowy, slight, small, subtle, tiny, undetectable, unnoticeable.

antonym perceptible.

imperfection *n*. blemish, blot, blotch, crack, defect, deficiency, dent, failing, fallibility, fault, flaw, foible, frailty, glitch, inadequacy, incompleteness, insufficiency, peccadillo, shortcoming, stain, taint, weakness.

antonyms asset, perfection.

imperil *v*. compromise, endanger, expose, hazard, jeopardize, risk, threaten.

impersonal *adj*. aloof, bureaucratic, businesslike, cold, detached, dispassionate, faceless, formal, frosty, glassy, inhuman, neutral, official, remote, unfriendly, unsympathetic.

antonym friendly.

impersonate *v*. act, ape, caricature, do, imitate, masquerade as, mimic, mock, parody, personate, pose as, take off.

impertinence *n*. assurance, audacity, backchat, boldness, brass, brazenness, cheek, discourtesy, disrespect, effrontery, forwardness, impoliteness, impudence, incivility, insolence, malapertness, nerve, pertness, politeness, presumption, rudeness, sauce, sauciness.

impertinent *adj*. bold, brattish, brazen, bumptious, cheeky, discourteous, disrespectful, forward, fresh, ill-mannered, impolite, impudent, insolent, interfering, malapert, pert, presumptuous, rude, saucy, uncivil, unmannerly.

antonym polite.

impetuous *adj*. ardent, bull-headed, eager, furious, hasty, headlong, impassioned, impulsive, overhasty, passionate, precipitate, rash, spontaneous, tearaway, unplanned, unpremeditated, unreflecting, unrestrained, unthinking.

antonym circumspect.

implacable *adj*. cruel, immovable, inappeasable, inexorable, inflexible, intractable, intransigent, irreconcilable, merciless, pitiless, rancorous, relentless, remorseless, ruthless, unappeasable, unbending, uncompromising, unforgiving, unrelenting, unyielding.

antonym placable.

implausible *adj*. dubious, far-fetched, flimsy, improbable, incredible, suspect, thin, transparent, unbeliev-

able, unconvincing, unlikely, unplausible, unreasonable, weak.
antonym plausible.

implicate *v.* associate, compromise, connect, embroil, entangle, include, incriminate, inculpate, involve, throw suspicion on.
antonyms absolve, exonerate.

implicit *adj.* absolute, constant, contained, entire, firm, fixed, full, implied, inherent, latent, presupposed, steadfast, tacit, total, undeclared, understood, unhesitating, unqualified, unquestioning, unreserved, unshakable, unshaken, unspoken, wholehearted.
antonym explicit.

implore *v.* ask, beg, beseech, crave, entreat, importune, plead, pray, solicit, supplicate, wheedle.

imply *v.* betoken, connote, denote, entail, evidence, hint, import, indicate, insinuate, intimate, involve, mean, point to, presuppose, require, signify, suggest.
antonym state.

impolite *adj.* abrupt, bad-mannered, boorish, churlish, clumsy, coarse, cross, discourteous, disrespectful, gauche, ill-bred, ill-mannered, indecorous, indelicate, inept, insolent, loutish, rough, rude, uncivil, uncourteous, ungallant, ungentlemanly, ungracious, unladylike, unmannerly, unrefined.
antonym polite.

import *n.* bearing, consequence, drift, essence, gist, implication, importance, intention, magnitude, meaning, message, moment, nub, purport, sense, significance, substance, thrust, weight.
v. betoken, bring in, imply, indicate, introduce, mean, purport, signify.

important *adj.* basic, eminent, essential, far-reaching, foremost, grave, heavy, high-level, high-ranking, influential, key, keynote, large, leading, material, meaningful, momentous, notable, noteworthy, on the map, outstanding, powerful, pre-eminent, primary, prominent, relevant, salient, seminal, serious, signal, significant, substantial, urgent, valuable, valued, weighty.
antonym unimportant.

impose[1] *v.* appoint, burden, charge (with), decree, dictate, encumber, enforce, enjoin, establish, exact, fix, impone, inflict, institute, introduce, lay, levy, ordain, place, prescribe, promulgate, put, saddle, set.

impose[2] *v.* butt in, encroach, foist, force oneself, gate crash, horn in, impone, interpose, intrude, obtrude, presume, take liberties, trespass.

imposing *adj.* august, commanding, dignified, distinguished, effective, grand, grandiose, impressive, majestic, ortund, pompous, stately, striking.
antonyms modest, unimposing.

imposition[1] *n.* application, decree, exaction, infliction, introduction, levying, promulgation.

imposition[2] *n.* burden, charge, cheek, constraint, deception, duty, encroachment, intrusion, levy, liberty, lines, presumption, punishment, task, tax.

impossible *adj.* absurd, hopeless, impracticable, inadmissible, inconceivable, insoluble, intolerable, ludicrous, outrageous, preposterous, unacceptable, unachievable, unattainable, ungovernable, unobtainable, unreasonable, untenable, unthinkable, unviable, unworkable.
antonym possible.

impractical *adj.* academic, idealistic, impossible,

impracticable, inoperable, ivory-tower, non-viable, romantic, starry-eyed, unbusinesslike, unrealistic, unserviceable, unworkable, visionary, wild.
antonym practical.

impregnable *adj.* fast, fortified, immovable, impenetrable, impugnable, indestructible, invincible, invulnerable, secure, solid, strong, unassailable, unbeatable, unconquerable.
antonym vulnerable.

impress *v.* affect, emboss, emphasize, engrave, excite, fix, grab, imprint, inculcate, indent, influence, inspire, instil, make one's mark, mark, move, namedrop, print, slay, stamp, stand out, stir, strike, sway, touch, wow.

impression[1] *n.* awareness, belief, concept, consciousness, conviction, effect, fancy, feeling, hunch, idea, impact, influence, memory, notion, opinion, reaction, recollection, sense, suspicion, sway.

impression[2] *n.* dent, edition, engram, engramma, hollow, impress, imprint, imprinting, incuse, indentation, issue, mark, niello, outline, pressure, printing, stamp, stamping.

impression[3] *n.* apery, aping, burlesque, imitation, impersonation, parody, send-up, take-off.

impressive *adj.* affecting, effective, exciting, forcible, foudroyant, frappant, imposing, moving, powerful, stirring, striking, touching.
antonym unimpressive.

impromptu *adj.* ad-lib, autoschediastic, extemporaneous, extempore, extemporised, improvised, off the cuff, off-hand, offhand, spontaneous, unpremeditated, unprepared, unrehearsed, unscripted, unstudied.
antonyms planned, rehearsed.
adv. ad lib, extempore, off the cuff, off the top of one's head, on the spur of the moment, spontaneously.
n. autoschediasm, extemporisation, improvisation, voluntary.

improper *adj.* abnormal, erroneous, false, illegitimate, ill-timed, impolite, inaccurate, inadmissible, inapplicable, inapposite, inappropriate, inapt, incongruous, incorrect, indecent, indecorous, indelicate, infelicitous, inopportune, irregular, malapropos, off-color, out of place, risqué, smutty, suggestive, unbecoming, uncalled-for, unfit, unfitting, unmaidenly, unparliamentary, unprintable, unquotable, unrepeatable, unseasonable, unseemly, unsuitable, unsuited, untoward, unwarranted, vulgar, wrong.
antonym proper.

improve *v.* advance, ameliorate, amend, augment, better, correct, culture, develop, embourgeoise, enhance, gentrify, help, increase, look up, meliorate, mend, mend one's ways, perk up, pick up, polish, progress, rally, recover, rectify, recuperate, reform, rise, touch up, turn over a new leaf, turn the corner, up, upgrade.
antonyms decline, diminish.

improvement *n.* advance, advancement, amelioration, amendment, augmentation, bettering, betterment, correction, development, embourgeoisement, enhancement, furtherance, gain, gentrification, increase, melioration, progress, rally, recovery, rectification, reformation, rise, upswing.

improvident *adj.* careless, feckless, heedless, imprudent, Micawberish, negligent, prodigal, profligate, reckless, shiftless, spendthrift, thoughtless, thriftless, underprepared, uneconomical, unprepared, unthrifty, wasteful.

antonym thrifty.

improvisation *n.* ad-lib, ad-libbing, autoschediasm, expedient, extemporising, impromptu, invention, makeshift, spontaneity, vamp.

imprudent *adj.* careless, foolhardy, foolish, hasty, heedless, ill-advised, ill-considered, ill-judged, impolitic, improvident, incautious, inconsiderate, indiscreet, injudicious, irresponsible, overhasty, rash, reckless, short-sighted, temerarious, unthinking, unwise.
antonym prudent.

impudence *n.* assurance, audacity, backchat, boldness, brass neck, brazenness, cheek, chutzpah, effrontery, face, impertinence, impudicity, insolence, lip, malapertness, neck, nerve, pertness, presumption, presumptuousness, rudeness, sauciness, shamelessness.
antonym politeness.

impudent *adj.* audacious, bold, bold-faced, brazen, brazen-faced, cheeky, cocky, forward, fresh, immodest, impertinent, insolent, malapert, pert, presumptuous, rude, saucy, shameless.
antonym polite.

impulse *n.* caprice, catalyst, conatus, desire, drive, feeling, force, impetus, incitement, inclination, influence, instinct, momentum, motive, movement, notion, passion, pressure, push, resolve, stimulus, surge, thrust, urge, whim, wish.

impulsive *adj.* hasty, headlong, impetuous, instinctive, intuitive, passionate, precipitant, precipitate, quick, rash, reckless, spontaneous, unconsidered, unpredictable, unpremeditated.
antonym cautious.

impure *adj.* admixed, adulterated, alloyed, carnal, coarse, contaminated, corrupt, debased, defiled, dirty, feculent, filthy, foul, gross, immodest, immoral, indecent, indelicate, infected, lascivious, lewd, licentious, lustful, mixed, obscene, polluted, prurient, salacious, smutty, sullied, tainted, turbid, unchaste, unclean, unrefined, unwholesome, vicious, vitiated.
antonyms chaste, pure.

imputation *n.* accusation, arrogation, ascription, aspersion, attribution, blame, censure, charge, insinuation, reproach, slander, slur, suggestion.

in abeyance dormant, hanging fire, on ice, pending, shelved, suspended.

in camera behind closed doors, hugger-mugger, in private, in secret, privately, secretly, sub rosa, under the rose.
antonym openly.

in confidence in private, privately, secretly, sub rosa, under the rose.

in depth comprehensively, exhaustively, extensively, in detail, intensively, thoroughly.
antonyms broadly, superficially.

in effect actually, effectively, essentially, for practical purposes, in actuality, in fact, in reality, in the end, in truth, really, to all intents and purposes, virtually, when all is said and done.

in force binding, current, effective, gregatim, in crowds, in droves, in flocks, in hordes, in large numbers, in operation, in strength, on the statute book, operative, valid, working.
antonym inoperative.

in good part cheerfully, cordially, good-naturedly, laughingly, well.
antonyms angrily, touchily.

in keeping appropriate, befitting, fit, fitting, harmonious, in harmony, of a piece, suitable.
antonym inappropriate.

in motion afoot, functioning, going, in progress, moving, on the go, operational, running, sailing, traveling, under way.
antonym stationary.

in order acceptable, all right, allowed, appropriate, arranged, called for, correct, done, fitting, in sequence, neat, OK, orderly, permitted, right, shipshape, suitable, tidy.
antonyms disallowed, out of order.

in order to intending to, so that, to, with a view to, with the intention of, with the purpose of.

in part a little, in some measure, part way, partially, partly, slightly, somewhat, to a certain extent, to some degree.
antonym wholly.

in passing accidentally, by the by(e), by the way, en passant, incidentally.

in person as large as life, bodily, in propria persona, personally.

in principle en principe, ideally, in essence, in theory, theoretically.

in spite of despite, notwithstanding.

in the light of bearing/keeping in mind, because of, considering, in view of, taking into account.

in the money affluent, flush, loaded, opulent, prosperous, rich, rolling in it, wealthy, well-heeled, well-off, well-to-do.
antonym poor.

in the mood disposed, in the right frame of mind, inclined, interested, keen, minded, of a mind, willing.

in the offing at hand, close at hand, coming up, imminent, in sight, on the horizon, on the way.
antonym far off.

in the red bankrupt, in arrears, in debt, insolvent, on the rocks, overdrawn.
antonym in credit.

in two minds dithering, hesitant, hesitating, shilly-shallying, swithering, uncertain, undecided, unsure, vacillating, wavering.
antonym certain.

in vain bootlessly, fruitlessly, ineffectually, to no avail, unsuccessfully, uselessly, vainly.
antonym successfully.

inability *n.* disability, disqualification, handicap, impotence, inadequacy, incapability, incapacity, incompetence, ineptitude, ineptness, powerlessness, weakness.
antonym ability.

inaccurate *adj.* careless, defective, discrepant, erroneous, faulty, imprecise, in error, incorrect, inexact, loose, mistaken, out, unfaithful, unreliable, unrepresentative, unsound, wide of the mark, wild, wrong.
antonym accurate.

inactive *adj.* abeyant, dormant, dull, idle, immobile, indolent, inert, inoperative, jobless, kicking one's heels, latent, lazy, lethargic, low-key, mothballed, out of service, out of work, passive, quiet, sedentary, sleepy, slothful, slow, sluggish, somnolent, stagnant, stagnating, torpid, unemployed, unoccupied, unused.
antonym active.

inactivity *n.* abeyance, abeyancy, dilatoriness, dolce far niente, dormancy, dullness, heaviness, hibernation,

idleness, immobility, inaction, indolence, inertia, inertness, languor, lassitude, laziness, lethargy, passivity, quiescence, sloth, sluggishness, stagnation, stasis, torpor, unemployment, vegetation.
antonym activeness.

inadequate *adj.* defective, deficient, faulty, imperfect, inapt, incapable, incommensurate, incompetent, incomplete, ineffective, ineffectual, inefficacious, inefficient, insubstantial, insufficient, leaving a little/a lot/much to be desired, meager, niggardly, scanty, short, sketchy, skimpy, sparse, unequal, unfitted, unqualified, wanting.
antonym adequate.

inadvertent *adj.* accidental, careless, chance, heedless, inattentive, negligent, thoughtless, unguarded, unheeding, unintended, unintentional, unplanned, unpremeditated, unthinking, unwitting.
antonym deliberate.

inane *adj.* asinine, daft, drippy, empty, fatuous, foolish, frivolous, futile, idiotic, imbecilic, mindless, nutty, puerile, senseless, silly, stupid, trifling, unintelligent, vacuous, vain, vapid, worthless.
antonym sensible.

inanimate *adj.* abiotic, dead, defunct, dormant, dull, exanimate, extinct, heavy, inactive, inert, inorganic, insensate, insentient, leaden, lifeless, listless, slow, spiritless, stagnant, torpid.
antonyms alive, animate, lively, living.

inappropriate *adj.* disproportionate, ill-fitted, ill-suited, ill-timed, improper, incongruous, infelicitous, malapropos, out of place, tactless, tasteless, unbecoming, unbefitting, unfit, unfitting, unseemly, unsuitable, untimely.
antonym appropriate.

inarticulate *adj.* blurred, dumb, dysarthric, dysphasic, dyspraxic, faltering, halting, hesitant, incoherent, incomprehensible, indistinct, muffled, mumbled, mute, silent, speechless, tongue-tied, unclear, unintelligible, unspoken, unuttered, unvoiced, voiceless, wordless.
antonym articulate.

inattentive *adj.* absent-minded, careless, deaf, distracted, distrait, dreaming, dreamy, heedless, inadvertent, neglectful, negligent, preoccupied, regardless, remiss, unheeding, unmindful, unobservant, vague.
antonym attentive.

inaugurate *v.* begin, christen, commence, commission, consecrate, dedicate, enthrone, han(d)sel, induct, initiate, install, instate, institute, introduce, invest, kick off, launch, open, ordain, originate, set up, start, start off, usher in.

incapable *adj.* disqualified, drunk, feeble, helpless, impotent, inadequate, incompetent, ineffective, ineffectual, inept, insufficient, powerless, tipsy, unable, unfit, unfitted, unqualified, weak.
antonyms capable, sober.

incarcerate *v.* cage, commit, confine, coop up, detain, encage, gaol, immure, impound, imprison, intern, jail, lock up, put away, restrain, restrict, send down, wall in.
antonym free.

incense[1] *n.* adulation, aroma, balm, bouquet, fragrance, homage, joss-stick, perfume, scent, worship.

incense[2] *v.* anger, enrage, exasperate, excite, inflame, infuriate, irritate, madden, make one see red, make

one's blood boil, make one's hackles rise, provoke, raise one's hackles, rile.
antonym calm.

incentive *n.* bait, carrot, cause, consideration, encouragement, enticement, impetus, impulse, inducement, lure, motivation, motive, reason, reward, spur, stimulant, stimulus.
antonym disincentive.

inception *n.* beginning, birth, commencement, dawn, inauguration, initiation, installation, kick-off, origin, outset, rise, start.
antonym end.

incessant *adj.* ceaseless, constant, continual, continuous, endless, eternal, everlasting, interminable, never-ending, non-stop, perpetual, persistent, relentless, unbroken, unceasing, unending, unrelenting, unremitting, weariless.
antonym intermittent.

incident *n.* adventure, affair(e), brush, circumstance, clash, commotion, confrontation, contretemps, disturbance, episode, event, fight, happening, mishap, occasion, occurrence, scene, skirmish.

incidental *adj.* accidental, accompanying, ancillary, attendant, casual, chance, concomitant, contingent, contributory, fortuitous, incident, inconsequential, inessential, irrelevant, minor, non-essential, occasional, odd, random, related, secondary, subordinate, subsidiary.
antonym essential.

incidentally *adv.* accidentally, by chance, by the by(e), by the way, casually, digressively, en passant, fortuitously, in passing, parenthetically.

incinerate *v.* burn, char, cremate, reduce to ashes.

incisive *adj.* acid, acute, astucious, astute, biting, caustic, cutting, keen, mordant, penetrating, perceptive, perspicacious, piercing, sarcastic, sardonic, satirical, severe, sharp, tart, trenchant.
antonym woolly.

incite *v.* abet, animate, drive, egg on, encourage, excite, foment, goad, impel, inflame, instigate, prompt, provoke, put up to, rouse, set on, solicit, spur, stimulate, stir up, urge, whip up.
antonym restrain.

incitement *n.* abetment, agitation, encouragement, goad, hortation, impetus, impulse, inducement, instigation, motivation, motive, prompting, provocation, spur, stimulus.
antonyms check, discouragement.

inclination[1] *n.* affection, aptitude, bent, bias, clinamen, desire, disposition, fancy, fondness, ingenium, leaning, liking, month's mind, partiality, penchant, predilection, predisposition, prejudice, proclivity, proneness, propensity, stomach, taste, tendency, turn, turn of mind, velleity, wish.
antonym disinclination.

inclination[2] *n.* angle, bend, bending, bow, bowing, clinamen, deviation, gradient, incline, leaning, nod, pitch, slant, slope, tilt.

incline[1] *v.* affect, bias, dispose, influence, nod, persuade, predispose, prejudice, stoop, sway.

incline[2] *v.* bend, bevel, bow, cant, deviate, diverge, lean, slant, slope, tend, tilt, tip, veer.
n. acclivity, ascent, brae, declivity, descent, dip, grade, gradient, hill, ramp, rise, slope.

inclose *see* enclose.

include v. add, allow for, comprehend, comprise, connote, contain, cover, embody, embrace, enclose, encompass, incorporate, involve, number among, rope in, subsume, take in, take into account.
antonyms exclude, ignore.

incoherent adj. confused, disconnected, disjointed, dislocated, disordered, inarticulate, inconsequent, inconsistent, jumbled, loose, muddled, rambling, stammering, stuttering, unconnected, unco-ordinated, unintelligible, unjointed, wandering, wild.
antonym coherent.

income n. earnings, gains, interest, means, pay, proceeds, profits, receipts, returns, revenue, salary, takings, wages, yield.
antonym expenses.

incomparable adj. brilliant, inimitable, matchless, paramount, peerless, superb, superlative, supreme, transcendent, unequaled, unmatched, unparalleled, unrivaled.
antonyms poor, run-of-the-mill.

incompetence n. bungling, inability, inadequacy, incapability, incapacity, incompetency, ineffectiveness, ineffectuality, ineffectualness, inefficiency, ineptitude, ineptness, insufficiency, stupidity, unfitness, uselessness.
antonym competence.

incomprehensible adj. above one's head, all Greek, arcane, baffling, beyond one's comprehension, beyond one's grasp, double-Dutch, enigmatic, impenetrable, inapprehensible, inconceivable, inscrutable, mysterious, obscure, opaque, perplexing, puzzling, unfathomable, unimaginable, unintelligible, unthinkable.
antonym comprehensible.

inconceivable adj. implausible, incogitable, incredible, mind-boggling, out of the question, staggering, unbelievable, unheard-of, unimaginable, unknowable, unthinkable.
antonym conceivable.

incongruous adj. absurd, conflicting, contradictory, contrary, disconsonant, discordant, dissociable, extraneous, improper, inappropriate, inapt, incoherent, incompatible, inconcinnous, inconsistent, out of keeping, out of place, unbecoming, unsuitable, unsuited.
antonyms consistent, harmonious.

inconsiderate adj. careless, imprudent, indelicate, insensitive, intolerant, rash, rude, self-centered, selfish, tactless, thoughtless, unconcerned, ungracious, unkind, unthinking.
antonym considerate.

inconsistency n. changeableness, contrariety, disagreement, discrepancy, disparity, divergence, fickleness, incompatibility, incongruity, inconsonance, inconstancy, instability, paradox, unpredictability, unreliability, unsteadiness, variance.
antonym consistency.

inconsistent adj. at odds, at variance, capricious, changeable, conflicting, contradictory, contrary, discordant, discrepant, erratic, fickle, incoherent, incompatible, incongruous, inconstant, irreconcilable, irregular, unpredictable, unstable, unsteady, variable, varying.
antonym constant.

inconspicuous adj. camouflaged, hidden, insignificant, low-key, modest, muted, ordinary, plain, quiet, retiring, unassuming, unnoticeable, unobtrusive, unostentatious.
antonym conspicuous.

inconstant adj. capricious, changeable, changeful, erratic, fickle, fluctuating, inconsistent, irresolute, mercurial, moonish, mutable, uncertain, undependable, unreliable, unsettled, unstable, unsteady, vacillating, variable, varying, volatile, wavering, wayward.
antonym constant.

inconvenient adj. annoying, awkward, bothersome, cumbersome, difficult, disadvantageous, disturbing, embarrassing, inopportune, tiresome, troublesome, unhandy, unmanageable, unseasonable, unsocial, unsuitable, untimely, untoward, unwieldy, vexatious.
antonym convenient.

incorrect adj. erroneous, false, faulty, flawed, illegitimate, imprecise, improper, inaccurate, inappropriate, inexact, mistaken, out, specious, ungrammatical, unidiomatic, unsuitable, untrue, wrong.
antonym correct.

incorruptible adj. everlasting, honest, honorable, imperishable, incorrupt, just, straight, trustworthy, unbribable, undecaying, upright.
antonym corruptible.

increase v. add to, advance, aggrandize, amplify, augment, boost, build up, develop, dilate, eke, eke out, enhance, enlarge, escalate, expand, extend, greaten, grow, heighten, inflate, intensify, magnify, mount, multiply, proliferate, prolong, pullulate, raise, snowball, soar, spread, step up, strengthen, swell, wax.
antonym decrease.
n. accrescence, addition, augment, augmentation, auxesis, boost, development, enlargement, escalation, expansion, extension, gain, growth, increment, intensification, proliferation, rise, step-up, surge, upsurge, upsurgence, upturn.
antonym decrease.

incredible adj. absurd, amazing, astonishing, astounding, extraordinary, fabulous, far-fetched, great, implausible, impossible, improbable, inconceivable, inspired, marvelous, preposterous, prodigious, superb, superhuman, unbelievable, unimaginable, unthinkable, wonderful.
antonyms believable, run-of-the-mill.

incriminate v. accuse, arraign, blame, charge, criminate, impeach, implicate, inculpate, indict, involve, point the finger at, recriminate, stigmatize.
antonym exonerate.

incurious adj. apathetic, careless, inattentive, indifferent, unconcerned, uncurious, unenquiring, uninquiring, uninquisitive, uninterested, unreflective.
antonym curious.

indebted adj. beholden, grateful, in debt, obligated, obliged, thankful.

indecency n. bawdiness, coarseness, crudity, foulness, grossness, immodesty, impropriety, impurity, indecorum, indelicacy, lewdness, licentiousness, obscenity, outrageousness, pornography, Rabelaisianism, smut, smuttiness, unseemliness, vileness, vulgarity.
antonyms decency, modesty.

indecent adj. blue, coarse, crude, dirty, filthy, foul, gross, immodest, improper, impure, indecorous, indelicate, lewd, licentious, near the knuckle, offensive, outrageous, pornographic, Rabelaisian, salacious,

scatological, smutty, tasteless, unbecoming, uncomely, unseemly, vile, vulgar.
antonyms decent, modest.

indecisive *adj.* doubtful, faltering, hesitating, hung, in two minds, inconclusive, indefinite, indeterminate, irresolute, pussyfooting, swithering, tentative, uncertain, unclear, undecided, undetermined, unsure, vacillating, wavering.
antonym decisive.

indeed *adv.* actually, certainly, doubtlessly, forsooth, positively, really, strictly, to be sure, truly, undeniably, undoubtedly, verily, veritably.

indefinite *adj.* ambiguous, confused, doubtful, equivocal, evasive, general, ill-defined, imprecise, indeterminate, indistinct, inexact, loose, obscure, uncertain, unclear, undecided, undefined, undetermined, unfixed, unfocus(s)ed, unformed, unformulated, unknown, unlimited, unresolved, unsettled, vague.
antonyms clear, limited.

indelicate *adj.* blue, coarse, crude, embarrassing, gross, immodest, improper, indecent, indecorous, low, obscene, off-color, offensive, risqué, rude, suggestive, tasteless, unbecoming, unmaidenly, unseemly, untoward, vulgar, warm.
antonym delicate.

indemnity *n.* amnesty, compensation, excusal, exemption, guarantee, immunity, impunity, insurance, privilege, protection, redress, reimbursement, remuneration, reparation, requital, restitution, satisfaction, security.

independent *adj.* absolute, autarchical, autocephalous, autogenous, autonomous, bold, crossbench, decontrolled, free, individualistic, liberated, non-aligned, one's own man, self-contained, self-determining, self-governing, self-reliant, self-sufficient, self-supporting, separate, separated, sovereign, unaided, unbiased, unconnected, unconstrained, uncontrolled, unconventional, unrelated, upon one's legs.
antonyms conventional, dependent, timid.

indestructible *adj.* abiding, durable, enduring, eternal, everlasting, immortal, imperishable, incorruptible, indissoluble, infrangible, lasting, permanent, unbreakable, unfading.
antonyms breakable, mortal.

indicate *v.* add up to, bespeak, betoken, denote, designate, display, evince, express, imply, manifest, mark, point out, point to, read, record, register, reveal, show, signify, specify, suggest, telegraph, tip.

indication *n.* clue, endeixis, evidence, explanation, forewarning, hint, index, inkling, intimation, manifestation, mark, note, omen, portent, prognostic, sign, signal, signpost, suggestion, symptom, warning.

indict *v.* accuse, arraign, charge, criminate, impeach, incriminate, prosecute, recriminate, summon, summons, tax.
antonym exonerate.

indictment *n.* accusation, allegation, charge, crimination, impeachment, incrimination, prosecution, recrimination, summons.
antonym exoneration.

indifference *n.* aloofness, apathy, callousness, coldness, coolness, detachment, disinterestedness, dispassion, disregard, equity, heedlessness, impartiality, inattention, insignificance, irrelevance, latitudinarianism, neg-

ligence, neutrality, objectivity, pococurant(e)ism, stoicalness, unconcern, unimportance.
antonyms bias, interest.

indifferent *adj.* aloof, apathetic, average, callous, careless, cold, cool, detached, disinterested, dispassionate, distant, equitable, fair, heedless, immaterial, impartial, impervious, inattentive, incurious, insignificant, jack easy, mediocre, middling, moderate, neutral, non-aligned, objective, ordinary, passable, perfunctory, pococurante, regardless, so-so, unbiased, uncaring, unconcerned, undistinguished, unenquiring, unenthusiastic, unexcited, unimportant, unimpressed, uninspired, uninterested, uninvolved, unmoved, unprejudiced, unresponsive, unsympathetic.
antonyms biased, interested.

indigence *n.* deprivation, destitution, distress, necessity, need, penury, poverty, privation, want.
antonym affluence.

indigenous *adj.* aboriginal, autochthonous, home-grown, indigene, local, native, original.
antonym foreign.

indigent *adj.* destitute, impecunious, impoverished, in forma pauperis, in want, necessitous, needy, penniless, penurious, poor, poverty-stricken, straitened.
antonym affluent.

indignant *adj.* angry, annoyed, disgruntled, exasperated, fuming, furibund, furious, heated, huffy, in a paddy, in a wax, incensed, irate, livid, mad, marked, miffed, peeved, provoked, resentful, riled, scornful, sore, waxy, wrathful, wroth.
antonym pleased.

indignation *n.* anger, exasperation, fury, ire, pique, rage, resentment, scorn, umbrage, wax, wrath.
antonym pleasure.

indignity *n.* abuse, affront, contempt, contumely, disgrace, dishonor, disrespect, humiliation, incivility, injury, insult, obloquy, opprobrium, outrage, reproach, slight, snub.
antonym honor.

indirect *adj.* ancillary, backhanded, circuitous, circumlocutory, collateral, contingent, crooked, devious, incidental, meandering, mediate, oblique, periphrastic, rambling, roundabout, secondary, slanted, subsidiary, tortuous, unintended, wandering, winding, zigzag.
antonym direct.

indiscretion *n.* boob, brick, error, faux pas, folly, foolishness, gaffe, imprudence, mistake, rashness, recklessness, slip, slip of the tongue, tactlessness, temerarity.
antonym discretion.

indispensable *adj.* basic, crucial, essential, imperative, key, necessary, needed, needful, required, requisite, vital.
antonym unnecessary.

indistinct *adj.* ambiguous, bleary, blurred, confused, dim, distant, doubtful, faint, fuzzy, hazy, ill-defined, indefinite, indeterminate, indiscernible, indistinguishable, misty, muffled, mumbled, obscure, shadowy, slurred, unclear, undefined, unintelligible, vague.
antonym distinct.

indistinguishable *adj.* alike, identical, interchangeable, same, tantamount, twin.
antonyms distinguishable, unalike.

individual *n.* being, bloke, body, chap, character, creature, fellow, individuum, mortal, party, person, personage, punter, soul.

adj. characteristic, discrete, distinct, distinctive, exclusive, identical, idiosyncratic, own, particular, peculiar, personal, personalized, proper, respective, separate, several, single, singular, special, specific, unique.

individuality *n.* character, discreteness, distinction, distinctiveness, haecceity, originality, peculiarity, personality, separateness, singularity, unicity, uniqueness.

antonym sameness.

indolent *adj.* fainéant, idle, inactive, inert, lackadaisical, languid, lazy, lethargic, listless, lumpish, slack, slothful, slow, sluggard, sluggish, torpid.

antonyms active, enthusiastic, industrious.

indomitable *adj.* bold, intrepid, invincible, resolute, staunch, steadfast, unbeatable, unconquerable, undaunted, unflinching, untameable, unyielding.

antonyms compliant, timid.

induce *v.* actuate, bring about, cause, convince, draw, effect, encourage, engender, generate, get, give rise to, impel, incite, influence, instigate, lead to, move, occasion, persuade, press, prevail upon, produce, prompt, talk into.

inducement *n.* attraction, bait, carrot, cause, come-on, consideration, encouragement, impulse, incentive, incitement, influence, lure, motive, reason, reward, spur, stimulus.

antonym disincentive.

induct *v.* consecrate, enthrone, inaugurate, initiate, install, introduce, invest, ordain, swear in.

indulge *v.* baby, cocker, coddle, cosset, favor, foster, give in to, go along with, gratify, humor, mollycoddle, pamper, pander to, pet, regale, satiate, satisfy, spoil, treat (oneself), yield to.

indulge in give free rein to, give oneself up to, give way to, luxuriate in, revel in, wallow in.

indulgent *adj.* complaisant, compliant, easy-going, favorable, fond, forbearing, gentle, gratifying, intemperate, kind, kindly, lenient, liberal, mild, permissive, prodigal, self-indulgent, tender, tolerant, understanding.

antonyms moderate, strict.

industrious *adj.* active, assiduous, busy, conscientious, deedy, diligent, energetic, hard-working, laborious, persevering, persistent, productive, purposeful, sedulous, steady, tireless, zealous.

antonym indolent.

industriously *adv.* assiduously, conscientiously, diligently, doggedly, hard, perseveringly, sedulously, steadily, with one's nose to the grindstone.

antonym indolently.

inebriated *adj.* befuddled, blind drunk, blotto, drunk, glorious, half seas over, half-cut, half-drunk, in one's cups, incapable, inebriate, intoxicated, legless, merry, paralytic, pie-eyed, plastered, sloshed, smashed, sozzled, stoned, stotious, three sheets in the wind, tight, tipsy, tired and emotional, under the influence.

antonym sober.

ineffective, ineffectual *adj.* abortive, barren, bootless, emasculate, feeble, fruitless, futile, idle, impotent, inadequate, incompetent, ineffective, ineffectual, inefficacious, inefficient, inept, lame, powerless, unavailing, unproductive, useless, vain, void, weak, worthless.

antonyms effective, effectual.

inefficient *adj.* incompetent, inept, inexpert, money-

wasting, negligent, slipshod, sloppy, time-wasting, unworkmanlike, wasteful.

antonym efficient.

ineligible *adj.* disqualified, improper, inappropriate, incompetent, objectionable, unacceptable, undesirable, unequipped, unfit, unfitted, unqualified, unsuitable, unworthy.

antonym eligible.

inept *adj.* absurd, awkward, bungling, cack-handed, clumsy, fatuous, futile, gauche, improper, inappropriate, inapt, incompetent, inexpert, infelicitous, irrelevant, maladroit, malapropos, meaningless, ridiculous, unfit, unhandy, unskilful, unworkmanlike.

antonyms adroit, apt.

inequity *n.* abuse, bias, discrimination, injustice, maltreatment, mistreatment, one-sidedness, partiality, prejudice, unfairness, unjustness.

antonym equity.

inert *adj.* apathetic, dead, dormant, dull, idle, immobile, inactive, inanimate, indolent, insensible, lazy, leaden, lifeless, motionless, nerveless, numb, passive, quiescent, senseless, slack, sleepy, slothful, sluggish, somnolent, static, still, torpid, unmoving, unreacting, unresponsive.

antonyms alive, animated.

inertia *n.* accedia, accidie, apathy, deadness, drowsiness, dullness, idleness, immobility, inactivity, indolence, insensibility, languor, lassitude, laziness, lethargy, listlessness, nervelessness, numbness, passivity, sleepiness, sloth, sluggishness, somnolence, stillness, stupor, torpor, unresponsiveness.

antonyms activity, liveliness.

inevitable *adj.* assured, automatic, certain, compulsory, decreed, destined, fated, fixed, ineluctable, inescapable, inexorable, irrevocable, mandatory, necessary, obligatory, ordained, settled, sure, unalterable, unavertable, unavoidable, unpreventable, unshunnable.

antonyms alterable, avoidable, uncertain.

inexorable *adj.* adamant, cruel, hard, harsh, immovable, implacable, ineluctable, inescapable, inflexible, intransigent, irreconcilable, irresistible, irrevocable, merciless, obdurate, pitiless, relentless, remorseless, severe, unalterable, unappeasable, unavertable, unbending, uncompromising, unrelenting, unyielding.

antonyms flexible, lenient, yielding.

inexperienced *adj.* amateur, callow, fresh, green, immature, inexpert, innocent, nescient, new, raw, unaccustomed, unacquainted, unbearded, unfamiliar, unpractical, unpracticed, unschooled, unseasoned, unskilled, unsophisticated, untrained, untraveled, untried, unused, unversed, verdant.

antonym experienced.

inexplicable *adj.* baffling, enigmatic, impenetrable, incomprehensible, incredible, inscrutable, insoluble, intractable, miraculous, mysterious, mystifying, puzzling, strange, unaccountable, unexplainable, unfathomable, unintelligible, unsolvable.

antonym explicable.

infallibility *n.* accuracy, dependability, faultlessness, impeccability, inerrancy, inevitability, irrefutability, irreproachability, omniscience, perfection, reliability, safety, supremacy, sureness, trustworthiness, unerringness.

antonym fallibility.

infamous *adj.* abhorrent, abominable, atrocious, base,

dastardly, despicable, detestable, discreditable, disgraceful, dishonorable, disreputable, egregious, execrable, facinorous, flagitious, hateful, heinous, ignoble, ignominious, ill-famed, iniquitous, knavish, loathsome, monstrous, nefarious, notorious, odious, opprobrious, outrageous, scandalous, scurvy, shameful, shocking, vile, villainous, wicked.
antonym glorious.

infantile *adj.* adolescent, babyish, childish, immature, juvenile, puerile, tender, undeveloped, young, youthful.
antonyms adult, mature.

infatuation *n.* besottedness, crush, dotage, engouement, fascination, fixation, folly, fondness, intoxication, madness, mania, obsession, passion, possession.
antonyms disenchantment, indifference.

infect *v.* affect, blight, canker, contaminate, corrupt, defile, enthuse, influence, inject, inspire, pervert, poison, pollute, taint, touch, vitiate.

infection *n.* contagion, contamination, corruption, defilement, disease, epidemic, illness, inflammation, influence, miasma, pestilence, poison, pollution, sepsis, septicity, taint, virus.

infectious *adj.* catching, communicable, contagious, contaminating, corrupting, deadly, defiling, epidemic, infective, miasmic, miasmous, pestilential, poisoning, poisonous, polluting, spreading, transmissible, transmittable, venemous, virulent, vitiating.

infer *v.* assume, conclude, conjecture, construe, deduce, derive, extract, extrapolate, gather, presume, surmise, understand.

inference *n.* assumption, conclusion, conjecture, consequence, construction, corollary, deduction, extrapolation, illation, interpretation, presumption, reading, surmise.

inferior *adj.* bad, crummy, dog, grotty, humble, imperfect, indifferent, junior, lesser, low, lower, low-grade, mean, mediocre, menial, minor, one-horse, paravail, poor, poorer, provant, schlock, secondary, second-class, second-rate, shoddy, slipshod, slovenly, subordinate, subsidiary, substandard, under, underneath, undistinguished, unsatisfactory, unworthy, worse.
antonym superior.
n. junior, menial, minion, subordinate, underling, understrapper, vassal.
antonym superior.

inferiority *n.* badness, baseness, deficiency, humbleness, imperfection, inadequacy, insignificance, lowliness, meanness, mediocrity, shoddiness, slovenliness, subordination, subservience, unimportance, unworthiness, worthlessness.
antonym superiority.

infernal *adj.* accursed, Acherontic, chthonian, chthonic, damnable, damned, demonic, devilish, diabolical, fiendish, Hadean, hellish, malevolent, malicious, Mephistophelian, Plutonian, satanic, Stygian, Tartarean, underworld.
antonym heavenly.

infiltrator *n.* entr(y)ist, insinuator, intruder, penetrator, seditionary, spy, subversive, subverter.

infinite *adj.* absolute, bottomless, boundless, countless, enormous, eternal, everlasting, fathomless, illimitable, immeasurable, immense, incomputable, inestimable, inexhaustible, interminable, limitless, measureless, never-ending, numberless, perpetual, stupendous,

total, unbounded, uncountable, uncounted, unfathomable, untold, vast, wide.
antonym finite.

infinitesimal *adj.* atomic, exiguous, imperceptible, inappreciable, inconsiderable, insignificant, microscopic, minuscule, minute, negligible, paltry, teeny, tiny, unnoticeable, wee.
antonyms significant, substantial.

infirm *adj.* ailing, crippled, debilitated, decrepit, dicky, doddering, doddery, enfeebled, failing, faltering, feeble, fickle, frail, hesitant, indecisive, insecure, irresolute, lame, poorly, sickly, unreliable, wavering, weak, wobbly.
antonyms healthy, strong.

infirmity *n.* ailment, complaint, debility, decrepitude, defect, deficiency, dickiness, disease, disorder, failing, fault, feebleness, foible, frailty, ill health, illness, imperfection, instability, malady, sickliness, sickness, vulnerability, weakness.
antonyms health, strength.

inflame *v.* aggravate, agitate, anger, arouse, embitter, enkindle, enrage, exacerbate, exasperate, excite, fan, fire, foment, fuel, galvanize, heat, ignite, impassion, incense, increase, infatuate, infuriate, intensify, intoxicate, kindle, madden, provoke, ravish, rile, rouse, stimulate, worsen.
antonyms cool, quench.

inflammation *n.* abscess, burning, empyema, erythema, heat, infection, painfulness, rash, redness, sepsis, septicity, sore, soreness, tenderness.

inflammatory *adj.* anarchic, demagogic, explosive, fiery, incendiary, incitative, inflaming, instigative, insurgent, intemperate, provocative, rabble-rousing, rabid, riotous, seditious.
antonyms calming, pacific.

inflate *v.* aerate, aggrandize, amplify, balloon, bloat, blow out, blow up, bombast, boost, dilate, distend, enlarge, escalate, exaggerate, expand, increase, puff out, puff up, pump up, swell, tumefy.
antonym deflate.

inflexible *adj.* adamant, dyed-in-the-wool, entrenched, fast, firm, fixed, hard, hardened, immovable, immutable, implacable, inelastic, inexorable, intractable, intransigent, iron, non-flexible, obdurate, obstinate, relentless, resolute, rigid, rigorous, set, steadfast, steely, stiff, strict, stringent, stubborn, taut, unaccommodating, unadaptable, unbending, unchangeable, uncompromising, unpliable, unpliant, unsupple, unyielding.
antonym flexible.

inflict *v.* administer, afflict, apply, burden, deal, deliver, enforce, exact, force, impose, lay, levy, mete, perpetrate, visit, wreak.

influence *n.* agency, ascendancy, authority, bias, charisma, clout, connections, control, credit, direction, domination, drag, effect, éminence grise, good offices, guidance, hold, importance, leverage, magnetism, mastery, power, pressure, prestige, pull, reach, rule, scope, spell, standing, strength, string-pulling, sway, teaching, training, weight, wire-pulling.
v. affect, alter, arouse, bias, change, control, direct, dispose, dominate, edge, guide, head, impel, impress, incite, incline, induce, instigate, maneuver, manipulate, modify, motivate, move, persuade, point, predis-

pose, prompt, pull, pull wires, rouse, strings, sway, teach, train, weigh with.

influential *adj.* ascendant, authoritative, charismatic, cogent, compelling, controlling, dominant, dominating, effective, efficacious, forcible, guiding, important, instrumental, leading, momentous, moving, persuasive, potent, powerful, significant, strong, telling, weighty, well-placed.

antonym ineffectual.

inform[1] *v.* acquaint, advise, apprize, brief, clue up, communicate, enlighten, fill in, illuminate, impart, instruct, intimate, leak, notify, teach, tell, tip off, wise up.

inform[2] *v.* animate, characterize, endue, fill, illuminate, imbue, inspire, invest, irradiate, light up, permeate, suffuse, typify.

informal *adj.* approachable, casual, colloquial, congenial, cosy, easy, familiar, free, homely, irregular, natural, relaxed, relaxing, simple, unbuttoned, unceremonious, unconstrained, unofficial, unorthodox, unpretentious, unsolemn.

antonym formal.

informality *n.* approachability, casualness, congeniality, cosiness, ease, familiarity, freedom, homeliness, irregularity, naturalness, relaxation, simplicity, unceremoniousness, unpretentiousness.

antonym formality.

information *n.* advices, blurb, briefing, bulletin, bumf, clues, communiqué, data, databank, database, dope, dossier, enlightenment, facts, gen, illumination, info, input, instruction, intelligence, knowledge, low-down, message, news, notice, report, tidings, word.

informative *adj.* chatty, communicative, constructive, edifying, educational, enlightening, forthcoming, gossipy, illuminating, informatory, instructive, newsy, revealing, revelatory, useful, valuable.

antonym uninformative.

informer *n.* betrayer, canary, denouncer, denunciator, fink, fiz(z)gig, grass, Judas, nark, singer, sneak, snitch(er), snout, squeak, squealer, stool pigeon, stoolie, supergrass.

infrequent *adj.* exceptional, intermittent, occasional, rare, scanty, sparse, spasmodic, sporadic, uncommon, unusual.

antonym frequent.

infringement *n.* breach, contravention, defiance, encroachment, evasion, infraction, intrusion, invasion, non-compliance, non-observance, transgression, trespass, violation.

ingenious *adj.* adroit, bright, brilliant, clever, crafty, creative, cunning, daedal, Daedalian, daedalic, dedalian, deft, dexterous, fertile, Gordian, imaginative, innovative, intricate, inventive, masterly, original, pretty, ready, resourceful, shrewd, skilful, sly, subtle.

antonyms clumsy, unimaginative.

ingenuity *n.* adroitness, cleverness, cunning, deftness, faculty, flair, genius, gift, ingeniousness, innovativeness, invention, inventiveness, knack, originality, resourcefulness, sharpness, shrewdness, skill, slyness, turn.

antonyms clumsiness, dullness.

ingenuous *adj.* artless, candid, childlike, frank, guileless, honest, innocent, naïf, naïve, open, plain, simple, sincere, trustful, trusting, unreserved, unsophisticated, unstudied.

antonyms artful, sly.

ingratiating *adj.* bland, bootlicking, crawling, fawning, flattering, obsequious, servile, smooth-tongued, suave, sycophantic, time-serving, toadying, unctuous, whilly, whillywha(w).

ingratitude *n.* thanklessness, unappreciativeness, ungraciousness, ungratefulness.

antonym gratitude.

ingredient *n.* component, constituent, element, factor, part.

inhabit *v.* abide, bide, dwell, habit, live, lodge, make one's home, occupy, people, populate, possess, reside, settle, settle in, stay, take up one's abode, tenant.

inhabitant *n.* aborigine, autochthon, burgher, citizen, denizen, dweller, habitant, indigene, indweller, inmate, lodger, native, occupant, occupier, resident, residentiary, resider, settler, tenant.

inherent *adj.* basic, characteristic, congenital, connate, essential, fundamental, hereditary, immanent, inborn, inbred, inbuilt, ingrained, inherited, innate, instinctive, intrinsic, inwrought, native, natural.

inheritance *n.* accession, bequest, birthright, descent, heredity, heritage, heritament, legacy, patrimony, succession.

inhibit *v.* arrest, bar, bridle, check, constrain, cramp, curb, debar, discourage, forbid, frustrate, hinder, hold, impede, interfere with, obstruct, prevent, prohibit, repress, restrain, stanch, stem, stop, suppress, thwart.

inhuman *adj.* animal, barbaric, barbarous, bestial, brutal, brutish, callous, cold-blooded, cruel, diabolical, fiendish, heartless, inhumane, insensate, merciless, pitiless, remorseless, ruthless, savage, sublime, unfeeling, vicious.

antonym human.

inimical *adj.* adverse, antagonistic, antipathetic, contrary, destructive, disaffected, harmful, hostile, hurtful, ill-disposed, inhospitable, injurious, intolerant, noxious, opposed, oppugnant, pernicious, repugnant, unfavorable, unfriendly, unwelcoming.

antonyms favorable, friendly, sympathetic.

inimitable *adj.* consummate, distinctive, exceptional, incomparable, matchless, nonpareil, peerless, sublime, superlative, supreme, unequaled, unexampled, unique, unmatched, unparalleled, unrivaled, unsurpassable, unsurpassed.

iniquitous *adj.* abominable, accursed, atrocious, awful, base, criminal, dreadful, evil, facinorous, flagitious, heinous, immoral, infamous, nefarious, nefast, reprehensible, reprobate, sinful, unjust, unrighteous, vicious, wicked.

antonym virtuous.

iniquity *n.* abomination, baseness, crime, enormity, evil, evil-doing, heinousness, impiety, infamy, injustice, misdeed, offence, sin, sinfulness, ungodliness, unrighteousness, vice, viciousness, wickedness, wrong, wrong-doing.

antonym virtue.

initial *adj.* beginning, commencing, early, embryonic, first, formative, inaugural, inauguratory, inceptive, inchoate, incipient, infant, introductory, opening, original, primary.

antonym final.

initiate *v.* activate, actuate, begin, cause, coach, commence, inaugurate, indoctrinate, induce, induct, instate, institute, instruct, introduce, invest, launch, open, originate, prompt, start, stimulate, teach, train.

n. authority, beginner, catechumen, cognoscente, connoisseur, convert, entrant, epopt, expert, insider, learner, member, newcomer, novice, novitiate, probationer, proselyte, recruit, sage, savant, tenderfoot, tiro.

initiative *n.* advantage, ambition, drive, dynamism, energy, enterprise, forcefulness, get-up-and-go, goeyness, innovativeness, inventiveness, lead, move, originality, prompting, push, recommendation, resource, resourcefulness, suggestion.

injure *v.* abuse, aggrieve, blemish, blight, break, cripple, damage, deface, disable, disfigure, disserve, harm, hurt, ill-treat, impair, maim, maltreat, mar, ruin, scathe, spoil, tarnish, undermine, vandalize, vitiate, weaken, wound, wrong.

injurious *adj.* adverse, bad, baneful, calumnious, corrupting, damaging, deleterious, destructive, detrimental, disadvantageous, harmful, hurtful, iniquitous, insulting, libelous, mischievous, noxious, pernicious, prejudicial, ruinous, slanderous, unconducive, unhealthy, unjust, wrongful.
antonyms beneficial, favorable.

injury *n.* abuse, annoyance, damage, damnification, detriment, disservice, evil, grievance, harm, hurt, ill, impairment, injustice, insult, lesion, loss, mischief, noyance, prejudice, ruin, scathe, trauma, vexation, wound, wrong.

injustice *n.* bias, discrimination, disparity, favoritism, imposition, inequality, inequitableness, inequity, iniquity, one-sidedness, oppression, partiality, partisanship, prejudice, unevenness, unfairness, unjustness, unlawfulness, unreason, wrong.
antonym justice.

inn *n.* albergo, alehouse, auberge, caravanserai, hostelry, hotel, howff, khan, local, public, public house, roadhouse, saloon, serai, tavern.

innate *adj.* basic, congenital, connate, constitutional, essential, fundamental, immanent, inborn, inbred, ingenerate, ingrained, inherent, inherited, instinctive, intrinsic, intuitive, native, natural.

innocent *adj.* Arcadian, artless, benign, bereft of, blameless, canny, chaste, childlike, clear, credulous, dewyeyed, faultless, frank, free of, fresh, green, guileless, guiltless, gullible, harmless, honest, immaculate, impeccable, incorrupt, ingenuous, innocuous, inoffensive, intact, irreproachable, naïve, natural, nescient, open, pristine, pure, righteous, simple, sinless, spotless, stainless, trustful, trusting, unblemished, uncontaminated, unimpeachable, unobjectionable, unoffending, unsullied, unsuspicious, untainted, untouched, unworldly, verdant, virginal, well-intentioned, well-meaning, well-meant.
antonyms experienced, guilty, knowing.

n. babe, babe in arms, beginner, child, greenhorn, infant, ingénu, ingénue, neophyte, tenderfoot.
antonyms connoisseur, expert.

innocuous *adj.* bland, harmless, hypo-allergenic, innocent, innoxious, inoffensive, non-irritant, safe, unimpeachable, unobjectionable.
antonym harmful.

innovative *adj.* adventurous, bold, daring, enterprising, fresh, go-ahead, goey, imaginative, inventive, moder-

nizing, new, on the move, original, progressive, reforming, resourceful, revolutionary.
antonyms conservative, unimaginative.

innuendo *n.* aspersion, hint, implication, imputation, insinuation, intimation, overtone, slant, slur, suggestion, whisper.

inoperative *adj.* broken, broken-down, defective, hors de combat, idle, ineffective, ineffectual, inefficacious, invalid, non-active, non-functioning, nugatory, out of action, out of commission, out of order, out of service, unserviceable, unused, unworkable, useless.
antonym operative.

inopportune *adj.* clumsy, ill-chosen, ill-timed, inappropriate, inauspicious, inconvenient, infelicitous, malapropos, mistimed, tactless, unfortunate, unpropitious, unseasonable, unsuitable, untimely, wrong-timed.
antonym opportune.

inquire *v.* ask, catechize, delve, enquire, examine, explore, inspect, interrogate, investigate, look into, probe, query, quest, question, reconnoiter, scout, scrutinize, search, speir.

inquiring *adj.* analytical, curious, doubtful, eager, inquisitive, interested, interrogatory, investigative, investigatory, nosy, outward-looking, probing, prying, questing, questioning, searching, skeptical, wondering, zetetic.
antonym incurious.

inquiry *n.* enquiry, examination, exploration, inquest, interrogation, investigation, perquisition, postmortem, probe, query, question, research, scrutiny, search, study, survey, witch-hunt, zetetic.

inquisitive *adj.* curious, eager, inquiring, intrusive, investigative, meddlesome, nosy, peeping, peering, probing, prying, questing, questioning, snooping, snoopy.
antonym incurious.

insane *adj.* barmy, batty, bizarre, bonkers, brainsick, cracked, crackers, crazed, cuckoo, daft, delirious, demented, deranged, distracted, disturbed, fatuous, foolish, idiotic, impractical, irrational, irresponsible, loony, loopy, lunatic, mad, manic, mental, mentally ill, non compos mentis, nuts, nutty, preposterous, psychotic, queer, schizoid, schizophrenic, screwy, senseless, stupid, touched, unbalanced, unhinged.
antonym sane.

insanity *n.* aberration, alienation, amentia, brainsickness, brainstorm, craziness, delirium, dementia, derangement, folly, frenzy, infatuation, irresponsibility, lunacy, madness, mania, mental illness, neurosis, preposterousness, psychoneurosis, psychosis, senselessness, stupidity.
antonym sanity.

insatiable *adj.* esurient, gluttonous, greedy, immoderate, incontrollable, inordinate, insatiate, intemperate, persistent, quenchless, rapacious, ravenous, unappeasable, uncurbable, unquenchable, unsatisfiable, voracious.
antonym moderate.

inscrutable *adj.* baffling, blank, cryptic, dead-pan, deep, enigmatic, esoteric, expressionless, hidden, impassive, impenetrable, incomprehensible, inexplicable, mysterious, poker-faced, sphinx-like, undiscoverable, unexplainable, unfathomable, unintelligible, unknowable, unsearchable.
antonyms clear, comprehensible, expressive.

insecure *adj.* afraid, anxious, apprehensive, dangerous, defenseless, diffident, exposed, expugnable, flimsy, frail, hazardous, insubstantial, jerry-built, loose, nervous, perilous, precarious, pregnable, rickety, rocky, shaky, shoogly, uncertain, unconfident, uneasy, unguarded, unprotected, unsafe, unshielded, unsound, unstable, unsteady, unsure, vulnerable, weak, wobbly, worried.
antonyms confident, safe, secure.

insensible[1] *adj.* anesthetized, apathetic, blind, callous, cataleptic, cold, deaf, dull, hard-hearted, impassive, impercipient, impervious, indifferent, inert, insensate, marble, nerveless, numb, numbed, oblivious, senseless, stupid, torpid, unaffected, unaware, unconscious, unfeeling, unmindful, unmoved, unnoticing, unobservant, unresponsive, unsusceptible, untouched.
antonyms conscious, sensible.

insensible[2] *adj.* imperceivable, imperceptible, inappreciable, minuscule, minute, negligible, tiny, unnoticeable.
antonym appreciable.

insensitive *adj.* blunted, callous, crass, dead, hardened, immune, impenetrable, imperceptive, impercipient, impervious, indifferent, insusceptible, obtuse, pachydermatous, proof, resistant, tactless, thick-skinned, tough, unaffected, uncaring, unconcerned, unfeeling, unimpressionable, unmoved, unreactive, unresponsive, unsensitive, unsusceptible.
antonym sensitive.

insight *n.* acumen, acuteness, apprehension, awareness, comprehension, discernment, grasp, ingenuity, intelligence, intuition, intuitiveness, judgment, knowledge, observation, penetration, perception, percipience, perspicacity, sensitivity, shrewdness, understanding, vision, wisdom.

insignificant *adj.* dinky, flimsy, humble, immaterial, inappreciable, inconsequential, inconsiderable, insubstantial, irrelevant, meager, meaningless, Mickey Mouse, minor, negligible, nondescript, nonessential, nugatory, paltry, petty, piddling, scanty, scrub, tiny, trifling, trivial, unimportant, unsubstantial.
antonym significant.

insincere *adj.* artificial, canting, deceitful, deceptive, devious, dishonest, disingenuous, dissembling, dissimulating, double-dealing, duplicitous, evasive, faithless, false, hollow, hypocritical, lip-deep, lying, mendacious, perfidious, phony, pretended, synthetic, two-faced, unfaithful, ungenuine, untrue, untruthful.
antonym sincere.

insinuate *v.* allude, get at, hint, imply, indicate, innuendo, intimate, suggest.

insipid *adj.* anemic, banal, bland, characterless, colorless, dilute, drab, dry, dull, fade, flat, flavorless, insulse, jejune, lash, lifeless, limp, missish, missy, monotonous, pointless, prosaic, prosy, savorless, spiritless, stale, tame, tasteless, trite, unappetizing, unimaginative, uninteresting, unsavory, vapid, watery, weak, wearish, weedy, wishy-washy.
antonyms appetizing, piquant, punchy, tasty.

insist *v.* assert, asseverate, aver, claim, contend, demand, dwell on, emphasize, harp on, hold, maintain, persist, reiterate, repeat, request, require, stand firm, stress, swear, urge, vow.

insolence *n.* abuse, arrogance, assurance, audacity, backchat, boldness, cheek, cheekiness, chutzpah, contemptuousness, contumely, defiance, disrespect,

effrontery, forwardness, gall, gum, hubris, impertinence, impudence, incivility, insubordination, lip, malapertness, offensiveness, pertness, presumption, presumptuousness, rudeness, sauce, sauciness.
antonyms politeness, respect.

insolent *adj.* abusive, arrogant, bold, brazen, cheeky, contemptuous, contumelious, defiant, disrespectful, forward, fresh, hubristic, impertinent, impudent, insubordinate, insulting, malapert, pert, presumptuous, rude, saucy, uncivil.
antonyms polite, respectful.

insoluble *adj.* baffling, impenetrable, indecipherable, inexplicable, inextricable, intractable, mysterious, mystifying, obscure, perplexing, unaccountable, unexplainable, unfathomable, unsolvable.
antonym explicable.

insolvent *adj.* bankrupt, broke, bust, defaulting, destitute, failed, flat broke, in queer street, on the rocks, ruined.
antonym solvent.

inspect *v.* audit, check, examine, give the once-over, investigate, look over, oversee, peruse, reconnoiter, scan, scrutinize, search, study, superintend, supervise, survey, vet, visit.

inspection *n.* audit, autopsy, check, check-up, examination, investigation, once-over, post-mortem, reconnaissance, review, scan, scrutiny, search, superintendence, supervision, surveillance, survey, vidimus, visitation.

inspiration *n.* afflation, afflatus, Aganippe, arousal, awakening, brainstorm, brain-wave, creativity, elevation, encouragement, enthusiasm, estro, exaltation, genius, Hippocrene, illumination, influence, insight, muse, Muse, revelation, spur, stimulation, stimulus, Svengali, taghairm.

inspire *v.* activate, animate, arouse, encourage, enkindle, enliven, enthuse, excite, fill, galvanize, hearten, imbue, influence, infuse, inhale, inspirit, instil, motivate, produce, quicken, spark off, spur, stimulate, stir, trigger.

inspiring *adj.* affecting, emboldening, encouraging, exciting, exhilarating, heartening, inspiriting, invigorating, moving, rousing, stimulating, stirring, uplifting.
antonyms dull, uninspiring.

instal(l) *v.* consecrate, ensconce, establish, fix, inaugurate, induct, instate, institute, introduce, invest, lay, locate, lodge, ordain, place, plant, position, put, set, set up, settle, site, situate, station.

installation *n.* base, consecration, equipment, establishment, fitting, inauguration, induction, instalment, instatement, investiture, location, machinery, ordination, placing, plant, positioning, post, siting, station, system.

instance[1] *n.* case, case in point, citation, example, illustration, occasion, occurrence, precedent, sample, situation, time.
v. adduce, cite, mention, name, point to, quote, refer to, specify.

instance[2] *n.* advice, application, behest, demand, entreaty, exhortation, importunity, impulse, incitement, initiative, insistence, instigation, pressure, prompting, request, solicitation, urging.

instant *n.* flash, jiffy, juncture, minute, mo, moment, occasion, point, second, shake, split second, tick, time, trice, twinkling, two shakes.

adj. convenience, direct, fast, immediate, instantaneous, on-the-spot, precooked, prompt, quick, rapid, ready-mixed, split-second, unhesitating, urgent.

instantaneous *adj.* direct, immediate, instant, on-the-spot, prompt, rapid, unhesitating.

antonym eventual.

instantly *adv.* at once, directly, forthwith, immediately, instantaneously, now, on the spot, pronto, quicksticks, right away, straight away, there and then, tout de suite, without delay.

antonym eventually.

instigate *v.* actuate, cause, encourage, excite, foment, generate, impel, incite, influence, initiate, inspire, kindle, move, persuade, prompt, provoke, rouse, set on, spur, start, stimulate, stir up, urge, whip up.

instinct *n.* ability, aptitude, faculty, feel, feeling, flair, gift, gut feeling, gut reaction, id, impulse, intuition, knack, nose, predisposition, proclivity, sixth sense, talent, tendency, urge.

instinctive *adj.* automatic, gut, immediate, impulsive, inborn, inherent, innate, instinctual, intuitional, intuitive, involuntary, mechanical, native, natural, reflex, spontaneous, unlearned, unpremeditated, unthinking, visceral.

antonyms conscious, deliberate, voluntary.

institute[1] *v.* appoint, begin, commence, constitute, create, enact, establish, fix, found, inaugurate, induct, initiate, install, introduce, invest, launch, open, ordain, organize, originate, pioneer, set up, settle, start.

antonyms abolish, cancel, discontinue.

institute[2] *n.* custom, decree, doctrine, dogma, edict, firman, indiction, irade, law, maxim, precedent, precept, principle, regulation, rescript, rule, tenet, ukase.

institute[3] *n.* academy, association, college, conservatory, foundation, guild, institution, organization, poly, polytechnic, school, seminary, society.

instruct *v.* acquaint, advise, apprize, bid, brief, catechize, charge, coach, command, counsel, direct, discipline, drill, educate, enjoin, enlighten, ground, guide, inform, mandate, notify, order, school, teach, tell, train, tutor.

instruction *n.* apprenticeship, briefing, catechesis, catechizing, coaching, command, direction, directive, discipline, drilling, education, enlightenment, grounding, guidance, information, injunction, lesson(s), mandate, order, preparation, ruling, schooling, teaching, training, tuition, tutelage.

instructions *n.* advice, book of words, commands, directions, guidance, handbook, information, key, legend, orders, recommendations, rules.

instrument *n.* agency, agent, apparatus, appliance, cat's-paw, channel, contraption, contrivance, device, doodad, dupe, factor, force, gadget, implement, means, mechanism, medium, organ, pawn, puppet, tool, utensil, vehicle, way, widget.

insubordinate *adj.* contumacious, defiant, disobedient, disorderly, fractious, impertinent, impudent, insurgent, mutinous, rebellious, recalcitrant, refractory, riotous, rude, seditious, turbulent, undisciplined, ungovernable, unruly.

antonyms docile, obedient.

insubstantial *adj.* chimerical, ephemeral, false, fanciful, feeble, flimsy, frail, idle, illusory, imaginary, immaterial, incorporeal, moonshine, poor, slight, tenuous, thin, unreal, vaporous, weak, windy, yeasty.

antonyms real, strong.

insufficient *adj.* deficient, inadequate, incapable, incommensurate, lacking, scanty, scarce, short, sparse, wanting.

antonyms excessive, sufficient.

insulation *n.* cushioning, deadening, deafening, padding, protection, stuffing.

insult *v.* abuse, affront, call names, fling/throw mud at, give offence to, injure, libel, miscall, offend, outrage, revile, slag, slander, slight, snub, vilify, vilipend.

antonyms compliment, honor.

n. abuse, affront, aspersion, contumely, indignity, insolence, libel, offence, outrage, rudeness, slander, slap in the face, slight, snub.

antonyms compliment, honor.

insulting *adj.* abusive, affronting, contemptuous, degrading, disparaging, insolent, libelous, offensive, rude, scurrilous, slanderous, slighting.

antonyms complimentary, respectful.

insurance *n.* assurance, cover, coverage, guarantee, indemnification, indemnity, policy, premium, protection, provision, safeguard, security, warranty.

insure *v.* assure, cover, guarantee, indemnify, protect, underwrite, warrant.

intact *adj.* all in one piece, complete, entire, inviolate, perfect, scatheless, sound, together, unbroken, undamaged, undefiled, unharmed, unhurt, unimpaired, uninjured, unscathed, untouched, unviolated, virgin, whole.

antonyms broken, damaged, harmed.

integrated *adj.* cohesive, concordant, connected, desegregated, harmonious, interrelated, part and parcel, unified, unsegregated, unseparated.

antonym unintegrated.

integration *n.* amalgamation, assimilation, blending, combining, commingling, desegregation, fusing, harmony, incorporation, mixing, unification.

antonym separation.

integrity *n.* candor, coherence, cohesion, completeness, entireness, goodness, honesty, honor, incorruptibility, principle, probity, purity, rectitude, righteousness, soundness, unity, uprightness, virtue, wholeness.

antonyms dishonesty, incompleteness, unreliability.

intellect *n.* brain, brain power, brains, egghead, genius, highbrow, intellectual, intelligence, judgment, mind, nous, reason, sense, thinker, understanding.

antonym dunce.

intellectual *adj.* bookish, cerebral, deep-browed, discursive, highbrow, intelligent, mental, noetic, rational, scholarly, studious, thoughtful.

antonym low-brow.

n. academic, egghead, headpiece, highbrow, mastermind, thinker.

antonym low-brow.

intelligence *n.* acuity, acumen, advice, alertness, aptitude, brain power, brains, brightness, capacity, cleverness, comprehension, data, discernment, disclosure, facts, findings, gen, gray matter, information, intellect, intellectuality, knowledge, low-down, mind, news, notice, notification, nous, penetration, perception, quickness, reason, report, rumor, tidings, tip-off, understanding, word.

antonym foolishness.

intelligent *adj.* acute, alert, apt, brainy, bright, clever, deep-browed, discerning, enlightened, instructed,

knowing, penetrating, perspicacious, quick, quick-witted, rational, razor-sharp, sharp, smart, thinking, well-informed.
antonyms foolish, unintelligent.

intend *v.* aim, consign, contemplate, design, destine, determine, earmark, have a mind, mark out, mean, meditate, plan, project, propose, purpose, scheme, set apart.

intense *adj.* acute, agonizing, ardent, burning, close, concentrated, consuming, eager, earnest, energetic, fanatical, fervent, fervid, fierce, forceful, forcible, great, harsh, heightened, impassioned, intensive, keen, passionate, powerful, profound, severe, strained, strong, vehement.
antonyms apathetic, mild.

intensify *v.* add to, aggravate, boost, concentrate, deepen, emphasize, enhance, escalate, exacerbate, fire, fuel, heighten, hot up, increase, magnify, quicken, redouble, reinforce, sharpen, step up, strengthen, whet, whip up.
antonyms damp down, die down.

intensity *n.* accent, ardor, concentration, depth, earnestness, emotion, energy, excess, extremity, fanaticism, fervency, fervor, fierceness, fire, force, intenseness, keenness, passion, potency, power, severity, strain, strength, tension, vehemence, vigor, voltage.

intent *adj.* absorbed, alert, attentive, bent, committed, concentrated, concentrating, determined, eager, earnest, engrossed, fixed, hell-bent, industrious, intense, mindful, occupied, piercing, preoccupied, rapt, resolute, resolved, set, steadfast, steady, watchful, wrapped up.
antonyms absent-minded, distracted.
n. aim, design, end, goal, intention, meaning, object, objective, plan, purpose.

intention *n.* aim, concept, design, end, end in view, goal, idea, intent, meaning, object, objective, plan, point, purpose, scope, target, view.

intentional *adj.* calculated, deliberate, designed, intended, meant, planned, prearranged, preconcerted, premeditated, purposed, studied, wilful.
antonym accidental.

intentionally *adv.* by design, deliberately, designedly, meaningly, on purpose, wilfully, with malice aforethought.
antonym accidentally.

intercept *v.* arrest, block, catch, check, cut off, deflect, delay, frustrate, head off, impede, interrupt, obstruct, retard, seize, stop, take, thwart.

intercourse¹ *n.* association, commerce, communication, communion, congress, connection, contact, conversation, converse, correspondence, dealings, intercommunication, traffic, truck.

intercourse² *n.* carnal knowledge, coition, coitus, copulation, embraces, intimacy, love-making, sex, sexual relations, venery.

interest *n.* activity, advantage, affair, affection, attention, attentiveness, attraction, authority, bag, benefit, business, care, claim, commitment, concern, consequence, curiosity, diversion, finger, gain, good, hobby, importance, influence, investment, involvement, line of country, matter, moment, note, notice, participation, pastime, portion, preoccupation, profit, pursuit, regard, relaxation, relevance, right, share, significance, stake, study, suspicion, sympathy, weight.

antonyms boredom, irrelevance.
v. affect, amuse, attract, concern, divert, engage, engross, fascinate, intrigue, involve, move, touch, warm.
antonym bore.

interested *adj.* affected, attentive, attracted, biased, concerned, curious, drawn, engrossed, fascinated, implicated, intent, involved, keen, partisan, predisposed, prejudiced, responsive, simulated.
antonyms apathetic, indifferent, unaffected.

interesting *adj.* absorbing, amusing, amusive, appealing, attractive, compelling, curious, engaging, engrossing, entertaining, gripping, intriguing, provocative, stimulating, thought-provoking, unusual, viewable, visitable.
antonym boring.

interfere *v.* block, butt in, clash, collide, conflict, cramp, frustrate, hamper, handicap, hinder, impede, inhibit, interlope, intermeddle, interpose, intervene, intrude, meddle, obstruct, poke one's nose in, stick one's oar in, tamper, trammel.
antonyms assist, forbear.

interference *n.* clashing, collision, conflict, do-goodery, do-goodism, impedance, intervention, intrusion, meddlesomeness, meddling, mush, obstruction, opposition, prying, statics, white noise.
antonyms assistance, forbearance.

interior *adj.* central, domestic, hidden, home, inland, inly, inner, inside, internal, intimate, inward, mental, pectoral, personal, private, remote, secret, spiritual, up-country.
antonyms exterior, external.
n. bowels, center, core, heart, heartland, hinterland, inside, up-country.

interject *v.* call, cry, exclaim, interjaculate, interpolate, interpose, interrupt, introduce, shout.

interlude *n.* break, breathing-space, breathing-time, breathing-while, delay, episode, halt, hiatus, intermission, interval, pause, respite, rest, spell, stop, stoppage, wait.

intermediate *adj.* halfway, in-between, intermediary, interposed, intervening, mean, medial, median, mid, middle, midway, transitional.
antonym extreme.

interminable *adj.* boundless, ceaseless, dragging, endless, everlasting, immeasurable, infinite, limitless, long, long-drawn-out, long-winded, never-ending, perpetual, prolix, protracted, unbounded, unlimited, wearisome.
antonym limited.

intermittent *adj.* broken, discontinuous, fitful, irregular, occasional, periodic, periodical, punctuated, recurrent, recurring, remittent, spasmodic, sporadic, stop-go.
antonym continuous.

internal *adj.* domestic, in-house, inner, inside, interior, intimate, inward, private, subjective.
antonym external.

interpose *v.* come between, insert, intercede, interfere, interjaculate, interject, interrupt, intervene, introduce, intrude, mediate, offer, place between, step in, thrust in.
antonym forbear.

interpret *v.* adapt, clarify, construe, decipher, decode, define, elucidate, explain, explicate, expound, paraphrase, read, render, solve, take, throw light on, translate, understand, unfold.

interpretation *n.* anagoge, anagogy, analysis, clarification, construction, diagnosis, elucidation, exegesis, explanation, explication, exposition, meaning, performance, portrayal, reading, rendering, rendition, sense, signification, translation, understanding, version.

interrogate *v.* ask, catechize, cross-examine, cross-question, debrief, enquire, examine, give (someone) the third degree, grill, inquire, investigate, pump, question, quiz.

interrupt *v.* barge in, break, break in, break off, butt in, check, cut, cut off, cut short, delay, disconnect, discontinue, disjoin, disturb, disunite, divide, heckle, hinder, hold up, interfere, interjaculate, interject, intrude, obstruct, punctuate, separate, sever, stay, stop, suspend.
antonym forbear.

interruption *n.* break, cessation, disconnection, discontinuance, disruption, dissolution, disturbance, disuniting, division, halt, hiatus, hindrance, hitch, impediment, intrusion, obstacle, obstruction, pause, separation, severance, stop, stoppage, suspension.

interval *n.* break, delay, distance, entr'acte, gap, hiatus, in-between, interim, interlude, intermission, interspace, interstice, meantime, meanwhile, opening, pause, period, playtime, rest, season, space, spell, term, time, wait.

intervene *v.* arbitrate, befall, ensue, happen, intercede, interfere, interpose oneself, interrupt, intrude, involve, mediate, occur, step in, succeed, supervene, take a hand.

interview *n.* audience, conference, consultation, dialogue, enquiry, evaluation, inquisition, meeting, oral, oral examination, press conference, talk, viva.
v. examine, interrogate, question, viva.

intimacy *n.* brotherliness, closeness, coition, coitus, confidence, confidentiality, copulating, copulation, familiarity, fornication, fraternization, friendship, intercourse, sexual intercourse, sisterliness, understanding.

intimate[1] *v.* allude, announce, communicate, declare, hint, impart, imply, indicate, insinuate, state, suggest, tell.

intimate[2] *adj.* as thick as thieves, bosom, cherished, close, confidential, cosy, dear, deep, deep-seated, detailed, exhaustive, friendly, gremial, informal, innermost, internal, near, palsy-walsy, penetrating, personal, private, privy, profound, secret, warm.
antonyms cold, distant, unfriendly.
n. Achates, associate, bosom buddy, buddy, china, chum, comrade, confidant, confidante, crony, familiar, friend, mate, mucker, pal, repository.
antonym stranger.

intimation *n.* allusion, announcement, communication, declaration, hint, indication, inkling, insinuation, notice, reminder, statement, suggestion, warning.

intimidate *v.* alarm, appal, browbeat, bulldoze, bully, coerce, cow, daunt, dishearten, dismay, dispirit, frighten, lean on, overawe, psych out, put the frighteners on, scare, subdue, terrify, terrorize, threaten.
antonym persuade.

intolerant *adj.* bigoted, chauvinistic, dictatorial, dogmatic, fanatical, illiberal, impatient, narrow, narrow-minded, opinionated, opinionative, opinioned, persecuting, prejudiced, racialist, racist, small-minded, uncharitable.

antonym tolerant.

intoxicated *adj.* blotto, canned, cut, disguised in liquor, dizzy, drunk, drunken, ebriate, ebriated, ebriose, elated, enraptured, euphoric, excited, exhilarated, fuddled, glorious, half seas over, high, in one's cups, incapable, inebriate, inebriated, infatuated, legless, lit up, looped, pickled, pissed, pixil(l)ated, plastered, sent, sloshed, smashed, sozzled, stewed, stiff, stimulated, stoned, stotious, three sheets in the wind, tight, tipsy, under the influence, up the pole, zonked.
antonym sober.

intransigent *adj.* hardline, immovable, intractable, irreconcilable, obdurate, obstinate, stubborn, tenacious, tough, unamenable, unbending, unbudgeable, uncompromising, unpersuadable, unyielding, uppity.
antonym amenable.

intrepid *adj.* audacious, bold, brave, courageous, daring, dashing, dauntless, doughty, fearless, gallant, game, gutsy, heroic, lion-hearted, nerveless, plucky, resolute, stalwart, stout-hearted, unafraid, undashed, undaunted, unflinching, valiant, valorous.
antonyms cowardly, timid.

intricate *adj.* Byzantine, complex, complicated, convoluted, daedal(e), Daedalian, daedalic, dedal, dedalian, difficult, elaborate, entangled, fancy, Gordian, involved, knotty, labyrinthine, perplexing, rococo, sophisticated, tangled, tortuous.
antonym simple.

intrigue[1] *v.* attract, charm, fascinate, interest, puzzle, rivet, tantalize, tickle one's fancy, titillate.
antonym bore.

intrigue[2] *n.* affair, amour, brigue, cabal, chicanery, collusion, conspiracy, double-dealing, intimacy, knavery, liaison, machination, machination(s), maneuver, manipulation, plot, romance, ruse, scheme, sharp practice, stratagem, string-pulling, trickery, wheeler-dealing, wile, wire-pulling.
v. connive, conspire, machinate, maneuver, plot, scheme.

intrinsic *adj.* basic, basically, built-in, central, congenital, constitutional, constitutionally, elemental, essential, essentially, fundamental, fundamentally, genuine, inborn, inbred, inherent, intrinsically, inward, native, natural, underlying.
antonym extrinsic.

introduce *v.* acquaint, add, advance, air, announce, begin, bring in, bring up, broach, commence, conduct, establish, familiarize, found, inaugurate, initiate, inject, insert, institute, interpolate, interpose, launch, lead in, lead into, moot, offer, open, organize, pioneer, preface, present, propose, put forward, put in, recommend, set forth, start, submit, suggest, throw in, ventilate.
antonym take away.

introduction *n.* addition, baptism, commencement, debut, establishment, exordium, foreword, inauguration, induction, initiation, insertion, institution, interpolation, intro, launch, lead-in, opening, overture, pioneering, preamble, preface, preliminaries, prelude, presentation, prodrome, prodromus, proem, prolegomena, prolegomenon, prologue, prooemion, pro-oemium.
antonym withdrawal.
vation, soul-searching.

introverted *adj.* indrawn, intervertive, introspective,

introversive, inward-looking, self-centered, self-contained, withdrawn.
antonym extroverted.

intrude *v.* aggress, butt in, encroach, infringe, interfere, interrupt, meddle, obtrude, trespass, violate.
antonyms stand back, withdraw.

intruder *n.* burglar, gate-crasher, infiltrator, interloper, invader, prowler, raider, snooper, trespasser.

intuition *n.* discernment, feeling, gut feeling, hunch, insight, instinct, perception, presentiment, sixth sense.
antonym reasoning.

invade *v.* assail, assault, attack, burst in, come upon, descend upon, encroach, enter, fall upon, infest, infringe, irrupt, occupy, overrun, overspread, penetrate, pervade, raid, rush into, seize, swarm over, violate.
antonym withdraw.

invalid¹ *adj.* ailing, bedridden, disabled, feeble, frail, ill, infirm, invalidish, poorly, sick, sickly, valetudinarian, valetudinary, weak.
antonym healthy.
n. case, convalescent, patient, sufferer, valetudinarian, valetudinary.

invalid² *adj.* baseless, fallacious, false, ill-founded, illogical, incorrect, inoperative, irrational, nugatory, null, null and void, unfounded, unscientific, unsound, untrue, void, worthless.
antonym valid.

invalidate *v.* abrogate, annul, cancel, nullify, overrule, overthrow, quash, rescind, undermine, undo, vitiate, weaken.
antonym validate.

invaluable *adj.* costly, exquisite, inestimable, precious, priceless, valuable.
antonym worthless.

invariable *adj.* changeless, consistent, constant, fixed, immutable, inflexible, permanent, regular, rigid, set, static, unalterable, unchangeable, unchanging, unfailing, uniform, unvarying, unwavering.
antonym variable.

invasion *n.* aggression, assault, attack, breach, encroachment, foray, incursion, infiltration, infraction, infringement, inroad, intrusion, irruption, offensive, onslaught, raid, seizure, usurpation, violation.
antonym withdrawal.

invective *n.* abuse, berating, castigation, censure, contumely, denunciation, diatribe, flyting, obloquy, philippic, philippic(s), reproach, revilement, sarcasm, scolding, tirade, tongue-lashing, vilification, vituperation.
antonym praise.

invent *v.* coin, conceive, concoct, contrive, cook up, create, design, devise, discover, dream up, fabricate, formulate, frame, imagine, improvise, make up, originate, think up, trump up.

invention *n.* brainchild, coinage, contraption, contrivance, contrivement, creation, creativeness, creativity, deceit, design, development, device, discovery, excogitation, fabrication, fake, falsehood, fantasy, fib, fiction, figment of (someone's) imagination, forgery, gadget, genius, imagination, ingenuity, inspiration, inventiveness, inveracity, lie, originality, prevarication, resourcefulness, sham, story, tall story, untruth, yarn.
antonym truth.

inventive *adj.* creative, daedal(e), Daedalian, daedalic,

dedal, excogitative, fertile, gifted, imaginative, ingenious, innovative, inspired, original, resourceful.
antonym uninventive.

inventor *n.* architect, author, builder, coiner, creator, designer, father, framer, inventress, maker, originator.

inventory *n.* account, catalog, equipment, file, list, listing, record, register, roll, roster, schedule, stock.

invert *v.* capsize, introvert, inverse, overturn, reverse, transpose, turn turtle, turn upside down, upset, upturn.
antonym right.

invest *v.* adopt, advance, authorize, charge, consecrate, devote, empower, endow, endue, enthrone, establish, inaugurate, induct, install, lay out, license, ordain, provide, put in, sanction, sink, spend, supply, vest.
antonym divest.

investigate *v.* consider, enquire into, examine, explore, go into, inspect, look into, probe, scrutinize, search, see how the land lies, sift, study, suss out.

investigation *n.* analysis, enquiry, examination, exploration, fact finding, hearing, inquest, inquiry, inspection, probe, research, review, scrutiny, search, study, survey, witch-hunt, zetetic.

investment *n.* ante, asset, besieging, blockade, contribution, investing, investiture, siege, speculation, stake, transaction, venture.

invidious *adj.* discriminating, discriminatory, hateful, objectionable, obnoxious, odious, offensive, repugnant, slighting, undesirable.
antonym desirable.

invigorating *adj.* bracing, energizing, exhilarating, fresh, generous, healthful, inspiriting, refreshing, rejuvenating, rejuvenative, restorative, salubrious, stimulating, tonic, uplifting, vivifying.
antonyms disheartening, wearying.

invincible *adj.* impenetrable, impregnable, indestructible, indomitable, inseparable, insuperable, invulnerable, irreducible, unassailable, unbeatable, unconquerable, unreducible, unsurmountable, unyielding.
antonym beatable.

invisible *adj.* concealed, disguised, hidden, imperceptible, inappreciable, inconspicuous, indetectable, indiscernible, infinitesimal, microscopic, out of sight, unperceivable, unseeable, unseen.
antonym visible.

invite *v.* allure, ask, ask for, attract, beckon, beg, bid, bring on, call, court, draw, encourage, entice, lead, provoke, request, seek, solicit, summon, tempt, welcome.
antonyms force, order.

inviting *adj.* alluring, appealing, appetizing, attractive, beguiling, captivating, delightful, engaging, enticing, fascinating, intriguing, magnetic, mouthwatering, pleasing, seductive, tantalizing, tempting, warm, welcoming, winning.
antonym uninviting.

involuntary *adj.* automatic, blind, compulsory, conditioned, forced, instinctive, instinctual, obligatory, reflex, reluctant, spontaneous, unconscious, uncontrolled, unintentional, unthinking, unwilled, unwilling, vegetative.
antonym voluntary.

involve *v.* absorb, affect, associate, bind, commit, comprehend, comprise, compromise, concern, connect, contain, cover, draw in, embrace, engage, engross,

entail, grip, hold, implicate, imply, include, incorporate, incriminate, inculpate, mean, mix up, necessitate,
number among, preoccupy, presuppose, require, rivet,
take in, touch.

involved *adj.* anfractuous, caught up/in, complex, complicated, concerned, confusing, convoluted, difficult,
elaborate, implicated, in on, intricate, knotty, labyrinthine, mixed up in/with, occupied, participating, sophisticated, tangled, tortuous.
antonyms simple, uninvolved.

invulnerable *adj.* impenetrable, indestructible, insusceptible, invincible, proof against, safe, secure, unassailable, unwoundable.
antonym vulnerable.

inward *adj.* confidential, entering, hidden, inbound,
incoming, inflowing, ingoing, inly, inmost, inner,
innermost, inpouring, inside, interior, internal, penetrating, personal, private, privy, secret.
antonyms external, outward.

inwardly *adv.* at heart, deep down, in gremio, in pectore,
in petto, inly, inside, privately, secretly, to oneself,
within.
antonyms externally, outwardly.

irate *adj.* angered, angry, annoyed, enraged, exasperated, fuming, furibund, furious, gusty, in a paddy,
incensed, indignant, infuriated, ireful, irritated, livid,
mad, piqued, provoked, riled, up in arms, waxy,
worked up, wrathful, wroth.
antonym calm.

ire *n.* anger, annoyance, choler, displeasure, exasperation, fury, indignation, passion, rage, wax, wrath.
antonym calmness.

irk *v.* aggravate, annoy, bug, disgust, distress, gall, get,
get to, irritate, miff, nettle, peeve, provoke, put out,
rile, rub up the wrong way, ruffle, vex, weary.
antonym please.

irksome *adj.* aggravating, annoying, boring, bothersome, burdensome, disagreeable, exasperating, infuriating, irritating, tedious, tiresome, troublesome, vexatious, vexing, wearisome.
antonym pleasing.

ironic *adj.* contemptuous, derisive, incongruous, ironical, irrisory, mocking, paradoxical, sarcastic, sardonic,
satirical, scoffing, scornful, sneering, wry.

irrational *adj.* aberrant, absurd, alogical, brainless,
crazy, demented, foolish, illogical, injudicious, insane,
mindless, muddle-headed, nonsensical, preposterous,
raving, senseless, silly, unreasonable, unreasoning,
unsound, unstable, unthinking, unwise, wild.
antonym rational.

irreconcilable *adj.* clashing, conflicting, hardline,
implacable, incompatible, incongruous, inconsistent,
inexorable, inflexible, intransigent, opposed, unappeasable, uncompromising, unreconcilable.
antonym reconcilable.

irregular *adj.* abnormal, anomalistic(al), anomalous,
asymmetrical, broken, bumpy, capricious, craggy,
crooked, difform, disconnected, disorderly, eccentric,
erratic, exceptional, extraordinary, extravagant, fitful,
fluctuating, fragmentary, haphazard, holey, immoderate, improper, inappropriate, incondite, inordinate,
intermittent, jagged, lop-sided, lumpy, occasional,
odd, patchy, peculiar, pitted, queer, quirky, ragged,
random, rough, serrated, shifting, snatchy, spasmodic,
sporadic, uncertain, unconventional, unequal, uneven,

unofficial, unorthodox, unprocedural, unpunctual,
unsteady, unsuitable, unsymmetrical, unsystematic,
unusual, variable, wavering.
antonyms conventional, regular, smooth.

irregularity *n.*. abberation, abnormality, anomaly, asymmetry, breach, bumpiness, confusion, crookedness,
desultoriness, deviation, difformity, disorderliness, disorganization, eccentricity, freak, haphazardness, het-
erodoxy, jaggedness, lop-sidedness, lumpiness, malfunction, malpractice, oddity, patchiness, peculiarity,
raggedness, randomness, roughness, singularity, uncertainty, unconventionality, unevenness, unorthodoxy,
unpunctuality, unsteadiness.
antonyms conventionality, regularity, smoothness.

irrelevant *adj.* alien, extraneous, foreign, immaterial,
impertinent, inapplicable, inapposite, inappropriate,
inapt, inconsequent, inessential, peripheral, tangential,
unapt, unconnected, unnecessary, unrelated.
antonym relevant.

irrepressible *adj.* boisterous, bubbling over, buoyant,
ebullient, effervescent, inextinguishable, insuppressible, resilient, uncontainable, uncontrollable,
ungovernable, uninhibited, unmanageable, unquenchable, unrestrainable, unstoppable.
antonyms depressed, depressive, despondent, resistible.

irresistible *adj.* alluring, beckoning, beguiling, charming, compelling, enchanting, fascinating, imperative,
ineluctable, inescapable, inevitable, inexorable, overm-
astering, overpowering, overwhelming, potent, pressing, ravishing, resistless, seductive, tempting, unavoidable, uncontrollable, urgent.
antonyms avoidable, resistible.

irresolute *adj.* dithering, doubtful, faint-hearted, fickle,
fluctuating, half-hearted, hesitant, hesitating, indecisive, infirm, shifting, shilly-shallying, swithering, tentative, undecided, undetermined, unsettled, unstable,
unsteady, vacillating, variable, wavering, weak.
antonym resolute.

irresponsible *adj.* carefree, careless, feather-brained,
feckless, flibbertigibbet, flighty, foot-loose, giddy, hare-
brained, harum-scarum, heedless, ill-considered,
immature, light-hearted, madcap, negligent, rash,
reckless, scatter-brained, shiftless, thoughtless, undependable, unreliable, untrustworthy, wild.
antonym responsible.

irreverent *adj.* blasphemous, cheeky, contemptuous,
derisive, discourteous, disrespectful, flip, flippant, godless, iconoclastic, impertinent, impious, impudent,
mocking, profane, rude, sacrilegious, saucy, tongue-in-
cheek.
antonym reverent.

irrevocable *adj.* changeless, fated, fixed, hopeless,
immutable, inexorable, invariable, irremediable, irre-
pealable, irretrievable, irreversible, predestined, predetermined, settled, unalterable, unchangeable.
antonyms alterable, flexible, mutable, reversible.

irritable *adj.* bad-tempered, cantankerous, captious,
choleric, crabbed, crabby, cross, crotchety, crusty,
edgy, feisty, fractious, fretful, hasty, hypersensitive,
ill-humored, ill-tempered, impatient, irascible, narky,
peevish, petulant, prickly, querulous, short, short-tempered, snappish, snappy, snarling, sore, tense, testy,
te(t)chy, thin-skinned, touchy.
antonyms cheerful, complacent.

irritant *n.* annoyance, bore, bother, goad, menace, nuisance, pain, pest, pin-prick, plague, provocation, rankle, tease, thorn in the flesh, trouble, vexation.

antonyms pleasure, sop, sweetness.

irritate v. acerbate, aggravate, anger, annoy, bedevil, bother, bug, chafe, emboil, enrage, exacerbate, exasperate, faze, fret, get on one's nerves, get to, give the pip, gravel, grig, harass, incense, inflame, infuriate, intensify, irk, needle, nettle, offend, pain, peeve, pester, pique, provoke, put out, rankle, rile, rouse, rub, ruffle, vex.

antonyms gratify, mollify, placate, please.

irritation n. aggravation, anger, annoyance, crossness, displeasure, dissatisfaction, exasperation, fury, goad, impatience, indignation, irritability, irritant, nuisance, pain, pain in the neck, pest, pin-prick, provocation, rankle, resentment, shortness, snappiness, tease, testiness, vexation, wrath.

antonyms pleasure, satisfaction.

isolate v. abstract, cut off, detach, disconnect, divorce, exclude, identify, insulate, keep apart, ostracize, pinpoint, quarantine, remove, seclude, segregate, separate, sequester, set apart.

antonyms assimilate, incorporate.

isolated adj. abnormal, anomalous, atypical, backwoods, deserted, detached, dissociated, eremitic, exceptional, freak, godforsaken, hermitical, hidden, incommunicado, insular, lonely, monastic, outlying, out-of-the-way, random, reclusive, remote, retired, secluded, single, solitary, special, sporadic, unfrequented, unique, unrelated, untrodden, untypical, unusual, unvisited.

antonyms populous, typical.

isolation n. aloofness, detachment, disconnection, dissociation, exile, insularity, insulation, lazaretto, loneliness, quarantine, reclusion, remoteness, retirement, seclusion, segregation, self-sufficiency, separation, solitariness, solitude, withdrawal.

issue[1] n. affair, argument, concern, controversy, crux, debate, matter, point, problem, question, subject, topic.

issue[2] n. announcement, broadcast, circulation, copy, delivery, dispersal, dissemination, distribution, edition, emanation, flow, granting, handout, impression, instalment, issuance, issuing, number, printing, promulgation, propagation, publication, release, supply, supplying, vent.

v. announce, broadcast, circulate, deal out, deliver, distribute, emit, give out, mint, produce, promulgate, publicize, publish, put out, release, supply.

issue[3] n. conclusion, consequence, culmination, dénouement, effect, end, finale, outcome, pay-off, product, result, termination, upshot.

v. arise, burst forth, debouch, emanate, emerge, flow, leak, originate, proceed, rise, spring, stem.

issue[4] n. brood, children, descendants, heirs, offspring, progeny, scions, seed, young.

itemize v. count, detail, document, enumerate, instance, inventory, list, mention, number, overname, particularize, record, specify, tabulate.

itinerant adj. ambulatory, drifting, journeying, migratory, nomadic, peregrinatory, peripatetic, rambling, roaming, rootless, roving, traveling, vagabond, vagrant, wandering, wayfaring.

antonyms settled, stationary.

n. diddicoy, dusty-foot, gypsy, hobo, nomad, perigrin-

ator, peripatetic, piepowder, pilgrim, Romany, tinker, toe-rag, tramp, traveler, vagabond, vagrant, wanderer, wayfarer.

itinerary n. circuit, course, journey, line, plan, program, route, schedule, tour.

J

jab v. dig, elbow, jag, lunge, nudge, poke, prod, punch, push, shove, stab, tap, thrust.

jabber v. babble, blather, blether, chatter, drivel, gab, gabble, gash, jaw, mumble, prate, rabbit, ramble, tattle, witter, yap.

jacket n. blouson, case, casing, coat, cover, covering, envelope, folder, jerkin, jupon, mackinaw, sheath, shell, skin, wrap, wrapper, wrapping.

jackpot n. award, big time, bonanza, kitty, pool, pot, prize, reward, stakes, winnings.

jade n. baggage, broad, draggle-tail, floosie, harridan, hussy, nag, shrew, slattern, slut, strumpet, tart, trollop, vixen, wench.

jaded adj. blunted, bored, cloyed, dulled, effete, exhausted, fagged, fatigued, played-out, satiated, spent, surfeited, tired, tired out, weary.

antonyms fresh, refreshed.

jag n. barb, denticle, dentil, notch, point, projection, protrusion, snag, spur, tooth.

jagged adj. barbed, broken, craggy, denticulate, hackly, indented, irregular, notched, pointed, ragged, ridged, rough, saw-edged, serrate, serrated, snagged, snaggy, spiked, spiky, toothed, uneven.

antonyms smooth.

jail, gaol n. borstal, bridewell, brig, calaboose, can, cells, choky, clink, cooler, coop, custody, guardhouse, hoos(e)gow, house of correction, inside, jailhouse, jankers, jug, lock-up, nick, pen, penitentiary, pokey, prison, quod, reformatory, slammer, stir, tollbooth.

v. confine, detain, immure, impound, imprison, incarcerate, intern, lock up, quod, send down.

jailer, gaoler n. captor, guard, keeper, prison officer, screw, turnkey, warden, warder.

jam[1] v. block, clog, compact, confine, congest, cram, crowd, crush, force, obstruct, pack, press, ram, sandwich, squash, squeeze, stall, stick, stuff, throng, thrust, vice, wedge.

n. bottle-neck, concourse, crowd, crush, gridlock, herd, horde, mass, mob, multitude, pack, press, swarm, throng, traffic jam.

jam[2] n. bind, contretemps, difficulty, dilemma, fix, hitch, hole, hot water, imbroglio, impasse, pickle, plight, predicament, quandary, scrape, spot, straits, tangle, tight corner, trouble.

jam[3] n. confiture, confyt, conserve, jelly, marmalade, preserve, spread.

jamboree n. carnival, carouse, celebration, convention, festival, festivity, fête, field day, frolic, gathering, get-together, jubilee, junket, merriment, party, potlatch, rally, revelry, shindig, spree.

jangle v. chime, clank, clash, clatter, jar, jingle, rattle, upset, vibrate.

n. cacophony, clang, clangor, clash, din, dissonance, jar, racket, rattle, reverberation, stridence, stridency, stridor.

antonyms euphony, harmony.

janitor *n.* caretaker, concierge, custodian, doorkeeper, doorman, janitress, janitrix, ostiary, porter.

jar¹ *n.* amphora, aquamanile, bellarmine, can, carafe, container, crock, cruet, cruse, ewer, flagon, jug, kang, mug, olla, pitcher, pot, receptacle, stamnos, stoup, urn, vase, vessel.

jar² *v.* agitate, annoy, clash, convulse, disagree, discompose, disturb, grate, grind, interfere, irk, irritate, jangle, jolt, nettle, offend, quarrel, rasp, rattle, rock, shake, upset, vibrate.

   n. clash, disagreement, discord, dissonance, grating, irritation, jangle, jolt, quarrel, rasping, wrangling.

jargon *n.* argot, balderdash, bunkum, cant, dialect, diplomatese, double-Dutch, drivel, gabble, gibberish, gobbledegook, gobbledygook, Greek, idiom, jive, lingo, mumbo-jumbo, nonsense, palaver, parlance, patois, rigmarole, slang, tongue, twaddle, vernacular.

jaundiced *adj.* biased, bitter, cynical, disbelieving, distorted, distrustful, envious, hostile, jaded, jealous, misanthropic, partial, pessimistic, preconceived, prejudiced, resentful, skeptical, suspicious.

antonyms fresh, naïve, optimistic.

jaunty *adj.* airy, breezy, buoyant, carefree, cheeky, chipper, dapper, debonair, gay, high-spirited, insouciant, lively, perky, self-confident, showy, smart, sparkish, sprightly, spruce, trim.

antonyms anxious, depressed, dowdy, seedy.

jazzy *adj.* animated, avant-garde, bold, fancy, flashy, gaudy, goey, lively, smart, snazzy, spirited, stylish, swinging, vivacious, wild, zestful.

antonyms conservative, prosaic, square.

jealous *adj.* anxious, apprehensive, attentive, careful, covetous, desirous, emulous, envious, green, green-eyed, grudging, guarded, heedful, invidious, mistrustful, possessive, proprietorial, protective, resentful, rival, solicitous, suspicious, vigilant, wary, watchful, zealous.

jealousy *n.* covetousness, distrust, emulation, envy, grudge, heart-burning, ill-will, mistrust, possessiveness, resentment, spite, suspicion, vigilance, watchfulness, zelotypia.

jeer *v.* banter, barrack, chaff, contemn, deride, explode, fleer, flout, flyte, gibe, heckle, hector, knock, mock, rail, razz, ridicule, scoff, sneer, taunt, twit.

   n. abuse, aspersion, catcall, chaff, derision, dig, fleer, flyte, flyting, gibe, hiss, hoot, mockery, raillery, raspberry, ridicule, scoff, sneer, taunt, thrust.

jeopardize *v.* chance, endanger, expose, gamble, hazard, imperil, jeopard, menace, risk, stake, threaten, venture.

antonyms protect, safeguard.

jerk¹ *n.* bounce, jog, jolt, lurch, pluck, pull, shrug, throw, thrust, tug, tweak, twitch, wrench, yank.

   v. bounce, flirt, jigger, jog, jolt, jounce, lurch, peck, pluck, pull, shrug, throw, thrust, tug, tweak, twitch, wrench, yank.

jerk² *n.* bum, clod, clot, clown, creep, dimwit, dolt, dope, fool, halfwit, idiot, klutz, ninny, prick, schlep, schmo, schmuck, twit.

jerky *adj.* bouncy, bumpy, convulsive, disconnected, fitful, incoherent, jolting, jumpy, rough, shaky, spasmodic, tremulous, twitchy, uncontrolled, unco-ordinated.

antonym smooth.

jest *n.* banter, bon mot, clowning, cod, crack, desipience, foolery, fooling, fun, gag, hoax, jape, jeu d'esprit, joke, josh, kidding, leg-pull, pleasantry, prank, quip, sally, sport, trick, trifling, waggery, wisecrack, witticism.

   v. banter, chaff, clown, deride, fool, gibe, jeer, joke, josh, kid, mock, quip, scoff, tease, trifle.

jester *n.* buffoon, clown, comedian, comic, droll, fool, goliard, harlequin, humorist, jocular, joker, juggler, merry-andrew, merryman, motley, mummer, pantaloon, patch, prankster, quipster, wag, wit, zany.

jet¹ *n.* atomizer, flow, fountain, gush, issue, nose, nozzle, rose, rush, spout, spray, sprayer, spring, sprinkler, spurt, squirt, stream, surge.

jet² *adj.* atramentous, black, coal-black, ebon, ebony, inky, jetty, pitch-black, pitchy, raven, sable, sloe, sooty.

jetsam *n.* jetsom, jetson, lagan, waif, wreckage.

jettison *v.* abandon, chuck, discard, ditch, dump, eject, expel, heave, offload, scrap, unload.

antonyms load, take on.

jetty *n.* breakwater, dock, groyne, jutty, mole, pier, quay, wharf.

jewel *n.* bijou, brilliant, charm, find, flower, gaud, gem, gemstone, humdinger, locket, masterpiece, ornament, paragon, pearl, precious stone, pride, prize, rarity, rock, sparkler, stone, treasure, wonder.

jib *v.* back off, balk, recoil, refuse, retreat, shrink, stall, stop short.

jibe, gibe *v.* deride, fleer, flout, jeer, mock, rail, ridicule, scoff, scorn, sneer, taunt, twit.

   n. barb, crack, derision, dig, fleer, fling, jeer, mockery, poke, quip, raillery, ridicule, sarcasm, scoff, slant, sneer, taunt, thrust.

jig *v.* bob, bobble, bounce, caper, hop, jerk, jiggle, jounce, jump, prance, shake, skip, twitch, wiggle, wobble.

jiggle *v.* agitate, bounce, fidget, jerk, jig, jog, joggle, shake, shift, shimmy, twitch, waggle, wiggle, wobble.

jilt *v.* abandon, betray, brush off, chuck, deceive, desert, discard, ditch, drop, forsake, reject, repudiate, spurn, throw over.

antonym cleave to.

jingle¹ *v.* chime, chink, clatter, clink, jangle, rattle, ring, tink, tinkle, tintinnabulate.

   n. clang, clangor, clink, rattle, reverberation, ringing, tink, tinkle, tintinnabulation.

jingle² *n.* chant, chime, chorus, couplet, ditty, doggerel, limerick, melody, poem, rhyme, song, tune, verse.

jinx *n.* black magic, charm, curse, evil eye, gremlin, hex, hoodoo, jettatura, Jonah, plague, spell, voodoo.

   v. bedevil, bewitch, curse, doom, hex, hoodoo, plague.

jittery *adj.* agitated, anxious, edgy, fidgety, flustered, jumpy, nervous, panicky, perturbed, quaking, quivering, shaky, shivery, trembling, uneasy.

antonyms calm, composed, confident.

job *n.* activity, affair, allotment, assignment, batch, business, calling, capacity, career, charge, chore, commission, concern, consignment, contract, contribution, craft, duty, employment, enterprise, errand, function, livelihood, lot, message, métier, mission, occupation, office, output, part, piece, place, portion, position, post, proceeding, product, profession, project, province, pursuit, responsibility, role, share, situation,

stint, task, trade, undertaking, venture, vocation, work.

jobless *adj.* idle, inactive, laid off, on the dole, out of work, unemployed, unoccupied, unused, workless.
antonym employed.

jocularity *n.* absurdity, comicality, desipience, drollery, facetiousness, fooling, gaiety, hilarity, humor, jesting, jocoseness, jocosity, jolliness, joviality, laughter, merriment, playfulness, pleasantry, roguishness, sport, sportiveness, teasing, waggery, waggishness, whimsicality, whimsy, wit.

jog[1] *v.* activate, arouse, bounce, jar, jerk, joggle, jolt, jostle, jounce, nudge, poke, prod, prompt, push, remind, rock, shake, shove, stimulate, stir.
n. jerk, jiggle, jolt, nudge, poke, prod, push, reminder, shake, shove.

jog[2] *v., n.* bump, canter, dogtrot, jogtrot, lope, lumber, pad, run, trot.

join *v.* abut, accompany, accrete, add, adhere, adjoin, affiliate, alligate, amalgamate, annex, append, associate, attach, border, border on, butt, cement, coincide, combine, compaginate, conglutinate, conjoin, conjugate, connect, couple, dock, enlist, enrol, enter, fasten, knit, link, march with, marry, meet, merge, reach, sign up, splice, team, tie, touch, unite, verge on, yoke.
antonyms leave, separate.

joint[1] *n.* articulation, commissure, connection, geniculation, gimmal, ginglymus, gomphosis, hinge, intersection, junction, juncture, knot, nexus, node, seam, union.
adj. adjunct, amalgamated, collective, combined, communal, concerted, consolidated, co-operative, co-ordinated, joined, mutual, shared, united.
v. articulate, carve, connect, couple, cut up, dismember, dissect, divide, fasten, fit, geniculate, join, segment, sever, sunder, unite.

joint[2] *n.* dance-hall, dive, haunt, honky-tonk, jerry-shop, night-club, place, pub.

joint[3] *n.* reefer, roach, stick.

joke *n.* buffoon, butt, clown, conceit, concetto, frolic, fun, funny, gag, guy, hoot, jape, jest, jeu d'esprit, lark, laughing-stock, play, pun, quip, sally, simpleton, sport, target, whimsy, wisecrack, witticism, yarn, yell.
v. banter, chaff, clown, deride, fool, frolic, gambol, jest, kid, laugh, mock, quip, ridicule, spoof, taunt, tease, wisecrack.

joker *n.* buffoon, card, character, clown, comedian, comic, droll, humorist, jester, joculator, jokesmith, kidder, prankster, sport, trickster, wag, wit.

jolly *adj.* blithe, blithesome, buxom, carefree, cheerful, cheery, convivial, exuberant, festive, frisky, frolicsome, funny, gay, gladsome, happy, hearty, hilarious, jaunty, jocund, jovial, joyful, joyous, jubilant, merry, mirthful, playful, sportive, sprightly, sunny.
antonym sad.

jolt *v.* astonish, bounce, bump, discompose, disconcert, dismay, disturb, jar, jerk, jog, jostle, jounce, knock, nonplus, perturb, push, shake, shock, shove, stagger, startle, stun, surprise, upset.
n. blow, bolt from the blue, bombshell, bump, hit, impact, jar, jerk, jog, jump, lurch, quiver, reversal, setback, shake, shock, start, surprise, thunderbolt.

jostle *v.* bump, butt, crowd, elbow, force, hustle, jog,

joggle, jolt, press, push, rough up, scramble, shake, shoulder, shove, squeeze, throng, thrust.

jot *n.* ace, atom, bit, detail, fraction, gleam, glimmer, grain, hint, iota, mite, morsel, particle, scintilla, scrap, smidgen, speck, tittle, trace, trifle, whit.

journal *n.* book, chronicle, commonplace, daily, daybook, diary, ephemeris, gazette, log, magazine, monthly, newspaper, organ, paper, periodical, publication, record, register, review, tabloid, waste-book, weekly.

journey *n.* career, course, excursion, expedition, eyre, hadj, itinerary, jaunt, odyssey, outing, passage, peregrination, pilgrimage, progress, raik, ramble, route, safari, tour, travel, trek, trip, voyage, wanderings.
v. fare, fly, gallivant, go, jaunt, peregrinate, proceed, ramble, range, roam, rove, safari, tour, tramp, travel, traverse, trek, voyage, wander, wend.

joust *n.* contest, encounter, engagement, pas d'armes, skirmish, tilt, tournament, tourney, trial.

jovial *adj.* affable, airy, animated, blithe, buoyant, cheery, convivial, cordial, ebullient, expansive, Falstaffian, gay, glad, happy, hilarious, jaunty, jocose, jocund, jolly, jubilant, merry, mirthful.
antonyms morose, sad, saturnine.

joy *n.* blessedness, bliss, charm, delight, ecstasy, elation, exaltation, exultation, felicity, festivity, gaiety, gem, gladness, gladsomeness, glee, gratification, happiness, hilarity, jewel, joyance, joyfulness, joyousness, pleasure, pride, prize, rapture, ravishment, satisfaction, seel, transport, treasure, treat, triumph, wonder.
antonyms mourning, sorrow.

joyful *adj.* blithe, blithesome, delighted, ecstatic, elated, enraptured, glad, gladsome, gratified, happy, jocund, jolly, jovial, jubilant, light-hearted, merry, pleased, rapturous, satisfied, seely, transported, triumphant.
antonyms mournful, sorrowful.

joyous *adj.* cheerful, ecstatic, festal, festive, frabjous, glad, gladsome, gleeful, happy, joyful, jubilant, merry, rapturous.
antonym sad.

jubilant *adj.* celebratory, delighted, elated, enraptured, euphoric, excited, exuberant, exultant, flushed, glad, gratified, joyous, over the moon, overjoyed, rejoicing, thrilled, triumphal, triumphant.
antonyms defeated, depressed.

jubilee *n.* anniversary, carnival, celebration, commemoration, festival, festivity, fête, gala, holiday.

judge *n.* adjudicator, alcalde, arbiter, arbiter elegantiae, arbitrator, arbitratrix, assessor, authority, beak, connoisseur, critic, Daniel, deemster, dempster, doomster, elegantiarum, evaluator, expert, hakim, justice, justiciar, justiciary, Law Lord, magistrate, mediator, moderator, pundit, referee, umpire, virtuoso, wig.
v. adjudge, adjudicate, appraise, appreciate, arbitrate, ascertain, assess, conclude, condemn, consider, criticize, decern, decide, decree, determine, dijudicate, discern, distinguish, doom, esteem, estimate, evaluate, examine, find, gauge, mediate, opine, rate, reckon, referee, review, rule, sentence, sit, try, umpire, value.

judgment *n.* acumen, appraisal, arbitration, arrêt, assessment, assize, award, belief, common sense, conclusion, conviction, damnation, decision, decree, decreet, deduction, determination, diagnosis, discernment, discretion, discrimination, doom, enlightenment, estimate, expertise, fate, fetwa, finding, intelligence, mediation, misfortune, opinion, order, penetration, perceptiveness, percipience, perspicacity, prudence, punishment, result, retribution, ruling, sagacity, sense, sentence, shrewdness, taste, understanding, valuation, verdict, view, virtuosity, wisdom.

judicial *adj.* critical, decretory, discriminating, distinguished, forensic, impartial, judiciary, juridical, legal, magisterial, magistral, official.

judicious *adj.* acute, astute, canny, careful, cautious, circumspect, considered, diplomatic, discerning, discreet, discriminating, enlightened, expedient, informed, percipient, perspicacious, politic, prescient, prudent, rational, reasonable, sagacious, sage, sane, sapient, sensible, shrewd, skilful, sober, sound, thoughtful, wary, well-advised, well-judged, well-judging, wise.
antonym injudicious.

jug *n.* amphora, aquamanile, bellarmine, blackjack, carafe, churn, container, crock, ewer, flagon, jar, pitcher, stoup, urn, vessel.

juice *n.* essence, extract, fluid, latex, liquid, liquor, nectar, sap, secretion, serum, succus.

jumble *v.* confuse, disarrange, disarray, disorder, disorganize, mingle-mangle, mix, mix up, muddle, shuffle, tangle, tumble, wuzzle.
antonym order.

n. agglomeration, chaos, clutter, collection, confusion, congeries, conglomeration, disarrangement, disarray, disorder, farrago, gallimaufry, hotch-potch, medley, mess, mingle-mangle, miscellany, mishmash, mixture, mix-up, muddle, olio, olla-podrida, pastiche, potpourri, raffle, salad.

jump¹ *v.* bounce, bound, caper, clear, dance, frisk, frolic, gambol, hop, hurdle, jig, leap, pounce, prance, skip, spring, vault.

n. bounce, bound, capriole, curvet, dance, frisk, frolic, gambado, hop, jeté, leap, pounce, prance, saltation, skip, spring, vault.

jump² *v.* avoid, bypass, digress, disregard, evade, ignore, leave out, miss, omit, overshoot, pass over, skip, switch.

n. breach, break, gap, hiatus, interruption, interval, lacuna, lapse, omission, saltation, saltus, switch.

jump³ *v.* advance, appreciate, ascend, boost, escalate, gain, hike, increase, mount, rise, spiral, surge.

n. advance, ascent, augmentation, boost, escalation, increase, increment, mounting, rise, upsurge, upturn.

jump⁴ *v.* flinch, jerk, jump out of one's skin, leap in the air, quail, recoil, resile, shrink, start, wince.

n. jar, jerk, jolt, lurch, quiver, shiver, shock, spasm, start, swerve, twitch, wrench.

jump⁵ *n.* barricade, barrier, fence, gate, hedge, hurdle, impediment, obstacle, pons asinorum, rail.

jumpy *adj.* agitated, anxious, apprehensive, discomposed, edgy, fidgety, jittery, nervous, nervy, restive, restless, shaky, tense, tremulous, uneasy.
antonyms calm, composed.

junction *n.* abutment, combination, confluence, conjunction, connection, coupling, disemboguement, intersection, interstice, join, joining, joint, juncture, linking, meeting-point, nexus, seam, union.

junior *adj.* inferior, lesser, lower, minor, puisne, secondary, subordinate, subsidiary, younger.
antonyms senior.

junk *n.* clutter, debris, detritus, dregs, garbage, litter,

oddments, refuse, rejectamenta, rubbish, rummage, scrap, trash, waste, wreckage.

jurisdiction *n.* area, authority, bailiwick, bounds, cognizance, command, control, domination, dominion, field, influence, judicature, orbit, power, prerogative, province, range, reach, rule, scope, sovereignty, sphere, sway, verge, zone.

just *adj.* accurate, apposite, appropriate, apt, blameless, condign, conscientious, correct, decent, deserved, disinterested, due, equitable, even-handed, exact, fair, fair-minded, faithful, fitting, four-square, good, honest, honorable, impartial, impeccable, irreproachable, justified, lawful, legitimate, merited, normal, precise, proper, pure, reasonable, regular, right, righteous, rightful, sound, suitable, true, unbiased, unimpeachable, unprejudiced, upright, virtuous, well-deserved.
antonym unjust.

justice¹ *n.* amends, appositeness, appropriateness, compensation, correction, dharma, equitableness, equity, fairness, honesty, impartiality, integrity, justifiableness, justness, law, legality, legitimacy, nemesis, penalty, propriety, reasonableness, recompense, rectitude, redress, reparation, requital, right, rightfulness, rightness, satisfaction.
antonym injustice.

justice² *n.* JP, judge, Justice of the Peace, justiciar, magistrate.

justifiable *adj.* acceptable, allowable, defensible, excusable, explainable, explicable, fit, forgivable, justified, lawful, legitimate, licit, maintainable, pardonable, proper, reasonable, right, sound, tenable, understandable, valid, vindicable, warrantable, warranted, well-founded.
antonyms culpable, illicit, unjustifiable.

justify *v.* absolve, acquit, condone, confirm, defend, establish, exculpate, excuse, exonerate, explain, forgive, legalize, legitimize, maintain, pardon, substantiate, support, sustain, uphold, validate, vindicate, warrant.

jut *v.* beetle, bulge, extend, impend, overhang, poke, project, protrude, stick out.
antonym recede.

juvenile *n.* adolescent, boy, child, girl, halfling, infant, kid, minor, young person, youngster, youth.
antonym adult.

adj. adolescent, babyish, boyish, callow, childish, girlish, immature, impressionable, inexperienced, infantile, jejune, puerile, tender, undeveloped, unsophisticated, young, youthful.
antonym mature.

K

keen *adj.* acid, acute, anxious, ardent, argute, assiduous, astute, avid, biting, brilliant, canny, caustic, clever, cutting, devoted, diligent, discerning, discriminating, eager, earnest, ebullient, edged, enthusiastic, fervid, fierce, fond, forthright, impassioned, incisive, industrious, intense, intent, mordant, penetrating, perceptive, perfervid, perspicacious, piercing, pointed, pungent, quick, razorlike, sagacious, sapient, sardonic, satirical, scathing, sedulous, sensitive, sharp, shrewd, shrill, tart, trenchant, wise, zealous.

antonyms apathetic, blunt, dull.

keep¹ *v.* accumulate, amass, carry, collect, conserve, control, deal in, deposit, furnish, garner, hang on to, heap, hold, hold on to, maintain, pile, place, possess, preserve, retain, stack, stock, store.

keep² *v.* be responsible for, board, care for, defend, feed, foster, guard, have charge of, have custody of, look after, maintain, manage, mind, nourish, nurture, operate, protect, provide for, provision, safeguard, shelter, shield, subsidize, support, sustain, tend, victual, watch, watch over.

n. board, food, livelihood, living, maintenance, means, nourishment, nurture, subsistence, support, upkeep.

keep³ *v.* arrest, block, check, constrain, control, curb, delay, detain, deter, hamper, hamstring, hinder, hold, hold back, hold up, impede, inhibit, interfere with, keep back, limit, obstruct, prevent, restrain, retard, shackle, stall, trammel, withhold.

keep⁴ *v.* adhere to, celebrate, commemorate, comply with, fulfil, hold, honor, keep faith with, keep up, maintain, obey, observe, perform, perpetuate, recognize, respect, ritualize, solemnize.

keep⁵ *n.* castle, citadel, donjon, dungeon, fastness, fort, fortress, motte, peel-house, peel-tower, stronghold, tower.

keeper *n.* attendant, caretaker, conservator, conservatrix, curator, custodian, defender, gaoler, governor, guard, guardian, inspector, jailer, mahout, nab, overseer, steward, superintendent, supervisor, surveyor, warden, warder.

keepsake *n.* emblem, favor, memento, pledge, relic, remembrance, reminder, souvenir, token.

keg *n.* barrel, butt, cask, drum, firkin, hogshead, puncheon, round, rundlet, tierce, tun, vat.

ken *n.* acquaintance, appreciation, awareness, cognizance, compass, comprehension, field, grasp, knowledge, notice, perception, range, reach, realization, scope, sight, understanding, view, vision.

kerchief *n.* babushka, bandana, cravat, fichu, headscarf, headsquare, kaffiyeh, madras, neck-cloth, neckerchief, scarf, shawl, square, sudary, veronica.

kernel *n.* core, essence, germ, gist, grain, heart, marrow, nitty-gritty, nub, pith, seed, substance.

key *n.* answer, clavis, clue, code, crib, cue, digital, explanation, glossary, guide, index, indicator, interpretation, lead, means, pointer, secret, sign, solution, table, translation.

adj. basic, cardinal, central, chief, core, crucial, decisive, essential, fundamental, hinge, important, leading, main, major, pivotal, principal, salient.

keynote *n.* accent, center, core, emphasis, essence, flavor, flavor of the month, gist, heart, kernel, leitmotiv, marrow, motif, pith, stress, substance, theme.

kick *v.* abandon, boot, break, desist from, drop, foot, give up, leave off, leave out, punt, quit, spurn, stop, toe.

n. bite, buzz, dash, élan, enjoyment, excitement, feeling, force, fun, gratification, gusto, intensity, panache, pep, pizzazz, pleasure, power, punch, pungency, relish, snap, sparkle, stimulation, strength, tang, thrill, verve, vitality, zest, zing, zip.

kick-off *n.* beginning, bully-off, commencement, face-off, inception, introduction, opening, outset, start, word go.

kid¹ *n.* babe, baby, bairn, bambino, boy, child, dandiprat, girl, halfling, infant, juvenile, kiddy, lad, nipper, shaver, stripling, teenager, tot, wean, whippersnapper, youngster, youth.

kid² *v.* bamboozle, befool, beguile, con, cozen, delude, dupe, fool, gull, have on, hoax, hoodwink, humbug, jest, joke, josh, mock, pretend, pull someone's leg, put one over on, rag, ridicule, tease, trick.

kidnap *v.* abduct, capture, hijack, rape, remove, seize, skyjack, snatch, steal.

kill *v.* abolish, annihilate, assassinate, beguile, bump off, butcher, cancel, cease, deaden, defeat, destroy, dispatch, do away with, do in, do to death, eliminate, eradicate, execute, exterminate, extinguish, extirpate, fill, finish off, halt, kibosh, knock off, knock on the head, liquidate, mar, martyr, massacre, murder, napoo, neutralize, nip in the bud, nullify, obliterate, occupy, pass, pip, put to death, quash, quell, rub out, ruin, scotch, slaughter, slay, smite, smother, spoil, stifle, still, stonker, stop, suppress, top, veto, vitiate, while away, zap.

n. climax, conclusion, coup de grâce, death, death-blow, dénouement, dispatch, end, finish, mop-up, shoot-out.

killing¹ *n.* assassination, bloodshed, carnage, elimination, ethnocide, execution, extermination, fatality, fratricide, homicide, infanticide, liquidation, mactation, manslaughter, massacre, matricide, murder, parricide, patricide, pogrom, regicide, slaughter, slaying, sororicide, thuggee, uxoricide.

adj. deadly, death-dealing, deathly, debilitating, enervating, exhausting, fatal, fatiguing, final, lethal, lethiferous, mortal, mortiferous, murderous, prostrating, punishing, tiring, vital.

killing² *n.* big hit, bonanza, bunce, clean-up, coup, fortune, gain, hit, lucky break, profit, smash, success, windfall, winner.

killing³ *adj.* absurd, amusing, comical, funny, hilarious, ludicrous, side-splitting, uproarious.

killjoy *n.* complainer, cynic, dampener, damper, grouch, misery, moaner, pessimist, prophet of doom, skeptic, spoil-sport, trouble-mirth, wet blanket, whiner.

antonyms enthusiast, optimist, sport.

kin *n.* affines, affinity, blood, clan, connection, connections, consanguinity, cousins, extraction, family, flesh and blood, kindred, kinsfolk, kinship, kinsmen, kith, lineage, people, relations, relationship, relatives, stock, tribe.

adj. affine, akin, allied, close, cognate, congener, connected, consanguine, consanguineous, interconnected, kindred, linked, near, related, similar, twin.

kind¹ *n.* brand, breed, category, character, class, description, essence, family, genus, habit, ilk, kidney, manner, mold, nature, persuasion, race, set, sort, species, stamp, style, temperament, type, variety.

kind² *adj.* accommodating, affectionate, altruistic, amiable, amicable, avuncular, beneficent, benevolent, benign, benignant, bonhomous, boon, bounteous, bountiful, brotherly, charitable, clement, compassionate, congenial, considerate, cordial, courteous, diplomatic, fatherly, friendly, generous, gentle, giving, good, gracious, hospitable, humane, indulgent, kind-hearted, kindly, lenient, loving, mild, motherly,

neighborly, obliging, philanthropic, propitious, sisterly, soft-boiled, soft-hearted, sweet, sympathetic, tactful, tender-hearted, thoughtful, understanding.
antonyms cruel, inconsiderate, unhelpful.

kindle *v.* activate, actuate, agitate, animate, arouse, awaken, deflagrate, enkindle, exasperate, excite, fan, fire, foment, ignite, incite, induce, inflame, initiate, inspire, inspirit, light, provoke, rouse, set alight, sharpen, stimulate, stir, thrill.

kindly *adj.* benefic, beneficent, beneficial, benevolent, benign, charitable, comforting, compassionate, cordial, favorable, generous, genial, gentle, giving, good-natured, good-willy, hearty, helpful, indulgent, kind, mild, patient, pleasant, polite, sympathetic, tender, warm.
adv. agreeably, charitably, comfortingly, considerately, cordially, generously, gently, graciously, indulgently, patiently, politely, tenderly, thoughtfully.
antonyms cruel, inconsiderate, uncharitable, unpleasant.

kindred *n.* affines, affinity, clan, connections, consanguinity, family, flesh, folk, kin, kinsfolk, kinship, kinsmen, lineage, people, relations, relationship, relatives.
adj. affiliated, affine, akin, allied, cognate, common, congenial, connected, corresponding, kin, like, matching, related, similar.

king *n.* boss, chief, chieftain, doyen, emperor, kingpin, leading light, luminary, majesty, monarch, overlord, paramount, patriarch, potentate, prince, royalet, ruler, sovereign, supremo, suzerain.

kingdom *n.* area, commonwealth, country, division, domain, dominion, dynasty, empire, field, land, monarchy, nation, palatinate, principality, province, realm, reign, royalty, sovereignty, sphere, state, territory, tract.

kingly *adj.* august, basilical, glorious, grand, grandiose, imperial, imperious, imposing, lordly, majestic, monarchical, noble, regal, royal, sovereign, splendid, stately, sublime, supreme.

kink[1] *n.* bend, coil, complication, corkscrew, crick, crimp, defect, dent, difficulty, entanglement, flaw, hitch, imperfection, indentation, knot, loop, tangle, twist, wrinkle.
v. bend, coil, crimp, curl, tangle, twist, wrinkle.

kink[2] *n.* caprice, crotchet, eccentricity, fetish, foible, freak, idiosyncracy, idiosyncrasy, oddity, quirk, singularity, vagary, whim.

kinship *n.* affinity, alliance, association, bearing, community, conformity, connection, consanguinity, correspondence, kin, relation, relationship, similarity.

kismet *n.* destiny, doom, fate, fortune, joss, karma, lot, portion, predestiny, providence, weird.

kiss[1] *v.* buss, canoodle, neck, osculate, peck, salute, smooch, snog.
n. buss, osculation, peck, plonker, salute, smack, smacker, snog.

kiss[2] *v.* brush, caress, fan, glance, graze, lick, scrape, touch.

kit *n.* accouterments, apparatus, appurtenances, baggage, effects, equipage, equipment, gear, impedimenta, implements, instruments, luggage, matériel, muniments, outfit, paraphernalia, provisions, rig, rig-out, set, supplies, tackle, tools, trappings, traps, utensils.

knack *n.* ability, adroitness, aptitude, bent, capacity,

dexterity, expertise, expertness, facility, faculty, flair, forte, genius, gift, handiness, hang, ingenuity, propensity, quickness, skilfulness, skill, talent, trick, trick of the trade, turn.

knave *n.* bastard, blackguard, blighter, bounder, cheat, dastard, drôle, fripon, rapscallion, rascal, reprobate, rogue, rotter, scallywag, scamp, scapegrace, scoundrel, stinker, swindler, swine, varlet, villain.

knead *v.* form, knuckle, manipulate, massage, mold, ply, press, rub, shape, squeeze, work.

knick-knack *n.* bagatelle, bauble, bibelot, bric-à-brac, gadget, gaud, gewgaw, gimcrack, gismo, jimjam, kickshaw, object of virtu, plaything, pretty, pretty-pretty, quip, rattle-trap, toy, trifle, trinket, whigmaleerie, whim-wham.

knife *n.* blade, carver, chiv, cutter, dagger, dah, flick-knife, jack-knife, machete, parang, pen-knife, pocket-knife, skean, skene, skene-dhu, skene-occle, switch-blade, whittle.
v. cut, impale, lacerate, pierce, rip, slash, stab, wound.

knightly *adj.* bold, chivalrous, courageous, courtly, dauntless, gallant, gracious, heroic, honorable, intrepid, noble, soldierly, valiant, valorous.
antonyms cowardly, ignoble, ungallant.

knit *v.* ally, bind, connect, crease, crotchet, fasten, furrow, heal, interlace, intertwine, join, knot, link, loop, mend, secure, tie, unite, weave, wrinkle.

knob *n.* boll, boss, bump, caput, door-handle, knot, knub, knurl, lump, nub, projection, protrusion, protuberance, snib, stud, swell, swelling, tuber, tumor, umbo.

knock[1] *v.* buffet, clap, cuff, ding, hit, knobble, (k)nubble, punch, rap, slap, smack, smite, strike, thump, thwack.
n. blow, box, chap, clip, clout, con, cuff, hammering, rap, slap, smack, thump.

knock[2] *v.* abuse, belittle, carp, cavil, censure, condemn, criticize, deprecate, disparage, find fault, lambaste, run down, slam, vilify, vilipend.
n. blame, censure, condemnation, criticism, defeat, failure, rebuff, rejection, reversal, setback, stricture.
antonyms boost, praise.

knockout *n.* bestseller, coup de grâce, hit, kayo, KO, sensation, smash, smash-hit, stunner, success, triumph, winner.
antonyms flop, loser.

knoll *n.* barrow, hill, hillock, hummock, knowe, koppie, mound.

knot *v.* bind, entangle, entwine, knit, loop, secure, tangle, tether, tie, weave.
n. aggregation, bond, bow, braid, bunch, burl, clump, cluster, collection, connection, gnar, gnarl, heap, hitch, joint, knag, knar, knarl, ligature, loop, mass, pile, rosette, tie, tuft.

know *v.* apprehend, comprehend, discern, distinguish, experience, fathom, identify, intuit, ken, learn, make out, notice, perceive, realize, recognize, see, tell, undergo, understand, wist.

knowing *adj.* acute, astute, aware, clever, competent, conscious, cunning, discerning, downy, eloquent, experienced, expert, expressive, gnostic, gnostical, hep, intelligent, meaningful, perceptive, qualified, sagacious, shrewd, significant, skilful, well-informed.
antonyms ignorant, obtuse.

knowledge *n.* ability, acquaintance, acquaintanceship,

apprehension, book-learning, booklore, cognition, cognizance, comprehension, consciousness, cum-savvy, discernment, education, enlightenment, erudition, familiarity, gnosis, grasp, information, instruction, intelligence, intimacy, judgment, know-how, learning, multiscience, notice, pansophy, recognition, scholarship, schooling, science, tuition, understanding, wisdom.

antonym ignorance.

knowledgeable *adj.* acquainted, au courant, au fait, aware, book-learned, bright, cognizant, conscious, conversant, educated, erudite, experienced, familiar, in the know, intelligent, learned, lettered, scholarly, well-informed.

antonym ignorant.

kowtow *v.* bow, court, cringe, defer, fawn, flatter, genuflect, grovel, kneel, pander, suck up, toady, truckle.

kudos *n.* acclaim, applause, distinction, esteem, fame, glory, honor, laudation, laurels, plaudits, praise, prestige, regard, renown, repute.

L

label *n.* badge, brand, categorization, characterization, classification, company, description, docket, epithet, mark, marker, sticker, tag, tally, ticket, trademark.

v. brand, call, categorize, characterize, class, classify, define, describe, designate, docket, dub, identify, mark, name, stamp, tag.

labor[1] *n.* chore, donkey-work, drudgery, effort, employees, exertion, grind, hands, industry, job, labor improbus, laborers, moil, pains, painstaking, slog, sweat, task, toil, undertaking, work, workers, workforce, workmen.

antonyms ease, leisure, relaxation, rest.

v. drudge, endeavor, grind, heave, moil, pitch, plod, roll, slave, strive, struggle, suffer, sweat, toil, toss, travail, work.

antonyms idle, laze, loaf, lounge.

labor[2] *n.* birth, childbirth, contractions, delivery, labor pains, pains, parturition, throes, travail.

v. dwell on, elaborate, overdo, overemphasize, overstress, strain.

labored *adj.* affected, awkward, complicated, contrived, difficult, forced, heavy, overdone, overwrought, ponderous, stiff, stilted, strained, studied, unnatural.

antonyms easy, natural.

laborer *n.* drudge, farm-hand, hand, hireling, hobbler, hobo, hodman, hunky, husbandman, manual worker, redneck, worker, working man, workman.

laborious *adj.* arduous, assiduous, backbreaking, burdensome, difficult, diligent, fatiguing, forced, hard, hard-working, heavy, herculean, indefatigable, industrious, labored, onerous, operose, painstaking, persevering, ponderous, sedulous, strained, strenuous, tireless, tiresome, toilsome, tough, unflagging, uphill, wearing, wearisome.

antonyms easy, effortless, relaxing, simple.

labyrinth *n.* circumvolution, coil, complexity, complication, convolution, entanglement, Gordian knot, intricacy, jungle, maze, perplexity, puzzle, riddle, tangle, windings.

lace[1] *n.* crochet, dentelle, filigree, mesh-work, netting, open-work, tatting.

lace[2] *n.* bootlace, cord, lanyard, shoe-lace, string, thong, tie.

v. attach, bind, close, do up, fasten, intertwine, interweave, interwork, string, thread, tie.

lace[3] *v.* add to, fortify, intermix, mix in, spike.

lacerate *v.* afflict, claw, cut, distress, gash, ga(u)nch, harrow, jag, lancinate, maim, mangle, rend, rip, slash, tear, torment, torture, wound.

laceration *n.* cut, gash, injury, lancination, maim, mutilation, rent, rip, slash, tear, wound.

lack *n.* absence, dearth, deficiency, deprivation, destitution, emptiness, insufficiency, need, privation, scantiness, scarcity, shortage, shortcoming, shortness, vacancy, void, want.

antonyms abundance, profusion.

v. miss, need, require, want.

lackey *n.* attendant, creature, fawner, flatterer, flunky, footman, gofer, hanger-on, instrument, manservant, menial, minion, parasite, pawn, servitor, sycophant, toady, tool, valet, yes-man.

lacking *adj.* defective, deficient, flawed, impaired, inadequate, minus, missing, needing, sans, short of, wanting, without.

lackluster *adj.* boring, dim, drab, dry, dull, flat, leaden, lifeless, lusterless, mundane, muted, prosaic, somber, spiritless, unimaginative, uninspired, vapid.

antonyms brilliant, polished.

laconic *adj.* brief, close-mouthed, compact, concise, crisp, curt, pithy, sententious, short, succinct, taciturn, terse.

antonyms garrulous, verbose, wordy.

lad *n.* boy, bucko, callant, chap, fellow, guy, halfling, juvenile, kid, laddie, schoolboy, shaver, stripling, youngster, youth.

laden *adj.* burdened, charged, chock-a-block, chock-full, encumbered, fraught, full, hampered, jammed, loaded, oppressed, packed, stuffed, taxed, weighed down, weighted.

antonym empty.

ladle *v.* bail, dip, dish, lade, scoop, shovel, spoon.

lady *n.* begum, dame, damsel, don(n)a, Frau, gentlewoman, hidalga, madam(e), matron, memsahib, milady, noblewoman, Señora, signora, woman.

ladylike *adj.* courtly, cultured, decorous, elegant, genteel, matronly, modest, polite, proper, queenly, refined, respectable, well-bred.

lag *v.* dawdle, delay, hang back, idle, linger, loiter, mosey, saunter, shuffle, straggle, tarry, trail.

antonym lead.

laggard *n.* dawdler, idler, lingerer, loafer, loiterer, lounger, saunterer, slowcoach, slowpoke, slug-a-bed, sluggard, snail, straggler.

antonyms dynamo, go-getter, livewire.

lair *n.* burrow, den, earth, form, hideout, hole, nest, refuge, retreat, roost, sanctuary, stronghold.

lake *n.* lagoon, loch, lochan, lough, mere, reservoir, tarn.

lambaste *v.* beat, berate, bludgeon, castigate, censure, cudgel, drub, flay, flog, leather, rebuke, reprimand, roast, scold, strike, thrash, upbraid, whip.

lame *adj.* crippled, defective, disabled, disappointing, feeble, flimsy, game, half-baked, halt, handicapped, hobbling, inadequate, insufficient, limping, poor, thin, unconvincing, unsatisfactory, weak.

v. cripple, damage, disable, hamstring, hobble, hurt, incapacitate, injure, maim, wing.

lament *v.* bemoan, bewail, beweep, complain, deplore, grieve, keen, mourn, regret, sorrow, wail, weep, yammer.

antonyms celebrate, rejoice.

n. complaint, coronach, dirge, dumka, elegy, jeremiad, keening, lamentation, moan, moaning, monody, plaint, requiem, threnody, ululation, wail, wailing.

lamentable *adj.* deplorable, disappointing, distressing, funest, grievous, inadequate, insufficient, low, meager, mean, miserable, mournful, pitiful, poor, regrettable, sorrowful, tragic, unfortunate, unsatisfactory, woeful, wretched.

lamp *n.* beacon, flare, floodlight, lampad, lantern, light, limelight, searchlight, torch, veilleuse.

lampoon *n.* burlesque, caricature, mickey-take, parody, Pasquil, Pasquin, pasquinade, satire, send-up, skit, spoof, squib, take-off.

v. burlesque, caricature, make fun of, mock, parody, Pasquil, Pasquin, pasquinade, ridicule, satirize, send up, spoof, squib, take off, take the mickey out of.

land[1] *n.* country, countryside, dirt, district, earth, estate, farmland, fatherland, ground, grounds, loam, motherland, nation, property, province, real estate, realty, region, soil, terra firma, territory, tract.

v. alight, arrive, berth, bring, carry, cause, come to rest, debark, deposit, disembark, dock, drop, end up, plant, touch down, turn up, wind up.

land[2] *v.* achieve, acquire, capture, gain, get, net, obtain, secure, win.

landlord *n.* freeholder, host, hotelier, hotel-keeper, innkeeper, lessor, letter, owner, proprietor, publican.

antonym tenant.

landmark *n.* beacon, boundary, cairn, feature, milestone, monument, signpost, turning-point, watershed.

landscape *n.* aspect, countryside, outlook, panorama, prospect, scene, scenery, view, vista.

landslide *n.* avalanche, earthfall, éboulement, landslip, rock-fall.

adj. decisive, emphatic, overwhelming, runaway.

lane *n.* alley(way), avenue, boreen, byroad, byway, channel, driveway, footpath, footway, gut, loan, passage(-way), path(way), towpath, vennel, way, wynd.

language *n.* argot, cant, conversation, dialect, diction, discourse, expression, idiolect, idiom, interchange, jargon, langue, lingo, lingua franca, parlance, parole, patois, phraseology, phrasing, speech, style, talk, terminology, tongue, utterance, vernacular, vocabulary, wording.

languid *adj.* debilitated, drooping, dull, enervated, faint, feeble, heavy, inactive, indifferent, inert, lackadaisical, languorous, lazy, lethargic, limp, listless, pining, sickly, slow, sluggish, spiritless, torpid, unenthusiastic, uninterested, weak, weary.

antonyms alert, lively, vivacious.

languish *v.* brood, decline, desire, despond, droop, fade, fail, faint, flag, grieve, hanker, hunger, long, mope, pine, repine, rot, sicken, sigh, sink, sorrow, suffer, sulk, want, waste, waste away, weaken, wilt, wither, yearn.

antonym flourish.

languor *n.* apathy, asthenia, calm, debility, dreaminess, drowsiness, enervation, ennui, faintness, fatigue, feebleness, frailty, heaviness, hush, indolence, inertia,

lassitude, laziness, lethargy, listlessness, lull, oppressiveness, relaxation, silence, sleepiness, sloth, stillness, torpor, weakness, weariness.

antonyms alacrity, gusto.

lanky *adj.* angular, bony, gangling, gangly, gaunt, loose-jointed, rangy, rawboned, scraggy, scrawny, spare, tall, thin, twiggy, weedy.

antonyms short, squat.

lap[1] *v.* drink, lick, sip, sup, tongue.

lap[2] *v.* gurgle, plash, purl, ripple, slap, slosh, splash, swish, wash.

lap[3] *n.* ambit, circle, circuit, course, distance, loop, orbit, round, tour.

v. cover, encase, enfold, envelop, fold, surround, swaddle, swathe, turn, twist, wrap.

lapse *n.* aberration, backsliding, break, caducity, decline, descent, deterioration, drop, error, failing, fall, fault, gap, indiscretion, intermission, interruption, interval, lull, mistake, negligence, omission, oversight, passage, pause, relapse, slip.

v. backslide, decline, degenerate, deteriorate, drop, end, expire, fail, fall, run out, sink, slide, slip, stop, terminate, worsen.

larceny *n.* burglary, expropriation, heist, misappropriation, pilfering, piracy, purloining, robbery, stealing, theft.

large *adj.* abundant, ample, big, broad, bulky, capacious, colossal, comprehensive, considerable, copious, decuman, enormous, extensive, full, generous, giant, gigantic, goodly, grand, grandiose, great, huge, immense, jumbo, king-sized, liberal, man-sized, massive, monumental, Patagonian, plentiful, plonking, roomy, sizeable, spacious, spanking, substantial, sweeping, swingeing, tidy, vast, wide.

antonyms diminutive, little, slight, small, tiny.

largely *adv.* abundantly, by and large, chiefly, considerably, extensively, generally, greatly, highly, mainly, mostly, predominantly, primarily, principally, widely.

largess(e) *n.* aid, allowance, alms, benefaction, bequest, bounty, charity, donation, endowment, generosity, gift, grant, handout, liberality, munificence, open-handedness, philanthropy, present.

antonym meanness.

lark *n.* antic, caper, escapade, fling, fredaine, frolic, fun, gambol, game, gammock, guy, jape, mischief, prank, revel, rollick, romp, skylark, spree.

v. caper, cavort, frolic, gambol, gammock, play, rollick, romp, skylark, sport.

lascivious *adj.* bawdy, blue, coarse, crude, dirty, horny, indecent, lecherous, lewd, libidinous, licentious, lustful, obscene, offensive, Paphian, pornographic, prurient, randy, ribald, salacious, scurrilous, sensual, smutty, suggestive, tentiginous, unchaste, voluptuous, vulgar, wanton.

lash[1] *n.* blow, cat, cat-o'-nine-tails, hit, quirt, stripe, stroke, swipe, whip.

v. attack, beat, belabor, berate, birch, buffet, castigate, censure, chastize, criticize, dash, drum, flagellate, flay, flog, hammer, hit, horsewhip, knock, lace, lam, lambaste, lampoon, larrup, pound, ridicule, satirize, scold, scourge, smack, strike, tear into, thrash, upbraid, welt, whip.

lash[2] *v.* affix, bind, fasten, join, make fast, rope, secure, strap, tether, tie.

lass *n.* bird, chick, colleen, damsel, girl, lassie, maid, maiden, miss, quean, quine, schoolgirl.

last¹ *adj.* aftermost, closing, concluding, conclusive, definitive, extreme, final, furthest, hindmost, latest, rearmost, remotest, terminal, ultimate, utmost.
antonyms first, initial.
adv. after, behind, finally, ultimately.
antonyms first, firstly.
n. close, completion, conclusion, curtain, end, ending, finale, finish, termination.
antonyms beginning, start.

last² *v.* abide, carry on, continue, endure, hold on, hold out, keep (on), perdure, persist, remain, stand up, stay, survive, wear.

latch *n.* bar, bolt, catch, fastening, hasp, hook, lock, sneck.

late¹ *adj.* behind, behind-hand, belated, delayed, dilatory, last-minute, overdue, slow, tardy, unpunctual.
antonyms early, punctual.
adv. behind-hand, belatedly, dilatorily, formerly, recently, slowly, tardily, unpunctually.
antonyms early, punctually.

late² *adj.* dead, deceased, defunct, departed, ex-, former, old, past, preceding, previous.

lately *adv.* formerly, heretofore, latterly, recently.

latent *adj.* concealed, delitescent, dormant, hidden, inherent, invisible, lurking, potential, quiescent, secret, underlying, undeveloped, unexpressed, unrealized, unseen, veiled.
antonyms active, live, patent.

lather¹ *n.* bubbles, foam, froth, shampoo, soap, soapsuds, suds.
v. foam, froth, shampoo, soap, whip up.

lather² *n.* agitation, dither, fever, flap, fluster, flutter, fuss, pother, state, stew, sweat, tizzy, twitter.

lather³ *v.* beat, cane, drub, flog, lambaste, lash, leather, strike, thrash, whip.

latitude *n.* breadth, clearance, compass, elbow-room, extent, field, freedom, indulgence, laxity, leeway, liberty, license, play, range, reach, room, scope, space, span, spread, sweep, width.

latter *adj.* closing, concluding, ensuing, last, last-mentioned, later, latest, modern, recent, second, succeeding, successive.
antonym former.

lattice *n.* espalier, fret-work, grate, grating, grid, grille, lattice-work, mesh, network, open-work, reticulation, tracery, trellis, web.

laud *v.* acclaim, applaud, approve, celebrate, extol, glorify, hail, honor, magnify, praise.
antonyms blame, condemn, curse, damn.

laudable *adj.* admirable, commendable, creditable, estimable, excellent, exemplary, meritorious, of note, praiseworthy, sterling, worthy.
antonyms damnable, execrable.

laudation *n.* acclaim, acclamation, accolade, adulation, blessing, celebrity, commendation, devotion, encomion, encomium, eulogy, extolment, glorification, glory, homage, kudos, paean, panegyric, praise, reverence, tribute, veneration.
antonyms condemnation, criticism.

laugh *v.* cachinnate, chortle, chuckle, crease up, fall about, giggle, guffaw, snicker, snigger, split one's sides, te(e)hee, titter.
antonym cry.

n. belly-laugh, card, case, caution, chortle, chuckle, clown, comedian, comic, cure, entertainer, giggle, guffaw, hoot, humorist, joke, lark, scream, snicker, snigger, te(e)hee, titter, wag, wit.

laughable *adj.* absurd, amusing, comical, derisive, derisory, diverting, droll, farcical, funny, gelastic, hilarious, humorous, laughworthy, ludicrous, mirthful, mockable, nonsensical, preposterous, ridiculous, risible.
antonyms impressive, serious, solemn.

launch *v.* begin, cast, commence, discharge, dispatch, embark on, establish, fire, float, found, inaugurate, initiate, instigate, introduce, open, project, propel, send off, set in motion, start, throw.

lavatory *n.* bathroom, bog, can, cloakroom, closet, cludge, comfort station, convenience, dike, draughthouse, dunnakin, dunny, dyke, garderobe, Gents, George, head(s), jakes, john, Ladies, latrine, lav, office, powder-room, privy, public convenience, restroom, smallest room, toilet, urinal, washroom, water-closet, WC.

lavish *adj.* abundant, bountiful, copious, effusive, exaggerated, excessive, extravagant, exuberant, free, generous, gorgeous, immoderate, improvident, intemperate, liberal, lush, luxuriant, munificent, open-handed, opulent, plentiful, princely, prodigal, profuse, prolific, sumptuous, thriftless, unlimited, unreasonable, unrestrained, unstinting, wasteful, wild.
antonyms economical, frugal, parsimonious, scanty, sparing, thrifty.
v. bestow, deluge, dissipate, expend, heap, pour, shower, spend, squander, waste.

law *n.* act, axiom, brocard, canon, charter, code, command, commandment, constitution, consuetudinary, covenant, criterion, decree, dharma, edict, enactment, formula, institute, jurisprudence, order, ordinance, precept, principle, regulation, rule, standard, statute.
antonym chance.

lawful *adj.* allowable, authorized, constitutional, hal(l)al, kosher, legal, legalized, legitimate, licit, permissible, proper, rightful, valid, warranted.
antonyms illegal, illicit, lawless, unlawful.

lawless *adj.* anarchic(al), chaotic, disorderly, felonious, insubordinate, insurgent, mutinous, rebellious, reckless, riotous, ruleless, seditious, unbridled, ungoverned, unrestrained, unruly, wild.
antonym lawful.

lawlessness *n.* anarchy, chaos, disorder, insurgency, mobocracy, mob-rule, ochlocracy, piracy, racketeering, rent-a-mob.
antonym order.

lawyer *n.* advocate, attorney, barrister, counsel, counsellor, jurisconsult, law-agent, lawmonger, legist, solicitor.

lax *adj.* broad, careless, casual, derelict, easy-going, flabby, flaccid, general, imprecise, inaccurate, indefinite, inexact, lenient, loose, neglectful, negligent, overindulgent, remiss, shapeless, slack, slipshod, soft, vague, wide, wide-open, yielding.
antonyms rigid, strict, stringent.

lay¹ *v.* advance, allay, alleviate, allocate, allot, appease, apply, arrange, ascribe, assess, assign, assuage, attribute, bet, burden, calm, charge, concoct, contrive, deposit, design, devise, dispose, encumber, establish, gamble, hatch, hazard, impose, impute, leave, locate, lodge, offer, organize, place, plan, plant, plot, posit, position, prepare, present, put, quiet, relieve, risk, saddle, set, set down, set out, settle, soothe, spread, stake, still, submit, suppress, tax, wager, work out.

lay[2] *adj.* amateur, inexpert, laic, laical, non-professional, non-specialist, secular.

lay[3] *n.* ballad, canzone(t), lyric, madrigal, ode, poem, roundelay, song.

lay-off *n.* discharge, dismissal, redundancy, unemployment.

layout *n.* arrangement, blueprint, design, draft, formation, geography, map, outline, plan, sketch.

lazy *adj.* dormant, drowsy, idle, inactive, indolent, inert, languid, languorous, lethargic, otiose, remiss, shiftless, slack, sleepy, slobby, slothful, slow, slow-moving, sluggish, somnolent, torpid, work-shy.
antonyms active, diligent, energetic, industrious.

leach *v.* drain, extract, filter, filtrate, lixiviate, osmose, percolate, seep, strain.

lead *v.* antecede, cause, command, conduct, direct, dispose, draw, escort, exceed, excel, experience, govern, guide, have, head, incline, induce, influence, live, manage, outdo, outstrip, pass, persuade, pilot, precede, preside over, prevail, prompt, spend, steer, supervise, surpass, transcend, undergo, usher.
antonym follow.

n. advance, advantage, clue, direction, edge, example, first place, guidance, guide, hint, indication, leadership, margin, model, precedence, primacy, principal, priority, protagonist, starring role, start, suggestion, supremacy, tip, title role, trace, van, vanguard.

adj. chief, first, foremost, head, leading, main, premier, primary, prime, principal, star.

leader *n.* bell-wether, boss, captain, chief, chieftain, commander, conductor, coryphaeus, counselor, director, doyen, figurehead, flagship, guide, head, mahatma, principal, ringleader, ruler, skipper, superior, supremo.
antonym follower.

leading *adj.* chief, dominant, first, foremost, governing, greatest, highest, main, number one, outstanding, paramount, pre-eminent, primary, principal, ruling, superior, supreme.
antonyms subordinate.

league *n.* alliance, association, band, Bund, cartel, category, class, coalition, combination, combine, compact, confederacy, confederation, consortium, federation, fellowship, fraternity, group, guild, level, partnership, sorority, syndicate, union.

v. ally, amalgamate, associate, band, collaborate, combine, confederate, consort, join forces, unite.

leak *n.* aperture, chink, crack, crevice, disclosure, divulgence, drip, fissure, hole, leakage, leaking, oozing, opening, percolation, perforation, puncture, seepage.

v. discharge, disclose, divulge, drip, escape, exude, give away, let slip, let the cat out of the bag, make known, make public, make water, ooze, pass, pass on, percolate, reveal, seep, spill, spill the beans, tell, trickle, weep.

lean[1] *v.* bend, confide, count on, depend, favor, incline, list, prefer, prop, recline, rely, repose, rest, slant, slope, tend, tilt, tip, trust.

lean[2] *adj.* angular, bare, barren, bony, emaciated, gaunt, inadequate, infertile, lank, meager, pitiful, poor, rangy, scanty, scragged, scraggy, scrawny, skinny,

slender, slim, slink(y), spare, sparse, thin, unfruitful, unproductive, wiry.
antonyms fat, fleshy.

lean on force, persuade, pressurize, put pressure on.

leaning *n.* aptitude, bent, bias, disposition, inclination, liking, partiality, penchant, predilection, proclivity, proneness, propensity, susceptibility, taste, tendency, velleity.

leap *v.* advance, bounce, bound, caper, capriole, cavort, clear, curvet, escalate, frisk, gambol, hasten, hop, hurry, increase, jump, jump (over), reach, rocket, rush, skip, soar, spring, surge, vault.
antonyms drop, fall, sink.

n. bound, caper, capriole, curvet, escalation, frisk, hop, increase, jump, rise, sally, skip, spring, surge, upsurge, upswing, vault, volt(e).

learn *v.* acquire, ascertain, assimilate, attain, cognize, con, detect, determine, discern, discover, find out, gather, get off pat, grasp, hear, imbibe, learn by heart, master, memorize, pick up, see, understand.

learned *adj.* academic, adept, blue, cultured, erudite, experienced, expert, highbrow, intellectual, lettered, literate, proficient, sage, scholarly, skilled, versed, well-informed, well-read, wise.
antonyms ignorant, illiterate, uneducated.

learning *n.* acquirements, attainments, culture, edification, education, enlightenment, erudition, information, knowledge, letters, literature, lore, research, scholarship, schoolcraft, schooling, study, tuition, wisdom.

lease *v.* charter, farm out, hire, let, loan, rent, sublet.

leash *n.* check, control, curb, discipline, hold, lead, lyam, rein, restraint, tether.

least *adj.* fewest, last, lowest, meanest, merest, minimum, minutest, poorest, slightest, smallest, tiniest.
antonym most.

leave[1] *v.* abandon, allot, assign, bequeath, cause, cease, cede, commit, consign, decamp, depart, deposit, desert, desist, disappear, do a bunk, drop, entrust, exit, flit, forget, forsake, generate, give over, give up, go, go away, hand down, leave behind, levant, move, produce, pull out, quit, refer, refrain, relinquish, renounce, retire, set out, stop, surrender, take off, transmit, will, withdraw.
antonyms arrive.

leave[2] *n.* allowance, authorization, concession, consent, dispensation, exeat, freedom, furlough, holiday, indulgence, liberty, permission, sabbatical, sanction, time off, vacation.
antonyms refusal, rejection.

lecherous *adj.* carnal, concupiscent, goatish, lascivious, lewd, libidinous, licentious, lickerish, liquorish, lubricous, lustful, prurient, randy, raunchy, salacious, unchaste, wanton, womanizing.

lecture *n.* address, castigation, censure, chiding, discourse, disquisition, dressing-down, going-over, harangue, instruction, lesson, prelection, rebuke, reprimand, reproof, scolding, speech, talk, talking-to, telling-off, wigging.

v. address, admonish, berate, carpet, castigate, censure, chide, discourse, expound, harangue, hold forth, lucubrate, prelect, rate, reprimand, reprove, scold, speak, talk, teach, tell off.

ledge *n.* berm, mantle, projection, ridge, shelf, shelve, sill, step.

leech *n.* bloodsucker, freeloader, hanger-on, parasite, sponger, sycophant, usurer.

leer *v.* eye, fleer, gloat, goggle, grin, ogle, smirk, squint, stare, wink.

n. grin, ogle, smirk, squint, stare, wink.

leeway *n.* elbow-room, latitude, play, room, scope, space.

left-overs *n.* dregs, fag-end, leavings, oddments, odds and ends, orts, refuse, remainder, remains, remnants, residue, scraps, surplus, sweepings.

legacy *n.* bequest, birthright, devise, endowment, estate, gift, heirloom, hereditament, heritage, heritance, inheritance, patrimony.

legal *adj.* above-board, allowable, allowed, authorized, constitutional, forensic, judicial, juridical, lawful, legalized, legitimate, licit, permissible, proper, rightful, sanctioned, valid, warrantable.
antonym illegal.

legalize *v.* allow, approve, authorize, decriminalize, legitimate, legitimize, license, permit, sanction, validate, warrant.

legate *n.* ambassador, delegate, depute, deputy, emissary, envoy, exarch, messenger, nuncio.

legend *n.* caption, celebrity, cipher, code, device, fable, fiction, folk-tale, household name, inscription, key, luminary, marvel, motto, myth, narrative, phenomenon, prodigy, saga, spectacle, story, tale, tradition, wonder.

legendary *adj.* apocryphal, celebrated, fabled, fabulous, famed, famous, fanciful, fictional, fictitious, illustrious, immortal, mythical, renowned, romantic, storied, story-book, traditional, unhistoric(al), well-known.

legible *adj.* clear, decipherable, discernible, distinct, intelligible, neat, readable.
antonym illegible.

legion *n.* army, battalion, brigade, cohort, company, division, drove, force, horde, host, mass, multitude, myriad, number, regiment, swarm, throng, troop.
adj. countless, illimitable, innumerable, multitudinous, myriad, numberless, numerous.

legislation *n.* act, authorization, bill, charter, codification, constitutionalization, enactment, law, lawmaking, measure, prescription, regulation, ruling, statute.

legislator *n.* law-giver, law-maker, nomothete, parliamentarian.

legitimate *adj.* acknowledged, admissible, authentic, authorized, correct, genuine, just, justifiable, kosher, lawful, legal, legit, licit, logical, proper, real, reasonable, rightful, sanctioned, sensible, statutory, true, true-born, valid, warranted, well-founded.
antonym illegitimate.
v. authorize, charter, entitle, legalize, legitimize, license, permit, sanction.

leisure *n.* breather, ease, freedom, holiday, let-up, liberty, opportunity, pause, quiet, recreation, relaxation, respite, rest, retirement, spare time, time off, vacation.
antonyms toil, work.

leisurely *adj.* carefree, comfortable, deliberate, easy, gentle, indolent, laid-back, lazy, lingering, loose, relaxed, restful, slow, tranquil, unhasty, unhurried.
antonyms hectic, hurried, rushed.

lend *v.* add, advance, afford, bestow, confer, contribute, furnish, give, grant, impart, lease, loan, present, provide, supply.

antonym borrow.

length *n.* distance, duration, elongation, extensiveness, extent, lengthiness, longitude, measure, operoseness, operosity, period, piece, portion, prolixity, protractedness, reach, section, segment, space, span, stretch, tediousness, term.

lengthen *v.* continue, draw out, eke, eke out, elongate, expand, extend, increase, pad out, prolong, prolongate, protract, spin out, stretch.
antonym shorten.

leniency *n.* clemency, compassion, forbearance, gentleness, indulgence, lenience, lenity, mercy, mildness, moderation, permissiveness, soft-heartedness, softness, tenderness, tolerance.
antonym severity.

lenient *adj.* clement, compassionate, easy-going, forbearing, forgiving, gentle, indulgent, kind, merciful, mild, soft, soft-hearted, sparing, tender, tolerant.
antonym severe.

lessen *v.* abate, abridge, bate, contract, curtail, deaden, decrease, de-escalate, degrade, die down, diminish, dwindle, ease, erode, fail, flag, impair, lighten, lower, minimize, moderate, narrow, reduce, shrink, slack, slow down, weaken.
antonym increase.

lesson *n.* admonition, assignment, censure, chiding, class, coaching, deterrent, drill, example, exemplar, exercise, homework, instruction, lection, lecture, message, model, moral, pericope, period, practice, precept, punishment, reading, rebuke, recitation, reprimand, reproof, schooling, scolding, task, teaching, tutorial, tutoring, warning.

let¹ *v.* agree to, allow, authorize, cause, charter, consent to, empower, enable, entitle, give leave, give permission, give the go-ahead, give the green light, grant, hire, lease, make, OK, permit, rent, sanction, tolerate.
antonym forbid.

let² *n.* check, constraint, hindrance, impediment, interference, obstacle, obstruction, prohibition, restraint, restriction.
antonym assistance.

let-down *n.* anticlimax, betrayal, blow, desertion, disappointment, disillusionment, frustration, lemon, setback, wash-out.
antonym satisfaction.

lethal *adj.* baleful, dangerous, deadly, deathful, deathly, destructive, devastating, fatal, lethiferous, mortal, mortiferous, murderous, noxious, pernicious, poisonous, virulent.
antonym harmless.

lethargic *adj.* apathetic, comatose, debilitated, drowsy, dull, enervated, heavy, hebetant, hebetated, hebetudinous, inactive, indifferent, inert, languid, lazy, listless, sleepy, slothful, slow, sluggish, somnolent, stupefied, torpid.
antonym lively.

lethargy *n.* apathy, drowsiness, dullness, hebetation, hebetude, hebetudinosity, inaction, indifference, inertia, languor, lassitude, listlessness, sleepiness, sloth, slowness, sluggishness, stupor, torpidity, torpor.
antonym liveliness.

letter¹ *n.* acknowledgment, answer, billet, chit, communication, da(w)k, dispatch, encyclical, epistle, epistolet, line, message, missive, note, reply.

letter² n. character, grapheme, lexigram, logogram, logograph, sign, symbol.

let-up n. abatement, break, breather, cessation, interval, lessening, lull, pause, recess, remission, respite, slackening.
antonym continuation.

level¹ adj. aligned, balanced, calm, champaign, commensurate, comparable, consistent, equable, equal, equivalent, even, even-tempered, flat, flush, horizontal, neck and neck, on a par, plain, proportionate, smooth, stable, steady, uniform.
antonyms behind, uneven, unstable.
v. aim, beam, bulldoze, couch, demolish, destroy, devastate, direct, equalize, even out, flatten, flush, focus, knock down, lay low, plane, point, pull down, raze, smooth, tear down, train, wreck.
n. altitude, bed, class, degree, echelon, elevation, floor, grade, height, horizontal, layer, plain, plane, position, rank, stage, standard, standing, status, story, stratum, zone.

level² v. admit, avow, come clean, confess, divulge, open up, tell.
antonym prevaricate.

level-headed adj. balanced, calm, collected, commonsensical, composed, cool, dependable, even-tempered, reasonable, sane, self-possessed, sensible, steady, together, unflappable.

leverage n. advantage, ascendancy, authority, clout, force, influence, pull, purchase, rank, strength, weight.

levity n. buoyancy, facetiousness, fickleness, flightiness, flippancy, frivolity, giddiness, irreverence, light-heartedness, silliness, skittishness, triviality, whifflery.
antonyms seriousness, sobriety.

levy v. assemble, call, call up, charge, collect, conscript, demand, exact, gather, impose, mobilize, muster, press, raise, summon, tax.
n. assessment, collection, contribution, duty, exaction, excise, fee, gathering, imposition, impost, subscription, tariff, tax, toll.

lewd adj. bawdy, blue, Cyprian, dirty, harlot, impure, indecent, lascivious, libidinous, licentious, loose, lubric, lubrical, lubricious, lubricous, lustful, obscene, pornographic, profligate, salacious, smutty, unchaste, vile, vulgar, wanton, wicked.
antonyms chaste, polite.

liability n. accountability, albatross, answerability, arrears, burden, culpability, debit, debt, disadvantage, drag, drawback, duty, encumbrance, handicap, hindrance, impediment, inconvenience, indebtedness, likeliness, millstone, minus, nuisance, obligation, onus, responsibility.
antonyms asset(s), unaccountability.

liable adj. accountable, amenable, answerable, apt, bound, chargeable, disposed, exposed, inclined, likely, obligated, open, predisposed, prone, responsible, subject, susceptible, tending, vulnerable.
antonyms unaccountable, unlikely.

liaison n. affair, amour, communication, conjunction, connection, contact, entanglement, interchange, intermediary, intrigue, link, love affair, romance, union.

liar n. Ananias, bouncer, deceiver, fabricator, falsifier, fibber, perjurer, prevaricator, storyteller.

libel n. aspersion, calumny, defamation, denigration, obloquy, slander, slur, smear, vilification, vituperation.
antonym praise.

v. blacken, calumniate, defame, derogate, malign, revile, slander, slur, smear, traduce, vilify, vilipend, vituperate.
antonym praise.

liberal adj. abundant, advanced, altruistic, ample, beneficent, bounteous, bountiful, broad, broad-minded, catholic, charitable, copious, enlightened, flexible, free, free-handed, general, generous, handsome, high-minded, humanistic, humanitarian, indulgent, inexact, kind, large-hearted, latitudinarian, lavish, lenient, libertarian, loose, magnanimous, munificent, open-handed, open-hearted, permissive, plentiful, profuse, progressive, radical, reformist, rich, tolerant, unbiased, unbigoted, unprejudiced, unstinting, verligte, Whig, Whiggish.
antonyms conservative, illiberal, mean, narrow-minded.

liberality n. altruism, beneficence, benevolence, bounty, breadth, broad-mindedness, candor, catholicity, charity, free-handedness, generosity, impartiality, kindness, large-heartedness, largess(e), latitude, liberalism, libertarianism, magnanimity, munificence, open-handedness, open-mindedness, permissiveness, philanthropy, progressivism, tolerance, toleration.
antonyms illiberality, meanness.

liberate v. affranchise, deliver, discharge, disenthral, emancipate, free, let go, let loose, let out, manumit, ransom, redeem, release, rescue, set free, uncage, unchain, unfetter, unpen, unshackle.
antonyms enslave, imprison, restrict.

liberation n. deliverance, emancipation, enfranchisement, freedom, freeing, liberating, liberty, manumission, ransoming, redemption, release, uncaging, unchaining, unfettering, unpenning, unshackling.
antonyms enslavement, imprisonment, restriction.

liberty n. authorization, autonomy, carte-blanche, dispensation, emancipation, exemption, franchise, free rein, freedom, immunity, independence, latitude, leave, liberation, license, permission, prerogative, privilege, release, right, sanction, self-determination, sovereignty.
antonyms imprisonment, restriction, slavery.

libretto n. book, lines, lyrics, script, text, words.

license¹ n. authorization, authority, carte blanche, certificate, charter, dispensation, entitlement, exemption, freedom, immunity, imprimatur, independence, indult, latitude, leave, liberty, permission, permit, privilege, right, self-determination, warrant.
antonyms banning, dependence, restriction.

license² n. abandon, amorality, anarchy, debauchery, disorder, dissipation, dissoluteness, excess, immoderation, impropriety, indulgence, intemperance, irresponsibility, lawlessness, laxity, profligacy, unruliness.
antonyms decorum, temperance.

license³ v. accredit, allow, authorize, certificate, certify, commission, empower, entitle, permit, sanction, warrant.
antonym ban.

lick¹ v. brush, dart, flick, lap, play over, smear, taste, tongue, touch, wash.
n. bit, brush, dab, hint, little, sample, smidgeon, speck, spot, stroke, taste, touch.

lick² v. beat, best, defeat, excel, flog, outdo, outstrip, overcome, rout, skelp, slap, smack, spank, strike, surpass, thrash, top, trounce, vanquish, wallop.

lick³ n. clip, gallop, pace, rate, speed.

lie[1] *v.* dissimulate, equivocate, fabricate, falsify, fib, forswear oneself, invent, misrepresent, perjure, prevaricate.

n. bam, bounce, caulker, cram, crammer, cretism, deceit, fabrication, falsehood, falsification, falsity, fib, fiction, flam, invention, inveracity, mendacity, plumper, prevarication, stretcher, tar(r)adiddle, untruth, whacker, white lie, whopper.

antonym truth.

lie[2] *v.* be, belong, couch, dwell, exist, extend, inhere, laze, loll, lounge, recline, remain, repose, rest, slump, sprawl, stretch out.

life *n.* activity, animation, autobiography, behavior, being, biography, breath, brio, career, conduct, confessions, continuance, course, creatures, duration, élan vital, energy, entity, essence, existence, fauna, flora and fauna, get-up-and-go, go, growth, heart, high spirits, history, life story, life-blood, life-style, lifetime, liveliness, memoirs, oomph, organisms, sentience, soul, span, sparkle, spirit, story, the world, this mortal coil, time, verve, viability, vigor, vita, vital flame, vital spark, vitality, vivacity, way of life, wildlife, zest.

lift[1] *v.* advance, ameliorate, annul, appropriate, arrest, ascend, boost, buoy up, cancel, climb, collar, copy, countermand, crib, dignify, disappear, disperse, dissipate, draw up, elevate, end, enhance, exalt, half-inch, heft, hoist, improve, mount, nab, nick, pick up, pilfer, pinch, pirate, plagiarize, pocket, promote, purloin, raise, rear, relax, remove, rescind, revoke, rise, steal, stop, take, terminate, thieve, up, upgrade, uplift, upraise, vanish.

antonyms drop, fall, impose, lower.

n. boost, encouragement, fillip, pick-me-up, reassurance, shot in the arm, spur, uplift.

antonym discouragement.

lift[2] *n.* drive, hitch, ride, run, transport.

light[1] *n.* beacon, blaze, brightness, brilliance, bulb, candle, cockcrow, dawn, day, daybreak, daylight, daytime, effulgence, flame, flare, flash, glare, gleam, glim, glint, glow, illumination, incandescence, lambency, lamp, lampad, lantern, lighter, lighthouse, luminescence, luminosity, luster, match, morn, morning, phosphorescence, radiance, ray, refulgence, scintillation, shine, sparkle, star, sunrise, sunshine, taper, torch, window, Yang.

antonym darkness.

v. animate, beacon, brighten, cheer, fire, floodlight, ignite, illuminate, illumine, inflame, irradiate, kindle, light up, lighten, put on, set alight, set fire to, switch on, turn on.

antonyms darken, extinguish.

adj. bleached, blond, bright, brilliant, faded, faint, fair, glowing, illuminated, lightful, lightsome, lucent, luminous, lustrous, pale, pastel, shining, sunny, well-lit.

antonym dark.

light[2] *n.* angle, approach, aspect, attitude, awareness, clue, comprehension, context, elucidation, enlightenment, example, exemplar, explanation, hint, illustration, information, insight, interpretation, knowledge, model, paragon, point of view, slant, understanding, viewpoint.

light[3] *adj.* agile, airy, amusing, animated, blithe, buoyant, carefree, cheerful, cheery, crumbly, delicate, delirious, digestible, diverting, dizzy, easy, effortless, entertaining, facile, faint, fickle, flimsy, friable, frivolous, frugal, funny, gay, gentle, giddy, graceful, humorous, idle, imponderous, inconsequential, inconsiderable, indistinct, insignificant, insubstantial, light-footed, light-headed, light-hearted, lightweight, lithe, lively, loose, manageable, merry, mild, minute, moderate, modest, nimble, pleasing, porous, portable, reeling, restricted, sandy, scanty, simple, slight, small, soft, spongy, sprightly, sunny, superficial, thin, tiny, trifling, trivial, unchaste, undemanding, underweight, unexacting, unheeding, unsteady, unsubstantial, untaxing, volatile, wanton, weak, witty, worthless.

antonyms clumsy, harsh, heavy, important, sad, severe, sober, solid, stiff.

lighten[1] *v.* beacon, brighten, illume, illuminate, illumine, light up, shine.

antonym darken.

lighten[2] *v.* alleviate, ameliorate, assuage, brighten, buoy up, cheer, disburden, disencumber, ease, elate, encourage, facilitate, gladden, hearten, inspire, inspirit, lessen, lift, mitigate, perk up, reduce, relieve, revive, unload, uplift.

antonyms burden, depress, oppress.

light-hearted *adj.* blithe, blithesome, bright, carefree, cheerful, effervescent, elated, frolicsome, gay, glad, gleeful, happy-go-lucky, insouciant, jocund, jolly, jovial, joyful, joyous, light-spirited, merry, perky, playful, sunny, untroubled, upbeat.

antonym sad.

like[1] *adj.* akin, alike, allied, analogous, approximating, cognate, corresponding, equivalent, homologous, identical, parallel, related, relating, resembling, same, similar.

antonym unlike.

n. counterpart, equal, fellow, match, opposite number, parallel, peer, twin.

prep. in the same manner as, on the lines of, similar to.

like[2] *v.* admire, adore, appreciate, approve, care to, cherish, choose, choose to, delight in, desire, dig, enjoy, esteem, fancy, feel inclined, go a bundle on, go for, hold dear, love, prefer, prize, relish, revel in, select, take a shine to, take kindly to, take to, want, wish.

antonym dislike.

n. favorite, liking, love, partiality, penchant, poison, predilection, preference.

antonym dislike.

likely *adj.* acceptable, agreeable, anticipated, appropriate, apt, befitting, believable, bright, credible, disposed, expected, fair, favorite, feasible, fit, foreseeable, hopeful, inclined, liable, odds-on, on the cards, plausible, pleasing, possible, predictable, probable, promising, prone, proper, qualified, reasonable, suitable, tending, up-and-coming, verisimilar.

antonyms unlikely, unsuitable.

adv. doubtlessly, in all probability, like as not, like enough, no doubt, odds on, presumably, probably, very like.

likeness *n.* affinity, appearance, copy, correspondence, counterpart, delineation, depiction, effigies, effigy, facsimile, form, guise, image, model, photograph, picture, portrait, replica, representation, reproduction, resemblance, semblance, similarity, similitude, simulacrum, study.

antonym unlikeness.

likewise *adv.* also, besides, by the same token, eke,

further, furthermore, in addition, moreover, similarly, too.
antonym contrariwise.

liking *n.* affection, affinity, appreciation, attraction, bent, bias, desire, favor, fondness, inclination, love, partiality, penchant, predilection, preference, proneness, propensity, satisfaction, soft spot, stomach, taste, tendency, weakness.
antonym dislike.

limb *n.* appendage, arm, bough, branch, extension, extremity, fork, leg, member, offshoot, part, projection, ramus, spur, wing.

limber *adj.* agile, elastic, flexible, flexile, graceful, lissom, lithe, loose-jointed, loose-limbed, plastic, pliable, pliant, supple.
antonym stiff.

limelight *n.* attention, big time, celebrity, fame, prominence, public notice, publicity, recognition, renown, stardom, the public eye, the spotlight.

limit *n.* bitter end, border, bound, boundary, bourne(e), brim, brink, ceiling, check, compass, confines, curb, cut-off point, deadline, edge, end, extent, frontier, limitation, maximum, mete, obstruction, outrance, perimeter, periphery, precinct, restraint, restriction, rim, saturation point, termination, terminus, terminus a quo, terminus ad quem, threshold, ultimate, utmost, verge.
v. bound, check, circumscribe, condition, confine, constrain, curb, delimit, delimitate, demarcate, fix, hem in, hinder, ration, restrain, restrict, specify.
antonyms extend, free.

limp[1] *v.* dot, falter, halt, hamble, hirple, hitch, hobble, hop, shamble, shuffle.
n. claudication, hitch, hobble, lameness.

limp[2] *adj.* debilitated, drooping, enervated, exhausted, flabby, flaccid, flexible, flexile, floppy, hypotonic, lax, lethargic, limber, loose, pliable, pooped, relaxed, slack, soft, spent, tired, toneless, weak, worn out.
antonym strong.

limpid *adj.* bright, clear, comprehensible, crystal-clear, crystalline, glassy, hyaline, intelligible, lucid, pellucid, pure, still, translucent, transparent, unruffled, untroubled.
antonyms muddy, ripply, turbid, unintelligible.

line[1] *n.* band, bar, border, borderline, boundary, cable, chain, channel, column, configuration, contour, cord, crease, crocodile, crow's foot, dash, demarcation, disposition, edge, features, figure, filament, file, firing line, formation, front, front line, frontier, furrow, groove, limit, mark, outline, position, procession, profile, queue, rank, rope, row, rule, score, scratch, sequence, series, silhouette, stipe, strand, streak, string, stroke, tail, thread, trail, trenches, underline, wire, wrinkle.
v. border, bound, crease, cut, draw, edge, fringe, furrow, hatch, inscribe, mark, rank, rim, rule, score, skirt, verge.

line up align, arrange, array, assemble, dispose, engage, fall in, form ranks, hire, lay on, marshal, obtain, order, organize, prepare, procure, produce, queue up, range, regiment, secure, straighten.

line[2] *n.* activity, approach, area, avenue, axis, belief, business, calling, course, course of action, department, direction, employment, field, forte, ideology, interest, job, line of country, method, occupation, path, policy, position, practice, procedure, profession, province,

pursuit, route, scheme, specialism, specialization, specialty, system, track, trade, trajectory, vocation.

line[3] *n.* ancestry, breed, family, lineage, pedigree, race, stirps, stock, strain, succession.

line[4] *n.* card, clue, hint, indication, information, lead, letter, memo, memorandum, message, note, postcard, report, word.

line[5] *v.* ceil, cover, encase, face, fill, reinforce, strengthen, stuff.

lineage *n.* ancestors, ancestry, birth, breed, descendants, descent, extraction, family, forebears, forefathers, genealogy, heredity, house, line, offspring, pedigree, progeny, race, stirp(s), stock, succession.

linger *v.* abide, continue, dally, dawdle, delay, dillydally, endure, hang around, hang on, hold out, idle, lag, last out, loiter, persist, procrastinate, remain, stay, stop, survive, tarry, wait.
antonyms leave, rush.

lingo *n.* argot, cant, dialect, idiom, jargon, language, parlance, patois, patter, speech, talk, terminology, tongue, vernacular, vocabulary.

link *n.* association, attachment, bond, communication, component, connection, constituent, division, element, joint, knot, liaison, member, part, piece, relationship, tie, tie-up, union.
v. associate, attach, bind, bracket, catenate, concatenate, connect, couple, fasten, identify, join, relate, tie, unite, yoke.
antonyms separate, unfasten.

lip[1] *n.* border, brim, brink, edge, margin, rim, verge.

lip[2] *n.* backchat, cheek, effrontery, impertinence, impudence, insolence, rudeness, sauce.
antonym politeness.

liquid *n.* drink, fluid, juice, liquor, lotion, potation, sap, solution.
adj. aqueous, clear, convertible, dulcet, flowing, fluid, limpid, liquefied, mellifluent, mellifluous, melted, molten, negotiable, running, runny, serous, shining, smooth, soft, sweet, thawed, translucent, transparent, watery, wet.
antonyms harsh, solid.

liquidate *v.* abolish, annihilate, annul, assassinate, bump off, cancel, cash, clear, destroy, discharge, dispatch, dissolve, do away with, do in, eliminate, exterminate, finish off, honor, kill, massacre, murder, pay, pay off, realize, remove, rub out, sell off, sell up, settle, silence, square, terminate, wipe out.

liquor[1] *n.* aguardiente, alcohol, booze, drink, fire-water, grog, hard stuff, hooch, intoxicant, juice, jungle juice, potation, rotgut, spirits, strong drink, tape.

liquor[2] *n.* broth, essence, extract, gravy, infusion, juice, liquid, stock.

lissom(e) *adj.* agile, flexible, graceful, light, limber, lithe, lithesome, loose-jointed, loose-limbed, nimble, pliable, pliant, supple, willowy.
antonym stiff.

list[1] *n.* catalog, directory, enumeration, file, index, inventory, invoice, leet, listing, litany, matricula, record, register, roll, schedule, series, syllabus, table, tabulation, tally.
v. alphabeticize, bill, book, catalog, enrol, enter, enumerate, file, index, itemize, note, record, register, schedule, set down, tabulate, write down.

list[2] *v.* cant, careen, heel, heel over, incline, lean, slope, tilt, tip.

n. cant, leaning, slant, slope, tilt.

listen *v.* attend, get a load of, give ear, give heed to, hang on (someone's) words, hang on (someone's) lips, hark, hear, hearken, heed, keep one's ears open, lend an ear, mind, obey, observe, pay attention, pin back one's ears, prick up one's ears, take notice.

listless *adj.* apathetic, bored, depressed, enervated, ennuyed, heavy, impassive, inattentive, indifferent, indolent, inert, languid, languishing, lethargic, lifeless, limp, lymphatic, mopish, sluggish, spiritless, supine, torpid, uninterested, vacant.

antonym lively.

literal *adj.* accurate, actual, boring, close, colorless, down-to-earth, dull, exact, factual, faithful, genuine, matter-of-fact, plain, prosaic, prosy, real, simple, strict, true, unexaggerated, unimaginative, uninspired, unvarnished, verbatim, word-for-word.

antonym loose.

literally *adv.* actually, closely, exactly, faithfully, literatim, plainly, precisely, really, simply, strictly, to the letter, truly, verbatim, word for word.

antonym loosely.

literary *adj.* bookish, cultivated, cultured, erudite, formal, learned, lettered, literate, refined, scholarly, well-read.

antonym illiterate.

literature *n.* belles-lettres, blurb, brochure(s), bumf, circular(s), hand-out(s), information, leaflet(s), letters, lore, pamphlet(s), paper(s), writings.

lithe *adj.* double-jointed, flexible, flexile, limber, lissom(e), lithesome, loose-jointed, loose-limbed, pliable, pliant, supple.

antonym stiff.

litigious *adj.* argumentative, belligerent, contentious, disputable, disputatious, quarrelsome.

antonym easy-going.

litter[1] *n.* clutter, confusion, debris, detritus, disarray, disorder, fragments, jumble, mess, muck, refuse, rubbish, scatter, scoria, shreds, untidiness, wastage.

v. bestrew, clutter, derange, disarrange, disorder, mess up, scatter, strew.

antonym tidy.

litter[2] *n.* brood, family, offspring, progeny, quiverful, young.

litter[3] *n.* couch, palanquin, stretcher.

little *adj.* babyish, base, brief, cheap, diminutive, dwarf, elfin, fleeting, hasty, immature, inconsiderable, infant, infinitesimal, insignificant, insufficient, junior, Lilliputian, meager, mean, microscopic, miniature, minor, minute, negligible, paltry, passing, petite, petty, piccaninny, pint-size(d), pygmy, scant, short, short-lived, skimpy, slender, sparse, tiny, transient, trifling, trivial, undeveloped, unimportant, wee, young.

antonyms important, large, long.

adv. barely, hardly, infrequently, rarely, scarcely, seldom.

antonyms frequently, greatly.

n. bit, dab, dash, drib, fragment, hint, modicum, particle, pinch, snippet, speck, spot, taste, touch, trace, trifle.

antonym lot.

liturgy *n.* celebration, ceremony, form, formula, office, rite, ritual, sacrament, service, usage, worship.

live[1] *v.* abide, breathe, continue, draw breath, dwell, earn a living, endure, exist, fare, feed, get along, hang out, inhabit, last, lead, lodge, make ends meet, pass, persist, prevail, remain, reside, settle, stay, subsist, survive.

antonyms cease, die.

live[2] *adj.* active, alert, alight, alive, animate, blazing, breathing, brisk, burning, connected, controversial, current, dynamic, earnest, energetic, existent, glowing, hot, ignited, lively, living, pertinent, pressing, prevalent, relevant, sentient, smoldering, topical, unsettled, vigorous, vital, vivid, wide-awake.

antonyms apathetic, dead, out.

livelihood *n.* employment, income, job, living, maintenance, means, occupation, subsistence, support, sustenance, work.

lively *adj.* active, agile, alert, animated, astir, blithe, blithesome, breezy, bright, brisk, buckish, bustling, busy, buxom, buzzing, canty, cheerful, chipper, chirpy, colorful, crowded, energetic, eventful, exciting, forceful, frisky, frolicsome, galliard, gay, invigorating, keen, lifesome, lightsome, merry, moving, nimble, perky, quick, racy, refreshing, skittish, sparkling, spirited, sprightly, spry, stimulating, stirring, swinging, tit(t)upy, vigorous, vivacious, vivid, zippy.

antonyms apathetic, inactive, moribund.

livid[1] *adj.* angry, beside oneself, boiling, enraged, exasperated, fuming, furibund, furious, incensed, indignant, infuriated, irate, ireful, mad, outraged, waxy.

antonym calm.

livid[2] *adj.* angry, ashen, black-and-blue, blanched, bloodless, bruised, contused, discolored, doughy, grayish, leaden, pale, pallid, pasty, purple, wan, waxen, waxy.

antonyms healthy, rosy.

living *adj.* active, alive, animated, breathing, existing, live, lively, strong, vigorous, vital.

antonyms dead, sluggish.

n. being, benefice, existence, income, job, life, livelihood, maintenance, occupation, profession, property, subsistence, support, sustenance, way of life, work.

load *n.* affliction, albatross, bale, burden, cargo, consignment, encumbrance, freight, goods, lading, millstone, onus, oppression, pressure, shipment, trouble, weight, worry.

v. adulterate, burden, charge, cram, doctor, drug, encumber, fill, fortify, freight, hamper, heap, lade, oppress, overburden, pack, pile, prime, saddle with, stack, stuff, trouble, weigh down, weight, worry.

loafer *n.* beachcomber, bludger, bum, bummer, burn, corner-boy, do-nothing, drone, idler, layabout, lazybones, lounge-lizard, lounger, ne'er-do-well, shirker, skiver, sluggard, time-waster, wastrel.

antonym worker.

loan *n.* accommodation, advance, allowance, calque, credit, lend-lease, loan translation, loan-word, mortgage, touch.

v. accommodate, advance, allow, credit, lend, let out, oblige.

antonym borrow.

loath *adj.* against, averse, backward, counter, disinclined, grudging, hesitant, indisposed, opposed, reluctant, resisting, unwilling.

antonym willing.

loathe *v.* abhor, abominate, despise, detest, dislike, execrate, hate, keck.

antonym like.

loathsome *adj.* abhorrent, abominable, detestable, disgusting, execrable, hateful, horrible, loathful, nasty, nauseating, obnoxious, odious, offensive, repellent, repugnant, repulsive, revolting, vile.
antonym likeable.

lob *v.* chuck, fling, heave, launch, lift, loft, pitch, shy, throw, toss.

lobby[1] *v.* call for, campaign for, demand, influence, persuade, press for, pressure, promote, pull strings, push for, solicit, urge.
n. ginger group, pressure group.

lobby[2] *n.* anteroom, corridor, entrance hall, foyer, hall, hallway, passage, passageway, porch, vestibule, waiting-room.

local *adj.* community, confined, district, limited, narrow, neighborhood, parish, parochial, provincial, pump, regional, restricted, small-town, vernacular, vicinal.
antonym far-away.
n. denizen, inhabitant, native, resident, yokel.
antonym incomer.

locality *n.* area, district, locale, location, neck of the woods, neighborhood, place, position, region, scene, settings, site, spot, vicinity, zone.

locate *v.* detect, discover, establish, find, fix, identify, lay one's hands on, pin-point, place, put, run to earth, seat, set, settle, situate, track down, unearth.

location *n.* bearings, locale, locus, place, point, position, site, situation, spot, ubiety, venue, whereabouts.

lock[1] *n.* bolt, clasp, fastening, padlock, sneck.
v. bolt, clasp, clench, close, clutch, disengage, embrace, encircle, enclose, engage, entangle, entwine, fasten, grapple, grasp, hug, join, latch, link, mesh, press, seal, secure, shut, sneck, unite, unlock.

lock out ban, bar, debar, exclude, keep out, ostracize, refuse admittance to, shut out.

lock together interdigitate, interlock.

lock up cage, close up, confine, detain, enlock, imprison, incarcerate, jail, pen, secure, shut, shut in, shut up.
antonym free.

lock[2] *n.* curl, plait, ringlet, strand, tress, tuft.

locomotion *n.* action, ambulation, headway, motion, movement, moving, progress, progression, travel, traveling.

locution *n.* accent, articulation, cliché, collocation, diction, expression, idiom, inflection, intonation, phrase, phrasing, style, term, turn of phrase, wording.

lodge *n.* abode, assemblage, association, branch, cabin, chalet, chapter, club, cot, cot-house, cottage, den, gang-hut, gatehouse, group, haunt, house, hunting-lodge, hut, lair, meeting-place, retreat, shelter, society.
v. accommodate, billet, board, deposit, dig, entertain, file, get stuck, harbor, imbed, implant, lay, place, put, put on record, put up, quarter, register, room, set, shelter, sojourn, stay, stick, stop, submit.

lodger *n.* boarder, guest, inmate, paying guest, renter, resident, roomer, tenant.

lofty *adj.* arrogant, condescending, dignified, disdainful, distinguished, elevated, esteemed, exalted, grand, haughty, high, high and mighty, illustrious, imperial, imposing, lordly, majestic, noble, patronizing, proud, raised, renowned, sky-high, snooty, soaring, stately, sublime, supercilious, superior, tall, toffee-nosed, towering.

antonyms humble, low(ly), modest.

log[1] *n.* billet, block, bole, chunk, loggat, stump, timber, trunk.

log[2] *n.* account, chart, daybook, diary, journal, listing, logbook, record, tally.
v. book, chart, note, record, register, report, tally, write down, write in, write up.

logic *n.* argumentation, deduction, dialectic(s), ratiocination, rationale, rationality, reason, reasoning, sense.

logistics *n.* co-ordination, engineering, management, masterminding, orchestration, organization, planning, plans, strategy.

loiter *v.* dally, dawdle, delay, dilly-dally, hang about, idle, lag, lallygag, linger, loaf, loll, lollygag, mooch, mouch, saunter, skulk, stroll.

loll *v.* dangle, depend, droop, drop, flap, flop, hang, lean, loaf, lounge, recline, relax, sag, slouch, slump, sprawl.

lone *adj.* deserted, isolated, lonesome, one, only, separate, separated, single, sole, solitary, unaccompanied, unattached, unattended.
antonym accompanied.

loneliness *n.* aloneness, desolation, forlornness, friendlessness, isolation, lonesomeness, seclusion, solitariness, solitude.

lonely *adj.* abandoned, alone, apart, companionless, destitute, estranged, forlorn, forsaken, friendless, isolated, lonely-heart, lonesome, outcast, out-of-the-way, remote, secluded, sequestered, solitary, unfrequented, uninhabited, untrodden.

loner *n.* hermit, individualist, lone wolf, maverick, outsider, pariah, recluse, solitary, solitudinarian.

lonesome *adj.* cheerless, companionless, deserted, desolate, dreary, forlorn, friendless, gloomy, isolated, lone, lonely, solitary.

long *adj.* dragging, elongated, expanded, expansive, extended, extensive, far-reaching, interminable, late, lengthy, lingering, long-drawn-out, marathon, prolonged, protracted, slow, spread out, stretched, sustained, tardy.
antonyms abbreviated, brief, fleeting, short.

long-standing *adj.* abiding, enduring, established, fixed, hallowed, long-established, long-lasting, long-lived, time-honored, traditional.

long-winded *adj.* circumlocutory, diffuse, discursive, garrulous, lengthy, long-drawn-out, overlong, prolix, prolonged, rambling, repetitious, tedious, verbose, voluble, wordy.
antonyms brief, compact, curt, terse.

look *v.* appear, behold, consider, contemplate, display, evidence, examine, exhibit, eye, gape, gawk, gawp, gaze, get a load of, glance, goggle, inspect, observe, ogle, peep, regard, rubberneck, scan, scrutinize, see, seem, show, stare, study, survey, view, watch.
n. air, appearance, aspect, bearing, cast, complexion, countenance, decko, demeanor, effect, examination, expression, eyeful, eye-glance, face, fashion, gaze, glance, glimpse, guise, inspection, look-see, manner, mien, observation, once-over, peek, review, semblance, sight, squint, survey, view.

loom *v.* appear, bulk, dominate, emerge, hang over, hover, impend, materialize, menace, mount, overhang, overshadow, overtop, rise, soar, take shape, threaten, tower.

loop *n.* arc, bend, circle, coil, convolution, curl, curve, eyelet, hoop, kink, loophole, noose, ring, spiral, turn, twirl, twist, whorl.

v. bend, braid, circle, coil, connect, curl, curve round, encircle, fold, gird, join, knot, roll, spiral, turn, twist.

loose¹ *adj.* baggy, crank, diffuse, disconnected, disordered, easy, floating, free, hanging, ill-defined, imprecise, inaccurate, indefinite, indistinct, inexact, insecure, loosened, movable, rambling, random, relaxed, released, shaky, slack, slackened, sloppy, solute, unattached, unbound, unconfined, unfastened, unfettered, unrestricted, unsecured, untied, vague, wobbly.

antonyms close, compact, precise, strict, taut, tense, tight.

v. absolve, detach, disconnect, disengage, ease, free, let go, liberate, loosen, release, set free, slacken, unbind, unbrace, unclasp, uncouple, undo, unfasten, unhand, unleash, unlock, unloose, unmew, unmoor, unpen, untie.

antonyms bind, fasten, fix, secure.

loose² *adj.* abandoned, careless, debauched, disreputable, dissipated, dissolute, fast, heedless, immoral, imprudent, lax, lewd, libertine, licentious, negligent, profligate, promiscuous, rash, thoughtless, unchaste, unmindful, wanton.

antonyms strict, stringent, tight.

loosen *v.* deliver, detach, free, let go, let out, liberate, release, separate, set free, slacken, unbind, undo, unfasten, unloose, unloosen, unstick, untie.

antonym tighten.

loot *n.* boodle, booty, cache, goods, haul, plunder, prize, riches, spoils, swag.

v. burglarize, despoil, maraud, pillage, plunder, raid, ransack, ravage, rifle, rob, sack.

lope *v.* bound, canter, gallop, lollop, run, spring, stride.

lop-sided *adj.* askew, asymmetrical, awry, cockeyed, crooked, disproportionate, ill-balanced, off balance, one-sided, out of true, squint, tilting, unbalanced, unequal, uneven, warped.

antonyms balanced, straight, symmetrical.

loquacious *adj.* babbling, blathering, chattering, chatty, gabby, garrulous, gassy, gossipy, multiloquent, multiloquous, talkative, voluble, wordy.

antonyms succinct, taciturn, terse.

lord *n.* baron, commander, count, daimio, duke, earl, governor, Herr, king, leader, liege, liege-lord, master, monarch, noble, nobleman, overlord, peer, potentate, prince, ruler, seigneur, seignior, sovereign, superior, suzerain, viscount.

lore *n.* beliefs, doctrine, erudition, experience, knowhow, knowledge, learning, letters, mythus, saws, sayings, scholarship, schooling, teaching, traditions, wisdom.

lose *v.* capitulate, come a cropper, come to grief, consume, default, deplete, displace, dissipate, dodge, drain, drop, duck, elude, escape, evade, exhaust, expend, fail, fall short, forfeit, forget, get the worst of, give (someone) the slip, lap, lavish, leave behind, lose out on, misfile, mislay, misplace, miss, misspend, outdistance, outrun, outstrip, overtake, pass, pass up, shake off, slip away, squander, stray from, suffer defeat, take a licking, throw off, use up, wander from, waste, yield.

antonyms gain, make, win.

loss *n.* bereavement, cost, damage, debit, debt, defeat,

deficiency, deficit, depletion, deprivation, destruction, detriment, disadvantage, disappearance, failure, forfeiture, harm, hurt, impairment, injury, losing, losings, misfortune, privation, ruin, shrinkage, squandering, waste, write-off.

antonyms benefit, gain.

lost *adj.* abandoned, abolished, absent, absorbed, abstracted, adrift, annihilated, astray, baffled, bewildered, confused, consumed, corrupt, damned, demolished, depraved, destroyed, devastated, disappeared, disoriented, dissipated, dissolute, distracted, dreamy, engrossed, entranced, eradicated, exterminated, fallen, forfeited, frittered away, irreclaimable, licentious, misapplied, misdirected, mislaid, misplaced, missed, missing, misspent, misused, mystified, obliterated, off-course, off-track, perished, perplexed, preoccupied, profligate, puzzled, rapt, ruined, spellbound, squandered, strayed, unrecallable, unrecapturable, unrecoverable, untraceable, vanished, wanton, wasted, wayward, wiped out, wrecked.

antonym found.

lot *n.* accident, allowance, assortment, batch, chance, collection, consignment, crowd, cut, destiny, doom, fate, fortune, group, hazard, jing-bang, parcel, part, percentage, piece, plight, portion, quantity, quota, ration, set, share, weird.

lottery *n.* chance, draw, gamble, hazard, raffle, risk, sweepstake, toss-up, uncertainty, venture.

loud *adj.* blaring, blatant, boisterous, booming, brash, brassy, brazen, clamorous, coarse, crass, crude, deafening, ear-piercing, ear-splitting, flamboyant, flashy, garish, gaudy, glaring, high-sounding, loud-mouthed, lurid, noisy, offensive, ostentatious, piercing, raucous, resounding, rowdy, showy, sonorous, stentorian, streperous, strepitant, strident, strong, tasteless, tawdry, thundering, tumultuous, turbulent, vehement, vocal, vociferous, vulgar.

antonyms low, quiet, soft.

lounge *v.* dawdle, idle, kill time, laze, lie about, lie back, loaf, loiter, loll, potter, recline, relax, slump, sprawl, take it easy, waste time.

n. day-room, drawing-room, parlor, sitting-room.

louring, lowering *adj.* black, brooding, browning, clouded, cloudy, dark, darkening, forbidding, foreboding, gloomy, glowering, gray, grim, heavy, impending, menacing, minatory, ominous, overcast, scowling, sullen, surly, threatening.

lousy *adj.* awful, bad, base, contemptible, crap, despicable, dirty, hateful, inferior, lice-infested, lice-ridden, low, mean, miserable, no good, pedicular, pediculous, poor, rotten, second-rate, shoddy, slovenly, terrible, trashy, vicious, vile.

antonyms excellent, superb.

lovable *adj.* adorable, amiable, attractive, captivating, charming, cuddly, delightful, enchanting, endearing, engaging, fetching, likable, lovely, pleasing, sweet, taking, winning, winsome.

antonym hateful.

love *v.* adore, adulate, appreciate, cherish, delight in, desire, dote on, enjoy, fancy, hold dear, idolize, like, prize, relish, savor, take pleasure in, think the world of, treasure, want, worship.

antonyms detest, hate, loathe.

n. adoration, adulation, affection, agape, aloha, amity, amorosity, amorousness, ardor, attachment, delight,

devotion, enjoyment, fondness, friendship, inclination, infatuation, liking, partiality, passion, rapture, regard, relish, soft spot, taste, tenderness, warmth, weakness.
antonyms detestation, hate, loathing.

loveless *adj.* cold, cold-hearted, disliked, forsaken, friendless, frigid, hard, heartless, icy, insensitive, lovelorn, passionless, unappreciated, uncherished, unfeeling, unfriendly, unloved, unloving, unresponsive, unvalued.
antonym passionate.

lovely *adj.* admirable, adorable, agreeable, amiable, attractive, beautiful, captivating, charming, comely, delightful, enchanting, engaging, enjoyable, exquisite, graceful, gratifying, handsome, idyllic, nice, pleasant, pleasing, pretty, sweet, taking, winning.
antonyms hideous, ugly, unlovely.

lover *n.* admirer, amoretto, amorist, amoroso, beau, beloved, bon ami, boyfriend, Casanova, fancy man, fancy woman, fiancé(e), flame, gigolo, girlfriend, inamorata, inamorato, mistress, paramour, philanderer, suitor, swain, sweetheart.

loving *adj.* affectionate, amative, amatorial, amatorian, amatorious, amorous, ardent, cordial, dear, demonstrative, devoted, doting, fond, friendly, kind, passionate, solicitous, tender, warm, warm-hearted.

low[1] *adj.* abject, base, base-born, blue, brassed off, browned off, cheap, coarse, common, contemptible, crude, dastardly, debilitated, deep, deficient, degraded, dejected, depleted, depraved, depressed, despicable, despondent, disgraceful, disheartened, dishonorable, disreputable, down, down in the dumps, downcast, dying, economical, exhausted, fed up, feeble, forlorn, frail, gloomy, glum, gross, humble, hushed, ignoble, ill, ill-bred, inadequate, inexpensive, inferior, insignificant, little, low-born, low-grade, lowly, low-lying, meager, mean, mediocre, meek, menial, miserable, moderate, modest, morose, muffled, muted, nasty, obscene, obscure, paltry, plain, plebeian, poor, prostrate, puny, quiet, reasonable, reduced, rough, rude, sad, scant, scurvy, second-rate, servile, shallow, shoddy, short, simple, sinking, small, soft, sordid, sparse, squat, stricken, stunted, subdued, substandard, sunken, trifling, unbecoming, undignified, unhappy, unpretentious, unrefined, unworthy, vile, vulgar, weak, whispered, worthless.
antonyms elevated, high, lofty, noble.

lower[1] *adj.* inferior, insignificant, junior, lesser, low-level, lowly, minor, secondary, second-class, smaller, subordinate, subservient, under, unimportant.
v. abase, abate, belittle, condescend, couch, curtail, cut, debase, decrease, degrade, deign, demean, demolish, depress, devalue, diminish, discredit, disgrace, downgrade, drop, fall, humble, humiliate, lessen, let down, minimize, moderate, prune, raze, reduce, sink, slash, soften, stoop, submerge, take down, tone down.
antonyms elevate, increase, raise, rise.

lower[2] *see* lour.

low-key *adj.* low-pitched, muffled, muted, quiet, restrained, slight, soft, subdued, understated.

lowly *adj.* average, common, docile, dutiful, homespun, humble, ignoble, inferior, low-born, mean, mean-born, meek, mild, modest, obscure, ordinary, plain, plebeian, poor, proletarian, simple, submissive, subordinate, unassuming, unexalted, unpretentious.
antonyms lofty, noble.

loyal *adj.* attached, constant, dependable, devoted, dutiful, faithful, honest, leal, patriotic, sincere, staunch, steadfast, true, true-blue, true-hearted, trustworthy, trusty, unswerving, unwavering.
antonyms disloyal, traitorous.

loyalty *n.* allegiance, constancy, dependability, devotion, faithfulness, fealty, fidelity, honesty, lealty, patriotism, reliability, sincerity, staunchness, steadfastness, trueheartedness, trueness, trustiness, trustworthiness.
antonyms disloyalty, treachery.

lubricate *v.* grease, lard, oil, smear, wax.

lucid *adj.* beaming, bright, brilliant, clear, clear-cut, clear-headed, compos mentis, comprehensible, crystalline, diaphanous, distinct, effulgent, evident, explicit, glassy, gleaming, intelligible, limpid, luminous, obvious, pellucid, perspicuous, plain, pure, radiant, rational, reasonable, resplendent, sane, sensible, shining, sober, sound, translucent, transparent.
antonyms dark, murky, unclear.

luck *n.* accident, blessing, break, chance, destiny, fate, fluke, fortuity, fortune, godsend, good fortune, hap, happenstance, hazard, jam, joss, prosperity, serendipity, stroke, success, windfall.
antonym misfortune.

lucky *adj.* advantageous, adventitious, auspicious, blessed, canny, charmed, favored, fluky, fortuitous, fortunate, jammy, opportune, propitious, prosperous, providential, serendipitous, successful, timely.
antonyms luckless, unlucky.

lucky dip bran tub, grab-bag.

lucrative *adj.* advantageous, fecund, fertile, fruitful, gainful, paying, productive, profitable, remunerative, well-paid.
antonym unprofitable.

ludicrous *adj.* absurd, amusing, burlesque, comic, comical, crazy, drôle, droll, farcical, funny, incongruous, laughable, nonsensical, odd, outlandish, preposterous, ridiculous, risible, silly, zany.

lug *v.* carry, drag, haul, heave, hump, humph, pull, tote, tow, yank.

lugubrious *adj.* dismal, doleful, dreary, funereal, gloomy, glum, melancholy, morose, mournful, sad, sepulchral, serious, somber, sorrowful, Wertherian, woebegone, woeful.
antonyms cheerful, jovial, merry.

lukewarm *adj.* apathetic, cold, cool, half-hearted, indifferent, laodicean, Laodicean, lew, phlegmatic, tepid, unconcerned, unenthusiastic, uninterested, unresponsive, warm.

lull *v.* abate, allay, calm, cease, compose, decrease, diminish, dwindle, ease off, hush, let up, lullaby, moderate, pacify, quell, quiet, quieten down, sedate, slacken, soothe, still, subdue, subside, tranquilize, wane.
antonym agitate.
n. calm, calmness, hush, let-up, pause, peace, quiet, respite, silence, stillness, tranquility.
antonym agitation.

lumber[1] *n.* bits and pieces, clutter, jumble, junk, odds and ends, refuse, rubbish, trash, trumpery.
v. burden, charge, encumber, hamper, impose, land, load, saddle.

lumber[2] *v.* clump, galumph, plod, shamble, shuffle, stump, trudge, trundle, waddle.

luminous *adj.* bright, brilliant, glowing, illuminated, lighted, lit, lucent, luminescent, luminiferous, lustrous, radiant, resplendent, shining, vivid.

lump[1] *n.* ball, bulge, bump, bunch, cake, chuck, chump, chunk, clod, cluster, cyst, dab, daud, dod, gob, gobbet, group, growth, hunch, hunk, (k)nub, (k)nubble, lob, mass, nugget, piece, protrusion, protuberance, spot, swelling, tuber, tumescence, tumor, wedge, wen, wodge.

v. coalesce, collect, combine, consolidate, group, mass, unite.

lump[2] *v.* bear (with), brook, endure, put up with, stand, stomach, suffer, swallow, take, thole, tolerate.

lunacy *n.* aberration, absurdity, craziness, dementia, derangement, folly, foolhardiness, foolishness, idiocy, imbecility, insanity, madness, mania, moon-madness, moonraking, psychosis, senselessness, stupidity, tomfoolery.

antonym sanity.

lunge *v.* bound, charge, cut, dash, dive, fall upon, grab (at), hit (at), jab, leap, pitch into, plunge, poke, pounce, set upon, stab, strike (at), thrust.

n. charge, cut, jab, pass, pounce, spring, stab, swing, swipe, thrust, venue.

lurch *v.* heave, lean, list, pitch, reel, rock, roll, stagger, stumble, sway, tilt, totter, wallow, weave, welter.

lure *v.* allure, attract, beckon, decoy, draw, ensnare, entice, inveigle, invite, lead on, seduce, tempt, trepan.

n. allurement, attraction, bait, carrot, come-on, decoy, enticement, inducement, magnet, siren, song, temptation, train.

lurid *adj.* ashen, bloody, disgusting, exaggerated, fiery, flaming, ghastly, glaring, glowering, gory, graphic, grim, grisly, gruesome, intense, livid, loud, macabre, melodramatic, pale, pallid, revolting, sallow, sanguine, savage, sensational, shocking, startling, unrestrained, violent, vivid, wan.

lurk *v.* crouch, hide, hide out, lie in wait, lie low, prowl, skulk, slink, sneak, snook, snoop.

luscious *adj.* appetizing, delectable, delicious, honeyed, juicy, luxuriant, luxurious, mouth-watering, palatable, rich, savory, scrumptious, succulent, sweet, tasty, toothsome, yummy.

antonym austere.

lush *adj.* abundant, dense, elaborate, extravagant, flourishing, grand, green, juicy, lavish, luxuriant, luxurious, opulent, ornate, overgrown, palatial, plush, prolific, rank, ripe, ritzy, succulent, sumptuous, superabundant, teeming, tender, verdant.

lust *n.* appetence, appetency, appetite, avidity, carnality, concupiscence, covetousness, craving, cupidity, desire, greed, Kama, Kamadeva, lasciviousness, lechery, lewdness, libido, licentiousness, longing, passion, prurience, randiness, salaciousness, sensuality, thirst, wantonness.

luster *n.* brightness, brilliance, burnish, dazzle, distinction, effulgence, fame, gleam, glint, glitter, glory, gloss, glow, gorm, honor, illustriousness, lambency, luminousness, prestige, radiance, renown, resplendence, sheen, shimmer, shine, sparkle, water.

lustful *adj.* carnal, concupiscent, craving, goatish, hankering, horny, lascivious, lecherous, lewd, libidinous, licentious, passionate, prurient, randy, raunchy, ruttish, sensual, unchaste, venerous, wanton.

lusty *adj.* blooming, brawny, energetic, gutsy, hale, healthy, hearty, in fine fettle, muscular, powerful, red-

blooded, robust, rugged, stalwart, stout, strapping, strong, sturdy, vigorous, virile.

antonyms effete, weak.

luxuriant *adj.* abundant, ample, baroque, copious, dense, elaborate, excessive, extravagant, exuberant, fancy, fecund, fertile, festooned, flamboyant, florid, flowery, lavish, lush, opulent, ornate, overflowing, plenteous, plentiful, prodigal, productive, profuse, prolific, rank, rich, riotous, rococo, sumptuous, superabundant, teeming, thriving.

antonyms barren, infertile.

luxurious *adj.* comfortable, costly, deluxe, epicurean, expensive, hedonistic, lavish, magnificent, opulent, pampered, plush, plushy, rich, ritzy, self-indulgent, sensual, splendid, sumptuous, sybaritic, voluptuous, well-appointed.

antonyms ascetic, austere, economical, frugal, scant(y), spartan.

luxury *n.* affluence, bliss, comfort, delight, dolce vita, enjoyment, extra, extravagance, flesh-pots, flesh-pottery, frill, gratification, hedonism, indulgence, milk and honey, non-essential, opulence, pleasure, richness, satisfaction, splendor, sumptuousness, treat, voluptuousness, well-being.

antonym essential.

lying *adj.* accumbent, deceitful, decumbent, dishonest, dissembling, double-dealing, duplicitous, false, guileful, mendacious, perfidious, treacherous, two-faced, untruthful.

antonyms honest, truthful.

n. deceit, dishonesty, dissimulation, double-dealing, duplicity, fabrication, falsity, fibbing, guile, mendacity, perjury, prevarication, pseudology, untruthfulness.

antonyms honesty, truthfulness.

lyrical *adj.* carried away, ecstatic, effusive, emotional, enthusiastic, expressive, impassioned, inspired, musical, passionate, poetic, rapturous, rhapsodic.

M

macabre *adj.* cadaverous, deathlike, deathly, dreadful, eerie, frightening, frightful, ghastly, ghostly, ghoulish, grim, grisly, gruesome, hideous, horrible, horrid, morbid, sick, weird.

macerate *v.* blend, liquefy, mash, pulp, soak, soften, steep.

Machiavellian *adj.* amoral, artful, astute, calculating, crafty, cunning, cynical, deceitful, designing, double-dealing, foxy, guileful, intriguing, opportunist, perfidious, scheming, shrewd, sly, underhand, unscrupulous, wily.

machine *n.* agency, agent, apparatus, appliance, automaton, contraption, contrivance, device, engine, gadget, gizmo, instrument, machinery, mechanism, organization, party, puppet, robot, set-up, structure, system, tool, zombi(e).

mad *adj.* abandoned, aberrant, absurd, agitated, angry, ardent, avid, bananas, barmy, bats, batty, berserk, boisterous, bonkers, crackers, crazed, crazy, cuckoo, daft, delirious, demented, deranged, devoted, distracted, dotty, ebullient, enamored, energetic, enraged, enthusiastic, exasperated, excited, fanatical, fond, foolhardy, foolish, frantic, frenetic, frenzied, fuming, furi-

ous, gay, have bats in the belfry, hooked, impassioned, imprudent, in a paddy, incensed, infatuated, infuriated, insane, irate, irrational, irritated, keen, livid, loony, loopy, ludicrous, lunatic, madcap, mental, moon-stricken, moon-struck, non compos mentis, nonsensical, nuts, nutty, off one's chump, off one's head, off one's nut, off one's rocker, off one's trolley, out of one's mind, possessed, preposterous, psychotic, rabid, raging, raving, resentful, riotous, round the bend, round the twist, screwball, screwy, senseless, unbalanced, uncontrolled, unhinged, unreasonable, unrestrained, unsafe, unsound, unstable, up the pole, waxy, wild, wrathful, zealous.
antonyms lucid, rational, sane.

madden *v.* annoy, craze, dement, dementate, derange, enrage, exasperate, incense, inflame, infuriate, irritate, provoke, unhinge, upset, vex.
antonyms calm, pacify, please.

madness *n.* abandon, aberration, absurdity, agitation, anger, ardor, craze, craziness, daftness, delusion, dementia, demoniacism, demonomania, derangement, distraction, enthusiasm, exasperation, excitement, fanaticism, folie, folly, fondness, foolhardiness, foolishness, frenzy, furore, fury, infatuation, insanity, intoxication, ire, keenness, lunacy, lycanthropy, mania, monomania, moon-madness, moonraking, nonsense, passion, preposterousness, psychopathy, psychosis, rage, raving, riot, unrestraint, uproar, wildness, wrath, zeal.
antonym sanity.

maelstrom *n.* bedlam, chaos, Charybdis, confusion, disorder, mess, pandemonium, tumult, turmoil, uproar, vortex, whirlpool.

magic *n.* allurement, black art, charm, conjuring, conjury, diablerie, enchantment, fascination, glamor, goety, gramary(e), hocus-pocus, hoodoo, illusion, jiggery-pokery, jugglery, legerdemain, magnetism, medicine, necromancy, occultism, prestidigitation, sleight of hand, sorcery, sortilege, spell, thaumaturgics, thaumaturgism, thaumaturgy, theurgy, trickery, voodoo, witchcraft, wizardry, wonder-work.
adj. bewitching, charismatic, charming, enchanting, entrancing, fascinating, goetic, hermetic, magical, magnetic, marvelous, miraculous, mirific, mirifical, sorcerous, spellbinding, spellful.

magician *n.* archimage, conjurer, conjuror, enchanter, enchantress, genius, illusionist, maestro, mage, Magian, magus, marvel, miracle-worker, necromancer, prestidigitator, prestigiator, sorcerer, spellbinder, thaumaturge, theurgist, virtuoso, warlock, witch, witch-doctor, wizard, wonder-monger, wonder-worker.

magistrate *n.* aedile, bailiff, bail(l)ie, beak, JP, judge, jurat, justice, justice of the peace, mittimus, stipendiary, tribune.

magnanimous *adj.* altruistic, beneficent, big, big-hearted, bountiful, charitable, free, generous, great-hearted, handsome, high-minded, kind, kindly, large-hearted, large-minded, liberal, munificent, noble, open-handed, philanthropic, selfless, ungrudging, unselfish, unstinting.
antonyms mean, paltry, petty.

magnate *n.* aristocrat, baron, bashaw, big cheese, big noise, big shot, big wheel, bigwig, captain of industry, chief, fat cat, grandee, leader, magnifico, merchant,

mogul, nabob, noble, notable, personage, plutocrat, prince, tycoon, VIP.

magnet *n.* appeal, attraction, bait, draw, enticement, lodestone, lure, solenoid.
antonym repellent.

magnetic *adj.* absorbing, alluring, attractive, captivating, charismatic, charming, enchanting, engrossing, entrancing, fascinating, gripping, hypnotic, irresistible, mesmerizing, seductive.
antonyms repellent, repugnant, repulsive.

magnetism *n.* allure, appeal, attraction, attractiveness, charisma, charm, draw, drawing power, enchantment, fascination, grip, hypnotism, lure, magic, mesmerism, power, pull, seductiveness, spell.

magnificence *n.* brilliance, glory, gorgeousness, grandeur, grandiosity, impressiveness, luxuriousness, luxury, majesty, nobility, opulence, pomp, resplendence, splendor, stateliness, sublimity, sumptuousness.
antonyms modesty, plainness, simplicity.

magnificent *adj.* august, brilliant, elegant, elevated, exalted, excellent, fine, glorious, gorgeous, grand, grandiose, imposing, impressive, lavish, luxurious, majestic, noble, opulent, outstanding, plush, posh, princely, regal, resplendent, rich, ritzy, splendid, stately, sublime, sumptuous, superb, superior, transcendent.
antonyms humble, modest, plain, simple.

magnify *v.* aggrandize, aggravate, amplify, augment, blow up, boost, build up, deepen, dilate, dramatize, enhance, enlarge, exaggerate, expand, greaten, heighten, increase, inflate, intensify, lionize, overdo, overemphasize, overestimate, overplay, overrate, overstate, praise.
antonyms belittle, play down.

magnitude *n.* amount, amplitude, bigness, brightness, bulk, capacity, consequence, dimensions, eminence, enormousness, expanse, extent, grandeur, greatness, hugeness, immensity, importance, intensity, largeness, mark, mass, measure, moment, note, proportions, quantity, significance, size, space, strength, vastness, volume, weight.
antonym smallness.

maid *n.* abigail, bonne, damsel, dresser, femme de chambre, fille de chambre, gentlewoman, girl, handmaiden, housemaid, lady's maid, lass, lassie, maiden, maid-of-all-work, maid-servant, miss, nymph, servant, serving-maid, soubrette, tirewoman, tiring-woman, virgin, waitress, wench.

maiden *n.* damozel, damsel, demoiselle, girl, lass, lassie, maid, may, miss, nymph, virgin, wench.
adj. chaste, female, first, fresh, inaugural, initial, initiatory, intact, introductory, new, pure, unbroached, uncaptured, undefiled, unmarried, unpolluted, untapped, untried, unused, unwed, virgin, virginal.
antonyms defiled, deflowered, unchaste.

mail *n.* correspondence, da(w)k, delivery, letters, packages, parcels, post.
v. air-mail, dispatch, forward, post, send.

maim *v.* cripple, disable, hack, haggle, hamstring, hurt, impair, incapacitate, injure, lame, mangle, mar, mutilate, savage, wound.
antonyms heal, repair.

main[1] *adj.* absolute, brute, capital, cardinal, central, chief, critical, crucial, direct, downright, entire, essential, extensive, first, foremost, general, great, head, leading, mere, necessary, outstanding, paramount, particular, predominant, pre-eminent, premier, primary, prime, principal, pure, sheer, special, staple, supreme, undisguised, utmost, utter, vital.

antonyms minor, unimportant.

n. effort, foison, force, might, potency, power, puissance, strength, vigor.

antonym weakness.

main[2] *n.* cable, channel, conduit, duct, line, pipe.

mainstay *n.* anchor, backbone, bulwark, buttress, linchpin, pillar, prop, support.

maintain *v.* advocate, affirm, allege, argue, assert, asseverate, aver, avouch, avow, back, care for, carry on, champion, claim, conserve, contend, continue, declare, defend, fight for, finance, hold, insist, justify, keep, keep up, look after, make good, nurture, observe, perpetuate, plead for, practice, preserve, profess, prolong, provide, retain, stand by, state, supply, support, sustain, take care of, uphold, vindicate.

antonyms deny, neglect, oppose.

maintenance *n.* aliment, alimony, allowance, care, conservation, continuance, continuation, defense, food, keep, keeping, livelihood, living, nurture, perpetuation, preservation, prolongation, protection, provision, repairs, retainment, subsistence, supply, support, sustainment, sustenance, sustention, upkeep.

antonym neglect.

majestic *adj.* august, awesome, dignified, distinguished, elevated, exalted, grand, grandiose, imperial, imperious, imposing, impressive, kingly, lofty, magisterial, magnificent, monumental, noble, pompous, princely, queenly, regal, royal, splendid, stately, sublime, superb.

antonyms unimportant, unimpressive.

majesty *n.* augustness, awesomeness, dignity, exaltedness, glory, grandeur, impressiveness, kingliness, loftiness, magnificence, majesticness, nobility, pomp, queenliness, regalness, resplendence, royalty, splendor, state, stateliness, sublimity.

antonyms unimportance, unimpressiveness.

major *adj.* better, bigger, chief, critical, crucial, elder, grave, great, greater, higher, important, key, keynote, larger, leading, main, most, notable, older, outstanding, pre-eminent, radical, senior, serious, significant, superior, supreme, uppermost, vital, weighty.

antonym minor.

make *v.* accomplish, acquire, act, add up to, amount to, appoint, arrive at, assemble, assign, attain, beget, bring about, build, calculate, carry out, catch, cause, clear, coerce, compel, compose, conclude, constitute, constrain, construct, contract, contribute, convert, create, designate, do, dragoon, draw up, drive, earn, effect, elect, embody, enact, engage in, engender, establish, estimate, execute, fabricate, fashion, fix, flow, force, forge, form, frame, gain, gar, gauge, generate, get, give rise to, impel, induce, install, invest, judge, lead to, manufacture, meet, mold, net, nominate, oblige, obtain, occasion, ordain, originate, pass, perform, practise, press, pressurize, prevail upon, proceed, produce, prosecute, put together, reach, reckon, render, require, secure, shape, smith(y), suppose, synthesize, take in, tend, think, turn, win.

antonyms dismantle, lose, persuade.

n. brand, build, character, composition, constitution, construction, cut, designation, disposition, form, formation, humor, kind, make-up, manner, manufacture,

mark, model, nature, shape, sort, stamp, structure, style, temper, temperament, texture, type, variety.

make-believe *n.* charade, dream, fantasy, imagination, play-acting, pretense, role-play, unreality.

antonym reality.

adj. dream, fantasized, fantasy, feigned, imaginary, imagined, made-up, mock, pretend, pretended, sham, simulated, unreal.

antonym real.

maker *n.* architect, author, builder, constructor, contriver, creator, director, fabricator, framer, manufacturer, producer.

antonym dismantler.

makeshift *adj.* band-aid, expedient, haywire, improvised, make-do, provisional, rough and ready, stopgap, substitute, temporary.

antonyms finished, permanent.

n. band-aid, expedient, fig-leaf, shift, stop-gap, substitute.

make-up[1] *n.* cosmetics, fard, fucus, greasepaint, maquillage, paint, powder, war paint, white-face.

make-up[2] *n.* arrangement, assembly, build, cast, character, complexion, composition, configuration, constitution, construction, disposition, figure, form, format, formation, make, nature, organization, stamp, structure, style, temper, temperament.

maladroit *adj.* awkward, bungling, cack-handed, clumsy, gauche, graceless, ham-fisted, ill-timed, inconsiderate, inelegant, inept, inexpert, insensitive, tactless, thoughtless, undiplomatic, unhandy, unskilful, untoward.

antonyms adroit, tactful.

malady *n.* affliction, ailment, breakdown, complaint, disease, disorder, illness, indisposition, infirmity, malaise, sickness.

antonym health.

malaise *n.* angst, anguish, anxiety, depression, discomfort, disquiet, distemper, doldrums, enervation, future shock, illness, indisposition, lassitude, melancholy, sickness, unease, uneasiness, weakness.

antonyms happiness, well-being.

malcontent *adj.* belly-aching, disaffected, discontented, disgruntled, dissatisfied, dissentious, factious, ill-disposed, morose, rebellious, resentful, restive, unhappy, unsatisfied.

antonym contented.

n. agitator, belly-acher, complainer, grouch, grouser, grumbler, mischief-maker, moaner, rebel, troublemaker.

male *adj.* bull, cock, dog, manlike, manly, masculine, virile.

antonym female.

n. boy, bull, cock, daddy, dog, father, man.

antonym female.

malefactor *n.* convict, criminal, crook, culprit, delinquent, evil-doer, felon, law-breaker, miscreant, misfeasor, offender, outlaw, transgressor, villain, wrongdoer.

malevolence *n.* bitterness, hate, hatred, hostility, illwill, malice, maliciousness, malignance, malignancy, malignity, rancor, spite, spitefulness, vengefulness, venom, viciousness, vindictiveness.

antonym benevolence.

malfunction *n.* breakdown, defect, failure, fault, flaw, glitch, impairment.

v. break down, fail, go wrong, misbehave.

malice *n.* animosity, animus, bad blood, bitterness, despite, enmity, hate, hatred, ill-will, malevolence, maliciousness, malignity, rancor, spite, spitefulness, spleen, vengefulness, venom, viciousness, vindictiveness.
antonym kindness.

malicious *adj.* baleful, bitchy, bitter, catty, despiteful, evil-minded, hateful, ill-natured, injurious, malevolent, malignant, mischievous, pernicious, rancorous, resentful, sham, spiteful, vengeful, venomous, vicious.
antonyms kind, thoughtful.

malign *adj.* bad, baleful, baneful, deleterious, destructive, evil, harmful, hostile, hurtful, injurious, malevolent, malignant, noxious, pernicious, venomous, vicious, wicked.
antonym benign.

v. abuse, badmouth, blacken the name of, calumniate, defame, denigrate, derogate, disparage, harm, injure, libel, revile, run down, slander, smear, traduce, vilify, vilipend.
antonym praise.

malignant *adj.* baleful, bitter, cancerous, cankered, dangerous, deadly, destructive, devilish, evil, fatal, harmful, hostile, hurtful, inimical, injurious, irremediable, malevolent, malicious, malign, pernicious, spiteful, uncontrollable, venomous, vicious, viperish, viperous, virulent.
antonyms harmless, kind.

malingerer *n.* dodger, lead-swinger, loafer, shirker, skiver, slacker.
antonym toiler.

malleable *adj.* adaptable, biddable, compliant, ductile, governable, impressionable, manageable, plastic, pliable, pliant, soft, tractable, tractile, workable.
antonyms intractable, unworkable.

malodorous *adj.* evil-smelling, fetid, foul-smelling, mephitic, miasmal, miasmatic, miasmatous, miasmic, miasmous, nauseating, niffy, noisome, offensive, putrid, rank, reeking, smelly, stinking.
antonym sweet-smelling.

malpractice *n.* abuse, dereliction, malversation, misbehavior, misconduct, misdeed, mismanagement, negligence, offence, transgression.

maltreat *v.* abuse, bully, damage, harm, hurt, ill-treat, injure, mistreat, misuse, mousle.
antonym care for.

maltreatment *n.* abuse, bullying, harm, ill-treatment, ill-usage, ill-use, injury, mistreatment, misuse.
antonym care.

mammoth *adj.* Brobdingnag, Brobdingnagian, colossal, enormous, formidable, gargantuan, giant, gigantic, herculean, huge, immense, leviathan, massive, mighty, monumental, mountainous, prodigious, rounceval, stupendous, titanic, vast.
antonym small.

man[1] *n.* adult, attendant, beau, bloke, body, boyfriend, cat, chap, employee, fellow, follower, gentleman, guy, hand, hireling, hombre, human, human being, husband, individual, lover, male, manservant, partner, person, retainer, servant, soldier, spouse, subject, subordinate, valet, vassal, worker, workman.

v. crew, fill, garrison, occupy, operate, people, staff, take charge of.

man[2] *n.* Homo sapiens, human race, humanity, humankind, humans, mankind, mortals, people.

manacle *v.* bind, chain, check, clap in irons, confine, constrain, curb, fetter, gyve, hamper, hamstring, handcuff, inhibit, put in chains, restrain, shackle, trammel.
antonym unshackle.

manage *v.* accomplish, administer, arrange, bring about, bring off, carry on, command, concert, conduct, contrive, control, cope, cope with, deal with, direct, dominate, effect, engineer, fare, get along, get by, get on, govern, guide, handle, influence, make do, make out, manipulate, muddle through, operate, oversee, pilot, ply, preside over, rule, run, shift, solicit, stage-manage, steer, succeed, superintend, supervise, survive, train, use, wield.
antonym fail.

manageable *adj.* amenable, biddable, compliant, controllable, convenient, docile, easy, governable, handy, submissive, tamable, tractable, wieldable, wieldy.
antonym unmanageable.

management *n.* administration, board, bosses, care, charge, command, conduct, control, direction, directorate, directors, employers, executive, executives, governance, government, governors, guidance, handling, managers, manipulation, operation, oversight, rule, running, stewardry, superintendence, supervision, supervisors.

manager *n.* administrator, boss, comptroller, conductor, controller, director, executive, factor, gaffer, governor, head, impresario, organizer, overseer, proprietor, steward, superintendent, supervisor.

mandate *n.* authorization, authority, bidding, charge, command, commission, decree, dedimus, directive, edict, fiat, firman, injunction, instruction, irade, order, precept, rescript, right, sanction, ukase, warrant.

mandatory *adj.* binding, compulsory, imperative, necessary, obligatory, required, requisite.
antonym optional.

maneuver *n.* action, artifice, device, dodge, exercise, gambit, intrigue, machination, move, movement, operation, plan, plot, ploy, ruse, scheme, stratagem, subterfuge, tactic, trick.

v. contrive, deploy, devise, direct, drive, engineer, exercise, guide, handle, intrigue, jockey, machinate, manage, manipulate, move, navigate, negotiate, pilot, plan, plot, pull strings, scheme, steer, wangle.

mangle *v.* butcher, crush, cut, deform, destroy, disfigure, distort, hack, haggle, lacerate, maim, mar, maul, mutilate, rend, ruin, spoil, tear, twist, wreck.

mangy *adj.* dirty, grotty, mean, moth-eaten, ratty, scabby, scruffy, seedy, shabby, shoddy, squalid, tatty.
antonyms clean, neat, spruce.

manhandle *v.* carry, haul, heave, hump, knock about, lift, maltreat, maneuver, maul, mishandle, mistreat, misuse, paw, pull, push, rough up, shove, tug.

manhood *n.* adulthood, bravery, courage, determination, firmness, fortitude, hardihood, machismo, manfulness, manliness, masculinity, maturity, mettle, resolution, spirit, strength, valor, virility.
antonym timidness.

mania *n.* aberration, cacoethes, compulsion, craving, craze, craziness, delirium, dementia, derangement, desire, disorder, enthusiasm, fad, fetish, fixation, frenzy, infatuation, insanity, itch, lunacy, madness, obsession, partiality, passion, preoccupation, rage, thing.

manifest *adj*. apparent, clear, conspicuous, distinct, evident, glaring, noticeable, obvious, open, palpable, patent, plain, unconcealed, undeniable, unmistakable, visible.

antonym unclear.

v. demonstrate, display, establish, evidence, evince, exhibit, expose, illustrate, prove, reveal, set forth, show.

antonym hide.

manifesto *n*. declaration, platform, policies, policy, pronunciamento.

manifold *adj*. abundant, assorted, copious, diverse, diversified, kaleidoscopic, many, multifarious, multifold, multiple, multiplex, multiplied, multitudinous, numerous, varied, various.

antonym simple.

manipulate *v*. conduct, control, cook, direct, employ, engineer, gerrymander, guide, handle, influence, juggle with, maneuver, negotiate, operate, ply, shuffle, steer, use, wield, work.

manly *adj*. bold, brave, courageous, daring, dauntless, fearless, gallant, hardy, heroic, macho, male, manful, masculine, muscular, noble, powerful, resolute, robust, stalwart, stout-hearted, strapping, strong, sturdy, valiant, valorous, vigorous, virile.

antonyms timid, unmanly.

man-made *adj*. artificial, ersatz, imitation, manufactured, simulated, synthetic.

antonym natural.

manner *n*. address, air, appearance, approach, aspect, bearing, behavior, brand, breed, category, character, comportment, conduct, custom, demeanor, deportment, description, fashion, form, genre, habit, kind, line, look, means, method, mien, mode, nature, practice, presence, procedure, process, routine, sort, style, tack, tenor, tone, type, usage, variety, way, wise, wont.

mannerism *n*. characteristic, feature, foible, habit, idiosyncrasy, peculiarity, quirk, stiltedness, trait, trick.

mannerly *adj*. civil, civilized, courteous, decorous, deferential, formal, genteel, gentlemanly, gracious, ladylike, polished, polite, refined, respectful, well-behaved, well-bred, well-mannered.

antonym unmannerly.

mantle *n*. blanket, canopy, cape, cloak, cloud, cover, covering, curtain, envelope, hood, mantlet, pall, pelerine, pelisse, screen, shawl, shroud, veil, wrap.

manual[1] *n*. bible, book of words, companion, enchi(e)ridion, guide, guide-book, handbook, instructions, primer, vade-mecum.

manual[2] *adj*. hand, hand-operated, human, physical.

manufacture *v*. assemble, build, churn out, compose, concoct, construct, cook up, create, devise, fabricate, forge, form, hatch, invent, make, make up, mass-produce, mold, process, produce, shape, think up, trump up, turn out.

n. assembly, construction, creation, fabrication, facture, formation, making, mass-production, production.

manure *n*. compost, droppings, dung, fertilizer, guano, muck, ordure.

manuscript *n*. autograph, deed, document, handwriting, holograph, palimpsest, parchment, scroll, text, vellum.

many *adj*. abundant, copious, countless, divers, frequent, innumerable, manifold, multifarious, multifold,

multitudinous, myriad, numerous, profuse, sundry, umpteen, umpty, varied, various, zillion.

antonym few.

map *n*. atlas, chart, graph, mappemond, plan, plot, street plan.

mar *v*. blemish, blight, blot, damage, deface, detract from, disfigure, foul up, harm, hurt, impair, injure, maim, mangle, mutilate, pollute, ruin, scar, spoil, stain, sully, taint, tarnish, temper, vitiate, wreck.

antonym enhance.

maraud *v*. depredate, despoil, forage, foray, harry, loot, pillage, plunder, raid, ransack, ravage, reive, sack, spoliate.

march *v*. countermarch, file, flounce, goose-step, pace, parade, slog, stalk, stride, strut, stump, tramp, tread, walk.

n. advance, career, demo, demonstration, development, evolution, footslog, gait, hike, pace, parade, passage, procession, progress, progression, step, stride, tramp, trek, walk.

margin *n*. allowance, border, bound, boundary, brim, brink, compass, confine, edge, extra, latitude, leeway, limit, marge, perimeter, periphery, play, rand, rim, room, scope, side, skirt, space, surplus, verge.

antonyms center, core.

marginal *adj*. bordering, borderline, doubtful, infinitesimal, insignificant, low, minimal, minor, negligible, peripheral, slight, small.

antonyms central, core.

marina *n*. dock, harbor, mooring, port, yacht station.

marine *adj*. maritime, nautical, naval, ocean-going, oceanic, pelagic, salt-water, sea, seafaring, sea-going, thalassian, thalassic.

n. galoot, leather-neck, sailor.

mariner *n*. bluejacket, deckhand, hand, Jack Tar, matelot, matlo(w), navigator, sailor, salt, sea-dog, seafarer, seaman, tar.

marital *adj*. conjugal, connubial, hymeneal, hymenean, married, matrimonial, nuptial, sponsal, spousal, wedded.

maritime *adj*. coastal, littoral, marine, nautical, naval, oceanic, pelagic, sea, seafaring, seaside, thalassian, thalassic.

mark *n*. aim, badge, blaze, blemish, blot, blotch, brand, bruise, character, characteristic, consequence, criterion, dent, device, dignity, distinction, earmark, emblem, eminence, end, evidence, fame, feature, fingermark, footmark, footprint, goal, hallmark, importance, impression, incision, index, indication, influence, label, level, line, lineament, marque, measure, nick, norm, notability, note, noteworthiness, notice, object, objective, pock, prestige, print, proof, purpose, quality, regard, scar, scratch, seal, sign, smudge, splotch, spot, stain, stamp, standard, standing, streak, symbol, symptom, target, token, trace, track, trail, vestige, yardstick.

v. appraise, assess, attend, betoken, blemish, blot, blotch, brand, bruise, characterize, correct, denote, dent, distinguish, evaluate, evince, exemplify, grade, hearken, heed, identify, illustrate, impress, imprint, label, list, listen, mind, nick, note, notice, observe, print, regard, remark, scar, scratch, show, smudge, splotch, stain, stamp, streak, take to heart, traumatize, watch.

marked *adj*. apparent, clear, considerable, conspicuous,

decided, distinct, doomed, emphatic, evident, glaring, indicated, manifest, notable, noted, noticeable, obvious, outstanding, patent, prominent, pronounced, remarkable, salient, signal, striking, strong, suspected, watched.
antonyms slight, unnoticeable.

market *n.* bazaar, demand, fair, market-place, mart, need, outlet, shop, souk.
v. hawk, peddle, retail, sell, vend.
antonym buy.

maroon *v.* abandon, cast away, desert, isolate, leave, put ashore, strand.
antonym rescue.

marriage *n.* alliance, amalgamation, association, confederation, coupling, espousal, link, match, matrimony, matronage, matronhood, merger, nuptials, spousage, spousals, union, wedding, wedlock.
antonym divorce.

marrow *n.* core, cream, essence, gist, heart, kernel, nub, pith, quick, quintessence, soul, spirit, stuff, substance.

marry *v.* ally, bond, espouse, get hitched, get spliced, join, jump the broomstick, knit, link, match, merge, splice, tie, tie the knot, unify, unite, wed, wive, yoke.
antonyms divorce, separate.

marsh *n.* bayou, bog, carr, fen, maremma, marshland, morass, moss, muskeg, quagmire, slough, slump, soak, swale, swamp, wetland.

marshal *v.* align, arrange, array, assemble, collect, conduct, convoy, deploy, dispose, draw up, escort, gather, group, guide, lead, line up, muster, order, organize, rank, shepherd, take, usher.

martial *adj.* bellicose, belligerent, brave, combative, heroic, militant, military, soldierly, warlike.
antonym pacific.

martyrdom *n.* agony, anguish, death, excruciation, ordeal, persecution, suffering, torment, torture, witness.

marvel *n.* genius, miracle, non(e)such, phenomenon, portent, prodigy, sensation, spectacle, whiz, wonder.
v. gape, gaze, goggle, wonder.

marvelous *adj.* amazing, astonishing, astounding, beyond belief, breathtaking, épatant, excellent, extraordinary, fabulous, fantastic, glorious, great, implausible, improbable, incredible, magnificent, miraculous, mirific(al), phenomenal, prodigious, remarkable, sensational, singular, smashing, spectacular, splendid, stupendous, super, superb, surprising, terrific, unbelievable, unlikely, wonderful, wondrous.
antonyms ordinary, plausible, run-of-the-mill.

masculine *adj.* bold, brave, butch, gallant, hardy, macho, male, manlike, manly, mannish, muscular, powerful, red-blooded, resolute, robust, stout-hearted, strapping, strong, tomboyish, vigorous, virile.
antonym feminine.

mash *v.* beat, champ, comminute, crush, grind, pound, pulverize, pummel, smash, triturate.

mask *n.* blind, camouflage, cloak, concealment, cover, cover-up, disguise, domino, façade, false face, front, guise, pretense, screen, semblance, show, veil, veneer, visard-mask, visor, vizard.
v. camouflage, cloak, conceal, cover, disguise, hide, obscure, screen, shield, veil.
antonym uncover.

masquerade *n.* cloak, costume, costume ball, counterfeit, cover, cover-up, deception, disguise, dissimul-

ation, domino, fancy dress party, front, guise, imposture, mask, masked ball, masque, mummery, pose, pretense, put-on, revel, screen, subterfuge.
v. disguise, dissemble, dissimulate, impersonate, mask, pass oneself off, play, pose, pretend, profess.

mass¹ *n.* accumulation, aggregate, aggregation, assemblage, band, batch, block, body, bulk, bunch, chunk, collection, combination, concretion, congeries, conglomeration, crowd, dimension, entirety, extensity, group, heap, horde, host, hunk, lion's share, load, lot, lump, magnitude, majority, mob, number, piece, pile, preponderance, quantity, size, stack, sum, sum total, throng, totality, troop, welter, whole.
adj. across-the-board, blanket, comprehensive, extensive, general, indiscriminate, large-scale, pandemic, popular, sweeping, wholesale, widespread.
antonym limited.
v. assemble, cluster, collect, congregate, crowd, for(e)-gather, gather, muster, rally.
antonym separate.

mass² *n.* communion, eucharist, holy communion, Lord's Supper, Lord's Table.

massacre *n.* annihilation, blood bath, butchery, carnage, decimation, extermination, holocaust, killing, murder, slaughter.
v. annihilate, butcher, decimate, exterminate, kill, mow down, murder, slaughter, slay, wipe out.

massage *n.* effleurage, kneading, malaxage, malaxation, manipulation, petrissage, rubbing, rub-down.
v. knead, manipulate, rub, rub down.

massive *adj.* big, bulky, colossal, cyclopean, enormous, extensive, gargantuan, gigantic, great, heavy, hefty, huge, hulking, immense, imposing, impressive, jumbo, mammoth, monster, monstrous, monumental, ponderous, rounceval, solid, substantial, titanic, vast, weighty, whacking, whopping.
antonyms slight, small.

master *n.* ace, adept, baas, boss, bwana, captain, chief, commander, controller, dab hand, deacon, director, doyen, employer, expert, genius, governor, guide, guru, head, Herr, instructor, lord, maestro, manager, overlord, overseer, owner, past master, pedagogue, preceptor, principal, pro, ruler, schoolmaster, skipper, superintendent, swami, teacher, tutor, virtuoso, wizard.
antonyms amateur, learner, pupil, servant, slave.
adj. ace, adept, chief, controlling, crack, expert, foremost, grand, great, leading, main, masterly, predominant, prime, principal, proficient, skilful, skilled.
antonyms copy, subordinate, unskilled.
v. acquire, bridle, check, command, conquer, control, curb, defeat, direct, dominate, get the hang of, govern, grasp, learn, manage, overcome, quash, quell, regulate, rule, subdue, subjugate, suppress, tame, triumph over, vanquish.

masterful *adj.* adept, adroit, arrogant, authoritative, autocratic, bossy, clever, consummate, crack, deft, despotic, dexterous, dictatorial, domineering, excellent, expert, exquisite, fine, finished, first-rate, high-handed, imperious, magisterial, masterly, overbearing, overweening, peremptory, powerful, professional, self-willed, skilful, skilled, superior, superlative, supreme, tyrannical.
antonyms clumsy, humble, unskilful.

masterly *adj.* adept, adroit, clever, consummate, crack,

dexterous, excellent, expert, exquisite, fine, finished, first-rate, magistral, masterful, skilful, skilled, superb, superior, superlative, supreme.
antonyms clumsy, poor, unskilled.
mastermind *v.* conceive, design, devise, direct, dream up, forge, frame, hatch, manage, organize, originate, plan.
n. architect, authority, brain(s), creator, director, engineer, genius, intellect, manager, organizer, originator, planner, prime mover, virtuoso.
masterpiece *n.* chef d'oeuvre, classic, jewel, magnum opus, master-work, museum-piece, pièce de résistance, tour de force.
mastery *n.* ability, acquirement, advantage, ascendancy, attainment, authority, cleverness, command, comprehension, conquest, control, conversancy, deftness, dexterity, domination, dominion, expertise, familiarity, finesse, grasp, know-how, knowledge, pre-eminence, proficiency, prowess, rule, skill, superiority, supremacy, sway, triumph, understanding, upper hand, victory, virtuosity, whip-hand.
antonyms clumsiness, unfamiliarity.
masticate *v.* champ, chew, crunch, eat, knead, manducate, munch, ruminate.
mat *n.* carpet, doormat, drugget, felt, rug, under-felt, underlay.
match[1] *n.* bout, competition, contest, game, main, test, trial, venue.
v. compete, contend, oppose, pit against, rival, vie.
match[2] *n.* affiliation, alliance, combination, companion, complement, copy, counterpart, couple, dead ringer, double, duet, duplicate, equal, equivalent, fellow, like, look-alike, marriage, mate, pair, pairing, parallel, partnership, peer, replica, ringer, rival, spit, spitting image, tally, twin, union.
v. accompany, accord, adapt, agree, ally, blend, combine, compare, co-ordinate, correspond, couple, emulate, equal, fit, gee, go together, go with, harmonize, join, link, marry, mate, measure up to, pair, relate, rival, suit, tally, team, tone with, unite, yoke.
antonyms clash, separate.
match[3] *n.* Congreve-match, fuse, fusee, light, lucifer, lucifer-match, safety match, spill, taper, vesta, vesuvian.
matchless *adj.* consummate, excellent, exquisite, incomparable, inimitable, nonpareil, peerless, perfect, superlative, supreme, unequaled, unique, unmatched, unparalleled, unrivaled, unsurpassed.
antonyms commonplace, poor.
mate *n.* assistant, associate, better half, buddy, china, chum, colleague, companion, compeer, comrade, confidant(e), co-worker, crony, double, fellow, fellow-worker, fere, friend, gossip, helper, helpmate, helpmeet, husband, match, pal, partner, repository, side-kick, spouse, subordinate, twin, wife.
v. breed, copulate, couple, join, marry, match, pair, wed, yoke.
material *n.* body, cloth, constituents, data, element, evidence, fabric, facts, information, literature, matter, notes, stuff, substance, textile, work.
adj. applicable, apposite, apropos, bodily, central, concrete, consequential, corporeal, essential, fleshly, germane, grave, gross, hylic, important, indispensable, key, meaningful, momentous, non-spiritual, palpable,

pertinent, physical, relevant, serious, significant, substantial, tangible, vital, weighty, worldly.
antonyms ethereal, immaterial.
materialize *v.* appear, arise, happen, occur, take shape, turn up.
antonym disappear.
maternal *adj.* loving, matronal, motherly, protective.
antonym paternal.
matrimony *n.* espousals, marriage, nuptials, sponsalia, spousage, spousal, wedlock.
matron *n.* dame, dowager, matriarch.
matted *adj.* knotted, tangled, tangly, tousled, uncombed.
antonyms tidy, untangled.
matter[1] *n.* affair, amount, argument, body, business, complication, concern, consequence, context, difficulty, distress, episode, event, hyle, import, importance, incident, issue, material, moment, note, occurrence, problem, proceeding, purport, quantity, question, sense, significance, situation, stuff, subject, substance, sum, text, thesis, thing, topic, transaction, trouble, upset, weight, worry.
antonym insignificance.
v. count, make a difference, mean something, signify.
matter[2] *n.* discharge, purulence, pus, secretion, suppuration.
v. discharge, secrete.
mature *adj.* adult, complete, due, fit, full-blown, full-grown, fully fledged, grown, grown-up, matured, mellow, nubile, perfect, perfected, prepared, ready, ripe, ripened, seasoned, well-thought-out.
antonym immature.
v. accrue, age, bloom, come of age, develop, fall due, grow up, maturate, mellow, perfect, ripen, season.
maudlin *adj.* drunk, emotional, fuddled, half-drunk, icky, lachrymose, mawkish, mushy, sentimental, sickly, slushy, soppy, tearful, tipsy, weepy.
antonym matter-of-fact.
maul *v.* abuse, batter, beat, beat up, claw, ill-treat, knock about, lacerate, maltreat, mangle, manhandle, molest, paw, pummel, rough up, thrash.
mawkish *adj.* disgusting, emotional, feeble, flat, foul, gushy, icky, insipid, jejune, loathsome, maudlin, mushy, nauseous, offensive, schmaltzy, sentimental, sickly, slushy, soppy, squeamish, stale, vapid.
antonyms matter-of-fact, pleasant.
maxim *n.* adage, aphorism, apophthegm, axiom, byword, epigram, gnome, mot, motto, precept, proverb, rule, saw, saying, sentence.
maximum *adj.* biggest, greatest, highest, largest, maximal, most, paramount, supreme, topmost, utmost.
antonym minimum.
n. apogee, ceiling, crest, extremity, height, most, ne plus ultra, peak, pinnacle, summit, top (point), upper limit, utmost, zenith.
antonym mimimum.
maybe *adv.* haply, happen, mayhap, peradventure, perchance, perhaps, possibly.
antonym definitely.
maze *n.* confusion, convolutions, imbroglio, intricacy, labyrinth, meander, mesh, mizmaze, puzzle, snarl, tangle, web.
meadow *n.* field, haugh, holm, inch, lea, ley, mead, pasture.
meager *adj.* barren, bony, deficient, emaciated, exigu-

ous, gaunt, hungry, inadequate, infertile, insubstantial, lank, lean, little, negligible, paltry, penurious, poor, puny, scanty, scraggy, scrawny, scrimpy, short, skimpy, skinny, slender, slight, small, spare, sparse, starved, thin, underfed, unfruitful, unproductive, weak.

antonyms fertile, substantial.

meal¹ *n.* banquet, barbecue, beanfeast, beano, blow-out, breakfast, brunch, collation, déjeuner, déjeuner à la fourchette, dinner, feast, lunch, luncheon, nosh, nosh-up, petit déjeuner, picnic, repast, scoff, snack, supper, tea, tuck-in.

meal² *n.* farina, flour, grits, oatmeal, powder.

mean¹ *adj.* abject, bad-tempered, base, base-born, beggarly, callous, cheese-paring, churlish, close, close-fisted, close-handed, common, contemptible, degraded, despicable, disagreeable, disgraceful, dishonorable, down-at-heel, excellent, fast-handed, good, great, hard-hearted, hostile, humble, ignoble, illiberal, inconsiderable, inferior, insignificant, low, low-born, lowly, malicious, malignant, mean-spirited, menial, mercenary, mingy, miserable, miserly, modest, narrow-minded, nasty, near, niggardly, obscure, one-horse, ordinary, paltry, parsimonious, penny-pinching, penurious, petty, plebeian, poor, proletarian, pusillanimous, rude, run-down, scrub, scurvy, seedy, selfish, servile, shabby, shameful, skilful, slink, small-minded, snippy, sordid, sour, squalid, stingy, tawdry, tight, tight-fisted, undistinguished, unfriendly, ungenerous, ungiving, unhandsome, unpleasant, vicious, vile, vulgar, wretched.

antonyms generous, kind, noble, superior.

mean² *v.* adumbrate, aim, aspire, augur, betoken, cause, connote, contemplate, convey, denote, design, desire, destine, drive at, engender, entail, express, fate, fit, foreshadow, foretell, get at, give rise to, herald, hint, imply, indicate, insinuate, intend, involve, lead to, make, match, necessitate, omen, plan, portend, predestine, preordain, presage, produce, promise, propose, purport, purpose, represent, result in, say, set out, signify, spell, stand for, suggest, suit, symbolize, want, wish.

mean³ *adj.* average, half-way, intermediate, medial, median, medium, middle, middling, moderate, normal, standard.

antonym extreme.

n. aurea mediocritas, average, balance, compromise, golden mean, happy medium, median, middle, middle course, middle way, mid-point, norm, via media.

antonym extreme.

meander *v.* amble, curve, ramble, snake, stravaig, stray, stroll, turn, twist, wander, wind, zigzag.

meaning *n.* aim, connotation, construction, denotation, design, drift, end, explanation, force, gist, goal, idea, implication, import, intention, interpretation, matter, message, object, plan, point, purport, purpose, sense, significance, signification, substance, thrust, trend, upshot, validity, value, worth.

meaningful *adj.* eloquent, expressive, important, material, meaningful, pointed, pregnant, purposeful, relevant, serious, significant, speaking, suggestive, useful, valid, warning, worthwhile.

meaningless *adj.* absurd, aimless, empty, expressionless, futile, hollow, inane, inconsequential, insignificant, insubstantial, nonsense, nonsensical, nugatory, point-

less, purposeless, senseless, trifling, trivial, unmeaning, useless, vain, valueless, worthless.

antonym meaningful.

means *n.* ability, affluence, agency, avenue, capacity, capital, channel, course, estate, expedient, fortune, funds, income, instrument, machinery, measure, medium, method, mode, money, process, property, resources, riches, substance, way, wealth, wherewithal.

measly *adj.* beggarly, contemptible, meager, mean, mingy, miserable, miserly, niggardly, paltry, pathetic, petty, piddling, pitiful, poor, puny, scanty, skimpy, stingy, trivial, ungenerous.

measure *n.* act, action, allotment, allowance, amount, amplitude, beat, bill, bounds, cadence, capacity, control, course, criterion, deed, degree, démarche, enactment, example, expedient, extent, foot, gauge, jigger, law, limit, limitation, magnitude, maneuver, means, method, meter, model, moderation, norm, portion, procedure, proceeding, proportion, quantity, quota, range, ration, reach, resolution, restraint, rhythm, rule, scale, scope, share, size, standard, statute, step, system, test, touchstone, verse, yardstick.

v. admeasure, appraise, assess, calculate, calibrate, choose, compute, determine, estimate, evaluate, fathom, gauge, judge, mark out, measure off, measure out, plumb, quantify, rate, size, sound, step, survey, value, weigh.

measureless *adj.* bottomless, boundless, endless, immeasurable, immense, incalculable, inestimable, infinite, innumerable, limitless, unbounded, vast.

antonym measurable.

meat¹ *n.* aliment, charqui, cheer, chow, comestibles, eats, fare, flesh, food, grub, jerk, nourishment, nutriment, provender, provisions, rations, subsistence, sustenance, viands, victuals.

meat² *n.* core, crux, essence, fundamentals, gist, heart, kernel, marrow, nub, nucleus, pith, point, substance.

mechanic *n.* artificer, engineer, machinist, mechanician, operative, operator, opificer, repairman, technician.

mechanism *n.* action, agency, apparatus, appliance, components, contrivance, device, execution, functioning, gadgetry, gears, innards, instrument, machine, machinery, means, medium, method, motor, operation, performance, procedure, process, structure, system, technique, tool, workings, works.

medal *n.* award, decoration, gong, honor, medalet, medallion, prize, reward, trophy.

meddle *v.* interfere, interlope, interpose, intervene, intrude, mell, pry, put one's oar in, tamper.

meddlesome *adj.* interfering, intruding, intrusive, meddling, mischievous, officious, prying, ultracrepidarian.

mediate *v.* arbitrate, conciliate, incubate, intercede, interpose, intervene, moderate, negotiate, reconcile, referee, resolve, settle, step in, umpire.

medicinal *adj.* adjuvant, analeptic, curative, healing, homeopathic, medical, medicamental, medicamentary, remedial, restorative, roborant, sanatory, therapeutic.

medicine¹ *n.* cure, diapente, diatessaron, drug, electuary, elixir, febrifuge, Galenical, materia medica, medicament, medication, nostrum, panacea, physic, remedy, specific, tincture, vermifuge.

medicine² *n.* acupuncture, allopathy, homeopathy, leech-craft, surgery, therapeutics.

mediocre *adj.* amateurish, average, commonplace, indifferent, inferior, insignificant, mean, medium, middling, ordinary, passable, pedestrian, run-of-the-mill, second-rate, so-so, undistinguished, unexceptional, uninspired.

antonyms excellent, exceptional, extraordinary.

meditate *v.* be in a brown study, cerebrate, cogitate, consider, contemplate, deliberate, devise, excogitate, intend, mull over, muse, plan, ponder, purpose, reflect, ruminate, scheme, speculate, study, think, think over.

medium[1] *adj.* average, fair, intermediate, mean, medial, median, mediocre, middle, middling, midway, standard.

n. aurea mediocritas, average, center, compromise, golden mean, happy medium, mean, middle, middle ground, midpoint, via media, way.

medium[2] *n.* agency, avenue, base, channel, excipient, form, instrument, instrumentality, means, mode, organ, vehicle, way.

medium[3] *n.* clairvoyant, psychic, spiritist, spiritualist.

medium[4] *n.* ambience, atmosphere, circumstances, conditions, element, environment, habitat, influences, milieu, setting, surroundings.

medley *n.* assortment, collection, confusion, conglomeration, farrago, galimatias, gallimaufry, hodge-podge, hotchpotch, jumble, macaroni, macédoine, mélange, mingle-mangle, miscellany, mishmash, mixture, olio, olla-podrida, omnium-gatherum, pastiche, patchwork, pot-pourri, quodlibet, salmagundi.

meek *adj.* acquiescent, compliant, deferential, docile, forbearing, gentle, humble, long-suffering, mild, modest, patient, peaceful, resigned, slavish, soft, spineless, spiritless, subdued, submissive, tame, timid, unambitious, unassuming, unpretentious, unresisting, weak, yielding.

antonyms arrogant, rebellious.

meet *v.* abut, adjoin, answer, assemble, bear, bump into, chance on, collect, come across, come together, comply, confront, congregate, connect, contact, convene, converge, cross, discharge, encounter, endure, equal, experience, face, find, forgather, fulfil, gather, go through, gratify, handle, happen on, intersect, join, link up, match, measure up to, muster, perform, rally, rencontre, rencounter, run across, run into, satisfy, suffer, touch, undergo, unite.

melancholy *adj.* blue, dejected, depressed, despondent, disconsolate, dismal, dispirited, doleful, down, down in the dumps, down in the mouth, downcast, downhearted, gloomy, glum, heavy-hearted, hipped, joyless, low, low-spirited, lugubrious, melancholic, miserable, moody, mournful, pensieroso, pensive, sad, somber, sorrowful, splenific, unhappy, woebegone, woeful.

antonyms cheerful, gay, happy, joyful.

n. blues, dejection, depression, despondency, dole, dolor, gloom, gloominess, glumness, low spirits, pensiveness, sadness, sorrow, unhappiness, woe.

antonym exhilaration.

mêlée *n.* affray, battle royal, brawl, broil, dogfight, donnybrook, fight, fracas, fray, free-for-all, ruckus, ruction, rumpus, scrimmage, scrum, scuffle, set-to, stramash, tussle.

mellow *adj.* cheerful, cordial, delicate, dulcet, elevated, expansive, full, full-flavored, genial, happy, jolly, jovial, juicy, mature, mellifluous, melodious, merry, perfect, placid, relaxed, rich, ripe, rounded, serene, smooth, soft, sweet, tipsy, tranquil, well-matured.

antonyms immature, unripe.

v. improve, mature, perfect, ripen, season, soften, sweeten, temper.

melodious *adj.* arioso, canorous, concordant, dulcet, euphonious, harmonious, melodic, musical, silvery, sonorous, sweet-sounding, tuneful.

antonyms discordant, grating, harsh.

melodramatic *adj.* blood-and-thunder, exaggerated, hammy, histrionic, overdone, overdramatic, overemotional, overwrought, sensational, stagy, theatrical.

melody *n.* air, aria, arietta, arriette, euphony, harmony, melisma, melodiousness, music, musicality, refrain, song, strain, theme, tune, tunefulness.

melt *v.* deliquesce, diffuse, disarm, dissolve, flux, fuse, liquate, liquefy, mollify, relax, soften, thaw, touch, uncongeal, unfreeze.

antonyms freeze, harden, solidify.

member *n.* appendage, arm, associate, component, constituent, element, extremity, fellow, initiate, leg, limb, organ, part, portion, representative.

membrane *n.* diaphragm, fell, film, hymen, integument, partition, septum, skin, tissue, veil, velum.

memento *n.* keepsake, memorial, record, relic, remembrance, reminder, souvenir, token, trophy.

memoirs *n.* annals, autobiography, chronicles, confessions, diary, experiences, journals, life, life story, memories, personalia, recollections, records, reminiscences, transactions.

memorable *adj.* catchy, celebrated, distinguished, extraordinary, famous, historic, illustrious, important, impressive, marvelous, momentous, notable, noteworthy, outstanding, remarkable, signal, significant, striking, unforgettable.

antonym forgettable.

memorial *n.* cairn, cromlech, dolmen, martyry, mausoleum, memento, menhir, monument, plaque, record, remembrance, souvenir, stone.

adj. celebratory, commemorative, monumental.

memorize *v.* con, learn, learn by heart, learn by rote, learn off, mug up, swot up.

antonym forget.

memory *n.* celebrity, commemoration, fame, glory, honor, memorial, name, recall, recollection, remembrance, reminiscence, renown, reputation, repute, retention.

antonym forgetfulness.

menace *v.* alarm, browbeat, bully, comminate, cow, frighten, impend, intimidate, loom, lour (lower), terrorize, threaten.

n. annoyance, commination, danger, hazard, intimidation, jeopardy, nuisance, peril, pest, plague, scare, terror, threat, troublemaker, warning.

mend *v.* ameliorate, amend, better, bushel, cobble, convalesce, correct, cure, darn, emend, fix, heal, improve, patch, recover, rectify, recuperate, refit, reform, remedy, renew, renovate, repair, restore, retouch, revise, solder.

antonyms break, destroy, deteriorate.

n. clout, darn, patch, repair, stitch.

mendacious *adj.* deceitful, deceptive, dishonest, duplicitous, fallacious, false, fraudulent, insincere, inveracious, lying, perfidious, perjured, untrue, untruthful, unveracious.

antonyms honest, truthful.

mendicant *adj.* begging, cadging, petitionary, scrounging, supplicant.

n. almsman, beachcomber, beggar, bum, cadger, hobo, moocher, panhandler, pauper, scrounger, tramp, vagabond, vagrant.

menial *adj.* abject, attending, base, boring, degrading, demeaning, dull, fawning, groveling, helping, humble, humdrum, ignoble, ignominious, low, lowly, mean, obsequious, routine, servile, slavish, sorry, subservient, sycophantic, unskilled, vile.

n. attendant, creature, dog's-body, domestic, drudge, eta, flunky, laborer, lackey, peon, serf, servant, skivvy, slave, underling.

mental[1] *adj.* abstract, cerebral, cognitive, conceptual, ideational, ideative, intellectual, noetic, rational, theoretical.

antonym physical.

mental[2] *adj.* crazy, deranged, disturbed, insane, loony, loopy, lunatic, mad, psychiatric, psychotic, unbalanced, unstable.

antonyms balanced, sane.

mentality *n.* attitude, brains, capacity, character, comprehension, disposition, endowment, faculty, frame of mind, intellect, IQ, make-up, mind, outlook, personality, psychology, rationality, understanding, wit.

mentally *adv.* emotionally, intellectually, inwardly, psychologically, rationally, subjectively, temperamentally.

mention *v.* acknowledge, adduce, advise, allude to, apprize, bring up, broach, cite, communicate, declare, disclose, divulge, hint at, impart, intimate, make known, name, point out, recount, refer to, report, reveal, speak of, state, tell, touch on.

n. acknowledgment, allusion, announcement, citation, indication, notification, observation, recognition, reference, remark, tribute.

mentor *n.* adviser, coach, counselor, guide, guru, instructor, pedagogue, swami, teacher, tutor.

merchandise *n.* cargo, commodities, freight, goods, produce, products, shipment, staples, stock, stock in trade, truck, vendibles, wares.

v. carry, deal in, distribute, market, peddle, retail, sell, supply, trade, traffic in, vend.

merchant *n.* broker, dealer, jobber, négociant, retailer, salesman, seller, shopkeeper, trader, tradesman, trafficker, vendor, wholesaler.

merciful *adj.* beneficent, benignant, clement, compassionate, condolent, forbearing, forgiving, generous, gracious, humane, humanitarian, kind, lenient, liberal, mild, pitying, soft, sparing, sympathetic, tenderhearted.

antonyms cruel, merciless.

merciless *adj.* barbarous, callous, cruel, hard, hardhearted, harsh, heartless, implacable, inexorable, inhuman, inhumane, pitiless, relentless, remorseless, ruthless, severe, unappeasable, unforgiving, unmerciful, unpitying, unsparing.

antonym merciful.

mercurial *adj.* active, capricious, changeable, erratic, fickle, flighty, gay, impetuous, impulsive, inconstant, irrepressible, light-hearted, lively, mobile, spirited, sprightly, temperamental, unpredictable, unstable, variable, volatile.

antonym saturnine.

mercy *n.* benevolence, blessing, boon, charity, clemency, compassion, favor, forbearance, forgiveness, god-

send, grace, humanitarianism, kindness, leniency, pity, quarter, relief.

antonyms cruelty, revenge.

mere *adj.* absolute, bare, common, complete, entire, paltry, petty, plain, pure, pure and simple, sheer, simple, stark, unadulterated, unmitigated, unmixed, utter, very.

merge *v.* amalgamate, blend, coalesce, combine, commingle, confederate, consolidate, converge, fuse, incorporate, intermix, join, liquesce, meet, meld, melt into, mingle, mix, unite.

merger *n.* amalgamation, coalescence, coalition, combination, confederation, consolidation, fusion, incorporation, union.

merit *n.* advantage, asset, claim, credit, desert, due, excellence, good, goodness, integrity, justification, quality, right, strong point, talent, value, virtue, worth, worthiness.

antonyms demerit, fault.

v. deserve, earn, incur, justify, rate, warrant.

merited *adj.* appropriate, condign, deserved, due, earned, entitled, fitting, just, justified, rightful, warranted, worthy.

antonyms inappropriate, unjustified.

meritorious *adj.* admirable, commendable, creditable, deserving, estimable, excellent, exemplary, good, honorable, laudable, praiseworthy, right, righteous, virtuous, worthful, worthy.

antonym unworthy.

merry *adj.* amusing, blithe, blithesome, boon, carefree, cheerful, chirpy, comic, comical, convivial, crank, elevated, facetious, festive, frolicsome, fun-loving, funny, gay, glad, gleeful, happy, heartsome, hilarious, humorous, jocular, jocund, jolly, joyful, joyous, light-hearted, mellow, mirthful, rollicking, rorty, saturnalian, sportful, sportive, squiffy, tiddly, tipsy, vivacious.

antonyms gloomy, glum, grave, melancholy, serious, sober, somber.

mesh *n.* entanglement, lattice, net, netting, network, plexus, reticulation, snare, tangle, toils, tracery, trap, web.

v. catch, combine, come together, connect, co-ordinate, dovetail, engage, enmesh, entangle, fit, harmonize, inmesh, interlock, knit.

mesmerize *v.* benumb, captivate, enthral, entrance, fascinate, grip, hypnotize, magnetize, spellbind, stupefy.

mess *n.* botch, chaos, clutter, cock-up, confusion, difficulty, dilemma, dirtiness, disarray, disorder, disorganization, fiasco, fix, guddle, hash, imbroglio, jam, jumble, litter, mishmash, mix-up, muddle, muss(e), perplexity, pickle, plight, predicament, shambles, shemozzle, soss, stew, turmoil, untidiness, yuck.

antonyms order, tidiness.

v. befoul, besmirch, clutter, dirty, disarrange, disarray, dishevel, foul, litter, muss(e), pollute, tousle.

antonyms order, tidy.

message *n.* bulletin, cable, commission, communication, communiqué, dépêche, dispatch, errand, idea, import, intimation, job, letter, meaning, memorandum, mission, missive, moral, note, notice, point, purport, send, task, theme, tidings, word.

messenger *n.* agent, ambassador, bearer, carrier, courier, delivery boy, emissary, envoy, errand-boy, go-between, harbinger, herald, in-between, internuncio, mercury, nuncio, runner, send, vaunt-courier.

messy *adj.* chaotic, cluttered, confused, dirty, dishevelled, disordered, disorganized, grubby, littered, muddled, shambolic, sloppy, slovenly, unkempt, untidy, yucky.

antonyms neat, ordered, tidy.

metamorphosis *n.* alteration, change, change-over, conversion, modification, mutation, rebirth, transfiguration, transformation, translation, transmogrification, transmutation, transubstantiation.

mete out administer, allot, apportion, assign, deal out, dispense, distribute, divide out, dole out, hand out, measure out, parcel out, portion, ration out, share out.

meteoric *adj.* brief, brilliant, dazzling, fast, instantaneous, momentary, overnight, rapid, spectacular, speedy, sudden, swift.

method *n.* approach, arrangement, course, design, fashion, form, manner, mode, modus operandi, order, orderliness, organization, pattern, plan, planning, practice, procedure, process, program, purpose, regularity, routine, rule, scheme, structure, style, system, technique, way.

methodical *adj.* business-like, deliberate, disciplined, efficient, meticulous, neat, ordered, orderly, organized, painstaking, planned, precise, punctilious, regular, scrupulous, structured, systematic, tidy.

antonyms confused, desultory, irregular.

meticulous *adj.* accurate, detailed, exact, fastidious, fussy, microscopic, nice, painstaking, particular, perfectionist, precise, punctilious, scrupulous, strict, thorough.

antonyms careless, slapdash.

mettle *n.* ardor, boldness, bottle, bravery, caliber, character, courage, daring, disposition, fire, fortitude, gallantry, gameness, ginger, grit, guts, hardihood, heart, indomitability, kidney, life, make-up, nature, nerve, pith, pluck, quality, resolution, resolve, spirit, spunk, stamp, temper, temperament, valor, vigor.

microscopic *adj.* imperceptible, indiscernible, infinitesimal, invisible, minuscule, minute, negligible, tiny.

antonyms huge, vast.

middle *adj.* central, halfway, inner, inside, intermediate, intervening, mean, medial, median, mediate, medium, mid, middle-bracket.

n. aurea mediocritas, center, focus, golden mean, halfway mark, halfway point, happy medium, heart, inside, mean, middle way, midpoint, midriff, midsection, midst, thick, via media, waist.

antonyms beginning, border, edge, end, extreme.

middleman *n.* broker, distributor, entrepreneur, fixer, go-between, intermediary, negotiator, retailer.

midget *n.* dwarf, gnome, homuncule, homunculus, manikin, minikin, minnow, pygmy, shrimp, Tom Thumb.

antonym giant.

adj. dwarf, Lilliputian, little, miniature, pocket, pocket-sized, pygmy, small, teeny, tiny.

antonym giant.

midst *n.* bosom, center, core, depths, epicenter, heart, hub, interior, middle, mid-point, thick.

midway *adv.* betwixt and between, halfway, in the middle, partially.

mien *n.* air, appearance, aspect, aura, bearing, carriage, complexion, countenance, demeanor, deportment, look, manner, presence, semblance.

miffed *adj.* aggrieved, annoyed, chagrined, disgruntled, displeased, hurt, in a huff, irked, irritated, narked, nettled, offended, piqued, put out, resentful, upset, vexed.

antonyms chuffed, delighted, pleased.

might *n.* ability, capability, capacity, clout, efficacy, efficiency, energy, force, heftiness, muscularity, potency, power, powerfulness, prowess, puissance, strength, sway, valor, vigor.

mighty *adj.* bulky, colossal, doughty, enormous, forceful, gigantic, grand, great, hardy, hefty, huge, immense, indomitable, large, lusty, manful, massive, monumental, muscular, potent, powerful, prodigious, puissant, robust, stalwart, stout, strapping, strenuous, strong, stupendous, sturdy, titanic, towering, tremendous, vast, vigorous.

antonyms frail, weak.

migrant *n.* drifter, emigrant, globe-trotter, gypsy, immigrant, itinerant, land-louper, nomad, rover, tinker, transient, traveler, vagrant, wanderer.

adj. drifting, globe-trotting, gypsy, immigrant, itinerant, migratory, nomadic, roving, shifting, transient, traveling, vagrant, wandering.

migrate *v.* drift, emigrate, journey, move, roam, rove, shift, transhume, travel, trek, voyage, wander.

migratory *adj.* gipsy, itinerant, migrant, nomadic, peripatetic, roving, shifting, transient, transitory, traveling, vagrant, wandering.

mild *adj.* amiable, balmy, bland, calm, clement, compassionate, docile, easy, easy-going, equable, forbearing, forgiving, gentle, indulgent, kind, lenient, meek, mellow, merciful, moderate, pacific, passive, peaceable, placid, pleasant, serene, smooth, soft, temperate, tender, tranquil, warm.

antonyms fierce, harsh, stormy, strong, violent.

milieu *n.* arena, background, element, environment, locale, location, medium, scene, setting, sphere, surroundings.

militant *adj.* active, aggressive, assertive, belligerent, combating, combative, contending, embattled, fighting, hawkish, pugnacious, vigorous, warring.

n. activist, aggressor, belligerent, combatant, fighter, partisan, struggler, warrior.

military *adj.* armed, martial, service, soldier-like, soldierly, warlike.

n. armed forces, army, forces, services, soldiers, soldiery.

milksop *n.* chinless wonder, coward, milquetoast, Miss Nancy, molly, mollycoddle, namby-pamby, pansy, sissy, weakling.

mill[1] *n.* ball-mill, crusher, grinder, quern.

v. comminute, crush, granulate, grate, grind, pound, powder, press, pulverize, roll.

mill[2] *n.* factory, foundry, plant, shop, works.

mill[3] *v.* crowd, scurry, seethe, swarm, throng, wander.

millstone *n.* affliction, burden, drag, encumbrance, grindstone, load, quernstone, weight.

mimic *v.* ape, caricature, echo, imitate, impersonate, look like, mirror, parody, parrot, personate, resemble, simulate, take off.

n. caricaturist, copy, copy-cat, imitator, impersonator, impressionist, parodist, parrot.

adj. echoic, fake, imitation, imitative, make-believe, mimetic, mock, pseudo, sham, simulated.

mince[1] *v.* chop, crumble, cut, dice, grind, hash.

n. hachis, hash.

mince[2] *v.* diminish, euphemize, extenuate, hold back, moderate, palliate, play down, soften, spare, suppress, tone down, weaken.

mince[3] *v.* attitudinize, ponce, pose, posture, simper.

mind[1] *n.* attention, attitude, belief, bent, brains, concentration, desire, disposition, fancy, feeling, genius, gray matter, head, imagination, inclination, inner, intellect, intellectual, intelligence, intention, judgment, leaning, marbles, memory, mentality, notion, opinion, outlook, point of view, psyche, purpose, rationality, reason, recollection, remembrance, sanity, sense, senses, sensorium, sensory, sentiment, spirit, tendency, thinker, thinking, thoughts, understanding, urge, view, will, wish, wits.

mind[2] *v.* care, demur, disapprove, dislike, object, resent, take offense.

mind[3] *v.* adhere to, attend, attend to, be careful, be on one's guard, comply with, ensure, follow, guard, have charge of, heed, keep an eye on, listen to, look after, make certain, mark, note, notice, obey, observe, pay attention, pay heed to, regard, respect, take care, take care of, take heed, tend, watch.

mindful *adj.* alert, alive (to), attentive, aware, careful, chary, cognizant, compliant, conscious, heedful, obedient, regardful, remindful, respectful, sensible, thoughtful, wary, watchful.

antonyms heedless, inattentive, mindless.

mine[1] *n.* abundance, coalfield, colliery, deposit, excavation, fund, hoard, lode, pit, reserve, sap, shaft, source, stock, store, supply, treasury, trench, tunnel, vein, wealth, wheal.

v. delve, dig for, dig up, excavate, extract, hew, quarry, remove, sap, subvert, tunnel, undermine, unearth, weaken.

mine[2] *n.* bomb, depth charge, egg, explosive, land-mine.

mingle *v.* alloy, associate, blend, circulate, coalesce, combine, commingle, compound, hobnob, intermingle, intermix, interweave, join, marry, mell, merge, mix, rub shoulders, socialize, unite.

miniature *adj.* baby, diminutive, dwarf, Lilliputian, little, midget, mini, minuscule, minute, pint-size(d), pocket, pocket-sized, pygmy, reduced, scaled-down, small, tiny, toy, wee.

antonym giant.

minimize *v.* abbreviate, attenuate, belittle, curtail, decrease, decry, deprecate, depreciate, diminish, discount, disparage, make light of, make little of, play down, prune, reduce, shrink, underestimate, underrate.

antonym maximize.

minimum *n.* bottom, least, lowest point, nadir, slightest.

antonym maximum.

adj. least, littlest, lowest, minimal, slightest, smallest, tiniest, weeniest, weest.

antonym maximum.

minister *n.* administrator, agent, aide, ambassador, assistant, churchman, clergyman, cleric, delegate, diplomat, divine, ecclesiastic, envoy, executive, Levite, office-holder, official, parson, pastor, plenipotentiary, preacher, priest, servant, subordinate, underling, vicar, vizier.

v. accommodate, administer, attend, cater to, nurse, pander to, serve, take care of, tend.

minor *adj.* inconsequential, inconsiderable, inferior, insignificant, junior, lesser, light, negligible, paltry, petty, piddling, secondary, second-class, slight, small, smaller, subordinate, trifling, trivial, unclassified, unimportant, younger.

antonym major.

minstrel *n.* bard, joculator, jongleur, musician, rhymer, rimer, singer, troubadour.

mint *v.* cast, coin, construct, devise, fabricate, fashion, forge, invent, make, make up, manufacture, monetize, produce, punch, stamp, strike.

adj. brand-new, excellent, first-class, fresh, immaculate, perfect, unblemished, undamaged, untarnished.

n. bomb, bundle, fortune, heap, million, packet, pile, stack.

minute[1] *n.* flash, instant, jiff, jiffy, mo, moment, sec, second, shake, tick, trice.

minute[2] *adj.* close, critical, detailed, diminutive, exact, exhaustive, fine, inconsiderable, infinitesimal, itsy-bitsy, Lilliputian, little, meticulous, microscopic, miniature, minim, minuscule, negligible, painstaking, paltry, petty, picayune, piddling, precise, punctilious, puny, slender, slight, small, tiny, trifling, trivial, unimportant.

antonyms gigantic, huge, immense.

miraculous *adj.* amazing, astonishing, astounding, extraordinary, incredible, inexplicable, magical, marvelous, otherworldly, phenomenal, preternatural, prodigious, stupendous, superhuman, supernatural, thaumaturgic, unaccountable, unbelievable, wonderful, wondrous.

antonyms natural, normal.

mirage *n.* fata Morgana, hallucination, illusion, optical illusion, phantasm.

mire *n.* bog, difficulties, dirt, fen, glaur, marsh, morass, muck, mud, ooze, quag, quagmire, slime, swamp, trouble.

mirror *n.* copy, double, glass, hand-glass, image, keeking-glass, likeness, looking-glass, pocket-glass, reflection, reflector, replica, representation, speculum, spit and image, spitting image, twin.

v. copy, depict, echo, emulate, follow, imitate, mimic, reflect, represent, show.

mirth *n.* amusement, cheerfulness, festivity, frolic, fun, gaiety, gladness, glee, hilarity, jocosity, jocularity, jocundity, jollity, joviality, joyousness, laughter, levity, merriment, merrymaking, pleasure, rejoicing, revelry, sport.

antonyms gloom, glumness, melancholy.

misadventure *n.* accident, calamity, cataclysm, catastrophe, debacle, disaster, failure, ill fortune, ill luck, mischance, misfortune, mishap, reverse, setback, tragedy.

misappropriate *v.* abuse, defalcate, embezzle, misapply, misspend, misuse, peculate, pervert, pocket, steal, swindle.

misbehave *v.* act up, carry on, get up to mischief, kick over the traces, mess about, muck about, offend, transgress, trespass.

antonym behave.

miscalculate *v.* blunder, boob, err, get wrong, misjudge, overestimate, overrate, overvalue, slip up, underestimate, underrate, undervalue.

miscarriage *n.* abortion, botch, breakdown, casualty, disappointment, error, failure, misadventure, mischance, misfire, mishap, mismanagement, perversion, thwarting, undoing.

antonym success.

miscarry v. abort, bite the dust, come to grief, come to nothing, fail, fall through, flounder, gang agley, misfire, warp.
antonym succeed.

miscellaneous adj. assorted, confused, diverse, diversified, farraginous, heterogeneous, indiscriminate, jumbled, manifold, many, mingled, mixed, motley, multifarious, multiform, omnifarious, promiscuous, sundry, varied, various.

miscellany n. anthology, assortment, collection, diversity, farrago, gallimaufry, hash, hotch-potch, jumble, medley, mélange, mixed bag, mixture, olla-podrida, omnium-gatherum, pot-pourri, salmagundi, variety.

mischief¹ n. bane, damage, detriment, devilment, deviltry, diablerie, disruption, evil, harm, hurt, impishness, injury, misbehavior, misfortune, monkey business, naughtiness, pranks, roguery, roguishness, shenanigans, trouble, waggery, waywardness.

mischief² n. devil, imp, monkey, nuisance, pest, rapscallion, rascal, rascallion, rogue, scallywag, scamp, tyke, villain.
antonym angel.

mischievous adj. arch, bad, damaging, deleterious, destructive, detrimental, elfish, elvan, elvish, evil, exasperating, frolicsome, harmful, hurtful, impish, injurious, malicious, malignant, naughty, pernicious, playful, puckish, rascally, roguish, sinful, spiteful, sportive, teasing, tricksy, troublesome, vexatious, vicious, wayward, wicked.
antonyms good, well-behaved.

misconduct n. delinquency, dereliction, hanky-panky, immorality, impropriety, malfeasance, malpractice, malversation, misbehavior, misdemeanor, misfeasance, mismanagement, naughtiness, rudeness, transgression, wrong-doing.

miscreant n. blackguard, caitiff, criminal, dastard, evildoer, knave, malefactor, mischief-maker, profligate, rascal, reprobate, rogue, scallywag, scamp, scapegrace, scoundrel, sinner, trouble-maker, vagabond, varlet, villain, wretch, wrong-doer.
antonym worthy.

misdemeanor n. delict, fault, indiscretion, infringement, lapse, malfeasance, misbehavior, misconduct, misdeed, offense, peccadillo, transgression, trespass.

miser n. cheapskate, curmudgeon, hunks, mammonist, meanie, money-grubber, muck-worm, niggard, pennypincher, pinchfist, pinchgut, pinchpenny, save-all, screw, Scrooge, skinflint, snudge, tightwad.
antonym spendthrift.

miserable adj. abject, anguished, bad, broken-hearted, caitiff, cheerless, contemptible, crestfallen, crushed, dejected, deplorable, depressed, depressive, desolate, despicable, despondent, destitute, detestable, disconsolate, disgraceful, dismal, distressed, doleful, dolorous, down, downcast, dreary, forlorn, gloomy, glum, griefstricken, hapless, heartbroken, ignominious, impoverished, indigent, joyless, lachrymose, lamentable, low, luckless, lugubrious, meager, mean, melancholic, melancholy, mournful, needy, niggardly, paltry, pathetic, penniless, piteous, pitiable, pitiful, poor, sad, scanty, scurvy, shabby, shameful, sordid, sorrowful, sorrowing, sorry, squalid, star-crossed, stricken, tearful, unhappy, vile, woebegone, worthless, wretched.
antonyms cheerful, comfortable, generous, honorable, noble.

miserly adj. avaricious, beggarly, cheese-paring, close, close-fisted, close-handed, covetous, curmudgeonly, gare, grasping, grudging, illiberal, mean, mercenary, mingy, money-grubbing, near, niggardly, parsimonious, penny-pinching, penurious, sordid, sparing, stingy, thrifty, tight-fisted, ungenerous.
antonyms generous, lavish, prodigal, spendthrift.

misery¹ n. abjectness, adversity, affliction, agony, anguish, bale, bane, bitter pill, blow, burden, calamity, catastrophe, cross, curse, depression, desolation, despair, destitution, disaster, discomfort, distress, dole, dolor, extremity, gloom, grief, hardship, heartache, heartbreak, humiliation, indigence, living death, load, melancholia, melancholy, misfortune, mortification, need, oppression, ordeal, penury, poverty, privation, prostration, sadness, sordidness, sorrow, squalor, suffering, torment, torture, trial, tribulation, trouble, unhappiness, want, woe, wretchedness.

misery² n. grouch, Jeremiah, Job's comforter, killjoy, moaner, pessimist, prophet of doom, ray of sunshine, sourpuss, spoil-sport, Weary Willie, wet blanket, whiner, whinger.
antonym sport.

misfit n. drop-out, eccentric, fish out of water, horse marine, individualist, lone wolf, loner, maverick, nonconformist, odd man out, oddball, rogue, square peg in a round hole, weirdo.
antonym conformist.

misfortune n. accident, adversity, affliction, bad luck, blow, buffet, calamity, catastrophe, disaster, failure, grief, hardship, harm, ill-luck, infelicity, infortune, loss, misadventure, mischance, misery, mishap, reverse, setback, sorrow, tragedy, trial, tribulation, trouble, woe.
antonyms luck, success.

misgiving n. anxiety, apprehension, backward glance, compunction, distrust, doubt, dubiety, fear, hesitation, misdoubt, niggle, presentiment, qualm, reservation, scruple, second thoughts, suspicion, uncertainty, unease, worry.
antonym confidence.

misguided adj. deluded, erroneous, foolish, ill-advised, ill-considered, ill-judged, imprudent, incautious, injudicious, misconceived, misled, misplaced, mistaken, rash, unreasonable, unsuitable, unwarranted, unwise.
antonym sensible.

mishap n. accident, adversity, balls-up, calamity, contretemps, disaster, hiccup, ill-fortune, ill-luck, misadventure, mischance, misfortune, misventure, setback.

mishmash n. conglomeration, farrago, gallimaufry, hash, hotchpotch, jumble, medley, mess, muddle, olio, olla-podrida, pastiche, pot-pourri, salad, salmagundi.

misjudge v. miscalculate, miscount, misestimate, misinterpret, misprize, mistake, overestimate, overrate, underestimate, underrate, undervalue.

mislay v. lose, lose sight of, misplace, miss.

mislead v. beguile, bluff, deceive, delude, fool, give a bum steer, hoodwink, lead up the garden path, misadvise, misdirect, misguide, misinform, mizzle, pull the wool over someone's eyes, snow, take for a ride, take in.

misleading adj. ambiguous, biased, casuistical, confusing, deceitful, deceptive, delusive, delusory, disingenuous, distorted, equivocatory, evasive, fallacious, false, falsidical, loaded, mendacious, sophistical, specious, spurious, tricky, unreliable.

antonyms authentic, authoritative, informative, plain, unequivocal.

mismatched *adj.* antipathetic, clashing, discordant, disparate, ill-assorted, incompatible, incongruous, irregular, misallied, mismated, unmatching, unreconcilable, unsuited.

antonyms compatible, matching.

misplace *v.* lose, misapply, misassign, misfile, mislay, miss.

misrepresent *v.* belie, bend, disguise, distort, exaggerate, falsify, garble, load, minimize, miscolor, misconstrue, misinterpret, misquote, misstate, pervert, slant, twist.

miss[1] *v.* avoid, bypass, circumvent, err, escape, evade, fail, forego, jump, lack, leave out, let go, let slip, lose, miscarry, mistake, obviate, omit, overlook, pass over, pass up, sidestep, skip, slip, trip.

n. blunder, error, failure, fault, fiasco, flop, lack, lacuna, loss, mistake, need, omission, oversight, want.

miss[2] *v.* grieve for, lack, lament, long for, mourn, need, pine for, regret, sorrow for, want, wish, yearn for.

miss[3] *n.* backfisch, child, damsel, demoiselle, flapper, Fraülein, girl, girly, Jungfrau, junior miss, kid, lass, lassie, mademoiselle, maid, maiden, missy, Ms, nymphet, schoolgirl, spinster, teenager, young thing.

misshapen *adj.* contorted, crippled, crooked, deformed, distorted, grotesque, ill-made, ill-proportioned, malformed, monstrous, thrawn, twisted, ugly, ungainly, unshapely, unsightly, warped, wry.

antonyms regular, shapely.

missile *n.* arrow, ball, bomb, dart, flying bomb, grenade, projectile, rocket, shaft, shell, shot, torpedo, V-bomb, weapon.

missing *adj.* absent, astray, disappeared, gone, lacking, lost, minus, misgone, mislaid, misplaced, strayed, unaccounted-for, wanting.

antonyms found, present.

mission *n.* aim, assignment, business, calling, campaign, charge, commission, crusade, delegation, deputation, duty, embassy, errand, goal, job, legation, mandate, ministry, object, office, operation, purpose, pursuit, quest, raison d'être, remit, task, task force, trust, undertaking, vocation, work.

missionary *n.* ambassador, apostle, campaigner, champion, crusader, emissary, envoy, evangelist, exponent, gospeller, preacher, promoter, propagandist, proselytizer, teacher.

mist *n.* brume, cloud, condensation, dew, dimness, drizzle, exhalation, film, fog, haar, haze, mizzle, roke, smir, smog, spray, steam, vapor, veil, water-smoke.

v. becloud, bedim, befog, blur, cloud, dim, film, fog, glaze, obscure, steam up, veil.

antonym clear.

mistake *n.* aberration, bêtise, bish, bloomer, blunder, boner, boob, boo-boo, clanger, clinker, corrigendum, erratum, error, fallacy, false move, fault, faux pas, floater, folly, gaffe, gaucherie, goof, howler, inaccuracy, indiscretion, inexactitude, lapse, lapsus, lapsus calami, lapsus linguae, lapsus memoriae, literal, malapropism, misapprehension, miscalculation, misconception, misjudgment, misprint, misprision, mispronunciation, misreading, misspelling, misunderstanding, mumpsimus, oversight, scape, slip, slip-up, solecism, stumer, tactlessness, trespass.

v. blunder, confound, confuse, err, get the wrong end

of the stick, goof, misapprehend, miscalculate, misconceive, misconstrue, misinterpret, misjudge, misobserve, misprize, misrate, misread, misreckon, misunderstand, slip up.

mistaken *adj.* deceived, deluded, erroneous, fallacious, false, faulty, ill-judged, inaccurate, inappropriate, inauthentic, incorrect, inexact, misguided, misinformed, misinstructed, mislead, misprized, off base, unfair, unfounded, unjust, unsound, untrue, wide of the mark, wrong.

antonyms correct, justified.

mistreat *v.* abuse, batter, brutalize, bully, harm, hurt, ill-treat, ill-use, injure, knock about, maltreat, manhandle, maul, mishandle, misuse, molest, rough up.

antonym pamper.

mistrust *n.* apprehension, caution, chariness, distrust, doubt, dubiety, fear, hesitancy, misdoubt, misgiving, reservations, skepticism, suspicion, uncertainty, wariness.

antonym trust.

v. be wary of, beware, disbelieve, distrust, doubt, fear, fight shy of, look askance at, misdoubt, mislippen, question, suspect.

antonym trust.

misunderstand *v.* get the wrong end of the stick, get wrong, misapprehend, miscomprehend, misconceive, misconstrue, misesteem, mishear, misinterpret, misjudge, misknow, misprize, misread, miss the point, mistake, take up wrong(ly).

antonyms grasp, understand.

misunderstanding *n.* argument, breach, clash, conflict, difference, difficulty, disagreement, discord, disharmony, dispute, dissension, error, malentendu, misacceptation, misapprehension, misconception, misconstruction, misinterpretation, misjudgment, misknowledge, misprision, misreading, mistake, mix-up, quarrel, rift, rupture, squabble, variance.

antonyms agreement, reconciliation.

misuse *n.* abusage, abuse, barbarism, catachresis, corruption, desecration, dissipation, distortion, exploitation, harm, ill-treatment, ill-usage, injury, malappropriation, malapropism, maltreatment, manhandling, misapplication, misappropriation, misemployment, mistreatment, misusage, perversion, profanation, prostitution, solecism, squandering, wastage, waste.

v. abuse, brutalize, corrupt, desecrate, dissipate, distort, exploit, harm, ill-treat, ill-use, injure, malappropriate, maltreat, manhandle, maul, misapply, misappropriate, misemploy, mistreat, molest, overload, overtax, pervert, profane, prostitute, squander, strain, waste, wrong.

mite *n.* atom, grain, iota, jot, modicum, morsel, ounce, scrap, smidgen, spark, trace, whit.

mitigate *v.* abate, allay, alleviate, appease, assuage, attemper, blunt, calm, check, decrease, diminish, dull, ease, extenuate, lenify, lessen, lighten, moderate, modify, mollify, pacify, palliate, placate, quiet, reduce, remit, slake, soften, soothe, still, subdue, temper, tone down, weaken.

antonyms aggravate, exacerbate, increase.

mix *v.* allay, alloy, amalgamate, associate, blend, coalesce, combine, commingle, commix, compound, consort, contemper, cross, dash, fold in, fraternize, fuse, hobnob, homogenize, immingle, incorporate,

intermingle, intermix, interweave, join, jumble, mell, merge, mingle, shuffle, socialize, synthesize, unite.
antonym separate.
n. alloy, amalgam, assortment, blend, combination, composite, compound, conglomerate, fusion, medley, mishmash, mixture, pastiche, synthesis.

mixture *n.* admixture, alloy, amalgam, amalgamation, association, assortment, blend, brew, coalescence, combination, combine, composite, compost, compound, concoction, conglomeration, cross, fusion, galimatias, gallimaufry, half-breed, hotchpotch, hybrid, jumble, macédoine, medley, mélange, miscegen, miscegenation, miscellany, mix, mixed bag, mongrel, olio, olla-podrida, omnium-gatherum, pastiche, pot-pourri, salad, salmagundi, synthesis, union, variety.

moan *n.* beef, belly-ache, bitch, complaint, gripe, groan, grouch, grouse, grumble, howl, keen, lament, lamentation, sigh, snivel, sob, sough, ululation, wail, whimper, whine, whinge.
v. beef, belly-ache, bemoan, bewail, bitch, carp, complain, deplore, grieve, gripe, groan, grouch, grouse, grumble, howl, keen, lament, mourn, sigh, snivel, sob, sough, ululate, wail, weep, whimper, whine, whinge, wuther.
antonym rejoice.

mob *n.* assemblage, bevy, body, canaille, class, collection, common herd, commonalty, company, crew, crowd, drove, faex populi, flock, galère, gang, gathering, great unwashed, group, herd, hoi polloi, horde, host, jingbang, lot, many-headed beast, many-headed monster, mass, masses, mobile, multitude, pack, plebs, populace, press, rabble, rent-a-crowd, rent-a-mob, riffraff, rout, scum, set, swarm, throng, tribe, troop, vulgus.
v. besiege, charge, cram, crowd, crowd round, descend on, fill, jam, jostle, overrun, pack, pester, set upon, surround, swarm round.
antonym shun.

mobile *adj.* active, agile, ambulatory, animated, changeable, changing, energetic, ever-changing, expressive, flexible, fluid, itinerant, lively, locomobile, locomotive, mercurial, migrant, motile, movable, moving, nimble, peripatetic, portable, roaming, roving, supple, traveling, vagile, vivacious, wandering.
antonym immobile.

mock *v.* ape, baffle, befool, burlesque, caricature, chaff, cheat, counterfeit, debunk, deceive, defeat, defy, delude, deride, disappoint, disparage, dupe, elude, explode, fleer, flout, foil, fool, frustrate, guy, imitate, insult, jeer, lampoon, laugh at, laugh in (someone's) face, laugh to scorn, make fun of, make sport of, mimic, parody, parrot, poke fun at, queer, quiz, ridicule, satirize, scoff, scorn, send up, sneer, take the mickey, taunt, tease, thwart, travesty, twit.
antonyms flatter, praise.
adj. artificial, bogus, counterfeit, dummy, ersatz, fake, faked, false, feigned, forged, fraudulent, imitation, phony, pinchbeck, pretended, pseudo, sham, simulated, spurious, synthetic.

mockery *n.* apology, burlesque, caricature, contempt, contumely, deception, derision, disappointment, disdain, disrespect, farce, fleer, gibes, iconoclasm, imitation, insults, invective, irrision, jeering, joke, lampoon, lampoonery, let-down, mickey-taking, mimesis, mimicry, misrepresentation, parody, pasquinade, pretence, quiz, ridicule, sarcasm, satire, scoffing, scorn, send-up, sham, spoof, take-off, travesty, wisecracks.

mode *n.* approach, condition, convention, course, craze, custom, dernier cri, fad, fashion, form, latest thing, look, manner, method, plan, practice, procedure, process, quality, rage, rule, state, style, system, technique, trend, vein, vogue, way.

model *n.* archetype, configuration, copy, criterion, design, draft, dummy, embodiment, epitome, example, exemplar, facsimile, form, gauge, ideal, image, imitation, kind, lodestar, manikin, mannequin, maquette, mark, miniature, mock-up, mode, mold, original, paradigm, paragon, pattern, personification, plan, poser, praxis, prototype, replica, representation, sitter, sketch, standard, style, subject, template, touchstone, type, variety, version, yardstick.
adj. archetypal, complete, consummate, dummy, exemplary, facsimile, ideal, illustrative, imitation, miniature, par excellence, paradigmatic, perfect, prototypal, prototypical, representative, standard, typical.
v. base, carve, cast, create, design, display, fashion, form, make, mold, pattern, plan, sculpt, shape, show off, sport, wear, work.

moderate *adj.* abstemious, average, calm, centrist, continent, controlled, cool, deliberate, disciplined, equable, fair, fairish, frugal, gentle, indifferent, judicious, limited, mediocre, medium, middle-of-the-road, middling, mild, modest, non-extreme, ordinary, passable, peaceable, quiet, rational, reasonable, restrained, sensible, sober, soft-shell(ed), so-so, steady, temperate, unexceptional, well-regulated.
v. abate, allay, alleviate, appease, assuage, attemper, blunt, calm, chasten, check, control, curb, cushion, decrease, diminish, dwindle, ease, lenify, lessen, mitigate, modify, modulate, pacify, palliate, play down, quiet, regulate, repress, restrain, slake, soften, softpedal, subdue, subside, tame, temper, tone down.

moderation *n.* abatement, abstemiousness, alleviation, aurea mediocritas, calmness, caution, chastity, composure, continence, control, coolness, decrease, diminution, discipline, discretion, easing, equanimity, extenuation, fairness, golden mean, judiciousness, justice, justness, let-up, mildness, mitigation, moderateness, modification, modulation, palliation, reasonableness, reduction, restraint, self-control, sobriety, temperance, via media.
antonyms increase, intemperance.

modern *adj.* advanced, avant-garde, contemporary, current, emancipated, fashionable, fresh, go-ahead, goey, innovative, inventive, jazzy, late, latest, mod, modernistic, modish, neoteric, new, newfangled, novel, present, present-day, progressive, recent, stylish, trendy, twentieth-century, up-to-date, up-to-the-minute, with it.
antonyms antiquated, old.

modernize *v.* do up, improve, modify, neoterize, progress, redesign, reform, refresh, refurbish, regenerate, rejuvenate, remake, remodel, renew, renovate, revamp, streamline, tart up, transform, update.
antonym regress.

modest *adj.* bashful, blushing, chaste, chastened, coy, demure, diffident, discreet, fair, humble, limited, maidenly, meek, middling, moderate, ordinary, proper, quiet, reserved, reticent, retiring, seemly, self-conscious, self-effacing, shamefaced, shy, simple, small, timid, unassuming, unexceptional, unpresuming, unpresumptuous, unpretending, unpretentious, verecund.

antonyms conceited, immodest, pretentious, vain.

modesty *n.* aidos, bashfulness, coyness, decency, demureness, diffidence, discreetness, humbleness, humility, meekness, propriety, quietness, reserve, reticence, seemliness, self-effacement, shamefacedness, shamefastness, shyness, simplicity, timidity, unobtrusiveness, unpretentiousness.

antonyms conceit, immodesty, vanity.

modicum *n.* atom, bit, crumb, dash, drop, fragment, grain, hint, inch, iota, little, mite, ounce, particle, pinch, scrap, shred, speck, suggestion, tinge, touch, trace.

modification *n.* adjustment, alteration, change, limitation, moderation, modulation, mutation, qualification, refinement, reformation, restriction, revision, tempering, variation.

modify *v.* abate, adapt, adjust, allay, alter, attemper, change, convert, improve, lessen, limit, lower, moderate, modulate, qualify, recast, redesign, redo, reduce, refashion, reform, remodel, reorganize, reshape, restrain, restrict, revise, rework, soften, temper, tone down, transform, vary.

modish *adj.* à la mode, all the rage, avant-garde, chic, contemporary, current, fashionable, goey, hip, in, jazzy, latest, mod, modern, modernistic, now, smart, stylish, trendy, up-to-the-minute, vogue, voguish, with-it.

antonyms dowdy, old-fashioned.

modulate *v.* adjust, alter, attune, balance, harmonize, inflect, lower, moderate, regulate, soften, tone, tune, vary.

antonyms increase, raise.

modus operandi manner, method, operation, plan, practice, praxis, procedure, process, rule, rule of thumb, system, technique, way.

mogul *n.* baron, bashaw, big cheese, big gun, big noise, big pot, big shot, big wheel, bigwig, grandee, magnate, magnifico, Mr Big, nabob, notable, panjandrum, personage, potentate, supremo, top dog, tycoon, VIP.

antonym nobody.

moist *adj.* clammy, damp, dampish, dampy, dank, dewy, dripping, drizzly, humid, marshy, muggy, rainy, soggy, swampy, tearful, vaporous, watery, wet, wettish.

antonyms arid, dry.

moisten *v.* bedew, damp, dampen, embrocate, humect, humectate, humidify, humify, imbue, irrigate, lick, madefy, moistify, moisturize, slake, soak, water, wet.

antonym dry.

moisture *n.* damp, dampness, dankness, dew, humidity, humor, liquid, mugginess, perspiration, sweat, tears, vapor, water, wateriness, wet, wetness.

antonym dryness.

mold¹ *n.* arrangement, brand, build, caliber, cast, character, configuration, construction, cut, design, die, fashion, form, format, frame, framework, ilk, kidney, kind, line, make, matrix, model, nature, pattern, quality, shape, sort, stamp, structure, style, template, type.

v. affect, carve, cast, construct, control, create, design, direct, fashion, fit, forge, form, hew, influence, make, model, sculpt, sculpture, shape, stamp, work.

mold² *n.* black, black spot, blight, fungus, mildew, moldiness, must, mustiness, rust.

mold³ *n.* clods, dirt, dust, earth, ground, humus, loam, soil.

moldy *adj.* bad, blighted, corrupt, decaying, fusty, mildewed, mucedinous, mucid, muggish, muggy, musty, putrid, rotten, rotting, spoiled, stale, vinewed.

antonyms fresh, wholesome.

molest *v.* abuse, accost, afflict, annoy, assail, attack, badger, beset, bother, bug, disturb, faze, harass, harm, harry, hassle, hector, hound, hurt, ill-treat, injure, irritate, maltreat, manhandle, mistreat, persecute, pester, plague, tease, torment, trouble, upset, vex, worry.

mollify *v.* abate, allay, appease, assuage, blunt, calm, compose, conciliate, cushion, ease, lessen, lull, mellow, mitigate, moderate, modify, pacify, placate, propitiate, quell, quiet, relax, relieve, soften, soothe, sweeten, temper.

antonyms aggravate, anger.

moment¹ *n.* breathing-while, flash, hour, instant, jiff, jiffy, juncture, less than no time, minute, mo, point, second, shake, split second, stage, tick, time, trice, twink, twinkling.

moment² *n.* concern, consequence, gravity, import, importance, note interest, seriousness, significance, substance, value, weight, weightiness, worth.

antonym insignificance.

momentary *adj.* brief, elusive, ephemeral, evanescent, fleeting, flying, fugitive, hasty, momentaneous, passing, quick, short, short-lived, temporary, transient, transitory.

antonyms lasting, permanent.

momentous *adj.* apocalyptic, consequential, critical, crucial, decisive, earth-shaking, epoch-making, eventful, fateful, grave, historic, important, major, pivotal, serious, significant, tremendous, vital, weighty.

antonym insignificant.

momentum *n.* drive, energy, force, impact, impetus, impulse, incentive, power, propulsion, push, speed, stimulus, strength, thrust, urge, velocity.

monarch *n.* despot, dynast, emperor, empress, king, potentate, prince, princess, queen, ruler, sovereign, tyrant.

money *n.* baksheesh, banco, banknotes, bankroll, boodle, brass, bread, capital, cash, chips, coin, currency, dough, dumps, fat, filthy lucre, fonds, funds, gelt, gold, gravy, greens, hard cash, hard money, legal tender, lolly, loot, mazuma, mint-sauce, money of account, moolah, oof, pelf, readies, ready money, riches, scrip, shekels, siller, silver, specie, spondulix (spondulicks), stumpy, sugar, the needful, the ready, the wherewithal, tin, wealth.

mongrel *n.* bigener, cross, crossbreed, half-breed, hybrid, lurcher, mule, mutt, yellow-dog.

adj. bastard, crossbred, half-breed, hybrid, ill-defined, mixed, mongrelly, nondescript.

antonyms pedigree, pure-bred.

monitor *n.* adviser, detector, guide, invigilator, overseer, prefect, recorder, scanner, screen, supervisor, watchdog.

v. check, detect, follow, keep an eye on, keep track of, keep under surveillance, note, observe, oversee, plot, record, scan, supervise, survey, trace, track, watch.

ite, contemplative, conventual, frate, frater, friar, gyrovague, hermit, mendicant, monastic, religieux, religionary, religioner, religious.

monkey[1] *n.* ape, primate, simian.

monkey[2] *n.* ass, butt, devil, dupe, fool, imp, jackanapes, laughing-stock, mug, rapscallion, rascal, rogue, scallywag, scamp.

v. fiddle, fidget, fool, interfere, meddle, mess, play, potter, tamper, tinker, trifle.

monogamous *adj.* monandrous, monogamic, monogynous.

antonyms bigamous, polygamous.

monologue *n.* harangue, homily, lecture, oration, sermon, soliloquy, speech, spiel.

antonyms conversation, dialogue, discussion.

monomania *n.* bee in one's bonnet, fanaticism, fetish, fixation, hobby-horse, idée fixe, mania, neurosis, obsession, ruling passion, thing.

monopoly *n.* ascendancy, control, corner, domination, exclusive right, monopsony, sole right.

monotonous *adj.* boring, colorless, droning, dull, flat, humdrum, monochrome, plodding, prosaic, repetitious, repetitive, routine, samey, soul-destroying, tedious, tiresome, toneless, unchanging, uneventful, uniform, uninflected, unvaried, unvarying, wearisome.

antonyms colorful, lively, varied.

monster *n.* abortion, barbarian, basilisk, beast, behemoth, bogeyman, brute, centaur, chimera, cockatrice, colossus, Cyclops, demon, devil, fiend, freak, giant, Gorgon, harpy, hellhound, hippocampus, hippogriff, Hydra, jabberwock, kraken, lamia, leviathan, lindworm, mammoth, manticore, Medusa, Minotaur, miscreation, monstrosity, mutant, ogre, ogress, prodigy, rye-wolf, savage, Sphinx, teratism, titan, villain, wivern.

adj. Brobdingnagian, colossal, cyclopean, enormous, gargantuan, giant, gigantic, huge, immense, jumbo, mammoth, massive, monstrous, prodigious, rounceval, stupendous, titanic, tremendous, vast.

antonym minute.

monstrous *adj.* abhorrent, abnormal, atrocious, colossal, criminal, cruel, cyclopean, deformed, devilish, diabolical, disgraceful, dreadful, egregious, elephantine, enormous, evil, fiendish, foul, freakish, frightful, gargantuan, giant, gigantic, great, grotesque, gruesome, heinous, hellish, hideous, horrendous, horrible, horrific, horrifying, huge, hulking, immense, infamous, inhuman, intolerable, loathsome, malformed, mammoth, massive, miscreated, misshapen, monster, obscene, odious, outrageous, prodigious, rounceval, satanic, scandalous, shocking, stupendous, teratoid, terrible, titanic, towering, tremendous, unnatural, vast, vicious, villainous, wicked.

monument *n.* ancient monument, antiquity, barrow, cairn, cenotaph, commemoration, cross, dolmen, evidence, gravestone, headstone, marker, martyry, mausoleum, memento, memorial, obelisk, pillar, prehistoric monument, record, relic, remembrance, reminder, shaft, shrine, statue, testament, token, tombstone, tumulus, witness.

monumental *adj.* abiding, awe-inspiring, awesome, catastrophic, classic, colossal, commemorative, conspicuous, cyclopean, durable, egregious, enduring, enormous, epoch-making, funerary, gigantic, great, historic, horrible, huge, immense, immortal, important, imposing, impressive, indefensible, lasting, magnificent, majestic, massive, memorable, memorial, monolithic, notable, outstanding, overwhelming, prodigious, significant, staggering, statuary, stupendous, terrible, tremendous, vast, whopping.

antonyms insignificant, unimportant.

mood *n.* blues, caprice, depression, disposition, doldrums, dumps, fit, frame of mind, grumps, humor, melancholy, pique, spirit, state of mind, sulk, temper, tenor, the sulks, vein, whim.

moody *adj.* angry, atrabilious, broody, cantankerous, capricious, cast-down, changeable, choleric, crabbed, crabby, cranky, cross, crotchety, crusty, dejected, depressive, dismal, doleful, dour, downcast, erratic, faddish, fickle, fitful, flighty, gloomy, glum, huffish, huffy, ill-humored, impulsive, inconstant, introspective, introvert, irascible, irritable, lugubrious, melancholy, mercurial, miserable, mopy, morose, peevish, pensive, petulant, piqued, sad, saturnine, short-tempered, splenetic, sulky, sullen, temperamental, testy, touchy, unpredictable, unsociable, unstable, unsteady, volatile, waspish.

antonyms cheerful, equable.

moor[1] *v.* anchor, berth, bind, dock, drop anchor, fasten, fix, hitch, lash, secure, tie up.

antonym loose.

moor[2] *n.* brae, downs, fell, heath, moorland, muir, upland, wold.

moot *v.* advance, argue, bring up, broach, debate, discuss, introduce, pose, propose, propound, put forward, submit, suggest, ventilate.

adj. academic, arguable, contestable, controversial, crucial, debatable, disputable, disputed, doubtful, insoluble, knotty, open, open to debate, problematic, questionable, undecided, undetermined, unresolvable, unresolved, unsettled, vexed.

mop *n.* head of hair, mane, mass, mat, shock, sponge, squeegee, swab, tangle, thatch.

v. absorb, clean, soak, sponge, swab, wash, wipe.

mope *v.* agonize, boody, brood, despair, despond, droop, fret, grieve, idle, languish, mooch, moon, pine, sulk.

n. depressive, grouch, grump, introvert, killjoy, melancholiac, melancholic, misery, moaner, moper, mopus, pessimist, Weary Willie.

moral *adj.* blameless, chaste, clean-living, decent, equitable, ethical, good, high-minded, honest, honorable, incorruptible, innocent, just, meritorious, moralistic, noble, principled, proper, pure, responsible, right, righteous, square, straight, temperate, upright, upstanding, virtuous.

antonym immoral.

n. adage, aphorism, apophthegm, dictum, epigram, gnome, import, lesson, maxim, meaning, message, motto, point, precept, proverb, saw, saying, significance, teaching.

morale *n.* confidence, esprit de corps, heart, mettle, mood, resolve, self-esteem, spirit, spirits, state of mind, temper.

morality *n.* chastity, conduct, decency, deontology, equity, ethicality, ethicalness, ethics, ethos, goodness, habits, honesty, ideals, integrity, justice, manners, morals, mores, philosophy, principle, principles, probity, propriety, rationale, rectitude, righteousness, standards, tightness, uprightness, virtue.

antonym immorality.

morals *n.* behavior, conduct, deontics, deontology, equity, ethics, ethos, habits, ideals, integrity, manners, morality, mores, principles, probity, propriety, rectitude, scruples, standards.

morass *n.* bog, can of worms, chaos, clutter, confusion, fen, flow, jam, jumble, marsh, marshland, mess, mire, mix-up, moss, muddle, quag, quagmire, quicksand, slough, swamp, tangle.

morbid *adj.* ailing, brooding, corrupt, deadly, diseased, dreadful, ghastly, ghoulish, gloomy, grim, grisly, gruesome, hideous, horrid, hypochondriacal, infected, lugubrious, macabre, malignant, melancholy, neurotic, pathological, peccant, pessimistic, putrid, sick, sickly, somber, unhealthy, unsalubrious, unsound, unwholesome, vicious, Wertherian.

more *adj.* added, additional, alternative, extra, fresh, further, increased, new, other, renewed, repeated, spare, supplementary.
adv. again, better, further, longer.

moreover *adv.* additionally, also, as well, besides, further, furthermore, in addition, into the bargain, likewise, may I add, more, more to the point, to boot, too, what is more, withal.

moron *n.* ass, blockhead, bonehead, clot, cretin, daftie, dimwit, dolt, dope, dumbbell, dummy, dunce, dunderhead, fool, halfwit, idiot, imbecile, klutz, mental defective, mooncalf, muttonhead, natural, numbskull, schmo, schmuck, simpleton, thickhead, vegetable, zombie.

morose *adj.* blue, cheerless, churlish, crabbed, crabby, cross, crusty, depressed, dour, down, gloomy, glum, grim, grouchy, gruff, grum, huffy, humorless, ill-humored, ill-natured, ill-tempered, low, melancholy, misanthropic, moody, mournful, perverse, pessimistic, saturnine, sour, stern, sulky, sullen, surly, taciturn, testy, unsociable.
antonyms cheerful, communicative.

morsel *n.* atom, bit, bite, bonne-bouche, crumb, fraction, fragment, grain, modicum, morceau, mouthful, nibble, part, piece, scrap, segment, slice, smidgen, snack, soupçon, taste, titbit.

mortal *adj.* agonizing, awful, bodily, corporeal, deadly, deathful, dire, earthly, enormous, ephemeral, extreme, fatal, fleshly, grave, great, human, impermanent, implacable, intense, irreconcilable, lethal, lethiferous, mortiferous, passing, perishable, relentless, remorseless, severe, sublunary, sworn, temporal, terrible, transient, unrelenting, worldly.
antonym immortal.
n. being, body, creature, earthling, human, human being, individual, man, person, sublunar, sublunary, woman.
antonyms god, immortal.

mortgage *v.* dip, pawn, pledge, put in hock.
n. bond, debenture, lien, loan, pledge, security, wadset.

mortified *adj.* abashed, affronted, annoyed, ashamed, chagrined, chastened, confounded, crushed, dead, decayed, deflated, discomfited, displeased, embarrassed, gangrenous, humbled, humiliated, necrotic, put out, put to shame, putrefied, putrid, rotted, rotten, shamed, vexed.
antonyms elated, jubilant.

mortify *v.* abase, abash, affront, annoy, chagrin, chasten, confound, conquer, control, corrupt, crush,

deflate, deny, die, disappoint, discipline, discomfit, embarrass, fester, gangrene, humble, humiliate, macerate, necrose, put to shame, putrefy, shame, subdue, vex.

mortuary *n.* deadhouse, funeral home, funeral parlor, morgue.

mostly *adv.* as a rule, characteristically, chiefly, commonly, customarily, feckly, for the most part, generally, largely, mainly, normally, on the whole, particularly, predominantly, primarily, principally, typically, usually.

mother *n.* dam, generatrix, genetrix, ma, mam, mama, mamma, mammy, mater, materfamilias, mom, momma, mommy, mum, mummy, old lady, old woman.
v. baby, bear, care for, cherish, cosset, foster, fuss over, indulge, nurse, nurture, overprotect, pamper, produce, protect, raise, rear, spoil, tend.
antonym neglect.

motif *n.* concept, decoration, design, device, figure, form, idea, leitmotiv, logo, notion, ornament, pattern, shape, strain, subject, theme.

motion *n.* action, change, dynamics, flow, flux, gesticulation, gesture, inclination, kinesics, kinetics, locomotion, mechanics, mobility, motility, move, movement, nod, passage, passing, progress, proposal, proposition, recommendation, sign, signal, submission, suggestion, transit, travel, wave.
v. beckon, direct, gesticulate, gesture, nod, sign, signal, usher, wave.

motionless *adj.* at a standstill, at rest, calm, fixed, frozen, halted, immobile, inanimate, inert, lifeless, moveless, paralyzed, resting, rigid, stagnant, standing, static, stationary, still, stock-still, transfixed, unmoved, unmoving.
antonym active.

motivate *v.* actuate, arouse, bring, cause, draw, drive, encourage, impel, incite, induce, inspire, inspirit, instigate, kindle, lead, move, persuade, prompt, propel, provoke, push, spur, stimulate, stir, trigger, urge.
antonyms deter, prevent.

motive *n.* cause, consideration, design, desire, encouragement, ground(s), impulse, incentive, incitement, inducement, influence, inspiration, intention, mainspring, motivation, object, occasion, purpose, rationale, reason, stimulus, thinking, urge.
antonyms deterrent, discouragement, disincentive.
adj. activating, actuating, agential, driving, impelling, initiating, motivating, moving, operative, prompting, propellent.
antonyms deterrent, inhibitory, preventive.

motley *adj.* assorted, checkered, disparate, dissimilar, diverse, diversified, haphazard, heterogeneous, ill-assorted, kaleidoscopic, mingled, miscellaneous, mixed, multicolored, particolored, patchwork, polychromatic, polychrome, polychromous, promiscuous, rainbow, unlike, varied, variegated.
antonyms homogeneous, monochrome, uniform.

mottled *adj.* blotchy, brindled, checkered, dappled, flecked, freaked, freckled, jaspé, marbled, piebald, pied, poikilitic, skewbald, speckled, spotted, stippled, streaked, tabby, variegated, veined, watered.
antonyms monochrome, plain, uniform.

motto *n.* adage, apophthegm, byword, catchword, cry, dictum, epigraph, formula, gnome, golden rule, ichthys, maxim, precept, proverb, rule, saw, saying, sentence, slogan, watchword.

mound *n.* agger, bank, barrow, bing, bulwark, drift, dune, earthwork, elevation, embankment, heap, hill, hillock, hummock, knoll, mote, motte, pile, rampart, rick, ridge, rise, stack, tuffet, tumulus, tussock, yardang.

mount *v.* accumulate, arise, ascend, bestride, build, clamber up, climb, climb on, climb up on, copulate, cover, deliver, display, emplace, enchase, escalade, escalate, exhibit, fit, frame, get astride, get on, get up, get up on, go up, grow, horse, increase, install, intensify, jump on, launch, lift, multiply, pile up, place, position, prepare, produce, put in place, put on, ready, ride, rise, rocket, scale, set, set in motion, set off, set up, soar, stage, straddle, swell, tower, tread.
n. backing, base, fixture, foil, frame, horse, monture, mounting, pedestal, podium, setting, stand, steed, support.

mountain *n.* abundance, alp, backlog, ben, berg, elevation, eminence, fell, heap, height, mass, massif, mound, mount, Munro, peak, pile, reserve, stack, ton.

mountebank *n.* charlatan, cheat, con man, confidence, fake, fraud, huckster, impostor, phony, pretender, pseud, quack, quacksalver, rogue, spieler, swindler, trickster.

mourn *v.* bemoan, bewail, beweep, deplore, grieve, keen, lament, miss, regret, rue, sorrow, wail, weep.
antonyms bless, rejoice.

mournful *adj.* afflicting, broken-hearted, calamitous, cast-down, cheerless, chopfallen, dearnful, dejected, deplorable, depressed, desolate, disconsolate, dismal, distressing, doleful, dolorous, downcast, funereal, gloomy, grief-stricken, grieving, grievous, heart-broken, heavy, heavy-hearted, joyless, lachrymose, lamentable, long-faced, long-visaged, lugubrious, melancholy, miserable, painful, piteous, plaintive, plangent, rueful, sad, somber, sorrowful, stricken, tragic, unhappy, woeful, woesome.
antonyms cheerful, joyful.

mourning *n.* bereavement, black, desolation, grief, grieving, keening, lamentation, sackcloth and ashes, sadness, sorrow, wailing, weeds, weeping, widow's weeds, woe.
antonym rejoicing.

mousy *adj.* brownish, characterless, colorless, diffident, drab, dull, indeterminate, ineffectual, mouse-like, plain, quiet, self-effacing, shy, timid, timorous, unassertive, unforthcoming, uninteresting, withdrawn.
antonyms assertive, bright, extrovert, irrepressible.

move *v.* activate, actuate, adjust, advance, advise, advocate, affect, agitate, budge, carry, cause, change, cover the ground, decamp, depart, disturb, drift, drive, ease, edge, excite, flit, get, give rise to, go, go away, gravitate, impel, impress, incite, induce, influence, inspire, instigate, jiggle, lead, leave, locomote, make strides, march, migrate, motivate, move house, operate, persuade, proceed, progress, prompt, propel, propose, pull, push, put forward, quit, recommend, relocate, remove, rouse, run, set going, shift, shove, start, stimulate, stir, submit, suggest, switch, take, touch, transfer, transport, transpose, turn, urge, walk.
n. act, action, deed, démarche, dodge, draft, flit, flitting, go, maneuver, measure, migration, motion, move-

ment, ploy, relocation, removal, ruse, shift, step, stratagem, stroke, tack, tactic, transfer, turn.

movement *n.* act, action, activity, advance, agitation, beat, cadence, campaign, change, crusade, current, development, displacement, division, drift, drive, evolution, exercise, faction, flow, front, gesture, ground swell, group, grouping, innards, machinery, maneuver, measure, mechanism, meter, motion, move, moving, operation, organization, pace, part, party, passage, progress, progression, rhythm, section, shift, steps, stir, stirring, swing, tempo, tendency, transfer, trend, workings, works.

moving *adj.* affecting, ambulant, ambulatory, arousing, dynamic, emotional, emotive, exciting, impelling, impressive, inspirational, inspiring, locomobile, mobile, motile, motivating, movable, pathetic, persuasive, poignant, portable, propelling, running, stimulating, stimulative, stirring, touching, unfixed.
antonyms fixed, stationary, unemotional.

mow *v.* clip, crop, cut, scythe, shear, trim.

much *adv.* considerably, copiously, decidedly, exceedingly, frequently, greatly, often.
adj. a lot of, abundant, ample, considerable, copious, great, plenteous, plenty of, sizable, substantial.
n. heaps, lashings, loads, lots, oodles, plenty, scads.
antonym little.

muck *n.* dirt, droppings, dung, feces, filth, gunge, gunk, manure, mire, mud, ooze, ordure, scum, sewage, slime, sludge.

muddle *v.* befuddle, bewilder, confound, confuse, daze, disarrange, disorder, disorganize, disorient(ate), fuddle, fuzzle, jumble, make a mess of, mess, mix up, mull, perplex, scramble, spoil, stupefy, tangle.
n. balls up, chaos, clutter, cock-up, confusion, daze, disarray, disorder, disorganization, fankle, guddle, jumble, mess, mix-up, mull, perplexity, pie, plight, predicament, puddle, snarl-up, tangle.

muddled *adj.* at sea, befuddled, bewildered, chaotic, confused, dazed, disarrayed, disordered, disorganized, disorient(at)ed, higgledy-piggledy, incoherent, jumbled, loose, messy, mixed-up, muddle-headed, perplexed, puzzle-headed, scrambled, stupefied, tangled, unclear, vague, woolly.

muff *v.* botch, bungle, fluff, mess up, mishit, mismanage, miss, spoil.

muffle *v.* cloak, conceal, cover, damp down, dampen, deaden, disguise, dull, envelop, gag, hood, hush, mask, mute, muzzle, quieten, shroud, silence, soften, stifle, suppress, swaddle, swathe, wrap up.
antonym amplify.

mug[1] *n.* beaker, cup, flagon, jug, pot, stoup, tankard, toby jug.

mug[2] *n.* chump, fool, gull, innocent, mark, muggins, sap, saphead, simpleton, soft touch, sucker.

mug[3] *n.* clock, countenance, dial, face, features, mush, phiz(og), puss, visage.

mug[4] *v.* attack, bash, batter, beat up, garrotte, jump (on), mill, rob, roll, set upon, steal from, waylay.

muggy *adj.* clammy, close, damp, humid, moist, oppressive, sticky, stuffy, sudorific, sultry, sweltering.
antonym dry.

mulish *adj.* bull-headed, cross-grained, defiant, difficult, headstrong, inflexible, intractable, intransigent, obstinate, perverse, pig-headed, recalcitrant, refractory, rigid, self-willed, stiff-necked, stubborn, unreasonable, wilful, wrong-headed.

multifarious *adj.* different, diverse, diversified, legion, manifold, many, miscellaneous, multiform, multiple, multiplex, multitudinous, numerous, sundry, varied, variegated.

multiply *v.* accumulate, augment, boost, breed, build up, expand, extend, increase, intensify, proliferate, propagate, reproduce, spread.
antonyms decrease, lessen.

multitude *n.* army, assemblage, assembly, collection, commonalty, concourse, congregation, crowd, herd, hive, hoi polloi, horde, host, legion, lot, lots, mass, mob, myriad, people, populace, proletariat, public, rabble, sea, swarm, throng.
antonyms handful, scattering.

mum *adj.* close-lipped, close-mouthed, dumb, mute, quiet, reticent, secretive, silent, tight-lipped, uncommunicative, unforthcoming.

mundane *adj.* banal, commonplace, day-to-day, earthly, everyday, fleshly, human, humdrum, material, mortal, ordinary, prosaic, routine, secular, subastral, sublunar(y), temporal, terrestrial, workaday, worldly.
antonyms cosmic, extraordinary, supernatural.

municipal *adj.* borough, burgh(al), city, civic, community, public, town, urban.

munificent *adj.* beneficent, benevolent, big-hearted, bounteous, bountiful, free-handed, generous, hospitable, lavish, liberal, magnanimous, open-handed, philanthropical, princely, rich, unstinting.
antonym mean.

murder *n.* agony, assassination, bloodshed, butchery, carnage, danger, deicide, difficulty, filicide, fractricide, hell, homicide, infanticide, killing, manslaughter, massacre, misery, ordeal, parricide, patricide, slaying, trial, trouble.
v. abuse, assassinate, bump off, burke, butcher, destroy, dispatch, do in, drub, eliminate, hammer, hit, kill, mangle, mar, massacre, misuse, rub out, ruin, slaughter, slay, spoil, thrash, waste.

murderer *n.* assassin, butcher, cut-throat, filicide, hitman, homicide, killer, matricide, parricide, patricide, slaughterer, slayer.

murky *adj.* cloudy, dark, dim, dismal, dreary, dull, dusky, enigmatic, foggy, gloomy, gray, misty, mysterious, obscure, overcast, veiled.
antonyms bright, clear.

murmur *n.* babble, brool, burble, buzz, buzzing, complaint, croon, drone, grumble, humming, moan, mumble, muttering, purl, purling, purr, rumble, susurrus, undertone, whisper, whispering.
v. babble, burble, burr, buzz, drone, gurgle, hum, mumble, mutter, purl, purr, rumble.

muscle *n.* brawn, clout, depressor, force, forcefulness, levator, might, potency, power, sinew, stamina, strength, sturdiness, tendon, thew, weight.

muse *v.* brood, chew, cogitate, consider, contemplate, deliberate, dream, meditate, mull over, ponder, reflect, review, ruminate, speculate, think, think over, weigh.

mushroom *v.* boom, burgeon, expand, flourish, grow, increase, luxuriate, proliferate, shoot up, spread, spring up, sprout.
n. champignon, chanterelle, fungus, morel, pixy-stool, puffball, toadstool.

musical *adj.* canorous, dulcet, euphonious, Euterpean,

harmonious, lilting, lyrical, melodic, melodious, sweet-sounding, tuneful.
antonym unmusical.

musician *n.* accompanist, bard, composer, conductor, instrumentalist, minstrel, performer, player, singer, vocalist.

musing *n.* absent-mindedness, abstraction, brown study, cerebration, cogitation, contemplation, daydreaming, dreaming, introspection, meditation, ponderment, reflection, reverie, rumination, thinking, wool-gathering.

must *n.* basic, duty, essential, fundamental, imperative, necessity, obligation, prerequisite, provision, requirement, requisite, sine qua non, stipulation.

muster *v.* assemble, call together, call up, collect, come together, congregate, convene, convoke, enrol, gather, group, marshal, mass, meet, mobilize, rally, round up, summon, throng.
n. assemblage, assembly, collection, concourse, congregation, convention, convocation, gathering, mass, meeting, mobilization, rally, round-up, throng.

musty *adj.* airless, ancient, antediluvian, antiquated, banal, clichéd, dank, decayed, dull, frowsty, fusty, hackneyed, hoary, mildewed, mildewy, moth-eaten, moldy, mucedinous, mucid, obsolete, old, old-fashioned, smelly, stale, stuffy, threadbare, trite, vinewed, worn-out.

mute *adj.* aphonic, dumb, mum, noiseless, silent, speechless, unexpressed, unpronounced, unspeaking, unspoken, voiceless, wordless.
antonyms articulate, vocal, voluble.
v. dampen, deaden, lower, moderate, muffle, silence, soften, soft-pedal, subdue, tone down.

mutilate *v.* adulterate, amputate, bowdlerize, butcher, censor, cut, cut to pieces, cut up, damage, detruncate, disable, disfigure, dismember, distort, expurgate, hack, hamble, injure, lacerate, lame, maim, mangle, mar, spoil.

mutinous *adj.* bolshie, bolshy, contumacious, disobedient, insubordinate, insurgent, rebellious, recusant, refractory, revolutionary, riotous, seditious, subversive, turbulent, ungovernable, unmanageable, unruly.
antonyms compliant, dutiful, obedient.

mutiny *n.* defiance, disobedience, insubordination, insurrection, putsch, rebellion, resistance, revolt, revolution, riot, rising, strike, uprising.
v. disobey, protest, rebel, resist, revolt, rise up, strike.

mutter *v.* chunter, complain, grouch, grouse, grumble, mumble, murmur, mussitate, rumble.

mutual *adj.* common, communal, complementary, exchanged, interchangeable, interchanged, joint, reciprocal, reciprocated, requited, returned, shared.

muzzle *n.* bit, curb, gag, guard, jaws, mouth, nose, snaffle, snout.
v. censor, choke, curb, gag, mute, restrain, silence, stifle, suppress.

myopic *adj.* half-blind, near-sighted, short-sighted.
antonym far-sighted.

myriad *adj.* boundless, countless, immeasurable, incalculable, innumerable, limitless, multitudinous, untold.
n. army, flood, horde, host, millions, mountain, multitude, scores, sea, swarm, thousands, throng.

mysterious *adj.* abstruse, arcane, baffling, concealed, covert, cryptic, curious, dark, enigmatic, furtive, hidden, impenetrable, incomprehensible, inexplicable, inscrutable, insoluble, mystical, mystifying, obscure, perplexing, puzzling, recondite, secret, secretive, strange, uncanny, unfathomable, unsearchable, veiled, weird.

antonyms comprehensible, frank, straightforward.

mystery *n.* arcanum, conundrum, enigma, problem, puzzle, question, riddle, secrecy, secret.

mystical *adj.* abstruse, arcane, cab(b)alistic(al), cryptic, enigmatical, esoteric, hidden, inscrutable, metaphysical, mysterious, mystic, occult, otherworldly, paranormal, preternatural, supernatural, transcendental.

mystify *v.* baffle, bamboozle, beat, befog, bewilder, confound, confuse, escape, perplex, puzzle, stump.

myth *n.* allegory, delusion, fable, fairy tale, fancy, fantasy, fiction, figment, illusion, legend, old wives' tale, parable, saga, story, superstition, tradition, untruism.

N

nag[1] *v.* annoy, badger, berate, chivvy, goad, harass, harry, henpeck, irritate, kvetch, pain, pester, plague, scold, torment, upbraid, vex.

n. harpy, harridan, kvetch(er), scold, shrew, tartar, termagant, virago.

nag[2] *n.* hack, horse, jade, plug, rip, Rosinante.

nail *v.* apprehend, attach, beat, capture, catch, clinch, collar, fasten, fix, hammer, join, nab, nick, pin, secure, seize, tack.

n. brad, hobnail, peg, pin, rivet, screw, skewer, spike, staple, tack, tacket.

naïve *adj.* artless, callow, candid, childlike, confiding, credulous, dewy-eyed, facile, frank, green, guileless, gullible, ingenuous, innocent, jejune, natural, open, simple, simplistic, trusting, unaffected, uncritical, unpretentious, unsophisticated, unsuspecting, unsuspicious, unworldly, verdant, wide-eyed.

antonyms experienced, sophisticated.

naked *adj.* adamic, bare, blatant, defenseless, denuded, disrobed, divested, evident, exposed, helpless, in puris naturalibus, in the altogether, in the buff, insecure, manifest, mother-naked, nude, open, overt, patent, plain, simple, skyclad, stark, starkers, stark-naked, stripped, unadorned, unarmed, unclothed, unconcealed, uncovered, undisguised, undraped, undressed, unexaggerated, unguarded, unmistakable, unprotected, unqualified, unvarnished, vulnerable.

antonyms clothed, concealed, covered.

name *n.* acronym, agname, agnomen, appellation, character, cognomen, compellation, compellative, credit, denomination, designation, distinction, eminence, epithet, esteem, fame, handle, honor, moni(c)ker, nickname, note, praise, renown, reputation, repute, sobriquet, stage name, term, title, to-name.

v. appoint, baptize, bename, betitle, call, choose, christen, cite, classify, cognominate, commission, denominate, designate, dub, entitle, identify, label, mention, nominate, select, specify, style, term, title.

nap[1] *v.* catnap, doze, drop off, drowse, kip, nod, nod off, rest, sleep, snooze.

n. catnap, forty winks, kip, rest, shuteye, siesta, sleep.

nap[2] *n.* down, downiness, fuzz, grain, pile, shag, weave.

narcissistic *adj.* conceited, egocentric, egomaniacal, ego(t)istic, self-centered, self-loving, vain.

narcotic *n.* anesthetic, analgesic, anodyne, drug, hop, kef, opiate, pain-killer, sedative, tranquilizer.

adj. analgesic, calming, dulling, hypnotic, Lethean, numbing, pain-killing, sedative, somniferous, somnific, soporific, stupefacient, stupefactive, stupefying.

narrate *v.* chronicle, describe, detail, recite, recount, rehearse, relate, repeat, report, set forth, state, tell, unfold.

narrative *n.* account, chronicle, detail, history, parable, report, statement, story, tale.

narrow *adj.* attenuated, avaricious, biased, bigoted, circumscribed, close, confined, constricted, contracted, cramped, dogmatic, exclusive, fine, illiberal, incapacious, intolerant, limited, meager, mean, mercenary, narrow-minded, near, niggardly, partial, pinched, prejudiced, reactionary, restricted, scanty, select, simplistic, slender, slim, small-minded, spare, straitened, tapering, thin, tight, ungenerous.

antonyms broad, liberal, tolerant, wide.

v. circumscribe, constrict, constringe, diminish, limit, reduce, simplify, straiten, tighten.

antonyms broaden, increase, loosen, widen.

antonyms broadening, widening.

narrow-minded *adj.* biased, bigoted, blinkered, borné, conservative, hidebound, illiberal, insular, intolerant, mean, opinionated, parochial, petty, prejudiced, provincial, reactionary, short-sighted, small-minded, straitlaced.

antonym broad-minded.

antonyms breadth, width.

nascent *adj.* advancing, budding, developing, embryonic, evolving, growing, incipient, naissant, rising, young.

antonym dying.

nasty *adj.* abusive, annoying, bad, bad-tempered, base, critical, dangerous, despicable, dirty, disagreeable, disgusting, distasteful, filthy, foul, gross, horrible, impure, indecent, lascivious, lewd, licentious, loathsome, low-down, malicious, malodorous, mean, mephitic, nauseating, noisome, objectionable, obnoxious, obscene, odious, offensive, painful, polluted, pornographic, repellent, repugnant, ribald, serious, severe, sickening, smutty, spiteful, unappetizing, unpleasant, unsavory, vicious, vile, waspish.

antonyms agreeable, clean, decent, pleasant.

nation *n.* citizenry, commonwealth, community, country, people, population, race, realm, society, state, tribe.

native *adj.* aboriginal, autochthonous, built-in, congenital, domestic, endemic, genuine, hereditary, home, home-born, home-bred, home-grown, home-made, inborn, inbred, indigene, indigenous, ingrained, inherent, inherited, innate, instinctive, intrinsic, inveterate, local, mother, natal, natural, original, real, vernacular.

n. aborigine, autochthon, citizen, countryman, dweller, indigene, inhabitant, national, resident.

antonyms foreigner, outsider, stranger.

natty *adj.* chic, dapper, elegant, fashionable, neat, ritzy, smart, snazzy, spruce, stylish, swanky, trim.

natural *adj.* artless, candid, characteristic, common, congenital, constitutional, essential, everyday, frank, genuine, inborn, indigenous, ingenuous, inherent, innate, instinctive, intuitive, legitimate, logical, natal, native, normal, open, ordinary, organic, plain, pure, real, regular, simple, spontaneous, typical, unaffected, unbleached, unforced, unlabored, unlearned, unmixed, unpolished, unpretentious, unrefined, unsophisticated, unstudied, untaught, usual, whole.

antonyms abnormal, affected, alien, artificial, pretended, unnatural.

naturally *adj.* absolutely, artlessly, as a matter of course, candidly, certainly, customarily, frankly, genuinely, informally, normally, of course, plainly, simply, spontaneously, typically, unaffectedly, unpretentiously.

nature[1] *n.* attributes, category, character, complexion, constitution, cosmos, creation, description, disposition, earth, environment, essence, features, humor, inbeing, inscape, kind, make-up, mood, outlook, quality, sort, species, style, temper, temperament, traits, type, universe, variety, world.

nature[2] *n.* country, countryside, landscape, natural history, scenery.

naught *n.* nil, nothing, nothingness, nought, zero, zilch.

naughty *adj.* annoying, bad, bawdy, blue, disobedient, exasperating, fractious, impish, improper, lewd, misbehaved, mischievous, obscene, off-color, perverse, playful, refractory, remiss, reprehensible, ribald, risqué, roguish, sinful, smutty, teasing, vulgar, wayward, wicked, worthless.

antonyms good, polite, well-behaved.

nausea *n.* abhorrence, aversion, biliousness, disgust, loathing, motion sickness, qualm(s), queasiness, repugnance, retching, revulsion, sickness, squeamishness, vomiting.

nauseating *adj.* abhorrent, detestable, disgusting, distasteful, fulsome, loathsome, nauseous, offensive, repugnant, repulsive, revolting, sickening.

nautical *adj.* boating, marine, maritime, naval, oceanic, sailing, seafaring, sea-going, yachting.

naval *adj.* marine, maritime, nautical, sea.

navigate *v.* con, cross, cruise, direct, drive, guide, handle, helm, journey, maneuver, pilot, plan, plot, sail, skipper, steer, voyage.

near *adj.* accessible, adjacent, adjoining, akin, allied, alongside, approaching, at close quarters, attached, beside, bordering, close, connected, contiguous, dear, familiar, forthcoming, handy, imminent, impending, in the offing, intimate, looming, near-at-hand, nearby, neighboring, next, nigh, on the cards, proximal, related, touching.

antonyms distant, far, remote.

near thing close shave, narrow escape, nasty moment, near miss.

nearly *adv.* about, all but, almost, approaching, approximately, as good as, closely, just about, not quite, practically, pretty much, pretty well, roughly, virtually, well-nigh.

neat *adj.* accurate, adept, adroit, agile, apt, clean-cut, clever, dainty, deft, dexterous, dinky, efficient, effortless, elegant, expert, fastidious, genty, graceful, handy, methodical, nice, nimble, orderly, practiced, precise, pure, shipshape, skilful, smart, spick-and-span, spruce, straight, stylish, systematic, tiddley, tidy, trig, trim, uncluttered, undi *antonyms* disordered, disorderly, messy, untidy.

nebulous *adj.* ambiguous, amorphous, cloudy, confused, dim, fuzzy, hazy, imprecise, indefinite, indeterminate,

indistinct, misty, murky, obscure, shadowy, shapeless, uncertain, unclear, unformed, unspecific, vague.

antonym clear.

necessary *adj.* certain, compulsory, de rigueur, essential, fated, imperative, indispensable, ineluctable, inescapable, inevitable, inexorable, mandatory, needed, needful, obligatory, required, requisite, unavoidable, vital.

antonyms inessential, unimportant, unnecessary.

necessity *n.* ananke, compulsion, demand, desideratum, destiny, destitution, essential, exigency, extremity, fate, fundamental, indigence, indispensability, inevitability, inexorableness, necessary, need, needfulness, obligation, penury, poverty, prerequisite, privation, requirement, requisite, sine qua non, want.

necromancy *n.* black art, black magic, conjuration, demonology, divination, enchantment, hoodoo, magic, sorcery, thaumaturgy, voodoo, witchcraft, witchery, wizardry.

need *v.* call for, crave, demand, lack, miss, necessitate, require, want.

n. besoin, demand, deprivation, desideratum, destitution, distress, egence, egency, emergency, essential, exigency, extremity, impecuniousness, inadequacy, indigence, insufficiency, lack, longing, necessity, neediness, obligation, paucity, penury, poverty, privation, requirement, requisite, shortage, urgency, want, wish.

antonym sufficiency.

needed *adj.* called for, compulsory, desired, essential, lacking, necessary, obligatory, required, requisite, wanted.

antonyms unnecessary, unneeded.

needle *v.* aggravate, annoy, bait, goad, harass, irk, irritate, nag, nettle, pester, prick, prod, provoke, rile, ruffle, spur, sting, taunt, torment.

needless *adj.* causeless, dispensable, excessive, expendable, gratuitous, groundless, inessential, non-essential, pointless, purposeless, redundant, superfluous, uncalled-for, unessential, unnecessary, unwanted, useless.

antonyms necessary, needful.

needy *adj.* deprived, destitute, disadvantaged, impecunious, impoverished, indigent, penniless, penurious, poor, poverty-stricken, underprivileged.

antonyms affluent, wealthy, well-off.

nefarious *adj.* abominable, atrocious, base, criminal, depraved, detestable, dreadful, evil, execrable, foul, heinous, horrible, infamous, infernal, iniquitous, monstrous, odious, opprobrious, satanic, shameful, sinful, unholy, vicious, vile, villainous, wicked.

antonym exemplary.

negate *v.* abrogate, annul, cancel, contradict, countermand, deny, disallow, disprove, gainsay, invalidate, neutralize, nullify, oppose, quash, refute, repeal, rescind, retract, reverse, revoke, void, wipe out.

antonym affirm.

antonyms optimistic, positive.

n. contradiction, denial, opposite, refusal.

neglect *v.* contemn, disdain, disprovide, disregard, forget, ignore, leave alone, let slide, omit, overlook, pass by, pigeon-hole, rebuff, scorn, shirk, skimp, slight, spurn.

antonyms cherish, nurture, treasure.

n. carelessness, default, dereliction, disdain, disregard, disrespect, failure, forgetfulness, heedlessness, inattention, indifference, laches, laxity, laxness, neglectfulness, negligence, oversight, slackness, slight, slovenliness, unconcern.

negligent *adj.* careless, cursory, disregardful, forgetful, inattentive, indifferent, lax, neglectful, nonchalant, offhand, regardless, remiss, slack, thoughtless, uncareful, uncaring, unmindful, unthinking.

antonyms attentive, careful, heedful, scrupulous.

negligible *adj.* imperceptible, inconsequential, insignificant, minor, minute, neglectable, nugatory, petty, small, trifling, trivial, unimportant.

antonym significant.

negotiate *v.* adjudicate, arbitrate, arrange, bargain, broke, clear, conciliate, confer, consult, contract, cross, deal, debate, discuss, get past, handle, manage, mediate, parley, pass, settle, surmount, transact, traverse, treat, work out.

neighborhood *n.* community, confines, district, environs, locale, locality, precincts, proximity, purlieus, quarter, region, surroundings, vicinage, vicinity.

neighboring *adj.* abutting, adjacent, adjoining, bordering, connecting, contiguous, near, nearby, nearest, next, surrounding, vicinal.

antonyms distant, faraway, remote.

neighborly *adj.* amiable, chummy, civil, companionable, considerate, friendly, genial, helpful, hospitable, kind, obliging, sociable, social, solicitous, well-disposed.

nerve *n.* audacity, boldness, bottle, brass, bravery, brazenness, cheek, chutzpah, coolness, courage, daring, determination, effrontery, endurance, energy, fearlessness, firmness, force, fortitude, gall, gameness, grit, guts, hardihood, impertinence, impudence, insolence, intrepidity, mettle, might, pluck, resolution, sauce, spirit, spunk, steadfastness, temerity, vigor, will.

antonyms cowardice, weakness.

v. bolster, brace, embolden, encourage, fortify, hearten, invigorate, steel, strengthen.

antonym unnerve.

nervous *adj.* agitated, anxious, apprehensive, edgy, excitable, fearful, fidgety, flustered, hesitant, highly-strung, high-strung, hysterical, jittery, jumpy, nervy, neurotic, on edge, shaky, tense, timid, timorous, twitchy, uneasy, uptight, weak, windy, worried.

antonyms bold, calm, confident, cool, relaxed.

nest *n.* breeding-ground, burrow, den, drey, earth, form, formicary, haunt, hideaway, hotbed, nid(e), nidus, refuge, resort, retreat.

nestle *v.* cuddle, curl up, ensconce, huddle, nuzzle, snuggle.

net[1] *n.* drag, drag-net, drift, drift-net, drop-net, lattice, mesh, netting, network, open-work, reticulum, tracery, web.

v. apprehend, bag, benet, capture, catch, enmesh, ensnare, entangle, nab, trap.

net[2] *adj.* after tax, clear, final, lowest, nett.

v. accumulate, bring in, clear, earn, gain, make, obtain, realize, reap, receive, secure.

nettle *v.* annoy, chafe, discountenance, exasperate, fret, goad, harass, incense, irritate, needle, pique, provoke, ruffle, sting, tease, vex.

neurotic *adj.* abnormal, anxious, compulsive, deviant, disordered, distraught, disturbed, maladjusted, manic, morbid, nervous, obsessive, overwrought, unhealthy, unstable, wearisome.

antonyms normal, stable.

neutral *adj.* colorless, disinterested, dispassionate, dull,

even-handed, expressionless, impartial, indeterminate, indifferent, indistinct, indistinguishable, intermediate, non-aligned, non-committal, nondescript, non-partisan, unbia(s)sed, uncommitted, undecided, undefined, uninvolved, unprejudiced.

antonyms biased, prejudiced.

nevertheless *adv.* anyhow, anyway, but, even so, however, nonetheless, notwithstanding, regardless, still, yet.

new *adj.* added, advanced, altered, changed, contemporary, current, different, extra, fresh, improved, latest, modern, modernistic, modernized, modish, more, newborn, newfangled, novel, original, recent, redesigned, renewed, restored, supplementary, topical, trendy, ultra-modern, unfamiliar, unknown, unused, unusual, up-to-date, up-to-the-minute, virgin.

antonyms hackneyed, old, outdated, out-of-date, usual.

newcomer *n.* alien, arrival, arriviste, beginner, colonist, foreigner, immigrant, incomer, Johnny-come-lately, novice, outsider, parvenu, settler, stranger.

news *n.* account, advice, bulletin, communiqué, disclosure, dispatch, exposé, gen, gossip, hearsay, information, intelligence, latest, leak, release, report, revelation, rumor, scandal, statement, story, tidings, update, word.

next *adj.* adjacent, adjoining, closest, consequent, ensuing, following, later, nearest, neighboring, sequent, sequential, subsequent, succeeding.

antonyms preceding, previous.

adv. afterwards, later, subsequently, then, thereafter.

nibble *n.* bit, bite, crumb, morsel, peck, piece, snack, soupçon, taste, titbit.

v. bite, eat, gnaw, knap, knapple, munch, nip, nosh, peck, pickle.

nice *adj.* accurate, agreeable, amiable, attractive, careful, charming, commendable, courteous, critical, cultured, dainty, delicate, delightful, discriminating, exact, exacting, fastidious, fine, finical, friendly, genteel, good, kind, likable, meticulous, neat, particular, pleasant, pleasurable, polite, precise, prepossessing, punctilious, purist, refined, respectable, rigorous, scrupulous, strict, subtle, tidy, trim, virtuous, well-bred, well-mannered.

antonyms careless, disagreeable, haphazard, nasty, unpleasant.

niche[1] *n.* alcove, corner, cubby, cubby-hole, hollow, nook, opening, recess.

niche[2] *n.* calling, métier, pigeon-hole, place, position, slot, vocation.

nick[1] *n.* chip, cut, damage, dent, indent, indentation, mark, notch, scar, score, scratch, snick.

v. chip, cut, damage, dent, indent, mark, notch, scar, score, scratch, snick.

nick[2] *v.* finger, knap, knock off, lag, pilfer, pinch, snitch, steal.

nickname *n.* cognomen, diminutive, epithet, familiarity, label, moni(c)ker, pet name, sobriquet.

niggardly *adj.* avaricious, beggarly, cheese-paring, close, covetous, frugal, grudging, hard-fisted, inadequate, insufficient, meager, mean, mercenary, miserable, miserly, near, paltry, parsimonious, penurious, scanty, skimpy, small, sordid, sparing, stinging, stingy, tight-fisted, ungenerous, ungiving, wretched.

antonyms bountiful, generous.

nightmare *n.* bad dream, ephialtes, hallucination,

horror, incubus, ordeal, succubus, torment, trial, tribulation.

nil *n.* duck, goose-egg, love, naught, nihil, none, nothing, zero.

nimble *adj.* active, agile, alert, brisk, deft, dexterous, light-foot(ed), lissom(e), lively, nippy, proficient, prompt, quick, quick-witted, ready, smart, sprightly, spry, swift, volant.
antonyms awkward, clumsy.

nincompoop *n.* blockhead, dimwit, dolt, dunce, fool, idiot, ignoramus, ninny, nitwit, noodle, numskull, sap, saphead, simpleton.

nip[1] *v.* bite, catch, check, clip, compress, grip, nibble, pinch, snag, snap, sneap, snip, squeeze, tweak, twitch.

nip[2] *n.* dram, draught, drop, finger, mouthful, peg, portion, shot, sip, slug, snifter, soupçon, sup, swallow, taste.

nippy[1] *adj.* astringent, biting, chilly, nipping, pungent, sharp, stinging.

nippy[2] *adj.* active, agile, fast, nimble, quick, speedy, sprightly, spry.
antonym slow.

nit-picking *adj.* captious, carping, caviling, finicky, fussy, hair-splitting, hypercritical, pedantic, pettifogging, quibbling.

noble *n.* aristocrat, baron, gentilhomme, grand seigneur, lord, nobleman, patrician, peer.
antonyms pleb, prole.
adj. aristocratic, august, blue-blooded, dignified, distinguished, elevated, eminent, excellent, generous, gentle, grand, great, high-born, honorable, honored, imposing, impressive, lofty, lordly, magnanimous, magnificent, majestic, patrician, splendid, stately, titled, upright, virtuous, worthy.
antonyms base, ignoble, low-born.

nobody *n.* also-ran, cipher, lightweight, man of straw, menial, minnow, nonentity, no-one, nothing, Walter Mitty.
antonym somebody.

nod *v.* acknowledge, agree, assent, beckon, bob, bow, concur, dip, doze, droop, drowse, duck, gesture, indicate, nap, salute, sign, signal, sleep, slip up, slump.
n. acknowledgment, beck, cue, gesture, greeting, indication, salute, sign, signal.

node *n.* bud, bump, burl, caruncle, growth, knob, knot, lump, nodule, process, protuberance, swelling.

noise *n.* babble, ballyhoo, blare, brattle, chirm, clamor, clash, clatter, coil, commotion, cry, din, fracas, hubbub, outcry, pandemonium, racket, row, sound, talk, tumult, uproar.
antonyms quiet, silence.
v. advertise, announce, bruit, circulate, gossip, publicize, repeat, report, rumor.

noisome *adj.* bad, baneful, deleterious, disgusting, fetid, foul, fulsome, harmful, hurtful, injurious, malodorous, mephitic, mischievous, noxious, offensive, pernicious, pestiferous, pestilential, poisonous, putrid, reeking, smelly, stinking, unhealthy, unwholesome.
antonyms balmy, pleasant, wholesome.

noisy *adj.* boisterous, cacophonous, chattering, clamorous, clangorous, deafening, ear-piercing, ear-splitting, horrisonant, loud, obstreperous, piercing, plangent, rackety, riotous, strepitant, strident, tumultuous, turbulent, uproarious, vocal, vociferous.
antonyms peaceful, quiet, silent.

nomad *n.* drifter, itinerant, migrant, rambler, roamer, rover, traveler, vagabond, vagrant, wanderer.

nominate *v.* appoint, assign, choose, commission, designate, elect, elevate, empower, mention, name, present, propose, put up, recommend, select, submit, suggest, term.

nomination *n.* appointment, choice, designation, election, proposal, recommendation, selection, submission, suggestion.

nominee *n.* appointee, assignee, candidate, contestant, entrant, protégé, runner.

nonchalant *adj.* airy, apathetic, blasé, calm, careless, casual, collected, cool, detached, dispassionate, impassive, indifferent, insouciant, offhand, pococurante, unconcerned, unemotional, unperturbed.
antonyms anxious, careful, concerned, worried.

non-committal *adj.* ambiguous, careful, cautious, circumspect, cunctatious, cunctative, cunctatory, discreet, equivocal, evasive, guarded, indefinite, neutral, politic, reserved, tactful, temporizing, tentative, unrevealing, vague, wary.

nonconformist *n.* deviant, dissenter, dissentient, eccentric, heretic, iconoclast, individualist, maverick, oddball, protester, radical, rebel, seceder, secessionist.
antonym conformist.

nondescript *adj.* commonplace, dull, featureless, indeterminate, mousy, ordinary, plain, unclassified, undistinctive, undistinguished, unexceptional, uninspiring, uninteresting, unmemorable, unremarkable, vague.

nonentity *n.* cipher, dandiprat, drip, drongo, earthworm, gnatling, lightweight, mediocrity, nobody.

non-essential *adj.* dispensable, excessive, expendable, extraneous, extrinsic(al), inessential, peripheral, superfluous, supplementary, unimportant, unnecessary.
antonym essential.

non-existent *adj.* chimerical, fancied, fictional, hallucinatory, hypothetical, illusory, imaginary, imagined, immaterial, incorporeal, insubstantial, legendary, missing, mythical, null, unreal.
antonyms actual, existing, real.

nonplus *v.* astonish, astound, baffle, bewilder, confound, confuse, discomfit, disconcert, discountenance, dismay, dumbfound, embarrass, flabbergast, flummox, mystify, perplex, puzzle, stump, stun, take aback.

nonsense *n.* absurdity, balderdash, balls, baloney, bilge, blah, blather, blethers, bollocks, bombast, bosh, bull, bullshit, bunk, bunkum, claptrap, cobblers, codswallop, crap, double-Dutch, drivel, fadaise, faddle, fandangle, fatuity, fiddle-de-dee, fiddle-faddle, fiddlesticks, flapdoodle, folly, foolishness, fudge, gaff, galimatias, gammon, gas and gaiters, gibberish, gobbledygook, havers, hogwash, hooey, inanity, jabberwock(y), jest, ludicrousness, moonshine, no-meaning, piffle, pulp, ridiculousness, rot, rubbish, senselessness, silliness, squish, squit, stuff, stultiloquence, stupidity, tar(r)adiddle, tommy-rot, tosh, trash, twaddle, twattle, unreason, waffle.
antonym sense.

nonsensical *adj.* absurd, crazy, daft, fatuous, foolish, inane, incomprehensible, irrational, ludicrous, meaningless, ridiculous, senseless, silly.
antonyms logical, sensible.

non-stop *adj.* ceaseless, constant, continuous, direct, endless, incessant, interminable, never-ending, ongoing, relentless, round-the-clock, steady, unbroken, unceasing, unending, unfaltering, uninterrupted, unrelenting, unremitting.

antonyms intermittent, occasional.

adv. ceaselessly, constantly, continuously, directly, endlessly, incessantly, interminably, relentlessly, round-the-clock, steadily, unbrokenly, unceasingly, unendingly, unfalteringly, uninterruptedly, unrelentingly, unremittingly.

antonyms imtermittently, occasionally.

nook *n.* alcove, cavity, corner, cranny, crevice, cubbyhole, hide-out, ingle-nook, nest, niche, opening, recess, retreat, shelter.

normal *adj.* accustomed, acknowledged, average, common, common-or-garden, conventional, habitual, mainstream, natural, ordinary, par for the course, popular, rational, reasonable, regular, routine, run-of-the-mill, sane, standard, straight, typical, usual, well-adjusted.

antonyms abnormal, irregular, odd, peculiar.

normally *adv.* as a rule, characteristically, commonly, habitually, ordinarily, regularly, straight, typically, usually.

antonym abnormally.

nos(e)y *adj.* curious, eavesdropping, inquisitive, interfering, intermeddling, intrusive, meddlesome, officious, prying, snooping.

nostalgia *n.* homesickness, longing, mal du pays, pining, regret, regretfulness, remembrance, reminiscence, wistfulness, yearning.

notable *adj.* celebrated, conspicuous, distinguished, eminent, evident, extraordinary, famous, impressive, manifest, marked, memorable, noteworthy, noticeable, notorious, outstanding, overt, pre-eminent, pronounced, rare, remarkable, renowned, signal, striking, uncommon, unusual, well-known.

antonyms commonplace, ordinary, usual.

n. celebrity, dignitary, luminary, notability, personage, somebody, VIP, worthy.

antonyms nobody, nonentity.

notch *n.* cleft, cut, degree, grade, incision, indentation, insection, kerf, level, mark, nick, score, sinus, snip, step.

v. cut, gimp, indent, mark, nick, raffle, scallop, score, scratch.

note *n.* annotation, apostil(le), billet, celebrity, character, comment, communication, consequence, distinction, eminence, epistle, epistolet, fame, gloss, heed, indication, jotting, letter, line, mark, memo, memorandum, message, minute, notice, observation, prestige, record, regard, remark, reminder, renown, reputation, signal, symbol, token.

v. denote, designate, detect, enter, indicate, mark, mention, notice, observe, perceive, record, register, remark, see, witness.

noted *adj.* acclaimed, celebrated, conspicuous, distinguished, eminent, famous, great, illustrious, notable, notorious, prominent, recognized, renowned, respected, well-known.

noteworthy *adj.* exceptional, extraordinary, important, notable, on the map, outstanding, remarkable, significant, unusual, visitable.

antonyms commonplace, ordinary, unexceptional, usual.

notice *v.* descry, detect, discern, distinguish, espy, heed, mark, mind, note, observe, perceive, remark, see, spot.

antonyms ignore, overlook.

n. advertisement, advice, affiche, announcement, attention, bill, civility, cognizance, comment, communication, consideration, criticism, heed, instruction, intelligence, intimation, news, note, notification, observation, order, poster, regard, respect, review, sign, warning.

notify *v.* acquaint, advise, alert, announce, apprize, declare, disclose, inform, publish, reveal, tell, warn.

notion *n.* apprehension, belief, caprice, conceit, concept, conception, concetto, construct, desire, fancy, idea, image, impression, impulse, inclination, inkling, judgment, knowledge, opinion, sentiment, understanding, view, whim, wish.

notorious *adj.* arrant, blatant, dishonorable, disreputable, egregious, flagrant, glaring, infamous, obvious, open, opprobrious, overt, patent, scandalous, undisputed.

nourish *v.* attend, cherish, comfort, cultivate, encourage, feed, foster, furnish, harbor, maintain, nurse, nurture, promote, supply, support, sustain, tend.

nourishment *n.* aliment, diet, food, goodness, nutriment, nutrition, pabulum, provender, sustenance, viands, victuals.

novel *adj.* different, fresh, imaginative, innovative, new, original, rare, singular, strange, surprising, uncommon, unconventional, unfamiliar, unusual.

antonyms familiar, ordinary.

n. fiction, narrative, romance, saga, story, tale, yarn.

novice *n.* amateur, apprentice, beginner, catechumen, convert, cub, griffin, Johnny-raw, learner, neophyte, newcomer, novitiate, probationer, proselyte, pupil, tiro.

antonyms doyen, expert, professional.

now *adv.* at once, at present, directly, immediately, instanter, instantly, next, nowadays, presently, promptly, straightaway, these days.

noxious *adj.* baneful, corrupting, deadly, deleterious, destructive, detrimental, foul, harmful, hurtful, injurious, insalubrious, mephitic(al), morbiferous, morbific, noisome, pernicious, pestilential, poisonous, unhealthy, unwholesome.

antonyms innocuous, wholesome.

nucleus *n.* basis, center, core, crux, focus, heart, heartlet, kernel, nub, pivot.

nude *adj.* au naturel, bare, disrobed, exposed, in one's birthday suit, in puris naturalibus, in the altogether, in the buff, naked, starkers, stark-naked, stripped, unattired, unclad, unclothed, uncovered, undraped, undressed, without a stitch.

antonyms clothed, covered, dressed.

nudge *v.*, *n.* bump, dig, jog, poke, prod, prompt, push, shove, touch.

nugget *n.* chunk, clump, hunk, lump, mass, piece, wodge.

nuisance *n.* annoyance, bore, bother, désagrément, drag, drawback, inconvenience, infliction, irritation, offence, pain, pest, plague, problem, trouble, vexation.

nullify *v.* abate, abolish, abrogate, annul, cancel, counteract, countervail, invalidate, negate, neutralize, quash, repeal, rescind, revoke, undermine, veto, vitiate, void.

antonym validate.

numb *adj.* benumbed, dead, deadened, frozen, immobilized, insensate, insensible, insensitive, paralyzed, stunned, stupefied, torpid, unfeeling.
antonym sensitive.
v. anesthetize, benumb, deaden, dull, freeze, immobilize, obtund, paralyze, stun, stupefy.
antonym sensitize.

number¹ *n.* aggregate, amount, character, collection, company, count, crowd, digit, figure, folio, horde, index, integer, many, multitude, numeral, quantity, several, sum, throng, total, unit.
v. account, add, apportion, calculate, compute, count, enumerate, include, inventory, reckon, tell, total.

number² *n.* copy, edition, impression, imprint, issue, printing, volume.

numeral *n.* character, cipher, digit, figure, folio, integer, number.

numerous *adj.* abundant, copious, divers, many, multitudinous, myriad, plentiful, profuse, several, sundry.
antonyms few, scanty.

numskull *n.* blockhead, bonehead, buffoon, clot, dimwit, dolt, dope, dullard, dummy, dunce, dunderhead, fathead, fool, sap, saphead, simpleton, thickhead, twit.

nuptials *n.* bridal, espousal, marriage, matrimony, spousals, wedding.

nurse *v.* breast-feed, care for, cherish, cultivate, encourage, feed, foster, harbor, keep, nourish, nurture, preserve, promote, succor, suckle, support, sustain, tend, treat, wet-nurse.
n. amah, district-nurse, home-nurse, mammy, nanny, nursemaid, sister of mercy, wet nurse.

nurture *n.* care, cultivation, development, diet, discipline, education, food, instruction, nourishment, rearing, training, upbringing.
v. bring up, care for, cultivate, develop, discipline, educate, feed, instruct, nourish, nurse, rear, school, support, sustain, tend, train.

nutriment *n.* aliment, diet, food, foodstuff, nourishment, nutrition, pabulum, provender, subsistence, support, sustenance.

nutrition *n.* eutrophy, food, nourishment, nutriment, sustenance.

O

oaf *n.* baboon, blockhead, bonehead, booby, brute, clod, dolt, dullard, dummy, dunce, fool, galoot, gawk, goon, gorilla, half-wit, hick, hobbledehoy, hulk, idiot, imbecile, lout, lummox, moron, nincompoop, oik, sap, schlemiel, schlep, simpleton, yob.

oasis *n.* enclave, haven, island, refuge, resting-place, retreat, sanctuary, sanctum, watering-hole.

oath *n.* affirmation, assurance, avowal, blasphemy, bond, curse, cuss, expletive, imprecation, malediction, pledge, plight, profanity, promise, swear-word, vow, word, word of honor.

obdurate *adj.* adamant, callous, dogged, firm, fixed, flinty, hard, hard-hearted, harsh, immovable, implac-

able, inexorable, inflexible, intransigent, iron, mulish, obstinate, perverse, pig-headed, relentless, stiff-necked, stony, stubborn, unbending, unfeeling, unrelenting, unshakable, unyielding.
antonyms submissive, tender.

obedience *n.* accordance, acquiescence, agreement, allegiance, amenableness, compliance, conformability, deference, docility, dutifulness, duty, observance, passivity, respect, reverence, submission, submissiveness, subservience, tractability.
antonym disobedience.

obedient *adj.* acquiescent, amenable, biddable, compliant, deferential, docile, duteous, dutiful, law-abiding, observant, passive, regardful, respectful, sequacious, submissive, subservient, tractable, unquestioning, unresisting, well-trained, yielding.
antonyms disobedient, rebellious, refractory, unruly, wilful.

obese *adj.* bulky, corpulent, Falstaffian, fat, fleshy, gross, heavy, outsize, overweight, paunchy, plump, podgy, ponderous, portly, pursy, roly-poly, rotund, stout, tubby.
antonyms skinny, slender, thin.

obey *v.* abide by, act upon, adhere to, be ruled by, bow to, carry out, comply, conform, defer (to), discharge, embrace, execute, follow, fulfil, give in, give way, heed, implement, keep, knuckle under, mind, observe, perform, respond, serve, submit, surrender, take orders from, toe the line, yield.
antonym disobey.

object¹ *n.* aim, article, body, butt, design, end, entity, fact, focus, goal, idea, intent, intention, item, motive, objective, phenomenon, point, purpose, raison d'être, reality, reason, recipient, target, thing, victim, visible.

object² *v.* argue, complain, demur, dissent, expostulate, oppose, protest, rebut, refuse, repudiate, take exception.
antonyms accede, acquiesce, agree, assent.

objection *n.* cavil, censure, challenge, complaint, counter-argument, demur, doubt, exception, niggle, opposition, protest, remonstrance, scruple.
antonyms agreement, assent.

objectionable *adj.* abhorrent, antisocial, deplorable, despicable, detestable, disagreeable, dislikable, displeasing, distasteful, exceptionable, indecorous, insufferable, intolerable, loathsome, noxious, obnoxious, offensive, regrettable, repugnant, unacceptable, undesirable, unpleasant, unseemly.
antonyms acceptable, pleasant, welcome.

objective *adj.* calm, detached, disinterested, dispassionate, equitable, even-handed, fair, impartial, impersonal, judicial, just, open-minded, sensible, sober, unbiased, uncolored, unemotional, unimpassioned, uninvolved, unprejudiced.
antonyms biased, subjective.
n. aim, ambition, aspiration, design, destination, end, goal, intention, mark, object, prize, purpose, target.

objectivity *n.* detachment, disinterest, disinterestedness, dispassion, equitableness, even-handedness, impartiality, impersonality, open mind, open-mindedness.
antonyms bias, subjectivity.

obligation *n.* accountability, accountableness, agreement, bond, burden, charge, commitment, compulsion, contract, debt, duty, engagement, indebtedness,

liability, must, obstriction, onus, promise, requirement, responsibility, stipulation, trust, understanding.
antonyms choice, discretion.

obligatory *adj.* binding, bounden, coercive, compulsory,
de rigueur, enforced, essential, imperative, mandatory,
necessary, required, requisite, statutory, unavoidable.
antonym optional.

oblige *v.* accommodate, assist, benefit, bind, coerce,
compel, constrain, do a favor, favor, force, gratify,
help, impel, indulge, make, necessitate, obligate,
please, require, serve.

obliging *adj.* accommodating, agreeable, aidful, amiable,
civil, complaisant, considerate, co-operative, courteous, eager, friendly, good-natured, helpful, kind,
polite, willing.
antonyms inconsiderate, unhelpful, unkind.

obliterate *v.* annihilate, blot out, cancel, delete, destroy,
efface, eradicate, erase, expunge, extirpate, rub out,
vaporize, wipe out.

oblivious *adj.* blind, careless, comatose, deaf, disregardful, forgetful, heedless, ignorant, inattentive, insensible, neglectful, negligent, nescient, regardless,
unaware, unconcerned, unconscious, unmindful,
unobservant.
antonyms aware, conscious.

obloquy *n.* abuse, animadversion, aspersion, attack, bad
press, blame, calumny, censure, contumely, criticism,
defamation, detraction, discredit, disfavor, disgrace,
dishonor, humiliation, ignominy, infamy, invective,
odium, opprobrium, reproach, shame, slander, stigma,
vilification.

obnoxious *adj.* abhorrent, abominable, detestable, disagreeable, disgusting, dislikable, foul, fulsome, hateful,
horrid, insufferable, loathsome, nasty, nauseating,
nauseous, noisome, objectionable, odious, offensive,
repellent, reprehensible, repugnant, repulsive, revolting, sickening, unpleasant.
antonyms agreeable, likable, pleasant.

obscene *adj.* atrocious, barrack-room, bawdy, blue,
coarse, dirty, disgusting, evil, Fescennine, filthy, foul,
gross, heinous, immodest, immoral, improper, impure,
indecent, lewd, licentious, loathsome, loose, offensive,
outrageous, pornographic, prurient, Rabelaisian,
ribald, salacious, scabrous, scurrilous, shameless,
shocking, sickening, smutty, suggestive, unchaste,
unwholesome, vile, wicked.
antonyms clean, decent, decorous.

obscure *adj.* abstruse, ambiguous, arcane, blurred,
caliginous, clear as mud, clouded, cloudy, concealed,
confusing, cryptic, deep, Delphic, dim, doubtful,
dusky, enigmatic, esoteric, faint, gloomy, hazy, hermetic, hidden, humble, incomprehensible, inconspicuous, indefinite, indistinct, inglorious, intricate,
involved, little-known, lowly, minor, misty, murky,
mysterious, nameless, obfuscated, occult, opaque,
oracular, out-of-the-way, recondite, remote, riddling,
shadowy, shady, somber, tenebr(i)ous, tenebrose, twilight, unclear, undistinguished, unheard-of, unhon-
ored, unimportant, unknown, unlit, unnoted, unobvious, unrenowned, unseen, unsung, vague, veiled.
antonyms clear, definite, explicit, famous, lucid.

v. bedim, befog, block out, blur, cloak, cloud, conceal,
cover, darken, dim, disguise, dull, eclipse, hide, mask,
muddy, obfuscate, overshadow, screen, shade, shadow,
shroud, veil.

antonyms clarify, illuminate.

obsequious *adj.* abject, cringing, deferential, dough-
faced, fawning, flattering, groveling, ingratiating, knee-
crooking, menial, oily, servile, slavish, slimy, smarmy,
submissive, subservient, sycophantic, toadying, unctuous.
antonym assertive.

observant *adj.* alert, attentive, eagle-eyed, eagle-sighted,
falcon-eyed, heedful, mindful, perceptive, percipient,
quick, sharp-eyed, vigilant, watchful, wide-awake.
antonyms inattentive, unobservant.

observation *n.* annotation, attention, cognition, comment, consideration, discernment, examination, experience, finding, information, inspection, knowledge,
monitoring, note, notice, obiter dictum, opinion, perception, pronouncement, reading, reflection, remark,
review, scrutiny, study, surveillance, thought, utterance, watching.

observe *v.* abide by, adhere to, animadvert, celebrate,
commemorate, comment, comply, conform to, contemplate, declare, detect, discern, discover, espy, follow,
fulfil, heed, honor, keep, keep an eye on, keep tabs on,
mention, mind, monitor, note, notice, obey, opine,
perceive, perform, regard, remark, remember, respect,
say, scrutinize, see, solemnize, spot, state, study, sur-
veille, survey, view, watch, witness.
antonyms break, miss, overlook, violate.

observer *n.* beholder, bystander, commentator, dis-
cerner, eyewitness, looker-on, noter, onlooker, spectator, spotter, viewer, watcher, witness.

obsession *n.* bee in one's bonnet, complex, enthusiasm,
fetish, fixation, hang-up, idée fixe, infatuation, mania,
monomania, phobia, preoccupation, ruling passion,
thing, zelotypia.

obsolete *adj.* anachronistic, ancient, antediluvian, antiquated, antique, archaic, bygone, dated, dead,
démodé, discarded, disused, extinct, fogram, horse-
and-buggy, musty, old, old hat, old-fashioned, out, out
of date, outmoded, outworn, passé, superannuated.
antonyms contemporary, current, modern, new, up-to-
date.

obstacle *n.* bar, barrier, boyg, catch, check, chicane,
difficulty, drawback, hindrance, hitch, hurdle, impediment, interference, interruption, obstruction, pons
asinorum, remora, snag, stop, stumbling-block, stum-
bling-stone.
antonyms advantage, help.

obstinate *adj.* bullet-headed, bull-headed, bullish,
camelish, contumacious, determined, dogged, firm,
headstrong, immovable, inflexible, intractable, intransigent, mulish, obdurate, opinionated, persistent, pertinacious, perverse, pervicacious, pig-headed, recalcitrant, refractory, restive, rusty, self-willed, steadfast,
stomachful, strong-minded, stubborn, sturdy, tenacious, unadvisable, unyielding, uppity, wilful, wrong-
headed.
antonyms co-operative, flexible, pliant, submissive.

obstruct *v.* arrest, bar, barricade, block, check, choke,
clog, crab, cumber, curb, cut off, frustrate, hamper,
hamstring, hide, hinder, hold up, impede, inhibit,
interfere with, interrupt, mask, obscure, occlude, prevent, restrict, retard, shield, shut off, slow down, stall,
stonewall, stop, stuff, thwart, trammel.
antonym help.

obstruction *n.* bar, barricade, barrier, blockage, check, difficulty, filibuster, hindrance, impediment, snag, stop, stoppage, trammel, traverse.

antonym help.

obtain[1] *v.* achieve, acquire, attain, come by, compass, earn, gain, get, impetrate, procure, secure.

obtain[2] *v.* be in force, be prevalent, be the case, exist, hold, prevail, reign, rule, stand.

obtrusive *adj.* blatant, forward, importunate, interfering, intrusive, manifest, meddling, nosy, noticeable, obvious, officious, prominent, protruding, protuberant, prying, pushy.

antonym unobtrusive.

obtuse *adj.* blunt, boneheaded, crass, dense, dopey, dull, dull-witted, dumb, imperceptive, impercipient, inattentive, insensitive, retarded, rounded, slow, stolid, stupid, thick, thick-skinned, uncomprehending, unintelligent.

antonyms bright, sharp.

obviate *v.* anticipate, avert, counter, counteract, divert, forestall, preclude, prevent, remove.

obvious *adj.* apparent, clear, conspicuous, discernible, distinct, evident, glaring, indisputable, manifest, noticeable, open, open-and-shut, overt, palpable, patent, perceptible, plain, prominent, pronounced, recognizable, self-evident, self-explanatory, straightforward, transparent, unconcealed, undeniable, undisguised, unmistakable, unsubtle, visible.

antonyms obscure, unclear.

obviously *adv.* certainly, clearly, distinctly, evidently, manifestly, of course, palpably, patently, plainly, undeniably, unmistakably, unquestionably, visibly, without doubt.

occasion *n.* affair, call, case, cause, celebration, chance, convenience, event, excuse, experience, ground(s), incident, inducement, influence, instance, justification, moment, motive, occurrence, opening, opportunity, prompting, provocation, reason, time.

v. bring about, bring on, cause, create, effect, elicit, engender, evoke, generate, give rise to, induce, influence, inspire, lead to, make, originate, persuade, produce, prompt, provoke.

occasional *adj.* casual, desultory, fitful, incidental, infrequent, intermittent, irregular, odd, periodic, rare, scattered, sporadic, uncommon.

antonym frequent.

occasionally *adv.* at intervals, at times, every so often, from time to time, infrequently, irregularly, now and again, now and then, off and on, on and off, on occasion, once in a while, periodically, sometimes, sporadically.

antonym frequently.

occult *adj.* abstruse, arcane, cabbalistic, concealed, esoteric, faint, hidden, impenetrable, invisible, magical, mysterious, mystic, mystical, mystifying, obscure, preternatural, recondite, secret, supernatural, unknown, unrevealed, veiled.

v. conceal, cover (up), enshroud, hide, mask, obscure, screen, shroud, veil.

antonym reveal.

occupant *n.* addressee, denizen, holder, householder, incumbent, indweller, inhabitant, inmate, lessee, occupier, resident, squatter, tenant, user.

occupation[1] *n.* absorption, activity, business, calling, craft, employment, job, line, post, profession, pursuit, trade, vocation, walk of life, work.

occupation[2] *n.* billet, conquest, control, habitation, holding, invasion, occupancy, possession, residence, seizure, subjugation, takeover, tenancy, tenure, use.

occupy *v.* absorb, amuse, beguile, busy, capture, conquer, cover, divert, dwell in, employ, engage, engross, ensconce oneself in, entertain, establish oneself in, fill, garrison, hold, immerse, inhabit, interest, invade, involve, keep, keep busy, live in, monopolize, overrun, own, permeate, pervade, possess, preoccupy, reside in, seize, stay in, take over, take possession of, take up, tenant, tie up, use, utilize.

occur *v.* appear, arise, be found, be met with, be present, befall, betide, chance, come about, come off, come to pass, crop up, develop, eventuate, exist, happen, intervene, manifest itself, materialize, obtain, result, show itself, take place, transpire, turn up.

occur to come to mind, come to one, cross one's mind, dawn on, enter one's head, present itself, spring to mind, strike one, suggest itself.

occurrence *n.* action, adventure, affair, appearance, case, circumstance, development, episode, event, existence, happening, incident, instance, manifestation, materialization, proceeding, transaction.

ocean *n.* briny, main, profound, sea, the deep, the drink.

odd[1] *adj.* abnormal, atypical, bizarre, curious, deviant, different, eccentric, exceptional, extraordinary, fantastic, freak, freakish, freaky, funky, funny, irregular, kinky, outlandish, peculiar, quaint, queer, rare, remarkable, singular, strange, uncanny, uncommon, unconventional, unexplained, unusual, weird, whimsical.

antonym normal.

odd[2] *adj.* auxiliary, casual, fragmentary, ill-matched, incidental, irregular, left-over, lone, miscellaneous, occasional, periodic, random, remaining, seasonal, single, solitary, spare, sundry, surplus, uneven, unmatched, unpaired, varied, various.

odious *adj.* abhorrent, abominable, annoying, detestable, disgusting, execrable, foul, hateful, heinous, horrible, horrid, insufferable, loathsome, obnoxious, offensive, repellent, repugnant, repulsive, revolting, unpleasant, vile.

antonym pleasant.

odium *n.* abhorrence, animosity, antipathy, censure, condemnation, contempt, detestation, disapprobation, disapproval, discredit, disfavor, disgrace, dishonor, dislike, disrepute, execration, hatred, infamy, obloquy, opprobrium, reprobation, shame.

odor *n.* air, aroma, atmosphere, aura, bouquet, breath, emanation, essence, exhalation, flavor, fragrance, perfume, quality, redolence, scent, smell, spirit, stench, stink.

odyssey *n.* journey, travels, wandering.

off *adj.* abnormal, absent, bad, below par, canceled, decomposed, disappointing, disheartening, displeasing, finished, gone, high, inoperative, moldy, poor, postponed, quiet, rancid, rotten, slack, sour, substandard, turned, unavailable, unsatisfactory, wrong.

adv. apart, aside, at a distance, away, elsewhere, out.

off-color *adj.* faded, ill, indecent, indisposed, off form, out of sorts, pasty-faced, peaky, peelie-wally, poorly, queasy, sick, under the weather, unwell.

offend *v.* affront, annoy, disgruntle, disgust, displease, fret, gall, hip, hurt, insult, irritate, miff, nauseate, outrage, pain, pique, provoke, repel, repulse, rile, sicken, slight, snub, transgress, turn off, upset, vex, violate, wound, wrong.

antonym please.

offender *n.* criminal, culprit, delinquent, guilty party, law-breaker, malefactor, miscreant, misfeasor, sinner, transgressor, wrong-doer.

offense *n.* affront, anger, annoyance, crime, delict, delinquency, displeasure, fault, hard feelings, harm, huff, hurt, indignation, indignity, infraction, infringement, injury, injustice, insult, ire, lapse, misdeed, misdemeanor, needle, outrage, peccadillo, pique, put-down, resentment, sin, slight, snub, transgression, trespass, umbrage, violation, wrath, wrong, wrong-doing.

offensive *adj.* abominable, abusive, aggressive, annoying, attacking, detestable, disagreeable, discourteous, disgusting, displeasing, disrespectful, embarrassing, grisly, impertinent, insolent, insulting, intolerable, invading, irritating, loathsome, nasty, nauseating, noisome, objectionable, obnoxious, odious, rank, repellent, repugnant, revolting, rude, sickening, uncivil, unmannerly, unpalatable, unpleasant, unsavory, vile.

antonyms defensive, pleasing.

n. attack, drive, onslaught, push, raid, sortie, thrust.

offer *v.* advance, afford, bid, extend, furnish, give, hold out, make available, move, present, proffer, propose, propound, provide, put forth, put forward, show, submit, suggest, tender, volunteer.

n. approach, attempt, bid, endeavor, essay, overture, presentation, proposal, proposition, submission, suggestion, tender.

offhand *adj.* abrupt, aloof, brusque, careless, casual, cavalier, curt, glib, informal, offhanded, perfunctory, take-it-or-leave-it, unappreciative, uncaring, unceremonious, unconcerned, uninterested.

antonyms calculated, planned.

adv. at once, extempore, immediately, off the cuff, off the top of one's head, straightaway.

office *n.* appointment, bath, business, capacity, charge, commission, duty, employment, function, obligation, occupation, place, post, responsibility, role, room, service, situation, station, trust, work.

officiate *v.* adjudicate, chair, conduct, emcee, manage, oversee, preside, referee, serve, superintend, umpire.

offset *v.* balance out, cancel out, compare, compensate for, counteract, counterbalance, counterpoise, countervail, juxtapose, make up for, neutralize.

n. balance, compensation, counterbalance, counterweight, equipoise, equivalent, redress.

offshoot *n.* adjunct, appendage, arm, branch, by-product, development, embranchment, limb, outgrowth, spin-off, sprout, spur.

offspring *n.* brood, child, children, creation, descendant, descendants, family, fry, heir, heirs, issue, kids, litter, progeny, quiverful, result, scion, seed, spawn, successor, successors, young.

antonym parent(s).

often *adv.* again and again, frequently, generally, habitually, many a time, much, oft, over and over, regularly, repeatedly, time after time, time and again.

antonym seldom.

ogle *v.* eye, eye up, leer, look, make eyes at, stare.

ogre *n.* bogey, bogeyman, bogle, boyg, bugaboo, bug-bear, demon, devil, giant, humgruffi(a)n, monster, specter.

ointment *n.* balm, balsam, cerate, cream, demulcent, embrocation, emollient, liniment, lotion, salve, unction, unguent.

old *adj.* aboriginal, aged, age-old, ancient, antediluvian, antiquated, antique, archaic, bygone, cast-off, crumbling, dated, decayed, decrepit, done, earlier, early, elderly, erstwhile, ex-, experienced, familiar, former, gray, gray-haired, grizzled, hackneyed, hardened, hoary, immemorial, long-established, long-standing, mature, obsolete, of old, of yore, Ogygian, olden, old-fashioned, one-time, original, out of date, outdated, outmoded, over the hill, passé, patriarchal, practiced, preadamic(al), prehistoric, previous, primeval, primitive, primordial, pristine, quondam, remote, senescent, senile, skilled, stale, superannuated, time-honored, time-worn, traditional, unfashionable, unoriginal, venerable, versed, veteran, vintage, worn-out.

antonym young.

old-fashioned *adj.* ancient, antiquated, archaic, arriéré, behind the times, corny, dated, dead, démodé, fog(e)yish, fusty, horse-and-buggy, musty, neanderthal, obsolescent, obsolete, old hat, old-fog(e)yish, old-time, out of date, outdated, outmoded, passé, past, retro, square, superannuated, unfashionable.

antonyms contemporary, modern, up-to-date.

old-world *adj.* archaic, ceremonious, chivalrous, conservative, courtly, formal, gallant, old-fashioned, picturesque, quaint, traditional.

omen *n.* augury, auspice, boding, foreboding, foretoken, indication, portent, premonition, presage, prognostic, prognostication, sign, straw in the wind, warning, writing on the wall.

ominous *adj.* baleful, bodeful, dark, fateful, inauspicious, menacing, minatory, portentous, premonitory, presageful, sinister, threatening, unpromising, unpropitious.

antonym auspicious.

omission *n.* avoidance, bowdlerization, default, ellipsis, exclusion, failure, forgetfulness, gap, lack, neglect, oversight.

antonyms addition, inclusion.

omit *v.* disregard, drop, edit out, eliminate, exclude, fail, forget, give something a miss, leave out, leave undone, let slide, miss out, neglect, overlook, pass over, pretermit, skip.

antonyms add, include.

omnipotent *adj.* all-powerful, almighty, plenipotent, supreme.

antonym impotent.

omnipresent *adj.* pervasive, ubiquitary, ubiquitous, universal.

omniscient *adj.* all-knowing, all-seeing, pansophic.

once *adv.*. at one time, formerly, heretofore, in the old days, in the past, in times gone by, in times past, long ago, once upon a time, previously.

oncoming *adj.* advancing, approaching, forthcoming, gathering, imminent, impending, looming, onrushing, upcoming.

oneness *n.* completeness, consistency, distinctness, identicalness, identity, individuality, sameness, singleness, unicity, unity, wholeness.

onerous *adj.* backbreaking, burdensome, crushing, demanding, difficult, exacting, exhausting, exigent, formidable, grave, hard, heavy, herculean, laborious, oppressive, responsible, taxing, troublesome, weighty. *antonyms* easy, light.

one-sided *adj.* asymmetrical, biased, colored, discriminatory, inequitable, lopsided, partial, partisan, prejudiced, unequal, unfair, unilateral, unjust. *antonym* impartial.

ongoing *adj.* advancing, continuing, continuous, current, developing, evolving, extant, growing, in progress, lasting, progressing, successful, unfinished, unfolding.

onlooker *n.* bystander, eye-witness, looker-on, observer, rubber-neck, spectator, viewer, watcher, witness.

only *adv.* at most, barely, exclusively, just, merely, purely, simply, solely.
adj. exclusive, individual, lone, single, sole, solitary, unique.

onset *n.* assault, attack, beginning, charge, commencement, inception, kick-off, onrush, onslaught, outbreak, outset, start. *antonyms* end, finish.

onslaught *n.* assault, attack, barrage, blitz, bombardment, charge, offensive, onrush, onset.

onus *n.* burden, duty, encumbrance, liability, load, obligation, responsibility, task.

onward(s) *adv.* ahead, beyond, forth, forward, frontward(s), in front, on. *antonym* backward(s).

ooze *v.* bleed, discharge, drain, dribble, drip, drop, emit, escape, exude, filter, leach, leak, osmose, overflow with, percolate, seep, strain, sweat, transude, weep.
n. alluvium, deposit, mire, muck, mud, sediment, silt, slime, sludge.

opacity *n.* cloudiness, density, dullness, filminess, impermeability, milkiness, murkiness, obfuscation, obscurity, opaqueness, unclearness. *antonym* transparency.

opaque *adj.* abstruse, baffling, clouded, cloudy, cryptic, difficult, dim, dull, enigmatic, filmy, fuliginous, hazy, impenetrable, incomprehensible, inexplicable, lusterless, muddied, muddy, murky, obfuscated, obscure, turbid, unclear, unfathomable, unintelligible. *antonym* transparent.

open *adj.* above-board, accessible, agape, airy, ajar, apparent, arguable, artless, available, avowed, bare, barefaced, blatant, bounteous, bountiful, candid, champaign, clear, conspicuous, debatable, disinterested, downright, evident, expanded, exposed, extended, extensive, fair, filigree, flagrant, frank, free, fretted, gaping, general, generous, guileless, holey, honest, honeycombed, impartial, ingenuous, innocent, lacy, liberal, lidless, loose, manifest, moot, munificent, natural, navigable, noticeable, objective, obvious, overt, passable, plain, porous, public, receptive, revealed, rolling, sincere, spacious, spongy, spread out, sweeping, transparent, unbarred, unbiased, unclosed, uncluttered, uncommitted, unconcealed, unconditional, uncovered, uncrowded, undecided, undefended, undisguised, unenclosed, unengaged, unfastened, unfenced, unfolded, unfortified, unfurled, unlidded, unlocked, unobstructed, unoccupied, unprejudiced, unprotected, unqualified, unreserved, unresolved, unrestricted, unroofed, unsealed, unsettled, unshel-

tered, unwalled, vacant, visible, wide, wide-open, yawning. *antonyms* closed, shut.
v. begin, clear, come apart, commence, crack, disclose, divulge, exhibit, explain, expose, inaugurate, initiate, launch, lay bare, ope, pour out, rupture, separate, set in motion, show, split, spread (out), start, throw wide, unbar, unbare, unblock, unclose, uncork, uncover, undo, unfasten, unfold, unfurl, unlatch, unlid, unlock, unroll, unseal, unshutter. *antonyms* close, shut.

open-handed *adj.* bountiful, eleemosynary, free, generous, large-hearted, lavish, liberal, munificent, unstinting. *antonym* tight-fisted.

opening *n.* adit, aperture, beginning, birth, breach, break, chance, chasm, chink, cleft, commencement, crack, dawn, fissure, fistula, foramen, gap, hole, inauguration, inception, initiation, interstice, kick-off, launch, launching, occasion, onset, opportunity, orifice, ostiole, outset, perforation, place, rent, rupture, slot, space, split, start, vacancy, vent, vista. *antonyms* closing, closure.
adj. beginning, commencing, early, first, inaugural, inauguratory, inceptive, initial, initiatory, introductory, maiden, primary. *antonym* closing.

openly *adv.* blatantly, brazenly, candidly, face to face, flagrantly, forthrightly, frankly, glaringly, in full view, in public, overtly, plainly, publicly, shamelessly, unabashedly, unashamedly, unhesitatingly, unreservedly, wantonly. *antonyms* secretly, slyly.

open-minded *adj.* broad, broad-minded, catholic, dispassionate, enlightened, free, impartial, latitudinarian, liberal, objective, reasonable, receptive, tolerant, unbiased, unprejudiced. *antonyms* bigoted, intolerant, prejudiced.

operate *v.* act, function, go, handle, manage, maneuver, perform, run, serve, use, utilize, work.

operation *n.* action, activity, affair, agency, assault, business, campaign, course, deal, effect, effort, employment, enterprise, exercise, force, influence, instrumentality, maneuver, manipulation, motion, movement, performance, procedure, proceeding, process, surgery, transaction, undertaking, use, utilization, working.

operative *adj.* active, crucial, current, effective, efficient, engaged, functional, functioning, important, in action, in force, in operation, indicative, influential, key, operational, relevant, serviceable, significant, standing, workable. *antonym* inoperative.
n. artisan, employee, hand, laborer, machinist, mechanic, operator, worker.

operator *n.* administrator, conductor, contractor, dealer, director, driver, handler, machinator, machinist, manager, manipulator, mechanic, mover, operant, operative, practitioner, punter, shyster, speculator, technician, trader, wheeler-dealer, worker.

opiate *n.* anodyne, bromide, depressant, downer, drug, narcotic, nepenthe, pacifier, sedative, soporific, stupefacient, tranquilizer.

opinion *n.* assessment, belief, conception, conjecture, conventional wisdom, doxy, estimation, feeling, idea, idée reçue, impression, judgment, mind, notion, perception, persuasion, point of view, sentiment, stance, tenet, theory, view, voice, vox pop, vox populi.

opinionated *adj.* adamant, biased, bigoted, bull-headed, cocksure, dictatorial, doctrinaire, dogmatic, high-dried, inflexible, obdurate, obstinate, overbearing, partisan, pig-headed, prejudiced, self-assertive, single-minded, stubborn, uncompromising, wilful.
antonym open-minded.

opponent *n.* adversary, antagonist, challenger, competitor, contestant, disputant, dissentient, dissident, enemy, foe, objector, opposer, opposition, rival.
antonyms ally, proponent.

opportune *adj.* advantageous, appropriate, apt, auspicious, convenient, favorable, felicitous, fit, fitting, fortunate, good, happy, lucky, pertinent, proper, propitious, seasonable, suitable, timely, well-timed.
antonym inopportune.

opportunity *n.* break, chance, convenience, hour, moment, occasion, opening, scope, shot, time, turn.

oppose *v.* bar, beard, breast, check, combat, compare, confront, contradict, contrary, contrast, contravene, controvert, counter, counterattack, counterbalance, defy, face, fight, fly in the face of, gainsay, hinder, obstruct, pit against, play off, prevent, recalcitrate, resist, stand up to, take a stand against, take issue with, thwart, withstand.
antonyms favor, support.

opposed *adj.* against, agin, antagonistic, anti, antipathetic, antithetical, clashing, conflicting, contrary, contrasted, dissentient, hostile, in opposition, incompatible, inimical, opposing, opposite.
antonym in favor.

opposite *adj.* adverse, antagonistic, antipodal, antipodean, antithetical, conflicting, contradictory, contrary, contrasted, corresponding, different, differing, diverse, facing, fronting, hostile, inconsistent, inimical, irreconcilable, opposed, reverse, unlike.
antonym same.

n. antipode(s), antipole, antithesis, contradiction, contrary, converse, inverse, reverse.
antonym same.

opposition *n.* antagonism, antagonist, clash, colluctation, competition, contraposition, contrariety, counteraction, counter-stand, counter-time, counter-view, disapproval, foe, hostility, obstruction, obstructiveness, opponent, other side, polarity, prevention, resistance, rival, syzygy, unfriendliness.
antonyms co-operation, support.

oppress *v.* abuse, afflict, burden, crush, depress, dispirit, harass, harry, lie hard on, lie heavy on, maltreat, overpower, overwhelm, persecute, sadden, subdue, subjugate, suppress, torment, trample, tyrannize, vex, weigh heavy.

oppression *n.* abuse, brutality, calamity, cruelty, hardship, harshness, injury, injustice, jackboot, liberticide, maltreatment, misery, persecution, severity, subjection, suffering, tyranny.

oppressive *adj.* airless, brutal, burdensome, close, cruel, despotic, grinding, harsh, heavy, inhuman, intolerable, muggy, onerous, overbearing, overpowering, overwhelming, repressive, severe, stifling, stuffy, suffocating, sultry, torrid, tyrannical, unendurable, unjust.
antonym gentle.

oppressor *n.* autocrat, bully, coercionist, despot, dictator, harrier, intimidator, liberticide, persecutor, scourge, slave-driver, taskmaster, tormentor, tyrant.

olic, vituperative.

opprobrium *n.* calumny, censure, contumely, debasement, degradation, discredit, disfavor, disgrace, dishonor, disrepute, ignominy, infamy, obloquy, odium, reproach, scurrility, shame, slur, stigma.

opt *v.* choose, decide (on), elect, go for, plump for, prefer, select, single out.

optimistic *adj.* assured, bright, bullish, buoyant, cheerful, confident, encouraged, expectant, heartened, hopeful, idealistic, Panglossian, Panglossic, positive, sanguine, upbeat, Utopian.
antonym pessimistic.

option *n.* alternative, choice, election, possibility, preference, selection.

optional *adj.* discretionary, elective, extra, open, possible, unforced, voluntary.
antonym compulsory.

opulence *n.* abundance, affluence, copiousness, cornucopia, easy street, fortune, fullness, lavishness, luxuriance, luxury, plenty, pleroma, profusion, prosperity, riches, richness, sumptuousness, superabundance, wealth.
antonyms penury, poverty.

opulent *adj.* abundant, affluent, copious, lavish, luxuriant, luxurious, moneyed, plentiful, profuse, prolific, prosperous, rich, sumptuous, superabundant, wealthy, well-heeled, well-off, well-to-do.
antonyms penurious, poor.

oracle *n.* adviser, answer, augur, augury, authority, divination, guru, high priest, mastermind, mentor, prediction, prognostication, prophecy, prophet, pundit, python, revelation, sage, seer, sibyl, soothsayer, vision, wizard.

oral *adj.* acroamatic(al), spoken, unwritten, verbal, vocal.
antonym written.

orate *v.* declaim, discourse, harangue, hold forth, pontificate, sermonize, speak, speechify, talk.

oration *n.* address, declamation, discourse, éloge, harangue, homily, lecture, sermon, speech, spiel.

orb *n.* ball, circle, globe, globule, mound, ring, round, sphere, spherule.

orbit *n.* ambit, circle, circumgyration, circumvolution, compass, course, cycle, domain, ellipse, influence, path, range, reach, revolution, rotation, scope, sphere, sphere of influence, sweep, track, trajectory.
v. circle, circumnavigate, circumvolve, encircle, revolve.

orchestrate *v.* arrange, compose, concert, co-ordinate, fix, integrate, organize, prepare, present, score, stage-manage.

ordain *v.* anoint, appoint, call, consecrate, decree, destine, dictate, elect, enact, enjoin, fate, fix, foredoom, foreordain, frock, instruct, intend, invest, lay down, legislate, nominate, order, predestine, predetermine, prescribe, pronounce, require, rule, set, will.

ordeal *n.* affliction, agony, anguish, nightmare, pain, persecution, suffering, test, torture, trial, tribulation(s), trouble(s).

order[1] *n.* application, arrangement, array, behest, booking, calm, categorization, chit, classification, codification, command, commission, control, cosmos, decree, dictate, diktat, direction, directive, discipline,

disposal, disposition, eutaxy, grouping, harmony, injunction, instruction, law, law and order, layout, line, line-up, mandate, method, neatness, ordering, orderliness, ordinance, organization, pattern, peace, placement, plan, precept, progression, propriety, quiet, regularity, regulation, request, requisition, reservation, rule, sequence, series, stipulation, structure, succession, symmetry, system, tidiness, tranquility.
antonym disorder.

v. adjure, adjust, align, arrange, authorize, bid, book, catalog, charge, class, classify, command, conduct, control, decree, direct, dispose, enact, engage, enjoin, group, instruct, lay out, manage, marshal, neaten, ordain, organize, prescribe, put to rights, regulate, request, require, reserve, sort out, systematize, tabulate, tidy.
antonym disorder.

order[2] *n.* association, breed, brotherhood, cast, caste, class, community, company, degree, family, fraternity, genre, genus, grade, guild, hierarchy, ilk, kind, league, lodge, organization, pecking order, phylum, position, rank, sect, sisterhood, society, sodality, sort, species, status, subclass, tribe, type, union.

orderly *adj.* businesslike, controlled, cosmic, decorous, disciplined, in order, law-abiding, methodical, neat, non-violent, peaceable, quiet, regular, restrained, ruly, scientific, shipshape, systematic, systematized, tidy, trim, well-behaved, well-organized, well-regulated.
antonym disorderly.

ordinarily *adv.* as a rule, commonly, conventionally, customarily, familiarly, generally, habitually, in general, normally, usually.

ordinary *adj.* accustomed, average, common, common-or-garden, commonplace, conventional, customary, established, everyday, fair, familiar, habitual, homespun, household, humble, humdrum, inconsequential, indifferent, inferior, mean, mediocre, modest, normal, pedestrian, plain, prevailing, prosaic, quotidian, regular, routine, run-of-the-mill, settled, simple, standard, stock, typical, undistinguished, unexceptional, unmemorable, unpretentious, unremarkable, usual, wonted, workaday.
antonyms extraordinary, special, unusual.

ordnance *n.* arms, artillery, big guns, cannon, guns, matériel, missil(e)ry, munitions, weapons.

organ *n.* agency, channel, device, element, forum, harmonium, hurdy-gurdy, implement, instrument, journal, kist of whistles, means, medium, member, mouthpiece, newspaper, paper, part, periodical, process, publication, structure, tool, unit, vehicle, viscus, voice.

organic *adj.* anatomical, animate, biological, biotic, constitutional, formal, fundamental, inherent, innate, integral, integrated, live, living, methodical, natural, ordered, organized, structural, structured, systematic, systematized.

organization *n.* arrangement, assembling, assembly, association, body, business, chemistry, combine, company, composition, concern, confederation, configuration, conformation, consortium, constitution, construction, co-ordination, corporation, design, disposal, federation, firm, format, formation, formulation, framework, group, grouping, institution, league, make-up, management, method, methodology, organism, outfit, pattern, plan, planning, regulation, running,

standardization, structure, structuring, syndicate, system, unity, whole.
antonym disorganization.

organize *v.* arrange, catalog, classify, codify, constitute, construct, co-ordinate, dispose, establish, form, frame, group, marshal, pigeonhole, regiment, run, see to, set up, shape, structure, systematize, tabulate.
antonym disorganize.

organized *adj.* arranged, neat, orderly, planned.
antonym disorganized.

orient *v.* acclimatize, accommodate, adapt, adjust, align, familiarize, get one's bearings, habituate, orientate.

orifice *n.* aperture, cleft, hole, inlet, mouth, opening, perforation, pore, rent, slit, vent.

origin *n.* ancestry, base, basis, beginning, beginnings, birth, cause, commencement, creation, dawning, derivation, descent, emergence, etymology, etymon, extraction, family, fons et origo, font, foundation, fountain, fountain-head, genesis, heritage, inauguration, inception, incunabula, launch, lineage, occasion, origination, outset, parentage, paternity, pedigree, provenance, root, roots, source, spring, start, stirps, stock, well-spring.
antonyms end, termination.

original *adj.* aboriginal, archetypal, authentic, autochthonous, commencing, creative, earliest, early, embryonic, fertile, first, first-hand, fresh, genuine, imaginative, infant, ingenious, initial, innovative, innovatory, introductory, inventive, master, new, novel, opening, primal, primary, primigenial, primitical, primitive, primordial, pristine, prototypical, resourceful, rudimentary, seminal, starting, unborrowed, unconventional, unhackneyed, unprecedented, unusual.
antonym unoriginal.

n. archetype, case, character, cure, eccentric, master, model, nonconformist, oddity, paradigm, pattern, prototype, queer fish, standard, type, weirdo.

originality *n.* boldness, cleverness, creative spirit, creativeness, creativity, daring, eccentricity, freshness, imagination, imaginativeness, individuality, ingenuity, innovation, innovativeness, inventiveness, newness, novelty, resourcefulness, singularity, unconventionality, unorthodoxy.

originate *v.* arise, be born, begin, come, commence, conceive, create, derive, develop, discover, emanate, emerge, establish, evolve, flow, form, formulate, generate, give birth to, inaugurate, initiate, institute, introduce, invent, issue, launch, pioneer, proceed, produce, result, rise, set up, spring, start, stem.
antonyms end, terminate.

originator *n.* architect, author, creator, designer, father, founder, generator, innovator, inventor, mother, pioneer, prime mover, the brains.

ornament *n.* accessory, adornment, bauble, decoration, doodah, embellishment, fallal, fandangle, figgery, flower, frill, furbelow, garnish, gaud, honor, jewel, leading light, pride, treasure, trimming, trinket.

v. adorn, beautify, bedizen, bespangle, brighten, caparison, deck, decorate, dress up, embellish, festoon, garnish, gild, grace, prettify, prink, trim.

ornamental *adj.* attractive, beautifying, decorative, embellishing, flashy, for show, grandiose, showy.

ornate *adj.* arabesque, aureate, baroque, beautiful, bedecked, busy, convoluted, decorated, elaborate, elegant,

fancy, florid, flowery, fussy, ornamented, rococo, sumptuous.
antonyms austere, plain.

orthodox *adj.* accepted, approved, conformist, conventional, correct, customary, doctrinal, established, kosher, official, received, sound, traditional, true, usual, well-established.
antonym unorthodox.

oscillate *v.* fluctuate, librate, seesaw, sway, swing, vacillate, vary, vibrate, waver, wigwag, yo-yo.

ostentation *n.* affectation, boasting, display, exhibitionism, flamboyance, flashiness, flaunting, flourish, foppery, pageantry, parade, pomp, pretension, pretentiousness, show, showiness, showing off, swank, tinsel, trappings, vaunting, window-dressing.
antonym unpretentiousness.

ostentatious *adj.* aggressive, boastful, conspicuous, extravagant, fastuous, flamboyant, flash, flashy, garish, gaudy, loud, obtrusive, pretentious, self-advertising, showy, splashy, swanking, swanky, vain, vulgar.
antonyms quiet, restrained.

ostracize *v.* avoid, banish, bar, black, blackball, blacklist, boycott, cast out, cold-shoulder, cut, debar, disfellowship, exclude, excommunicate, exile, expatriate, expel, reject, segregate, send to Coventry, shun, snub.
antonyms accept, receive, reinstate, welcome.

other *adj.* added, additional, alternative, auxiliary, contrasting, different, differing, dissimilar, distinct, diverse, extra, fresh, further, more, new, remaining, separate, spare, supplementary, unrelated.

oust *v.* depose, disinherit, dislodge, displace, dispossess, drive out, eject, evict, expel, overthrow, replace, supplant, throw out, topple, turn out, unseat, upstage.
antonyms ensconce, install, reinstate, settle.

out¹ *adj.* abroad, absent, away, disclosed, elsewhere, evident, exposed, gone, manifest, not at home, outside, public, revealed.

out² *adj.* antiquated, banned, blacked, dated, dead, démodé, disallowed, ended, excluded, exhausted, expired, extinguished, finished, forbidden, impossible, not on, old hat, old-fashioned, out of date, passé, square, taboo, unacceptable, unfashionable, used up.
antonyms acceptable, fashionable, in.

outbreak *n.* burst, ebullition, epidemic, eruption, excrescence, explosion, flare-up, flash, outburst, pompholyx, rash, spasm, upsurge.

outburst *n.* access, attack, boutade, discharge, eruption, explosion, fit, fit of temper, flare-up, gale, gush, outbreak, outpouring, paroxysm, seizure, spasm, storm, surge, volley.

outcast *n.* abject, castaway, derelict, exile, leper, outsider, pariah, persona non grata, refugee, reject, reprobate, unperson, untouchable, vagabond, wretch.
antonyms favorite, idol.

outclass *v.* beat, eclipse, excel over, leave standing, outdistance, outdo, outrank, outrival, outshine, outstrip, overshadow, put in the shade, surpass, top, transcend.

outcome *n.* after-effect, aftermath, conclusion, consequence, effect, end, end result, harvest, issue, pay-off, result, sequel, upshot.

outcry *n.* clamor, commotion, complaint, cry, exclamation, flap, howl, hue and cry, hullaballoo, noise, outburst, protest, row, scream, screech, uproar, vociferation, yell.

outdated *adj.* antediluvian, antiquated, antique, archaic,

behind the times, dated, démodé, fogram, obsolescent, obsolete, old-fashioned, out of date, out of style, outmoded, passé, square, unfashionable, unmodish.
antonyms fashionable, modern, modish.

outdo *v.* beat, best, eclipse, excel over, get the better of, outclass, outdistance, outfox, out-Herod, outmaneuver, outshine, outsmart, outstrip, outwit, overcome, surpass, top, transcend.

outer *adj.* distal, distant, exterior, external, further, outlying, outside, outward, peripheral, remote, superficial, surface.
antonyms central, inner, mesial, proximal.

outfit¹ *n.* accouterments, clothes, costume, ensemble, equipage, equipment, garb, gear, get-up, kit, paraphernalia, rig, rig-out, set-out, suit, togs, trappings, turn-out.
v. accouter, apparel, appoint, attire, equip, fit out, fit up, furnish, kit out, provision, stock, supply, turn out.

outfit² *n.* business, clan, clique, company, corps, coterie, crew, firm, galère, gang, group, organization, set, set-out, set-up, squad, team, unit.

outgoing *adj.* affable, approachable, chatty, communicative, cordial, demonstrative, departing, easy, ex-, expansive, extrovert, former, friendly, genial, gregarious, informal, last, open, past, retiring, sociable, sympathetic, unreserved, warm, withdrawing.
antonyms incoming, introvert, new, unsociable.

outgrowth *n.* consequence, effect, emanation, excrescence, offshoot, product, protuberance, shoot, sprout, swelling.

outing *n.* excursion, expedition, jaunt, picnic, pleasure trip, ramble, spin, trip, wayzgoose.

outlandish *adj.* alien, barbarous, bizarre, eccentric, exotic, extraordinary, fantastic, foreign, grotesque, odd, outré, preposterous, queer, strange, unheard-of, weird.
antonyms familiar, ordinary.

outlandishness *n.* bizarreness, eccentricity, exoticness, grotesqueness, oddness, peregrinity, queerness, strangeness, weirdness.
antonyms commonplaceness, familiarity.

outlast *v.* come through, outlive, outstay, ride, survive, weather.

outlaw *n.* bandit, brigand, bushranger, cateran, dacoit, desperado, freebooter, fugitive, highwayman, marauder, outcast, outsider, pariah, proscript, robber.
v. ban, banish, bar, condemn, debar, decitizenize, disallow, embargo, exclude, excommunicate, forbid, illegalize, illegitimate, interdict, prohibit, proscribe, waive.
antonyms allow, legalize.

outlay *n.* cost, disbursal, disbursement, expenditure, expenses, investment, outgoings, payment, price.
antonym income.

outlet *n.* avenue, channel, débouché, debouchment, duct, egress, emissary, exit, femerall, market, opening, orifice, outfall, release, safety valve, vent, way out.
antonyms entry, inlet.

outline *n.* bare facts, configuration, contorno, contour, croquis, delineation, draft, drawing, figure, form, frame, framework, lay-out, lineament(s), plan, profile, recapitulation, résumé, rough, run-down, scenario, schema, shape, silhouette, skeleton, sketch, summary, synopsis, thumbnail sketch, tracing.

v. adumbrate, delineate, draft, plan, recapitulate, rough out, sketch, summarize, trace.

outlook *n.* angle, aspect, attitude, expectations, forecast, frame of mind, future, look-out, panorama, perspective, point of view, prognosis, prospect, scene, slant, standpoint, vantage-point, view, viewpoint, views, vista.

outlying *adj.* distant, far-away, far-flung, far-off, further, outer, outlandish, peripheral, provincial, remote.
antonyms central, inner.

outmoded *adj.* anachronistic, antediluvian, antiquated, antique, archaic, behind the times, bygone, dated, démodé, fogram, fossilized, horse-and-buggy, obsolescent, obsolete, olden, old-fashioned, old-fogeyish, out of date, outworn, passé, square, superannuated, superseded, unfashionable, unmodish, unusable.
antonyms fashionable, fresh, modern, modish, new.

output *n.* achievement, manufacture, outturn, print-out, product, production, productivity, read-out, yield.
antonyms input, outlay.

outrage *n.* hurt, abuse, affront, anger, atrocity, barbarism, crime, desecration, disgrace, enormity, evil, fury, grand guignol, horror, indignation, indignity, inhumanity, injury, insult, offence, profanation, rape, ravishing, resentment, scandal, shock, violation, violence, wrath.
v. abuse, affront, astound, defile, desecrate, disgust, épater le bourgeois, incense, infuriate, injure, insult, madden, make someone's blood boil, maltreat, offend, rape, ravage, ravish, repel, scandalize, shock, violate.

outrageous *adj.* abominable, atrocious, barbaric, beastly, disgraceful, egregious, excessive, exorbitant, extortionate, extravagant, flagrant, godless, heinous, horrible, immoderate, infamous, inhuman, iniquitous, inordinate, monstrous, nefarious, offensive, preposterous, scandalous, shocking, steep, turbulent, unconscionable, ungodly, unholy, unreasonable, unspeakable, villainous, violent, wicked.
antonyms acceptable, irreproachable.

outright *adj.* absolute, arrant, categorical, complete, consummate, definite, direct, downright, flat, out-and-out, perfect, point-blank, pure, straightforward, thorough, thoroughgoing, total, uncompromising, unconditional, undeniable, unequivocal, unmitigated, unqualified, utter, wholesale.
antonyms ambiguous, indefinite, provisional.
adv. absolutely, at once, cleanly, completely, directly, explicitly, immediately, instantaneously, instantly, on the spot, openly, positively, straight away, straightaway, straightforwardly, there and then, thoroughly, unhesitatingly, without restraint.

outset *n.* beginning, commencement, early days, forthgoing, inauguration, inception, kick-off, opening, start.
antonyms conclusion, end, finish.

outside[1] *adj.* exterior, external, extramural, extraneous, extreme, outdoor, outer, outermost, outward, superficial, surface.
antonym inside.
n. cover, exterior, façade, face, front, skin, superficies, surface, topside.
antonym inside.
prep. furth, outwith, without.

outside[2] *adj.* distant, faint, infinitesimal, marginal, minute, negligible, remote, slight, slim, small, unlikely.

antonyms likely, real, substantial.

outsider *n.* alien, foreigner, immigrant, incomer, interloper, intruder, layman, misfit, newcomer, non-member, non-resident, observer, odd man out, outcast, outlander, outlier, settler, stranger.
antonyms inhabitant, insider, local, member, native, resident, specialist.

outsmart *v.* beat, best, deceive, dupe, get the better of, outfox, outmaneuver, outperform, out-think, outwit, trick.

outspoken *adj.* abrupt, blunt, candid, direct, explicit, forthright, frank, free, open, plain-spoken, pointed, Rabelaisian, rude, sharp, trenchant, unceremonious, unequivocal, unreserved.
antonyms diplomatic, tactful.

outstanding[1] *adj.* ace, arresting, celebrated, conspicuous, distinguished, egregious, eminent, excellent, exceptional, extraordinary, eye-catching, great, important, impressive, marked, memorable, notable, noteworthy, pre-eminent, prominent, prosilient, remarkable, salient, signal, singular, special, striking, superior, superlative, surpassing.
antonyms ordinary, unexceptional.

outstanding[2] *adj.* due, left, ongoing, open, over, owing, payable, pending, remaining, uncollected, undone, unpaid, unresolved, unsettled.

outward *adj.* alleged, apparent, avowed, evident, exterior, external, noticeable, observable, obvious, ostensible, outer, outside, professed, public, superficial, supposed, surface, visible.
antonyms inner, private.

outweigh *v.* cancel out, compensate for, eclipse, make up for, outbalance, overcome, override, overrule, predominate, preponderate, prevail over, take precedence over, tip the scales in favor of, transcend.

outwit *v.* beat, best, better, cheat, circumvent, deceive, defraud, dupe, get the better of, gull, make a monkey of, outfox, outmaneuver, outsmart, outthink, swindle, trick.

oval *adj.* egg-shaped, ellipsoidal, elliptical, lens-shaped, lenticular, lentiform, lentoid, obovate, obovoid, ovate, oviform, ovoid, ovoidal, vulviform.

ovation *n.* acclaim, acclamation, applause, bravos, cheering, cheers, clapping, éclat, laudation, plaudits, praises, tribute.
antonyms abuse, boos, catcalls, mockery.

over[1] *adj.* accomplished, bygone, closed, completed, concluded, done with, ended, finished, forgotten, gone, in the past, past, settled, up.

over[2] *prep.* above, exceeding, in charge of, in command of, in excess of, more than, on, on top of, superior to, upon.
adv. above, aloft, beyond, extra, in addition, in excess, left, on high, overhead, remaining, superfluous, surplus, unclaimed, unused, unwanted.

overall *adj.* all-embracing, all-inclusive, all-over, blanket, broad, complete, comprehensive, general, global, inclusive, total, umbrella.
antonyms narrow, short-term.
adv. by and large, generally speaking, in general, in the long term, on the whole.

overbearing *adj.* arrogant, autocratic, bossy, cavalier, despotic, dictatorial, dogmatic, domineering, haughty, high and mighty, high-handed, imperious, lordly,

magisterial, officious, oppressive, overweening, peremptory, pompous, supercilious, superior, tyrannical.
antonyms modest, unassertive, unassuming.

overcast *adj.* black, clouded, clouded over, cloudy, dark, darkened, dismal, dreary, dull, gray, hazy, leaden, lowering, murky, somber, sunless, threatening.
antonyms bright, clear, sunny.

overcome *v.* beat, best, better, conquer, crush, defeat, expugn, lick, master, overpower, overthrow, overwhelm, prevail, rise above, subdue, subjugate, surmount, survive, triumph over, vanquish, weather, worst.
adj. affected, beaten, bowled over, broken, defeated, exhausted, overpowered, overwhelmed, speechless, swept off one's feet.

over-confident *adj.* arrogant, brash, cocksure, cocky, foolhardy, hubristic, incautious, over-optimistic, overweening, presumptuous, rash, sanguine, temerarious, uppish.
antonyms cautious, diffident.

overdo *v.* do to death, exaggerate, gild the lily, go to extremes, go too far, labor, lay it on thick, overact, overexert, overindulge, overplay, overreach, overstate, overtax, overuse, overwork.
antonyms neglect, underuse.

overdue *adj.* behind schedule, behindhand, belated, delayed, late, owing, slow, tardy, unpunctual.
antonym early.

overemphasize *v.* belabor, exaggerate, labor, overdramatize, overstress.
antonyms belittle, minimize, underplay, understate.

overflow *v.* brim over, bubble over, cover, deluge, discharge, drown, flood, inundate, pour over, shower, soak, spill, spray, submerge, surge, swamp, well over.
n. flood, inundation, overabundance, overspill, spill, superfluity, surplus.

overflowing *adj.* abounding, bountiful, brimful, copious, inundant, plenteous, plentiful, profuse, rife, superabundant, swarming, teeming, thronged.
antonyms lacking, scarce.

overhang *v.* beetle, bulge, extend, impend, jut, loom, menace, project, protrude, stick out, threaten.

overhaul[1] *v.* check, do up, examine, fix, inspect, mend, recondition, re-examine, repair, restore, service, survey.
n. check, check-up, examination, going-over, inspection, reconditioning, repair, restoration, service.

overhaul[2] *v.* gain on, outpace, outstrip, overtake, pass, pull ahead of.

overhead *adv.* above, aloft, on high, up above, upward.
antonyms below, underfoot.
adj. aerial, elevated, overhanging, roof, upper.
antonyms floor, ground, underground.

overjoyed *adj.* delighted, delirious, ecstatic, elated, enraptured, euphoric, in raptures, joyful, jubilant, on cloud nine, over the moon, rapturous, thrilled, tickled pink, transported.
antonyms disappointed, sad.

overlap *v.* coincide, cover, flap over, imbricate, overlay, overlie, shingle.

overload *v.* burden, encumber, oppress, overburden, overcharge, overtax, saddle, strain, surcharge, tax, weigh down.

overlook[1] *v.* condone, disregard, excuse, forget, forgive, ignore, let pass, let ride, miss, neglect, omit, pardon,

pass, pass over, skip, slight, turn a blind eye to, wink at.
antonyms animadvert, note, notice, penalize, record, remember.

overlook[2] *v.* command a view of, face, front on to, give upon, look on to.

overly *adv.* exceedingly, excessively, immoderately, inordinately, over, too, unduly, unreasonably.
antonyms inadequately, insufficiently.

overpower *v.* beat, best, conquer, crush, defeat, floor, immobilize, master, overcome, overthrow, overwhelm, quell, subdue, subjugate, vanquish.

overpowering *adj.* compelling, convincing, extreme, forceful, insuppressible, invincible, irrefutable, irrepressible, irresistible, nauseating, oppressive, overwhelming, powerful, sickening, strong, suffocating, telling, unbearable, uncontrollable.

overrate *v.* blow up, magnify, make too much of, overestimate, overpraise, overprize, oversell, overvalue.
antonym underrate.

override *v.* abrogate, annul, cancel, countermand, disregard, ignore, nullify, outweigh, overrule, quash, rescind, reverse, ride roughshod over, set aside, supersede, trample, upset, vanquish.

overrule *v.* abrogate, annul, cancel, countermand, disallow, invalidate, outvote, override, overturn, recall, repeal, rescind, reverse, revoke, set aside, veto, vote down.
antonyms allow, approve.

overrun[1] *v.* choke, infest, inundate, invade, occupy, overflow, overgrow, overspread, overwhelm, permeate, ravage, run riot, spread over, surge over, swamp, swarm over.
antonyms desert, evacuate.

overrun[2] *v.* exceed, overdo, overshoot, overstep.

overseas *adj.* exotic, foreign, outland, outlandish, ultramarine.
antonyms domestic, home.
adv. abroad, in/to foreign climes, in/to foreign parts.
n. foreign climes, foreign parts, outland, outremer.
antonym home.

overseer *n.* boss, chief, foreman, forewoman, gaffer, headman, manager, master, super, superintendent, superior, supervisor, surveyor, workmaster, workmistress.

overshadow *v.* adumbrate, becloud, bedim, blight, cloud, darken, dim, dominate, dwarf, eclipse, excel, mar, obfuscate, obscure, outshine, outweigh, protect, put in the shade, rise above, ruin, shelter, spoil, surpass, tower above, veil.

oversight[1] *n.* administration, care, charge, control, custody, direction, guidance, handling, inspection, keeping, management, responsibility, superintendence, supervision, surveillance.

oversight[2] *n.* blunder, boob, carelessness, delinquency, error, fault, inattention, lapse, laxity, mistake, neglect, omission, slip, slip-up.

overt *adj.* apparent, avowed, evident, manifest, observable, obvious, open, patent, plain, professed, public, unconcealed, undisguised, visible.
antonyms covert, secret.

overtake *v.* befall, catch up with, come upon, draw level with, engulf, happen, hit, outdistance, outdo, outstrip, overhaul, pass, pull ahead of, strike.

overthrow *v.* abolish, beat, bring down, conquer, crush, defeat, demolish, depose, destroy, dethrone, displace, knock down, level, master, oust, overcome, overpower, overturn, overwhelm, raze, ruin, subdue, subjugate, subvert, topple, unseat, upset, vanquish.

antonyms install, reinstate.

n. bouleversement, confounding, defeat, deposition, destruction, dethronement, discomfiture, disestablishment, displacement, dispossession, downfall, end, fall, humiliation, labefactation, labefaction, ousting, prostration, rout, ruin, subjugation, subversion, suppression, undoing, unseating.

overture *n.* advance, approach, introduction, invitation, motion, move, offer, opening, (opening) gambit, opening move, prelude, proposal, proposition, signal, suggestion, tender.

overturn *v.* abolish, abrogate, annul, capsize, countermand, depose, destroy, invalidate, keel over, knock down, knock over, overbalance, overset, overthrow, quash, repeal, rescind, reverse, set aside, spill, tip over, topple, tumble, unseat, upend, upset, upturn.

overweight *adj.* ample, bulky, buxom, chubby, chunky, corpulent, fat, flabby, fleshy, gross, heavy, hefty, huge, massive, obese, outsize, plump, podgy, portly, potbellied, stout, tubby, well-padded, well-upholstered.

antonyms emaciated, skinny, thin, underweight.

overwhelm *v.* bowl over, bury, confuse, crush, cut to pieces, defeat, deluge, destroy, devastate, engulf, floor, inundate, knock for six, massacre, overcome, overpower, overrun, prostrate, rout, snow under, stagger, submerge, swamp.

overwrought *adj.* agitated, beside oneself, distracted, emotional, excited, frantic, keyed up, on edge, overcharged, overexcited, overheated, overworked, stirred, strung up, tense, uptight, worked up, wound up.

antonyms calm, cool, impassive.

owing *adj.* due, in arrears, outstanding, overdue, owed, payable, unpaid, unsettled.

own¹ *adj.* idiosyncratic, individual, inimitable, particular, personal, private.

own² *v.* acknowledge, admit, agree, allow, avow, concede, confess, disclose, enjoy, grant, have, hold, keep, possess, recognize, retain.

owner *n.* franklin, freeholder, holder, laird, landlady, landlord, lord, master, mistress, possessor, proprietor, proprietress, proprietrix.

P

pace *n.* celerity, clip, gait, lick, measure, momentum, motion, movement, progress, quickness, rapidity, rate, speed, step, stride, tempo, time, tread, velocity, walk.

v. count, determine, march, mark out, measure, pad, patrol, pound, step, stride, tramp, tread, walk.

pacific *adj.* appeasing, calm, complaisant, conciliatory, diplomatic, dovelike, dovish, eirenic, equable, friendly, gentle, halcyon, irenic, mild, nonbelligerent, nonviolent, pacificatory, pacifist, peaceable, peaceful, peace-loving, peacemaking, placatory, placid, propitiatory, quiet, serene, smooth, still, tranquil, unruffled.

antonyms aggressive, belligerent, contentious, pugnacious.

pacify *v.* allay, ameliorate, appease, assuage, calm, chasten, compose, conciliate, crush, humor, lull, mod-

erate, mollify, placate, propitiate, put down, quell, quiet, repress, silence, smooth down, soften, soothe, still, subdue, tame, tranquilize.

antonyms aggravate, anger.

pack *n.* assemblage, back-pack, bale, band, boodle, bunch, bundle, burden, collection, company, crew, crowd, deck, drove, fardel, flock, galère, gang, group, haversack, herd, kit, kitbag, knapsack, load, lot, Matilda, mob, outfit, package, packet, parcel, rucksack, set, troop, truss.

v. batch, bundle, burden, charge, compact, compress, cram, crowd, empocket, fill, jam, load, mob, package, packet, press, ram, steeve, store, stow, stuff, tamp, throng, thrust, wedge.

package *n.* agreement, amalgamation, arrangement, bale, box, carton, combination, consignment, container, deal, entity, kit, pack, packet, parcel, proposal, proposition, unit, whole.

v. batch, box, pack, pack up, packet, parcel, parcel up, wrap, wrap up.

packed *adj.* brimful, brim-full, chock-a-block, chock-full, congested, cram-full, crammed, crowded, filled, full, hotching, jammed, jam-packed, overflowing, overloaded, seething, swarming.

antonyms deserted, empty.

packet¹ *n.* bag, carton, case, container, pack, package, packing, parcel, poke, wrapper, wrapping.

packet² *n.* bomb, bundle, fortune, king's ransom, lot, lots, mint, pile, pot, pots, pretty penny, small fortune, tidy sum.

pact *n.* agreement, alliance, arrangement, bargain, bond, cartel, compact, concord, concordat, contract, convention, covenant, deal, entente, league, protocol, treaty, understanding.

antonyms breach, disagreement, quarrel.

pad¹ *n.* block, buffer, cushion, jotter, notepad, pillow, protection, pulvillus, pulvinar, stiffening, stuffing, tablet, wad, writing-pad.

v. cushion, fill, line, pack, protect, shape, stuff, wrap.

pad² *n.* foot, footprint, paw, print, sole.

pad³ *n.* apartment, flat, hang-out, home, penthouse, place, quarters, room, rooms.

pad⁴ *v.* lope, move, run, step, tiptoe, tramp, tread, trudge, walk.

padding *n.* bombast, circumlocution, filling, hot air, packing, perissology, prolixity, stuffing, verbiage, verbosity, wadding, waffle, wordiness.

paddle¹ *n.* oar, scull, sweep.

v. oar, ply, propel, pull, row, scull, steer.

paddle² *v.* dabble, plash, slop, splash, stir, trail, wade.

pageant *n.* display, extravaganza, masque, parade, play, procession, representation, ritual, scene, show, spectacle, tableau, tableau vivant.

pain *n.* ache, affliction, aggravation, agony, anguish, annoyance, bitterness, bore, bother, burden, cramp, discomfort, distress, dole, dolor, drag, grief, gyp, headache, heartache, heartbreak, hurt, irritation, lancination, misery, nuisance, pang, pest, smart, soreness, spasm, suffering, tenderness, throb, throe, torment, torture, tribulation, trouble, twinge, vexation, woe, wretchedness.

v. afflict, aggrieve, agonize, annoy, chagrin, cut to the quick, disappoint, disquiet, distress, exasperate, gall, grieve, harass, hurt, irritate, nettle, rile, sadden, torment, torture, vex, worry, wound, wring.

antonyms gratify, please.

painful *adj.* aching, achy, afflictive, agonizing, arduous, difficult, disagreeable, distasteful, distressing, doloriferous, dolorific, excruciating, grievous, hard, harrowing, laborious, lancinating, saddening, severe, smarting, sore, tedious, tender, troublesome, trying, unpleasant, vexatious.

antonyms easy, painless.

painstaking *adj.* assiduous, careful, conscientious, dedicated, devoted, diligent, earnest, exacting, hardworking, industrious, meticulous, perfectionist, persevering, punctilious, scrupulous, sedulous, strenuous, thorough, thoroughgoing.

antonyms careless, negligent.

painting *n.* aquarelle, daubery, depiction, fresco, illustration, kakemono, landscape, miniature, mural, oil, oil-painting, picture, portrait, portraiture, portrayal, representation, scene, seascape, still life, tablature, water-color.

pair *n.* brace, combination, couple, doublet, doubleton, duad, duo, dyad, match, span, twins, two of a kind, twosome, yoke.

v. bracket, couple, join, link, marry, match, match up, mate, pair off, put together, splice, team, twin, wed, yoke.

antonyms dissever, sever.

pal *n.* amigo, buddy, chum, companion, comrade, confidant(e), crony, friend, gossip, intimate, mate, partner, side-kick, soul mate.

antonym enemy.

palatial *adj.* de luxe, grand, grandiose, illustrious, imposing, luxurious, magnificent, majestic, opulent, plush, posh, regal, spacious, splendid, stately, sumptuous, swanky.

antonyms cramped, poky.

pale *adj.* anemic, ashen, ashy, bleached, bloodless, chalky, colorless, dim, etiolated, faded, faint, feeble, inadequate, light, lily-livered, pallid, pasty, poor, sallow, thin, wan, washed-out, waxy, weak, wheyfaced, white, white-livered, whitish.

antonym ruddy.

v. blanch, decrease, dim, diminish, dull, etiolate, fade, lessen, whiten.

antonyms blush, color.

pallid *adj.* anemic, ashen, ashy, bloodless, cadaverous, colorless, doughy, etiolated, insipid, lifeless, livid, pale, pasty, pasty-faced, peelie-wally, sallow, spiritless, sterile, tame, tired, uninspired, vapid, wan, waxen, waxy, whey-faced, whitish.

antonyms high-complexioned, ruddy, vigorous.

pally *adj.* affectionate, chummy, close, familiar, friendly, intimate, palsy, palsy-walsy, thick.

antonym unfriendly.

palpable *adj.* apparent, blatant, clear, concrete, conspicuous, evident, manifest, material, obvious, open, overt, patent, plain, real, solid, substantial, tangible, touchable, unmistakable, visible.

antonyms elusive, impalpable, imperceptible, intangible.

paltry *adj.* base, beggarly, contemptible, derisory, despicable, inconsiderable, insignificant, jitney, low, meager, mean, minor, miserable, negligible, pettifogging, petty, picayunish, piddling, piffling, pimping, pitiful, poor, puny, rubbishy, slight, small, sorry,

tinpot, trifling, trivial, two-bit, unimportant, worthless, wretched.

antonyms significant, substantial.

pamper *v.* baby, cocker, coddle, cosset, fondle, gratify, humor, indulge, mollycoddle, mother, overindulge, pet, spoil.

antonyms ill-treat, neglect.

pamphlet *n.* booklet, broadside, brochure, chapbook, folder, leaflet, tract, tractate, treatise.

panacea *n.* catholicon, cure-all, diacatholicon, elixir, nostrum, panpharmacon, theriac, treacle.

panache *n.* brio, dash, élan, enthusiasm, flair, flamboyance, flourish, grand manner, ostentation, pizzazz, spirit, style, swagger, theatricality, verve, vigor, zest.

pang *n.* ache, agony, anguish, crick, discomfort, distress, gripe, pain, prick, spasm, stab, sting, stitch, throe, twinge, twitch, wrench.

panic *n.* agitation, alarm, consternation, dismay, fear, fright, hassle, horror, hysteria, scare, terror, tizzy, to-do.

antonyms assurance, confidence.

v. alarm, get one's knickers in a twist, go to pieces, lose one's cool, lose one's nerve, overreact, put the wind up, scare, startle, terrify, unnerve.

antonyms reassure, relax.

pant *v.* ache, blow, breathe, covet, crave, desire, flaff, gasp, hanker, heave, huff, hunger, long, palpitate, pine, puff, sigh, thirst, throb, want, wheeze, yearn, yen.

n. gasp, huff, puff, throb, wheeze.

pants *n.* briefs, drawers, knickers, panties, shorts, slacks, trews, trousers, trunks, underpants, undershorts, Y-fronts.

paper *n.* analysis, archive, article, assignment, authorization, certificate, composition, credential, critique, daily, deed, diary, dissertation, document, dossier, essay, examination, file, gazette, instrument, journal, letter, monograph, news, newspaper, notepaper, organ, rag, record, report, script, stationery, study, thesis, treatise.

papery *adj.* delicate, flimsy, fragile, frail, insubstantial, light, lightweight, paper-thin, thin, translucent.

parable *n.* allegory, apologue, exemplum, fable, homily, lesson, story.

parade *n.* array, cavalcade, ceremony, column, corso, display, exhibition, flaunting, march, motorcade, ostentation, pageant, panache, pizzazz, pomp, procession, promenade, review, show, spectacle, train, vaunting.

v. air, brandish, defile, display, exhibit, flaunt, make a show of, march, peacock, process, show, show off, strut, swagger, vaunt.

paradise *n.* bliss, City of God, delight, Eden, Elysian fields, Elysium, felicity, garden of delights, Garden of Eden, heaven, heavenly kingdom, Land o' the Leal, Olympus, Promised Land, seventh heaven, utopia, Valhalla, Zion.

antonyms Hades, hell.

paradoxical *adj.* absurd, ambiguous, baffling, conflicting, confounding, contradictory, enigmatic, equivocal, Gilbertian, illogical, impossible, improbable, incongruous, inconsistent, puzzling, self-contradictory.

paragon *n.* apotheosis, archetype, crème de la crème, criterion, cynosure, epitome, exemplar, ideal, jewel, masterpiece, model, non(e)such, nonpareil, paradigm, pattern, prototype, quintessence, standard, the bee's knees.

parallel *adj.* akin, aligned, alongside, analogous, co-extensive, collateral, connate, correspondent, corresponding, equidistant, homologous, like, matching, resembling, similar, uniform.
antonyms divergent, separate.

n. analog, analogy, comparison, corollary, correlation, correspondence, counterpart, duplicate, equal, equivalent, homologue, likeness, match, parallelism, resemblance, similarity, twin.

v. agree, compare, conform, correlate, correspond, duplicate, emulate, equal, match.
antonyms diverge, separate.

paramount *adj.* capital, cardinal, chief, dominant, eminent, first, foremost, highest, main, outstanding, predominant, pre-eminent, premier, primary, prime, principal, superior, supreme, topmost, top-rank.
antonyms inferior, last, lowest.

paraphernalia *n.* accessories, accouterments, apparatus, appurtenances, baggage, belongings, bits and pieces, clobber, clutter, effects, equipage, equipment, gear, impedimenta, material, odds and ends, stuff, tackle, things, trappings, traps.

parasite *n.* bloodsucker, cadger, endophyte, endozoon, entozoon, epiphyte, epizoan, epizoon, free-loader, hanger-on, leech, lick-trencher, scrounger, sponge, sponger, sucker.

parcel *n.* band, batch, bunch, bundle, carton, collection, company, crew, crowd, da(w)k, gang, group, lot, pack, package, packet, plot, portion, property, quantity, set, tract.

v. bundle, collect, pack, package, tie up, wrap.

parched *adj.* arid, dehydrated, dried up, drouthy, dry, scorched, shriveled, thirsty, waterless, withered.

pardon *v.* absolve, acquit, amnesty, condone, emancipate, exculpate, excuse, exonerate, forgive, free, let off, liberate, overlook, release, remit, reprieve, respite, vindicate.

n. absolution, acquittal, allowance, amnesty, compassion, condonation, discharge, excuse, exoneration, forgiveness, grace, humanity, indulgence, mercy, release, remission, reprieval, reprieve.

pare *v.* clip, crop, cut, cut back, decrease, diminish, dock, flaught, float, lop, peel, prune, reduce, retrench, shave, shear, skin, skive, trim.

parent *n.* architect, author, begetter, cause, creator, father, forerunner, generant, genetrix, genitor, guardian, mother, origin, originator, procreator, progenitor, progenitress, progenitrix, prototype, root, sire, source.

pariah *n.* black sheep, castaway, exile, Ishmael, leper, outcast, outlaw, undesirable, unperson, untouchable.

parity *n.* affinity, agreement, analogy, conformity, congruence, congruity, consistency, consonance, correspondence, equality, equivalence, likeness, par, parallelism, resemblance, sameness, semblance, similarity, similitude, uniformity, unity.

parley *n.* colloquy, confab, conference, council, deliberation, dialogue, discussion, get-together, meeting, negotiation, palaver, powwow, talk(s), tête-à-tête.

v. confabulate, confer, consult, deliberate, discuss, get together, negotiate, palaver, powwow, speak, talk.

parody *n.* burlesque, caricature, imitation, lampoon, mimicry, pasquinade, satire, send-up, skit, spoof, take-off.

v. burlesque, caricature, lampoon, mimic, pasquinade, satirize, send up, spoof, take off, travesty.

paroxysm *n.* attack, convulsion, eruption, explosion, fit, flare-up, outbreak, outburst, seizure, spasm, tantrum.

parry *v.* avert, avoid, block, circumvent, deflect, divert, dodge, duck, evade, fence, fend off, field, forestall, obviate, rebuff, repel, repulse, shun, sidestep, stave off, ward off.

parsimonious *adj.* cheese-paring, close, close-fisted, close-handed, frugal, grasping, mean, mingy, miserable, miserly, money-grubbing, niggardly, penny-pinching, penny-wise, penurious, saving, scrimpy, sparing, stingy, stinting, tight-fisted.
antonyms generous, liberal, open-handed.

part *n.* airt, area, behalf, bit, branch, business, capacity, cause, character, charge, clause, complement, component, concern, constituent, department, district, division, duty, element, faction, factor, fraction, fragment, function, heft, ingredient, interest, involvement, limb, lines, lot, member, module, neck of the woods, neighborhood, office, organ, particle, partwork, party, piece, place, portion, quarter, region, responsibility, role, scrap, section, sector, segment, share, side, slice, task, territory, tip of the iceberg, unit, vicinity, work.

v. break, break up, cleave, come apart, depart, detach, disband, disconnect, disjoin, dismantle, disperse, disunite, divide, go, go away, leave, part company, quit, rend, scatter, separate, sever, split, split up, sunder, take leave, tear, withdraw.

partake *v.* be involved, engage, enter, participate, share, take part.

partial[1] *adj.* fragmentary, imperfect, incomplete, inexhaustive, limited, part, uncompleted, unfinished.
antonyms complete, exhaustive, total.

partial[2] *adj.* affected, biased, colored, discriminatory, ex parte, influenced, interested, one-sided, partisan, predisposed, prejudiced, tendentious, unfair, unjust.
antonyms disinterested, fair, unbiased.

partiality *n.* affinity, bias, discrimination, favoritism, fondness, inclination, liking, love, partisanship, penchant, predilection, predisposition, preference, prejudice, proclivity, propensity, soft spot, taste, weakness.
antonyms dislike, justice.

partially *adv.* fractionally, in part, incompletely, partly, somewhat.

participant *n.* associate, contributor, co-operator, helper, member, partaker, participator, party, shareholder, worker.

participation *n.* a piece of the action, assistance, contribution, co-operation, involvement, mucking in, partaking, partnership, sharing.

particle *n.* atom, atom(y), bit, corn, crumb, drop, electron, grain, iota, jot, kaon, mite, molecule, morsel, mote, neutrino, neutron, piece, pion, proton, scrap, shred, sliver, smidgen, speck, tittle, whit.

particular[1] *adj.* blow-by-blow, circumstantial, detailed, distinct, especial, exact, exceptional, express, itemized, marked, minute, notable, noteworthy, painstaking, peculiar, precise, remarkable, selective, several, singular, special, specific, thorough, uncommon, unique, unusual, very.
antonym general.

n. circumstance, detail, fact, feature, item, point, specific, specification.

particular[2] *adj.* choosy, critical, dainty, demanding, discriminating, exacting, fastidious, finical, finicky, fussy, meticulous, nice, overnice, perjink, pernickety, picky. *antonym* casual.

particularity *n.* accuracy, carefulness, characteristic, choosiness, circumstance, detail, distinctiveness, fact, fastidiousness, feature, fussiness, idiosyncrasy, individuality, instance, item, mannerism, meticulousness, peculiarity, point, precision, property, quirk, singularity, thoroughness, trait, uniqueness.

particularly *adv.* decidedly, distinctly, especially, exceptionally, explicitly, expressly, extraordinarily, in particular, markedly, notably, noticeably, outstandingly, peculiarly, remarkably, singularly, specifically, surprisingly, uncommonly, unusually.

partisan *n.* adherent, backer, champion, devotee, disciple, factionary, factionist, follower, guerrilla, irregular, party-man, stalwart, supporter, upholder, votary.
adj. biased, discriminatory, factional, guerrilla, interested, irregular, one-sided, partial, predisposed, prejudiced, resistance, sectarian, tendentious, underground.

partisanship *n.* bias, factionalism, fanaticism, partiality, partyism, sectarianism.

partition[1] *n.* allocation, allotment, apportionment, distribution, dividing, division, part, portion, rationing out, section, segregation, separation, severance, share, splitting.
v. allocate, allot, apportion, assign, divide, parcel out, portion, section, segment, separate, share, split up, subdivide.

partition[2] *n.* barrier, diaphragm, dissepiment, divider, membrane, room-divider, screen, septum, traverse, wall.
v. bar, divide, fence off, screen, separate, wall off.

partly *adv.* halfway, in part, incompletely, moderately, partially, relatively, slightly, somewhat, to a certain degree, to a certain extent, up to a point.
antonyms completely, in toto, totally.

partner *n.* accomplice, ally, associate, bedfellow, butty, collaborator, colleague, companion, comrade, confederate, consort, co-partner, gigolo, helper, helpmate, helpmeet, husband, mate, participant, side-kick, spouse, team-mate, wife.

party[1] *n.* assembly, at-home, bash, beanfeast, beano, ceilidh, celebration, do, drag, drum, entertainment, fest, festivity, function, gathering, get-together, hooley, hoot(e)nanny, housewarming, hurricane, jollification, knees-up, rave-up, reception, rout, shindig, social, soirée, thrash.

party[2] *n.* alliance, association, band, body, bunch, cabal, caucus, clique, coalition, combination, company, confederacy, contingent, contractor, coterie, crew, defendant, detachment, faction, gang, gathering, group, grouping, individual, junto, league, litigant, participant, person, plaintiff, set, side, squad, team, unit.

pass[1] *v.* accept, adopt, answer, approve, authorize, beat, befall, beguile, blow over, cease, come up, come up to scratch, convey, declare, decree, defecate, delate, deliver, depart, develop, devote, die, die away, disappear, discharge, disregard, dissolve, do, dwindle, ebb, elapse, eliminate, employ, empty, enact, end, establish, evacuate, evaporate, exceed, excel, exchange, excrete, expel, experience, expire, express, fade, fall out, fill, flow, get through, give, go, go beyond, go by, go past, graduate, hand, happen, ignore, impersonate, lapse, leave, legislate, melt away, miss, move, neglect, occupy, occur, omit, ordain, outdistance, outdo, outstrip, overlook, overtake, pass muster, proceed, pronounce, qualify, ratify, roll, run, sanction, send, serve as, skip, spend, succeed, suffer, suffice, suit, surmount, surpass, take place, terminate, throw, transcend, transfer, transmit, undergo, utter, validate, vanish, void, waft, wane, while away.

pass[2] *n.* advances, approach, authorization, chit, condition, feint, identification, jab, juncture, laissez-passer, license, lunge, overture, passport, permission, permit, pinch, play, plight, predicament, proposition, push, safe-conduct, situation, stage, state, state of affairs, straits, suggestion, swing, thrust, ticket, warrant.

pass[3] *n.* canyon, col, defile, gap, gorge, nek, ravine.

passable *adj.* acceptable, adequate, admissible, all right, allowable, average, clear, fair, mediocre, middling, moderate, navigable, OK, open, ordinary, presentable, so-so, tolerable, traversable, unblocked, unexceptional, unobstructed.

passage *n.* acceptance, access, adit, advance, allowance, authorization, avenue, change, channel, citation, clause, close, communication, conduit, conversion, corridor, course, crossing, deambulatory, doorway, drift, dromos, duct, enactment, entrance, entrance hall, establishment, excerpt, exit, extract, fistula, flow, freedom, gallery, gut, hall, hallway, journey, lane, legalization, legislation, lobby, motion, movement, opening, orifice, paragraph, part, passageway, passing, path, permission, piece, portion, progress, progression, quotation, ratification, reading, right, road, route, safe-conduct, section, sentence, spiracle, text, thorough, thoroughfare, tour, transit, transition, trek, trip, vent, verse, vestibule, visa, vista, voyage, warrant, way.

passenger *n.* commuter, fare, hitch-hiker, pillionist, pillion-rider, rider, traveler.

passer-by *n.* bystander, looker-on, onlooker, spectator, witness.

passion *n.* adoration, affection, anger, animation, ardor, attachment, avidity, bug, chafe, concupiscence, craving, craze, dander, desire, eagerness, emotion, enthusiasm, excitement, fancy, fascination, feeling, fervency, fervor, fire, fit, flare-up, fondness, frenzy, fury, heat, idol, indignation, infatuation, intensity, ire, itch, joy, keenness, love, lust, mania, monomania, obsession, outburst, paroxysm, rage, rapture, resentment, spirit, storm, transport, vehemence, verve, vivacity, warmth, wax, wrath, zeal, zest.
antonyms calm, coolness, self-possession.

passionate *adj.* amorous, animated, ardent, aroused, choleric, desirous, eager, emotional, enthusiastic, erotic, excitable, excited, fervent, fervid, fierce, fiery, frenzied, heartfelt, hot, hot-headed, hot-tempered, impassioned, impetuous, impulsive, incensed, inflamed, inspirited, intense, irascible, irate, irritable, loving, lustful, peppery, quick-tempered, sensual, sexy, stormy, strong, sultry, tempestuous, torrid, vehement, violent, wanton, warm, wild, zealous.
antonyms frigid, laid-back, phlegmatic.

passive *adj.* acquiescent, compliant, docile, enduring, impassive, inactive, indifferent, indolent, inert, lifeless, long-suffering, non-participating, non-violent, patient, quiescent, receptive, resigned, submissive, supine, unaffected, unassertive, uninvolved, unresisting.
antonyms active, involved, lively.

password n. countersign, open sesame, parole, shibboleth, signal, watchword.

past adj. accomplished, ancient, bygone, completed, defunct, done, early, elapsed, ended, erstwhile, extinct, finished, foregone, forgotten, former, gone, gone by, late, long-ago, no more, olden, over, over and done with, preceding, previous, prior, quondam, recent, spent, vanished.

n. antiquity, auld lang syne, background, days of yore, dossier, experience, former times, good old days, history, life, old times, olden days, track record, yesteryear.

pastiche n. blend, composition, farrago, gallimaufry, hotchpotch, medley, mélange, miscellany, mixture, motley, olla-podrida, patchwork, pot-pourri.

pastime n. activity, amusement, avocation, distraction, diversion, divertisement, entertainment, game, hobby, play, recreation, relaxation, sport.

antonyms business, employment, occupation, vocation, work.

pat v. caress, clap, dab, fondle, pet, rub, slap, stroke, tap, touch.

n. cake, caress, clap, dab, lump, piece, portion, slap, stroke, tap, touch.

adv. exactly, faultlessly, flawlessly, fluently, glibly, just right, off pat, opportunely, perfectly, plumb, precisely, relevantly, seasonably.

antonyms imprecisely, wrongly.

adj. apposite, appropriate, apropos, apt, automatic, easy, facile, felicitous, fitting, glib, happy, neat, pertinent, ready, relevant, right, simplistic, slick, smooth, spot-on, suitable, to the point, well-chosen.

antonyms irrelevant, unsuitable.

patch n. area, bit, clout, ground, land, lot, parcel, piece, plot, scrap, shred, spot, stretch, tract.

v. botch, cover, fix, mend, reinforce, repair, sew up, stitch, vamp.

patent adj. apparent, blatant, clear, clear-cut, conspicuous, downright, evident, explicit, flagrant, glaring, indisputable, manifest, obvious, open, ostensible, overt, palpable, transparent, unconcealed, unequivocal, unmistakable.

antonyms hidden, opaque.

n. certificate, copyright, invention, license, privilege, registered trademark.

path n. avenue, course, direction, footpath, footway, gate, pad, passage, pathway, procedure, ridgeway, road, route, towpath, track, trail, walk, walkway, way.

pathetic adj. affecting, contemptible, crummy, deplorable, dismal-looking, distressing, feeble, heartbreaking, heart-rending, inadequate, lamentable, meager, melting, miserable, moving, paltry, petty, piteous, pitiable, pitiful, plaintive, poignant, poor, puny, rubbishy, sad, sorry, tender, touching, trashy, uninteresting, useless, woebegone, woeful, worthless.

antonyms admirable, cheerful.

patience n. calmness, composure, constancy, cool, diligence, endurance, equanimity, forbearance, fortitude, long-suffering, perseverance, persistence, resignation, restraint, self-control, serenity, stoicism, submission, sufferance, tolerable, toleration.

antonyms impatience, intolerance.

patient[1] adj. accommodating, calm, composed, enduring, even-tempered, forbearing, forgiving, indulgent, lenient, long-suffering, mild, persevering, persistent,

philosophical, quiet, resigned, restrained, self-controlled, self-possessed, serene, stoical, submissive, tolerant, uncomplaining, understanding, untiring.

antonyms impatient, intolerant.

patient[2] n. case, client, invalid, sufferer.

patriotism n. chauvinism, flag-waving, jingoism, loyalty, nationalism.

patrol n. defence, garrison, guard, guarding, policing, protecting, roundvigilance, sentinel, surveillance, watch, watching, watchman.

v. cruise, go the rounds, guard, inspect, perambulate, police, range, tour.

patron n. advocate, backer, benefactor, buyer, champion, client, customer, defender, fautor, frequenter, friend, guardian, habitué, helper, Maecenas, partisan, philanthropist, protector, regular, shopper, sponsor, subscriber, supporter, sympathizer.

patronize v. assist, back, befriend, encourage, foster, frequent, fund, habituate, help, humor, maintain, promote, shop at, sponsor, support, talk down to.

pattern n. archetype, arrangement, criterion, cynosure, decoration, delineation, design, device, diagram, examplar, example, figuration, figure, Gestalt, guide, instructions, kind, method, model, motif, norm, order, orderliness, original, ornament, ornamentation, paradigm, paragon, plan, prototype, sample, sequence, shape, sort, specimen, standard, stencil, style, system, template, type, variety.

v. copy, decorate, design, emulate, follow, form, imitate, match, model, mold, order, shape, stencil, style, trim.

paunchy adj. adipose, corpulent, fat, podgy, portly, pot-bellied, pudgy, rotund, tubby.

pause v. break, cease, cut, delay, desist, discontinue, halt, hesitate, interrupt, rest, take a break, take a breather, take five, wait, waver.

n. abatement, break, breather, caesura, cessation, delay, discontinuance, dwell, gap, halt, hesitation, interlude, intermission, interruption, interval, let-up, lull, respite, rest, slackening, stay, stoppage, suspension, wait.

pawn[1] n. cat's-paw, creature, dupe, instrument, plaything, puppet, stooge, tool, toy.

pawn[2] v. deposit, dip, gage, hazard, hock, impawn, impignorate, lay in lavender, mortgage, pledge, pop, stake, wager.

n. hostage, security.

pay v. ante, benefit, bestow, bring in, clear, compensate, cough up, disburse, discharge, extend, foot, get even with, give, grant, honor, indemnify, liquidate, meet, offer, pay out, present, produce, proffer, profit, punish, reciprocate, recompense, reimburse, remit, remunerate, render, repay, requite, return, reward, serve, settle, square, square up, yield.

n. allowance, compensation, consideration, earnings, emoluments, fee, hire, honorarium, income, payment, recompense, reimbursement, remuneration, reward, salary, stipend, takings, wages.

payable adj. due, in arrears, mature, obligatory, outstanding, owed, owing, receivable, unpaid.

peace n. accord, agreement, amity, armistice, calm, calmness, cease-fire, composure, conciliation, concord, contentment, frith, harmony, hush, pacification, pax, peacefulness, placidity, quiet, quietude, relaxation, repose, rest, serenity, silence, stillness, tranquility, treaty, truce.

antonyms disagreement, disturbance, war

peace studies irenology.

peaceable *adj.* amiable, amicable, compatible, conciliatory, douce, dovish, easy-going, friendly, gentle, inoffensive, mild, non-belligerent, pacific, peaceful, peace-loving, placid, unwarlike.

antonyms belligerent, offensive.

peaceful *adj.* amicable, at peace, becalmed, calm, conciliatory, friendly, gentle, halcyon, harmonious, irenic (eirenic), non-violent, pacific, peaceable, peace-loving, placatory, placid, quiet, restful, serene, still, tranquil, unagitated, undisturbed, unruffled, untroubled, unwarlike.

antonyms disturbed, noisy, troubled.

peak *n.* acme, aiguille, apex, apogee, brow, climax, crest, crown, culmination, cuspid, high point, maximum, ne plus ultra, pinnacle, point, summit, tip, top, visor, zenith.

antonyms nadir, trough.

v. climax, come to a head, culminate, spire, tower.

peccadillo *n.* boob, delinquency, error, fault, indiscretion, infraction, lapse, misdeed, misdemeanor, slip, slip-up.

peculiar[1] *adj.* abnormal, bizarre, curious, eccentric, exceptional, extraordinary, far-out, freakish, funky, funny, odd, offbeat, outlandish, out-of-the-way, quaint, queer, singular, strange, uncommon, unconventional, unusual, way-out, weird.

antonyms normal, ordinary.

peculiar[2] *adj.* appropriate, characteristic, discriminative, distinct, distinctive, distinguishing, endemic, idiosyncratic, individual, local, particular, personal, private, quintessential, restricted, special, specific, unique.

antonyms general, uncharacteristic.

peculiarity *n.* abnormality, attribute, bizarreness, characteristic, distinctiveness, eccentricity, exception, feature, foible, freakishness, idiosyncrasy, kink, mannerism, mark, oddity, particularity, property, quality, queerness, quirk, singularity, specialty, trait, whimsicality.

pedantic *adj.* abstruse, academic, bookish, caviling, didactic, donnish, erudite, finical, formal, fussy, hair-splitting, learned, nit-picking, particular, pedagogic, perfectionist, pompous, precise, punctilious, scholastic, schoolmasterly, sententious, stilted.

antonyms casual, imprecise, informal.

peddle *v.* dilly-dally, flog, hawk, huckster, idle, loiter, market, piddle, push, retail, sell, tout, trade, trifle, vend.

pedestrian *n.* footslogger, foot-traveler, voetganger, walker.

adj. banal, boring, commonplace, dull, flat, humdrum, indifferent, mediocre, mundane, ordinary, plodding, prosaic, run-of-the-mill, stodgy, tolerable, unimaginative, uninspired, uninteresting.

antonyms bright, brilliant, exciting, imaginative.

pedigree *n.* ancestry, blood, breed, derivation, descent, dynasty, extraction, family, family tree, genealogy, heritage, line, lineage, parentage, race, stemma, stirps, stock, succession.

peek *v.* glance, keek, look, peep, peer, spy.

n. blink, dekko, gander, glance, glimpse, keek, look, look-see, peep.

peel *v.* decorticate, denude, desquamate, flake (off), pare, scale, skin, strip (off), undress.

n. epicarp, exocarp, integument, peeling, rind, skin, zest.

peep *v.* blink, emerge, glimpse, issue, keek, peek, peer.

n. blink, dekko, gander, glim, glimpse, keek, look, look-see, peek.

peer[1] *v.* appear, blink, emerge, examine, gaze, inspect, peep, scan, scrutinize, snoop, spy, squint.

peer[2] *n.* aristocrat, baron, count, duke, earl, lord, marquess, marquis, noble, nobleman, thane, viscount.

peer[3] *n.* compeer, counterpart, equal, equipollent, equivalent, fellow, like, match.

peevish *adj.* acrimonious, cantankerous, captious, childish, churlish, crabbed, cross, crotchety, crusty, fractious, franzy, fretful, grumpy, hipped, ill-natured, ill-tempered, irritable, miffy, perverse, pettish, petulant, querulous, ratty, short-tempered, snappy, splenetic, sulky, sullen, surly, testy, touchy, waspish.

antonym good-tempered.

peevishness *n.* acrimony, captiousness, ill-temper, irritability, perversity, pet, petulance, pique, protervity, querulousness, testiness.

peg *v.* attach, control, fasten, fix, freeze, insert, join, limit, mark, pierce, score, secure, set, stabilize.

n. dowel, hook, knob, marker, pin, post, stake, thole(-pin), toggle.

pejorative *adj.* bad, belittling, condemnatory, damning, debasing, deprecatory, depreciatory, derogatory, detractive, detractory, disparaging, negative, slighting, uncomplimentary, unflattering, unpleasant.

antonyms complimentary, laudatory.

pen *n.* cage, coop, crib, cru(i)ve, enclosure, fold, hutch, stall, sty.

v. cage, confine, coop, corral, crib, enclose, fence, hedge, hem in, hurdle, mew (up), shut up.

penalize *v.* amerce, correct, disadvantage, discipline, handicap, mulct, punish.

antonym reward.

penalty *n.* amende, amercement, disadvantage, fine, forfeit, forfeiture, handicap, mulct, price, punishment, retribution.

antonym reward.

penchant *n.* affinity, bent, bias, disposition, fondness, inclination, leaning, liking, partiality, predilection, predisposition, preference, proclivity, proneness, propensity, soft spot, taste, tendency, turn.

antonym dislike.

penetrate *v.* affect, bore, come across, come home, comprehend, decipher, diffuse, discern, enter, fathom, get through to, get to the bottom of, grasp, impress, infiltrate, perforate, permeate, pervade, pierce, prick, probe, seep, sink, stab, strike, suffuse, touch, understand, unravel.

penetrating *adj.* acute, astute, biting, carrying, critical, discerning, discriminating, harsh, incisive, intelligent, intrusive, keen, observant, penetrative, perceptive, percipient, perspicacious, pervasive, piercing, profound, pungent, quick, sagacious, searching, sharp, sharp-witted, shrewd, shrill, stinging, strong.

antonyms gentle, obtuse, soft.

peninsula *n.* cape, chersonese, doab, mull, point, tongue.

penitent *adj.* abject, apologetic, atoning, conscience-stricken, contrite, humble, in sackcloth and ashes, regretful, remorseful, repentant, rueful, sorrowful, sorry.

antonym unrepentant.

penniless *adj.* bankrupt, broke, bust(ed), cleaned out, destitute, flat broke, impecunious, impoverished, indigent, moneyless, necessitous, needy, obolary, on one's uppers, on the rocks, penurious, poor, poverty-stricken, ruined, skint, stony-broke, strapped.

antonyms rich, wealthy.

pensive *adj.* absent-minded, absorbed, cogitative, contemplative, dreamy, grave, meditative, melancholy, musing, preoccupied, reflective, ruminative, serious, sober, solemn, thoughtful, wistful.

penurious *adj.* beggarly, bust(ed), cheeseparing, close, close-fisted, deficient, destitute, flat broke, frugal, grudging, impecunious, impoverished, inadequate, indigent, meager, mean, miserable, miserly, near, needy, niggardly, obolary, paltry, parsimonious, penniless, poor, poverty-stricken, scanty, skimping, stingy, tight-fisted, ungenerous.

antonyms generous, wealthy.

penury *n.* beggary, dearth, deficiency, destitution, indigence, lack, mendicancy, mendicity, need, paucity, pauperism, poverty, privation, scantiness, scarcity, shortage, sparseness, straitened circumstances, straits, want.

antonym prosperity.

people *n.* citizens, clan, commonalty, community, crowd, demos, family, folk, general public, gens, grass roots, hoi polloi, human beings, humanity, humans, inhabitants, mankind, many-headed beast, many-headed monster, masses, mob, mortals, multitude, nation, persons, plebs, populace, population, public, punters, rabble, race, rank and file, the herd, the million, tribe.

v. colonize, inhabit, occupy, populate, settle, tenant.

perceive *v.* appreciate, apprehend, be aware of, behold, catch, comprehend, conclude, deduce, descry, discern, discover, distinguish, espy, feel, gather, get, grasp, intuit, know, learn, make out, note, observe, realize, recognize, remark, see, sense, spot, understand.

perceptible *adj.* apparent, appreciable, clear, conspicuous, detectable, discernible, distinct, distinguishable, evident, noticeable, observable, obvious, palpable, perceivable, recognizable, salient, tangible, visible.

antonym imperceptible.

perception *n.* apprehension, awareness, conception, consciousness, discernment, feeling, grasp, idea, impression, insight, intellection, notion, observation, recognition, sensation, sense, taste, understanding, uptake.

perceptive *adj.* able to see through a millstone, acute, alert, astute, aware, discerning, insightful, observant, penetrating, percipient, perspicacious, quick, responsive, sagacious, sapient, sensitive, sharp.

antonym unobservant.

percipient *adj.* alert, alive, astute, aware, discerning, discriminating, intelligent, judicious, knowing, penetrating, perceptive, perspicacious, quick-witted, sharp, wide-awake.

antonyms obtuse, unaware.

perfect *adj.* absolute, accomplished, accurate, adept, blameless, close, complete, completed, consummate, copybook, correct, entire, exact, excellent, experienced, expert, faithful, faultless, finished, flawless, full,

ideal, immaculate, impeccable, irreproachable, masterly, model, polished, practiced, precise, pure, right, sheer, skilful, skilled, splendid, spotless, spot-on, strict, sublime, superb, superlative, supreme, true, unadulterated, unalloyed, unblemished, unerring, unimpeachable, unmarred, unmitigated, untarnished, utter, whole.

antonyms flawed, imperfect.

v. accomplish, achieve, carry out, complete, consummate, effect, elaborate, finish, fulfil, perfectionate, perform, realize, refine.

perfection *n.* accomplishment, achievement, acme, completeness, completion, consummation, crown, evolution, exactness, excellence, exquisiteness, flawlessness, fulfilment, ideal, integrity, maturity, nonpareil, paragon, perfectness, pinnacle, precision, purity, realization, sublimity, superiority, wholeness.

antonyms flaw, imperfection.

perfectly *adv.* absolutely, admirably, altogether, completely, consummately, entirely, exquisitely, faultlessly, flawlessly, fully, ideally, impeccably, incomparably, irreproachably, quite, superbly, superlatively, supremely, thoroughly, to perfection, totally, unimpeachably, utterly, wholly, wonderfully.

antonyms imperfectly, partially.

perform *v.* accomplish, achieve, act, appear as, bring about, bring off, carry out, complete, depict, discharge, do, effect, enact, execute, fulfil, function, functionate, manage, observe, play, present, produce, pull off, put on, render, represent, satisfy, stage, transact, work.

performance *n.* accomplishment, account, achievement, act, acting, action, appearance, behavior, bother, business, carrying out, carry-on, completion, conduct, consummation, discharge, efficiency, execution, exhibition, exploit, feat, fulfilment, functioning, fuss, gig, implementation, interpretation, melodrama, operation, play, portrayal, practice, presentation, production, rendition, representation, rigmarole, running, show, to-do, work, working.

performer *n.* actor, actress, artiste, moke, mummer, play-actor, player, Thespian, trouper.

perfume *n.* aroma, attar, balm, balminess, bouquet, cologne, essence, fragrance, incense, odor, redolence, scent, smell, sweetness, toilet water.

perfunctory *adj.* automatic, brief, careless, cursory, heedless, hurried, inattentive, indifferent, mechanical, negligent, offhand, routine, sketchy, slipshod, slovenly, stereotyped, superficial, wooden.

antonym cordial.

perhaps *adv.* conceivably, feasibly, happen, maybe, mayhap, peradventure, perchance, possibly, you never know.

peril *n.* danger, exposure, hazard, imperilment, insecurity, jeopardy, menace, pitfall, risk, threat, uncertainty, vulnerability.

antonyms safety, security.

perilous *adj.* chancy, dangerous, desperate, dicey, difficult, dire, exposed, hairy, hazardous, menacing, parlous, precarious, risky, threatening, unsafe, unsure, vulnerable.

antonyms safe, secure.

period[1] *n.* age, course, cycle, date, days, end, eon, epoch, era, generation, interval, season, space, span, spell, stage, stint, stop, stretch, term, time, turn, while, years.

period² n. menses, menstrual flow, menstruation, monthlies, the curse.

periodical n. gazette, journal, magazine, monthly, organ, paper, publication, quarterly, review, serial, weekly.

perish v. collapse, croak, crumble, decay, decline, decompose, decrease, die, disappear, disintegrate, end, expire, fall, molder, pass away, rot, vanish, waste, wither.

perishable adj. biodegradable, corruptible, decomposable, destructible, fast-decaying, fast-deteriorating, short-lived, unstable.

perjury n. false oath, false statement, false swearing, false witness, falsification, forswearing, mendacity.

permanent adj. abiding, constant, durable, enduring, everlasting, fixed, immutable, imperishable, indestructible, ineffaceable, ineradicable, inerasable, invariable, lasting, long-lasting, perennial, perpetual, persistent, stable, standing, steadfast, unchanging, unfading.
antonyms ephemeral, fleeting, temporary.

permeate v. charge, fill, filter through, imbue, impenetrate, impregnate, infiltrate, interfuse, interpenetrate, pass through, penetrate, percolate, pervade, saturate, seep through, soak through.

permissible adj. acceptable, admissible, all right, allowable, allowed, authorized, kosher, lawful, leal, legit, legitimate, licit, OK, permitted, proper, sanctioned.
antonym prohibited.

permission n. allowance, approval, assent, authorization, consent, dispensation, freedom, go-ahead, green light, imprimatur, indult, leave, liberty, license, permit, sanction, sufferance.
antonym prohibition.

permissive adj. acquiescent, complaisant, easy-going, forbearing, free, indulgent, latitudinarian, lax, lenient, liberal, open-minded, overindulgent, tolerant.
antonym strict.

permit v. admit, agree, allow, authorize, consent, empower, enable, endorse, endure, give leave, grant, let, warrant.
antonym prohibit.
n. authorization, carnet, liberty, license, pass, passport, permission, sanction, visa, warrant.
antonym prohibition.

perpetrate v. carry out, commit, do, effect, enact, execute, inflict, perform, practice, wreak.

perpetual adj. abiding, ceaseless, constant, continual, continuous, deathless, endless, enduring, eternal, everlasting, immortal, incessant, infinite, interminable, lasting, never-ending, never-failing, perennial, permanent, persistent, recurrent, repeated, sempiternal, unceasing, unchanging, undying, unending, unfailing, unflagging, uninterrupted, unremitting, unvarying.
antonyms ephemeral, intermittent, transient.

perpetuate v. commemorate, continue, eternalize, immortalize, keep alive, keep up, maintain, preserve, protract, sustain.

perplex v. baffle, befuddle, beset, bewilder, complicate, confound, confuse, dumbfound, embrangle, encumber, entangle, gravel, hobble, involve, jumble, mix up, muddle, mystify, nonplus, pother, pudder, puzzle, stump, tangle, thicken, throw.

perplexed adj. at a loss, baffled, bamboozled, bewildered, confounded, disconcerted, fuddled, muddled, mystified, puzzled, worried.

perplexing adj. amazing, baffling, bewildering, complex, complicated, confusing, difficult, distractive, enigmatic, hard, inexplicable, intricate, involved, knotty, labyrinthine, mysterious, mystifying, paradoxical, puzzling, strange, taxing, thorny, unaccountable, vexatious, weird.
antonyms easy, simple.

persecute v. afflict, annoy, badger, bait, bother, castigate, crucify, distress, dragoon, harass, haze, hound, hunt, ill-treat, injure, maltreat, martyr, molest, oppress, pester, pursue, tease, torment, torture, tyrannize, vex, victimize, worry.
antonyms accommodate, humor, indulge, pamper.

persevere v. adhere, carry on, continue, endure, go on, hang on, hold fast, hold on, keep going, persist, plug away, pursue, remain, soldier on, stand firm, stick at.
antonyms desist, discontinue, give up, stop.

persist v. abide, carry on, continue, endure, insist, keep at it, last, linger, perdure, persevere, remain, stand fast, stand firm.
antonyms desist, stop.

persistence n. assiduity, assiduousness, constancy, determination, diligence, doggedness, endurance, grit, indefatigableness, perseverance, pertinacity, pluck, resolution, sedulity, stamina, steadfastness, tenacity, tirelessness.

persistent adj. assiduous, constant, continual, continuous, determined, dogged, endless, enduring, fixed, hydra-headed, immovable, incessant, indefatigable, indomitable, interminable, never-ending, obdurate, obstinate, perpetual, persevering, pertinacious, relentless, repeated, resolute, steadfast, steady, stubborn, tenacious, tireless, unflagging, unrelenting, unremitting, zealous.

person n. being, bod, body, cat, character, codger, cookie, customer, human, human being, individual, individuum, living soul, party, soul, specimen, type, wight.

personable adj. affable, agreeable, amiable, attractive, charming, good-looking, handsome, likable, nice, outgoing, pleasant, pleasing, presentable, warm, winning.
antonyms disagreeable, unattractive.

personal adj. bodily, corporal, corporeal, derogatory, disparaging, exclusive, exterior, idiosyncratic, individual, inimitable, insulting, intimate, material, nasty, offensive, own, particular, peculiar, pejorative, physical, private, privy, slighting, special, tête-à-tête.
antonyms general, public, universal.

personality n. attraction, attractiveness, celebrity, character, charisma, charm, disposition, dynamism, humor, identity, individuality, likableness, magnetism, make-up, nature, notable, personage, pleasantness, psyche, selfhood, selfness, star, temper, temperament, traits.

perspicacity n. acuity, acumen, acuteness, brains, cleverness, discernment, discrimination, insight, keenness, penetration, perceptiveness, percipience, perspicaciousness, perspicuity, sagaciousness, sagacity, sharpness, shrewdness, wit.

persuade v. actuate, advise, allure, bring round, cajole, coax, convert, convince, counsel, entice, impel, incite, induce, influence, inveigle, lead on, lean on, prevail upon, prompt, satisfy, sway, sweet-talk, talk into, urge, win over.
antonyms discourage, dissuade.

persuasion n. belief, blandishment, cajolery, camp, certitude, cogency, come-on, conversion, conviction, credo, creed, cult, denomination, enticement, exhortation, faction, faith, force, inducement, influence, inveiglement, opinion, party, persuasiveness, potency, power, pull, school (of thought), sect, side, suasion, sweet talk, tenet, views, wheedling.

persuasive adj. cogent, compelling, convincing, credible, effective, eloquent, forceful, honeyed, impelling, impressive, inducing, influential, logical, moving, persuasory, plausible, potent, sound, telling, touching, valid, weighty, whilly, whillywha(w), winning.

pertain v. appertain, apply, be appropriate, be part of, be relevant, bear on, befit, belong, come under, concern, refer, regard, relate.

pertinacious adj. determined, dogged, headstrong, inflexible, intractable, mulish, obdurate, obstinate, persevering, persistent, perverse, purposeful, relentless, resolute, self-willed, strong-willed, stubborn, tenacious, uncompromising, unyielding, wilful.

pertinent adj. ad rem, admissible, analogous, applicable, apposite, appropriate, apropos, apt, befitting, fit, fitting, germane, material, pat, proper, relevant, suitable, to the point, to the purpose.

antonyms inappropriate, irrelevant, unsuitable.

perturbed adj. agitated, alarmed, anxious, discomposed, disconcerted, disturbed, fearful, flurried, flustered, nervous, restless, shaken, troubled, uncomfortable, uneasy, unsettled, upset, worried.

antonym unperturbed.

pervade v. affect, charge, diffuse, extend, fill, imbue, infuse, osmose, overspread, penetrate, percolate, permeate, saturate, suffuse.

perverse adj. abnormal, balky, cantankerous, churlish, contradictory, contrary, contumacious, crabbed, cross, cross-grained, cussed, delinquent, depraved, deviant, disobedient, dogged, fractious, froward, headstrong, ill-natured, ill-tempered, improper, incorrect, intractable, intransigent, miscreant, mulish, obdurate, obstinate, peevish, petulant, pig-headed, rebellious, recalcitrant, refractory, spiteful, stroppy, stubborn, surly, thrawn, thwart, troublesome, unhealthy, unmanageable, unreasonable, unyielding, uppity, wayward, wilful, wrong-headed, wry.

antonyms normal, reasonable.

perversion n. aberration, abnormality, anomaly, corruption, debauchery, depravity, deviance, deviancy, deviation, distortion, falsification, immorality, kink, kinkiness, misapplication, misinterpretation, misrepresentation, misuse, paraphilia, twisting, unnaturalness, vice, vitiation, wickedness.

pervert v. abuse, bend, corrupt, debase, debauch, degrade, deprave, distort, divert, falsify, garble, lead astray, misapply, misconstrue, misinterpret, misrepresent, misuse, subvert, twist, vitiate, warp, wrest.

n. debauchee, degenerate, deviant, paraphiliac, vert, weirdo.

perverted adj. aberrant, abnormal, corrupt, debased, debauched, depraved, deviant, distorted, evil, freakish, immoral, impaired, kinky, misguided, queer, sick, twisted, unhealthy, unnatural, vicious, vitiated, warped, wicked.

pest n. annoyance, bane, blight, bore, bother, bug, canker, curse, irritation, nuisance, pain (in the neck), scourge, thorn in one's flesh, trial, vexation.

pester v. annoy, badger, bedevil, bother, bug, chivvy, disturb, dog, drive round the bend, drive up the wall, fret, get at, harass, harry, hassle, hector, hound, irk, nag, pick on, plague, ride, torment, worry.

pet n. darling, dilling, doll, duck, ewe-lamb, favorite, idol, jewel, treasure, whitehead.

adj. cherished, dearest, favored, favorite, particular, preferred, special.

v. baby, canoodle, caress, coddle, cosset, cuddle, dote on, fondle, indulge, kiss, mollycoddle, neck, pamper, pat, smooch, snog, spoil, stroke.

petition n. address, appeal, application, boon, entreaty, imploration, invocation, plea, prayer, request, rogation, round robin, solicitation, suit, supplication.

v. appeal, ask, beg, beseech, bid, call upon, crave, entreat, implore, memorialize, plead, pray, press, solicit, sue, supplicate, urge.

petrify v. amaze, appal, astonish, astound, benumb, calcify, confound, dumbfound, fossilize, gorgonize, harden, horrify, immobilize, numb, paralyze, set, solidify, stun, stupefy, terrify, transfix, turn to stone.

petty adj. cheap, contemptible, grudging, inconsiderable, inessential, inferior, insignificant, junior, lesser, little, lower, mean, measly, minor, negligible, one-horse, paltry, picayune, picayunish, piddling, pimping, poking, poky, secondary, shabby, slight, small, small-minded, spiteful, stingy, subordinate, trifling, trivial, ungenerous, unimportant.

antonyms generous, important, large-hearted, significant, vital.

petulant adj. bad-tempered, captious, caviling, crabbed, cross, crusty, fretful, ill-humored, impatient, irascible, irritable, moody, peevish, perverse, pettish, procacious, querulous, snappish, sour, sulky, sullen, ungracious, waspish.

phantom n. apparition, chimera, eidolon, figment (of the imagination), ghost, hallucination, illusion, manes, phantasm(a), revenant, shade, simulacrum, specter, spirit, spook, vision, wraith.

phase n. aspect, chapter, condition, development, juncture, period, point, position, season, spell, stage, state, step, time.

phenomenon n. appearance, circumstance, curiosity, episode, event, fact, happening, incident, marvel, miracle, occurrence, prodigy, rarity, sensation, sight, spectacle, wonder.

philanthropy n. agape, alms-giving, altruism, beneficence, benevolence, benignity, bounty, brotherly love, charitableness, charity, generosity, humanitarianism, kind-heartedness, liberality, munificence, open-handedness, patronage, public-spiritedness, unselfishness.

philosophical adj. abstract, analytical, calm, collected, composed, cool, dispassionate, equanimous, erudite, impassive, imperturbable, learned, logical, metaphysical, patient, philosophic, rational, resigned, sagacious, serene, stoical, theoretical, thoughtful, tranquil, unruffled, wise.

phlegmatic adj. apathetic, bovine, cold, dull, frigid, heavy, impassive, imperturbable, indifferent, lethargic, listless, lymphatic, matter-of-fact, nonchalant, placid, sluggish, stoical, stolid, unconcerned, undemonstrative, unemotional.

antonyms demonstrative, passionate.

phony adj. affected, assumed, bogus, counterfeit, fake,

false, forged, imitation, pseudo, put-on, quack, quack-salving, sham, spurious, trick.

antonyms real, true.

n. counterfeit, fake, faker, forgery, fraud, humbug, impostor, mountebank, pretender, pseud, quack, sham.

phrase *n.* construction, expression, idiom, locution, mention, motto, remark, saying, tag, utterance.

v. couch, express, formulate, frame, present, pronounce, put, say, style, term, utter, voice, word.

physical *adj.* actual, bodily, carnal, concrete, corporal, corporeal, earthly, fleshly, incarnate, material, mortal, natural, palpable, real, sensible, solid, somatic, substantial, tangible, visible.

antonyms mental, spiritual.

physique *n.* body, build, chassis, constitution, figure, form, frame, make-up, shape, structure.

pick *v.* break into, break open, choose, collect, crack, cull, cut, decide on, elect, embrace, espouse, fix upon, foment, gather, harvest, incite, instigate, opt for, pluck, prize, provoke, pull, screen, select, settle on, sift out, single out, start.

antonym reject.

n. best, brightest and best, choice, choicest, choosing, cream, crème de la crème, decision, elect, élite, flower, option, preference, pride, prize, selection, tops.

picket *n.* demonstrator, dissenter, guard, look-out, outpost, pale, paling, palisade, patrol, peg, picketer, post, protester, scout, sentinel, sentry, spotter, stake, stanchion, upright, vedette, watchman.

v. blockade, boycott, corral, demonstrate, enclose, fence, hedge in, palisade, pen in, protest.

pictorial *adj.* diagrammatic, expressive, graphic, illustrated, picturesque, representational, scenic, schematic, striking, vivid.

picture *n.* account, archetype, carbon copy, copy, dead ringer, delineation, depiction, description, double, drawing, duplicate, effigy, embodiment, engraving, epitome, essence, film, flick, graphic, illustration, image, impression, kakemono, likeness, living image, lookalike, motion picture, movie, painting, personification, photograph, portrait, portrayal, print, re-creation, replica, report, representation, ringer, scene, similitude, sketch, spit, spitting image, tablature, table, twin, vraisemblance.

v. conceive of, delineate, depict, describe, draw, envisage, envision, illustrate, image, imagine, paint, photograph, portray, render, represent, see, show, sketch, visualize.

piece *n.* allotment, article, bit, case, chunk, component, composition, constituent, creation, division, element, example, fraction, fragment, instance, item, length, mammock, morsel, mouthful, objet d'art, occurrence, offcut, part, piecemeal, portion, production, quantity, sample, scrap, section, segment, share, shred, slice, snippet, specimen, stroke, study, work, work of art.

piecemeal *adv.* at intervals, bit by bit, by degrees, fitfully, in dribs and drabs, in penny numbers, intermittently, little by little, parcel-wise, partially, slowly.

antonyms completely, entirely, wholly.

adj. discrete, fragmentary, intermittent, interrupted, partial, patchy, scattered, unsystematic.

antonyms complete, entire, whole, wholesale.

pierce *v.* affect, barb, bore, comprehend, discern, discover, drift, drill, enter, excite, fathom, grasp, gride,

hurt, impale, lancinate, move, pain, penetrate, perforate, pink, prick, probe, prog, puncture, realize, rouse, run through, see, spike, stab, stick into, sting, stir, strike, thrill, thrust, touch, transfix, transpierce, understand, wound.

piercing *adj.* acute, agonizing, alert, algid, arctic, aware, biting, bitter, cold, ear-piercing, ear-splitting, excruciating, exquisite, fierce, freezing, frore, frosty, gelid, high-pitched, intense, keen, loud, nipping, nippy, numbing, painful, penetrating, perceptive, perspicacious, powerful, probing, quick-witted, racking, raw, searching, severe, sharp, shattering, shooting, shrewd, shrill, Siberian, stabbing, wintry.

pig-headed *adj.* bull-headed, contrary, cross-grained, dense, froward, inflexible, intractable, intransigent, mulish, obstinate, perverse, self-willed, stiff-necked, stubborn, stupid, unyielding, wilful, wrong-headed.

antonyms flexible, tractable.

pigment *n.* color, colorant, coloring, coloring matter, dye, dyestuff, hue, paint, stain, tempera, tincture, tint.

pile¹ *n.* accumulation, assemblage, assortment, bing, bomb, building, cock, collection, edifice, erection, fortune, heap, hoard, mass, mint, money, mound, mountain, mow, packet, pot, stack, stockpile, structure, wealth.

v. accumulate, amass, assemble, build up, charge, climb, collect, crowd, crush, flock, flood, gather, heap, hoard, jam, load up, mass, pack, rush, stack, store, stream.

pile² *n.* bar, beam, column, foundation, pier, piling, pill, post, rib, stanchion, support, upright.

pile³ *n.* down, fur, fuzz, fuzziness, hair, nap, plush, shag.

pilgrim *n.* crusader, hadji, palmer, peregrine, traveler, wanderer, wayfarer.

pilgrimage *n.* crusade, excursion, expedition, hadj, journey, mission, odyssey, peregrination, tour, trip.

pillar *n.* balluster, bastion, cippus, column, leader, leading light, mainstay, mast, pier, pilaster, piling, post, prop, rock, shaft, stanchion, support, supporter, tower of strength, upholder, upright, worthy.

pilot *n.* airman, aviator, captain, conductor, coxswain, director, flier, guide, helmsman, hobbler, leader, lodesman, navigator, steersman.

v. boss, conduct, control, direct, drive, fly, guide, handle, lead, manage, navigate, operate, run, shepherd, steer.

adj. experimental, model, test, trial.

pimp *n.* bawd, fancy man, fleshmonger, go-between, mack, pander, panderer, procurer, white-slaver, whoremaster, whoremonger.

pin *v.* affix, attach, fasten, fix, hold down, hold fast, immobilize, join, nail, pinion, press, restrain, secure, tack.

n. bolt, breastpin, brooch, clip, fastener, nail, peg, rivet, screw, spike, spindle, stick pin, tack, tie-pin.

pinch *v.* afflict, apprehend, arrest, bust, chafe, check, collar, compress, confine, cramp, crush, distress, do, economize, filch, grasp, hurt, knap, knock off, lay, lift, nab, nick, nip, oppress, pain, pick up, pilfer, press, prig, pull in, purloin, rob, run in, scrimp, skimp, snaffle, snatch, sneap, snitch, spare, squeeze, steal, stint, swipe, tweak.

n. bit, crisis, dash, difficulty, emergency, exigency, hardship, jam, jot, mite, necessity, nip, oppression, pass, pickle, plight, predicament, pressure, soupçon, speck, squeeze, strait, stress, taste, tweak.

pinion v. bind, chain, confine, fasten, fetter, hobble, immobilize, manacle, pin down, shackle, tie, truss.

pinnacle n. acme, apex, apogee, cap, cone, crest, crown, eminence, height, needle, obelisk, peak, pyramid, spire, steeple, summit, top, turret, vertex, zenith.

pioneer n. colonist, colonizer, developer, explorer, founder, founding father, frontiersman, innovator, leader, settler, trail-blazer, voortrekker, way-maker.

v. blaze a trail, create, develop, discover, establish, found, initiate, instigate, institute, invent, launch, lead, open up, originate, prepare, start.

pious adj. dedicated, devoted, devout, God-fearing, godly, good, goody-goody, holier-than-thou, holy, hypocritical, moral, pietistic, religiose, religious, reverent, righteous, saintly, sanctimonious, self-righteous, spiritual, unctuous, virtuous.

antonyms impious.

piquant adj. biting, interesting, lively, peppery, poignant, provocative, pungent, racy, salty, savory, scintillating, sharp, sparkling, spicy, spirited, stimulating, stinging, tangy, tart, zesty.

antonyms banal, jejune.

pirate n. buccaneer, corsair, filibuster, freebooter, infringer, marauder, marque, picaroon, plagiarist, plagiarizer, raider, rover, sallee-man, sea-rat, sea-robber, sea-rover, sea-wolf, water-rat.

v. appropriate, borrow, copy, crib, lift, nick, pinch, plagiarize, poach, reproduce, steal.

pistol n. dag, derringer, gat, gun, hand-gun, iron, Luger, piece, revolver, rod, sidearm, six-shooter.

pit n. abyss, alveole, alveolus, cavity, chasm, coal-mine, crater, dent, depression, dimple, excavation, gulf, hole, hollow, indentation, mine, oubliette, pock-mark, pothole, trench, variole.

pitch v. bung, cast, chuck, dive, drop, erect, fall headlong, fix, fling, flounder, heave, hurl, launch, lob, locate, lurch, peck, place, plant, plunge, raise, roll, set up, settle, sling, stagger, station, throw, topple, toss, tumble, wallow, welter.

n. angle, cant, degree, dip, gradient, ground, harmonic, height, incline, level, line, modulation, park, patter, playing-field, point, sales talk, slope, sound, spiel, sports field, steepness, summit, tilt, timbre, tone.

pitcher n. bottle, can, container, crock, ewer, jack, jar, jug, urn, vessel.

piteous adj. affecting, deplorable, distressing, doleful, doloriferous, dolorific, grievous, heartbreaking, heart-rending, lamentable, miserable, mournful, moving, pathetic, pitiable, pitiful, plaintive, poignant, sad, sorrowful, touching, woeful, wretched.

pitfall n. catch, danger, difficulty, downfall, drawback, hazard, peril, pit, snag, snare, stumbling-block, trap.

pitiable adj. contemptible, distressed, distressful, distressing, doleful, grievous, lamentable, miserable, mournful, pathetic, piteous, poor, sad, sorry, woeful, woesome, wretched.

pitiful adj. abject, base, beggarly, contemptible, deplorable, despicable, distressing, grievous, heartbreaking, heart-rending, hopeless, inadequate, insignificant, lamentable, low, mean, miserable, paltry, pathetic, piteous, pitiable, ruthful, sad, scurvy, shabby, sorry, vile, woeful, worthless, wretched.

pitiless adj. brutal, callous, cold-blooded, cold-hearted, cruel, flinty, hard-hearted, harsh, heartless, implacable, inexorable, inhuman, merciless, obdurate, relentless, ruthless, uncaring, unfeeling, unmerciful, unpitying, unsympathetic.

antonyms compassionate, gentle, kind, merciful.

pity n. charity, clemency, commiseration, compassion, condolence, crime, crying shame, fellow-feeling, forbearance, kindness, mercy, misfortune, regret, ruth, shame, sin, sympathy, tenderness, understanding.

antonyms cruelty, disdain, scorn.

v. absolve, bleed for, commiserate with, condole with, feel for, forgive, grieve for, pardon, reprieve, sympathize with, weep for.

pivotal adj. axial, central, climactic, critical, crucial, decisive, determining, focal, vital.

place n. abode, accommodation, affair, apartment, appointment, area, berth, billet, charge, city, concern, district, domicile, duty, dwelling, employment, flat, function, grade, home, house, job, locale, locality, location, locus, manor, mansion, neighborhood, pad, point, position, post, prerogative, property, quarter, rank, region, residence, responsibility, right, role, room, seat, site, situation, space, spot, station, status, stead, town, venue, vicinity, village, whereabouts.

v. allocate, appoint, arrange, assign, associate, bung, charge, class, classify, commission, deposit, dispose, dump, entrust, establish, fix, give, grade, group, identify, install, know, lay, locate, order, plant, position, put, put one's finger on, rank, recognize, remember, rest, set, settle, situate, sort, stand, station, stick.

placid adj. calm, collected, composed, cool, equable, even, even-tempered, gentle, halcyon, imperturbable, level-headed, mild, peaceful, quiet, reposeful, restful, self-possessed, serene, still, tranquil, undisturbed, unexcitable, unmoved, unruffled, untroubled.

antonyms agitated, jumpy.

plagiarize v. appropriate, borrow, counterfeit, crib, infringe, lift, pirate, reproduce, steal, thieve.

plague n. affliction, aggravation, annoyance, bane, blight, bother, calamity, cancer, contagion, curse, death, disease, epidemic, evil, infection, irritant, nuisance, pain, pandemic, pest, pestilence, problem, scourge, thorn in the flesh, torment, trial, vexation, visitation.

v. afflict, annoy, badger, bedevil, bother, distress, disturb, fret, harass, harry, hassle, haunt, hound, molest, pain, persecute, pester, tease, torment, torture, trouble, vex.

plain adj. apparent, artless, austere, bare, basic, blunt, candid, clear, clinical, common, commonplace, comprehensible, direct, discreet, distinct, downright, even, everyday, evident, flat, forthright, frank, frugal, guileless, home-bred, homely, homespun, honest, ill-favored, ingenuous, legible, level, lowly, lucid, manifest, modest, muted, obvious, open, ordinary, outspoken, patent, penny-plain, plane, pure, restrained, self-colored, severe, simple, sincere, smooth, Spartan, stark, straightforward, transparent, ugly, unadorned, unaffected, unambiguous, unattractive, unbeautiful, understandable, undistinguished, unelaborate, unembellished, unfigured, unhandsome, unlovely, unmistakable, unobstructed, unornamented, unpatterned, unprepossessing, unpretentious, untrimmed, unvarnished, visible, whole-colored, workaday.

antonyms abstruse, attractive, elaborate, exaggerated, ostentatious, rich, striking, unclear.

n. flat, grassland, llano, lowland, maidan, plateau, prairie, steppe, tableland, vega, veld(t).

plan *n.* blueprint, chart, contrivance, delineation, design, device, diagram, drawing, idea, illustration, layout, map, method, plot, procedure, program, project, proposal, proposition, representation, scenario, schedule, scheme, sketch, strategy, suggestion, system.
v. aim, arrange, complot, concoct, conspire, contemplate, contrive, design, devise, draft, envisage, foreplan, foresee, formulate, frame, intend, invent, mean, organize, outline, plot, prepare, propose, purpose, represent, scheme.

plane¹ *n.* class, condition, degree, echelon, footing, level, position, rank, rung, stage, stratum.
adj. even, flat, flush, horizontal, level, plain, planar, regular, smooth, uniform.

plane² *n.* aircraft, airliner, airplane, bomber, fighter, glider, jet, jumbo, jumbo jet, sea-plane, swing-wing, VTOL.
v. fly, glide, sail, skate, skim, volplane, wing.

plastic *adj.* compliant, docile, ductile, fictile, flexible, impressionable, malleable, manageable, moldable, pliable, pliant, receptive, responsive, soft, supple, tractable.
antonyms inflexible, rigid.

plasticity *n.* flexibility, malleability, pliability, pliableness, pliancy, softness, suppleness, tractability.
antonyms inflexibility, rigidity.

platform *n.* dais, estrade, gantry, manifesto, objective(s), party line, podium, policy, principle, program, rostrum, stage, stand, tenet(s).

platitude *n.* banality, bromide, chestnut, cliché, commonplace, inanity, stereotype, truism.

plausible *adj.* believable, colorable, conceivable, convincing, credible, facile, fair-spoken, glib, likely, persuasive, possible, probable, reasonable, smooth, smooth-talking, smooth-tongued, specious, tenable, voluble.
antonyms implausible, improbable, unlikely.

play *v.* act, bet, caper, challenge, chance, compete, contend, execute, fiddle, fidget, flirt, fool around, frisk, frolic, gamble, gambol, hazard, impersonate, interfere, lilt, participate, perform, personate, portray, punt, represent, revel, risk, rival, romp, speculate, sport, string along, take, take on, take part, take the part of, trifle, vie with, wager.
antonym work.
n. action, activity, amusement, caper, comedy, diversion, doodle, drama, elbowroom, employment, entertainment, exercise, farce, foolery, frolic, fun, function, gambling, gambol, game, gaming, give, humor, jest, joking, lark, latitude, leeway, margin, masque, motion, movement, operation, pastime, performance, piece, prank, range, recreation, romp, room, scope, show, space, sport, sweep, swing, teasing, tragedy, transaction, working.

playful *adj.* arch, cheerful, coltish, coquettish, coy, espiègle, flirtatious, frisky, frolicsome, gamesome, gay, good-natured, humorous, impish, jesting, joking, joyous, kittenish, kitteny, larkish, larky, lively, merry, mischievous, puckish, reasing, roguish, rollicking, spirited, sportive, sprightly, tongue-in-cheek, toyish, toysome, vivacious, waggish.

antonyms serious, stern.

plaything *n.* amusement, bauble, game, gewgaw, gimcrack, pastime, puppet, toy, trifle, trinket.

playwright *n.* dramatist, dramaturge, dramaturgist, screen-writer, scriptwriter.

plea *n.* action, allegation, apology, appeal, begging, cause, claim, defense, entreaty, excuse, explanation, extenuation, imploration, intercession, invocation, justification, overture, petition, placit(um), prayer, pretext, request, suit, supplication, vindication.

plead *v.* adduce, allege, appeal, argue, ask, assert, beg, beseech, crave, entreat, implore, importune, maintain, moot, petition, put forward, request, solicit, supplicate.

pleasant *adj.* acceptable, affable, agreeable, amene, amiable, amusing, charming, cheerful, cheery, congenial, cool, delectable, delightful, delightsome, engaging, enjoyable, fine, friendly, genial, good-humored, gratifying, likable, listenable, lovely, nice, pleasing, pleasurable, refreshing, satisfying, sunshiny, toothsome, welcome, winsome.
antonyms distasteful, nasty, repugnant, unpleasant.

please *v.* amuse, captivate, charm, cheer, choose, content, delight, desire, enchant, entertain, gladden, go for, gratify, humor, indulge, like, opt, prefer, rejoice, satisfy, see fit, suit, think fit, tickle, tickle pink, want, will, wish.
antonyms anger, annoy, displease.

pleasing *adj.* acceptable, agreeable, amiable, amusing, attractive, charming, congenial, delightful, engaging, enjoyable, entertaining, good, gratifying, likable, nice, pleasurable, polite, satisfying, welcome, winning.
antonym unpleasant.

pleasure *n.* amusement, bliss, choice, comfort, command, complacency, contentment, delectation, delight, desire, diversion, ease, enjoyment, gladness, gratification, happiness, inclination, joy, mind, option, preference, purpose, recreation, satisfaction, solace, will, wish.
antonyms displeasure, pain, sorrow, trouble.

plebiscite *n.* ballot, poll, referendum, straw poll, vote.

pledge *n.* assurance, bail, bond, collateral, covenant, deposit, earnest, gage, guarantee, health, oath, pawn, promise, security, surety, toast, undertaking, vow, warrant, word, word of honor.
v. bind, contract, drink to, engage, ensure, gage, guarantee, mortgage, plight, promise, secure, swear, toast, undertake, vouch, vow.

plentiful *adj.* abounding, abundant, ample, bounteous, bountiful, bumper, complete, copious, fertile, fruitful, generous, inexhaustible, infinite, lavish, liberal, luxuriant, overflowing, plenteous, productive, profuse, prolific.
antonyms rare, scanty, scarce.

plenty *n.* abundance, affluence, copiousness, enough, fertility, fruitfulness, fund, heap(s), lots, luxury, mass, masses, milk and honey, mine, mountain(s), oodles, opulence, pile(s), plenitude, plenteousness, plentifulness, plethora, profusion, prosperity, quantities, quantity, stack(s), store, sufficiency, volume, wealth.
antonyms lack, need, scarcity, want.

pliable *adj.* accommodating, adaptable, bendable, bendy, compliant, docile, ductile, flexible, impressionable, influenceable, limber, lithe, malleable, manage-

able, persuadable, plastic, pliant, receptive, responsive, suggestible, supple, susceptible, tractable, yielding.
antonyms inflexible, rigid.

pliant *adj.* adaptable, bendable, bendy, biddable, compliant, ductile, easily led, flexible, impressionable, influenceable, lithe, manageable, persuadable, plastic, pliable, supple, susceptible, tractable, whippy, yielding.
antonyms inflexible, intractable.

plight[1] *n.* case, circumstances, condition, difficulty, dilemma, extremity, galère, hole, jam, perplexity, pickle, predicament, quandary, scrape, situation, spot, state, straits, trouble.

plight[2] *n.* affiance, contract, covenant, engage, guarantee, pledge, promise, propose, swear, vouch, vow.

plot[1] *n.* action, cabal, conspiracy, covin, design, intrigue, machination(s), narrative, outline, plan, scenario, scheme, story, story line, stratagem, subject, theme, thread.
v. brew, cabal, calculate, chart, collude, compass, compute, conceive, concoct, conspire, contrive, cook up, design, devise, draft, draw, frame, hatch, imagine, intrigue, lay, locate, machinate, maneuver, map, mark, outline, plan, project, scheme.

plot[2] *n.* allotment, area, green, ground, lot, parcel, patch, tract.

plotter *n.* caballer, conspirator, intriguer, Machiavellian, machinator, schemer, strategist.

ploy *n.* artifice, contrivance, device, dodge, gambit, game, maneuver, move, ruse, scheme, strategem, subterfuge, tactic, trick, wile.

pluck[1] *n.* backbone, boldness, bottle, bravery, courage, determination, fortitude, gameness, grit, guts, hardihood, heart, intrepidity, mettle, nerve, resolution, spirit, spunk, tenacity.

pluck[2] *v.* catch, clutch, collect, depilate, deplume, displume, draw, evulse, gather, harvest, jerk, pick, plunk, pull, pull off, pull out, snatch, strum, thrum, tug, twang, tweak, unplume, yank.

plug *n.* advert, advertisement, bung, cake, chew, cork, dossil, dottle, good word, hype, mention, pigtail, publicity, puff, push, quid, spigot, spile, stopper, stopple, studdle, tamp(i)on, twist, wad.
v. advertise, block, build up, bung, choke, close, cork, cover, drudge, fill, grind, hype, labor, mention, pack, peg away, plod, promote, publicize, puff, push, seal, slog, stop, stop up, stopper, stopple, stuff, tamp, toil.

plump[1] *adj.* beefy, burly, buxom, chopping, chubby, corpulent, dumpy, embonpoint, endomorphic, fat, fleshy, full, matronly, obese, podgy, portly, roly-poly, rotund, round, stout, tubby, well-upholstered.
antonyms skinny, thin.

plump[2] *v.* collapse, descend, drop, dump, fall, flop, sink, slump.
adv. abruptly, directly, straight.

plunder *v.* depredate, despoil, devastate, loot, pillage, raid, ransack, ravage, reive, rifle, rob, sack, spoil, spoliate, steal, strip.
n. booty, despoilment, ill-gotten gains, loot, pickings, pillage, prey, prize, rapine, spoils, swag.

plunge *v.* career, cast, charge, dash, demerge, demerse, descend, dip, dive, dive-bomb, dook, douse, drop, fall, go down, hurtle, immerse, jump, lurch, nose-dive, pitch, plummet, rush, sink, submerge, swoop, tear, throw, tumble.

n. collapse, descent, dive, dook, drop, fall, immersion, jump, submersion, swoop, tumble.

plurality *n.* bulk, diversity, galaxy, majority, mass, most, multiplicity, multitudinousness, numerousness, preponderance, profusion, variety.

pocketbook *n.* bag, handbag, purse, wallet.

podium *n.* dais, platform, rostrum, stage, stand.

poem *n.* acrostic, ballad(e), dit(t), ditty, eclogue, elegy, epicede, epicedium, epinicion, epithalamion, epithalamium, fabliau, genethliac(on), idyll, jingle, lay, limerick, lipogram, lyric, madrigal, monody, ode, palinode, rhyme, song, sonnet, verse, verselet, verset, versicle.

poetry *n.* free verse, gay science, iambics, lyrics, macaronics, muse, Parnassus, pennill, poems, poesy, rhyme, rhyming, vers libre, verse, versing.

poignant *adj.* acrid, acute, affecting, agonizing, biting, bitter, caustic, distressing, heartbreaking, heart-rending, intense, keen, moving, painful, pathetic, penetrating, piercing, piquant, pointed, pungent, sad, sarcastic, severe, sharp, stinging, tender, touching, upsetting.

point[1] *n.* aim, aspect, attribute, burden, characteristic, circumstance, condition, core, crux, degree, design, detail, dot, drift, end, essence, extent, facet, feature, full stop, gist, goal, import, instance, instant, intent, intention, item, juncture, location, mark, marrow, matter, meaning, moment, motive, nicety, nub, object, objective, particular, peculiarity, period, pith, place, position, property, proposition, purpose, quality, question, reason, respect, score, side, site, speck, spot, stage, station, stop, subject, tally, text, theme, thrust, time, trait, unit, use, usefulness, utility.
v. aim, denote, designate, direct, draw attention to, hint, indicate, level, show, signal, signify, suggest, train.

point[2] *n.* apex, bill, cacumen, cape, end, fastigium, foreland, head, headland, neb, ness, nib, promontory, prong, spike, spur, summit, tang, tine, tip, top.

pointed *adj.* accurate, acicular, aciform, aculeate(d), acuminate, acute, barbed, biting, cuspidate, cutting, edged, fastigiate(d), incisive, keen, lanceolate(d), lancet, lanciform, mucronate, penetrating, pertinent, sharp, telling, trenchant.

pointless *adj.* absurd, aimless, bootless, fruitless, futile, inane, ineffectual, irrelevant, meaningless, nonsensical, profitless, senseless, silly, stupid, unavailing, unbeneficial, unproductive, unprofitable, useless, vague, vain, worthless.
antonyms meaningful, profitable.

poise *n.* aplomb, assurance, calmness, collectedness, composure, cool, coolness, dignity, elegance, equanimity, equilibrium, grace, presence, presence of mind, sangfroid, savoir-faire, self-possession, serenity.
v. balance, float, hang, hold, hover, librate, position, support, suspend.

poison *n.* aconite, aconitum, bane, blight, cancer, canker, contagion, contamination, corruption, malignancy, miasma, toxin, venom, virus.
v. adulterate, contaminate, corrupt, defile, deprave, empoison, envenom, infect, kill, murder, pervert, pollute, subvert, taint, undermine, vitiate, warp.

poke *v.* butt, butt in, dig, elbow, hit, interfere, intrude, jab, meddle, nose, nudge, peek, prod, prog, pry, punch, push, shove, snoop, stab, stick, tamper, thrust.

n. butt, dig, dunt, jab, nudge, prod, punch, shove, thrust.

pole¹ *n.* bar, lug, mast, post, rod, shaft, spar, staff, stake, standard, stang, stick.

pole² *n.* antipode, extremity, limit, terminus, (ultima) Thule.

policy *n.* action, approach, code, course, custom, discretion, good sense, guideline, line, plan, position, practice, procedure, program, protocol, prudence, rule, sagacity, scheme, shrewdness, stance, stratagem, theory, wisdom.

polish *v.* brighten, brush up, buff, burnish, clean, correct, cultivate, emend, emery, enhance, file, finish, furbish, improve, luster, perfect, planish, refine, rub, rub up, shine, shine up, slick, slicken, smooth, touch up, wax.

antonyms dull, tarnish.

n. breeding, brightness, brilliance, class, cultivation, elegance, eutrapelia, expertise, finesse, finish, glaze, gloss, grace, luster, perfectionism, politesse, proficiency, refinement, savoir-faire, sheen, smoothness, sophistication, sparkle, style, suavity, urbanity, varnish, veneer, wax.

antonyms clumsiness, dullness, gaucherie.

polished *adj.* accomplished, adept, bright, burnished, civilized, courtly, cultivated, educated, elegant, expert, faultless, fine, finished, flawless, furbished, genteel, glassy, gleaming, glossy, graceful, gracious, impeccable, lustrous, masterly, outstanding, perfected, polite, professional, refined, sheeny, shining, skilful, slippery, smooth, sophisticated, suave, superlative, urbane, well-bred.

antonyms clumsy, dull, gauche, inexpert, tarnished.

polite *adj.* affable, attentive, civil, civilized, complaisant, considerate, cordial, courteous, courtly, cultured, deferential, diplomatic, discreet, elegant, genteel, gentlemanly, gracious, ladylike, mannerly, obliging, polished, refined, respectful, tactful, thoughtful, urbane, well-behaved, well-bred, well-mannered.

antonyms impolite, uncultivated.

politic *adj.* advantageous, advisable, artful, astute, canny, crafty, cunning, designing, diplomatic, discreet, expedient, ingenious, intriguing, judicious, Machiavellian, opportune, prudent, sagacious, sage, scheming, sensible, shrewd, sly, subtle, tactful, unscrupulous, wise.

antonym impolitic.

pollute *v.* adulterate, befoul, besmirch, canker, contaminate, corrupt, debase, debauch, defile, deprave, desecrate, dirty, dishonor, foul, infect, mar, poison, profane, soil, spoil, stain, sully, taint, violate, vitiate.

pomp *n.* ceremonial, ceremoniousness, ceremony, display, éclat, flourish, formality, grandeur, grandiosity, magnificence, ostentation, pageant, pageantry, parade, pomposity, ritual, show, solemnity, splendor, state, vainglory.

antonyms austerity, simplicity.

pompous *adj.* affected, aldermanlike, aldermanly, arrogant, bloated, bombastic, budge, chesty, euphuistic, flatulent, fustian, grandiloquent, grandiose, high-flown, imperious, inflated, magisterial, magniloquent, oro(ro)-tund, ostentatious, overbearing, overblown, pontifical, portentous, pretentious, prosy, ranting, self-important, stilted, supercilious, turgid, vainglorious, windy.

antonyms economical, modest, simple, unaffected, unassuming.

ponder *v.* analyze, brood, cerebrate, cogitate, contemplate, consider, deliberate, examine, excogitate, give thought to, incubate, meditate, mull over, muse, ponderate, puzzle over, ratiocinate, reason, reflect, ruminate over, study, think, volve, weigh.

ponderous *adj.* awkward, bulky, clumsy, cumbersome, cumbrous, dreary, dull, elephantine, graceless, heavy, heavy-footed, heavy-handed, hefty, huge, humorless, labored, laborious, lifeless, long-winded, lumbering, massive, pedantic, pedestrian, plodding, portentous, prolix, slow-moving, stilted, stodgy, stolid, tedious, unwieldy, verbose, weighty.

antonyms delicate, light, simple.

pool¹ *n.* dub, lake, lasher, leisure pool, linn, mere, pond, puddle, splash, stank, swimming bath, swimming pool, tarn, water-hole, watering-hole.

pool² *n.* accumulation, bank, cartel, collective, combine, consortium, funds, group, jackpot, kitty, pot, purse, reserve, ring, stakes, syndicate, team, trust.

v. amalgamate, chip in, combine, contribute, dob in, merge, muck in, put together, share.

poor¹ *adj.* badly off, bankrupt, beggared, beggarly, broke, deficient, destitute, distressed, embarrassed, exiguous, hard up, impecunious, impoverished, in reduced circumstances, inadequate, indigent, insufficient, lacking, meager, miserable, moneyless, necessitious, needy, niggardly, obolary, on one's beam-ends, on one's uppers, on the rocks, pauperized, penniless, penurious, pinched, pitiable, poverty-stricken, reduced, scanty, skimpy, skint, slight, sparse, stony-broke, straitened, without means, without the wherewithal.

antonyms affluent, opulent, rich, wealthy.

poor² *adj.* bad, bare, barren, below par, depleted, exhausted, faulty, feeble, fruitless, grotty, humble, imperfect, impoverished, inferior, infertile, insignificant, jejune, low-grade, lowly, mean, mediocre, modest, paltry, pathetic, pitiful, plain, ropy, rotten, rubbishy, second-rate, shabby, shoddy, sorry, spiritless, sterile, substandard, third-rate, trivial, unfruitful, unimpressive, unproductive, unsatisfactory, valueless, weak, worthless.

antonym superior.

poor³ *adj.* accursed, cursed, forlorn, hapless, ill-fated, luckless, miserable, pathetic, pitiable, star-crossed, unfortunate, unhappy, unlucky, wretched.

antonym lucky.

poppycock *n.* babble, balderdash, balls, baloney, bullshit, bunk, bunkum, drivel, eyewash, gibberish, gobbledegook, guff, hooey, nonsense, rot, rubbish, tommyrot, tosh, trash, twaddle.

antonym sense.

popular *adj.* accepted, approved, celebrated, common, conventional, current, democratic, demotic, famous, fashionable, favored, favorite, fêted, general, household, idolized, in, in demand, in favor, liked, lionized, modish, overpopular, overused, prevailing, prevalent, public, sought-after, standard, stock, trite, ubiquitous, universal, vernacular, voguey, voguish, vulgar, well-liked, widespread.

antonyms exclusive, unpopular, unusual.

popularity *n.* acceptance, acclaim, adoration, adulation, approbation, approval, celebrity, currency, esteem, fame, favor, glory, idolization, kudos, lionization, mass appeal, recognition, regard, renown, reputation, repute, vogue, worship.

antonym unpopularity.

population *n.* citizenry, citizens, community, denizens, folk, inhabitants, natives, occupants, people, populace, residents, society.

pornographic *adj.* bawdy, blue, coarse, dirty, filthy, girlie, gross, indecent, lewd, nudie, obscene, off-color, offensive, porn, porno, prurient, risqué, salacious, smutty.

antonyms innocent, inoffensive.

port *n.* anchorage, harbor, harborage, haven, hithe, roads, roadstead, seaport.

portable *adj.* carriageable, compact, convenient, handy, light, lightweight, manageable, movable, portatile, portative, transportable.

antonyms fixed, immovable.

portend *v.* adumbrate, announce, augur, bespeak, betoken, bode, forebode, forecast, foreshadow, foretell, foretoken, forewarn, harbinger, herald, indicate, omen, point to, predict, presage, prognosticate, promise, signify, threaten, warn of.

portentous *adj.* alarming, amazing, astounding, awe-inspiring, bloated, charged, consequential, crucial, earth-shaking, epoch-making, extraordinary, fateful, heavy, important, menacing, minatory, miraculous, momentous, ominous, phenomenal, pompous, ponderous, pontifical, pregnant, prodigious, remarkable, significant, sinister, solemn, threatening.

antonyms insignificant, unimportant, unimpressive.

portion *n.* allocation, allotment, allowance, assignment, bit, cup, destiny, division, fate, fortune, fraction, fragment, helping, kismet, lot, luck, measure, meed, moiety, morsel, parcel, part, piece, quantity, quota, rake-off, ration, scrap, section, segment, serving, share, slice, something, tranche, whack.

v. allocate, allot, apportion, assign, carve up, deal, distribute, divide, divvy up, dole, parcel, partion, partition, share out, slice up.

portly *adj.* ample, beefy, bulky, chubby, corpulent, dumpy, embonpoint, fat, fleshy, full, heavy, large, obese, overweight, paunchy, plump, rotund, round, stout, tubby.

antonyms slight, slim.

portrait *n.* account, caricature, characterization, depiction, description, icon, image, likeness, miniature, mug shot, painting, photograph, picture, portraiture, portrayal, profile, representation, sketch, thumbnail, vignette.

portray *v..* act, capture, characterize, delineate, depict, describe, draw emblazon, encapsulate, evoke figure, illustrate, impersonate, limn, paint, personate, personify, picture, play, present, render, represent, sketch, suggest.

pose *v.* advance, affect, arrange, assert, attitudinize, claim, feign, impersonate, masquerade, model, pass oneself off, place, posit, position, posture, present, pretend, profess to be, propound, put, put forward, put on an act, set, sham, sit, state, strike an attitude, submit.

n. act, affectation, air, attitude, bearing, con, façade, front, mark, masquerade, mien, position, posture, pretense, role, sham, stance, take-in.

poseur *n.* attitudinizer, charlatan, con, exhibitionist,

impostor, masquerader, mountebank, phony, poser, poseuse, posturer, posturist, pseud, quack.

position *n.* angle, area, arrangement, attitude, bearings, belief, berth, billet, capacity, character, circumstances, condition, deployment, disposition, duty, employment, function, grade, importance, job, level, locale, locality, location, niche, occupation, office, opinion, outlook, pass, perspective, pinch, place, placement, placing, plight, point, point of view, pose, positioning, post, posture, predicament, prestige, rank, reference, reputation, role, set, setting, site, situation, slant, slot, spot, stance, stand, standing, standpoint, state, station, stature, status, ubiety, view, viewpoint, whereabouts.

v. arrange, array, deploy, dispose, fix, lay out, locate, place, pose, put, range, set, settle, stand, stick.

positive *adj.* absolute, actual, affirmative, arrant, assertive, assured, authoritative, beneficial, categorical, certain, clear, clear-cut, cocksure, complete, conclusive, concrete, confident, constructive, consummate, convinced, decided, decisive, definite, direct, dogmatic, downright, effective, efficacious, emphatic, explicit, express, firm, forceful, forward-looking, helpful, hopeful, incontestable, incontrovertible, indisputable, irrefragable, irrefutable, open-and-shut, opinionated, optimistic, out-and-out, peremptory, perfect, practical, productive, progressive, promising, rank, real, realistic, resolute, secure, self-evident, sheer, stubborn, sure, thorough, thoroughgoing, uncompromising, undeniable, unequivocal, unmistakable, unmitigated, unquestioning, useful, utter.

antonyms indecisive, indefinite, negative, uncertain.

positively *adv.* absolutely, assuredly, authoritatively, categorically, certainly, conclusively, constructively, decisively, definitely, dogmatically, emphatically, expressly, finally, firmly, incontestably, incontrovertibly, indisputably, surely, uncompromisingly, undeniably, unequivocally, unmistakably, unquestionably.

possess *v.* acquire, be endowed with, control, dominate, enjoy, have, hold, obtain, occupy, own, possess oneself of, seize, take, take over, take possession of.

possessed *adj.* bedeviled, berserk, besotted, bewitched, consumed, crazed, cursed, demented, dominated, enchanted, frenzied, hag-ridden, haunted, infatuated, maddened, mesmerized, obsessed, raving.

possession *n.* colony, control, custody, dependency, dominion, enjoyment, fruition, hold, mandate, occupancy, occupation, ownership, proprietorship, protectorate, province, tenure, territory, title.

possessions *n.* assets, belongings, chattels, effects, estate, goods, goods and chattels, junk, meum et tuum, movables, paraphernalia, property, riches, stuff, things, traps, wealth, worldly wealth.

possibility *n.* achievability, chance, conceivability, feasibility, hazard, hope, liability, likelihood, odds, plausibility, potentiality, practicability, probability, prospect, realizability, risk, workableness.

antonym impossibility.

possible *adj.* accomplishable, achievable, alternative, attainable, available, conceivable, credible, doable, feasible, hopeful, hypothetical, imaginable, likely, on, potential, practicable, probable, promising, realizable, tenable, viable, workable.

antonym impossible.

possibly *adv.* at all, by any chance, by any means, Deo volente, DV, God willing, haply, happen, hopefully, in any way, maybe, mayhap, peradventure, perchance, perhaps, very like(ly).

post[1] *n.* baluster, banister, column, leg, newel, pale, palisade, picket, pier, pillar, pin, pole, shaft, stake, stanchion, standard, stock, strut, support, upright.

v. advertise, affix, announce, denounce, display, make known, placard, preconize, proclaim, promulgate, publicize, publish, report, stick up.

post[2] *n.* appointment, assignment, beat, berth, billet, employment, incumbency, job, office, place, position, situation, station, vacancy.

v. appoint, assign, establish, locate, move, place, position, put, second, send, shift, situate, station, transfer.

post[3] *n.* collection, delivery, dispatch, mail, postal service, uplifting.

v. acquaint, advise, apprize, brief, dispatch, fill in on, inform, keep posted, mail, notify, report to, send, transmit.

postpone *v.* adjourn, defer, delay, freeze, hold over, pigeonhole, prorogue, put back, put off, put on ice, shelve, suspend, table, waive.

antonyms advance, forward.

postulate *v.* advance, assume, hypothesize, lay down, posit, predicate, presuppose, propose, stipulate, suppose, take for granted, theorize.

posture *n.* attitude, bearing, carriage, decubitus, disposition, mien, port, pose, position, set, stance.

v. affect, attitudinize, pose, put on airs, show off, strike attitudes, strut.

potency *n.* authority, capacity, cogency, control, effectiveness, efficaciousness, efficacy, energy, force, headiness, influence, kick, might, muscle, persuasiveness, potential, power, puissance, punch, strength, sway, vigor.

antonyms impotence, weakness.

potential *adj.* budding, concealed, conceivable, dormant, embryonic, future, hidden, imaginable, in embryo, in posse, inherent, latent, likely, possible, probable, promising, prospective, undeveloped, unrealized.

n. ability, aptitude, capability, capacity, flair, possibility, potentiality, power, talent, the makings, what it takes, wherewithal.

potion *n.* beverage, brew, concoction, cup, dose, draught, drink, electuary, elixir, medicine, mixture, philter, potation, tonic, treacle.

pouch *n.* bag, container, marsupium, pocket, poke, purse, reticule, sac, sack, sporran, wallet.

pounce *v.* ambush, attack, dash at, dive on, drop, fall upon, grab, jump, leap at, lunge at, snatch, spring, strike, swoop.

n. assault, attack, bound, dive, grab, jump, leap, lunge, spring, swoop.

pound[1] *v.* bang, bash, baste, batter, beat, belabor, bray, bruise, clobber, clomp, clump, comminute, crush, drum, hammer, levigate, march, palpitate, pelt, powder, pulsate, pulse, pulverize, pummel, smash, stomp, strike, strum, thrash, throb, thrum, thud, thump, thunder, tramp, triturate.

pound[2] *n.* compound, corral, enclosure, fank, fold, pen, yard.

pour *v.* bucket, cascade, course, crowd, decant, effuse, emit, exude, flow, gush, rain, rain cats and dogs, run, rush, sheet, spew, spill, spout, stream, swarm, teem, throng, tumble.

pout *v.* glower, grimace, lower, mope, pull a face, scowl, sulk.

antonyms grin, smile.

n. glower, grimace, long face, moue, scowl.

antonyms grin, smile.

poverty *n.* aridity, bareness, barrenness, beggary, dearth, deficiency, depletion, destitution, distress, exhaustion, hardship, ill-being, impoverishment, inadequacy, indigence, infertility, insolvency, insufficiency, jejuneness, lack, meagerness, necessitousness, necessity, need, paucity, pauperism, pennilessness, penury, poorness, privation, proletarianism, scarcity, shortage, sterility, thinness, unfruitfulness, want.

antonyms affluence, fertility, fruitfulness, riches, richness.

power *n.* ability, ascendancy, autarchy, authorization, authority, brawn, capability, capacity, clout, clutches, command, competence, competency, control, dominance, domination, dominion, efficience, energy, faculty, force, forcefulness, heavy metal, hegemony, imperium, influence, intensity, juice, kami, license, mana, mastery, might, muscle, omnipotence, plenipotence, potency, potential, prerogative, privilege, right, rule, sovereignty, strength, supremacy, sway, teeth, vigor, virtue, vis, voltage, vroom, warrant, weight.

dominant, effective, effectual, energetic, forceful, forcible, impressive, influential, leading, masterful, mighty, muscular, omnipotent, persuasive, plutocratic, potent, pre-eminent, prepotent, prevailing, puissant, robust, souped-up, sovereign, stalwart, strapping, strong, sturdy, supreme, telling, vigorous, weighty, winning.

antonyms impotent, ineffective, weak.

practical *adj.* accomplished, active, applicative, applied, businesslike, commonsense, commonsensical, down-to-earth, efficient, empirical, everyday, expedient, experienced, experimental, factual, feasible, functional, hardheaded, hard-nosed, material, matter-of-fact, mundane, nuts-and-bolts, ordinary, practicable, practive, pragmatic, proficient, qualified, realistic, seasoned, sensible, serviceable, skilled, sound, trained, unsentimental, useful, utilitarian, workable, workaday, working.

antonym impractical.

practically[1] *adv.* actually, all but, almost, essentially, fundamentally, in effect, in practice, in principle, just about, nearly, not quite, pretty nearly, pretty well, very nearly, virtually, well-nigh.

practically[2] *adv.* clearly, from a commonsense angle, matter-of-factly, rationally, realistically, reasonably, sensibly, unsentimentally.

practice[1] *n.* action, application, business, career, clientèle, convention, custom, discipline, drill, dry run, dummy run, effect, exercise, experience, habit, ism, method, mode, modus operandi, operation, patronage, performance, policy, practic, practicalities, practicum, praxis, preparation, procedure, profession, rehearsal, repetition, routine, rule, run-through, study, system, tradition, training, usage, use, vocation, way, wont, work, work-out.

practice[2] *v.* apply, carry out, discipline, do, drill, enact, engage in, execute, exercise, follow, implement, live up to, observe, perfect, perform, ply, prepare, pursue, put into practice, rehearse, repeat, run through, study, train, undertake, warm up.

practiced *adj.* able, accomplished, consummate, experienced, expert, finished, highly-developed, knowing, knowledgeable, perfected, proficient, qualified, refined, seasoned, skilled, trained, versed, veteran, well-trained.
antonyms inexpert, unpracticed.

pragmatic *adj.* businesslike, efficient, factual, hard-headed, opportunistic, practical, realistic, sensible, unidealistic, unsentimental, utilitarian.
antonyms idealistic, romantic, unrealistic.

praise *n.* acclaim, acclamation, accolade, acknowledgment, adoration, adulation, applause, approbation, approval, bouquet, cheering, commend, commendation, compliment, compliments, congratulation, devotion, encomium, eulogium, eulogy, extolment, flattery, glory, homage, honor, kudos, laud, laudation, ovation, panegyric, plaudit, puff, rave, recognition, salvoes, testimonial, thanks, thanksgiving, tribute, worship.
antonyms criticism, revilement.
v. acclaim, acknowledge, admire, adore, applaud, approve, belaud, bless, celebrate, cheer, compliment, congratulate, cry up, eulogize, exalt, extol, flatter, give thanks to, glorify, hail, honor, laud, magnify, panegyrize, pay tribute to, promote, puff, rave over, recognize, tout, wax lyrical, worship.
antonyms criticize, revile.

praiseworthy *adj.* admirable, commendable, creditable, deserving, estimable, excellent, exemplary, fine, honorable, laudable, meritorious, reputable, sterling, worthy.
antonyms discreditable, dishonorable, ignoble.

pray *v.* adjure, ask, beg, beseech, call on, crave, entreat, implore, importune, invoke, obsecrate, petition, plead, press, request, solicit, sue, supplicate, urge.

prayer *n.* appeal, collect, communion, devotion, entreaty, invocation, kyrie, kyrie eleison, litany, orison, paternoster, petition, plea, request, solicitation, suffrage, suit, supplication.

preach *v.* address, admonish, advocate, ethicize, evangelize, exhort, harangue, lecture, moralize, orate, pontificate, pontify, preachify, prose, sermonize, urge.

preamble *n.* exordium, foreword, introduction, lead-in, overture, preface, preliminaries, prelude, preparation, proem, prolegomenon, prologue.
antonyms epilogue, postscript.

precarious *adj.* chancy, dangerous, delicate, dicey, dodgy, doubtful, dubious, hairy, hazardous, iffy, insecure, parlous, periculous, perilous, problematic, risky, shaky, slippery, ticklish, tricky, uncertain, unpredictable, unreliable, unsafe, unsettled, unstable, unsteady, unsure, vulnerable.
antonyms certain, safe, secure.

precaution *n.* anticipation, backstop, buffer, care, caution, circumspection, foresight, forethought, insurance, preparation, prophylaxis, protection, providence, provision, prudence, safeguard, safety measure, security, surety, wariness.

precedence *n.* antecedence, first place, lead, pre-eminence, preference, pride of place, primacy, priority, rank, seniority, superiority, supremacy.

precedent *n.* antecedent, authority, citation, criterion, example, exemplar, guideline, instance, judgment, model, paradigm, past instance, pattern, prototype, ruling, standard, yardstick.

precept *n.* axiom, behest, bidding, byword, canon, charge, command, commandment, convention, decree, dictum, direction, directive, guideline, injunction, institute, instruction, law, mandate, maxim, motto, order, ordinance, principle, regulation, rubric, rule, saying, sentence, statute.

precious *adj.* adored, affected, artificial, beloved, cherished, chichi, choice, costly, darling, dear, dearest, expensive, exquisite, fastidious, favorite, fine, flowery, greenery-yallery, idolized, inestimable, invaluable, irreplaceable, loved, namby-pamby, overnice, overrefined, priceless, prized, rare, recherché, treasured, twee, valuable, valued.

precipice *n.* bluff, brink, cliff, cliff face, crag, drop, escarp, escarpment, height, scarp, steep.

precipitate *v.* accelerate, advance, bring on, cast, cause, chuck, discharge, drive, expedite, fling, further, hasten, hurl, hurry, induce, launch, occasion, pitch, press, project, quicken, speed, throw, trigger.
adj. abrupt, breakneck, brief, frantic, Gadarene, hasty, headlong, heedless, hot-headed, hurried, impatient, impetuous, impulsive, incautious, indiscreet, madcap, pell-mell, plunging, precipitous, quick, quixotic, rapid, rash, reckless, rushing, sudden, swift, unannounced, unexpected, violent.
antonym cautious.

precise *adj.* absolute, accurate, actual, authentic, blow-by-blow, buckram, careful, ceremonious, clear-cut, correct, definite, delimitative, determinate, distinct, exact, explicit, express, expressis verbis, factual, faithful, fastidious, finical, finicky, fixed, formal, identical, literal, meticulous, minute, nice, particular, prim, punctilious, puritanical, rigid, scrupulous, specific, strict, succinct, unequivocal, verbatim, word-for-word.
antonym imprecise.

precisely *adv.* absolutely, accurately, bang, blow by blow, correctly, dead, distinctly, exactly, expressis verbis, just, just so, literally, minutely, plumb, slap, smack, square, squarely, strictly, verbatim, word for word.

precision *n.* accuracy, care, correctness, definiteness, detail, exactitude, exactness, explicitness, expressness, faithfulness, fastidiousness, fidelity, meticulousness, minuteness, neatness, niceness, nicety, particularity, preciseness, punctilio, punctiliousness, rigor, scrupulosity, specificity.
antonym imprecision.

preclude *v.* avoid, check, debar, eliminate, exclude, forestall, hinder, inhibit, obviate, prevent, prohibit, restrain, rule out, stop.
antonyms incur, involve.

precocious *adj.* advanced, ahead, bright, clever, developed, fast, forward, gifted, mature, precocial, premature, quick, smart.
antonym backward.

predatory *adj.* acquisitive, avaricious, carnivorous, covetous, despoiling, greedy, hunting, lupine, marauding, pillaging, plundering, predacious, predative, preying, rapacious, raptatorial, raptorial, ravaging, ravening, thieving, voracious, vulturine, vulturous, wolfish.

predestination *n.* ananke, destiny, doom, election, fate, foreordainment, foreordination, karma, lot, necessity, portion, predestiny, predetermination, preordainment, preordination, weird.

predicament *n.* can of worms, corner, crisis, dilemma,

embarrassment, emergency, fix, galère, hole, hot water, impasse, jam, kettle of fish, mess, pickle, pinch, plight, quandary, scrape, situation, spot, state, trouble.

predict v. augur, auspicate, divine, forebode, forecast, foresay, foresee, foreshow, forespeak, foretell, portend, presage, prognosticate, project, prophesy, second-guess, soothsay, vaticinate.

prediction n. augury, auspication, divination, forecast, fortune-telling, prognosis, prognostication, prophecy, second sight, soothsaying, vaticination.

predilection n. affection, affinity, bent, bias, enthusiasm, fancy, fondness, inclination, leaning, liking, love, partiality, penchant, predisposition, preference, proclivity, proneness, propensity, soft spot, taste, tendency, weakness.

antonyms antipathy, disinclination.

predisposed adj. agreeable, amenable, biased, disposed, favorable, inclined, liable, minded, not unwilling, nothing loth, prejudiced, prepared, prone, ready, subject, susceptible, well-disposed, willing.

predominant adj. ascendant, capital, chief, controlling, dominant, forceful, important, influential, leading, main, paramount, potent, powerful, prepollent, preponderant, prepotent, prevailing, prevalent, primary, prime, principal, prominent, ruling, sovereign, strong, superior, supreme.

antonyms ineffective, lesser, minor, weak.

predominate v. dominate, obtain, outnumber, outweigh, override, overrule, overshadow, preponderate, prevail, reign, rule, tell, transcend.

pre-eminent adj. chief, consummate, distinguished, excellent, exceptional, facile princeps, foremost, incomparable, inimitable, leading, matchless, nonpareil, outstanding, paramount, passing, peerless, predominant, prominent, renowned, superior, superlative, supreme, surpassing, transcendent, unequaled, unmatched, unrivaled, unsurpassed.

antonyms undistinguished, unknown.

pre-empt v. acquire, anticipate, appropriate, arrogate, assume, bag, forestall, secure, seize, usurp.

preface n. exordium, foreword, intro, introduction, preamble, preliminaries, prelims, prelude, proem, prolegomena, prolegomenon, prologue, prooemion, prooemium.

antonyms afterthought, epilogue, postscript.

v. begin, introduce, launch, lead up to, open, precede, prefix, prelude, premise, start.

antonyms append, complete, finish.

prefer[1] v. adopt, advocate, back, be partial to, choose, desire, elect, endorse, fancy, favor, go for, incline towards, like better, opt for, pick, plump for, recommend, select, single out, support, want, wish, would rather, would sooner.

antonym reject.

prefer[2] v. bring, file, lodge, place, present, press.

prefer[3] v. advance, aggrandize, dignify, elevate, exalt, promote, raise, upgrade.

antonym demote.

preference[1] n. choice, desire, election, fancy, favorite, first choice, inclination, liking, option, partiality, pick, predilection, selection, wish.

preference[2] n. advantage, favor, favoritism, precedence, preferential treatment, priority, special consideration, special treatment.

pregnant[1] adj. big, big-bellied, enceinte, expectant,

expecting, gravid, impregnated, in an interesting condition, in the club, in the family way, in the pudding club, parturient, preggers, teeming, with child.

pregnant[2] adj. charged, eloquent, expressive, full, heavy, loaded, meaning, meaningful, ominous, pithy, pointed, significant, suggestive, telling, weighty.

antonym jejune.

prejudice[1] n. bias, bigotry, chauvinism, discrimination, injustice, intolerance, narrow-mindedness, partiality, partisanship, preconception, prejudgment, racism, sexism, unfairness, viewiness, warp.

antonyms fairness, tolerance.

v. bias, color, condition, distort, incline, indoctrinate, influence, jaundice, load, poison, predispose, prepossess, slant, sway, warp, weight.

prejudice[2] n. damage, detriment, disadvantage, harm, hurt, impairment, injury, loss, mischief, ruin, vitiation, wreck.

antonyms advantage, benefit.

v. damage, harm, hinder, hurt, impair, injure, mar, ruin, spoil, undermine, vitiate, wreck.

antonyms advance, benefit, help.

prejudiced adj. biased, bigoted, chauvinist, conditioned, discriminatory, distorted, ex parte, illiberal, influenced, intolerant, jaundiced, loaded, narrow-minded, one-sided, opinionated, partial, partisan, prepossessed, racist, sexist, subjective, unenlightened, unfair, verkrampte, viewy, warped, weighted.

antonyms fair, tolerant.

preliminary adj. earliest, early, embryonic, exordial, experimental, exploratory, first, inaugural, initial, initiative, initiatory, introductory, opening, pilot, precursory, prefatory, prelusive, preparatory, primary, prior, qualifying, test, trial.

antonyms closing, final.

premature adj. abortive, early, embryonic, forward, green, half-formed, hasty, ill-considered, ill-timed, immature, imperfect, impulsive, incomplete, inopportune, overhasty, precipitate, precocious, preterm, previous, rash, raw, undeveloped, unfledged, unripe, unseasonable, untimely.

antonyms late, tardy.

premeditated adj. aforethought, calculated, cold-blooded, conscious, considered, contrived, deliberate, intended, intentional, planned, plotted, prearranged, predetermined, prepense, preplanned, studied, wilful.

antonyms spontaneous, unpremeditated.

premeditation n. deliberateness, deliberation, design, determination, forethought, intention, malice aforethought, planning, plotting, prearrangement, predetermination, purpose, scheming.

antonyms impulse, spontaneity.

premise v. assert, assume, hypothesize, lay down, posit, postulate, predicate, presuppose, state, stipulate, take as true.

n. argument, assertion, assumption, ground, hypothesis, postulate, postulation, predication, premiss, presupposition, proposition, statement, stipulation, supposition, thesis.

preoccupied adj. absent-minded, absorbed, abstracted, daydreaming, distracted, distrait, engrossed, entêté, faraway, fixated, heedless, immersed, intent, oblivious, obsessed, pensive, rapt, taken up, unaware, visited, wrapped up.

preparation[1] n. alertness, anticipation, arrangement,

assignment, basics, development, expectation, foresight, foundation, groundwork, homework, imposition, lesson, measure, plan, precaution, preliminaries, prep, preparedness, provision, readiness, revision, rudiments, safeguard, schoolwork, study, task.

preparation² *n.* application, composition, compound, concoction, lotion, medicine, mixture, potion, tincture.

prepare *v.* accouter, adapt, adjust, anticipate, arrange, assemble, boun, brace, brief, busk, coach, compose, concoct, confect, construct, contrive, develop, devise, dispose, do one's homework, draft, draw up, dress, equip, fashion, fettle, fit, fit out, fix up, forearm, form, fortify, furnish, get up, gird, groom, instruct, limber up, make, make ready, outfit, plan, practice, predispose, prime, produce, provide, psych up, ready, rehearse, rig out, steel, strengthen, supply, train, trim, warm up.

prepared *adj.* able, arranged, briefed, disposed, expectant, fit, forearmed, inclined, minded, planned, predisposed, primed, psyched up, ready, set, waiting, well-rehearsed, willing, word-perfect.

antonyms unprepared, unready.

preponderance *n.* ascendancy, bulk, dominance, domination, dominion, extensiveness, force, lion's share, majority, mass, power, predominance, prevalence, superiority, supremacy, sway, weight.

prepossessing *adj.* alluring, amiable, appealing, attractive, beautiful, bewitching, captivating, charming, delightful, disarming, enchanting, engaging, fair, fascinating, fetching, good-looking, handsome, inviting, likable, lovable, magnetic, pleasing, striking, taking, winning, winsome.

antonyms unattractive, unprepossessing.

preposterous *adj.* absurd, asinine, bizarre, crazy, derisory, excessive, exorbitant, extravagant, extreme, fatuous, foolish, imbecile, impossible, inane, incredible, insane, intolerable, irrational, laughable, ludicrous, monstrous, nonsensical, outrageous, ridiculous, risible, senseless, shocking, unbelievable, unconscionable, unreasonable, unthinkable.

antonym reasonable.

prerequisite *adj.* basic, essential, fundamental, imperative, indispensable, mandatory, necessary, needed, needful, obligatory, required, requisite, vital.

antonym unnecessary.

n. condition, essential, imperative, must, necessity, precondition, provision, proviso, qualification, requirement, requisite, sine qua non.

antonym extra.

prerogative *n.* advantage, authority, birthright, carte blanche, choice, claim, droit, due, exemption, immunity, liberty, license, perquisite, privilege, right, sanction, title.

prescribe *v.* appoint, assign, command, decree, define, dictate, direct, enjoin, fix, impose, lay down, limit, ordain, order, require, rule, set, set bounds to, specify, stipulate.

presence *n.* air, apparition, appearance, aspect, attendance, aura, bearing, carriage, closeness, companionship, company, comportment, demeanor, ease, existence, ghost, habitation, inhabitance, manifestation, mien, nearness, neighborhood, occupancy, personality, poise, propinquity, proximity, residence, revenant, self-assurance, shade, specter, spirit, statuesqueness, vicinity.

antonym absence.

present¹ *adj.* at hand, attending, available, contemporary, current, existent, extant, here, immediate, instant, near, ready, there, to hand.

antonyms absent, out-of-date, past.

present² *v.* acquaint with, adduce, advance, award, bestow, confer, declare, demonstrate, display, donate, entrust, exhibit, expound, extend, furnish, give, grant, hand over, hold out, introduce, mount, offer, porrect, pose, produce, proffer, put on, raise, recount, relate, show, stage, state, submit, suggest, tender.

antonym take.

n. benefaction, boon, bounty, cadeau, compliment, donation, endowment, favor, gift, grant, gratuity, largess, nuzzer, offering, prezzie, refresher.

presentable *adj.* acceptable, becoming, clean, decent, neat, passable, proper, respectable, satisfactory, suitable, tidy, tolerable.

antonyms unpresentable, untidy.

presently *adv.* anon, before long, by and by, directly, immediately, in a minute, shortly, soon.

preserve *v.* care for, confect, conserve, continue, defend, embalm, entreasure, guard, keep, maintain, perpetuate, protect, retain, safeguard, save, secure, shelter, shield, store, sustain, uphold.

antonyms destroy, ruin.

n. area, confection, confiture, conserve, domain, field, game park, game reserve, jam, jelly, konfyt, marmalade, realm, reservation, reserve, safari park, sanctuary, specialism, specialty, sphere, thing.

preside *v.* administer, chair, conduct, control, direct, govern, head, lead, manage, officiate, run, supervise.

press¹ *v.* adpress, afflict, appress, assail, beg, beset, besiege, calendar, clasp, cluster, compel, compress, condense, constrain, crowd, crush, demand, depress, disquiet, dun, embrace, encircle, enfold, enforce, enjoin, entreat, exhort, finish, flatten, flock, force, force down, gather, harass, hasten, herd, hug, hurry, implore, importune, insist on, iron, jam, mangle, mash, mill, petition, plague, plead, pressurize, push, reduce, rush, seethe, smooth, squeeze, steam, stuff, sue, supplicate, surge, swarm, throng, torment, trouble, urge, vex, worry.

antonyms expand, hang back, lighten, relieve.

n. bunch, bustle, crowd, crush, demand, flock, hassle, herd, horde, host, hurry, mob, multitude, pack, pressure, push, strain, stress, swarm, throng, urgency.

press² *n.* columnists, correspondents, fourth estate, hacks, journalism, journalists, news media, newsmen, newspapers, paparazzi, papers, photographers, pressmen, reporters, writers.

pressing *adj.* burning, constraining, crowding, crucial, essential, exigent, high-priority, imperative, important, importunate, serious, thronging, urgent, vital.

antonyms trivial, unimportant.

pressure *n.* adversity, affliction, burden, coercion, compressing, compression, compulsion, constraint, crushing, demands, difficulty, distress, exigency, force, hassle, heat, heaviness, hurry, influence, load, obligation, power, press, pression, squeezing, strain, stress, sway, urgency, weight.

v. browbeat, bulldoze, bully, coerce, compel, constrain, dragoon, drive, force, impel, induce, lean on, oblige, persuade, press, pressurize, squeeze.

prestige *n.* authority, cachet, celebrity, clout, credit, distinction, eminence, esteem, fame, honor, importance, influence, kudos, pull, regard, renown, reputation, standing, stature, status, weight.

antonyms humbleness, unimportance.

presume *v.* assume, bank on, believe, conjecture, count on, dare, depend on, go so far, have the audacity, hypothesize, hypothetize, infer, make bold, make so bold, posit, postulate, presuppose, rely on, suppose, surmise, take for granted, take it, take the liberty, think, trust, undertake, venture.

presumption[1] *n.* assurance, audacity, boldness, brass, brass neck, cheek, effrontery, forwardness, gall, impudence, insolence, neck, nerve, presumptuousness, temerity.

antonyms humility, politeness.

presumption[2] *n.* anticipation, assumption, basis, belief, chance, conjecture, grounds, guess, hypothesis, likelihood, opinion, plausibility, premiss, presupposition, probability, reason, supposition, surmise.

presumptuous *adj.* arrogant, audacious, big-headed, bold, conceited, foolhardy, forward, impertinent, impudent, insolent, over-confident, over-familiar, overweening, presuming, pushy, rash, uppish.

antonym modest.

presupposition *n.* assumption, belief, hypothesis, preconception, premise, premiss, presumption, supposition, theory.

pretend *v.* act, affect, allege, aspire, assume, claim, counterfeit, dissemble, dissimulate, fake, falsify, feign, go through the motions, imagine, impersonate, make believe, pass oneself off, profess, purport, put on, sham, simulate, suppose.

pretense *n.* acting, affectation, aim, allegation, appearance, artifice, blague, bounce, charade, claim, cloak, color, cover, deceit, deception, display, excuse, fabrication, façade, faking, falsehood, feigning, garb, guise, humbug, invention, make-believe, mask, masquerade, posing, posturing, pretentiousness, pretext, profession, pseudery, purpose, ruse, semblance, sham, show, simulation, subterfuge, trickery, veil, veneer, wile.

antonyms honesty, openness, reason.

pretentious *adj.* affected, ambitious, assuming, bombastic, chichi, conceited, euphemistic, exaggerated, extravagant, flaunting, grandiloquent, grandiose, highfalutin, high-flown, high-sounding, hollow, inflated, magniloquent, mannered, oro(ro)tund, ostentatious, overambitious, overassuming, pompous, showy, snobbish, specious, uppish, vainglorious.

antonyms humble, modest, simple, straightforward.

pretty *adj.* appealing, attractive, beautiful, bijou, bonny, charming, comely, cute, dainty, delicate, elegant, fair, fine, good-looking, graceful, lovely, neat, nice, personable, pleasing, sightly, tasteful, trim.

antonyms tasteless, ugly.

adv. fairly, moderately, passably, quite, rather, reasonably, somewhat, tolerably.

prevail *v.* abound, obtain, overcome, overrule, predominate, preponderate, reign, rule, succeed, triumph, win.

antonym lose.

prevailing *adj.* common, controlling, current, customary, dominant, established, fashionable, general, in style, in vogue, influential, main, mainstream, operative, ordinary, popular, predominating, preponderating, prepotent, prevalent, principal, ruling, set, usual, widespread.

antonyms minor, uncommon.

prevalent *adj.* accepted, ascendant, common, commonplace, compelling, current, customary, dominant, epidemic, established, everyday, extensive, frequent, general, governing, habitual, popular, powerful, predominant, prevailing, rampant, regnant, rife, successful, superior, ubiquitous, universal, usual, victorious, widespread.

antonyms subordinate, uncommon.

prevaricate *v.* cavil, deceive, dodge, equivocate, evade, fib, hedge, lie, palter, quibble, shift, shuffle, temporize, tergiversate.

prevent *v.* anticipate, avert, avoid, balk, bar, block, check, counteract, debar, defend against, foil, forestall, frustrate, hamper, head off, hinder, impede, inhibit, intercept, obstruct, obviate, preclude, restrain, stave off, stop, stymie, thwart, ward off.

antonyms cause, foster, help.

preventive *adj.* counteractive, deterrent, hampering, hindering, impeding, inhibitory, obstructive, precautionary, prevenient, preventative, prophylactic, protective, shielding.

antonyms causative, fostering.

n. block, condom, deterrent, hindrance, impediment, neutralizer, obstacle, obstruction, prevention, prophylactic, protection, protective, remedy, safeguard, shield.

antonyms cause, encouragement, incitement.

previous *adj.* antecedent, anterior, arranged, earlier, erstwhile, ex-, foregoing, former, one-time, past, preceding, precipitate, premature, prior, quondam, sometime, umwhile, untimely, whilom.

antonyms later, timely.

prey *n.* booty, dupe, fall guy, game, kill, mark, mug, plunder, quarry, target, victim.

prey on blackmail, bleed, bully, burden, devour, distress, eat, eat away, exploit, feed on, gnaw at, haunt, hunt, intimidate, live off, moth-eat, oppress, seize, take advantage of, terrorize, trouble, victimize, waste, weigh down, weigh heavily, worry.

price *n.* amount, assessment, bill, bounty, charge, consequences, cost, damage, estimate, expenditure, expense, fee, figure, levy, odds, outlay, payment, penalty, rate, reward, sacrifice, sum, toll, valuation, value, worth.

v. assess, cost, estimate, evaluate, offer, put, rate, valorize, value.

priceless[1] *adj.* beyond price, cherished, costly, dear, expensive, incalculable, incomparable, inestimable, invaluable, irreplaceable, precious, prized, rare, rich, treasured, without price.

antonyms cheap, run-of-the-mill.

priceless[2] *adj.* a hoot, a scream, absurd, amusing, comic, droll, funny, hilarious, killing, rib-tickling, ridiculous, riotous, risible, side-splitting.

pride *n.* amour-propre, arrogance, best, big-headedness, boast, choice, conceit, cream, delight, dignity, egotism, élite, flower, gem, glory, gratification, haughtiness, hauteur, high spirits, honor, hubris, jewel, joy, loftiness, magnificence, mettle, morgue, ostentation, pick, pleasure, presumption, pretension, pretensiousness, pride and joy, prize, satisfaction, self-esteem, self-importance, self-love, self-respect, smugness, snobbery, splendor, superciliousness, treasure, vainglory, vanity.

antonym humility.

prim *adj*. demure, fastidious, formal, fussy, governessy, old-maidish, old-maidist, particular, perjink, po-faced, precise, priggish, prissy, proper, prudish, pudibund, puritanical, school-marmish, sedate, starchy, stiff, strait-laced.
antonyms broad-minded, informal.

primarily *adv*. at first, basically, chiefly, especially, essentially, fundamentally, generally, initially, mainly, mostly, originally, principally.
antonym secondarily.

primary *adj*. aboriginal, basic, beginning, best, capital, cardinal, chief, dominant, earliest, elemental, elementary, essential, first, first-formed, first-made, fundamental, greatest, highest, initial, introductory, leading, main, original, paramount, primal, prime, primeval, primigenial, primitial, primitive, primordial, principal, pristine, radical, rudimentary, simple, top, ultimate, underlying.
antonym secondary.

prime[1] *adj*. basic, best, capital, chief, choice, earliest, excellent, first-class, first-rate, fundamental, highest, leading, main, original, predominant, pre-eminent, primary, principal, quality, ruling, select, selected, senior, superior, top, underlying.
antonyms minor, secondary, second-rate.
n. beginning, flowering, height, heyday, maturity, morning, opening, peak, perfection, spring, springtide, springtime, start, zenith.

prime[2] *v*. brief, charge, clue up, coach, cram, fill, fill in, gen up, groom, inform, notify, post up, prepare, train.

primeval *adj*. ancient, earliest, early, first, Ogygian, old, original, prehistoric, primal, primitial, primitive, primordial, pristine.
antonyms developed, later, modern.

primitive *adj*. aboriginal, barbarian, barbaric, childlike, crude, earliest, early, elementary, first, naïve, neanderthal, original, primal, primary, primeval, primordial, pristine, rough, rude, rudimentary, savage, simple, uncivilized, uncultivated, undeveloped, unrefined, unsophisticated, untrained, untutored.
antonyms advanced, civilized, developed.

primordial *adj*. basic, earliest, elemental, first, first-formed, first-made, fundamental, original, prehistoric, primal, primeval, primigenial, primitial, primitive, pristine, radical.
antonyms developed, later, modern.

principal[1] *adj*. capital, cardinal, chief, controlling, decuman, dominant, essential, first, foremost, highest, key, leading, main, paramount, pre-eminent, primary, prime, strongest, truncal.
antonyms least, lesser, minor.
n. boss, chief, dean, director, first violin, head, head teacher, headmaster, headmistress, lead, leader, master, prima ballerina, prima donna, rector, star, superintendent.

principal[2] *n*. assets, capital, capital funds, money.

principle *n*. assumption, attitude, axiom, belief, canon, code, conscience, credo, criterion, dictum, doctrine, dogma, duty, element, ethic, formula, fundamental, golden rule, honor, institute, integrity, law, maxim, moral, morality, morals, opinion, precept, principium, probity, proposition, rectitude, rule, scruples, standard, tenet, truth, uprightness, verity.
antonyms corruption, wickedness.

print *v*. engrave, impress, imprint, issue, mark, produce, publish, put to bed, reproduce, run off, stamp, write.
n. book, characters, copy, dab, engraving, face, fingerprint, font, fount, impression, lettering, letters, magazine, mold, newspaper, newsprint, periodical, photo, photograph, picture, publication, reproduction, stamp, type, typeface, typescript.

prior *adj*. aforementioned, antecedent, anterior, earlier, foregoing, former, preceding, pre-existent, previous.
antonym later.

prison *n*. bagnio, bastille, brig, cage, calaboose, can, cell, chok(e)y, clink, confinement, cooler, coop, dungeon, glasshouse, guardhouse, gulag, hoos(e)gow, house of correction, house of detention, imprisonment, jail, jug, lock-up, panopticon, penal institution, penitentiary, pokey, prison-house, prison-ship, quod, reformatory, slammer, slink, stalag, stir, stockade, tank.

pristine *adj*. earliest, first, former, initial, original, primal, primary, primeval, primigenial, primitial, primitive, primordial, uncorrupted, undefiled, unspoiled, unsullied, untouched, virgin.
antonyms developed, later, spoiled.

private *adj*. clandestine, closet, concealed, confidential, exclusive, home-felt, hush-hush, in camera, independent, individual, inside, intimate, intraparietal, inward, isolated, off the record, own, particular, personal, privy, reserved, retired, secluded, secret, separate, sequestrated, solitary, special, unofficial, withdrawn.
antonyms open, public.
n. buck private, common soldier, enlisted man, private soldier.

privation *n*. affliction, austerity, destitution, distress, hardship, indigence, lack, loss, misery, necessary, need, neediness, penury, poverty, suffering, want.
antonyms affluence, wealth.

privilege *n*. advantage, benefit, birthright, claim, concession, droit, due, entitlement, franchise, freedom, immunity, liberty, license, prerogative, right, sanction, title.
antonym disadvantage.

prize[1] *n*. accolade, aim, ambition, award, conquest, desire, gain, goal, haul, honor, hope, jackpot, premium, purse, reward, stake(s), trophy, windfall, winnings.
adj. award-winning, best, champion, excellent, first-rate, outstanding, top, top-notch, winning.
antonym second-rate.
v. appreciate, cherish, esteem, hold dear, revere, reverence, set store by, treasure, value.
antonyms despise, undervalue.

prize[2] *n*. booty, capture, loot, pickings, pillage, plunder, spoils, trophy.

prize[3], prise *v*. force, jemmy, lever, pry, winkle.

probable *adj*. apparent, credible, feasible, likely, odds-on, on the cards, plausible, possible, presumed, reasonable, seeming, verisimilar.
antonym improbable.

probe *v*. examine, explore, go into, investigate, look into, pierce, poke, prod, query, scrutinize, search, sift, sound, test, verify.
n. bore, detection, drill, examination, exploration, inquest, inquiry, investigation, research, scrutiny, study, test.

problem *n*. boyg, brain-teaser, complication, conundrum, difficulty, dilemma, disagreement, dispute, doubt, enigma, no laughing matter, poser, predicament, puzzle, quandary, question, riddle, trouble, vexata quaestio, vexed question.

adj. delinquent, difficult, intractable, perverse, refractory, uncontrollable, unmanageable, unruly.

antonyms manageable, well-behaved.

procedure *n.* action, conduct, course, custom, form, formula, method, modus operandi, move, operation, performance, plan of action, policy, practice, process, routine, scheme, step, strategy, system, transaction.

proceed *v.* advance, arise, carry on, come, continue, derive, emanate, ensue, flow, follow, go ahead, issue, move on, originate, press on, progress, result, set in motion, spring, start, stem.

antonyms retreat, stop.

proceedings *n.* account, action, affair, affairs, annals, archives, business, course of action, dealings, deeds, doings, event(s), matters, measures, minutes, moves, procedure, process, records, report, steps, transactions, undertaking.

proceeds *n.* earnings, emoluments, gain, income, motser, motza, produce, products, profit, receipts, returns, revenue, takings, yield.

antonyms losses, outlay.

process[1] *n.* action, advance, case, course, course of action, development, evolution, formation, growth, manner, means, measure, method, mode, movement, operation, performance, practice, procedure, proceeding, progress, progression, stage, step, suit, system, transaction, trial, unfolding.

v. alter, convert, deal with, digitize, dispose of, fulfil, handle, prepare, refine, transform, treat.

process[2] *n.* node, nodosity, nodule, projection, prominence, protuberance, protusion.

procession *n.* cavalcade, column, concatenation, cortege, course, cycle, file, march, motorcade, parade, run, sequence, series, string, succession, train.

proclaim *v.* advertise, affirm, announce, annunciate, blaze, blazon, circulate, declare, enounce, enunciate, give out, herald, indicate, make known, preconize, profess, promulgate, publish, show, testify, trumpet.

proclamation *n.* announcement, annunciation, ban, declaration, decree, edict, indiction, interlocution, irade, manifesto, notice, notification, proclaim, promulgation, pronouncement, pronunciamento, publication, ukase.

procrastinate *v.* adjourn, dally, defer, delay, dilly-dally, drag one's feet, gain time, penelopize, play for time, postpone, prolong, protract, put off, retard, stall, temporize.

antonyms advance, proceed.

procreate *v.* beget, breed, conceive, engender, father, generate, mother, produce, propagate, reproduce, sire, spawn.

procure *v.* acquire, appropriate, bag, buy, come by, earn, effect, find, gain, get, induce, lay hands on, obtain, pander, pick up, pimp, purchase, secure, win.

antonym lose.

prod *v.* dig, drive, egg on, elbow, goad, impel, incite, jab, motivate, move, nudge, poke, prick, prog, prompt, propel, push, rouse, shove, spur, stimulate, urge.

n. boost, cue, dig, elbow, jab, nudge, poke, prog, prompt, push, reminder, shove, signal, stimulus.

prodigious *adj.* abnormal, amazing, astounding, colossal, enormous, exceptional, extraordinary, fabulous,

fantastic, flabbergasting, giant, gigantic, huge, immeasurable, immense, impressive, inordinate, mammoth, marvelous, massive, miraculous, monstrous, monumental, phenomenal, remarkable, spectacular, staggering, startling, striking, stupendous, tremendous, unusual, vast, wonderful.

antonyms commonplace, small, unremarkable.

produce[1] *v.* advance, afford, bear, beget, breed, bring forth, cause, compose, construct, create, deliver, demonstrate, develop, direct, effect, facture, fabricate, factify, factuate, furnish, generate, give, give rise to, invent, make, manufacture, mount, occasion, offer, originate, present, provoke, put forward, put on, render, result in, show, stage, supply, throw, yield.

antonyms consume, result from.

n. crop, harvest, product, yield.

produce[2] *v.* continue, elongate, extend, lengthen, prolong, protract.

product *n.* artefact, commodity, concoction, consequence, creation, effect, facture, fruit, goods, invention, issue, legacy, merchandise, offshoot, offspring, outcome, output, produce, production, result, returns, spin-off, upshot, work, yield.

antonym cause.

productive *adj.* advantageous, beneficial, constructive, creative, dynamic, effective, energetic, fecund, fertile, fructiferous, fructuous, fruitful, gainful, generative, gratifying, inventive, plentiful, producing, profitable, prolific, rewarding, rich, teeming, uberous, useful, valuable, vigorous, voluminous, worthwhile.

antonyms fruitless, unproductive.

profanity *n.* abuse, blasphemy, curse, cursing, execration, expletive, four-letter word, impiety, imprecation, inquination, irreverence, malediction, obscenity, profaneness, sacrilege, swearing, swearword.

antonyms politeness, reverence.

profess *v.* acknowledge, admit, affirm, allege, announce, assert, asseverate, aver, avow, certify, claim, confess, confirm, declare, enunciate, fake, feign, maintain, make out, own, pretend, proclaim, propose, propound, purport, sham, state, vouch.

profession *n.* acknowledgment, affirmation, assertion, attestation, avowal, business, calling, career, claim, confession, declaration, employment, job, line (of work), manifesto, métier, occupation, office, position, sphere, statement, testimony, vocation, vow, walk of life.

professional *adj.* adept, competent, crack, efficient, experienced, expert, finished, masterly, polished, practiced, proficient, qualified, skilled, slick, trained, virtuose, virtuosic, well-skilled.

antonyms amateur, unprofessional.

n. adept, authority, dab hand, expert, maestro, master, pastmaster, pro, proficient, specialist, virtuoso, wizard.

proffer *v.* advance, extend, hand, hold out, offer, present, propose, propound, submit, suggest, tender, volunteer.

proficient *adj.* able, accomplished, adept, apt, capable, clever, competent, conversant, efficient, experienced, expert, gifted, masterly, qualified, skilful, skilled, talented, trained, versed, virtuose, virtuosic.

antonyms clumsy, incompetent.

profile *n.* analysis, biography, biopic, characterization, chart, contour, diagram, drawing, examination, fig▪

form, graph, outline, portrait, review, shape, side view, silhouette, sketch, study, survey, table, thumbnail sketch, vignette.

profit n. a fast buck, advancement, advantage, avail, benefit, boot, bottom line, bunce, earnings, emoluments, fruit, gain, gelt, good, graft, gravy, grist, interest, melon, percentage, proceeds, receipts, return, revenue, surplus, takings, use, value, velvet, winnings, yield.
antonym loss.
v. advance, advantage, aid, avail, benefit, better, boot, contribute, gain, help, improve, line one's pockets, promote, serve, stand in good stead.
antonyms harm, hinder.

profitable adj. advanteageable, advantageous, beneficial, commercial, cost-effective, emolumental, emolumentary, fruitful, gainful, lucrative, money-making, paying, plummy, productive, remunerative, rewarding, serviceable, useful, utile, valuable, worthwhile.
antonym unprofitable.

profligate adj. abandoned, corrupt, Cyprian, debauched, degenerate, depraved, dissipated, dissolute, extravagant, immoderate, immoral, improvident, iniquitous, libertine, licentious, loose, prodigal, promiscuous, reckless, shameless, spendthrift, squandering, unprincipled, vicious, vitiated, wanton, wasteful, whorish, wicked, wild.
antonyms moral, parsimonious, thrifty, upright.
n. debauchee, degenerate, libertine, prodigal, racketeer, rake, reprobate, roué, spendthrift, squanderer, waster, wastrel.

profound adj. abject, absolute, abstruse, abysmal, acute, awful, bottomless, cavernous, complete, consummate, deep, deep-seated, discerning, erudite, exhaustive, extensive, extreme, far-reaching, fathomless, great, heartfelt, heart-rending, hearty, intense, keen, learned, penetrating, philosophical, pronounced, recondite, sagacious, sage, serious, sincere, skilled, subtle, thoroughgoing, thoughtful, total, utter, weighty, wise, yawning.
antonyms mild, shallow, slight.

profuse adj. abundant, ample, bountiful, copious, excessive, extravagant, exuberant, fulsome, generous, immoderate, large-handed, lavish, liberal, luxuriant, open-handed, over the top, overflowing, plentiful, prodigal, prolific, teeming, unstinting.
antonyms sparing, sparse.

profusion n. abundance, bounty, copiousness, cornucopia, excess, extravagance, exuberance, glut, lavishness, luxuriance, multitude, plenitude, pleroma, plethora, prodigality, quantity, riot, superabundance, superfluity, surplus, wealth.
antonyms sparingness, sparsity.

program n. agenda, broadcast, curriculum, design, lineup, list, listing, order of events, order of the day, performance, plan, plan of action, presentation, procedure, production, project, schedule, scheme, show, syllabus, transmission.
v. arrange, bill, book, brainwash, design, engage, formulate, itemize, lay on, line up, list, map out, plan, prearrange, schedule, work out.

progress n. advance, advancement, amelioration, betterment, breakthrough, circuit, continuation, course, development, gain, growth, headway, improvement,

increase, journey, movement, passage, procession, progression, promotion, step forward, way.
antonyms decline, deterioration.
v. advance, ameliorate, better, blossom, come on, continue, develop, forge ahead, gain, gather momentum, grow, improve, increase, make headway, make strides, mature, proceed, prosper, travel.
antonyms decline, deteriorate.

progression n. advance, advancement, chain, concatenation, course, cycle, furtherance, gain, headway, order, progress, sequence, series, string, succession.
antonyms decline, deterioration.

prohibit v. ban, bar, constrain, debar, disallow, forbid, hamper, hinder, impede, interdict, obstruct, outlaw, preclude, prevent, proscribe, restrict, rule out, stop, veto.
antonym permit.

prohibition n. ban, bar, constraint, disallowance, embargo, exclusion, forbiddal, forbiddance, injunction, interdict, interdiction, negation, obstruction, prevention, proscription, restruction, veto.
antonym permission.

prohibitive adj. excessive, exorbitant, extortionate, forbidding, impossible, preposterous, prohibiting, prohibitory, proscriptive, repressive, restraining, restrictive, sky-high, steep, suppressive.
antonyms encouraging, reasonable.

project n. activity, assignment, conception, design, enterprise, idea, job, occupation, plan, program, proposal, purpose, scheme, task, undertaking, venture, work.
v. beetle, bulge, calculate, cast, contemplate, contrive, design, devise, discharge, draft, estimate, exsert, extend, extrapolate, extrude, fling, forecast, frame, gauge, hurl, jut, launch, map out, outline, overhang, plan, predetermine, predict, propel, prophesy, propose, protrude, purpose, reckon, scheme, shoot, stand out, stick out, throw, transmit.

prolific adj. abounding, abundant, bountiful, copious, fecund, fertile, fertilizing, fruitful, generative, luxuriant, productive, profuse, rank, reproductive, rich, teeming, voluminous.
antonyms infertile, scarce.

prolong v. continue, delay, drag out, draw out, extend, lengthen, lengthen out, perpetuate, produce, protract, spin out, stretch.
antonym shorten.

prominent adj. beetling, bulging, celebrated, chief, conspicuous, distinguished, eminent, eye-catching, famous, foremost, important, jutting, leading, main, noted, noticeable, obtrusive, obvious, outstanding, popular, pre-eminent, projecting, pronounced, protruding, protrusive, protuberant, remarkable, renowned, respected, salient, standing out, striking, top, unmistakable, weighty, well-known.
antonyms inconspicuous, unimportant.

promiscuity n. abandon, amorality, debauchery, depravity, dissipation, immorality, laxity, laxness, lechery, libertinism, licentiousness, looseness, permissiveness, profligacy, promiscuousness, protervity, wantonness, whoredom, whoring, whorishness.
antonym chastity.

promise v. assure, augur, bespeak, betoken, bid fair, contract, denote, engage, guarantee, hint at, indicate, look like, pledge, plight, predict, presage, prophesy, stipulate, suggest, swear, take an oath, undertake, vouch, vow, warrant.

n. ability, aptitude, assurance, bond, capability, capacity, commitment, compact, covenant, engagement, flair, guarantee, oath, pledge, pollicitation, potential, talent, undertaking, vow, word, word of honor.

promote *v.* advance, advertise, advocate, aggrandize, aid, assist, back, blazon, boost, champion, contribute to, develop, dignify, elevate, encourage, endorse, espouse, exalt, forward, foster, further, help, honor, hype, kick upstairs, nurture, plug, popularize, prefer, publicize, puff, push, raise, recommend, sell, sponsor, stimulate, support, trumpet, upgrade, urge.

antonyms demote, disparage, obstruct.

prompt[1] *adj.* alert, brisk, eager, early, efficient, expeditious, immediate, instant, instantaneous, on time, punctual, quick, rapid, ready, responsive, smart, speedy, swift, timely, timeous, unhesitating, willing.

antonym slow.

adv. exactly, on the dot, promptly, punctually, sharp, to the minute.

prompt[2] *v.* advise, assist, call forth, cause, cue, elicit, evoke, give rise to, impel, incite, induce, inspire, instigate, motivate, move, occasion, prod, produce, provoke, remind, result in, spur, stimulate, urge.

antonym dissuade.

n. cue, help, hint, instigation, jog, jolt, prod, reminder, spur, stimulus.

promptly *adv.* directly, forthwith, immediately, instantly, on time, posthaste, pronto, punctually, quickly, speedily, swiftly, unhesitatingly.

promulgate *v.* advertise, announce, broadcast, circulate, communicate, declare, decree, disseminate, issue, notify, preconize, proclaim, promote, publicize, publish, spread.

prone[1] *adj.* apt, bent, disposed, given, inclined, liable, likely, predisposed, propense, subject, susceptible, tending, vulnerable.

antonym unlikely.

prone[2] *adj.* face down, flat, full-length, horizontal, procumbent, prostrate, recumbent, stretched.

antonym upright.

pronounce *v.* accent, affirm, announce, articulate, assert, breathe, declaim, declare, decree, deliver, enunciate, judge, proclaim, say, sound, speak, stress, utter, vocalize, voice.

pronounced *adj.* broad, clear, conspicuous, decided, definite, distinct, evident, marked, noticeable, obvious, positive, striking, strong, unmistakable.

antonyms unnoticeable, vague.

proof *n.* assay, attestation, authentication, certification, confirmation, corroboration, demonstration, documentation, evidence, examination, experiment, ordeal, scrutiny, substantiation, test, testimony, trial, verification, voucher.

adj. impenetrable, impervious, proofed, rainproof, repellent, resistant, strong, tight, treated, waterproof, weatherproof, windproof.

antonyms permeable, untreated.

propagate *v.* beget, breed, broadcast, circulate, diffuse, disseminate, engender, generate, increase, multiply, proclaim, procreate, produce, proliferate, promote, promulgate, publicize, publish, reproduce, spawn, spread, transmit.

propel *v.* drive, force, impel, launch, push, send, shoot, shove, start, thrust, waft.

antonyms slow, stop.

propensity *n.* aptness, bent, bias, disposition, foible, inclination, leaning, liability, penchant, predisposition, proclivity, proneness, readiness, susceptibility, tendency, weakness.

antonym disinclination.

proper *adj.* accepted, accurate, appropriate, apt, becoming, befitting, characteristic, conventional, correct, decent, decorous, established, exact, fit, fitting, formal, genteel, gentlemanly, gradely, individual, kosher, ladylike, legitimate, mannerly, meet, orthodox, own, particular, peculiar, perjink, personal, polite, precise, prim, prissy, punctilious, refined, respectable, respective, right, sedate, seemly, special, specific, suitable, suited, well-becoming, well-beseeming.

antonyms common, general, improper.

property[1] *n.* acres, assets, belongings, building(s), capital, chattels, effects, estate, freehold, goods, holding, holdings, house(s), land, means, meum et tuum, possessions, real estate, realty, resources, riches, title, wealth.

property[2] *n.* ability, affection, attribute, characteristic, feature, hallmark, idiosyncrasy, mark, peculiarity, quality, trait, virtue.

prophecy *n.* augury, divination, forecast, foretelling, hariolation, prediction, prognosis, prognostication, revelation, second-sight, soothsaying, taghairm, vaticination.

prophesy *v.* augur, divine, forecast, foresee, foretell, forewarn, hariolate, predict, presage, prognosticate, soothsay, vaticinate.

prophet *n.* augur, Cassandra, clairvoyant, divinator, diviner, forecaster, foreteller, Nostradamus, oracle, prognosticator, prophesier, seer, sibyl, soothsayer, tipster, vaticinator.

propitious *adj.* advantageous, auspicious, beneficial, benevolent, benign, bright, encouraging, favorable, fortunate, friendly, gracious, happy, kindly, lucky, opportune, promising, prosperous, reassuring, rosy, timely, well-disposed.

antonym inauspicious.

proportion *n.* agreement, amount, balance, congruity, correspondence, cut, distribution, division, eurhythmy, fraction, harmony, measure, part, percentage, quota, ratio, relationship, segment, share, symmetry.

antonyms disproportion, imbalance.

proportional *adj.* balanced, commensurate, comparable, compatible, consistent, correspondent, corresponding, equitable, even, fair, just, logistical, proportionate.

antonyms disproportionate, unjust.

proposal *n.* bid, design, draft, manifesto, motion, offer, outline, overture, plan, platform, presentation, proffer, program, project, proposition, recommendation, scheme, sketch, suggestion, suit, tender, terms.

propose *v.* advance, aim, bring up, design, enunciate, have in mind, intend, introduce, invite, lay before, mean, move, name, nominate, pay suit, plan, pop the question, present, proffer, propound, purpose, put forward, put up, recommend, scheme, submit, suggest, table, tender.

antonyms oppose, withdraw.

proposition *n.* manifesto, motion, plan, program, project, proposal, recommendation, scheme, suggestion, tender.

v. accost, solicit.

propound *v.* advance, advocate, contend, enunciate, lay down, move, postulate, present, propose, put forward, set forth, submit, suggest.

antonym oppose.

proprietor *n.* châtelaine, deed holder, freeholder, landlady, landlord, landowner, owner, possessor, proprietary, proprietress, proprietrix, title-holder.

prosaic *adj.* banal, boring, bromidic, commonplace, dry, dull, everyday, flat, hackneyed, humdrum, matter-of-fact, mundane, ordinary, pedestrian, routine, stale, tame, trite, unimaginative, uninspired, uninspiring, unpoetical, vapid, workaday.

antonyms imaginative, interesting.

proscribe *v.* attaint, ban, banish, bar, black, blackball, boycott, censure, condemn, damn, denounce, deport, doom, embargo, exclude, excommunicate, exile, expatriate, expel, forbid, interdict, ostracize, outlaw, prohibit, reject.

antonyms admit, allow.

prosecute *v.* arraign, bring suit against, bring to trial, carry on, conduct, continue, direct, discharge, engage in, execute, follow through, indict, litigate, manage, perform, persevere, persist, practice, prefer charges, pursue, put on trial, see through, sue, summon, take to court, try, work at.

antonym desist.

prospect *n.* calculation, chance, contemplation, expectation, future, hope, landscape, likelihood, odds, opening, outlook, panorama, perspective, plan, possibility, presumption, probability, promise, proposition, scene, sight, spectacle, thought, view, vision, vista.

antonym unlikelihood.

v. explore, fossick, nose, quest, search, seek, survey.

prospective *adj.* anticipated, approaching, awaited, coming, designate, designated, destined, eventual, expected, forthcoming, future, imminent, intended, likely, possible, potential, soon-to-be, to come, -to-be.

antonyms agreed, current.

prosper *v.* advance, bloom, boom, burgeon, fare well, flourish, flower, get on, grow rich, make good, progress, succeed, thrive, turn out well.

antonym fail.

prosperous *adj.* affluent, blooming, booming, burgeoning, flourishing, fortunate, in the money, lucky, moneyed, opulent, palmy, profitable, rich, successful, thriving, wealthy, well-heeled, well-off, well-to-do.

antonym poor.

prostrate *adj.* abject, brought to one's knees, crushed, defenseless, dejected, depressed, desolate, disarmed, done, drained, exhausted, fagged, fallen, flat, helpless, horizontal, impotent, inconsolable, knackered, kowtowing, overcome, overwhelmed, paralyzed, pooped, powerless, procumbent, prone, reduced, shattered, spent, worn out.

antonyms elated, erect, hale, happy, strong, triumphant.

v. crush, depress, disarm, drain, exhaust, fag out, fatigue, knacker, lay low, overcome, overthrow, overturn, overwhelm, paralyze, poop, reduce, ruin, sap, shatter, tire, wear out, weary.

antonyms elate, exalt, strengthen.

protagonist *n.* advocate, champion, chief character,

exponent, hero, heroine, lead, leader, mainstay, prime mover, principal, proponent, standard-bearer, supporter.

protect *v.* care for, chaperon, convoy, cover, cover up for, defend, escort, guard, harbor, keep, look after, preserve, safeguard, save, screen, secure, shelter, shield, stand guard over, support, watch over.

antonyms attack, threaten.

protection *n.* aegis, armor, backstop, barrier, buffer, bulwark, care, charge, cover, custody, defense, guard, guardianship, guarding, preservation, protecting, refuge, safeguard, safekeeping, safety, screen, security, shelter, shield, umbrella, wardship.

antonyms attack, threat.

protest *n.* complaint, declaration, demur, demurral, dharna, disapproval, dissent, formal complaint, objection, obtestation, outcry, protestation, remonstrance.

antonym acceptance.

v. affirm, argue, assert, asseverate, attest, avow, complain, contend, cry out, declare, demonstrate, demur, disagree, disapprove, expostulate, insist, maintain, object, obtest, oppose, profess, remonstrate, squawk, take exception, testify, vow.

antonym accept.

prototype *n.* archetype, example, exemplar, mock-up, model, original, paradigm, pattern, precedent, standard, type.

protract *v.* continue, draw out, extend, keep going, lengthen, prolong, spin out, stretch out, sustain.

antonym shorten.

protuberance *n.* apophysis, bulb, bulge, bump, excrescence, knob, lump, mamelon, mamilla, outgrowth, process, projection, prominence, protrusion, swelling, tuber, tubercle, tumor, umbo, venter, wart, welt.

proud *adj.* appreciative, arrogant, august, boastful, conceited, content, contented, disdainful, distinguished, egotistical, eminent, exalted, glad, glorious, grand, gratified, gratifying, great, haughty, high and mighty, honored, illustrious, imperious, imposing, lofty, lordly, magnificent, majestic, memorable, misproud, noble, orgulous, overbearing, overweening, pleased, pleasing, presumptuous, prideful, red-letter, rewarding, satisfied, satisfying, self-important, self-respecting, snobbish, snobby, snooty, splendid, stately, stuck-up, supercilious, toffee-nosed, vain.

antonym humble.

prove *v.* analyze, ascertain, assay, attest, authenticate, bear out, check, confirm, corroborate, demonstrate, determine, document, establish, evidence, evince, examine, experience, experiment, justify, show, substantiate, suffer, test, try, turn out, verify.

antonyms discredit, disprove, falsify.

proverb *n.* adage, aphorism, apophthegm, bromide, byword, dictum, gnome, maxim, precept, saw, saying.

proverbial *adj.* accepted, acknowledged, apophthegmatic, archetypal, axiomatic, bromidic, conventional, current, customary, famed, famous, legendary, notorious, self-evident, time-honored, traditional, typical, unquestioned, well-known.

provide *v.* accommodate, add, afford, anticipate, arrange for, bring, cater, contribute, determine, equip, forearm, furnish, give, impart, lay down, lend, outfit, plan for, prepare for, present, produce, provision, render,

require, serve, specify, state, stipulate, stock up, suit, supply, take measures, take precautions, yield.
antonyms remove, take.

provident *adj.* canny, careful, cautious, discreet, economical, equipped, far-seeing, far-sighted, frugal, imaginative, long-sighted, prudent, sagacious, shrewd, thrifty, vigilant, wary, well-prepared, wise.
antonym improvident.

provision *n.* accouterment, agreement, arrangement, catering, clause, condition, demand, equipping, fitting out, furnishing, plan, prearrangement, precaution, preparation, prerequisite, providing, proviso, purveyance, purveying, requirement, specification, stipulation, supplying, term, victualing.
antonyms neglect, removal.

provisions *n.* comestibles, eatables, eats, edibles, fare, food, foodstuff, groceries, grub, piece, prog, provand, provender, proviant, rations, stores, supplies, sustenance, viands, viaticum, victualage, victuals, vittles.

proviso *n.* clause, condition, limitation, provision, qualification, requirement, reservation, restriction, rider, small print, stipulation.

provoke *v.* affront, aggravate, anger, annoy, cause, chafe, elicit, enrage, evoke, exasperate, excite, fire, gall, generate, give rise to, incense, incite, induce, inflame, infuriate, inspire, instigate, insult, irk, irritate, kindle, madden, motivate, move, occasion, offend, pique, precipitate, produce, promote, prompt, put out, rile, rouse, stimulate, stir, vex.
antonyms pacify, please, result.

prowess *n.* ability, accomplishment, adeptness, adroitness, aptitude, attainment, bravery, command, daring, dauntlessness, dexterity, doughtiness, excellence, expertise, expertness, facility, genius, heroism, mastery, skill, talent, valor.
antonyms clumsiness, mediocrity.

prowl *v.* creep, cruise, hunt, lurk, nose, patrol, range, roam, rove, scavenge, search, skulk, slink, sneak, snook, stalk, steal.

proximity *n.* adjacency, closeness, contiguity, juxtaposition, nearness, neighborhood, propinquity, proximation, vicinity.
antonym remoteness.

proxy *n.* agent, attorney, delegate, deputy, factor, representative, stand-in, substitute, surrogate.

prudence *n.* canniness, care, caution, circumspection, common sense, discretion, economy, far-sightedness, foresight, forethought, frugality, good sense, heedfulness, husbandry, judgment, judiciousness, planning, policy, precaution, preparedness, providence, sagacity, saving, thrift, vigilance, wariness, wisdom.
antonym imprudence.

prudent *adj.* canny, careful, cautious, circumspect, discerning, discreet, economical, far-sighted, frugal, judicious, politic, provident, sagacious, sage, sensible, shrewd, sparing, thrifty, vigilant, wary, well-advised, wise, wise-hearted.
antonym imprudent.

prudish *adj.* demure, narrow-minded, old-maidish, overmodest, overnice, po-faced, priggish, prim, prissy, proper, pudibund, puritanical, school-marmish, squeamish, starchy, strait-laced, stuffy, ultra-virtuous, Victorian.
antonyms easy-going, lax.

pry *v.* delve, dig, ferret, interfere, intrude, meddle, nose, peep, peer, poke, poke one's nose in, snoop.
antonym mind one's own business.

prying *adj.* curious, inquisitive, interfering, intrusive, meddlesome, meddling, nosy, peering, peery, snooping, snoopy, spying.
antonym uninquisitive.

psyche *n.* anima, awareness, consciousness, individuality, intellect, intelligence, mind, personality, pneuma, self, soul, spirit, subconscious, understanding.

psychiatrist *n.* analyst, headshrinker, psychoanalyzer, psychoanalyst, psychologist, psychotherapist, shrink, therapist, trick-cyclist.

psychic *adj.* clairvoyant, cognitive, extra-sensory, intellectual, mental, mystic, mystical, occult, preternatural, psychogenic, psychological, spiritual, spiritualistic, supernatural, telekinetic, telepathic.

psychological *adj.* affective, cerebral, cognitive, emotional, imaginary, intellectual, irrational, mental, psychosomatic, subconscious, subjective, unconscious, unreal.

psychotic *adj.* certifiable, demented, deranged, insane, lunatic, mad, mental, psychopathic, unbalanced.
antonym sane.

public *adj.* accessible, acknowledged, circulating, civic, civil, common, communal, community, exposed, general, important, known, national, notorious, obvious, open, overt, patent, plain, popular, prominent, published, recognized, respected, social, state, universal, unrestricted, well-known, widespread.
antonym private.

n. audience, buyers, citizens, clientèle, commonalty, community, country, electorate, everyone, followers, following, masses, multitude, nation, patrons, people, populace, population, punters, society, supporters, voters.

publicize *v.* advertise, blaze, blazon, broadcast, hype, plug, promote, puff, push, spotlight, spread about, write off.
antonym keep secret.

publish *v.* advertise, announce, bring out, broadcast, circulate, communicate, declare, diffuse, disclose, distribute, divulgate, divulge, evulgate, issue, leak, part, print, proclaim, produce, promulgate, publicize, reveal, spread, vent.
antonym keep secret.

puerile *adj.* babyish, childish, foolish, immature, inane, infantile, irresponsible, jejune, juvenile, naïve, petty, ridiculous, silly, trifling, trivial, weak.
antonym mature.

pugnacious *adj.* aggressive, antagonistic, argumentative, bellicose, belligerent, choleric, combative, contentious, disputatious, hostile, hot-tempered, irascible, petulant, quarrelsome.
antonym easy-going.

pull *v.* attract, cull, dislocate, drag, draw, draw out, entice, extract, gather, haul, jerk, lure, magnetize, pick, pluck, remove, rend, rip, schlep, sprain, strain, stretch, take out, tear, tow, track, trail, tug, tweak, uproot, weed, whang, wrench, yank.
antonyms deter, push, repel.

n. advantage, allurement, attraction, clout, drag, drawing power, effort, exertion, force, forcefulness, influence, inhalation, jerk, leverage, lure, magnetism,

muscle, power, puff, seduction, tug, twitch, weight, yank.
antonyms deterring, push, repelling.

pulsate *v.* beat, drum, hammer, oscillate, palpitate, pound, pulse, quiver, throb, thud, thump, tick, vibrate.

pulse *n.* beat, beating, drumming, oscillation, pulsation, rhythm, stroke, throb, throbbing, thudding, vibration.
v. beat, drum, pulsate, throb, thud, tick, vibrate.

pummel *v.* bang, batter, beat, fib, hammer, knock, nevel, pound, punch, strike, thump.

pump *v.* catechize, cross-examine, debrief, drive, force, grill, inject, interrogate, pour, probe, push, question, quiz, send, supply.

pun *n.* clinch, double entendre, equivoke, jeu de mots, paronomasia, paronomasy, play on words, quip, witticism.

punch[1] *v.* bash, biff, bop, box, clout, fib, hit, plug, pummel, slam, slug, smash, sock, strike, wallop.
n. bash, biff, bite, blow, bop, clout, drive, effectiveness, force, forcefulness, hit, impact, jab, knock, knuckle sandwich, lander, muzzler, panache, pizzazz, plug, point, sock, thump, verve, vigor, wallop.
antonym feebleness.

punch[2] *v.* bore, cut, drill, perforate, pierce, pink, prick, puncture, stamp.

punctilious *adj.* careful, ceremonious, conscientious, exact, finicky, formal, formalist, fussy, meticulous, nice, overnice, particular, precise, proper, scrupulous, strict.
antonyms boorish, easy-going, informal.

punctual *adj.* early, exact, in good time, on the dot, on time, precise, prompt, punctilious, strict, timely, up to time.
antonym unpunctual.

pungent *adj.* acid, acrid, acrimonious, acute, aromatic, barbed, biting, bitter, caustic, cutting, fell, hot, incisive, keen, mordant, painful, penetrating, peppery, piercing, piquant, poignant, pointed, sarcastic, scathing, seasoned, sharp, sour, spicy, stinging, stringent, strong, tangy, tart, telling, trenchant.
antonyms feeble, mild, tasteless.

punish *v.* abuse, amerce, batter, beat, castigate, chasten, chastise, correct, crucify, discipline, flog, give a lesson to, give someone laldie, harm, hurt, injure, keelhaul, knee-cap, lash, maltreat, manhandle, masthead, misuse, oppress, penalize, rough up, scour, scourge, sort, strafe, trounce.

punishment *n.* abuse, beating, chastening, chastisement, come-uppance, correction, damnation, deserts, discipline, jankers, knee-capping, laldie, maltreatment, manhandling, medicine, pain, pay-off, penalty, penance, punition, retribution, sanction, toco, torture, victimization.

puny *adj.* diminutive, dwarfish, feeble, frail, inconsequential, inferior, insignificant, little, meager, minor, paltry, petty, piddling, pimping, reckling, runted, runtish, runty, sickly, stunted, tiny, trifling, trivial, underfed, undersized, undeveloped, weak, weakly, worthless.
antonyms important, large, strong.

pupil *n.* beginner, catechumen, disciple, learner, neophyte, novice, protégé, scholar, schoolboy, schoolgirl, student, tiro, tutee.
antonym teacher.

purchase *v.* achieve, acquire, attain, buy, earn, gain, invest in, obtain, pay for, procure, ransom, realize, secure, win.
antonym sell.
n. acquisition, advantage, asset, buy, edge, emption, foothold, footing, gain, grasp, grip, hold, influence, investment, lever, leverage, possession, property, ransoming, support, toehold.
antonym sale.

pure *adj.* absolute, abstract, academic, antiseptic, authentic, blameless, chaste, clean, clear, disinfected, flawless, genuine, germ-free, guileless, high-minded, honest, hygienic, immaculate, innocent, intemerate, maidenly, modest, natural, neat, pasteurized, perfect, philosophical, real, refined, sanitary, Saturnian, sheer, simple, sincere, snow-white, speculative, spiritous, spotless, stainless, sterile, sterilized, straight, taintless, theoretical, thorough, true, unadulterate, unadulterated, unalloyed, unblemished, uncontaminated, uncorrupted, undefiled, unmingled, unmitigated, unmixed, unpolluted, unqualified, unsoiled, unspoilt, unspotted, unstained, unsullied, untainted, untarnished, upright, utter, virgin, virginal, virginly, virtuous, wholesome.
antonyms adulterated, applied, defiled, immoral, impure, polluted, tainted.

purely *adv.* absolutely, completely, entirely, exclusively, just, merely, only, plainly, sheerly, simply, solely, thoroughly, totally, utterly, wholly.

purify *v.* absolve, beneficiate, catharize, chasten, clarify, clean, cleanse, decontaminate, deodorize, depurate, desalinate, disinfect, epurate, filter, fumigate, furbish, lustrate, mundify, redeem, refine, sanctify, sanitize, shrive, sublimize, wash.
antonyms contaminate, defile, pollute.

purist *n.* Atticist, classicist, formalist, grammaticaster, grammatist, mandarin, nit-picker, pedant, precisian, precisianist, precisionist, quibbler, stickler, vocabularian.
antonym liberal.
adj. austere, captious, fastidious, finicky, fussy, hypercritical, nit-picking, over-exact, over-fastidious, over-meticulous, over-particular, over-precise, pedantic, puristic, quibbling, strict, uncompromising.
antonyms liberal, open-minded, tolerant.

puritanical *adj.* abstemious, abstinent, ascetic, austere, bigoted, disapproving, disciplinarian, fanatical, narrow, narrow-minded, prim, proper, prudish, puritan, rigid, severe, stern, stiff, strait-laced, strict, stuffy, uncompromising, zealous.
antonyms broad-minded, hedonistic, indulgent, liberal.

purity *n.* blamelessness, chasteness, chastity, clarity, classicism, cleanliness, clearness, decency, faultlessness, fineness, genuineness, immaculateness, incorruption, innocence, integrity, morality, piety, pureness, rectitude, refinement, sanctity, simplicity, sincerity, spotlessness, stainlessness, truth, unspottedness, untaintedness, uprightness, virginity, virtue, virtuousness, wholesomeness.
antonyms immorality, impurity.

purloin *v.* abstract, appropriate, filch, finger, half-inch, lift, nick, nobble, palm, pilfer, pinch, pocket, prig, remove, rob, snaffle, snitch, steal, swipe, take, thieve.

purport *v.* allege, argue, assert, betoken, claim, convey, declare, denote, express, give out, imply, import, indicate, intend, maintain, mean, portend, pose as, pretend, proclaim, profess, seem, show, signify, suggest.

n. bearing, direction, drift, gist, idea, implication, import, meaning, point, significance, spirit, substance, tendency, tenor, theme, thrust.

purpose *n.* advantage, aim, ambition, aspiration, assiduity, ·avail, benefit, constancy, contemplation, decision, dedication, design, determination, devotion, drive, effect, end, firmness, function, gain, goal, good, hope, idea, ideal, intention, motive, object, objective, outcome, persistence, pertinacity, plan, point, principle, profit, project, rationale, reason, resolution, resolve, result, return, scheme, service, single-mindedness, steadfastness, target, telos, tenacity, use, usefulness, utility, view, vision, will, wish, zeal.

v. aim, aspire, contemplate, decide, design, desire, determine, ettle, intend, mean, meditate, plan, propose, resolve.

purposely *adv..* by design, calculatedly, consciously, deliberately, designedly, expressly, intentionally, knowingly, on purpose, premeditatedly, specifically, wilfully, with malice aforethought.

antonyms impulsively, spontaneously, unpremeditatedly.

pursue *v.* accompany, adhere to, aim at, aim for, aspire to, attend, bedevil, beset, besiege, carry on, chase, check out, conduct, continue, course, court, cultivate, desire, dog, engage in, follow, follow up, go for, gun for, harass, harry, haunt, hold to, hound, hunt, inquire into, investigate, keep on, maintain, perform, persecute, persevere in, persist in, plague, ply, practice, proceed, prosecute, purpose, seek, set one's cap at, shadow, stalk, strive for, tackle, tail, track, trail, try for, wage, woo.

antonyms eschew, shun.

pursuit[1] *n.* chase, chevy, hounding, hue and cry, hunt, hunting, inquiry, investigation, quest, search, seeking, stalking, tracking, trail, trailing.

pursuit[2] *n.* activity, craft, hobby, interest, line, occupation, parergon, pastime, pleasure, side-line, specialty, vocation.

push *v.* advance, advertise, boost, browbeat, bulldoze, bully, coerce, constrain, depress, dragoon, drive, edge, egg on, elbow, encourage, expedite, force, hurry, hype, incite, influence, inveigle, jockey, jog, joggle, jostle, maneuver, manhandle, oblige, peddle, persuade, plug, poke, press, prod, promote, propagandize, propel, publicize, puff, ram, shoulder, shove, speed, spur, squeeze, thrust, urge, wedge, whang.

n. advance, ambition, assault, attack, bunt, butt, charge, determination, discharge, dismissal, drive, dynamism, effort, energy, enterprise, go, impetus, impulse, initiative, jolt, knock, notice, nudge, offensive, one's books, one's cards, one's marching orders, onset, onslaught, poke, pressure, prod, shove, the axe, the boot, the bum's rush, the chop, the sack, thrust, vigor, vim, vitality, zip.

push-over *n.* child's play, cinch, doddle, dupe, easy mark, fall guy, gull, mug, picnic, piece of cake, sinecure, sitting duck, sitting target, soft mark, soft touch, stooge, sucker, walk-over.

antonyms challenge, labor.

pushy *adj.* aggressive, ambitious, arrogant, assertive, assuming, bold, bossy, brash, bumptious, forceful, forward, loud, obtrusive, offensive, officious, over-confident, presumptuous, pushing, self-assertive.

antonyms quiet, restrained, unassertive, unassuming.

pusillanimous *adj.* caitiff, chicken, chicken-hearted, cowardly, craven, faint-hearted, fearful, feeble, gutless, lily-livered, mean-spirited, poltroon, recreant, scared, spineless, timid, timorous, unassertive, unenterprising, weak, weak-kneed, yellow.

antonyms ambitious, courageous, forceful, strong.

put *v.* advance, apply, assign, bring, bring forward, cast, commit, condemn, consign, constrain, couch, deploy, deposit, dispose, drive, employ, enjoin, establish, express, fit, fix, fling, force, formulate, forward, frame, heave, hurl, impel, impose, induce, inflict, land, lay, levy, lob, make, oblige, offer, park, phrase, pitch, place, plonk, pose, position, post, present, propose, push, render, require, rest, send, set, set down, settle, situate, state, station, subject, submit, suggest, tender, throw, thrust, toss, utter, voice, word, write.

putative *adj.* alleged, assumed, conjectural, hypothetical, imputed, presumed, presumptive, reported, reputative, reputed, supposed, suppositional, supposititious.

put-down *n.* affront, dig, disparagement, gibe, humiliation, insult, rebuff, sarcasm, slap in the face, slight, sneer, snub.

putrefy *v.* addle, corrupt, decay, decompose, deteriorate, fester, foost, gangrene, go bad, mortify, mold, necrose, perish, rot, spoil, stink, taint.

putrid *adj.* addle, addled, bad, contaminated, corrupt, decayed, decomposed, fetid, foosty, foul, gangrenous, mephitic, moldy, necrosed, noisome, off, putrefied, rancid, rank, reeking, rotten, rotting, sphacelate(d), spoiled, stinking, tainted.

antonyms fresh, wholesome.

puzzle[1] *v.* baffle, bamboozle, beat, bewilder, confound, confuse, fickle, floor, flummox, metagrobolize, mystify, nonplus, perplex, pother, stump, worry.

n. acrostic, anagram, brain-teaser, confusion, conundrum, crossword, difficulty, dilemma, enigma, knot, koan, logogram, logograph, logogriph, maze, mindbender, mystery, paradox, poser, problem, quandary, question, rebus, riddle, Sphinx, tickler.

puzzle[2] *v.* brood, cogitate, consider, deliberate, figure, meditate, mull over, muse, ponder, rack one's brains, ratiocinate, reason, ruminate, study, think, wonder, worry.

puzzled *adj.* at a loss, at sea, baffled, bamboozled, beaten, bemused, bewildered, confounded, confused, disorientated, doubtful, flummoxed, in a haze, lost, mixed up, mizzled, mystified, nonplused, perplexed, stuck, stumped, stymied, uncertain.

antonyms certain, clear.

puzzling *adj.* abstruse, ambiguous, baffling, bewildering, bizarre, cabalistic, circuitous, confusing, cryptic, curious, enigmatic, equivocal, impenetrable, inexplicable, intricate, involved, knotty, labyrinthine, mind-bending, mind-boggling, misleading, mysterious, mystical, mystifying, peculiar, perplexing, queer, riddling, Sphinx-like, strange, tangled, tortuous, unaccountable, unclear, unfathomable.

Q

quack *n.* charlatan, cowboy, empiric, fake, fraud, humbug, impostor, masquerader, medicaster, mountebank, phony, pretender, pseud, quacksalver, sham, spieler, swindler, trickster, witch-doctor.
adj. bogus, counterfeit, fake, false, fraudulent, phony, pretended, sham, so-called, spurious, supposed, unqualified.
antonym genuine.

quackery *n.* charlatanism, charlatanry, empiricism, fraud, fraudulence, humbug, imposture, mountebankery, mountebankism, phoniness, sham.

quaff *v.* booze, carouse, down, drain, drink, gulp, guzzle, imbibe, knock back, swallow, swig, swill, tipple, tope, toss off.
n. bevvy, cup, dram, draught, drink, jorum, slug, snifter, swig.

quagmire *n.* bog, everglade, fen, marsh, mire, morass, moss, mudflat, quag, quicksand, slough, swamp.

quail *v.* back away, blanch, blench, cower, droop, faint, falter, flinch, quake, recoil, shake, shrink, shudder, shy away, tremble, wince.

quaint *adj.* absurd, antiquated, antique, bizarre, charming, curious, droll, eccentric, fanciful, fantastic, freaky, funky, ingenious, odd, old-fashioned, old-time, old-world, peculiar, picturesque, queer, rum, singular, strange, unconventional, unusual, weird, whimsical.

quake *v.* convulse, heave, jolt, move, pulsate, quail, quiver, rock, shake, shiver, shudder, sway, throb, totter, tremble, vibrate, waver, wobble.

qualification[1] *n.* ability, accomplishment, adequacy, aptitude, attribute, capability, capacity, certification, competence, eligibility, fitness, skill, suitability, suitableness, training.

qualification[2] *n.* adaptation, adjustment, allowance, caveat, condition, criterion, exception, exemption, limitation, modification, objection, provision, proviso, reservation, restriction, stipulation.

qualified[1] *adj.* able, accomplished, adept, adequate, capable, certificated, certified, competent, efficient, eligible, equipped, experienced, expert, fit, habilitated, knowledgeable, licensed, practiced, proficient, skilful, talented, trained.
antonym unqualified.

qualified[2] *adj.* bounded, cautious, circumscribed, conditional, confined, contingent, equivocal, guarded, limitative, limited, modificatory, modified, provisional, qualificatory, reserved, restricted.

qualify[1] *v.* authorize, capacitate, certificate, empower, endow, equip, fit, graduate, habilitate, permit, prepare, sanction, shape, train.
antonym unfit.

qualify[2] *v.* abate, adapt, adjust, alleviate, assuage, categorize, characterize, circumscribe, classify, define, delimit, describe, designate, diminish, distinguish, ease, lessen, limit, mitigate, moderate, modify, modulate, reduce, regulate, restrain, restrict, soften, temper, vary, weaken.

quality *n.* aspect, attribute, caliber, character, characteristic, class, complexion, condition, constitution, deal, description, distinction, essence, excellence, feature, fineness, grade, kidney, kind, make, mark, merit, nature, peculiarity, position, pre-eminence, property, rank, refinement, sort, standing, status, superiority, talent, timbre, tone, trait, value, water, worth.

qualm *n.* anxiety, apprehension, compunction, disquiet, doubt, fear, hesitation, misgiving, pang, presentiment, regret, reluctance, remorse, scruple, twinge, uncertainty, unease, uneasiness, worry.

quandary *n.* bewilderment, confusion, corner, difficulty, dilemma, doubt, embarrassment, entanglement, fix, hole, imbroglio, impasse, jam, kettle of fish, mess, perplexity, plight, predicament, problem, puzzle, uncertainty.

quantity *n.* aggregate, allotment, amount, breadth, bulk, capacity, content, dosage, expanse, extent, greatness, length, lot, magnitude, mass, measure, number, part, portion, proportion, quantum, quota, share, size, spread, strength, sum, total, volume, weight.

quarantine *n.* detention, isolation, lazaret, lazaretto, segregation.

quarrel *n.* affray, altercation, argument, barney, beef, bicker, brattle, brawl, breach, breeze, broil, clash, commotion, conflict, contention, controversy, coolness, debate, difference, disagreement, discord, disputation, dispute, dissension, dissidence, disturbance, dust-up, estrangement, feud, fight, fracas, fray, misunderstanding, row, rupture, schism, scrap, shouting match, slanging match, spat, split, squabble, strife, tiff, tumult, vendetta, wrangle.
antonyms agreement, harmony.
v. altercate, argue, be at loggerheads, be at variance, bicker, brawl, carp, cavil, clash, contend, differ, disagree, dispute, dissent, fall out, fight, find fault, object, pick holes, question, row, spar, spat, squabble, take exception, tiff, vitilitigate, wrangle.
antonym agree.

quarrelsome *adj.* altercative, antagonistic, argumentative, bellicose, belligerent, cantankerous, captious, choleric, combative, contentious, contrary, cross, disputatious, fractious, ill-tempered, irascible, irritable, peevish, perverse, petulant, pugnacious, querulous, stroppy, testy, truculent, turbulent, wranglesome.
antonyms peaceable, placid.

quarry *n.* game, goal, kill, object, objective, prey, prize, target, victim.

quarter[1] *n.* area, direction, district, division, locality, location, neighborhood, part, place, point, position, province, quartier, region, section, sector, side, spot, station, territory, vicinity, zone.

quarter[2] *n.* clemency, compassion, favor, forgiveness, grace, indulgence, leniency, mercy, pardon, pity.

quarter[3] *n.* fourth, quartern, term.
v. decussate, divide in four, quadrisect.

quarter[4] *v.* accommodate, bed, billet, board, house, install, lodge, place, post, put up, shelter, station.

quarters *n.* abode, accommodation, apartment, barracks, billet, cantonment, caserne, chambers, digs, domicile, dwelling, habitation, lodging, lodgings, post, quarterage, residence, rooms, station.

quash *v.* annul, cancel, crush, declare null and void, defeat, disannul, disenact, invalidate, nullify, overrule, overthrow, quell, repress, rescind, reverse, revoke, set aside, squash, subdue, suppress, void.
antonyms confirm, justify, reinstate, vindicate.

quaver *v.* break, crack, flicker, flutter, oscillate, pulsate, quake, quiver, shake, shudder, tremble, trill, twitter, vibrate, warble.

n. break, quaveriness, quiver, shake, sob, throb, tremble, trembling, tremolo, tremor, trill, vibration, vibrato, warble.

quay *n.* dock, harbor, jetty, levee, pier, wharf.

queasy *adj.* bilious, dizzy, faint, giddy, green, groggy, ill, indisposed, nauseated, off-color, qualmish, qualmy, queer, sick, sickened, squeamish, unwell.

queen *n.* beauty, belle, consort, diva, doyenne, empress, goddess, grande dame, idol, maharani, mistress, monarch, nonpareil, prima donna, princess, rani, ruler, sovereign, star, sultana, tsarina, Venus.

queer *adj.* aberrant, abnormal, absurd, anomalous, atypical, bizarre, cranky, crazy, curious, daft, demented, deranged, deviant, disquieting, dizzy, doubtful, droll, dubious, eccentric, eerie, eldritch, erratic, exceptional, extraordinary, faint, fanciful, fantastic, fey, fishy, freakish, funny, giddy, grotesque, homosexual, idiosyncratic, ill, irrational, irregular, light-headed, mad, mysterious, odd, offbeat, outlandish, outré, peculiar, preternatural, puzzling, quaint, queasy, questionable, reeling, remarkable, rum, screwy, shady, shifty, singular, strange, suspect, suspicious, touched, unaccountable, unbalanced, uncanny, uncommon, unconventional, uneasy, unhinged, unnatural, unorthodox, unusual, unwell, unwonted, weird.
antonyms common, ordinary, straightforward, unexceptional, usual.
v. botch, cheat, endanger, foil, frustrate, harm, impair, imperil, injure, jeopardize, mar, ruin, spoil, stymie, thwart, upset, wreck.

queerness *n.* aberrance, abnormality, absurdity, anomalousness, atypicalness, bizarreness, crankiness, craziness, curiousness, deviance, drollness, dubiety, dubiousness, eccentricity, eeriness, fishiness, grotesqueness, idiosyncrasy, individuality, irrationality, irregularity, light-headedness, madness, mysteriousness, mystery, oddity, oddness, outlandishness, peculiarity, puzzle, quaintness, shadiness, shiftiness, singularity, strangeness, suspiciousness, uncanniness, uncommonness, unconventionality, unnaturalness, unorthodoxy, unusualness, unwontedness.

quell *v.* allay, alleviate, appease, assuage, blunt, calm, compose, conquer, crush, deaden, defeat, dull, extinguish, hush, mitigate, moderate, mollify, overcome, overpower, pacify, put down, quash, quench, quiet, reduce, silence, soothe, squash, stifle, subdue, subjugate, suppress, vanquish.

quench *v.* allay, appease, check, cool, crush, damp down, destroy, douse, end, extinguish, overcome, put out, quash, quell, sate, satisfy, silence, slake, smother, snuff out, stifle, suppress.

querulous *adj.* cantankerous, captious, carping, caviling, censorious, complaining, crabbed, critical, cross, cross-grained, crusty, discontented, dissatisfied, exacting, fault-finding, fretful, fussy, grouchy, grumbling, hypercritical, intolerant, irascible, irritable, peevish, perverse, petulant, plaintive, quarrelsome, querimonious, sour, testy, thrawn, waspish, whingeing, whining.
antonyms contented, equable, placid, uncomplaining.

query *v.* ask, be skeptical of, call in question, challenge, disbelieve, dispute, distrust, doubt, enquire, misdoubt, mistrust, quarrel with, question, suspect.
antonym accept.
n. demand, doubt, hesitation, inquiry, misdoubt, misgiving, objection, problem, quaere, question, quibble, reservation, skepticism, suspicion, uncertainty.

quest *n.* adventure, crusade, enterprise, expedition, exploration, hunt, inquiry, investigation, journey, mission, pilgrimage, pursuit, search, undertaking, venture, voyage.

question *v.* ask, be skeptical of, catechize, challenge, controvert, cross-examine, debrief, disbelieve, dispute, distrust, doubt, enquire, examine, grill, impugn, interpellate, interrogate, interview, investigate, misdoubt, mistrust, oppose, probe, pump, quarrel with, query, quiz, suspect.
n. argument, confusion, contention, controversy, debate, difficulty, dispute, doubt, dubiety, erotema, erotesis, examination, inquiry, interpellation, interrogation, investigation, issue, misdoubt, misgiving, motion, point, problem, proposal, proposition, quaere, query, quibble, skepsis, subject, theme, topic, uncertainty.

questionable *adj.* arguable, borderline, controversial, debatable, disputable, doubtful, dubious, dubitable, equivocal, fishy, iffy, impugnable, moot, problematical, queer, shady, suspect, suspicious, uncertain, undetermined, unproven, unreliable, unsettled, vexed.
antonyms certain, indisputable, straightforward.

queue *n.* file, line, line-up, order, procession, sequence, series, string, succession, tail, tail-back, train.

quibble *v.* carp, cavil, chop logic, equivocate, pettifog, prevaricate, shift, split hairs.
n. carriwitchet, casuistry, cavil, complaint, criticism, equivocation, equivoke, evasion, niggle, objection, pettifoggery, prevarication, query, quiddit, quiddity, quillet, quip, quirk, sophism, subterfuge.

quibbler *n.* casuist, caviler, chop-logic, criticaster, equivocator, hair-splitter, logic-chopper, niggler, nitpicker, pettifogger, sophist.

quick *adj.* able, active, acute, adept, adroit, agile, alert, animated, apt, astute, awake, brief, bright, brisk, clever, cursory, deft, dexterous, discerning, energetic, expeditious, express, fast, fleet, flying, hasty, headlong, hurried, immediate, instant, instantaneous, intelligent, keen, lively, nifty, nimble, nippy, penetrating, perceptive, perfunctory, precipitate, prompt, quick-witted, rapid, ready, receptive, responsive, sharp, shrewd, skilful, smart, snappy, speedy, spirited, sprightly, spry, sudden, summary, swift, unhesitating, vivacious, wide-awake, winged.
antonyms dull, slow.

quicken *v.* accelerate, activate, advance, animate, arouse, dispatch, energize, enliven, excite, expedite, galvanize, hasten, hurry, impel, incite, inspire, invigorate, kindle, precipitate, reactivate, refresh, reinvigorate, resuscitate, revitalize, revive, revivify, rouse, sharpen, speed, stimulate, strengthen, vitalize, vivify.
antonyms dull, retard.

quickly *adv.* abruptly, at a rate of knots, at the double, before you can say Jack Robinson, briskly, by leaps and bounds, cursorily, expeditiously, express, fast, hastily, hell for leather, hotfoot, hurriedly, immediately, instantaneously, instantly, lickety-split, like a bat out of hell, perfunctorily, posthaste, promptly, pronto, quick, rapidly, readily, soon, speedily, swiftly, unhesitatingly.
antonyms slowly, tardily, thoroughly.

quickness *n.* acuteness, agility, alertness, aptness, astuteness, briskness, deftness, dexterity, expedition,

hastiness, immediacy, instantaneousness, intelligence, keenness, liveliness, nimbleness, penetration, precipitation, promptitude, promptness, quick-wittedness, rapidity, readiness, receptiveness, sharpness, shrewdness, speed, speediness, suddenness, summariness, swiftness, turn of speed.
antonyms dullness, slowness, tardiness.

quick-witted *adj.* acute, alert, astute, bright, clever, crafty, ingenious, intelligent, keen, nimble-witted, penetrating, perceptive, ready-witted, resourceful, sharp, shrewd, smart, wide-awake, witty.
antonyms dull, slow, stupid.

quiescent *adj.* asleep, calm, dormant, in abeyance, inactive, inert, latent, motionless, passive, peaceful, placid, quiet, reposeful, resting, serene, silent, sleeping, smooth, still, tranquil, undisturbed, untroubled.
antonym active.

quiet *adj.* calm, composed, conservative, contemplative, contented, docile, dumb, even-tempered, gentle, hushed, inaudible, isolated, lonely, low, low-pitched, meek, mild, modest, motionless, noiseless, pacific, passive, peaceable, peaceful, placid, plain, private, removed, reserved, restful, restrained, retired, retiring, secluded, secret, sedate, self-contained, sequestered, serene, shy, silent, simple, smooth, sober, soft, soundless, still, stilly, subdued, taciturn, thoughtful, tranquil, uncommunicative, unconversable, undisturbed, uneventful, unexcitable, unexciting, unforthcoming, unfrequented, uninterrupted, unobtrusive, untroubled.
antonyms busy, noisy, obtrusive.
n. calm, calmness, ease, hush, lull, peace, quiescence, quietness, quietude, repose, rest, serenity, silence, stillness, tranquility.
antonyms bustle, disturbance, noise.

quietness *n.* calm, calmness, composure, dullness, hush, inactivity, inertia, lull, peace, placidity, quiescence, quiet, quietude, repose, serenity, silence, still, stillness, tranquility, uneventfulness.
antonyms activity, bustle, commotion, disturbance, noise, racket.

quintessence *n.* core, distillation, embodiment, essence, exemplar, extract, gist, heart, kernel, marrow, pattern, pith, quiddity, soul, spirit, sum and substance.

quip *n.* bon mot, carriwitchet, crack, epigram, gag, gibe, jest, jeu d'esprit, joke, mot, one-liner, pleasantry, quirk, retort, riposte, sally, wisecrack, witticism.
v. gag, gibe, jest, joke, quirk, retort, riposte, wisecrack.

quirk *n.* aberration, caprice, characteristic, curiosity, eccentricity, fancy, fetish, foible, freak, habit, idiosyncrasy, kink, mannerism, oddity, oddness, peculiarity, singularity, trait, turn, twist, vagary, warp, whim.

quit *v.* abandon, abdicate, apostatize, cease, conclude, decamp, depart, desert, disappear, discontinue, drop, end, exit, forsake, give up, go, halt, leave, relinquish, renege, renounce, repudiate, resign, retire, stop, surrender, suspend, vamoose, vanish, withdraw.

quite *adv.* absolutely, comparatively, completely, entirely, exactly, fairly, fully, moderately, perfectly, precisely, rather, relatively, somewhat, totally, utterly, wholly.

quits *adj.* equal, even, level, square.

quitter *n.* apostate, defector, delinquent, deserter, rat, recreant, renegade, shirker, skiver.

quiver *v.* agitate, bicker, convulse, flichter, flicker, flutter, oscillate, palpitate, pulsate, quake, quaver, shake, shiver, shudder, tremble, vibrate, wobble.
n. convulsion, flicker, flutter, oscillation, palpitation, pulsation, shake, shiver, shudder, spasm, throb, tic, tremble, tremor, vibration, wobble.

quixotic *adj.* chivalrous, extravagant, fanciful, fantastical, idealistic, impetuous, impracticable, impulsive, romantic, starry-eyed, unrealistic, unworldly, Utopian, visionary.
antonyms hard-headed, practical, realistic.

quiz *n.* catechism, examination, investigation, questioning, questionnaire, test.
v. ask, catechize, cross-examine, cross-question, debrief, examine, grill, interrogate, investigate, pump, question.

quizzical *adj.* amused, arch, bantering, curious, humorous, inquiring, mocking, questioning, sardonic, satirical, skeptical, teasing, waggish, whimsical.

quota *n.* allocation, allowance, assignment, cut, part, percentage, portion, proportion, quotum, ration, share, slice, whack.

quotation[1] *n.* citation, crib, cutting, excerpt, extract, gobbet, locus classicus, passage, piece, quote, reference, remnant.

quotation[2] *n.* charge, cost, estimate, figure, price, quote, rate, tender.

quote *v.* adduce, attest, cite, detail, echo, instance, name, parrot, recall, recite, recollect, refer to, repeat, reproduce, retell.

R

rabble *n.* canaille, clamjamphrie, colluvies, commonalty, commoners, crowd, doggery, dregs, faex populi, galère, herd, hoi polloi, horde, masses, mob, peasantry, plebs, populace, proles, proletariat, raffle, raggletaggle, rag-tag (and bobtail), rascality, riffraff, scum, swarm, tagrag, throng, trash.
antonyms aristocracy, elite, nobility.

rabid *adj.* berserk, bigoted, crazed, extreme, fanatical, fervent, frantic, frenzied, furious, hydrophobic, hysterical, infuriated, intemperate, intolerant, irrational, mad, maniacal, narrow-minded, obsessive, overzealous, raging, unreasoning, violent, wild, zealous.

race[1] *n.* chase, competition, contention, contest, corso, dash, derby, foot-race, marathon, pursuit, quest, rat race, regatta, rivalry, scramble, sprint, steeplechase.
v. career, compete, contest, dart, dash, fly, gallop, hare, hasten, hurry, run, rush, speed, sprint, tear, zoom.

race[2] *n.* ancestry, blood, breed, clan, descent, family, folk, house, issue, kin, kindred, line, lineage, nation, offspring, people, progeny, seed, stirps, stock, strain, tribe, type.

racial *adj.* ancestral, avital, ethnic, ethnological, folk, genealogical, genetic, inherited, national, tribal.

rack[1] *n.* frame, framework, gantry, gondola, hack, shelf, stand, structure.

rack[2] *n.* affliction, agony, anguish, distress, misery, pain, pangs, persecution, suffering, torment, torture.
v. afflict, agonize, convulse, crucify, distress, excruciate, harass, harrow, lacerate, oppress, pain, shake,

strain, stress, stretch, tear, torment, torture, wrench, wrest, wring.

acket *n.* babel, ballyhoo, clamor, clangor, commotion, din, disturbance, fuss, hubbub, hullabaloo, hurly-burly, kerfuffle, noise, outcry, pandemonium, row, shouting, tumult, uproar.

acket² *n.* business, con, deception, dodge, fiddle, fraud, game, scheme, swindle, trick.

acy *adj.* animated, bawdy, blue, boisterous, breezy, broad, buoyant, distinctive, doubtful, dubious, dynamic, ebullient, energetic, entertaining, enthusiastic, exciting, exhilarating, gamy, heady, immodest, indecent, indelicate, jaunty, lewd, lively, naughty, piquant, pungent, Rabelaisian, ribald, rich, risqué, salacious, sharp, smutty, sparkling, spicy, spirited, stimulating, strong, suggestive, tangy, tasty, vigorous, zestful.
antonyms dull, ponderous.

adiance *n.* brightness, brilliance, delight, effulgence, gaiety, glare, gleam, glitter, glow, happiness, incandescence, joy, lambency, light, luminosity, luster, pleasure, rapture, refulgence, resplendence, shine, splendor, warmth.

adiant *adj.* aglow, alight, beaming, beamish, beamy, beatific, blissful, bright, brilliant, delighted, ecstatic, effulgent, gleaming, glittering, glorious, glowing, happy, illuminated, incandescent, joyful, joyous, lambent, luminous, lustrous, profulgent, rapturous, refulgent, resplendent, shining, sparkling, splendid, sunny.
antonym dull.

adiate *v.* branch, diffuse, disseminate, divaricate, diverge, emanate, emit, eradiate, gleam, glitter, issue, pour, scatter, shed, shine, spread, spread out.

adical *adj.* basic, complete, comprehensive, constitutional, deep-seated, entire, essential, excessive, extreme, extremist, fanatical, far-reaching, fundamental, inherent, innate, intrinsic, native, natural, organic, primary, profound, revolutionary, rooted, severe, sweeping, thorough, thoroughgoing, total, violent.
antonym superficial.

n. extremist, fanatic, jacobin, left-winger, militant, reformer, reformist, revolutionary.

ag *v.* badger, bait, bullyrag, chaff, haze, jeer, mock, rib, ridicule, taunt, tease, torment, twit.

agamuffin *n.* dandiprat, gamin, guttersnipe, mudlark, scarecrow, street arab, tatterdemalion, urchin, waif.

age *n.* agitation, anger, bate, chafe, conniption, craze, dernier cri, enthusiasm, fad, fashion, frenzy, fury, ire, madness, mania, obsession, paddy, passion, style, tantrum, vehemence, violence, vogue, wrath.

v. chafe, explode, fret, fulminate, fume, inveigh, ramp, rampage, rant, rave, seethe, storm, surge, thunder.

aging *adj.* enraged, fizzing, frenzied, fulminating, fuming, furibund, furious, incensed, infuriated, irate, ireful, mad, rabid, rampageous, raving, seething, wrathful.

aid *n.* attack, break-in, bust, descent, foray, incursion, inroad, invasion, irruption, onset, onslaught, sally, seizure, sortie, strike, swoop.

v. attack, bust, descend on, do, forage, foray, invade, loot, maraud, pillage, plunder, ransack, reive, rifle, rush, sack.

ail *v.* abuse, arraign, attack, castigate, censure, criticize, decry, denounce, fulminate, inveigh, jeer, mock, revile, ridicule, scoff, upbraid, vituperate, vociferate.

railing *n.* balustrade, barrier, fence, paling, parapet, rail, rails.

rain *n.* cloudburst, deluge, downpour, drizzle, fall, flood, hail, mizzle, precipitation, raindrops, rainfall, rains, serein, shower, spate, squall, stream, torrent, volley.

v. bestow, bucket, deluge, deposit, drizzle, drop, expend, fall, heap, lavish, mizzle, pour, shower, spit, sprinkle, teem.

raise *v.* abandon, activate, advance, aggrade, aggrandize, aggravate, amplify, arouse, assemble, augment, awaken, boost, breed, broach, build, cause, collect, construct, create, cultivate, develop, discontinue, elate, elevate, emboss, embourgeoise, end, engender, enhance, enlarge, erect, escalate, evoke, exaggerate, exalt, excite, foment, form, foster, gather, gentrify, get, grow, heave, heighten, hoist, incite, increase, inflate, instigate, intensify, introduce, kindle, levy, lift, loft, magnify, mass, mobilize, moot, motivate, muster, nurture, obtain, occasion, originate, pose, prefer, produce, promote, propagate, provoke, rally, rear, recruit, reinforce, relinquish, remove, sky, start, strengthen, sublime, suggest, terminate, up, upgrade, uplift.
antonyms debase, decrease, degrade, dismiss, lower, reduce, suppress.

rakish *adj.* abandoned, breezy, dapper, dashing, debauched, debonair, degenerate, depraved, devil-may-care, dissipated, dissolute, flamboyant, flashy, immoral, jaunty, lecherous, libertine, licentious, loose, natty, prodigal, profligate, raffish, sharp, sinful, smart, snazzy, sporty, stylish, wanton.

rally¹ *v.* assemble, bunch, cheer, cluster, collect, congregate, convene, embolden, encourage, gather, hearten, improve, marshal, mass, mobilize, muster, organize, pick up, rally round, reassemble, recover, recuperate, re-form, regroup, reorganize, revive, round up, summon, unite.

n. assembly, comeback, concourse, conference, congregation, convention, convocation, gathering, improvement, jamboree, meeting, recovery, recuperation, regrouping, renewal, reorganization, resurgence, reunion, revival, stand.

rally² *v.* chaff, mock, rag, rib, ridicule, send up, taunt, tease, twit.

ramble *v.* amble, babble, chatter, digress, divagate, dodder, drift, expatiate, maunder, meander, perambulate, peregrinate, range, roam, rove, saunter, snake, straggle, stravaig, stray, stroll, traipse, walk, wander, wind, zigzag.

n. divagation, excursion, hike, perambulation, peregrination, roaming, roving, saunter, stroll, tour, traipse, trip, walk.

rambling *adj.* circuitous, desultory, diffuse, digressive, disconnected, discursive, disjointed, excursive, incoherent, irregular, long-drawn-out, long-winded, periphrastic, prolix, sprawling, spreading, straggling, trailing, wordy.
antonym direct.

ramification *n.* branch, complication, consequence, development, dichotomy, divarication, division, excrescence, extension, fork, offshoot, outgrowth, ramulus, ramus, result, sequel, subdivision, upshot.

rampage *v.* rage, rant, rave, run amuck, run riot, run wild, rush, storm, tear.

n. destruction, frenzy, furore, fury, rage, storm, tempest, tumult, uproar, violence.

rampant *adj.* aggressive, dominant, epidemic, erect, excessive, exuberant, fierce, flagrant, luxuriant, outrageous, prevalent, prodigal, profuse, raging, rampaging, rank, rearing, rife, riotous, standing, unbridled, unchecked, uncontrollable, uncontrolled, ungovernable, unrestrained, upright, vehement, violent, wanton, widespread, wild.

ramshackle *adj.* broken-down, crumbling, decrepit, derelict, dilapidated, flimsy, haywire, jerry-built, rickety, shaky, tottering, tumbledown, unsafe, unsteady.

antonyms solid, stable.

rancid *adj.* bad, fetid, foul, frowsty, fusty, musty, off, putrid, rank, reasty, rotten, sour, stale, strong-smelling, tainted.

antonym sweet.

rancor *n.* acrimony, animosity, animus, antipathy, bitterness, enmity, grudge, hate, hatred, hostility, ill-feeling, ill-will, malevolence, malice, malignity, resentfulness, resentment, spite, spleen, venom, vindictiveness.

random *adj.* accidental, adventitious, aimless, arbitrary, casual, chance, desultory, fortuitous, haphazard, incidental, indiscriminate, purposeless, scattershot, spot, stray, unfocused, unplanned, unpremeditated.

antonyms deliberate, systematic.

range *n.* amplitude, area, assortment, band, bounds, chain, class, collection, compass, confines, diapason, distance, domain, extent, field, file, gamut, kind, latitude, limits, line, lot, orbit, order, palette, parameters, province, purview, radius, raik, rank, reach, row, scale, scope, selection, sequence, series, sort, span, spectrum, sphere, string, sweep, tessitura, tier, variety.
v. aim, align, arrange, array, bracket, catalog, categorize, class, classify, cruise, direct, dispose, explore, extend, file, fluctuate, go, grade, group, level, order, pigeonhole, point, raik, ramble, rank, reach, roam, rove, run, straggle, stravaig, stray, stretch, stroll, sweep, train, traverse, wander.

rank[1] *n.* caste, class, classification, column, condition, degree, dignity, division, echelon, estate, état, file, formation, grade, group, level, line, nobility, order, position, quality, range, row, series, sort, standing, station, status, stratum, tier, type.
v. align, arrange, array, class, classify, dispose, grade, locate, marshal, order, organize, place, position, range, sort.

rank[2] *adj.* absolute, abundant, abusive, arrant, atrocious, bad, blatant, coarse, complete, crass, dense, disagreeable, disgusting, downright, egregious, excessive, extravagant, exuberant, fetid, filthy, flagrant, flourishing, foul, fusty, gamy, glaring, gross, indecent, lush, luxuriant, mephitic, musty, nasty, noisome, noxious, obscene, off, offensive, out-and-out, outrageous, productive, profuse, pungent, putrid, rampant, rancid, repulsive, revolting, scurrilous, sheer, shocking, stale, stinking, strong-smelling, thorough, thoroughgoing, total, undisguised, unmitigated, utter, vigorous, vulgar.

antonyms sparse, sweet.

ransack *v.* comb, depredate, despoil, explore, gut, loot, maraud, pillage, plunder, raid, rake, ravage, rifle, rummage, sack, scour, search, strip.

ransom *n.* deliverance, liberation, money, payment, payoff, price, redemption, release, rescue.

v. buy out, deliver, extricate, liberate, redeem, releas⟨e⟩ rescue.

rant *v.* bellow, bluster, cry, declaim, mouth it, ra⟨v⟩ roar, shout, slang-whang, spout, vociferate, yell.
n. bluster, bombast, declamation, diatribe, fanfar⟨e⟩ nade, harangue, philippic, rhetoric, storm, tirad⟨e⟩ vociferation.

rap *v.* bark, castigate, censure, chat, confabulate, co⟨n⟩ verse, crack, criticize, discourse, flirt, hit, knock, pa⟨t⟩ reprimand, scold, strike, talk, tap.
n. blame, blow, castigation, censure, chat, chidin⟨g⟩ clout, colloquy, confabulation, conversation, crac⟨k⟩ dialogue, discourse, discussion, knock, punishmen⟨t⟩ rebuke, reprimand, responsibility, sentence, talk, tap.

rapacious *adj.* avaricious, esurient, extortionate, gras⟨p⟩ ing, greedy, insatiable, marauding, plundering, pred⟨a⟩ tory, preying, ravening, ravenous, usurious, voraciou⟨s⟩ vulturine, vulturish, vulturous, wolfish, wolvish.

rapid *adj.* brisk, expeditious, express, fast, fleet, flyin⟨g⟩ hasty, headlong, hurried, precipitate, prompt, quic⟨k⟩ speedy, swift, tantivy.

antonyms leisurely, slow, sluggish.

rapidity *n.* alacrity, briskness, celerity, dispatc⟨h⟩ expedition, expeditiousness, fleetness, haste, hurr⟨y⟩ precipitateness, promptitude, promptness, quicknes⟨s⟩ rush, speed, speediness, swiftness, velocity.

antonym slowness.

rapids *n.* dalles, white water, wild water.

rapine *n.* depredation, despoilment, despoliation, loo⟨t⟩ ing, marauding, pillage, plunder, ransacking, rape, ra⟨v⟩ aging, robbery, sack, sacking, seizure, spoliation, thef⟨t⟩

rapport *n.* affinity, bond, compatibility, empathy, ha⟨r⟩ mony, link, relationship, sympathy, understanding.

rapture *n.* beatitude, bliss, delectation, delight, ecstas⟨y⟩ enthusiasm, entrancement, euphoria, exaltation, fe⟨l⟩ icity, happiness, joy, ravishment, rhapsody, spel⟨l⟩ transport.

rare *adj.* admirable, choice, curious, excellent, exce⟨p⟩ tional, exquisite, extreme, few, fine, great, incompar⟨⟩ able, infrequent, invaluable, peerless, precious, pric⟨e⟩ less, recherché, rich, scarce, singular, sparse, sporadi⟨c⟩ strange, superb, superlative, uncommon, unusual.

antonyms abundant, common, usual.

rarely *adv.* atypically, exceptionally, extraordinaril⟨y⟩ finely, hardly, infrequently, little, notably, remarkabl⟨y⟩ seldom, singularly, uncommonly, unusually.

antonyms frequently, often.

rascal *n.* blackguard, caitiff, cullion, devil, disgrac⟨e⟩ good-for-nothing, hellion, imp, knave, loon, miscrean⟨t⟩ ne'er-do-well, rake, ra(p)scallion, reprobate, rogu⟨e⟩ scallywag, scamp, scoundrel, skeesicks, spalpeen, to⟨e⟩ rag, toe-ragger, varmint, villain, wastrel, wretch.

rash[1] *adj.* adventurous, audacious, brash, careless, foo⟨l⟩ hardy, harebrained, harum-scarum, hasty, headlon⟨g⟩ headstrong, heedless, helter-skelter, hot-headed, il⟨l⟩ advised, ill-considered, impetuous, imprudent, impu⟨l⟩ sive, incautious, indiscreet, injudicious, insipien⟨t⟩ madcap, precipitant, precipitate, premature, reckles⟨s⟩ slap-dash, temerarious, temerous, thoughtles⟨s⟩ unguarded, unthinking, unwary, venturesome.

antonyms calculating, careful, considered, wary.

rash[2] *n.* epidemic, eruption, exanthem(a), flood, hive⟨s⟩ nettlerash, outbreak, plague, pompholyx, series, spat⟨e⟩ succession, urticaria, wave.

rashness *n.* adventurousness, audacity, brashness, car⟨e⟩

lessness, foolhardiness, hastiness, heedlessness, incaution, incautiousness, indiscretion, precipitance, precipitation, precipitency, recklessness, temerity, thoughtlessness.

antonyms carefulness, cautiousness.

rasp *n.* croak, grating, grinding, harshness, hoarseness, scrape, scratch.

v. abrade, croak, excoriate, file, grate, grind, irk, irritate, jar, rub, sand, scour, scrape.

rasping *adj.* creaking, croaking, croaky, grating, gravelly, gruff, harsh, hoarse, husky, jarring, raspy, raucous, rough, scratchy, stridulant.

rate[1] *n.* basis, charge, class, classification, cost, degree, dues, duty, fee, figure, gait, grade, hire, measure, pace, percentage, position, price, proportion, quality, rank, rating, ratio, reckoning, relation, scale, speed, standard, status, tariff, tax, tempo, time, toll, value, velocity, worth.

v. adjudge, admire, appraise, assess, class, classify, consider, count, deserve, esteem, estimate, evaluate, figure, grade, judge, measure, measure up, merit, perform, rank, reckon, regard, respect, value, weigh.

rate[2] *v.* admonish, berate, blame, castigate, censure, chide, criticize, lecture, rebuke, reprimand, reprove, roast, scold, tongue-lash, upbraid.

ratify *v.* affirm, approve, authenticate, authorize, bind, certify, confirm, corroborate, endorse, establish, homologate, legalize, recognize, sanction, sign, uphold, validate.

antonyms reject, repudiate.

rating[1] *n.* class, classification, degree, designation, estimate, evaluation, grade, grading, order, placing, position, rank, rate, sort, sorting, standing, status.

rating[2] *n.* castigation, chiding, dressing-down, lecture, rebuke, reprimand, reproof, roasting, row, scolding, telling-off, ticking-off, tongue-lashing, upbraiding, wigging.

ration *n.* allocation, allotment, allowance, amount, dole, helping, measure, part, portion, provision, quota, share.

v. allocate, allot, apportion, budget, conserve, control, deal, dispense, distribute, dole, issue, limit, mete, restrict, save, supply.

rational *adj.* balanced, cerebral, cognitive, compos mentis, dianoetic, enlightened, intelligent, judicious, logical, lucid, normal, ratiocinative, realistic, reasonable, reasoning, sagacious, sane, sensible, sound, thinking, well-founded, well-grounded, wise.

antonyms crazy, illogical, irrational.

rationalize *v.* elucidate, excuse, extenuate, justify, reason out, reorganize, resolve, streamline, trim, vindicate.

raucous *adj.* grating, harsh, hoarse, husky, loud, noisy, rasping, rough, rusty, strident.

ravage *v.* demolish, depredate, desolate, despoil, destroy, devastate, gut, lay waste, loot, pillage, plunder, ransack, raze, ruin, sack, shatter, spoil, wreck.

n. damage, defilement, demolition, depredation, desecration, desolation, destruction, devastation, havoc, pillage, plunder, rapine, ruin, ruination, spoliation, waste, wreckage.

rave *v.* babble, declaim, fulminate, fume, harangue, rage, ramble, rant, roar, splutter, storm, thunder.

adj. ecstatic, enthusiastic, excellent, fantastic, favorable, laudatory, wonderful.

ravenous *adj.* avaricious, covetous, devouring, esurient, famished, ferocious, gluttonous, grasping, greedy, insatiable, insatiate, predatory, rapacious, ravening, starved, starving, voracious, wolfish, wolvish.

ravine *n.* arroyo, canyon, chine, clough, defile, flume, gap, gorge, grike, gulch, gully, kloof, linn, lin(n), pass.

ravish *v.* abuse, captivate, charm, deflorate, deflower, delight, enchant, enrapture, entrance, fascinate, outrage, overjoy, rape, spellbind, transport, violate.

ravishing *adj.* alluring, beautiful, bewitching, charming, dazzling, delightful, enchanting, entrancing, gorgeous, lovely, radiant, seductive, stunning.

raw *adj.* abraded, bare, basic, biting, bitter, bleak, bloody, blunt, brutal, callow, candid, chafed, chill, chilly, coarse, cold, crude, damp, frank, freezing, fresh, grazed, green, harsh, ignorant, immature, inexperienced, naked, natural, new, open, organic, piercing, plain, realistic, rough, scraped, scratched, sensitive, skinned, sore, tender, unadorned, uncooked, undisciplined, undisguised, undressed, unfinished, unpleasant, unpracticed, unprepared, unprocessed, unrefined, unripe, unseasoned, unskilled, untrained, untreated, untried, unvarnished, verdant, wet.

antonyms cooked, experienced, refined.

ray *n.* bar, beam, flash, flicker, gleam, glimmer, glint, hint, indication, scintilla, shaft, spark, stream, trace.

raze *v.* bulldoze, delete, demolish, destroy, dismantle, efface, erase, expunge, extinguish, extirpate, flatten, level, obliterate, remove, ruin.

reach *v.* amount to, arrive at, attain, contact, drop, fall, get to, grasp, hand, land at, make, move, pass, rise, sink, stretch, strike, touch.

n. ambit, capacity, command, compass, distance, extension, extent, grasp, influence, jurisdiction, latitude, mastery, power, purview, range, scope, spread, stretch, sweep.

react *v.* acknowledge, act, answer, behave, emote, function, operate, proceed, reply, respond, work.

reaction *n.* acknowledgment, answer, antiperistasis, backwash, compensation, conservatism, counteraction, counterbalance, counterbuff, counterpoise, counter-revolution, feedback, obscurantism, recoil, reply, response, swing-back.

readable *adj.* clear, compelling, comprehensible, compulsive, decipherable, enjoyable, entertaining, enthralling, gripping, intelligible, interesting, legible, plain, pleasant, understandable, unputdownable.

antonyms illegible, unreadable.

readily *adv.* cheerfully, eagerly, easily, effortlessly, fain, freely, gladly, lief, promptly, quickly, smoothly, speedily, unhesitatingly, voluntarily, willingly.

ready *adj.* à la main, about, accessible, acute, ad manum, adroit, agreeable, alert, apt, arranged, astute, available, bright, clever, close, completed, convenient, deft, dexterous, disposed, eager, expert, facile, fit, game, glad, handy, happy, inclined, intelligent, keen, liable, likely, minded, near, on call, on tap, organized, overflowing, perceptive, predisposed, prepared, present, primed, prompt, prone, quick, quick-witted, rapid, resourceful, ripe, set, sharp, skilful, smart, willing.

antonyms unprepared, unready.

v. alert, arrange, equip, order, organize, prepare, prime, set.

real *adj.* absolute, actual, authentic, bona fide, certain, dinkum, dinky-di(e), essential, existent, factual, genuine, heartfelt, honest, intrinsic, legitimate, positive, right, rightful, simon-pure, sincere, substantial, substantive, sure-enough, tangible, thingy, true, unaffected, unfeigned, valid, veritable.

antonyms imaginary, unreal.

realization *n.* accomplishment, achievement, actualization, appreciation, apprehension, awareness, cognizance, completion, comprehension, conception, consciousness, consummation, effectuation, fulfilment, grasp, imagination, perception, recognition, understanding.

realize *v.* accomplish, achieve, acquire, actualize, appreciate, apprehend, catch on, clear, complete, comprehend, conceive, consummate, do, earn, effect, effectuate, fulfil, gain, get, grasp, imagine, implement, make, net, obtain, perform, produce, recognize, reify, take in, twig, understand.

really *adv.* absolutely, actually, assuredly, categorically, certainly, essentially, genuinely, indeed, intrinsically, positively, surely, truly, undoubtedly, verily.

realm *n.* area, bailiwick, branch, country, department, domain, dominion, empire, field, jurisdiction, kingdom, land, monarchy, orbit, principality, province, region, sphere, state, territory, world, zone.

reap *v.* acquire, collect, crop, cut, derive, gain, garner, gather, get, harvest, mow, obtain, realize, secure, win.

rear[1] *n.* back, backside, bottom, buttocks, croup, end, hindquarters, posterior, rearguard, rump, stern, tail.

antonym front.

adj. aft, after, back, following, hind, hindmost, last.

antonym front.

rear[2] *v.* breed, build, construct, cultivate, educate, elevate, erect, fabricate, foster, grow, hoist, lift, loom, nurse, nurture, parent, raise, rise, soar, tower, train.

reason *n.* aim, apologia, apology, apprehension, argument, basis, bounds, brains, case, cause, common sense, comprehension, consideration, defense, design, end, excuse, explanation, exposition, goal, ground, grounds, gumption, impetus, incentive, inducement, intellect, intention, judgment, justification, limits, logic, mentality, mind, moderation, motive, nous, object, occasion, propriety, purpose, ratiocination, rationale, rationality, reasonableness, reasoning, sanity, sense, sensibleness, soundness, target, understanding, vindication, warrant, wisdom.

v. conclude, deduce, infer, intellectualize, ratiocinate, resolve, solve, syllogize, think, work out.

reasonable *adj.* acceptable, advisable, arguable, average, believable, credible, equitable, fair, fit, honest, inexpensive, intelligent, judicious, just, justifiable, logical, moderate, modest, OK, passable, plausible, possible, practical, proper, rational, reasoned, right, sane, satisfactory, sensible, sober, sound, tenable, tolerable, viable, well-advised, well-thought-out, wise.

antonyms crazy, extravagant, irrational, outrageous, unreasonable.

rebel *v.* defy, disobey, dissent, flinch, kick over the traces, mutiny, recoil, resist, revolt, rise up, run riot, shrink.

n. apostate, dissenter, heretic, insurgent, insurrectionary, Jacobin, malcontent, mutineer, nonconformist, revolutionary, revolutionist, schismatic, secessionist.

adj. insubordinate, insurgent, insurrectionary, malcontent(ed), mutinous, rebellious, revolutionary.

rebellion *n.* apostasy, defiance, disobedience, dissent,

heresy, insubordination, insurgence, insurgency, insurrection, Jacquerie, mutiny, nonconformity, resistance, revolt, revolution, rising, schism, uprising.

rebellious *adj.* contumacious, defiant, difficult, disaffected, disloyal, disobedient, disorderly, incorrigible, insubordinate, insurgent, insurrectionary, intractable, malcontent(ed), mutinous, obstinate, rebel, recalcitrant, refractory, resistant, revolutionary, seditious, turbulent, ungovernable, unmanageable, unruly.

antonyms obedient, submissive.

rebirth *n.* reactivation, reanimation, regeneration, reincarnation, rejuvenation, renaissance, renascence, renewal, restoration, resurgence, resurrection, revitalization, revival.

rebuff *v.* cold-shoulder, cut, decline, deny, discourage, put someone's nose out of joint, refuse, reject, repulse, resist, slight, snub, spurn, turn down.

n. brush-off, check, cold shoulder, defeat, denial, discouragement, flea in one's ear, noser, opposition, refusal, rejection, repulse, rubber, set-down, slight, snub.

rebuild *v.* reassemble, reconstruct, re-edify, refashion, remake, remodel, renovate, restore.

antonyms demolish, destroy.

rebuke *v.* admonish, berate, blame, carpet, castigate, censure, chide, countercheck, jobe, keelhaul, lecture, lesson, rate, reprehend, reprimand, reproach, reprove, scold, slap down, tell off, tick off, trim, trounce, upbraid.

antonyms compliment, praise.

n. admonition, blame, castigation, censure, countercheck, dressing-down, lecture, reprimand, reproach, reproof, reproval, row, slap, telling-off, ticking-off, tongue-lashing, wigging.

antonyms compliment, praise.

rebuttal *n.* confutation, defeat, disproof, invalidation, negation, overthrow, refutation.

recall *v.* abjure, annul, cancel, cast one's mind back, countermand, evoke, mind, nullify, place, recognize, recollect, remember, repeal, rescind, retract, revoke, withdraw.

n. abrogation, annulment, cancellation, memory, nullification, recision, recollection, remembrance, repeal, rescission, retraction, revocation, withdrawal.

recapitulate *v.* give a resumé, recap, recount, reiterate, repeat, restate, review, summarize.

recede *v.* abate, decline, decrease, diminish, dwindle, ebb, fade, lessen, regress, retire, retreat, retrogress, return, shrink, sink, slacken, subside, wane, withdraw.

antonyms advance, proceed.

receive *v.* accept, accommodate, acquire, admit, apprehend, bear, collect, derive, encounter, entertain, experience, gather, get, greet, hear, meet, obtain, perceive, pick up, react to, respond to, suffer, sustain, take, undergo, welcome.

antonyms donate, give.

recent *adj.* contemporary, current, fresh, late, latter, latter-day, modern, neoteric(al), new, novel, present-day, up-to-date, young.

antonyms dated, old, out-of-date.

reception *n.* acceptance, acknowledgment, admission, do, durbar, entertainment, function, greeting, levee, party, reaction, receipt, receiving, recipience, recognition, response, shindig, soirée, treatment, welcome.

recess *n.* alcove, apse, apsidiole, bay, break, cavity, cessation, closure, corner, depression, embrasure, holiday, hollow, indentation, intermission, interval, loculus, niche, nook, oriel, respite, rest, vacation.

recession *n.* decline, depression, downturn, slump, stagflation.

antonyms boom, upturn.

recipe *n.* directions, formula, ingredients, instructions, method, prescription, procedure, process, program, receipt, system, technique.

recital *n.* account, convert, description, detailing, enumeration, interpretation, narration, narrative, performance, reading, recapitulation, recitation, rehearsal, relation, rendering, rendition, repetition, statement, story, tale, telling.

recite *v.* articulate, declaim, deliver, describe, detail, enumerate, itemize, narrate, orate, perform, recapitulate, recount, rehearse, relate, repeat, speak, tell.

reckless *adj.* careless, daredevil, devil-may-care, foolhardy, harebrained, hasty, headlong, heedless, ill-advised, imprudent, inattentive, incautious, indiscreet, irresponsible, madcap, mindless, negligent, precipitate, rantipole, rash, regardless, tearaway, thoughtless, wild.

antonyms calculating, careful, cautious.

recklessness *n.* carelessness, foolhardiness, gallowsness, heedlessness, imprudence, inattention, incaution, irresponsibleness, irresposibility, madness, mindlessness, negligence, rashness, thoughtlessness.

antonym carefulness.

reckon *v.* account, add up, adjudge, appraise, assess, assume, believe, calculate, compute, conjecture, consider, count, deem, enumerate, esteem, estimate, evaluate, expect, fancy, gauge, guess, hold, imagine, judge, number, opine, rate, regard, suppose, surmise, tally, think, total.

reclaim *v.* impolder, recapture, recover, redeem, reform, regain, regenerate, reinstate, rescue, restore, retrieve, salvage.

recline *v.* couch, lean, lie, loll, lounge, repose, rest, sprawl, stretch out.

recluse *n.* anchoress, anchoret, anchorite, ancress, ascetic, eremite, hermit, monk, solitaire, solitarian, solitary, stylite.

recognize *v.* accept, acknowledge, admit, allow, appreciate, approve, avow, concede, confess, grant, greet, honor, identify, know, notice, own, perceive, place, realize, recall, recollect, remember, respect, salute, see, spot, understand, wot.

recollect *v.* call up, cast one's mind back, mind, place, recall, remember, reminisce.

recollection *n.* image, impression, memory, recall, remembrance, reminiscence, souvenir.

recommend *v.* advance, advise, advocate, approve, commend, counsel, endorse, enjoin, exhort, plug, praise, propose, puff, suggest, urge, vouch for.

antonyms disapprove, veto.

recommendation *n.* advice, advocacy, approbation, approval, blessing, commendation, counsel, endorsement, plug, praise, proposal, puff, reference, sanction, suggestion, testimonial, urging.

antonyms disapproval, veto.

reconcile *v.* accept, accommodate, accord, adjust, appease, compose, conciliate, harmonize, pacify, placate, propitiate, rectify, resign, resolve, reunite, settle, square, submit, yield.

antonym estrange.

recondition *v.* fix, overhaul, refurbish, remodel, renew, renovate, repair, restore, revamp, sort.

reconsider *v.* modify, reassess, re-examine, rethink, review, revise, think better of, think over, think twice.

record *n.* account, album, annals, archives, background, career, chronicle, curriculum vitae, diary, disc, document, documentation, dossier, entry, EP, evidence, file, form, forty-five, gramophone record, history, journal, log, LP, memoir, memorandum, memorial, minute, noctuary, performance, platter, recording, register, release, remembrance, report, single, talkie, testimony, trace, tracing, track record, witness.

v. annalize, chalk up, chronicle, contain, cut, diarize, document, enregister, enrol, enter, indicate, inscribe, log, minute, note, preserve, read, register, report, say, score, show, tape, tape-record, transcribe, video, videotape, wax.

recount *v.* communicate, delineate, depict, describe, detail, enumerate, narrate, portray, recite, rehearse, relate, repeat, report, tell.

recoup *v.* compensate, indemnify, make good, recover, redeem, refund, regain, reimburse, remunerate, repay, requite, retrieve, satisfy.

recover *v.* convalesce, heal, improve, mend, pick up, pull through, rally, recapture, reclaim, recoup, recuperate, redeem, regain, repair, replevy, repossess, restore, retake, retrieve, revive.

antonyms forfeit, lose, worsen.

recreation *n.* amusement, distraction, diversion, enjoyment, entertainment, exercise, fun, games, hobby, leisure activity, pastime, play, pleasure, refreshment, relaxation, relief, sport.

recrimination *n.* accusation, bickering, counter-attack, counterblast, countercharge, name-calling, quarrel, retaliation, retort, squabbling.

recruit *v.* augment, draft, engage, enlist, enrol, gather, headhunt, impress, levy, mobilize, muster, obtain, procure, proselytize, raise, refresh, reinforce, renew, replenish, restore, strengthen, supply, trawl.

n. apprentice, beginner, conscript, convert, draftee, greenhorn, helper, initiate, learner, neophyte, novice, proselyte, rookie, trainee, tyro, yob.

recuperate *v.* convalesce, get better, improve, mend, pick up, rally, recoup, recover, regain, revive.

antonym worsen.

recur *v.* persist, reappear, repeat, return.

redeem *v.* absolve, acquit, atone for, cash (in), change, compensate for, defray, deliver, discharge, emancipate, exchange, extricate, free, fulfil, keep, liberate, make good, make up for, meet, offset, outweigh, perform, ransom, reclaim, recoup, recover, recuperate, redress, regain, rehabilitate, reinstate, repossess, repurchase, rescue, retrieve, salvage, satisfy, save, trade in.

redolent *adj.* aromatic, evocative, fragrant, odorous, perfumed, remindful, reminiscent, scented, suggestive, sweet-smelling.

reduce *v.* abate, abridge, bankrupt, break, cheapen, conquer, contract, curtail, cut, debase, decimate, decrease, degrade, demote, deoxidate, deoxidize, depress, diet, dilute, diminish, discount, downgrade, drive, force, humble, humiliate, impair, impoverish, lessen, lower, master, moderate, overpower, pauperize, rebate, ruin, scant, shorten, slake, slash, slenderize, slim, subdue, trim, truncate, vanquish, weaken.

antonyms boost, fatten, increase, upgrade.

reduction *n.* abbreviation, abridgment, abstraction, alleviation, attenuation, compression, condensation, constriction, contraction, curtailment, cut, cutback, decline, decrease, deduction, degradation, demotion, deoxidation, deoxidization, deposal, depreciation, devaluation, diminution, discount, drop, easing, ellipsis, limitation, loss, miniature, mitigation, moderation, modification, muffling, muting, narrowing, rebate, rebatement, refund, restriction, shortening, shrinkage, slackening, softening, subtraction, summarization, summary, syncope.
antonyms enlargement, improvement, increase.

redundant *adj.* de trop, diffuse, excessive, extra, inessential, inordinate, padded, periphrastic, pleonastical, prolix, repetitious, supererogatory, superfluous, supernumerary, surplus, tautological, unemployed, unnecessary, unneeded, unwanted, verbose, wordy.
antonyms concise, essential, necessary.

reek *v.* exhale, fume, hum, pong, smell, smoke, stink.
n. effluvium, exhalation, fetor, fume(s), malodor, mephitis, odor, pong, smell, smoke, stench, stink, vapor.

refer *v.* accredit, adduce, advert, allude, apply, ascribe, assign, attribute, belong, cite, commit, concern, consign, consult, credit, deliver, direct, go, guide, hint, impute, invoke, look up, mention, pertain, point, recommend, relate, send, speak of, submit, touch on, transfer, turn to.

referee *n.* adjudicator, arbiter, arbitrator, arbitratrix, arbitress, judge, ref, umpire.
v. adjudicate, arbitrate, judge, ref, umpire.

reference *n.* allusion, applicability, bearing, certification, character, citation, concern, connection, consideration, credentials, endorsement, illustration, instance, mention, note, quotation, recommendation, regard, relation, remark, respect, testimonial.

refine *v.* chasten, civilize, clarify, cultivate, distil, elevate, exalt, filter, hone, improve, perfect, polish, process, purify, rarefy, spiritualize, sublimize, subtilize, temper.

refined *adj.* Attic, Augustan, civil, civilized, clarified, clean, courtly, cultivated, cultured, delicate, discerning, discriminating, distilled, elegant, exact, fastidious, filtered, fine, genteel, gentlemanly, gracious, ladylike, nice, polished, polite, precise, processed, punctilious, pure, purified, sensitive, sophisticated, sublime, subtle, urbane, well-bred, well-mannered.
antonyms brutish, coarse, earthy, rude, vulgar.

refinement *n.* breeding, chastity, civilization, civility, clarification, cleansing, courtesy, courtliness, cultivation, culture, delicacy, discrimination, distillation, elegance, fastidiousness, filtering, fineness, finesse, finish, gentility, grace, graciousness, manners, nicety, nuance, polish, politeness, politesse, precision, processing, purification, rarefaction, rectification, sophistication, style, subtlety, taste, urbanity.
antonyms coarseness, earthiness, vulgarity.

reflect *v.* bespeak, cogitate, communicate, consider, contemplate, deliberate, demonstrate, display, echo, evince, exhibit, express, imitate, indicate, manifest, meditate, mirror, mull (over), muse, ponder, reproduce, return, reveal, ruminate, show, think, wonder.

reflection *n.* aspersion, censure, cerebration, cogitation, consideration, contemplation, counterpart, criticism, deliberation, derogation, echo, idea, image,

impression, imputation, meditation, musing, observation, opinion, pondering, reflex, reproach, rumination, slur, study, thinking, thought, view.

reform *v.* ameliorate, amend, better, correct, emend, improve, mend, purge, rebuild, reclaim, reconstitute, reconstruct, rectify, regenerate, rehabilitate, remodel, renovate, reorganize, repair, restore, revamp, revolutionize.
n. amelioration, amendment, betterment, correction, improvement, purge, rectification, rehabilitation, renovation, shake-out.

refractory *adj.* balky, cantankerous, contentious, contumacious, difficult, disobedient, disputatious, headstrong, intractable, mulish, obstinate, perverse, recalcitrant, resistant, restive, stubborn, uncontrollable, unco-operative, unmanageable, unruly, wilful.
antonyms co-operative, malleable, obedient.

refrain[1] *v.* abstain, avoid, cease, desist, eschew, forbear, leave off, quit, renounce, stop, swear off.

refrain[2] *n.* burden, chorus, epistrophe, falderal, melody, song, tune, undersong, wheel.

refresh *v.* brace, cheer, cool, energize, enliven, freshen, inspirit, jog, prod, prompt, reanimate, reinvigorate, rejuvenate, renew, renovate, repair, replenish, restore, revitalize, revive, revivify, stimulate.
antonyms exhaust, tire.

refreshing *adj.* bracing, cooling, different, energizing, fresh, inspiriting, invigorating, new, novel, original, refrigerant, restorative, revivifying, stimulating, thirst-quenching.
antonyms exhausting, tiring.

refreshment *n.* enlivenment, freshening, reanimation, reinvigoration, renewal, renovation, repair, restoration, revitalization, revival, stimulation.

refuge *n.* asylum, bolthole, funk-hole, harbor, haven, hide-away, hideout, holt, protection, resort, retreat, sanctuary, security, shelter.

refuse[1] *v.* decline, deny, nay-say, reject, repel, repudiate, spurn, withhold.
antonyms accept, allow.

refuse[2] *n.* chaff, dregs, dross, excrementa, garbage, hogwash, husks, junk, lag(s), landfill, leavings, lees, leftovers, litter, mullock, offscourings, rejectamenta, riddlings, rubbish, scum, sediment, slops, sordes, sullage, sweepings, tailings, trash, waste, wastrel.

refute *v.* confute, counter, discredit, disprove, give the lie to, negate, overthrow, rebut, silence.

regain *v.* reattain, recapture, reclaim, recoup, recover, redeem, re-establish, repossess, retake, retrieve, return to.

regal *adj.* kingly, magnificent, majestic, monarch(i)al, monarchic(al), noble, princely, proud, queenly, royal, sovereign, stately.

regale *v.* amuse, captivate, delight, divert, entertain, fascinate, feast, gratify, ply, refresh, serve.

regard *v.* account, adjudge, attend, behold, believe, concern, consider, deem, esteem, estimate, eye, heed, hold, imagine, interest, judge, mark, mind, note, notice, observe, pertain to, rate, relate to, remark, respect, scrutinize, see, suppose, think, treat, value, view, watch.
antonyms despise, disregard.
n. account, advertence, advertency, affection, aspect, attachment, attention, bearing, care, concern, connection, consideration, deference, detail, esteem, feature,

gaze, glance, heed, honor, item, look, love, matter, mind, note, notice, particular, point, reference, relation, relevance, reputation, repute, respect, scrutiny, stare, store, sympathy, thought.

antonyms contempt, disapproval, disregard.

regardless *adj.* disregarding, heedless, inattentive, inconsiderate, indifferent, neglectful, negligent, nonchalant, rash, reckless, remiss, uncaring, unconcerned, unmindful.

antonyms attentive, heedful, regardful.

adv. anyhow, anyway, come what may, despite everything, in any case, nevertheless, no matter what, nonetheless, willy-nilly.

regards *n.* compliments, devoirs, greetings, respects, salutations.

regenerate *v.* change, inspirit, invigorate, reawaken, reconstitute, reconstruct, re-establish, refresh, reinvigorate, rejuvenate, renew, renovate, reproduce, restore, revive, revivify, uplift.

regime *n.* administration, command, control, establishment, government, leadership, management, reign, rule, system.

regimented *adj.* controlled, co-ordinated, disciplined, methodical, ordered, organized, regulated, severe, standardized, stern, strict, systematic.

antonyms disorganized, free, lax, loose.

region *n.* area, clime, country, district, division, domain, expanse, field, land, locality, neighborhood, part, place, province, quarter, range, realm, scope, section, sector, sphere, terrain, terrene, territory, tract, vicinity, world, zone.

register *n.* almanac, annals, archives, catalog, chronicle, diary, file, ledger, list, log, matricula, memorandum, notitia, record, roll, roster, schedule.

v. bespeak, betray, catalog, chronicle, display, enlist, enrol, enter, exhibit, express, indicate, inscribe, list, log, manifest, mark, note, read, record, reflect, reveal, say, score, show, sign on.

regress *v.* backslide, degenerate, deteriorate, ebb, lapse, recede, relapse, retreat, retrocede, retrogress, return, revert, wane.

antonym progress.

regret *v.* bemoan, bewail, deplore, grieve, lament, miss, mourn, repent, rue, sorrow.

n. bitterness, compunction, contrition, disappointment, grief, lamentation, penitence, remorse, repentance, ruefulness, self-reproach, shame, sorrow.

regrettable *adj.* deplorable, disappointing, distressing, ill-advised, lamentable, pitiable, sad, shameful, sorry, unfortunate, unhappy, unlucky, woeful, wrong.

antonyms fortunate, happy.

regular *adj.* approved, balanced, bona fide, classic, common, commonplace, consistent, constant, consuetudinary, conventional, correct, customary, daily, dependable, efficient, established, even, everyday, fixed, flat, formal, habitual, level, methodical, normal, official, ordered, orderly, ordinary, orthodox, periodic, prevailing, proper, rhythmic, routine, sanctioned, set, smooth, standard, standardized, stated, steady, straight, symmetrical, systematic, time-honored, traditional, typical, uniform, unvarying, usual.

antonyms irregular, sporadic, unconventional.

regulate *v.* adjust, administer, arrange, balance, conduct, control, direct, fit, govern, guide, handle, manage, moderate, modulate, monitor, order, organ-

ize, oversee, regiment, rule, run, settle, square, superintend, supervise, systematize, tune.

regulation *n.* adjustment, administration, arrangement, commandment, control, decree, dictate, direction, edict, governance, government, law, management, modulation, order, ordinance, precept, prodecure, regimentation, requirement, rule, statute, supervision, tuning.

adj. accepted, customary, mandatory, normal, official, prescribed, required, standard, stock, usual.

rehabilitate *v.* adjust, clear, convert, mend, normalize, rebuild, recondition, reconstitute, reconstruct, redeem, redintegrate, re-establish, reform, reinstate, reintegrate, reinvigorate, renew, renovate, restore, save.

rehearse *v.* act, delineate, depict, describe, detail, drill, enumerate, list, narrate, practice, prepare, ready, recite, recount, relate, repeat, review, run through, spell out, study, tell, train, trot out.

reign *n.* ascendancy, command, control, dominion, empire, hegemony, influence, monarchy, power, rule, sovereignty, supremacy, sway.

v. administer, authority, command, govern, influence, kingship, obtain, predominate, prevail, rule.

reimburse *v.* compensate, indemnify, recompense, refund, remunerate, repay, requite, restore, return, square up.

rein *n.* brake, bridle, check, check-rein, control, curb, harness, hold, overcheck, restraint, restriction.

v. arrest, bridle, check, control, curb, halt, hold, hold back, limit, restrain, restrict, stop.

reinforce *v.* augment, bolster, buttress, emphasize, fortify, harden, increase, prop, recruit, steel, stiffen, strengthen, stress, supplement, support, toughen, underline.

antonyms undermine, weaken.

reiterate *v.* ding, iterate, recapitulate, repeat, resay, restate, retell.

reject *v.* athetize, condemn, decline, deny, despise, disallow, discard, eliminate, exclude, explode, jettison, jilt, pip, rebuff, refuse, renounce, repel, reprobate, repudiate, repulse, scrap, spike, spurn, veto.

antonyms accept, select.

n. cast-off, discard, failure, second.

rejection *n.* athetesis, brush-off, dear John letter, denial, dismissal, elimination, exclusion, rebuff, refusal, renunciation, repudiation, veto.

antonyms acceptance, selection.

rejoice *v.* celebrate, delight, exult, glory, joy, jubilate, revel, triumph.

rejuvenate *v.* reanimate, recharge, refresh, regenerate, reinvigorate, rekindle, renew, restore, revitalize, revivify.

relapse *v.* backslide, degenerate, deteriorate, fade, fail, lapse, regress, retrogress, revert, sicken, sink, weaken, worsen.

n. backsliding, deterioration, hypostrophe, lapse, recidivism, recurrence, regression, retrogression, reversion, setback, weakening, worsening.

relate *v.* ally, appertain, apply, associate, chronicle, concern, connect, co-ordinate, correlate, couple, describe, detail, empathize, feel for, identify with, impart, join, link, narrate, pertain, present, recite, recount, refer, rehearse, report, sympathize, tell, understand.

relation *n.* account, affiliation, affine, affinity, agnate, agnation, application, bearing, bond, comparison, connection, consanguinity, correlation, description, german, interdependence, kin, kindred, kinship, kinsman, kinswoman, link, narration, narrative, pertinence, propinquity, recital, recountal, reference, regard, relationship, relative, report, sib, similarity, story, tale, tie-in.

relationship n. affaire, association, bond, communications, conjunction, connection, contract, correlation, dealings, exchange, intercourse, kinship, liaison, link, parallel, proportion, rapport, ratio, similarity, tie-up.

relative adj. allied, applicable, apposite, appropriate, appurtenant, apropos, associated, comparative, connected, contingent, correlative, corresponding, dependent, germane, interrelated, pertinent, proportionate, reciprocal, related, relevant, respective.

n. cognate, connection, german, kinsman, kinswoman, relation, sib.

relatively adv. comparatively, fairly, quite, rather, somewhat.

relax v. abate, diminish, disinhibit, ease, ebb, lessen, loosen, lower, mitigate, moderate, reduce, relieve, remit, rest, slacken, soften, tranquilize, unbend, unclench, unwind, weaken.

antonyms intensify, tighten.

relaxation n. abatement, amusement, délassement, détente, diminution, disinhibition, distraction, easing, emollition, enjoyment, entertainment, fun, leisure, lessening, let-up, moderation, pleasure, recreation, reduction, refreshment, rest, slackening, weakening.

antonyms intensification, tension.

relaxed adj. calm, carefree, casual, collected, composed, cool, down-beat, easy-going, even-tempered, happy-go-lucky, informal, insouciant, laid-back, mellow, mild, nonchalant, placid, serene, together, tranquil, unhurried.

antonyms edgy, nervous, stiff, tense, uptight.

release v. absolve, acquit, break, circulate, declassify, decontrol, deliver, discage, discharge, disengage, disenthral, disimprison, disinhibit, disoblige, dispense, disprison, disseminate, distribute, drop, emancipate, exempt, excuse, exonerate, extricate, free, furlough, issue, launch, liberate, loose, manumit, present, publish, unbind, uncage, unchain, undo, unfasten, unfetter, unhand, unleash, unloose, unmew, unpen, unshackle, untie, unveil.

antonyms check, detain.

n. absolution, acquittal, acquittance, announcement, deliverance, delivery, discharge, disimprisonment, disinhibition, dispensation, emancipation, exemption, exoneration, freedom, issue, let-off, liberation, liberty, manumission, offering, proclamation, publication, quittance, relief.

antonym detention.

relegate v. assign, banish, consign, delegate, demote, deport, dispatch, downgrade, eject, entrust, exile, expatriate, expel, refer, transfer.

antonym promote.

relent v. acquiesce, capitulate, drop, ease, fall, forbear, give in, melt, relax, slacken, slow, soften, unbend, weaken, yield.

relentless adj. cruel, fierce, grim, hard, harsh, implacable, incessant, inexorable, inflexible, merciless, nonstop, persistent, pitiless, punishing, remorseless, ruthless, stern, sustained, unabated, unbroken, uncompromising, undeviating, unfaltering, unflagging, unforgiv-

ing, unrelenting, unrelieved, unremitting, unstoppable, unyielding.

antonyms submissive, yielding.

relevant adj. ad rem, admissible, applicable, apposite, appropriate, appurtenant, apt, congruous, fitting, germane, material, pertinent, proper, related, relative, significant, suitable, suited.

antonym irrelevant.

reliable adj. certain, constant, copper-bottomed, dependable, faithful, honest, predictable, regular, responsible, safe, solid, sound, stable, staunch, sure, true, trustworthy, trusty, unfailing, upright, white.

antonyms doubtful, suspect, unreliable, untrustworthy.

reliance n. assurance, belief, confidence, credence, credit, dependence, faith, trust.

relic n. fragment, keepsake, memento, potsherd, remembrance, remnant, scrap, souvenir, survival, token, trace, vestige.

relief n. abatement, aid, alleviation, assistance, assuagement, balm, break, breather, comfort, cure, deliverance, diversion, ease, easement, help, let-up, load off one's mind, mitigation, palliation, refreshment, relaxation, release, remedy, remission, respite, rest, solace, succor, support, sustenance.

relieve v. abate, aid, alleviate, appease, assist, assuage, break, brighten, calm, comfort, console, cure, deliver, diminish, discharge, disembarrass, disencumber, dull, ease, exempt, free, help, interrupt, lighten, mitigate, mollify, palliate, relax, release, salve, slacken, soften, solace, soothe, spell, stand in for, substitute for, succor, support, sustain, take over from, take the place of, unburden, vary.

antonyms aggravate, intensify.

religious adj. church-going, conscientious, devotional, devout, divine, doctrinal, exact, faithful, fastidious, God-fearing, godly, holy, meticulous, pious, punctilious, pure, reverent, righteous, rigid, rigorous, sacred, scriptural, scrupulous, sectarian, spiritual, strict, theological, unerring, unswerving.

antonyms irreligious, lax, ungodly.

relinquish n. abandon, abdicate, cede, desert, discard, drop, forgo, forsake, hand over, leave, quit, release, renounce, repudiate, resign, surrender, vacate, waive, yield.

antonyms keep, retain.

relish v. appreciate, degust, enjoy, fancy, lap up, like, prefer, revel in, savor, taste.

n. appetizer, appetite, appreciation, condiment, enjoyment, fancy, flavor, fondness, gout, gusto, liking, love, partiality, penchant, piquancy, predilection, sauce, savor, seasoning, smack, spice, stomach, tang, taste, trace, zest.

reluctance n. aversion, backwardness, disinclination, dislike, distaste, hesitancy, indisposition, loathing, recalcitrance, repugnance, unwillingness.

antonyms eagerness, willingness.

reluctant adj. averse, backward, disinclined, grudging, hesitant, indisposed, loath, loathful, loth, recalcitrant, renitent, slow, squeamish, unenthusiastic, unwilling.

antonyms eager, willing.

rely v. bank, bet, count, depend, lean, reckon, swear by, trust.

remain v. abide, bide, cling, continue, delay, dwell, endure, last, linger, persist, prevail, rest, sojourn, stand, stay, survive, tarry, wait.

antonyms depart, go, leave.

remainder *n.* balance, dregs, excess, leavings, remanent, remanet, remnant, residuum, rest, surplus, trace, vestige(s).

remains *n.* ashes, balance, body, cadaver, carcass, corpse, crumbs, debris, detritus, dregs, fragments, leavings, left-overs, oddments, pieces, relics, reliquiae, remainder, remnants, residue, rest, scraps, traces, vestiges.

remark *v.* animadvert, comment, declare, espy, heed, mark, mention, note, notice, observe, perceive, reflect, regard, say, see, state.

n. acknowledgment, assertion, attention, comment, consideration, declaration, heed, mention, notice, observation, opinion, recognition, reflection, regard, say, statement, thought, utterance, word.

remarkable *adj.* amazing, conspicuous, distinguished, exceptional, extraordinary, famous, impressive, miraculous, notable, noteworthy, odd, outstanding, phenomenal, pre-eminent, prominent, rare, signal, singular, strange, striking, surprising, unco, uncommon, unusual, wonderful.

antonyms average, commonplace, ordinary.

remedy *n.* antidote, corrective, counteractive, countermeasure, cure, magistery, medicament, medicine, nostrum, panacea, physic, prescript, redress, relief, restorative, solution, specific, therapy, treatment.

v. alleviate, ameliorate, assuage, control, correct, counteract, cure, ease, fix, heal, help, mitigate, palliate, put right, rectify, redress, reform, relieve, repair, restore, solve, soothe, treat.

remember *v.* commemorate, place, recall, recognize, recollect, reminisce, retain, summon up, think back.

antonym forget.

remembrance *n.* anamnesis, commemoration, keepsake, memento, memorial, memory, mind, monument, recall, recognition, recollection, recordation, regard, relic, remembrancer, reminder, reminiscence, retrospect, souvenir, testimonial, thought, token.

remiss *adj.* careless, culpable, delinquent, derelict, dilatory, fainéant, forgetful, heedless, inattentive, indifferent, lackadaisical, lax, neglectful, negligent, regardless, slack, slipshod, sloppy, slothful, slow, tardy, thoughtless, unmindful.

antonyms careful, scrupulous.

remit *v.* abate, alleviate, cancel, decrease, defer, delay, desist, desist from, diminish, dispatch, dwindle, forbear, forward, halt, mail, mitigate, moderate, post, postpone, put back, reduce, relax, repeal, rescind, send, send back, shelve, sink, slacken, soften, stop, suspend, transfer, transmit, wane, weaken.

n. authorization, brief, guidelines, instructions, orders, responsibility, scope, terms of reference.

remittance *n.* allowance, consideration, dispatch, fee, payment, sending.

remnant *n.* balance, bit, end, fent, fragment, hangover, left-overs, piece, remainder, remains, remane(n)t, residue, residuum, rest, rump, scrap, shred, survival, trace, vestige.

remonstrate *v.* argue, challenge, complain, dispute, dissent, expostulate, gripe, object, protest.

remorse *n.* anguish, bad conscience, compassion, compunction, contrition, grief, guilt, penitence, pity, regret, repentance, ruefulness, ruth, self-reproach, shame, sorrow.

remorseless *adj.* callous, cruel, hard, hard-hearted, harsh, implacable, inexorable, inhumane, merciless, pitiless, relentless, ruthless, savage, stern, undeviating, unforgiving, unmerciful, unrelenting, unremitting, unstoppable.

antonyms remorseful, sorry.

remote *adj.* abstracted, alien, aloof, backwoods, cold, detached, distant, doubtful, dubious, extraneous, extrinsic, faint, far, faraway, far-off, foreign, god-forsaken, immaterial, implausible, inaccessible, inconsiderable, indifferent, introspective, introverted, irrelevant, isolated, lonely, meager, negligible, outlying, out-of-the-way, outside, poor, removed, reserved, secluded, slender, slight, slim, small, standoffish, unconnected, uninterested, uninvolved, unlikely, unrelated, withdrawn.

antonyms adjacent, close, nearby, significant.

remove *v.* ablate, abolish, abstract, amove, amputate, assassinate, delete, depart, depose, detach, dethrone, discharge, dislodge, dismiss, displace, doff, efface, eject, eliminate, erase, execute, expunge, extract, flit, flit (move house), guy, kill, liquidate, move, murder, oust, purge, quit, relegate, relocate, shave, shear, shed, shift, sideline, strike, subduct, transfer, transmigrate, transport, unseat, vacate, withdraw.

remuneration *n.* compensation, earnings, emolument, fee, guerdon, income, indemnity, pay, payment, profit, recompense, reimbursement, remittance, reparation, repayment, retainer, return, reward, salary, stipend, wages.

render *v.* act, cede, clarify, construe, contribute, deliver, depict, display, do, evince, exchange, exhibit, explain, furnish, give, give back, give up, hand over, interpret, leave, make, make up, manifest, melt, pay, perform, play, portray, present, provide, put, relinquish, repay, represent, reproduce, restate, restore, return, show, show forth, submit, supply, surrender, swap, tender, trade, transcribe, translate, yield.

rendition *n.* arrangement, construction, delivery, depiction, execution, explanation, interpretation, metaphrase, metaphrasis, performance, portrayal, presentation, reading, rendering, transcription, translation, version.

renegade *n.* apostate, backslider, betrayer, defector, deserter, dissident, mutineer, outlaw, rebel, recreant, renegado, renegate, runaway, tergiversator, traitor, turncoat.

antonyms adherent, disciple, follower.

adj. apostate, backsliding, disloyal, dissident, mutinous, outlaw, perfidious, rebel, rebellious, recreant, runaway, traitorous, unfaithful.

renege *v.* apostatize, cross the floor, default, renegue, renig, repudiate, welsh.

renew *v.* continue, extend, mend, modernize, overhaul, prolong, reaffirm, recommence, recreate, re-establish, refashion, refit, refresh, refurbish, regenerate, rejuvenate, remodel, renovate, reopen, repair, repeat, replace, replenish, restate, restock, restore, resume, revitalize, transform.

renounce *v.* abandon, abdicate, abjure, abnegate, decline, deny, discard, disclaim, disown, disprofess, eschew, forgo, forsake, forswear, put away, quit, recant, reject, relinquish, repudiate, resign, spurn.

renovate *v.* do up, furbish, improve, modernize, overhaul, recondition, reconstitute, recreate, refit, reform, refurbish, rehabilitate, remodel, renew, repair, restore, revamp.

renown *n.* acclaim, celebrity, distinction, eminence, fame, glory, honor, illustriousness, kudos, luster, mark, note, reputation, repute, stardom.
antonyms anonymity, obscurity.

renowned *adj.* acclaimed, celebrated, distinguished, eminent, esteemed, famed, famous, illustrious, notable, noted, pre-eminent, supereminent, well-known.
antonyms anonymous, obscure, unknown.

rent[1] *n.* fee, gale, hire, lease, payment, rental, tariff.
v. charter, farm out, hire, lease, let, sublet, take.

rent[2] *n.* breach, break, chink, cleavage, crack, dissension, disunion, division, flaw, gash, hole, opening, perforation, rift, rip, rupture, schism, slash, slit, split, tear.

repair[1] *v.* debug, fix, heal, mend, patch up, recover, rectify, redress, renew, renovate, restore, retrieve, square.
n. adjustment, condition, darn, fettle, form, improvement, mend, nick, overhaul, patch, restoration, shape, state.

repair[2] *v.* go, wend one's way, move, remove, resort, retire, turn, withdraw.

repartee *n.* badinage, banter, jesting, persiflage, pleasantry, raillery, riposte, sally, waggery, wit, witticism, wittiness, wordplay.

repast *n.* collation, feed, food, meal, nourishment, refection, snack, spread, victuals.

repeal *v.* abolish, abrogate, annul, cancel, countermand, invalidate, nullify, quash, recall, rescind, reverse, revoke, set aside, void, withdraw.
antonyms enact, establish.
n. abolition, abrogation, annulment, cancellation, invalidation, nullification, quashing, rescinding, rescindment, rescission, reversal, revocation, withdrawal.
antonyms enactment, establishment.

repeat *v.* duplicate, echo, iterate, quote, rebroadcast, recapitulate, recite, re-do, rehearse, reiterate, relate, renew, replay, reproduce, rerun, reshow, restate, retell.
n. duplicate, echo, rebroadcast, recapitulation, reiteration, repetition, replay, reproduction, rerun, reshowing.

repeatedly *adv.* again and again, frequently, often, oftentimes, ofttimes, over and over, recurrently, time after time, time and (time) again.

repel *v.* check, confront, decline, disadvantage, disgust, fight, hold off, nauseate, offend, oppose, parry, rebuff, refuse, reject, repulse, resist, revolt, sicken, ward off.
antonym attract.

repellent *adj.* abhorrent, abominable, discouraging, disgusting, distasteful, hateful, horrid, loathsome, nauseating, noxious, obnoxious, odious, offensive, off-putting, rebarbative, repugnant, repulsive, revolting, sickening.
antonym attractive.

repent *n.* atone, bewail, deplore, lament, regret, relent, rue, sorrow.

repentance *n.* compunction, contrition, grief, guilt, metanoia, penitence, regret, remorse, self-reproach, sorriness, sorrow.

repentant *adj.* apologetic, ashamed, chastened, compunctious, contrite, penitent, regretful, remorseful, rueful, sorry.
antonym unrepentant.

repetitious *adj.* battological, long-winded, pleonastic(al), prolix, redundant, tautological, tedious, verbose, windy, wordy.

repine *v.* beef, brood, complain, fret, grieve, grouse, grumble, lament, languish, moan, mope, murmur, sulk.

replace *v.* deputize, follow, make good, oust, re-establish, reinstate, restore, substitute, succeed, supersede, supplant, supply.

replacement *n.* double, fill-in, proxy, replacer, stand-in, substitute, succedaneum, successor, surrogate, understudy.

replenish *v.* fill, furnish, provide, recharge, recruit, refill, reload, renew, replace, restock, restore, stock, supply, top up.

replica *n.* clone, copy, duplicate, facsimile, imitation, model, reproduction.

reply *v.* acknowledge, answer, counter, echo, react, reciprocate, rejoin, repartee, respond, retaliate, retort, return, riposte.
n. acknowledgment, answer, comeback, counter, echo, reaction, reciprocation, rejoinder, repartee, response, retaliation, retort, return, riposte.

report *n.* account, announcement, article, bang, blast, boom, bruit, character, communication, communiqué, crack, crash, declaration, description, detail, detonation, discharge, dispatch, esteem, explosion, fame, gossip, hearsay, information, message, narrative, news, noise, note, paper, piece, procès-verbal, recital, record, regard, relation, reputation, repute, reverberation, rumor, sound, statement, story, summary, tale, talk, tidings, version, word, write-up.
v. air, announce, appear, arrive, broadcast, bruit, circulate, come, communicate, cover, declare, describe, detail, document, mention, narrate, note, notify, proclaim, publish, recite, record, recount, relate, relay, state, tell.

reporter *n.* announcer, correspondent, hack, journalist, leg-man, newscaster, newshound, newspaperman, newspaperwoman, pressman, stringer, writer.

repose[1] *n.* aplomb, calm, calmness, composure, dignity, ease, equanimity, inactivity, peace, poise, quiet, quietness, quietude, relaxation, respite, rest, restfulness, self-possession, serenity, sleep, slumber, stillness, tranquility.
antonyms activity, strain, stress.
v. laze, recline, relax, rest, sleep, slumber.

repose[2] *v.* confide, deposit, entrust, invest, lodge, place, put, set, store.

reprehensible *adj.* bad, blamable, blameworthy, censurable, condemnable, culpable, delinquent, discreditable, disgraceful, errant, erring, ignoble, objectionable, opprobrious, remiss, shameful, unworthy.
antonyms creditable, good, praiseworthy.

represent *v.* act, appear as, be, betoken, delineate, denote, depict, depicture, describe, designate, embody, enact, epitomize, equal, evoke, exemplify, exhibit, express, illustrate, mean, outline, perform, personify, picture, portray, produce, render, reproduce, show, sketch, stage, symbolize, typify.

representation *n.* account, argument, bust, committee, delegates, delegation, delineation, depiction, description, embassy, exhibition, explanation, exposition, expostulation, icon, idol, illustration, image, likeness, model, narration, narrative, performance, petition, picture, play, portrait, portrayal, production, relation, remonstrance, resemblance, show, sight, sketch, spectacle, statue.

representative *n.* agent, archetype, commissioner, congressman, congresswoman, councillor, delegate, depute, deputy, embodiment, epitome, exemplar, member, personification, proxy, rep, representant, salesperson, senator, spokesperson, traveler, type.

adj. archetypal, characteristic, chosen, delegated, elected, elective, emblematic, evocative, exemplary, illustrative, normal, symbolic, typical, usual.

antonyms atypical, unrepresentative.

repress *v.* bottle up, chasten, check, control, crush, curb, hamper, hinder, impede, inhibit, master, muffle, overcome, overpower, quash, quell, reprime, restrain, silence, smother, stifle, subdue, subjugate, suppress, swallow.

reprimand *n.* admonition, blame, castigation, censure, dressing-down, jawbation, jobation, lecture, rebuke, reprehension, reproach, reproof, row, schooling, talking-to, telling-off, ticking-off, tongue-lashing, wigging.

v. admonish, bawl out, blame, bounce, castigate, censure, check, chide, jobe, keelhaul, lecture, lesson, rebuke, reprehend, reproach, reprove, scold, slate, tongue-lash, upbraid.

reproach *v.* abuse, blame, censure, chide, condemn, criticize, defame, discredit, disparage, dispraise, rebuke, reprehend, reprimand, reprove, scold, upbraid.

n. abuse, blame, blemish, censure, condemnation, contempt, disapproval, discredit, disgrace, dishonor, disrepute, ignominy, indignity, nayword, obloquy, odium, opprobrium, reproof, scorn, shame, slight, slut, stain, stigma, upbraiding.

reproduction *n.* amphimixis, breeding, copy, duplicate, ectype, facsimile, fructuation, gamogenesis, generation, imitation, increase, multiplication, picture, print, procreation, proliferation, propagation, replica.

antonym original.

reproof *n.* admonition, blame, castigation, censure, chiding, condemnation, criticism, dressing-down, rebuke, reprehension, reprimand, reproach, reproval, reproving, scolding, ticking-off, tongue-lashing, upbraiding.

antonym praise.

repugnance *n.* abhorrence, abhorring, antipathy, aversion, disgust, dislike, disrelish, distaste, hatred, inconsistency, loathing, reluctance, repugnancy, repulsion, revulsion.

antonyms liking, pleasure.

repulsive *adj.* abhorrent, abominable, cold, disagreeable, disgusting, distasteful, forbidding, foul, hateful, hideous, horrid, ill-faced, loathsome, nauseating, objectionable, obnoxious, odious, offensive, repellent, reserved, revolting, sickening, ugly, unpleasant, vile.

antonyms friendly, pleasant.

reputable *adj.* creditable, dependable, estimable, excellent, good, honorable, honored, irreproachable, legitimate, principled, reliable, respectable, trustworthy, unimpeachable, upright, worthy.

antonyms disreputable, infamous.

reputation *n.* bad name, character, credit, distinction, esteem, estimation, fame, good name, honor, infamy, name, opinion, renown, repute, standing, stature.

repute *n.* celebrity, distinction, esteem, estimation, fame, good name, name, renown, reputation, standing, stature.

antonym infamy.

request *v.* ask, ask for, beg, beseech, demand, desire, entreat, impetrate, importune, petition, pray, requisition, seek, solicit, supplicate.

n. appeal, application, asking, begging, call, demand, desire, entreaty, impetration, petition, prayer, representation, requisition, solicitation, suit, supplication.

require *v.* ask, beg, beseech, bid, command, compel, constrain, crave, demand, desire, direct, enjoin, exact, force, instruct, involve, lack, make, miss, necessitate, need, oblige, order, request, take, want, wish.

requirement *n.* demand, desideratum, essential, lack, must, necessity, need, precondition, prerequisite, provision, proviso, qualification, requisite, sine qua non, specification, stipulation, term, want.

antonym inessential.

requisite *adj.* essential, imperative, indispensable, mandatory, necessary, needed, needful, obligatory, prerequisite, required, vital.

antonyms inessential, optional.

n. condition, desiderative, desideratum, essential, must, necessity, need, precondition, prerequisite, requirement, sine qua non.

antonym inessential.

rescind *v.* abrogate, annul, cancel, countermand, invalidate, negate, nullify, overturn, quash, recall, repeal, retract, reverse, revoke, void.

antonym enforce.

rescue *v.* deliver, extricate, free, liberate, ransom, recover, redeem, release, salvage, save.

antonym capture.

n. deliverance, delivery, extrication, liberation, recovery, redemption, release, relief, salvage, salvation, saving.

antonym capture.

research *n.* analysis, delving, examination, experimentation, exploration, fact-finding, groundwork, inquiry, investigation, probe, quest, scrutiny, search, study.

v. analyze, examine, experiment, explore, ferret, investigate, probe, scrutinize, search, study.

resemblance *n.* affinity, analogy, assonance, closeness, comparability, comparison, conformity, correspondence, counterpart, facsimile, image, kinship, likeness, parallel, parity, sameness, semblance, similarity, similitude.

antonym dissimilarity.

resemble *v.* approach, duplicate, echo, favor, mirror, parallel, take after.

antonym differ from.

resentful *adj.* aggrieved, angry, bitter, embittered, exasperated, grudging, huffish, huffy, hurt, incensed, indignant, irate, ireful, jealous, miffed, offended, peeved, piqued, put out, resentive, revengeful, stomachful, unforgiving, wounded.

antonym contented.

resentment *n.* anger, animosity, bitterness, disaffection, discontentment, displeasure, fury, grudge, huff, hurt, ill-feeling, ill-will, indignation, ire, irritation, malice, pique, rage, rancor, umbrage, vexation, vindictiveness, wrath.

antonym contentment.

reservation[1] *n.* arrière pensée, condition, demur, doubt, hesitancy, hesitation, inhibition, proviso, qualification, restraint, scruple, second thought, skepticism, stipulation.

reservation[2] enclave, homeland, park, preserve, reserve, sanctuary, territory, tract.

reserve[1] *v.* bespeak, book, conserve, defer, delay, engage, hoard, hold, husband, keep, postpone, prearrange, preserve, retain, save, secure, set apart, spare, stockpile, store, withhold.

antonym use up.

n. backlog, cache, capital, fund, hoard, park, preserve, reservation, reservoir, sanctuary, savings, stock, stockpile, store, substitute, supply, tract.

reserve[2] aloofness, constraint, coolness, formality, limitation, modesty, reluctance, reservation, restraint, restriction, reticence, secretiveness, shyness, silence, taciturnity.

antonyms friendliness, informality.

adj. additional, alternate, auxiliary, extra, secondary, spare, substitute.

reserved[1] *adj.* booked, bound, designated, destined, earmarked, engaged, fated, held, intended, kept, meant, predestined, restricted, retained, set aside, spoken for, taken.

antonym unreserved.

reserved[2] aloof, cautious, close-mouthed, cold, cool, demure, formal, modest, prim, restrained, reticent, retiring, secretive, shy, silent, stand-offish, taciturn, unapproachable, unclub(b)able, uncommunicative, uncompanionable, unconversable, undemonstrative, unforthcoming, unresponsive, unsociable.

antonyms friendly, informal.

reside *v.* abide, consist, dwell, exist, inhabit, inhere, lie, live, lodge, remain, settle, sit, sojourn, stay.

residence *n.* abode, country-house, country-seat, domicile, dwelling, habitation, hall, home, house, household, lodging, manor, mansion, occupancy, occupation, pad, palace, place, quarters, seat, sojourn, stay, tenancy, villa.

residue *n.* balance, difference, dregs, excess, extra, leftovers, overflow, overplus, remainder, remains, remnant, residuum, rest, surplus.

antonym core.

resign *v.* abandon, abdicate, cede, forgo, forsake, leave, quit, relinquish, renounce, sacrifice, stand down, surrender, vacate, waive, yield.

antonyms join, maintain.

resignation *n.* abandonment, abdication, acceptance, acquiescence, compliance, defeatism, demission, departure, endurance, forbearing, fortitude, leaving, non-resistance, notice, passivity, patience, relinquishment, renunciation, retirement, submission, sufferance, surrender.

antonym resistance.

resigned *adj.* acquiescent, compliant, defeatist, long-suffering, patient, stoical, subdued, submissive, unprotesting, unresisting.

antonym resisting.

resilience *n.* adaptability, bounce, buoyancy, elasticity, flexibility, give, hardiness, plasticity, pliability, recoil,

spring, springiness, strength, suppleness, toughness, unshockability.

antonyms inflexibility, rigidity.

resist *v.* avoid, battle, check, combat, confront, counteract, countervail, curb, defy, dispute, fight back, forbear, forgo, hinder, oppose, recalcitrate, refuse, repel, thwart, weather, withstand.

antonyms accept, submit.

resolute *adj.* bold, constant, determined, dogged, firm, fixed, indissuadable, indivertible, inflexible, obstinate, persevering, purposeful, relentless, set, staunch, steadfast, stout, strong-minded, strong-willed, stubborn, sturdy, tenacious, unbending, undaunted, unflinching, unshakable, unshaken, unwavering.

antonym irresolute.

resolution *n.* aim, answer, boldness, constancy, courage, decision, declaration, dedication, dénouement, determination, devotion, doggedness, earnestness, end, energy, finding, firmness, fortitude, intent, intention, judgment, motion, obstinacy, outcome, perseverance, pertinacity, purpose, relentlessness, resoluteness, resolve, settlement, sincerity, solution, solving, staunchness, steadfastness, stubbornness, tenacity, unraveling, verdict, will power, zeal.

antonym indecision.

resolve *v.* agree, alter, analyze, anatomize, answer, banish, break up, change, clear, conclude, convert, crack, decide, design, determine, disentangle, disintegrate, dispel, dissect, dissipate, dissolve, elucidate, explain, fathom, fix, intend, liquefy, melt, metamorphose, purpose, reduce, relax, remove, separate, settle, solve, transform, transmute, undertake, unravel.

antonyms blend, waver.

n. boldness, conclusion, conviction, courage, decision, design, determination, earnestness, firmness, intention, objective, project, purpose, resoluteness, resolution, sense of purpose, steadfastness, undertaking, will power.

antonym indecision.

resort *v.* frequent, go, haunt, hie, repair, visit.

antonym avoid.

n. alternative, chance, course, expedient, haunt, health resort, hope, howf(f), possibility, recourse, reference, refuge, retreat, spa, spot, watering-place.

resound *v.* boom, echo, re-echo, resonate, reverberate, ring, sound, thunder.

resource *n.* ability, appliance, cache, capability, cleverness, contrivance, course, device, expedient, hoard, ingenuity, initiative, inventiveness, means, quick-wittedness, reserve, resort, resourcefulness, shift, source, stockpile, supply, talent.

antonym unimaginativeness.

resourceful *adj.* able, bright, capable, clever, creative, fertile, imaginative, ingenious, innovative, inventive, originative, quick-witted, sharp, slick, talented.

respect *n.* admiration, appreciation, approbation, aspect, bearing, characteristic, connection, consideration, deference, detail, esteem, estimation, facet, feature, homage, honor, matter, particular, point, recognition, reference, regard, relation, reverence, sense, veneration, way.

antonym disrespect.

v. admire, appreciate, attend, esteem, follow, heed, honor, notice, obey, observe, pay homage to, recognize, regard, revere, reverence, value, venerate.

antonym scorn.

respectable *adj.* admirable, ample, appreciable, clean-living, considerable, decent, decorous, dignified, estimable, fair, good, goodly, honest, honorable, large, passable, presentable, proper, reasonable, reputable, respected, seemly, sizable, substantial, tidy, tolerable, upright, venerable, well-to-do, worthy.
antonyms disreputable, miserly, unseemly.

respectful *adj.* civil, courteous, courtly, deferential, dutiful, filial, gracious, humble, mannerly, obedient, polite, regardful, reverent, reverential, self-effacing, solicitous, submissive, subservient, well-mannered.
antonym disrespectful.

respite *n.* adjournment, break, breather, cessation, delay, gap, halt, hiatus, intermission, interruption, interval, let-up, lull, moratorium, pause, postponement, recess, relaxation, relief, remission, reprieve, rest, stay, suspension.

response *n.* acknowledgment, answer, comeback, counterblast, feedback, reaction, rejoinder, reply, respond, retort, return, riposte.
antonym query.

responsibility *n.* accountability, amenability, answerability, authority, blame, burden, care, charge, conscientiousness, culpability, dependability, duty, fault, guilt, importance, level-headedness, liability, maturity, obligation, onus, power, rationality, reliability, sense, sensibleness, soberness, stability, trust, trustworthiness.
antonym irresponsibility.

responsible *adj.* accountable, adult, amenable, answerable, authoritative, bound, chargeable, conscientious, culpable, decision-making, dependable, duty-bound, ethical, executive, guilty, high, important, level-headed, liable, mature, public-spirited, rational, reliable, right, sensible, sober, sound, stable, steady, subject, trustworthy.
antonym irresponsible.

rest[1] *n.* base, break, breather, breathing-space, breathing-time, breathing-while, calm, cessation, cradle, doze, halt, haven, holiday, idleness, inactivity, interlude, intermission, interval, leisure, lie-down, lie-in, lodging, lull, motionlessness, nap, pause, prop, refreshment, refuge, relaxation, relief, repose, retreat, shelf, shelter, shut-eye, siesta, sleep, slumber, snooze, somnolence, spell, stand, standstill, stillness, stop, support, tranquility, trestle, vacation.
antonyms action, activity, restlessness.

v. alight, base, cease, continue, depend, desist, discontinue, doze, found, halt, hang, hinge, idle, keep, land, lay, laze, lean, lie, lie back, lie down, lie in, perch, prop, recline, relax, rely, remain, repose, reside, settle, sit, sleep, slumber, snooze, spell, stand, stay, stop, turn.
antonyms change, continue, work.

rest[2] *n.* balance, core, excess, left-overs, majority, others, remainder, remains, remnants, residue, residuum, rump, surplus.

restful *adj.* calm, calming, comfortable, easeful, languid, pacific, peaceful, placid, quiet, relaxed, relaxing, serene, sleepy, soothing, tranquil, tranquilizing, undisturbed, unhurried.
antonyms disturbed, disturbing.

restitution *n.* amends, compensation, damages, indemnification, indemnity, recompense, redress, refund,

reimbursement, remuneration, reparation, repayment, requital, restoration, restoring, return, satisfaction.

restive *adj.* agitated, edgy, fidgety, fractious, fretful, impatient, jittery, jumpy, nervous, obstinate, recalcitrant, refractory, restless, uneasy, unquiet, unruly.
antonyms calm, relaxed.

restless *adj.* active, agitated, anxious, bustling, changeable, disturbed, edgy, fidgety, fitful, footloose, fretful, hurried, inconstant, irresolute, jumpy, moving, nervous, nomadic, restive, roving, shifting, sleepless, transient, troubled, turbulent, uneasy, unquiet, unresting, unruly, unsettled, unstable, unsteady, wandering, worried.
antonyms calm, relaxed.

restore *v.* fix, mend, reanimate, rebuild, recondition, reconstitute, reconstruct, recover, recruit, redintegrate, re-enforce, re-establish, refresh, refurbish, rehabilitate, reimpose, reinstate, reintroduce, rejuvenate, renew, renovate, repair, replace, retouch, return, revitalize, revive, revivify, strengthen.
antonyms damage, remove, weaken.

restrain *v.* arrest, bind, bit, bridle, chain, check, cohibit, confine, constrain, control, curb, curtail, debar, detain, fetter, govern, hamper, hamshackle, handicap, harness, hinder, hold, imprison, inhibit, jail, keep, limit, manacle, muzzle, pinion, prevent, repress, restrict, stay, subdue, suppress, tie.
antonyms encourage, liberate.

restraint *n.* arrest, ban, bondage, bonds, bridle, captivity, chains, check, coercion, cohibition, command, compulsion, confinement, confines, constraint, control, cramp, curb, curtailment, dam, detention, embargo, fetters, grip, hindrance, hold, imprisonment, inhibition, interdict, lid, limit, limitation, manacles, moderation, pinions, prevention, rein, restriction, self-control, self-discipline, self-possession, self-restraint, stint, straitjacket, suppression, taboo, tie.
antonym freedom.

restrict *v.* astrict, bound, circumscribe, condition, confine, constrain, contain, cramp, demarcate, hamper, handicap, impede, inhibit, limit, regulate, restrain, restringe, scant, thirl, tie.
antonyms broaden, encourage, free.

restriction *n.* check, condition, confinement, constraint, containment, control, curb, demarcation, handicap, inhibition, limitation, regulation, restraint, rule, squeeze, stint, stipulation.
antonyms broadening, encouragement, freedom.

result *n.* conclusion, consequence, decision, development, effect, end, end-product, event, fruit, issue, outcome, produce, reaction, sequel, termination, upshot.
antonyms beginning, cause.

v. appear, arise, culminate, derive, develop, emanate, emerge, end, ensue, eventuate, finish, flow, follow, happen, issue, proceed, spring, stem, terminate.
antonyms begin, cause.

resume *v.* continue, pick up, proceed, recommence, reinstitute, reopen, restart, take up.
antonym cease.

resurgence *n.* rebirth, recrudescence, re-emergence, renaissance, renascence, resumption, resurrection, return, revival, revivification, risorgimento.
antonym decrease.

resuscitate *v.* quicken, reanimate, reinvigorate, renew, rescue, restore, resurrect, revitalize, revive, revivify, save.

retain v. absorb, commission, contain, detail, employ, engage, grasp, grip, hire, hold, hold back, keep, keep in mind, keep up, maintain, memorize, pay, preserve, recall, recollect, remember, reserve, restrain, save.
antonyms release, spend.

retainer[1] n. attendant, dependant, domestic, galloglass, henchman, lackey, minion, servant, satellite, subordinate, supporter.

retainer[2] n. advance, deposit, fee, retaining fee.

retaliate v. fight back, get back at, get even with, get one's own back, give as good as one gets, hit back, reciprocate, repay in kind, return like for like, revenge oneself, strike back, take revenge.
antonyms accept, submit.

retard v. arrest, brake, check, clog, decelerate, defer, delay, detain, encumber, handicap, hinder, impede, keep back, obstruct, slow, stall.
antonym advance.

reticent adj. boutonné, close-lipped, close-mouthed, mum, mute, quiet, reserved, restrained, secretive, silent, taciturn, tight-lipped, uncommunicative, unforthcoming, unspeaking.
antonyms communicative, forward, frank.

retire v. decamp, depart, draw back, ebb, exit, leave, recede, remove, retreat, withdraw.
antonyms enter, join.

retiring adj. bashful, coy, demure, diffident, humble, meek, modest, mousy, quiet, reclusive, reserved, reticent, self-effacing, shamefaced, shrinking, shy, timid, timorous, unassertive, unassuming.
antonyms assertive, forward.

retort v. answer, counter, rejoin, repartee, reply, respond, retaliate, return, riposte.
n. answer, backword, come-back, quip, rejoinder, repartee, reply, response, riposte, sally.

retreat v. depart, ebb, leave, quit, recede, recoil, retire, shrink, turn tail, withdraw.
antonym advance.
n. asylum, den, departure, ebb, evacuation, flight, funk-hole, growlery, haunt, haven, hibernacle, hibernaculum, hideaway, privacy, refuge, resort, retirement, sanctuary, seclusion, shelter, withdrawal.
antonyms advance, company, limelight.

retrench v. curtail, cut, decrease, diminish, economize, husband, lessen, limit, pare, prune, reduce, save, slim down, trim.
antonym increase.

retribution n. compensation, justice, Nemesis, payment, punishment, reckoning, recompense, redress, repayment, reprisal, requital, retaliation, revenge, reward, satisfaction, talion, vengeance.

retrieve v. fetch, make good, recall, recapture, recoup, recover, redeem, regain, repair, repossess, rescue, restore, return, salvage, save.
antonym lose.

retrograde adj. backward, declining, degenerative, denigrating, deteriorating, downward, inverse, negative, regressive, relapsing, retreating, retrogressive, reverse, reverting, waning, worsening.
antonym progressive.

return v. announce, answer, choose, communicate, convey, deliver, earn, elect, make, net, pick, reappear, rebound, reciprocate, recoil, recompense, recur,

redound, re-establish, refund, reimburse, reinstate, rejoin, remit, render, repair, repay, replace, reply, report, requite, respond, restore, retort, retreat, revert, send, submit, transmit, volley, yield.
antonyms leave, take.
n. account, advantage, answer, benefit, comeback, compensation, form, gain, home-coming, income, interest, list, proceeds, profit, quip, reappearance, rebound, reciprocation, recoil, recompense, recrudescence, recurrence, redound, re-establishment, reimbursement, reinstatement, rejoinder, reparation, repayment, replacement, reply, report, requital, response, restoration, retaliation, retort, retreat, revenue, reversion, reward, riposte, sally, statement, summary, takings, yield.
antonyms disappearance, expense, loss, payment.

reveal v. announce, bare, betray, broadcast, communicate, disbosom, disclose, dismask, display, divulge, exhibit, expose, impart, leak, lift the lid off, manifest, open, proclaim, publish, show, tell, unbare, unbosom, uncover, unearth, unfold, unmask, unshadow, unveil.
antonym hide.

revel v. carouse, celebrate, live it up, make merry, paint the town red, push the boat out, raise the roof, roist, roister, whoop it up.
n. bacchanal, carousal, carouse, celebration, comus, debauch, festivity, gala, jollification, merry-make, merrymaking, party, saturnalia, spree.

revel in bask, crow, delight, gloat, glory, indulge, joy, lap up, luxuriate, rejoice, relish, savor, take pleasure, thrive on, wallow.
antonym dislike.

revelation n. announcement, apocalypse, betrayal, broadcasting, communication, disclosure, discovery, display, exhibition, exposé, exposition, exposure, giveaway, leak, manifestation, news, proclamation, publication, telling, uncovering, unearthing, unveiling.

revelry n. carousal, carouse, celebration, debauch, debauchery, festivity, fun, jollification, jollity, merrymaking, party, revel-rout, riot, roistering, saturnalia, spree, wassail, wassailing, wassailry.
antonym sobriety.

revenge n. a dose/taste of one's own medicine, ravanche, reprisal, requital, retaliation, retribution, revengement, satisfaction, ultion, vengeance, vindictiveness.
v. avenge, even the score, get one's own back, get satisfaction, repay, requite, retaliate, vindicate.

revenue n. gain, income, interest, proceeds, profits, receipts, returns, rewards, take, takings, yield.
antonym expenditure.

revere v. adore, defer to, exalt, honor, pay homage to, respect, reverence, venerate, worship.
antonyms despise, scorn.

reverence n. admiration, adoration, awe, deference, devotion, dulia, esteem, genuflection, homage, honor, hyperdulia, latria, respect, veneration, worship.
antonym scorn.
v. acknowledge, admire, adore, honor, respect, revere, venerate, worship.
antonyms despise, scorn.

reverent adj. adoring, awed, decorous, deferential, devout, dutiful, humble, loving, meek, pious, respectful, reverential, solemn, submissive.
antonym irreverent.

reverse v. alter, annul, back, backtrack, cancel, change, countermand, hark back, invalidate, invert, negate, overrule, overset, overthrow, overturn, quash, repeal, rescind, retract, retreat, revert, revoke, transpose, undo, up-end, upset.

antonym enforce.

n. adversity, affliction, antithesis, back, blow, check, contradiction, contrary, converse, defeat, disappointment, failure, hardship, inverse, misadventure, misfortune, mishap, opposite, rear, repulse, reversal, setback, trial, underside, verso, vicissitude, woman.

adj. backward, contrary, converse, inverse, inverted, opposite, verso.

revert *v.* backslide, lapse, recur, regress, relapse, resume, retrogress, return, reverse.

antonym progress.

review *v.* assess, criticize, discuss, evaluate, examine, inspect, judge, reassess, recall, recapitulate, recollect, reconsider, re-evaluate, re-examine, rehearse, remember, rethink, revise, scrutinize, study, weigh.

n. analysis, assessment, commentary, criticism, critique, evaluation, examination, journal, judgment, magazine, notice, periodical, reassessment, recapitulation, recension, reconsideration, re-evaluation, re-examination, report, rethink, retrospect, revision, scrutiny, study, survey.

revile *v.* abuse, blackguard, calumniate, defame, denigrate, libel, malign, miscall, reproach, scorn, slander, smear, traduce, vilify, vilipend, vituperate.

antonym praise.

revise *v.* alter, amend, change, correct, edit, emend, memorize, modify, recast, recense, reconsider, reconstruct, redo, re-examine, reread, revamp, review, rewrite, study, swot up, update.

revision *n.* alteration, amendment, change, correction, editing, emendation, homework, memorizing, modification, recast, recasting, recension, reconstruction, re-examination, rereading, review, rewriting, rifacimento, studying, swotting, updating.

revival *n.* awakening, quickening, reactivation, reanimation, reawakening, rebirth, recrudescence, renaissance, renascence, renewal, restoration, resurgence, resurrection, resuscitation, revitalization, revivification, risorgimento.

antonym suppression.

revive *v.* animate, awaken, cheer, comfort, invigorate, quicken, rally, reactivate, reanimate, recover, refresh, rekindle, renew, renovate, restore, resuscitate, revitalize, revivify, rouse.

antonyms suppress, weary.

revoke *v.* abolish, abrogate, annul, cancel, countermand, disclaim, dissolve, invalidate, negate, nullify, quash, recall, recant, renounce, repeal, repudiate, rescind, retract, reverse, withdraw.

antonym enforce.

revolt[1] *n.* breakaway, defection, insurgency, insurrection, Jacquerie, mutiny, putsch, rebellion, revolution, rising, secession, sedition, uprising.

v. defect, mutiny, rebel, resist, riot, rise.

antonym submit.

revolt[2] *v.* disgust, nauseate, offend, outrage, repel, repulse, scandalize, shock, sicken.

antonym please.

revolting *adj.* abhorrent, abominable, appalling, disgusting, distasteful, fetid, foul, horrible, horrid, loathsome, nasty, nauseating, nauseous, noisome, obnoxious,

obscene, offensive, repellent, repugnant, repulsive, shocking, sickening, sickly.

antonym pleasant.

revolution *n.* cataclysm, change, circle, circuit, coup, coup d'état, cycle, gyration, innovation, insurgency, Jacquerie, lap, metamorphosis, metanoia, mutiny, orbit, putsch, rebellion, reformation, revolt, rising, rotation, round, shift, spin, transformation, turn, upheaval, uprising, volution, wheel, whirl.

revolutionary *n.* anarchist, insurgent, insurrectionary, insurrectionist, Jacobin, mutineer, rebel, revolutionist, Trot, Trotskyite.

adj. anarchistic, avant-garde, different, drastic, experimental, extremist, fundamental, innovative, insurgent, insurrectionary, mutinous, new, novel, progressive, radical, rebel, seditious, subversive, thoroughgoing.

antonyms commonplace, establishment.

revolve *v.* circle, circumgyrate, circumvolve, gyrate, orbit, rotate, spin, turn, wheel, whirl.

revolver *n.* air-gun, firearm, gun, hand-gun, heater, peace-maker, piece, pistol, rod, shooter, six-shooter.

revulsion *n.* abhorrence, abomination, aversion, detestation, disgust, dislike, distaste, hatred, loathing, recoil, repugnance, repulsion.

antonym pleasure.

reward *n.* benefit, bonus, bounty, come-up(p)ance, compensation, desert, gain, guerdon, honor, meed, merit, payment, pay-off, premium, prize, profit, punishment, recompense, remuneration, repayment, requital, retribution, return, wages.

antonym punishment.

v. compensate, guerdon, honor, pay, recompense, remunerate, repay, requite.

antonym punish.

rewarding *adj.* advantageous, beneficial, edifying, enriching, fruitful, fulfilling, gainful, gratifying, pleasing, productive, profitable, remunerative, rewardful, satisfying, valuable, worthwhile.

antonym unrewarding.

rhetorical *adj.* artificial, bombastic, declamatory, false, flamboyant, flashy, florid, flowery, grandiloquent, high-flown, high-sounding, hyperbolic, inflated, insincere, linguistic, magniloquent, oratorical, over-decorated, pompous, pretentious, rhetoric, showy, silver-tongued, stylistic, verbal, verbose, windy.

antonyms simple.

rhythm *n.* accent, beat, cadence, cadency, eurhythmy, flow, lilt, measure, meter, movement, pattern, periodicity, pulse, rhythmicity, swing, tempo, time.

ribald *adj.* base, bawdy, blue, broad, coarse, derisive, earthy, filthy, foul-mouthed, gross, indecent, irrisory, jeering, licentious, low, mean, mocking, naughty, obscene, off-color, Rabelaisian, racy, risqué, rude, scurrilous, smutty, vulgar.

antonym polite.

rich *adj.* abounding, abundant, affluent, ample, bright, copious, costly, creamy, deep, delicious, dulcet, elaborate, elegant, expensive, exquisite, exuberant, fatty, fecund, fertile, fine, flavorsome, flush, fruitful, full, full-bodied, full-flavored, full-toned, gay, gorgeous, heavy, highly-flavored, humorous, in the money, intense, juicy, laughable, lavish, loaded, ludicrous, luscious, lush, luxurious, mellifluous, mellow, moneyed, opulent, palatial, pecunious, plenteous, plentiful, plutocratic, precious, priceless, productive, prolific, propertied, property, prosperous, resonant, ridiculous, risible, rolling, savory, side-splitting, spicy, splendid, strong, succulent, sumptuous, superb, sweet, tasty, uberous, valuable, vibrant, vivid, warm, wealthy, well-heeled, well-off, well-provided, well-stocked, well-supplied, well-to-do.

antonyms harsh, miserly, plain, poor, simple, tasteless, thin, unfertile.

rickety *adj.* broken, broken-down, decrepit, derelict, dilapidated, feeble, flimsy, frail, imperfect, infirm, insecure, jerry-built, precarious, ramshackle, shaky, shoogly, tottering, tottery, unsound, unstable, unsteady, weak, wobbly.

antonyms stable, strong.

rid *v.* clear, deliver, disabuse, disburden, disembarrass, disencumber, expel, free, purge, relieve, unburden.

antonym burden.

riddle¹ *n.* brain-teaser, charade, conundrum, enigma, logogram, logograph, logogriph, mystery, poser, problem, puzzle, rebus.

riddle² *v.* corrupt, damage, fill, filter, impair, infest, invade, mar, pepper, perforate, permeate, pervade, pierce, puncture, screen, sieve, sift, spoil, strain, winnow.

n. sieve, strainer.

ride *v.* control, dominate, enslave, float, grip, handle, haunt, hurl, journey, manage, move, oppress, progress, sit, survive, travel, weather.

n. drive, hurl, jaunt, journey, lift, outing, spin, trip, whirl.

ridge *n.* arête, band, costa, crinkle, drum, drumlin, escarpment, eskar, hill, hog's back, hummock, lump, reef, ripple, saddle, wale, weal, welt, zastruga.

ridicule *n.* banter, chaff, derision, gibe, irony, irrision, jeering, jeers, laughter, mockery, raillery, sarcasm, satire, scorn, sneers, taunting.

antonym praise.

v. banter, burlesque, caricature, cartoon, chaff, crucify, deride, humiliate, jeer, josh, lampoon, mock, parody, pillory, pooh-pooh, queer, quiz, rib, satirize, scoff, send up, sneer at, take the mickey out of, taunt.

antonym praise.

ridiculous *adj.* absurd, comical, contemptible, damfool, derisory, farcical, foolish, funny, hilarious, incredible, laughable, laughworthy, ludicrous, nonsensical, outrageous, preposterous, risible, silly, stupid, unbelievable.

antonym sensible.

rife *adj.* abounding, abundant, common, commonplace, current, epidemic, frequent, general, plentiful, prevailing, prevalent, raging, rampant, teeming, ubiquitous, universal, widespread.

antonym scarce.

rifle¹ *v.* burgle, despoil, gut, loot, maraud, pillage, plunder, ransack, rob, rummage, sack, strip.

rifle² *n.* air-gun, carbine, firearm, firelock, flintlock, fusil, gun, musket, shotgun.

rift *n.* alienation, beach, breach, break, chink, cleavage, cleft, crack, cranny, crevice, difference, disaffection, disagreement, dissure, division, estrangement, fault, flaw, fracture, gap, opening, quarrel, schism, separation, space, split.

antonym unity.

right *adj.* absolute, accurate, admissible, advantageous, appropriate, authentic, balanced, becoming, character-

istic, comme il faut, complete, compos mentis, conservative, correct, deserved, desirable, dexter, dextral, direct, done, due, equitable, ethical, exact, factual, fair, favorable, fine, fit, fitting, genuine, good, healthy, honest, honorable, ideal, just, lawful, lucid, moral, normal, opportune, out-and-out, perpendicular, precise, proper, propitious, rational, reactionary, real, reasonable, righteous, rightful, rightist, rightward, right-wing, sane, satisfactory, seemly, sound, spot-on, straight, suitable, thorough, thoroughgoing, Tory, true, unerring, unimpaired, upright, utter, valid, veracious, veritable, virtuous, well.

antonyms left, left-wing, mad, unfit, wrong.

adv. absolutely, accurately, advantageously, altogether, appropriate, aptly, aright, bang, befittingly, beneficially, completely, correctly, directly, entirely, ethically, exactly, factually, fairly, favorably, fittingly, fortunately, genuinely, honestly, honorably, immediately, instantly, justly, morally, perfectly, precisely, promptly, properly, quickly, quite, righteously, rightward(s), satisfactorily, slap-bang, squarely, straight, straightaway, suitably, thoroughly, totally, truly, utterly, virtuously, well, wholly.

antonyms incorrectly, left, unfairly, wrongly.

n. authority, business, claim, droit, due, equity, freedom, good, goodness, honor, integrity, interest, justice, lawfulness, legality, liberty, licence, morality, permission, power, prerogative, privilege, propriety, reason, rectitude, righteousness, rightfulness, rightness, title, truth, uprightness, virtue.

antonyms depravity, wrong.

v. avenge, correct, fix, rectify, redress, repair, righten, settle, stand up, straighten, vindicate.

righteous *adj.* blameless, equitable, ethical, fair, God-fearing, good, guiltless, honest, honorable, incorrupt, just, law-abiding, moral, pure, saintly, sinless, upright, virtuous.

antonym unrighteous.

n. Holy Willies, just, Pharisees, saints, unco guid, well-doers.

antonym unrighteous.

rigid *adj.* adamant, austere, cast-iron, exact, fixed, harsh, inflexible, intransigent, invariable, rigorous, set, severe, starch(y), stern, stiff, stony, strict, stringent, tense, unalterable, unbending, uncompromising, undeviating, unrelenting, unyielding.

antonym flexible.

rigorous *adj.* accurate, austere, challenging, conscientious, demanding, exact, exacting, extreme, firm, hard, harsh, inclement, inflexible, inhospitable, meticulous, nice, painstaking, precise, punctilious, Rhadamanthine, rigid, scrupulous, severe, stern, strict, stringent, thorough, tough, unsparing.

antonyms lenient, mild.

rile *v.* anger, annoy, bug, exasperate, gall, get, irk, irritate, miff, nark, nettle, peeve, pique, provoke, put out, upset, vex.

antonym soothe.

rim *n.* border, brim, brink, circumference, edge, lip, margin, skirt, verge.

antonym center.

rind *n.* crust, epicarp, husk, integument, peel, skin, zest.

ring¹ *n.* annulation, annulet, annulus, arena, association, band, cabal, cartel, cell, circle, circuit, circus, clique, collar, collet, combine, coterie, crew, enclosure, gang, group, gyre, halo, hoop, knot, loop, mob, organization, rink, round, rundle, syndicate.

v. circumscribe, encircle, enclose, encompass, gash, gird, girdle, mark, score, surround.

ring² *v.* bell, buzz, call, chime, clang, clink, peal, phone, resonate, resound, reverberate, sound, tang, telephone, ting, tinkle, tintinnabulate, toll.

n. buzz, call, chime, clang, clink, knell, peal, phone-call, tang, ting, tinkle, tintinnabulation.

ringleader *n.* bell-wether, brains, chief, fugleman, leader, spokesman.

rinse *v.* bathe, clean, cleanse, dip, sluice, splash, swill, synd, wash, wet.

n. bath, dip, dye, splash, tint, wash, wetting.

riot *n.* anarchy, bagarre, boisterousness, carousal, commotion, confusion, debauchery, disorder, display, disturbance, Donnybrook, émeute, excess, extravaganza, festivity, flourish, fray, frolic, high, insurrection, jinks, jollification, lawlessness, merry-make, merrymaking, quarrel, revelry, riotousness, riotry, romp, rookery, rout, row, ruction, ruffle, shindig, shindy, show, splash, strife, tumult, turbulence, turmoil, uproar.

antonyms calm, order.

v. carouse, frolic, rampage, rebel, revel, revolt, rise up, roister, romp, run riot, run wild.

riotous *adj.* anarchic, boisterous, disorderly, insubordinate, insurrectionary, lawless, loud, luxurious, mutinous, noisy, orgiastic, rambunctious, rampageous, rebellious, refractory, roisterous, rollicking, rowdy, saturnalian, side-splitting, tumultuous, ungovernable, unrestrained, unruly, uproarious, violent, wanton, wild.

antonyms orderly, restrained.

rip *v.* burst, claw, cut, gash, hack, lacerate, rend, rupture, score, separate, slash, slit, split, tear.

n. cleavage, cut, gash, hole, laceration, rent, rupture, slash, slit, split, tear.

ripe *adj.* accomplished, auspicious, complete, developed, favorable, finished, grown, ideal, mature, mellow, opportune, perfect, prepared, promising, propitious, ready, right, ripened, seasoned, suitable, timely.

antonyms inopportune, untimely.

ripen *v.* age, burgeon, develop, mature, mellow, prepare, season.

rip-off *n.* cheat, con, con trick, daylight robbery, diddle, exploitation, fraud, robbery, sting, swindle, theft.

riposte *n.* answer, come-back, quip, rejoinder, repartee, reply, response, retort, return, sally.

v. answer, quip, reciprocate, rejoin, reply, respond, retort, return.

ripple *n.* babble, burble, disturbance, eddy, gurgle, lapping, pirl, purl, ripplet, undulation, wave, wimple.

rise *v.* advance, appear, arise, ascend, buoy, climb, crop up, emanate, emerge, enlarge, eventuate, flow, get up, grow, happen, improve, increase, intensify, issue, levitate, lift, mount, mutiny, occur, originate, progress, prosper, rebel, resist, revolt, slope, slope up, soar, spring, spring up, stand up, surface, swell, tower, volume, wax.

antonyms descend, fall.

n. acclivity, advance, advancement, aggrandizement, ascent, climb, elevation, hillock, improvement, incline, increase, increment, origin, progress, promotion, raise, rising, upsurge, upswing, upturn, upward turn.

antonyms descent, fall.

risk *n.* adventure, chance, danger, gamble, hazard, jeopardy, peril, possibility, speculation, uncertainty, venture.

antonyms certainty, safety.

v. adventure, chance, dare, endanger, gamble, hazard, imperil, jeopardize, speculate, venture.

risky *adj.* chancy, dangerous, dicey, dodgy, fraught, hazardous, perilous, precarious, riskful, touch-and-go, tricky, uncertain, unsafe.

antonym safe.

rite *n.* act, ceremonial, ceremony, custom, form, formality, liturgy, mystery, observance, office, ordinance, practice, procedure, ritual, sacrament, service, solemnity, usage, worship.

ritual *n.* ceremonial, ceremony, communion, convention, custom, form, formality, habit, liturgy, mystery, observance, ordinance, practice, prescription, procedure, rite, routine, sacrament, service, solemnity, tradition, usage, wont.

adj. ceremonial, ceremonious, conventional, customary, formal, formulary, habitual, prescribed, procedural, routine, stereotyped.

antonyms informal, unusual.

rival *n.* adversary, antagonist, challenger, collateral, compeer, competitor, contender, contestant, corrival, emulator, equal, equivalent, fellow, match, opponent, peer, rivaless.

antonyms associate, colleague, co-worker.

adj. competing, competitive, conflicting, corrival, emulating, emulous, opposed, opposing.

antonyms associate, co-operating.

v. compete, contend, emulate, equal, match, oppose, rivalize, vie with.

antonym co-operate.

rivalry *n.* antagonism, competition, competitiveness, conflict, contention, contest, duel, emulation, opposition, rivality, rivalship, struggle, vying.

antonym co-operation.

river *n.* beck, burn, creek, ea, flood, flow, gush, riverway, rush, spate, stream, surge, tributary, waterway.

adj. fluvial, riverain, riverine.

riveting *adj.* absorbing, arresting, captivating, engrossing, enthralling, fascinating, gripping, hypnotic, magnetic, spellbinding.

antonym boring.

road *n.* Autobahn, autopista, autoroute, autostrada, avenue, boulevard, camino real, carriageway, clearway, course, crescent, direction, drift, drive, driveway, freeway, highway, lane, path, pathway, roadway, route, street, thoroughfare, thruway, track, way.

roam *v.* drift, meander, peregrinate, prowl, ramble, range, rove, squander, stravaig, stray, stroll, travel, walk, wander.

antonym stay.

roar *v.* bawl, bay, bell, bellow, blare, clamor, crash, cry, guffaw, hoot, howl, rumble, shout, thunder, vociferate, wuther, yell.

antonym whisper.

n. bellow, belly-laugh, blare, clamor, crash, cry, guffaw, hoot, howl, outcry, rumble, shout, thunder, yell.

antonym whisper.

rob *v.* bereave, bunko, cheat, con, defraud, deprive, despoil, dispossess, do, flake, flimp, gyp, heist, hold

up, loot, mill, pillage, plunder, raid, ramp, ransack, reive, rifle, rip off, roll, sack, sting, strip, swindle.
antonyms give, provide.

robbery *n.* burglary, dacoitage, dacoity, depredation, embezzlement, filching, fraud, heist, hold-up, larceny, pillage, plunder, purse-snatching, purse-taking, raid, rapine, rip-off, spoliation, stealing, stick-up, swindle, theft, thievery.

robe *n.* bathrobe, costume, dressing-gown, gown, habit, housecoat, peignoir, vestment, wrap, wrapper.
v. apparel, attire, clothe, drape, dress, garb, vest.

robot *n.* android, automaton, golem, machine, zombie.

robust *adj.* able-bodied, athletic, boisterous, brawny, coarse, down-to-earth, earthy, fit, hale, hard-headed, hardy, healthy, hearty, husky, indecorous, lusty, muscular, over-hearty, powerful, practical, pragmatic, raw, realistic, robustious, roisterous, rollicking, rough, rude, rugged, sensible, sinewy, sound, staunch, sthenic, stout, straightforward, strapping, strong, sturdy, thick-set, tough, unsubtle, vigorous, well.
antonyms mealy-mouthed, unhealthy, unrealistic, weak.

rock[1] *n.* anchor, boulder, bulwark, cornerstone, danger, foundation, hazard, logan, log(g)an-stone, mainstay, obstacle, pebble, problem, protection, stone, support.

rock[2] *v.* astonish, astound, daze, dumbfound, jar, lurch, pitch, reel, roll, shake, shock, stagger, stun, surprise, sway, swing, tilt, tip, toss, wobble.

rocky[1] *adj.* craggy, flinty, hard, pebbly, rocklike, rough, rugged, stony.
antonyms smooth, soft.

rocky[2] *adj.* dizzy, doubtful, drunk, ill, inebriated, intoxicated, rickety, shaky, sick, sickly, staggering, tipsy, tottering, uncertain, undependable, unpleasant, unreliable, unsatisfactory, unstable, unsteady, unwell, weak, wobbly, wonky.
antonyms dependable, steady, well.

rod *n.* bar, baton, birch, cane, dowel, ferula, ferule, mace, pole, scepter, shaft, spoke, staff, stick, strut, switch, verge, wand.

rogue *n.* blackguard, charlatan, cheat, con man, crook, deceiver, devil, fraud, knave, miscreant, mountebank, nasty piece/bit of work, ne'er-do-well, picaroon, rapscallion, rascal, reprobate, scamp, scapegallows, scoundrel, sharper, swindler, vagrant, villain, wag.
antonym saint.

roguish *adj.* arch, bantering, cheeky, confounded, coquettish, criminal, crooked, deceitful, deceiving, dishonest, espiègle, fraudulent, frolicsome, hempy, impish, knavish, mischievous, playful, puckish, raffish, rascally, roguing, shady, sportive, swindling, unprincipled, unscrupulous, villainous, waggish.
antonyms honest, serious.

roister *v.* bluster, boast, brag, carouse, celebrate, frolic, make merry, paint the town red, revel, roist, rollick, romp, strut, swagger, whoop it up.

role *n.* capacity, character, duty, function, impersonation, job, job of work, part, portrayal, position, post, representation, task.

roll *v.* billow, bind, boom, coil, curl, drum, echo, elapse, enfold, entwine, envelop, even, flatten, flow, furl, grumble, gyrate, level, lumber, lurch, pass, peel, pivot, press, reel, resound, reverberate, revolve, roar, rock, rotate, rumble, run, smooth, spin, spread, stagger, swagger, swathe, sway, swing, swivel, thunder, toss, trill, trindle, trundle, tumble, turn, twirl, twist, undu-

late, volume, waddle, wallow, wander, welter, wheel, whirl, wind, wrap.

n. annals, ball, bobbin, boom, catalog, census, chronicle, cycle, cylinder, directory, drumming, growl, grumble, gyration, index, inventory, list, notitia, record, reel, register, resonance, reverberation, revolution, roar, roller, roster, rotation, rumble, run, schedule, scroll, spin, spool, table, thunder, turn, twirl, undulation, volume, wheel, whirl.

rollicking *adj.* boisterous, carefree, cavorting, devil-may-care, exuberant, frisky, frolicsome, hearty, jaunty, jovial, joyous, lively, merry, playful, rip-roaring, roisterous, roisting, romping, spirited, sportive, sprightly, swashbuckling.
antonyms restrained, serious.

romance *n.* absurdity, adventure, affair(e), amour, attachment, charm, color, exaggeration, excitement, fabrication, fairy tale, falsehood, fantasy, fascination, fiction, gest(e), glamor, idyll, intrigue, invention, legend, liaison, lie, love affair, love story, melodrama, mystery, novel, passion, relationship, sentiment, story, tale, tear-jerker.
v. exaggerate, fantasize, lie, overstate.

romantic *adj.* amorous, charming, chimerical, colorful, dreamy, exaggerated, exciting, exotic, extravagant, fabulous, fairy-tale, fanciful, fantastic, fascinating, fictitious, fond, glamorous, high-flown, idealistic, idyllic, imaginary, imaginative, impractical, improbable, legendary, lovey-dovey, loving, made-up, mushy, mysterious, passionate, picturesque, quixotic, romantical, sentimental, sloppy, soppy, starry-eyed, tender, unrealistic, utopian, visionary, whimsical, wild.
antonyms humdrum, practical, real, sober, unromantic.
n. Don Quixote, dreamer, idealist, romancer, sentimentalist, utopian, visionary.
antonym realist.

romp *v.* caper, cavort, frisk, frolic, gambol, revel, rig, roister, rollick, skip, sport.
n. caper, frolic, lark, rig, spree.

room *n.* allowance, apartment, area, capacity, chamber, chance, compartment, compass, elbow-room, expanse, extent, house-room, latitude, leeway, margin, occasion, office, opportunity, play, range, salon, saloon, scope, space, territory, volume.

roomy *adj.* ample, broad, capacious, commodious, extensive, generous, large, sizable, spacious, voluminous, wide.
antonym cramped.

root[1] *n.* base, basis, beginnings, bottom, cause, core, crux, derivation, essence, foundation, fountainhead, fundamental, germ, heart, mainspring, more, nub, nucleus, occasion, origin, radicle, radix, rhizome, root-cause, rootlet, seat, seed, source, starting point, stem, tuber.
v. anchor, embed, entrench, establish, fasten, fix, ground, implant, moor, set, sink, stick.

root[2] *v.* burrow, delve, dig, ferret, forage, grout, hunt, nose, poke, pry, rootle, rummage.

rooted *adj.* confirmed, deep, deeply, deep-seated, entrenched, established, felt, firm, fixed, ingrained, radical, rigid, root-fast.
antonyms superficial, temporary.

rope *n.* cable, cord, fake, hawser, lariat, lasso, line, marline, strand, warp, widdy.

v. bind, catch, fasten, hitch, lash, lasso, moor, pinion, tether, tie.

ropy *adj.* below par, deficient, inadequate, indifferent, inferior, off-color, poorly, rough, sketchy, stringy, substandard, unwell.

antonyms good, well.

roster *n.* bead-roll, list, listing, register, roll, rota, schedule, table.

rosy *adj.* auspicious, blooming, blushing, bright, cheerful, encouraging, favorable, fresh, glowing, healthy-looking, hopeful, optimistic, pink, promising, reassuring, red, reddish, rose, roseate, rose-colored, rose-hued, roselike, rose-pink, rose-red, rose-scented, rosy-fingered, rubicund, ruddy, sunny.

antonyms depressed, depressing, sad.

rot *v.* corrode, corrupt, crumble, decay, decline, decompose, degenerate, deteriorate, disintegrate, fester, go bad, languish, molder, perish, putrefy, ret, spoil, taint.
n. balderdash, blight, bosh, bunk, bunkum, canker, claptrap, codswallop, collapse, corrosion, corruption, decay, decomposition, deterioration, disintegration, drivel, flapdoodle, guff, hogwash, moonshine, mold, nonsense, poppycock, putrefaction, putrescence, rubbish, tommyrot, tosh, twaddle.

rotary *adj.* gyrating, gyratory, revolving, rotating, rotational, rotatory, spinning, turning, whirling.

antonym fixed.

rotate *v.* alternate, gyrate, interchange, pirouette, pivot, reel, revolve, spell, spin, switch, swivel, turn, twiddle, wheel.

rotation *n.* alternation, cycle, gyration, interchanging, orbit, pirouette, reel, revolution, sequence, spin, spinning, succession, switching, turn, turning, volution, wheel.

rotten *adj.* addle(d), bad, base, below par, bent, contemptible, corroded, corrupt, crooked, crumbling, crummy, decayed, decaying, deceitful, decomposed, decomposing, degenerate, deplorable, despicable, dirty, disagreeable, disappointing, dishonest, dishonorable, disintegrating, disloyal, faithless, festering, fetid, filthy, foul, grotty, ill-considered, ill-thought-out, immoral, inadequate, inferior, lousy, low-grade, manky, mean, mercenary, moldering, moldy, nasty, off-color, perfidious, perished, poor, poorly, punk, putid, putrescent, putrid, rank, regrettable, ropy, rough, scurrilous, sick, sorry, sour, stinking, substandard, tainted, treacherous, unacceptable, unfortunate, unlucky, unpleasant, unsatisfactory, unsound, untrustworthy, unwell, venal, vicious, vile, wicked.

antonyms good, honest, practical, sensible, well.

rotund *adj.* bulbous, chubby, corpulent, fat, fleshy, full, globular, grandiloquent, heavy, magniloquent, obese, orbed, orbicular, orby, oro(ro)tund, plump, podgy, portly, resonant, rich, roly-poly, rotundate, round, rounded, sonorous, spheral, spheric, spherical, spherular, sphery, stout, tubby.

antonyms flat, gaunt, slim.

rough *adj.* agitated, amorphous, approximate, arduous, austere, basic, bearish, bluff, blunt, boisterous, bristly, broken, brusque, bumpy, bushy, cacophonous, choppy, churlish, coarse, craggy, crude, cruel, cursory, curt, discordant, discourteous, disheveled, disordered, drastic, estimated, extreme, foggy, formless, fuzzy, general, grating, gruff, hairy, hard, harsh, hasty, hazy, husky, ill, ill-bred, ill-mannered, imperfect, impolite,

imprecise, inclement, incomplete, inconsiderate, indelicate, inexact, inharmonious, irregular, jagged, jarring, loutish, nasty, off-color, poorly, quick, rasping, raspy, raucous, raw, rocky, ropy, rotten, rough-and-ready, rowdy, rude, rudimentary, rugged, rusty, scabrous, severe, shaggy, shapeless, sharp, sick, sketchy, spartan, squally, stony, stormy, tangled, tempestuous, tough, tousled, tousy, turbulent, unceremonious, uncivil, uncomfortable, uncouth, uncultured, uncut, undressed, uneven, unfeeling, unfinished, ungracious, unjust, unmannerly, unmusical, unpleasant, unpolished, unprocessed, unrefined, unshaven, unshorn, untutored, unwell, unwrought, upset, vague, violent, wild.

antonyms accurate, calm, harmonious, mild, polite, smooth, well.

n. boor, bruiser, bully, hooligan, keelie, lout, mock-up, model, outline, roughneck, rowdy, ruffian, sketch, thug, tough, yob, yobbo.

round *adj.* ample, annular, ball-shaped, blunt, bowed, bulbous, candid, circular, complete, curved, curvilinear, cylindrical, direct, discoid, disc-shaped, entire, fleshy, frank, full, full-fleshed, globular, mellifluous, orbed, orbicular, orby, orotund, outspoken, plain, plump, resonant, rich, ring-shaped, roly-poly, rotund, rotundate, rounded, solid, sonorous, spheral, spheric, spherical, spherular, sphery, straightforward, unbroken, undivided, unmodified, whole.

antonyms evasive, niggardly, partial, thin.

n. ambit, ball, band, beat, bout, bullet, cartridge, circle, circuit, compass, course, cycle, disc, discharge, division, globe, lap, level, orb, period, ring, routine, schedule, sequence, series, session, shell, shot, sphere, spheroid, spherule, stage, succession, tour, turn.

v. bypass, circle, circumnavigate, encircle, flank, sail round, skirt, turn.

roundabout *adj.* ambagious, circuitous, circumlocutory, devious, discursive, evasive, indirect, meandering, oblique, periphrastic, tortuous, twisting, winding.

antonyms direct, straight, straightforward.

roundly *adv.* bluntly, completely, fiercely, forcefully, frankly, intensely, openly, outspokenly, rigorously, severely, sharply, thoroughly, vehemently, violently.

antonym mildly.

rouse *v.* agitate, anger, animate, arouse, awaken, bestir, call, disturb, enkindle, excite, exhilarating, firk, flush, galvanize, incite, inflame, instigate, move, provoke, rise, start, startle, stimulate, stir, suscitate, unbed, wake, whip up.

antonym calm.

rousing *adj.* brisk, electrifying, excitant, excitative, excitatory, exciting, exhilarating, hypnopompic, inflammatory, inspiring, lively, moving, spirited, stimulating, stirring, vigorous.

antonym calming.

rout *n.* beating, brawl, clamor, crowd, debacle, defeat, disturbance, Donnybrook, drubbing, flight, fracas, fuss, herd, hiding, licking, mob, overthrow, pack, rabble, riot, rookery, ruffle, ruin, shambles, stampede, thrashing.

antonyms calm, win.

v. beat, best, chase, conquer, crush, defeat, destroy, discomfit, dispel, drub, hammer, lick, overthrow, scatter, thrash, worst.

route *n.* avenue, beat, circuit, course, direction, flight-path, itinerary, journey, passage, path, road, round, run, way.

v. convey, direct, dispatch, forward, send.

routine *n.* act, bit, custom, formula, grind, groove, heigh, jog-trot, line, method, order, pattern, performance, piece, practice, procedure, program, spiel, usage, way, wont.

adj. banal, boring, clichéd, conventional, customary, day-by-day, dull, everyday, familiar, habitual, hackneyed, humdrum, mundane, normal, ordinary, predictable, run-of-the-mill, standard, tedious, tiresome, typical, unimaginative, uninspired, unoriginal, usual, wonted, workaday.

antonyms exciting, unusual.

rover *n.* drifter, gadabout, gypsy, itinerant, nomad, rambler, ranger, stravaiger, transient, traveler, vagrant, wanderer.

antonym stay-at-home.

row[1] *n.* bank, colonnade, column, file, line, queue, range, rank, sequence, series, string, tier.

row[2] *n.* altercation, brawl, castigation, commotion, controversy, dispute, disturbance, Donnybrook, dressing-down, falling-out, fracas, fray, fuss, lecture, noise, quarrel, racket, rammy, reprimand, reproof, rhubarb, rollicking, rookery, rout, ruckus, ruction, ruffle, rumpus, scrap, shemozzle, shindig, shindy, slanging match, squabble, talking-to, telling-off, ticking-off, tiff, tongue-lashing, trouble, tumult, uproar.

antonym calm.

v. argue, argufy, brawl, dispute, fight, scrap, squabble, wrangle.

rowdy *adj.* boisterous, disorderly, loud, loutish, noisy, obstreperous, roisterous, roisting, rorty, rough, rumbustious, stroppy, unruly, uproarious, wild.

antonyms quiet, restrained.

n. brawler, hoodlum, hooligan, keelie, lout, rough, ruffian, tearaway, tough, yahoo, yob, yobbo.

royal *adj.* august, basilical, grand, imperial, impressive, kinglike, kingly, magnificent, majestic, monarchical, princely, queenlike, queenly, regal, sovereign, splendid, stately, superb, superior.

rub *v.* abrade, apply, caress, chafe, clean, embrocate, fray, grate, knead, malax, malaxate, massage, polish, put, scour, scrape, shine, smear, smooth, spread, stroke, wipe.

n. caress, catch, difficulty, drawback, hindrance, hitch, impediment, kneading, malaxage, malaxation, massage, obstacle, polish, problem, shine, snag, stroke, trouble, wipe.

rubbish *n.* balderdash, balls, baloney, bosh, bunkum, clamjamphrie, claptrap, cobblers, codswallop, crap, dead-wood, debris, draff, drivel, dross, flotsam and jetsam, garbage, gibberish, gobbledegook, guff, havers, hogwash, junk, kibosh, kitsch, landfill, leavings, litter, lumber, moonshine, mullock, nonsense, offal, offscourings, offscum, piffle, poppycock, raffle, refuse, riddlings, rot, scoria, scrap, stuff, sullage, sweepings, tommyrot, tosh, trash, trashery, truck, trumpery, twaddle, vomit, waste.

antonym sense.

ruddy *adj.* blooming, blushing, crimson, flammulated, florid, flushed, fresh, glowing, healthy, pink, red, reddish, roseate, rose-hued, rose-pink, rosy, rosy-cheeked, rubicund, rubineous, rubious, ruby, sanguine, scarlet, sunburnt.

antonyms pale, unhealthy.

rude *adj.* abrupt, abusive, artless, barbarous, blunt, boorish, brusque, brutish, cheeky, churlish, coarse, crude, curt, discourteous, disrespectful, graceless, gross, harsh, ignorant, illiterate, ill-mannered, impertinent, impolite, impudent, inartistic, inconsiderate, inelegant, insolent, insulting, loutish, low, makeshift, oafish, obscene, offhand, peremptory, primitive, raw, rough, savage, scurrilous, sharp, short, simple, startling, sudden, uncivil, uncivilized, uncouth, uncultured, uneducated, ungracious, unmannerly, unpleasant, unpolished, unrefined, untutored, violent, vulgar.

antonyms graceful, polished, polite, smooth.

rudimentary *adj.* abecedarian, basic, early, elementary, embryonic, fundamental, germinal, immature, inchoate, initial, introductory, primary, primitive, primordial, undeveloped, vestigial.

antonyms advanced, developed.

rue *v.* bemoan, bewail, beweep, deplore, grieve, lament, mourn, regret, repent.

antonym rejoice.

ruffian *n.* apache, bruiser, brute, bully, bully-boy, cutthroat, hoodlum, hooligan, keelie, lout, miscreant, Mohock, myrmidon, plug-ugly, rascal, rogue, rough, roughneck, rowdy, scoundrel, thug, tough, villain, yob, yobbo.

ruffle *v.* agitate, annoy, confuse, derange, disarrange, discompose, disconcert, dishevel, disorder, disquiet, disturb, fluster, harass, irritate, mess up, muss up, muss(e), nettle, peeve, perturb, rattle, rumple, stir, torment, tousle, trouble, unsettle, upset, vex, worry, wrinkle.

antonym smooth.

rugged *adj.* arduous, austere, barbarous, beefy, blunt, brawny, broken, bumpy, burly, churlish, crabbed, craggy, crude, demanding, difficult, dour, exacting, graceless, gruff, hale, hard, hard-featured, hardy, harsh, husky, irregular, jagged, laborious, muscular, ragged, rigorous, robust, rocky, rough, rude, severe, sour, stark, stern, strenuous, strong, sturdy, surly, taxing, tough, trying, uncompromising, uncouth, uncultured, uneven, unpolished, unrefined, vigorous, weather-beaten, weathered, worn.

antonyms easy, refined, smooth.

ruin *n.* bankruptcy, bouleversement, breakdown, collapse, crash, damage, decay, defeat, destitution, destruction, devastation, disintegration, disrepair, dissolution, downfall, failure, fall, havoc, heap, insolvency, nemesis, overthrow, ruination, subversion, undoing, Waterloo, wreck, wreckage.

antonyms development, reconstruction.

v. banjax, bankrupt, botch, break, crush, damage, defeat, demolish, destroy, devastate, disfigure, impoverish, injure, jigger, mangle, mar, mess up, overthrow, overturn, overwhelm, pauperize, raze, scupper, scuttle, shatter, smash, spoil, unmake, unshape, wreck.

antonyms develop, restore.

ruinous *adj.* baleful, baneful, broken-down, calamitous, cataclysmic, catastrophic, crippling, deadly, decrepit, deleterious, derelict, destructive, devastating, dilapidated, dire, disastrous, extravagant, fatal, immoderate, injurious, murderous, noxious, pernicious, ramshackle, ruined, shattering, wasteful, withering.

antonym beneficial.

rule *n.* administration, ascendancy, authority, axiom, canon, command, condition, control, convention, course, criterion, custom, decree, direction, domination, dominion, empire, form, formula, governance, government, guide, guideline, habit, influence, institute, jurisdiction, law, leadership, mastery, maxim, method, order, ordinance, policy, power, practice, precept, prescript, principle, procedure, raj, regime, regulation, reign, routine, ruling, standard, supremacy, sway, tenet, way, wont.

v. adjudge, adjudicate, administer, command, control, decide, decree, determine, direct, dominate, establish, find, govern, guide, judge, lead, manage, obtain, predominate, preponderate, prevail, pronounce, regulate, reign, resolve, settle.

ruler *n.* commander, controller, emperor, empress, gerent, governor, gubernator, head of state, imperator, king, leader, lord, monarch, potentate, prince, princess, queen, sovereign, suzerain.

antonym subject.

ruling *n.* adjudication, decision, decree, finding, indiction, interlocution, irade, judgment, pronouncement, resolution, ukase, verdict.

adj. boss, chief, commanding, controlling, dominant, governing, leading, main, predominant, pre-eminent, preponderant, prevailing, prevalent, principal, regnant, reigning, supreme, upper.

ruminate *v.* brood, chew over, chew the cud, cogitate, consider, contemplate, deliberate, meditate, mull over, muse, ponder, reflect, revolve, think.

rummage *v.* delve, examine, explore, hunt, poke around, ransack, root, rootle, rout, search.

rumor *n.* breeze, bruit, bush telegraph, buzz, canard, fame, gossip, grapevine, hearsay, kite, news, on-dit, report, story, talk, tidings, underbreath, whisper, word.

v. bruit, circulate, gossip, publish, put about, report, say, tell, whisper.

rumple *v.* crease, crinkle, crumple, crush, derange, dishevel, disorder, muss up, muss(e), pucker, ruffle, scrunch, tousle, wrinkle.

antonym smooth.

rumpus *n.* bagarre, barney, brouhaha, commotion, confusion, disruption, disturbance, Donnybrook, fracas, furore, fuss, kerfuffle, noise, rhubarb, rookery, rout, row, ruction, shemozzle, shindig, shindy, tumult, uproar.

antonym calm.

run *v.* abscond, administer, bear, beat it, bleed, bolt, boss, career, carry, cascade, challenge, circulate, clear out, climb, compete, conduct, contend, continue, control, convey, co-ordinate, course, creep, dart, dash, decamp, depart, direct, discharge, display, dissolve, drive to, escape, extend, feature, flee, flow, function, fuse, gallop, glide, go, gush, hare, hasten, head, hie, hotfoot, hurry, issue, jog, ladder, last, lead, leak, lie, liquefy, lope, manage, maneuver, mastermind, melt, mix, move, operate, oversee, own, pass, perform, ply, pour, print, proceed, propel, publish, race, range, reach, regulate, roll, rush, scamper, scarper, scramble, scud, scurry, skedaddle, skim, slide, speed, spill, spout, spread, sprint, stand, stream, stretch, superintend, supervise, tear, tick, trail, transport, unravel, work.

antonyms stay, stop.

n. application, category, chain, class, coop, course, current, cycle, dash, demand, direction, drift, drive, enclosure, excursion, flow, gallop, jaunt, jog, journey, joy, kind, ladder, lift, motion, movement, order, outing, passage, path, pen, period, pressure, progress, race, ride, rip, round, rush, season, sequence, series, snag, sort, spell, spin, sprint, spurt, streak, stream, stretch, string, tear, tendency, tenor, tide, trend, trip, type, variety, way.

runaway *n.* absconder, deserter, escapee, escaper, fleer, fugitive, refugee, truant.

adj. escaped, fleeing, fugitive, loose, uncontrolled, wild.

rundown *n.* briefing, cut, decrease, drop, lessening, outline, précis, recap, reduction, résumé, review, runthrough, sketch, summary, synopsis.

run-down *adj.* broken-down, debilitated, decrepit, dilapidated, dingy, drained, enervated, exhausted, fatigued, grotty, peaky, ramshackle, scabby, seedy, shabby, tumble-down, unhealthy, weak, weary, worn-out.

antonym well-kept.

rupture *n.* altercation, breach, break, breaking, burst, bust-up, cleavage, cleft, contention, crack, disagreement, disruption, dissolution, estrangement, falling-out, feud, fissure, fracture, hernia, hostility, quarrel, rent, rift, schism, split, splitting, tear.

v. break, burst, cleave, crack, disrupt, dissever, divide, fracture, puncture, rend, separate, sever, split, sunder, tear.

rural *adj.* agrarian, agrestic, agricultural, Arcadian, bucolic, countrified, country, forane, pastoral, predial, rustic, sylvan, yokelish.

antonym urban.

ruse *n.* artifice, blind, deception, device, dodge, hoax, imposture, maneuver, ploy, sham, stall, stratagem, subterfuge, trick, wile.

rush *v.* accelerate, attack, bolt, capture, career, charge, dart, dash, dispatch, expedite, fly, hasten, hightail it, hotfoot, hurry, hustle, overcome, press, push, quicken, race, run, scour, scramble, scurry, shoot, speed, speed up, sprint, stampede, storm, tear, wallop, w(h)oosh.

n. assault, charge, dash, dispatch, expedition, flow, haste, hurry, onslaught, push, race, scramble, speed, stampede, storm, streak, surge, swiftness, tantivy, tear, urgency.

adj. brisk, careless, cursory, emergency, expeditious, fast, hasty, hurried, prompt, quick, rapid, superficial, swift, urgent.

S

sabotage *v.* cripple, damage, destroy, disable, disrupt, incapacitate, mar, nullify, ratten, scupper, subvert, thwart, undermine, vandalize, vitiate, wreck.

n. damage, destruction, disablement, disruption, impairment, marring, rattening, subversion, treachery, treason, undermining, vandalism, vitiation, wrecking.

sack[1] *v.* axe, discharge, dismiss, fire, lay off, make redundant.

n. discharge, dismissal, notice, one's books, one's cards, one's marching orders, the ax, the boot, the bum's rush, the chop, the elbow, the push.

sack² *v.* demolish, depredate, desecrate, despoil, destroy, devastate, lay waste, level, loot, maraud, pillage, plunder, raid, rape, ravage, raze, rifle, rob, ruin, spoil, strip, waste.

n. depredation, desecration, despoliation, destruction, devastation, leveling, looting, marauding, pillage, plunder, plundering, rape, rapine, ravage, razing, ruin, waste.

sacred *adj.* blessed, consecrated, dedicated, devotional, divine, ecclesiastical, godly, hallowed, heavenly, holy, inviolable, inviolate, invulnerable, priestly, protected, religious, revered, sacrosanct, saintly, sanctified, secure, solemn, venerable, venerated.

antonyms mundane, profane, temporal.

sad *adj.* bad, blue, calamitous, cheerless, chopfallen, crestfallen, crushed, dark, dejected, deplorable, depressed, depressing, desolated, despondent, disastrous, disconsolate, dismal, dispirited, distressed, distressing, doleful, dolesome, doloriferous, dolorific, doughy, dour, dowie, downcast, down-hearted, drear, dreary, gloomy, glum, grave, grief-stricken, grieved, grieving, grievous, heart-rending, heavy, heavy-hearted, jaw-fallen, joyless, lachrymose, lamentable, long-faced, low, low-spirited, lugubrious, melancholy, miserable, mournful, moving, painful, pathetic, pensive, piteous, pitiable, pitiful, poignant, regrettable, serious, shabby, sober, sober-minded, somber, sorrowful, sorry, sportless, stiff, tearful, touching, tragic, triste, uncheerful, unfortunate, unhappy, unsatisfactory, upsetting, wan, wistful, woebegone, woeful, wretched.

antonyms cheerful, fortunate, happy, lucky.

safe *adj.* alive and well, all right, cautious, certain, circumspect, conservative, dependable, discreet, foolproof, guarded, hale, harmless, immune, impregnable, innocuous, intact, invulnerable, non-poisonous, nontoxic, OK, out of harm's way, protected, proven, prudent, pure, realistic, reliable, scatheless, secure, sound, sure, tame, tested, tried, trustworthy, unadventurous, uncontaminated, undamaged, unfailing, unharmed, unhurt, uninjured, unscathed, wholesome.

antonyms exposed, harmful, unsafe, vulnerable.

n. cash-box, chest, coffer, deposit box, peter, repository, strongbox, vault.

safeguard *v.* assure, defend, guard, insure, preserve, protect, screen, secure, shelter, shield.

antonyms endanger, jeopardize.

n. armor, assurance, bulwark, convoy, cover, defense, escort, guarantee, guard, insurance, long-stop, Palladium, precaution, preventive, protection, security, shield, surety.

sag *v.* bag, decline, dip, drag, droop, drop, dwindle, fail, fall, flag, give, give way, hang, settle, sink, slide, slip, slump, wane, weaken, wilt.

antonyms bulge, rise.

n. decline, depression, dip, downturn, drop, dwindling, fall, low, low point, reduction, slide, slip, slump.

antonyms peak, rise.

sagacity *n.* acumen, acuteness, astuteness, canniness, discernment, foresight, insight, judgment, judiciousness, knowingness, penetration, percipience, perspicacity, prudence, sapience, sense, sharpness, shrewdness, understanding, wariness, wiliness, wisdom.

antonyms folly, foolishness, obtuseness.

sage *adj.* astute, canny, discerning, intelligent, judicious, knowing, knowledgeable, learned, perspicacious, politic, prudent, sagacious, sapient, sensible, wise.

antonym foolish.

n. authority, elder, expert, guru, hakam, maharishi, mahatma, master, Nestor, oracle, philosopher, pundit, rishi, savant, Solomon, Solon, teacher, wise man.

antonym ignoramus.

saintly *adj.* angelic, beatific, blameless, blessed, blest, celestial, devout, god-fearing, godly, holy, immaculate, innocent, pious, pure, religious, righteous, sainted, saintlike, seraphic, sinless, spotless, stainless, upright, virtuous, worthy.

antonyms godless, unholy, unrighteous, wicked.

sake *n.* account, advantage, aim, behalf, benefit, cause, consideration, end, gain, good, interest, motive, object, objective, principle, profit, purpose, reason, regard, respect, score, welfare, wellbeing.

salary *n.* earnings, emolument, honorarium, income, pay, remuneration, screw, stipend, wage, wages.

salient *adj.* arresting, chief, conspicuous, important, jutting, main, marked, noticeable, obvious, outstanding, principal, projecting, prominent, pronounced, protruding, remarkable, signal, significant, striking.

salubrious *adj.* beneficial, bracing, healthful, health-giving, healthy, hygienic, invigorating, refreshing, restorative, salutary, sanitary, wholesome.

antonyms insalubrious, unwholesome.

salutary *adj.* advantageous, beneficial, good, healthful, healthy, helpful, much-needed, practical, profitable, salubrious, seasonable, timely, useful, valuable, wholesome.

salute *v.* accost, acknowledge, address, bow, greet, hail, honor, kiss, knuckle, nod, recognize, salaam, wave, welcome.

n. acknowledgment, address, bow, gesture, greeting, hail, handclap, handshake, hello, kiss, nod, obeisance, recognition, reverence, salaam, salutation, salve, salvo, tribute, wave.

salvage *v.* conserve, glean, preserve, reclaim, recover, recuperate, redeem, repair, rescue, restore, retrieve, salve, save.

antonyms abandon, lose, waste.

salvation *n.* deliverance, escape, liberation, lifeline, preservation, reclamation, redemption, rescue, restoration, retrieval, safety, saving, soteriology.

antonyms damnation, loss.

same *adj.* aforementioned, aforesaid, alike, analogous, changeless, comparable, consistent, corresponding, duplicate, equal, equivalent, homologous, identical, indistinguishable, interchangeable, invariable, matching, mutual, reciprocal, selfsame, similar, substitutable, synonymous, twin, unaltered, unchanged, undiminished, unfailing, uniform, unvarying, very.

antonyms changeable, different, incompatible, inconsistent, variable.

n. ditto, the above-mentioned, the above-named, the aforementioned, the aforesaid.

sample *n.* cross-section, demonstration, ensample, example, exemplification, foretaste, free sample, freebie, illustration, indication, instance, model, pattern, representative, sign, specimen, swatch.

v. experience, inspect, investigate, pree, sip, taste, test, try.

adj. demonstration, illustrative, pilot, representative, specimen, test, trial.

sanction *n.* accreditation, agreement, allowance, approbation, approval, authorization, authority, backing, cachet, confirmation, countenance, endorsement, go-ahead, green light, imprimatur, license, OK, permission, ratification, seal, support.
antonyms disapproval, veto.
v. accredit, allow, approve, authorize, back, confirm, countenance, countersign, endorse, fiat, license, permit, ratify, support, underwrite, warrant.
antonyms disallow, disapprove, veto.

sanctuary *n.* adytum, altar, ark, asylum, chancel, church, delubrum, frith, grith, harborage, haven, holy of holies, naos, presbytery, protection, refuge, retreat, sacrarium, sanctum, sanctum sanctorum, seclusion, shelter, shrine, tabernacle, temple.

sane *adj.* all there, balanced, compos mentis, dependable, judicious, level-headed, lucid, moderate, normal, rational, reasonable, reliable, right-minded, sensible, sober, sound, stable.

sanguinary *adj.* bloodied, bloodthirsty, bloody, brutal, cruel, fell, gory, grim, merciless, murderous, pitiless, ruthless, savage.

sanguine[1] *adj.* animated, ardent, assured, buoyant, cheerful, confident, expectant, hopeful, lively, optimistic, over-confident, over-optimistic, Panglossian, roseate, spirited, unabashed, unappalled, unbowed.
antonyms cynical, depressive, gloomy, melancholy, pessimistic, realistic.

sanguine[2] *adj.* florid, flushed, fresh, fresh-complexioned, pink, red, rosy, rubicund, ruddy.
antonyms pale, sallow.

sanitary *adj.* aseptic, clean, disinfected, germ-free, healthy, hygienic, pure, salubrious, uncontaminated, unpolluted, wholesome.
antonyms insanitary, unwholesome.

sap *v.* bleed, deplete, devitalize, diminish, drain, enervate, exhaust, impair, reduce, rob, undermine, weaken.
antonyms build up, increase, strengthen.

sarcastic *adj.* acerbic, acid, acrimonious, biting, caustic, contemptuous, cutting, cynical, derisive, disparaging, incisive, ironical, mocking, mordant, sardonic, sarky, satirical, scathing, sharp, sharp-tongued, sneering, taunting, withering.

sardonic *adj.* biting, bitter, cynical, derisive, dry, heartless, ironical, jeering, malevolent, malicious, malignant, mocking, mordant, quizzical, sarcastic, satirical, scornful, sneering, wry.

satanic *adj.* accursed, black, demoniac, demoniacal, demonic, devilish, diabolic, diabolical, evil, fell, fiendish, hellish, infernal, inhuman, iniquitous, malevolent, malignant, Mephistophelian, satanical, wicked.
antonyms benevolent, benign, divine, godlike, godly, heavenly, holy.

sate *v.* cloy, fill, glut, gorge, gratify, overfill, satiate, satisfy, saturate, sicken, slake, surfeit, weary.
antonyms deprive, dissatisfy, starve.

satiate *v.* cloy, engorge, glut, gorge, jade, nauseate, overfeed, overfill, sate, satisfy, slake, stuff, surfeit.
antonyms deprive, dissatisfy, underfeed.

satire *n.* burlesque, caricature, diatribe, invective, irony, lampoon, parody, Pasquil, Pasquin, pasquinade, raillery, ridicule, sarcasm, send-up, skit, spoof, squib, takeoff, travesty, wit.

satirical *adj.* biting, bitter, burlesque, caustic, cutting, cynical, derisive, Hudibrastic, iambic, incisive, ironical, irreverent, mocking, mordant, pungent, sarcastic, sardonic, satiric, taunting.

satisfaction *n.* achievement, amends, appeasing, assuaging, atonement, comfort, compensation, complacency, content, contentedness, contentment, conviction, damages, ease, enjoyment, fulfilment, fullness, gratification, guerdon, happiness, indemnification, justice, payment, pleasure, pride, quittance, recompense, redress, reimbursement, remuneration, reparation, repleteness, repletion, requital, resolution, restitution, reward, satiety, self-satisfaction, sense of achievement, settlement, vindication, well-being.
antonyms discontent, displeasure, dissatisfaction, frustration.

satisfactory *adj.* acceptable, adequate, all right, average, competent, fair, fit, OK, passable, proper, sufficient, suitable, tickety-boo, up to the mark.
antonyms inadequate, unacceptable, unsatisfactory.

satisfy *v.* answer, appease, assuage, assure, atone, compensate, content, convince, delight, discharge, do, fill, fulfil, glut, gratify, guerdon, indemnify, indulge, meet, mollify, pacify, pay, persuade, placate, please, qualify, quench, quiet, reassure, recompense, reimburse, remunerate, replete, requite, reward, sate, satiate, serve, settle, slake, square up, suffice, surfeit.
antonyms disappoint, dissatisfy, fail, frustrate, thwart.

saturate *v.* douse, drench, drouk, imbue, impregnate, infuse, permeate, ret, soak, souse, steep, suffuse, waterlog.

saucy *adj.* arch, audacious, cheeky, dashing, disdainful, disrespectful, flip, flippant, forward, fresh, gay, impertinent, impudent, insolent, irreverent, jaunty, lippy, malapert, natty, perky, pert, presumptuous, provocative, rakish, rude, sassy, sporty.
antonyms polite, respectful.

savage *adj.* barbarous, beastly, bestial, blistering, bloodthirsty, bloody, brutal, brutish, catamountain, cruel, devilish, diabolical, dog-eat-dog, fell, feral, ferocious, fierce, harsh, immane, inhuman, merciless, murderous, pitiless, primitive, ravening, rough, rude, rugged, ruthless, sadistic, sanguinary, uncivilized, uncultivated, undomesticated, uneducated, unenlightened, unsparing, untamed, untaught, vicious, wild.
antonyms benign, civilized, humane.
n. aboriginal, aborigine, ape, autochthon, barbarian, bear, beast, boor, brute, fiend, heathen, illiterate, indigene, lout, monster, native, oaf, philistine, primitive, roughneck, yahoo, yobbo.
v. attack, claw, hammer, lacerate, mangle, maul, pan, scarify, tear.

save *v.* cache, collect, conserve, cut back, deliver, economize, free, gather, guard, hinder, hoard, hold, husband, keep, lay up, liberate, obviate, preserve, prevent, protect, put aside, put by, reclaim, recover, redeem, rescue, reserve, retain, retrench, safeguard, salt away, salvage, screen, shield, spare, squirrel, stash, store.
antonyms discard, spend, squander, waste.

savory *adj.* agreeable, appetizing, aromatic, dainty, decent, delectable, delicious, edifying, full-flavored, gamy, good, gusty, honest, luscious, mouthwatering, palatable, piquant, reputable, respectable, rich, salubrious, scrumptious, spicy, tangy, tasty, toothsome, wholesome.

antonyms insipid, tasteless, unappetizing.

n. appetizer, bonne bouche, canapé, hors d'oeuvre.

say *v.* add, affirm, allege, announce, answer, assert, assume, bruit, claim, comment, communicate, conjecture, convey, declare, deliver, disclose, divulge, do, enunciate, estimate, express, guess, imagine, imply, intimate, judge, maintain, mention, opine, orate, perform, presume, pronounce, read, recite, reckon, rehearse, rejoin, remark, render, repeat, reply, report, respond, retort, reveal, rumor, signify, speak, state, suggest, surmise, tell, utter, voice.

n. authority, chance, clout, crack, go, influence, power, sway, turn, voice, vote, weight, word.

saying *n.* adage, aphorism, apophthegm, axiom, byword, dictum, gnome, maxim, mot, motto, precept, proverb, remnant, saw, slogan.

scald *v.* blister, burn, sear.

scale[1] *n.* calibration, compass, continuum, degree, degrees, extent, gamut, gradation, grading, graduation, hierarchy, ladder, measure, order, progression, proportion, range, ranking, ratio, reach, register, scope, sequence, series, spectrum, spread, steps.

v. adjust, level, move, proportion, prorate, regulate, shift.

scale[2] *n.* crust, encrustation, film, flake, furfur, lamella, lamina, layer, plate, scutellum, shield, squama, squamella, squamula, squamule.

v. clean, desquamate, exfoliate, flake, peel, scrape.

scale[3] *v.* ascend, clamber, climb, escalade, mount, scramble, shin up, surmount, swarm.

scamp *n.* blighter, caitiff, devil, fripon, imp, knave, mischief-maker, monkey, prankster, rascal, rogue, ruffian, scallywag, scapegrace, tyke, whippersnapper, wretch.

scan *v.* check, con, examine, glance through, investigate, pan, pan over, scrutinize, search, skim, survey, sweep.

n. check, examination, investigation, probe, review, screening, scrutiny, search, survey.

scandal *n.* abuse, aspersion, backbiting, calumniation, calumny, crime, defamation, detraction, dirt, discredit, disgrace, dishonor, embarrassment, enormity, evil, furore, gossip, gossiping, ignominy, infamy, muckraking, obloquy, odium, offense, opprobrium, outcry, outrage, reproach, rumors, shame, sin, slander, stigma, talk, tattle, traducement, uproar, Watergate, wrongdoing.

scandalize *v.* affront, appal, astound, disgust, dismay, horrify, nauseate, offend, outrage, repel, revolt, shock, sicken.

scandalous *adj.* abominable, atrocious, calumnious, defamatory, disgraceful, disreputable, evil, exorbitant, extortionate, gamy, gossiping, immoderate, improper, infamous, libelous, monstrous, odious, opprobrious, outrageous, scurrilous, shameful, shocking, slanderous, unseemly, unspeakable, untrue.

scant *adj.* bare, deficient, hardly any, inadequate, insufficient, limited, little, little or no, minimal, sparse.

antonyms adequate, ample, sufficient.

scanty *adj.* bare, beggarly, deficient, exiguous, inadequate, insubstantial, insufficient, light, meager, narrow, parsimonious, poor, restricted, scant, scrimp,

scrimpy, short, shy, skimped, skimpy, slender, sparing, sparse, thin.

antonyms ample, plentiful, substantial.

scarce *adj.* deficient, few, infrequent, insufficient, lacking, rare, scanty, sparse, thin on the ground, uncommon, unusual, wanting.

antonyms common, copious, plentiful.

scarcely *adv.* barely, hardly, just and no more, not readily, not willingly, only just, scarce.

scarcity *n.* dearth, deficiency, infrequency, insufficiency, lack, niggardliness, paucity, poverty, rareness, rarity, scantiness, shortage, sparseness, uncommonness, want.

antonyms abundance, enough, glut, plenty, sufficiency.

scare *v.* affright, alarm, appal, daunt, dismay, frighten, gally, intimidate, panic, shock, startle, terrify, terrorize, unnerve.

antonym reassure.

n. agitation, alarm, alarm and despondency, alert, consternation, dismay, fright, hysteria, panic, shock, start, terror.

antonym reassurance.

scared *adj.* affrighted, affrightened, agitated, anxious, appalled, dismayed, fearful, frightened, nervous, panicky, panic-stricken, petrified, shaken, startled, terrified, worried.

antonyms confident, reassured.

scarf *n.* babushka, boa, cravat, fichu, headscarf, headsquare, kerchief, muffler, neckerchief, necktie, shawl, stole, tawdry-lace.

scatter *v.* bestrew, break up, broadcast, diffuse, disband, disintegrate, disject, dispel, disperse, disseminate, dissipate, disunite, divide, fling, flurr, litter, propagate, separate, shower, sow, spatter, splutter, spread, sprinkle, squander, strew.

antonyms collect, concentrate.

scene *n.* act, area, arena, backdrop, background, business, carry-on, chapter, circumstances, commotion, confrontation, display, disturbance, division, drama, environment, episode, exhibition, focus, fuss, incident, landscape, locale, locality, location, melodrama, milieu, mise en scène, outburst, pageant, panorama, part, performance, picture, place, position, prospect, representation, row, set, setting, show, sight, site, situation, spectacle, spot, stage, tableau, tantrum, to-do, upset, view, vista, whereabouts, world.

scent *n.* aroma, bouquet, fragrance, fumet, odor, perfume, redolence, smell, spoor, trace, track, trail, waft, whiff.

antonym stink.

v. detect, discern, nose, nose out, perceive, recognize, sense, smell, sniff, sniff out.

schedule *n.* agenda, calendar, catalog, diary, form, inventory, itinerary, list, plan, program, scheme, scroll, table, timetable.

v. appoint, arrange, book, list, organize, plan, program, slot, table, time.

scheme *n.* arrangement, blueprint, chart, codification, configuration, conformation, conspiracy, contrivance, dart, design, device, diagram, disposition, dodge, draft, game, idea, intrigue, lay-out, machinations, maneuver, method, outline, pattern, plan, plot, ploy, procedure, program, project, proposal, proposition, racket, ruse, schedule, schema, shape, shift, stratagem, strategy, subterfuge, suggestion, system, tactics, theory.

v. collude, conspire, contrive, design, devise, frame, imagine, intrigue, machinate, manipulate, maneuver, mastermind, plan, plot, project, pull strings, pull wires, work out.

scheming *adj.* artful, calculating, conniving, crafty, cunning, deceitful, designing, devious, duplicitous, foxy, insidious, Machiavellian, slippery, sly, tricky, underhand, unscrupulous, wily.

antonyms artless, honest, open, transparent.

scholar *n.* academe, academic, authority, bookman, bookworm, egghead, intellectual, man of letters, pupil, savant, scholastic, schoolboy, schoolchild, schoolgirl, schoolman, student.

antonyms dullard, dunce, ignoramus, illiterate, philistine.

scholarly *adj.* academic, analytical, bookish, clerk-like, clerkly, conscientious, critical, erudite, intellectual, knowledgeable, learned, lettered, scholastic, scientific, studious, well-read, wissenschaftlich.

antonyms illiterate, unscholarly.

scholarship[1] *n.* attainments, book-learning, education, erudition, insight, knowledge, learnedness, learning, lore, scholarliness, wisdom, Wissenschaft.

scholarship[2] *n.* award, bursary, endowment, exhibition, fellowship, grant.

science *n.* art, discipline, knowledge, ology, proficiency, skill, specialization, technique, technology, Wissenschaft.

scoff[1] *v.* belittle, deride, despise, fleer, flout, geck, gibe, jeer, knock, mock, poke fun, pooh-pooh, rail, revile, rib, ridicule, scorn, sneer, taunt, twit.

antonyms compliment, flatter, praise.

scoff[2] *v.* bolt, consume, cram, devour, fill one's face, gobble, gulp, guzzle, pig, put away, shift, wolf.

antonym abstain.

n. chow, comestibles, commons, eatables, eats, edibles, fare, feed, fodder, food, grub, meal, nosh, nosh-up, provisions, rations, scran, tuck, victuals.

scold *v.* admonish, bawl out, berate, blame, castigate, censure, chide, find fault with, flyte, jaw, lecture, nag, rate, rebuke, remonstrate, reprimand, reproach, reprove, take to task, tell off, tick off, upbraid, vituperate, wig.

antonyms commend, praise.

n. battle-ax, beldam, fishwife, Fury, harridan, nag, shrew, termagant, virago, vixen, Xanthippe.

scope *n.* ambit, application, area, breadth, capacity, compass, competence, confines, coverage, elbow-room, extent, freedom, latitude, liberty, opportunity, orbit, outlook, purview, range, reach, remit, room, space, span, sphere, terms of reference, tessitura.

scorch *v.* blacken, blister, burn, char, parch, roast, scald, sear, shrivel, singe, sizzle, torrefy, wither.

score *n.* a bone to pick, account, amount, basis, bill, cause, charge, debt, due, gash, grade, gravamen, grievance, ground, grounds, grudge, injury, injustice, line, mark, notch, obligation, outcome, points, reason, reckoning, record, result, scratch, sum total, tab, tally, total, wrong.

v. achieve, adapt, amass, arrange, attain, be one up, benefit, chalk up, count, cut, deface, earn, engrave, furrow, gain, gouge, grave, graze, groove, hatch, have the advantage, have the edge, impress, incise, indent, knock up, make, make a hit, mark, nick, notch, notch up, orchestrate, profit, realize, record, register, scrape, scratch, set, slash, tally, total, win.

scorn *n.* contempt, contemptuousness, contumely, derision, despite, disdain, disgust, dismissiveness, disparagement, geck, mockery, sarcasm, scornfulness, slight, sneer.

antonyms admiration, respect.

v. contemn, deride, despise, disdain, dismiss, flout, hold in contempt, laugh at, laugh in the face of, look down on, misprize, pooh-pooh, refuse, reject, scoff at, slight, sneer at, spurn.

antonyms admire, respect.

scornful *adj.* arrogant, contemptuous, contumelious, defiant, derisive, disdainful, dismissive, disparaging, haughty, insulting, jeering, mocking, sarcastic, sardonic, scathing, scoffing, slighting, sneering, supercilious, withering.

antonyms admiring, complimentary, respectful.

scoundrel *n.* blackguard, blighter, bounder, caitiff, cheat, cur, dastard, good-for-nothing, heel, hound, knave, louse, miscreant, ne'er-do-well, picaroon, rascal, rat, reprobate, rogue, rotter, ruffian, scab, scallywag, scamp, scapegrace, stinker, swine, vagabond, villain.

scour[1] *v.* abrade, buff, burnish, clean, cleanse, flush, furbish, polish, purge, rub, scrape, scrub, wash, whiten.

scour[2] *v.* beat, comb, drag, forage, go over, hunt, rake, ransack, search, turn upside-down.

scourge *n.* affliction, bane, cat, cat-o'-nine-tails, curse, evil, flagellum, infliction, knout, lash, menace, misfortune, penalty, pest, pestilence, plague, punishment, strap, switch, terror, thong, torment, visitation, whip.

antonyms benefit, blessing, boon, godsend.

v. afflict, beat, belt, cane, castigate, chastize, curse, devastate, discipline, excoriate, flagellate, flail, flog, harass, horsewhip, lambaste, lash, lather, leather, plague, punish, tan, terrorize, thrash, torment, trounce, verberate, visit, wallop, whale, whip.

scowl *v.* frown, glare, glower, grimace, lower.

n. frown, glare, glower, grimace, moue.

antonyms beam, grin, smile.

scramble *v.* clamber, climb, contend, crawl, hasten, jostle, jumble, push, run, rush, scale, scrabble, shuffle, sprawl, strive, struggle, swarm, vie.

n. climb, commotion, competition, confusion, contention, free-for-all, hustle, mêlée, muddle, race, rat race, rivalry, rush, strife, struggle, trek, trial, tussle.

scrap[1] *n.* atom, bit, bite, crumb, fraction, fragment, grain, iota, junk, mite, modicum, morsel, mouthful, part, particle, piece, portion, remnant, shard, shred, sliver, snap, snatch, snippet, trace, vestige, waste, whit.

v. abandon, ax, break up, cancel, chuck, demolish, discard, ditch, drop, jettison, junk, shed, throw out, write off.

antonyms reinstate, restore, resume.

scrap[2] *n.* argument, bagarre, barney, battle, brawl, disagreement, dispute, dust-up, fight, quarrel, row, ruckus, ruction, rumpus, scuffle, set-to, shindy, squabble, tiff, wrangle.

antonyms agreement, peace.

v. argue, argufy, bicker, clash, fall out, fight, spat, squabble, wrangle.

antonym agree.

scrape *v.* abrade, bark, claw, clean, erase, file, grate, graze, grind, pinch, rasp, remove, rub, save, scour, scrabble, scratch, screech, scrimp, scuff, skimp, skin, squeak, stint.

n. abrasion, difficulty, dilemma, distress, fix, graze, mess, pickle, plight, predicament, pretty kettle of fish, rub, scratch, scuff, shave, spot, trouble.

scratch *v.* annul, cancel, claw, curry, cut, damage, delete, eliminate, erase, etch, grate, graze, incise, lacerate, mark, race, retire, rub, scarify, score, scrab, scrabble, scrape, withdraw.

n. blemish, claw mark, gash, graze, laceration, mark, race, scrape, streak.

adj. haphazard, impromptu, improvised, rough, rough-and-ready, unrehearsed.

antonym polished.

scrawny *adj.* angular, bony, emaciated, gaunt, lanky, lean, rawboned, scraggy, skeletal, skinny, thin, underfed, under-nourished.

antonym plump.

scream[1] *v.* bawl, clash, cry, holler, jar, roar, screak, screech, shriek, shrill, squeal, wail, yell, yelp, yowl.

n. howl, outcry, roar, screak, screech, shriek, squeal, wail, yell, yelp, yowl.

antonym whisper.

scream[2] *n.* card, caution, character, comedian, comic, cure, hoot, joker, laugh, riot, sensation, wit.

antonym bore.

screech *v.* cry, screak, scream, shriek, squawk, squeal, ululate, yelp.

antonym whisper.

screen *v.* broadcast, cloak, conceal, cover, cull, defend, evaluate, examine, filter, gauge, grade, guard, hide, mask, present, process, protect, riddle, safeguard, scan, shade, shelter, shield, show, shroud, sieve, sift, sort, veil, vet.

n. abat-jour, awning, canopy, cloak, concealment, cover, divider, guard, hallan, hedge, hoarding, mantle, mesh, net, partition, shade, shelter, shield, shroud, uncover.

scrimp *v.* curtail, economize, limit, pinch, reduce, restrict, save, scrape, shorten, skimp, stint.

antonym spend.

script *n.* book, calligraphy, cheirography, copy, hand, handwriting, letters, libretto, lines, longhand, manuscript, penmanship, text, words, writing.

scrounge *v.* beg, bludge, bum, cadge, freeload, purloin, sponge, wheedle.

scrub *v.* abandon, abolish, cancel, clean, cleanse, delete, discontinue, ditch, drop, forget, give up, rub, scour.

scrupulous *adj.* careful, conscientious, conscionable, exact, fastidious, honorable, meticulous, minute, moral, nice, painstaking, precise, principled, punctilious, rigorous, strict, upright.

antonym careless.

scrutinize *v.* analyze, dissect, examine, explore, give a once-over, inspect, investigate, peruse, probe, scan, search, sift, study.

scurrilous *adj.* abusive, coarse, defamatory, Fescennial, foul, foul-mouthed, gross, indecent, insulting, low, nasty, obscene, offensive, Rabelaisian, ribald, rude, salacious, scabrous, scandalous, slanderous, vituperative, vulgar.

antonym polite.

scurry *v.* dart, dash, fly, hurry, race, scamper, scoot,

scud, scuttle, skedaddle, skelter, skim, sprint, trot, whisk.

antonym stroll.

n. flurry, hustle and bustle, scampering, whirl.

antonym calm.

scuttle *v.* bustle, hare, hasten, hurry, run, rush, scamper, scoot, scramble, scud, scurry, scutter, trot.

antonym stroll.

seal *v.* assure, attest, authenticate, bung, clinch, close, conclude, confirm, consummate, cork, enclose, establish, fasten, finalize, plug, ratify, secure, settle, shake hands on, shut, stamp, stop, stopper, validate, waterproof.

antonym unseal.

n. assurance, attestation, authentication, bulla, confirmation, imprimatur, insignia, notification, ratification, sigil, signet, stamp.

search *v.* check, comb, examine, explore, ferret, frisk, inquire, inspect, investigate, jerque, look, probe, pry, quest, ransack, rifle, rummage, scour, scrutinize, sift, test.

n. examination, exploration, going-over, hunt, inquiry, inspection, investigation, perquisition, perscrutation, pursuit, quest, researches, rummage, scrutiny, zetetic.

searching *adj.* close, intent, keen, minute, penetrating, piercing, probing, quizzical, severe, sharp, thorough, zetetic.

antonyms superficial, vague.

season *n.* division, interval, period, span, spell, term, time.

v. acclimatize, accustom, anneal, color, condiment, condition, discipline, enliven, flavor, habituate, harden, imbue, inure, lace, leaven, mature, mitigate, moderate, prepare, qualify, salt, spice, temper, toughen, train.

seasoned *adj.* acclimatized, battle-scarred, experienced, hardened, long-serving, mature, old, practiced, time-served, veteran, weathered, well-versed.

antonym novice.

secede *v.* apostatize, disaffiliate, leave, quit, resign, retire, separate, split off, withdraw.

antonyms join, unite with.

secluded *adj.* claustral, cloistered, cloistral, cut off, isolated, lonely, out-of-the-way, private, reclusive, remote, retired, sequestered, sheltered, solitary, umbratile, umbratilous, unfrequented.

antonyms busy, public.

seclusion *n.* concealment, hiding, isolation, privacy, purdah, recluseness, remoteness, retirement, retreat, shelter, solitude.

secondary *adj.* alternate, auxiliary, back-up, consequential, contingent, derivative, derived, extra, indirect, inferior, lesser, lower, minor, relief, reserve, resultant, resulting, second, second-hand, second-rate, spare, subordinate, subsidiary, supporting, unimportant.

antonym primary.

secret *adj.* abstruse, arcane, back-door, backstairs, cabbalistic(al), camouflaged, clandestine, classified, cloak-and-dagger, close, closet, concealed, conspiratorial, covered, covert, cryptic, deep, discreet, disguised, esoteric, furtive, hidden, hole-and-corner, hush-hush, inly, mysterious, occult, out-of-the-way, private, privy, recondite, reticent, retired, secluded, secretive, sensitive, shrouded, sly, stealthy, tête-à-tête, undercover, underground, underhand, under-the-counter, undisclosed, unfrequented, unknown, unpublished, unrevealed, unseen.

antonyms open, public.

n. arcanum, code, confidence, enigma, formula, key, mystery, recipe.

secrete[1] *v.* appropriate, bury, cache, conceal, cover, disguise, harbor, hide, screen, secure, shroud, stash away, stow, veil.

antonym reveal.

secrete[2] *v.* emanate, emit, extravasate, extrude, exude, osmose, secern, separate.

sect *n.* camp, denomination, division, faction, group, party, school, splinter group, subdivision, wing.

section *n.* area, article, component, cross section, department, district, division, fraction, fractionlet, fragment, instalment, part, passage, piece, portion, region, sample, sector, segment, slice, subdivision, wing, zone.

antonym whole.

secular *adj.* civil, laic, laical, lay, non-religious, profane, state, temporal, worldly.

antonym religious.

secure *adj.* absolute, assured, certain, conclusive, confident, definite, dependable, easy, fast, fastened, firm, fixed, fortified, immovable, immune, impregnable, on velvet, over-confident, protected, reassured, reliable, safe, sheltered, shielded, solid, stable, steadfast, steady, sure, tight, unassailable, undamaged, unharmed, well-founded.

antonyms insecure, uncertain.

v. acquire, assure, attach, batten down, bolt, chain, ensure, fasten, fix, gain, get, get hold of, guarantee, insure, land, lash, lock, lock up, moor, nail, obtain, padlock, procure, rivet, seize.

antonyms lose, unfasten.

security *n.* assurance, asylum, care, certainty, collateral, confidence, conviction, cover, custody, defense, gage, guarantee, guards, hostage, immunity, insurance, pawn, pledge, positiveness, precautions, preservation, protection, refuge, reliance, retreat, safeguards, safekeeping, safety, sanctuary, sureness, surety, surveillance, warranty.

antonym insecurity.

sedate *adj.* calm, collected, composed, cool, decorous, deliberate, demure, dignified, douce, earnest, grave, imperturbable, middle-aged, placed, proper, quiet, seemly, serene, serious, slow-moving, sober, solemn, staid, tranquil, unflappable, unruffled.

antonyms flippant, hasty, undignified.

sediment *n.* deposit, draff, dregs, feces, fecula, grounds, lees, precipitate, residuum, settlings, warp.

seductive *adj.* alluring, attractive, beguiling, bewitching, captivating, come-hither, come-on, enticing, flirtatious, honeyed, inviting, irresistible, provocative, ravishing, seducing, sexy, siren, specious, tempting.

antonym unattractive.

see *v.* accompany, anticipate, appreciate, ascertain, attend, behold, comprehend, consider, consult, court, date, decide, deem, deliberate, descry, determine, discern, discover, distinguish, divine, encounter, ensure, envisage, escort, espy, experience, fathom, feel, follow, foresee, foretell, get, glimpse, grasp, guarantee, heed, identify, imagine, interview, investigate, judge, know, lead, learn, look, make out, mark, meet, mind, note, notice, observe, perceive, picture, realize, receive, reco-

gnize, reflect, regard, show, sight, spot, take, understand, usher, view, visit, visualize, walk, witness.

seek *v.* aim, ask, aspire to, attempt, beg, busk, desire, endeavor, entreat, essay, follow, hunt, inquire, invite, petition, pursue, request, solicit, strive, try, want.

seem *v.* appear, look, look like, pretend, sound like.

seemly *adj.* appropriate, attractive, becoming, befitting, comely, comme il faut, decent, decorous, fit, fitting, handsome, maidenly, meet, nice, proper, suitable, suited.

antonym unseemly.

segment *n.* articulation, bit, compartment, division, part, piece, portion, section, slice, wedge.

antonym whole.

v. anatomize, cut up, divide, halve, separate, slice, split.

segregate *v.* cut off, discriminate against, dissociate, isolate, quarantine, separate, set apart.

antonym unite.

seize *v.* abduct, annex, apprehend, appropriate, arrest, capture, catch, claw, clutch, cly, collar, commandeer, confiscate, crimp, distrain, distress, fasten, fix, get, grab, grasp, grip, hijack, impound, nab, prehend, smug, snatch, take.

antonym let go.

seldom *adv.* infrequently, occasionally, rarely, scarcely.

antonym often.

select *v.* choose, cull, pick, prefer, single out.

adj. choice, élite, excellent, exclusive, first-class, first-rate, hand-picked, limited, picked, posh, preferable, prime, privileged, rare, selected, special, superior, top, top-notch.

antonyms general, second-rate.

selection *n.* anthology, assortment, choice, choosing, collection, line-up, medley, miscellany, option, palette, pick, potpourri, preference, range, variety.

self-confident *adj.* assured, confident, fearless, poised, secure, self-assured, self-collected, self-possessed, self-reliant.

antonyms humble, unsure.

self-conscious *adj.* affected, awkward, bashful, coy, diffident, embarrassed, ill at ease, insecure, nervous, retiring, self-effacing, shamefaced, sheepish, shrinking, uncomfortable.

antonyms natural, unaffected.

self-denial *n.* abstemiousness, asceticism, moderation, renunciation, self-abandonment, self-abnegation, selflessness, self-renunciation, self-sacrifice, temperance, unselfishness.

antonym self-indulgence.

self-evident *adj.* axiomatic, clear, incontrovertible, inescapable, manifest, obvious, undeniable, unquestionable.

self-important *adj.* arrogant, big-headed, bumptious, cocky, conceited, consequential, overbearing, pompous, pushy, self-consequent, strutting, swaggering, swollen-headed, vain.

antonym humble.

self-indulgence *n.* dissipation, dissoluteness, excess, extravagance, high living, incontinence, intemperance, profligacy, self-gratification, sensualism.

antonym self-denial.

selfish *adj.* egoistic, egoistical, egotistic, egotistical, greedy, mean, mercenary, narrow, self-centered, self-interested, self-seeking, self-serving.

self-possessed *adj.* calm, collected, composed, confident, cool, poised, self-assured, self-collected, together, unruffled.

antonym worried.

self-respect *n.* amour-propre, dignity, pride, self-assurance, self-confidence, self-esteem, self-pride, self-regard.

antonym self-doubt.

self-righteous *adj.* complacent, goody-goody, holier-than-thou, hypocritical, pharisaical, pi, pietistic(al), pious, priggish, sanctimonious, self-satisfied, smug, superior, Tartuffian, Tartuffish.

antonym understanding.

self-sacrifice *n.* altruism, generosity, self-abandonment, self-abnegation, self-denial, selflessness, self-renunciation.

antonym selfishness.

self-satisfied *adj.* complacent, puffed up, self-approving, self-congratulatory, self-righteous, smug.

antonym humble.

self-seeking *adj.* acquisitive, calculating, careerist, fortune-hunting, gold-digging, mercenary, on the make, opportunistic, self-endeared, self-interested, selfish, self-loving, self-serving.

antonym altruistic.

sell *v.* barter, cheat, convince, deal in, exchange, handle, hawk, impose on, market, merchandise, peddle, persuade, promote, retail, sell out, stock, surrender, trade, trade in, traffic in, trick, vend.

antonym buy.

send *v.* broadcast, cast, charm, communicate, consign, convey, delight, deliver, direct, discharge, dispatch, electrify, emit, enrapture, enthrall, excite, exude, fire, fling, forward, grant, hurl, intoxicate, move, please, propel, radiate, ravish, remit, shoot, stir, thrill, titillate, transmit.

senile *adj.* anile, decrepit, doddering, doited, doting, failing, imbecile, senescent.

senior *adj.* aîné(e), elder, first, higher, high-ranking, major, older, superior.

antonym junior.

sensation *n.* agitation, awareness, commotion, consciousness, emotion, Empfindung, excitement, feeling, furore, hit, impression, perception, scandal, sense, stir, surprise, thrill, tingle, vibes, vibrations, wow.

sensational *adj.* amazing, astounding, blood-and-thunder, breathtaking, dramatic, electrifying, excellent, exceptional, exciting, fabulous, gamy, hair-raising, horrifying, impressive, lurid, marvelous, melodramatic, mind-blowing, revealing, scandalous, sensationalistic, shocking, smashing, spectacular, staggering, startling, superb, thrilling.

antonym run-of-the-mill.

sense *n.* advantage, appreciation, atmosphere, aura, awareness, brains, clear-headedness, cleverness, consciousness, definition, denotation, direction, discernment, discrimination, drift, faculty, feel, feeling, gist, good, gumption, implication, import, impression, intelligence, interpretation, intuition, judgment, logic, marbles, meaning, message, mother wit, nous, nuance, opinion, perception, point, premonition, presentiment, purport, purpose, quickness, reason, reasonableness, sagacity, sanity, savvy, sensation, sensibility, sentiment, sharpness, significance, signification, smeddum,

substance, tact, understanding, use, value, wisdom, wit(s), worth.

antonym foolishness.

v. appreciate, comprehend, detect, divine, feel, grasp, notice, observe, perceive, realize, suspect, understand.

senseless *adj.* absurd, anesthetized, asinine, crazy, daft, deadened, dotty, fatuous, foolish, halfwitted, idiotic, illogical, imbecilic, inane, incongruous, inconsistent, insensate, insensible, irrational, ludicrous, mad, meaningless, mindless, moronic, nonsensical, numb, numbed, out, out for the count, pointless, ridiculous, silly, simple, stunned, stupid, unconscious, unfeeling, unintelligent, unreasonable, unwise.

antonym sensible.

sensibility *n.* appreciation, awareness, delicacy, discernment, insight, intuition, perceptiveness, responsiveness, sensitiveness, sensitivity, susceptibility, taste.

antonym insensibility.

sensible *adj.* appreciable, canny, considerable, delicate, discernible, discreet, discriminating, down-to-earth, far-sighted, intelligent, judicious, level-headed, matter-of-fact, noticeable, palpable, perceptible, practical, prudent, rational, realistic, reasonable, right-thinking, sagacious, sage, sane, senseful, shrewd, significant, sober, solid, sound, tangible, visible, well-advised, well-thought-out, wise.

antonyms imperceptible, senseless.

sensible of acquainted with, alive to, aware of, cognizant of, conscious of, convinced of, mindful of, observant of, sensitive to, understanding.

antonym unaware of.

sensitive *adj.* acute, controversial, delicate, fine, hyperesthesic, hyperesthetic, hyperconscious, impressionable, irritable, keen, perceptive, precise, reactive, responsive, secret, sensitized, sentient, susceptible, temperamental, tender, thin-skinned, touchy, umbrageous.

antonym insensitive.

sensual *adj.* animal, bodily, carnal, epicurean, erotic, fleshly, lascivious, lecherous, lewd, libidinous, licentious, lustful, luxurious, pandemian, physical, randy, raunchy, self-indulgent, sexual, sexy, voluptuous, worldly.

antonyms ascetic, Puritan.

sentence *n.* aphorism, apophthegm, condemnation, decision, decree, doom, gnome, judgment, maxim, opinion, order, pronouncement, ruling, saying, verdict.

v. condemn, doom, judge, pass judgment on, penalize, pronounce judgment on.

sentiment *n.* attitude, belief, emotion, emotionalism, feeling, idea, judgment, mawkishness, maxim, opinion, persuasion, romanticism, saying, sensibility, sentimentalism, sentimentality, slush, soft-heartedness, tenderness, thought, view.

antonyms hard-heartedness, straightforwardness.

sentimental *adj.* corny, dewy-eyed, drippy, emotional, gushing, gushy, gutbucket, impressionable, lovey-dovey, maudlin, mawkish, mushy, nostalgic, pathetic, romantic, rose-water, schmaltzy, simpering, sloppy, slushy, soft-hearted, tearful, tear-jerking, tender, too-too, touching, treacly, weepy, Wertherian.

antonym unsentimental.

separate *v.* abstract, bifurcate, deglutinate, departmentalize, detach, disaffiliate, disally, discerp, disconnect, disentangle, disjoin, dislink, dispart, dissever, distance,

disunite, divaricate, diverge, divide, divorce, eloi(g)n, estrange, exfoliate, isolate, part, part company, prescind, remove, secede, secern, seclude, segregate, sever, shear, split, split up, sunder, uncouple, winnow, withdraw.
antonyms join, unite.

adj. alone, apart, autonomous, detached, disconnected, discrete, disjointed, disjunct, disparate, distinct, divided, divorced, independent, individual, isolated, particular, several, single, solitary, sundry, unattached, unconnected.
antonyms attached, together.

separation *n.* break, break-up, detachment, diaeresis, dialysis, diaspora, diastasis, discerption, disconnection, disengagement, disgregation, disjunction, disjuncture, disseverance, disseveration, disseverment, dissociation, disunion, division, divorce, estrangement, farewell, gap, leave-taking, parting, rift, segregation, severance, solution, split, split-up.
antonyms togetherness, unification.

sequence *n.* arrangement, chain, consequence, course, cycle, order, procession, progression, series, set, succession, track, train.

serene *adj.* calm, composed, cool, halcyon, imperturbable, peaceful, placid, tranquil, unclouded, undisturbed, unflappable, unruffled, untroubled.
antonym troubled.

serenity *n.* calm, calmness, composure, cool, peace, peacefulness, placidity, quietness, quietude, stillness, tranquility, unflappability.
antonyms anxiety, disruption.

series *n.* arrangement, catena, chain, concatenation, consecution, course, cycle, enfilade, line, order, progression, run, scale, sequence, set, string, succession, train.

serious *adj.* acute, alarming, critical, crucial, dangerous, deep, deliberate, determined, difficult, earnest, far-reaching, fateful, genuine, grave, grim, heavy, honest, humorless, important, long-faced, momentous, pensive, pressing, resolute, resolved, sedate, severe, significant, sincere, sober, solemn, staid, stern, thoughtful, unsmiling, urgent, weighty, worrying.
antonyms facetious, light, slight, smiling, trivial.

servant *n.* aia, amah, ancillary, attendant, ayah, bearer, boy, butler, daily, day, day-woman, domestic, drudge, flunky, footman, garçon, gentleman's gentleman, gossoon, gyp, haiduk, handmaid, handmaiden, help, helper, hind, hireling, Jeeves, kitchen-maid, knave, lackey, lady's maid, livery-servant, maid, maid of all work, maître d'hôtel, major-domo, man, manservant, menial, ministrant, retainer, scout, seneschal, servitor, skivvy, slave, slavey, steward, valet, vassal, woman.
antonyms master, mistress.

serve *v.* act, aid, answer, arrange, assist, attend, avail, complete, content, dance attendance, deal, deliver, discharge, distribute, do, fulfil, further, handle, help, minister to, oblige, observe, officiate, pass, perform, present, provide, satisfy, succor, suffice, suit, supply, undergo, wait on, work for.

service *n.* advantage, assistance, avail, availability, benefit, business, ceremony, check, disposal, duty, employ, employment, expediting, function, help, labor, maintenance, ministrations, observance, office, overhaul, performance, rite, servicing, set, supply, use, usefulness, utility, work, worship.

v. check, maintain, overhaul, recondition, repair, tune.

serviceable *adj.* advantageous, beneficial, convenient, dependable, durable, efficient, functional, hard-wearing, helpful, operative, plain, practical, profitable, simple, strong, tough, unadorned, usable, useful, utilitarian.
antonym unserviceable.

servile *adj.* abject, base, bootlicking, controlled, craven, cringing, fawning, groveling, humble, low, mean, menial, obsequious, slavish, subject, submissive, subservient, sycophantic, toadying, toadyish, unctuous.
antonyms aggressive, bold.

servitude *n.* bondage, bonds, chains, enslavement, obedience, serfdom, slavery, subjugation, thraldom, thrall, vassalage, villeinage.
antonym freedom.

set[1] *v.* adjust, aim, allocate, allot, apply, appoint, arrange, assign, cake, conclude, condense, congeal, coordinate, crystallize, decline, decree, deposit, designate, determine, dip, direct, disappear, embed, establish, fasten, fix, fix up, gelatinize, harden, impose, install, jell, lay, locate, lodge, mount, name, ordain, park, place, plant, plonk, plump, position, prepare, prescribe, propound, put, rectify, regulate, resolve, rest, schedule, seat, settle, sink, situate, solidify, specify, spread, stake, station, stick, stiffen, subside, synchronize, thicken, turn, vanish.

n. attitude, bearing, carriage, fit, hang, inclination, mise-en-scène, position, posture, scene, scenery, setting, turn.

adj. agreed, appointed, arranged, artificial, conventional, customary, decided, definite, deliberate, entrenched, established, firm, fixed, formal, hackneyed, immovable, inflexible, intentional, prearranged, predetermined, prescribed, regular, rehearsed, rigid, routine, scheduled, settled, standard, stereotyped, stock, strict, stubborn, traditional, unspontaneous, usual.
antonyms free, movable, spontaneous, undecided.

set[2] *n.* apparatus, assemblage, assortment, band, batch, circle, class, clique, collection, company, compendium, coterie, covey, crew, crowd, faction, gang, group, kit, outfit, sect, sequence, series.

settle *v.* adjust, agree, alight, appoint, arrange, bed, calm, choose, clear, colonize, compact, complete, compose, conclude, confirm, decide, decree, descend, determine, discharge, dispose, dower, drop, dwell, endow, establish, fall, fix, found, hush, inhabit, land, light, liquidate, live, lower, lull, occupy, ordain, order, pacify, pay, people, pioneer, plant, plump, populate, quell, quiet, quieten, quit, reassure, reconcile, relax, relieve, reside, resolve, sedate, sink, soothe, square, square up, subside, tranquilize.

settlement[1] *n.* accommodation, adjustment, agreement, allowance, arrangement, clearance, clearing, completion, conclusion, confirmation, decision, defrayal, diktat, discharge, disposition, establishment, income, liquidation, payment, resolution, satisfaction, termination.

settlement[2] *n.* colonization, colony, community, encampment, hamlet, immigration, kibbutz, nahal, occupation, outpost, peopling, plantation, population.

settlement[3] *n.* compacting, drop, fall, sinkage, subsidence.

sever *v.* alienate, bisect, cleave, cut, detach, disconnect, disjoin, dissever, dissociate, dissolve, dissunder, disunite, divide, estrange, part, rend, separate, split, sunder, terminate.

antonyms join, unite.

several *adj.* assorted, different, discrete, disparate, distinct, divers, diverse, individual, many, particular, respective, separate, single, some, some few, specific, sundry, various.

severe *adj.* acute, arduous, ascetic, astringent, austere, biting, bitter, Catonian, caustic, chaste, classic, classical, cold, critical, cruel, cutting, dangerous, demanding, difficult, disapproving, distressing, dour, Draconian, Draconic, Dracontic, eager, exacting, extreme, fierce, flinty, forbidding, functional, grave, grim, grinding, hard, harsh, inclement, inexorable, intense, iron-handed, oppressive, pitiless, plain, punishing, relentless, restrained, Rhadamanthine, rigid, rigorous, satirical, scathing, serious, shrewd, simple, sober, Spartan, stern, strait-laced, strict, stringent, taxing, tight-lipped, tough, trying, unadorned, unbending, unembellished, ungentle, unrelenting, unsmiling, unsparing, unsympathetic, violent.

antonyms compassionate, kind, lenient, mild, sympathetic.

sex *n.* coition, coitus, congress, copulation, desire, fornication, gender, intercourse, intimacy, libido, lovemaking, nookie, reproduction, screw, sexual intercourse, sexual relations, sexuality, union, venery.

sexual *adj.* carnal, coital, erotic, gamic, genital, intimate, procreative, reproductive, sensual, sex, sex-related, venereal.

antonym asexual.

sexy *adj.* arousing, beddable, come-hither, cuddly, curvaceous, epigamic, erotic, flirtatious, inviting, kissable, naughty, nubile, pornographic, provocative, provoking, seductive, sensual, sensuous, slinky, suggestive, titillating, virile, voluptuous.

antonym sexless.

shabby *adj.* cheap, contemptible, dastardly, despicable, dilapidated, dingy, dirty, dishonorable, disreputable, dog-eared, down-at-heel, faded, frayed, ignoble, low, low-down, low-life, low-lived, mangy, mean, moth-eaten, neglected, paltry, poking, poky, poor, ragged, raunchy, rotten, run-down, scruffy, seedy, shameful, shoddy, tacky, tattered, tatty, threadbare, ungentlemanly, unworthy, worn, worn-out.

antonyms honorable, smart.

shack *n.* bothy, but and ben, cabin, dump, hole, hovel, hut, hutch, lean-to, shanty, shed, shiel, shieling.

shackle *n.* bond, bracelets, chain, darbies, fetter, gyve, hamper, handcuff, hobble, iron, leg-iron, manacle, rope, shackles, tether, trammel.

v. bind, chain, constrain, embarrass, encumber, fetter, gyve, hamper, hamstring, handcuff, handicap, hobble, hogtie, impede, inhibit, limit, manacle, obstruct, pinion, restrain, restrict, secure, tether, thwart, tie, trammel.

shade *n.* amount, apparition, blind, canopy, color, coolness, cover, covering, curtain, darkness, dash, degree, difference, dimness, dusk, eidolon, ghost, gloaming, gloom, gloominess, gradation, hint, hue, manes, murk, nuance, obscurity, phantasm, phantom, screen, semblance, semi-darkness, shadiness, shadow, shadows, shelter, shield, shroud, specter, spirit, stain, suggestion, suspicion, tinge, tint, tone, trace, twilight, umbra, umbrage, variation, variety, veil, wraith.

v. cloud, conceal, cover, darken, dim, hide, inumbrate, mute, obscure, overshadow, protect, screen, shadow, shield, shroud, veil.

shadowy *adj.* caliginous, crepuscular, dark, dim, dream-like, dusky, faint, ghostly, gloomy, half-remembered, hazy, illusory, imaginary, impalpable, indistinct, intangible, murky, nebulous, obscure, shaded, shady, spectral, tenebrious, tenebrose, tenebrous, umbratile, umbratilous, undefined, unreal, unsubstantial, vague, wraithlike.

shady[1] *adj.* bosky, bowery, caliginous, cool, dark, dim, leafy, shaded, shadowy, tenebrous, umbrageous, umbratile, umbratilous, umbriferous, umbrose, umbrous.

antonyms bright, sunlit, sunny.

shady[2] *adj.* crooked, discreditable, dishonest, disreputable, dubious, fishy, louche, questionable, shifty, slippery, suspect, suspicious, underhand, unethical, unscrupulous, untrustworthy.

antonyms honest, trustworthy.

shaggy *adj.* crinose, hairy, hirsute, long-haired, nappy, rough, tousled, tousy, unkempt, unshorn.

antonyms bald, shorn.

shake *n.* agitation, convulsion, disturbance, instant, jar, jerk, jiffy, jolt, jounce, moment, no time, pulsation, quaking, second, shiver, shock, shudder, tick, trembling, tremor, trice, twitch, vellication, vibration.

v. agitate, brandish, bump, churn, concuss, convulse, didder, discompose, distress, disturb, flourish, fluctuate, frighten, heave, impair, intimidate, jar, joggle, jolt, jounce, move, oscillate, quake, quiver, rattle, rock, rouse, shimmy, shiver, shock, shog, shudder, split, stir, succuss, sway, totter, tremble, twitch, undermine, unnerve, unsettle, upset, vellicate, vibrate, wag, waggle, wave, waver, weaken, wobble.

shaky *adj.* dubious, faltering, inexpert, insecure, precarious, questionable, quivery, rickety, rocky, shoogly, suspect, tottering, tottery, uncertain, undependable, unreliable, unsound, unstable, unsteady, unsupported, untrustworthy, weak, wobbly.

antonyms firm, strong.

shallow *adj.* empty, flimsy, foolish, frivolous, idle, ignorant, meaningless, puerile, simple, skin-deep, slight, superficial, surface, trivial, unanalytical, unintelligent, unscholarly.

antonyms analytical, deep.

sham *n.* charlatan, counterfeit, feint, forgery, fraud, gold-brick, hoax, humbug, imitation, impostor, imposture, mountebank, phony, pretense, pretender, pseud, stumer.

adj. artificial, bogus, counterfeit, ersatz, faked, false, feigned, imitation, mock, pasteboard, phony, pinch-beck, pretended, pseud, pseudo, put-on, simulated, snide, spurious, synthetic.

antonym genuine.

v. affect, counterfeit, fake, feign, malinger, pretend, put on, simulate.

shame *n.* aidos, bashfulness, blot, chagrin, compunction, contempt, degradation, derision, discredit, disgrace, dishonor, disrepute, embarrassment, humiliation, ignominy, infamy, mortification, obloquy, odium, opprobrium, reproach, scandal, shamefacedness, stain, stigma.

antonyms distinction, honor, pride.

v. abash, blot, confound, debase, defile, degrade, discomfit, disconcert, discredit, disgrace, dishonor, embarrass, humble, humiliate, mortify, put to shame, reproach, ridicule, show up, smear, stain, sully, taint. *interj*. fi donc, fie, fie upon you, for shame, fy, shame on you.

shameful *adj*. abominable, atrocious, base, contemptible, dastardly, degrading, discreditable, disgraceful, dishonorable, embarrassing, humiliating, ignominious, indecent, infamous, low, mean, mortifying, outrageous, reprehensible, scandalous, shaming, unbecoming, unworthy, vile, wicked.
antonyms creditable, honorable.

shameless *adj*. abandoned, abashless, audacious, barefaced, blatant, brash, brazen, corrupt, defiant, depraved, dissolute, flagrant, hardened, immodest, improper, impudent, incorrigible, indecent, insolent, ithyphallic, profligate, reprobate, unabashed, unashamed, unblushing, unprincipled, unscrupulous, wanton.
antonyms ashamed, contrite, shamefaced.

shape *n*. apparition, appearance, aspect, build, condition, configuration, conformation, contours, cut, dimensions, fettle, figure, form, format, frame, Gestalt, guise, health, kilter, likeness, lines, make, model, mold, outline, pattern, physique, profile, semblance, silhouette, state, template, trim.
v. accommodate, adapt, construct, create, define, develop, devise, embody, fashion, forge, form, frame, guide, make, model, modify, mold, plan, prepare, produce, redact, regulate, remodel.

shapeless *adj*. amorphous, asymmetrical, battered, characterless, dumpy, embryonic, formless, inchoate, indeterminate, indigest, irregular, misshapen, nebulous, undeveloped, unformed, unshapely, unstructured.
antonym shapely.

shapely *adj*. comely, curvaceous, elegant, featous, gainly, graceful, neat, pretty, trim, voluptuous, well-formed, well-proportioned, well-set-up, well-turned.
antonym shapeless.

share *v*. allot, apportion, assign, chip in, distribute, divide, divvy, divvy up, go Dutch, go fifty-fifty, go halves, muck in, partake, participate, split, whack.
n. a piece of the action, allotment, allowance, contribution, cut, dividend, division, divvy, due, finger, lot, part, portion, proportion, quota, ration, snap, snip, stint, whack.

sharp *adj*. abrupt, acerbic, acicular, acid, acidulous, acrid, acrimonious, acute, alert, apt, artful, astute, barbed, biting, bitter, bright, burning, canny, caustic, chic, chiseled, classy, clear, clear-cut, clever, crafty, crisp, cunning, cutting, discerning, dishonest, distinct, dressy, eager, edged, excruciating, extreme, fashionable, fierce, fit, fly, harsh, honed, hot, hurtful, incisive, intense, jagged, keen, knife-edged, knifelike, knowing, long-headed, marked, natty, nimble-witted, noticing, observant, painful, penetrating, peracute, perceptive, piercing, piquant, pointed, pungent, quick, quick-witted, rapid, razor-sharp, ready, sarcastic, sardonic, saw-edged, scathing, serrated, severe, sharpened, shooting, shrewd, sly, smart, snappy, snazzy, sour, spiky, stabbing, stinging, stylish, subtle, sudden, tart, trenchant, trendy, unblurred, undulled, unscrupulous, vinegary, violent, vitriolic, waspish, wily.
antonyms blunt, dull, mild, obtuse, slow, stupid.

adv. abruptly, exactly, on the dot, out of the blue, precisely, promptly, punctually, suddenly, unexpectedly.

sharpen *v*. acuminate, edge, file, grind, hone, strop, taper, whet.
antonym blunt.

shatter *v*. blast, blight, break, burst, crack, crush, demolish, destroy, devastate, disable, disshiver, dumbfound, exhaust, explode, impair, implode, overturn, overwhelm, pulverize, ruin, shiver, smash, split, stun, torpedo, undermine, upset, wreck.

shattered *adj*. all in, crushed, dead beat, devastated, dog-tired, done in, exhausted, jiggered, knackered, overwhelmed, undermined, weary, worn out, zonked.

sheepish *adj*. abashed, ashamed, chagrined, chastened, embarrassed, foolish, mortified, self-conscious, shamefaced, silly, uncomfortable.
antonym unabashed.

sheer[1] *adj*. abrupt, absolute, arrant, complete, downright, mere, out-and-out, perpendicular, precipitous, pure, rank, steep, thorough, thoroughgoing, total, unadulterated, unalloyed, unmingled, unmitigated, unqualified, utter, vertical.

sheer[2] diaphanous, fine, flimsy, gauzy, gossamer, pellucid, see-through, thin, translucent, transparent.
antonyms heavy, thick.

sheet *n*. blanket, broadsheet, broadside, circular, coat, covering, expanse, film, flyer, folio, handbill, handout, lamina, layer, leaf, leaflet, membrane, nappe, newssheet, overlay, pane, panel, piece, plate, shroud, skin, slab, stratum, surface, veneer.

shelf *n*. bank, bar, bench, bracket, ledge, mantel, mantelpiece, platform, projection, reef, sandbank, sandbar, shoal, step, terrace.

shelter *v*. accommodate, cover, defend, ensconce, guard, harbor, hide, protect, put up, safeguard, screen, shade, shadow, shield, shroud, skug.
antonym expose.
n. accommodation, aegis, asylum, bield, bunker, cover, covert, coverture, defense, dugout, funk-hole, guard, harborage, haven, lean-to, lee, lodging, protection, refuge, retreat, roof, safety, sanctuary, sconce, screen, screening, security, shade, shadow, shiel, umbrage, umbrella.
antonym exposure.

shield *n*. aegis, ancile, buckler, bulwark, cover, defense, escutcheon, guard, pelta, protection, rampart, safeguard, screen, scutum, shelter, targe, ward.
v. cover, defend, guard, protect, safeguard, screen, shade, shadow, shelter.
antonym expose.

shift *v*. adjust, alter, budge, change, dislodge, displace, fluctuate, maneuver, move, quit, rearrange, relocate, remove, reposition, rid, scoff, swallow, swerve, switch, transfer, transpose, vary, veer, wolf.
n. alteration, artifice, change, contrivance, craft, device, displacement, dodge, equivocation, evasion, expedient, fluctuation, maneuver, modification, move, permutation, rearrangement, removal, resource, ruse, shifting, sleight, stratagem, subterfuge, switch, transfer, trick, veering, wile.

shifty *adj*. contriving, crafty, deceitful, devious, dishonest, disingenuous, dubious, duplicitous, evasive, fly-by-night, furtive, scheming, shady, slippery, tricky, underhand, unprincipled, untrustworthy, wily.

antonyms honest, open.

shilly-shally *v.* dilly-dally, dither, falter, fluctuate, haver, hem and haw, hesitate, mess about, prevaricate, seesaw, shuffle, swither, teeter, vacillate, waver.

shimmer *v.* coruscate, gleam, glisten, glitter, phosphoresce, scintillate, twinkle.

n. coruscation, gleam, glimmer, glitter, glow, incandescence, iridescence, luster, phosphorescence.

shine *v.* beam, brush, buff, burnish, coruscate, effulge, excel, flash, glare, gleam, glimmer, glisten, glitter, glow, luster, polish, radiate, resplend, scintillate, shimmer, sparkle, stand out, star, twinkle.

n. brightness, burnish, effulgence, glare, glaze, gleam, gloss, glow, lambency, light, luminosity, luster, patina, polish, radiance, sheen, shimmer, sparkle.

shining *adj.* beaming, bright, brilliant, celebrated, conspicuous, distinguished, effulgent, eminent, fulgent, gleaming, glistening, glittering, glorious, glowing, illustrious, lamping, leading, lucent, luminous, nitid, outstanding, profulgent, radiant, resplendent, rutilant, shimmering, sparkling, splendid, twinkling.

shiny *adj.* agleam, aglow, bright, burnished, gleaming, glistening, glossy, lustrous, nitid, polished, satiny, sheeny, shimmery, sleek.

antonyms dark, dull.

shipshape *adj.* businesslike, neat, orderly, seamanlike, spick-and-span, spruce, tidy, trig, trim, well-organized, well-planned, well-regulated.

antonyms disorderly, untidy.

shiver *v.* palpitate, quake, quiver, shake, shudder, tremble, vibrate.

n. flutter, frisson, grue, quiver, shudder, start, thrill, tremble, trembling, tremor, twitch, vibration.

shock *v.* agitate, appal, astound, confound, disgust, dismay, disquiet, horrify, jar, jolt, nauseate, numb, offend, outrage, paralyze, revolt, scandalize, shake, sicken, stagger, stun, stupefy, traumatize, unnerve, unsettle.

antonyms delight, gratify, please, reassure.

n. blow, bombshell, breakdown, clash, collapse, collision, concussion, consternation, dismay, distress, disturbance, encounter, fright, impact, jarring, jolt, perturbation, prostration, stupefaction, stupor, succussion, thunderbolt, trauma, turn, upset.

antonyms delight, pleasure.

shocking *adj.* abhorrent, abominable, appalling, astounding, atrocious, deplorable, detestable, disgraceful, disgusting, disquieting, distressing, dreadful, execrable, foul, frightful, ghastly, hideous, horrible, horrific, horrifying, insufferable, intolerable, loathsome, monstrous, nauseating, nefandous, odious, offensive, outrageous, repugnant, repulsive, revolting, scandalous, sickening, stupefying, unbearable, unspeakable.

antonyms acceptable, delightful, pleasant, satisfactory.

shore[1] *n.* beach, coast, foreshore, lakeside, littoral, margin, offing, promenade, rivage, sands, seaboard, sea-front, seashore, strand, waterfront, water's edge, waterside.

shore[2] *v.* brace, buttress, hold, prop, reinforce, shore up, stay, strengthen, support, underpin.

short *adj.* abbreviated, abridged, abrupt, blunt, brief, brittle, brusque, compendious, compressed, concise, crisp, crumbly, crusty, curt, curtailed, deficient, diminutive, direct, discourteous, dumpy, ephemeral, evanescent, fleeting, friable, gruff, impolite, inadequate, insufficient, lacking, laconic, limited, little, low, meager, momentary, murly, offhand, passing, petite, pithy, poor, précised, sawn-off, scant, scanty, scarce, sententious, sharp, shortened, short-handed, short-lived, short-term, slender, slim, small, snappish, snappy, sparse, squat, straight, succinct, summarized, summary, tart, terse, tight, tiny, transitory, uncivil, understaffed, unplentiful, wanting, wee.

antonyms adequate, ample, expansive, large, lasting, long, long-lived, polite, tall.

shortage *n.* absence, dearth, deficiency, deficit, failure, inadequacy, insufficiency, lack, leanness, meagerness, paucity, poverty, scantiness, scarcity, shortfall, sparseness, want, wantage.

antonyms abundance, sufficiency.

shortcoming *n.* defect, drawback, faible, failing, fault, flaw, foible, frailty, imperfection, inadequacy, weakness.

shorten *v.* abbreviate, abridge, crop, curtail, cut, decrease, diminish, dock, foreshorten, lessen, lop, précis, prune, reduce, take up, telescope, trim, truncate.

antonyms amplify, enlarge, lengthen.

short-lived *adj.* brief, caducous, ephemeral, evanescent, fleeting, fugacious, impermanent, momentary, passing, short, temporary, transient, transitory.

antonyms abiding, enduring, lasting, long-lived.

shortly *adv.* abruptly, anon, briefly, concisely, curtly, directly, laconically, presently, sharply, soon, succinctly, tartly, tersely.

short-sighted *adj.* careless, hasty, ill-advised, ill-considered, impolitic, impractical, improvident, imprudent, injudicious, myopic, near-sighted, unimaginative, unthinking.

antonyms far-sighted, hypermetropic, long-sighted.

short-tempered *adj.* choleric, crusty, fiery, hot-tempered, impatient, irascible, irritable, peppery, quick-tempered, ratty, testy, touchy.

antonyms calm, patient, placid.

shout *n.* bay, bellow, belt, call, cheer, cry, roar, scream, shriek, yell.

v. bawl, bay, bellow, call, cheer, cry, holler, roar, scream, shriek, yell.

shove *v.* barge, crowd, drive, elbow, force, impel, jostle, press, propel, push, shoulder, thrust.

shovel *n.* backhoe, bail, bucket, scoop, spade.

v. convey, dredge, heap, ladle, load, move, scoop, shift, spade, spoon, toss.

show *v.* accompany, accord, assert, attend, attest, bestow, betray, clarify, conduct, confer, demonstrate, disclose, display, divulge, elucidate, escort, evidence, evince, exemplify, exhibit, explain, grant, guide, illustrate, indicate, instruct, lead, manifest, offer, present, prove, register, reveal, teach, usher, witness.

n. affectation, air, appearance, array, dash, demonstration, display, éclat, élan, entertainment, exhibition, exhibitionism, expo, exposition, extravaganza, façade, fair, féerie, flamboyance, gig, illusion, indication, likeness, manifestation, ostentation, pageant, pageantry, panache, parade, performance, pizzazz, plausibility, pose, presentation, pretence, pretext, production, profession, razzle-dazzle, representation, semblance, sight, sign, spectacle, swagger, view.

show-down n. clash, climax, confrontation, crisis, culmination, dénouement, exposé, face-off.

show-off n. boaster, braggadocio, braggart, egotist, exhibitionist, peacock, self-advertiser, swaggerer, swanker, vaunter.

showy adj. epideictic, euphuistic, flamboyant, flash, flashy, florid, flossy, garish, gaudy, glitzy, loud, ostentatious, pompous, pretentious, sparkish, specious, splashy, swanking, swanky, tawdry, tinselly.
antonyms quiet, restrained.

shred n. atom, bit, fragment, grain, iota, jot, mammock, mite, piece, rag, ribbon, scrap, sliver, snippet, tatter, trace, whit, wisp.

shrewd adj. acute, arch, argute, artful, astucious, astute, calculated, calculating, callid, canny, clever, crafty, cunning, discerning, discriminating, downy, far-seeing, far-sighted, fly, gnostic, intelligent, judicious, keen, knowing, long-headed, observant, perceptive, perspicacious, sagacious, sharp, sly, smart, well-advised, wily.
antonyms naïve, obtuse, unwise.

shriek v. bellow, caterwaul, cry, holler, howl, scream, screech, shout, squeal, wail, yell.
n. bellow, caterwaul, cry, howl, scream, screech, shout, squeal, wail.

shrill adj. acute, argute, carrying, ear-piercing, ear-splitting, high, high-pitched, penetrating, piercing, piping, screaming, screeching, screechy, sharp, strident, treble.
antonyms gentle, low, soft.

shrink v. back away, balk, contract, cower, cringe, decrease, deflate, diminish, dwindle, flinch, lessen, narrow, quail, recoil, retire, shorten, shrivel, shun, shy away, wince, withdraw, wither, wrinkle.
antonyms embrace, expand, stretch, warm to.

shrivel v. burn, dehydrate, desiccate, dwindle, frizzle, gizzen, parch, pucker, scorch, sear, shrink, wilt, wither, wizen, wrinkle.

shun v. avoid, cold-shoulder, elude, eschew, evade, ignore, ostracize, shy away from, spurn, steer clear of.
antonyms accept, embrace.

shut v. bar, bolt, cage, close, fasten, latch, lock, seal, secure, slam, spar.
antonym open.

shy adj. backward, bashful, cautious, chary, coy, diffident, distrustful, farouche, hesitant, inhibited, modest, mousy, nervous, reserved, reticent, retiring, self-conscious, self-effacing, shrinking, suspicious, timid, unassertive, wary.
antonyms bold, confident.
v. back away, balk, buck, flinch, quail, rear, recoil, shrink, start, swerve, wince.

sick adj. ailing, black, blasé, bored, diseased, disgusted, displeased, dog-sick, fed up, feeble, ghoulish, glutted, ill, indisposed, jaded, laid up, morbid, mortified, nauseated, pining, poorly, puking, qualmish, queasy, sated, satiated, sickly, tired, under the weather, unwell, vomiting, weak, weary.
antonyms healthy, well.

sickness n. affliction, ailment, bug, complaint, derangement, disease, disorder, dwam, ill-health, illness, indisposition, infirmity, insanity, malady, nausea, pestilence, qualmishness, queasiness, vomiting.
antonym health.

side n. airs, angle, arrogance, aspect, bank, border,

boundary, brim, brink, camp, cause, department, direction, division, edge, elevation, face, facet, faction, flank, flitch, fringe, gang, hand, insolence, light, limit, margin, opinion, ostentation, page, part, party, perimeter, periphery, position, pretentiousness, quarter, region, rim, sect, sector, slant, stand, standpoint, surface, team, twist, verge, view, viewpoint.
adj. flanking, incidental, indirect, irrelevant, lateral, lesser, marginal, minor, oblique, roundabout, secondary, subordinate, subsidiary.

sidle v. creep, edge, inch, ingratiate, insinuate, slink, sneak, steal, wriggle.

sieve v. boult, remove, riddle, separate, sift, strain.
n. boulter, colander, riddle, screen, sifter, strainer.

sight n. appearance, apprehension, decko, display, estimation, exhibition, eye, eyes, eye-shot, eyeshot, eyesight, eyesore, field of vision, fright, gander, glance, glimpse, judgment, ken, look, mess, monstrosity, observation, opinion, pageant, perception, range, scene, seeing, show, spectacle, view, viewing, visibility, vision, vista.
v. behold, discern, distinguish, glimpse, observe, perceive, see, spot.

sightseer n. excursionist, holidaymaker, rubber-neck, tourist, tripper, visitor.

sign n. augury, auspice, badge, beck, betrayal, board, character, cipher, clue, device, emblem, ensign, evidence, figure, foreboding, forewarning, gesture, giveaway, grammalogue, hierogram, hint, indication, indicium, insignia, intimation, lexigram, logo, logogram, logograph, manifestation, mark, marker, miracle, note, notice, omen, placard, pointer, portent, presage, proof, reminder, representation, rune, signal, signature, signification, signpost, spoor, suggestion, symbol, symptom, token, trace, trademark, vestige, warning.
v. autograph, beckon, endorse, gesticulate, gesture, indicate, initial, inscribe, motion, signal, subscribe, wave.

signal n. alarm, alert, beacon, beck, cue, flare, flash, gesture, go-ahead, griffin, impulse, indication, indicator, light, mark, OK, password, rocket, sign, tip-off, token, transmitter, waft, warning, watchword.
adj. conspicuous, distinguished, eminent, exceptional, extraordinary, famous, glorious, impressive, memorable, momentous, notable, noteworthy, outstanding, remarkable, significant, striking.
v. beckon, communicate, gesticulate, gesture, indicate, motion, nod, sign, telegraph, waft, wave.

significance n. consequence, consideration, force, implication, implications, import, importance, impressiveness, interest, matter, meaning, message, moment, point, purport, relevance, sense, signification, solemnity, weight.
antonym unimportance.

significant adj. critical, denoting, eloquent, expressing, expressive, important, indicative, knowing, material, meaning, meaningful, momentous, noteworthy, ominous, pregnant, senseful, serious, solemn, suggestive, symbolic, symptomatic, vital, weighty.
antonyms meaningless, unimportant.

signify v. announce, augur, betoken, carry weight, communicate, connote, convey, count, denote, evidence, exhibit, express, imply, indicate, intimate, matter, mean, omen, portend, presage, proclaim, represent, show, stand for, suggest, symbolize, transmit.

silence *n*. calm, dumbness, hush, lull, muteness, noiselessness, obmutescence, peace, quiescence, quiet, quietness, reserve, reticence, secretiveness, speechlessness, stillness, taciturnity, uncommunicativeness.

v. deaden, dumbfound, extinguish, gag, muffle, muzzle, quell, quiet, quieten, stifle, still, strike dumb, subdue, suppress.

silent *adj*. aphonic, aphonous, dumb, hushed, idle, implicit, inaudible, inoperative, mum, mute, muted, noiseless, quiet, reticent, soundless, speechless, still, stilly, tacit, taciturn, tongue-tied, uncommunicative, understood, unexpressed, unforthcoming, unpronounced, unsounded, unspeaking, unspoken, voiceless, wordless.

antonyms loud, noisy, talkative.

silhouette *n*. configuration, delineation, form, outline, profile, shadow-figure, shadowgraph, shape.

silly *adj*. absurd, addled, asinine, benumbed, birdbrained, brainless, childish, cuckoo, daft, dazed, dopey, drippy, fatuous, feather-brained, flighty, foolhardy, foolish, frivolous, giddy, groggy, hen-witted, idiotic, illogical, immature, imprudent, inane, inappropriate, inept, irrational, irresponsible, meaningless, mindless, muzzy, pointless, preposterous, puerile, ridiculous, scatter-brained, senseless, spoony, stunned, stupefied, stupid, unwise, witless.

antonyms collected, mature, sane, sensible, wise.

n. clot, dope, duffer, goose, half-wit, ignoramus, ninny, silly-billy, simpleton, twit, wally.

similar *adj*. alike, analogous, close, comparable, compatible, congruous, corresponding, homogeneous, homogenous, homologous, related, resembling, self-like, uniform.

antonym different.

similarity *n*. affinity, agreement, analogy, closeness, coincidence, comparability, compatibility, concordance, congruence, correspondence, equivalence, homogeneity, likeness, relation, resemblance, sameness, similitude, uniformity.

antonym difference.

simple *adj*. artless, bald, basic, brainless, childlike, classic, classical, clean, clear, credulous, dense, direct, dumb, easy, elementary, feeble, feeble-minded, foolish, frank, green, guileless, half-witted, homely, honest, humble, idiot-proof, inelaborate, ingenuous, innocent, inornate, intelligible, lowly, lucid, manageable, modest, moronic, naïf, naive, naïve, naked, natural, obtuse, one-fold, plain, pure, rustic, Saturnian, shallow, silly, sincere, single, slow, Spartan, stark, straightforward, stupid, thick, unadorned, unaffected, unalloyed, unblended, uncluttered, uncombined, uncomplicated, undeniable, understandable, undisguised, undivided, unelaborate, unembellished, unfussy, uninvolved, unlearned, unmixed, unornate, unpretentious, unschooled, unskilled, unsophisticated, unsuspecting, unvarnished.

antonyms artful, clever, complicated, difficult, fancy, intricate.

simpleton *n*. Abderite, blockhead, booby, daftie, dizzard, dolt, dope, dullard, dunce, dupe, flat, flathead, fool, gaby, gander, gomeril, goon, goop, goose, goosecap, goosy, Gothamist, Gothamite, green goose, greenhorn, gump, gunsel, idiot, imbecile, jackass, Johnny, juggins, maffling, moron, nincompoop, ninny, ninnyhammer, numskull, soft-head, spoon, stupid, twerp.

antonym brain.

simulate *v*. act, affect, assume, counterfeit, duplicate, echo, fabricate, fake, feign, imitate, mimic, parrot, pretend, put on, reflect, reproduce, sham.

sin *n*. crime, damnation, debt, error, evil, fault, guilt, hamartia, impiety, iniquity, lapse, misdeed, offense, sinfulness, transgression, trespass, ungodliness, unrighteousness, wickedness, wrong, wrongdoing.

v. err, fall, fall from grace, go astray, lapse, misbehave, offend, stray, transgress, trespass.

sincere *adj*. artless, bona fide, candid, deep-felt, earnest, frank, genuine, guileless, heartfelt, heart-whole, honest, natural, open, plain-hearted, plain-spoken, pure, real, serious, simple, simple-hearted, single-hearted, soulful, straightforward, true, true-hearted, truthful, unadulterated, unaffected, unfeigned, unmixed, wholehearted.

antonym insincere.

sincerity *n*. artlessness, bona fides, candor, earnestness, frankness, genuineness, good faith, guilelessness, honesty, plain-heartedness, probity, seriousness, straightforwardness, truth, truthfulness, wholeheartedness.

antonym insincerity.

sinful *adj*. bad, corrupt, criminal, depraved, erring, fallen, guilty, immoral, impious, iniquitous, irreligious, peccable, peccant, ungodly, unholy, unrighteous, unvirtuous, wicked, wrongful.

antonyms righteous, sinless.

sing *v*. betray, bizz, blow the whistle, cantillate, carol, caterwaul, chant, chirp, croon, finger, fink, grass, hum, inform, intone, lilt, melodize, peach, pipe, purr, quaver, rat, render, serenade, spill the beans, squeal, talk, trill, vocalize, warble, whine, whistle, yodel.

singe *v*. blacken, burn, cauterize, char, scorch, sear.

single *adj*. celibate, distinct, exclusive, free, individual, lone, man-to-man, one, one-fold, one-to-one, only, particular, separate, simple, sincere, single-minded, singular, sole, solitary, unattached, unblended, unbroken, uncombined, uncompounded, undivided, unique, unmarried, unmixed, unshared, unwed, wholehearted.

singular *adj*. atypical, conspicuous, curious, eccentric, eminent, exceptional, extraordinary, individual, noteworthy, odd, out-of-the-way, outstanding, peculiar, pre-eminent, private, prodigious, proper, puzzling, queer, rare, remarkable, separate, single, sole, strange, uncommon, unique, unparalleled, unusual.

antonyms normal, usual.

sink *v*. abandon, abate, abolish, bore, collapse, conceal, decay, decline, decrease, defeat, degenerate, degrade, delapse, descend, destroy, dig, diminish, dip, disappear, drill, drive, droop, drop, drown, dwindle, ebb, engulf, excavate, fade, fail, fall, finish, flag, founder, invest, lapse, lay, lessen, lower, merge, overwhelm, pay, penetrate, plummet, plunge, relapse, retrogress, ruin, sag, scupper, slip, slope, slump, stoop, submerge, subside, succumb, suppress, weaken, worsen.

antonyms float, rise, uplift.

sinless *adj*. faultless, guiltless, immaculate, impeccable, innocent, pure, unblemished, uncorrupted, undefiled, unspotted, unsullied, virtuous.

antonym sinful.

sip *v*. delibate, sample, sup, taste.

n. drop, mouthful, spoonful, swallow, taste, thimbleful.

sit *v*. accommodate, assemble, befit, brood, contain, con vene, deliberate, hold, meet, officiate, perch, pose, preside, reside, rest, seat, settle.

site *n.* ground, location, lot, place, plot, position, setting, spot, station.

v. dispose, install, locate, place, position, set, situate, station.

situation *n.* ball-game, berth, case, circumstances, condition, employment, galère, job, kettle of fish, lie of the land, locale, locality, location, office, place, plight, position, post, predicament, rank, scenario, seat, setting, set-up, site, sphere, spot, state, state of affairs, station, status.

size *n.* amount, amplitude, bigness, bulk, dimensions, extent, greatness, height, hugeness, immensity, largeness, magnitude, mass, measurement(s), proportions, range, vastness, volume.

skeletal *adj.* cadaverous, drawn, emaciated, fleshless, gaunt, haggard, hollow-cheeked, shrunken, skin-and-bone, wasted.

sketch *v.* block out, delineate, depict, draft, draw, outline, paint, pencil, plot, portray, represent, rough out.

n. croquis, delineation, design, draft, drawing, ébauche, esquisse, outline, plan, scenario, skeleton, vignette.

sketchy *adj.* bitty, crude, cursory, imperfect, inadequate, incomplete, insufficient, outline, perfunctory, rough, scrappy, skimpy, slight, superficial, unfinished, vague.

antonym full.

skill *n.* ability, accomplishment, adroitness, aptitude, art, cleverness, competence, dexterity, experience, expertise, expertness, facility, finesse, handiness, ingenuity, intelligence, knack, proficiency, quickness, readiness, savoir-faire, savvy, skilfulness, talent, technique, touch.

skilled *adj.* able, accomplished, crack, experienced, expert, masterly, practiced, professional, proficient, schooled, skilful, trained.

antonym unskilled.

skimpy *adj.* beggarly, exiguous, inadequate, insufficient, meager, measly, miserly, niggardly, scanty, short, sketchy, sparse, thin, tight.

antonym generous.

skin *n.* casing, coating, crust, deacon, epidermis, fell, film, hide, husk, integument, membrane, outside, peel, pellicle, pelt, rind, tegument.

v. abrade, bark, excoriate, flay, fleece, graze, peel, scrape, strip.

skinny *adj.* attenuate(d), emaciated, lean, scragged, scraggy, skeletal, skin-and-bone, thin, twiggy, underfed, undernourished, weedy.

antonym fat.

skip *v.* bob, bounce, caper, cavort, cut, dance, eschew, flisk, flit, frisk, gambol, hop, miss, omit, overleap, play truant, prance, trip.

skirmish *n.* affair, affray, battle, brush, clash, combat, conflict, contest, dust-up, encounter, engagement, fracas, incident, scrap, scrimmage, set-to, spat, tussle, velitation.

v. clash, collide, pickeer, scrap, tussle.

slack *adj.* baggy, crank, dull, easy, easy-going, flaccid, flexible, idle, inactive, inattentive, lax, lazy, limp, loose, neglectful, negligent, permissive, quiet, relaxed, remiss, slow, slow-moving, sluggish, tardy.

antonyms busy, diligent, quick, rigid, stiff, taut.

n. excess, give, inactivity, leeway, looseness, play, relaxation, room.

v. dodge, idle, malinger, neglect, relax, shirk, slacken.

slander *n.* aspersion, backbiting, calumniation, calumny, defamation, detraction, libel, misrepresentation, muck-raking, obloquy, scandal, smear, traducement, traduction.

v. asperse, backbite, calumniate, decry, defame, detract, disparage, libel, malign, muck-rake, scandalize, slur, smear, traduce, vilify, vilipend.

antonyms glorify, praise.

slang *v.* abuse, berate, castigate, excoriate, insult, lambaste, malign, revile, scold, slag, vilify, vituperate.

antonym praise.

slant *v.* angle, bend, bevel, bias, cant, color, distort, incline, lean, list, shelve, skew, slope, tilt, twist, warp, weight.

n. angle, attitude, bias, camber, declination, diagonal, emphasis, gradient, incline, leaning, obliquity, pitch, prejudice, rake, ramp, slope, tilt, viewpoint.

slanting *adj.* angled, askew, aslant, asymmetrical, bent, canted, cater-cornered, diagonal, inclined, oblique, sideways, skew-whiff, slanted, slantwise, sloping, tilted, tilting.

antonyms level.

slap-dash *adj.* careless, clumsy, disorderly, haphazard, hasty, hurried, last-minute, messy, negligent, offhand, perfunctory, rash, slipshod, sloppy, slovenly, thoughtless, thrown-together, untidy.

antonyms careful, orderly.

slash *v.* criticize, cut, drop, gash, hack, lacerate, lash, lower, reduce, rend, rip, score, slit.

n. cut, gash, incision, laceration, lash, rent, rip, slit.

slaughter *n.* battue, blood-bath, bloodshed, butchery, carnage, extermination, holocaust, killing, liquidation, massacre, murder, slaying.

v. butcher, crush, defeat, destroy, exterminate, halal, hammer, kill, liquidate, massacre, murder, overwhelm, rout, scupper, slay, thrash, trounce, vanquish.

slave *n.* abject, bondservant, bond-slave, bond(s)man, bond(s)woman, captive, drudge, peon, scullion, serf, servant, skivvy, slavey, thrall, vassal, villein.

v. drudge, grind, labor, skivvy, slog, struggle, sweat, toil.

slavery *n.* bondage, captivity, duress(e), enslavement, impressment, serfdom, servitude, subjugation, thraldom, thrall, vassalage, yoke.

antonym freedom.

slay *v.* amuse, annihilate, assassinate, butcher, destroy, dispatch, eliminate, execute, exterminate, impress, kill, massacre, murder, rub out, slaughter, wow.

sleek *adj.* glossy, insinuating, lustrous, plausible, shiny, smooth, smug, well-fed, well-groomed.

sleep *v.* catnap, doss (down), doze, drop off, drowse, hibernate, nod off, repose, rest, slumber, snooze, snore.

n. coma, dormancy, doss, doze, forty winks, hibernation, nap, repose, rest, shut-eye, siesta, slumber(s), snooze, sopor.

sleepy *adj.* drowsy, dull, heavy, hypnotic, inactive, lethargic, quiet, slow, sluggish, slumb(e)rous, slumbersome, slumbery, somnolent, soporific, soporose, soporous, torpid.

antonyms alert, awake, restless, wakeful.

slender *adj.* acicular, faint, feeble, flimsy, fragile, gra-

cile, inadequate, inconsiderable, insufficient, lean, little, meager, narrow, poor, remote, scanty, slight, slim, small, spare, svelte, sylph-like, tenuous, thin, thready, wasp-waisted, weak, willowish, willowy.
antonyms considerable, fat, thick.

slide *v.* coast, glide, glissade, lapse, skate, skim, slidder, slip, slither, toboggan, veer.

slight *adj.* delicate, feeble, flimsy, fragile, gracile, inconsiderable, insignificant, insubstantial, meager, minor, modest, negligible, paltry, scanty, slender, slim, small, spare, superficial, trifling, trivial, unimportant, weak.
antonyms considerable, large, major, significant.
v. affront, cold-shoulder, cut, despise, disdain, disparage, disrespect, ignore, insult, neglect, scorn, snub.
antonyms compliment, flatter.
n. affront, contempt, discourtesy, disdain, disregard, disrespect, inattention, indifference, insult, neglect, rebuff, rudeness, slur, snub.

slim *adj.* ectomorphic, faint, gracile, lean, narrow, poor, remote, slender, slight, svelte, sylph-like, thin, trim.
antonyms chubby, fat, strong.
v. bant, diet, lose weight, reduce, slenderize.

slip[1] *v.* blunder, boob, conceal, creep, disappear, discharge, dislocate, elude, err, escape, fall, get away, glide, hide, lapse, loose, miscalculate, misjudge, mistake, skate, skid, slidder, slide, slink, slither, sneak, steal, trip.
n. bloomer, blunder, boob, error, failure, fault, imprudence, indiscretion, lapsus, lapsus calami, lapsus linguae, lapsus memoriae, mistake, omission, oversight, slip-up.

slip[2] *n.* certificate, coupon, cutting, offshoot, pass, piece, runner, scion, shoot, sliver, sprig, sprout, strip.

slipshod *adj.* careless, casual, loose, negligent, slap-dash, sloppy, slovenly, unsystematic, untidy.
antonyms careful, fastidious, neat, tidy.

slit *v.* cut, gash, knife, lance, pierce, rip, slash, slice, split.
n. cut, fent, fissure, gash, incision, opening, rent, split, tear, vent.
adj. cut, pertusate, pertuse(d), rent, split, torn.

slogan *n.* battle-cry, catch-phrase, catchword, chant, jingle, motto, rallying-cry, war cry, watchword.

slope *v.* batter, delve, fall, incline, lean, pitch, rise, slant, tilt, verge, weather.
n. bajada, brae, cant, declination, declivity, descent, downgrade, escarp, glacis, gradient, inclination, incline, ramp, rise, scarp, slant, tilt, versant.

sloth *n.* accidie, acedia, fainéance, idleness, inactivity, indolence, inertia, laziness, listlessness, slackness, slothfulness, sluggishness, torpor.
antonyms diligence, industriousness, sedulity.

slothful *adj.* do-nothing, fainéant, idle, inactive, indolent, inert, lazy, listless, slack, sluggish, torpid, workshy.
antonyms diligent, industrious, sedulous.

slouching *adj.* careless, disorderly, heedless, loose, negligent, shambling, shuffling, slack, slap-dash, slatternly, slipshod, sloppy, unkempt, untidy.

slow *adj.* adagio, backward, behind, behindhand, boring, bovine, conservative, creeping, dawdling, dead, dead-and-alive, delayed, deliberate, dense, dilatory, dim, dull, dull-witted, dumb, easy, gradual, inactive, lackadaisical, laggard, lagging, late, lazy, leaden, leisurely, lingering, loitering, long-drawn-out, meas-

ured, obtuse, one-horse, pedetentous, plodding, ponderous, prolonged, protracted, quiet, retarded, slack, sleepy, slow-moving, slow-witted, sluggardly, sluggish, stagnant, stupid, tame, tardy, tedious, thick, time-consuming, uneventful, unhasty, unhurried, uninteresting, unproductive, unprogressive, unpunctual, unresponsive, wearisome.
antonyms active, fast, quick, rapid, swift.
v. brake, check, curb, decelerate, delay, detain, draw rein, handicap, hold up, lag, relax, restrict, retard.

sluggish *adj.* dull, heavy, inactive, indolent, inert, lethargic, lifeless, listless, lurdan, lymphatic, phlegmatic, slothful, slow, slow-moving, torpid, unresponsive.
antonyms brisk, dynamic, eager, quick, vigorous.

slumber *v.* doze, drowse, nap, repose, rest, sleep, snooze.

slump *v.* bend, collapse, crash, decline, deteriorate, droop, drop, fall, hunch, loll, plummet, plunge, sag, sink, slip, slouch, worsen.
n. collapse, crash, decline, depreciation, depression, downturn, drop, failure, fall, falling-off, low, recession, reverse, stagnation, trough, worsening.
antonym boom.

sly *adj.* arch, artful, astute, canny, clever, conniving, covert, crafty, cunning, devious, foxy, furtive, guileful, impish, insidious, knowing, mischievous, peery, roguish, scheming, secret, secretive, shifty, sleeky, stealthy, subtle, surreptitious, underhand, vulpine, wily.
antonyms frank, honest, open, straightforward.

small *adj.* bantam, base, dilute, diminutive, dwarf(ish), grudging, humble, illiberal, immature, inadequate, incapacious, inconsiderable, insignificant, insufficient, itsy-bitsy, lesser, limited, little, meager, mean, mignon(ne), mini, miniature, minor, minuscule, minute, modest, narrow, negligible, paltry, petite, petty, pigmean, pint-size(d), pocket, pocket-sized, puny, pygmaean, pygmean, scanty, selfish, slight, small-scale, tiddl(e)y, tiny, trifling, trivial, undersized, unimportant, unpretentious, wee, young.
antonyms big, huge, large.

smart[1] *adj.* acute, adept, agile, apt, astute, bright, brisk, canny, chic, clever, cracking, dandy, effective, elegant, fashionable, fine, impertinent, ingenious, intelligent, jaunty, keen, lively, modish, natty, neat, nimble, nimble-witted, nobby, pert, pointed, quick, quick-witted, rattling, ready, ready-witted, saucy, sharp, shrewd, smart-alecky, snappy, spanking, spirited, spruce, stylish, swagger, swish, tippy, trim, vigorous, vivacious, well-appointed, witty.
antonyms dowdy, dumb, slow, stupid, unfashionable, untidy.

smart[2] *v.* burn, hurt, nip, pain, sting, throb, tingle, twinge.
adj. hard, keen, nipping, nippy, painful, piercing, resounding, sharp, stinging.
n. nip, pain, pang, smarting, soreness, sting, twinge.

smash *v.* break, collide, crash, crush, defeat, demolish, destroy, disintegrate, lay waste, overthrow, prang, pulverize, ruin, shatter, shiver, squabash, wreck.
n. accident, collapse, collision, crash, defeat, destruction, disaster, downfall, failure, pile-up, prang, ruin, shattering, smash-up.

smear *v.* asperse, bedaub, bedim, besmirch, blacken, blur, calumniate, coat, cover, dab, daub, dirty, drag (someone's) name through the mud, gaum, malign, patch, plaster, rub on, slubber, smarm, smudge, soil, spread over, stain, sully, tarnish, traduce, vilify.

n. blot, blotch, calumny, daub, defamation, gaum, libel, mudslinging, slander, smudge, splodge, streak, vilification, whispering campaign.

smell *n.* aroma, bouquet, fetor, fragrance, fumet(te), funk, malodor, mephitis, nose, odor, perfume, pong, redolence, scent, sniff, stench, stink, whiff.

v. be malodorous, hum, inhale, nose, pong, reek, scent, sniff, snuff, stink, stink to high heaven, whiff.

smelly *adj.* bad, evil-smelling, fetid, foul, foul-smelling, frowsty, funky, graveolent, high, malodorous, mephitic, noisome, off, pongy, putrid, reeking, stinking, strong, strong-smelling, whiffy.

smitten *adj.* afflicted, beguiled, beset, bewitched, bowled over, burdened, captivated, charmed, enamored, infatuated, plagued, struck, troubled.

smoke *n.* exhaust, film, fog, fume, funk, gas, mist, reek, roke, smog, vapor.

v. cure, dry, fume, fumigate, reek, roke, smolder, vent.

smooth *adj.* agreeable, bland, calm, classy, easy, effortless, elegant, equable, even, facile, fair-spoken, flat, flowing, fluent, flush, frictionless, glassy, glib, glossy, hairless, horizontal, ingratiating, level, levigate, mellow, mild, mirror-like, peaceful, persuasive, plain, plane, pleasant, polished, regular, rhythmic, serene, shiny, silken, silky, sleek, slick, slippery, smarmy, smug, soft, soothing, steady, suave, tranquil, unbroken, unctuous, undisturbed, uneventful, uniform, uninterrupted, unpuckered, unruffled, unrumpled, untroubled, unwrinkled, urbane, velvety, well-ordered.

antonyms coarse, harsh, irregular, rough, unsteady.

v. allay, alleviate, appease, assuage, calm, dub, ease, emery, extenuate, facilitate, flatten, iron, level, levigate, mitigate, mollify, palliate, plane, polish, press, slicken, soften, unknit, unwrinkle.

antonym roughen.

smother *v.* choke, cocoon, conceal, cover, envelop, extinguish, heap, hide, inundate, muffle, overlie, overwhelm, repress, shower, shroud, snuff, stifle, strangle, suffocate, suppress, surround.

smug *adj.* cocksure, complacent, conceited, holier-than-thou, priggish, self-opinionated, self-righteous, self-satisfied, superior, unctuous.

antonym modest.

smutty *adj.* bawdy, blue, coarse, crude, dirty, filthy, gross, improper, indecent, indelicate, lewd, obscene, off-color, pornographic, prurient, racy, raunchy, ribald, risqué, salacious, suggestive, vulgar.

antonyms clean, decent.

snag *n.* bug, catch, complication, difficulty, disadvantage, drawback, hitch, inconvenience, obstacle, problem, snub, stick, stumbling block.

v. catch, hole, ladder, rip, tear.

snap *v.* bark, bite, break, catch, chop, click, crack, crackle, crepitate, flash, grip, growl, knap, nip, pop, retort, seize, separate, snarl, snatch.

n. bite, break, crack, crackle, energy, fillip, flick, get-up-and-go, go, grabe, liveliness, nip, pizazz, pop, vigor, zip.

adj. abrupt, immediate, instant, offhand, on-the-spot, sudden, unexpected, unpremeditated.

snappy *adj.* brusque, chic, crabbed, cross, dapper, edgy, fashionable, hasty, ill-natured, irritable, modish, natty,

quick-tempered, smart, snappish, stylish, tart, testy, touchy, trendy, up-to-the-minute, waspish.

snare *v.* catch, ensnare, entrap, illaqueate, net, seize, springe, trap, trepan, wire.

n. catch, cobweb, gin, lime, lime-twig, net, noose, pitfall, springe, springle, toils, trap, wire.

snarl[1] *v.* complain, gnarl, gnar(r), growl, grumble, knar.

snarl[2] *v.* complicate, confuse, embroil, enmesh, entangle, entwine, jam, knot, muddle, ravel, tangle.

snatch *v.* clutch, gain, grab, grasp, grip, kidnap, nab, pluck, pull, ramp, rap, rescue, seize, spirit, take, win, wrench, wrest.

n. bit, fraction, fragment, part, piece, section, segment, smattering, snippet, spell.

sneak *v.* cower, cringe, grass on, inform on, lurk, pad, peach, sidle, skulk, slink, slip, smuggle, spirit, steal, tell tales.

n. informer, snake in the grass, sneaker, telltale.

adj. clandestine, covert, furtive, quick, secret, stealthy, surprise, surreptitious.

sneer *v.* deride, disdain, fleer, gibe, jeer, laugh, look down on, mock, ridicule, scoff, scorn, sniff at, snigger.

n. derision, disdain, fleer, gibe, jeer, mockery, ridicule, scorn, smirk, snidery, snigger.

sniff *v.* breathe, inhale, nose, smell, snuff, snuffle, vent.

snigger *v.*, *n.* giggle, laugh, sneer, snicker, snort, titter.

sniveling *adj.* blubbering, crying, girning, grizzling, mewling, moaning, sniffling, snuffling, weeping, whimpering, whingeing, whining.

snobbish *adj.* arrogant, condescending, high and mighty, high-hat, hoity-toity, lofty, lordly, patronizing, pretentious, snooty, stuck-up, superior, toffee-nosed, uppish, uppity, upstage.

snoop *v.* interfere, pry, sneak, spy.

snooze *v.* catnap, doze, drowse, kip, nap, nod off, sleep.

n. catnap, doze, forty winks, kip, nap, shut-eye, siesta, sleep.

snub *v.* check, cold-shoulder, cut, humble, humiliate, mortify, rebuff, rebuke, shame, slight, sneap, squash, squelch, wither.

n. affront, brush-off, check, humiliation, insult, put-down, rebuff, rebuke, slap in the face, sneap.

snug *adj.* close, close-fitting, comfortable, comfy, compact, cosy, homely, intimate, neat, sheltered, trim, warm.

soak *v.* bathe, damp, drench, imbue, immerse, infuse, interfuse, marinate, moisten, penetrate, permeate, saturate, sog, souse, steep, wet.

soar *v.* ascend, climb, escalate, fly, mount, plane, rise, rocket, tower, wing.

antonym plummet.

sob *v.* bawl, blubber, boohoo, cry, greet, howl, mewl, moan, shed tears, snivel, weep.

sober *adj.* abstemious, abstinent, calm, clear-headed, cold, composed, cool, dark, dispassionate, douce, drab, grave, level-headed, lucid, moderate, peaceful, plain, practical, quiet, rational, realistic, reasonable, restrained, sedate, serene, serious, severe, solemn, somber, sound, staid, steady, subdued, temperate, unexcited, unruffled.

antonyms drunk, excited, frivolous, gay, intemperate, irrational.

sobriety *n.* abstemiousness, abstinence, calmness, composure, continence, coolness, gravity, level-headedness, moderation, reasonableness, restraint, sedateness, self-restraint, seriousness, soberness, solemnity, staidness, steadiness, temperance.

antonyms drunkenness, excitement, frivolity.

social *adj.* collective, common, communal, community, companionable, friendly, general, gregarious, group, neighborly, organized, public, sociable, societal.

n. ceilidh, do, gathering, get-together, hoolly, hoot(e)nanny, party.

society *n.* association, beau monde, brotherhood, camaraderie, circle, civilization, club, companionship, company, corporation, culture, elite, fellowship, fraternity, fratry, friendship, gentry, Gesellschaft, group, guild, haut monde, humanity, institute, league, mankind, organization, people, population, sisterhood, the public, the smart set, the swells, the top drawer, the world, union, upper classes, upper crust, Verein.

soft *adj.* balmy, bendable, bland, caressing, comfortable, compassionate, cottony, creamy, crumby, cushioned, cushiony, cushy, daft, delicate, diffuse, diffused, dim, dimmed, doughy, downy, ductile, dulcet, easy, easy-going, effeminate, elastic, faint, feathery, feeble-minded, flabby, flaccid, fleecy, flexible, flowing, fluid, foolish, furry, gelatinous, gentle, impressible, indulgent, kind, lash, lax, lenient, liberal, light, limp, low, malleable, mellifluous, mellow, melodious, mild, moldable, murmured, muted, namby-pamby, non-alcoholic, overindulgent, pale, pampered, pastel, permissive, pitying, plastic, pleasant, pleasing, pliable, pulpy, quaggy, quiet, restful, sensitive, sentimental, shaded, silky, silly, simple, smooth, soothing, soppy, spineless, spongy, squashy, subdued, supple, swampy, sweet, sympathetic, temperate, tender, tender-hearted, undemanding, understated, unprotected, velvety, weak, whispered, yielding.

antonyms hard, harsh, heavy, loud, rigid, rough, severe, strict.

soften *v.* abate, allay, alleviate, anneal, appease, assuage, calm, cushion, digest, diminish, ease, emolliate, intenerate, lessen, lighten, lower, macerate, malax, malaxate, melt, mitigate, moderate, modify, mollify, muffle, palliate, quell, relax, soothe, still, subdue, temper.

soil¹ *n.* clay, country, dirt, dust, earth, glebe, ground, humus, land, loam, region, terra firma.

soil² *v.* bedaggle, bedraggle, befoul, begrime, besmirch, besmut, defile, dirty, foul, maculate, muddy, pollute, smear, spatter, spot, stain, sully, tarnish.

solace *n.* alleviation, assuagement, comfort, consolation, relief, succor, support.

v. allay, alleviate, comfort, console, mitigate, soften, soothe, succor, support.

sole *adj.* alone, exclusive, individual, one, only, single, singular, solitary, unique.

antonyms multiple, shared.

solemn *adj.* august, awed, awe-inspiring, ceremonial, ceremonious, devotional, dignified, earnest, formal, glum, grand, grave, hallowed, holy, imposing, impressive, majestic, momentous, pompous, portentous, religious, reverential, ritual, sacred, sanctified, sedate, serious, sober, somber, staid, stately, thoughtful, venerable.

antonyms frivolous, gay, light-hearted.

solicit *v.* ask, beg, beseech, canvass, crave, entreat, implore, importune, petition, pray, seek, sue, supplicate.

solicitous *adj.* anxious, apprehensive, ardent, attentive,

careful, caring, concerned, eager, earnest, fearful, troubled, uneasy, worried, zealous.

solicitude *n.* anxiety, attentiveness, care, concern, considerateness, consideration, disquiet, regard, uneasiness, worry.

solid *adj.* agreed, compact, complete, concrete, constant, continuous, cubic(al), decent, dense, dependable, estimable, firm, genuine, good, hard, law-abiding, level-headed, massed, pure, real, reliable, sensible, serious, sober, sound, square, stable, stocky, strong, sturdy, substantial, trusty, unalloyed, unanimous, unbroken, undivided, uninterrupted, united, unmixed, unshakeable, unvaried, upright, upstanding, wealthy, weighty, worthy.

antonyms broken, insubstantial, liquid.

solitary *adj.* alone, cloistered, companionless, de(a)rnful, desolate, friendless, hermitical, hidden, isolated, lone, lonely, lonesome, out-of-the-way, reclusive, remote, retired, secluded, separate, sequestered, single, sole, unfrequented, unsociable, unsocial, untrodden, unvisited.

antonyms accompanied, gregarious.

solitude *n.* aloneness, desert, emptiness, isolation, loneliness, privacy, reclusiveness, retirement, seclusion, waste, wasteland, wilderness.

antonym companionship.

solution *n.* answer, blend, clarification, compound, decipherment, dénouement, disconnection, dissolution, elucidation, emulsion, explanation, explication, key, liquefaction, melting, mix, mixture, resolution, result, solvent, solving, suspension, unfolding, unraveling.

solve *v.* answer, clarify, crack, decipher, disentangle, dissolve, elucidate, explain, expound, interpret, resolve, settle, unbind, unfold, unravel, work out.

somber *adj.* dark, dim, dismal, doleful, drab, dull, dusky, funereal, gloomy, grave, joyless, lugubrious, melancholy, mournful, obscure, sad, sepulchral, shadowy, shady, sober, sombrous, subfusc.

antonyms bright, cheerful, happy.

sometimes *adv.* at times, from time to time, now and again, now and then, occasionally, off and on, once in a while, otherwhiles.

antonyms always, never.

soon *adv.* anon, betimes, in a minute, in a short time, in the near future, presently, shortly.

soothe *v.* allay, alleviate, appease, assuage, calm, coax, comfort, compose, ease, hush, lull, mitigate, mollify, pacify, quiet, relieve, salve, settle, soften, still, tranquilize.

antonyms annoy, irritate, vex.

soothing *adj.* anetic, assuasive, balmy, balsamic, calming, demulcent, easeful, emollient, lenitive, palliative, relaxing, restful.

antonyms annoying, irritating, vexing.

sophisticated *adj.* advanced, blasé, citified, complex, complicated, cosmopolitan, couth, cultivated, cultured, delicate, elaborate, highly-developed, intricate, jet-set, multifaceted, refined, seasoned, subtle, urbane, worldly, worldly-wise, world-weary.

antonyms artless, naïve, simple, unsophisticated.

sorcery *n.* black art, black magic, charm, diablerie, divination, enchantment, hoodoo, incantation, magic, necromancy, pishogue, spell, voodoo, warlockry, witchcraft, witchery, witching, wizardry.

sordid *adj.* avaricious, base, corrupt, covetous, debauched, degenerate, degraded, despicable, dingy, dirty, disreputable, filthy, foul, grasping, low, mean, mercenary, miserly, niggardly, rapacious, seamy, seedy, selfish, self-seeking, shabby, shameful, sleazy, slovenly, slummy, squalid, tawdry, unclean, ungenerous, venal, vicious, vile, wretched.

sore adj. acute, afflicted, aggrieved, angry, annoyed, annoying, burning, chafed, critical, desperate, dire, distressing, extreme, grieved, grievous, harrowing, hurt, inflamed, irked, irritable, irritated, pained, painful, peeved, pressing, raw, reddened, resentful, sensitive, severe, sharp, smarting, stung, tender, touchy, troublesome, upset, urgent, vexed.
n. abscess, boil, canker, carbuncle, chafe, gathering, inflammation, swelling, ulcer, wound.

sorrow n. affliction, anguish, blow, distress, dole, grief, hardship, heartache, heartbreak, lamentation, misery, misfortune, mourning, regret, ruth, sadness, trial, tribulation, trouble, unhappiness, woe, worry.
antonyms happiness, joy.
v. agonize, bemoan, bewail, beweep, grieve, lament, moan, mourn, pine, weep.
antonym rejoice.

sorrowful adj. affecting, afflicted, dejected, depressed, disconsolate, distressing, doleful, grievous, heartbroken, heart-rending, heavy-hearted, lamentable, lugubrious, melancholy, miserable, mournful, painful, piteous, rueful, ruthful, sad, sorry, tearful, unhappy, wae, woebegone, woeful, wretched.
antonyms happy, joyful.

sorry adj. abject, apologetic, base, commiserative, compassionate, conscience-stricken, contrite, deplorable, disconsolate, dismal, distressed, distressing, grieved, guilt-ridden, mean, melancholy, miserable, mournful, moved, paltry, pathetic, penitent, piteous, pitiable, pitiful, pitying, poor, regretful, remorseful, repentant, ruthful, sad, self-reproachful, shabby, shamefaced, sorrowful, sympathetic, unhappy, unworthy, vile, wretched.
antonym glad.

sort n. brand, breed, category, character, class, denomination, description, family, genre, genus, group, ilk, kidney, kind, make, nature, order, quality, race, species, stamp, style, type, variety.
v. arrange, assort, catalog, categorize, choose, class, classify, distribute, divide, file, grade, group, neaten, order, rank, screen, select, separate, systematize, tidy.

sound[1] *n.* description, din, earshot, hearing, idea, implication, impression, look, noise, range, report, resonance, reverberation, tenor, tone, utterance, voice.
v. announce, appear, articulate, chime, declare, echo, enunciate, express, knell, look, peal, pronounce, resonate, resound, reverberate, ring, seem, signal, toll, utter, voice.

sound[2] *adj.* complete, copper-bottomed, correct, deep, entire, established, fair, fere, firm, fit, hale, healthy, hearty, intact, just, level-headed, logical, orthodox, peaceful, perfect, proper, proven, prudent, rational, reasonable, recognized, reliable, reputable, responsible, right, right-thinking, robust, safe, secure, sensible, solid, solvent, stable, sturdy, substantial, thorough, tried-and-true, true, trustworthy, unbroken, undamaged, undisturbed, unhurt, unimpaired, uninjured, untroubled, valid, vigorous, wakeless, well-founded, well-grounded, whole, wise.

antonyms shaky, unfit, unreliable, unsound.
sound[3] *v.* examine, fathom, inspect, investigate, measure, plumb, probe, test.
sound[4] *n.* channel, estuary, firth, fjord, inlet, passage, strait, voe.

sour adj. acerb(ic), acetic, acid, acidulated, acrid, acrimonious, bad, bitter, churlish, crabbed, curdled, cynical, disagreeable, discontented, embittered, fermented, grouchy, grudging, ill-natured, ill-tempered, inharmonious, jaundiced, off, peevish, pungent, rancid, rank, sharp, tart, turned, ungenerous, unpleasant, unsavory, unsuccessful, unsweet, unwholesome, vinegarish, vinegary, waspish.
antonyms good-natured, sweet.
v. alienate, curdle, disenchant, embitter, envenom, exacerbate, exasperate, spoil.

source n. author, authority, begetter, beginning, cause, commencement, derivation, fons et origo, fountainhead, informant, klondike, milch-cow, mine, origin, originator, primordium, quarry, rise, spring, waterhead, well-head, ylem.

souvenir n. fairing, gift, keepsake, memento, memory, relic, remembrance(r), reminder, token.

sovereign n. autarch, chief, dynast, emperor, empress, kaiser, king, monarch, potentate, prince, queen, ruler, shah, tsar.
adj. absolute, august, chief, dominant, effectual, efficacious, efficient, excellent, imperial, kingly, majestic, monarch(ic)al, paramount, predominant, principal, queenly, regal, royal, ruling, supreme, unlimited.

sovereignty n. ascendancy, domination, imperium, kingship, primacy, raj, regality, supremacy, suzerainty, sway.

space n. accommodation, amplitude, berth, blank, capacity, chasm, diastema, distance, duration, elbowroom, expanse, extension, extent, gap, house-room, interval, lacuna, leeway, margin, omission, period, place, play, room, scope, seat, spaciousness, span, time, volume.

spacious adj. ample, big, broad, capacious, comfortable, commodious, expansive, extensive, huge, large, roomy, sizable, uncrowded, vast, wide.
antonyms confined, cramped, narrow, small.

span n. amount, compass, distance, duration, extent, length, period, reach, scope, spell, spread, stretch, term.
v. arch, bridge, cover, cross, encompass, extend, link, overarch, traverse, vault.

spare adj. additional, economical, emergency, extra, free, frugal, gash, gaunt, lank, lean, leftover, meager, modest, odd, over, remaining, scanty, slender, slight, slim, sparing, superfluous, supernumerary, surplus, unoccupied, unused, unwanted, wiry.
antonyms corpulent, necessary, profuse.
v. afford, allow, bestow, give quarter, grant, leave, let off, pardon, part with, refrain from, release, relinquish.

sparing adj. careful, chary, cost-conscious, economical, frugal, lenten, prudent, saving, thrifty.
antonyms lavish, liberal, unsparing.

sparkle v. beam, bubble, coruscate, dance, effervesce, emicate, fizz, fizzle, flash, gleam, glint, glisten, glister, glitter, glow, scintillate, shimmer, shine, spark, twinkle, wink.
n. animation, brilliance, coruscation, dash, dazzle, effervescence, élan, emication, flash, flicker, gaiety,

gleam, glint, glitter, life, panache, pizzazz, radiance, scintillation, spark, spirit, twinkle, vim, vitality, vivacity, wit, zip.

spartan *adj.* abstemious, abstinent, ascetic, austere, bleak, disciplined, extreme, frugal, hardy, joyless, plain, rigorous, self-denying, severe, stern, strict, stringent, temperate, unflinching.

spasm *n.* access, burst, contraction, convulsion, eruption, fit, frenzy, jerk, outburst, paroxysm, seizure, throe, twitch.

speak *v.* address, advert to, allude to, argue, articulate, breathe, comment on, communicate, converse, deal with, declaim, declare, discourse, discuss, enunciate, express, harangue, lecture, mention, plead, pronounce, refer to, say, speechify, spiel, state, talk, tell, utter, voice.

special *adj.* appropriate, certain, characteristic, chief, choice, detailed, distinctive, distinguished, especial, exceptional, exclusive, extraordinary, festive, gala, important, individual, intimate, main, major, memorable, momentous, particular, peculiar, precise, primary, red-letter, select, significant, specialized, specific, uncommon, unique, unusual.

antonyms common, normal, ordinary, usual.

specialist *n.* adept, authority, connoisseur, consultant, expert, master, professional, proficient.

species *n.* breed, category, class, collection, denomination, description, genus, group, kind, sort, type, variety.

specific *adj.* characteristic, clear-cut, definite, delimitative, distinguishing, especial, exact, explicit, express, limited, particular, peculiar, precise, special, unambiguous, unequivocal.

antonyms general, vague.

specify *v.* cite, define, delineate, describe, designate, detail, enumerate, indicate, individualize, itemize, list, mention, name, particularize, spell out, stipulate.

specimen *n.* copy, embodiment, ensample, example, exemplar, exemplification, exhibit, illustration, individual, instance, model, paradigm, pattern, person, proof, representative, sample, type.

speck *n.* atom, bit, blemish, blot, defect, dot, fault, flaw, fleck, grain, iota, jot, macula, mark, mite, modicum, mote, particle, shred, speckle, spot, stain, tittle, trace, whit.

spectacle *n.* curiosity, display, event, exhibition, extravaganza, marvel, pageant, parade, performance, phenomenon, scene, show, sight, wonder.

spectator *n.* beholder, bystander, eye-witness, looker-on, observer, onlooker, passer-by, viewer, watcher, witness.

antonyms contestant, participant, player.

speculate *v.* cogitate, conjecture, consider, contemplate, deliberate, gamble, guess, hazard, hypothesize, meditate, muse, reflect, risk, scheme, suppose, surmise, theorize, venture, wonder.

speech *n.* address, articulation, colloquy, communication, conversation, dialect, dialogue, diction, discourse, discussion, disquisition, enunciation, harangue, homily, idiom, intercourse, jargon, language, lecture, lingo, oration, parlance, parole, peroration, say, spiel, talk, tongue, utterance, voice, winged words.

speed *n.* acceleration, celerity, dispatch, expedition, fleetness, haste, hurry, lick, momentum, pace, precipi-

tation, quickness, rapidity, rush, swiftness, tempo, velocity.

v. advance, aid, assist, belt, bomb, boost, bowl along, career, dispatch, expedite, facilitate, flash, fleet, further, gallop, hasten, help, hurry, impel, lick, press on, promote, put one's foot down, quicken, race, rush, sprint, step on it, step on the gas, step on the juice, tear, urge, vroom, zap, zoom.

antonyms delay, hamper, restrain, slow.

spell[1] *n.* bout, course, innings, interval, patch, period, season, stint, stretch, term, time, turn.

spell[2] *n.* abracadabra, allure, bewitchment, charm, conjuration, enchantment, exorcism, fascination, glamor, hex, incantation, jettatura, love-charm, magic, open sesame, paternoster, philter, rune, sorcery, trance, weird, witchery.

spell[3] *v.* augur, herald, imply, indicate, mean, portend, presage, promise, signal, signify, suggest.

spellbound *adj.* bemused, bewitched, captivated, charmed, enchanted, enthralled, entranced, fascinated, gripped, hooked, mesmerized, possessed, rapt, transfixed, transported.

spend *v.* apply, bestow, blow, blue, concentrate, consume, cough up, deplete, devote, disburse, dispense, dissipate, drain, employ, empty, exhaust, expend, fill, fork out, fritter, invest, lavish, lay out, occupy, pass, pay out, shed, shell out, splash out, squander, use, use up, waste.

antonyms hoard, save.

spendthrift *n.* big spender, prodigal, profligate, spendall, spender, squanderer, unthrift, waster, wastrel.

antonyms hoarder, miser, saver.

adj. extravagant, improvident, prodigal, profligate, thriftless, wasteful.

sphere *n.* ball, capacity, circle, compass, department, domain, employment, field, function, globe, globule, milieu, orb, province, range, rank, realm, scope, spheroid, spherule, station, stratum, territory.

spherical *adj.* globate, globed, globe-shaped, globoid, globose, globular, orbicular, rotund, round.

spicy *adj.* aromatic, flavorsome, fragrant, hot, improper, indecorous, indelicate, off-color, piquant, pointed, pungent, racy, ribald, risqué, savory, scandalous, seasoned, sensational, showy, suggestive, tangy, titillating, unseemly.

antonym bland.

spin *v.* birl, concoct, develop, gyrate, gyre, hurtle, invent, narrate, pirouette, purl, recount, reel, relate, revolve, rotate, spirt, swim, swirl, tell, turn, twirl, twist, unfold, wheel, whirl.

n. agitation, commotion, drive, flap, gyration, hurl, panic, pirouette, revolution, ride, roll, run, state, tizzy, turn, twist, whirl.

spine *n.* backbone, barb, needle, quill, rachis, ray, spicule, spiculum, spike, spur, vertebrae, vertebral column.

spineless *adj.* cowardly, faint-hearted, feeble, gutless, inadequate, ineffective, irresolute, lily-livered, soft, spiritless, squeamish, submissive, vacillating, weak, weak-kneed, weak-willed, wet, wishy-washy, yellow.

antonyms brave, strong.

spirit *n.* air, animation, apparition, ardor, Ariel, atmosphere, attitude, backbone, bravura, breath, brio, character, complexion, courage, daemon, dauntlessness, deva, disposition, div, djinni, earnestness energy, enterprise, enthusiasm, entrain, Erdgeist, esprit follet, essence, familiar, faun, feeling, feelings, fire, foison, force, gameness, geist, genie, genius, genius loci, ghost, ghoul, gist, grit, guts, humor, intent, intention, jinnee, jinni, ka, kobold, life, liveliness, manito(u), marid, meaning, mettle, mood, morale, motivation, outlook, phantom, pneuma, psyche, purport, purpose, python, quality, resolution, resolve, revenant, sense, shade, shadow, soul, sparkle, specter, spook, sprite, spunk, stout-heartedness, substance, sylph, temper, temperament, tenor, tone, verve, vigor, vision, vivacity, warmth, water-horse, water-nymph, water-rixie, water-sprite, Weltgeist, wili, will, will power, Zeitgeist, zest.

v. abduct, abstract, capture, carry, convey, kidnap, purloin, remove, seize, snaffle, steal, whisk.

spirited *adj.* active, animated, ardent, bold, courageous, energetic, game, gamy, high-spirited, lively, mettlesome, plucky, sparkling, sprightly, spunky, stomachful, vigorous, vivacious.

antonyms lazy, spiritless, timid.

spiritless *adj.* anemic, apathetic, dejected, depressed, despondent, dispirited, droopy, dull, lackluster, languid, lifeless, listless, low, melancholic, melancholy, mopy, torpid, unenthusiastic, unmoved, wishy-washy.

antonym spirited.

spiritual *adj.* aery, devotional, divine, ecclesiastical, ethereal, ghostly, holy, immaterial, incorporeal, otherwordly, pneumatic, pure, religious, sacred, unfleshly, unworldly.

antonyms material, physical.

spit *v.* discharge, drizzle, eject, expectorate, hawk, hiss, spew, splutter, sputter.

n. dribble, drool, expectoration, phlegm, saliva, slaver, spittle, sputum.

spite *n.* animosity, bitchiness, despite, gall, grudge, hate, hatred, ill-nature, malevolence, malice, malignity, pique, rancor, spitefulness, spleen, venom, viciousness.

antonyms affection, goodwill.

v. annoy, discomfit, gall, harm, hurt, injure, irk, irritate, needle, nettle, offend, peeve, pique, provoke, put out, vex.

spiteful *adj.* barbed, bitchy, catty, cruel, ill-disposed, ill-natured, malevolent, malicious, malignant, nasty, rancorous, snide, splenetic, vengeful, venomous, vindictive, waspish.

antonyms affectionate, charitable.

splendid *adj.* admirable, beaming, bright, brilliant, costly, dazzling, excellent, exceptional, fantastic, fine, first-class, glittering, glorious, glowing, gorgeous, grand, great, heroic, illustrious, imposing, impressive, lavish, lustrous, luxurious, magnificent, marvelous, ornate, outstanding, pontific(al), radiant, rare, refulgent, remarkable, renowned, resplendent, rich, splendiferous, splend(o)rous, sterling, sublime, sumptuous, superb, supreme, tiptop, top-hole, top-notch, topping, wonderful.

antonyms drab, ordinary, run-of-the-mill.

splendor *n.* brightness, brilliance, ceremony, dazzle, display, effulgence, fulgor, glory, gorgeousness, grandeur, luster, magnificence, majesty, pomp, radiance, refulgence, renown, resplendence, richness, show, solemnity, spectacle, stateliness, sumptuousness.

splinter *n.* chip, flake, flinder, fragment, needle, paring, shaving, sliver, spall, spicule, stob.

v. disintegrate, fracture, fragment, shatter, shiver, smash, split.

split *v.* allocate, allot, apportion, betray, bifurcate, branch, break, burst, cleave, crack, delaminate, disband, distribute, disunite, divaricate, diverge, divide, divulge, fork, gape, grass, halve, inform on, open, parcel out, part, partition, peach, rend, rip, separate, share out, slash, slice up, slit, sliver, snap, spell, splinter, squeal.

n. breach, break, break-up, cleft, crack, damage, dichotomy, difference, discord, disruption, dissension, disunion, divergence, division, estrangement, fissure, gap, partition, race, rent, rift, rip, rupture, schism, scissure, separation, slash, slit, tear.

adj. ambivalent, bisected, broken, cleft, cloven, cracked, divided, dual, fractured, ruptured, twofold.

spoil *v.* addle, baby, blemish, bugger, butcher, cocker, coddle, cosset, curdle, damage, debase, decay, decompose, deface, despoil, destroy, deteriorate, disfigure, go bad, go off, harm, impair, indulge, injure, jigger, louse up, mar, mildew, mollycoddle, pamper, plunder, putrefy, queer, rot, ruin, screw, spoon-feed, turn, upset, wreck.

spoken *adj.* declared, expressed, oral, phonetic, said, stated, told, unwritten, uttered, verbal, viva voce, voiced.

antonyms unspoken, written.

spontaneous *adj.* extempore, free, impromptu, impulsive, instinctive, natural, ultroneous, unbidden, uncompelled, unconstrained, unforced, unhesitating, unlabored, unpremeditated, unprompted, unstudied, untaught, voluntary, willing.

antonyms forced, planned, studied.

sport *n.* activity, amusement, badinage, banter, brick, buffoon, butt, dalliance, derision, diversion, entertainment, exercise, fair game, frolic, fun, game, jest, joking, kidding, laughing-stock, merriment, mirth, mockery, pastime, play, plaything, raillery, recreation, ridicule, sportsman, teasing.

v. caper, dally, display, disport, exhibit, flirt, frolic, gambol, philander, play, romp, show off, toy, trifle, wear.

sporting *adj.* considerate, fair, gentlemanly, sportsmanlike.

antonyms unfair, ungentlemanly, unsporting.

spot *n.* bit, blemish, blot, blotch, daub, difficulty, discoloration, flaw, little, locality, location, macula, maculation, macule, mark, mess, morsel, pimple, place, plight, plook, point, position, predicament, pustule, quandary, scene, site, situation, smudge, speck, splash, stain, stigma, taint, trouble.

v. besmirch, blot, descry, detect, dirty, discern, dot, espy, fleck, identify, maculate, mark, mottle, observe, recognize, see, sight, soil, spatter, speckle, splodge, splotch, stain, sully, taint, tarnish.

spotty *adj.* blotchy, pimpled, pimply, plooky, speckled, spotted.

spout *v.* declaim, discharge, emit, erupt, expatiate, gush, jet, orate, pontificate, rabbit on, ramble (on), rant, sermonize, shoot, speechify, spiel, spray, spurt, squirt, stream, surge.

n. chute, fistula, fountain, gargoyle, geyser, jet, nozzle, outlet, rose, spray.

spray[1] *v.* atomize, diffuse, douse, drench, scatter, shower, sprinkle, wet.

n. aerosol, atomizer, drizzle, droplets, foam, froth, mist, moisture, spindrift, spoondrift, sprinkler.

spray² *n.* bough, branch, corsage, garland, shoot, sprig, wreath.

spread *v.* advertise, arrange, array, blazon, bloat, broadcast, broaden, bruit, cast, circulate, couch, cover, diffuse, dilate, dispread, disseminate, distribute, divulgate, divulge, effuse, escalate, expand, extend, fan out, furnish, lay, metastasize, multiply, mushroom, open, overlay, prepare, proclaim, proliferate, promulgate, propagate, publicize, publish, radiate, scatter, set, shed, sprawl, stretch, strew, swell, transmit, unfold, unfurl, unroll, widen.

antonyms close, compress, contain, fold.

n. advance, advancement, array, banquet, blow-out, compass, cover, development, diffusion, dispersion, dissemination, divulgation, divulgence, escalation, expanse, expansion, extent, feast, increase, period, proliferation, ranch, reach, repast, span, spreading, stretch, suffusion, sweep, term, transmission.

sprightly *adj.* active, agile, airy, alert, animated, blithe, brisk, cheerful, energetic, frolicsome, gamesome, gay, hearty, jaunty, joyous, lively, nimble, perky, playful, spirited, sportive, spry, vivacious.

antonym inactive.

spring¹ *v.* appear, arise, bounce, bound, burgeon, come, dance, derive, descend, develop, emanate, emerge, grow, hop, issue, jump, leap, mushroom, originate, proceed, rebound, recoil, shoot up, sprout, start, stem, vault.

n. bounce, bounciness, bound, buck, buoyancy, elasticity, flexibility, gambado, give, hop, jump, leap, rebound, recoil, resilience, saltation, springiness, vault.

spring² *n.* beginning, cause, eye, fountain-head, origin, root, source, well, well-spring.

sprinkle *v.* asperge, diversify, dot, dredge, dust, pepper, powder, scatter, seed, shower, sparge, spatter, spray, strew.

spruce *adj.* dainty, dapper, elegant, natty, neat, sleek, slick, smart, smirk, trig, trim, well-groomed, well-turned-out.

antonyms disheveled, untidy.

spry *adj.* active, agile, alert, brisk, energetic, nimble, nippy, peppy, quick, ready, sprightly, supple.

antonyms doddering, inactive, lethargic.

spur *v.* animate, drive, goad, impel, incite, poke, press, prick, prod, prompt, propel, stimulate, urge.

antonym curb.

n. fillip, goad, impetus, impulse, incentive, incitement, inducement, motive, prick, rowel, stimulus.

antonym curb.

spurious *adj.* adulterate, adulterine, apocryphal, artificial, bastard, bogus, contrived, counterfeit, deceitful, dog, fake, false, feigned, forged, illegitimate, imitation, mock, phony, pretended, pseudo, sham, simulated, specious, supposititious, unauthentic.

antonyms authentic, genuine, real.

squabble *v.* argue, bicker, brawl, clash, dispute, fall out, fight, quarrel, row, scrap, spat, tiff, wrangle.

n. argument, barney, clash, disagreement, dispute, fight, rhubarb, row, scrap, set-to, spat, tiff.

squalid *adj.* broken-down, decayed, dingy, dirty, disgusting, fetid, filthy, foul, low, nasty, neglected, poverty-stricken, repulsive, run-down, seedy, sleazy, slovenly, slummy, sordid, uncared-for, unclean, unkempt.

antonyms clean, pleasant.

squander *v.* blow, blue, consume, dissipate, expend, fritter away, lavish, misspend, misuse, scatter, spend, splurge, throw away, waste.

square *v.* accommodate, accord, adapt, adjust, agree, align, appease, balance, bribe, conform, correspond, corrupt, discharge, fit, fix, harmonize, level, liquidate, match, quit, reconcile, regulate, rig, satisfy, settle, suborn, suit, tailor, tally, true.

adj. above-board, bourgeois, broad, complete, conservative, conventional, decent, equitable, ethical, even, exact, fair, fitting, full, genuine, honest, just, old-fashioned, on the level, opposed, orthodox, quadrate, right-angled, satisfying, solid, straight, straightforward, strait-laced, stuffy, suitable, thick-set, traditional, true, unequivocal, upright.

n. antediluvian, conformer, conformist, conservative, conventionalist, die-hard, fuddy-duddy, (old) fogy, stick-in-the-mud, traditionalist.

squeamish *adj.* coy, delicate, fastidious, finicky, nauseous, particular, prissy, prudish, punctilious, qualmish, queasy, queer, reluctant, scrupulous, sick, sickish, strait-laced.

squeeze *v.* bleed, chirt, clasp, clutch, compress, cram, crowd, crush, cuddle, embrace, enfold, extort, force, grip, hug, jam, jostle, lean on, milk, nip, oppress, pack, pinch, press, pressurize, ram, scrounge, squash, strain, stuff, thrust, wedge, wrest, wring.

n. clasp, congestion, crowd, crush, embrace, grasp, handclasp, hold, hug, jam, press, pressure, restriction, squash.

stability *n.* constancy, durability, firmness, fixity, permanence, solidity, soundness, steadfastness, steadiness, strength, sturdiness.

antonyms insecurity, instability, unsteadiness, weakness.

stable *adj.* abiding, constant, deep-rooted, durable, enduring, established, fast, firm, fixed, immutable, invariable, lasting, permanent, reliable, secure, self-balanced, sound, static, steadfast, steady, strong, sturdy, sure, unalterable, unchangeable, unwavering, well-founded.

antonyms shaky, unstable, weak, wobbly.

stack *n.* accumulation, clamp, cock, heap, hoard, load, mass, mound, mountain, pile, ruck, stockpile.

v. accumulate, amass, assemble, gather, load, pile, save, stockpile, store.

staff *n.* caduceus, cane, crew, employees, lecturers, lituus, officers, organization, personnel, pole, prop, rod, stave, teachers, team, wand, workers, workforce.

stage *n.* division, floor, juncture, lap, leg, length, level, period, phase, point, shelf, step, story, subdivision, tier.

v. arrange, do, engineer, give, mount, orchestrate, organize, perform, present, produce, put on, stage-manage.

stagger *v.* alternate, amaze, astonish, astound, confound, daddle, daidle, dumbfound, falter, flabbergast, hesitate, lurch, nonplus, overlap, overwhelm, reel, shake, shock, step, stun, stupefy, surprise, sway, teeter, titubate, totter, vacillate, waver, wobble, zigzag.

staid *adj.* calm, composed, decorous, demure, grave, quiet, sedate, self-restrained, serious, sober, sober-blooded, solemn, steady, Victorian.

antonyms debonair, frivolous, jaunty, sportive.

stain v. bedye, besmirch, blacken, blemish, blot, color, contaminate, corrupt, defile, deprave, dirty, discolor, disgrace, distain, dye, imbue, mark, smutch, soil, spot, sully, taint, tarnish, tinge.

n. blemish, blot, discoloration, disgrace, dishonor, dye, infamy, reproach, shame, slur, smirch, smutch, soil, splodge, spot, stigma, tint.

stake[1] n. loggat, pale, paling, picket, pile, pole, post, spike, standard, stang, stave, stick.

v. brace, fasten, pierce, prop, secure, support, tether, tie, tie up.

stake[2] n. ante, bet, chance, claim, concern, hazard, interest, investment, involvement, peril, pledge, prize, risk, share, venture, wager.

v. ante, bet, chance, gage, gamble, hazard, imperil, jeopardize, pledge, risk, venture, wager.

stale adj. antiquated, banal, cliché'd, cliché-ridden, common, commonplace, decayed, drab, dry, effete, faded, fetid, flat, fozy, fusty, hackneyed, hard, insipid, musty, old, old hat, overused, platitudinous, repetitious, sour, stagnant, stereotyped, tainted, tasteless, threadbare, trite, unoriginal, vapid, worn-out.

antonym fresh.

stalk[1] v. approach, follow, haunt, hunt, march, pace, pursue, shadow, stride, strut, tail, track.

stalk[2] n. bole, branch, kex, shoot, spire, stem, sterigma, trunk.

stall[1] v. delay, equivocate, hedge, obstruct, penelopize, play for time, prevaricate, stonewall, temporize.

antonym advance.

stall[2] n. bay, bench, booth, compartment, cowshed, pew, seat, stable, table.

stammer v. falter, gibber, hesitate, splutter, stumble, stutter.

stamp v. beat, brand, bray, categorize, characterize, crush, engrave, exhibit, fix, identify, impress, imprint, inscribe, label, mark, mint, mold, pound, print, pronounce, reveal, strike, trample.

n. attestation, authorization, brand, breed, cast, character, cut, description, earmark, evidence, fashion, form, hallmark, impression, imprint, incuse, kind, mark, mold, sign, signature, sort, stomp, type.

stand v. abide, allow, bear, belong, brook, continue, cost, countenance, demur, endure, erect, exist, experience, halt, handle, hold, mount, obtain, pause, place, position, prevail, put, rank, remain, rest, rise, scruple, set, stay, stomach, stop, suffer, support, sustain, take, thole, tolerate, undergo, wear, weather, withstand.

antonym advance.

n. attitude, base, booth, bracket, cradle, dais, determination, erection, frame, grandstand, halt, holder, loss, opinion, place, platform, position, rack, rank, resistance, rest, stage, staging, stall, stance, standpoint, standstill, stay, stop, stop-over, stoppage, support, table, tub, vat, witness-box.

antonym progress.

standard[1] n. average, bench-mark, canon, criterion, example, exemplar, gauge, grade, guide, guideline, level, measure, model, norm, norma, pattern, principle, requirement, rule, sample, specification, touchstone, type, yardstick.

adj. accepted, approved, authoritative, average, basic, classic, customary, definitive, established, mainstream, normal, official, orthodox, popular, prevailing, recognized, regular, set, staple, stock, typical, usual.

antonyms abnormal, irregular, unusual.

standard[2] n. banner, colors, ensign, flag, gonfalon, gonfanon, labarum, pennant, pennon, rallying-point, streamer, vexillum.

standing n. condition, continuance, credit, duration, eminence, estimation, existence, experience, footing, position, rank, reputation, repute, seniority, station, status.

adj. erect, fixed, lasting, on one's feet, permanent, perpendicular, perpetual, rampant, regular, repeated, upended, upright, vertical.

antonyms horizontal, lying.

standpoint n. angle, point of view, position, post, stance, station, vantage-point, viewpoint, Weltanschauung.

staple adj. basic, chief, essential, fundamental, key, leading, main, major, predominant, primary, principle.

antonym minor.

stare v. gape, gawk, gawp, gaze, glare, goggle, look, watch.

n. fish-eye, gaze, glare, glower, leer, look, ogle, scowl.

stark adj. absolute, arrant, austere, bald, bare, barren, bleak, blunt, cold, consummate, depressing, desolate, downright, drear, dreary, entire, flagrant, forsaken, grim, harsh, out-and-out, palpable, patent, plain, pure, severe, sheer, simple, solitary, stern, stiff, strong, unadorned, unalloyed, unmitigated, unyielding, utter.

antonyms mild, slight.

adv. absolutely, altogether, clean, completely, entirely, quite, stoutly, totally, utterly, wholly.

antonyms mildly, slightly.

start v. activate, appear, arise, begin, blench, break away, commence, create, dart, depart, engender, establish, father, flinch, found, inaugurate, initiate, instigate, institute, introduce, issue, jerk, jump, kick off, launch, leave, open, originate, pioneer, recoil, sally forth, set off, set out, set up, shoot, shy, spring forward, twitch.

antonyms finish, stop.

n. advantage, backing, beginning, birth, break, chance, commencement, convulsion, dawn, edge, fit, foundation, inauguration, inception, initiation, introduction, jar, jump, kick-off, lead, onset, opening, opportunity, outburst, outset, spasm, sponsorship, spurt, twitch.

antonyms finish, stop.

startle v. affray, agitate, alarm, amaze, astonish, astound, electrify, flush, frighten, scare, shock, spook, start, surprise.

antonym calm.

starving adj. famished, hungering, hungry, ravenous, sharp-set, starved, underfed, undernourished.

antonym fed.

state[1] v. affirm, articulate, assert, asseverate, aver, declare, enumerate, explain, expound, express, formalize, formulate, formulize, present, propound, put, report, say, specify, voice.

n. attitude, bother, case, category, ceremony, circumstances, condition, dignity, display, flap, glory, grandeur, humor, majesty, mode, mood, panic, pass, phase, plight, pomp, position, pother, predicament, shape, situation, spirits, splendor, stage, station, style, tizzy.

antonym calmness.

state[2] n. body politic, commonwealth, country, federation, government, kingdom, land, leviathan, nation, republic, territory.

adj. ceremonial, ceremonious, formal, governmental, magnificent, national, official, pompous, public, solemn.

stately *adj.* august, ceremonious, deliberate, dignified, elegant, grand, imperial, imposing, impressive, Junoesque, kingly, lofty, majestic, measured, noble, pompous, princely, queenly, regal, royal, solemn.
antonyms informal, unimpressive.

statement *n.* account, announcement, bulletin, communication, communiqué, constatation, declaration, explanation, ipse dixit, ipsissima verba, proclamation, recital, relation, report, testimony, utterance, verbal.

station *n.* appointment, base, business, calling, depot, employment, grade, habitat, head-quarters, location, occupation, office, place, position, post, rank, seat, situation, sphere, stance, standing, standing-place, status, stopping-place.
v. appoint, assign, establish, fix, garrison, install, locate, post, send, set.

statuesque *adj.* dignified, imposing, majestic, regal, stately, statuary.
antonym small.

status *n.* character, condition, consequence, degree, distinction, eminence, grade, importance, position, prestige, rank, standing, state, weight.
antonym unimportance.

statute *n.* act, decree, edict, enactment, indiction, interlocution, irade, law, ordinance, regulation, rescript, rule, ukase.

staunch[1] *adj.* constant, dependable, faithful, firm, hearty, loyal, reliable, resolute, sound, steadfast, stout, strong, sure, true, true-blue, trustworthy, trusty, watertight, yeomanly, zealous.
antonyms unreliable, wavering, weak.

staunch[2] *same as* **stanch**.

stay[1] *v.* abide, adjourn, allay, arrest, check, continue, curb, defer, delay, detain, discontinue, dwell, endure, halt, hinder, hold, hold out, hover, impede, last, linger, live, lodge, loiter, obstruct, pause, prevent, prorogue, remain, reside, restrain, settle, sojourn, stand, stop, suspend, tarry, visit, wait.
antonyms advance, leave.
n. continuance, deferment, delay, halt, holiday, pause, postponement, remission, reprieve, sojourn, stop, stopover, stopping, suspension, visit.

stay[2] *n.* brace, buttress, prop, reinforcement, shoring, stanchion, support.
v. buttress, prop, prop up, shore up, support, sustain.

steadfast *adj.* constant, dedicated, dependable, established, faithful, fast, firm, fixed, intent, loyal, perseverant, persevering, reliable, resolute, single-minded, stable, staunch, steady, unfaltering, unflinching, unswerving, unwavering.
antonyms unreliable, wavering, weak.

steady *adj.* balanced, calm, ceaseless, confirmed, consistent, constant, continuous, dependable, equable, even, faithful, firm, fixed, habitual, immovable, imperturbable, incessant, industrious, level-headed, non-stop, persistent, regular, reliable, rhythmic, safe, sedate, sensible, serene, serious-minded, settled, sober, stable, staid, steadfast, substantial, unbroken, unchangeable, unfaltering, unfluctuating, unhasting, unhasty, unhurried, uniform, uninterrupted, unremitting, unswerving, unvarying, unwavering.
antonyms unsteady, wavering.

v. balance, brace, firm, fix, secure, stabilize, support.

steal *v.* appropriate, bone, cly, convey, creep, embezzle, filch, flit, half-inch, heist, knap, knock off, lag, lift, mill, misappropriate, nab, nick, peculate, pilfer, pinch, pirate, plagiarize, poach, purloin, relieve someone of, rip off, shoplift, slink, slip, smouch, smug, snaffle, snatch, sneak, snitch, swipe, take, thieve, tiptoe.
antonym return.

stealthy *adj.* cat-like, clandestine, covert, furtive, quiet, secret, secretive, skulking, sly, sneaking, sneaky, surreptitious, underhand.
antonym open.

steamy *adj.* close, damp, gaseous, hazy, humid, misty, muggy, roky, steaming, stewy, sticky, sultry, sweaty, sweltering, vaporiform, vaporous, vaporish, vapory.

steep[1] *adj.* abrupt, bluff, excessive, exorbitant, extortionate, extreme, headlong, high, overpriced, precipitious, sheer, stiff, uncalled-for, unreasonable.
antonyms gentle, moderate.

steep[2] *v.* brine, damp, drench, fill, imbrue, imbue, immerse, infuse, macerate, marinate, moisten, permeate, pervade, pickle, saturate, seethe, soak, souse, submerge, suffuse.

steer *v.* con, conduct, control, direct, govern, guide, pilot.

stem[1] *n.* axis, branch, family, house, line, lineage, peduncle, race, shoot, stalk, stock, trunk.

stem[2] *v.* check, contain, curb, dam, oppose, resist, restrain, stanch, stay, stop, tamp.
antonyms encourage, increase.

stench *n.* mephitis, odor, pong, reek, stink, whiff.

step *n.* act, action, advance, advancement, deed, degree, demarche, doorstep, expedient, footfall, footprint, footstep, gait, halfpace, impression, level, maneuver, means, measure, move, pace, phase, point, print, procedure, proceeding, process, progression, rank, remove, round, rung, stage, stair, stride, trace, track, tread, walk.
v. move, pace, stalk, stamp, tread, walk.

stereotyped *adj.* banal, cliché'd, cliché-ridden, conventional, corny, hackneyed, mass-produced, overused, platitudinous, stale, standard, standardized, stock, threadbare, tired, trite, unoriginal.
antonyms different, unconventional.

sterile *adj.* abortive, acarpous, antiseptic, aseptic, bare, barren, disinfected, dry, empty, fruitless, germ-free, infecund, pointless, sterilized, unfruitful, unimaginative, unproductive, unprofitable, unprolific.
antonyms fruitful, septic.

stern *adj.* austere, authoritarian, bitter, cruel, flinty, forbidding, frowning, grim, hard, harsh, inflexible, relentless, rigid, rigorous, serious, severe, stark, steely, strict, unrelenting, unsmiling, unsparing, unyielding.
antonym mild.

stew *v.* agonize, boil, braise, fret, fricassee, fuss, jug, perspire, seethe, simmer, sweat, swelter, worry.
n. agitation, bother, bouillabaisse, chowder, daube, fluster, fret, fuss, goulash, hash, lobscouse, pot-au-feu, pother, ragout, tizzy, worry.

stick[1] *v.* abid, adhere, affix, attach, bind, bond, bulge, catch, cement, cleave, cling, clog, deposit, dig, drop, endure, extend, fasten, fix, fuse, glue, gore, hold, insert, install, jab, jam, join, jut, lay, linger, lodge, obtrude, paste, penetrate, persist, pierce, pin, place, plant, plonk, poke, position, prod, project, protrude,

puncture, put, put up with, remain, set, show, snag, spear, stab, stand, stay, stomach, stop, store, stuff, take, thole, thrust, tolerate, transfix, weld.
antonym unstick.

stick² *n.* baton, bavin, birch, bludgeon, branch, cane, lathi, lug, pole, quarterstaff, rod, scepter, staff, stake, stave, switch, twig, wand, whip, withy.

stick³ *n.* abuse, blame, criticism, flak, hostility, punishment, reproof.
antonym praise.

stickler *n.* fanatic, fusspot, maniac, martinet, nut, pedant, perfectionist, precisianist, purist.

sticky *adj.* adhesive, awkward, claggy, clammy, clinging, clingy, cloggy, close, dauby, delicate, difficult, discomforting, embarrassing, gluey, glutinous, gooey, gummy, hairy, humid, muggy, nasty, oppressive, painful, smeary, sultry, sweltering, syrupy, tacky, tenacious, thorny, tricky, unpleasant, viscid, viscous.
antonyms cool, dry, easy.

stiff *adj.* arduous, arthritic, artificial, austere, awkward, brisk, brittle, buckram, budge, ceremonious, chilly, clumsy, cold, constrained, creaky, crude, cruel, difficult, drastic, exacting, excessive, extreme, fatiguing, firm, forced, formal, formidable, fresh, graceless, great, hard, hardened, harsh, heavy, inelastic, inelegant, inexorable, inflexible, jerky, laborious, labored, mannered, oppressive, pertinacious, pitiless, pokerish, pompous, powerful, priggish, prim, punctilious, resistant, rheumaticky, rigid, rigorous, severe, sharp, solid, solidified, stand-offish, starch(y), stark, stilted, strict, stringent, strong, stubborn, taut, tense, tight, toilsome, tough, trying, unbending, uneasy, ungainly, ungraceful, unnatural, unrelaxed, unsupple, unyielding, uphill, vigorous, wooden.
antonyms flexible, graceful, informal, mild.

stifle *v.* asphyxiate, check, choke, curb, dampen, extinguish, hush, muffle, prevent, repress, restrain, silence, smother, stop, strangle, suffocate, suppress.
antonym encourage.

stigma *n.* blemish, blot, brand, disgrace, dishonor, imputation, mark, reproach, shame, slur, smirch, spot, stain.
antonym credit.

still *adj.* calm, hushed, inert, lifeless, motionless, noiseless, pacific, peaceful, placid, quiet, restful, serene, silent, smooth, stagnant, stationary, stilly, tranquil, undisturbed, unruffled, unstirring.
antonyms agitated, busy, disturbed, noisy.

v. allay, alleviate, appease, calm, hold back, hush, lull, pacify, quiet, quieten, restrain, settle, silence, smooth, soothe, subdue, tranquilize.
antonyms agitate, stir up.

n. hush, peace, peacefulness, quiet, quietness, silence, stillness, tranquility.
antonyms agitation, disturbance, noise.

adv. but, even so, even then, however, nevertheless, nonetheless, notwithstanding, yet.

stimulate *v.* animate, arouse, encourage, fan, fire, foment, get psyched up, goad, hop up, hype up, impel, incite, inflame, instigate, jog, prompt, provoke, psych oneself up, quicken, rouse, spur, titillate, urge, whet.
antonym discourage.

stimulus *n.* carrot, encouragement, fillip, ginger, goad, incentive, incitement, inducement, prick, provocation, spur.

antonym discouragement.

stingy *adj.* avaricious, cheeseparing, close-fisted, covetous, illiberal, inadequate, insufficient, meager, mean, measly, mingy, miserly, near, niggardly, parsimonious, penny-pinching, penurious, save-all, scanty, scrimping, small, tightfisted, ungenerous, ungiving.
antonym generous.

stinking *adj.* boozed, canned, contemptible, disgusting, drunk, fetid, foul-smelling, graveolent, grotty, ill-smelling, intoxicated, low, low-down, malodorous, mean, mephitic, noisome, pissed, plastered, pongy, reeking, rotten, smashed, smelly, sozzled, stenchy, stewed, stoned, unpleasant, vile, whiffy, wretched.
antonyms good, pleasant, sober.

stipulate *v.* agree, contract, covenant, engage, guarantee, insist upon, lay down, pledge, postulate, promise, provide, require, settle, specify.
antonym imply.

stir *v.* affect, agitate, beat, bestir, budge, disturb, electrify, emove, excite, fire, flutter, hasten, inspire, look lively, mix, move, quiver, rustle, shake, shake a leg, thrill, touch, tremble.
antonyms bore, calm, stay.

n. activity, ado, agitation, bustle, commotion, disorder, disturbance, excitement, ferment, flurry, fuss, hustle and bustle, movement, to-do, toing and froing, tumult, uproar.
antonym calm.

stock *n.* ancestry, array, assets, assortment, background, beasts, block, breed, cache, capital, cattle, choice, commodities, descent, equipment, estimation, extraction, family, flocks, forebears, fund, funds, goods, handle, herds, hoard, horses, house, inventory, investment, kindred, line, lineage, livestock, log, merchandise, parentage, pedigree, post, property, race, range, repertoire, repute, reserve, reservoir, selection, sheep, source, stem, stockpile, store, strain, stump, supply, trunk, type, variety, wares.

adj. banal, basic, bromidic, clichéd, commonplace, conventional, customary, formal, hackneyed, ordinary, overused, regular, routine, run-of-the-mill, set, standard, staple, stereotyped, traditional, trite, usual, worn-out.
antonym original.

v. deal in, handle, keep, sell, supply, trade in.

stoical *adj.* calm, cool, dispassionate, impassive, imperturbable, indifferent, long-suffering, patient, philosophic(al), phlegmatic, resigned, stoic, stolid.
antonyms anxious, depressed, furious, irascible.

stolid *adj.* apathetic, beefy, blockish, bovine, doltish, dull, heavy, impassive, lumpish, obtuse, slow, stoic(al), stupid, unemotional, wooden.
antonyms interested, lively.

stone *n.* boulder, cobble, concretion, endocarp, flagstone, gem, gemstone, gravestone, headstone, jewel, kernel, lapis, pebble, pip, pit, rock, seed, set(t), slab, tombstone.

stony *adj.* adamant, blank, callous, chilly, expressionless, frigid, hard, heartless, hostile, icy, indifferent, inexorable, lapideous, lapilliform, lithoid(al), merciless, obdurate, pitiless, steely, stonelike, unfeeling, unforgiving, unresponsive.
antonyms forgiving, friendly, soft-hearted.

stoop *v.* bend, bow, couch, crouch, descend, duck, hunch, incline, kneel, lean, squat.

n. droop, inclination, round-shoulderedness, sag, slouch, slump.

stop *v.* arrest, bar, block, break, cease, check, close, conclude, desist, discontinue, embar, end, finish, forestall, frustrate, halt, hinder, impede, intercept, intermit, interrupt, knock off, leave off, lodge, obstruct, pack (it) in, pack in, pack up, pause, plug, poop out, prevent, quit, refrain, repress, rest, restrain, scotch, seal, silence, sojourn, stall, staunch, stay, stem, stymie, suspend, tarry, terminate.

antonyms advance, continue, start.

n. bar, block, break, bung, cessation, check, conclusion, control, depot, destination, discontinuation, end, finish, halt, hindrance, impediment, plug, rest, sojourn, stage, standstill, station, stay, stop-over, stoppage, termination, terminus, ventage, visit.

antonyms continuation, start.

interj. avast, cease, cut it out, desist, easy, give over, halt, hang on, hold it, hold on, hold your horses, lay off, leave it out, refrain, stop it, wait, wait a minute, whoa.

store *v.* accumulate, cupboard, deposit, garner, hive, hoard, husband, keep, lay aside, lay by, lay in lavender, lay up, put aside, reserve, salt away, save, stash, stock, stockpile, treasure.

antonym use.

n. abundance, accumulation, cache, cupboard, depository, emporium, esteem, fund, hoard, keeping, lot, market, mart, mine, outlet, panary, plenty, plethora, provision, quantity, repository, reserve, reservoir, shop, stock, stockpile, storehouse, storeroom, supermarket, supply, value, warehouse, wealth.

antonym scarcity.

storm *n.* agitation, anger, assault, attack, blast, blitz, blitzkrieg, blizzard, clamor, commotion, cyclone, disturbance, dust-devil, furore, gale, gust, hubbub, hurricane, offensive, onset, onslaught, outbreak, outburst, outcry, paroxysm, passion, roar, row, rumpus, rush, sandstorm, squall, stir, strife, tempest, tornado, tumult, turmoil, violence, whirlwind.

antonym calm.

v. assail, assault, beset, bluster, charge, complain, expugn, flounce, fly, fume, rage, rant, rave, rush, scold, stalk, stamp, stomp, thunder.

stormy *adj.* blustering, blustery, boisterous, choppy, dirty, foul, gustful, gusty, oragious, raging, rough, squally, tempestuous, turbulent, wild, windy.

antonym calm.

story[1] *n.* account, ancedote, article, chronicle, episode, fable, fairy-tale, falsehood, feature, fib, fiction, historiette, history, legend, lie, Märchen, myth, narration, narrative, news, novel, plot, recital, record, relation, report, romance, scoop, spiel, tale, untruth, version, yarn.

story[2] *n.* deck, étage, flight, floor, level, stage, stratum, tier.

stout *adj.* able-bodied, athletic, beefy, big, bold, brave, brawny, bulky, burly, chopping, corpulent, courageous, dauntless, doughty, embonpoint, enduring, fat, fearless, fleshy, gallant, hardy, heavy, hulking, husky, intrepid, lion-hearted, lusty, manly, muscular, obese, overweight, plucky, plump, portly, resolute, robust, rotund, stalwart, strapping, strong, sturdy, substantial, thick, tough, tubby, valiant, valorous, vigorous.

antonyms slim, timid, weak.

straight *adj.* accurate, aligned, arranged, authentic, balanced, blunt, bourgeois, candid, consecutive, conservative, continuous, conventional, decent, direct, downright, equitable, erect, even, fair, forthright, frank, honest, honorable, horizontal, just, law-abiding, level, near, neat, non-stop, normal, orderly, organized, orthodox, outright, perpendicular, plain, plumb, point-blank, pure, reliable, respectable, right, running, settled, shipshape, short, smooth, solid, square, straightforward, successive, sustained, through, tidy, traditional, true, trustworthy, unadulterated, undeviating, undiluted, uninterrupted, unmixed, unqualified, unrelieved, unswerving, upright, vertical.

antonyms circuitous, dilute, dishonest, evasive, indirect, roundabout.

adv. candidly, directly, frankly, honestly, outspokenly, point-blank, upright.

straightforward *adj.* candid, clear-cut, direct, easy, elementary, forthright, genuine, guileless, honest, open, open-and-shut, penny-plain, routine, simple, sincere, truthful, uncomplicated, undemanding.

antonyms complicated, devious, evasive.

strain[1] *v.* compress, distend, drive, embrace, endeavor, exert, express, extend, fatigue, filter, injure, labor, overtax, overwork, percolate, pull, purify, restrain, retch, riddle, screen, seep, separate, sieve, sift, sprain, squeeze, stretch, strive, struggle, tauten, tax, tear, tighten, tire, tug, twist, weaken, wrench, wrest, wrick.

n. anxiety, burden, effort, exertion, force, height, injury, key, pitch, pressure, pull, sprain, stress, struggle, tautness, tension, wrench.

strain[2] *n.* ancestry, blood, descent, extraction, family, humor, lineage, manner, pedigree, race, spirit, stem, stock, streak, style, suggestion, suspicion, temper, tendency, tone, trace, trait, vein, way.

strained *adj.* artificial, awkward, constrained, difficult, embarrassed, epitonic, false, forced, labored, self-conscious, stiff, tense, uncomfortable, uneasy, unnatural, unrelaxed.

antonym natural.

straitened *adj.* difficult, distressed, embarrassed, impoverished, limited, poor, reduced, restricted.

antonyms easy, well-off.

strait-laced *adj.* moralistic, narrow, narrow-minded, old-maidish, prim, proper, prudish, puritanical, strict, stuffy, upright, Victorian.

antonyms broad-minded, easy-going.

strange *adj.* abnormal, alien, astonishing, awkward, bewildered, bizarre, curious, disorientated, disoriented, eccentric, eerie, exceptional, exotic, extraordinary, fantastic(al), foreign, funny, irregular, lost, marvelous, mystifying, new, novel, odd, out-of-the-way, peculiar, perplexing, queer, rare, remarkable, remote, singular, sinister, unaccountable, unacquainted, uncanny, unco, uncomfortable, uncommon, unexplained, unexplored, unfamiliar, unheard of, unknown, untried, unversed, weird, wonderful.

antonyms comfortable, common, familiar, ordinary.

stranger *n.* alien, foreigner, guest, incomer, newcomer, non-member, outlander, unknown, visitor.

antonyms local, native.

strap *n.* belt, leash, thong, tie, vitta.

v. beat, belt, bind, buckle, fasten, flog, lash, scourge, secure, tie, truss, whip.

stratagem *n*. artifice, device, dodge, feint, fetch, intrigue, maneuver, plan, plot, ploy, ruse, ruse de guerre, scheme, subterfuge, trick, wile.

strategy *n*. approach, design, maneuvering, plan, planning, policy, procedure, program, scheme, way.

stray *v*. deviate, digress, diverge, drift, err, get lost, meander, ramble, range, roam, rove, straggle, wander (off).

adj. abandoned, accidental, chance, erratic, forwandered, freak, homeless, lost, odd, random, roaming, scattered, vagrant.

stream *n*. beck, brook, burn, course, creek, current, drift, flow, freshet, ghyll, gill, gush, outpouring, rill, rillet, river, rivulet, run, runnel, rush, surge, tide, torrent, tributary.

v. cascade, course, emit, flood, flow, glide, gush, issue, pour, run, shed, spill, spout, surge, well out.

streamer *n*. banner, ensign, flag, gonfalon, gonfanon, pennant, pennon, plume, ribbon, standard.

street *n*. avenue, boulevard, corso, crescent, drive, expressway, freeway, highway, lane, main drag, parkway, road, roadway, row, terrace, thoroughfare, thruway, turnpike.

strength *n*. advantage, anchor, asset, backbone, brawn, brawniness, cogency, concentration, courage, effectiveness, efficacy, energy, firmness, foison, force, fortitude, fushion, health, intensity, lustiness, mainstay, might, muscle, potency, power, resolution, robustness, security, sinew, spirit, stamina, stoutness, sturdiness, thew, toughness, vehemence, vigor, virtue.

antonyms timidity, weakness.

strengthen *v*. afforce, bolster, brace, buttress, confirm, consolidate, corroborate, edify, encourage, enhance, establish, fortify, harden, hearten, heighten, increase, intensify, invigorate, justify, nerve, nourish, reinforce, rejuvenate, restore, steel, stiffen, substantiate, support, toughen.

antonym weaken.

strenuous *adj*. active, arduous, bold, demanding, determined, eager, earnest, energetic, exhausting, hard, Herculean, laborious, persistent, resolute, spirited, strong, taxing, tireless, toilful, toilsome, tough, uphill, urgent, vigorous, warm, zealous.

antonyms easy, effortless.

stress *n*. accent, accentuation, anxiety, beat, burden, emphasis, emphaticalness, force, hassle, importance, oppression, pressure, significance, strain, tautness, tension, trauma, urgency, weight, worry.

antonym relaxation.

v. accentuate, belabor, emphasize, repeat, strain, tauten, underline, underscore.

antonym relax.

stretch *n*. area, bit, distance, exaggeration, expanse, extensibility, extension, extent, period, reach, run, space, spell, spread, stint, strain, sweep, term, time, tract.

v. cover, distend, elongate, expand, extend, inflate, lengthen, pull, rack, reach, spread, strain, swell, tauten, tighten, unfold, unroll.

antonyms relax, squeeze.

strict *adj*. absolute, accurate, austere, authoritarian, close, complete, exact, faithful, firm, harsh, meticulous, no-nonsense, particular, perfect, precise, religious, restricted, rigid, rigorous, scrupulous,

severe, stern, stringent, thoroughgoing, total, true, unsparing, utter, Victorian.

antonyms easy-going, flexible, mild.

strident *adj*. cacophonous, clamorous, clashing, discordant, grating, harsh, jangling, jarring, loud, rasping, raucous, screeching, shrill, stridulant, stridulous, unmusical, vociferous.

antonyms quiet, sweet.

strife *n*. animosity, battle, bickering, brigue, colluctation, combat, conflict, contention, contest, contestation, controversy, discord, dissension, friction, quarrel, rivalry, row, squabbling, struggle, warfare, wrangling.

antonym peace.

strike *n*. attack, buffet, hit, mutiny, raid, refusal, stoppage, thump, walk-out, wallop, work-to-rule.

v. achieve, affect, afflict, arrange, assail, assault, assume, attack, attain, bang, beat, bop, box, buff, buffet, cancel, chastise, clap, clash, clobber, clout, clump, cob, coin, collide with, cuff, dart, dash, delete, devastate, discover, dismantle, douse, down tools, drive, dunt, effect, encounter, find, force, hammer, hit, impel, impress, interpose, invade, knock, mutiny, penetrate, pierce, pound, print, punish, ratify, reach, register, remove, revolt, seem, shoot, slap, slat, smack, smite, sock, stamp, stumble across, stumble upon, surrender, swap, swipe, swop, thrust, thump, touch, trap, turn up, uncover, unearth, walk out, wallop, wham, work to rule, zap.

striking *adj*. arresting, astonishing, conspicuous, dazzling, distingué(e), extraordinary, forcible, foudroyant, frappant, impressive, memorable, noticeable, outstanding, salient, stunning, wonderful.

antonym unimpressive.

stringent *adj*. binding, demanding, exacting, flexible, inflexible, mild, rigid, rigorous, severe, strict, tight, tough.

strip[1] *v*. bare, clear, defoliate, denude, deprive, despoil, devest, disadorn, disembellish, disgarnish, disinvest, disleaf, disleave, dismantle, displenish, disrobe, divest, doff, empty, excoriate, excorticate, expose, gut, husk, lay bare, loot, peel, pillage, plunder, ransack, rob, sack, skin, spoil, unclothe, uncover, undress, widow.

antonyms cover, provide.

strip[2] *n*. band, belt, bit, fillet, lath, list, piece, ribbon, sash, screed, shred, slat, slip, spline, strake, strap, swathe, thong, tongue, vitta.

stripe *n*. band, bar, belt, chevron, flash, fleck, striation, vitta.

strive *v*. attempt, compete, contend, endeavor, fight, labor, push oneself, strain, struggle, toil, try, work.

stroke *n*. accomplishment, achievement, apoplexy, attack, blow, clap, collapse, effleurage, feat, fit, flourish, hit, knock, move, movement, pat, rap, seizure, shock, swap, swop, thump.

v. caress, clap, fondle, pat, pet, rub.

stroll *v*. amble, dander, dawdle, mosey, promenade, ramble, saunter, stooge, toddle, wander.

n. airing, constitutional, dawdle, excursion, promenade, ramble, saunter, toddle, turn, walk.

strong *adj*. acute, aggressive, athletic, beefy, biting, bold, brave, brawny, bright, brilliant, burly, capable, clear, clear-cut, cogent, compelling, competent, concentrated, convincing, courageous, dazzling, dedicated, deep, deep-rooted, determined, distinct, drastic, durable, eager, effective, efficient, emphasized, excelling, extreme, fast-moving, fervent, fervid, fierce, firm, forceful, forcible, formidable, glaring, great, grievous, gross, hale, hard, hard-nosed, hard-wearing, hardy, heady, healthy, hearty, heavy-duty, Herculean, highly-flavored, highly-seasoned, hot, intemperate, intense, intoxicating, keen, loud, lusty, marked, muscular, nappy, numerous, offensive, overpowering, persuasive, petrous, piquant, pithy, plucky, pollent, potent, powerful, pungent, pure, rank, redoubtable, reinforced, resilient, resolute, resourceful, robust, self-assertive, severe, sharp, sinewy, sound, spicy, stalwart, stark, staunch, steadfast, sthenic, stout, stout-hearted, strapping, stressed, sturdy, substantial, telling, tenacious, thewy, tough, trenchant, undiluted, unmistakable, unseemly, unyielding, urgent, vehement, violent, virile, vivid, weighty, well-armed, well-built, well-established, well-founded, well-knit, well-protected, well-set, well-versed, zealous.

antonyms mild, weak.

structure *n.* arrangement, building, compages, configuration, conformation, construction, contexture, design, edifice, erection, fabric, form, formation, make-up, organization, pile, set-up.

v. arrange, assemble, build, construct, design, form, organize, shape.

struggle *v.* agonize, battle, compete, contend, fight, grapple, labor, scuffle, strain, strive, toil, work, wrestle.

antonyms give in, rest.

n. agon, agony, battle, brush, clash, combat, conflict, contest, effort, encounter, exertion, grind, hostilities, labor, luctation, pains, scramble, skirmish, strife, toil, tussle, work.

antonyms ease, submission.

stubborn *adj.* bull-headed, contumacious, cross-grained, difficult, dogged, dour, fixed, headstrong, inflexible, intractable, intransigent, mulish, obdurate, obstinate, opinionated, persistent, pertinacious, pig-headed, recalcitrant, refractory, rigid, self-willed, stiff, stiff-necked, tenacious, unbending, unmanageable, unshakable, unyielding, wilful.

antonym compliant.

student *n.* apprentice, bajan, bejant, bookman, chela, co-ed, collegianer, contemplator, disciple, fresher, freshman, learner, observer, pupil, scholar, seminarist, soph, sophomore, undergraduate, undergraduette.

studio *n.* atelier, school, workroom, workshop.

study *v.* analyze, cogitate, con, consider, contemplate, cram, deliberate, dig, examine, investigate, learn, lucubrate, meditate, mug up, peruse, ponder, pore over, read, read up, research, scan, scrutinize, survey, swot.

n. analysis, application, attention, cogitation, consideration, contemplation, cramming, critique, examination, inclination, inquiry, inspection, interest, investigation, learning, lessons, lucubration, memoir, monograph, prolusion, reading, report, research, reverie, review, scrutiny, survey, swotting, thesis, thought, zeal.

stuff *v.* binge, bombast, compress, cram, crowd, fill, force, gobble, gorge, gormandize, guzzle, jam, load, overindulge, pack, pad, push, ram, sate, satiate, shove, squeeze, steeve, stodge, stow, trig, wedge.

antonyms nibble, unload.

n. belongings, clobber, cloth, effects, equipment,

essence, fabric, furniture, gear, goods, impedimenta, junk, kit, luggage, material, materials, matériel, matter, objects, paraphernalia, pith, possessions, provisions, quintessence, staple, substance, tackle, textile, things, trappings.

stumble *v.* blunder, fall, falter, flounder, fluff, hesitate, lurch, reel, slip, stagger, stammer, stutter, titubate, trip.

stun *v.* amaze, astonish, astound, bedeafen, bewilder, confound, confuse, daze, deafen, dumbfound, flabbergast, overcome, overpower, shock, stagger, stupefy.

stunning *adj.* beautiful, brilliant, dazing, dazzling, devastating, gorgeous, great, heavenly, impressive, lovely, marvelous, ravishing, remarkable, sensational, smashing, spectacular, stotting, striking, wonderful.

antonyms poor, ugly.

stunt[1] *n.* act, campaign, deed, enterprise, exploit, feat, feature, gest(e), performance, tour de force, trick, turn.

stunt[2] *v.* arrest, check, dwarf, hamper, hinder, impede, restrict, slow, stop.

antonym promote.

stupefy *v.* amaze, astound, baffle, benumb, bewilder, confound, daze, drowse, dumbfound, hocus, numb, shock, stagger, stun.

stupid *adj.* anserine, asinine, beef-brained, beef-witted, blockish, Boeotian, boobyish, boring, bovine, brainless, clueless, crackbrained, cretinous, cuckoo, damfool, dazed, deficient, dense, dim, doltish, dopey, dovie, dozy, drippy, dull, dumb, fat-witted, foolish, fozy, futile, gaumless, glaikit, gormless, groggy, gullible, half-baked, half-witted, hammer-headed, idiotic, ill-advised, imbecilic, inane, indiscreet, insensate, insensible, insulse, irrelevant, irresponsible, laughable, ludicrous, lumpen, lurdan, meaningless, mindless, moronic, naïve, nonsensical, obtuse, opaque, pointless, puerile, punch-drunk, rash, semiconscious, senseless, short-sighted, simple, simple-minded, slow, slow-witted, sluggish, stolid, stunned, stupefied, thick, thick-headed, thick-witted, trivial, unintelligent, unthinking, vacuous, vapid, witless, wooden-headed.

antonyms alert, clever.

stupor *n.* coma, daze, inertia, insensibility, kef, lethargy, numbness, stupefaction, torpor, trance, unconsciousness, wonder.

antonym alertness.

sturdy *adj.* athletic, brawny, determined, durable, firm, flourishing, hardy, hearty, husky, lusty, muscular, obstinate, powerful, resolute, robust, secure, solid, stalwart, staunch, steadfast, stout, strong, substantial, vigorous, well-built, well-made.

antonyms decrepit, puny.

style *n.* affluence, appearance, approach, bon ton, category, chic, comfort, cosmopolitanism, custom, cut, dash, design, diction, dressiness, dress-sense, ease, élan, elegance, expression, fashion, fashionableness, flair, flamboyance, form, genre, grace, grandeur, hand, haut ton, kind, luxury, manner, method, mode, panache, pattern, phraseology, phrasing, pizzazz, polish, rage, refinement, savoir-faire, smartness, sophistication, sort, spirit, strain, stylishness, taste, technique, tenor, tone, treatment, trend, type, urbanity, variety, vein, vogue, way, wording.

antonym inelegance.

v. adapt, address, arrange, call, christen, create, cut,

denominate, design, designate, dress, dub, entitle, fashion, label, name, shape, tailor, term, title.

suave *adj.* affable, agreeable, bland, charming, civilized, courteous, diplomatic, gracious, obliging, pleasing, polite, smooth, smooth-tongued, soft-spoken, sophisticated, unctuous, urbane, worldly.
antonym unsophisticated.

subdue *v.* allay, break, check, conquer, control, crush, damp, dampen, daunt, defeat, discipline, humble, master, mellow, moderate, overcome, overpower, overrun, quell, quieten, reduce, repress, soften, soft-pedal, subact, subject, suppress, tame, trample, vanquish.
antonym arouse.

subject *n.* affair, business, case, chapter, citizen, client, dependant, ground, issue, liegeman, matter, mind, national, object, participant, patient, point, question, subordinate, substance, theme, topic, vassal, victim.
antonym master.
adj. answerable, captive, cognizable, conditional, contingent, dependent, disposed, enslaved, exposed, heteronomous, inferior, liable, obedient, open, prone, satellite, subjugated, submissive, subordinate, subservient, susceptible, vulnerable.
antonyms free, insusceptible, superior.
v. expose, lay open, subdue, submit, subordinate, treat.

sublime *adj.* Dantean, Dantesque, elevated, eminent, empyreal, empyrean, exalted, glorious, grand, great, high, imposing, lofty, magnificent, majestic, noble, transcendent.
antonym lowly.

submerge *v.* deluge, demerge, dip, drown, duck, dunk, engulf, flood, immerse, implunge, inundate, overflow, overwhelm, plunge, sink, submerse, swamp.
antonym surface.

submissive *adj.* abject, accommodating, acquiescent, amenable, biddable, bootlicking, complaisant, compliant, deferential, docile, dutiful, humble, ingratiating, malleable, meek, obedient, obeisant, obsequious, passive, patient, pliant, resigned, subdued, subservient, supine, tractable, uncomplaining, unresisting, yielding.
antonym intractable.

submit *v.* accede, acquiesce, advance, agree, argue, assert, bend, bow, capitulate, claim, commit, comply, contend, defer, endure, knuckle under, move, present, proffer, propose, propound, put, refer, state, stoop, succumb, suggest, surrender, table, tender, tolerate, volunteer, yield.
antonym struggle.

subordinate *adj.* ancillary, auxiliary, dependent, inferior, junior, lesser, lower, menial, minor, secondary, servient, subject, subservient, subsidiary, supplementary.
antonym superior.
n. adjunct, aide, assistant, attendant, dependant, inferior, junior, second, second banana, stooge, sub, subaltern, underdog, underling, underman, underworkman, weakling.
antonym superior.
antonym superiority.

subpoena *n.* court order, decree, summons, writ.

subsequent *adj.* after, consequent, consequential, ensuing, following, later, postliminary, postliminous, resulting, succeeding.

antonym previous.

subside *v.* abate, collapse, decline, decrease, descend, diminish, drop, dwindle, ease, ebb, fall, lessen, lower, moderate, quieten, recede, settle, sink, slacken, slake, wane.
antonym increase.

subsidy *n.* aid, allowance, assistance, backing, contribution, finance, grant, help, sponsorship, subvention, support.

subsist *v.* continue, endure, exist, hold out, inhere, last, live, remain, survive.

substance *n.* actuality, affluence, assets, body, burden, concreteness, consistence, element, entity, essence, estate, fabric, force, foundation, gist, gravamen, ground, hypostasis, import, material, matter, meaning, means, nitty-gritty, pith, property, reality, resources, significance, solidity, stuff, subject, subject-matter, texture, theme, wealth.

substantial *adj.* actual, ample, big, bulky, considerable, corporeal, durable, enduring, essential, existent, firm, full-bodied, generous, goodly, hefty, important, large, massive, material, positive, real, significant, sizable, solid, sound, stout, strong, sturdy, tidy, true, valid, weighty, well-built, worthwhile.
antonyms insignificant, small.

substantiate *v.* affirm, authenticate, confirm, corroborate, embody, establish, prove, support, validate, verify.
antonym disprove.

substitute *v.* change, commute, exchange, interchange, replace, subrogate, swap, switch.
n. agent, alternate, depute, deputy, equivalent, ersatz, locum, locum tenens, makeshift, proxy, relief, replacement, replacer, reserve, stand-by, stop-gap, sub, succedaneum, supply, surrogate, temp, vicar.
adj. acting, additional, alternative, ersatz, proxy, replacement, reserve, second, surrogate, temporary, vicarious.

substitution *n.* change, exchange, interchange, replacement, swap, swapping, switch, switching.

subterfuge *n.* artifice, deception, deviousness, dodge, duplicity, evasion, excuse, expedient, machination, maneuver, ploy, pretense, pretext, quibble, ruse, scheme, shift, stall, stratagem, trick.
antonyms honesty, openness.

subtle *adj.* artful, astute, crafty, cunning, deep, delicate, designing, devious, discriminating, elusive, faint, fine-drawn, fine-spun, impalpable, implied, indirect, ingenious, insinuated, intriguing, keen, Machiavellian, nice, obstruse, over-refined, penetrating, profound, rarefied, refined, scheming, shrewd, slight, sly, sophisticated, tenuous, understated, wily.
antonyms open, unsubtle.

subtract *v.* debit, deduct, detract, diminish, remove, withdraw.
antonyms add, add to.

subvert *v.* confound, contaminate, corrupt, debase, demolish, demoralize, deprave, destroy, disrupt, invalidate, overturn, pervert, poison, raze, ruin, sabotage, undermine, upset, vitiate, wreck.
antonyms boost, uphold.

succeed *v.* arrive, ensue, fadge, flourish, follow, make good, make it, prosper, result, supervene, thrive, triumph, work.
antonyms fail, precede.

success *n.* ascendancy, bestseller, celebrity, eminence,

fame, fortune, happiness, hit, luck, prosperity, sensation, somebody, star, triumph, VIP, well-doing, winner.
antonym failure.

successful *adj.* acknowledged, bestselling, booming, efficacious, favorable, flourishing, fortunate, fruitful, lucky, lucrative, moneymaking, paying, profitable, prosperous, rewarding, satisfactory, satisfying, thriven, thriving, top, unbeaten, victorious, wealthy, well-doing.
antonym unsuccessful.

succession *n.* accession, assumption, chain, concatenation, continuation, course, cycle, descendants, descent, elevation, flow, inheritance, line, lineage, order, procession, progression, race, run, sequence, series, train.

successive *adj.* consecutive, following, in succession, sequent, succeeding.

succinct *adj.* brief, compact, compendious, concise, condensed, gnomic, laconic, pithy, short, summary, terse.
antonym wordy.

succor *v.* aid, assist, befriend, comfort, encourage, foster, help, help out, nurse, relieve, support.
antonym undermine.
n. aid, assistance, comfort, help, helping hand, ministrations, relief, support.

sudden *adj.* abrupt, hasty, hurried, impulsive, prompt, quick, rapid, rash, snap, startling, subitaneous, swift, unexpected, unforeseen, unusual.
antonym slow.

suffer *v.* ache, agonize, allow, bear, brook, deteriorate, endure, experience, feel, grieve, hurt, let, permit, sorrow, support, sustain, tolerate, undergo.

suffering *n.* ache, affliction, agony, anguish, discomfort, distress, hardship, martyrdom, misery, ordeal, pain, pangs, torment, torture.

sufficient *adj.* adequate, competent, effective, enough, satisfactory, sufficing, well-off, well-to-do.
antonyms insufficient, poor.

suffocate *v.* asphyxiate, choke, smother, stifle, strangle, throttle.

suggest *v.* advise, advocate, connote, evoke, hint, imply, indicate, inkle, innuendo, insinuate, intimate, move, propose, recommend.
antonyms demonstrate, order.

suggestion *n.* breath, hint, incitement, indication, innuendo, insinuation, intimation, motion, plan, proposal, proposition, recommendation, suspicion, temptation, trace, whisper.
antonyms demonstration, order.

suit *v.* accommodate, adapt, adjust, agree, answer, become, befit, correspond, do, fashion, fit, gee, gratify, harmonize, match, modify, please, proportion, satisfy, tailor, tally.
antonyms clash, displease.
n. action, addresses, appeal, attentions, case, cause, clothing, costume, courtship, dress, ensemble, entreaty, get-up, habit, invocation, kind, lawsuit, outfit, petition, prayer, proceeding, prosecution, request, rig-out, series, trial, type.

suitable *adj.* acceptable, accordant, adequate, applicable, apposite, appropriate, apt, becoming, befitting, competent, conformable, congenial, congruent, consonant, convenient, correspondent, due, fit, fitting, opportune, pertinent, proper, relevant, right, satisfac-

tory, seemly, square, suited, well-becoming, well-beseeming.
antonym unsuitable.

sulky *adj.* aloof, churlish, cross, disgruntled, grouty, ill-humored, moody, morose, perverse, pettish, petulant, put out, resentful, sullen.
antonym cheerful.

sullen *adj.* baleful, brooding, cheerless, cross, dark, dismal, dull, farouche, gloomy, glowering, glum, heavy, lumpish, malignant, moody, morose, obstinate, perverse, silent, somber, sour, stubborn, sulky, surly, unsociable.
antonym cheerful.

sultry *adj.* close, come-hither, erotic, hot, humid, indecent, lurid, muggy, oppressive, passionate, provocative, seductive, sensual, sexy, sticky, stifling, stuffy, sweltering, torrid, voluptuous.
antonyms cold, cool.

sum *n.* aggregate, amount, completion, culmination, entirety, height, quantity, reckoning, result, score, substance, sum total, summary, tally, total, totality, whole.

summarize *v.* abbreviate, abridge, condense, encapsulate, epitomize, outline, précis, review, shorten, sum up.
antonym expand (on).

summary *n.* abridgment, abstract, compendium, digest, epitome, essence, extract, outline, précis, recapitulation, résumé, review, rundown, summation, summing-up, synopsis.
adj. arbitrary, brief, compact, compendious, concise, condensed, cursory, expeditious, hasty, laconic, perfunctory, pithy, short, succinct.
antonym lengthy.

summit *n.* acme, apex, apogee, crown, culmination, head, height, peak, pinnacle, point, top, zenith.
antonyms bottom, nadir.

summon *v.* accite, arouse, assemble, beckon, bid, call, cite, convene, convoke, gather, hist, invite, invoke, mobilize, muster, preconize, rally, rouse.
antonym dismiss.

sundry *adj.* a few, assorted, different, divers, miscellaneous, separate, several, some, varied, various.

sunny *adj.* beaming, blithe, bright, brilliant, buoyant, cheerful, cheery, clear, cloudless, fine, genial, happy, joyful, light-hearted, luminous, optimistic, pleasant, radiant, smiling, summery, sun-bright, sunlit, sunshiny.
antonym gloomy.

superannuated *adj.* aged, antiquated, decrepit, fogram, moribund, obsolete, old, past it, pensioned off, put out to grass, retired, senile, superannuate.
antonym young.

superb *adj.* admirable, breathtaking, choice, clipping, excellent, exquisite, fine, first-rate, gorgeous, grand, magnificent, marvelous, splendid, superior, unrivaled.
antonym poor.

supercilious *adj.* arrogant, condescending, contemptuous, disdainful, haughty, highty-tighty, hoity-toity, imperious, insolent, lofty, lordly, overbearing, patronizing, proud, scornful, snooty, snotty, snouty, stuck-up, toffee-nosed, uppish, uppity, upstage, vainglorious.
antonym humble.

superficial *adj.* apparent, casual, cosmetic, cursory,

desultory, empty, empty-headed, evident, exterior, external, frivolous, hasty, hurried, lightweight, nodding, ostensible, outward, passing, perfunctory, peripheral, seeming, shallow, silly, sketchy, skin-deep, slapdash, slight, surface, trivial, unanalytical, unreflective.

antonym detailed.

superintend *v.* administer, control, direct, guide, inspect, manage, overlook, oversee, run, steer, supervise.

superintendence *n.* administration, care, charge, control, direction, government, guidance, inspection, management, supervision, surveillance.

superintendent *n.* administrator, chief, conductor, controller, curator, director, gaffer, governor, inspector, manager, overseer, supervisor.

superior *adj.* admirable, airy, better, choice, condescending, de luxe, disdainful, distinguished, excellent, exceptional, exclusive, fine, first-class, first-rate, good, grander, greater, haughty, high-class, higher, hightytighty, hoity-toity, lofty, lordly, par excellence, patronizing, predominant, preferred, pretentious, prevailing, respectable, snobbish, snooty, snotty, snouty, stuck-up, supercilious, superordinate, surpassing, top-flight, top-notch, transcendent, unrivaled, upper, uppish, uppity, upstage, worthy.

antonyms humble, inferior.

n. boss, chief, director, foreman, gaffer, manager, principal, senior, supervisor.

antonyms inferior, junior.

superiority *n.* advantage, ascendancy, edge, excellence, lead, predominance, pre-eminence, preponderance, prevalence, supremacy, vis major.

antonym inferiority.

superlative *adj.* consummate, crack, excellent, greatest, highest, magnificent, matchless, nonpareil, outstanding, peerless, supreme, surpassing, transcendent, unbeatable, unbeaten, unparalleled, unrivaled, unsurpassed.

antonym poor.

supernatural *adj.* abnormal, dark, ghostly, hidden, hyperphysical, metaphysical, miraculous, mysterious, mystic, occult, paranormal, phantom, preternatural, psychic, spectral, spiritual, superlunary, supersensible, supersensory, uncanny, unearthly, unnatural.

antonym natural.

supervise *v.* administer, conduct, control, direct, general, handle, inspect, keep tabs on, manage, oversee, preside over, run, superintend.

supervision *n.* administration, auspices, care, charge, control, direction, guidance, instruction, leading-strings, management, oversight, stewardship, superintendence, surveillance.

supervisor *n.* administrator, boss, chief, foreman, gaffer, inspector, manager, overseer, steward, superintendent.

supplant *v.* displace, dispossess, oust, overthrow, remove, replace, supersede, topple, undermine, unseat.

supple *adj.* bending, double-jointed, elastic, flexible, limber, lithe, loose-limbed, plastic, pliable, pliant, whippy, willowish, willowy.

antonym rigid.

supplement *n.* addendum, addition, appendix, codicil, complement, extra, insert, postscript, pull-out, sequel, supplemental, supplementary, suppletion.

v. add, add to, augment, complement, eke, eke out, extend, fill up, reinforce, supply, top up.

antonym deplete.

supplication *n.* appeal, entreaty, invocation, orison, petition, plea, pleading, prayer, request, rogation, solicitation, suit, supplicat.

supply *v.* afford, contribute, endow, equip, fill, furnish, give, grant, minister, outfit, produce, provide, purvey, replenish, satisfy, stock, store, victual, yield.

antonym take.

n. cache, fund, hoard, materials, necessities, provender, provisions, quantity, rations, reserve, reservoir, service, source, stake, stock, stockpile, store, stores.

antonym lack.

support *v.* adminiculate, advocate, aid, appui, appuy, assist, authenticate, back, bear, bolster, brace, brook, buttress, carry, champion, cherish, confirm, corroborate, countenance, crutch, defend, document, endorse, endure, finance, foster, fund, help, hold, keep, maintain, nourish, promote, prop, rally round, reinforce, second, stand (for), stay, stomach, strengthen, strut, submit, subsidize, substantiate, succor, suffer, sustain, take (someone's) part, thole, tolerate, underpin, underwrite, uphold, verify.

antonyms contradict, oppose.

n. abutment, adminicle, aid, aidance, approval, appui, assistance, back, backbone, backer, backing, back-stays, backstop, blessing, brace, championship, comfort, comforter, crutch, encouragement, foundation, friendship, fulcrum, furtherance, help, jockstrap, keep, lining, livelihood, loyalty, mainstay, maintenance, patronage, pillar, post, prop, protection, relief, second, sheet-anchor, shore, stanchion, stay, stiffener, subsistence, succor, supporter, supportment, supporture, sustenanace, sustenance, underpinning, upkeep.

antonym opposition.

supporter *n.* adherent, advocate, ally, apologist, bottle-holder, champion, co-worker, defender, fan, follower, friend, heeler, helper, patron, seconder, sponsor, upholder, well-wisher.

antonym opponent.

suppose *v.* assume, believe, calculate, conceive, conclude, conjecture, consider, expect, fancy, guess, hypothesize, hypothetize, imagine, infer, judge, opine, posit, postulate, presume, presuppose, pretend, surmise, think.

antonym know.

supposition *n.* assumption, conjecture, doubt, guess, guesstimate, guesswork, hypothesis, idea, notion, opinion, postulate, presumption, speculation, surmise, theory.

antonym knowledge.

suppress *v.* censor, check, conceal, conquer, contain, crush, extinguish, muffle, muzzle, overpower, overthrow, quash, quell, repress, restrain, silence, smother, snuff out, squelch, stamp out, stifle, stop, strangle, subdue, submerge, vote down, withhold.

antonyms encourage, incite.

supremacy *n.* ascendancy, dominance, domination, dominion, hegemony, lordship, mastery, paramountcy, predominance, pre-eminence, primacy, sovereignty, sway.

supreme *adj.* cardinal, chief, consummate, crowning, culminating, extreme, final, first, foremost, greatest, head, highest, incomparable, leading, matchless, nonpareil, paramount, peerless, predominant, pre-eminent, prevailing, prime, principal, second-to-none, sovereign, superlative, surpassing, top, transcendent, ultimate, unbeatable, unbeaten, unsurpassed, utmost, world-beating.

antonyms lowly, poor, slight.

sure *adj.* accurate, assured, bound, certain, clear, confident, convinced, decided, definite, dependable, effective, fast, firm, fixed, foolproof, guaranteed, honest, indisputable, ineluctable, inescapable, inevitable, infallible, irrevocable, persuaded, positive, precise, reliable, safe, satisfied, secure, solid, stable, steadfast, steady, sure-fire, trustworthy, trusty, undeniable, undoubted, unerring, unfailing, unmistakable, unswerving, unwavering.

antonyms doubtful, unsure.

surface *n.* covering, day, exterior, façade, face, facet, grass, outside, plane, side, skin, superficies, top, veneer, working-surface, worktop.

antonym interior.

adj. apparent, exterior, external, outer, outside, outward, superficial.

antonym interior.

v. appear, come to light, emerge, materialize, rise, transpire.

antonyms disappear, sink.

surge *v.* billow, eddy, gush, heave, rise, roll, rush, seethe, swell, swirl, tower, undulate.

n. access, billow, breaker, efflux, flood, flow, gurgitation, gush, intensification, outpouring, roller, rush, swell, uprush, upsurge, wave.

surly *adj.* bearish, brusque, chuffy, churlish, crabbed, cross, crusty, curmudgeonly, grouchy, gruff, grum, gurly, ill-natured, morose, perverse, sulky, sullen, testy, uncivil, ungracious.

antonym pleasant.

surmise *v.* assume, conclude, conjecture, consider, deduce, fancy, guess, imagine, infer, opine, presume, speculate, suppose, suspect.

antonym know.

n. assumption, conclusion, conjecture, deduction, guess, hypothesis, idea, inference, notion, opinion, possibility, presumption, speculation, supposition, suspicion, thought.

antonym certainty.

surmount *v.* conquer, exceed, get over, master, overcome, surpass, triumph over, vanquish.

surpass *v.* beat, best, ding, eclipse, exceed, excel, outdo, outshine, outstrip, override, overshadow, surmount, top, tower above, transcend.

surplus *n.* balance, excess, overplus, remainder, residue, superabundance, superfluity, surfeit, surplusage.

antonym lack.

adj. excess, extra, odd, redundant, remaining, spare, superfluous, unused.

antonym essential.

surprise *v.* amaze, astonish, astound, bewilder, confuse, disconcert, dismay, flabbergast, nonplus, stagger, startle, stun.

n. amazement, astonishment, bewilderment, bombshell, dismay, eye-opener, incredulity, jolt, revelation, shock, start, stupefaction, wonder.

antonym composure.

surrender *v.* abandon, capitulate, cede, concede, forego,

give in, give up, quit, relinquish, remise, renounce, resign, submit, succumb, waive, yield.

antonyms fight on.

n. appeasement, capitulation, déchéance, delivery, Munich, relinquishment, remise, rendition, renunciation, resignation, submission, white flag, yielding.

surreptitious *adj.* behind-door, clandestine, covert, fraudulent, furtive, secret, sly, sneaking, stealthy, unauthorized, underhand, veiled.

antonym open.

surround *v.* begird, besiege, compass, embosom, encase, encincture, encircle, enclose, encompass, envelop, environ, girdle, invest, ring.

surveillance *n.* care, charge, check, control, direction, guardianship, inspection, monitoring, observation, regulation, scrutiny, stewardship, superintendence, supervision, vigilance, watch.

survey *v.* appraise, assess, consider, contemplate, estimate, examine, inspect, measure, observe, peruse, plan, plot, prospect, reconnoiter, research, review, scan, scrutinize, study, supervise, surview, triangulate, view.

n. appraisal, assessment, conspectus, examination, geodesy, inquiry, inspection, measurement, overview, perusal, review, sample, scrutiny, study, triangulation.

survive *v.* endure, exist, last, last out, live, live out, live through, outlast, outlive, ride, stay, subsist, weather, withstand.

antonym succumb.

susceptible *adj.* defenseless, disposed, given, impressible, impressionable, inclined, liable, open, predisposed, pregnable, prone, receptive, responsive, sensitive, subject, suggestible, tender, vulnerable.

antonyms impregnable, resistant.

suspect *v.* believe, call in question, conclude, conjecture, consider, distrust, doubt, fancy, feel, guess, infer, mistrust, opine, speculate, suppose, surmise.

adj. debatable, dodgy, doubtful, dubious, fishy, questionable, suspicious, unauthoritative, unreliable.

antonyms acceptable, innocent, straightforward.

suspend *v.* adjourn, append, arrest, attach, cease, dangle, debar, defer, delay, disbar, discontinue, dismiss, expel, freeze, hang, hold off, interrupt, postpone, shelve, sideline, stay, swing, unfrock, withhold.

antonyms continue, expedite, reinstate, restore.

suspicious *adj.* apprehensive, chary, distrustful, dodgy, doubtful, dubious, fishy, incredulous, irregular, jealous, louche, mistrustful, peculiar, queer, questionable, shady, skeptical, suspect, suspecting, unbelieving, uneasy, wary.

antonyms innocent, trustful, unexceptionable.

sustain *v.* aid, approve, assist, bear, carry, comfort, confirm, continue, endorse, endure, experience, feel, foster, help, hold, keep going, maintain, nourish, nurture, prolong, protract, provide for, ratify, relieve, sanction, stay, suffer, support, survive, sustenate, undergo, uphold, validate, verify, withstand.

sustenance *n.* aliment, board, comestibles, commons, eatables, edibles, étape, fare, food, freshments, livelihood, maintenance, nourishment, nutriment, pabulum, provender, provisions, rations, refection, subsistence, support, viands, victuals.

swagger *v.* bluster, boast, brag, brank, bully, cock, crow, gasconade, hector, parade, prance, roist, roister, strut, swank.

n. arrogance, bluster, boastfulness, boasting, braggadocio, display, fanfaronade, gasconade, gasconism, ostentation, rodomontade, show, showing off, swank, vainglory.
antonyms diffidence, modesty, restraint.

swallow *v.* absorb, accept, assimilate, believe, buy, consume, devour, down, drink, eat, englut, engulf, gulp, imbibe, ingest, ingurgitate, knock back, quaff, stifle, suppress, swig, swill, wash down.

swamp *n.* bog, dismal, everglades, fen, marsh, mire, morass, moss, quagmire, quicksands, slough, vlei.
v. beset, besiege, capsize, deluge, drench, engulf, flood, inundate, overload, overwhelm, saturate, sink, submerge, waterlog.

swank *v.* attitudinize, boast, parade, posture, preen oneself, show off, strut, swagger.
n. boastfulness, conceit, conceitedness, display, ostentation, pretentiousness, self-advertisement, show, showing-off, swagger, vainglory.
antonyms modesty, restraint.

swarm *n.* army, bevy, concourse, crowd, drove, flock, herd, horde, host, mass, mob, multitude, myriad, shoal, throng.
v. congregate, crowd, flock, flood, mass, stream, throng.

swarthy *adj.* black, brown, dark, dark-complexioned, dark-skinned, dusky, swart, swarth, tawny.
antonyms fair, pale.

sway *v.* affect, bend, control, direct, divert, dominate, fluctuate, govern, guide, incline, induce, influence, lean, lurch, oscillate, overrule, persuade, rock, roll, swerve, swing, titter, veer, wave.
n. ascendency, authority, cloud, command, control, dominion, government, hegemony, influence, jurisdiction, leadership, power, predominance, preponderance, rule, sovereignty, sweep, swerve, swing.

swear¹ *v.* affirm, assert, asseverate, attest, avow, declare, depose, insist, promise, testify, vow, warrant.

swear² *v.* blaspheme, blind, curse, cuss, eff, imprecate, maledict, take the Lord's name in vain, turn the air blue.

sweat *n.* agitation, anxiety, chore, dew, diaphoresis, distress, drudgery, effort, exudation, fag, flap, hidrosis, labor, panic, perspiration, strain, sudation, sudor, worry.
v. agonize, chafe, exude, fret, glow, perspirate, perspire, swelter, worry.

sweeping *adj.* across-the-board, all-embracing, all-inclusive, blanket, broad, comprehensive, exaggerated, extensive, far-reaching, global, indiscriminate, overdrawn, oversimplified, overstated, radical, simplistic, thoroughgoing, unanalytical, unqualified, wholesale, wide, wide-ranging.

sweet¹ *adj.* affectionate, agreeable, amiable, appealing, aromatic, attractive, balmy, beautiful, beloved, benign, charming, cherished, clean, cloying, darling, dear, dearest, delightful, dulcet, engaging, euphonic, euphonious, fair, fragrant, fresh, gentle, gracious, harmonious, honeyed, icky, kin, lovable, luscious, mellow, melodious, melting, mild, musical, new, perfumed, pet, precious, pure, redolent, saccharine, sickly, silver-toned, silvery, soft, suave, sugary, sweetened, sweet-smelling, sweet-sounding, sweet-tempered, syrupy, taking, tender, toothsome, treasured, tuneful, unselfish, wholesome, winning, winsome.

antonyms acid, bitter, cacophonous, discordant, malodorous, salty, sour, unpleasant.
n. afters, dessert, pudding, second course, sweet course.

sweet² *n.* bonbon, candy, comfit, confect, confection, confectionery, sweetie, sweetmeat.

swell¹ *v.* aggravate, augment, balloon, belly, billow, blab, bloat, boll, bulb, bulge, dilate, distend, enhance, enlarge, expand, extend, fatten, grow, heave, heighten, hove, increase, intensify, intumesce, louden, mount, protrude, reach a crescendo, rise, strout, surge, tumefy, volume.
antonyms contract, dwindle, shrink.
n. billow, bore, bulge, distension, eagre, enlargement, loudening, rise, surge, swelling, undulation, wave.

swell² *n.* adept, beau, bigwig, blade, cockscomb, dandy, dude, fop, nob, popinjay, toff.
antonyms down-and-out, scarecrow, tramp.
adj. de luxe, dude, exclusive, fashionable, flashy, grand, posh, ritzy, smart, stylish, swanky.
antonyms seedy, shabby.

swift *adj.* abrupt, agile, expeditious, express, fast, fleet, fleet-footed, flying, hurried, light-heeled, light-legged, limber, nimble, nimble-footed, nippy, precipitate, prompt, quick, rapid, ready, short, spanking, speedy, sudden, winged.
antonyms slow, sluggish, tardy.

swindle *v.* bamboozle, bilk, bunko, cheat, chicane, chouse, con, deceive, defraud, diddle, do, dupe, finagle, financier, fleece, grift, gyp, hand someone a lemon, hornswoggle, overcharge, ramp, rip off, rook, sell smoke, sell someone a pup, skelder, trick.
n. chicanery, con, deceit, deception, double-dealing, fiddle, fraud, gold-brick, gyp, imposition, knavery, racket, rip-off, roguery, scam, sharp practice, shenanigans, skin-game, swizz, swizzle, trickery.

swing *v.* arrange, brandish, control, dangle, fix, fluctuate, hang, hurl, influence, librate, oscillate, pendulate, rock, suspend, sway, swerve, vary, veer, vibrate, wave, whirl.
n. fluctuation, impetus, libration, motion, oscillation, rhythm, scope, stroke, sway, swaying, sweep, sweeping, vibration, waving.

switch¹ *v.* change, change course, change direction, chop and change, deflect, deviate, divert, exchange, interchange, put, rearrange, replace, shift, shunt, substitute, swap, trade, turn, veer.
n. about-turn, alteration, change, change of direction, exchange, interchange, shift, substitution, swap.

switch² *v.* birch, flog, jerk, lash, swish, twitch, wave, whip, whisk.
n. birch, cane, jerk, rod, whip, whisk.

swivel *v.* gyrate, pirouette, pivot, revolve, rotate, spin, swing round, turn, twirl, wheel.

sycophantic *adj.* ass-licking, backscratching, bootlicking, cringing, fawning, flattering, groveling, ingratiating, obsequious, parasitical, servile, slavish, slimy, smarmy, timeserving, toad-eating, toadying, truckling, unctuous.

symbol *n.* badge, character, emblem, figure, grammalogue, ideogram, ideograph, image, logo, logogram, logograph, mandala, mark, representation, rune, sign, token, type.

symmetry *n.* agreement, balance, correspondence, evenness, form, harmony, isometry, order, parallelism, proportion, regularity.

antonyms asymmetry, irregularity.

sympathetic *adj.* affectionate, agreeable, appreciative, caring, comforting, commiserating, companionable, compassionate, compatible, concerned, congenial, consoling, empathetic, empathic, exorable, feeling, friendly, interested, kind, kindly, like-minded, pitying, responsive, supportive, tender, understanding, warm, warm-hearted, well-intentioned.

antonyms antipathetic, callous, indifferent, unsympathetic.

sympathize *v.* agree, commiserate, condole, empathize, feel for, identify with, pity, rap, respond to, side with, understand.

antonyms disapprove, dismiss, disregard, ignore, oppose.

sympathy *n.* affinity, agreement, comfort, commiseration, compassion, condolement, condolence, condolences, congeniality, correspondence, empathy, fellow-feeling, harmony, pity, rapport, responsiveness, tenderness, thoughtfulness, understanding, warmth.

antonyms callousness, disharmony, incompatibility, indifference.

symptom *n.* concomitant, diagnostic, evidence, expression, feature, indication, manifestation, mark, note, sign, syndrome, token, warning.

symptomatic *adj.* associated, characteristic, indicative, suggestive, typical.

synonymous *adj.* co-extensive, comparable, corresponding, equal, equivalent, exchangeable, identical, identified, interchangeable, parallel, similar, substitutable, tantamount, the same.

antonyms antonymous, dissimilar, opposite.

synopsis *n.* abridgment, abstract, aperçu, compendium, condensation, conspectus, digest, epitome, outline, précis, recapitulation, résumé, review, run-down, sketch, summary, summation.

synthetic *adj.* artificial, bogus, ersatz, fake, imitation, man-made, manufactured, mock, pseud, pseudo, put-on, sham, simulated.

antonyms genuine, real.

system *n.* arrangement, classification, co-ordination, logic, method, methodicalness, methodology, mode, modus operandi, orderliness, organization, plan, practice, procedure, process, regularity, routine, rule, scheme, set-up, structure, systematization, tabulation, taxis, taxonomy, technique, theory, usage.

systematic *adj.* businesslike, efficient, habitual, intentional, logical, methodical, ordered, orderly, organized, planned, precise, standardized, systematical, systematized, well-ordered, well-planned.

antonyms disorderly, inefficient, unsystematic.

T

table *n.* agenda, altar, bench, board, catalog, chart, counter, diagram, diet, digest, fare, flat, flatland, food, graph, index, inventory, list, mahogany, paradigm, plain, plan, plateau, record, register, roll, schedule, slab, spread, stall, stand, syllabus, synopsis, tableland, victuals.

v. postpone, propose, put forward, submit, suggest.

tableau *n.* diorama, picture, portrayal, representation, scene, spectacle, tableau vivant, vignette.

taboo *adj.* accursed, anathema, banned, forbidden, inviolable, outlawed, prohibited, proscribed, sacrosanct, unacceptable, unmentionable, unthinkable, verboten.

antonym acceptable.

n. anathema, ban, curse, disapproval, interdict, interdiction, prohibition, proscription, restriction.

tacit *adj.* implicit, implied, inferred, silent, ulterior, undeclared, understood, unexpressed, unprofessed, unspoken, unstated, unuttered, unvoiced, voiceless, wordless.

antonyms explicit, express, spoken, stated.

taciturn *adj.* aloof, antisocial, cold, distant, dumb, mute, quiet, reserved, reticent, saturnine, silent, tight-lipped, uncommunicative, unconversable, unforthcoming, withdrawn.

antonyms communicative, forthcoming, sociable, talkative.

tack *n.* approach, attack, bearing, course, direction, drawing-pin, heading, line, loop, method, nail, path, pin, plan, procedure, route, staple, stitch, tactic, thumbtack, tin-tack, way.

v. add, affix, annex, append, attach, baste, fasten, fix, join, nail, pin, staple, stitch, tag.

tackle[1] *n.* accouterments, apparatus, equipment, gear, harness, implements, outfit, paraphernalia, rig, rigging, tackling, tools, trappings.

v. harness.

tackle[2] *n.* attack, block, challenge, interception, intervention, stop.

v. attempt, begin, block, challenge, clutch, confront, deal with, embark upon, encounter, engage in, essay, face up to, grab, grapple with, grasp, halt, intercept, seize, set about, stop, take on, throw, try, undertake, wade into.

antonyms avoid, side-step.

tacky *adj.* adhesive, cheap, gimcrack, gluey, gummy, messy, nasty, scruffy, seedy, shabby, shoddy, sleazy, sticky, tasteless, tatty, tawdry, vulgar, wet.

tact *n.* address, adroitness, consideration, delicacy, diplomacy, discernment, discretion, finesse, grace, judgment, perception, prudence, savoir-faire, sensitivity, skill, thoughtfulness, understanding.

antonyms clumsiness, indiscretion, tactlessness.

tactful *adj.* careful, considerate, delicate, diplomatic, discerning, discreet, graceful, judicious, perceptive, polished, polite, politic, prudent, sensitive, skilful, subtle, thoughtful, understanding.

antonym tactless.

tactical *adj.* adroit, artful, calculated, clever, cunning, diplomatic, judicious, politic, prudent, shrewd, skilful, smart, strategic.

antonym impolitic.

tactics *n.* approach, campaign, game plan, line of attack, maneuvers, moves, plan, plan of campaign, plans, ploys, policy, procedure, shifts, stratagems, strategy.

tag[1] *n.* aglet, aiglet, aiguillette, appellation, dag, designation, docket, epithet, flap, identification, label, mark, marker, name, note, slip, sticker, tab, tally, ticket.

v. add, adjoin, affix, annex, append, call, christen, designate, dub, earmark, fasten, identify, label, mark, name, nickname, style, tack, term, ticket.

tag[2] *n.* dictum, fadaise, gnome, gobbet, maxim, moral, motto, proverb, quotation, quote, remnant, saw, saying.

tail *n.* appendage, backside, behind, bottom, bum, buttocks, conclusion, croup, detective, empennage, end, extremity, file, follower, fud, line, posterior, queue, rear, rear end, retinue, rump, scut, suite, tailback, tailpiece, tailplane, train.

v. dog, follow, keep with, shadow, spy on, stalk, track, trail.

tailor *n.* clothier, costumer, costumier, couturier, couturière, dressmaker, modiste, outfitter, seamstress, whipcat, whip-stitch.

v. accommodate, adapt, adjust, alter, convert, cut, fashion, fit, modify, mold, shape, style, suit, trim.

taint *v.* adulterate, besmirch, blacken, blemish, blight, blot, brand, contaminate, corrupt, damage, defile, deprave, dirty, disgrace, dishonor, envenom, foul, infect, muddy, poison, pollute, ruin, shame, smear, smirch, soil, spoil, stain, stigmatize, sully, tarnish, vitiate.

n. blemish, blot, contagion, contamination, corruption, defect, disgrace, dishonor, fault, flaw, infamy, infection, obloquy, odium, opprobium, pollution, shame, smear, smirch, spot, stain, stigma.

take *v.* abduct, abide, abstract, accept, accommodate, accompany, acquire, adopt, appropriate, arrest, ascertain, assume, attract, bear, believe, betake, bewitch, blight, book, brave, bring, brook, buy, call for, captivate, capture, carry, cart, catch, charm, clutch, conduct, consider, consume, contain, convey, convoy, deduct, deem, delight, demand, derive, detract, do, drink, eat, effect, eliminate, enchant, endure, engage, ensnare, entrap, escort, execute, fascinate, ferry, fetch, filch, gather, glean, grasp, grip, guide, haul, have, have room for, hire, hold, imbibe, ingest, inhale, lead, lease, make, measure, misappropriate, necessitate, need, nick, observe, obtain, operate, perceive, perform, photograph, pick, pinch, please, pocket, portray, presume, purchase, purloin, receive, regard, remove, rent, require, reserve, secure, seize, select, stand, steal, stomach, strike, subtract, succeed, suffer, swallow, swipe, thole, tolerate, tote, transport, undergo, understand, undertake, usher, weather, win, withstand, work.

n. catch, gate, haul, income, proceeds, profits, receipts, return, revenue, takings, yield.

take-off *n.* burlesque, caricature, imitation, lampoon, mickey-take, mimicry, parody, spoof, travesty.

taking *adj.* alluring, appealing, attractive, beguiling, captivating, catching, charming, compelling, delightful, enchanting, engaging, fascinating, fetching, intriguing, pleasing, prepossessing, winning, winsome.

antonyms repellent, repulsive, unattractive.

n. agitation, alarm, coil, commotion, consternation, flap, fuss, panic, passion, pother, state, sweat, tiz-woz, tizzy, turmoil, wax.

tale *n.* account, anecdote, fable, fabrication, falsehood, fib, fiction, legend, lie, Märchen, Munchausen, myth, narration, narrative, old wives' tale, relation, report, rigmarole, romance, rumor, saga, spiel, story, superstition, tall story, tradition, untruth, yarn.

talent *n.* ability, aptitude, bent, capacity, endowment, faculty, feel, flair, forte, genius, gift, knack, long suit, nous, parts, power, strength.

antonyms inability, ineptitude, weakness.

talented *adj.* able, accomplished, adept, adroit, apt,

artistic, brilliant, capable, clever, deft, gifted, ingenious, inspired, well-endowed.

antonyms clumsy, inept, maladroit.

talk *v.* articulate, blab, blether, chat, chatter, chinwag, commune, communicate, confabulate, confer, converse, crack, gab, gossip, grass, inform, jaw, natter, negotiate, palaver, parley, prate, prattle, rap, say, sing, speak, squeak, squeal, utter, verbalize, witter.

n. address, argot, bavardage, blather, blether, causerie, chat, chatter, chinwag, chitchat, clash, claver, colloquy, conclave, confab, confabulation, conference, consultation, conversation, crack, dialect, dialogue, discourse, discussion, disquisition, dissertation, gab, gossip, harangue, hearsay, jargon, jaw, jawing, language, lecture, lingo, meeting, natter, negotiation, oration, palabra, palaver, parley, patois, rap, rumor, seminar, sermon, slang, speech, spiel, symposium, tittle-tattle, utterance, words.

talkative *adj.* chatty, communicative, conversational, effusive, expansive, forthcoming, gabby, garrulous, gossipy, long-tongued, long-winded, loquacious, prating, prolix, unreserved, verbose, vocal, voluble, wordy.

antonyms reserved, taciturn.

tall *adj.* absurd, big, dubious, elevated, embellished, exaggerated, far-fetched, giant, grandiloquent, great, high, implausible, improbable, incredible, lanky, leggy, lofty, overblown, preposterous, remarkable, soaring, steep, topless, towering, unbelievable, unlikely.

antonyms low, reasonable, short, small.

tally *v.* accord, agree, coincide, compute, concur, conform, correspond, figure, fit, harmonize, jibe, mark, match, parallel, reckon, record, register, square, suit, tie in, total.

antonyms differ, disagree.

n. account, count, counterfoil, counterpart, credit, duplicate, label, mark, match, mate, notch, reckoning, record, score, stub, tab, tag, tick, total.

tame *adj.* amenable, anemic, biddable, bland, bloodless, boring, broken, compliant, cultivated, disciplined, docile, domesticated, dull, feeble, flat, gentle, humdrum, insipid, lifeless, manageable, meek, obedient, prosaic, spiritless, subdued, submissive, tedious, tractable, unadventurous, unenterprising, unexciting, uninspired, uninspiring, uninteresting, unresisting, vapid, wearisome.

antonyms exciting, rebellious, unmanageable, wild.

v. break in, bridle, calm, conquer, curb, discipline, domesticate, enslave, gentle, house-train, humble, master, mellow, mitigate, mute, pacify, quell, repress, soften, subdue, subjugate, suppress, temper, train.

tamper *v.* alter, bribe, cook, corrupt, damage, fiddle, fix, influence, interfere, intrude, juggle, manipulate, meddle, mess, rig, tinker.

tang *n.* aroma, bite, flavor, hint, kick, overtone, piquancy, pungency, reek, savor, scent, smack, smell, suggestion, taste, tinge, touch, trace, whiff.

tangible *adj.* actual, concrete, corporeal, definite, discernible, evident, manifest, material, objective, observable, palpable, perceptible, physical, positive, real, sensible, solid, substantial, tactile, touchable.

antonym intangible.

tangle *n.* burble, coil, complication, confusion, convolution, embroglio, embroilment, entanglement, fankle, fix, imbroglio, jam, jumble, jungle, knot, labyrinth, mass, mat, maze, mesh, mess, mix-up, muddle, raffle, snarl, snarl-up, twist, web.

v. catch, coil, confuse, convolve, embroil, enmesh, ensnare, entangle, entrap, hamper, implicate, interlace, interlock, intertwine, intertwist, interweave, involve, jam, knot, mat, mesh, muddle, snarl, trap, twist.

antonym disentangle.

tangy *adj.* biting, bitter, fresh, gamy, piquant, pungent, savory, sharp, spicy, strong, tart.

antonym insipid.

tantalize *v.* baffle, bait, balk, disappoint, entice, frustrate, lead on, play upon, provoke, taunt, tease, thwart, titillate, torment, torture.

antonym satisfy.

tantrum *n.* bate, fit, flare-up, fury, hysterics, outburst, paddy, paroxysm, rage, scene, storm, temper, wax.

tap[1] *v.* beat, chap, drum, knock, pat, rap, strike, tat, touch.

n. beat, chap, knock, pat, rap, rat-tat, touch.

tap[2] *n.* bug, bung, faucet, plug, receiver, spigot, spile, spout, stop-cock, stopper, valve.

v. bleed, broach, bug, drain, exploit, milk, mine, open, pierce, quarry, siphon, unplug, use, utilize, wiretap.

tape *n.* band, binding, magnetic tape, riband, ribbon, strip, tape-measure.

v. assess, bind, measure, record, seal, secure, stick, tape-record, video, wrap.

taper[2] *v.* attenuate, decrease, die away, die out, dwindle, fade, lessen, narrow, peter out, reduce, slim, subside, tail off, thin, wane, weaken.

antonyms increase, swell, widen.

taper[1] *n.* bougie, candle, spill, wax-light, wick.

tardy *adj.* backward, behindhand, belated, dawdling, delayed, dilatory, eleventh-hour, lag, last-minute, late, loitering, overdue, procrastinating, retarded, slack, slow, sluggish, unpunctual.

antonyms prompt, punctual.

target *n.* aim, ambition, bull's-eye, butt, destination, end, goal, intention, jack, mark, object, objective, prey, prick, purpose, quarry, scapegoat, victim.

tariff *n.* assessment, bill of fare, charges, customs, duty, excise, impost, levy, menu, price list, rate, schedule, tax, toll.

tarnish *v.* befoul, blacken, blemish, blot, darken, dim, discolor, disluster, dull, mar, rust, soil, spoil, spot, stain, sully, taint.

antonyms brighten, enhance, polish up.

n. blackening, blemish, blot, discoloration, film, patina, rust, spot, stain, taint.

antonyms brightness, polish.

tarry *v.* abide, bide, dally, dawdle, delay, dwell, lag, linger, loiter, pause, remain, rest, sojourn, stay, stop, wait.

tart[1] *n.* pastry, pie, quiche, tartlet.

tart[2] *adj.* acerb, acerbic, acid, acidulous, acrimonious, astringent, barbed, biting, bitter, caustic, cutting, incisive, piquant, pungent, sardonic, scathing, sharp, short, sour, tangy, trenchant, vinegary.

tart[3] *n.* broad, call girl, drab, fallen woman, fille de joie, fille publique, floosie, harlot, hooker, prostitute, slut, street-walker, strumpet, tramp, trollop, whore.

task *n.* assignment, aufgabe, burden, business, charge, chore, darg, duty, employment, enterprise, exercise, imposition, job, job of work, labor, mission, occupation, pensum, toil, undertaking, work.

v. burden, charge, commit, encumber, entrust, exhaust, load, lumber, oppress, overload, push, saddle, strain, tax, test, weary.

taste *n.* appetite, appreciation, bent, bit, bite, choice, correctness, cultivation, culture, dash, decorum, delicacy, desire, discernment, discretion, discrimination, drop, elegance, experience, fancy, finesse, flavor, fondness, gout, grace, gustation, inclination, judgment, leaning, liking, morsel, mouthful, nibble, nicety, nip, palate, partiality, penchant, perception, polish, politeness, predilection, preference, propriety, refinement, relish, restraint, sample, sapor, savor, sensitivity, sip, smack, smatch, soupçon, spoonful, style, swallow, tact, tactfulness, tang, tastefulness, titbit, touch.

v. assay, degust, degustate, differentiate, discern, distinguish, encounter, experience, feel, know, meet, nibble, perceive, relish, sample, savor, sip, smack, test, try, undergo.

tasteful *adj.* aesthetic, artistic, beautiful, charming, comme il faut, correct, cultivated, cultured, delicate, discreet, discriminating, elegant, exquisite, fastidious, graceful, handsome, harmonious, judicious, polished, refined, restrained, smart, stylish, well-judged.

antonym tasteless.

tasteless *adj.* barbaric, bland, boring, cheap, coarse, crass, crude, dilute, dull, flashy, flat, flavorless, garish, gaudy, graceless, gross, improper, inartistic, indecorous, indelicate, indiscreet, inelegant, inharmonious, insipid, low, mild, rude, stale, tacky, tactless, tame, tatty, tawdry, thin, uncouth, undiscriminating, uninspired, uninteresting, unseemly, untasteful, vapid, vulgar, watered-down, watery, weak, wearish.

antonym tasteful.

tasty *adj.* appetizing, delectable, delicious, flavorful, flavorous, flavorsome, gusty, luscious, mouthwatering, palatable, piquant, sapid, saporous, savory, scrumptious, succulent, toothsome, yummy.

antonyms disgusting, insipid, tasteless.

tattered *adj.* duddie, frayed, in shreds, lacerated, ragged, raggy, rent, ripped, tatty, threadbare, torn.

antonyms neat, trim.

tattle *v.* babble, blab, blather, blether, chat, chatter, clash, claver, gab, gash, gossip, jabber, natter, prate, prattle, talk, tittle-tattle, yak, yap.

n. babble, blather, blether, chat, chatter, chitchat, clash, claver, gossip, hearsay, jabber, prattle, rumor, talk, tittle-tattle, yak, yap.

taunt *v.* bait, chiack, deride, fleer, flout, flyte, gibe, insult, jeer, mock, provoke, reproach, revile, rib, ridicule, sneer, tease, torment, twit.

n. barb, catcall, censure, cut, derision, dig, fling, gibe, insult, jeer, poke, provocation, reproach, ridicule, sarcasm, sneer, teasing.

taut *adj.* contracted, rigid, strained, stressed, stretched, tense, tensed, tight, tightened, unrelaxed.

antonyms loose, relaxed, slack.

tautology *n.* duplication, iteration, otioseness, perissology, pleonasm, redundancy, repetition, repetitiousness, repetitiveness, superfluity.

antonyms economy, succinctness.

tavern *n.* alehouse, bar, boozer, bush, dive, doggery, fonda, hostelry, inn, joint, local, pub, roadhouse, saloon, tap-house.

tawdry *adj.* cheap, cheap-jack, flashy, garish, gaudy, gimcrack, gingerbread, glittering, meretricious, pinch-

beck, plastic, raffish, showy, tacky, tasteless, tatty, tinsel, tinsely, vulgar.
antonyms excellent, fine, superior.

tax *n.* agistment, assessment, burden, charge, contribution, customs, demand, drain, duty, excise, geld, imposition, impost, levy, load, octroi, pressure, rate, scat, scot, strain, tariff, tithe, toll, tribute, weight.

v. accuse, arraign, assess, blame, burden, censure, charge, demand, drain, enervate, exact, exhaust, extract, geld, impeach, impose, impugn, incriminate, load, overburden, overtax, push, rate, reproach, sap, strain, stretch, task, tithe, try, weaken, weary.

taxi *n.* cab, fiacre, hack, hansom-cab, taxicab.

teach *v.* accustom, advise, coach, counsel, demonstrate, direct, discipline, drill, edify, educate, enlighten, ground, guide, impart, implant, inculcate, inform, instil, instruct, school, show, train, tutor, verse.

teacher *n.* abecedarian, coach, dominie, don, educator, guide, guru, instructor, khodja, kindergartener, kindergärtner, lecturer, luminary, maharishi, master, mentor, mistress, pedagogue, professor, pundit, school-marm, schoolmaster, schoolmistress, schoolteacher, trainer, tutor, usher.

team *n.* band, body, bunch, company, crew, écurie, équipe, gang, group, line-up, pair, set, shift, side, span, squad, stable, troupe, yoke.

v. combine, couple, join, link, match, yoke.

teamwork *n.* collaboration, co-operation, co-ordination, esprit de corps, fellowship, joint effort, team spirit.
antonyms disharmony, disunity.

tear *v.* belt, bolt, career, charge, claw, dart, dash, dilacerate, divide, drag, fly, gallop, gash, grab, hurry, lacerate, mangle, mutilate, pluck, pull, race, rend, rip, rive, run, rupture, rush, scratch, seize, sever, shoot, shred, snag, snatch, speed, split, sprint, sunder, wrench, wrest, yank, zoom.

n. hole, laceration, rent, rip, run, rupture, scratch, snag, split.

tearful *adj.* blubbering, crying, distressing, dolorous, emotional, lachrymose, lamentable, maudlin, mournful, pathetic, pitiable, pitiful, poignant, sad, sobbing, sorrowful, upsetting, weeping, weepy, whimpering, woeful.

tease *v.* aggravate, annoy, badger, bait, banter, bedevil, chaff, chip, gibe, goad, grig, guy, irritate, josh, mock, needle, pester, plague, provoke, rag, rib, ridicule, take a rise out of, tantalize, taunt, torment, twit, vex, worry.

technique *n.* address, adroitness, approach, art, artistry, course, craft, craftsmanship, delivery, executancy, execution, expertise, facility, fashion, knack, know-how, manner, means, method, mode, modus operandi, performance, procedure, proficiency, skill, style, system, touch, way.

tedious *adj.* annoying, banal, boring, deadly, drab, dreary, dreich, dull, fatiguing, humdrum, irksome, laborious, lifeless, long-drawn-out, longsome, long-spun, monotonous, prosaic, prosy, soporific, tiring, unexciting, uninteresting, vapid, wearisome.
antonyms exciting, interesting.

tedium *n.* banality, boredom, drabness, dreariness, dullness, ennui, lifelessness, monotony, prosiness, routine, sameness, tediousness, vapidity.

teem *v.* abound, bear, brim, bristle, burst, increase, multiply, overflow, overspill, produce, proliferate, pullulate, swarm.

antonyms lack, want.

teeming *adj.* abundant, alive, brimful, brimming, bristling, bursting, chock-a-block, chock-full, crawling, fruitful, full, numerous, overflowing, packed, pregnant, proliferating, pullulating, replete, swarming, thick.
antonyms lacking, rare, sparse.

teeter *v.* balance, lurch, pitch, pivot, rock, seesaw, stagger, sway, titubate, totter, tremble, waver, wobble.

teetotaller *n.* abstainer, nephalist, non-drinker, Rechabite, water-drinker.

telephone *n.* blower, handset, line, phone.

v. buzz, call, call up, contact, dial, get in touch, get on the blower, give someone a tinkle, phone, ring (up).

telescope *v.* abbreviate, abridge, compress, concertina, condense, contract, crush, curtail, cut, reduce, shorten, shrink, squash, trim, truncate.

television *n.* boob tube, goggle-box, idiot box, receiver, set, small screen, the box, the tube, TV, TV set.

tell *v.* acquaint, announce, apprize, authorize, bid, calculate, chronicle, command, communicate, comprehend, compute, confess, count, depict, describe, differentiate, direct, discern, disclose, discover, discriminate, distinguish, divulge, enjoin, enumerate, express, foresee, identify, impart, inform, instruct, mention, militate, narrate, notify, number, order, portray, predict, proclaim, reckon, recount, register, rehearse, relate, report, require, reveal, say, see, speak, state, summon, tally, understand, utter, weigh.

temerity *n.* assurance, audacity, boldness, brass neck, chutzpah, daring, effrontery, forwardness, gall, heedlessness, impudence, impulsiveness, intrepidity, nerve, pluck, rashness, recklessness.
antonym caution.

temper *n.* anger, annoyance, attitude, bate, calm, calmness, character, composure, constitution, cool, coolness, disposition, equanimity, fury, heat, humor, ill-humor, irascibility, irritability, irritation, mind, moderation, mood, nature, paddy, passion, peevishness, pet, petulance, rage, resentment, sang-froid, self-control, surliness, taking, tantrum, temperament, tenor, tranquility, vein, wax, wrath.

v. abate, admix, allay, anneal, assuage, calm, harden, indurate, lessen, mitigate, moderate, modify, mollify, palliate, restrain, soften, soothe, strengthen, toughen.

temperament *n.* anger, bent, character, complexion, constitution, crasis, disposition, excitability, explosiveness, hot-headedness, humor, impatience, make-up, mettle, moodiness, moods, nature, outlook, personality, petulance, quality, soul, spirit, stamp, temper, tendencies, tendency, volatility.

temperamental *adj.* capricious, congenital, constitutional, emotional, erratic, excitable, explosive, fiery, highly-strung, hot-headed, hypersensitive, impatient, inborn, inconsistent, ingrained, inherent, innate, irritable, mercurial, moody, natural, neurotic, overemotional, passionate, petulant, sensitive, touchy, undependable, unpredictable, unreliable, volatile, volcanic.

antonyms calm, serene, steady.

temperance *n.* abstemiousness, abstinence, continence, discretion, forbearance, moderation, prohibition, restraint, self-abnegation, self-control, self-denial, self-discipline, self-restraint, sobriety, teetotalism.
antonyms excess, intemperance.

temperate *adj.* abstemious, abstinent, agreeable, balanced, balmy, calm, clement, composed, continent, controlled, cool, dispassionate, equable, even-tempered, fair, gentle, mild, moderate, pleasant, reasonable, restrained, sensible, sober, soft, stable.
antonyms excessive, extreme, intemperate.

tempest *n.* bourasque, commotion, cyclone, disturbance, ferment, furore, gale, hurricane, squall, storm, tornado, tumult, typhoon, upheaval, uproar.

tempo *n.* beat, cadence, measure, meter, pace, pulse, rate, rhythm, speed, time, velocity.

temporal *adj.* carnal, civil, earthly, evanescent, fleeting, fleshly, fugacious, fugitive, impermanent, lay, material, momentary, mortal, mundane, passing, profane, secular, short-lived, sublunary, temporary, terrestrial, transient, transitory, unspiritual, worldly.
antonym spiritual.

temporary *adj.* brief, ephemeral, evanescent, fleeting, fugacious, fugitive, impermanent, interim, makeshift, momentary, passing, pro tem, pro tempore, provisional, short-lived, stop-gap, transient, transitory.
antonyms everlasting, permanent.

tempt *v.* allure, attract, bait, coax, dare, decoy, draw, enamor, entice, incite, inveigle, invite, lure, provoke, risk, seduce, tantalize, test, try, woo.
antonyms discourage, dissuade.

tenacious *adj.* adamant, adhesive, clinging, coherent, cohesive, determined, dogged, fast, firm, forceful, gluey, glutinous, inflexible, intransigent, mucilaginous, obdurate, obstinate, persistent, pertinacious, resolute, retentive, single-minded, solid, staunch, steadfast, sticky, strong, strong-willed, stubborn, sure, tight, tough, unshakeable, unswerving, unwavering, unyielding, viscous.
antonyms loose, slack, weak.

tenacity *n.* adhesiveness, application, clinginess, coherence, cohesiveness, determination, diligence, doggedness, fastness, firmness, force, forcefulness, indomitability, inflexibility, intransigence, obduracy, obstinacy, perseverance, persistence, pertinacity, power, resoluteness, resolution, resolve, retention, retentiveness, single-mindedness, solidity, solidness, staunchness, steadfastness, stickiness, strength, stubbornness, toughness, viscosity.
antonyms looseness, slackness, weakness.

tenant *n.* gavelman, inhabitant, landholder, leaseholder, lessee, occupant, occupier, renter, resident.

tend[1] *v.* affect, aim, bear, bend, conduce, contribute, go, gravitate, head, incline, influence, lead, lean, move, point, trend, verge.

tend[2] *v.* attend, comfort, control, cultivate, feed, guard, handle, keep, maintain, manage, minister to, nurse, nurture, protect, serve, succor.
antonym neglect.

tendency *n.* bearing, bent, bias, conatus, course, direction, disposition, drift, drive, heading, inclination, leaning, liability, movement, partiality, penchant, predilection, predisposition, proclivity, proneness, propensity, purport, readiness, susceptibility, tenor, thrust, trend, turning.

tender[1] *adj.* aching, acute, affectionate, affettuoso, amoroso, amorous, benevolent, breakable, bruised, callow, caring, chary, compassionate, complicated, considerate, dangerous, delicate, difficult, emotional, evocative, feeble, fond, fragile, frail, gentle, green, humane,

immature, impressionable, inexperienced, inflamed, irritated, kind, loving, merciful, moving, new, painful, pathetic, pitiful, poignant, raw, risky, romantic, scrupulous, sensitive, sentimental, smarting, soft, softhearted, sore, sympathetic, tender-hearted, ticklish, touching, touchy, tricky, vulnerable, warm, warmhearted, weak, young, youthful.
antonyms callous, chewy, hard, harsh, rough, severe, tough.

tender[2] *v.* advance, extend, give, offer, present, proffer, propose, submit, suggest, volunteer.
n. bid, currency, estimate, medium, money, offer, payment, proffer, proposal, proposition, specie, submission, suggestion.

tender-hearted *adj.* affectionate, benevolent, benign, caring, compassionate, considerate, feeling, fond, gentle, humane, kind, kind-hearted, kindly, loving, merciful, mild, pitying, responsive, sensitive, sentimental, soft-hearted, sympathetic, warm, warmhearted.
antonyms callous, cruel, hard-hearted, unfeeling.

tenderness *n.* ache, aching, affection, amorousness, attachment, benevolence, bruising, callowness, care, compassion, consideration, delicateness, devotion, discomfort, feebleness, fondness, fragility, frailness, gentleness, greenness, humaneness, humanity, immaturity, impressionableness, inexperience, inflammation, irritation, kindness, liking, love, loving-kindness, mercy, newness, pain, painfulness, pity, rawness, sensitiveness, sensitivity, sentimentality, soft-heartedness, softness, soreness, sweetness, sympathy, tender-heartedness, vulnerability, warm-heartedness, warmth, weakness, youth, youthfulness.
antonyms cruelty, hardness, harshness.

tenet *n.* article of faith, belief, canon, conviction, credo, creed, doctrine, dogma, maxim, opinion, precept, presumption, principle, rule, teaching, thesis, view.

tense *adj.* anxious, apprehensive, edgy, electric, exciting, fidgety, jittery, jumpy, moving, nerve-racking, nervous, overwrought, restless, rigid, strained, stressful, stretched, strung up, taut, tight, uneasy, uptight, worrying.
antonyms calm, lax, loose, relaxed.
v. brace, contract, strain, stretch, tauten, tighten.
antonyms loosen, relax.

tension *n.* anxiety, apprehension, edginess, hostility, nervousness, pressure, restlessness, rigidity, stiffness, strain, straining, stress, stretching, suspense, tautness, tightness, tone, unease, worry.
antonyms calm(ness), laxness, looseness, relaxation.

tentative *adj.* cautious, conjectural, diffident, doubtful, experimental, faltering, hesitant, indefinite, peirastic, provisional, speculative, timid, uncertain, unconfirmed, undecided, unformulated, unsettled, unsure.
antonyms conclusive, decisive, definite, final.

tenure *n.* habitation, holding, incumbency, occupancy, occupation, possession, proprietorship, residence, tenancy, term, time.

tepid *adj.* apathetic, cool, half-hearted, indifferent, lew, lukewarm, unenthusiastic, warmish.
antonyms animated, cold, hot, passionate.

term[1] *n.* appellation, denomination, designation, epithet, epitheton, expression, locution, name, phrase, title, word.

v. call, denominate, designate, dub, entitle, label, name, style, tag, title.

term² *n.* bound, boundary, close, conclusion, confine, course, culmination, duration, end, finish, fruition, half, interval, limit, period, season, semester, session, space, span, spell, terminus, time, while.

terminal *adj.* bounding, concluding, deadly, desinent, desinential, extreme, fatal, final, incurable, killing, last, lethal, limiting, mortal, ultimate, utmost.

antonym initial.

n. boundary, depot, end, extremity, limit, termination, terminus.

terminate *v.* abort, cease, close, complete, conclude, cut off, discontinue, drop, end, expire, finish, issue, lapse, result, stop, wind up.

antonyms begin, initiate, start.

terminology *n.* argot, cant, jargon, language, lingo, nomenclature, patois, phraseology, terms, vocabulary, words.

terms *n.* agreement, charges, compromise, conditions, fees, footing, language, particulars, payment, phraseology, position, premises, price, provisions, provisos, qualifications, rates, relations, relationship, specifications, standing, status, stipulations, terminology, understanding.

terrible *adj.* abhorrent, appalling, awful, bad, beastly, dangerous, desperate, dire, disgusting, distressing, dread, dreaded, dreadful, extreme, fearful, foul, frightful, god-awful, gruesome, harrowing, hateful, hideous, horrendous, horrible, horrid, horrific, horrifying, loathsome, monstrous, obnoxious, odious, offensive, outrageous, poor, repulsive, revolting, rotten, serious, severe, shocking, unpleasant, vile.

antonyms great, pleasant, superb, wonderful.

terrific *adj.* ace, amazing, awesome, awful, breathtaking, brilliant, dreadful, enormous, excellent, excessive, extreme, fabulous, fantastic, fearful, fierce, fine, gigantic, great, harsh, horrific, huge, intense, magnificent, marvelous, monstrous, outstanding, prodigious, sensational, severe, smashing, stupendous, super, superb, terrible, tremendous, wonderful.

terrify *v.* affright, alarm, appal, awe, dismay, frighten, horrify, intimidate, petrify, scare, shock, terrorize.

territory *n.* area, bailiwick, country, dependency, district, domain, jurisdiction, land, park, preserve, province, region, sector, state, terrain, tract, zone.

terror *n.* affright, alarm, anxiety, awe, blue funk, bogeyman, bugbear, consternation, devil, dismay, dread, fear, fiend, fright, horror, intimidation, monster, panic, rascal, rogue, scourge, shock, tearaway.

terse *adj.* abrupt, aphoristic, brief, brusque, clipped, compact, concise, condensed, crisp, curt, economical, elliptical, epigrammatic, gnomic, incisive, laconic, neat, pithy, sententious, short, snappy, succinct.

antonyms long-winded, prolix, repetitious.

test *v.* analyze, assay, assess, check, examine, experiment, investigate, prove, screen, try, verify.

n. analysis, assessment, attempt, catechism, check, evaluation, examination, hurdle, investigation, moment of truth, ordeal, pons asinorum, probation, proof, shibboleth, trial, try-out.

testify *v.* affirm, assert, asseverate, attest, avow, certify, corroborate, declare, depone, depose, evince, show, state, swear, vouch, witness.

testimony *n.* affidavit, affirmation, asseveration, attest-ation, avowal, confirmation, corroboration, declaration, demonstration, deposition, evidence, indication, information, manifestation, profession, proof, statement, submission, support, verification, witness.

testy *adj.* bad-tempered, cantankerous, captious, carnaptious, crabbed, cross, crusty, fretful, grumpy, impatient, inflammable, irascible, irritable, peevish, peppery, petulant, quarrelsome, quick-tempered, short-tempered, snappish, snappy, splenetic, sullen, tetchy, touchy, waspish.

antonyms even-tempered, good-humored.

tether *n.* bond, chain, cord, fastening, fetter, halter, lead, leash, line, restraint, rope, shackle.

v. bind, chain, fasten, fetter, lash, leash, manacle, picket, restrain, rope, secure, shackle, tie.

text *n.* argument, body, contents, lection, libretto, matter, motif, paragraph, passage, reader, reading, script, sentence, source, subject, textbook, theme, topic, verse, wordage, wording, words.

texture *n.* character, composition, consistency, constitution, fabric, feel, grain, quality, structure, surface, tissue, weave, weftage, woof.

thankful *adj.* appreciative, beholden, contented, grateful, indebted, obliged, pleased, relieved.

antonyms thankless, unappreciative, ungrateful.

thaw *v.* defreeze, defrost, dissolve, liquefy, melt, soften, unbend, uncongeal, unfreeze, unthaw, warm.

antonym freeze.

theater *n.* amphitheater, auditorium, hall, lyceum, odeon, opera house, playhouse.

theatrical *adj.* affected, artificial, ceremonious, dramatic, dramaturgic, exaggerated, extravagant, hammy, histrionic, mannered, melodramatic, ostentatious, overdone, pompous, scenic, showy, stagy, stilted, theatric, Thespian, unreal.

theft *n.* abstraction, embezzlement, fraud, heist, kleptomania, larceny, pilfering, plunderage, purloining, rip-off, robbery, stealing, thievery, thieving.

theme *n.* argument, burden, composition, dissertation, essay, exercise, idea, keynote, leitmotiv, lemma, matter, motif, mythos, paper, subject, subject-matter, text, thesis, topic, topos.

theoretical *adj.* abstract, academic, conjectural, doctrinaire, doctrinal, hypothetical, ideal, impractical, on paper, pure, speculative.

antonyms applied, concrete, practical.

theory *n.* abstraction, assumption, conjecture, guess, hypothesis, ism, philosophy, plan, postulation, presumption, proposal, scheme, speculation, supposition, surmise, system, thesis.

antonyms certainty, practice.

therefore *adv.* accordingly, as a result, consequently, ergo, for that reason, hence, so, then, thence, thus.

thick *adj.* abundant, brainless, brimming, bristling, broad, bulky, bursting, chock-a-block, chock-full, chummy, close, clotted, coagulated, compact, concentrated, condensed, confidential, covered, crass, crawling, crowded, decided, deep, dense, devoted, dimwitted, distinct, distorted, dopey, dull, excessive, familiar, fat, foggy, frequent, friendly, full, gross, guttural, heavy, hoarse, husky, impenetrable, inarticulate, indistinct, insensitive, inseparable, intimate, marked, matey, moronic, muffled, numerous, obtuse, opaque, packed, pally, pronounced, replete, rich, slow, slow-witted, solid, soupy, squabbish, strong, stupid, substantial, swarming, teeming, thick-headed, throaty, turbid, wide.

antonyms brainy, clever, slender, slight, slim, thin, watery.

n. center, focus, heart, hub, middle, midst.

thief *n.* abactor, Autolycus, bandit, burglar, cheat, cracksman, crook, cut-purse, embezzler, filcher, house-breaker, kleptomaniac, ladrone, land-rat, larcener, larcenist, latron, mugger, pickpocket, pilferer, plunderer, prigger, purloiner, robber, shop-lifter, snatch-purse, St Nicholas's clerk, stealer, swindler.

thin *adj.* attenuate, attenuated, bony, deficient, delicate, diaphanous, dilute, diluted, emaciated, feeble, filmy, fine, fine-drawn, flimsy, gaunt, gossamer, inadequate, insubstantial, insufficient, lanky, lean, light, meager, narrow, poor, rarefied, runny, scant, scanty, scarce, scattered, scragged, scraggy, scrawny, see-through, shallow, sheer, skeletal, skimpy, skinny, slender, slight, slim, spare, sparse, spindly, superficial, tenuous, translucent, transparent, unconvincing, under-nourished, underweight, unsubstantial, washy, watery, weak, wishy-washy, wispy.

antonyms broad, dense, fat, solid, strong, thick.

v. attenuate, decrassify, dilute, diminish, emaciate, extenuate, prune, rarefy, reduce, refine, trim, water down, weaken, weed out.

think *v.* anticipate, be under the impression, believe, brood, calculate, cerebrate, cogitate, conceive, conclude, consider, contemplate, deem, deliberate, design, determine, envisage, esteem, estimate, expect, foresee, hold, ideate, imagine, intellectualize, judge, meditate, mull over, muse, ponder, presume, purpose, ratiocinate, reason, recall, reckon, recollect, reflect, regard, remember, revolve, ruminate, suppose, surmise.

n. assessment, cogitation, consideration, contemplation, deliberation, meditation, reflection.

thirst *n.* appetite, craving, desire, drought, drouth, drouthiness, dryness, eagerness, hankering, hunger, hydromania, keenness, longing, lust, passion, thirstiness, yearning, yen.

thirsty *adj.* adry, appetitive, arid, athirst, avid, burning, craving, dehydrated, desirous, drouthy, dry, drying, eager, greedy, hankering, hungry, hydropic, itching, longing, lusting, parched, thirsting, yearning.

thorn *n.* acantha, affliction, annoyance, bane, barb, bother, curse, doorn, irritant, irritation, nuisance, pest, plague, prickle, scourge, spike, spine, torment, torture, trouble.

thorough *adj.* absolute, all-embracing, all-inclusive, arrant, assiduous, careful, complete, comprehensive, conscientious, deep-seated, downright, efficient, entire, exhaustive, full, in-depth, intensive, meticulous, out-and-out, painstaking, perfect, pure, root-and-branch, scrupulous, sheer, sweeping, thoroughgoing, total, unmitigated, unqualified, utter.

antonyms careless, haphazard, partial.

thoroughfare *n.* access, avenue, boulevard, concourse, expressway, freeway, highway, motorway, passage, passageway, road, roadway, street, thruway, turnpike, way.

though *conj.* albeit, allowing, although, even if, granted, howbeit, notwithstanding, while.

adv. all the same, even so, for all that, however, in spite of that, nevertheless, nonetheless, notwithstanding, still, yet.

thought *n.* aim, anticipation, anxiety, aspiration, assessment, attention, attentiveness, belief, brainwork, care, cerebration, cogitation, compassion, concept, conception, concern, conclusion, conjecture, considerateness, consideration, contemplation, conviction, dash, deliberation, design, dream, estimation, excogitation, expectation, heed, hope, idea, intention, introspection, jot, judgment, kindness, little, meditation, mentation, muse, musing, notion, object, opinion, plan, prospect, purpose, reflection, regard, resolution, rumination, scrutiny, solicitude, study, sympathy, thinking, thoughtfulness, touch, trifle, view, whisker.

thoughtful *adj.* absorbed, abstracted, astute, attentive, canny, careful, caring, cautious, circumspect, considerate, contemplative, deliberate, deliberative, discreet, heedful, helpful, introspective, kind, kindly, meditative, mindful, musing, pensieroso, pensive, prudent, rapt, reflective, ruminative, serious, solicitous, studious, thinking, unselfish, wary, wistful.

antonym thoughtless.

thoughtless *adj.* absent-minded, careless, étourdi(e), foolish, heedless, ill-considered, impolite, imprudent, inadvertent, inattentive, inconsiderate, indiscreet, injudicious, insensitive, mindless, neglectful, negligent, rash, reckless, regardless, remiss, rude, selfish, silly, stupid, tactless, uncaring, undiplomatic, unkind, unmindful, unobservant, unreflecting, unthinking.

antonym thoughtful.

thrash *v.* beat, belt, bethump, bethwack, birch, cane, chastise, clobber, crush, defeat, drub, flagellate, flail, flog, hammer, heave, horse-whip, jerk, lam, lambaste, larrup, lather, lay into, leather, maul, overwhelm, paste, plunge, punish, quilt, rout, scourge, slaughter, spank, squirm, swish, tan, thresh, toss, towel, trim, trounce, wallop, whale, whap, whip, writhe.

thread *n.* cotton, course, direction, drift, fiber, filament, film, fimbria, line, motif, plot, story-line, strain, strand, string, tenor, theme, yarn.

v. ease, inch, meander, pass, string, weave, wind.

threadbare *adj.* clichéd, cliché-ridden, commonplace, conventional, corny, down-at-heel, frayed, hackneyed, moth-eaten, old, overused, overworn, ragged, scruffy, shabby, stale, stereotyped, stock, tattered, tatty, tired, trite, used, well-worn, worn, worn-out.

antonyms fresh, luxurious, new, plush.

threat *n.* commination, danger, foreboding, foreshadowing, frighteners, hazard, menace, omen, peril, portent, presage, risk, saber-rattling, warning.

threaten *v.* browbeat, bully, comminate, cow, endanger, forebode, foreshadow, impend, imperil, intimidate, jeopardize, menace, portend, presage, pressurize, terrorize, warn.

threatening *adj.* baleful, bullying, cautionary, comminatory, Damoclean, grim, inauspicious, intimidatory, menacing, minacious, minatory, ominous, sinister, terrorizing, warning.

threshold *n.* beginning, brink, dawn, door, door-sill, door-stead, doorstep, doorway, entrance, inception, minimum, opening, outset, sill, start, starting-point, verge.

thrift *n.* carefulness, conservation, economy, frugality, husbandry, parsimony, prudence, saving, thriftiness.

antonyms profligacy, waste.

thrifty *adj.* careful, conserving, economical, frugal, parsimonious, provident, prudent, saving, sparing.

antonyms prodigal, profligate, thriftless, wasteful.

thrill *n.* adventure, buzz, charge, flutter, fluttering, frisson, glow, kick, pleasure, quiver, sensation, shudder, stimulation, throb, tingle, titillation, tremble, tremor, vibration.

v. arouse, electrify, excite, flush, flutter, glow, move, quake, quiver, send, shake, shudder, stimulate, stir, throb, tingle, titillate, tremble, vibrate, wow.

thrive *v.* advance, bloom, blossom, boom, burgeon, develop, flourish, gain, grow, increase, profit, prosper, succeed, wax.

antonyms die, fail, languish, stagnate.

throb *v.* beat, palpitate, pound, pulsate, pulse, thump, vibrate.

n. beat, palpitation, pounding, pulsating, pulsation, pulse, thump, thumping, vibration, vibrato.

throe *n.* convulsion, fit, pain, pang, paroxysm, seizure, spasm, stab.

throng *n.* assemblage, bevy, concourse, congregation, crowd, crush, flock, herd, horde, host, jam, mass, mob, multitude, pack, press, swarm.

v. bunch, congregate, converge, cram, crowd, fill, flock, herd, jam, mill around, pack, press, swarm.

throttle *v.* asphyxiate, choke, control, gag, garrotte, inhibit, silence, smother, stifle, strangle, strangulate, suppress.

through *prep.* as a result of, because of, between, by, by means of, by reason of, by virtue of, by way of, during, in, in and out of, in consequence of, in the middle of, past, thanks to, throughout, using, via.

adj. completed, direct, done, ended, express, finished, non-stop, terminated.

throughout *adv.* everywhere, extensively, ubiquitously, widely.

throw *v.* astonish, baffle, bemuse, bring down, cast, chuck, confound, confuse, defeat, discomfit, disconcert, dislodge, dumbfound, elance, execute, fell, fling, floor, heave, hurl, jaculate, launch, lob, overturn, perform, perplex, pitch, produce, project, propel, put, send, shy, sling, slug, toss, unhorse, unsaddle, unseat, upset, whang.

n. attempt, cast, chance, essay, fling, gamble, hazard, heave, lob, pitch, projection, put, shy, sling, spill, toss, try, venture, wager.

thrust *v.* bear, butt, drive, force, impel, intrude, jab, jam, lunge, pierce, plunge, poke, press, prod, propel, push, ram, shove, stab, stick, urge, wedge.

n. drive, flanconade, impetus, lunge, momentum, poke, prod, prog, push, shove, stab, stoccado.

thug *n.* animal, assassin, bandit, bangster, bruiser, bullyboy, cut-throat, gangster, goon, gorilla, heavy, highbinder, hood, hoodlum, hooligan, killer, mugger, murderer, robber, ruffian, tough.

thump *n.* bang, blow, box, clout, clunk, crash, cuff, knock, rap, smack, thud, thwack, wallop, whack.

v. bang, batter, beat, belabor, box, clout, crash, cuff, daud, ding, dunt, dush, hit, knock, lambaste, pound, rap, smack, strike, thrash, throb, thud, thwack, wallop, whack.

thunderstruck *adj.* agape, aghast, amazed, astonished, astounded, dazed, dumbfounded, flabbergasted, floored, flummoxed, nonplused, open-mouthed, paralyzed, petrified, shocked, staggered, stunned.

thus *adv.* accordingly, as follows, consequently, ergo, hence, in this way, like so, like this, so, then, therefore, thuswise.

thwart *v.* baffle, balk, check, defeat, foil, frustrate, hinder, impede, obstruct, oppose, outwit, prevent, spite, stonker, stop, stymie, transverse, traverse.

antonyms abet, aid, assist.

ticket *n.* card, certificate, coupon, docket, label, marker, pass, slip, sticker, tab, tag, tessera, token, voucher.

tickle *v.* amuse, cheer, delight, divert, enchant, entertain, excite, gratify, please, thrill, titillate.

ticklish *adj.* awkward, critical, delicate, difficult, dodgy, hazardous, nice, precarious, risky, sensitive, thorny, touchy, tricky, uncertain, unstable, unsteady.

antonyms easy, straightforward.

tidings *n.* advice, bulletin, communication, dope, gen, greetings, information, intelligence, message, news, report, word.

tidy *adj.* ample, businesslike, clean, cleanly, considerable, fair, generous, good, goodly, handsome, healthy, large, largish, methodical, neat, ordered, orderly, respectable, shipshape, sizable, spick, spick-and-span, spruce, substantial, systematic, trim, uncluttered, well-groomed, well-kept.

antonyms disorganized, untidy.

v. arrange, clean, fettle, groom, neaten, order, spruce up, straighten.

tie *v.* attach, bind, confine, connect, draw, equal, fasten, hamper, hinder, hold, interlace, join, knot, lash, ligature, limit, link, match, moor, oblige, restrain, restrict, rope, secure, strap, tether, truss, unite.

n. affiliation, allegiance, band, bond, commitment, connection, contest, copula, cord, dead heat, deadlock, draw, duty, encumbrance, fastening, fetter, fixture, game, hindrance, joint, kinship, knot, liaison, ligature, limitation, link, match, obligation, relationship, restraint, restriction, rope, stalemate, string.

tier *n.* band, belt, echelon, floor, gradin(e), layer, level, line, rank, row, stage, story, stratification, stratum, zone.

tiff *n.* barney, difference, disagreement, dispute, falling-out, huff, ill-humor, pet, quarrel, row, scrap, set-to, spat, squabble, sulk, tantrum, temper, words.

tight[1] *adj.* close, close-fitting, compact, competent, constricted, cramped, dangerous, difficult, even, evenly-balanced, fast, firm, fixed, grasping, harsh, hazardous, hermetic, impervious, inflexible, mean, miserly, narrow, near, niggardly, parsimonious, penurious, perilous, precarious, precise, problematic, proof, rigid, rigorous, sealed, secure, severe, snug, sound, sparing, stern, sticky, stiff, stretched, strict, stringent, taut, tense, ticklish, tight-fisted, tough, tricky, trig, troublesome, uncompromising, unyielding, watertight, well-matched, worrisome.

antonyms lax, loose, slack.

tight[2] *adj.* blotto, drunk, half cut, half-seas-over, in one's cups, inebriated, intoxicated, pickled, pie-eyed, pissed, plastered, smashed, sozzled, stewed, stoned, three sheets in the wind, tiddly, tipsy, under the influence.

antonym sober.

till *v.* cultivate, dig, dress, plow, work.

tilt *v.* attack, cant, clash, contend, duel, encounter, fight, heel, incline, joust, lean, list, overthrow, pitch, slant, slope, spar, tip.

n. angle, cant, clash, combat, duel, encounter, fight,

inclination, incline, joust, list, lists, pitch, set-to, slant, slope, thrust, tournament, tourney.

timber n. beams, boarding, boards, forest, logs, planking, planks, trees, wood.

time n. age, beat, chronology, date, day, duration, epoch, era, generation, heyday, hour, instance, interval, juncture, life, lifespan, lifetime, measure, meter, occasion, peak, period, point, rhythm, season, space, span, spell, stage, stretch, tempo, term, tide, while.

v. clock, control, count, judge, measure, meter, regulate, schedule, set.

timeless adj. abiding, ageless, amaranthine, ceaseless, changeless, deathless, endless, enduring, eternal, everlasting, immortal, immutable, imperishable, indestructible, lasting, permanent, perpetual, persistent, undying.

timely adj. appropriate, convenient, judicious, opportune, prompt, propitious, punctual, seasonable, suitable, tempestive, well-timed.

antonyms ill-timed, inappropriate, unfavorable.

timetable n. agenda, calendar, curriculum, diary, list, listing, program, roster, rota, schedule.

time-worn adj. aged, ancient, broken-down, bromidic, clichéd, dated, decrepit, dog-eared, hackneyed, hoary, lined, old hat, out of date, outworn, passé, ragged, ruined, run-down, shabby, stale, stock, threadbare, tired, trite, weathered, well-worn, worn, wrinkled.

antonyms fresh, new.

timid adj. afraid, apprehensive, bashful, cowardly, coy, diffident, faint-hearted, fearful, hen-hearted, irresolute, modest, mousy, nervous, pavid, pusillanimous, retiring, shrinking, shy, spineless, timorous.

antonyms audacious, bold, brave.

tinge n. bit, cast, color, dash, drop, dye, flavor, pinch, shade, smack, smatch, smattering, sprinkling, stain, suggestion, tinct, tincture, tint, touch, trace, wash.

v. color, dye, encolor, imbue, shade, stain, suffuse, tint.

tingle v. dindle, itch, prickle, ring, sting, thrill, throb, tickle, vibrate.

n. frisson, gooseflesh, goose-pimples, itch, itching, pins and needles, prickling, quiver, shiver, stinging, thrill, tickle, tickling.

tinker v. dabble, fiddle, meddle, monkey, play, potter, putter, toy, trifle.

n. botcher, bungler, diddicoy, fixer, itinerant, mender.

tint n. cast, color, dye, hint, hue, rinse, shade, stain, streak, suggestion, tinct, tincture, tinge, tone, touch, trace, wash.

v. affect, color, dye, influence, rinse, stain, streak, taint, tincture, tinge.

tiny adj. diminutive, dwarfish, infinitesimal, insignificant, itsy-bitsy, Lilliputian, little, microscopic, mini, miniature, minute, negligible, petite, pint-size(d), pocket, puny, pygmy, slight, small, teensy, teentsy, teeny, teeny-weeny, tiddl(e)y, tottie, totty, trifling, wee, weeny.

antonyms big, immense.

tip[1] n. acme, apex, cap, crown, end, extremity, ferrule, head, nib, peak, pinnacle, point, summit, top.

v. cap, crown, finish, pinnacle, poll, pollard, prune, surmount, top.

tip[2] v. cant, capsize, ditch, dump, empty, heel, incline, lean, list, overturn, pour out, slant, spill, tilt, topple over, unload, up-end, upset.

n. bing, coup, dump, midden, refuse-heap, rubbish-heap, slag-heap.

tip[3] n. baksheesh, clue, forecast, gen, gift, gratuity, hint, information, inside information, lagniappe, perquisite, pointer, pourboire, refresher, suggestion, tip-off, warning, word, word of advice, wrinkle.

v. advise, caution, forewarn, inform, remunerate, reward, suggest, tell, warn.

tipsy adj. a peg too low, a pip out, cockeyed, corny, drunk, elevated, fuddled, happy, mellow, merry, moony, moppy, mops and brooms, nappy, pixil(l)ated, rocky, screwed, screwy, slewed, sprung, squiff(y), tiddled, tiddley, tiddly, tight, totty, wet, woozy.

antonym sober.

tirade n. abuse, denunciation, diatribe, fulmination, harangue, invective, lecture, outburst, philippic, rant.

tire v. annoy, betoil, bore, cook, drain, droop, enervate, exasperate, exhaust, fag, fail, fatigue, flag, harass, irk, irritate, jade, knacker, sink, weary.

antonyms energize, enliven, exhilarate, invigorate, refresh.

tired adj. all in, awearied, aweary, beat, bone-weary, bushed, clapped-out, clichéd, conventional, corny, dead-beat, disjaskit, dog-tired, drained, drooping, drowsy, enervated, épuisé(e), exhausted, fagged, familiar, fatigued, flagging, forfairn, forfough(t)en, forjeskit, hackneyed, jaded, knackered, old, outworn, shagged, shattered, sleepy, spent, stale, stock, threadbare, trite, weary, well-worn, whacked, worn out.

antonyms active, energetic, fresh, lively, rested.

tireless adj. determined, diligent, energetic, indefatigable, industrious, resolute, sedulous, unflagging, untiring, unwearied, vigorous.

antonyms tired, unenthusiastic, weak.

tiresome adj. annoying, boring, bothersome, dull, exasperating, fatiguing, flat, irksome, irritating, laborious, monotonous, pesky, tedious, troublesome, trying, uninteresting, vexatious, wearing, wearisome.

antonyms easy, interesting, stimulating.

tiring adj. arduous, demanding, draining, enervating, enervative, exacting, exhausting, fagging, fatiguing, laborious, strenuous, tough, wearing, wearying.

titan n. Atlas, colossus, giant, Hercules, leviathan, superman.

titillating adj. arousing, captivating, exciting, interesting, intriguing, lewd, lurid, provocative, sensational, stimulating, suggestive, teasing, thrilling.

title n. appellation, caption, championship, claim, crown, denomination, designation, entitlement, epithet, handle, heading, inscription, label, laurels, legend, letter-head, moniker, name, nickname, nom de plume, ownership, prerogative, privilege, pseudonym, right, sobriquet, style, term.

v. call, christen, designate, dub, entitle, label, name, style, term.

toast[1] v. broil, brown, grill, heat, roast, warm.

toast[2] n. compliment, darling, drink, favorite, grace cup, health, hero, heroine, pledge, salutation, salute, tribute, wassail.

together adv. all at once, arranged, as one, as one man, at the same time, cheek by jowl, closely, collectively, concurrently, consecutively, contemporaneously, continuously, en masse, fixed, hand in glove, hand in hand, in a body, in a row, in concert, in co-operation, in fere, in mass, in succession, in unison, jointly, mutually, on end, ordered, organized, pari passu, settled, shoulder to shoulder, side by side, simultaneously, sorted out, straight, successively.

antonym separately.

adj. calm, commonsensical, composed, cool, down-to-earth, level-headed, sensible, stable, well-adjusted, well-balanced, well-organized.

toil *n.* application, donkey-work, drudgery, effort, elbow grease, exertion, graft, industry, labor, labor improbus, pains, slog, sweat, travail.

v. drudge, graft, grind, grub, labor, persevere, plug away, slave, slog, strive, struggle, sweat, tew, work.

token *n.* badge, clue, demonstration, earnest, evidence, expression, index, indication, keepsake, manifestation, mark, memento, memorial, note, proof, remembrance, reminder, representation, sign, souvenir, symbol, tessera, testimony, voucher, warning.

adj. emblematic, hollow, inconsiderable, minimal, nominal, perfunctory, superficial, symbolic.

tolerant *adj.* biddable, broad-minded, catholic, charitable, complaisant, compliant, easy-going, fair, forbearing, indulgent, kind-hearted, latitudinarian, lax, lenient, liberal, long-suffering, magnanimous, open-minded, patient, permissive, soft, sympathetic, understanding, unprejudiced.

antonyms biased, bigoted, intolerant, prejudiced, unsympathetic.

tolerate *v.* abear, abide, accept, admit, allow, bear, brook, condone, connive at, countenance, endure, indulge, permit, pocket, put up with, receive, sanction, stand, stomach, suffer, swallow, take, thole, turn a blind eye to, undergo, wear, wink at.

toll[1] *v.* announce, call, chime, clang, knell, peal, ring, send, signal, sound, strike, summon, warn.

toll[2] *n.* assessment, charge, cost, customs, damage, demand, duty, fee, impost, inroad, levy, loss, payment, penalty, rate, tariff, tax, tithe, tribute.

tomb *n.* burial-place, catacomb, cenotaph, crypt, dolmen, grave, mastaba, mausoleum, sepulcher, sepulture, speos, vault.

tone *n.* accent, air, approach, aspect, attitude, cast, character, color, drift, effect, emphasis, feel, force, frame, grain, harmony, hue, inflection, intonation, klang, manner, modulation, mood, note, pitch, quality, shade, spirit, strength, stress, style, temper, tenor, timbre, tinge, tint, tonality, vein, volume.

v. blend, harmonize, intone, match, sound, suit.

tongue *n.* argot, articulation, clack, clapper, dialect, discourse, idiom, language, languet(te), lath, lingo, parlance, patois, red rag, speech, talk, utterance, vernacular, voice.

tongue-tied *adj.* dumb, dumbstruck, inarticulate, mute, silent, speechless, voiceless.

antonyms garrulous, talkative, voluble.

too[1] *adv.* also, as well, besides, further, in addition, into the bargain, likewise, moreover, to boot, what's more.

too[2] *adv.* excessively, exorbitantly, extremely, immoderately, inordinately, over, overly, ridiculously, to excess, to extremes, unduly, unreasonably, very.

tool *n.* agency, agent, apparatus, appliance, cat's-paw, contraption, contrivance, creature, device, dupe, flunkey, front, gadget, hireling, implement, instrument, intermediary, jackal, lackey, machine, means, medium, minion, pawn, puppet, stooge, toady, utensil, vehicle, weapon, widget.

v. chase, cut, decorate, fashion, machine, ornament, shape, work.

top *n.* acme, apex, apogee, cacumen, cap, cop, cork, cover, crest, crown, culmen, culmination, head, height, high point, hood, lead, lid, meridian, peak, pinnacle, roof, stopper, summit, upside, vertex, zenith.

antonyms base, bottom, nadir.

adj. best, chief, crack, crowning, culminating, dominant, elite, finest, first, foremost, greatest, head, highest, lead, leading, pre-eminent, prime, principal, ruling, sovereign, superior, topmost, upmost, upper, uppermost.

v. ascend, beat, best, better, cap, climb, command, cover, crest, crown, decorate, eclipse, exceed, excel, finish, finish off, garnish, head, lead, outdo, outshine, outstrip, roof, rule, scale, surmount, surpass, tip, transcend.

topic *n.* issue, lemma, matter, motif, point, question, subject, subject-matter, talking-point, text, theme, thesis.

topical *adj.* contemporary, current, familiar, newsworthy, popular, relevant, up-to-date, up-to-the-minute.

topple *v.* capsize, collapse, oust, overbalance, overthrow, overturn, totter, tumble, unseat, upset.

torment *v.* afflict, agitate, agonize, annoy, bedevil, bother, chivvy, crucify, devil, distort, distress, excruciate, harass, harrow, harry, hound, irritate, nag, pain, persecute, pester, plague, provoke, rack, tease, torture, trouble, vex, worry, wrack.

n. affliction, agony, angst, anguish, annoyance, bane, bother, distress, harassment, hassle, hell, irritation, misery, nag, nagging, nuisance, pain, persecution, pest, plague, provocation, scourge, suffering, torture, trouble, vexation, worry.

torpid *adj.* apathetic, benumbed, dormant, drowsy, dull, fainéant, hebetudinous, inactive, indolent, inert, lackadaisical, languid, languorous, lazy, lethargic, listless, lymphatic, motionless, numb, passive, slothful, slow, slow-moving, sluggish, somnolent, stagnant, supine.

antonyms active, lively, vigorous.

torpor *n.* accidie, acedia, apathy, dormancy, drowsiness, dullness, hebetude, inactivity, inanition, indolence, inertia, inertness, languor, laziness, lethargy, listlessness, numbness, passivity, sloth, sluggishness, somnolence, stagnancy, stupidity, stupor, torpidity.

antonyms activity, animation, vigor.

torrent *n.* barrage, cascade, deluge, downpour, effusion, flood, flow, gush, outburst, rush, spate, stream, tide, volley.

torrid *adj.* ardent, arid, blistering, boiling, broiling, burning, dried, dry, emotional, erotic, fervent, fiery, hot, intense, parched, parching, passionate, scorched, scorching, sexy, sizzling, steamy, stifling, sultry, sweltering, tropical.

antonym arctic.

tortuous *adj.* ambagious, ambiguous, bent, Byzantine, circuitous, complicated, convoluted, crooked, cunning, curved, deceptive, devious, indirect, involved, mazy, meandering, misleading, roundabout, serpentine, sinuous, tricky, twisted, twisting, winding, zigzag.

antonyms straight, straightforward.

torture *v.* afflict, agonize, crucify, distress, excruciate, harrow, lacerate, martyr, martyrize, pain, persecute, rack, torment, wrack.

n. affliction, agony, anguish, distress, gyp, hell, laceration, martyrdom, misery, pain, pang(s), persecution, rack, suffering, torment.

toss *v.* agitate, cant, cast, chuck, disturb, fling, flip, heave, hurl, jiggle, joggle, jolt, labor, launch, lob, lurch, pitch, project, propel, rock, roll, shake, shy, sling, thrash, throw, tumble, wallow, welter, wriggle, writhe.

n. cast, chuck, fling, lob, pitch, shy, sling, throw.

total *n.* aggregate, all, amount, ensemble, entirety, lot, mass, sum, totality, whole.

adj. absolute, all-out, complete, comprehensive, consummate, downright, entire, full, gross, integral, out-and-out, outright, perfect, root-and-branch, sheer, sweeping, thorough, thoroughgoing, unconditional, undisputed, undivided, unmitigated, unqualified, utter, whole, whole-hog.

antonyms limited, partial, restricted.

v. add (up), amount to, come to, count (up), reach, reckon, sum (up), tot up.

totalitarian *adj.* authoritarian, despotic, dictatorial, monocratic, monolithic, omnipotent, one-party, oppressive, tyrannous, undemocratic.

antonym democratic.

totter *v.* daddle, daidle, falter, lurch, quiver, reel, rock, shake, stagger, stumble, sway, teeter, titter, tremble, waver.

touch *n.* ability, acquaintance, adroitness, approach, art, artistry, awareness, bit, blow, brush, caress, characteristic, command, communication, contact, correspondence, dash, deftness, detail, direction, drop, effect, facility, familiarity, feel, feeling, flair, fondling, hand, handiwork, handling, hint, hit, influence, intimation, jot, knack, manner, mastery, method, palpation, pat, pinch, push, skill, smack, smattering, soupçon, speck, spot, stroke, style, suggestion, suspicion, tactility, tap, taste, technique, tig, tincture, tinge, trace, trademark, understanding, virtuosity, way, whiff.

v. abut, adjoin, affect, attain, border, brush, caress, cheat, compare with, concern, consume, contact, converge, disturb, drink, eat, equal, feel, finger, fondle, graze, handle, hit, hold a candle to, impress, influence, inspire, interest, mark, match, meet, melt, move, palp, palpate, parallel, pat, pertain to, push, reach, regard, rival, soften, stir, strike, stroke, tap, tat, tinge, upset, use, utilize.

touch-and-go *adj.* close, critical, dangerous, dodgy, hairy, hazardous, near, nerve-racking, offhand, parlous, perilous, precarious, risky, sticky, tricky.

touching *adj.* affecting, emotional, emotive, haptic, heartbreaking, libant, melting, moving, pathetic, piteous, pitiable, pitiful, poignant, sad, stirring, tender.

touchy *adj.* bad-tempered, captious, crabbed, cross, feisty, grouchy, grumpy, huffy, irascible, irritable, miffy, peevish, pettish, petulant, querulous, quick-tempered, snippety, snuffy, sore, splenetic, surly, testy, tetchy, thin-skinned.

antonyms calm, imperturbable, serene, unflappable.

tough *adj.* adamant, arduous, bad, baffling, brawny, butch, callous, cohesive, difficult, durable, exacting, exhausting, firm, fit, hard, hard-bitten, hard-boiled, hardened, hard-nosed, hardy, herculean, inflexible, intractable, irksome, knotty, laborious, lamentable, leathery, merciless, obdurate, obstinate, perplexing, pugnacious, puzzling, refractory, regrettable, resilient, resistant, resolute, rigid, rough, ruffianly, rugged, ruth-

less, seasoned, severe, solid, stalwart, stern, stiff, stout, strapping, strenuous, strict, strong, stubborn, sturdy, tenacious, thorny, troublesome, unbending, unforgiving, unfortunate, unlucky, unyielding, uphill, vicious, vigorous, violent.

antonyms brittle, delicate, fragile, liberal, soft, tender, vulnerable, weak.

n. bravo, bruiser, brute, bully, bully-boy, bully-rook, gorilla, hooligan, rough, roughneck, rowdy, ruffian, thug, yob, yobbo.

toughness *n.* arduousness, callousness, difficulty, durability, firmness, fitness, grit, hardiness, hardness, inflexibility, intractability, laboriousness, obduracy, obstinacy, pugnacity, resilience, resistance, rigidity, roughness, ruggedness, ruthlessness, severity, solidity, sternness, stiffness, strength, strenuousness, strictness, sturdiness, tenacity, viciousness.

antonyms fragility, liberality, softness, vulnerability, weakness.

tour *n.* circuit, course, drive, excursion, expedition, jaunt, journey, outing, peregrination, progress, ride, round, trip.

v. drive, explore, journey, ride, sightsee, travel, visit.

tourist *n.* excursionist, globe-trotter, holidaymaker, journeyer, rubber-neck, sightseer, sojourner, traveler.

tournament *n.* championship, competition, contest, event, joust, lists, match, meeting, series, tourney.

tousled *adj.* disarranged, disheveled, disordered, messed up, ruffled, rumpled, tangled, tumbled.

tow *v.* drag, draw, haul, lug, pull, tote, trail, transport, trawl, tug, yank.

towering *adj.* burning, colossal, elevated, excessive, extraordinary, extreme, fiery, gigantic, great, high, immoderate, imposing, impressive, inordinate, intemperate, intense, lofty, magnificent, mighty, monumental, outstanding, overpowering, paramount, passionate, prodigious, soaring, sublime, superior, supreme, surpassing, tall, transcendent, vehement, violent.

antonyms minor, small, trivial.

town *n.* borough, bourg, burg, burgh, city, metropolis, municipality, settlement, township.

antonym country.

toxic *adj.* baneful, deadly, harmful, lethal, morbific, noxious, pernicious, pestilential, poisonous, septic, unhealthy.

antonym harmless.

toy *n.* bauble, doll, game, gewgaw, kickshaw(s), knick-knack, plaything, trifle, trinket.

v. dally, fiddle, flirt, play, potter, putter, sport, tinker, trifle, wanton.

trace *n.* bit, dash, drop, evidence, footmark, footprint, footstep, hint, indication, iota, jot, mark, path, record, relic, remains, remnant, scintilla, shadow, sign, smack, soupçon, spoor, spot, suggestion, survival, suspicion, tincture, tinge, token, touch, track, trail, trifle, vestige, whiff.

v. ascertain, chart, copy, delineate, depict, detect, determine, discover, draw, find, follow, map, mark, outline, pursue, record, seek, shadow, show, sketch, stalk, track, trail, traverse, unearth, write.

track *n.* course, drift, footmark, footprint, footstep, line, mark, orbit, path, pathway, piste, rail, rails, ridgeway, road, scent, sequence, slot, spoor, tack, trace, trail, train, trajectory, wake, wavelength, way.

v. chase, dog, follow, hunt, pursue, shadow, spoor, stalk, tail, trace, trail, travel, traverse.

tract¹ *n.* area, district, estate, expanse, extent, lot, plot, quarter, region, section, stretch, territory, zone.

tract² *n.* booklet, brochure, discourse, disquisition, dissertation, essay, homily, leaflet, monograph, pamphlet, sermon, tractate, treatise.

tractable *adj.* amenable, biddable, complaisant, compliant, controllable, docile, ductile, fictile, governable, malleable, manageable, obedient, persuadable, plastic, pliable, pliant, submissive, tame, tractile, willing, workable, yielding.
antonyms headstrong, intractable, obstinate, refractory, stubborn, unruly, wilful.

trade *n.* avocation, barter, business, calling, clientele, commerce, commodities, craft, custom, customers, deal, dealing, employment, exchange, interchange, job, line, market, métier, occupation, patrons, profession, public, pursuit, shopkeeping, skill, swap, traffic, transactions, truck.
v. bargain, barter, commerce, deal, do business, exchange, peddle, swap, switch, traffic, transact, truck.

trademark *n.* badge, brand, crest, emblem, hallmark, identification, idiograph, insignia, label, logo, logotype, name, sign, symbol.

tradition *n.* convention, custom, customs, folklore, habit, institution, lore, praxis, ritual, usage, usance, way, wony.

traduce *v.* abuse, asperse, blacken, calumniate, decry, defame, denigrate, deprecate, depreciate, detract, disparage, knock, malign, misrepresent, revile, run down, slag, slander, smear, vilify.

tragedy *n.* adversity, affliction, blow, calamity, catastrophe, disaster, misfortune, unhappiness.
antonyms prosperity, success, triumph.

tragic *adj.* anguished, appalling, awful, calamitous, catastrophic, deadly, dire, disastrous, doleful, dreadful, fatal, grievous, heartbreaking, heart-rending, ill-fated, ill-starred, lamentable, miserable, mournful, pathetic, pitiable, ruinous, sad, shocking, sorrowful, thespian, unfortunate, unhappy, woeful, wretched.
antonyms comic, successful, triumphant.

trail *v.* chase, dangle, dawdle, drag, draw, droop, extend, follow, hang, haul, hunt, lag, linger, loiter, pull, pursue, shadow, stalk, straggle, stream, sweep, tail, tow, trace, track, traipse.
n. abature, appendage, drag, footpath, footprints, footsteps, mark, marks, path, road, route, scent, spoor, stream, tail, trace, track, train, wake, way.

train *v.* aim, coach, direct, discipline, drill, educate, exercise, focus, guide, improve, instruct, lesson, level, point, prepare, rear, rehearse, school, teach, tutor.
n. appendage, attendants, caravan, chain, choo-choo, column, concatenation, convoy, cortege, course, court, entourage, file, followers, following, household, lure, order, process, procession, progression, retinue, sequence, series, set, staff, string, succession, suite, tail, trail.

traipse *v.* plod, slouch, trail, tramp, trudge.
n. plod, slog, tramp, trek, trudge.

trait *n.* attribute, characteristic, feature, idiosyncrasy, lineament, mannerism, peculiarity, quality, quirk, thew.

traitor *n.* apostate, -back-stabber, betrayer, deceiver, defector, deserter, double-crosser, fifth columnist,

informer, Judas, miscreant, nithing, proditor, quisling, rebel, renegade, turncoat.

traitorous *adj.* apostate, dishonorable, disloyal, double-crossing, double-dealing, faithless, false, perfidious, proditorious, renegade, seditious, treacherous, treasonable, unfaithful, untrue.
antonyms faithful, loyal, patriotic.

trajectory *n.* course, flight, line, path, route, track, trail.

tramp *v.* crush, footslog, hike, march, plod, ramble, range, roam, rove, slog, stamp, stomp, stump, toil, traipse, trample, tread, trek, trudge, walk, yomp.
n. call girl, clochard, derelict, dosser, down-and-out, drifter, drummer, footfall, footstep, hike, hobo, hooker, march, piker, plod, ramble, slog, stamp, street walker, toe-rag(ger), tread, trek, vagabond, vagrant, weary willie.

trample *v.* crush, flatten, hurt, infringe, insult, squash, stamp, tread, violate.

tranquil *adj.* at peace, calm, composed, cool, disimpassioned, dispassionate, pacific, peaceful, placid, quiet, reposeful, restful, sedate, serene, still, undisturbed, unexcited, unperturbed, unruffled, untroubled.
antonyms agitated, disturbed, noisy, troubled.

tranquility *n.* ataraxia, ataraxy, calm, calmness, composure, coolness, equanimity, hush, imperturbability, peace, peacefulness, placidity, quiet, quietness, quietude, repose, rest, restfulness, sedateness, serenity, silence, stillness.
antonyms agitation, disturbance, noise.

transact *v.* accomplish, carry on, carry out, conclude, conduct, discharge, dispatch, do, enact, execute, handle, manage, negotiate, perform, prosecute, settle.

transaction *n.* action, affair, arrangement, bargain, business, coup, deal, deed, enterprise, event, execution, matter, negotiation, occurrence, proceeding, undertaking.

transcend *v.* eclipse, exceed, excel, outdo, outrival, outshine, outstrip, overleap, overstep, overtop, surmount, surpass.

transcribe *v.* copy, engross, exemplify, interpret, note, record, render, reproduce, rewrite, take down, tape, tape-record, transfer, translate, transliterate.

transfer *v.* carry, cede, change, consign, convey, decal, decant, demise, displace, grant, hand over, move, relocate, remove, second, shift, translate, transmit, transplant, transport, transpose.
n. change, changeover, crossover, decantation, displacement, handover, move, relocation, removal, shift, switch, switch-over, transference, translation, transmission, transposition, virement.

transform *v.* alter, change, convert, metamorphose, reconstruct, remodel, renew, revolutionize, transfigure, translate, transmogrify, transmute, transverse.
antonym preserve.

transgression *n.* breach, contravention, crime, debt, encroachment, error, fault, infraction, infringement, iniquity, lapse, misbehavior, misdeed, misdemeanor, offence, peccadillo, peccancy, sin, trespass, violation, wrong, wrongdoing.

transient *adj.* brief, caducous, deciduous, ephemeral, evanescent, fleeting, flying, fugacious, fugitive, impermanent, momentary, passing, short, short-lived, short-term, temporary, transitory.
antonym permanent.

transition n. alteration, change, changeover, conversion, development, evolution, flux, metabasis, metamorphosis, metastasis, passage, passing, progress, progression, shift, transformation, transit, transmutation, upheaval.
antonyms beginning, end.

translate v. alter, carry, change, construe, convert, convey, decipher, decode, do, do up, elucidate, enrapture, explain, improve, interpret, metamorphose, move, paraphrase, remove, render, renovate, send, simplify, spell out, transcribe, transfer, transfigure, transform, transliterate, transmogrify, transmute, transplant, transport, transpose, turn.

translucent adj. clear, diaphanous, limpid, lucent, pellucid, translucid, transparent.
antonym opaque.

transmit v. bear, broadcast, carry, communicate, convey, diffuse, dispatch, disseminate, forward, impart, network, radio, relay, remit, send, spread, traject, transfer, transport.
antonym receive.

transparent adj. apparent, candid, clear, crystalline, diaphanous, dioptric, direct, distinct, easy, evident, explicit, filmy, forthright, frank, gauzy, hyaline, hyaloid, ingenuous, limpid, lucent, lucid, manifest, obvious, open, patent, pellucid, perspicuous, plain, plain-spoken, recognizable, see-through, sheer, straight, straightforward, translucent, transpicuous, unambiguous, understandable, undisguised, unequivocal, visible.
antonyms ambiguous, opaque, unclear.

transpire v. appear, arise, befall, betide, chance, come out, come to light, emerge, happen, leak out, occur, take place, turn up.

transport v. banish, bear, bring, captivate, carry, carry away, convey, delight, deport, ecstasize, electrify, enchant, enrapture, entrance, exile, fetch, haul, move, ravish, remove, run, ship, spellbind, take, transfer, waft.
antonyms bore, leave.
n. bliss, carriage, cartage, carting, conveyance, delight, ecstasy, enchantment, euphoria, happiness, haulage, heaven, rapture, ravishment, removal, shipment, shipping, transference, transportation, vehicle, waterage.
antonym boredom.

transpose v. alter, change, exchange, interchange, metathesize, move, rearrange, relocate, reorder, shift, substitute, swap, switch, transfer.
antonym leave.

trap n. ambush, artifice, bunker, danger, deception, device, gin, hazard, net, noose, pitfall, ruse, snare, spring, springe, springle, strategem, subterfuge, toils, trap-door, trepan, trick, trickery, wile.
v. ambush, beguile, benet, catch, corner, deceive, dupe, enmesh, ensnare, entrap, illaqueate, inveigle, lime, snare, take, tangle, trepan, trick.

trash n. balderdash, draff, dregs, drivel, dross, garbage, hogwash, inanity, junk, kitsch, litter, nonsense, offscourings, offscum, refuse, riddlings, rot, rubbish, scoria, sullage, sweepings, trashery, tripe, trumpery, twaddle, waste.
antonym sense.

trashy adj. catchpenny, cheap, cheap-jack, flimsy, grotty, inferior, kitschy, meretricious, pinchbeck, rubbishy, shabby, shoddy, tawdry, third-rate, tinsel, worthless.

antonym first-rate.

trauma n. agony, anguish, damage, disturbance, hurt, injury, jolt, lesion, ordeal, pain, scar, shock, strain, suffering, torture, upheaval, upset, wound.
antonyms healing, relaxation.

travail n. birth-pangs, childbirth, distress, drudgery, effort, exertion, grind, hardship, labor, labor pains, pain, slavery, slog, strain, stress, suffering, sweat, tears, throes, toil, tribulation.
antonym rest.

travel v. carry, commute, cross, excursionize, go, journey, locomote, move, peregrinate, proceed, progress, ramble, roam, rove, tour, traverse, trek, voyage, walk, wander, wayfare, wend.
antonym stay.

travesty n. apology, botch, burlesque, caricature, distortion, lampoon, mockery, parody, perversion, send-up, sham, take-off.
v. burlesque, caricature, deride, distort, lampoon, mock, parody, pervert, pillory, ridicule, send up, sham, spoof, take off.

treachery n. betrayal, disloyalty, double-cross, double-dealing, duplicity, faithlessness, falseness, infidelity, Judas-kiss, laesa Medism, perfidiousness, perfidy, Punic faith, Punica fides, trahison, treason.
antonyms dependability, loyalty.

treason n. disaffection, disloyalty, duplicity, laesa majestas, lese-majesty, mutiny, perfidy, sedition, subversion, trahison, traitorousness, treachery.
antonym loyalty.

treasure n. cash, darling, ewe-lamb, flower, fortune, funds, gem, gold, jewel, jewels, money, nonpareil, paragon, pearl, precious, pride and joy, prize, riches, valuables, wealth.
v. adore, cherish, esteem, idolize, love, preserve, prize, revere, value, venerate, worship.
antonym disparage.

treat n. banquet, celebration, delight, enjoyment, entertainment, excursion, feast, fun, gift, gratification, joy, outing, party, pleasure, refreshment, satisfaction, surprise, thrill, wayzgoose.
antonym drag.
v. attend to, bargain, care for, confer, consider, contain, deal with, discourse upon, discuss, doctor, entertain, feast, give, handle, manage, medicament, medicate, medicine, negotiate, nurse, parley, provide, regale, regard, stand, use.

treaty n. agreement, alliance, bargain, bond, compact, concordat, contract, convention, covenant, entente, negotiation, pact.

trek n. expedition, footslog, hike, journey, march, migration, odyssey, safari, slog, tramp, walk.
v. footslog, hike, journey, march, migrate, plod, range, roam, rove, slog, traipse, tramp, trudge, yomp.

tremble v. heave, oscillate, quake, quiver, rock, shake, shiver, shudder, teeter, totter, vibrate, wobble.
n. heart-quake, oscillation, quake, quiver, shake, shiver, shudder, tremblement, tremor, vibration.
antonym steadiness.

trembling n. heart-quake, oscillation, quaking, quavering, quivering, rocking, shakes, shaking, shivering, shuddering, tremblement, trepidation, vibration.
antonym steadiness.

tremendous adj. ace, amazing, appalling, awe-inspiring, awesome, awful, colossal, deafening, dreadful, enor-

mous, excellent, exceptional, extraordinary, fabulous, fantastic, fearful, formidable, frightful, gargantuan, gigantic, great, herculean, huge, immense, incredible, mammoth, marvelous, monstrous, prodigious, sensational, spectacular, stupendous, super, terrible, terrific, titanic, towering, vast, whopping, wonderful.
antonyms boring, dreadful, run-of-the-mill, tiny.

tremor *n.* agitation, earthquake, quake, quaking, quaver, quavering, quiver, quivering, shake, shaking, shiver, shock, thrill, tremble, trembling, trepidation, trillo, vibration, wobble.
antonym steadiness.

tremulous *adj.* afraid, agitated, agog, anxious, aspen, excited, fearful, frightened, jittery, jumpy, nervous, quavering, quivering, quivery, scared, shaking, shivering, timid, trembling, trembly, tremulant, trepid, trepidant, vibrating, wavering.
antonyms calm, firm.

trenchant *adj.* acerbic, acid, acidulous, acute, astringent, biting, caustic, clear, clear-cut, cogent, crisp, cutting, distinct, driving, effective, effectual, emphatic, energetic, explicit, forceful, forthright, hurtful, incisive, keen, mordant, penetrating, piquant, pointed, potent, powerful, pungent, sarcastic, scratching, severe, sharp, strong, tart, unequivocal, vigorous.
antonym woolly.

trend *n.* bias, course, crazed, current, dernier cri, direction, fad, fashion, flow, inclination, leaning, look, mode, rage, style, tendency, thing, vogue.

trendy *adj.* fashionable, funky, groovy, in, latest, modish, stylish, up to the minute, voguish, with it.
antonym unfashionable.

trepidation *n.* agitation, alarm, anxiety, apprehension, butterflies, cold sweat, consternation, dismay, disquiet, disturbance, dread, emotion, excitement, fear, fright, jitters, misgivings, nervousness, palpitation, perturbation, qualms, quivering, shaking, trembling, tremor, unease, uneasiness, worry.
antonym calm.

trespass *v.* encroach, err, infringe, injure, intrude, invade, obtrude, offend, poach, sin, transgress, violate, wrong.
antonyms keep to, obey.

n. breach, contravention, crime, debt, delinquency, encroachment, error, evil-doing, fault, infraction, infringement, iniquity, injury, intrusion, invasion, misbehavior, misconduct, misdeed, misdemeanor, offense, poaching, sin, transgression, wrong-doing.

trespasser *n.* criminal, debtor, delinquent, evil-doer, infringer, interloper, intruder, invader, malefactor, offender, poacher, sinner, transgressor, wrong-doer.

tribe *n.* blood, branch, caste, clan, class, division, dynasty, family, gens, group, house, ilk, nation, people, phratry, race, seed, sept, stock.

tribulation *n.* adversity, affliction, blow, burden, care, curse, distress, grief, heartache, misery, misfortune, ordeal, pain, reverse, sorrow, suffering, travail, trial, trouble, unhappiness, vexation, woe, worry, wretchedness.
antonyms happiness, rest.

tribunal *n.* bar, bench, court, examination, hearing, inquisition, trial.

tribute *n.* accolade, acknowledgment, annates, applause, charge, commendation, compliment, contribution, cornage, credit, customs, duty, encomium, esteem,

eulogy, excise, first-fruits, gavel, gift, gratitude, homage, honor, horngeld, impost, laudation, offering, panegyric, payment, praise, ransom, recognition, respect, subsidy, tax, testimonial, testimony, toll.
antonyms blame.

trick *n.* antic, art, artifice, cantrip, caper, characteristic, chicane, command, con, craft, deceit, deception, device, dodge, dog-trick, expedient, expertise, feat, feint, foible, fraud, frolic, gag, gambol, gift, gimmick, habit, hang, hoax, idiosyncrasy, imposition, imposture, jape, joke, josh, knack, know-how, legerdemain, leg-pull, maneuver, mannerism, peculiarity, ploy, practical joke, practice, prank, put-on, quirk, quiz, rig, ruse, secret, shot, skill, sleight, spell, stall, stratagem, stunt, subterfuge, swindle, technique, toy, trait, trap, trinket, turn, wile.
adj. artificial, bogus, counterfeit, ersatz, fake, false, feigned, forged, imitation, mock, pretend, sham.
antonym genuine.
v. bamboozle, beguile, cheat, con, cozen, deceive, defraud, delude, diddle, dupe, fool, gull, hoax, hocus-pocus, hoodwink, hornswoggle, illude, lead on, mislead, outwit, pull a fast one on, pull someone's leg, sell, swindle, trap.

trickle *v.* dribble, drip, drop, exude, filter, gutter, leak, ooze, percolate, run, seep.
antonyms gush, stream.
n. drib, dribble, driblet, dribs and drabs, drip, seepage.
antonyms gush, stream.

tricky *adj.* artful, complicated, crafty, cunning, deceitful, deceptive, delicate, devious, difficult, foxy, Gordian, knotty, legerdemain, problematic, risky, scheming, slippery, sly, sticky, subtle, thorny, ticklish, touch-and-go, trickish, tricksome, tricksy, wily.
antonyms easy, honest.

trifling *adj.* empty, footling, foozling, fribbling, fribblish, frivolous, idle, inconsiderable, insignificant, minuscule, negligible, nugatory, paltry, petty, piddling, piffling, puny, shallow, silly, slight, small, tiny, trivial, unimportant, valueless, worthless.
antonym important.
n. desipience, fiddling, fooling, footling, frivolity, piddling, piffling, whifflery.

trigger *v.* activate, actuate, cause, elicit, generate, initiate, produce, prompt, provoke, set off, spark off, start.
n. catch, goad, lever, release, spur, stimulus, switch.

trim *adj.* clean-limbed, compact, dapper, natty, neat, orderly, shipshape, slender, slim, smart, smirk, soigné, spick-and-span, spruce, streamlined, svelte, trig, well-dressed, well-groomed, willowy.
antonym scruffy.
v. adjust, adorn, arrange, array, balance, barb, barber, beautify, bedeck, clip, crop, curtail, cut, decorate, distribute, dock, dress, dub, embellish, embroider, garnish, lop, order, ornament, pare, prepare, prune, settle, shave, shear, tidy, trick.
n. adornment, array, attire, border, clipping, condition, crop, cut, decoration, disposition, dress, edging, embellishment, equipment, fettle, fitness, fittings, form, frill, fringe, garnish, gear, health, humor, nick, order, ornament, ornamentation, piping, pruning, repair, shape, shave, shearing, situation, state, temper, trappings, trimming.

trimmings *n.* accessories, accompaniments, additions,

appurtenances, clippings, cuttings, ends, extras, frills, garnish, ornaments, paraphernalia, parings, remnants, shavings, trappings.

trinket *n.* bagatelle, bauble, bibelot, bijou, doodad, fairing, gewgaw, gimcrack, kickshaws, knick-knack, nothing, ornament, toy, trifle, trinkum-trankum, whig-maleerie, whim-wham.

trio *n.* terzetto, threesome, triad, trilogy, trine, trinity, triple, triplet, triptych, triumvirate, triune.

trip *n.* blunder, boob, errand, error, excursion, expedition, fall, faux pas, foray, indiscretion, jaunt, journey, lapse, misstep, outing, ramble, run, skip, slip, step, stumble, tour, travel, voyage.
v. activate, blunder, boob, caper, confuse, dance, disconcert, engage, err, fall, flip, flit, frisk, gambol, go, hop, lapse, miscalculate, misstep, pull, ramble, release, set off, skip, slip, slip up, spring, stumble, switch on, throw, tilt up, tip up, tour, trap, travel, tumble, unsettle, voyage.

trite *adj.* banal, bromidic, clichéd, common, commonplace, corny, dull, hack, hackneyed, Mickey Mouse, ordinary, overworn, pedestrian, routine, run-of-the-mill, stale, stereotyped, stock, threadbare, tired, uninspired, unoriginal, well-trodden, well-worn, worn, worn out.
antonym original.

triumph *n.* accomplishment, achievement, ascendancy, attainment, conquest, coup, elation, exultation, feat, happiness, hit, joy, jubilation, masterstroke, mastery, pride, rejoicing, sensation, smash, smash-hit, success, tour de force, victory, walk-away, walk-over, win.
antonym disaster.
v. best, celebrate, crow, defeat, dominate, exult, gloat, glory, have the last laugh, humble, humiliate, jubilate, overcome, overwhelm, prevail, prosper, rejoice, revel, subdue, succeed, swagger, vanquish, win.
antonym fail.

triumphant *adj.* boastful, celebratory, cock-a-hoop, conquering, dominant, elated, epinikian, exultant, gloating, glorious, joyful, jubilant, proud, rejoicing, successful, swaggering, triumphal, undefeated, victorious, winning.
antonyms defeated, humble.

trivial *adj.* commonplace, dinky, everyday, frivolous, incidental, inconsequential, inconsiderable, insignificant, little, meaningless, Mickey Mouse, minor, negligible, nugatory, paltry, pettifogging, petty, piddling, piffling, puny, slight, small, snippety, trifling, trite, unimportant, valueless, worthless.
antonym significant.

troops *n.* army, forces, men, military, servicemen, soldiers, soldiery.

trophy *n.* award, booty, cup, laurels, memento, memorial, prize, souvenir, spoils.

tropical *adj.* equatorial, hot, humid, lush, luxuriant, steamy, stifling, sultry, sweltering, torrid.
antonyms arctic, cold, cool, temperate.

trouble *n.* affliction, agitation, ailment, annoyance, anxiety, attention, bother, care, commotion, complaint, concern, danger, defect, difficulty, dilemma, disability, discontent, discord, disease, disorder, disquiet, dissatisfaction, distress, disturbance, effort, exertion, failure, grief, heartache, illness, inconvenience, irritation, labor, malfunction, mess, misfortune, nuisance, pain, pains, pest, pickle, predicament, problem, row, scrape,

solicitude, sorrow, spot, strife, struggle, suffering, thought, torment, travail, trial, tribulation, tumult, uneasiness, unrest, upheaval, upset, vexation, woe, work, worry.
antonyms calm, peace.
v. afflict, agitate, annoy, bother, burden, discomfort, discommode, discompose, disconcert, disquiet, distress, disturb, fash, fret, grieve, harass, incommode, inconvenience, molest, muddy, pain, perplex, perturb, pester, plague, sadden, torment, upset, vex, worry.
antonyms help, reassure.

troublemaker *n.* agent provocateur, agitator, bellwether, bolshevik, firebrand, heller, incendiary, instigator, meddler, mischief-maker, rabble-rouser, ringleader, stirrer, tub-thumper.
antonym peace-maker.

troublesome *adj.* annoying, arduous, bothersome, burdensome, demanding, difficult, disorderly, fashious, harassing, hard, importunate, inconvenient, insubordinate, irksome, irritating, laborious, oppressive, pestilential, plaguesome, plaguey, rebellious, recalcitrant, refractory, rowdy, spiny, taxing, thorny, tiresome, tricky, trying, turbulent, unco-operative, undisciplined, unruly, upsetting, vexatious, violent, wearisome, worrisome, worrying.
antonyms easy, helpful, polite.

trounce *v.* beat, best, censure, clobber, crush, drub, hammer, lick, overwhelm, paste, punish, rebuke, rout, slaughter, thrash, whale, whitewash.

truant *n.* absentee, deserter, dodger, hookey, malingerer, runaway, shirker, skiver, wag.
adj. absent, malingering, missing, runaway, skiving.
v. desert, dodge, malinger, play truant, shirk.

truce *n.* armistice, break, cease-fire, cessation, intermission, interval, let-up, lull, moratorium, peace, respite, rest, stay, suspension, treaty, Truce of God.
antonym hostilities.

truculent *adj.* aggressive, antagonistic, bad-tempered, bellicose, belligerent, combative, contentious, cross, defiant, fierce, hostile, ill-tempered, obstreperous, pugnacious, quarrelsome, savage, scrappy, sullen, violent.
antonyms co-operative, good-natured.

trudge *v.* clump, footslog, hike, labor, lumber, march, mush, plod, slog, stump, traipse, tramp, trek, walk.
n. footslog, haul, hike, march, mush, slog, traipse, tramp, trek, walk.

true *adj.* absolute, accurate, actual, apod(e)ictic, authentic, bona fide, confirmed, conformable, constant, correct, corrected, dedicated, devoted, dutiful, exact, factual, faithful, fast, firm, genuine, honest, honorable, legitimate, loyal, natural, perfect, precise, proper, pure, real, right, rightful, sincere, sooth, spot-on, square, staunch, steady, true-blue, true-born, true-hearted, trustworthy, trusty, truthful, typical, unerring, unswerving, upright, valid, veracious, veridical, veritable.
antonyms faithless, false, inaccurate.
adv. accurately, correctly, exactly, faithfully, honestly, perfectly, precisely, properly, rightly, truly, truthfully, unerringly, veraciously, veritably.
antonyms falsely, inaccurately.

truly *adv.* accurately, authentically, constantly, correctly, devotedly, dutifully, en verité, exactly, exceptionally, extremely, factually, faithfully, firmly, genuinely, greatly, honestly, honorably, in good sooth, in

reality, in truth, indeed, indubitably, legitimately, loyally, precisely, properly, really, rightly, sincerely, soothly, staunchly, steadfastly, steadily, truthfully, undeniably, veraciously, verily, veritably, very.
antonyms faithlessly, falsely, incorrectly, slightly.

truncate *v.* abbreviate, clip, crop, curtail, cut, cut short, lop, maim, pare, prune, shorten, trim.
antonym lengthen.

truss *v.* bind, bundle, fasten, hogtie, pack, pinion, secure, strap, tether, tie.
antonym untie.
n. bale, bandage, beam, binding, brace, bundle, buttress, joist, prop, shore, stanchion, stay, strut, support.

trust *n.* affiance, assurance, belief, care, certainty, certitude, charge, confidence, conviction, credence, credit, custody, duty, expectation, faith, fidelity, guard, guardianship, hope, obligation, protection, reliance, responsibility, safekeeping, trusteeship, uberrima fides.
antonym mistrust.
v. assign, assume, bank on, believe, command, commit, confide, consign, count on, credit, delegate, depend on, entrust, expect, give, hope, imagine, presume, rely on, suppose, surmise, swear by.
antonym mistrust.

trusting *adj.* confiding, credulous, gullible, innocent, naïve, optimistic, simple, trustful, unguarded, unquestioning, unsuspecting, unsuspicious, unwary.
antonyms cautious, distrustful.

trustworthy *adj.* authentic, dependable, ethical, foursquare, honest, honorable, level-headed, mature, principled, reliable, responsible, righteous, sensible, steadfast, true, trusty, truthful, upright.
antonym unreliable.

truth *n.* accuracy, actuality, axiom, candor, certainty, constancy, dedication, devotion, dutifulness, exactness, fact, facts, factuality, factualness, faith, faithfulness, fidelity, frankness, genuineness, historicity, honesty, integrity, law, legitimacy, loyalty, maxim, naturalism, precision, realism, reality, sooth, truism, truthfulness, uprightness, validity, veracity, verdicality, verity.
antonym falsehood.

truthful *adj.* accurate, candid, correct, exact, faithful, forthright, frank, honest, literal, naturalistic, plainspoken, precise, realistic, reliable, sincere, sooth, soothfast, soothful, straight, straightforward, true, trustworthy, veracious, veridicous, verist, veristic, veritable.
antonym untruthful.

try *v.* adjudge, adjudicate, afflict, aim, annoy, appraise, attempt, catechize, endeavor, essay, evaluate, examine, experiment, hear, inconvenience, inspect, investigate, irk, irritate, pain, plague, prove, sample, seek, strain, stress, strive, struggle, taste, tax, test, tire, trouble, undertake, upset, venture, vex, wear out, weary.
n. appraisal, attempt, bash, crack, effort, endeavor, essay, evaluation, experiment, fling, go, inspection, sample, shot, stab, taste, taster, test, trial, whack.

trying *adj.* aggravating, annoying, arduous, bothersome, difficult, distressing, exasperating, fatiguing, hard, irksome, irritating, searching, severe, stressful, taxing, testing, tiresome, tough, troublesome, upsetting, vexing, wearisome.
antonym calming.

tub *n.* back, barrel, basin, bath, bathtub, bucket, butt,

cask, hogshead, keeve, keg, kid, kit, pail, puncheon, stand, tun, vat.

tube *n.* channel, conduit, cylinder, duct, hose, inlet, main, outlet, pipe, shaft, spout, trunk, valve, vas.

tubular *adj.* pipelike, pipy, tubate, tubelike, tubiform, tubulate, tubulous, vasiform.

tuck[1] *v.* cram, crease, fold, gather, insert, push, stuff.
n. crease, fold, gather, pinch, pleat, pucker.

tuck[2] *n.* comestibles, eats, food, grub, nosh, prog, scoff, victuals, vittles.

tuft *n.* beard, bunch, clump, cluster, collection, crest, dag, daglock, dollop, floccule, flocculus, floccus, flock, knot, shock, tassle, topknot, truss, tussock.

tug *v.* drag, draw, haul, heave, jerk, jigger, lug, pluck, pull, tow, wrench, yank.
n. drag, haul, heave, jerk, pluck, pull, tow, traction, wrench, yank.

tuition *n.* education, instruction, lessons, pedagogics, pedagogy, schooling, teaching, training, tutelage, tutoring.

tumble *v.* disorder, drop, fall, flop, jumble, overthrow, pitch, plummet, roll, rumple, stumble, topple, toss, trip up.
n. collapse, drop, fall, flop, plunge, roll, spill, stumble, toss, trip.

tumbledown *adj.* broken-down, crumbling, crumbly, decrepit, dilapidated, disintegrating, ramshackle, rickety, ruined, ruinous, shaky, tottering.
antonym well-kept.

tumult *n.* ado, affray, agitation, altercation, bedlam, brattle, brawl, brouhaha, bustle, clamor, coil, commotion, deray, din, disorder, disturbance, Donnybrook, émeute, excitement, fracas, hubbub, hullabaloo, outbreak, pandemonium, quarrel, racket, riot, rookery, rout, row, ruction, ruffle, stir, stramash, strife, turmoil, unrest, upheaval, uproar.
antonym calm.

tune *n.* agreement, air, attitude, concert, concord, consonance, demeanor, disposition, euphony, frame of mind, harmony, melisma, melody, mood, motif, pitch, song, strain, sympathy, temper, theme, unison.
v. adapt, adjust, attune, harmonize, pitch, regulate, set, synchronize, temper.

tunnel *n.* burrow, channel, chimney, drift, flue, gallery, hole, passage, passageway, sap, shaft, subway, underpass.
v. burrow, dig, excavate, mine, penetrate, sap, undermine.

turbid *adj.* clouded, cloudy, confused, dense, dim, disordered, feculent, foggy, foul, fuzzy, hazy, impure, incoherent, muddled, muddy, murky, opaque, roily, thick, unclear, unsettled.
antonym clear.

turbulent *adj.* agitated, anarchic, blustery, boiling, boisterous, choppy, confused, disordered, disorderly, foaming, furious, insubordinate, lawless, mutinous, obstreperous, raging, rebellious, refractory, riotous, rough, rowdy, seditious, stormy, tempestuous, tumultuous, unbridled, undisciplined, ungovernable, unruly, unsettled, unstable, uproarious, violent, wild.
antonym calm.

turf *n.* clod, divot, glebe, grass, green, sod, sward.

turmoil *n.* agitation, bedlam, brouhaha, bustle, chaos, combustion, commotion, confusion, disorder, disquiet, disturbance, Donnybrook, dust, émeute, ferment, flurry, hubbub, hubbuboo, noise, pandemonium, pother, pudder, rookery, rout, row, ruffle, stir, stour, stramash, strife, tracasserie, trouble, tumult, turbulence, uproar, violence, welter.

antonym calm.

turn v. adapt, alter, apostatize, appeal, apply, approach, become, caracol, change, circle, construct, convert, corner, curdle, defect, deliver, depend, desert, divert, double, execute, fashion, fit, form, frame, go, gyrate, hang, hinge, infatuate, influence, issue, look, make, metamorphose, mold, move, mutate, nauseate, negotiate, pass, perform, persuade, pivot, prejudice, remodel, renege, resort, retract, return, reverse, revolve, roll, rotate, shape, shift, sicken, sour, spin, spoil, swerve, switch, swivel, taint, transfigure, transform, translate, transmute, twirl, twist, upset, veer, wheel, whirl, write.

n. act, action, airing, aptitude, bend, bent, bias, bout, caracol, cast, chance, change, circle, circuit, constitutional, crack, crankle, crisis, culmination, curve, cycle, deed, departure, deviation, direction, distortion, drift, drive, excursion, exigency, fashion, favor, fling, form, format, fright, gesture, go, guise, gyration, heading, innings, jaunt, make-up, manner, mode, mold, occasion, opportunity, outing, performance, performer, period, pivot, promenade, reversal, revolution, ride, rotation, round, saunter, scare, service, shape, shift, shock, shot, spell, spin, start, stint, stroll, style, succession, surprise, swing, tendency, time, trend, trick, try, turning, twist, uey, U-turn, vicissitude, walk, warp, way, whack, whirl.

turncoat n. apostate, backslider, blackleg, defector, deserter, fink, rat, recreant, renegade, renegate, scab, seceder, tergiversator, traitor.

turning n. bend, crossroads, curve, flexure, fork, junction, turn, turn-off.

turning-point n. change, climacteric, crisis, crossroads, crux, cusp, moment of truth, watershed.

turnover n. business, change, flow, income, movement, output, outturn, production, productivity, profits, replacement, volume, yield.

tussle v. battle, brawl, compete, contend, fight, grapple, scramble, scrap, scuffle, struggle, vie, wrestle.

n. battle, bout, brawl, competition, conflict, contention, contest, dust-up, fight, fracas, fray, mêlée, punch-up, race, scramble, scrap, scrimmage, scrum, scuffle, set-to, struggle.

tutor n. coach, director of studies, educator, governor, guardian, guide, guru, instructor, lecturer, master, mentor, preceptor, répétiteur, supervisor, teacher.

v. coach, control, direct, discipline, drill, edify, educate, guide, instruct, lecture, school, supervise, teach, train.

tweak v., n. jerk, nip, pull, punch, snatch, squeeze, tug, twist, twitch.

twig[1] n. branch, offshoot, ramulus, shoot, spray, spring, stick, wattle, whip, withe, withy.

twig[2] v. catch on, comprehend, cotton on, fathom, get, grasp, rumble, savvy, see, tumble to, understand.

twilight n. crepuscle, crepuscule, decline, demi-jour, dimness, dusk, ebb, evening, eventide, gloaming, half-light, sundown, sunset.

adj. crepuscular, darkening, declining, dim, dying, ebbing, evening, final, last, shadowy.

twin n. clone, corollary, counterpart, doppelgänger,

double, duplicate, fellow, gemel, likeness, lookalike, match, mate, ringer.

adj. balancing, corresponding, didymous, double, dual, duplicate, geminate, geminous, identical, matched, matching, paired, parallel, symmetrical, twofold.

v. combine, couple, join, link, match, pair, yoke.

twine n. cord, string, twist, yarn.

v. bend, braid, coil, curl, encircle, entwine, interlace, interweave, knit, loop, meander, plait, snake, spiral, splice, surround, tie, twist, weave, wind, wrap, wreathe, wriggle, zigzag.

twinge n. bite, gripe, pain, pang, pinch, prick, qualm, spasm, stab, stitch, throb, throe, tweak, twist, twitch.

twinkle v. blink, coruscate, flash, flicker, gleam, glint, glisten, glitter, scintillate, shimmer, shine, sparkle, vibrate, wink.

n. amusement, blink, coruscation, flash, flicker, gleam, glimmer, glistening, glitter, glittering, light, quiver, scintillation, shimmer, shine, spark, sparkle, wink.

twirl v. birl, coil, gyrate, gyre, pirouette, pivot, revolve, rotate, spin, swivel, turn, twiddle, twist, wheel, whirl, wind.

n. coil, convulution, gyration, gyre, helix, pirouette, revolution, rotation, spin, spiral, turn, twiddle, twist, wheel, whirl, whorl.

twist v. alter, change, coil, contort, corkscrew, crankle, crinkle, crisp, curl, distort, encircle, entangle, entwine, garble, intertwine, misquote, misrepresent, pervert, pivot, revolve, rick, screw, spin, sprain, squirm, strain, swivel, turn, tweak, twine, warp, weave, wigwag, wind, wrap, wreathe, wrench, wrest, wrick, wriggle, wring, writhe.

n. aberration, arc, bend, bent, braid, break, change, characteristic, coil, confusion, contortion, convolution, crankle, curl, curlicue, curve, defect, deformation, development, distortion, eccentricity, entanglement, fault, flaw, foible, hank, idiosyncrasy, imperfection, intortion, jerk, kink, knot, meander, mess, mix-up, nuance, oddity, peculiarity, plug, proclivity, pull, quid, quirk, revelation, roll, screw, slant, snarl, spin, sprain, squiggle, surprise, swivel, tangle, tortion, trait, turn, twine, undulation, variation, warp, wind, wrench, wrest, zigzag.

twitch v. blink, flutter, jerk, jump, pinch, pluck, pull, snatch, tug, tweak, vellicate, yank.

n. blink, convulsion, flutter, jerk, jump, pluck, pull, spasmytic, subsultus, tremor, tweak, twinge, vellication.

two-faced adj. deceitful, deceiving, devious, dissembling, double-dealing, double-tongued, duplicitous, false, hypocritical, insincere, Janus-faced, lying, mendacious, perfidious, treacherous, untrustworthy.

antonyms candid, frank, honest.

tycoon n. baron, big cheese, big noise, big shot, capitalist, captain of industry, Croesus, Dives, entrepreneur, fat cat, financier, gold-bug, industrialist, magnate, mogul, nabob, plutocrat, potentate, supremo.

type[1] n. archetype, breed, category, class, classification, description, designation, emblem, embodiment, epitome, essence, example, exemplar, form, genre, group, ilk, insignia, kidney, kind, mark, model, order, original, paradigm, pattern, personification, prototype, quintessence, sort, species, specimen, stamp, standard, strain, subdivision, variety.

type[2] *n.* case, characters, face, font, fount, lettering, print, printing.

typhoon *n.* baguio, cordonazo, cyclone, hurricane, squall, storm, tempest, tornado, twister, whirlwind, willy-willy.

typical *adj.* archetypal, average, characteristic, classic, conventional, distinctive, essential, illustrative, indicative, model, normal, orthodox, quintessential, representative, standard, stock, symptomatic, usual, vintage.
antonyms atypical, untypical.

typify *v.* characterize, embody, encapsulate, epitomize, exemplify, illustrate, incarnate, personify, represent, symbolize.

tyrannical *adj.* absolute, arbitrary, authoritarian, autocratic, coercive, despotic, dictatorial, domineering, high-handed, imperious, inexorable, iron-handed, magisterial, Neronian, oppressive, overbearing, overpowering, overweening, peremptory, ruthless, severe, tyrannous, unjust, unreasonable.
antonyms liberal, tolerant.

tyrannize *v.* browbeat, bully, coerce, crush, dictate, domineer, enslave, intimidate, lord it, oppress, subjugate, terrorize.

U

ubiquitous *adj.* all-over, common, commonly-encountered, ever-present, everywhere, frequent, global, omnipresent, pervasive, universal.
antonym rare.

ugly *adj.* angry, bad-tempered, dangerous, dark, disagreeable, disgusting, distasteful, evil, evil-favored, forbidding, frightful, hagged, haggish, hard-favored, hard-featured, hideous, homely, horrid, ill-faced, ill-favored, ill-looking, malevolent, menacing, misshapen, monstrous, nasty, objectionable, offensive, ominous, plain, repugnant, repulsive, revolting, shocking, sinister, spiteful, sullen, surly, terrible, threatening, truculent, unattractive, unlovely, unpleasant, unprepossessing, unsightly, vile.
antonyms beautiful, charming, good, pretty.

ultimate *adj.* basic, conclusive, consummate, decisive, elemental, end, eventual, extreme, final, fundamental, furthest, greatest, highest, last, maximum, paramount, perfect, primary, radical, remotest, superlative, supreme, terminal, topmost, utmost.
n. consummation, culmination, daddy of them all, dinger, epitome, extreme, granddaddy, greatest, height, peak, perfection, summit.

umbrage *n.* anger, chagrin, disgruntlement, displeasure, grudge, high dudgeon, huff, indignation, offence, pique, resentment, sulks.

umpire *n.* adjudicator, arbiter, arbitrator, daysman, judge, linesman, mediator, moderator, ref, referee.
v. adjudicate, arbitrate, call, control, judge, moderate, ref, referee.

umpteen *adj.* a good many, a thousand, considerable, countless, innumerable, millions, numerous, plenty, uncounted.
antonym few.

unabashed *adj.* blatant, bold, brazen, composed, confi-

dent, unawed, unblushing, unconcerned, undaunted, undismayed, unembarrassed.
antonyms abashed, sheepish.

unaccountable *adj.* astonishing, baffling, extraordinary, impenetrable, incomprehensible, inexplicable, inscrutable, mysterious, odd, peculiar, puzzling, singular, strange, uncommon, unexplainable, unfathomable, unheard-of, unintelligible, unusual, unwonted.
antonyms accountable, explicable.

unaffected[1] *adj.* aloof, impervious, naïf, natural, proof, spontaneous, unaltered, unchanged, unimpressed, unmoved, unresponsive, untouched.
antonyms affected, unnatural.

unaffected[2] *adj.* artless, blasé, genuine, honest, indifferent, ingenuous, naive, plain, simple, sincere, straightforward, unassuming, unconcerned, unpretentious, unsophisticated, unspoilt, unstudied.
antonyms affected, impressed, moved.

unalterable *adj.* final, fixed, immutable, inflexible, invariable, permanent, rigid, steadfast, unchangeable, unchanging, unyielding.
antonyms alterable, flexible.

unanimous *adj.* agreed, common, concerted, concordant, harmonious, in accord, in agreement, joint, united.
antonyms disunited, split.

unapproachable *adj.* aloof, distant, forbidding, formidable, frigid, godforsaken, inaccessible, remote, reserved, stand-offish, unbending, unfriendly, un-get-at-able, unreachable, unsociable, withdrawn.
antonym approachable.

unassailable *adj.* absolute, conclusive, impregnable, incontestable, incontrovertible, indisputable, invincible, inviolable, invulnerable, irrefutable, positive, proven, sacrosanct, secure, sound, undeniable, well-armed, well-fortified.
antonym assailable.

unassuming *adj.* diffident, humble, meek, modest, natural, quiet, restrained, retiring, self-effacing, simple, unassertive, unobtrusive, unostentatious, unpresuming, unpretentious.
antonyms assuming, presumptuous, pretentious.

unattached *adj.* autonomous, available, fancy-free, footloose, free, independent, non-aligned, single, unaffiliated, uncommitted, unengaged, unmarried, unspoken for.
antonyms attached, committed, engaged.

unavailing *adj.* abortive, barren, bootless, fruitless, futile, idle, ineffective, ineffectual, inefficacious, pointless, unproductive, unprofitable, unsuccessful, useless, vain.
antonyms productive, successful.

unavoidable *adj.* certain, compulsory, fated, ineluctable, inescapable, inevitable, inexorable, mandatory, necessary, obligatory.
antonym avoidable.

unawares *adv.* aback, abruptly, accidentally, by surprise, imperceptibly, inadvertently, insidiously, mistakenly, off guard, on the hop, suddenly, unconsciously, unexpectedly, unintentionally, unknowingly, unprepared, unthinkingly, unwittingly.

unbalanced *adj.* asymmetrical, biased, crazy, demented, deranged, disturbed, dysharmonic, eccentric, erratic, inequitable, insane, irrational, irregular, lopsided, lunatic, mad, off-balance, off-center, one-sided, partial, partisan, prejudiced, shaky, touched, unequal, uneven, unfair, unhinged, unjust, unsound, unstable, unsteady, wobbly.

antonym balanced.

unbearable *adj.* insufferable, insupportable, intolerable, outrageous, unacceptable, unendurable, unspeakable.

antonyms acceptable, bearable.

unbecoming *adj.* discreditable, dishonorable, ill-suited, improper, inappropriate, incongruous, indecorous, indelicate, offensive, tasteless, unattractive, unbefitting, unfit, unflattering, unmaidenly, unmeet, unseemly, unsightly, unsuitable, unsuited.

antonyms becoming, seemly.

unbelievable *adj.* astonishing, far-fetched, implausible, impossible, improbable, inconceivable, incredible, outlandish, preposterous, questionable, staggering, unconvincing, unimaginable, unlikely, unthinkable.

antonyms believable, credible.

unbending *adj.* aloof, distant, firm, forbidding, formal, formidable, hard-line, inflexible, intransigent, reserved, resolute, Rhadamanthine, rigid, severe, stiff, strict, stubborn, tough, uncompromising, unyielding.

antonyms approachable, friendly, relaxed.

unbiased *adj.* disinterested, dispassionate, equitable, even-handed, fair, fair-minded, impartial, independent, just, neutral, objective, open-minded, uncolored, uninfluenced, unprejudiced.

antonym biased.

unbidden *adj.* free, spontaneous, unasked, unforced, uninvited, unprompted, unsolicited, unwanted, unwelcome, voluntary, willing.

antonyms invited, solicited.

unblemished *adj.* clear, flawless, immaculate, irreproachable, perfect, pure, spotless, unflawed, unimpeachable, unspotted, unstained, unsullied, untarnished.

antonyms blemished, flawed, imperfect.

unbosom *v.* admit, bare, confess, confide, disburden, disclose, divulge, lay bare, let out, pour out, reveal, tell, unburden, uncover.

antonyms conceal, suppress.

unbridled *adj.* excessive, immoderate, intemperate, licentious, profligate, rampant, riotous, unchecked, unconstrained, uncontrolled, uncurbed, ungovernable, ungoverned, unrestrained, unruly, violent, wanton.

unbroken *adj.* ceaseless, complete, constant, continuous, endless, entire, incessant, intact, integral, perpetual, progressive, serried, solid, successive, total, unbowed, unceasing, undivided, unimpaired, uninterrupted, unremitting, unsubdued, untamed, whole.

antonyms cowed, fitful, intermittent.

unburden *v.* confess, confide, disburden, discharge, disclose, discumber, disencumber, empty, lay bare, lighten, offload, pour out, relieve, reveal, tell all, unbosom, unload.

antonyms conceal, hide, suppress.

uncalled-for *adj.* gratuitous, inappropriate, needless, undeserved, unheeded, unjust, unjustified, unmerited, unnecessary, unprovoked, unwanted, unwarranted, unwelcome.

antonym timely.

uncanny *adj.* astonishing, astounding, bizarre, creepy, eerie, eldritch, exceptional, extraordinary, fantastic, incredible, inspired, miraculous, mysterious, preternatural, prodigious, queer, remarkable, scary, singular, spooky, strange, supernatural, unaccountable, unco,

unearthly, unerring, unheard-of, unnatural, unusual, weird.

uncertain *adj.* ambiguous, ambivalent, chancy, changeable, conjectural, dicky, doubtful, dubious, erratic, fitful, hazardous, hazy, hesitant, iffy, in the lap of the gods, incalculable, inconstant, indefinite, indeterminate, indistinct, insecure, irregular, irresolute, on the knees of the gods, precarious, problematic, questionable, risky, shaky, slippy, speculative, unclear, unconfirmed, undecided, undetermined, unfixed, unforeseeable, unpredictable, unreliable, unresolved, unsettled, unsure, vacillating, vague, variable, wavering.

antonym certain.

uncertainty *n.* ambiguity, bewilderment, confusion, diffidence, dilemma, doubt, dubiety, hesitancy, hesitation, incalculability, inconclusiveness, indecision, insecurity, irresolution, misgiving, peradventure, perplexity, puzzlement, qualm, quandary, risk, skepticism, unpredictability, vagueness.

antonym certainty.

uncharitable *adj.* callous, captious, cruel, hard-hearted, hypercritical, inhumane, insensitive, mean, merciless, pitiless, stingy, unchristian, unfeeling, unforgiving, unfriendly, ungenerous, unkind, unsympathetic.

antonym charitable.

uncharted *adj.* foreign, mysterious, new, novel, strange, undiscovered, unexplored, unfamiliar, unknown, unplumbed, virgin.

antonyms familiar, well-known.

uncivil *adj.* abrupt, bad-mannered, bearish, boorish, brusque, churlish, curt, discourteous, disrespectful, gruff, ill-bred, ill-mannered, impolite, rude, surly, uncouth, ungracious, unmannerly.

antonym civil.

uncivilized *adj.* antisocial, barbarian, barbaric, barbarous, boorish, brutish, churlish, coarse, gross, heathenish, ill-bred, illiterate, philistine, primitive, savage, tramontane, uncouth, uncultivated, uncultured, uneducated, unpolished, unsophisticated, untamed, vulgar, wild.

antonym civilized.

unclean *adj.* contaminated, corrupt, defiled, dirty, evil, filthy, foul, impure, insalubrious, nasty, polluted, soiled, spotted, stained, sullied, tainted, unhygienic, unwholesome.

antonym clean.

uncomfortable *adj.* awkward, bleak, confused, conscience-stricken, cramped, disagreeable, discomfited, discomfortable, discomposed, disquieted, distressed, disturbed, embarrassed, hard, ill-fitting, incommodious, irritating, painful, poky, self-conscious, sheepish, troubled, troublesome, uneasy.

antonyms comfortable, easy.

uncommon *adj.* abnormal, atypical, bizarre, curious, distinctive, exceptional, extraordinary, incomparable, infrequent, inimitable, notable, noteworthy, novel, odd, outstanding, peculiar, queer, rare, recherché, remarkable, scarce, singular, special, strange, superior, unfamiliar, unparalleled, unprecedented, unusual, unwonted.

antonym common.

uncompromising *adj.* decided, die-hard, firm, hardcore, hard-line, hardshell, inexorable, inflexible, intransigent, obdurate, obstinate, rigid, steadfast, strict,

stubborn, tough, unaccommodating, unbending, unyielding.
antonyms flexible, open-minded.

unconcerned *adj.* aloof, apathetic, blithe, callous, carefree, careless, complacent, composed, cool, detached, dispassionate, distant, easy, incurious, indifferent, insouciant, joco, nonchalant, oblivious, pococurante, relaxed, serene, uncaring, uninterested, uninvolved, unmoved, unperturbed, unruffled, unsympathetic, untroubled, unworried.
antonym concerned.

unconditional *adj.* absolute, categorical, complete, downright, entire, full, implicit, out-and-out, outright, plenary, positive, thoroughgoing, total, unequivocal, unlimited, unqualified, unreserved, unrestricted, utter, whole-hearted.
antonym conditional.

uncongenial *adj.* antagonistic, antipathetic, disagreeable, discordant, displeasing, distasteful, incompatible, unappealing, unattractive, uninviting, unpleasant, unsavory, unsuited, unsympathetic.
antonym congenial.

unconscious *adj.* accidental, automatic, blind to, comatose, concussed, deaf to, heedless, ignorant, inadvertent, innate, insensible, instinctive, involuntary, knocked out, latent, oblivious, out, out cold, out for the count, reflex, repressed, senseless, stunned, subconscious, subliminal, suppressed, unaware, unintended, unintentional, unknowing, unmindful, unsuspecting, unwitting.
antonym conscious.

unconventional *adj.* abnormal, alternative, atypical, bizarre, bohemian, different, eccentric, freakish, idiosyncratic, individual, individualistic, informal, irregular, nonconforming, odd, offbeat, original, spacy, unconformable, unorthodox, unusual, way-out, wayward.
antonym conventional.

uncouth *adj.* awkward, barbarian, barbaric, boorish, clownish, clumsy, coarse, crude, gauche, gawky, graceless, gross, ill-mannered, loutish, lubberly, oafish, rough, rude, rustic, uncivilized, uncultivated, ungainly, unrefined, unseemly, vulgar.
antonyms polished, polite, refined, urbane.

uncover *v.* bare, detect, disclose, discover, dismask, disrobe, divulge, exhume, expose, leak, lift the lid off, open, reveal, show, strip, unearth, unmask, unveil, unwrap.
antonyms conceal, cover, suppress.

unctuous *adj.* fawning, glib, greasy, gushing, ingratiating, insincere, obsequious, oily, pietistic, plausible, religiose, sanctimonious, slick, smarmy, smooth, suave, sycophantic.

undaunted *adj.* bold, brave, courageous, dauntless, fearless, gallant, indomitable, intrepid, resolute, steadfast, unbowed, undashed, undeterred, undiscouraged, undismayed, unfaltering, unflinching, unperturbed, unshrinking.
antonyms cowed, timorous.

undefined *adj.* formless, hazy, ill-defined, imprecise, indefinite, indeterminate, indistinct, inexact, nebulous, shadowy, tenuous, unclear, unexplained, unspecified, vague, woolly.
antonyms definite, precise.

undependable *adj.* capricious, changeable, erratic, fair-

weather, fickle, inconsistent, inconstant, irresponsible, mercurial, treacherous, uncertain, unpredictable, unreliable, unstable, untrustworthy, variable.
antonyms dependable, reliable.

under *prep.* belonging to, below, beneath, governed by, included in, inferior to, junior to, lead by, less than, lower than, secondary to, subject to, subordinate to, subservient to, underneath.
adv. below, beneath, down, downward, less, lower.

undercover *adj.* clandestine, concealed, confidential, covert, furtive, hidden, hush-hush, intelligence, private, secret, spy, stealthy, surreptitious, underground.
antonyms open, unconcealed.

undercurrent *n.* atmosphere, aura, cross-current, drift, eddy, feeling, flavor, hint, movement, murmur, overtone, rip, riptide, sense, suggestion, tendency, tenor, tide, tinge, trend, underflow, undertone, undertow, vibes, vibrations.

undergo *v.* bear, brook, endure, experience, run the gauntlet, stand, submit to, suffer, sustain, weather, withstand.

underhand *adj.* clandestine, crafty, crooked, deceitful, deceptive, devious, dishonest, dishonorable, fraudulent, furtive, immoral, improper, shady, shifty, sly, sneaky, stealthy, surreptitious, treacherous, underhanded, unethical, unscrupulous.
antonym above board.

undermine *v.* debilitate, disable, erode, excavate, impair, mar, mine, sabotage, sap, subvert, threaten, tunnel, undercut, vitiate, weaken, wear away.
antonyms fortify, strengthen.

underprivileged *adj.* deprived, destitute, disadvantaged, impecunious, impoverished, needy, poor, poverty-stricken.
antonyms affluent, fortunate, privileged.

understand *v.* accept, appreciate, apprehend, assume, believe, commiserate, comprehend, conceive, conclude, cotton on, discern, fathom, follow, gather, get, get the message, get the picture, grasp, hear, know, learn, penetrate, perceive, presume, realize, recognize, savvy, see, see daylight, suppose, sympathize, think, tolerate, tumble, twig.
antonym misunderstand.

understanding *n.* accord, agreement, appreciation, awareness, belief, comprehension, conclusion, discernment, estimation, grasp, idea, impression, insight, intellect, intellection, intelligence, interpretation, judgment, knowledge, notion, opinion, pact, penetration, perception, reading, sense, view, viewpoint, wisdom.
adj. accepting, compassionate, considerate, discerning, forbearing, forgiving, kind, kindly, loving, patient, perceptive, responsive, sensitive, sympathetic, tender, tolerant.
antonyms impatient, insensitive, intolerant, unsympathetic.

understudy *n.* alternate, deputy, double, fill-in, replacement, reserve, stand-in, substitute.

undertake *v.* accept, agree, assume, attempt, bargain, begin, commence, contract, covenant, embark on, endeavor, engage, guarantee, pledge, promise, shoulder, stipulate, tackle, try.

undertaking *n.* adventure, affair, assurance, attempt, business, commitment, effort, emprise, endeavor, enterprise, game, operation, pledge, project, promise, task, venture, vow, word.

undervalue v. depreciate, discount, dismiss, disparage, disprize, minimize, misjudge, misprice, misprize, underestimate, underrate.
antonyms exaggerate, overrate.

underwrite v. approve, authorize, back, consent, countenance, countersign, endorse, finance, fund, guarantee, initial, insure, okay, sanction, sign, sponsor, subscribe, subsidize, validate.

undesirable adj. disagreeable, disliked, disreputable, distasteful, dreaded, objectionable, obnoxious, offensive, repugnant, unacceptable, unattractive, unpleasant, unpopular, unsavory, unsuitable, unwanted, unwelcome, unwished-for.
antonym desirable.

undignified adj. foolish, improper, inappropriate, indecorous, inelegant, infra dig, petty, unbecoming, ungentlemanly, unladylike, unrefined, unseemly, unsuitable.
antonym dignified.

undisciplined adj. disobedient, disorganized, obstreperous, uncontrolled, unpredictable, unreliable, unrestrained, unruly, unschooled, unsteady, unsystematic, untrained, wayward, wild, wilful.
antonym disciplined.

undivided adj. combined, complete, concentrated, concerted, entire, exclusive, full, individuate, solid, thorough, tight-knit, unanimous, unbroken, united, whole, whole-hearted.

undoing n. besetting sin, blight, collapse, curse, defeat, destruction, disgrace, downfall, hamartia, humiliation, misfortune, overthrow, overturn, reversal, ruin, ruination, shame, tragic fault, trouble, weakness.

undoubtedly adv. assuredly, certainly, definitely, doubtless, indubitably, of course, surely, undeniably, unmistakably, unquestionably.

undreamed-of adj. astonishing, inconceivable, incredible, miraculous, undreamt, unexpected, unforeseen, unheard-of, unhoped-for, unimagined, unsuspected.

undulating adj. billowing, flexuose, flexuous, rippling, rolling, sinuous, undate, undulant, wavy.
antonym flat.

unduly adv. disproportionately, excessively, extravagantly, immoderately, inordinately, over, overly, overmuch, too, unjustifiably, unnecessarily, unreasonably.
antonym reasonably.

undying adj. abiding, constant, continuing, deathless, eternal, everlasting, immortal, imperishable, indestructible, inextinguishable, infinite, lasting, perennial, permanent, perpetual, sempiternal, undiminished, unending, unfading.
antonyms impermanent, inconstant.

unearthly adj. abnormal, eerie, eldritch, ethereal, extraordinary, ghostly, haunted, heavenly, nightmarish, other-worldly, phantom, preternatural, spectral, spine-chilling, strange, sublime, supernatural, uncanny, ungodly, unreasonable, weird.

uneasy adj. agitated, anxious, apprehensive, awkward, constrained, discomposed, disquieting, disturbed, disturbing, edgy, impatient, insecure, jittery, nervous, niggling, on edge, perturbed, precarious, restive, restless, shaky, strained, tense, troubled, troubling, uncomfortable, unquiet, unsettled, unstable, upset, upsetting, worried, worrying.
antonyms calm, composed.

uneconomic adj. loss-making, non-profit-making, uncommercial, unprofitable.
antonyms economic, profitable.

unemotional adj. apathetic, cold, cool, dispassionate, impassive, indifferent, laid-back, low-key, objective, passionless, phlegmatic, reserved, undemonstrative, unexcitable, unfeeling, unimpassioned, unresponsive.
antonyms emotional, excitable.

unemployed adj. idle, jobless, out of employ, out of work, redundant, resting, unoccupied, workless.
antonym employed.

unenviable adj. disagreeable, painful, thankless, uncomfortable, uncongenial, undesirable, unpalatable, unpleasant, unsavory.
antonyms desirable, enviable.

unequal adj. asymmetrical, different, differing, disparate, disproportionate, dissimilar, ill-equipped, ill-matched, inadequate, incapable, incompetent, insufficient, irregular, unbalanced, uneven, unlike, unmatched, variable, varying.
antonym equal.

unequivocal adj. absolute, certain, clear, clear-cut, crystal-clear, decisive, definite, direct, distinct, evident, explicit, express, incontrovertible, indubitable, manifest, plain, positive, straight, unambiguous, uncontestable, unmistakable.
antonyms ambiguous, vague.

unerring adj. accurate, certain, dead, exact, faultless, impeccable, infallible, perfect, sure, uncanny, unfailing.
antonym fallible.

unethical adj. dirty, discreditable, dishonest, dishonorable, disreputable, illegal, illicit, immoral, improper, shady, underhand, unfair, unprincipled, unprofessional, unscrupulous, wrong.
antonym ethical.

uneven adj. accidented, asymmetrical, broken, bumpy, changeable, desultory, disparate, erratic, fitful, fluctuating, ill-matched, inconsistent, intermittent, irregular, jerky, lopsided, odd, one-sided, patchy, rough, spasmodic, unbalanced, unequal, unfair, unsteady, variable.
antonym even.

unexceptional adj. average, commonplace, conventional, indifferent, insignificant, mediocre, normal, ordinary, pedestrian, run-of-the-mill, typical, undistinguished, unimpressive, unmemorable, unremarkable, usual.
antonyms exceptional, impressive.

unexpected adj. abrupt, accidental, amazing, astonishing, chance, fortuitous, startling, sudden, surprising, unaccustomed, unanticipated, unforeseen, unlooked-for, unpredictable, unusual, unwonted.
antonyms expected, normal, predictable.

unfair adj. arbitrary, biased, bigoted, crooked, discriminatory, dishonest, dishonorable, inequitable, one-sided, partial, partisan, prejudiced, uncalled-for, undeserved, unethical, unjust, unmerited, unprincipled, unscrupulous, unsporting, unwarranted, wrongful.
antonym fair.

unfaithful adj. adulterous, deceitful, dishonest, disloyal, faithless, false, false-hearted, fickle, godless, inconstant, perfidious, recreant, traitorous, treacherous, treasonable, two-timing, unbelieving, unchaste, unreliable, untrue, untrustworthy.

antonyms faithful, loyal.

unfamiliar *adj*. alien, curious, different, foreign, new, novel, out-of-the-way, strange, unaccustomed, unacquainted, uncharted, uncommon, unconversant, unexplored, unknown, unpracticed, unskilled, unusual, unversed.

antonyms customary, familiar.

unfasten *v*. detach, disconnect, loosen, open, separate, uncouple, undo, unlace, unlock, unloose, unloosen, untie.

antonym fasten.

unfavorable *adj*. adverse, bad, contrary, critical, disadvantageous, discouraging, hostile, ill-suited, inauspicious, infelicitous, inimical, inopportune, low, negative, ominous, poor, threatening, uncomplimentary, unfortunate, unfriendly, unlucky, unpromising, unpropitious, unseasonable, unsuited, untimely, untoward.

antonym favorable.

unfeeling *adj*. apathetic, callous, cold, cruel, hard, hardened, hard-hearted, harsh, heartless, inhuman, insensitive, pitiless, soulless, stony, uncaring, unsympathetic.

antonym concerned.

unfeigned *adj*. frank, genuine, heartfelt, natural, pure, real, sincere, spontaneous, unaffected, unforced, whole-hearted.

antonyms feigned, insincere, pretended.

unfit *adj*. debilitated, decrepit, feeble, flabby, flaccid, hypotonic, ill-adapted, ill-equipped, inadequate, inappropriate, incapable, incompetent, ineffective, ineligible, unequal, unhealthy, unprepared, unqualified, unsuitable, unsuited, untrained, useless.

antonyms competent, fit, suitable.

unfold *v*. clarify, describe, develop, disclose, disentangle, divulge, elaborate, evolve, expand, explain, flatten, grow, illustrate, mature, open, present, reveal, show, spread, straighten, stretch out, uncoil, uncover, undo, unfurl, unravel, unroll, unwrap.

antonyms fold, suppress, withhold, wrap.

unforeseen *adj*. abrupt, accidental, fortuitous, startling, sudden, surprise, surprising, unanticipated, unavoidable, unexpected, unheralded, unlooked-for, unpredicted.

antonyms expected, predictable.

unfortunate *adj*. adverse, calamitous, cursed, deplorable, disadventurous, disastrous, doomed, hapless, hopeless, ill-advised, ill-fated, ill-starred, ill-timed, inappropriate, infelicitous, inopportune, lamentable, luckless, poor, regrettable, ruinous, star-crossed, tactless, unbecoming, unfavorable, unhappy, unlucky, unprosperous, unsuccessful, unsuitable, untimely, untoward, wretched.

antonym fortunate.

unfriendly *adj*. alien, aloof, antagonistic, chilly, cold, critical, disagreeable, distant, hostile, ill-disposed, inauspicious, inhospitable, inimical, quarrelsome, sour, stand-offish, surly, unapproachable, unbending, uncongenial, unfavorable, unneighborly, unsociable, unwelcoming.

antonyms agreeable, amiable, friendly.

ungainly *adj*. awkward, clumsy, gangling, gauche, gawky, inelegant, loutish, lubberly, lumbering, slouching, unco-ordinated, uncouth, unwieldy.

antonyms elegant, graceful.

ungodly *adj*. blasphemous, corrupt, depraved, dreadful, godless, horrendous, immoral, impious, intolerable,

irreligious, outrageous, profane, sinful, unearthly, unreasonable, unseasonable, unseemly, unsocial, vile, wicked.

ungrateful *adj*. heedless, ill-mannered, ingrate, selfish, thankless, unappreciative, ungracious, unmindful.

antonym grateful.

unguarded[1] *adj*. careless, foolhardy, foolish, heedless, ill-considered, impolitic, imprudent, incautious, indiscreet, rash, thoughtless, uncircumspect, undiplomatic, unheeding, unthinking, unwary.

antonyms cautious, guarded.

unguarded[2] *adj*. defenseless, exposed, pregnable, undefended, unpatrolled, unprotected, vulnerable.

antonyms guarded, protected.

unhappy *adj*. awkward, blue, clumsy, contentless, crestfallen, cursed, dejected, depressed, despondent, disconsolate, dismal, dispirited, down, downcast, gauche, gloomy, hapless, ill-advised, ill-chosen, ill-fated, ill-omened, ill-timed, inappropriate, inapt, inept, infelicitous, injudicious, long-faced, luckless, lugubrious, malapropos, melancholy, miserable, mournful, sad, sorrowful, sorry, tactless, uneasy, unfortunate, unlucky, unsuitable, wretched.

antonyms fortunate, happy.

unhealthy *adj*. ailing, bad, baneful, corrupt, corrupting, degrading, deleterious, delicate, demoralizing, detrimental, epinosic, feeble, frail, harmful, infirm, insalubrious, insalutary, insanitary, invalid, morbid, noisome, noxious, polluted, poorly, sick, sickly, undesirable, unhygienic, unsound, unwell, unwholesome, weak.

antonyms healthy, hygienic, robust, salubrious.

unheard-of *adj*. disgraceful, extreme, inconceivable, new, novel, obscure, offensive, out of the question, outrageous, preposterous, shocking, singular, unacceptable, unbelievable, undiscovered, undreamed-of, unexampled, unfamiliar, unimaginable, unique, unknown, unprecedented, unregarded, unremarked, unsung, unthinkable, unthought-of, unusual.

antonyms famous, normal, usual.

unhurried *adj*. calm, deliberate, easy, easy-going, laid-back, leisurely, relaxed, sedate, slow.

antonyms hasty, hurried.

uniform *n*. costume, dress, garb, gear, habit, insignia, livery, outfit, regalia, regimentals, rig, robes, suit.

adj. alike, consistent, constant, equable, equal, even, homochromous, homogeneous, homomorphic, homomorphous, identical, like, monochrome, montonous, of a piece, regular, same, selfsame, similar, smooth, unbroken, unchanging, undeviating, unvarying.

antonyms changing, colorful, varied.

unify *v*. amalgamate, bind, combine, confederate, consolidate, federate, fuse, join, marry, merge, unite, weld.

antonyms separate, split.

unimaginable *adj*. fantastic, impossible, inconceivable, incredible, indescribable, ineffable, mind-boggling, unbelievable, undreamed-of, unheard-of, unhoped-for, unknowable, unthinkable.

unimportant *adj*. immaterial, inconsequential, insignificant, irrelevant, low-ranking, Mickey Mouse, minor, minuscule, negligible, nugatory, off the map, paltry, paravail, petty, slight, small-time, trifling, trivial, worthless.

antonym important.

unimpressive *adj.* average, commonplace, dull, indifferent, mediocre, undistinguished, unexceptional, uninteresting, unremarkable, unspectacular.
antonyms impressive, memorable, notable.

uninhibited *adj.* abandoned, candid, emancipated, frank, free, informal, instinctive, liberated, natural, open, relaxed, spontaneous, unbridled, unchecked, unconstrained, uncontrolled, uncurbed, unrepressed, unreserved, unrestrained, unrestricted, unselfconscious.
antonyms constrained, inhibited, repressed.

uninspired *adj.* boring, commonplace, dull, humdrum, indifferent, ordinary, pedestrian, prosaic, stale, stock, trite, undistinguished, unexciting, unimaginative, uninspiring, uninteresting, unoriginal.
antonyms inspired, original.

unintelligent *adj.* brainless, dense, dull, dumb, empty-headed, fatuous, foolish, gormless, half-witted, obtuse, silly, slow, stupid, thick, unreasoning, unthinking.
antonym intelligent.

unintelligible *adj.* double Dutch, garbled, illegible, inapprehensible, inarticulate, incoherent, incomprehensible, indecipherable, indistinct, jumbled, meaningless, muddled, unfathomable.
antonym intelligible.

unintentional *adj.* accidental, fortuitous, inadvertent, involuntary, unconscious, undeliberate, unintended, unpremeditated, unthinking, unwitting.
antonyms deliberate, intentional.

uninviting *adj.* disagreeable, distasteful, offensive, off-putting, repellent, repulsive, unappealing, unappetizing, unattractive, undesirable, unpleasant, unsavory, unwelcoming.
antonyms inviting, welcome.

union *n.* accord, agreement, alliance, amalgam, amalgamation, Anschluss, association, blend, Bund, coalition, coition, coitus, combination, compact, concord, concrescence, concurrence, confederacy, confederation, conjugation, conjunction, copulation, couplement, coupling, enosis, federation, fusion, harmony, intercourse, junction, juncture, league, marriage, matrimony, mixture, symphysis, synthesis, unanimity, unison, uniting, unity, wedlock.
antonyms alienation, disunity, estrangement, separation.

unique *adj.* incomparable, inimitable, lone, matchless, nonpareil, one-off, only, peerless, single, sole, solitary, sui generis, unequaled, unexampled, unmatched, unparalleled, unprecedented, unrivaled.
antonym commonplace.

unison *n.* accord, accordance, aggreement, concert, concord, co-operation, harmony, homophony, monophony, unanimity, unity.
antonyms disharmony, polyphony.

unit *n.* ace, assembly, component, constituent, detachment, element, entity, Gestalt, group, item, measure, measurement, member, module, monad, monas, one, part, piece, portion, quantity, section, segment, system, whole.

unite *v.* accrete, ally, amalgamate, associate, band, blend, coadunate, coalesce, combine, confederate, conglutinate, conjoin, conjugate, consolidate, cooperate, couple, fay, fuse, incorporate, join, join forces, league, link, marry, merge, pool, splice, unify, wed.
antonyms separate, sever.

universal *adj.* across-the-board, all-embracing, all-inclusive, all-round, catholic, common, ecumenic, ecumenical, entire, general, global, omnipresent, total, ubiquitous, unlimited, whole, widespread, worldwide.

unjustifiable *adj.* excessive, immoderate, indefensible, inexcusable, outrageous, steep, unacceptable, unforgivable, unjust, unpardonable, unreasonable, unwarrantable, wrong.
antonym justifiable.

unkempt *adj.* bedraggled, blowsy, disarranged, disheveled, disordered, frowsy, mal soigné, messy, mop-headed, ratty, rumpled, scruffy, shabby, shaggy, slatternly, sloppy, slovenly, sluttish, tousled, uncombed, ungroomed, untidy.
antonyms neat, tidy.

unkind *adj.* callous, cruel, disobliging, hard-hearted, harsh, inconsiderate, inhuman, inhumane, insensitive, malevolent, malicious, mean, nasty, spiteful, thoughtless, unamiable, uncaring, uncharitable, unchristian, unfeeling, unfriendly, unsympathetic.
antonyms considerate, kind.

unknown *adj.* alien, anonymous, concealed, dark, foreign, hidden, humble, incognito, mysterious, nameless, new, obscure, secret, strange, uncharted, undisclosed, undiscovered, undistinguished, unexplored, unfamiliar, unheard-of, unidentified, unnamed, unrecognized, unsung, untold.
antonyms familiar, known.

unlawful *adj.* actionable, banned, criminal, forbidden, illegal, illegitimate, illicit, outlawed, prohibited, unauthorized, unconstitutional, unlicensed, unsanctioned.
antonym lawful.

unlike *adj.* contrasted, different, difform, disparate, dissimilar, distinct, divergent, diverse, ill-matched, incompatible, opposed, opposite, unequal, unrelated.
antonyms related, similar.

unlimited *adj.* absolute, all-encompassing, boundless, complete, countless, endless, extensive, full, great, illimitable, immeasurable, immense, incalculable, infinite, limitless, total, unbounded, uncircumscribed, unconditional, unconstrained, unfettered, unhampered, unqualified, unrestricted, vast.
antonyms circumscribed, limited.

unlooked-for *adj.* chance, fortuitous, fortunate, lucky, surprise, surprising, unanticipated, undreamed-of, unexpected, unforeseen, unhoped-for, unpredicted, unthought-of.
antonyms expected, predictable.

unlucky *adj.* cursed, disastrous, doomed, hapless, ill-fated, ill-omened, ill-starred, inauspicious, infaust, jinxed, left-handed, luckless, mischanceful, miserable, ominous, unfavorable, unfortunate, unhappy, unsuccessful, untimely, wretched.
antonym lucky.

unmanageable *adj.* awkward, bulky, cumbersome, difficult, disorderly, fractious, inconvenient, intractable, obstreperous, recalcitrant, refractory, stroppy, uncontrollable, unco-operative, unhandy, unruly, unwieldy, wild.
antonyms docile, manageable.

unmannerly *adj.* badly-behaved, bad-mannered, boorish, discourteous, disrespectful, graceless, ill-bred, ill-mannered, impolite, low-bred, rude, uncivil, uncouth, ungracious.
antonym polite.

unmatched *adj.* beyond compare, consummate, incomparable, matchless, nonpareil, paramount, peerless, supreme, unequaled, unexampled, unparalleled, unrivaled, unsurpassed.

unmerciful *adj.* brutal, callous, cruel, hard, heartless, implacable, merciless, pitiless, relentless, remorseless, ruthless, sadistic, uncaring, unfeeling, unrelenting, unsparing.
antonym merciful.

unmistakable *adj.* certain, clear, conspicuous, crystal-clear, decided, distinct, evident, explicit, glaring, indisputable, manifest, obvious, palpable, patent, plain, positive, pronounced, sure, unambiguous, undeniable, undisputed, unequivocal, unquestionable.
antonyms ambiguous, unclear.

unmitigated *adj.* absolute, arrant, complete, consummate, downright, grim, harsh, intense, oppressive, out-and-out, outright, perfect, persistent, pure, rank, relentless, sheer, thorough, thoroughgoing, unabated, unalleviated, unbroken, undiminished, unmodified, unqualified, unredeemed, unrelenting, unrelieved, unremitting, utter.

unnatural *adj.* aberrant, abnormal, absonant, affected, anomalous, artificial, assumed, bizarre, brutal, callous, cataphysical, cold-blooded, contrived, cruel, disnatured, evil, extraordinary, factitious, false, feigned, fiendish, forced, freakish, heartless, inhuman, insincere, irregular, labored, mannered, monstrous, odd, outlandish, perverse, perverted, phony, queer, ruthless, sadistic, savage, self-conscious, stagy, stiff, stilted, strained, strange, studied, supernatural, theatrical, unaccountable, uncanny, unfeeling, unspontaneous, unusual, wicked.
antonyms acceptable, natural, normal.

unnecessary *adj.* dispensable, expendable, inessential, needless, non-essential, otiose, pleonastic, redundant, supererogatory, superfluous, supernumerary, tautological, uncalled-for, unjustified, unneeded, useless.
antonyms indispensable, necessary.

unobtrusive *adj.* humble, inconspicuous, low-key, meek, modest, quiet, restrained, retiring, self-effacing, subdued, unassertive, unassuming, unemphatic, unnoticeable, unostentatious, unpretentious.
antonyms obtrusive, ostentatious.

unoccupied *adj.* disengaged, empty, free, idle, inactive, jobless, unemployed, uninhabited, untenanted, vacant, workless.
antonyms busy, occupied.

unofficial *adj.* confidential, illegal, informal, personal, private, ulterior, unauthorized, unconfirmed, undeclared, wildcat.
antonym official.

unorthodox *adj.* abnormal, alternative, fringe, heterodox, irregular, nonconformist, unconventional, unusual, unwonted.
antonyms conventional, orthodox.

unparalleled *adj.* consummate, exceptional, incomparable, matchless, peerless, rare, singular, superlative, supreme, surpassing, unequaled, unexampled, unique, unmatched, unprecedented, unrivaled, unsurpassed.

unpleasant *adj.* abhorrent, bad, disagreeable, displeasing, distasteful, god-awful, ill-natured, irksome, nasty, objectionable, obnoxious, repulsive, rocky, sticky, traumatic, troublesome, unattractive, unpalatable.
antonym pleasant.

unpopular *adj.* avoided, detested, disliked, hated, neglected, rejected, shunned, undesirable, unfashionable, unloved, unsought-after, unwanted, unwelcome.
antonyms fashionable, popular.

unprecedented *adj.* abnormal, exceptional, extraordinary, freakish, new, novel, original, remarkable, revolutionary, singular, unexampled, unheard-of, unknown, unparalleled, unrivaled, unusual.

unpredictable *adj.* chance, changeable, doubtful, erratic, fickle, fluky, iffy, in the lap of the gods, inconstant, on the knees of the gods, random, scatty, unforeseeable, unreliable, unstable, variable.
antonym predictable.

unprejudiced *adj.* balanced, detached, dispassionate, enlightened, even-handed, fair, fair-minded, impartial, just, non-partisan, objective, open-minded, unbiased, uncolored.
antonyms narrow-minded, prejudiced.

unpremeditated *adj.* extempore, fortuitous, impromptu, impulsive, offhand, off-the-cuff, spontaneous, spur-of-the-moment, unintentional, unplanned, unprepared, unrehearsed.
antonym premeditated.

unprincipled *adj.* amoral, corrupt, crooked, deceitful, devious, discreditable, dishonest, dishonorable, immoral, underhand, unethical, unprofessional, unscrupulous.
antonym ethical.

unprofessional *adj.* amateur, amateurish, improper, inadmissible, incompetent, inefficient, inexperienced, inexpert, lax, negligent, unacceptable, unbecoming, unethical, unfitting, unprincipled, unseemly, unskilled, untrained, unworthy.
antonyms professional, skilful.

unprotected *adj.* defenseless, exposed, helpless, inerm, liable, naked, open, pregnable, unarmed, unattended, undefended, unfortified, unguarded, unsheltered, unshielded, unvaccinated, vulnerable.
antonyms immune, protected, safe.

unqualified *adj.* absolute, categorical, complete, consummate, downright, ill-equipped, incapable, incompetent, ineligible, out-and-out, outright, thorough, thoroughgoing, total, uncertificated, unconditional, unfit, unmitigated, unmixed, unprepared, unreserved, unrestricted, untrained, utter, whole-hearted.
antonyms conditional, tentative.

unreal *adj.* academic, artificial, chimerical, fabulous, fairy-tale, fake, false, fanciful, fantastic, fictitious, hypothetical, illusory, imaginary, immaterial, impalpable, insincere, insubstantial, intangible, made-up, make-believe, mock, moonshiny, mythical, nebulous, ostensible, phantasmagorical, pretended, seeming, sham, storybook, synthetic, vaporous, visionary.
antonyms genuine, real.

unrealistic *adj.* half-baked, idealistic, impracticable, impractical, improbable, quixotic, romantic, starry-eyed, theoretical, unworkable.
antonyms pragmatic, realistic.

unreasonable *adj.* absurd, arbitrary, biased, blinkered, capricious, cussed, erratic, excessive, exorbitant, extortionate, extravagant, far-fetched, foolish, froward, headstrong, illogical, immoderate, inconsistent, irrational, mad, nonsensical, opinionated, perverse, preposterous, quirky, senseless, silly, steep, stupid,

thrawn, uncalled-for, undue, unfair, unjust, unjustifiable, unjustified, unwarranted.
antonyms moderate, rational, reasonable.

unregenerate *adj.* abandoned, hardened, impenitent, incorrigible, intractable, obdurate, obstinate, persistent, recalcitrant, refractory, shameless, sinful, stubborn, unconverted, unreformed, unrepentant, wicked.
antonyms reformed, repentant.

unrelenting *adj.* ceaseless, constant, continual, continuous, cruel, endless, implacable, incessant, inexorable, insistent, intransigent, merciless, perpetual, pitiless, relentless, remorseless, ruthless, steady, stern, tough, unabated, unalleviated, unbroken, unceasing, uncompromising, unmerciful, unremitting, unsparing.
antonyms intermittent, spasmodic.

unreliable *adj.* deceptive, delusive, disreputable, erroneous, fair-weather, fallible, false, implausible, inaccurate, inauthentic, irresponsible, mistaken, specious, uncertain, unconvincing, undependable, unsound, unstable, untrustworthy.
antonym reliable.

unrepentant *adj.* callous, hardened, impenitent, incorrigible, obdurate, shameless, unabashed, unashamed, unregenerate, unremorseful, unrepenting.
antonyms penitent, repentant.

unresponsive *adj.* aloof, apathetic, cool, echoless, indifferent, unaffected, uninterested, unmoved, unsympathetic.
antonyms responsive, sympathetic.

unrest *n.* agitation, anxiety, apprehension, disaffection, discontent, discord, disquiet, dissatisfaction, dissension, distress, perturbation, protest, rebellion, restlessness, sedition, strife, tumult, turmoil, unease, uneasiness, worry.
antonyms calm, peace.

unrestrained *adj.* abandoned, boisterous, free, immoderate, inordinate, intemperate, irrepressible, natural, rampant, unbounded, unbridled, unchecked, unconstrained, uncontrolled, unhindered, uninhibited, unrepressed, unreserved, uproarious.
antonym inhibited.

unruffled *adj.* calm, collected, composed, cool, even, imperturbable, level, peaceful, placid, serene, smooth, tranquil, unbroken, undisturbed, unflustered, unmoved, unperturbed, untroubled.
antonyms anxious, troubled.

unruly *adj.* camstairy, disobedient, disorderly, fractious, headstrong, insubordinate, intractable, lawless, mutinous, obstreperous, rebellious, refractory, riotous, rowdy, ruleless, turbulent, uncontrollable, ungovernable, unmanageable, wayward, wild, wilful.
antonym manageable.

unsafe *adj.* dangerous, exposed, hazardous, insecure, parlous, perilous, precarious, risky, threatening, treacherous, uncertain, unreliable, unsound, unstable, vulnerable.
antonyms safe, secure.

unsatisfactory *adj.* deficient, disappointing, displeasing, dissatisfying, frustrating, inadequate, inferior, insufficient, leaving a lot to be desired, mediocre, poor, rocky, thwarting, unacceptable, unsatisfying, unsuitable, unworthy, weak.
antonym satisfactory.

unscrupulous *adj.* corrupt, crooked, cynical, discredi-

table, dishonest, dishonorable, immoral, improper, ruthless, shameless, unethical, unprincipled.
antonym scrupulous.

unseemly *adj.* discreditable, disreputable, improper, inappropriate, indecorous, indelicate, shocking, unbecoming, unbefitting, undignified, undue, ungentlemanly, unladylike, unrefined, unsuitable.
antonyms decorous, seemly.

unselfish *adj.* altruistic, charitable, dedicated, devoted, disinterested, generous, humanitarian, kind, liberal, magnanimous, noble, philanthropic, self-denying, selfless, self-sacrificing, single-eyed, ungrudging, unstinting.
antonym selfish.

unsentimental *adj.* cynical, hard as nails, hard-headed, level-headed, practical, pragmatic, realistic, shrewd, tough.
antonyms sentimental, soft.

unsettled *adj.* agitated, anxious, changeable, changing, confused, debatable, disorderly, disoriented, disturbed, doubtful, due, edgy, flustered, iffy, inconstant, insecure, moot, open, outstanding, overdue, owing, payable, pending, perturbed, problematical, restive, restless, shaken, shaky, tense, troubled, uncertain, undecided, undetermined, uneasy, unnerved, unpredictable, unresolved, unstable, unsteady, upset, variable.
antonyms certain, composed, settled.

unsightly *adj.* disagreeable, displeasing, hideous, horrid, off-putting, repellent, repugnant, repulsive, revolting, ugly, unattractive, unpleasant, unprepossessing.
antonym pleasing.

unsolicited *adj.* gratuitous, spontaneous, unasked, uncalled-for, unforced, uninvited, unrequested, unsought, unwanted, unwelcome, voluntary.
antonyms invited, solicited.

unsophisticated *adj.* artless, childlike, funky, guileless, hick, homespun, inexperienced, ingenuous, innocent, naïve, natural, plain, simple, straightforward, unaffected, uncomplicated, uninvolved, unpretentious, unrefined, unspecialized, unspoilt, untutored, unworldly.
antonyms complex, pretentious, sophisticated.

unsound *adj.* ailing, defective, delicate, deranged, dicky, diseased, erroneous, fallacious, fallible, false, faulty, flawed, frail, ill, ill-founded, illogical, insecure, invalid, shaky, specious, unbalanced, unhealthy, unhinged, unreliable, unsafe, unstable, unsteady, unwell, weak, wobbly.
antonyms safe, sound.

unspeakable *adj.* abhorrent, abominable, appalling, dreadful, evil, execrable, frightful, heinous, horrible, inconceivable, indescribable, ineffable, inexpressible, loathsome, monstrous, nefandous, odious, overwhelming, repellent, shocking, unbelievable, unimaginable, unutterable, wonderful.

unstable *adj.* astable, capricious, changeable, erratic, fitful, fluctuating, inconsistent, inconstant, insecure, irrational, labile, precarious, rickety, risky, shaky, shoogly, slippy, ticklish, tottering, unpredictable, unsettled, unsteady, untrustworthy, vacillating, variable, volatile, wobbly.
antonyms stable, steady.

unsteady *adj.* changeable, dicky, erratic, flickering, flighty, fluctuating, frail, inconstant, infirm, insecure, irregular, precarious, reeling, rickety, shaky, shoogly,

skittish, tittupy, tottering, totty, treacherous, tremulous, unreliable, unsafe, unstable, unsteeled, vacillating, variable, volatile, wavering, wobbly.
antonyms firm, steady.

unsubstantiated *adj.* debatable, dubious, questionable, unattested, unconfirmed, uncorroborated, unestablished, unproved, unproven, unsupported, unverified.
antonyms proved, proven.

unsuccessful *adj.* abortive, bootless, failed, foiled, fruitless, frustrated, futile, ill-fated, inadequate, ineffective, ineffectual, losing, luckless, manqué, otiose, sterile, thwarted, unavailing, unfortunate, unlucky, unproductive, unsatisfactory, useless, vain.
antonyms effective, successful.

unsuitable *adj.* improper, inapposite, inappropriate, inapt, incompatible, incongruous, inconsistent, indecorous, ineligible, infelicitous, malapropos, unacceptable, unbecoming, unbefitting, unfitting, unlikely, unseasonable, unseemly, unsuited.
antonyms seemly, suitable.

unsuspecting *adj.* childlike, confiding, credulous, green, gullible, inexperienced, ingenuous, innocent, naïve, trustful, trusting, unconscious, uncritical, unsuspicious, unwary, unwitting.
antonyms conscious, knowing.

unswerving *adj.* constant, dedicated, devoted, direct, firm, fixed, immovable, resolute, single-minded, staunch, steadfast, steady, sure, true, undeviating, unfaltering, unflagging, untiring, unwavering.
antonyms irresolute, tentative.

unsympathetic *adj.* antagonistic, antipathetic, apathetic, callous, cold, compassionless, cruel, hard, hard as nails, hard-hearted, harsh, heartless, indifferent, inhuman, insensitive, soulless, stony, uncharitable, uncompassionate, unconcerned, unfeeling, unkind, unmoved, unpitying, unresponsive.
antonyms compassionate, sympathetic.

untamed *adj.* barbarous, ferae naturae, feral, fierce, haggard, savage, unbroken, undomesticated, unmellowed, untameable, wild.
antonyms domesticated, tame.

untenable *adj.* fallacious, flawed, illogical, indefensible, insupportable, rocky, shaky, unmaintainable, unreasonable, unsound, unsustainable.
antonyms sound, tenable.

untidy *adj.* bedraggled, chaotic, cluttered, disheveled, disorderly, higgledy-piggledy, jumbled, littered, messy, muddled, ratty, raunchy, rumpled, scruffy, shambolic, slatternly, slipshod, sloppy, slovenly, sluttish, topsy-turvy, unkempt, unsystematic.
antonyms systematic, tidy.

untimely *adj.* awkward, early, ill-timed, inappropriate, inauspicious, inconvenient, inopportune, intempestive, malapropos, mistimed, premature, unfortunate, unseasonable, unsuitable.
antonyms opportune, timely.

untold *adj.* boundless, countless, hidden, incalculable, indescribable, inexhaustible, inexpressible, infinite, innumerable, measureless, myriad, numberless, private, secret, uncountable, uncounted, undisclosed, undreamed-of, unimaginable, unknown, unnumbered, unpublished, unreckoned, unrecounted, unrelated, unrevealed, unthinkable, unutterable.

untoward *adj.* adverse, annoying, awkward, contrary, disastrous, ill-timed, improper, inappropriate, inaus-

picious, inconvenient, indecorous, inimical, inopportune, irritating, ominous, troublesome, unbecoming, unexpected, unfavorable, unfitting, unfortunate, unlucky, unpropitious, unseemly, unsuitable, untimely, vexatious, worrying.
antonyms auspicious, suitable.

untrustworthy *adj.* capricious, deceitful, devious, dishonest, disloyal, dubious, duplicitous, fair-weather, faithless, false, fickle, fly-by-night, shady, slippery, treacherous, tricky, two-faced, undependable, unfaithful, unreliable, unsafe, untrue, untrusty.
antonyms reliable, trustworthy.

untruthful *adj.* crooked, deceitful, deceptive, dishonest, dissembling, false, hypocritical, lying, mendacious, untrustworthy, unveracious.
antonym truthful.

untutored *adj.* artless, ignorant, illiterate, inexperienced, inexpert, simple, uneducated, unlearned, unlessoned, unpracticed, unrefined, unschooled, unsophisticated, untrained, unversed.
antonyms educated, trained.

unusual *adj.* abnormal, anomalous, atypical, bizarre, curious, different, eccentric, exceptional, extraordinary, odd, phenomenal, queer, rare, remarkable, singular, strange, surprising, uncommon, unconventional, unexpected, unfamiliar, unwonted.
antonyms normal, usual.

unutterable *adj.* egregious, extreme, indescribable, ineffable, nefandous, overwhelming, unimaginable, unspeakable.

unwarranted *adj.* baseless, gratuitous, groundless, indefensible, inexcusable, uncalled-for, unjust, unjustified, unprovoked, unreasonable, vain, wrong.
antonyms justifiable, warranted.

unwary *adj.* careless, credulous, hasty, heedless, imprudent, incautious, indiscreet, rash, reckless, thoughtless, unchary, uncircumspect, unguarded, unthinking, unwatchful.
antonyms cautious, wary.

unwieldy *adj.* awkward, bulky, burdensome, clumsy, cumbersome, cumbrous, gangling, hefty, hulking, inconvenient, massive, ponderous, ungainly, unhandy, unmanageable, weighty.
antonyms dainty, neat, petite.

unwilling *adj.* averse, disinclined, grudging, indisposed, laggard, loath, loathful, opposed, reluctant, resistant, slow, unenthusiastic.
antonyms enthusiastic, willing.

unwise *adj.* foolhardy, foolish, ill-advised, ill-considered, ill-judged, impolitic, improvident, imprudent, inadvisable, indiscreet, inexpedient, injudicious, irresponsible, rash, reckless, senseless, short-sighted, silly, stupid, thoughtless, unintelligent.
antonyms prudent, wise.

unwitting *adj.* accidental, chance, ignorant, inadvertent, innocent, involuntary, unaware, unconscious, unintended, unintentional, unknowing, unmeant, unplanned, unsuspecting, unthinking.
antonyms conscious, deliberate, knowing, witting.

unwonted *adj.* atypical, exceptional, extraordinary, infrequent, peculiar, rare, singular, strange, unaccustomed, uncommon, uncustomary, unexpected, unfamiliar, unheard-of, unusual.
antonyms usual, wonted.

unyielding *adj.* adamant, determined, firm, hardline,

immovable, implacable, inexorable, inflexible, intractable, intransigent, obdurate, obstinate, relentless, resolute, rigid, solid, staunch, steadfast, stubborn, tough, unbending, uncompromising, unrelenting, unwavering.
antonyms flexible, yielding.

upbeat *adj.* bright, bullish, buoyant, cheerful, cheery, encouraging, favorable, forward-looking, heartening, hopeful, optimistic, positive, promising, rosy.
antonyms down-beat, gloomy.

upbraid *v.* admonish, berate, blame, carpet, castigate, censure, chide, condemn, criticize, dress down, jaw, lecture, rate, rebuke, reprimand, reproach, reprove, scold, take to task, tell off, tick off.
antonyms commend, praise.

upbringing *n.* breeding, bringing-up, care, cultivation, education, instruction, nurture, parenting, raising, rearing, tending, training.

upgrade *v.* advance, ameliorate, better, elevate, embourgeoise, enhance, gentilize, gentrify, improve, promote, raise.
antonyms degrade, downgrade.

uphold *v.* advocate, aid, back, champion, countenance, defend, encourage, endorse, fortify, hold to, justify, maintain, promote, stand by, stengthen, support, sustain, vindicate.

upkeep *n.* care, conservation, expenditure, expenses, keep, maintenance, oncosts, operating costs, outgoing, outlay, overheads, preservation, repair, running, running costs, subsistence, support, sustenance.
antonym neglect.

uppish *adj.* affected, arrogant, assuming, big-headed, bumptious, cocky, conceited, hoity-toity, impertinent, overweening, presumptuous, self-important, snobbish, stuck-up, supercilious, swanky, toffee-nosed, uppity.
antonyms diffident, unassertive.

upright *adj.* arrect, bluff, conscientious, erect, ethical, faithful, four-square, good, high-minded, honest, honorable, incorruptible, just, noble, perpendicular, principled, righteous, straight, straightforward, true, trustworthy, unimpeachable, upstanding, vertical, virtuous.
antonyms dishonest, flat, horizontal, prone, supine.

uprising *n.* insurgence, insurgency, insurrection, mutiny, putsch, rebellion, revolt, revolution, rising, sedition, upheaval.

uproar *n.* brawl, brouhaha, clamor, commotion, confusion, din, disorder, furore, noise, hubbub, hullabaloo, hurly-burly, katzenjammer, noise, outcry, pandemonium, racket, rammy, randan, riot, ruckus, ruction, rumpus, stramash, tumult, turbulence, turmoil.

uproarious *adj.* boisterous, clamorous, confused, convulsive, deafening, disorderly, gleeful, hilarious, hysterical, killing, loud, noisy, rib-tickling, riotous, riproaring, roistering, rollicking, rowdy, rowdy-dowdy, side-splitting, tempestuous, tumultuous, turbulent, unrestrained, wild.
antonym sedate.

upset *v.* agitate, bother, capsize, change, conquer, defeat, destabilize, discombobulate, discompose, disconcert, dismay, disorder, disorganize, disquiet, distress, disturb, fluster, grieve, hip, overcome, overset, overthrow, overturn, perturb, ruffle, shake, spill, spoil, tip, topple, trouble, unnerve, unsteady.
n. agitation, bother, bug, complaint, defeat, disorder, disruption, disturbance, illness, indisposition, malady,

purl, reverse, shake-up, shock, sickness, surprise, trouble, upheaval, worry.
adj. agitated, bothered, capsized, chaotic, choked, confused, disconcerted, dismayed, disordered, disquieted, distressed, disturbed, frantic, gippy, grieved, hurt, ill, messed up, muddled, overturned, overwrought, pained, poorly, qualmish, queasy, ruffled, shattered, sick, spilled, toppled, topsy-turvy, troubled, tumbled, worried.

upshot *n.* conclusion, consequence, culmination, end, event, finale, finish, issue, outcome, pay-off, result.

urbane *adj.* bland, civil, civilized, cosmopolitan, courteous, cultivated, cultured, debonair, easy, elegant, mannerly, polished, refined, smooth, sophisticated, suave, well-bred, well-mannered.
antonyms gauche, uncouth.

urge *v.* advise, advocate, beg, beseech, champion, compel, constrain, counsel, drive, emphasize, encourage, entreat, exhort, force, goad, hasten, hist, impel, implore, incite, induce, instigate, nag, plead, press, propel, push, recommend, solicit, spur, stimulate, support, underline, underscore.
antonyms deter, dissuade.
n. compulsion, desire, drive, eagerness, fancy, impulse, inclination, itch, libido, longing, wish, yearning, yen.
antonym disinclination.

urgency *n.* exigence, exigency, extremity, gravity, hurry, imperativeness, importance, importunity, instancy, necessity, need, pressure, seriousness, stress.

urgent *adj.* clamorous, cogent, compelling, critical, crucial, eager, earnest, emergent, exigent, immediate, imperative, important, importunate, insistent, instant, intense, persistent, persuasive, pressing, top-priority.

usage *n.* application, control, convention, custom, employment, etiquette, form, habit, handling, management, method, mode, operation, practice, procedure, protocol, régime, regulation, routine, rule, running, tradition, treatment, use, wont.

use *v.* apply, bring, consume, employ, enjoy, exercise, exhaust, expend, exploit, handle, manipulate, misuse, operate, ply, practice, spend, treat, usufruct, utilize, waste, wield, work.
n. advantage, application, avail, benefit, call, cause, custom, employment, end, enjoyment, exercise, good, habit, handling, help, meaning, mileage, necessity, need, object, occasion, operation, point, practice, profit, purpose, reason, service, treatment, usage, usefulness, usufruct, utility, value, way, wont, worth.

useful *adj.* advantageous, all-purpose, beneficial, convenient, effective, fruitful, general-purpose, handy, helpful, practical, productive, profitable, salutary, serviceable, valuable, worthwhile.
antonym useless.

useless *adj.* bootless, clapped-out, disadvantageous, effectless, feckless, fruitless, futile, hopeless, idle, impractical, incompetent, ineffective, ineffectual, inefficient, inept, of no use, pointless, profitless, shiftless, stupid, unavailing, unproductive, unworkable, vain, valueless, weak, worthless.
antonym useful.

usher *n.* attendant, doorkeeper, escort, guide, huissier, usherette.
v. conduct, direct, escort, guide, lead, pilot, shepherd, steer.

usual *adj.* accepted, accustomed, common, constant,

conventional, customary, everyday, expected, familiar, fixed, general, habitual, nomic, normal, ordinary, recognized, regular, routine, standard, stock, typical, unexceptional, wonted.
antonyms unheard-of, unusual.

usually *adv.* as a rule, by and large, chiefly, commonly, customarily, generally, generally speaking, habitually, in the main, mainly, mostly, normally, on the whole, ordinarily, regularly, routinely, traditionally, typically.
antonym exceptionally.

utensil *n.* apparatus, contrivance, device, gadget, gismo, implement, instrument, tool.

utility *n.* advantage, advantageousness, avail, benefit, convenience, efficacy, expedience, fitness, point, practicality, profit, satisfactoriness, service, serviceableness, use, usefulness, value.
antonym inutility.

utilize *v.* adapt, appropriate, employ, exploit, make use of, put to use, resort to, take advantage of, turn to account, use.

Utopian *adj.* airy, chimerical, dream, Elysian, fanciful, fantastic, ideal, idealistic, illusory, imaginary, impractical, perfect, romantic, unworkable, visionary, wishful.

utter¹ *adj.* absolute, arrant, complete, consummate, dead, downright, entire, out-and-out, perfect, sheer, stark, thorough, thoroughgoing, total, unalleviated, unmitigated, unqualified.

utter² *v.* articulate, declare, deliver, divulge, enounce, enunciate, express, proclaim, promulgate, pronounce, publish, reveal, say, sound, speak, state, tell, tongue, verbalize, vocalize, voice.

V

vacancy *n.* accommodation, emptiness, gap, job, opening, opportunity, place, position, post, room, situation, space, vacuity, vacuousness, vacuum, void.

vacant *adj.* absent, absent-minded, abstracted, available, blank, disengaged, dreaming, dreamy, empty, expressionless, free, idle, inane, inattentive, incurious, thoughtless, to let, unemployed, unengaged, unfilled, unoccupied, untenanted, unthinking, vacuous, void.
antonyms engaged, occupied.

vacate *v.* abandon, depart, evacuate, leave, quit, withdraw.

vacillate *v.* fluctuate, haver, hesitate, oscillate, shilly-shally, shuffle, sway, swither, temporize, tergiversate, waver.

vacillating *adj.* hesitant, irresolute, oscillating, shilly-shallying, shuffling, swithering, temporizing, uncertain, unresolved, wavering.
antonyms resolute, unhesitating.

vacuity *n.* apathy, blankness, emptiness, inanity, incognizance, incomprehension, incuriosity, nothingness, space, vacuousness, vacuum, void.

vacuous *adj.* apathetic, blank, empty, idle, inane, incurious, stupid, uncomprehending, unfilled, unintelligent, vacant, void.

vacuum *n.* chasm, emptiness, gap, nothingness, space, vacuity, void.

vagabond *n.* beggar, bo, bum, down-and-out, hobo, itinerant, knight of the road, migrant, nomad, outcast,

rascal, rover, runabout, runagate, tramp, vagrant, wanderer, wayfarer.

vagary *n.* caprice, crotchet, fancy, fegary, humor, megrim, notion, prank, quirk, whim, whimsy.

vagrant *n.* beggar, bum, gangrel, hobo, itinerant, rolling stone, stroller, tramp, wanderer.
adj. footloose, homeless, itinerant, nomadic, roaming, rootless, roving, shiftless, traveling, vagabond, wandering.

vague *adj.* amorphous, blurred, dim, doubtful, evasive, fuzzy, generalized, hazy, ill-defined, imprecise, indefinite, indeterminate, indistinct, inexact, lax, loose, misty, nebulous, obscure, shadowy, uncertain, unclear, undefined, undetermined, unknown, unspecific, unspecified, woolly.
antonyms certain, clear, definite.

vain *adj.* abortive, affected, arrogant, baseless, big-headed, conceited, egotistical, empty, fruitless, futile, groundless, hollow, idle, inflated, mindless, narcissistic, nugatory, ostentatious, overweening, peacockish, pointless, pretentious, proud, purposeless, self-important, self-satisfied, senseless, stuck-up, swaggering, swanky, swollen-headed, time-wasting, trifling, trivial, unavailing, unimportant, unproductive, unprofitable, unsubstantial, useless, vainglorious, vaporous, worthless.
antonyms modest, self-effacing.

valet *n.* body servant, gentleman's gentleman, man, man-servant, valet de chambre.

valiant *adj.* bold, brave, courageous, dauntless, doughty, fearless, gallant, heroic, indomitable, intrepid, plucky, redoubtable, stalwart, staunch, stout, stout-hearted, valorous, worthy.
antonym cowardly.

valid *adj.* approved, authentic, binding, bona fide, cogent, conclusive, convincing, efficacious, efficient, genuine, good, just, lawful, legal, legitimate, logical, official, potent, powerful, proper, rational, reliable, sound, substantial, telling, weighty, well-founded, well-grounded.
antonym invalid.

validate *v.* attest, authenticate, authorize, certify, confirm, corroborate, endorse, legalize, ratify, substantiate, underwrite.

validity *n.* authority, cogency, force, foundation, grounds, justifiability, lawfulness, legality, legitimacy, logic, point, power, soundness, strength, substance, weight.
antonym invalidity.

valley *n.* arroyo, canyon, cwm, dale, dell, depression, dingle, draw, glen, gorge, gulch, hollow, hope, slade, strath, vale.

valor *n.* boldness, bravery, courage, derring-do, doughtiness, fearlessness, fortitude, gallantry, hardiness, heroism, intrepidity, lion-heartedness, mettle, spirit.
antonyms cowardice, weakness.

valuable *adj.* advantageous, beneficial, blue-chip, cherished, costly, dear, esteemed, estimable, expensive, fruitful, handy, helpful, high-priced, important, invaluable, precious, prizable, prized, productive, profitable, serviceable, treasured, useful, valued, worthwhile, worthy.
antonyms useless, valueless.

value *n.* account, advantage, avail, benefit, cost, desirability, equivalent, good, help, importance, merit, price, profit, rate, significance, use, usefulness, utility, worth.

v. account, appraise, appreciate, apprize, assess, cherish, compute, esteem, estimate, evaluate, hold dear, price, prize, rate, regard, respect, survey, treasure. *antonyms* disregard, neglect, undervalue.

vanish *v.* dematerialize, depart, die out, disappear, disperse, dissolve, evanesce, evaporate, exit, fade, fizzle out, melt, peter out.
antonyms appear, materialize.

vanity *n.* affectation, airs, arrogance, bigheadedness, conceit, conceitedness, egotism, emptiness, frivolity, fruitlessness, fume, futility, hollowness, idleness, inanity, narcissism, ostentation, peacockery, pointlessness, pretension, pride, self-admiration, self-conceit, self-love, self-satisfaction, swollen-headedness, triviality, unreality, unsubstantiality, uselessness, vainglory, worthlessness.
antonyms modesty, worth.

vanquish *v.* beat, confound, conquer, crush, defeat, humble, master, overcome, overpower, overwhelm, quell, reduce, repress, rout, subdue, subjugate, triumph over.

vapid *adj.* banal, bland, bloodless, boring, colorless, dead, dull, flat, flavorless, insipid, jejune, lifeless, limp, stale, tame, tasteless, tedious, tiresome, trite, uninspiring, uninteresting, watery, weak, wishy-washy.
antonyms interesting, vigorous.

vapor *n.* breath, brume, damp, dampness, exhalation, fog, fumes, halitus, haze, miasm, miasma, mist, reek, roke, smoke, steam.

variable *adj.* capricious, chameleonic, changeable, fickle, fitful, flexible, fluctuating, inconstant, mercurial, moonish, mutable, protean, shifting, temperamental, unpredictable, unstable, unsteady, vacillating, varying, versiform, wavering.
antonym invariable.

n. factor, parameter.

variant *adj.* alternative, derived, deviant, different, divergent, exceptional, modified.
antonyms normal, standard, usual.

n. alternative, development, deviant, modification, rogue, sport, variation.

variation *n.* alteration, change, departure, deviation, difference, discrepancy, diversification, diversity, elaboration, inflection, innovation, modification, modulation, novelty, variety.
antonyms monotony, similitude, uniformity.

variety *n.* array, assortment, brand, breed, category, change, class, collection, difference, discrepancy, diversification, diversity, intermixture, kind, make, manifoldness, many-sidedness, medley, miscellany, mixture, multifariousness, multiplicity, olio, olla-podrida, order, pot-pourri, range, sort, species, strain, type, variation.
antonyms monotony, similitude, uniformity.

various *adj.* assorted, different, differing, disparate, distinct, divers, diverse, diversified, heterogeneous, many, many-sided, miscellaneous, multifarous, omnifarious, several, sundry, varied, variegated, varying.

vary *v.* alter, alternate, change, depart, differ, disagree, diverge, diversify, fluctuate, inflect, intermix, modify, modulate, permutate, reorder, transform.

vassalage *n.* bondage, dependence, serfdom, servitude, slavery, subjection, subjugation, thraldom, villeinage.

vast *adj.* astronomical, boundless, capacious, colossal, cyclopean, enormous, extensive, far-flung, fathomless, gigantic, great, huge, illimitable, immeasurable, immense, limitless, mammoth, massive, measureless, monstrous, monumental, never-ending, prodigious, stupendous, sweeping, tremendous, unbounded, unlimited, vasty, voluminous, wide.

vault[1] *v.* bound, clear, hurdle, jump, leap, leap-frog, spring.

vault[2] *n.* arch, camera, cavern, cellar, concave, crypt, depository, mausoleum, repository, roof, span, strong-room, tomb, undercroft, wine-cellar.

vaunt *v.* blazon, boast, brag, crow, exult in, flaunt, parade, show off, trumpet.
antonyms belittle, minimize.

veer *v.* change, sheer, shift, swerve, tack, turn, wheel.

vehement *adj.* animated, ardent, eager, earnest, emphatic, enthusiastic, fervent, fervid, fierce, forceful, forcible, heated, impassioned, impetuous, intense, passionate, powerful, strong, urgent, violent, zealous.
antonyms apathetic, indifferent.

veil *v.* cloak, conceal, cover, dim, disguise, dissemble, dissimulate, hide, mantle, mask, obscure, screen, shade, shadow, shield.
antonyms expose, uncover.

n. blind, cloak, cover, curtain, disguise, film, humeral, integument, mask, screen, shade, shroud, velum.

venal *adj.* bent, bribable, buyable, corrupt, corruptible, grafting, mercenary, purchasable, simoniacal.
antonym incorruptible.

venerable *adj.* aged, august, dignified, esteemed, grave, honored, respected, revered, reverenced, reverend, sage, sedate, venerated, wise, worshipful.

venerate *v.* adore, esteem, hallow, honor, respect, revere, reverence, worship.
antonyms anathematize, disregard, execrate.

vengeance *n.* avengement, lex talionis, reprisal, requital, retaliation, retribution, revanche, revenge, talion, tit for tat.
antonym forgiveness.

venom *n.* acrimony, bane, bitterness, gall, grudge, hate, hatred, ill-will, malevolence, malice, maliciousness, malignity, poison, rancor, spite, spitefulness, spleen, toxin, venin, vindictiveness, virulence, virus, vitrio.

vent *n.* aperture, blowhole, duct, hole, opening, orifice, outlet, passage, spiracle, split.

v. air, discharge, emit, express, let fly, release, unloose, utter, voice.

venture *v.* advance, adventure, chance, dare, endanger, hazard, imperil, jeopardize, make bold, presume, put forward, risk, speculate, stake, suggest, take the liberty, volunteer, wager.

n. adventure, chance, endeavor, enterprise, fling, gamble, hazard, operation, project, risk, speculation, undertaking.

verbal *adj.* lexical, oral, spoken, unwritten, verbatim, word-of-mouth.

verbatim *adv.* exactly, literally, precisely, to the letter, (verbatim et) literatim, word for word.

verbose *adj.* ambagious, circumlocutory, diffuse, garrulous, long-winded, loquacious, multiloquent, periphrastic, phrasy, pleonastic, prolix, windy, wordy.
antonyms economical, laconic, succinct.

verbosity *n.* garrulity, logorrhoea, long-windedness,

loquaciousness, loquacity, multiloquy, prolixity, verbiage, verboseness, windiness, wordiness.
antonyms economy, succinctness.

verdict *n.* adjudication, assessment, conclusion, decision, finding, judgment, opinion, sentence.

verge *n.* border, boundary, brim, brink, edge, edging, extreme, limit, lip, margin, roadside, threshold.

verification *n.* attestation, authentication, checking, confirmation, corroboration, proof, substantiation, validation.

verify *v.* attest, authenticate, check, confirm, corroborate, prove, substantiate, support, testify, validate.
antonyms discredit, invalidate.

vernacular *adj.* colloquial, common, endemic, indigenous, informal, local, mother, native, popular, vulgar.
n. argot, cant, dialect, idiom, jargon, language, lingo, parlance, patois, speech, tongue.

versatile *adj.* adaptable, adjustable, all-round, flexible, functional, general-purpose, handy, many-sided, multifaceted, multipurpose, protean, Renaissance, resourceful, variable.
antonym inflexible.

versed *adj.* accomplished, acquainted, au fait, competent, conversant, experienced, familiar, knowledgeable, learned, practiced, proficient, qualified, seasoned, skilled.

version *n.* account, adaptation, design, form, interpretation, kind, model, paraphrase, portrayal, reading, rendering, rendition, style, translation, type, variant.

vertical *adj.* erect, on end, perpendicular, upright, upstanding.
antonym horizontal.

verve *n.* animation, brio, dash, élan, energy, enthusiasm, force, gusto, life, liveliness, pizzazz, punch, relish, sparkle, spirit, vigor, vim, vitality, vivacity, zeal, zip.
antonym apathy.

very *adv.* absolutely, acutely, awfully, decidedly, deeply, dogged, dooms, eminently, exceeding(ly), excessively, extremely, fell, gey, greatly, highly, jolly, noticeably, particularly, passing, rattling, really, remarkably, superlatively, surpassingly, terribly, truly, uncommonly, unusually, wonderfully.
antonyms hardly, scarcely, slightly.
adj. actual, appropriate, bare, exact, express, identical, mere, perfect, plain, precise, pure, real, same, self-same, sheer, simple, unqualified, utter.

vessel *n.* barque, boat, canister, container, craft, holder, jar, pot, receptacle, ship, utensil.

vestige *n.* evidence, glimmer, hint, indication, print, relic, remainder, remains, remnant, residue, scrap, sign, suspicion, token, trace, track, whiff.

veto *v.* ban, blackball, disallow, forbid, interdict, kill, negative, prohibit, reject, rule out, turn down.
antonyms approve, sanction.
n. ban, embargo, interdict, prohibition, rejection, thumbs down.
antonyms approval, assent.

vex *v.* afflict, aggravate, agitate, annoy, bother, bug, chagrin, deave, displease, distress, disturb, exasperate, fret, gall, get (to), harass, hump, irritate, molest, needle, nettle, offend, peeve, perplex, pester, pique, plague, provoke, rile, spite, tease, torment, trouble, upset, worry.
antonym soothe.

vexation *n.* aggravation, anger, annoyance, bore, bother,

chagrin, difficulty, displeasure, dissatisfaction, exasperation, frustration, fury, headache, irritant, misfortune, nuisance, pique, problem, trouble, upset, worry.

viable *adj.* achievable, applicable, feasible, operable, possible, practicable, usable, workable.
antonyms impossible, unworkable.

vibrate *v.* fluctuate, judder, oscillate, pendulate, pulsate, pulse, quiver, resonate, reverberate, shake, shimmy, shiver, shudder, sway, swing, throb, tremble, undulate.

vice *n.* bad habit, besetting sin, blemish, corruption, defect, degeneracy, depravity, evil, evil-doing, failing, fault, hamartia, immorality, imperfection, iniquity, profligacy, shortcoming, sin, venality, weakness, wickedness.
antonym virtue.

vicinity *n.* area, circumjacency, district, environs, locality, neighborhood, precincts, propinquity, proximity, purlieus, vicinage.

vicious *adj.* abhorrent, atrocious, backbiting, bad, barbarous, bitchy, brutal, catty, corrupt, cruel, dangerous, debased, defamatory, depraved, diabolical, fiendish, foul, heinous, immoral, infamous, malicious, mean, monstrous, nasty, perverted, profligate, rancorous, savage, sinful, slanderous, spiteful, unprincipled, venomous, vile, vindictive, violent, virulent, vitriolic, wicked, worthless, wrong.
antonyms gentle, good, virtuous.

victimize *v.* bully, cheat, deceive, defraud, discriminate against, dupe, exploit, fool, gull, hoodwink, oppress, persecute, pick on, prey on, swindle, use.

victor *n.* champ, champion, conqueror, first, prize-winner, subjugator, top dog, vanquisher, victor ludorum, victrix, winner.
antonyms loser, vanquished.

victory *n.* conquest, laurels, mastery, palm, prize, subjugation, success, superiority, triumph, vanquishment, win.
antonyms defeat, loss.

view *n.* aspect, attitude, belief, contemplation, conviction, display, estimation, examination, feeling, glimpse, impression, inspection, judgment, landscape, look, notion, opinion, outlook, panorama, perception, perspective, picture, prospect, scan, scene, scrutiny, sentiment, sight, spectacle, survey, viewing, vision, vista.
v. behold, consider, contemplate, deem, examine, explore, eye, inspect, judge, observe, perceive, read, regard, scan, speculate, survey, watch, witness.

viewpoint *n.* angle, Anschauung, attitude, feeling, opinion, perspective, position, slant, stance, standpoint.

vigilant *adj.* alert, Argus-eyed, attentive, careful, cautious, circumspect, guarded, on one's guard, on one's toes, on the alert, on the lookout, on the qui vive, sleepless, unsleeping, wakeful, watchful, wide-awake.
antonyms careless, forgetful, lax, negligent.

vigor *n.* activity, animation, dash, dynamism, energy, force, forcefulness, gusto, health, liveliness, might, oomph, pep, potency, power, punch, robustness, snap, soundness, spirit, stamina, strength, verve, vim, virility, vitality, zip.
antonyms impotence, sluggishness, weakness.

vigorous *adj.* active, brisk, dynamic, effective, efficient, energetic, enterprising, flourishing, forceful, forcible,

full-blooded, hale, hardy, healthy, hearty, intense, lively, lusty, mettlesome, powerful, red-blooded, robust, sound, spanking, spirited, stout, strenuous, strong, virile, vital, zippy.
antonyms feeble, lethargic, weak.

vile *adj.* abandoned, abject, appalling, bad, base, coarse, contemptible, corrupt, debased, degenerate, degrading, depraved, despicable, disgraceful, disgusting, earthly, evil, foul, horrid, humiliating, ignoble, impure, loathsome, low, mean, miserable, nasty, nauseating, nefarious, noxious, offensive, perverted, repellent, repugnant, repulsive, revolting, scabbed, scabby, scandalous, scurvy, shocking, sickening, sinful, ugly, vicious, vulgar, wicked, worthless, wretched.

vilify *v.* abuse, asperse, bad-mouth, berate, calumniate, criticize, debase, decry, defame, denigrate, denounce, disparage, malign, revile, slander, smear, stigmatize, traduce, vilipend, vituperate.
antonyms adore, compliment, eulogize, glorify.

village *n.* clachan, community, district, dorp, hamlet, kraal, pueblo, settlement, township.

villain *n.* anti-hero, baddy, blackguard, bravo, caitiff, criminal, devil, evil-doer, heavy, knave, libertine, malefactor, miscreant, profligate, rapscallion, rascal, reprobate, rogue, scoundrel, wretch.
antonyms angel, goody, hero, heroine.

villainous *adj.* atrocious, bad, base, blackguardly, criminal, cruel, debased, degenerate, depraved, detestable, diabolical, disgraceful, evil, fiendish, hateful, heinous, ignoble, infamous, inhuman, malevolent, mean, nefarious, opprobrious, outrageous, ruffianly, scoundrelly, sinful, terrible, thievish, vicious, vile, wicked.
antonyms angelic, good, heroic.

vindication *n.* apology, assertion, defence, exculpation, excuse, exoneration, extenuation, justification, maintenance, plea, rehabilitation, substantiation, support, verification.
antonyms accusation, conviction.

violate *v.* abuse, assault, befoul, break, contravene, debauch, defile, desecrate, dishonor, disobey, disregard, flout, infract, infringe, invade, outrage, pollute, profane, rape, ravish, transgress.
antonyms obey, observe, uphold.

violence *n.* abandon, acuteness, bestiality, bloodshed, bloodthirstiness, boisterousness, brutality, conflict, cruelty, destructiveness, ferocity, fervor, fierceness, fighting, force, frenzy, fury, harshness, hostilities, intensity, murderousness, passion, power, roughness, savagery, severity, sharpness, storminess, terrorism, thuggery, tumult, turbulence, vehemence, wildness.
antonyms passivity, peacefulness.

violent *adj.* acute, agonizing, berserk, biting, bloodthirsty, blustery, boisterous, brutal, cruel, destructive, devastating, excruciating, extreme, fiery, forceful, forcible, furious, harsh, headstrong, homicidal, hot-headed, impetuous, intemperate, intense, maddened, maniacal, murderous, outrageous, painful, passionate, peracute, powerful, raging, riotous, rough, ruinous, savage, severe, sharp, strong, tempestuous, tumultuous, turbulent, uncontrollable, ungovernable, unrestrained, vehement, vicious, wild.
antonyms calm, gentle, moderate, passive, peaceful.

virgin *n.* bachelor, celibate, damsel, girl, maid, maiden, spinster, vestal, virgo intacta.
adj. chaste, fresh, immaculate, intact, maidenly,

modest, new, pristine, pure, snowy, spotless, stainless, uncorrupted, undefiled, unsullied, untouched, unused, vestal, virginal.

virile *adj.* forceful, husky, lusty, macho, male, manlike, manly, masculine, potent, red-blooded, robust, rugged, strong, vigorous.
antonyms effeminate, impotent, weak.

virtue *n.* advantage, asset, attribute, chastity, credit, excellence, goodness, high-mindedness, honor, incorruptibility, innocence, integrity, justice, merit, morality, plus, probity, purity, quality, rectitude, redeeming feature, righteousness, strength, uprightness, virginity, worth, worthiness.
antonym vice.

virtuous *adj.* blameless, celibate, chaste, clean-living, continent, ethical, excellent, exemplary, good, high-principled, honest, honorable, incorruptible, innocent, irreproachable, moral, praiseworthy, pure, righteous, spotless, unimpeachable, upright, virginal, worthy.
antonyms bad, dishonest, immoral, vicious, wicked.

virulent *adj.* acrimonious, baneful, bitter, deadly, envenomed, hostile, infective, injurious, lethal, malevolent, malicious, malignant, noxious, pernicious, poisonous, rancorous, resentful, septic, spiteful, splenetic, toxic, venomous, vicious, vindictive, vitriolic.

vision *n.* apparition, chimera, concept, conception, construct, daydream, delusion, discernment, dream, eyes, eyesight, fantasy, far-sightedness, foresight, ghost, hallucination, idea, ideal, illusion, image, imagination, insight, intuition, mirage, penetration, perception, phantasm, phantasma, phantom, picture, prescience, revelation, seeing, sight, spectacle, specter, view, wraith.

visionary *adj.* chimerical, delusory, dreaming, dreamy, fanciful, fantastic, ideal, idealized, idealistic, illusory, imaginary, impractical, moonshiny, prophetic, quixotic, romantic, speculative, starry-eyed, unreal, unrealistic, unworkable, utopian.
n. daydreamer, Don Quixote, dreamer, enthusiast, fantasist, idealist, mystic, prophet, rainbow-chaser, romantic, seer, theorist, utopian, zealot.
antonym pragmatist.

visit *v.* afflict, assail, attack, befall, call in, call on, drop in on, haunt, inspect, look in, look up, pop in, punish, see, smite, stay at, stay with, stop by, take in, trouble.
n. call, excursion, sojourn, stay, stop.

visitor *n.* caller, company, guest, holidaymaker, tourist, visitant.

vista *n.* enfilade, panorama, perspective, prospect, view.

vital *adj.* alive, animate, animated, animating, basic, cardinal, critical, crucial, decisive, dynamic, energetic, essential, forceful, fundamental, generative, imperative, important, indispensable, invigorating, key, life-giving, life-or-death, live, lively, living, necessary, quickening, requisite, significant, spirited, urgent, vibrant, vigorous, vivacious, zestful.
antonyms inessential, peripheral, unimportant.

vitality *n.* animation, energy, exuberance, foison, go, life, liveliness, lustiness, oomph, pep, robustness, sparkle, stamina, strength, vigor, vim, vivaciousness, vivacity.

vitiate *v.* blemish, blight, contaminate, corrupt, debase, defile, deprave, deteriorate, devalue, harm, impair, injure, invalidate, mar, nullify, pervert, pollute, ruin spoil, sully, taint, undermine.

antonym purify.

vituperation *n.* abuse, blame, castigation, censure, contumely, diatribe, fault-finding, flak, invective, objurgation, obloquy, phillipic, rebuke, reprimand, reproach, revilement, scurrility, stick, vilification.
antonyms acclaim, eulogy, praise.

vivacious *adj.* animated, bubbling, bubbly, cheerful, chipper, ebullient, effervescent, frisky, frolicsome, gay, high-spirited, jolly, light-hearted, lively, merry, scintillating, sparkling, spirited, sportive, sprightly, vital.
antonym languid.

vivid *adj.* active, animated, bright, brilliant, clear, colorful, distinct, dramatic, dynamic, eidetic, energetic, expressive, flamboyant, glowing, graphic, highly-colored, intense, lifelike, lively, memorable, powerful, quick, realistic, rich, sharp, spirited, stirring, striking, strong, telling, vibrant, vigorous.
antonyms dull, lifeless.

vocal *adj.* articulate, clamorous, eloquent, expressive, forthright, frank, free-spoken, noisy, oral, outspoken, plain-spoken, said, shrill, spoken, strident, uttered, vociferous, voiced.
antonyms inarticulate, quiet.

vocation *n.* bag, business, calling, career, employment, job, métier, mission, niche, office, post, profession, pursuit, role, trade, work.

void *adj.* bare, blank, canceled, clear, dead, drained, emptied, empty, free, inane, ineffective, ineffectual, inoperative, invalid, nugatory, null, tenantless, unenforceable, unfilled, unoccupied, useless, vacant, vain, worthless.
antonyms full, valid.
n. blank, blankness, cavity, chasm, emptiness, gap, hiatus, hollow, lack, opening, space, vacuity, vacuum, want.
v. abnegate, annul, cancel, defecate, discharge, drain, eject, elimate, emit, empty, evacuate, invalidate, nullify, rescind.
antonyms fill, validate.

volatile *adj.* airy, changeable, erratic, explosive, fickle, flighty, gay, giddy, hot-headed, hot-tempered, inconstant, lively, mercurial, sprightly, temperamental, unsettled, unstable, unsteady, variable, volcanic.
antonyms constant, steady.

volition *n.* choice, choosing, determination, discretion, election, option, preference, purpose, resolution, taste, velleity, will.

voluble *adj.* articulate, fluent, forthcoming, garrulous, glib, loquacious, talkative.

volume *n.* aggregate, amount, amplitude, bigness, body, book, bulk, capacity, compass, dimensions, fascic(u)le, heft, mass, part, publication, quantity, tome, total, treatise.

voluminous *adj.* abounding, ample, big, billowing, bulky, capacious, cavernous, commodious, copious, full, large, massive, prolific, roomy, vast.
antonyms scanty, slight.

voluntary *adj.* conscious, deliberate, discretional, free, gratuitous, honorary, intended, intentional, optional, purposeful, purposive, spontaneous, unconstrained, unforced, unpaid, volunteer, wilful, willing.
antonyms compulsory, forced, involuntary, unwilling.

voluptuous *adj.* ample, buxom, curvaceous, effeminate, enticing, epicurean, erotic, goluptious, hedonistic, licentious, luscious, luxurious, pleasure-loving, pro-

vocative, seductive, self-indulgent, sensual, shapely, sybaritic.
antonym ascetic.

voracious *adj.* acquisitive, avid, devouring, edacious, gluttonous, greedy, hungry, insatiable, omnivorous, pantophagous, prodigious, rapacious, ravening, ravenous, uncontrolled, unquenchable.

vouch for affirm, assert, asseverate, attest to, avouch, back, certify, confirm, endorse, guarantee, support, swear to, uphold.

vouchsafe *v.* accord, bestow, cede, confer, deign, grant, impart, yield.

vow *v.* affirm, avouch, bename, consecrate, dedicate, devote, maintain, pledge, profess, promise, swear.
n. avouchment, oath, pledge, promise, troth.

voyage *n.* crossing, cruise, expedition, journey, passage, peregrination, travels, trip.

vulgar *adj.* banausic, blue, boorish, cheap and nasty, coarse, common, crude, dirty, flashy, gaudy, general, gross, ill-bred, impolite, improper, indecent, indecorous, indelicate, low, low-life, low-lived, low-minded, low-thoughted, nasty, native, naughty, ordinary, pandemian, plebby, plebeian, ribald, risqué, rude, suggestive, tacky, tasteless, tawdry, uncouth, unmannerly, unrefined, vernacular.
antonyms correct, decent, elegant, noble, polite, refined.

vulnerable *adj.* accessible, assailable, defenseless, exposed, expugnable, pregnable, sensitive, susceptible, tender, thin-skinned, unprotected, weak, wide open.
antonyms protected, strong.

W

wacky *adj.* crazy, daft, eccentric, erratic, goofy, irrational, loony, loopy, nutty, odd, screwy, silly, unpredictable, wild, zany.
antonym sensible.

wad *n.* ball, block, bundle, chunk, hump, hunk, mass, pledget, plug, roll.

waffle *v.* blather, fudge, jabber, prate, prattle, prevaricate, rabbit on, spout, witter on.
n. blather, gobbledegook, guff, jabber, nonsense, padding, prating, prattle, prolixity, verbiage, verbosity, wordiness.

waft *v.* bear, carry, convey, drift, float, ride, transmit, transport, whiffle, winnow.
n. breath, breeze, current, draft, puff, scent, whiff.

wage *n.* allowance, compensation, earnings, emolument, fee, guerdon, hire, pay, payment, penny-fee, recompense, remuneration, reward, salary, screw, stipend, wage-packet, wages.
v. carry on, conduct, engage in, practice, prosecute, pursue, undertake.

wager *n.* bet, flutter, gage, gamble, hazard, pledge, punt, speculation, stake, venture.
v. bet, chance, gamble, hazard, lay, lay odds, pledge, punt, risk, speculate, stake, venture.

waggish *adj.* amusing, arch, bantering, comical, droll, espiègle, facetious, frolicsome, funny, humorous, impish, jesting, jocose, jocular, merry, mischievous, playful, puckish, risible, roguish, sportive, witty.
antonyms grave, serious, staid.

wagon *n.* buggy, carriage, cart, float, pushcart, train, truck, wain.

waif *n.* foundling, orphan, stray, wastrel.

wail *v.* bemoan, bewail, complain, cry, deplore, grieve, howl, keen, lament, mewl, moan, ululate, weep, yammer, yowl.

n. caterwaul, complaint, cry, grief, howl, keen, lament, lamentation, moan, ululation, weeping, yowl.

wait *v.* abide, dally, delay, hang fire, hesitate, hold back, hover, linger, loiter, mark time, pause, remain, rest, stay, tarry.

antonyms depart, go, leave.

n. delay, halt, hesitation, hiatus, hold-up, interval, pause, rest, stay.

waive *v.* abandon, defer, disclaim, forgo, postpone, relinquish, remit, renounce, resign, surrender.

antonyms claim, maintain.

wake[1] *v.* activate, animate, arise, arouse, awake, awaken, bestir, enliven, excite, fire, galvanize, get up, kindle, provoke, quicken, rise, rouse, stimulate, stir, unbed.

antonyms relax, sleep.

n. death-watch, funeral, pernoctation, vigil, watch.

wake[2] *n.* aftermath, backwash, path, rear, track, trail, train, wash, waves.

waken *v.* activate, animate, arouse, awake, awaken, enliven, fire, galvanize, get up, ignite, kindle, quicken, rouse, stimulate, stir, whet.

walk *v.* accompany, advance, amble, convoy, escort, go by Shanks's pony, hike, hoof it, march, move, pace, pedestrianize, perambulate, plod, promenade, saunter, step, stride, stroll, take, traipse, tramp, tread, trek, trog, trudge.

n. aisle, alley, ambulatory, avenue, carriage, constitutional, esplanade, footpath, frescade, gait, hike, lane, mall, march, pace, path, pathway, pavement, pawn, perambulation, promenade, ramble, saunter, sidewalk, step, stride, stroll, trail, traipse, tramp, trek, trudge, turn.

wall *n.* bailey, barricade, barrier, block, breastwork, bulk-head, bulwark, dike, divider, dyke, embankment, enclosure, fence, fortification, hedge, impediment, membrane, obstacle, obstruction, palisade, panel, parapet, partition, rampart, screen, septum, stockade.

wallow *v.* bask, delight, enjoy, flounder, glory, indulge, lie, lurch, luxuriate, relish, revel, roll, splash, stagger, stumble, tumble, wade, welter.

wan *adj.* anemic, ashen, bleak, bloodless, cadaverous, colorless, dim, discolored, faint, feeble, ghastly, livid, lurid, mournful, pale, pallid, pasty, sickly, waxen, weak, weary, whey-faced, white.

wander *v.* aberrate, babble, cruise, depart, deviate, digress, divagate, diverge, drift, err, hump the bluey, lapse, meander, mill around, peregrinate, ramble, range, rave, roam, rove, saunter, squander, straggle, stravaig, stray, stroll, swerve, traipse, veer, wilder.

n. cruise, excursion, meander, peregrination, ramble, saunter, stroll, traipse.

wane *v.* abate, atrophy, contract, decline, decrease, dim, diminish, droop, drop, dwindle, ebb, fade, fail, lessen, shrink, sink, subside, taper off, weaken, wither.

antonyms increase, wax.

n. abatement, atrophy, contraction, decay, decline, decrease, diminution, drop, dwindling, ebb, fading, failure, fall, lessening, sinking, subsidence, tapering off, weakening.

antonym increase.

want *v.* call for, covet, crave, demand, desiderate, desire, fancy, hanker after, hunger for, lack, long for, miss, need, pine for, require, thirst for, wish, yearn for, yen.

n. absence, appetite, besoin, craving, dearth, default, deficiency, demand, desideratum, desire, destitution, famine, fancy, hankering, hunger, indigence, insufficiency, lack, longing, necessity, need, neediness, paucity, pauperism, penury, poverty, privation, requirement, scantiness, scarcity, shortage, thirst, wish, yearning, yen.

antonyms abundance, plenty, riches.

wanton *adj.* abandoned, arbitrary, careless, coltish, cruel, dissipated, dissolute, evil, extravagant, fast, gratuitous, groundless, heedless, immoderate, immoral, intemperate, lavish, lecherous, lewd, libertine, libidinous, licentious, loose, lubricious, lustful, malevolent, malicious, motiveless, needless, outrageous, promiscuous, rakish, rash, reckless, senseless, shameless, spiteful, uncalled-for, unchaste, unjustifiable, unjustified, unprovoked, unrestrained, vicious, wicked, wild, wilful.

n. baggage, Casanova, debauchee, Don Juan, floozy, harlot, hussy, lecher, libertine, loose woman, profligate, prostitute, rake, roué, slut, strumpet, tart, trollop, voluptuary, wench, whore.

war *n.* battle, bloodshed, combat, conflict, contention, contest, enmity, fighting, hostilities, hostility, jihad, strife, struggle, ultima ratio regum, warfare.

antonym peace.

v. battle, clash, combat, contend, contest, fight, skirmish, strive, struggle, take up arms, wage war.

ward *n.* apartment, area, care, charge, cubicle, custody, dependant, district, division, guardianship, keeping, minor, precinct, protection, protégé, pupil, quarter, room, safe-keeping, vigil, watch, zone.

warden *n.* administrator, captain, caretaker, castellan, châtelaine, concierge, curator, custodian, guardian, janitor, keeper, ranger, steward, superintendent, warder, watchman.

wardrobe *n.* apparel, attire, closet, clothes, cupboard, garderobe, outfit.

warehouse *n.* depository, depot, entrepot, freightshed, godown, hong, repository, stockroom, store, storehouse.

wares *n.* commodities, goods, lines, manufactures, merchandise, produce, products, stock, stuff, vendibles.

wariness *n.* alertness, apprehension, attention, caginess, care, carefulness, caution, circumspection, discretion, distrust, foresight, heedfulness, hesitancy, mindfulness, prudence, suspicion, unease, vigilance, watchfulness.

antonyms heedlessness, recklessness, thoughtlessness.

warlike *adj.* aggressive, antagonistic, bellicose, belligerent, bloodthirsty, combative, hawkish, hostile, inimical, jingoistic, martial, militaristic, military, pugnacious, saber-rattling, truculent, unfriendly.

antonym peaceable.

warm *adj.* affable, affectionate, amiable, amorous, animated, ardent, balmy, calid, cheerful, cordial, dangerous, disagreeable, earnest, effusive, emotional, enthusiastic, excited, fervent, friendly, genial, glowing, happy, hazardous, hearty, heated, hospitable, impassioned, incalescent, intense, irascible, irritable, keen, kindly, lively, loving, lukewarm, passionate, perilous, pleasant,

quick, sensitive, short, spirited, stormy, sunny, tender, tepid, thermal, touchy, tricky, uncomfortable, unpleasant, vehement, vigorous, violent, zealous.
antonyms cool, indifferent, unfriendly.

v. animate, awaken, excite, heat, heat up, interest, melt, mull, put some life into, reheat, rouse, stimulate, stir, thaw, turn on.
antonym cool.

warm-hearted *adj.* affectionate, ardent, compassionate, cordial, generous, genial, kind-hearted, kindly, loving, sympathetic, tender, tender-hearted.
antonyms cold, unsympathetic.

warmth *n.* affability, affection, amorousness, animation, ardor, calidity, cheerfulness, cordiality, eagerness, earnestness, effusiveness, empressement, enthusiasm, excitement, fervency, fervor, fire, happiness, heartiness, heat, hospitableness, hotness, intensity, kindliness, love, passion, spirit, tenderness, transport, vehemence, vigor, violence, warmness, zeal, zest.
antonyms coldness, coolness, unfriendliness.

warn *v.* admonish, advise, alert, apprize, caution, counsel, forewarn, inform, notify, put on one's guard, tip off.

warning *n.* admonishment, admonition, advance notice, advice, alarm, alert, augury, caution, caveat, forenotice, foretoken, forewarning, griffin, hint, larum, larum-bell, lesson, monition, notice, notification, omen, premonition, presage, prodrome, sign, signal, siren, threat, tip, tip-off, token, vigia, word, word to the wise.
adj. admonitory, apposematic, cautionary, in terrorem, monitive, monitory, ominous, premonitory, prodromal, prodromic, threatening.

warp *v.* bend, contort, deform, deviate, distort, kink, misshape, pervert, twist.
antonym straighten.

n. bend, bent, bias, contortion, deformation, deviation, distortion, irregularity, kink, perversion, quirk, turn, twist.

warranty *n.* assurance, authorization, bond, certificate, contract, covenant, guarantee, justification, pledge.

warrior *n.* champion, combatant, fighter, fighting man, knight, man-at-arms, soldier, wardog, war-horse.

wary *adj.* alert, apprehensive, attentive, cagey, careful, cautious, chary, circumspect, distrustful, guarded, hawk-eyed, heedful, leery, on one's guard, on the lookout, on the qui vive, prudent, suspicious, vigilant, watchful, wide-awake.
antonyms careless, foolhardy, heedless, reckless, unwary.

wash¹ *v.* bath, bathe, clean, cleanse, launder, moisten, rinse, scrub, shampoo, shower, sluice, swill, wet.

n. a lick and a promise, ablution, bath, bathe, cleaning, cleansing, coat, coating, ebb and flow, film, flow, laundering, layer, overlay, rinse, roll, screen, scrub, shampoo, shower, souse, stain, suffusion, surge, sweep, swell, washing, wave.

wash² *v.* bear examination, bear scrutiny, carry weight, hold up, hold water, pass muster, stand up, stick.

washed-out *adj.* all in, blanched, bleached, colorless, dead on one's feet, dog-tired, drained, drawn, etiolated, exhausted, faded, fatigued, flat, haggard, knackered, lackluster, mat, pale, pallid, peelie-wally, spent, tiredout, wan, weary, worn-out.

waspish *adj.* bad-tempered, bitchy, cantankerous, cap-

tious, crabbed, crabby, cross, crotchety, fretful, grouchy, grumpy, ill-tempered, irascible, irritable, peevish, peppery, pettish, petulant, prickly, snappish, splenetic, testy, touchy, waxy.

waste *v.* atrophy, blow, consume, corrode, crumble, debilitate, decay, decline, deplete, despoil, destroy, devastate, disable, dissipate, drain, dwindle, eat away, ebb, emaciate, enfeeble, exhaust, fade, fritter away, gnaw, lavish, lay waste, misspend, misuse, perish, pillage, prodigalize, rape, ravage, raze, rig, ruin, sack, sink, spend, spoil, squander, tabefy, throw away, undermine, wane, wanton, wear out, wither.

n. debris, desert, desolation, destruction, devastation, dissipation, dregs, dross, effluent, expenditure, extravagance, garbage, havoc, leavings, leftovers, litter, loss, misapplication, misuse, mullock, offal, offscouring(s), prodigality, ravage, recrement, refuse, rubbish, ruin, scrap, slops, solitude, spoilage, squandering, sweepings, trash, void, wastefulness, wasteland, wild, wilderness.

adj. bare, barren, desolate, devastated, dismal, dreary, empty, extra, left-over, superfluous, supernumerary, uncultivated, uninhabited, unproductive, unprofitable, unused, unwanted, useless, wild, worthless.

wasteful *adj.* dissipative, extravagant, improvident, lavish, prodigal, profligate, ruinous, spendthrift, thriftless, uneconomical, unthrifty.
antonyms economical, frugal, thrifty.

watch¹ *v.* attend, contemplate, eye, gaze at, guard, keep, keep an eye open, look, look after, look at, look on, look out, mark, mind, note, observe, ogle, pay attention, peer at, protect, regard, see, spectate, stare at, superintend, take care of, take heed, tend, view, wait.
n. alertness, attention, eye, heed, inspection, lookout, notice, observation, pernoctation, supervision, surveillance, vigil, vigilance, wake, watchfulness.

watch² *n.* chronometer, clock, ticker, tick-tick, ticktock, timepiece, wristwatch.

watch-dog *n.* custodian, guard dog, guardian, housedog, inspector, monitor, ombudsman, protector, scrutineer, vigilante.

watchful *adj.* alert, attentive, cautious, circumspect, guarded, heedful, observant, on one's guard, on the lookout, on the qui vive, on the watch, suspicious, unmistaking, vigilant, wary, wide awake.
antonym inattentive.

water *n.* Adam's ale, Adam's wine, aqua, lake, ocean, rain, river, saliva, sea, stream, sweat, tears, urine.
v. adulterate, damp, dampen, dilute, douse, drench, drink, flood, hose, irrigate, moisten, soak, souse, spray, sprinkle, thin, water down, weaken.
antonyms dry out, purify, strengthen.

waterfall *n.* cascade, cataract, chute, fall, force, lash, lin(n), torrent.

watery *adj.* adulterated, aqueous, damp, dilute, diluted, flavorless, fluid, humid, hydatoid, insipid, liquid, marshy, moist, poor, rheumy, runny, soggy, squelchy, tasteless, tear-filled, tearful, thin, washy, watereddown, waterish, weak, weepy, wet, wishy-washy.
antonyms solid, strong.

wave¹ *v.* beckon, brandish, direct, flap, flourish, flutter, gesticulate, gesture, indicate, oscillate, quiver, ripple, shake, sign, signal, stir, sway, swing, undulate, waft, wag, waver, weave, wield.

wave² *n.* billow, breaker, comber, current, drift, flood, ground swell, movement, outbreak, rash, ripple, roller, rush, stream, surge, sweep, swell, tendency, tidal wave, trend, tsunami, undulation, unevenness, upsurge, water-wave, wavelet, white horse.

waver *v.* blow hot and cold, dither, falter, flicker, fluctuate, haver, hesitate, hum and haw, quiver, reel, rock, seesaw, shake, shilly-shally, sway, swither, totter, tremble, undulate, vacillate, vary, waffle, wave, weave, wobble.

antonyms decide, stand.

wavering *adj.* dithering, dithery, doubtful, doubting, havering, hesitant, in two minds, shilly-shallying.

antonym determined.

wavy *adj.* curly, curvy, flamboyant, ridged, ridgy, rippled, ripply, sinuate(d), sinuous, undate, undulate, undulated, winding, wrinkled, zigzag.

antonyms flat, smooth.

wax *v.* become, develop, dilate, enlarge, expand, fill out, grow, increase, magnify, mount, rise, swell.

antonym wane.

way *n.* access, advance, aim, ambition, approach, aspect, avenue, channel, characteristic, choice, circumstance, condition, conduct, course, custom, demand, desire, detail, direction, distance, elbow-room, fashion, feature, fettle, gate, goal, habit, headway, highway, idiosyncrasy, journey, lane, length, manner, march, means, method, mode, movement, nature, opening, particular, passage, path, pathway, personality, plan, pleasure, point, practice, procedure, process, progress, respect, road, room, route, scheme, sense, shape, situation, space, state, status, street, stretch, style, system, technique, thoroughfare, track, trail, trait, usage, will, wish, wont.

waylay *v.* accost, ambush, attack, buttonhole, catch, hold up, intercept, lie in wait for, seize, set upon, surprise.

way-out *adj.* advanced, amazing, avant-garde, bizarre, crazy, eccentric, excellent, experimental, fantastic, far-out, freaky, great, marvelous, off-beat, outlandish, progressive, satisfying, tremendous, unconventional, unorthodox, unusual, weird, wild, wonderful.

antonym ordinary.

wayward *adj.* capricious, changeable, contrary, contumacious, cross-grained, disobedient, erratic, fickle, flighty, froward, headstrong, inconstant, incorrigible, insubordinate, intractable, mulish, obdurate, obstinate, perverse, rebellious, refractory, self-willed, stubborn, undependable, ungovernable, unmanageable, unpredictable, unruly, uppity, wilful.

antonyms complaisant, good-natured.

weak *adj.* anemic, asthenic, atonic, cowardly, debile, debilitated, decrepit, defenseless, deficient, delicate, diluted, disturbant, dull, effete, enervated, exhausted, exposed, faint, faulty, feeble, fiberless, flimsy, fragile, frail, helpless, hollow, imperceptible, impotent, inadequate, inconclusive, indecisive, ineffective, ineffectual, infirm, insipid, invalid, irresolute, lacking, lame, languid, low, milk-and-water, muffled, namby-pamby, pathetic, poor, powerless, puny, quiet, runny, shaky, shallow, sickly, slight, small, soft, spent, spineless, substandard, tasteless, tender, thin, timorous, toothless, unconvincing, under-strength, unguarded, unprotected, unresisting, unsafe, unsatisfactory, unsound, unsteady, unstressed, untenable, vulnerable, wanting,

wasted, watery, weak-hearted, weak-kneed, weakly, weak-minded, weak-spirited, wishy-washy.

antonym strong.

weaken *v.* abate, adulterate, craze, cut, debase, debilitate, depress, dilute, diminish, disinvigorate, droop, dwindle, ease up, effeminate, effeminize, emasculate, enervate, enfeeble, fade, fail, flag, give way, impair, invalidate, lessen, lower, mitigate, moderate, reduce, sap, soften up, temper, thin, tire, undermine, wane, water down.

antonym strengthen.

weakling *n.* coward, doormat, drip, milksop, mouse, namby-pamby, puff, pushover, sissy, softling, underdog, underling, wally, weed, wet, wimp, wraith.

antonyms hero, stalwart.

weakness *n.* Achilles' heel, asthenia, atonicity, atony, blemish, debility, decrepitude, defect, deficiency, enervation, enfeeblement, faible, failing, faintness, fault, feebleness, flaw, foible, fondness, fragility, frailty, imperfection, impotence, inclination, infirmity, irresolution, lack, liking, passion, penchant, powerlessness, predilection, proclivity, proneness, shortcoming, soft spot, soft underbelly, underbelly, vulnerability, weakpoint, weediness.

antonyms dislike, strength.

wealth *n.* abundance, affluence, assets, bounty, capital, cash, copiousness, cornucopia, estate, fortune, fullness, funds, golden calf, goods, klondike, lucre, mammon, means, money, opulence, pelf, plenitude, plenty, possessions, profusion, property, prosperity, resources, riches, richness, store, substance.

antonym poverty.

wealthy *adj.* affluent, comfortable, easy, filthy rich, flush, living in clover, loaded, moneyed, opulent, prosperous, rich, rolling in it, well-heeled, well-off, well-to-do.

antonym poor.

wear *v.* abrade, accept, allow, annoy, bear, bear up, believe, brook, carry, consume, corrode, countenance, deteriorate, display, don, drain, dress in, endure, enervate, erode, exasperate, exhibit, fall for, fatigue, fly, fray, grind, harass, have on, hold up, irk, last, permit, pester, put on, put up with, rub, show, sport, stand for, stand up, stomach, swallow, take, tax, tolerate, undermine, use, vex, waste, weaken, weary.

n. abrasion, apparel, attire, attrition, clothes, corrosion, costume, damage, depreciation, deterioration, dress, durability, employment, erosion, friction, garb, garments, gear, habit, mileage, outfit, service, things, use, usefulness, utility, wear and tear.

weariness *n.* drowsiness, enervation, ennui, exhaustion, fatigue, languor, lassitude, lethargy, listlessness, prostration, sleepiness, tiredness.

antonym freshness.

wearisome *adj.* annoying, boring, bothersome, burdensome, dreary, dull, ennuying, exasperating, exhausting, fatiguing, humdrum, irksome, monotonous, oppressive, pestilential, prolix, prosaic, protracted, tedious, troublesome, trying, vexatious, weariful, wearing.

antonym refreshing.

weary *adj.* all in, arduous, awearied, aweary, beat, bored, browned-off, dead beat, dead on one's feet, discontented, dog-tired, drained, drooping, drowsy, enervated, enervative, ennuied, ennuyé, exhausted, fagged, fatigued, fed up, flagging, impatient, indifferent, irksome, jaded, knackered, laborious, sick, sick and tired, sleepy, spent, taxing, tired, tiresome, tiring, wayworn, wearied, wearing, wearisome, whacked, worn out.

antonyms excited, fresh, lively.

v. annoy, betoil, bore, bug, burden, debilitate, drain, droop, enervate, ennui, exasperate, fade, fag, fail, fatigue, irk, irritate, jade, plague, sap, sicken, tax, tire, tire out, wear out.

weather *n.* climate, conditions, rainfall, temperature.

v. brave, come through, endure, expose, harden, live through, overcome, pull through, resist, ride out, rise above, season, stand, stick out, suffer, surmount, survive, toughen, weather out, withstand.

antonym succumb.

weave *v.* blend, braid, build, construct, contrive, create, criss-cross, entwine, fabricate, fuse, incorporate, intercross, interdigitate, interlace, intermingle, intertwine, introduce, knit, make, mat, merge, plait, put together, spin, twist, unite, wind, zigzag.

web *n.* interlacing, lattice, mesh, mesh-work, net, netting, network, palama, screen, snare, tangle, tela, texture, toils, trap, weave, webbing, weft.

wed *v.* ally, blend, coalesce, combine, commingle, dedicate, espouse, fuse, get hitched, interweave, join, jump the broomstick, link, marry, merge, splice, tie the knot, unify, unite, wive, yoke.

antonym divorce.

wedlock *n.* holy matrimony, marriage, matrimony, union.

wee *adj.* diminutive, insignificant, itsy-bitsy, Lilliputian, little, microscopic, midget, miniature, minuscule, minute, negligible, small, teeny, teeny-weeny, tiny, weeny.

antonym large.

weep *v.* bemoan, bewail, blub, blubber, boo-hoo, bubble, complain, cry, drip, exude, greet, keen, lament, leak, moan, mourn, ooze, pipe, pipe one's eye, pour forth, pour out, rain, snivel, sob, tune one's pipes, ululate, whimper, whinge.

antonym rejoice.

n. blub, bubble, cry, greet, lament, moan, snivel, sob.

weigh *v.* bear down, burden, carry weight, consider, contemplate, count, deliberate, evaluate, examine, give thought to, impress, matter, meditate on, mull over, oppress, ponder, ponderate, prey, reflect on, study, tell, think over.

antonyms cut no ice, hearten.

weight *n.* authority, avoirdupois, ballast, burden, clout, consequence, consideration, efficacy, emphasis, force, gravity, heaviness, heft, impact, import, importance, impressiveness, influence, load, mass, millstone, moment, onus, oppression, persuasiveness, ponderance, ponderancy, poundage, power, preponderance, pressure, significance, strain, substance, tonnage, value.

antonym lightness.

v. ballast, bias, burden, charge, encumber, freight, handicap, hold down, impede, keep down, load, oppress, overburden, slant, unbalance, weigh down.

antonym lighten.

weird *adj.* bizarre, creepy, eerie, eldritch, freakish, ghostly, grotesque, mysterious, odd, outlandish, preternatural, queer, spooky, strange, superlunar, supernatural, uncanny, unco, unearthly, unnatural, witching.

antonym normal.

welcome *adj.* able, acceptable, accepted, agreeable, allowed, appreciated, delightful, desirable, entitled, free, gratifying, permitted, pleasant, pleasing, refreshing.

antonym unwelcome.

n. acceptance, greeting, hospitality, reception, red carpet, salaam, salutation.

v. accept, approve of, embrace, greet, hail, meet, receive, roll out the red carpet for.

antonyms reject, snub.

weld *v.* bind, bond, cement, connect, fuse, join, link, seal, solder, unite.

antonym separate.

n. bond, joint, seal, seam.

welfare *n.* advantage, benefit, good, happiness, heal, health, interest, profit, prosperity, success, weal, well-being.

antonym harm.

well[1] *n.* bore, cavity, fount, fountain, hole, lift-shaft, mine, pit, pool, repository, shaft, source, spring, water-hole, well-spring.

v. brim over, flood, flow, gush, jet, ooze, pour, rise, run, seep, spout, spring, spurt, stream, surge, swell, trickle.

well[2] *adv.* ably, abundantly, accurately, adeptly, adequately, admirably, agreeably, amply, approvingly, attentively, capitally, carefully, clearly, closely, comfortably, completely, conscientiously, considerably, correctly, deeply, easily, effectively, efficiently, expertly, fairly, famously, favorably, fittingly, flourishingly, fully, glowingly, graciously, greatly, happily, heartily, highly, intimately, justly, kindly, nicely, personally, pleasantly, possibly, proficiently, profoundly, properly, prosperously, readily, rightly, satisfactorily, skilfully, smoothly, splendidly, substantially, successfully, sufficiently, suitably, thoroughly, warmly.

antonym badly.

adj. A1, able-bodied, advisable, agreeable, bright, fine, fit, fitting, flourishing, fortunate, good, great, hale, happy, healthy, hearty, in fine fettle, in good health, lucky, on the top of the world, pleasing, profitable, proper, prudent, right, robust, satisfactory, sound, strong, thriving, up to par, useful.

antonyms bad, ill.

well-being *n.* comfort, contentment, good, happiness, prosperity, weal, welfare.

antonyms discomfort, harm.

well-bred *adj.* aristocratic, blue-blooded, civil, courteous, courtly, cultivated, cultured, gallant, genteel, gentle, gentlemanly, highborn, ladylike, mannerly, noble, patrician, polished, polite, refined, titled, uppercrust, urbane, well-born, well-brought-up, well-mannered.

antonym ill-bred.

well-known *adj.* celebrated, famed, familiar, famous, illustrious, notable, noted, popular, renowned.

antonym unknown.

well-off *adj.* affluent, comfortable, flourishing, flush, fortunate, in the money, loaded, lucky, moneyed, prosperous, rich, successful, thriving, warm, wealthy, well-heeled, well-to-do.

antonym poor.

well-thought-of *adj.* admired, esteemed, highly regarded, honored, reputable, respected, revered, venerated, weighty.
antonym despised.

well-to-do *adj.* affluent, comfortable, flush, loaded, moneyed, prosperous, rich, warm, wealthy, well-heeled, well-off.
antonym poor.

welsh *v.* cheat, defraud, diddle, do, swindle, welch.

wet *adj.* boggy, clammy, damp, dank, drenched, dripping, drizzling, effete, feeble, foolish, humid, ineffectual, irresolute, misty, moist, moistened, namby-pamby, pouring, raining, rainy, saturated, showery, silly, sloppy, soaked, soaking, sodden, soft, soggy, sopping, soppy, soused, spineless, spongy, teeming, timorous, waterlogged, watery, weak, weedy.
antonyms dry, resolute, strong.

n. clamminess, condensation, damp, dampness, drip, drizzle, humidity, liquid, milksop, moisture, rain, rains, sap, water, weakling, weed, wetness, wimp.
antonyms dryness.

v. bedabble, bedew, bedrench, damp, dampen, dip, douse, drench, humidify, imbue, irrigate, moisten, saturate, sluice, soak, splash, spray, sprinkle, steep, water.
antonym dry.

wharf *n.* dock, dockyard, jetty, landing-stage, marina, pier, quay, quayside.

wheedle *v.* cajole, charm, coax, court, draw, entice, flatter, importune, inveigle, persuade, whilly, whil-lywha(w).
antonym force.

whereabouts *n.* location, place, position, site, situation, vicinity.

wherewithal *n.* capital, cash, funds, means, money, necessary, readies, resources, supplies.

whim *n.* caprice, chimera, conceit, concetto, crank, craze, crotchet, fad, fancy, fizgig, flam, freak, humor, impulse, maggot, notion, quirk, sport, urge, vagary, whims(e)y.

whimper *v.* blub, blubber, cry, girn, grizzle, mewl, moan, pule, snivel, sob, weep, whine, whinge.
n. girn, moan, snivel, sob, whine.

whimsical *adj.* capricious, chimeric(al), crotchety, curious, dotty, droll, eccentric, fanciful, fantastic(al), freakish, funny, maggoty, mischievous, odd, peculiar, playful, quaint, queer, singular, unusual, waggish, weird, whimmy.
antonym sensible.

whine *n.* beef, belly-ache, complaint, cry, girn, gripe, grouch, grouse, grumble, moan, sob, wail, whimper.
v. beef, belly-ache, carp, complain, cry, girn, gripe, grizzle, grouch, grouse, grumble, kvetch, moan, sob, wail, whimper, whinge.

whip *v.* agitate, beat, best, birch, cane, castigate, clobber, compel, conquer, dart, dash, defeat, dive, drive, drub, flagellate, flash, flit, flog, flounce, fly, foment, goad, hammer, hound, incite, instigate, jambok, jerk, knout, lash, leather, lick, outdo, overcome, overpower, overwhelm, paddle, prick, prod, produce, provoke, pull, punish, push, quirt, remove, rout, rush, scourge, shoot, sjambok, snatch, spank, spur, stir, strap, switch, tan, tear, thrash, trounce, urge, whale, whisk, whop, worst.
n. birch, bullwhip, cane, cat, cat-o'-nine-tails, crop,

flagellum, horsewhip, jambok, knout, lash, paddle, quirt, rawhide, riding-crop, scourge, sjambok, switch, thong.

whirl *v.* birl, circle, gyrate, gyre, pirouette, pivot, reel, revolve, roll, rotate, spin, swirl, swivel, turn, twirl, twist, wheel.
n. agitation, birl, bustle, circle, commotion, confusion, daze, dither, flurry, giddiness, gyration, gyre, hubbub, hubbuboo, hurly-burly, merry-go-round, pirouette, reel, revolution, roll, rotation, round, series, spin, stir, succession, swirl, tumult, turn, twirl, twist, uproar, vortex, wheel, whorl.
antonym calm.

whisk *v.* beat, brush, dart, dash, flick, fly, grab, hasten, hurry, race, rush, scoot, shoot, speed, sweep, swipe, tear, twitch, whip, wipe.
n. beater, brush, swizzle-stick.

whisk(e)y *n.* barley-bree, bourbon, Canadian, corn, John Barleycorn, Irish, malt, mountain dew, peat-reek, rye, Scotch, usquebaugh.

whisper *v.* breathe, buzz, divulge, gossip, hint, hiss, insinuate, intimate, murmur, rustle, sigh, sough, susurrate, tittle.
antonym shout.
n. breath, buzz, gossip, hint, hiss, innuendo, insinuation, murmur, report, rumor, rustle, shadow, sigh, sighing, soughing, soupçon, suggestion, suspicion, susurration, susurrus, swish, tinge, trace, underbreath, undertone, whiff, word.
antonym roar.

whistle *n.* call, cheep, chirp, hooter, siren, song, warble.
v. call, cheep, chirp, pipe, siffle, sing, warble, wheeze, whiss.

whole *adj.* better, complete, cured, entire, faultless, fit, flawless, full, good, hale, healed, healthy, in one piece, intact, integral, integrate, inviolate, mint, perfect, recovered, robust, sound, strong, total, unabbreviated, unabridged, unbroken, uncut, undamaged, undivided, unedited, unexpurgated, unharmed, unhurt, unimpaired, uninjured, unmutilated, unscathed, untouched, well.
antonyms damaged, ill, partial.
n. aggregate, all, ensemble, entirety, entity, everything, fullness, Gestalt, lot, piece, total, totality, unit, unity.
antonym part.

wholesome *adj.* advantageous, beneficial, clean, decent, edifying, exemplary, good, healthful, health-giving, healthy, helpful, honorable, hygienic, improving, innocent, invigorating, moral, nice, nourishing, nutritious, propitious, pure, respectable, righteous, salubrious, salutary, sanitary, uplifting, virtuous, worthy.
antonym unwholesome.

wholly *adv.* absolutely, all, altogether, completely, comprehensively, entirely, exclusively, fully, in toto, only, perfectly, solely, thoroughly, through and through, totally, utterly.
antonym partly.

wicked *adj.* abandoned, abominable, acute, agonizing, amoral, arch, atrocious, awful, bad, black-hearted, bothersome, corrupt, debased, depraved, destructive, devilish, difficult, dissolute, distressing, dreadful, egregious, evil, facinorous, fearful, fiendish, fierce, flagitious, foul, galling, guilty, harmful, heinous, immoral, impious, impish, incorrigible, inexpiable, iniquitous, injurious, intense, irreligious, mighty, mischievous, nasty, naughty, nefarious, nefast, offensive, painful, piacular, rascal-like, rascally, roguish, scandalous, severe, shameful, sinful, spiteful, terrible, troublesome, trying, ungodly, unpleasant, unprincipled, unrighteous, vicious, vile, villainous, worthless.

antonyms good, harmless, modest, upright.

wide *adj.* ample, away, baggy, broad, capacious, catholic, commodious, comprehensive, diffuse, dilated, distant, distended, encyclopedic, expanded, expansive, extensive, far-reaching, full, general, immense, inclusive, large, latitudinous, loose, off, off-course, off-target, outspread, outstretched, remote, roomy, spacious, sweeping, vast.

antonyms limited, narrow.

adv. aside, astray, off course, off target, off the mark, out.

antonym on target.

wide-awake *adj.* alert, astute, aware, conscious, fully awake, heedful, keen, observant, on one's toes, on the alert, on the ball, on the qui vive, quick-witted, roused, sharp, vigilant, wakened, wary, watchful.

antonym asleep.

width *n.* amplitude, beam, breadth, compass, diameter, extent, girth, measure, range, reach, scope, span, thickness, wideness.

wield *v.* apply, brandish, command, control, employ, exercise, exert, flourish, handle, have, hold, maintain, manage, manipulate, ply, possess, swing, use, utilize, wave, weave.

wild *adj.* agrest(i)al, barbaric, barbarous, berserk, blustery, boisterous, brutish, chaotic, chimeric(al), choppy, crazed, crazy, daft, delirious, demented, desert, deserted, desolate, disheveled, disordered, disorderly, eager, empty, enthusiastic, excited, extravagant, fantastic, ferae naturae, feral, feralized, ferine, ferocious, fierce, flighty, foolhardy, foolish, frantic, free, frenzied, furious, giddy, god-forsaken, howling, hysterical, ill-considered, impetuous, impracticable, imprudent, inaccurate, indigenous, intense, irrational, lawless, mad, madcap, maniacal, native, natural, noisy, nuts, outrageous, potty, preposterous, primitive, rabid, raging, rash, raving, reckless, riotous, rough, rowdy, rude, savage, self-willed, tempestuous, tousled, trackless, turbulent, unbridled, unbroken, uncheated, uncivilized, uncontrollable, uncontrolled, uncultivated, undisciplined, undomesticated, unfettered, ungovernable, uninhabited, unjustified, unkempt, unmanageable, unpopulated, unpruned, unrestrained, unruly, unsubstantiated, untamed, untidy, uproarious, violent, virgin, wayward, woolly.

antonyms civilized, peaceful, sane, sensible, tame, unenthusiastic.

wilderness *n.* clutter, confusion, congeries, desert, jumble, jungle, mass, maze, muddle, tangle, waste, wasteland, welter, wild, wild-land.

wile *n.* artfulness, artifice, cheating, chicanery, contrivance, craft, craftiness, cunning, deceit, device, dodge, expedient, fraud, guile, hanky-panky, imposition, lure, maneuver, ploy, ruse, slyness, stratagem, subterfuge, trick, trickery.

antonym guilelessness.

wilful *adj.* adamant, bloody-minded, bull-headed, conscious, deliberate, determined, dogged, froward, headstrong, inflexible, intended, intentional, intractable, intransigent, mulish, obdurate, obstinate, persistent,

perverse, pig-headed, purposeful, refractory, self-willed, stubborn, thrawn, uncompromising, unyielding, volitional, voluntary.

antonyms complaisant, good-natured.

will *n.* aim, attitude, choice, command, decision, declaration, decree, desire, determination, discretion, disposition, fancy, feeling, inclination, intention, mind, option, pleasure, preference, prerogative, purpose, resolution, resolve, testament, velleity, volition, will power, wish, wishes.

v. bequeath, bid, cause, choose, command, confer, decree, desire, determine, devise, direct, dispose of, elect, give, leave, opt, ordain, order, pass on, resolve, transfer, want, wish.

willing *adj.* agreeable, amenable, biddable, compliant, consenting, content, desirous, disposed, eager, enthusiastic, favorable, game, happy, inclined, nothing lo(a)th, pleased, prepared, ready, so-minded, volitient, willing-hearted.

antonym unwilling.

wilt *v.* atrophy, diminish, droop, dwindle, ebb, fade, fail, flag, flop, languish, melt away, sag, shrivel, sink, wane, weaken, wither.

antonym perk up.

wily *adj.* arch, artful, astute, cagey, crafty, crooked, cunning, deceitful, deceptive, designing, fly, foxy, guileful, intriguing, long-headed, Machiavellian, scheming, sharp, shifty, shrewd, sly, tricky, underhand, versute, wileful.

antonym guileless.

win *v.* accomplish, achieve, acquire, attain, bag, capture, catch, collect, come away with, conquer, earn, gain, get, net, obtain, overcome, pick up, prevail, procure, receive, secure, succeed, sweep the board, triumph.

antonym lose.

n. conquest, mastery, success, triumph, victory.

antonym defeat.

wind[1] *n.* air, air-current, babble, blast, blather, bluster, boasting, breath, breeze, clue, current, cyclone, draft, flatulence, flatus, gab, gale, gas, gust, hint, hot air, humbug, hurricane, idle talk, inkling, intimation, northeaster, notice, puff, report, respiration, rumor, sirocco, southwester, suggestion, talk, tidings, tornado, twister, typhoon, warning, whisper, williwaw, windiness, zephyr.

wind[2] *v.* bend, coil, curl, curve, deviate, encircle, furl, loop, meander, ramble, reel, roll, serpent, serpentine, serpentinize, snake, spiral, turn, twine, twist, wreath, zigzag.

n. bend, curve, meander, turn, twist, zigzag.

windfall *n.* bonanza, find, godsend, jackpot, manna, pennies from heaven, stroke of luck, treasure-trove.

windy *adj.* afraid, blowy, blustering, blustery, boastful, boisterous, bombastic, breezy, changeable, chicken, conceited, cowardly, diffuse, empty, fearful, flatulent, flatuous, frightened, garrulous, gusty, long-winded, loquacious, meandering, nervous, pompous, prolix, rambling, scared, squally, stormy, tempestuous, thrasonic, timid, turgid, ventose, verbose, wild, windswept, wordy.

antonyms calm, fearless, modest.

wing *n.* adjunct, annexe, arm, branch, circle, clique, coterie, extension, faction, fender, flank, group, grouping, pinion, protection, section, segment, set, side.

v. clip, fleet, flit, fly, glide, hasten, hit, hurry, move, nick, pass, race, soar, speed, travel, wound, zoom.

wink *v.* bat, blink, flash, flicker, flutter, gleam, glimmer, glint, nictate, nictitate, pink, sparkle, twinkle.

n. blink, flash, flutter, gleam, glimmering, glint, hint, instant, jiffy, moment, nictation, nictitation, second, sparkle, split second, twinkle, twinkling.

winnow *v.* comb, cull, diffuse, divide, fan, part, screen, select, separate, sift, waft.

winsome *adj.* agreeable, alluring, amiable, attractive, bewitching, captivating, charming, cheerful, comely, delectable, disarming, enchanting, endearing, engaging, fair, fascinating, fetching, graceful, pleasant, pleasing, prepossessing, pretty, sweet, taking, winning.
antonym unattractive.

wire-pulling *n.* clout, conspiring, influence, intrigue, Machiavellianism, manipulation, plotting, pull, scheming.

wisdom *n.* anthroposophy, astuteness, circumspection, comprehension, discernment, enlightenment, erudition, foresight, gnosis, intelligence, judgment, judiciousness, knowledge, learning, penetration, prudence, reason, sagacity, sapience, sense, sophia, understanding.
antonym folly.

wise *adj.* aware, clever, discerning, enlightened, erudite, informed, intelligent, judicious, knowing, long-headed, long-sighted, perceptive, politic, prudent, rational, reasonable, sagacious, sage, sapient, sensible, shrewd, sound, understanding, well-advised, well-informed.
antonym foolish.

wish *v.* ask, aspire, bid, command, covet, crave, desiderate, desire, direct, greet, hanker, hope, hunger, instruct, long, need, order, require, thirst, want, whim, yearn, yen.
antonyms dislike, fear.

n. aspiration, bidding, command, desire, hankering, hope, hunger, inclination, intention, liking, order, request, thirst, urge, velleity, voice, want, whim, will, yearning, yen.
antonyms dislike, fear.

wispy *adj.* attenuate, attenuated, delicate, diaphanous, ethereal, faint, fine, flimsy, flyaway, fragile, frail, gossamer, insubstantial, light, thin, unsubstantial.
antonym substantial.

wistful *adj.* contemplative, disconsolate, dreaming, dreamy, forlorn, longing, meditative, melancholy, mournful, musing, pensive, reflective, sad, soulful, thoughtful, wishful, yearning.

wit *n.* acumen, badinage, banter, brains, card, cleverness, comedian, common sense, comprehension, conceit, discernment, drollery, epigrammatist, eutrapelia, facetiousness, farceur, fun, homme d'esprit, humorist, humor, ingenuity, insight, intellect, intelligence, jocularity, joker, judgment, levity, merum sal, mind, nous, perception, pleasantry, punster, quipster, raillery, reason, repartee, sense, smeddum, understanding, wag, wisdom, wit-cracker, wordplay.
antonyms seriousness, stupidity.

witch *n.* enchantress, hag, hex, lamia, magician, necromancer, occultist, pythoness, sorceress, sortileger, weird, wise woman, witch-wife.

witchcraft *n.* black magic, conjuration, divination, enchantment, glamor, goety, incantation, invultuation, magic, myalism, necromancy, occultism, pishogue, sorcery, sortilege, sortilegy, spell, the black art, the occult, voodoo, witchery, witching, wizardry.

withdraw *v.* abjure, absent oneself, back out, depart, disavow, disclaim, disengage, disenrol, disinvest, draw back, draw out, drop out, extract, fall back, go, go away, hive off, leave, pull back, pull out, recall, recant, remove, repair, rescind, retire, retract, retreat, revoke, secede, subduct, subtract, take away, take back, take off, unsay, waive.
antonyms advance, deposit, persist.

wither *v.* abash, blast, blight, decay, decline, desiccate, disintegrate, droop, dry, fade, humiliate, languish, miff, mortify, perish, put down, shame, shrink, shrivel, snub, wane, waste, welt, wilt.
antonyms boost, thrive.

withhold *v.* check, conceal, deduct, detain, hide, keen, keep back, refuse, repress, reserve, resist, restrain, retain, sit on, suppress, suspend.
antonyms accord, give.

withstand *v.* bear, brave, combat, confront, cope with, defy, endure, face, grapple with, hold off, hold one's ground, hold out, last out, oppose, put up with, resist, stand, stand fast, stand one's ground, stand up to, survive, take, take on, thwart, tolerate, weather.
antonyms collapse, yield.

witness *n.* attestant, beholder, bystander, corroborator, deponent, eye-witness, looker-on, observer, onlooker, spectator, testifier, viewer, vouchee, voucher, watcher, witnesser.
v. attend, attest, bear out, bear witness, confirm, corroborate, countersign, depone, depose, endorse, look on, mark, note, notice, observe, perceive, see, sign, testify, view, watch.

wits *n.* acumen, astuteness, brains, cleverness, comprehension, faculties, gumption, ingenuity, intelligence, judgment, marbles, mother-wit, nous, reason, sense, understanding.
antonym stupidity.

witty *adj.* amusing, brilliant, clever, comic, droll, epigrammatic, facetious, fanciful, funny, humorous, ingenious, jocular, lively, original, piquant, salty, sparkling, waggish, whimsical.
antonyms dull, unamusing.

wizard[1] *n.* conjurer, enchanter, mage, magician, magus, necromancer, occultist, shaman, sorcerer, sortileger, thaumaturge, warlock, witch.

wizard[2] *n.* ace, adept, dabster, deacon, expert, genius, hotshot, maestro, master, prodigy, star, virtuoso, whiz.
antonym duffer.
adj. ace, brilliant, enjoyable, fab, fantastic, good, great, marvelous, sensational, smashing, super, superb, terrif, terrific, tiptop, topping, tremendous, wonderful.
antonym rotten.

wizardry *n.* black magic, conjuration, divination, enchantment, glamor, goety, incantation, invultuation, magic, myalism, necromancy, occultism, pishogue, sorcery, sortilege, sortilegy, the black art, the occult, voodoo, warlockry, witchcraft, witchery, witching.

woe *n.* adversity, affliction, agony, anguish, burden, curse, dejection, depression, disaster, distress, dole, dolor, dule, gloom, grief, hardship, heartache, heartbreak, melancholy, misery, misfortune, pain, sadness, sorrow, suffering, tears, trial, tribulation, trouble, unhappiness, wretchedness.
antonym joy.

woebegone *adj.* blue, crestfallen, dejected, disconsolate, dispirited, doleful, down in the mouth, downcast, downhearted, forlorn, gloomy, grief-stricken, hangdog, long-faced, lugubrious, miserable, mournful, sad, sorrowful, tearful, tear-stained, troubled, wretched. *antonym* joyful.

woman *n.* bride, broad, chambermaid, char, charwoman, chick, dame, daughter, domestic, fair, female, feme, femme, Frau, girl, girlfriend, handmaiden, housekeeper, kept woman, lady, lady-in-waiting, ladylove, lass, lassie, maid, maiden, maidservant, mate, miss, mistress, old lady, partner, piece, she, sheila, spouse, sweetheart, vrouw, wife, woman-body. *antonym* man.

womanly *adj.* female, feminine, ladylike, matronly, motherly, weak, womanish. *antonym* manly.

wonder *n.* admiration, amaze, amazement, astonishment, awe, bewilderment, curiosity, fascination, marvel, miracle, nonpareil, phenomenon, portent, prodigy, rarity, sight, spectacle, stupefaction, surprise, wonderment, wunderkind. *antonyms* disinterest, ordinariness.
v. ask oneself, boggle, conjecture, doubt, gape, gaup, gawk, inquire, marvel, meditate, ponder, puzzle, query, question, speculate, stare, think.

wonderful *adj.* ace, admirable, amazing, astonishing, astounding, awe-inspiring, awesome, brilliant, épatant, excellent, extraordinary, fab, fabulous, fantastic, great, incredible, magnificent, marvelous, miraculous, mirific(al), odd, oustanding, peculiar, phenomenal, remarkable, sensational, smashing, staggering, startling, strange, stupendous, super, superb, surprising, terrif, terrific, tiptop, top-hole, topping, tremendous, unheard-of, wizard, wondrous. *antonyms* ordinary, rotten.

wont *adj.* accustomed, given, habituated, used.
n. custom, habit, practice, routine, rule, use, way.

wooden *adj.* awkward, blank, clumsy, colorless, deadpan, dense, dim, dim-witted, dull, dull-witted, emotionless, empty, expressionless, gauche, gawky, glassy, graceless, inelegant, inflexible, lifeless, ligneous, maladroit, muffled, oaken, obstinate, obtuse, rigid, slow, spiritless, stiff, stupid, thick, timber, treen, unbending, unemotional, ungainly, unresponsive, unyielding, vacant, woody, xyloid. *antonyms* bright, lively.

word *n.* account, advice, affirmation, assertion, assurance, bidding, bulletin, chat, colloquy, command, commandment, comment, communication, communiqué, confab, confabulation, consultation, conversation, countersign, declaration, decree, discussion, dispatch, edict, expression, firman, go-ahead, green light, guarantee, hint, information, intelligence, interlocution, intimation, lexigram, locution, mandate, message, news, notice, oath, order, palabra, parole, password, pledge, promise, remark, report, rescript, rumor, sign, signal, slogan, talk, term, tête-à-tête, tidings, ukase, undertaking, utterance, vocable, vow, war-cry, watch-word, will.
v. couch, explain, express, phrase, put, say, write.

wordy *adj.* diffuse, discursive, garrulous, longiloquent, long-winded, loquacious, phrasy, pleonastic, prolix, rambling, verbose, windy. *antonyms* concise, laconic.

work *n.* achievement, art, assignment, book, business, calling, chore, commission, composition, craft, creation, darg, deed, doings, drudgery, duty, effort, elbow grease, employ, employment, exertion, graft, grind, handiwork, industry, job, labor, line, livelihood, métier, occupation, oeuvre, office, opus, ouvrage, performance, piece, play, poem, production, profession, pursuit, service, skill, slog, stint, sweat, task, toil, trade, travail, undertaking, workload, workmanship. *antonyms* hobby, play, rest.
v. accomplish, achieve, act, arrange, beaver, bring about, bring off, cause, contrive, control, convulse, create, cultivate, dig, direct, drive, drudge, effect, encompass, execute, exploit, farm, fashion, fiddle, fix, force, form, function, go, graft, handle, implement, knead, labor, make, manage, maneuver, manipulate, mold, move, operate, peg away, perform, ply, process, progress, pull off, run, shape, slave, slog, sweat, swing, till, toil, twitch, use, wield, writhe. *antonyms* fail, play, rest.

workable *adj.* doable, effectible, feasible, possible, practicable, practical, realistic, viable. *antonym* unworkable.

working *n.* action, functioning, manner, method, operation, routine, running.
adj. active, employed, functioning, going, laboring, operational, operative, running. *antonyms* idle, inoperative, retired, unemployed.

workmanlike *adj.* adept, careful, efficient, expert, masterly, painstaking, professional, proficient, satisfactory, skilful, skilled, thorough, workmanly. *antonym* amateurish.

workmanship *n.* art, artistry, craft, craftsmanship, execution, expertise, facture, finish, handicraft, handiwork, manufacture, skill, technique, work.

world *n.* age, area, class, creation, days, division, domain, earth, environment, epoch, era, existence, field, globe, human race, humanity, humankind, kingdom, life, man, mankind, men, nature, people, period, planet, province, public, realm, society, sphere, star, system, terrene, times, universe, Welt.

worldly *adj.* ambitious, avaricious, blasé, carnal, cosmopolitan, covetous, earthly, experienced, fleshly, grasping, greedy, knowing, lay, materialistic, mundane, physical, politic, profane, secular, selfish, sophisticated, sublunary, temporal, terrene, terrestrial, unspiritual, urbane, worldly-minded, worldly-wise. *antonym* unworldly.

worn *adj.* attrite, bromidic, careworn, clichéd, drawn, exhausted, fatigued, frayed, hackneyed, haggard, jaded, lined, pinched, played-out, ragged, shabby, shiny, spent, tattered, tatty, threadbare, tired, trite, wearied, weary, wizened, woe-wearied, woe-worn, worn-out. *antonyms* fresh, new.

worried *adj.* afraid, agonized, anxious, apprehensive, bothered, concerned, distracted, distraught, distressed, disturbed, fearful, frabbit, fretful, frightened, ill at ease, nervous, on edge, overwrought, perturbed, strained, tense, tormented, troubled, uneasy, unquiet, upset. *antonyms* calm, unconcerned, unworried.

worry *v.* agonize, annoy, attack, badger, bite, bother, brood, disquiet, distress, disturb, faze, fret, get one's knickers in a twist, gnaw at, go for, harass, harry, hassle, hector, importune, irritate, kill, lacerate, nag, perturb, pester, plague, savage, tantalize, tear, tease, torment, trouble, unsettle, upset, vex.

antonyms comfort, reassure.

n. agitation, annoyance, anxiety, apprehension, care, concern, disturbance, fear, irritation, misery, misgiving, perplexity, pest, plague, problem, stew, tew, tizz, tizzy, torment, trial, trouble, unease, vexation, woe, worriment.

antonyms comfort, reassurance.

worsen *v.* aggravate, damage, decay, decline, degenerate, deteriorate, disimprove, exacerbate, go downhill, pejorate, retrogress, sink, take a turn for the worse.

antonym improve.

worship *v.* adore, adulate, deify, exalt, glorify, honor, idolatrize, idolize, kanticoy, laud, love, misworship, praise, pray to, respect, revere, reverence, venerate.

antonym despise.

n. adoration, adulation, deification, devotion(s), dulia, exaltation, glorification, glory, homage, honor, hyperdulia, image-worship, knee-drill, latria, latry, laudation, love, misdevotion, misworship, monolatry, praise, prayer(s), regard, respect, reverence, willworship.

antonym vilification.

worth *n.* aid, assistance, avail, benefit, cost, credit, desert(s), excellence, goodness, help, importance, merit, price, quality, rate, significance, use, usefulness, utility, value, virtue, worthiness.

antonym worthlessness.

worthless *adj.* abandoned, abject, base, beggarly, contemptible, depraved, despicable, draffish, draffy, futile, good-for-nothing, grotty, ignoble, ineffectual, insignificant, littleworth, meaningless, miserable, no use, no-account, nugatory, paltry, pointless, poor, rubbishy, scabbed, scabby, screwy, stramineous, trashy, trifling, trivial, unavailing, unimportant, unusable, useless, valueless, vaurien, vile, wretched.

antonym valuable.

worthy *adj.* admirable, appropriate, commendable, creditable, decent, dependable, deserving, estimable, excellent, fit, good, honest, honorable, laudable, meritorious, praiseworthy, reliable, reputable, respectable, righteous, suitable, upright, valuable, virtuous, worthwhile.

antonyms disreputable, unworthy.

n. big cheese, big noise, big pot, big shot, big-wig, dignitary, luminary, name, notable, personage.

wound *n.* anguish, cut, damage, distress, gash, grief, harm, heartbreak, hurt, injury, insult, laceration, lesion, offense, pain, pang, scar, shock, slash, slight, torment, torture, trauma.

v. annoy, bless, cut, cut to the quick, damage, distress, gash, grieve, harm, hit, hurt, injure, irritate, lacerate, mortify, offend, pain, pierce, pip, shock, slash, sting, traumatize, wing, wring someone's withers.

wrangle *n.* altercation, argument, argy-bargy, barney, bickering, brawl, clash, contest, controversy, dispute, quarrel, row, set-to, slanging match, squabble, tiff, tussle.

antonym agreement.

v. altercate, argue, argufy, bicker, brawl, contend, digladiate, disagree, dispute, ergotize, fall out, fight, quarrel, row, scrap, squabble.

antonym agree.

wrap *v.* absorb, bind, bundle up, cloak, cocoon, cover, encase, enclose, enfold, envelop, fold, hap, immerse, muffle, pack, package, roll up, sheathe, shroud, surround, swathe, wind.

antonym unwrap.

n. cape, cloak, mantle, pelisse, robe, shawl, stole.

wrath *n.* anger, bitterness, choler, displeasure, exasperation, fury, indignation, ire, irritation, passion, rage, resentment, spleen, temper.

antonyms calm, pleasure.

wreck *v.* break, crab, demolish, destroy, devastate, mar, play havoc with, ravage, ruin, shatter, smash, spoil, torpedo, write off.

antonyms repair, save.

n. derelict, desolation, destruction, devastation, disruption, hulk, mess, overthrow, ruin, ruination, shipwreck, undoing, write-off.

wrench *v.* distort, force, jerk, pull, rax, rick, rip, sprain, strain, tear, tug, twist, wrest, wring, yank.

n. ache, blow, jerk, monkey-wrench, pain, pang, pliers, pull, sadness, shock, sorrow, spanner, sprain, tear, tug, twist, upheaval, uprooting.

wrestle *v.* battle, combat, contend, contest, fight, grapple, scuffle, strive, struggle, tussle, vie.

wretch *n.* blackguard, cad, caitiff, cullion, cur, good-for-nothing, insect, miscreant, outcast, profligate, rapscallion, rascal, rascallion, rat, rogue, rotter, ruffian, scoundrel, swine, vagabond, villain, wight, worm.

wretched *adj.* abject, base, broken-hearted, caitiff, calamitous, cheerless, comfortless, contemptible, crestfallen, dejected, deplorable, depressed, despicable, disconsolate, distressed, doggone, doleful, downcast, forlorn, gloomy, grotty, hapless, hopeless, inferior, low, low-down, mean, melancholy, miserable, paltry, pathetic, pesky, pitiable, pitiful, poor, ratty, scurvy, shabby, shameful, sorry, unfortunate, unhappy, vile, woebegone, woeful, worthless.

antonyms excellent, happy.

writ *n.* court order, decree, subpoena, summons.

write *v.* compose, copy, correspond, create, draft, draw up, indite, inscribe, jot down, pen, record, screeve, scribble, scribe, set down, take down, tell, transcribe.

writer *n.* amanuensis, author, authoress, clerk, columnist, copyist, crime writer, detectivist, dialogist, diarist, diatribist, dramatist, dramaturg, dramaturgist, elegiast, elegist, encomiast, epigrammatist, epistler, epistolarian, epistoler, epistolist, epitapher, epitaphist, epitomist, essayist, farceur, fictionist, hack, librettist, littérateur, man of letters, memoirist, novelist, panegyrist, paper-stainer, pen, penman, penny-a-liner, penpusher, penwoman, periodicalist, playwright, prosaist, proseman, proser, prose-writer, quill-driver, scribbler, scribe, secretary, wordsmith, writeress.

writhe *v.* coil, contort, jerk, squirm, struggle, thrash, thresh, toss, twist, wiggle, wreathe, wriggle.

wrong *adj.* abusive, askew, awry, bad, blameworthy, criminal, crooked, defective, dishonest, dishonorable, erroneous, evil, fallacious, false, faulty, felonious, funny, illegal, illicit, immoral, improper, in error, in the wrong, inaccurate, inappropriate, inapt, incongruous, incorrect, indecorous, infelicitous, iniquitous, inner, inside, inverse, malapropos, misinformed, mistaken, off beam, off target, off-base, opposite, out, out of commission, out of order, reprehensible, reverse, sinful, unacceptable, unbecoming, unconventional,

under, undesirable, unethical, unfair, unfitting, unhappy, unjust, unlawful, unseemly, unsound, unsuitable, untrue, wicked, wide of the mark, wrongful, wrongous.
antonym right.

adv. amiss, askew, astray, awry, badly, erroneously, faultily, improperly, inaccurately, incorrectly, mistakenly, wrongly.
antonym right.

n. abuse, crime, error, grievance, immorality, inequity, infraction, infringement, iniquity, injury, injustice, misdeed, offense, sin, sinfulness, transgression, trespass, unfairness, wickedness, wrong-doing.
antonym right.

v. abuse, cheat, discredit, dishonor, harm, hurt, ill-treat, ill-use, impose on, injure, malign, maltreat, misrepresent, mistreat, oppress, traduce.

wry *adj.* askew, aslant, awry, contorted, crooked, deformed, distorted, droll, dry, ironic, mocking, pawky, perverse, sarcastic, sardonic, thrawn, twisted, uneven, warped.
antonym straight.

Y

yank *v., n.* haul, heave, jerk, pull, snatch, tug, wrench.

yap *v.* babble, blather, chatter, go on, gossip, jabber, jaw, prattle, talk, tattle, twattle, ya(c)k, yammer, yatter, yelp, yip.

yard *n.* court, court-yard, garden, garth, Hof, hypaethron, quad, quadrangle.

yardstick *n.* benchmark, comparison, criterion, gauge, measure, standard, touchstone.

yarn[1] *n.* abb, fiber, fingering, gimp, lisle, thread.

yarn[2] *n.* anecdote, cock-and-bull story, fable, fabrication, story, tale, tall story.

yawn *v.* gape, ga(u)nt, open, split.

yearly *adj.* annual, per annum, per year.
adv. annually, every year, once a year.

yearn for ache for, covet, crave, desire, hanker for, hunger for, itch for, languish for, long for, lust for, pant for, pine for, want, wish for, yen for.
antonym dislike.

yell *v.* bawl, bellow, holler, hollo, howl, roar, scream, screech, shout, shriek, squawl, squeal, whoop, yelp, yowl.
antonym whisper.

n. bellow, cry, holler, hollo, howl, roar, scream, screech, shriek, squawl, whoop, yelp.
antonym whisper.

yellow *adj.* flavescent, flaxen, fulvid, fulvous, gold, golden, lemon, primrose, saffron, vitellary, vitelline, xanthic, xanthochroic, xanthomelanous, xanthous.

yelp *v.* bark, bay, cry, yap, yell, yip, yowl.

n. bark, cry, yap, yell, yip, yowl.

yen *n.* craving, desire, hankering, hunger, itch, longing, lust, passion, thing, yearning.
antonym dislike.

yield[1] *v.* abandon, abdicate, accede, acquiesce, admit defeat, agree, allow, bow, capitulate, cave in, cede, comply, concede, consent, cry quits, give, give in, give way, go along with, grant, knuckle under, part with,

permit, relinquish, resign, resign oneself, submit, succumb, surrender, throw in the towel.
antonym withstand.

yield[2] *v.* afford, bear, bring forth, bring in, earn, fructify, fructuate, fruit, furnish, generate, give, net, pay, produce, provide, return, supply.

n. crop, earnings, harvest, income, output, proceeds, produce, product, profit, return, revenue, takings.

yielding *adj.* accommodating, acquiescent, amenable, biddable, complaisant, compliant, docile, easy, elastic, flexible, obedient, obliging, pliable, pliant, quaggy, resilient, soft, spongy, springy, submissive, supple, tractable, unresisting.
antonyms obstinate, solid.

yoke *n.* bond, bondage, burden, chain, coupling, enslavement, helotry, ligament, link, oppression, serfdom, service, servility, servitude, slavery, subjugation, thraldom, tie, vassalage.

v. bracket, connect, couple, enslave, harness, hitch, inspan, join, link, tie, unite.
antonym unhitch.

yokel *n.* boor, bucolic, bumpkin, clodhopper, corn-ball, country cousin, hick, hillbilly, jake, peasant, rustic.
antonyms sophisticate, towny.

young *adj.* adolescent, baby, callow, cub, early, fledgling, green, growing, immature, infant, junior, juvenile, little, new, recent, unblown, unfledged, youthful.
antonym old.

n. babies, brood, chicks, cubs, family, fledglings, issue, litter, little ones, offspring, progeny, quiverful.
antonym parents.

youngster *n.* boy, girl, juvenile, kid, lad, laddie, lass, lassie, nipper, shaver, teenybopper, urchin, young pup, youth.
antonym oldie.

youthful *adj.* active, boyish, childish, ephebic, fresh, girlish, immature, inexperienced, juvenescent, juvenile, lively, pubescent, puerile, sprightly, spry, vigorous, vivacious, well-preserved, young.
antonyms aged, languorous.

youthfulness *n.* freshness, juvenileness, juvenility, liveliness, sprightliness, spryness, vigor, vivaciousness, vivacity.
antonyms agedness, languor.

yowl *v.* bay, caterwaul, cry, howl, screech, squall, ululate, wail, yell, yelp.

n. cry, howl, screech, wail, yell, yelp.

Z

zany *adj.* amusing, clownish, comical, crazy, daft, droll, eccentric, funny, goofy, kooky, loony, madcap, nutty, screwy, wacky.
antonym serious.

n. buffoon, card, clown, comedian, cure, droll, fool, jester, joker, kook, laugh, merry-andrew, nut, nutcase, nutter, screwball, wag.

zeal *n.* ardor, dedication, devotion, eagerness, earnestness, enthusiasm, fanaticism, fervency, fervor, fire, gusto, keenness, militancy, passion, spirit, verve, warmth, zelotypia, zest.
antonym apathy.

zealot *n.* bigot, devotee, enthusiast, extremist, fanatic, fiend, freak, maniac, militant.

zealous *adj.* ardent, burning, devoted, eager, earnest, enthusiastic, fanatical, fervent, fervid, fired, gung-ho, impassioned, keen, militant, passionate, rabid, spirited.

antonym apathetic.

zenith *n.* acme, apex, apogee, climax, culmination, height, high point, meridian, peak, pinnacle, summit, top, vertex.

antonym nadir.

zero *n.* bottom, cipher, duck, goose-egg, love, nadir, naught, nil, nothing, nought.

zest *n.* appetite, charm, delectation, élan, enjoyment, flavor, gusto, interest, joie de vivre, keenness, kick, peel, piquancy, pungency, relish, rind, savor, smack, spice, tang, taste, zeal, zing.

zip *n.* brio, drive, élan, energy, enthusiasm, get-up-and-go, go, gusto, life, liveliness, oomph, pep, pizzazz, punch, sparkle, spirit, verve, vigor, vim, vitality, zest, zing.

antonym listlessness.

v. dash, flash, fly, gallop, hurry, race, rush, scoot, shoot, speed, tear, whiz, whoosh, zoom.

zone *n.* area, belt, district, region, section, sector, sphere, stratum, territory, tract, zona, zonule, zonulet.

zoo *n.* animal park, aquarium, aviary, menagerie, safari park, zoological gardens.

Appendix I

Classified word-lists

air and space vehicles aerobus, airdrome, aerodyne, aerohydroplane, airplane, aerostat, air-ambulance, air-bus, airship, all-wing airplane, amphibian, autogiro, balloon, biplane, blimp, bomber, cable-car, camel, canard, chopper, comsat, convertiplane, crate, delta-wing, dirigible, dive bomber, fan-jet, fighter, fire-balloon, flying boat, flying saucer, flying wing, glider, gondola, gyrocopter, gyroplane, helibus, helicopter, hoverbus, hovercar, hovercraft, hovertrain, hydro-airplane, hydrofoil, hydroplane, intercepter, jet, jetliner, jetplane, lem, mictolight, module, monoplane, multiplane, plane, rocket, rocket-plane, runabout, sailplane, satellite, seaplane, space platform, space probe, space shuttle, spacecraft, spaceship, spitfire, sputnik, step-rocket, stol, strato-cruiser, stratotanker, swingtail cargo aircraft, swing-wing, tanker, taube, téléférique, tow-plane, tractor, triplane, troop-carrier, tube, tug, turbojet, twoseater, UFO, warplane, zeppelin.

alphabets and writing systems Chalcidian alphabet, cuneiform, Cyrillic, devanagari, estrang(h)elo, finger-alphabet, futhark, Glagol, Glossic, Greek, Gurmukhi, hieroglyphs, hiragana, ideograph, kana, katakana, Kuffic, linear A, linear B, logograph, nagari, naskhi, og(h)am, pictograph, Roman, runic, syllabary.

anatomical abductor, acromion, adductor, alvine, ancon, astragalus, atlas, aural, auricular, axilla, biceps, blade-bone, bone, brachial, bregma, buccal, calcaneum, calcaneus, capitate, cardiac, carpal, carpus, cartilage, cephalic, cerebral, cholecyst, clavicle, coccyx, celiac, collar-bone, concha, coracoid, crural, cuboid, cuneiform, deltoid, dental, derm, derma, dermal, dermic, diaphragm, diencephalon, digital, diploe, diverticulum, dorsal, dorsolumbar, dorsum, duodenal, duodenum, dura mater, earlap, elbow, enarthrosis, encephalic, encephalon, endocardiac, endocardial, endocardium, endocrinal, endocrine, epencephalic, epencephalon, epidermal, epidermic, epidermis, epididymis, epigastric, epigastrium, epiglottic, epiglottis, epithelium, eponychium, erythrocyte, esophagus, ethmoid, extensor, Fallopian tubes, false rib, femur, fenestra ovalis, fenestra rotunda, fibula, flexor, floating rib, fontanel(le), fonticulus, foramen magnum, forearm, forebrain, forefinger, foreskin, fourchette, frenum, frontal, funiculus, funny bone, gastric, gastrocnemius, gena, genal, genial, genitalia, genu, gingival, glabella, glabellar, gladiolus, glossa, glossal, glottal, glottic, glottis, gluteus, gnathal, gnathic, gonion, gracilis, gremial, gristle, groin, gula, gular, gullet, guttural, hallux, ham, hamate, hamstring, helix, hemal, hematic, hepatic, hind-brain, hindhead, hip-bone, hip-girdle, hock, huckle-bone, humeral, humerus, hyoid, hypogastrium, hypothalamus, iliac, ilium, incus, inguinal, innominate, innominate bone, intercostal, ischium, jugular, labial, lachrymal, lacrimal, leucocyte, ligament, lumbar, lumbrical, lunate, luz, malar, malleolus, malleus, mamillar(y), mammary, mandible, mandibular, manubrium, marriage-bone, mastoid, maxilla, maxillary, membral, mental, merrythought, metacarpal, metatarsal, mons veneris, mount of Venus, muscle, nasal, nates, navicular, neural, obturators, occipital, occiput, occlusal, occlusion, occlusor, ocular, odontic, omentum, omohyoid, omoplate, optical, orbicularis, orbit(a), origin, os innominatum, oscheal, oscular, ossicle, otic, otolith, palatal, palatine, palpebral, parasphenoid, parietal, paroccipital, parotid, patela, patellar, pecten, pectoral, pedal, pelvic girdle, pelvis, periotic, perone, phalanges, pisiform, plantar, popliteal, poplitic, prefrontal, premaxilla, premaxillary, pronator, prootic, prosencephalon, psoas, pubis, pudenda, pulmonary, quadriceps, radius, renal, rhomboid, rib, rictal, sacrocostal, sacrum, sartorius, scaphoid, scapula, sesamoid, shoulder-blade, shoulder-bone, skull, soleus, spade-bone, sphenoid, spine, splinter-bone, stapes, sternum, stirrup-bone, supinator, sural, talus, tarsal, temporal, tendon, thigh-bone, tibia, trapezium, trapezius, trapezoid, triceps, triquetral, turbinal, tympanic, ulna, umbilicus, unguis, urachus, uterus, uvula, vagus, vas deferens, velum, vermis, vertebra, vertebrae, vertex, vesica, voice-box, vomer, vulva, windpipe, wisdom tooth, womb, wrist, xiphisternum, xiphoid, zygapophysis, zygoma, zygomatic.

architecture and building abacus, abutment, acrolith, acroter, acroterial, acroterion, acroterium, alcove, annulet, anta, antefix, areostyle, architrave, ashlar, ashler, astragal, baguette, bandelet, banderol(e), barge-board, barge-couple, barge-stones, battlement, bellcote, bema, bratticing, canephor, canton, cartouche, caryatid, Catherine-wheel, cavetto, centering, cinque-foil, concha, corbeil, corbel, corner-stone, corona, cradling, crenel, crocket, crossette, cruck, cul-de-four, dado, decorated, demi-bastion, demi-lune, dentil, diaconicon, diaper, diastyle, diglyph, dimension work, dinette, dipteros, distyle, ditriglyph, dodecastyle, dog-leg(ged), dogtooth, dome, domed, domical, donjon, Doric, dormer, double-glazing, doucine, drawbridge, drawing-room, dreamhole, dressing, drip, dripstone, dromic, dromos, drum, dry-stone, duplex, Early English, eaves, echinus, egg-and-anchor, egg-and-dart, egg-and-tongue, egg-box, el, elevation, Elizabethan, embattlement, embrasure, emplection, encarpus, engage, engaged, engrail, enneastyle, entresol, epaule, epaulement, epistyle, eustyle, exedra, extrados, eye-catcher, façade, fan tracery, fan vaulting, fanlight, fascia, fastigium, feathering, fenestella, fenestra, fenestral, fenestration, festoon, fillet, finial, flamboyant, flèche, Flemish bond, fletton, fleuron, foliation, fornicate, fortalice, French sash/window, frieze, fronton, furring, fusarol(e), fust, gable, gablet, galilee, gambrel roof, gargoyle, gatehouse, glacis, glyph, gopura(m), gorgerin, Gothic, gradin(e), griff(e), groin, groundplan, groundsel, guilloche, gutta, hagioscope, half-timbered, hammer-beam, hammer-brace, hance, hanging buttress, harling, haunch, haute époque, headstone, heart, helix, herringbone, hexastyle, hip, hip-knob, holderbat, hood-mold(ing), hypostyle, imbrex, imbricate, imbrication, imperial, impost, impostume, intercolumniation, intrados, jamb, javelin, jerkinhead, knosp, lierne, linen-fold, linen-scroll, lintel, mansard(-roof), mascaron, merlon, metope, modillion, monostyle, mullion, muntin(g), mutule, Norman, oeil-de-boeuf, ogee, opisthodomos, oriel, out-wall, ovolo, ox-eye, pagoda, pantile, pargret, patera, paternoster, patten, pediment, pilaster, pineapple, pinnacle, plafond, platband, plateresque, plinth, poppy-head, predella, propylaeum, propylon, prostyle, pylon, quatrefeuille, quatrefoil, queen-post, quirk, rear-arch, reglet, regula, rere-arch, retrochoir, reredos, revet, rocaille, rococo, Romanesque, rood-loft, rood-screen, rood-steeple, rood tower, roof, roof-tree, rosace, rose, rosette, rotunda, roughcast, sacristy, skew-back, socle, soffit, solidum, spandrel, strap-work, stria, string-course, subbasal, surbase, swag, systyle, tabernacle-work, table, telamon, terrazzo, tierceron, tondino, toroid, torsel, torus, trabeation, tracery, triforium, trumeau, tympanum, vault, vaultage, vaulted, vaulting, Venetian mosaic, vermiculate(d), vice, vitrail, vitrailled, Vitruvian, volute, voussoir, wainscot, wall-plate, water-joint, water-table, weathering, xystus.

art abstract, abstraction, action painting, anaglyph, anastasis, anastatic, anthemion, aquarelle, bas relief, Bauhaus, camaieu, cire perdue, dadaism, decal, decoupage, Der Blaue Reiter, diaglyph, Die Brücke, diptych, dry-point, duotone, écorché, enamel, encaustic, engraving, etch, etchant, faience, fashion-plate, Fauve, Fauvism, fête champêtre, figurine, filigree, flambé, flannelgraph, Flemish, flesh-tint, Florentine, free-hand, fresco, fret, frit, futurism, futurist, gadroon, genre, gesso, glyptics, glyptography, Gobelin, gouache, graphic, graphics, graphium, graticulation, gravure, grecque, grisaille, gumption, hachure, hatch, hatching, haut relief, herm(a), historiated, hound's-tooth, intaglio, linocut, literalism, litho, lithochromatic(s), lithchromy, lithograph, lithoprint, lost wax, mandorla, meander, monotint, monotype, morbidezza, Parian, paysage, phylactery, pietra-dura, piqué, pochoir, pompier, putto, quattrocento, relievo, repoussage, repoussé, reserved, retroussage, rilievo, sculp(t), scumble, sea-piece, seascape, secco, serigraph, statuary, stipple, stylus, surrealism, symbolism, tachism(e), tempera, tenebrism, tessellated, tessera, tondo, trecento, triptych, ukiyo-e, velatura, Venetian mosaic, Venetian red, verditer, verism, vermiculate(d), versal, vitrail, vitraillist, vitrifacture, vitrine, vitro-di-trina, volute, vorticism, woodblock, wood-carving, woodcut, wood-engraving, xoanon, zoomorphic.

canonical hours compline, lauds, matins, none, orthros, prime, sext, terce, undern, vespers.

cattle breeds Africander, Alderney, Angus, Ankole, Ayrshire, Blonde d'Aquitaine, Brahman, Brown Swiss, cattabu, cattalo, Charol(l)ais, Chillingham, Devon, dexter, Durham, Friesian, Galloway, Guernsey, Hereford, Highland, Holstein, Jersey, Latvian, Limousin, Luing, Red Poll, Romagnola, Santa Gertrudis, short-horn, Simmenthaler, Teeswater, Ukrainian, Welsh Black.

cheeses Amsterdam, Bel Paese, Blarney, Bleu d'Auvergne, Blue Vinny, Boursin, Brie, Caboc, Caerphilly, Camembert, Carré, Cheddar, Cheshire, Chevrotin, Colwick, Coulommiers, Crowdie, Danish blue, Derby, Dolcelatte, Dorset Blue, double Gloucester, Dunlop, Edam, Emmental, Emment(h)al(er), Esrom, ewe-cheese, Feta, Fynbo, Gammelost, G(j)etost, Gloucester, Gorgonzola, Gouda, Grana, Grevé, Gruyère,

cheeses *contd.*
Handkäse, Havarti, Herrgårdsost, Herve, Huntsman, Hushållsost, Islay, Jarlsberg, Killarney, Kryddost, Lancashire, Leicester, Limburg(er), Lymeswold, mouse-trap, mozzarella, Munster, Mysost, Neufchâtel, Parmesan, Petit Suisse, pipo creme, Pont-l'Éveque, Port(-du-)Salut, Prästost, Provolone, Pultost, Raclette, Red Windsor, Reggiano, ricotta, Romadur, Roquefort, sage Derby, Saint-Paulin, Samsø, sapsago, Stilton, stracchino, Tilsit(er), Vacherin, Wensleydale, Wexford.

chemical elements Actinium, Aluminum, Americium, Antimony, Argon, Arsenic, Astatine, Barium, Berkelium, Beryllium, Bismuth, Boron, Bromine, Cadmium, Calcium, Californium, Carbon, Cerium, Cesium, Chlorine, Chromium, Cobalt, Copper, Curium, Dysprosium, Einsteinium, Erbium, Europium, Fermium, Fluorine, Francium, Gadolinium, Gallium, Germanium, Gold, Hafnium, Hahnium, Helium, Holmium, Hydrogen, Indium, Iodine, Iridium, Iron, Krypton, Lanthanum, Lawrencium, Lead, Lithium, Lutetium, Magnesium, Manganese, Mendelevium, Mercury, Molybdenum, Neodymium, Neon, Neptunium, Nickel, Niobium, Nitrogen, Nobelium, Osmium, Oxygen, Palladium, Phosphorus, Platinum, Plutonium, Polonium, Potassium, Praseodymium, Promethium, Protoactinium, Radium, Radon, Rhenium, Rhodium, Rubidium, Ruthenium, Rutherfordium, Samarium, Scandium, Selenium, Silicon, Silver, Sodium, Strontium, Sulfur, Tantalum, Technetium, Tellurium, Terbium, Thallium, Thorium, Thulium, Tin, Titanium, Tungsten, Uranium, Vanadium, Xenon, Ytterbium, Yttrium, Zinc, Zirconium.

cloths, fabrics abaca, abb, alamonde, alepine, alpaca, American cloth, angora, armozine, armure, arrasene, astrakhan, atlas, baft, bagging, Balbriggan, baldachin, balzarine, barathea, barege, barracan, batiste, batting, bayadère, bearskin, beaver, beige, bengaline, Binca®, blanket, blanketing, blonde(e)-lace, bobbinet, bobbin-lace, bombasine, bone-lace, botany, bouclé, bolting cloth, box-cloth, broadcloth, brocade, brocatel(le), broché, Brussels lace, buckram, buckskin, budge, buff, bunting, Burberry, burlap, burnet, burrel, butter-cloth, butter-muslin, byssus, caddis, calamanco, calico, cambric, cameline, camlet, candlewick, canvas, carmelite, carpeting, casement-cloth, cashmere, cassimere, catgut, (cavalry) twill, challis, chamois, chantilly (lace), charmeuse, cheesecloth, damask, damassin, delaine, denim, devil's dust, dhoti, d(h)urrie, diamanté, diaper, dimity, doe-skin, doily, domett, dornick, dowlas, drab, drabbet, drap-de-Berry, dreadnought, drill, droguet, drugget, duchesse lace, duck, duffel, dungaree, dupion, durant, Dutch carpet, ecru, éolienne, façonné, faille, far(r)andine, fearnought, felt, ferret, filet, flannel, flannelette, foulard, foulé, frieze, frocking, fustian, gaberdine, galatea, galloon, gambroon, gauze, genappe, georgette, gingham, Gobelini(s), gold-cloth, gold-lace, grass cloth, grenadine, grogram, grosgrain, guipure, gunny, gurrah, habit-cloth, haircloth, harn, Hessian, hodden, holland, homespun, Honiton, hopsack, horsehair, huckaback, humhum, jaconet, Jaeger®, jamdani, jean, jeanette, jersey, kalamkari, karakul, kente cloth, kersey, kerseymere, khader, khaki, kid, kidskin, kilt, kincob, kip-skin, lamé, lampas, lawn, leather, leather-cloth, leatherette, leghorn, leno, levant, linen, linsey, linsey-woolsey, llama, lockram, loden, longcloth, lovat, Lurex®, luster, lustring, lutestring, mac(k)intosh, madras, mantling, marcella, marocain, maroquin, marquisette, mazarine, Mechlin, medley, melton, merino, Mexican, mignonette, mohair, moire, moleskin, monk's cloth, moreen, morocco, mourning-stuff, mousseline, mousseline-de-laine, mousseline-de-soie, Moygashel®, mull, mulmul(l), mungo, musk-rat, muslin, muslinet, musquash, nacarat, nainsook, nankeen, ninon, nitro-silk, nun's-veiling, nylon, oilcloth, organdie, organza, organzine, orleans, osnaburg, orris, ottoman, overcoating, paduasoy, paisley, panne, paper-cloth, paper-muslin, par(r)amatta, peau-de-soie, penistone, percale, percaline, perse, petersham, piña-cloth, pin-stripe, piqué, plaid, plush, point-lace, polycotton, poplin, poplinette, prunella, purple, quilting, rabanna, ratine(ratteen), raven('s)-duck, rep (repp), roan, russel, russel-cord, russet, sackcloth, sacking, sagathy, sail-cloth, samite, sarsenet, satara, sateen, satin, satinette, satin-sheeting, saxony, say, scarlet, schappe, scrim, seersucker, sendal, serge, shagreen, shalloon, shammy(-leather), shantung, sharkskin, sheepskin, Shetland wool, shoddy, Sicilian, sicilienne, silesia, silk, slipper satin, soneri, split, sponge-cloth, spun silk, stammel, strouding, suede, suedette, suiting, surah, surat, swansdown, swan-skin, tabaret, tabbinet, tabby, taffeta, tamin(e), tamise, tammy, tarlatan, tarpaulin, tartan, tat, Tattersall (check), T-cloth, tentage, tent-cloth, terry, Terylene®, thibet, thickset, thrown-silk, thunder-and-lightning, ticken, tick(ing), tiffany, toile, toilinet(te), torchon lace, toweling, tram, tricot, troll(e)y, tulle, tusser(-silk), tweed, union, Valenciennes, veiling, Velcro®, velour(s), veloutine, velveret, velvet, velveteen, velveting, vicuña, voile, wadmal, waistcoating, watchet, waterwork, waxcloth, webbing, whipcord, wigan, wild silk, wincey, winceyette, wire gauze, woolsey, worcester, worsted, zanella, zephyr.

coins, currencies agora, antoninianus, as, asper, aureus, baht, balboa, bawbee, bekah, belga, bezant, bit, bod(d)le, bolivar, boliviano, bonnet-piece, broad(piece), buck, cardecu(e), Carolus, cash, cent, centavo,

coins, currencies *contd.*

centime, chiao, colon, conto, cordoba, couter, crown, crusado, cruzeiro, dam, daric, deaner, décime, denarius, denier, Deutschmark, didrachm(a), dime, dinar, dirham, doit, dollar, double, doubloon, drachma, ducat, dupondius, duro, eagle, écu, eighteen-penny piece, escudo, farthing, fen, fifty-pence piece, fifty-penny piece, five-pence piece, five-penny piece, florin, forint, franc, geordie, gerah, gourde, groat, groschen, guinea, gulden, haler, half-crown, half-dollar, halfpenny, half-sovereign, heller, jacobus, jane, jitney, joe, joey, jo(h)annes, kina, knife-money, koban(g), kopeck, koruna, kreutzer, krona, krone, Krugerrand, kwacha, kyat, lek, lepton, leu, lev, lion, lira, litre, livre, louis, louis-d'or, mag, maik, make, manch, mancus, maravedi, mark, mawpus, merk, mil, millième, millime, milreis, mina, mite, mna, mohur, moidore, mopus, naira, napoleon, (naya) paisa, (new) cedi, ngwee, nickel, obang, obol, obolus, öre, øre, Paduan, pagoda, paolo, para, patrick, paul, peseta, pesewa, peso, pfennig, piastre, picayune, pice, piece of eight, pine-tree money, pistareen, pistole, pistolet, plack, portague, portcullis, pound, punt, qintar, quetzal, quid, rag, rand, real, red, red cent, reichsmark, reis, rial, rider, riel, ringgit, rix-dollar, riyal, rose-noble, r(o)uble, royal, ruddock, ruddy, rupee, rupiah, ryal, saw-buck, sceat(t), schilling, scudo, semis, semuncia, sen, sequin, sesterce, sestertium, sextans, shekel, shilling, silverling, sixpence, skilling, smacker, sol, soldo, solidus, sou, sovereign, spade-guinea, spur-royal, stater, sterling, stiver, sucre, sword-dollar, sycee, tael, taka, talent, tanner, tenner, tenpence, ten-pence piece, ten-penny piece, tester(n), testo(o)n, testril(l), tetradrachm, thaler, thick'un, thin'un, three-farthings, three-halfpence, threepence, threepenny bit/piece, tical, tick(e)y, tizzy, toman, turner, twenty-pence piece, twenty-penny piece, two bits, twopence, two-pence piece, two-penny piece, unicorn, ure, vellon, wakiki, wampum, won, xerafin, yen, yuan, zack, zecchino, zimbi, zloty, zuz, zwanziger.

collective nouns building of rooks, cast of hawks, cete of badgers, charm of goldfinches, chattering of choughs, clamor of rooks, clowder of cats, covert of coots, covey of partridges, down of hares, drift of swine, drove of cattle, dule of doves, exaltation of larks, fall of woodcock, fesnyng of ferrets, gaggle of geese, gam of whales, gang of elks, grist of bees, husk of hares, kindle of kittens, leap of leopards, leash of bucks, murder of crows, murmuration of starlings, muster of peacocks, mute of hounds, nide of pheasants, pace of asses, pod of seals, pride of lions, school of porpoises, siege (or sedge) of bitterns, skein of geese, skulk of foxes, sloth of bears, sounder of boars, spring of teals, stud of mares, team of ducks, tok of capercailzies, troop of kangaroos, walk of snipe, watch of nightingales.

collectors, enthusiasts abolitionist, ailurophile, antiquary, antivaccinationist, antivivisectionist, arachnologist, arctophile, audiophil(e), balletomane, bibliolatrist, bibliomane, bibliopegist, bibliophagist, bibliophile, bibliophilist, bicameralist, campanologist, canophilist, cartophile, cartophilist, cheirographist, coleopterist, conservationist, cynophilist, Dantophilist, deltiologist, discophile, dog-fancier, ecclesiologist, egger, enophile, enophilist, entomologist, environmentalist, ephemerist, epicure, ex-librist, feminist, Francophile, Gallophile, gastronome, gemmologist, Germanophil(e), gourmet, herpetologist, hippophile, homoeopathist, iconophilist, incunabulist, Kremlinologist, lepidopterist, medallist, miscegenationist, monarchist, myrmecologist, negrophile, negrophilist, notaphilist, numismatist, ophiophilist, orchidomaniac, ornithologist, orthoepist, orthographist, ostreiculturist, pangrammatist, Panhellenist, panislamist, Pan-Slavist, paragrammatist, paroemographer, perfectionist, philanthrope, philatelist, philhellene, phillumenist, philogynist, philologist, philologue, prohibitionist, pteridophilist, reincarnationist, Russophile, Russophilist, scripophile, scripophilist, sericulturist, Sinophile, Slavophile, speleologist, steganographist, stegophilist, supernaturalist, tege(s)tologist, timbrologist, timbromaniac, timbrophilist, tulipomane, tulipomaniac, Turcophile, ufologist, ultramontanist, vexillologist, virtuoso, vulcanologist, xenophile, zoophile, zoophilist.

colors anthochlore, anthocyan(in), anthoxanthin, aquamarine, argent, aurora, avocado, badious, Berlin blue, beryl, biscuit, black, blae, blood-red, blue, bottle-green, brick-red, buff, canary, caramel, carmine, carnation, celadon, celeste, cerise, cerulean, cervine, cesious, champagne, charcoal, cobalt-blue, coral, cyan, dove, drab, dun, Dutch pink, dwale, eau de Nil, ebony, emerald, fawn, feldgrau, ferrugin(e)ous, filemot, flame, flavescent, flaxen, flesh-color, fulvous, fuscous, ginger, glaucous, gold, golden, gray, green, greige (grège), gridelin, griseous, grizzle(d), gules, guly, hoar, horse-flesh, hyacinth, hyacinthine, ianthine, icterine, icteritious, incarnadine, indigo, isabel, isabella, isabelline, jacinth, khaki, lake, lateritious, lemon, lilac, lovat, lurid, luteolous, luteous, magenta, mahogany, maize, mandarin(e), maroon, mauve, mazarine, miniate, minium, modena, morel, mouse-color(ed), mous(e)y, mulberry, murrey, nacarat, Naples-yellow, nattier blue, Nile green, nut-brown, ochroleucous, off-white, orange, oxblood, Oxford blue, palatinate, pansy, peach, peach-bloom, peacock, peacock-blue, perse, philomot, piceous, pink, plum,

colors *contd.*

plumbeous, pompadour, ponceau, pongee, porphyry, porraceous, puce, purple, purpure, pyrrhous, red, reseda, roan, rose, rose-colored, rose-pink, rose-red, rosy, rubicund, rubied, rubiginous, rubineous, rubious, ruby, ruby-red, ruddy, rufescent, rufous, russet, rust-colored, rusty, sable, saffron, sage, salmon, sand, sapphire, saxe blue, scarlet, sepia, siena, silver, sky, slate, smalt, straw, tan, taupe, tawny, tenné, Titian, tomato, tusser, Tyrian, ultramarine, vermeil, vermilion, vinous, violet, virescent, vitellary, vitreous, watchet, white, wine, xanthic, xanthous, yellow.

confections, dishes, foods angels-on-horseback, battalia pie, bir(i)yani, blanquette, Bombay duck, borsch(t), bouillabaisse, bubble-and-squeak, bummalo, burgoo, cannelloni, carbon(n)ade, cassoulet, cecils, charlotte russe, chilli con carné, chocolate vermicelli, chop-suey, chowder, chow-mein, cockaleekie, colcannon, consommé, Danish pastry, dariole, devil, devil's food cake, devils-on-horseback, Devonshire cream, diet-bread, dika-bread, dimsum, dough-boy, doughnut, dragée, drammock, duff, dumpling, dunderfunk, Eccles cake, éclair, Edinburgh rock, egg custard, enchilada, eryngo, escalope, escargot, faggot, fancy-bread, farle, fedelini, felafel, fettuc(c)ine, fishball, fishcake, fishfinger, flan, flapjack, floater, flummery, foie gras, fondant, fondue, forcemeat, fortune cookie, fraise, frankfurter, French bread, French dressing, French fry, French stick, French toast, fricandeau, fricassee, friedcake, fritter, fritto misto, friture, froise, fruit cocktail, fruit salad, fruitcake, frumenty, fu yung, fudge, fumado, galantine, game chips, garam masala, Garibaldi biscuit, gateau, gazpacho, gefilte fish, Genoa cake, ghee, ginger nut, gingerbread, gingersnap, gnocchi, gofer, goulash, graham bread, graham crackers, grits, gruel, guacamole, gumdrop, gundy, haberdine, haggis, halva(h), hamburger, hard sauce, hardbake, hardtack, hoe-cake, hominy, hoosh, hot dog, hot-cross-bun, hotpot, howtowdie, humbug, hummus, hundreds-and-thousands, hyson, jemmy, kedgeree, lardy-cake, laverbread, matelote, millefeuille(s), minestrone, mous(s)aka, na(a)n, navarin, olla-podrida, opsonium, paella, panada, pastrami, pavlova, pem(m)ican, pettitoes, pilaff, pilau, pinole, pirozhki, pizza, plowman's lunch, plum-duff, plum-porridge, plum-pudding, poi, polenta, polony, popover, pop(p)adum, porterhouse(-steak), pot-au-feu, prairie-oyster, profiterole, prosciutto, pumpernickel, queen of puddings, queen's pudding, quenelle, quiche, ragout, ramekin, ratatouille, ravioli, remoulade, risotto, roly-poly pudding, Sachertorte, salmagundi, salmi(s), saltimbocca, sauce hollandaise, sauerkraut, scampi, schnitzel, sch(t)chi, Scotch woodcock, shepherd's pie, smørbrød, smörgåsbord, soufflé, spaghetti (alla) bolognese, spotted dick, spring roll, stovies, stroganoff, succotash, sukiyaki, summer pudding, sundae, sup(p)awn, sushi, syllabub, Tabasco®, tablet, taco, tamal(e), tandoori, tapioca, taramasalata, tempura, timbale, toad-in-the-hole, torte, tortellini, tortilla, trifle, tsamba, turtle-soup, tutti-frutti, tzimmes, velouté sauce, vermicelli, vichyssoise, vienna loaf, vienna steak, vindaloo, vol-au-vent, wafer, waffle, warden pie, wastel-bread, water-biscuit, water-gruel, welsh rabbit (rarebit), white sauce, white-pot, white-pudding, Wiener schnitzel, Wimpy®, wine-biscuit, wonder, Worcestershire sauce, wurst, yoghurt, Yorkshire pudding, zabaglione, Zwieback.

dances allemande, beguine, belly-dance, bergamask, black bottom, bolero, bossanova, bourree, branle, breakdown, bunny-hug, cachucha, cakewalk, canary, cancan, carioca, carmagnole, carol, cha-cha, chaconne, Charleston, cinque-pace, Circassian, circle, clogdance, conga, coranto, corroboree, cotill(i)on, country-dance, courant, cracovienne, csárdás (czardas), dos-à-dos (dosi-do) dump, écossaise, egg-dance, fading, fado, fandango, farruca, figure-dance, flamenco, fling, flip-flap(-flop), forlana, fox-trot, galliard, gallopade, galop, gavotte, gigue, gopak, habanera, haka, halling, haymaker, hey (hay), hey-de-guy, Highland fling, hoedown, hoolachan, hula-hula, jig, jitterbug, jive, jota, juba, kolo, lancers, loure, malagueña, mambo, matachin, maxixe, mazurka, minuet, Moresco, morris-dance, musette, onestep, Paduan, paso doble, passacaglia, passepied, passy-measure, Paul Jones, pavan(e), petronella, planxty, polacca, polka, polo, polonaise, poule, poussette, quadrille, quickstep, redowa, reel, r(h)umba, rigadoon, ring-dance, romaika, roundel, roundelay, roundle, rumba, saltarello, samba, sand-dance, saraband, schottische, sequidilla, shimmy(-shake), siciliano, spring, square-dance, stomp, strathspey, sword-dance, tamborin, tango, tap-dance, tarantella, the twist, toe-dance, tripudium, turkey-trot, two-step, Tyrolienne, valeta, valse, varsovienne, volta, waltz, war dance, zapateado, ziganka.

dog-breeds affenpinscher, badger-dog, basenji, basset(-hound), Bedlington (terrier), Blenheim spaniel, boar-hound, Border terrier, borzoi, Boston terrier, Briard, Brussels griffon, bull mastiff, bulldog, bull-terrier, cairn terrier, Cavalier King Charles spaniel, chihuahua, chow, clumber spaniel, coach-dog, cocker spaniel, collie, corgi, dachshund, Dalmatian, Dandie Dinmont, Dane, deerhound, dhole, dingo, Doberman(n) pinscher, elkhound, Eskimo dog, foxhound, fox-terrier, German police dog, German Shepherd dog, Great

dog-breeds *contd.*

Dane, greyhound, griffon, harlequin, (Irish) water-spaniel, Jack Russell, keeshond, King Charles spaniel, Labrador, laika, lhasa apso, lurcher, lyam-hound, malemute, Maltese, mastiff, peke, Pekin(g)ese, pinscher, pointer, Pomeranian, poodle, pug, pug-dog, retriever, Rottweiler, saluki, Samoyed(e), sausage-dog, schipperke, schnauzer, Scotch-terrier, Sealyham, setter, sheltie, Shetland sheepdog, shih tzu, shough, Skye (terrier), spaniel, Spartan, spitz, St Bernard, staghound, Sussex spaniel, talbot, teckel, terrier, vizsla, volpino, warragal, water-dog, Weimaraner, whippet, wire-hair(ed terrier), wolf-dog, wolf-hound, Yorkshire terrier, zorro.

drinks, alcoholic absinth(e), aguardiente, akvavit, amontillado, anisette, apple-jack, aqua-mirabilis, aquavit, aqua-vitae, arak, Armagnac, arrack, audit ale, ava, bacharach, badminton, barley-bree, Beaujolais, Beaune, Benedictine, bingo, bishop, black velvet, bloody Mary, blue ruin, bourbon, brandy-pawnee, bride-ale, Bristol-milk, bucellas, bumbo, burgundy, Calvados, Campari, canary, catawba, Chablis, chain-lightning, Chambertin, Champagne, Chartreuse, cherry brandy, cherry-bounce, Chianti, chicha, cider, claret, claret-cup, cobbler, cobbler's punch, Cognac, Cointreau®, cold-without, Constantia, cool-tankard, cooper, cordial, corn-brandy, daiquiri, demerara, dog's nose, dop, eau de vie, eau des creoles, egg-flap, eggnog, enamel, enzian, fine, fino, four-ale, geneva, genevrette, geropiga, gimlet, gin, gin and it, gin-fizz, ginger wine, ginsling, glogg, gooseberry wine, grappa, Graves, grog, haoma, heavy wet, herb-beer, hermitage, hippocras, hock, hollands, hoo(t)ch, it, Johannisberger, John Barleycorn, John Collins, kaoliang, kava, kefir, kirsch, kirschwasser, k(o)umiss, kümmel, kvass, London particular, manzanilla, maraschino, marc brandy, Marcobrunner, Marsala, Martini®, Médoc, metheglin, mirabelle, mobbie, Moselle, mountain, mountain dew, muscat, muscatel, negus, Nipa, noyau, Old Tom, oloroso, olykoek, Orvieto, ouzo, pastis, peach-brandy, Pernod®, perry, persico(t), Peter-see-me, pils(e)ner, plottie, pombe, port, pot(h)een, pousse-café, pulque, punch, purl, quetsch, ratafia, resinata, retsina, Rhine-wine, Riesling, Rioja, rosé, Rudesheimer, Rüdesheimer, rum, rumbo, rumfustian, rum-punch, rum-shrub, rye, rye-whisky, sack, sack-posset, sake, samshoo, sangaree, sangria, Sauterne(s), schiedam, schnapps, Scotch, shandy, sherry, sherry-cobbler, shrub, sidecar, Sillery, sling, slivovitz, sloe-gin, small beer, small-ale, sour, spruce-beer, St Julien, Steinberger, stengah, stinger, stingo, swipes, swizzle, tafia, Tarragona, tent, tequil(l)a, tipper, toddy, Tokay, Tom Collins, Tom-and-Jerry, twankay, twopenny, usquebaugh, vermouth, vin blanc, vin ordinaire, vin rosé, vinho verde, vodka, wassail, water-brose, whisk(e)y, whisky toddy, white wine, white-ale, Xeres, zythum.

French Revolutionary calendar Brumaire, Floréal, Frimaire, Fructidor, Germinal, Messidor, Nivôse, Pluviôse, Prairiel, Thermidor, Vendémiaire, Ventôse.

furniture, furnishings andiron, banquette, basket-chair, basketwork, bergama, bergamot, bolster, bonheur-du-jour, box-bed, bracket clock, brise-soleil, buffet, buhl, bureau, cabriolet, camp-bed, canterbury, chair-bed, chaise-longue, chesterfield, cheval-glass, chiffonier, coaster, commode, continental quilt, credence (table/shelf), credenza, davenport, day-bed, desk, dinner-table, dinner-wagon, divan, dos-à-dos, drape, drawer, drawing-table, draw-leaf table, dresser, dressing-table, dumb-waiter, easy-chair, elbow-chair, electrolier, encoignure, escritoire, étagere, faldstool, fauteuil, fender, fender-stool, festoon-blind, fire-dog, fireguard, firescreen, four-poster, gasalier, girandole, girnel, guéridon, hallstand, hassock, hearth-rug, highboy, high-chair, hip-bath, humpty, jardinière, lectern, looking-glass, lounge, lounger, love-seat, lowboy, lug-chair, mirror, mobile, ottoman, overmantel, pelmet, pembroke (table), picture rail, piecrust table, pier-glass, pier-table, plaque, plenishings, pouf(fe), prie-dieu, pulpit, pulvinar, radiator, rocking chair, sag-bag, scatter rug/cushion, sconce, secretaire, settee, settle, settle-bed, sideboard, side-table, sofa, sofa-bed, sofa-table, squab, standard lamp, studio couch, swivel-chair, table, tallboy, tapestry, tatami, teapoy, tea-service, tea-set, tea-table, tea-tray, tea-trolley, tent-bed, tête-à-tête, toilet-table, toilet(te), torchère, tridarn, tringle, umbrella-stand, Vanitory®, vanity unit, vargueño, veilleuse, vis-à-vis, vitrine, wall-unit, wardrobe, washhand-stand, wash-stand, water bed, Welsh dresser, whatnot, writing-desk, writing-table.

garments, vestments aba, abaya, abba, abolla, achkan, acton, Afghan, alb, alpargata, amice, anorak, antigropelo(e)s, babouche, babushka, balaclava, Balbriggan, balibuntal, balmoral, bandan(n)a, bania(n), barret, basher, bashlyk, basinet, basque, basquine, bathing-costume, bauchle, beanie, bearskin, beaver, bed-jacket, bedsocks, beetle-crushers, belcher, benjamin, Bermuda shorts, Bermudas, bertha, bikini, billycock, biretta, blanket, blouson, blucher, boa, boater, bobbysock, bodice, body stocking, bolero, bomber

353

jacket, bongrace, bonnet, bonnet-rouge, boob-tube, bootee, bottine, box-coat, bow-tie, bra, brassière, breeches, breeks, breton, broad-brim, brogue(s), buckskins, buff, buffalo-robe, buff-coat, buff-jerkin, bumfreezer, Burberry, burdash, burk(h)a, burnous(e), busby, bush jacket, bush shirt, buskin, bustle, bustle, bycoket, caftan, cagoul(e), calamanco, calash, calceamentum, calotte, calyptra, camiknickers, camise, camisole, capa, cape, capel(l)ine, capote, capuche, capuchin, carcanet, car-coat, cardigan, cardinal, carmagnole, cashmere, casque, cassock, casuals, catsuit, caul, cere-cloth, cerement, chadar, chaparajos, chapeau, chapeau-bras, chaperone, chapka, chaplet, chaps, chasuble, collar of esses, corset, corslet, cummerbund, dalmahoy, Dalmatic, décolletage, derby, diadem, diaper, dick(e)y, dinner-gown, dinner-jacket, dirndl, dishabille, dittos, divided skirt, djellaba(h), djibbah, dog-collar, Dolly Varden, dolman, donkey jacket, doublet, drainpipes, drapesuit, drawers, dreadnought, dress uniform, dress-coat, dress-improver, dressing-gown, dressing-jacket, dressing-sack, dress-shirt, dress-suit, dress-tie, duffel coat, dungarees, earmuffs, encolpion, epaulet(te), ephod, epitrachelion, espadrille, Eton collar, Eton jacket, Etons, evening dress, evening-dress, exomis, faldetta, falling band, fannel(l), fanon, farthingale, fascinator, fatigues, fedora, ferronnière, fez, fibula, fichu, filibeg, fillet, finnesko, flat-cap, flip-flop, fob, fontange, fore-and-after, fraise, French knickers, frock, frock-coat, frog, frontlet, fustanella, gaberdine, gaiter, galligaskins, galoshes, gamash, gambeson, garibaldi, gauchos, gay deceivers, gee-string (G-string), geneva bands, geta, gibus, gi(e), gilet, girandole, gizz, grego, gremial, g-suit, guernsey, gumboot, gum(shoe), habergeon, hacqueton, haik, hair-net, hair-piece, half-boot, hat, hatband, hatpin, hattock, hauberk, havelock, headcloth, head-hugger, headsquare, himation, hip-huggers, hipsters, hogger, Homburg, hood, hotpants, housecoat, hug-me-tight, humeral veil, hummel, hunting cap, ihram, indescribables, jabot, jacket, Jap-silk, jeans, jersey, jiz, jubbah (djibḅah), jumper, jump-suit, jupon, kabaya, kaffiyeh, kaftan, kagoul, kalpak, kalyptra, kamees, kanzu, kell, kerchief, k(h)anga, k(h)urta, Kilmarnock, Kilmarnock cowl, kimono, kirtle, kiss-me, kiss-me-quick, knickerbockers, knickers, lammy, lava-lava, lederhosen, leggings, leghorn, leg-warmers, leotard, Levis®, liberty bodice, lingerie, loden, lounger, lounge-suit, lungi, mac(k), mackinaw, mac(k)intosh, madras, manta, manteau, mantilla, mantle, mantlet, manto, matinee, matinee jacket/coat, maud, mazarine, mazarine hood, middy (blouse), mink, miter, mitt, mitten, mob, mob-cap, mode, modius, mohair, moleskins, monkey-jacket, monteith, montero, montero-cap, morning-dress, morning-gown, mortar-board, Mother Hubbard, mourning-cloak, mousquetaire, moz(z)etta, muff, muffin-cap, muffler, mutch, muu-muu, netherstock, newmarket, nightingale, Nithsdale, Norfolk jacket, nubia, obi, omophorion, orarion, orarium, overcoat, overgarment, Oxonian, paduasoy, paenula, pagri, paletot, pall, palla, pallium, paludament, pantable, pantalets, pantaloons, panties, pantihose, pantof(f)le, panton, pantoufle, pants, pants suit, pea-coat, pea-jacket, pearlies, pectoral, pedal-pushers, pelerine, pelisse, pencil skirt, penitentials, peplos, peplum, petasos, petersham, petticoat, petticoat, petticoat-breeches, ph(a)elonion, Phrygian cap, picture-hat, pierrot, pilch, pileus, pill-box, pinafore, pinafore-dress, pinafore-skirt, pinner, pixie-hood, plaid, plimsoll, plus-fours, plushes, pneumonia-blouse, poke-bonnet, polonaise, polo-neck, poncho, pontificals, pos(h)teen, powdering-gown, pressure-helmet, pressure-suit, pressure-waistcoat, princess(e), pumps, puttee, rabato, raglan, raincoat, rami(e), Ramil(l)ie(s), ra-ra skirt, rat-catcher, rational, rationals, rebater, rebato, redingote, reefer, reefing-jacket, riding-breeches, riding-cloak, riding-clothes, riding-coat, riding-glove, riding-habit, riding-hood, riding-robe, riding-skirt, riding-suit, robe, robe-de-chambre, rochet, roll-neck sweater, roll-on, rompers, romper-suit, roquelaure, ruff, rug-gown, sabot, sack, sack-coat, safari jacket, safari suit, sagum, sailor-hat, sakkos, salopette, samfoo, sanbenito, sandal, sarafan, sari, sarong, sash, sayon, scapular, scarf, scarpetto, schema, scotch bonnet, screen, sea-boots, sealskin, semmit, separates, shako, shaps, shauchle, shawl, shawl-waistcoat, shift, shirt, shirt dress, shirtwaist, shirtwaister, shoe, shooting-jacket, short-clothes, short-coats, shortgown, shorts, shovel-hat, silk-hat, silly-how, singlet, siren suit, skeleton suit, skin-tights, skirt, skullcap, slacks, slicker, sling-back, slip, slip-over, slipper(s), slipslop, sloppy Joe, slop(s), slouch(-hat), small-clothes, smalls, smicket, smock, smock-frock, smoking cap, smoking jacket, sneaker(s), snood, snow-boots, snow-shoe(s), sock, sola(r) topi/helmet, solitaire, solleret, sombrero, sontag, soubise, soutane, sou'-wester, space-suit, spat, spattee, spatterdash, spencer, sphendone, sponge-bags, sporran, sports jacket, sports shirt, start-up, stays, steenkirk, steeple-crown, steeple-hat, stephane, step-in, Stetson, sticharion, stock, stockinet(te), stockingette, stocking(s), stola, stole, stomacher, stovepipe (hat), strait-jacket, strait-waistcoat, straw (hat), string vest, string-tie, strip, stuff-gown, subfusc, subucula, succinctorium, sun-bonnet, sundown, sun-dress, sunhat, sunsuit, superhumeral, surcingle, surcoat, surplice, surtout, suspender-belt, suspenders, swaddling-band/cloth/clothes, swagger-coat, swallow-tail, sweat band, sweat suit, sweater, sweat-shirt, swimming costume, swimsuit, swimwear, sword-belt, tabard, taglioni, tail-coat, tails, taj, talar, talaria, tall hat, tallith, talma, tam, Tam O'Shanter, tammy, tanga, tank top, tarboosh, tarpaulin, tasse, tawdry-lace, tea-gown,

garments, vestments *contd.*
Teddy suit, tee-shirt, ten-gallon hat, terai, thrum-cap, tiar(a), tie, tights, tile(-hat), tippet, toga, tonnag, top-boots, topcoat, topee, topi, topper, tops, toque, toreador pants, tournure, tower, toy, tozie, track shoe, track suit, trenchard, trench-coat, trencher-cap, trews, tricorn(e), trilby, trollopee, trot-cozy, trouser suit, trousers, trouse(s), trunk-breeches, trunk-hose, trunks, truss(es), trusty, T-shirt, tube-skirt, tunic, tunicle, tuque, turban, turtle-neck, tuxedo, twin-set, ugly, ulster, ulsterette, undercoat, underpants, undershorts, undervest, upper-stock, Vandyke (collar), vareuse, veil, veld(-)schoen, vest, victorine, visite, vitta, volet, waistcloth, waistcoat, wam(p)us, war bonnet, warm, watch cap, watch chain, Watteau bodice, weeper, wellie, wellington, wet-suit, whisk, white tie, wide-awake, wig, wimple, windcheater, windjammer, wing collar, winkle-pickers, woggle, wrap, wraparound, wrapover, wrapper, wrap-rascal, wristlet, wylie-coat, yarmulka, yashmak, Y-fronts, zamarra, zoot suit, zoster, zucchetto.

heraldry abatement, addorsed, affrontee, Albany Herald, allusive, annulet, armorist, assurgent, augmentation, baton-sinister, bendlet, bend-sinister, bendwise, bendy, bezant, bicorporate, billet, bordure, botoné, brisure, caboched, cabré, cadency, canting, canton, catherine-wheel, champ, chequy, chevron, chevrony, chief, coupé, debased, debruised, declinant, delf, device, dexter, difference, dimidiate, dismembered, displayed, dormant, double, doubling, dragonné, dwale, eightfoil, embattled, emblaze, emblazon, emblazoner, emblazonment, emblazonry, enarched, enarmed, engouled, engrail, engrailed, engrailment, enveloped, escrol(l), escutcheon, extendant, fess(e), fesse-point, fetterlock, field, fimbriate, fitché(e), flanch, flanched, flotant, fracted, fret, fructed, fur, fusil, gale, gamb, garb(e), gemel, gerbe, golp(e), gorged, grieced, g(u)ardant, gules, gyron, gyronny, hatchment, haurient, herisson, honor-point, impale, impalement, increscent, inescutcheon, interfretted, invected, jessant, langued, lioncel, lis, lozenge, lozengy, manche, mantling, martlet, mascle, mascled, masculy, moline, morné, morned, mounted, mullet, naiant, naissant, nombril, nowed, nowy, opinicus, or, orle, palewise, pall, passant, patonce, patté(e), pean, percussant, pheon, pile, point, pommelé, pommeled, pommetty, portate, portcullis, posé, potencé, potent, primrose, quarter, quartering, quarterly, queue, ragged staff, raguled, raguly, rampant, raping, rebate, regardant, respect, respectant, roundel, rustre, saltire, sans nombre, satyral, scarp, segreant, sej(e)ant, semé(e), square-pierced, statant, tenné, trangle, tressure, trippant, umbrated, undee, undifferenced, unguled, urinant, vair, vairé, verdoy, vert, voided, vol, volant, vorant, vuln, vulned, waved, weel, wivern, woodwose (wood-house).

herbs, spices amaracus, basil thyme, caraway seeds, cardamom, cassia, cayenne, chĕrvil, chilli, chive, cinnamon, cloves, coriander, cum(m)in, dill, dittany, endive, eyebright, fennel, fenugreek, finoc(c)hio, galega, garlic, gentian, ginger, groundsel, hellebore, henbane, horehound, horseradish, Hyoscyamus, hyssop, isatis, juniper, lemon thyme, licorice, lovage, lungwort, mace, marjoram, mint, motherwort, mustard, myrrh, nutmeg, oregano, orpine, paprika, parsley, peppermint, purslane, rampion, rape, rosemary, rue, saffron, sage, savory, stacte, tarragon, thyme, turmeric, vanilla, verbena, watercress, wintergreen, wormwood, woundwort, yerba.

jewels, gems agate, amber, amethyst, aquamarine, asteria, balas ruby, baroque, beryl, bloodstone, brilliant, cairngorm, cameo, carbuncle, chalcedony, chrysolite, coral, cornelian, crystal, diamond, draconites, emerald, fire-opal, garnet, girasol(e), grossular(ite), heliodor, hyacinth, hyalite, hydrophane, intaglio, jacinth, jade, jango(o)n, jasper, jet, lapis lazuli, ligure, marcasite, marquise, Mocha stone, moonstone, morganite, mother-of-pearl, nacre, olivet, olivine, onyx, opal, oriental amethyst, paragon, pearl, peridot(e), pyreneite, pyrope, Rhinestone, rhodolite, rose, rose-cut, rose-diamond, ruby, sapphire, sard, sardine, sardonyx, smaragd, topaz, tourmaline, turquoise, water-sapphire, wood-opal, yu, yu-stone, zircon.

Jewish calendar Ab, Abib, Adar, Adar Sheni, Elul, Hes(h)van, Iy(y)ar, Kislev, Nisan, S(h)ebat, Sivan, Tammuz, Tebet(h), Tis(h)ri, Veadar.

languages Aeolic, Afghan, Afrikaans, Akkadian, Albanian, Alemannic, Algonki(a)n, Altaic, Ameslan, Amharic, Anatolian, Anglo-Saxon, Arabic, Aramaic, Armenian, Armoric, Aryan, Assyrian, Attic, Austric, Austroasiatic, Austronesian, Avestan, Bahasa Indonesia, Balinese, Baltoslav(on)ic, Baluch(i), Bantu, Basque, Basuto, Bengali, Berber, Bohemian, bohunk, Breton, Brezonek, British, Brythonic, Bulgarian, Bulgaric, Burmese, B(y)elorussian, Cajun, Carib, Catalan, Celtic, Chaldaic, Cherokee, Chinese, Choctaw, Circassian, Cornish, creole, Croat(ian), Cushitic, Czech, Danish, Dardic, Doric, Dravidian, Dutch, Early English, English, Erse, Eskimo, Esperanto, Est(h)onian, Ethiopic, Etruscan, Euskarian, Fanti, Farsi,

languages *contd.*

Finnish, Finno-Ugric(-Ugrian), Flemish, Franglais, French, Frisian, Gadhelic (Goidelic), Gaelic, Gaulish, Geëz (Giz), Gentoo, Georgian, German, Germanic, Greek, Guarani, Gujarat(h)i, Gullah, Hausa, Hawaiian, Hebrew, Hellenic, Herero, High German, Hindi, Hindustani, Hittite, Hottentot, Hungarian, Icelandic, Idiom Neutral, Ido, I(g)bo, Indian, Indic, Indo-European, Indo-Germanic, In(n)uit, Interlingua, Ionic, Iranian, Iraqi, Irish, Iroquoian, Italian, Italic, Japanese, Kalmuck, Kanarese, Kannada, Karen, Kennick, Khmer, Koine, Kolarian, Kuo-yü, Kurdish, Ladin, Ladino, Lallans, Landsmaal, Langue d'oc, Langue d'oil, Langue d'oui, Laplandish, Lapp, Lappish, Latin, Latvian, Lettic, Lettish, lingua franca, lingua geral, Lithuanian, Low German, Magyar, Malagasy, Malay, Malayala(a)m, Maltese, Manchu, Mandaean, Mandarin, Mandingo, Manx, Maori, Marathi, Median, Melanesian, Mexican, Micmac, Middle English, Moeso-gothic, Mohawk, Mohican, Mon, Mongolian, Munda, Nahuati, Neo, Newspeak, Norwegian, Novial, Nynorsk, Old English, Old Norse, Oriya, Oscan, Ostyak, Pali, Pawnee, Pehlevi, Pekin(g)ese, Pennsylvania Dutch, Persian, Persic, Phoenician, Pictish, pig Latin, Pilipino, Platt-Deutsch, Polabian, Polish, Portuguese, Prakrit, Provençal Provinçal, Prussian, Punic, Punjabi, Pushtu, Quechua, Rabbinic, Rhaetic, Rhaeto-Romance, Rhaeto-Romanic, Rock English, rogues' Latin, Romaic, Romance, Romanes, Romanic, Roman(n)y, Romans(c)h, Rumanian, Russian, Russniak, Ruthenian, Sakai, Samnite, Samoyed(e), Sanskrit, Saxon, Scots, Scythian, Semitic, Serb(ian), Serbo-Croat(ian), Shan, Shona, Siamese, Sinhalese, Siouan, Slavonic, Slovak, Slovenian, Somali, Sorbian, Sorbish, Spanish, Sudanic, Sumerian, Suomi, Swahili, Swedish, Swiss, Syriac, Taal, Tagálog, Taino, Tamil, Tataric, Telugu, Teutonic, Thai, Tibetan, Tocharian, Tswana, Tuareg, Tungus(ian), Tupi, Turki, Turkish, Twi, Ugrian, Ugro-finnic, Ukrainian, Umbrian, Uralic, Urdu, Uzbeg, Vaudois, Vietnamese, Volapük, Volga-Baltic, Volscian, Welsh, Wendic, Wendish, West-Saxon, Wolof, Xhosa, Yakut, Yiddish, Yoruba, Zulu.

legal abate, abatement, absolvitor, abstract of title, acceptilation, accession, accessory, accessory after the fact, accessory before the fact, Acts of Adjournal, (ad)avizandum, adeem, adhere, adjudication, adminicle, administrator, afforce, alienee, alienor, allenarly, allodial, amicus curiae, amove, appointer, apprize, apprizer, assumpsit, attorn, back-bond, bairn's-part, capias, certiorari, chaud-mellé, cognosce, cognovit, compear, compulsitor, copyhold, cross-examine, decree absolute, decree nisi, decreet, decretals, decretist, dedimus, deed, deed of accession, defalcate, defeasance, defeasanced, defeasible, defendant, defender, deforce, deforcement, deforciant, delapidation, delate, delation, delator, delict, demurrer, deodand, detainer, detinue, devastavit, devest, diet, dimissory, disapply, disbar, disbench, discovert, discoverture, disentail, disgavel, disinherison, dispone, disponee, disposition, disseise, disseisin, disseisor, distinguish, distrain, distrainee, distrainer, distrainment, distrainor, distraint, distress, distringas, dittay, dole, donatary, droit, droit du Seigneur, duplicand, duply, dying declaration, easement, ejectment, embracer, embracery, emendals, emphyteusis, en ventre sa mère, enfeoff, enfeoffment, enjoin, enlevé, enlevement, entry, eric, escheat, escrow (escroll), escuage, esnecy, esrepe, essoin, estate, estop, estoppel, estover, estray, estreat, estrepement, examination, excamb, excambion, excambium, executry, exemplify, expromission, extend, extent, extinguishment, extract, extradition, facile, facility, factorize, faldage, felo de se, felony, feme, feme covert, feme sole, feoff, feoffee, feoffer (feoffor), feoffment, feu, feuar, fief, filacer, fire-bote, fiscal, folio, force and fear, force majeure, foreclose, foreclosure, forinsec, forisfamiliate, forjudge, frankalmoign, french-bench, frontager, fugitation, fungibles, garnishee, garnisheement, garnisher, gavelkind, gavelman, granter (grantor), grassum, hamesucken, hedge-bote, hide, homologation, horning, house-bote, hypothec, hypothecary, hypothecate, hypothecation, improbation, indenture, indict, indictee, indictment, induciae, infangthief, infeft, inquirendo, institorial, insucken, interlocutor, interplead, interpleader, interpose, irrepleviable, irreplevisable, ish, John Doe and Richard Roe, joinder, jointure, jus primae noctis, laches, law-agent, law-burrows, legitim, lenocinium, letters of administration, lien, life-rent, malfeasance, mens rea, mesne, messuage, misdemeanant, misfeasance, misfeasor, misprison, mittimus, mora, mortmain, multiplepoinding, nolle prosequi, nolo contendere, non-access, nonage, non-compearance, non-entry, nonsuit, non-user, notour, novalia, noverint, novodamus, noxal, obligant, obligation, obligor, obreption, onus probandi, ouster, outfangthief, overt act, owelty, oyer, pactum nudum, Pandect, panel, pernancy, personalty, pickery, plaint, plaintiff, porteous roll, portioner, practic, prima facie, privy, prorogate, pupil, quadruply, realty, recaption, recusation, reddendo, relator, relaxation, remise, replevin, replevy, repone, reprobator, res gestae, retour, retroact, retroactive, reverser, right of drip, rout, scutage, stillicide, supersedeas, supplicavit, surrebut, surrebuttal, surrebutter, surrejoin, surrejoinder, terminer, tolt, tort, tortfeasor, tortious, udal, udaller, ultimus haeres, unlaw, uses, usucapient, usucapion (usucaption), usucapt, usucaptible, usufruct, usufructuary, ultimogeniture, vacatur, venire (facias), venter, venue, vert, vest, vested, visne, voidable, voir dire, volunteer, wage, waive, waste, watch, watching brief, water-privilege, wit.

minerals adularia, aegirine, aegirite, alabandine, almandine, alum-shale, alum-slate, alum-stone, alunite, amazonite, amazon-stone, amianthus, amphibole, analcime, anatase, andesine, argil, arkose, asbestos, asparagus-stone, asphalt(um), aventurine, baetyl, balas, Barbados earth, barilla, baryta, barytes, basalt, Bath stone, bath-brick, bezoar, bitter-earth, bitter-spar, bitumen, blackjack, blacklead, blaes, blende, bloodstone, blue ground, blue John, blue vitriol, bluestone, Bologna phosphorous, borane, borax, borazon, boride, bornite, boulder-clay, breccia, Bristol-brick, Bristol-diamond, brown spar, brownstone, buhrstone, cacholong, caen-stone, cairngorm, calamine, calc-sinter, calcspar, calc-tuff, caliche, calp, Carborundum®, cat's-eye, cat-silver, cauk, celestine, cement-stone, ceruse, chalcedony, chalcodonyx, chalk, chert, Chile saltpeter, china clay, china stone, chrome-alum, chrome-spinel, chrysoberyl, chrysocolla, chrysoprase, chrysotile, cinnabar, cinnamon-stone, cipollino, corundum, cryolite, cymophane, dacite, dendrite, Derbyshire spar, diabase, diallage, dialogite, diaspore, diatomite, dice-coal, diopside, dioptase, diorite, dogger, dogtooth-spar, dolerite, dolomite, dopplerite, dropstone, dunite, dyscrasite, dysodyle, eagle-stone, earthflax, earthwax, eclogite, electric calamine, elvan, emery, encrinite, enhydrite, enhydros, epidiorite, epidosite, epidote, epistilbite, epsomite, erinite, erubescite, erythrite, euclase, eucrite, eudialyte, eutaxite, euxenite, fahlerz, fahlore, fakes, fayalite, fel(d)spar, felsite, felstone, flint, fluorite, fluorspar, franklinite, French chalk, fuchsite, fulgurite, fuller's earth, gabbro, gadolinite, gahnite, galena, galenite, gangue, gan(n)ister, garnet-rock, gibbsite, glance, glauberite, glauconite, glimmer, gmelinite, gneiss, goldstone, goslarite, gossan, göthite, granite, granitite, granodiorite, granophyre, granulite, graphic granite, graphite, green earth, greenockite, greensand, greenstone, greisen, greywacke, gummite, gypsum, hälleflinta, halloysite, harmotome, hatchettite, haüyne, heavy spar, hedyphane, hematite, hemimorphite, hepatite, hercynite, (h)essonite, heulandite, hiddenite, honey-stone, hornblende, hornfels, hornstone, horseflesh ore, humite, hyacinth, hyalophane, hypersthene, ice-spar, ice-stone, idocrase, ironstone, jacinth, keratophyre, kermes, kermesite, kieselguhr, kunkur, kupferschiefer, lamprophyre, lapis lazuli, lepidomelane, limestone, lithomarge, marlstone, meerschaum, mellite, mica, microlite, microlith, mispickel, morion, moss-agate, mundic, nail-head-spar, needle-tin, nepheline, nickel-bloom, nickel-ocher, Norway saltpeter, nosean, noselite, obsidian, omphacite, onyx, onyx-marble, orthoclase, orthophyre, ottrelite, ozokerite, peacock-ore, pencil-ore, pencil-stone, peperino, periclase, pericline, petuntse, pipeclay, pipestone, plagioclose, pleonaste, porphyry, potstone, prase, protogine, pyrites, quartz, realgar, rock-oil, rubicelle, ruby-spinel, rutile, saltpeter, sandstone, sanidine, sapphire, sapphire-quartz, sapphirine, sard, sardonyx, satin-spar, satin-stone, scaglia, schalstein, schiller-spar, schist, schorl, serpentine, serpentine(-rock), shale, shell-limestone, shell-marl, silica, silver-glance, sinter, slate, soapstone, spar, speiss-cobalt, spelter, sphene, spiegeleisen, spinel, spinel-ruby, spodumene, stinkstone, sunstone, surturbrand, swinestone, sylvine, tabular spar, tachylite, talc, talc-schist, terne, terpene, terpineol, terra alba, terracotta, terra-japonica, terramara, terra-rossa, terra-sigillata, terts, thulia, tiger(s)-eye, till, tin-stone, toad-stone, tombac, touchstone, tourmaline, trass, travertin(e), tripoli, troutstone, tufa, tuff, Turkey hone, Turkey stone, turquoise, tutty, uinta(h)ite, umber, Uralian emerald, uralite, uraninite, uranite, uvarovite, vanadinite, variolite, variscite, veinstone, veinstuff, Venice talc, verd-antique, vesuvianite, vitrain, vivianite, vulpinite, wacke, wad(d), wallsend, wavellite, Wernerite, whet-slate, whewellite, whinstone, white pyrites, willemite, witherite, wolfram, wollastonite, wood-coal, wulfenite, wurtzite, zaratite, zarnich, zeolite, zeuxite, zinkenite, zircon, zoisite, zorgite.

musical instruments aeolian harp, aerophone, alpenhorn, alphorn, althorn, alto, Amati, American organ, apollonicon, archlute, arpeggione, atabal, autoharp, balalaika, bandore, banjulele, baryton(e), bass clarinet, bass drum, bass fiddle, bass horn, bass tuba, bass viol, basset horn, bazooka, bombard, bombardon, bongo (drum), bouzouki, buccina, bugle, buglet, bull fiddle, calliope, castanets, celeste, cello, cembalo, chair-organ, chalumeau, chamber organ, chikara, Chinese pavilion, chitarrone, chordophone, cinema-organ, cithara, cither(n), citole, cittern, clarichord, clarinet, clarion, clarsach, clave, clavichord, crwth, cymbal, cymbalo, decachord, dichord, didgeridoo, digitorium, double bass, drum, dulcimer, Dulcitone®, dumb-piano, echo, electric guitar, electric organ, euphonium, fagotto, fife, fipple-flute, flageolet, flügel, flügelhorn, flute, flûte-à-bec, flutina, French horn, gamelan, German flute, gimbard, gittern, glass harmonica, glockenspiel, grand piano, gu, guitar, gusla, Hammerklavier, hand-horn, hand-organ, harmonica, harmonicon, harmoniphone, harmonium, harp, harpsichord, hautboy, heckelphone, heptachord, horn, hornpipe, humstrum, hunting-horn, hurdy-gurdy, idiophone, jingling Johnny, kazoo, kent-bugle, keyboard(s), keybugle, klavier, koto, krummhorn, Kuh-horn, langsp(i)el, lituus, lur(e), lyra-viol, lyre, mandola, mandolin(e), mandora, maraca, marimba, marine trumpet, melodeon, metallophone, mirliton, monochord, Moog synthesizer, mouth-harp, mouth-organ, musette, musical glasses, naker, nose-flute, nun's-fiddle, oboe, oboe d'amore, oboe di caccia, ocarina, octachord, octave-flute, ophicleide,

musical instruments *contd.*

organ-harmonium, orpharion, orpheorion, pandora, panharmonicon, Pan-pipes, Pan's pipes, pantaleon, pianette, pianino, piano, piano-accordion, pianoforte, Pianola®, piano-organ, piffero, pipe, pipeless organ, pipe-organ, player piano, polyphon(e), posaune, psaltery, pyrophone, quint(e), racket(t), rebec(k), regal, rote, sackbut, salpinx, sambuca, sancho, sang, santir, sarangi, sarrusophone, sausage-bassoon, saxhorn, saxophone, seraphine, serinette, serpent, s(h)amisen, shawm, side-drum, sitar, small-pipes, sourdeline, sousaphone, spinet(te), squeeze-box, squiffer, steel drum, sticcado, stock-and-horn, strad, Stradivari(us), string bass, sultana, symphonion, symphony, synthesizer, syrinx, tabla, tabor, tabo(u)rin, tabret, tambour, tamboura, tambourine, tam-tam, testudo, tetrachord, theater organ, theorbo, timbal, timbrel, timpano, tin whistle, traps, triangle, trichord, tromba marina, trombone, trump, trumpet, trumpet marine, tuba, tubular bells, tympan, uillean pipes, ukulele, vibraharp, vibraphone, vielle, vihuela, vina, viol, viola, viola da braccio, (viola da) gamba, viola da gamba, viola da spalla, viola d'amore, violin, violoncello, violone, virginal(s), vocalion, waldflute, waldhorn, Welsh harp, xylophone, zambomba, zampogna, zanze, zel, zinke, zither, zufolo.

parliaments Althing (Iceland), Congress (USA), Cortes (Spain, Portugal), Dáil (Ireland), d(o)uma (Russia), ecclesia (Athens), Folketing (Denmark), House of Commons (UK), House of Keys (Isle of Man), House of Lords (UK), Knesset (Israel), Lagt(h)ing (Norway), Lagting (Norway), Landst(h)ing (Denmark), Landtag (Germany), Lok Sabha (India), Majlis (Iran), Odelst(h)ing (Norway), Oireachtas (Ireland), Parliament (UK), Pnyx (Athens), Porte (Turkey), Rajya Sabha (India), Reichsrat(h) (Austria), Reichstag (Germany), Rigsdag (Denmark), Riksdag (Sweden), Seanad (Ireland), Senate (Rome, USA, etc.), Skupshtina (Yugoslavia), Sobranje (Bulgaria), Stort(h)ing (Norway), Tynwald (Isle of Man), witenagemot (England).

prosody Alcaic, alexandrine, amphibrach, amphibrachic, amphimacer, Anacreontic, anacrusis, anacrustic, anapaest, anapaestic, antibacchius, antispast, antispastic, antistrophe, Archilochian, arsis, Asclepiad, asynartete, atonic, bacchius, catalectic, choliamb, choree, choriamb, cinquain, cretic, dactyl, decastich, decasyllabic, decasyllable, dipody, dispondaic, dispondee, distich, disyllable, ditrochean, ditrochee, dizain, dochmiac, dochmius, dodecasyllabic, dodecasyllable, dolichurus, duan, ectasis, ecthlipsis, elide, elision, enjamb(e)ment, envoy, epic, epirrhema, epistrophe, epitrite, epode, epopee, epopoeia, epos, epyllion, extrametrical, eye-rhyme, false quantity, feminine caesura, feminine ending, feminine rhyme, fifteener, free verse, galliambic, g(h)azal, glyconic, gradus, haiku, head-rhyme, hendecasyllabic, hendecasyllable, hephthemimer, heptameter, heptapody, heptasyllabic, heterostrophic, heterostrophy, hexameter, hexametric(al), hexapody, hexastich, Hudibrastic, huitain, hypercatalectic, hypercatalexis, hypermetrical, iamb, iambus, ictus, Ionic, irrational, kyrielle, laisse, Leonine, limerick, limma, linked verse, logaoedic, long-measure, macaronic(s), masculine ending, masculine rhyme, meliboean, miurus, monometer, monorhyme, monostich, monostrophic, mora, outride, oxytone, pantoum, pentameter, pentastich, penthemimer, Pherecratean, Pherecratic, Pindaric, poulters' measure, proceleusmatic, pyrrhic, Pythian, quatorzain, quatrain, reported verses, rhopalic, rhyme-royal, rich rhyme, riding-rhyme, rime riche, rime suffisante, rondeau, rondel, rove-over, rubaiyat, run-on, Sapphics, scazon, semeion, senarius, septenarius, sestina, spondee, strophe, synaphe(i)a, tetrameter, tetrapody, tetrasemic, tetrastich, thesis, tirade, tribrach, trimeter, tripody, triseme, trochee, villanelle, virelay.

ranks in armed forces able seaman, acting sub-lieutenant, admiral, admiral of the fleet, air chief marshal, air commandant, air commodore, air vice marshal, aircraftsman, air-marshal, brigadier, captain, chief officer, chief petty officer, chief technician, colonel, commandant, commander, commodore, corporal, field marshal, first officer, fleet chief petty officer, flight lieutenant, flight officer, flight sergeant, flying officer, general, group captain, group officer, junior seaman, junior technician, lance-corporal, lance-jack, lance-sergeant, leading aircraftsman, leading seaman, lieutenant, lieutenant-colonel, lieutenant-commander, lieutenant-general, major, major-general, marshal, marshal of the Royal Air Force, master-at-arms, midshipman, ordinary seaman, petty officer, pilot officer, post-captain, private, purser, quartermaster, quartermaster-general, quartermaster-sergeant, quartermistress, rear-admiral, risaldar, ritt-master, second lieutenant, second officer, senior aircraftsman, sergeant, sergeant-major, squadron leader, squadron officer, staff sergeant, sub-lieutenant, superintendent, third officer, vice admiral, warrant officer, wing commander, wing officer.

rhetoric abscission, alliteration, amoebaean, anacoluthia, anacoluthon, anadiplosis, anaphora, anaphoric, anastrophe, antimetabole, antimetathesis, antiphrasis, antiphrastic(al), antithesis, antithetic(al),

rhetoric *contd.*

antonomasia, aporia, asteism, asyndeton, auxesis, catachresis, chiasmus, climax, diallage, diegesis, dissimile, double entendre, dramatic irony, dysphemism, ecbole, echoic, ecphonesis, ellipsis, enallage, enantiosis, enumeration, epanadiplosis, epanalepsis, epanaphora, epanodos, epanorthosis, epexegesis, epiphonema, epizeuxis, erotema, erotetic, figure, flower, head-rhyme, hendiadys, holophrase, hypallage, hyperbaton, hyperbole, hypobole, hypostrophe, hypotyposis, hysteron-proteron, increment, irony, litotes, meiosis, metalepsis, metaphor, metonym, metonymy, mixed metaphor, onomatopoeia, oxymoron, parabole, paral(e)ipsis, parenthesis, prolepsis, simile, syllepsis, symploce, synchoresis, synchysis, synedoche, synoeciosis, trope, vicious circle, zeugma.

titles of rulers abuna, adelantado, ag(h)a, alderman, amir, amman, amtman, ard-ri(gh), atabeg, atabek, ataman, atheling, ayatollah, Ban, beglerbeg, begum, bey, boyar, burgrave, caboceer, cacique, caliph, caudillo, Cid, Dan, Dauphin, Dauphine, Dauphiness, dey, diadochus, doge, duce, duke, ealdorman, elector, emir, emperor, empress, ethnarch, exarch, gospodar, Graf, Gräfin, grave, Great Mogul, harmost, heptarch, hospodar, huzoor, imperator, Inca, infanta, infante, jarl, kaid, kaiser, kalif, khan, khedive, king, kinglet, kingling, landgrave, landgravine, maharaja(h), maharani, mandarin, marchesa, marchese, marchioness, margrave, margravine, marquess, marquis, marquise, mikado, Mirza, Monseigneur, monsieur, Monsignor, Monsignore, mormaor, mpret, nabob, naik, nawab, nizam, nomarch, omrah, padishah, palatine, palsgrave, pasha, pendragon, pentarch, pharaoh, prince, prince-bishop, prince-imperial, princess, raja(h), rajpramukh, rana, rani, Rhinegrave, Rhinegravine, sachem, sagamore, satrap, shah, sheik(h), sherif, shogun, sirdar, sovereign, stad(t)holder, starosta, suba(h)dar, sultan, suzerain, taoiseach, theocrat, toiseach, toparch, tsar, tuchun, voivode, waldgrave.

tools about-sledge, aiguille, auger, auger-bit, awl, boaster, bodkin, bolster, bradawl, broach, bucksaw, burin, burr, buzz-saw, card, caschrom, caulking-iron, celt, center-bit, chaser, chisel, chopper, clamp, cleaver, cold-chisel, cradle-scythe, crosscut-saw, crown-saw, diamond-drill, dibble, dividers, dolly, drawing-knife, draw-knife, drill, drove, els(h)in, extirpator, fillister, float, forceps, forfex, fork, fraise, frame-saw, fretsaw, gad, gang-saw, gavelock, gimlet, gouge, grapnel, grapple, graver, gurlet, hacksaw, hammer, handsaw, hawk, hay fork, hay knife, helve-hammer, hod, hoe, holing-axe, jackhammer, jack-plane, jointer, laster, level, leveling rod, leveling staff, loy, mace, madge, maker, mall, mallet, mattock, maul, monkey, moon-knife, mortar, muller, oliver, oustiti, pachymeter, pad-saw, palstave, panel saw, panga, paper-cutter, paper-knife, pattle, pecker, peel, pestle, pick, pickaxe, pincers, pinch, pinking-shears, piolet, pitchfork, plane, planer, plessor, plexor, pliers, plow, plugger, plumb, plumb-line, plumb-rule, plummet, pocket-knife, pointel, pricker, priest, priming-iron, priming-wire, probang, probe, probing-scissors, prod, prog, pruning-bill, pruning-hook, pruning-knife, pruning-shears, prunt, punch, puncheon, punty, quadrant, quannet, rabble, rake, raspatory, reed-knife, repositor, retractor, ricker, rickstick, riddle, riffle, ripper, ripping-saw, ripple, rip-saw, risp, router, rule, ruler, sash-tool, saw, sax, scalpel, scauper, scissors, scoop, scooper, scorper, scraper, screwdriver, screwjack, screw-wrench, scribe(r), scutch(er), scythe, seam-set, serving-mallet, shave, shears, shovel, sickle, slane, slate-axe, slater, slicker, smoother, snap, snarling-iron, snarling-rod, snips, soldering-bolt, soldering-iron, spade, spanner, spider, spokeshave, spud, squeegee, stadda, stake, stapler, stapling-machine, steel, stithy, stone-hammer, stretching-iron, strickle, strigil, stubble-rake, style, stylet, swage, swingle(-hand), switch, tedder, tenon-saw, threshel, thresher, thrust-hoe, tint-tool, tongs, trepan, trowel, T-square, turfing-iron, turf-spade, turning-saw, tweezers, twist drill, upright, van, vice, vulsella, waster, whip-saw, widener, wimble, wood-shears, wortle, xyster, Y-level.

units of measurement acre, ampere, angstrom, anker, ardeb, are, arpent, arroba, arshin, as, bar, barleycorn, barn, barrel, bath, baud, becquerel, bel, bigha, bit, board-foot, boll, bolt, braccio, bushel, butt, cab, cable, calorie, candela, candle, candy, carat, catty, cell, cental, centner, chain, chalder, chaldron, chenix, chopin, chronon, clove, co(o)mb, cor, cord, coss, coulumb, cran, crith, cubit, cumec, curie, cusec, cyathus, daraf, Debye (unit), degree, demy, dessiatine, digit, dirham, dra(ch)m, dyne, ell, em, en, epha(h), erg, farad, faraday, fathom, fermium, firkin, firlot, foot, fother, fou, furlong, gal, gallon, gerah, gilbert, gill, grain, gram, hectare, henry, hertz, hin, hogshead, homer, hoppus foot, hundredweight, inch, joule, kaneh, kantar, kelvin, k(h)at, kilderkin, kin, knot, league, leaguer, li, liang, liard, ligne, link, lippy, lire lisp(o)und, liter, log, lux, maneh, maund, meter, mho, micrometer, micron, mile, mil(l), mina, minim, minute, mna, modius, mole, morgen, muid, mutchkin, nail, neper, nepit, newton, nit (information), nit (luminance), noggin, obol, oersted, ohm, oke, omer, ounce, oxgang, parasang, pascal, peck, perch, picul, pin, pint, pipe, poise, pole, pood, pound, poundal, quart, quarter, quartern, quintal, quire, radian, ream,

359

units of measurement *contd.*

rem, rod, rood, rote, rotolo, run(d)let, rutherford, sabin, s(a)eculum, sazhen, scruple, second, seer, semuncia, shekel, shippound, siemens, sievert, sone, span, square, stadium, steradian, stere, stilb, stoke(s), stone, tael, talent, tare, tesla, therm, tical, tierce, tod, toise, tola, ton, tonne, tonneau, tor, truss, tun, vara, verst, virgate, volt, watt, weber, wey, yard, yardland, yojan.

vehicles aerotrain, air-car, amtrack, araba, arba, aroba, automobile, barouche, Bath chair, berlin(e), bicycle, biga, bobsled, bobsleigh, bogie, boneshaker, brake, britzka, brougham, bubble-car, buckboard, buckcart, buck-wagon, buggy, bus, cab, caboose, cabriolet, caisson, calash, camper, caravan, caravanette, caroche, car(r)iole, carry-all, catafalque, chair, chaise, chaise-cart, chapel cart, charabanc, chariot, clarence, coach, convertible, conveyance, cycle, dandy-cart, dandy-horse, dennet, désobligeante, dhooly, diesel, diligence, dilly, Dodgem(s)®, dog-cart, dogcart, dolly, doolie, dormitory-car, drag, dray, dros(h)ky, duck, ekka, fiacre, fly, fork-lift truck, four-in-hand, gharri, gig, glass-coach, go-kart, Green Goddess, gyrocar, gyrodyne, hack, hackery, hackney-carriage/coach, hatchback, herdic, honey-cart, honey-wagon, hurley-hacket, ice-yacht, inside-car, jeep, jingle, jinricksha(w), jitney, juggernaut, kago, kajawah, kart, kibitka, landau, landaulet(te), limousine, litter, lorry, mail-cart, minibus, monorail, motor caravan, motor-bicycle, motor-bike, motor-bus, motor-car, motor-coach, motor-cycle, motor-lorry, motor-scooter, norimon, omnibus, outside-car, palanquin (palankeen), palki, pantechnicon, pedal cycle, pedicab, people mover, phaeton, pick-up, pill-box, pincers, post-chaise, prairie schooner, pulka, quadriga, rail-bus, rail-car, rail-motor, ricksha(w), roadster, rockaway, runabout, safety bicycle, saloon-car, saloon-carriage, scooter, sedan, sedan-chair, shandry(dan), shooting-brake, sidecar, single-decker, skateboard, ski-bob, sled, sledge, sleeper, sleeping-car, sleeping-carriage, sleeping-coach, sleigh, slip-carriage, slip-coach, slipe, snowmobile, snow-plow, sociable, solo, speedster, spider, spring-carriage, spring-cart, squad car, stage-coach, stage-wagon, stanhope, station-wagon, steam-car, steam-carriage, steamer, steam-roller, stillage, stone boat, straddle carrier, street-car, sulky, surrey, tally-ho, tandem, tank, tank-car, tank-engine, tanker, tank-wagon, tarantas(s), tartana, tax(ed)-cart, taxi, taxicab, T-cart, telega, telpher, tender, thoroughbrace, through-train, tilbury, tim-whisk(e)y, tin Lizzie, tip, tip-cart, tipper, toboggan, tonga, tourer, touring-car, tractor, trailer, train, tram, tramway-car, transporter, transport-rider, trap, tricar, tricycle, trike, triplet, trishaw, troika, trolley, trolley-bus, trolley-car, troop-carrier, truck, tube, tumble-car(t), tumbrel, turbocar, two-decker, twoseater, two-wheeler, velocipede, vettura, victoria, village cart, vis-à-vis, volante, wagon, wagonette, wagon-lit, wain, water-cart, water-wagon, weasel, wheelbarrow, wheel-chair, whisk(e)y, Whitechapel cart.

vessels, ships argosy, barca, barque, barquentine, bateau, bawley, Berthon-boat, bilander, billyboy, bireme, birlinn, boat, bomb-ketch, bomb-vessel, brig, brigantine, Bucentaur, budgerow, bum-boat, buss, butty, cabin cruiser, caique, canal-boat, canoe, caravel, Carley float, carrack, casco, cat, catamaran, catboat, clipper, coaster, cob(b)le, cockboat, cockleshell, cog, collier, commodore, coracle, corocore, corvette, cot, crare, crayer, currach, cutter, dandy, deep-sinker, destroyer, d(h)ow, dinghy, diving-bell, dogger, drake, dreadnought, dredger, drog(h)er, dromond, dugout, East-Indiaman, E-boat, faltboat, felucca, flatboat, floating battery, flyboat, flying bridge, fore-and-after, frigate, frigatoon, funny, gabbart, galleass, galleon, galley, gal(l)iot, gallivat, gay-you, geordie, gondola, grab, hatch-boat, herringer, hooker, hovercraft, hoy, hydrofoil, hydroplane, hydrovane, ice-boat, Indiaman, iron-clad, jigger, jollyboat, junk, kayak, ketch, koff, laker, landing-craft, lapstreak, launch, liberty-ship, lighter, line-of-battle-ship, liner, long-boat, longship, lorcha, lugger, lymphad, mackinaw, masoolah, merchantman, mistico, monitor, monkey-boat, monohull, monoxylon, montaria, motor-boat, motor-launch, motor-ship, motoscafo, mud-boat, mudscow, multihull, nacelle, nuggar, outrigger, packet, packet-boat, packet-ship, pair-oar, patamar, pedalo, penteconter, periagua, peter-boat, pink, pinkie, pinky, pinnace, piragua, pirogue, pleasure-boat, pocket battleship, polacca, polacre, pontoon, powerboat, praam, pra(h)u, pram, privateer, puffer, pulwar, punt, puteli, quadrireme, quinquereme, randan, razee, river-boat, river-craft, row-barge, row-boat, rowing-boat, saic, sail-boat, sailing-boat, sailing-ship, salmon-coble, sampan, schooner, schuit, scooter, scow, scull, sculler, sea-boat, seaplane-carrier, settee, shallop, ship, ship-of-the-line, shore-boat, show-boat, skiff, sloop, sloop-of-war, smack, smuggler, snow, speed-boat, speedster, square rigger, steamboat, steamer, steam-launch, steam-packet, steamship, steam-tug, steam-vessel, steam-yacht, stern-wheeler, stew-can, sub, submarine, super-Dreadnought, supertanker, surface-craft, surf-board, surf-boat, surf-canoe, surfing-board, swamp boat, tanker, tartane(e), tender, tern, three-decker, three-master, tilt-boat, torpedo-boat, torpedo-boat destroyer, track-boat, tracker, trader, train ferry, tramp, transport-ship, trawler, trek-schuit, triaconter, trimaran, trireme, troop-carrier, trooper, troop-ship, tub, tug, tug-boat, turbine-steamer, turret-ship,

vessels, ships *contd.*
two-decker, two-master, U-boat, umiak, vaporetto, vedette(-boat), vessel, wager-boat, warship, water-bus, well-boat, well-smack, whaleboat, whaler, wherry, whiff, windjammer, xebec, yacht, yawl, zabra.

weapons, armor A-bomb, ack-ack, aerodart, ailette, air rifle, amusette, an(e)lace, arbalest, arblast, Archibald, Archie, arcubalist, armet, arquebus(e), baldric(k), ballista, ballistic missile, bandolier, Bangalore torpedo, basilisk, baton gun, bazooka, beaver, bill, Biscayan, blackjack, blowgun, blowpipe, bludgeon, blunderbuss, boarding-pike, bodkin, Bofors gun, bolas, bomb, bombard, boomerang, bowie knife, brassard, breastplate, breech-loader, Bren(gun), bricole, brigandine, broadsword, brown Bess, brown bill, buckler, buckshot, bulldog, bullet, bundook, burganet, byrnie, caltrop, cannon, carbine, carronade, casque, cataphract, catapult, chain-armor, chain-mail, chamfrain, Chassepot, chausses, cheval-de-frise, chokebore, claymore, cluster-bomb, coal-box, co(e)horn, Colt, Congreve, corium, dag, dagger, dah, Damascus blade, Damascus sword, demi-cannon, demi-culverin, demi-lance, depth-bomb, depth-charge, dirk, dragoon, elephant gun, épée, escopette, Exocet®, express rifle, falchion, falconet, field gun, fire-arm, fire-arrow, firebomb, firelock, firepot, fission bomb, flail, flame-thrower, flick-knife, flintlock, foil, fougade, fougasse, four-pounder, fusee, fusil, Garand rifle, gatling-gun, gavelock, genouillère, gisarme, gladius, gorget, grapeshot, greave, Greek fire, grenade, gun, habergeon, hackbut, hacqueton, hailshot, halberd, half-pike, hand-grenade, hand-gun, han(d)jar, handstaff, harquebus, hauberk, H-bomb, heaume, helm, helmet, hielaman, howitzer, jack, jamb(e), jazerant, jesserant, Jethart staff, kris, lamboys, lame, lance, Lochaber-axe, Long Tom, machete, machine-gun, mangonel, martel, Martini(-Henry), matchlock, Mauser, Maxim(-gun), mesail, Mills bomb, Mills grenade, mine, mine-thrower, mini-rocket launcher, minnie, mitrailleur, mitrailleuse, morgenstern, morglay, morning-star, mor(r)ion, mortar, musket, musketoon, nulla-nulla, oerlikon, panga, partisan, pauldron, pavis(e), peasecod-cuirass, pederero, pelican, pelta, perrier, petrary, petronel, pickelhaube, pike, pilum, pistol, pistolet, placket, plastron, plate-armor, pocket-pistol, poitrel, pole-ax(e), poleyn, pompom, poniard, potgun, quarter-staff, queen's-arm, rapier, rerebrace, rest, revolver, rifle, rifle-grenade, sabaton, saber, saker, sallet, saloon-pistol, saloon-rifle, sap, sarbacane, schiavone, schläger, scimitar, scorpion, scutum, serpentine, sharp, shell, shield, shillela(g)h, shortsword, shotgun, shrapnel, siege-artillery, siege-gun, siege-piece, singlestick, six-gun, six-shooter, skean(dhu), sling, slung-shot, small-arm, small-sword, smoke-ball, smoke-bomb, snickersnee, spadroon, sparth(e), spear, spear gun, splint-armor, spontoon, spring-gun, squid, steel, sten gun, Sterling, stern-chaser, stiletto, stone axe, stone-bow, stylet, submachine-gun, sumpit(an), switch-blade (knife), swivel-gun, sword, sword bayonet, sword-cane, sword-stick, tace, targe, target, taslet, tasse, tasset, testudo, three-pounder, threshel, throw-stick, time-bomb, toc emma, toggle-iron, tomahawk, tomboc, tommy-gun, tormentum, torpedo, tortoise, trecento, trench-mortar, trident, truncheon, tuille, tuillette, tulwar, turret-gun, twibill, vambrace, vamplate, V-bomb, visor, vou(l)ge, war-wolf, waster, water-cannon, water-pistol, Welsh hook, white-arm, Winchester (rifle), wind-gun, wo(o)mera(ng), yatag(h)an, zumbooruk.

wine-bottle sizes baby, balthasar, jeroboam, magnum, Methuselah, nebuchadnezzar, nip, rehoboam, Salmanazar.

zodiac signs Aquarius, Aries, Cancer, Capricorn, Gemini, Leo, Libra, Pisces, Sagittarius, Scorpio, Taurus, Virgo.

Appendix II

Words listed by suffix

-ast chiliast, diaskeuast, dicast, dikast, dynast, ecclesiast, ecdysiast, elegiast, encomiast, enthusiast, fantast, gymnasiast, gymnast, Hesychast, hypochondriast, iconoclast, idoloclast, metaphrast, orgiast, pancratiast, paraphrast, pederast, peltast, phantasiast, pleonast, scholiast, utopiast.

-aster criticaster, grammaticaster, medicaster, philosophaster, poetaster, politicaster, theologaster.

-cide aborticide, acaricide, algicide, aphicide, aphidicide, bacillicide, bactericide, biocide, deicide, ecocide, ethnocide, feticide, filicide, foeticide, fratricide, fungicide, genocide, germicide, giganticide, herbicide, homicide, infanticide, insecticide, larvicide, liberticide, matricide, menticide, molluscicide, ovicide, parasiticide, parasuicide, parricide, patricide, pesticide, prolicide, regicide, rodenticide, sororicide, spermicide, suicide, taeniacide, trypanocide, tyrannicide, uxoricide, vaticide, verbicide, vermicide, viricide, viticide, vulpicide, weedicide,

-cracy aristocracy, autocracy, bureaucracy, chrysocracy, cottonocracy, democracy, demonocracy, despotocracy, dollarocracy, doulocracy, dulocracy, ergatocracy, Eurocracy, gerontocracy, gynecocracy, hagiocracy, hierocracy, isocracy, kakistocracy, meritocracy, millocracy, mobocracy, monocracy, nomocracy, ochlocracy, pantisocracy, pedantocracy, physiocracy, plantocracy, plutocracy, plutodemocracy, pornocracy, ptochocracy, slavocracy, snobocracy, squattocracy, stratocracy, technocracy, thalassocracy, thalattocracy, theocracy, timocracy.

-crat aristocrat, autocrat, bureaucrat, cosmocrat, democrat, hierocrat, meritocrat, millocrat, mobocrat, monocrat, ochlocrat, pantisocrat, pedantocrat, physiocrat, plutocrat, slavocrat, stratocrat, technocrat, theocrat.

-cratic aristocratic, autocratic, bureaucratic, cosmocratic, democratic, Eurocratic, gerontocratic, gynecocratic, hierocratic, isocratic, meritocratic, mobocratic, monocratic, ochlocratic, pancratic, pantisocratic, pedantocratic, physiocratic, plutocratic, stratocratic, technocratic, theocratic, timocratic, undemocratic.

-cultural accultural, agricultural, arboricultural, crinicultural, cultural, floricultural, horticultural, piscicultural, subcultural, vinicultural, vocicultural.

-culture agriculture, apiculture, aquaculture, aquiculture, arboriculture, aviculture, culture, electroculture, floriculture, horticulture, mariculture, monoculture, ostreiculture, pisciculture, pomiculture, self-culture, sericiculture, sericulture, silviculture, stirpiculture, subculture, sylviculture, viniculture, viticulture, water-culture, zooculture.

-cyte athrocyte, cyte, erythrocyte, fibrocyte, gonocyte, granulocyte, hemocyte, leucocyte, lymphocyte, macrocyte, microcyte, oocyte, phagocyte, poikilocyte, spermatocyte, thrombocyte, thymocyte.

-dom Anglo-Saxondom, apedom, archdukedom, attorneydom, babeldom, babudom, bachelordom, beadledom, beggardom, birthdom, bishopdom, boredom, Bumbledom, chiefdom, Christendom, clerkdom, cockneydom, crippledom, cuckoldom, czardom, demirepdom, devildom, Dogberrydom, dolldom, dufferdom, dukedom, dancedom, earldom, enthraldom, fairydom, fandom, filmdom, flunkeydom,

-dom *contd.*

fogydom, freedom, fresherdom, Greekdom, gypsydom, halidom, heathendom, heirdom, hobbledehoydom, hobodom, junkerdom, kaiserdom, kingdom, kitchendom, leechdom, liegedom, mandom, martyrdom, masterdom, newspaperdom, noodledom, noveldom, officialdom, overfreedom, penny-wisdom, popedom, princedom, puppydom, puzzledom, Quakerdom, queendom, queerdom, rascaldom, rebeldom, sachemdom, saintdom, savagedom, Saxondom, scoundreldom, serfdom, sheikdom, sheikhdom, sheriffdom, Slavdom, spinsterdom, squiredom, stardom, subkingdom, swelldom, thanedom, thraldom, thralldom, topsyturvydom, tsardom, underkingdom, unwisdom, villadom, whoredom, wisdom, Yankeedom.

-ferous aluminiferous, amentiferous, antenniferous, argentiferous, auriferous, bacciferous, balsamiferous, bulbiferous, calciferous, carboniferous, celliferous, celluliferous, cheliferous, cobaltiferous, conchiferous, coniferous, coralliferous, corniferous, cruciferous, culmiferous, cupriferous, cupuliferous, diamantiferous, diamondiferous, doloriferous, dorsiferous, ferriferous, flagelliferous, flammiferous, floriferous, foraminiferous, fossiliferous, frondiferous, fructiferous, frugiferous, furciferous, garnetiferous, gemmiferous, glandiferous, glanduliferous, globuliferous, glumiferous, granuliferous, guaniferous, gummiferous, guttiferous, lactiferous, laniferous, laticiferous, lethiferous, luciferous, luminiferous, mammaliferous, mammiferous, manganiferous, manniferous, margaritiferous, melliferous, metalliferous, morbiferous, mortiferous, moschiferous, muciferous, nectariferous, nickeliferous, nubiferous, nuciferous, odoriferous, oleiferous, omniferous, ossiferous, oviferous, ovuliferous, ozoniferous, papilliferous, papuliferous, Permo-Carboniferous, pestiferous, petaliferous, petroliferous, piliferous, platiniferous, plumbiferous, polliniferous, pomiferous, poriferous, proliferous, pyritiferous, quartziferous, reptiliferous, resiniferous, rotiferous, sacchariferous, saliferous, salutiferous, sanguiferous, sebiferous, seminiferous, septiferous, siliciferous, soboliferous, somniferous, soporiferous, spiniferous, spinuliferous, splendiferous, staminiferous, stanniferous, stelliferous, stigmatiferous, stoloniferous, strombuliferous, styliferous, sudoriferous, tentaculiferous, thuriferous, titaniferous, tuberiferous, umbelliferous, umbriferous, unfossiliferous, uriniferous, vitiferous, vociferous, yttriferous, zinciferous, zinkiferous.

-gamy allogamy, apogamy, autogamy, bigamy, chalazogamy, chasmogamy, cleistogamy, clistogamy, cryptogamy, deuterogamy, dichogamy, digamy, endogamy, exogamy, geitonogamy, hercogamy, herkogamy, heterogamy, homogamy, hypergamy, isogamy, misogamy, monogamy, oogamy, pangamy, pantagamy, plasmogamy, plastogamy, polygamy, porogamy, siphonogamy, syngamy, trigamy, xenogamy, zoogamy.

-genesis abiogenesis, agamogenesis, anthropogenesis, autogenesis, biogenesis, blastogenesis, carcinogenesis, chondrogenesis, cytogenesis, diagenesis, diplogenesis, dynamogenesis, ectogenesis, electrogenesis, embryogenesis, epeirogenesis, epigenesis, gametogenesis, gamogenesis, hematogenesis, heterogenesis, histogenesis, homogenesis, hylogenesis, hypogenesis, merogenesis, metagenesis, monogenesis, morphogenesis, mythogenesis, neogenesis, noogenesis, ontogenesis, oogenesis, organogenesis, orogenesis, orthogenesis, osteogenesis, palingenesis, pangenesis, paragenesis, parthenogenesis, pathogenesis, pedogenesis, perigenesis, petrogenesis, phylogenesis, phytogenesis, polygenesis, psychogenesis, pyogenesis, schizogenesis, spermatogenesis, sporogenesis, syngenesis, thermogenesis, xenogenesis.

-genic aesthesiogenic, allergenic, androgenic, anthropogenic, antigenic, biogenic, blastogenic, carcinogenic, cariogenic, cryogenic, dysgenic, ectogenic, electrogenic, endogenic, epeirogenic, erogenic, erotogenic, eugenic, genic, glycogenic, hallucinogenic, histogenic, hypnogenic, hysterogenic, iatrogenic, lactogenic, lysigenic, mammogenic, mutagenic, myogenic, neurogenic, odontogenic, oestrogenic, oncogenic, ontogenic, orogenic, orthogenic, osteogenic, pathogenic, photogenic, phytogenic, polygenic, psychogenic, pyogenic, pyrogenic, pythogenic, radiogenic, rhizogenic, saprogenic, schizogenic, somatogenic, spermatogenic, telegenic, teratogenic, thermogenic, tumorgenic, tumorigenic, visiogenic, zoogenic, zymogenic.

-gon chiliagon, decagon, dodecagon, endecagon, enneagon, hendecagon, heptagon, hexagon, isogon, nonagon, octagon, pentagon, perigon, polygon, tetragon, trigon.

-gram airgram, anagram, anemogram, angiogram, audiogram, ballistocardiogram, barogram, cablegram, calligram, cardiogram, cartogram, centigram, centimeter-gram, chromatogram, chromogram, chronogram, cryptogram, dactylogram, decagram, decigram, dendrogram, diagram, echogram, electrocardiogram, electroencephalogram, encephalogram, engram, epigram, ergogram, ferrogram, harmonogram, hectogram, hexagram, hierogram, histogram, hologram, ideogram, indicator-diagram, isogram, kilogram, lexigram,

-gram *contd.*

lipogram, logogram, lymphogram, marconigram, marigram, meteorogram, micrograrn, monogram, myogram, nanogram, nephogram, neurogram, nomogram, organogram, oscillogram, pangram, paragram, parallelogram, pentagram, phonogram, photogram, phraseogram, pictogram, program, psychogram, pyelogram, radiogram, radiotelegram, röntgenogram, scintigram, seismogram, sialogram, skiagram, sociogram, spectrogram, spectroheliogram, sphenogram, sphymogram, steganogram, stereogram, tachogram, telegram, tephigram, tetragram, thermogram, tomogram, trigram.

-graph Addressograph®, airgraph, allograph, anemograph, apograph, audiograph, autograph, autoradiograph, ballistocardiograph, bar-graph, barograph, biograph, cardiograph, cathodograph, cerograph, chirograph, choreograph, chromatograph, chromolithograph, chromoxylograph, chronograph, cinematograph, coronagraph, coronograph, cryptograph, cyclograph, cymagraph, cymograph, diagraph, Dictograph®, digraph, dynamograph, eidograph, electrocardiograph, electroencephalograph, electrograph, electromyograph, ellipsograph, encephalograph, epigraph, ergograph, evaporograph, flannelgraph, glyphograph, harmonograph, hectograph, helicograph, heliograph, hierograph, hodograph, holograph, homograph, hydrograph, hyetograph, hyetometrograph, hygrograph, ideograph, idiograph, jellygraph, keraunograph, kinematograph, kinetograph, kymograph, lithograph, logograph, magnetograph, marconigraph, marigraph, meteorograph, micrograph, microphotograph, microseismograph, mimeograph, monograph, myograph, nephograph, nomograph, odograph, odontograph, oleograph, opisthograph, orthograph, oscillograph, pantograph, paragraph, pentagraph, phonautograph, phonograph, photograph, photolithograph, photomicrograph, phototelegraph, photozincograph, phraseograph, pictograph, planigraph, plethysmograph, polygraph, pseudograph, psychograph, pyrophotograph, radioautograph, radiograph, radiometeorograph, radiotelegraph, rotograph, seismograph, salenograph, serigraph, shadowgraph, skiagraph, spectrograph, spectroheliograph, sphygmograph, spirograph, steganograph, stenograph, stereograph, Stevengraph, stylograph, syngraph, tachograph, tachygraph, Telautograph®, telegraph, telephotograph, thermograph, thermometrograph, tomograph, torsiograph, trigraph, vectograph, vibrograph, xylograph, zincograph.

-graphy aerography, ampelography, angiography, anthropogeography, anthropography, areography, autobiography, autography, autoradiography, autotypography, ballistocardiography, bibliography, biogeography, biography, brachygraphy, cacography, calligraphy, cardiography, cartography, cathodography, ceramography, cerography, chalcography, chartography, chirography, cholangiography, choregraphy, choreography, chorography, chromatography, chromolithography, chromotypography, chromoxylography, chronography, cinematography, cinemicrography, climatography, cometography, cosmography, cryptography, crystallography, dactyliography, dactylography, demography, dermatography, dermography, discography, dittography, doxography, echocardiography, ectypography, electrocardiography, electroencephalography, electrography, electromyography, electrophotography, encephalography, enigmatography, epigraphy, epistolography, ethnography, ferrography, filmography, geography, glossography, glyphography, glyptography, hagiography, haplography, heliography, heresiography, hierography, historiography, holography, horography, hydrography, hyetography, hymnography, hypsography, ichnography, ichthyography, iconography, ideography, lexicography, lexigraphy, lipography, lithography, logography, lymphography, mammography, metallography, microcosmography, micrography, microphotography, mimography, monography, morphography, myography, mythography, nomography, nosography, oceanography, odontography, oleography, opisthography, orchesography, oreography, organography, orography, orthography, osteography, paleogeography, paleography, paleontography, pantography, paroemiography, pasigraphy, pathography, petrography, phonography, photography, photolithography, photomicrography, phototelegraphy, photoxylography, photozincography, physiography, phytogeography, phytography, pictography, polarography, polygraphy, pornography, prosopography, pseudepigraphy, pseudography, psychobiography, psychography, pterylography, pyelography, pyrography, pyrophotography, radiography, radiotelegraphy, reprography, rhyparography, röntgenography, scenography, scintigraphy, seismography, selenography, serigraphy, sialography, snobography, spectrography, sphygmography, steganography, stenography, stereography, stratigraphy, stylography, symbolography, tachygraphy, telautography, telegraphy, telephotography, thalassography, thanatography, thaumatography, thermography, tomography, topography, typography, ultrasonography, uranography, urography, ventriculography, xerography, xeroradiography, xylography, xylopyrography, xylotypography, zincography, zoogeography, zoography.

-graphical autobiographical, bathygraphical, bathyorographical, bibliographical, biobibliographical, biogeographical, biographical, cacographical, calligraphical, cartographical, cerographical, chorographical, cinematographical, climatographical, cosmographical, geographical, glossographical, graphical, hagiographical, hierographical, historiographical, hydrographical, hyetographical, hygrographical, ichnographical, ideographical, lexicographical, lexigraphical, lithographical, logographical, monographical, myographical, oceanographical, oreographical, orographical, orthographical, paleographical, paleontographical, pantographical, paragraphical, pasigraphical, petrographical, photographical, physiographical,prosopographical, pseudepigraphical, psychobiographical, psychographical, pterylographical, seismographical, selenographical, spectrographical, stenographical, stereographical, stratigraphical, tachygraphical, topographical, typographical, xylographical, zincographical, zoogeographical, zoographical.

-hedron chiliahedron, decahedron, dihedron, dodecahedron, enneahedron, hemihedron, hexahedron, holohedron, icosahedron, icositetrahedron, leucitohedron, octahedron, octohedron, pentahedron, polyhedron, pyritohedron, rhombohedron, scalenohedron, tetrahedron, tetrakishexahedron, trapezohedron, triakisoctahedron, trihedron, trisoctahedron.

-hood adulthood, angelhood, apehood, apprenticehood, babyhood, bachelorhood, beadlehood, beasthood, bountihood, boyhood, brotherhood, cathood, childhood, Christhood, companionhood, cousinhood, cubhood, deaconhood, dollhood, drearihood, elfhood, fairyhood, falsehood, fatherhood, flapperhood, flesh-hood, gawkihood, gentlehood, gentlemanhood, gianthood, girlhood, godhood, hardihood, high-priesthood, hobbledehoyhood, hoghood, hoydenhood, idlehood, invalidhood, jealoshood, kinghood, kinglihood, knighthood, ladyhood, likelihood, livelihood, lustihood, maidenhood, maidhood, manhood, masterhood, matronhood, misshood, monkhood, motherhood, nationhood, needy-hood, neighborhood, novicehood, nunhood, old-maidhood, orphanhood, pagehood, parenthood, popehood, priesthood, princehood, prophethood, puppyhood, queenhood, sainthood, selfhood, serfhood, sisterhood, spinsterhood, squirehood, statehood, swinehood, tabbyhood, thanehood, thinghood, traitorhood, unlikelihood, virginhood, waiterhood, widowerhood, widowhood, wifehood, wivehood, womanhood, youthhood.

-iac ammoniac, amnesiac, anaphrodisiac, anglomaniac, Anglophobiac, antaphrodisiac, anthomaniac, aphasiac, aphrodisiac, archgenethliac, bacchiac, bibliomaniac, cardiac, celiac, Cluniac, coprolaliac, demoniac, dextrocardiac, Dionysiac, dipsomaniac, dochmiac, dysthymiac, egomaniac, elegiac, endocardiac, erotomaniac, etheromaniac, Genesiac, genethliac, hebephreniac, heliac, hemophiliac, hypochondriac, iliac, insomniac, intracardiac, Isiac, kleptomaniac, maniac, megalomaniac, meloncholiac, melomaniac, monomaniac, morphinomaniac, mythomaniac, necrophiliac, neurastheniac, nymphomaniac, opsomaniac, orchidomaniac, Pandemoniac, paradisiac, paranoiac, paraphiliac, paroemiac, pedophiliac, pericardiac, phrenesiac, pyromaniac, sacroiliac, scopophiliac, scoriac, simoniac, symposiac, Syriac, theomaniac, theriac, timbromaniac, toxiphobiac, zodiac, zygocardiac.

-iatric chemiatric, chemopsychiatric, geriatric, hippiatric, kinesiatric, pediatric, psychiatric, psychogeriatric.

-iatry chemopsychiatry, geriatry, hippiatry, neuropsychiatry, orthopsychiatry, pediatry, podiatry, psychiatry.

-ician academician, acoustician, aeroelastician, aesthetician, arithmetician, audiometrician, beautician, biometrician, clinician, cosmetician, diagnostician, dialectician, dietician, econometrician, ekistician, electrician, geometrician, geopolitician, geriatrician, informatician, linguistician, logician, logistician, magician, magnetician, mathematician, mechanician, metaphysician, metrician, mortician, musician, obstetrician, optician, pediatrician, patrician, Paulician, phonetician, physician, politician, practician, psychogeriatrician, psychometrician, rhetorician, rubrician, statistician, systematician, tactician, technician, theoretician.

-ics acoustics, acrobatics, aerobatics, aerobics, aerodynamics, aeronautics, aerostatics, aesthetics, agogics, agnostics, ambisonics, apologetics, aquabatics, aquanautics, astrodynamics, astronautics, astrophysics, athletics, atmospherics, autonomics, avionics, axiomatics, ballistics, bioastronautics, biodynamics, bioethics, biomathematics, biomechanics, biometrics, bionics, bionomics, biophysics, biorhythmics, biosystematics, cacogenics, calisthenics, callisthenics, catacoustics, catallactics, cataphonics, catechetics, catoptrics, ceroplastics, chemotherapeutics, chremastics, chromatics, civics, cliometrics, conics,

-ics *contd.*

cosmonautics, cosmopolitics, cryogenics, cryonics, cryophysics, cybernetics, cytogenetics, deontics, dermatoglyphics, diacoustics, diagnostics, dialectics, dianetics, didactics, dietetics, dioptrics, dogmatics, dramatics, dynamics, dysgenics, eclectics, econometrics, economics, ecumenics, ekistics, electrodynamics, electrokinetics, electromechanics, electronics, electrostatics, electrotechnics, electrotherapeutics, electrothermics, energetics, entoptics, environics, epigenetics, epistemics, epizootics, ergonomics, ethics, ethnolinguistics, eudaemonics, eudemonics, eugenics, eurhythmics, euthenics, exegetics, floristics, fluidics, forensics, genetics, geodetics, geodynamics, geophysics, geopolitics, geoponics, geostatics, geotectonics, geriatrics, gerontotherapeutics, glyptics, gnomonics, gnotobiotics, graphemics, graphics, gyrostatics, halieutics, haptics, harmonics, hedonics, hermeneutics, hermetics, hippiatrics, histrionics, homiletics, hydraulics, hydrodynamics, hydrokinetics, hydromagnetics, hydromechanics, hydroponics, hydrostatics, hydrotherapeutics, hygienics, hypersonics, hysterics, informatics, irenics, isagogics, isometrics, kinematics, kinesics, kinetics, linguistics, lithochromatics, liturgics, logistics, loxodromics, macrobiotics, macroeconomics, magnetics, magneto-hydrodynamics, magneto-optics, maieutics, mathematics, mechanics, melodics, metalinguistics, metamathematics, metaphysics, metapsychics, meteoritics, microeconomics, microelectronics, microphysics, mnemotechnics, mole-electronics, monostrophics, morphemics, morphophonemics, nautics, nucleonics, numismatics, obstetrics, olympics, onomastics, optics, optoelectronics, orchestics, orthodontics, orthodromics, orthogenics, orthopedics, orthoptics, orthotics, paideutics, pantopragmatics, paralinguistics, party-politics, pataphysics, patristics, pedagogics, pedentics, pediatrics, pedodontics, peptics, periodontics, pharmaceutics, pharmacodynamics, pharmacokinetics, phelloplastics, phonemics, phonetics, phonics, phonocamptics, phonotactics, photics, photochromics, photoelectronics, phototherapeutics, photovoltaics, physics, physiotherapeutics, plastics, pneumatics, pneumodynamics, polemics, politico-economics, politics, power-politics, problematics, prosthetics, prosthodontics, psychics, psychodynamics, psychogeriatrics, psycholinguistics, psychometrics, psychonomics, psychophysics, psychosomatics, psychotherapeutics, pyrotechnics, quadraphonics, quadrophonics, radionics, radiophonics, radiotherapeutics, rhythmics, robotics, semantics, semeiotics, semiotics, Semitics, sferics, significs, sociolinguistics, sonics, sophistics, spherics, sphragistics, statics, stereoptics, strategics, stylistics, subatomics, subtropics, syllabics, symbolics, synectics, systematics, tactics, technics, tectonics, telearchics, thaumaturgics, theatrics, therapeutics, thermionics, thermodynamics, thermotics, toponymics, toreutics, transonics, transsonics, ultrasonics, vitrics, zoiatrics, zootechnics, zymotechnics.

-iform aciform, acinaciform, aciniform, aeriform, alphabetiform, amoebiform, anguiform, anguilliform, antenniform, asbestiform, auriform, aviform, bacciform, bacilliform, biform, bursiform, cactiform, calcariform, calceiform, calyciform, cambiform, campaniform, campodeiform, cancriform, capriform, cauliform, cerebriform, cirriform, claviform, clypeiform, cobriform, cochleariform, coliform, colubriform, conchiform, coniform, coralliform, cordiform, corniform, corolliform, cotyliform, crateiform, cribriform, cristiform, cruciform, cteniform, cubiform, cucumiform, culiciform, cultriform, cumuliform, cuneiform, curviform, cyathiform, cylindriform, cymbiform, cystiform, deiform, dendriform, dentiform, digitiform, dolabriform, elytriform, ensiform, equisetiform, eruciform, falciform, fibriform, filiform, flabelliform, flagelliform, floriform, fringilliform, fungiform, fusiform, gangliform, gasiform, glandiform, granitiform, granuliform, hydatidiform, incisiform, infundibuliform, insectiform, janiform, jelliform, lamelliform, lanciform, lapilliform, larviform, lentiform, limaciform, linguiform, lumbriciform, lyriform, malleiform, mamilliform, mammiform, maniform, medusiform, mitriform, monadiform, moniliform, morbilliform, multiform, mummiform, muriform, mytiliform, napiform, natiform, naupliiform, nubiform, omniform, oviform, paliform, panduriform, papilliform, patelliform, pelviform, penicilliform, penniform, perciform, phialiform, piliform, pisciform, pisiform, placentiform, planuliform, plexiform, poculiform, proteiform, pulvilliform, pyriform, quadriform, radiciform, raduliform, raniform, reniform, restiform, retiform, sacciform, sagittiform, salpiform, scalariform, scalpelliform, scalpriform, scoleciform, scolopendriform, scutiform, scyphiform, securiform, septiform, serpentiform, spiniform, spongiform, squamiform, stalactiform, stalactitiform, stelliform, stratiform, strigiform, strobiliform, strombuliform, styliform, tauriform, tectiform, telescopiform, thalliform, triform, tuberiform, tubiform, tympaniform, umbraculiform, unciform, unguiform, uniform, vaporiform, variform, vasculiform, vasiform, vermiform, verruciform, versiform, villiform, viperiform, vitriform, vulviform, ypsiliform, zeolitiform.

-ism abnormalism, abolitionism, aboriginalism, absenteeism, absolutism, academicalism, academicism, accidentalism, achromatism, acosmism, acrobatism, acotism, actinism, activism, Adamitism, adiaphorism, adoptianism, Adopttionism, adventurism, aeroembolism, aerotropism, aestheticism, Africanism, ageism, agnosticism, agrarianism, Albigensianism, albinism, albinoism, alcoholism, algorism, alienism, allelomorphism, allotropism, alpinism, altruism, amateurism, Americanism, ametabolism, amoralism, amorism, amorphism, anabaptism, anabolism, anachronism, anagrammatism, anarchism, anastigmatism, androdioecism, andromonoecism, aneurism, Anglicanism, anglicism, Anglo-Catholicism, aniconism, animalism, animatism, animism, annihilationism, antagonism, anthropomorphism, anthropomorphitism, anthropopathism, anthropophuism, anthropopsychism, antichristianism, anticivism, anticlericalism, antidisestablishmentarianism, anti-federalism, anti-Gallicanism, anti-Jacobinism, antinomianism, antiochianism, antiquarianism, anti-Semitism, antisepticism, antisocialism, antitheism, antitrinitarianism, antivaccinationism, antivivisectionism, anythingarianism, apheliotropism, aphorism, apism, aplanatism, apochromatism, apogeotropism, apoliticism, Apollinarianism, apostolicism, apriorism, Arabism, Aramaism, Arcadianism, archaicism, archaism, Arianism, aristocratism, Aristotelianism, Aristotelism, Arminianism, asceticism, asepticism, Asiaticism, aspheterism, asteism, asterism, astigmatism, asynchronism, asystolism, atavism, atheism, athleticism, Atlanticism, atomism, atonalism, atropism, Atticism, attorneyism, Augustinianism, Australianism, authorism, authoritarianism, autism, autochthonism, autoeroticism, autoerotism, automatism, automobilism, automorphism, autotheism, avant-gardism, Averrhoism, Averroism, Baalism, Baathism, Ba'athism, Babbitism, Babeeism, babelism, Babiism, Babism, babuism, bacchanalianism, bachelorism, Baconianism, Bahaism, bantingism, baptism, barbarism, bashawism, bastardism, bathmism, bedlamism, behaviorism, Benthamism, Bergsonism, Berkeleianism, bestialism, betacism, biblicism, bibliophilism, bilateralism, bilingualism, bimetallism, bipedalism, blackguardism, blepharism, bogeyism, bogyism, Bohemianism, bolshevism, Bonapartism, bonism, boobyism, Boswellism, botulism, Bourbonism, bowdlerism, bradyseism, braggartism, Brahmanism, Brahminism, Braidism, Briticism, Britishism, Brownism, bruxism, Buchmanism, Buddhism, bullyism, Burschenism, Byronism, Byzantinism, cabalism, cabbalism, Caesarism, caesaropapism, caffeinism, caffeism, Calvinism, cambism, Camorrism, cannibalism, capitalism, Carbonarism, careerism, Carlism, Carlylism, carnalism, Cartesianism, casualism, catabolism, catastrophism, catechism, catechumenism, Catharism, catheterism, catholicism, causationism, cauterism, cavalierism, Celticism, cenobitism, centenarianism, centralism, centripetalism, centrism, cerebralism, ceremonialism, chaldaism, characterism, charism, charlatanism, chartism, Chasidism, Chassidism, Chaucerism, chauvinism, chemism, chemotropism, chloralism, Christianism, chromaticism, churchism, Ciceronianism, cicisbeism, cinchonism, civism, classicism, clericalism, cliquism, clubbism, coalitionism, Cobdenism, cocainism, cockneyism, collectivism, collegialism, colloquialism, colonialism, commensalism, commercialism, communalism, communism, compatriotism, comstockism, Comtism, conacreism, conceptualism, concettism, concretism, confessionalism, confrontationism, Confucianism, Congregationalism, conservatism, consortism, constitutionalism, constructionism, constructivism, consubstantialism, consumerism, contact-metamorphism, continentalism, contortionism, contrabandism, conventionalism, conversationism, convictism, copyism, corporatism, corporealism, corybantism, cosmeticism, cosmism, cosmopolitanism, cosmopolitism, cosmotheism, cottierism, Couéism, courtierism, creatianism, creationism, cretinism, cretism, criticism, crotalism, cubism, cultism, curialism, cyclicism, cynicism, czarism, Dadaism, Daltonism, dandyism, Darwinism, deaf-mutism, decimalism, defeatism, deism, demagogism, demagoguism, demoniacism, demonianism, demonism, denominationalism, departmentalism, descriptivism, depotism, deteriorism, determinism, deviationism, devilism, diabolism, diachronism, diageotropism, diaheliotropism, dialecticism, diamagnetism, diaphototropism, diastrophism, diatropism, dichroism, dichromatism, dichromism, diclinism, dicrotism, didacticism, diffusionism, dilettanteism, dilettantism, dimerism, dimorphism, diocism, diorism, diothelism, diphysitism, dirigism, dissenterism, dissolutionism, disyllabism, ditheism, ditheletism, dithelism, dithelitism, divisionism, Docetism, doctrinairism, doctrinarianism, Dogberryism, dogmatism, do-goodism, dolichocephalism, donatism, donnism, do-nothingism, Doricism, Dorism, dowdyism, draconism, dragonism, dramaticism, drudgism, druidism, dualism, dudism, dufferism, dunderheadism, dynamism, dyotheletism, dyothelism, dysphemism, ebionism, ebionitism, echoism, eclecticism, ecumenicalism, ecumenicism, ecumenism, Edwardianism, egalitarianism, egoism, egotheism, egotism, electromagnetism, electromerism, elementalism, elitism, Elizabethanism, embolism, emotionalism, empiricism, enantiomorphism, Encratism, encyclopedism, endemism, Englishism, entrism, environmentalism, eonism, epicism, Epicureanism, epicurism, epiphenomenalism, epiphytism, epipolism, episcopalianism, episcopalism, equalitarianism, equestrianism, Erastianism, eremitism, erethism, ergotism, eroticism, erotism, erythrism, escapism, esotericism, esoterism, Essenism, essentialism, etacism, etherism, ethicism, ethnicism, ethnocentrism, eudemonism, eugenism, euhemerism, eumerism, eunuchism, eunuchoidism,

-ism *contd.*

euphemism, euphuism, Eurocommunism, Europeanism, evangelicalism, evangelicism, evangelism, evolutionism, exclusionism, exclusivism, exhibitionism, existentialism, ex-librism, exorcism, exotericism, exoticism, expansionism, experientialism, experimentalism, expressionism, extensionalism, externalism, extremism, Fabianism, factionalism, faddism, fairyism, fakirism, falangism, familism, fanaticism, fantasticism, faradism, fascism, fatalism, Fauvism, favism, favoritism, Febronianism, federalism, femininism, feminism, Fenianism, fetichism, fetishism, feudalism, feuilletonism, fideism, fifthmonarchism, filibusterism, finalism, fissiparism, flagellantism, flunkeyism, fogyism, formalism, fortuitism, Fourierism, fractionalism, Froebelism, functionalism, fundamentalism, fusionism, futurism, gaelicism, Galenism, Gallicanism, gallicism, galvanism, gamotropism, ganderism, gangsterism, Gargantuism, gargarism, gargoylism, Gasconism, Gaullism, generationism, Genevanism, genteelism, gentilism, geocentricism, geomagnetism, geophagism, geotropism, Germanism, giantism, gigantism, Girondism, Gnosticism, Gongorism, gormandism, Gothicism, gradualism, Graecism, grammaticism, Grangerism, Grecism, gregarianism, griffinism, Grobianism, Grundyism, gynandrism, gynandromophism, gynodioecism, gynomonoecism, gypsyism, gyromagnetism, haptotropism, Hasidism, Hassidism, heathenism, Hebraicism, Hebrewism, hectorism, hedonism, Hegelianism, hegemonism, heliotropism, Hellenism, helotism, hemihedrism, hemimorphism, henotheism, hermaphroditism, heroism, hetaerism, hetairism, heterochronism, heteroecism, heteromorphism, heterostylism, heterothallism, heurism, Hibernianism, Hibernicism, hidalgoism, hierarchism, highbrowism, High-Churchism, Hildebrandism, Hinduism, Hippocratism, hispanicism, historicism, historism, histrionicism, histrionism, Hitlerism, Hobbesianism, Hobbianism, Hobbism, hobbledehoyism, hobbyism, hobgoblinism, hoboism, holism, holohedrism, holometabolism, holophytism, homeomorphism, homoeroticism, homoerotism, homomorphism, homothallism, hooliganism, hoydenism, humanism, humanitarianism, Humism, humoralism, hybridism, hydrargyrism, hydrotropism, hylicism, hylism, hylomorphism, hylopathism, hylotheism, hylozoism, hyperadrenalism, hyperbolism, hypercriticism, hyperthyroidism, hyphenism, hypnotism, hypochondriacism, hypocorism, hypognathism, hypothyroidism, Ibsenism, iconomaticism, iconophilism, idealism, idiotism, idolism, illuminism, illusionism, imagism, immanentism, immaterialism, immediatism, immersionism, immobilism, immoralism, imperialism, impossibilism, impressionism, incendiarism, incivism, incorporealism, indeterminism, indifferentism, individualism, industrialism, infallibilism, infantilism, inflationism, Infralapsarianism, inquilinism, inspirationism, institutionalism, instrumentalism, insularism, insurrectionism, intellectualism, interactionism, internationalism, interventionism, intimism, intransigentism, intuitionalism, intuitionism, intuitivism, invalidism, iodism, Ionism, iotacism, irenicism, Irishism, irrationalism, irredentism, Irvingism, Islamism, ism, Ismailism, isochronism, isodimorphism, isolationism, isomerism, isomorphism, isotropism, itacism, Italianism, italicism, Jacobinism, Jacobitism, Jainism, Jansenism, Jesuitism, jingoism, jockeyism, Johnsonianism, Johnsonism, journalism, Judaism, junkerism, kaiserism, Kantianism, Kantism, katabolism, Kelticism, Keynesianism, klephtism, know-nothingism, Krishnaism, labdacism, labialism, laborism, laconicism, laconism, ladyism, Lamaism, Lamarckianism, Lamarckism, lambdacism, landlordism, Laodiceanism, larrikinism, lathyrism, Latinism, latitudinarianism, laxism, leftism, legalism, leggism, Leibnitzianism, Leibnizianism, Leninism, lesbianism, liberalism, liberationism, libertarianism, libertinism, lichenism, lionism, lipogrammatism, Listerism, literalism, literaryism, localism, Lollardism, Londonism, Low-Churchism, Luddism, luminarism, Lutheranism, Lutherism, lyricism, lyrism, Lysenkoism, macarism, Machiavellianism, Machiavellism, Magianism, Magism, magnetism, Magyarism, Mahdiism, Mahdism, maidism, malapropism, Malthusianism, mammonism, Manichaeism, Manicheanism, Manicheism, mannerism, Maoism, Marcionitism, Marinism, martialism, martinetism, Marxianism, Marxism, masochism, materialism, mathematicism, matriarchalism, maudlinism, Mazdaism, Mazdeism, McCarthyism, mechanism, medievalism, Medism, melanism, meliorism, memoirism, Mendelism, mentalism, mephitism, mercantilism, mercenarism, mercurialism, merism, merycism, mescalism, mesmerism, mesocephalism, mesomerism, Messianism, metabolism, metachronism, metamerism, metamorphism, metasomatism, metempiricism, meteorism, methodism, metopism, Micawberism, Michurinism, micro-organism, microseism, militarism, millenarianism, millenarism, millennianism, millenniarism, Miltonism, minimalism, minimism, misoneism, Mithraicism, Mithraism, mithridatism, modalism, moderatism, modernism, Mohammedanism, Mohammedism, Molinism, monachism, monadism, monarchianism, monarchism, monasticism, monergism, monetarism, mongolism, mongrelism, monism, monkeyism, monochromatism, monoecism, monogenism, monolingualism, monometallism, monophysitism, monorchism, monosyllabism, monotheism, monotheletism, monothelism, monothelitism, Monroeism, Montanism, moralism, Moravianism, Morisonianism, Mormonism, morphinism, mosaicism,

Mosaism, Moslemism, mountebankism, multiracialism, Munichism, municipalism, Muslimism, mutism, mutualism, myalism, mysticism, mythicism, mythism, namby-pambyism, nanism, Napoleonism, narcissism, narcotism, nationalism, nativism, naturalism, naturism, navalism, Nazaritism, Naziism, Nazism, necessarianism, necessitarianism, necrophilism, negativism, negroism, negrophilism, neoclassicism, neocolonialism, Neo-Darwinism, Neofascism, Neohellenism, Neo-Impressionism, Neo-Kantianism, Neo-Lamarckism, neologism, Neo-Malthusianism, neo-Nazism, neonomianism, neopaganism, neoplasticism, Neo-Plasticism, Neoplatonism, Neopythagoreanism, neoterism, neovitalism, nephalism, Nestorianism, neuroticism, neutralism, newspaperism, nicotinism, Nietzscheanism, nihilism, noctambulism, Noetianism, nomadism, nominalism, nomism, northernism, notaphilism, nothingarianism, nothingism, Novatianism, novelism, nudism, nyctitropism, obeahism, obeism, obiism, objectivism, obscurantism, obsoletism, Occamism, occasionalism, Occidentalism, occultism, Ockhamism, odism, odylism, officialism, old-maidism, onanism, onirocriticism, Ophism, Ophitism, opportunism, optimism, Orangeism, Orangism, organicism, organism, Orientalism, Origenism, Orleanism, orphanism, Orphism, orthognathism, orthotropism, ostracism, ostrichism, Owenism, pacificism, pacifism, Paddyism, paganism, paleomagnetism, palladianism, paludism, panaesthetism, Pan-Africanism, Pan-Americanism, Pan-Arabian, panchromatism, pancosmism, panderism, panegoism, Pan-Germanism, Panhellenism, panislamism, panlogism, panpsychism, pansexualism, Pan-Slavism, pansophism, panspermatism, panspermism, Pantagruelism, pantheism, papalism, papism, parabaptism, parachronism, paragnathism, paraheliotropism, parallelism, paralogism, paramagnetism, paramorphism, parapsychism, parasitism, Parkinsonism, parliamentarism, Parnassianism, Parnellism, parochialism, Parseeism, Parsiism, Parsism, partialism, particularism, partyism, passivism, pasteurism, pastoralism, paternalism, patrialism, patriarchalism, patriarchism, patriotism, Patripassianism, patristicism, Paulinism, pauperism, pedagogism, pedagoguism, pedanticism, pedantism, pedestrianism, pedobaptism, pedomorphism, Pelagianism, pelmanism, pelorism, pennalism, penny-a-linerism, pentadactylism, pentamerism, pentaprism, peonism, perfectibilism, perfectionism, peripateticism, perpetualism, Persism, personalism, perspectivism, pessmism, petalism, Petrarchianism, Petrarchism, Petrinism, phagocytism, phalansterianism, phalansterism, phallicism, phallism, pharisaism, phariseeism, pheism, phenakism, phenomenalism, phenomenism, philhellenism, philistinism, philosophism, phobism, phoneticism, phonetism, phosphorism, photism, photochromism, photoperiodism, phototropism, physicalism, physicism, physitheism, pianism, pietism, piezomagnetism, Pindarism, Pittism, plagiarism, plagiotropism, Platonicism, Platonism, plebeianism, pleiotropism, pleochroism, pleomorphism, plumbism, pluralism, Plutonism, Plymouthism, pococuranteism, pococurantism, poeticism, pointillism, polonism, polychroism, polycrotism, polydactylism, polygenism, polymastism, polymerism, polymorphism, polynomialism, polysyllabicism, polysyllabism, polysyllogism, polysyntheticism, polysynthetism, polytheism, Pooterism, populism, porism, Porphyrogenitism, positivism, possibilism, Post-Impressionism, post-millennialism, Poujadism, Powellism, practicalism, pragmatism, precisianism, predestinarianism, predeterminism, preferentialism, preformationism, prelatism, premillenarianism, premillennialism, Pre-Raphaelism, Pre-Raphaelitism, Presbyterianism, presentationism, preternaturalism, prettyism, priapism, priggism, primitivism, primordialism, probabiliorism, probablism, prochronism, professionalism, prognathism, progressionism, progressism, progressivism, prohibitionism, proletarianism, propagandism, prophetism, prosaicism, prosaism, proselytism, prostatism, prosyllogism, protectionism, Protestantism, proverbialism, provincialism, prudentialism, Prussianism, psellism, psephism, pseudo-archaism, pseudoclassicism, pseudomorphism, psilanthropism, psychism, psychologism, psychopannychism, psychoticism, ptyalism, puerilism, pugilism, puppyism, purism, puritanism, Puseyism, pyrrhonism, Pythagoreanism, Pythagorism, Quakerism, quattrocentism, quietism, quixotism, rabbinism, Rabelaisianism, racemism, Rachmanism, racialism, racism, radicalism, Ramism, ranterism, rascalism, rationalism, reactionarism, realism, rebaptism, Rebeccaism, Rechabitism, recidivism, red-tapism, reductionism, reformism, regalism, regionalism, reincarnationism, relationism, relativism, religionism, Rembrandtism, representationalism, representationism, republicanism, restitutionism, restorationism, resurrectionism, reunionism, revanchism, revisionism, revivalism, revolutionism, rheotropism, rheumatism, rhopalism, rhotacism, Ribbonism, rigorism, ritualism, Romanism, romanticism, Rosicrucianism, Rosminianism, Rotarianism, routinism, rowdyism, royalism, ruffianism, ruralism, Russianism, Russophilism, Sabaism, Sabbatarianism, sabbatism, Sabellianism, Sabianism, sacerdotalism, sacramentalism, sacramentarianism, Sadduceeism, Sadducism, sadism, sado-masochism, saintism, Saint-Simonianism, Saint-Simonism, Saivism, Saktism, salvationism, Samaritanism, sanitarianism, sansculottism, sapphism, saprophytism, Saracenism, satanism, saturnism, Saxonism, schematism, scholasticism, scientism, sciolism, Scotism, Scotticism, scoundrelism, scribism, scripturalism, scripturism,

-ism *contd.*

secessionism, sectarianism, sectionalism, secularism, self-criticism, self-hypnotism, selfism, semi-Arianism, semi-barbarism, Semi-Pelagianism, Semitism, sensationalism, sensationism, sensism, sensualism, sensuism, sentimentalism, separatism, serialism, servilism, servo-mechanism, sesquipedalianism, sexism, sexualism, Shaivism, shakerism, Shaktism, shamanism, shamateurism, Shiism, Shintoism, Shivaism, shunamitism, sigmatism, Sikhism, simplism, sinapism, sinecurism, singularism, Sinicism, Sinophilism, Sivaism, skepticism, Slavism, snobbism, socialism, Socinianism, sociologism, Sofism, solarism, solecism, sol-faism, solidarism, solidism, solifidianism, solipsism, somatism, somnambulism, somniloquism, sophism, southernism, sovietism, specialism, speciesism, Spencerianism, Spinozism, spiritism, spiritualism, spoonerism, spread-eagleism, Stahlianism, Stahlism, Stakhanovism, Stalinism, stand-pattism, statism, stercoranism, stereoisomerism, stereotropism, stibialism, stigmatism, stoicism, strabism, structuralism, strychninism, strychnism, Stundism, subjectivism, sublapsarianism, subordinationism, substantialism, suburbanism, suffragism, Sufiism, Sufism, suggestionism, supernationalism, supernaturalism, superrealism, Supralapsarianism, supremacism, suprematism, surrealism, sutteeism, Swadeshism, swarajism, Swedenborgianism, swingism, sybaritism, sybotism, syllabism, syllogism, symbolism, symphilism, synaposematism, synchronism, syncretism, syndactylism, syndicalism, synecdochism, synergism, synoecism, syntheticism, Syriarcism, Syrianism, systematism, tachism, tactism, Tammanyism, tantalism, Tantrism, Taoism, tarantism, Tartuffism, Tartufism, tautochronism, tautologism, tautomerism, teetotalism, teleologism, tenebrism, teratism, terminism, territorialism, terrorism, tetramerism, tetratheism, Teutonicism, Teutonism, textualism, thanatism, thaumaturgism, theanthropism, theatricalism, theatricism, theism, theomorphism, Theopaschitism, theophilanthropism, theosophism, therianthropism, theriomorphism, thermotropism, thigmotropism, Thomism, thrombo-embolism, thuggism, tigerism, Timonism, Titanism, Titoism, toadyism, tokenism, Toryism, totalitarianism, totemism, tourism, tractarianism, trade-unionism, traditionalism, Traducianism, traitorism, transcendentalism, transformism, transmigrationism, transsexualism, tranvestism, transvestitism, traumatism, trialism, tribadism, tribalism, trichroism, trichromatism, tricrotism, triliteralism, trimorphism, Trinitarianism, trinomialism, tripersonalism, tritheism, triticism, trituberculism, trivialism, troglodytism, troilism, trophotropism, tropism, Trotskyism, truism, tsarism, tuism, Turcophilism, tutiorism, tutorism, tychism, ultra-Conservatism, ultraism, ultramontanism, undenominationalism, unicameralism, unidealism, uniformitarianism, unilateralism, unionism, unitarianism, unversalism, unrealism, unsectarianism, unsocialism, untuism, uranism, utilitarianism, utopianism, utopism, Utraquism, vagabondism, Valentinianism, valetudinarianism, vampirism, vandalism, Vansittartism, Vaticanism, Vedism, veganism, vegetarianism, ventriloquism, verbalism, verism, vernacularism, Victorianism, vigilantism, vikingism, virilism, virtualism, vitalism, viviparism, vocalism, vocationalism, volcanism, Voltaireanism, Voltairianism, Voltairism, voltaism, voltinism, voluntarism, voluntaryism, voodooism, vorticism, voyeurism, vulcanism, vulgarism, vulpinism, vulturism, Wagnerianism, Wagnerism, Wahabiism, Wahabism, welfarism, werewolfism, Wertherism, werwolfism, Wesleyanism, westernism, Whiggism, wholism, witticism, Wodenism, Wolfianism, xanthochroism, Yankeeism, yogism, zanyism, Zarathustrianism, Zarathustrism, zealotism, Zionism, Zoilism, zoism, Zolaism, zombiism, zoomagnetism, zoomorphism, zoophilism, zootheism, Zoroastrianism, Zwinglianism, zygodactylism, zygomorphism.

-itis adenitis, antiaditis, aortitis, appendicitis, arteritis, arthritis, balanitis, blepharitis, bronchitis, bursitis, carditis, cellulitis, cephalitis, ceratitis, cerebritis, cholecystitis, colitis, conchitis, conjunctivitis, crystallitis, cystitis, dermatitis, diaphragmatitis, diphtheritis, diverticulitis, duodenitis, encephalitis, endocarditis, endometritis, enteritis, fibrositis, gastritis, gastroenteritis, gingivitis, glossitis, hamarthritis, hepatitis, hysteritis, ileitis, iritis, keratitis, labyrinthitis, laminitis, laryngitis, lymphangitis, mastitis, mastoiditis, meningitis, metritis, myelitis, myocarditis, myositis, myringitis, nephritis, neuritis, onychitis, oophoritis, ophthalmitis, orchitis, osteitis, osteo-arthritis, osteomyelitis, otitis, ovaritis, panarthritis, pancreatitis, panophthalmitis, papillitis, parotiditis, parotitis, pericarditis, perigastritis, perihepatitis, perinephritis, perineuritis, periostitis, peritonitis, perityphlitis, pharnygitis, phlebitis, phrenitis, pleuritis, pneumonitis, poliomyelitis, polyneuritis, proctitis, prostatitis, pyelitis, pyelonephritis, rachitis, rectitis, retinitis, rhachitis, rhinitis, rhinopharyngitis, salpingitis, scleritis, sclerotitis, sinuitis, splenitis, spondylitis, staphylitis, stomatitis, strumitis, synovitis, syringitis, thrombo-phlebitis, thyroiditis, tonsilitis, tonsillitis, tracheitis, trachitis, tympanitis, typhlitis, ulitis, ureteritis, urethritis, uteritis, uveitis, uvulitis, vaginitis, valvulitis, vulvitis.

-latrous bibliolatrous, heliolatrous, ichthyolatrous, idolatrous, litholatrous, Mariolatrous, Maryolatrous, monolatrous, ophiolatrous, zoolatrous.

-latry angelolatry, anthropolatry, astrolatry, autolatry, bardolatry, bibliolatry, Christolatry, cosmolatry, demonolatry, dendrolatry, ecclesiolatry, epeolatry, geolatry, hagiolatry, heliolatry, hierolatry, ichthyolatry, iconolatry, idolatry, litholatry, lordolatry, Mariolatry, Maryolatry, monolatry, necrolatry, ophiolatry, physiolatry, plutolatry, pylolatry, symbololatry, thaumatolatry, theriolatry, zoolatry.

-logical aerobiological, aerological, aetiological, agrobiological, agrological, agrostological, algological, alogical, amphibological, analogical, anthropological, arachnological, archaeological, astrological, atheological, audiological, autecological, axiological, bacteriological, batological, battological, biological, bryological, campanological, carcinological, cartological, chorological, Christological, chronological, climatological, codicological, conchological, cosmological, craniological, cryobiological, cryptological, cytological, demonological, dendrological, deontological, dermatological, dysteleological, ecclesiological, ecological, Egyptological, electrophysiological, embryological, enological, entomological, epidemiological, epistemological, eschatological, ethnological, ethological, etymological, futurological, gastrological, gemmological, gemological, genealogical, genethlialogical, geochronological, geological, geomorphological, gerontological, glaciological, glossological, gnotobiological, graphological, gynecological, hagiological, helminthological, hepaticological, herpetological, histological, histopathological, homological, horological, hydrobiological, hydrological, ichthyological, ideological, illogical, immunological, laryngological, limnological, lithological, logical, malacological, mammalogical, martyrological, metapsychological, meteorological, micrological, mineralogical, monological, morphological, musicological, mycological, myological, myrmecological, mythological, necrological, neological, nephological, nephrological, neurological, nomological, nosological, nostological, oceanological, odontological, ontological, ophiological, ophthalmological, oreological, ornithological, orological, osteological, paleontological, paleozoological, palynological, parapsychological, pathological, pedological, penological, pestological, petrological, phenological, phenomenological, philological, phonological, phraseological, phrenological, phycological, physiological, phytological, phytopathological, pneumatological, pomological, posological, potamological, protozoological, psephological, psychobiological, psychological, radiological, reflexological, rheumatological, rhinological, scatological, sedimentological, seismological, selenological, serological, Sinological, sociobiological, sociological, somatological, soteriological, Sovietological, spectrological, speleological, stoechiological, stoicheiological, stoichiological, synecological, tautological,technological, teleological, teratological, terminological, theological, topological, toxicological, traumatological, trichological, tropological, typological, unlogical, untheological, urological, virological, volcanological, vulcanological, zoological, zoophytological, zymological.

-logous analogous, antilogous, dendrologous, heterologous, homologous, isologous, tautologous.

-logue apologue, collogue, decalogue, dialogue, duologue, eclogue, epilogue, grammalogue, homologue, idealogue, ideologue, isologue, monologue, philologue, prologue, Sinologue, theologue, travelogue, trialogue.

-logy acarology, aerobiology, aerolithology, aerology, aetiology, agriology, agrobiology, agrology, agrostology, algology, amphibology, anesthesiology, analogy, andrology, anemology, angelology, anthology, anthropobiology, anthropology, antilogy, apology, arachnology, archaeology, archology, aristology, Assyriology, astrogeology, astrology, atheology, atmology, audiology, autecology, autology, axiology, bacteriology, balneology, batology, battology, bibliology, bioecology, biology, biotechnology, brachylogy, bryology, bumpology, cacology, caliology, campanology, carcinology, cardiology, carphology, cartology, cetology, cheirology, chirology, choreology, chorology, Christology, chronobiology, chronology, cine-biology, climatology, codicology, cometology, conchology, coprology, cosmetology, cosmology, craniology, criminology, cryobiology, cryptology, cytology, dactyliology, dactylology, deltiology, demology, demonology, dendrochronology, dendrology, deontology, dermatology, diabology, diabolology, dialectology, diplomatology, dittology, docimology, dogmatology, dosiology, dosology, doxology, dyslogy, dysteleology, ecclesiology, eccrinology, ecology, edaphology, Egyptology, electrobiology, electrology, electrophysiology, electrotechnology, elogy, embryology, emmenology, endemiology, endocrinology, enology, entomology, enzymology, epidemiology, epistemology, escapology, eschatology, ethnology, ethnomusicology, ethology, Etruscology, etymology, euchology, eulogy, exobiology, festilogy, festology, folk-etymology, futurology, gastroenterology, gastrology, gemmology, gemology, genealogy, genethlialogy, geochronology, geology, geomorphology, gerontology, gigantology, glaciology, glossology, glottology, gnomonology, gnoseology, gnosiology, gnotobiology, graphology, gynecology, hematology, hagiology, hamartiology, haplology,

-logy *contd.*

heliology, helminthology, heorology, hepaticology, hepatology, heresiology, herpetology, heterology, hierology, hippology, histiology, histology, histopathology, historiology, homology, hoplology, horology, hydrobiology, hydrogeology, hydrology, hydrometeorology, hyetology, hygrology, hymnology, hypnology, ichnology, ichthyology, iconology, ideology, immunology, insectology, irenology, kidology, kinesiology, koniology, Kremlinology, laryngology, lepidopterology, lexicology, lichenology, limnology, lithology, liturgiology, macrology, malacology, malariology, mammalogy, Mariology, martyrology, Maryology, Mayology, menology, metapsychology, meteorology, methodology, microbiology, microclimatology, micrology, micro-meteorology, microtechnology, mineralogy, misology, monadology, monology, morphology, muscology, museology, musicology, mycetology, mycology, myology, myrmecology, mythology, necrology, nematology, neology, nephology, nephrology, neurobiology, neurohypnology, neurology, neuropathology, neurophysiology, neuroradiology, neurypnology, nomology, noology, nosology, nostology, numerology, numisatology, oceanology, odontology, olfactology, oncology, onirology, ontology, oology, ophiology, ophthalmology, optology, orchidology, oreology, ornithology, orology, orthopterology, oryctology, osteology, otolaryngology, otology, otorhinolaryngology, ourology, paleanthropology, paleethnology,paleichthyology, paleoclimatology, paleolimnology, paleontology, paleopelology, paleophytology, paleozoology, palillogy, palynology, pantheology, papyrology, paradoxology, paralogy, parapsychology, parasitology, paroemiology, pathology, patrology, pedology, pelology, penology, periodontology, perissology, pestology, petrology, phenology, pharmacology, pharyngology, phenology, phenomenology, philology, phonology, photobiology, photogeology, phraseology, phrenology, phycology, physiology, phytology, phytopathology, planetology, plutology, pneumatology, prodology, pomology, ponerology, posology, potamology, primatology, protistology, protozoology, psephology, pseudology, psychobiology, psychology, psychopathology, psychophysiology, pteridology, pyretology, pyroballogy, radiobiology, radiology, reflexology, rheology, rheumatology, rhinology, röntgenology, sacrology, satanology, scatology, Scientology, sedimentology, seismology, selenology, selenomorphology, semasiology, semeiology, semiology, serology, sexology, sindonology, Sinology, sitiology, sitology, skatology, sociobiology, sociology, somatology, soteriology, spectrology, speleology, sphagnology, sphygmology, spongology, stichology, stoechiology, stoichiology, stomatology, storiology, symbology, symbolology, symptomatology, synchronology, synecology, syphilology, systematology, tautology, technology, teleology, teratology, terminology, terotechnology, tetralogy, thanatology, theology, thermology, therology, thremmatology, timbrology, tocology, tokology, topology, toxicology, traumatology, tribology, trichology, trilogy, trophology, tropology, typhlology, typology, ufology, uranology, urbanology, urinology, urology, venereology, vexillology, victimology, vinology, virology, volcanology, vulcanology, xylology, zoopathology, zoophytology, zoopsychology, zymology.

-lysis analysis, atmolysis, autocatalysis, autolysis, bacteriolysis, catalysis, cryptanalysis, cytolysis, dialysis, electroanalysis, electrolysis, hematolysis, hemodialysis, hemolysis, histolysis, hydrolysis, hypno-analysis, leucocytolysis, microanalysis, nacro-analysis, neurolysis, paralysis, photolysis, plasmolysis, pneumatolysis, proteolysis, psephoanalysis, psychoanalysis, pyrolysis, radiolysis, thermolysis, uranalysis, urinalysis, zincolysis, zymolysis.

-lytic analytic, anxiolytic, autocatalytic, autolytic, bacteriolytic, catalytic, dialytic, electrolytic, hemolytic, histolytic, hydrolytic, paralytic, photolytic, plasmolytic, pneumatolytic, proteolytic, psychoanalytic, pyrolytic, sympatholytic, tachylytic, thermolytic, unanalytic.

-mania acronymania, anglomania, anthomania, balletomania, bibliomania, Celtomania, demonomania, dipsomania, egomania, enomania, erotomania, etheromania, francomania, gallomania, hydromania, hypomania, hysteromania, Keltomania, kleptomania, mania, megalomania, melomania, methomania, metromania, monomania, morphinomania, mythomania, nostomania, nymphomania, opsomania, orchidomania, petalomania, phyllomania, potichomania, pteridomania, pyromania, squandermania, theatromania, theomania, timbromania, toxicomania, tulipomania, typomania, xenomania.

-mancy aeromancy, axinomancy, belomancy, bibliomancy, botanomancy, capnomancy, cartomancy, ceromancy, chiromancy, cleromancy, coscinomancy, crithomancy, crystallomancy, dactyliomancy, enomancy, gastromancy, geomancy, gyromancy, hieromancy, hydromancy, lampadomancy, lithomancy, myomancy, necromancy, nigromancy, omphalomancy, oniromancy, onychomancy, ornithomancy, pyromancy, rhabdomancy, scapulimancy, spodomancy, tephromancy, theomancy, zoomancy.

-mantic chiromantic, geomantic, hydromantic, myomantic, necromantic, ornithomantic, pyromantic, scapulimantic, spodomantic, theomantic, zoomantic.

-mathic chrestomathic, philomathic, polymathic.

-mathy chrestomathy, opsimathy, philomathy, polymathy.

-meter absorptiometer, accelerometer, acidimeter, actinometer, aerometer, alcoholometer, alkalimeter, altimeter, ammeter, anemometer, areometer, arithmometer, atmometer, audiometer, auxanometer, auxometer, barometer, bathometer, bathymeter, bolometer, bomb-calorimeter, calorimeter, cathetometer, centimeter, chlorimeter, chlorometer, chronometer, clinometer, colorimeter, Comptometer®, coulombmeter, coulometer, craniometer, cryometer, cyanometer, cyclometer, decelerometer, declinometer, dendrometer, densimeter, densitometer, diagometer, diameter, diaphanometer, diffractometer, dimeter, dose-meter, dosimeter, drosometer, dynamometer, effusiometer, electrodynamometer, electrometer, endosmometer, enometer, ergometer, eriometer, evaporimeter, extensimeter, extensometer, fathometer, flowmeter, fluorimeter, fluorometer, focimeter, galactometer, galvanometer, gas-meter, gasometer, geometer, geothermometer, goniometer, gradiometer, gravimeter, harmonometer, heliometer, heptameter, hexameter, hodometer, hydrometer, hyetometer, hygrometer, hypsometer, iconometer, inclinometer, interferometer, isoperimeter, katathermometer, konimeter, kryometer, lactometer, luxmeter, lysimeter, machmeter, magnetometer, manometer, mekometer, meter, micrometer, microseismometer, mileometer, milometer, monometer, nephelometer, Nilometer, nitrometer, octameter, odometer, ohmmeter, ombrometer, oncometer, ophthalmometer, opisometer, opsiometer, optometer, osmometer, oximeter, pachymeter, parameter, passimeter, pedometer, pelvimeter, pentameter, perimeter, permeameter, phonmeter, phonometer, photometer, piezometer, planimeter, planometer, plessimeter, pleximeter, pluviometer, pneumatometer, polarimeter, potentiometer, potometer, psychometer, psychrometer, pulsimeter, pulsometer, pycnometer, pyknometer, pyrheliometer, pyrometer, quantometer, radiogoniometer, radiometer, radiotelemeter, refractometer, rheometer, rhythmometer, saccharimeter, saccharometer, salimeter, salinometer, scintillometer, sclerometer, seismometer, semi-diameter, semiperimeter, sensitometer, slot-meter, solarimeter, spectrophotometer, speedometer, spherometer, sphygmomanometer, sphygmometer, stactometer, stalagometer, stereometer, strabismometer, strabometer, swingometer, sympiesometer, tacheometer, tachometer, tachymeter, taseometer, tasimeter, taximeter, telemeter, tellurometer, tetrameter, thermometer, Tintometer®, tonometer, torque-meter, tribometer, trigonometer, trimeter, trocheameter, trochometer, tromometer, udometer, urinometer, vaporimeter, variometer, viameter, vibrometer, viscometer, viscosimeter, voltameter, voltmeter, volumenometer, volumeter, volumometer, water-barometer, water-meter, water-thermometer, wattmeter, wavemeter, weathermeter, xylometer, zymometer, zymosimeter.

-metry acidimetry, aerometry, alcoholometry, alkalimetry, anemometry, anthropometry, areometry, asymmetry, barometry, bathymetry, biometry, bolometry, calorimetry, chlorimetry, chlorometry, chronometry, clinometry, colorimetry, coulometry, craniometry, densimetry, densitometry, dissymmetry, dosimetry, dynamometry, electrometry, galvanometry, gasometry, geometry, goniometry, gravimetry, hodometry, horometry, hydrometry, hygometry, hypsometry, iconometry, interferometry, isometry, isoperimetry, micrometry, microseismometry, nephelometry, noometry, odometry, ophthalmometry, optometry, pelvimetry, perimetry, photometry, planimetry, plessimetry, pleximetry, polarimetry, pseudosymmetry, psychometry, psychrometry, pyrometry, saccharimetry, seismometry, sociometry, spectrometry, spectrophotometry, spirometry, stalagmometry, stereometry, stichometry, stoechiometry, stoichiometry, symmetry, tacheometry, tachometry, tachymetry, telemetry, tensiometry, thermometry, trigonometry, unsymmetry, uranometry, viscometry, viscosimetry, zoometry.

-monger balladmonger, barber-monger, borough-monger, carpetmonger, cheese-monger, costardmonger, costermonger, fellmonger, fishmonger, flesh-monger, gossip-monger, ironmonger, lawmonger, love-monger, maxim-monger, meal-monger, miracle-monger, mystery-monger, newsmonger, panic-monger, peace-monger, pearmonger, peltmonger, phrasemonger, place-monger, prayer-monger, relic-monger, scandalmonger, scaremonger, sensation-monger, species-monger, starmonger, state-monger, system-monger, verse-monger, warmonger, whoremonger, wit-monger, wonder-monger.

-morphic actinomorphic, allelomorphic, allotriomorphic, anamorphic, anthropomorphic, automorphic, biomorphic, dimorphic, ectomorphic, enantiomorphic, endomorphic, ergatomorphic, gynandromorphic,

-morphic *contd.*
hemimorphic, heteromorphic, homeomorphic, homomorphic, hylomorphic, idiomorphic, isodimorphic, isomorphic, lagomorphic, mesomorphic, metamorphic, monomorphic, morphic, ophiomorphic, ornithomorphic, paramorphic, pedomorphic, perimorphic, pleomorphic, polymorphic, protomorphic, pseudomorphic, tetramorphic, theomorphic, theriomorphic, trimorphic, xenomorphic, xeromorphic, zoomorphic, zygomorphic.

-morphous amorphous, anamorphous, anthropomorphous, dimorphous, enantiomorphous, gynandromorphous, heteromorphous, homeomorphous, homomorphous, isodimorphous, isomorphous, lagomorphous, mesomorphous, monomorphous, ophiomorphous, perimorphous, pleomorphous, polymorphous, pseudomorphous, rhizomorphous, tauromorphous, theriomorphous, trimorphous, xeromorphous, zygomorphous.

-onym acronym, anonym, antonym, autonym, cryptonym, eponym, exonym, heteronym, homonym, metonym, paronym, polyonym, pseudonym, synonym, tautonym, toponym, trionym.

-onymic acronymic, Hieronymic, homonymic, matronymic, metonymic, metronymic, patronymic, polyonymic, synonymic, toponymic.

-osis abiosis, acidosis, actinobacillosis, actinomycosis, aerobiosis, aeroneurosis, alkalosis, amaurosis, amitosis, anabiosis, anadiplosis, anamorphosis, anaplerosis, anastomosis, anchylosis, anerobiosis, ankylosis, anthracosis, anthropomorphosis, antibiosis, apodosis, aponeurosis, apotheosis, arteriosclerosis, arthrosis, asbestosis, aspergillosis, ateleiosis, atherosclerosis, athetosis, autohypnosis, avitaminosis, bacteriosis, bagassosis, bilharziosis, biocoenosis, bromhidrosis, bromidrosis, brucellosis, byssinosis, carcinomatosis, carcinosis, chlorosis, cirrhosis, coccidiosis, cyanosis, cyclosis, dermatosis, diarthrosis, diorthosis, diverticulosis, dulosis, ecchymosis, enantiosis, enarthrosis, endometriosis, endosmosis, enosis, enteroptosis, epanadiplosis, epanorthosis, exosmosis, exostosis, fibrosis, fluorosis, furunculosis, gliomatosis, gnotobiosis, gomphosis, gummosis, halitosis, hallucinosis, heliosis, hematosis, heterosis, hidrosis, homeosis, homomorphosis, homozygosis, hydronephrosis, hyperhidrosis, hyperidrosis, hyperinosis, hypersacosis, hypervitaminosis, hypinosis, hypnosis, hypotyposis, ichthyosis, kenosis, keratosis, ketosis, kurtosis, kyllosis, kyphosis, leishmaniosis, leptospirosis, leucocytosis, limosis, lipomatosis, lordosis, madarosis, marmarosis, meiosis, melanosis, metachrosis, metamorphosis, metempsychosis, miosis, mitosis, molybdosis, mononucleosis, monosis, morphosis, mucoviscidosis, mycosis, mycotoxicosis, myosis, myxomatosis, narcohypnosis, narcosis, necrobiosis, necrosis, nephroptosis, nephrosis, neurosis, onychocryptosis, ornithosis, osmidrosis, osmosis, osteoarthrosis, osteoporosis, otosclerosis, parabiosis, paraphimosis, parapsychosis, parasitosis, pedamorphosis, pediculosis, phagocytosis, phimosis, pholidosis, phytosis, pneumoconiosis, pneumokoniosis, pneumonokoniosis, pneumonoultramicroscopicsilicovolcanoconiosis, pollenosis, polyposis, porosis, proptosis, psilosis, psittacosis, psychoneurosis, psychosis, pterylosis, ptilosis, ptosis, pyrosis, resinosis, salmonellosis, sarcoidosis, sarcomatosis, sclerosis, scoliosis, self-hypnosis, siderosis, silicosis, sorosis, spirillosis, spirochetosis, steatosis, stegnosis, stenosis, strongylosis, sycosis, symbiosis, symptosis, synarthrosis, synchrondrosis, syndesmosis, synociosis, synostosis, syntenosis, syssarcosis, thanatosis, theriomorphosis, thrombosis, thylosis, thyrotoxicosis, torulosis, toxoplasmosis, trichinosis, trichophytosis, trichosis, trophobiosis, trophoneurosis, tuberculosis, tylosis, ulosis, urosis, virosis, visceroptosis, xerosis, zoonosis, zygosis, zymosis.

-path allopath, homeopath, kinesipath, naturopath, neuropath, osteopath, psychopath, sociopath, telepath.

-pathic allopathic, anthropopathic, antipathic, empathic, homoeopathic, hydropathic, idiopathic, kinesipathic, naturopathic, neuropathic, osteopathic, protopathic, psychopathic, sociopathic, telepathic.

-pathy allopathy, anthropopathy, antipathy, apathy, cardiomyopathy, dyspathy, empathy, enantiopathy, homeopathy, hydropathy, idiopathy, kinesipathy, myocardiopathy, naturopathy, neuropathy, nostopathy, osteopathy, psychopathy, sociopathy, sympathy, telepathy, theopathy, zoopathy.

374

-phage bacteriophage, macrophage, ostreophage, xylophage.

-phagous anthropophagous, autophagous, carpophagous, coprophagous, creophagous, endophagous, entomophagous, exophagous, geophagous, hippophagous, hylophagous, ichthyophagous, lithophagous, mallophagous, meliphagous, monophagous, myrmecophagous, necrophagous, omophagous ophiophagous, ostreophagous, pantophagous, phyllophagous, phytophagous, polyphagous, rhizophagous, saprophagous, sarcophagous, scatophagous, theophagous, toxicophagous, toxiphagous, xylophagous, zoophagous.

-phagy anthropophagy, autophagy, coprophagy, dysphagy, endophagy, entomophagy, exophagy, hippophagy, ichthyophagy, monophagy, mycophagy, omophagy, ostreophagy, pantophagy, polyphagy, sacrophagy, scatophagy, theophagy, xerophagy.

-phile ailurophile, arctophile, audiophile, bibliophile, cartophile, discophile, enophile, francophile, gallophile, Germanophile, gerontophile, halophile, hippophile, homophile, iodophile, lyophile, myrmecophile, necrophile, negrophile, ombrophile, pedophile, psammophile, Russophile, scripophile, Sinophile, Slavophile, spermophile, thermophile, Turcophile, xenophile, zoophile.

-philia ailurophilia, anglophilia, canophilia, coprophilia, ephebophilia, Germanophilia, gerontophilia, hemophilia, necrophilia, paraphilia, pedophilia, scopophilia, scoptophilia, zoophilia.

-philist bibliophilist, canophilist, cartophilist, Dantophilist, enophilist, iconophilist, negrophilist, notaphilist, ophiophilist, pteridophilist, Russophilist, scripophilist, stegophilist, timbrophilist, zoophilist.

-phily acarophily, anemophily, bibliophily, cartophily, enophily, entomophily, halophily, hydrophily, myrmecophily, necrophily, notaphily, ornithophily, photophily, scripophily, Sinophily, symphily, timbrophily, toxophily, xerophily.

-phobe ailurophobe, anglophobe, francophobe, gallophobe, Germanophobe, hippophobe, hygrophobe, lyophobe, negrophobe, ombrophobe, photophobe, Russophobe, Slavophobe, Turcophobe, xenophobe.

-phobia acrophobia, aerophobia, agoraphobia, ailurophobia, algophobia, anglophobia, astraphobia, astrapophobia, bathophobia, bibliophobia, canophobia, claustrophobia, cynophobia, dromophobia, ecophobia, ergophobia, gallophobia, hydrophobia, hypsophobia, monophobia, mysophobia, necrophobia, negrophobia, neophobia, nosophobia, nyctophobia, ochlophobia, panophobia, pantophobia, pathophobia, phonophobia, photophobia, Russophobia, satanophobia, scopophobia, sitiophobia, sitophobia, symmetrophobia, syphilophobia, taphephobia, taphophobia, thanatophobia, theophobia, toxicophobia, toxiphobia, triskaidecaphobia, triskaidekaphobia, xenophobia, zoophobia.

-phobic aerophobic, agoraphobic, anglophobic, claustrophobic, heliophobic, hydrophobic, lyophobic, monophobic, phobic, photophobic.

-phone aerophone, allophone, anglophone, Ansaphone®, audiophone, chordophone, detectophone, diaphone, dictaphone, diphone, earphone, Entryphone®, francophone, geophone, gramophone, harmoniphone, headphone, heckelphone, homophone, hydrophone, idiophone, interphone, kaleidophone, megaphone, metallophone, microphone, monotelephone, optophone, phone, photophone, Picturephone®, polyphone, pyrophone, radiogramophone, radiophone, radiotelephone, sarrusophone, saxophone, sousaphone, speakerphone, sphygmophone, stentorphone, telephone, theatrophone, triphone, vibraphone, videophone, videotelephone, viewphone, zylophone.

-phonic acrophonic, allophonic, anglophonic, antiphonic, aphonic, cacophonic, cataphonic, chordophonic, dodecaphonic, dysphonic, euphonic, gramophonic, homophonic, microphonic, monophonic, paraphonic,

-phonic *contd.*
photophonic, quadraphonic, quadrophonic, radiophonic, stentorophonic, stereophonic, symphonic, telephonic, xylophonic.

-phony acrophony, antiphony, aphony, autophony, cacophony, colophony, dodecaphony, euphony, gramophony, homophony, laryngophony, monophony, photophony, polyphony, quadraphony, quadrophony, radiophony, radiotelephony, stereophony, symphony, tautophony, telephony.

-phorous discophorous, Eriophorous, galactophorous, hypophosphorous, mastigophorous, necrophorous, odontophorous, phosphorous, pyrophorous, rhynchophorous, sporophorous.

-phyte aerophyte, bryophyte, cormophyte, dermatophyte, ectophyte, endophyte, entophyte, epiphyte, gametophyte, geophyte, halophyte, heliophyte, heliosciophyte, holophyte, hydrophyte, hygrophyte, hylophyte, lithophyte, mesophyte, microphyte, neophyte, oophyte, osteophyte, phanerophyte, phreatophyte, protophyte, psammophyte, pteridophyte, saprophyte, schizophyte, spermaphyte, spermatophyte, spermophyte, sporophyte, thallophyte, tropophyte, xerophyte, zoophyte, zygophyte.

-saurus Allosaurus, Ankylosaurus, Apatosaurus, Atlantosaurus, brachiosaurus, brontosaurus, Ceteosaurus, Dolichosaurus, Ichthyosaurus, megalosaurus, Plesiosaurus, Stegosaurus, Teleosaurus, Titanosaurus, tyrannosaurus.

-scope aethrioscope, auriscope, baroscope, bathyscope, benthoscope, bioscope, bronchoscope, chromoscope, chronoscope, colposcope, cryoscope, cystoscope, dichrooscope, dichroscope, dipleidoscope, ebullioscope, electroscope, endoscope, engiscope, engyscope, epidiascope, episcope, fluoroscope, galvanoscope, gastroscope, gyroscope, hagioscope, helioscope, hodoscope, horoscope, hydroscope, hygroscope, iconoscope, iriscope, kaleidoscope, kinetoscope, koniscope, lactoscope, laparoscope, laryngoscope, lychnoscope, megascope, microscope, mutoscope, myringoscope, myrioscope, nephoscope, opeidoscope, ophthalmoscope, oscilloscope, otoscope, pantoscope, periscope, pharyngoscope, phenakistoscope, phonendoscope, polariscope, poroscope, praxinoscope, proctoscope, pseudoscope, pyroscope, radarscope, radioscope, rhinoscope, scintilloscope, scope, seismoscope, sigmoidoscope, somascope, spectrohelioscope, spectroscope, sphygmoscope, spinthariscope, statoscope, stereofluoroscope, stereoscope, stethoscope, stroboscope, tachistoscope, teinoscope, telescope, thermoscope, triniscope, ultramicroscope, vectorscope, Vertoscope®, vitascope.

-scopic autoscopic, bronchoscopic, cryoscopic, deuteroscopic, dichroscopic, ebullioscopic, electroscopic, endoscopic, gyroscopic, hagioscopic, helioscopic, horoscopic, hygroscopic, kaleidoscopic, laryngoscopic, macroscopic, megascopic, metoscopic, microscopic, necroscopic, ophthalmoscopic, orthoscopic, pantoscopic, periscopic, poroscopic, rhinoscopic, seismoscopic, spectroscopic, stethoscopic, stroboscopic, submicroscopic, tachistoscopic, telescopic, thermoscopic, ultramicroscopic, zooscopic.

-scopy autoscopy, bronchoscopy, colposcopy, cranioscopy, cryoscopy, cystoscopy, dactyloscopy, deuteroscopy, ebullioscopy, endoscopy, episcopy, fluoroscopy, hepatoscopy, hieroscopy, horoscopy, laparoscopy, laryngoscopy, metoposcopy, microscopy, necroscopy, omoplatoscopy, oniroscopy, ophthalmoscopy, ornithoscopy, ouroscopy, pharyngoscopy, poroscopy, proctoscopy, radioscopy, retinoscopy, rhinoscopy, röntgenoscopy, skiascopy, spectroscopy, stereoscopy, stethoscopy, telescopy, tracheoscopy, ultramicroscopy, urinoscopy, uroscopy, zooscopy.

-ship abbotship, accountantship, acquaintanceship, administratorship, admiralship, advisership, aedileship, airmanship, aldermanship, amateurship, ambassadorship, apostleship, apprenticeship, archonship, assessorship, associateship, attorneyship, auditorship, augurship, authorship, bachelorship, bailieship, baillieship, bardship, barristership, bashawship, batmanship, beadleship, bedellship, bedelship, benchership, bondmanship, brinkmanship, bursarship, bushmanship, butlership, cadetship, Caesarship, candidateship, captainship, cardinalship, catechumenship, censorship, chairmanship, chamberlainship, championship, chancellorship, chaplainship, chelaship, chiefship, chieftainship, citizenship, clanship,

-ship *contd.*

clerkship, clientship, clownship, coadjutorship, colleagueship, collectorship, colonelship, commandantship, commandership, commissaryship, commissionership, committeeship, companionship, compotationship, comradeship, conductorship, confessorship, connoisseurship, conservatorship, constableship, consulship, controllership, copartnership, co-rivalship, corporalship, counsellorship, countship, courtship, cousinship, cowardship, craftmanship, craftsmanship, creatorship, creatureship, curateship, curatorship, custodianship, deaconship, dealership, deanship, demyship, denizenship, devilship, dictatorship, directorship, discipleship, disfellowship, doctorship, dogeship, dogship, dollarship, donship, draftsmanship, dukeship, editorship, eldership, electorship, emperorship, endship, ensignship, entrepreneurship, envoyship, executorship, factorship, fathership, fellowship, foxship, freshmanship, friendship, gamesmanship, generalship, gentlemanship, giantship, gladiatorship, goddess-ship, godship, good-fellowship, governor-generalship, governorship, grandeeship, guardianship, guideship, hardship, headship, hectorship, heirship, heraldship, heroship, hership, hetmanship, horsemanship, hostess-ship, housewifeship, huntsmanship, inspectorship, interpretership, interrelationship, janitorship, jockeyship, judgeship, justiceship, kaisership, keepership, kindredship, kingship, kinship, knaveship, ladyship, lairdship, land-ownership, laureateship, leadership, lectorship, lectureship, legateship, legislatorship, librarianship, lieutenant-commandership, lieutenant-generalship, lieutenant-governorship, lieutenantship, lifemanship, logship, lordship, ludship, mageship, major-generalship, majorship, managership, marshalship, mastership, matronship, mayorship, mediatorship, membership, Messiahship, milk-kinship, minorship, mistress-ship, moderatorship, monitorship, multi-ownership, musicianship, noviceship, nunship, oarsmanship, one-upmanship, overlordship, ownership, partisanship, partnership, pastorship, patroonship, peatship, pendragonship, penmanship, physicianship, poetship, popeship, possessorship, postmastership, praetorship, preachership, precentorship, perfectship, prelateship, premiership, prenticeship, presbytership, presidentship, pretendership, priestship, primateship, primogenitureship, principalship, priorship, probationership, proconsulship, proctorship, procuratorship, professorship, progenitorship, prolocutorship, prophetship, proprietorship, prosectorship, protectorship, provostship, pursership, quaestorship, queenship, rajahship, rajaship, rangership, readership, recordership, rectorship, regentship, registrarship, relationship, residentiaryship, residentship, retainership, rivalship, rogueship, rulership, sachemship, saintship, salesmanship, scholarship, school-friendship, schoolmastership, scrivenership, seamanship, secretaryship, seigniorship, sempstress-ship, senatorship, seneschalship, serfship, sergeantship, serjeantship, servantship, servitorship, sextonship, sheriffship, showmanship, sibship, sizarship, soldiership, solicitorship, sonship, speakership, spectatorship, spinstership, sponsorship, sportsmanship, squireship, statesmanship, stewardship, studentship, subahship, subdeaconship, subeditorship, subinspectorship, subjectship, successorship, suffraganship, sultanship, superintendentship, superiorship, supervisorship, suretyship, surgeonship, surrogateship, surveyorship, survivorship, swordsmanship, teachership, tellership, tenantship, thaneship, thwartship, tide-waitership, township, traineeship, traitorship, treasurership, treeship, tribuneship, truantship, trusteeship, tutorship, twinship, umpireship, uncleship, under-clerkship, undergraduateship, under-secretaryship, unfriendship, ushership, vaivodeship, vergership, vicarship, vice-chairmanship, vice-chancellorship, vice-consulship, viceroyship, virtuosoship, viscountship, viziership, vizirship, voivodeship, waivodeship, wardenship, wardship, watermanship, Whigship, workmanship, worship, wranglership, writership, yachtsmanship.

-sophy anthroposophy, gastrosophy, gymnosophy, pansophy, philosophy, sciosophy, theosophy.

-stat aerostat, antistat, appestat, bacteriostat, barostat, celostat, chemostat, coccidiostat, cryostat, gyrostat, heliostat, hemostat, humidistat, hydrostat, hygrostat, klinostat, pyrostat, rheostat, siderostat, thermostat.

-therapy actinotherapy, balneotherapy, chemotherapy, cryotherapy, curietherapy, electrotherapy, heliotherapy, hydrotherapy, hypnotherapy, immunotherapy, kinesitherapy, musicotherapy, narcotherapy, opotherapy, organotherapy, pelotherapy, phototherapy, physiotherapy, psychotherapy, pyretotherapy, radiotherapy, röntgenotherapy, serotherapy, serum-therapy, zootherapy.

-tomy adenectomy, adenoidectomy, anatomy, anthropotomy, appendectomy, appendicectomy, arteriotomy, autotomy, cephalotomy, cholecystectomy, cholecystotomy, colotomy, cordotomy, craniectomy, craniotomy, cystotomy, dichotomy, duodenectomy, embryotomy, encephalotomy, enterectomy, enterotomy, gastrectomy, gingivectomy, glossectomy, hepatectomy, herniotomy, hysterectomy, hysterotomy, iridectomy, laparotomy, laryngectomy, laryngotomy, leucotomy, lipectomy, lithotomy, lobectomy, lobotomy, ...omy, mastectomy, microtomy, myringotomy, necrotomy, nephrectomy, nephrotomy, neurectomy, neuroanatomy, neurotomy, oophorectomy, orchidectomy, orchiectomy, osteotomy, ovariotomy, pharyngotomy, phlebotomy, phytotomy, pleurotomy, pneumonectomy, pogonotomy, prostatectomy, rhytidectomy, salpingectomy, sclerotomy, splenectomy, stapedectomy, stereotomy, strabotomy, sympathectomy, symphyseotomy, symphsiotomy, syringotomy, tenotomy, tetrachotomy, thymectomy, tonsillectomy, tonsillotomy, topectomy, tracheotomy, trichotomy, tubectomy, ultramicrotomy, uterectomy, uterotomy, varicotomy, vasectomy, zootomy.

-urgy chemurgy, dramaturgy, electrometallurgy, hierurgy, hydrometallurgy, liturgy, metallurgy, micrurgy, theurgy, zymurgy.

-vorous apivorous, baccivorous, carnivorous, fructivorous, frugivorous, graminivorous, granivorous, herbivorous, insectivorous, lignivorous, mellivorous, myristicivorous, nucivorous, omnivorous, ossivorous, piscivorous, radicivorous, ranivorous, sanguinivorous, sanguivorous, vermivorous.